C000076587

GEORGINA CAMPBELL'S
ireland

the guide
2008

All the best places to eat, drink and stay

Georgina Campbell Guides

Editor: Georgina Campbell
Production Editor: Bob Nixon

Epicure Press,
PO Box 6173
Dublin 13
Ireland

website: www.ireland-guide.com
email: info@ireland-guide.com

The contents of this book are believed to be correct at the time of going to
press. Nevertheless the publisher can accept no responsibility for errors or
omissions or changes in the details given.

Front cover photographs: Newforge House, Co Armagh

Hayfield Manor Hotel, Cork City

Rhodes D7, Dublin

Back cover top, (left to right):   Olive, Co Dublin

Gregans Castle, Co Clare

Carlow Tourism

Merchant Hotel, Belfast

Ashford Castle, Co Mayo

Back cover bottom, (left to right): Carlow Tourism

Dromhall Hotel, Co Kerry

Hayfield Manor Hotel, Cork

BrookLodge Hotel, Co Wicklow

Carlow Tourism

City and county introductions © W.M. Nixon
Design and Artwork by Brian Darling of The Design Station, Dublin
Printed and bound in Spain
First published 2007 by Georgina Campbell Guides Ltd.

ISBN: 978-1-903164-26-6

Georgina Campbell Guides Awards

The Merrion Hotel, Dublin
Hotel of the Year

Deanes Restaurant, Belfast
Restaurant of the Year

Paul Flynn
Chef of the Year

The Olde Glen Bar, Co Donegal
Pub of the Year

Chart House Restaurant, Co Kerry
Féile Bia Award

O'Grady's on the Pier, Co Galway
Seafood Restaurant of the Year

The full list of awards is on page 9

Georgina Campbell Guides Awards

Mary Ann's, Co Cork
Seafood Bar of the Year

Enniscoe House, Co Mayo
Food EXTRA Award

Jacques Restaurant, Cork
Natural Food Award

Coxtown Manor, Co Donegal
Hideaway of the Year

Furama, Dublin
Ethnic Restaurant of the Year

Waterford Castle Hotel, Waterford
Irish Breakfast Award

The full list of awards is on page 9

GEORGINA CAMPBELL'S ireland

The Best of the Best
STARRED RESTAURANTS

★★ / ★ / ☆

REPUBLIC OF IRELAND

2 Star: ★★
Dublin, Mint
Dublin, Restaurant Patrick Guilbaud

1 Star: ★
Dublin, Chapter One
Dublin, The Tea Room @ The Clarence Hotel
Dublin, l'Ecrivain
Dublin, One Pico Restaurant
Dublin, Thornton's
Co Cavan, MacNean Bistro, Blacklion
Co Clare, Dromoland Castle
Co Cork, Ballymaloe House, Shanagarry
Co Cork, Longueville House, Mallow
Co Kerry, Park Hotel Kenmare
Co Kerry, Killarney Park Hotel, Killarney
Co Kerry, Sheen Falls Lodge, Kenmare
Co Mayo, Ashford Castle, Cong
Co Sligo, Cromleach Lodge, Castlebaldwin
Co Waterford, The Tannery, Dungarvan

Demi-Star: ☆
Dublin, Balzac
Dublin, Bang Café
Dublin, First Floor @ Harvey Nichols
Dublin, Locks Restaurant
Dublin, Mermaid Café
Dublin, Pearl Brasserie
Dublin, Roly's Bistro
Dublin, Still @ Dylan Hotel
Dublin, The Merrion Hotel
Dublin, The Winding Stair
Co Dublin, Bon Appetit, Malahide
Co Dublin, King Sitric Seafood Restaurant &
   Accommodation, Howth
Cork City, Café Paradiso
Cork City, Fleming's
Cork City, Isaacs
Cork City, Jacob's on the Mall
Cork City, Jacques
Cork City, Les Gourmandises Restaurant
Co Cork, Capricho @ Bayview Hotel, Ballycotton

Demi-Star (continued): ☆
Co Cork, Casino House, Kilbrittain
Co Cork, Gleeson's, Clonakilty
Co Cork, Good Things Café, Durrus
Co Cork, Toddies, Kinsale
Co Carlow, Sha-Roe Bistro, Clonegal
Co Cavan, The Olde Post Inn, Cloverhill
Co Clare, Cherry Tree Restaurant, Killaloe
Co Clare, Sheedy's Hotel, Lisdoonvarna
Co Donegal, The Mill Restaurant, Dunfanaghy
Co Galway, St. Clerans Country House,
   Craughwell
Co Kerry, The Chart House Restaurant, Dingle
Co Kerry, The Lime Tree Restaurant, Kenmare
Co Kerry, Mulcahys Restaurant, Kenmare
Co Kerry, Packie's Restaurant, Kenmare
Co Kerry, Restaurant David Norris, Tralee
Co Kildare, The Mill Restaurant @ Lyons
   Demesne, Celbridge
Co Kildare, Kildare Hotel, Straffan
Co Limerick, The Mustard Seed @ Echo
   Lodge, Ballingarry
Co Monaghan, The Nuremore Hotel,
   Carrickmacross
Co Tipperary, Chez Hans, Cashel
Co Tipperary, The Old Convent Gourmet
   Hideaway, Clogheen
Co Waterford, Waterford Castle Hotel, Waterford
Co Westmeath, Wineport Lodge, Glasson
Co Wexford, Dunbrody House, Arhurstown
Co Wexford, Marlfield House, Gorey

NORTHERN IRELAND

2 Star: ★★
Belfast, Deane's Restaurant

1 Star: ★
Shu, Belfast

Demi-Star: ☆
Belfast, Aldens Restaurant
Belfast, Cayenne
Belfast, James Street South

DELUXE HOTELS

REPUBLIC OF IRELAND

Dublin, The Clarence, Temple Bar
Dublin, Conrad Dublin, Earlsfort Terrace
Dublin, The Fitzwilliam Hotel,
    St. Stephen's Green
Dublin, The Dylan Hotel, Dublin 4
Dublin, Four Seasons Hotel, Ballsbridge
Dublin, The Merrion, Merrion Street
Dublin, The Shelbourne, St. Stephen's Green
Dublin, The Westbury, Grafton Street
Dublin, The Westin Hotel, College Green
Cork City, Hayfield Manor Hotel
Cork City, Kingsley Hotel
Co Cork, Capella Castlemartyr, Castlemartyr
Co Cork, Sheraton Fota Island, Cobh
Co Clare, Dromoland Castle,
    Newmarket-on-Fergus
Co Galway, Glenlo Abbey Hotel

Co Kerry, Aghadoe Heights Hotel, Killarney
Co Kerry, Killarney Park Hotel, Killarney
Co Kerry, Hotel Europe, Killarney
Co Kerry, Dunloe Castle Hotel, Killarney
Co Kerry, Park Hotel Kenmare
Co Kerry, Sheen Falls Lodge, Kenmare
Co Kildare, Kildare Hotel, Straffan
Co Kilkenny, Mount Juliet Conrad,
    Thomastown
Co Laois, Heritage Golf & Spa Resort, Killenard
Co Limerick, Adare Manor, Adare
Co Mayo, Ashford Castle, Cong
Co Wexford, Marlfield House, Gorey
Co Wicklow, The Ritz Carlton Powerscort,
    Enniskerry

NORTHERN IRELAND

Belfast, The Merchant Hotel
Co Down, Culloden Hotel, Holywood

OUTSTANDING PUBS (for good food & atmosphere)

REPUBLIC OF IRELAND

Dublin, Café en Seine
Dublin, Clarendon Café Bar
Dublin, The Porterhouse
Dublin, The Purty Kitchen, Monkstown
Co Carlow, Lennon's Café Bar, Carlow
Co Clare, Vaughans Anchor Inn, Liscannor
Co Cork, The Bosun, Monkstown
Co Cork, Bushe's Bar, Baltimore
Co Cork, Hayes' Bar, Glandore
Co Cork, Mary Ann's Bar & Restaurant,
    Castletownshend
Co Cork, The Poachers Inn, Bandon
Co Donegal, Olde Glen Pub, Carrigart
Co Galway, Moran's Oyster Cottage, Kilcolgan
Co Kerry, QC's Seafood Bar & Restaurant,
    Cahirciveen
Co Kerry, Lord Baker's Restaurant & Bar, Dingle

Co Kildare, The Ballymore Inn, Ballymore
    Eustace
Co Kildare, Fallons Café & Bar, Kilcullen
Co Kilkenny, Marble City Bar, Kilkenny
Co Leitrim, The Oarsman Bar & Café, Carrick
    on Shannon
Co Louth, Fitzpatrick's Bar & Restaurant,
    Dundalk
Co Offaly, The Wolftrap, Tullamore
Co Roscommon, Keenans Bar & Restaurant,
    Tarmonbarry
Co Waterford, The Glencairn Inn, Lismore
Co Wexford, The Lobster Pot, Carne
Co Wicklow, Roundwood Inn, Roundwood

NORTHERN IRELAND

Belfast, Crown Liquor Salon
Co Down, The Plough Inn, Hillsborough
Co Down, Balloo House, Killinchy

For further accreditations, see symbols on listed entries.

Introduction
by Georgina Campbell, Editor

Welcome to the 2008 edition of the Guide - this is the tenth edition of our comprehensive flagship guide to the best of Irish hospitality and, as usual, we have visited every county in Ireland to find you the very best places to stay and to eat, or to relax over a drink, for both business and leisure. No matter what the occasion or the area, we are uniquely placed to help you to find just the right place for your holiday, short break, meeting or meal out, and the most atmospheric pub for a pint or a music session. This is the only guide of its kind, offering recommendations across a very wide range of categories and price ranges - and, most importantly, our selections are made entirely on merit: unlike most other 'guides', establishments do not pay to be included in any of the Georgina Campbell guide books.

Major anniversaries mark milestones in all areas of life and are inevitably cause for reflection so, on our travels this year, we have been thinking especially about the changes we've seen in the last decade. Fast-growing development is the most obvious physical change of course, the result of a period of unprecedented prosperity, and many places in Ireland previously untouched by change would now be almost unrecognisable to anyone revisiting Ireland after an absence of five or ten years. While this clearly has a downside it has also brought benefits, including a much better choice of quality accommodation in areas where there was very little until recently and - thanks to a new focus on providing activities and amenities for guests, including luxurious spa facilities, golf and a wide range of other outdoor activities - many holiday areas now enjoy a longer season, which is good for business and also for the legions of city folk who love nothing better than to escape for short breaks as often as possible. The arrival of so many appealing new establishments has also raised the bar for all working in hospitality, so standards continue to rise. And, interestingly, although there has been much talk of competition from new inexpensive midmarket hotels bringing about the demise of the small family-run establishments, especially guesthouses and B&Bs, what we've observed is an even higher level of dedication, and determination from owner-managers to offer something unique and personal to guests, and the quality in this area is truly outstanding. These are also the people who really know their own area and, through genuine hospitality, can help ensure their guests enjoy the full range of experiences each area has to offer.

In all areas of hospitality, and perhaps especially on the food side, there is a feeling that we are on the cusp of big changes in Ireland as we become more environmentally aware and learn to treasure the small and the particular. The growing importance of small scale and artisan food production during the last decade is nothing short of sensational: at the Great Taste Awards in London this year, for example, a total of 39 Irish artisan food and drink producers won no less than 68 gold awards, which is a phenomenal achievement by any standards. In parallel developments, there is also a growing interest in food tourism and - most interestingly - eco-tourism, as Ireland's 'Greenbox' in the northwest of the country begins to capture the public imagination, and a growing number of establishments of all sizes throughout the country choose to develop their 'green' credentials and offer a different kind of experience to guests. Chefs are gradually responding too, as they recognise the strength of the good-tasting seasonal ingredients which are increasingly easy to source locally, and consumers tired of complicated and over-presented food begin to demand simpler fare with real flavour. Interesting times ahead, then, and exciting too: as I look into my emerald crystal ball, I think I can make out the future for hospitality in Ireland - and it is green.

I hope that you will enjoy using the guide on your own travels, and that it will lead you to many wonderful places. Don't forget to check our website (www.ireland-guide.com), where you will find constant updates - and if you would like to share your experiences, good or bad, we would love to hear from you.

Georgina Campbell.

Awards of Excellence

Annual awards for outstanding establishments and individuals

Georgina Campbell Guides
gratefully acknowledges the support of the following sponsors:

GEORGINA CAMPBELL'S ireland

Hotel of the Year

The Merrion Hotel
Dublin

See page 86

2007 WINNER:
Mount Juliet Conrad, Co Kilkenny

GEORGINA CAMPBELL'S ireland

Restaurant of the Year

Deanes Restaurant
Belfast

See page 557

2007 WINNER:
MacNean House & Bistro, Co Cavan

GEORGINA CAMPBELL'S ireland

Chef of the Year

Paul Flynn
The Tannery, Dungarvan,
Co Waterford

See page 497

2007 WINNER:
Stefan Matz, Ashford Castle, Co Mayo

GEORGINA CAMPBELL'S ireland

Pub of the Year

The Olde Glen Bar
Carrigart, Co Donegal

See page 272

2007 WINNER:

The Roundwood Inn, Co Wicklow

Irish Food Board

Féile Bia Award

The Chart House Restaurant
Dingle, Co Kerry

See page 332

2007 WINNER:

Ballymore Inn, Co Kildare

Fáilte Ireland
National Tourism Development Authority

Food EXTRA Award

Enniscoe House
Crossmolina, Co Mayo

See page 434

Fáilte Ireland
National Tourism Development Authority

Natural Food Award

Jacques Restaurant
Cork

See page 209

2007 WINNER:
Farmgate, Co Cork

Fáilte Ireland
National Tourism Development Authority

Hideaway of the Year

Coxtown Manor
Laghey, Co Donegal

See page 278

2007 WINNER:
Gregans Castle Hotel, Co Clare

Bord Iascaigh Mhara
Irish Sea Fisheries Board

Seafood Bar of the Year

Mary Ann's Bar & Restaurant

Castletownshend, Co Cork

See page 231

2007 WINNER:

Aherne's Seafood Bar & Restaurant, Co Cork

Bord Iascaigh Mhara
Irish Sea Fisheries Board

Seafood Restaurant
of the Year

O'Grady's on the Pier
Barna, Co Galway

See page 305

2007 WINNER:
Fishy Fishy Café, Co Cork

TASTE AND TRADITION

Rudd's

SPONSORS OF

Georgina Campbell's
Irish Breakfast Awards

— Hotel —
Waterford Castle
Waterford, Co Waterford

— Country House —
Old Convent
Gourmet Hideaway
Clogheen, Co Tipperary

— Guesthouse —
Number 31
Dublin 2

— B&B —
Marble Hall
Dublin 4

SPONSORS OF

Georgina Campbell's Irish Breakfast Awards
— National Winner —

Waterford Castle Hotel
Waterford, Co Waterford

See page 508

2007 WINNER:

Farmgate Café, Cork

Ethnic Restaurant
of the Year

Furama
Dublin 4

See page 113

2007 WINNER:

Rasam, Co Dublin

GEORGINA CAMPBELL'S ireland

Atmospheric Establishment of the Year

Hunters Hotel
Rathnew, Co Wicklow

See page 548

2007 WINNER:

La Péniche, Dublin

GEORGINA CAMPBELL'S ireland

Wine Award of the Year

Ashford Castle
Cong, Co Mayo

See page 439

2007 WINNER:
Ely CHQ, Dublin

GEORGINA CAMPBELL'S ireland

Host of the Year

Martina Sheedy
Sheedys Hotel, Lisdoonvarna, Co Clare

See page 192

2007 WINNER:

Seamus & Aoife Brock, Teach de Broc, Co Kerry

GEORGINA CAMPBELL'S ireland

Business Hotel
of the Year

Clontarf Castle Hotel
Dublin 3

See page 105

2007 WINNER:
Brooks Hotel, Dublin

GEORGINA CAMPBELL'S ireland

Family Friendly Hotel of the Year

Ferrycarrig Hotel
Wexford, Co Wexford

See page 535

2007 WINNER:

Dingle Skellig Hotel, Co Kerry

GEORGINA CAMPBELL'S ireland

Newcomer of the Year

Inis Meáin Restaurant
Aran Islands, Co Galway

See page 299

2007 WINNER:
Sha-Roe Bistro, Co Carlow

GEORGINA CAMPBELL'S ireland

Country House of the Year

Echo Lodge
Ballingarry, Co Limerick

See page 415

2007 WINNER:

Rathmullan House, Co Donegal

GEORGINA CAMPBELL'S ireland

Guesthouse of the Year

Whitepark House
Ballintoy, Co Antrim

See page 572

GEORGINA CAMPBELL'S ireland

B&B of the Year

McMenamin's Townhouse
Wexford, Co Wexford

See page 533

2007 WINNER:

Killyon House, Co Meath

GEORGINA CAMPBELL'S ireland

Farmhouse of the Year

Castle Farm Country House
Millstreet, Co Waterford

See page 501

2007 WINNER:

Glasha, Co Waterford

A Bite
of the Best...

..*Irish Hospitality*

Ireland today is a prosperous country, where visitors will find that - as in other modern societies - urban life is fast paced and the streets are traffic laden; but, although the Irish work hard to maintain the vibrant economy that they have created in recent years, they still make time to enjoy the good things in life, especially good food and breaks taken with family and friends. Irish hospitality is legendary and, although the pace of modern life does take its toll, rumours of its demise have been exaggerated: there are many, many people offering food, drink and accommodation all over Ireland who love nothing better than getting to know their guests, spending time with them, and helping them to get every last drop of enjoyment out of a visit to this country and - most patricularly - to their own area. They say all politics is local and the same is true of hospitality - in a world of increasing sameness, it's the local differences that count and the most rewarding way to travel in Ireland is by visiting the people who care about the area they live in. And, despite the huge amount of development that has taken place in recent years, you will still find that, beyond the bustle of urban centres, lies stunningly beautiful countryside: lakes, rivers, picturesque villages, and the gentler pace of life in rural Ireland.

Trends

Ireland has never been a low cost destination, and there are many reasons for prices that may seem high in comparison with other European countries; but independent travellers visiting Ireland today will find that the quality of accommodation and food is generally high, and that a growing number of estabishments are specialising in providing for the most discerning of guests, and giving value at all price levels - as the wide-ranging entries in this guide clearly demonstrate, this is true at every level, whether you seek a luxurious place to stay, a small but special retreat, a fine meal for a special occasion or a simple bite to eat based on the highest quality local and speciality foods.

Irish society is becoming increasingly cosmopolitan and this - plus the influence of international food fashion - has led to multi-cultural cooking styles in many restaurants, and rapid growth in the number and variety of ethnic restaurants and shops. All the main food cultures are well represented and the best restaurants - where you will find an emphasis on authenticity, rather than westernised versions of ethnic cuisines - are included in the guide. While Italian, Chinese and Indian/Pakistani restaurants are common in every corner of the island, you'll also find many others including regional French, Greek, Moroccan, Thai, Nepalese, Cuban, Filipino, Malaysian, and, since the enlargement of the European Union, an increasing number of Eastern European cuisines. Spanish food is enjoying a surge of popularity and influence - with tapas and other similar 'small bites' a fast growing trend, matching the growth of a new café-bar culture.

On the other hand - perhaps partly in response to the inevitable internationalism of food products and cooking styles that creates a disappointing sameness in many mid range restaurants everywhere - there is enormous interest in Irish food and, particularly, the artisan food products that are flourishing throughout the country. Over the last twenty years, the influence and strength of Euro-Toques (The European Community of Chefs) has been a real force for good in reawakening interest and pride in the value of locally produced, traditional foodstuffs and the leading chefs have put a creative, often innovative, spin on traditional Irish dishes. The result is a very attractive if, so far, limited contemporary Irish cuisine that is "entirely itself" - an Irish idiom that indicates our high regard for an individual approach to life and living.

Style and Value

Some welcome current trends are resulting from a higher value placed on seasonal, naturally produced and local food - including a gradual move away from the very complex dishes that have been fashionable in recent years, towards a simpler style with more emphasis on the taste and flavour of top quality ingredients. This trend is slower to develop than many food critics and regular diners out would like, but the wider availability of local speciality foods with real depth of flavour is gradually encouraging chefs to allow these ingredients to take pride of place instead of relying on fancy footwork in the kitchen for effect. The growth of interest in wine is also continue to be very noticeable, with many restaurants offering an extensive choice of good value house wines and half bottles on their wine lists - and, most interestingly, many more are now offering an increasingly wide selection of wines by the glass, sometimes a range of 50 or even more is offered. Giving value for money is also a high priority, and visitors who wish to eat well without breaking the budget will often find that the best value is offered on early dinner menus and fixed price two-course menus - and lunchtime remains the least costly way of enjoying a meal in our leading restaurants, where a stunning meal may often be found at a surprisngly reasonable price. A Sunday curiosity worth keeping an eye out for is the extended lunch hour, sometimes running from noon to seven in the evening.

The Irish Breakfast

Traditional Irish breakfasts, known as "the full Irish", are substantial and lingering over a leisurely breakfast remains an essential part of being on holiday. In some establishments the traditional morning meal of porridge or cereals and fruit followed by bacon, sausage, black and white pudding, eggs, mushrooms, and tomatoes, accompanied by Irish soda bread and scones, has become just one choice from an elaborate menu, and you'll often also be offered fresh or smoked fish dishes, vegetarian dishes, local farmhouse cheeses, traditional cured hams and other cured meats and salamis.

BLT with a Fried Egg

This mixture of the popular sandwich and elements of the traditional Irish breakfast is good at any time of day. Serves 1

A slice of good bread, preferably an artisan loaf with good texture

Drizzle of olive oil

Rocket leaves

3 or 3 cherry tomatoes, sliced

Two slices streaky bacon, cooked crispy

1 egg, fried

Grill the bread with the olive oil, top with the rocket, tomatoes and bacon slices, finish with the fried egg. Simple and delicious!

Artisan and Speciality Foods

"Ireland the food island" is more than a clever sales slogan - we are a food producing nation and, in support of their mission to promote Irish food, Bord Bia (The Irish Food Board) has initiated programmes that have had a genuinely beneficial effect on the quality and diversity of Irish foods available to chefs and their customers. The Féile Bia programme (a celebration of food) is a partnership initiative between Bord Bia, The Restaurants Association of Ireland and The Hotels Federation of Ireland, supported by the farming community. The scheme covers beef, lamb, pork, bacon, chicken and eggs, produced under Quality Assurance schemes, or sourced from small scale suppliers, including butchers, with appropriate regulatory approval.

The developments in promotion of food and horticulture as a result of the amalgamation of Bord Bia and Bord Glas (Irish Horticulture Board) allows the joint expertise of both organisations to promote and market food and horticulture at home and to encourage the development of speciality food production. Certainly, it's likely to underpin the trend towards offering creative vegetarian dishes, the increased use of seasonal fruit and vegetables from named local growers, and the increasing popularity of organic vegetables.

An initiative to support the development of small food producers is also in operation, the TASTE Council (acronym for traditional, artisan, speciality, trade expertise) is coordinated by Bord Bia. Its main aim is to support the growing number of craft food producers to develop, distribute and market their products; also to offer a focus for small food producers that allows them to draw on expertise within the group itself. Membership of the council includes small food producers, organic growers, representatives of relevant organisations like Cáis (the Irish Farmhouse Cheesemakers Association), Euro-Toques (The European Community of Chefs), and retailers and distributors who specialise in traditional, artisan and speciality foods.

Bord Bia works with over 300 small speciality food producers (just part of a growing number of artisan food producers), a sector that continues to expand, driven by consumer demand at home and abroad. EU agricultural reforms, particularly de-coupling, has concentrated farmers' minds on ways and means to survive in the leaner, meaner climate. Those who believe they have the capacity to expand profitably can do so without the need to acquire quotas, or rights to trade. Adaptable farmers see this as an opportunity to cut out the middle man and sell direct to the customer by turning their produce into consumer goods that can be sold locally and at food markets. Markets are a great place for producers and farmers to get mutual support from fellow producers, to get feedback on their produce and ideas for improvement, and just interact with consumers in a way that Irish farmers have not done for generations.

Bacon and Regato Scramble

This tasty dish is perfect for a weekend brunch or midweek supper. 'Farl' means a quarter, and soda farls are triangular sections of traditional round soda bread that has been cooked on a skillet, making it shallower than oven-baked bread so it is split horizontally rather than sliced - but any good soda bread can be used instead. Regato is a hard parmesan-style cheese made in Ireland, and widely available. Serves 2

2 lean bacon rashers, diced

6 cherry tomatoes

4 free range eggs

2 tablesp. milk

1 tablesp. grated Regato cheese

2 tablesp. chives, chopped

Salt and freshly ground black pepper

Soda bread/farls to serve

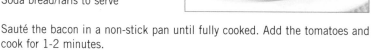

Sauté the bacon in a non-stick pan until fully cooked. Add the tomatoes and cook for 1-2 minutes.

Beat the eggs with the milk, cheese, chives and seasoning. Add the mixture to the cooked bacon and continue cooking over a gentle heat until just scrambled - they should be creamy but still a little runny as they continue to cook as you serve them. Serve on toasted buttered soda bread.

The Local Food Market Revolution

The widespread revival of local food markets has been one of the most exciting achievements of recent years. If you come from anywhere else in Europe you will wonder why they were in need of reviving. For historical reasons (you'd almost need a degree in Irish history to understand them) local food markets, widespread and highly organised since Norman times had, apart a few, all but died out. Now, to the delight of food lovers, all that has changed. For a nation that treasures individualism there is a remarkable degree of mutual support between artisan food producers and other interested parties. The Irish Food Market Traders Association addresses the many and varied needs of food market traders - spread around the country by their very nature, there was little contact with each other, so the association was set up to give strength, structure and negotiating power to this disparate group of individuals and protect their historical and legal rights to sell food direct to the public at local markets. They have established a safety committee who try to maintain meaningful dialogue with local health and safety officers; Bord Bia lend a helping hand with a web-based service offering advice and assistance for people wishing to establish a market and also (via the internet) promoting the all of the regular farmers' markets and one held in September during the Food At Farmleigh month - this is one of the events when the state guest house (normally devoted to offering hospitality to state guests) is open to the public.

Irish Farmers Markets

Markets are a wonderful way of experiencing Irish food - a chance to buy food for a picnic, to taste traditional and innovative food products from traditional smoked wild salmon, trout, mackerel, smoked mussels, or smoked scallops,

fish patés, seafood soups and seaweeds (an ancient tradition in Ireland). Farmhouse cheeses are one of the glories of artisan producers and there are over 70 farmhouse cheesemakers, each producing cheeses that are unique to the family and farmland. Here, too, you will find distinctive Irish breads, biscuits and cakes. A surprising Irish speciality is handcrafted chocolates filled with cream and Irish liqueurs; fine examples are winners of Irish Food Writers Guild Chocolate Lovers' Awards: Gallwey's made in Co Waterford and Eve's made in Cork. Soft fruit and wild berries are often made into gorgeous preserves, chutneys and liqures. Traditional dry cures of bacon and ham are found alongside innovative smoked and cured meats, like the award-winning smoked Connemara lamb and smoked Irish beef, both creations of young craft butcher James McGeough of Oughterard, who has already won many awards including the top prizes at both The Irish Food Writers Guild Food Awards and The Craft Butchers Speciality Foods Competition.

The Bord Bia guide to farmers food markets, held regularly in many cities, towns and villages:

Co. Antrim
- Origin Farmers Market Ballymoney Castlecroft, Main St., Last Saturday of month 11-2pm
- City Food & Garden Market, Belfast, St George's Street, Saturday 9-4pm
- Templepatrick Farmers Market Colmans Garden Centre
- Lisburn Market, Saturday
- Portadown Market. Last Saturday of month

Co. Carlow
- Carlow Farmers Market, Potato Market Carlow, Saturday 9-2pm
- Cavan Farmers Market, McCarren's, Farham Road, Saturday 10am - 4pm
- Belturbet Farmers Market. McGowan's Garden, (Beside carpark) Fridays 4-7pm (May to October)

Co. Clare
- Ballyvaughan Farmers Market, Village Hall Car Park, Saturdays - 10am - 2pm
- Ennis Farmers Market, Car Park, Upr Main Street. Friday 8-2pm
- Killaloe Farmers Market, Between the Waters, Sunday 11-3pm
- Kilrush Farmers Market, The Square, Thursday 9-2pm
- Shannon Farmers Market, Town Centre, next to Skycourt Shopping Centre Friday 12.30-7pm

Co. Cork
- Ballydehob Food Market, Community Hall. Friday 10.30-12pm
- Hosfords Market, Hosfords Garden Centre, Bandon-Clonakilty Rd (N71). 5 miles west of Bandon, First Sunday of every month June -September, 12-5pm
- Bandon Market, Bandon Friday 10.30-1pm
- Bantry Market, Main Square 1st Friday of month
- Blackwater Valley Farmers Market Nano Nagle Centre, Mallow. Every 2nd Saturday 10.30-1pm
- Castletownbere. 1st Thursday of month
- Clonakilty Farmers Market, McCurtain Hill. Thursdays & Sundays 10-2pm
- Cobh Market, Sea Front. Friday 10-1pm
- Cornmarket Street Market, Cornmarket Street. Saturday 9-3pm
- Douglas Food Market, Douglas Community Park. Saturday 9.30-2pm
- Duhallow Farmers Market, Kanturk Thursday and Saturday morning 10.30- 1.30pm
- Dunmanway, The Old Mill, Castle St. Fridays 10-2pm
- English Market. Entrances on Princes St & Grand Parade. Daily
- Fermoy Farmers Market, Opposite Cork Marts. Saturday 9-1pm
- Inchigeelagh Market, Creedons Hotel. Last Saturday of month

- Kanturk Food Market, Behind Supervalu, Kanturk. Thursday & Saturday, 10.30-1pm
- Mahon Point Farmers Market, West Entrance, Mahon Point Shopping Centre. Thursday 10-2pm
- Macroom Farmers Market, The Square. Tuesday 9-3pm
- Midleton Farmers Market, Hospital Road. Saturday
- Schull Farmers Market, Car Park, Near Pier. Sunday 10-3pm
- Skibbereen Farmers Market, Old Market Square. Saturday 10-2pm

Co. Derry
- Guildhall Country Fair. Last Saturday in month

Co. Donegal
- Ballybofey Farmers Market, GAA grounds. Friday 12-4pm
- Donegal Town Farmers Market, Diamond. 3rd Saturday of Month

Co. Down
- Castlewellan Farmers Market, Castlewellan Community Centre. Saturday 10am - 1pm
- Newry Dundalk Farmers Market, Newry Marketplace, John Mitchell Place. Friday 9am-2pm

Co. Dublin
- Anglesea Road Village Market, Grounds of St Mary's Church at junction of Anglesea Road & Simmonscourt Road. Thursday 10am - 4pm
- Ballymun Farmers Market, Ballymun Civic Centre. 1st Thursday of month 11am-2.30pm
- Dalkey Market, Dalkey Town Hall. Friday 10-4pm
- Dundrum Farmers Market, Airfield House. Saturday 10-4pm
- Dun Laoghaire Harbour Market, Dun Laoghaire Harbour. Saturday 10-4pm
- Dun Laoghaire People's Park Market, People's Park. Sunday 11-4pm
- Dun Laoghaire Shopping Centre Thursdays 10-5pm
- Farmleigh Food Market, Farmleigh House. See www.farmleigh.ie
- Fingal Food Fayre, Fingal Arts Centre. Last Sunday every month 12-5pm
- Howth Harbour Market, The Harbour, Howth. Sunday 10-4pm
- Liffey Valley Shopping Centre, Quarryvale, D.22. Fridays 10-4pm
- Powerscourt Town Centre Market, Powerscourt Town Centre, D.2. Fridays 10-4pm
- Docklands Market, Mayor Square, IFSC. Wednesday 11-3pm
- Leopardstown Farmers Market, Leopardstown Racecourse. Friday 10-4pm
- Malahide Market, GAA facility, Church Rd. Saturday 11-5pm
- Marley Park Food Market, Marlay Park Craft Courtyard. Saturday 10-4pm
- Monkstown Village Market, Monkstown Parish Church. Saturday 10-4pm
- Phibsborough Farmers Market, Near Doyle's Corner. Saturday 10-5pm (from July 21st)
- Pearse Street Market, St Andrews Centre. Saturday 9.30-3.30pm
- Ranelagh Market, Multi Denominational School. Sunday 10-4pm
- South Dublin Co. Market, High St, Tallaght. Friday 10-4pm
- Swords Farmers Market, St Colmcilles GAA Club, near Applewood Village. Thursday 10am- 4pm
- Temple Bar Market, Meeting House Square. Saturday 9-5pm
- The Red Stables Food Market. St Anne's Park, Clontarf (beside the Rose Garden). Saturday 10am-5pm

Co. Galway
- Athenry Farmers Market, 100% Organic, Market Cross. Friday 9.30-4pm
- Ballinasloe Farmers Market, Croffy's Centre, Main Street. Fridays 10-3pm
- Galway Market, Beside St Nicholas Church. Saturday, 8.30-4pm & Sunday 2-6pm
- Tuam Farmer's Market, 100% Organic, Market Cross. Friday 9.30-4pm
- Loughrea Market, Barrack Street. Thursdays 10am-2pm

Co. Kerry
- Cahirciveen Market, Community Centre. Thursday 10-2pm (Jun-Sept)
- Caherdaniel Market, Village Hall. Friday 10-12am (Jun-Sept & Christmas)
- Dingle Farm Produce & Craft Market, By the fishing harbour, near bus stop, Friday 9.30-4pm
- Dunloe Farmers Market, Dunloe Golf Course. Sundays 1-5pm
- Kenmare Farmers Market. Wed - Sun 10-6pm (7 days Jul-Aug)
- Listowel Farmers Market, The Square, Listowel. Fridays, 10am-2pm
- Listowel Food Fair, Seanchai Centre Thursday 10-1pm
- Milltown Market, Old Church, Sat 10-2pm
- Milltown Market, Organic Centre. Tuesday - Friday, 2-5pm
- Sneem Market, Community Centre, Tuesday 11-2pm (Jun-Sept & Christmas)
- Tralee Farmers Market. Friday 9-5pm

Co. Kildare
- Athy Farmers Market, Emily Square. Sunday 10-2pm
- Kildare Folly Market, Kildare Town, 3rd Sunday in month, 11am-6pm
- Maynooth Farmer's Market, Maynooth, Co. Kildare. Saturday, 10-4 pm
- Naas Farmers Market, The Storehouse Restaurant, Saturday 10-3pm
- Kildare Farmers Market, Kildare Town. Friday 10-3pm
- Whitewater Farmers Market, Whitewater Shopping Centre, Newbridge, Co. Kildare. Wednesdays 10-4pm

Co. Kilkenny

- Gowran Farmers Market, Gowran Community Hall, 3rd Sunday of month 10am-2pm
- Callan Farmers Market, Main St., Callan. Every Saturday 10am-12pm
- Kilkenny Farmers Market, The Parade, Kilkenny. Every Thursday 9.30am-2.30pm

Co. Laois

- Portlaoise, Market Square. Friday 10-3pm

Co. Leitrim

- Origin Farmers Market (Manorhamilton) Beepark Resource Centre. Friday 9-2pm

Co. Limerick

- Abbeyfeale Farmers Market, Parish Hall Friday 9-1pm
- Kilmallock Farmers Market, The Kilmallock GAA Club. Friday 9-1pm
- Limerick Milk Market, Limerick Milk Market, Saturday 8-1.30pm

Co. Longford

- Longford Farmers Market, Temperance Hall. Saturday 9.30-1pm

Co. Louth

- Castlebellingham Farmers Market, Bellingham Castle Hotel. 1st Sunday of month
- Newry Dundalk Farmers Market, The County Museum, Jocelyn Street, Dundalk. Saturday 10-2pm
- Dundalk Town Producers Market, The Square, Dundalk. Friday 10am -2pm (from 4th August 06)

Co. Meath

- Kells Farmers Market, FBD Insurance Grounds, Saturday 10-1pm
- Sonairte Farmers Market, Laytown, The Ecology Centre. 3rd Sunday in month, 10.30am -5pm

Co. Monaghan

- Monaghan Farmers / Country Market Castleblayney Livestock Salesyard, Last Saturday of month, 9-1pm

Co. Offaly

- The Full Moon Market, The Chestnut Courtyard. Every 3rd Sunday
- Tullamore Country Fair, Millenium Square. Saturday 9-4pm

Co. Roscommon

- Origin Farmers Market (Boyle), Grounds of King House. Saturday, 10-2pm

Co. Sligo

- Origin Farmers Market, IT Sports Field Car Park, Saturdays 9am-1pm

Co. Tipperary

- Cahir Farmers Market, Beside The Craft Granary. Saturday 9-1pm
- Clonmel Farmers Market, St. Peter & Paul's Primary School, Kickham Street, beside Oakville Shopping Centre. Saturday 10-2pm
- Carrick-on-Suir, Heritage Centre, Main St. Friday 10-2pm
- Nenagh Farmers Market, Teach an Lean 1st Saturday of month 10-2pm

Co. Tyrone

- Origin Farmers Market, Strabane, The Score Centre, Dock Rd. Last Saturday of month
- Tyrone Farmers Market, Tesco Carpark, Dungannon. 1st Saturday of month 8.30-1pm

Co. Waterford

- Ardkeen Producers Market, Ardkeen Quality Food Store. 2nd Sunday of every month
- Dunhill Farmers Market, Parish Hall. Last Sunday of month 11.30-2pm
- Dungarvan Farmers Market, The Square Thursday 9.30-2pm
- Lismore Farmers Market, Blackwater Valley.
- Stradbally Community Market. 1st Saturday of month 10-12.30pm
- Waterford Farmers Market, Jenkins Lane. Saturday 10-4pm

Co. Westmeath

- Athlone Farmers Market, Market Square, Athlone. Saturday 10-3pm
- Mullingar, Fairgreen (Adjacent to Lifestyle and Penneys). Every Sunday 10.30-2.30 p.m

Co. Wexford

- New Ross Farmers Market, Conduit Lane. Saturday 9-2pm
- Wexford Farmers Market, Dunbrody Abbey Centre. 15th July-19th August
- Wexford Farmers Market Community Partnership, Enniscorthy, The Abbey Square Carpark. Saturday 9-2pm
- Gorey Farmers Market, Gorey Community School Car Park, Esmonde Street, Saturday 9-2pm
- Wexford Farmers Market, Trimmers Lane West (beside La Dolce Vitae Restaurant). Friday 9-2pm

Co. Wicklow

- Brooklodge Organic Market, Macreddin Village. 1st & 3rd Sunday of month
- Glendalough Farmers Market, Brockagh Resource Centre. 2nd Sunday of month 11-6pm
- Greystones Market, Meridian Point Shopping Centre. Saturday 10-4pm
- Kilcoole. Saturdays 10.30-11.30am
- Bray Farmers Market, Outside Bray Heritage Centre, Main St. Saturday 11-3pm
- Wicklow Town, Market Square, Main St. Saturday 11-3pm

NB: Times, days and locations of markets do sometimes change; be sure to check locally or log on to: www.bordbia.ie/go/Consumers/Buying_Food/farmers_markets

Féile Bia - Certified Farm to Fork

Féile Bia is a year round programme that emphasises the importance of food sourcing in hotels, restaurants, pubs and workplaces throughout the country. Féile Bia was introduced in 2001 in response to growing consumer concerns on the origins of food offered when eating out.

Féile Bia is the consumer's reassurance that the fresh beef, lamb, pork, bacon, chicken and eggs being served are fully traceable from farm to fork and have been produced under a Quality Assurance Scheme.

When you see the Féile Bia logo displayed in a restaurant, hotel or pub you can be sure of the origin of the food being served. Those establishments recommended by the guide which have signed up to the charter are listed below and are identified within the body of the guide by the use of the Féile Bia logo.

The Féile Bia Award

Each year, in the Guide, we single out for the Féile Bia Award an establishment that we feel is interpeting the Féile Bia message especially well and not only putting into practice the principles of Quality Assurance and traceability, but doing so in a creative and pro-active manner, with the enthusiastic inclusion of local and speciality foods on their menus. This year's winner is **The Chart House Restaurant** in Dingle, County Kerry-and this award-winning recipe using Kerry mountain lamb is typical of the delicious food they serve...

Roast Rack of Kerry Lamb with Fondant Potato and Redcurrant & Rosemary Jus

4 baking potatoes, washed & peeled

Butter, as required

2 racks of lamb, seasoned

120ml/ 6 fl oz veal jus, or well reduced beef stock

1 teasp. redcurrant jelly

2 sprigs of rosemary

100g/4oz baby spinach, washed and drained

Salt & freshly ground pepper

Preheat a fan assisted oven at a moderate temperature, 150°C/gas mark 2.

Slice the potatoes thickly and, using a circular pastry cutter, cut the potato into discs ('fondants'). Rinse and pat dry. Melt some butter in a heavy-based ovenproof frying pan and cook the fondants in it over a low heat for 20 minutes. Turn over in the pan and place in oven at 150°C/gas mark 2 for 60 minutes.

Turn the oven up high, 220°C/gas mark 7, and cook the seasoned racks of racks of lamb until pink (approx. 15-20 minutes). Remove from the oven and allow to rest.

Heat the veal jus or reduced stock with the redcurrant jelly, and infuse with the rosemary sprigs for 2 minutes. In a hot pan, heat the spinach briefly with a little butter, to wilt. Assemble the dish on heated plates and serve.

Noel Enright, 31, leads a talented kitchen team at The Chart House Restaurant and sources many of his ingredients from the area, taking advantage of the great local meat and produce available on his doorstep. This very simple dish is easy to make and depends on the quality of its ingredients for success.

Noel Enright
The Chart House Restaurant
Dingle, Co. Kerry

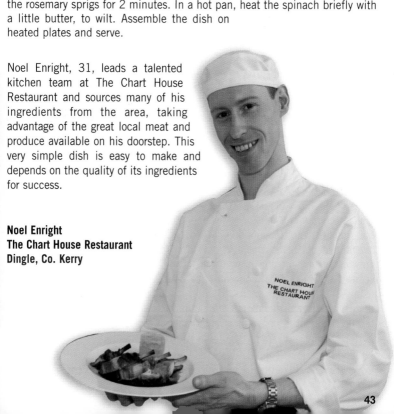

Euro-Toques (The European Community of Chefs)

Local sourcing from small, artisan producers is central to the ethos of Euro-Toques chefs. One of their principal aims is to protect the quality, diversity and flavour of our food and to promote indigenous and traditional production methods. Euro-Toques have been diligent in representing the interests of their own members, but also those of the network of small producers who supply them and the consumers they cater for. With over two hundred members and an energetic and vibrant organisation presently led by Lorcan Cribben, Commissioner-General of Euro-Toques Ireland. The Euro-Toque ethos has been of immeasurable value in the creation of a unique contemporary Irish cuisine that many Irish people now take for granted. Creative and dedicated they may be, but they come out of their kitchens when needs be, and they are active in lobbying (and encouraging other organisations to lobby) against any threat to the diversity and quality of Irish food. At their annual Food Forum they tackle major issues, such as the dangers of introducing genetically modified food crops into Ireland. Calling on the government to make Ireland a GM-free zone, the Euro-Toques statement said: "Cross contamination of organic and conventional crops will inevitably occur and consumers will have no choice about eating GM foods. In our experience people are increasingly looking for traditionally and naturally produced foods. They simply don't want GM foods." Euro-Toques are also diligent in developing young chefs, nurturing the particularly talented through the annual Bailey's/Euro-Toques Young Chef of the Year Competition and coaching Ireland's representatives at international cooking competitions including the prestigious Bocuse d'Or.

The **Small Foods Initiative** is another interesting programme that has run in recent years. Focused on the border counties and Northern Ireland, it is an INTERREG IIIA project (Ireland/Northern Ireland) to foster communication between chefs and small food producers and develop the latter's ability to supply and aid chefs in sourcing quality ingredients. They hope, in time, this will have a positive influence on the standard of food generally available in Ireland.

Slow Food

The international Slow Food Movement has caught the imagination of food lovers - despite the name it's a fast-growing movement and over the last two years many more local convivia have been established; it is open to both food professionals and members of the public, and the involvement of consumers helps make it a very potent force in the movement towards smaller production methods and artisan foods. Its emblem, the snail (a small, cosmopolitan and prudent animal), stands as the symbol of a movement that exists to spread awareness of food culture, to safeguard agricultural heritage techniques, to defend biodiversity in crops, craft techniques, food traditions, and eating places. Members are free to attend international Slow Food events but, probably, what appeals even more to the Irish independence of spirit is that local activities are led from the bottom up- local - convivia meet regularly to explore their own small corner with like-minded people. It provides a meeting ground with artisan food producers, with growers and traditional farmers, to share knowledge and support those who work in harmony with the principles of the movement.

Bord Iascaigh Mhara (BIM)

Bord Iascaigh Mhara (The Irish Sea Fisheries Board- BIM) is dedicated to promoting the sustainable development of the Irish seafood industry at sea and ashore, working closely with all sectors from fisherman to fish farmer, processor, retailer and chef. BIM also plays a vital role in the development of aquaculture, supporting the trend towards environmentally friendly and organic fish farming, as well as the cultivation of shellfish like oysters, clams, scallops and mussels.

Irish Seafood - Something Special

Luscious Dublin Bay prawns, succulent oysters, melt in the mouth mussels, tempting smoked salmon, mouth-watering mackerel, tantalising monkfish... just some of the delicious seafood you'll find on menus right round Ireland. Irish people love to eat seafood when dining out; in fact, unlike our European neighbours, we eat more seafood outside the home than in it (perhaps this is a testament to the quality of our restaurants). Visitors to Ireland also place a high value on the range and quality of Irish seafood. For many, a trip to Ireland wouldn't be complete without sampling a few oysters and sinking a pint of the black stuff.

Wonderful seafood is found in a vast range of establishments, from award winning restaurants to hotels, little bistros and pubs. Locally caught seafood is especially good and is often flagged on the menu. Seafood is incredibly versatile, allowing chefs to creative innovative dishes suitable

for all meal occasions whether it's a breakfast, light lunch, quick snack or gourmet dinner. Irish seafood is renowned for its quality and flavour and is much sought after in markets worldwide. Smoked Irish salmon finds a ready market in France, Italy and Germany while Irish mussels are enjoyed as far afield as the west coast of America. Pub goers in Toyko are snacking on Irish crab, salmon and mussels and in Spain monkfish and hake from Irish waters are snapped up.

BIM Seafood Circle

Looking for delicious moules marinière in a seafront restaurant, a sumptuous seafood platter in a cosy pub or just a hearty bowl of chowder at lunchtime? For the best places to buy and enjoy seafood just look for the Seafood Circle.

Bord Iascaigh Mhara (Irish Sea Fisheries Board) initially developed the BIM Seafood Circle initiative to encourage publicans to serve seafood dishes at lunchtime, a meal at which many people prefer to choose lighter, healthier dishes. This initiative has been further developed in conjunction with Georgina Campbell Guides to encompass not only pubs, but also restaurants and hotels. Seafood Circle membership is awarded on an annual basis and is subject to meeting the necessary criteria.

Check out the listings in this guide and you'll find top quality, innovative, delicious seafood dishes in the establishments carrying the distinctive Seafood Circle logo.

And if you fancy yourself as a seafood chef then watch out for the Seafood Circle specialist/

seafood counter logos in fish shops around the country or check **www.seafoodcircle.ie** for a listing. Shops displaying the logo offer a range of top quality seafood and you'll be assisted by knowledgeable, professional staff.

Seafood, the healthy option

Nutritionists recommend that we eat seafood at least twice a week. Apart from tasting great, it is packed with protein, minerals, vitamins and essential Omega 3's, providing many of the nutrients we need for good health. BIM has developed a range of information materials on the health benefits of fish consumption. Visit **www.bim.ie/wellbeing** for nutritional information and great recipe ideas.

Old-fashioned Fish Bake

The timelessness of simple, traditional seafood dishes explains their enduring popularity. Almost every seafood restaurant will have its own a speciality chowder, for e xample, and many will also have a unique recipe for a fish pie or bake. Serves 4

450-675g/1-1½ lbs smoked cod fillet

30g/1oz butter

2 leeks - washed well and thinly sliced

30g/1oz flour

300ml/½ pint milk

2 tablespoons cream

Freshly milled pepper

Bay leaf

Chopped parsley

30g/1oz grated cheddar cheese

Generously grease a pie dish with butter.

Cut the fish in portions and place in the pie dish.

Melt the weighed butter in a saucepan, then add the leeks. Cook gently for 2 minutes until softening slightly.

Add in the flour, blend in with a wooden spoon and cook gently for 1 minute.

Gradually add the milk and cream, and bring to the boil over moderate heat, whisking to blend and prevent lumps forming. Season with a grinding of pepper.

Pour the sauce over fish, and add the bay leaf.

Cover and bake in a moderate oven 180°C/350°F/Gas 4 for 25 minutes

Remove the cover, sprinkle cheese over the fish, and return to oven to brown.

Garnish with chopped parsley, then serve with boiled potatoes and fresh vegetables.

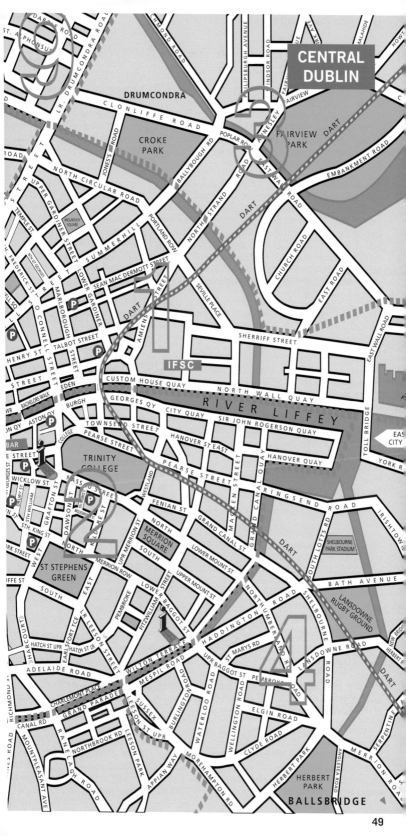

DRUMCONDRA

CROKE PARK

FAIRVIEW PARK

DART

DART

DART

DART

DART

DART

MOUNTJOY SQUARE

KING GEORGES

IFSC

RIVER LIFFEY

EAST CITY

TEMPLE BAR

TRINITY COLLEGE

MERRION SQUARE

NORTH

SOUTH

ST STEPHENS GREEN

SHELBOURNE PARK STADIUM

LANSDOWNE RUGBY GROUND

HERBERT PARK

BALLSBRIDGE

Streets and roads (as labelled):

DART ROAD, ST. ALPHONSU, LR. DRUMCONDRA ROAD, DRUMCONDRA ROAD, CLONLIFFE ROAD, RICHMOND ROAD, PHILIPSBURGH AVENUE, WINDSOR ROAD, FAIRVIEW, HOWTH, CLONLIFFE ROAD, POPLAR RD, ANNESLEY, FAIRVIEW, EMBANKMENT ROAD, NORTH CIRCULAR ROAD, JONES'S ROAD, BALLYBOUGH RD, ANNESLEY ROAD, EAST WALL, UPPER GARDINER STREET, TEMPLE ST, SUMMERHILL, PORTLAND ROW, NORTH STRAND, CHURCH ROAD, EAST ROAD, SEVILLE PLACE, SEAN MAC DERMOTT STREET, LOWER GARDINER, AMIENS STREET, SHERRIFF STREET, EAST WALL ROAD, MARLBOROUGH STREET, TALBOT STREET, HENRY ST, EDEN, CUSTOM HOUSE QUAY, NORTH WALL QUAY, BACHELORS WALK, BURGH, GEORGES QY, CITY QUAY, SIR JOHN ROGERSON QUAY, TOLL BRIDGE, YORK R, ASTON QY, TOWNSEND STREET, HANOVER ST EAST, HANOVER QUAY, PEARSE STREET, COLLEGE, WESTLAND, FENIAN ST, GRAND CANAL QUAY, MACKEN STREET, RINGSEND ROAD, LOTTS RD, IRISHTOWN, WICKLOW ST, DRURY ST, STH WILLIAM, KILDARE ST, DAWSON, GRAFTON ST, STH KING ST, NASSAU STREET, MOLESWORTH, NORTH MERRION SQUARE SOUTH, LOWER MOUNT ST, UPPER MOUNT ST, NORTH UMBERLAND ROAD, SHELBOURNE ROAD, BATH AVENUE, YORK STREET, WEST, MERRION ROW, PEMBROKE, LR LEESON STREET, FITZWILLIAM STREET, LOWER BAGGOT ST, HADDINGTON ROAD, ST MARYS RD, LANSDOWNE ROAD, HATCH ST UPR, HATCH ST LR, EARLSFORT TCE, WILTON TERRACE, UPR BAGGOT ST, PEMBROKE ROAD, ELGIN ROAD, ADELAIDE ROAD, MESPIL ROAD, WATERLOO ROAD, WELLINGTON ROAD, CLYDE ROAD, HERBERT PARK, MERRION ROAD, ANGLESEA ROAD, SERPENTINE, CHARLEMONT PLACE, GRAND PARADE, SUSSEX, BURLINGTON ROAD, MORE HAMPTON RD, CANAL RD, LEESON ST UPR, SUSSEX RD, RICHMOND, MOUNTPLEASANT AVE, NORTHBROOK RD, LEESON PARK, RANELAGH ROAD, APPIAN WAY

DUBLIN *A Town for our Times*

As one of Europe's fastest expanding economic centres, Dublin's commercial and creative energy is matched by the vibrancy of its everyday life and hospitality. It's an old town where many meandering stories have interacted and combined to create today's busy riverside and coastal metropolis. Through a wide variety of circumstances, it has become an entertaining place suited to the civilised enjoyment of life in the 21st Century. That said, there's no doubting the edge there is to life in Dublin today - international business news and global movements in property values attract as much popular interest as sport, politics and gossip.

With so much of it about, most Dubliners wear their city's history lightly in an environment where the past lives with the present in ancient monuments, historic buildings, gracious squares and fine old urban style that still manages to be gloriously alive. This if anything is emphasised by the city's modern architecture, seen particularly in the area around the International Financial Services Centre north of the river, and across the Liffey on George's Quay. Further development is taking place along both sides of the Liffey towards the Bay. And though the city's official municipal spirit is expressed through The Spire in O'Connell Street, Dubliners themselves prefer to take their inspiration from the twin powerstation smokestacks of 1974 vintage – Laurel and Hardy - down at the rivermouth on the sea. Needless to say they caused disputation when they were being built, but now it seems most Dubs are quite fond of them.

The city and Ireland's spirit is also expressed in the Gaelic Athletic Association's impressive headquarters stadium at Croke Park which can accommodate over 80,000 spectators for several sports, while the legendary Lansdowne Road rugby stadium south of the river is being completely re-built as a 50,000 seater.

Dubliners may seem to take this dynamic interaction of ancient, classic and modern for granted, but then they have to get on with life. They've a vigorous appetite for it. So they'll quickly deflate any visitor's excessive enthusiasm about their city's significance with some throwaway line of Dublin wit, or sweep aside some highfalutin notions about legendary figures of supposed cultural importance by recalling how their grandfathers had the measure of that same character when he was still no more than a pup making a nuisance of himself in the neighbourhood pub. Dubliners are well aware that it's a good thing for writers to be unhappy, but you can have too much of a good thing.

The origins of the city's name are in keeping with this downbeat approach. From the ancient Irish there came something which derived from a makeshift solution to local inconvenience. Baile Atha Cliath - the official name in recent times - means nothing more exciting than "the townland of the hurdle ford". Ancient Ireland being an open plan sort of place without towns, the site of the future city was no more than a river crossing with several comfortable monasteries in the neighbourhood

But where the residents saw some inconvenience in the river, the Vikings sensed an opportunity. When they brought their longships up the River Liffey around 837AD having first raided at nearby Lambay in 795, they knew of a sheltered berth in a place which the locals of the hurdle ford called Dubh Linn - "the black pool". The Vikings settled along Wood Quay and around Dublin Castle. This living memory of this busy Viking capital was celebrated in 2006 with the arrival under sail and oar in Dublin from Denmark of the 29.4 metres longship Sea Stallion of Glendalough, which had been re-created at the ancient Viking central capital of Roskilde as a remarkably exact facsimile of the original, built in Dublin in 1042 with timber from County Wicklow

Exhibited in the impressive museum in Collins Barrack until July 2008, Sea Stallion represents a Dublin creation of the 11th Century in an 18th Century setting. With a voyage back to Denmark scheduled for July 2008, the beautiful vessel's hull resemblance to a Venetian gondola is a tangible reminder of the enormous extent of the Viking world at its peak, though it was already declining in Ireland in 1042 as the raiders became absorbed into the population. Dublin was the Viking trading empire's western capital at a time when the eastern capital was to be found far into Russia, with sea power extended deep into the Mediterranean and through the Adriatic to the future location of Venice.

Although the name of Ireland's main Viking port was to go through mutations as the Vikings were succeeded in mnanagement by the Normans who in turn were in the business of becoming English and then more Irish than the Irish themselves, today's name of Dublin is the one the Vikings came upon - though the pre-Viking Irish would have pronounced it as something more like "doo-lin". With the Normans putting manners about the place, the descendants of Vikings and their Irish kinsfolk tended to move north of the Liffey where Oxmantown was Eastmantown – the Danes were the Eastmen while the Norwegian were the Northmen or Norsemen or Normans, and sometimes all three.

It was confusing for those who wanted to get on with day-to-day life in Dublin, but some sense of it was made with the Liffey divide which still prevails today in Dublin's northside-southside interface, though analysts suggest that it is now becoming more east-west, with the M50 and Dublin's coastal regions providing a barrier which the Normans knew as The Pale, a name which in itself has survived through various permutations of English power.

Be that as it may, the name Dublin still works best, for it was thanks to the existence of the black pool in the Liffey that Dublin became the port, trading base and cultural focus which evolved as the country's natural administrative centre. Thus your Dubliner may well think that the persistent official use of Baile Atha Cliath was an absurdity. But it isn't the business of any visitor to say so, for although Dublin came into existence through socioeconomic and historical pressures, it has been around for quite some time, and Dubliners have developed their own attitudes and their own way of doing things.

As for their seaport, it is still very much part of the city, and has never been busier – with forty major ship movements every day, sea and city are closely intertwined. However, Dublin Port is becoming a people-oriented transit focus, a giant ferry and cruise-liner port in the midst of residential, hospitality, administrative, business, service, entertainment and cultural centres. The opening of the Port Tunnel at the end of 2006 is ultimately about providing convenient access for city folk to Dublin Airport north of the city. In time, container freight will go to other developing purpose-built facilities, such as Bremore north along the east coast between Balbriggan and Drogheda, and several established ports to the southeast such as Rosslare, New Ross, and Bellview near Waterford.

Located beside a wide bay with some extraordinarily handsome hills and mountains near at hand, the city has long had as an important part of its makeup the dictates of stylish living, and the need to cater efficiently for individual tastes and requirements. From time to time the facade has been maintained through periods of impoverishment, but even in the earliest Mediaeval period this was already a major centre of craftsmanship and innovative shop-keeping. Today, the Dublin craftsmen and shop-keepers and their assistants are characterful subjects worthy of respectful academic study. And in an age when "going shopping" has become the world's favourite leisure activity, this old city has reinvented herself in the forefront of international trends.

Dublin virtually shunned the heavier side of the Industrial Revolution, or at least took some care to ensure that it happened elsewhere. More recently, the growth of computer-related industries was a very Dublin thing – what better way to deal with the vagaries of the Irish weather than in a workplace which had to be climate-controlled? And in times past, the city's few large enterprises tended to be aimed at personal needs and the consumer market, rather than some aspiration towards heavy industry. Typical of them was Guinness's Brewery, founded in 1759. Today, its work-force may be much slimmed in every sense, but it still creates the black nectar, and if a new mash is under way up at the brewery and the wind is coming damply across Ireland from the west, the aroma of Guinness in the making will be wafted right into the city centre, the moist evocative essence of Anna Livia herself. Doubtless the aroma can be re-created should it prove economically necessary to move the brewing to an out-of-town site, meanwhile the imaginatively renovated Guinness Storehouse - with its interactive museums, restaurants and bars - provides a visitor centre of international quality.

Although some of the vitality of the city faded in the periods when the focus of power had been moved elsewhere, today Dublin thrives as one of Europe's more entertaining capitals. While it may be trite to suggest that her history has been a fortuitous preparation for the needs of modern urban life in all its variety of work and relaxation, there is no denying Dublin's remarkable capacity to provide the ideal circumstances for fast-moving people-orientated modern industries, even if those same people find at times that their movement within the city is hampered by weight of traffic. Nevertheless it's a civilised city where the importance of education is a central theme of the strong family ethos, this high level of education making it a place of potent attraction in the age of information technology.

Such a city naturally has much of interest for historians of all kinds, and a vibrant cultural life is available for visitors and Dubliners alike. You can immerse yourself in it all as much or as little as you prefer, for today's Dublin is a city for all times and all tastes, and if you're someone who hopes to enjoy Dublin as we know Dubliners enjoy it, we know you'll find much of value here. And don't forget that there's enjoyment in Dublin well hidden from the familiar tourist trails.

History is well-matched by modernity, or a mixture of both. The glass palaces of the International Financial Services Centre point the way to a maturing new business district which is a village in itself. Upriver to the westward, the award-winning transformation of the Smithfield area encompasses the popular Old Jameson Distillery Visitor Centre, another magnet for the discerning visitor - particularly someone who enjoys a sense of the past interacting with the present, not least in the age-old story of the creation of whiskey. The revitalisation of the Smithfield area has succeeded in creating its own special dynamic, and it's clearly attractive for today's new Dubliners.

When Dublin was starting to expand to its present size during the mid-20th Century, with people flocking in from all over Ireland to work in the city, it was said that the only "real Dub" was someone who didn't go home to the country for the weekend. Nowadays, with Dublin so popular with visitors, the more cynical citizens have suggested that the surest test of a real Dub is someone who avoids Temple Bar, but here too the city's instinct for community has re-asserted itself.

So it's rather unfair of any Dubliner to dismiss Temple Bar's bustling riverside hotbed of musical pubs, ethnic restaurants, cultural events and nightclubs as being no more than a tourist ghetto. After all, in addition to its many places of entertainment and hospitality, Temple Bar is also home to at least 1,300 people, and they've their own neighbourhood Food Fairs and Specialist Markets like all other Dublin villages.

So there's real life here too. And at the very least, it is Temple Bar which maintains Dubliners' international reputation as round-the-clock party animals, which they're quite happy to acknowledge - just don't expect them to do it themselves. Another thing they don't do is form an orderly queue. In fact, they don't queue at all. Any real Dub reckons that queuing is a clear sign of mismanagement of personal time and endeavour. They make alternative arrangements.

As to meeting them if you haven't made prior rendezvous arrangements, well – perhaps. Come nightfall, and your discerning Dubliner is more likely to be found in a pleasant pub or restaurant in one of the city's many urban villages, places such as Ranelagh or Rathmines or Templeogue or Stoneybatter or Phibsborough or Donnybrook or Glasnevin or Ringsend or Dundrum or Clontarf or Drumcondra or Chapelizod. And then there are places like Stepaside or Howth or Glasthule or Foxrock or Dalkey which are at sufficient distance as scarcely to think of themselves as being part of Dublin at all.

Or perhaps your Dubliner is into sport – nearly everyone is. If it's a stadium sport – fine, you pay your way in like everyone else. There's horse racing and greyhound racing too. That's where you'll find today's real Dubs enjoying their fair city every bit as much as city centre folk. That is, if they're not sailing on The Bay or playing golf. There are so many golf links and courses that it might be possible to play from one side of the city to the other, and as for boating and sailing – well, Dublin is only half of a circle, the other half is the sea, and the interaction between the two is mighty, as they'd say in Dublin.

Happy is the visitor who is able to savour it all, in and around this town for our times. If you do see it all, don't tell us – we haven't seen the most of it ourselves.

Local Attractions & Information

Abbey & Peacock Theatres Lower Abbey Street, Dublin 1	01 878 7222
The Ark Arts Centre Eustace Street, Temple Bar, Dublin 2	01 670 7788
Bank of Ireland (historic), College Green, Dublin 2	01 661 5933
Botanic Gardens Glasnevin, Dublin 9	01 837 4388 / 804 0300
Christchurch Cathedral Christchurch Place, Dublin 8	01 677 8099
City Arts Centre 23-25 Moss Street, Dublin 2	01 677 0643
Croke Park GAA Stadium and Museum, Dublin 3	01 819 2300
Drimnagh Castle (moat, formal 17c gardens) Longmile Road	01 450 2530
Dublin Airport	01 814 4222
Dublin Castle, Dame Street	01 677 7129 / 645 8813
Dublin Film Festival (April)	01 635 0290
Dublin Garden Festival, RDS (June)	01 668 0866
Dublin International Horse Show, RDS (August)	01 668 0866
Dublin International Organ & Choral Festival (June)	01 677 3066
Dublin Theatre Festival (October)	01 677 8439 / 677 8899
Dublin Tourism Centre (restored church) Suffolk Street	01 605 7700
Dublin Writer's Museum, Parnell Square	01 872 2077
Dublinia (living history) Christchurch	01 679 4611
Farmleigh House, Phoenix Park	01 815 5900
Farmleigh House, Boathouse Restaurant	01 815 7255 / 815 7250
Gaiety Theatre, South King Street	01 677 1717
Gate Theatre, Cavendish Row	01 874 4045

Guinness Brewery, St Jame's Gate	01 453 6700 ext 5155
Guinness Storehouse	01 408 4800
Helix DCU Performing Arts Centre, Collins Avenue, Dublin 9	01 700 7000
Hugh Lane Municipal Gallery, Parnell Square	01 874 1903
Irish Antique Dealers Fair, RDS (October)	01 668 0866
Irish Film Centre, Eustace Street	01 679 3477
Irish Museum of Modern Art/Royal Hospital Kilmainham	01 612 9900
Irish Music Hall of Fame, Middle Abbey Street	01 878 3345
Irish Tourist Board/Failte Ireland, Baggot Street Bridge	01 602 4000
Iveagh Gardens, Earlsfort Terrace	01 475 7816
Jameson Distillery Smithfield, Dublin 7	01 807 2355
Kilmainham Gaol, Kilmainham	01 453 5984
Irish Rugby Football Union, Ballsbridge	01 668 4601
Mother Redcaps Market, nr St Patricks/Christchurch (Fri-Sun 10am-5.30pm)	01 454 0656
National Botanic Gardens, Glasnevin	01 837 7596
National Concert Hall, Earlsfort Terrace	01 417 0077
National Gallery of Ireland, Merrion Square West	01 661 5133
National Museum of Ireland, Kildare Street	01 677 7444
National Museum of Ireland, Collins Barracks	01 677 7444
Natural History Museum, Merrion Street	01 677 7444
Newman House, St Stephen's Green	01 475 7255
Northern Ireland Tourist Board, Nassau Street	01 679 1977
Number 29, (18c House) Lower Fitzwilliam Street	01 702 6165
Olympia Theatre, Dame Street	01 679 3323
Pearse Street Market, (St Andrew's Cntr.) Sats 9am-3pm	01 087 630 3839
Point Depot (Concerts & Exhibitions), North Wall Quay	01 836 6777
Powerscourt Townhouse, South William Street	01 671 7000
Pro Cathedral, Marlborough Street	01 874 5441
Project Arts Centre, 39 East Sussex Street, Dublin 2	01 881 9613
RDS (Royal Dublin Society), Ballsbridge	01 668 0866
Royal Hospital Kilmainham	01 679 8666
St Michans Church (mummified remains), Dublin 7	01 872 4154
St Patrick's Cathedral, Patrick's Close	01 475 4817
Shaw birthplace, 33 Synge Street, Dublin 8	01 475 0854
Shelbourne Park, Greyhound Stadium	01 668 3502
Temple Bar Foodmarket (Saturday morning)	01 677 2255
Tivoli Theatre, Francis Street	01 454 4472
Trinity College (Book of Kells & Dublin Experience)	01 608 2308 / 896 1000
Viking Adventure, Essex Street W, Temple Bar	01 679 6040
Viking Splash (Amphibious Tours)	01 453 9185
War Memorial Gardens (Sir Edwin Lutyens), Islandbridge	01 677 0236
Zoological Gardens, Phoenix Park	01 474 8900

DUBLIN 1

Newly re-opened in the area after a multi-million Euro revamp, the **Accademy Plaza Hotel** (01 878 0666; www.academyplazahotel.ie) offers excellent facilities in a prime location off O'Connell Street; also in the area are budget hotels **Comfort Inn** (Parnell Square; 01 873 7700) and **Jurys Inn** (Parnell Street; 01 878 4900); the **Hugh Lane Gallery** on Parnell Square has a restaurant, **Blas** (Mon-Sat 10-6 pm, Sun 10.30-5) and there is also a café at the **Writers' Museum** (Mon-Sat 10-5). The Moore Street/Parnell Street area is well known for its street markets and specialist food shops catering for an increasingly cosmopolitan population - it has become a hothouse of international flavours and is a place to wander for authentic, keenly priced food from different cultures. The area has many great value ethnic restaurants, including: **Cactus Jack's** (Millennium Way; 01 874 6198): one of a small chain of above average Tex-Mex restaurants (also at Tallaght & Galway City). **China House** (Parnell Street, 01 873 3870); friendly, authentic, very good value Chinese; **Hanyang** (Parnell Street 01 874 6144): authentic Korean cuisine & hospitality, beside the **Ice Bar** Asian pub; **Alilang Korean Restaurant** (Parnell Street; 01 874 6766) serves tasty and exceptionally reasonably priced food endorsed by the local Asian community who frequent it. **Radha Govinda's** (Middle Abbey Street; 01 872 9861) Hare Krishna restaurant serving wholesome, inexpensive vegetarian food. While in this part of town be sure to drop into **Sheridans Foodhall** (Henry Street; 01 804 5878) in Arnotts department store, they have wonderful range of meats, cheeses and other artisan products to take away - a picnic in one of the many parks nearby may be just the ticket. Alternatively **Ristorante Romano** (Capel Street; 01 872 6868) is a simple cafe-style restaurant with great home cooking that is widely recognised as one the best value Italian restaurants in town, especially at lunch. For those with a thirst that needs quenching in interesting surroundings, the **John M. Keating Pub** (Mary Street; 01 828 0102) is in an old converted church with an impressive contemporary interior. The old has been meticulously restored and the new sits easily against it, a testament to brilliant design.

Dublin 1
RESTAURANT
🍴 🄴 🅢🄵

101 Talbot Restaurant

100-102 Talbot Street Dublin 1 **Tel: 01 874 5011**
www.101talbot.com

féile bia Here a decade ahead of the gold rush to service the growing needs of the International Financial Services Centre, good cooking, good value and promising menus are at the heart of Margaret Duffy and Pascal Bradley's pioneering northside restaurant. While the nearby Abbey and Gate Theatres and the constantly changing art exhibitions in the restaurant are partly responsible for drawing an artistic/theatrical crowd, it is essentially their creative and healthy food that has earned the 101 such a fine reputation. Mediterranean/Middle Eastern influences explain the unique wholesomeness across the range of dishes, with six to eight choices on each course, always including strong vegetarian options. Dietary requirements are always willingly met. Interesting food, friendly staff, good complimentary breads, helpful menu advice - and very reasonable prices - ensure the continuing success of this popular restaurant. Don't expect lavish decor - and try to ignore the drabness of Talbot Street. Children welcome before 8pm. **Seats 80.** Open Tue-Sat, 5-11. A la carte. Early D €21.50 (5-8, all evening Wed), Set D 2/3 course €30/35. House Wine €18.95. Closed Sun & Mon, Christmas. Amex, MasterCard, Visa, Laser. **Directions:** 5 minutes walk between Connolly Station and O'Connell Street. Straight down from the Spire.

BLOOMS LANE

Known variously as the Italian Quarter (reflecting the collection of Italian-inspired establishments that have congregated here), occasionally as 'Quartier Bloom', sometimes as 'Mick Wallaces' (after the inspired developer who created it), or, more usually, simply by its address, this stylish food court off the north quays is home to some interesting restaurants, cafés and shops. It's at its best on Friday night or Saturday lunchtime; on Saturday evening (unless the Italians have won a huge sporting event that day) it's more 'gloom' than 'Bloom', the street is dark and uninviting, and some atmospheric lighting is needed, to dispel a spooky 'Victorian Whitechapel' feeling. **Enoteca delle Langhe** (01 888 0834), an appealing shop-cum-wine bar, was one of the first to open; food, while not exactly incidental, plays second fiddle to the wines here, but they carry a good range of dried Italian meats, cheeses, panini etc, and you can sit at a sturdy wooden table and have something by the glass (or choose any bottle, plus 10%), and a bite from a limited but interesting selection of quality food. It's all very relaxed and sociable, prices are reasonable - and it's a pleasant way to shop for wine. Nearby you will also find other like-minded outlets like **Wallaces Italian Food Shop**, **Café Cagliostro** (great coffees), a juice café and **Taverna di Bacco** (01 873 0040), a dark and atmospheric restaurant, which offers an interesting menu and authentic ingredient-led Italian food, including great antipasta, unusual variations on risotto, handmade pasta dishes and really good coffees And many people head here specially to eat in **Bar Italia** (01 874 1000) chaotic, warm, real food, great coffee, it's the essence of Italy minus cheap local wine. With good restaurants, an excellent deli and the bustling daytime café, Blooms Lane makes a great addition to the atmospherics of Dublin.

WWW.IRELAND-GUIDE.COM FOR THE BEST PLACES TO EAT, DRINK & STAY

Dublin 1
RESTAURANT
★ ☺ ☺

Chapter One Restaurant

18/19 Parnell Square Dublin 1 **Tel: 01 873 2266**
info@chapteronerestaurant.com www.chapteronerestaurant.com

téile *bia* In the former home of the great John Jameson of whiskey fame, Chapter One was our Restaurant of the Year way back in 2001 when everybody thought southside was the place to be. Since then many others have discovered that one of Ireland's finest restaurant resides in this arched basement beneath the Irish Writers Museum and - despite being the darling of the media these days - it remains the Guide's favourite when dining out in Dublin. Together with an exceptional team including head chef Garrett Byrne, restaurant manager Declan Maxwell and sommelier Ian Brosnan, the proprietors - chef-patron Ross Lewis and front of house manager Martin Corbett - have earned an enviable reputation here, for outstanding modern Irish cooking and superb service from friendly and well-informed staff. It's an atmospheric room with original granite walls and old brickwork contrasting with elegant modern décor. A recent revamp has seen the comfy reception area halved in size: it's still a smart place for an aperitif but has made way for a larger dining room and a few more tables - good news indeed for those struggling to get a booking. The cooking - classic French lightly tempered by modern influences - showcases specialist Irish produce whenever possible, notably on a magnificent charcuterie trolley, which showcases West Cork producer Fingal Ferguson, among others, and is a treat not to be missed. Another unusual speciality is a fish plate which is a carefully balanced compilation of five individual fish and seafood dishes, served with melba toast. Other specialities include slow cooked meat - a sweet-flavoured shoulder of spring lamb, for example, with creamed onion and curry spice, roast carrot and garlic, kidney, and boulangère potato - and, of course, a cheese menu offering farmhouse cheeses in peak condition. But many guests will stall at dessert, as an utterly irresistible choice of half a dozen delectable dishes is offered, each with its own dessert wine or champagne... An excellent wine list leans towards the classics and offers many fairly priced treats for the wine buff, and also carefully selected house wines and wines by the glass, including a range of dessert wines. Another special treat is the perfectly timed pre-theatre menu, for which Chapter One is rightly renowned: depart for one of the nearby theatres after your main course, and return for dessert after the performance - perfect timing, every time. Like the lunch menu, early dinner offers outstanding value. Small conferences. Air conditioning. Children welcome. **Seats 85** (private rooms,16 & 20). L Tue-Fri, 12.30-2.30, D Tue-Sat, 6-10.45. Set L €35. Pre-theatre menu €32.50 (6-6.30); Set D €57.50; also à la carte (Tasting Menu, for entire parties, €70). House wine €24.50. SC discretionary. Closed L Sat, all Sun & Mon, 2 weeks Christmas, 2 weeks August. MasterCard, Visa, Laser. **Directions:** Top of O'Connell Street, north side of Parnell Square, opposite Garden of Remembrance, beside Hugh Lane Gallery.

Dublin 1
HOTEL/RESTAURANT
☺ 🏛

Clarion Hotel IFSC

Excise Walk IFSC Dublin 1 **Tel: 01 433 8800**
info@clarionhotelifsc.com www.clarionhotelsireland.com

téile *bia* This dashing contemporary hotel on the river side of the International Financial Services Centre was the first in the area to be built specifically for the mature 'city' district and its high standards and central location have proved very popular with leisure guests, as well as business guests and the financial community, especially at weekends. Bright, airy and spacious, the style is refreshingly clean-lined yet comfortable, with lots of gentle neutrals and a somewhat eastern feel that is emphasised by the food philosophy of the hotel - a waft of lemongrass and ginger in the open plan public areas entices guests through to the Kudos Bar, where Asian wok cooking is served; the smart casual Kudos Restaurant also features world cuisine, but with more European influences. Uncluttered suites and bedrooms have everything the modern traveller could want, including a high level of security, air conditioning, generous semi-orthopaedic beds and excellent bathrooms with top quality toiletries. There is a sense of thoughtful planning to every aspect of the hotel, and helpful, well-trained staff show a real desire to ensure the comfort of guests. Clarion Hotel Dublin IFSC was our Business Hotel of the Year in 2002. **Rooms 163** (17 suites, 50 executive, 80 no smoking, 8 disabled, 5 family rooms). B&B about €132.50 pps. Room rate €265, no SC. **Kudos Bar & Restaurant:** Mon-Fri,12-8; **Sinergie Restaurant:** L Mon-Fri 12.30-2.30, D daily, 6-9.45. Set L about €12.95; Early D about €19.95 (6-7.30); D about €19.95-€24.95, also à la carte. House wines, from €23. Sinergie closed L Sat. Kudos no food Sun. [* Comfort Inn, Talbot Street (Tel: 01-874 9202) is in the same group and offers budget accommodation near the IFSC.] Amex, Diners, MasterCard, Visa, Laser. **Directions:** Overlooking the River Liffey in the IFSC. ◇

Dublin 1

RESTAURANT/WINE BAR

ely chq

CHQ IFSC Dublin 1 **Tel: 01 672 0010**
chq@elywinebar.com   www.elywinebar.ie

Ely CHQ (Customs House Quay) is a younger sister of the original Ely off St Stephen's Green and older one to Ely HQ on the south quay (see entries); the style reflects the dashing contemporary architecture of the IFSC and the (very large) space includes an authentic expansive vaulted basement area, as well as a bright, open ground floor space and a covered terrace where tables are in great demand in summer. The successful Ely theme of simple organic food appealingly presented (including meats from the Robson family farm in County Clare) has been continued at the new venue: the burger is quite simply the best in town; pure unadulterated prime meat. Seafood is zingingly sea-fresh and you could even be lucky enough to have a pleasant, efficient Italian waiter commandeer an 'espresso' with thick crema that would be appreciated in Naples or Milan, let alone Dublin's northside. But it is their great wine list and, especially, an unrivalled choice of nearly a hundred wines offered by the glass - that makes Ely such an exceptional dining destination. This allows diners to taste a huge range of wines that might otherwise be inaccessible - and every dish offered on the lunch and à la carte menus has a suggested glass of wine to accompany. The wine list runs to over 500 bottles and mirrors that of the original Ely, being both well thought out and comprehensive, with many old favourites available. There is also a carefully selected beer list and you can even buy a Laguiole corkscrew ('guaranteed for life') and machine washable wine glasses to take home. Dine outside if the weather allows, with bright views of the dock and the Liffey it can be a magic spot. * Ely chq was the winner of our 2007 Wine Award of the Year. **Seats 150** (private rooms to 100, outdoors, 50); children welcome before; Food served all day 12-11pm; L&D daily: Mon-Sat 12-3 & 4.30-11.00; Sun 12-4 & 6-10; set L, €35, set D €45; also a la carte; SC 12.5% on groups 6+. Closed Christmas week. Amex, Diners, MasterCard, Visa, Laser. **Directions:** On the banks of the Liffey, overlooking Georges Dock, 2 mins from Connolly Station.

Dublin 1

EPICUREAN FOOD HALL

Lr Liffey Street Dublin 1

On the corner of Liffey Street and Middle Abbey Street, The Epicurean Food Hall is a buzzy place bringing together a collection of small units with a common seating area where you will find a wide range of gourmet foods, cooked and uncooked - and the wines to go with them. The hall is open during the day every day (opens later on Sunday, remains open for late shoppers on Thursday evening); it's an enjoyable place to browse - there are lots of lovely little shops and cafés in the hall, including a good choice of ethnic ones, and they quite often change so these long-established tenants are just a taster: **La Corte** (01 873 4200) is one of two north river outposts of Stefano Crescenzi and David Izzo's smart Italian café (see entry). **Itsabagel** (Tel 01 874 0486): Domini and Peaches Kemps' classy bagel bar offeres authentic New York bagels, savoury breads with fillings, juices, muffins and cookies and is very popular with discerning lunchtime browsers (also at The Pavilion, Dun Laoghaire). **Directions:** On the corner of Liffey Street and Middle Abbey Street.

Dublin 1
RESTAURANT

Floridita

Irish Life Mall Lower Abbey Street Dublin 1 **Tel: 01 878 1032**
info@floriditadublin.com www.floridita.co.uk/dublin

téile bia Located in the Irish Life Mall, probably the least likely spot for an exotic Cuban restaurant, Floridita is the fifth of the successful Floridita chains with branches in London, Madrid, Moscow and Cuba. Marketed as a bar and music venue as well as a restaurant, the first floor dining room features a giant tilted mirror which reflects the live bands from downstairs to the restaurant above. The décor evokes some of the 1950s style of Cuba, and the atmosphere reflects that of high octane Celtic Cubs at play. The traditional cocktail of choice is the mojito criollo made with churned fresh mint, lime juice and sugar, although there are plenty of other cocktails on offer. Traditional Cuban cuisine tends to reflect its peasant history so the menu borrows from further afield with South American and Spanish influences; Cuban dishes to try include deep fried tostones (plantains pounded flat and deep fried) and moros y christanos (Moors and Christians) a mix of black beans and rice. A great venue for a celebration especially when visiting Cuban bands are playing. **Seats 100.** Average starter €9.60, average main course €20 and average dessert €7. House wines from €26; by the glass from €6.50; cocktails from €9. SC 12.5% added to all bills. Open L Mon- Fri 12 to 3, D Mon Fri 5 to 9.30, Sat 5 to 10.30. Closed Sunday. Amex, MasterCard, Visa, Laser. **Directions:** In the Irish Life Mall off Abbey Street. ◇

Dublin 1
HOTEL/RESTAURANT

The Gresham

23 Upper O'Connell Street Dublin 1 **Tel: 01 874 6881**
info@thegresham.com www.gresham-hotels.com

téile bia At the centre of Dublin society since the early nineteenth century, the Gresham is one of the city's best business hotels. A recent makeover has transformed the ground floor, including the lobby lounge, a favourite meeting place renowned for its traditional afternoon tea; the Gresham and Toddy's bars are both popular meeting places and Toddy's, in particular, offers the kind of comfortable casual eating that was once the norm but is now increasingly hard to find in this busy city. Business guests will appreciate the refurbished bedrooms: 108 rooms have been transformed in executive contemporary style and all have good amenities. **Restaurant "23":** Dining options in the hotel include this smart and welcoming restaurant which offers good cooking and interested service. Knowledgeable young staff make this a useful place to know about, and the 2-course 'city' dinner menu offers good value. Conference/banqueting (350/280). Business centre; secretarial services; video conferencing. Fitness suite. Wheelchair access. Secure multi-storey parking. **Rooms 288** (4 suites, 2 junior suites, 96 executive, 60 no-smoking, 3 disabled); Children welcome (u12s €40 sharing with parents); Lifts. B&B about €175pps, ss up to €175. [Restaurant "23":D Mon-Sat 5.30-10.15, Early D about €26 5.30-7, also á la carte] Hotel open all year. Amex, Diners, MasterCard, Visa, Laser. **Directions:** City centre, on north side of the River Liffey. ◇

Dublin 1
BAR/RESTAURANT

The Harbourmaster Bar and Restaurant

IFSC Dublin 1
Tel: 01 670 1688

téile bia In a waterside setting at Dublin's thriving financial services centre, this old Dock Offices building has genuine character and makes a fine restaurant and bar. The bar itself is very busy at times, but there is also an impressive contemporary upstairs restaurant, The Greenhouse, in a modern extension which has been designed in sympathy with the original building. Most tables have an interesting (and increasingly attractive) view of the development outside but, as there are now several dining areas, it is wise to ensure you get to the right one on arrival. For fine weather, there's also a decked outdoor area overlooking the inner harbour and fountain, with extra seating. The Harbourmaster has that indefinable buzz that comes from being in the financial centre of a capital city and, while not necessarily a destination dining experience, the food is appropriately international and contemporary in style. **The Greenhouse Restaurant:** L, Mon-Fri. Restaurant closed evenings and weekends (except for functions). Bar open Mon-Wed, noon-closing daily (Sun 12.30-11) Brasserie food all day, daily. Closed 25 Dec & Good Fri. Amex, Diners, MasterCard, Visa. **Directions:** In IFSC, near Connolly train station. ◇

IFSC

The International Financial Services Centre (IFSC) is Dublin's relatively new banking and financial district that is situated between the River Liffey and Connolly Station. It is a bustling, lively area during the week with tens of thousands of people working there, and although at the weekends the area can be fairly quiet it is frequently livened up by a concert at the nearby Point Theatre or through festivals and similar activities that are held around the Docklands. The area has seen many restaurants and pubs mushroom over the last few years including: **Il Fornaio** (Valentia House Square; 01 672 1852): new and equally informal branch of the long-established authentic Italian pizzeria/restaurant in Kilbarrack, Dublin 5. **Insomnia** (Lr Mayor St, Custom House Quay; 01 671 8651): one of an excellent small chain of speciality coffee outlets around Dublin (some under the Bendini & Shaw brand), whose complementary speciality is sandwiches. Also at: Charlotte Way, Dublin 1; Ballsbridge, Dublin 4; Main Street Blackrock, Co Dublin; Pavilion SC Swords; Malahide. **Milano** (Clarion Quay; 01 611 9012): north quays branch of the stylish and reliable pizza & pasta restaurant chain. **Bar Italia IFSC** (Custom House Square; 01 670 2887) is the most recent arrival in the area; it is a little Italian café in the traditional trattoria style that is part of a popular small restaurant chain where prompt, efficient service and flavoursome food are the hallmarks. Recommended accommodation in the IFSC is in the **Clarion Hotel** (see entry) and **Jurys Custom House Inn** (see entry).

WWW.IRELAND-GUIDE.COM FOR THE BEST PLACES TO EAT, DRINK & STAY

Dublin 1   # Jurys Custom House Inn
HOTEL   Custom House Quay Dublin 1
Tel: 01 607 5000

féile bía Right beside the International Financial Services Centre, overlooking the Liffey and close to train, Luas and bus stations, this hotel meets the requirements of business guests with better facilities than is usual in budget hotels. Large bedrooms have all the expected facilities, but with a higher standard of finish than most of its sister hotels; fabrics and fittings are good quality and neat bathrooms are thoughtfully designed, with generous shelf space. As well as a large bar, there is a full restaurant on site, plus conference facilities for up to 100 and a staffed business centre. No room service. Adjacent multi-storey car park has direct access to the hotel. **Rooms 239.** Room Rate from c. €108 (max 3 guests); breakfast c. €8-10. Closed 24-26 Dec. Amex, Diners, MasterCard, Visa. **Directions:** IFSC, overlooking River Liffey. ◇

Dublin 1   # The Morrison Hotel & Halo Restaurant
HOTEL/RESTAURANT   Lower Ormond Quay Dublin 1 **Tel: 01 887 2400**
reservations@morrisonhotel.ie www.morrisonhotel.ie

féile bía Centrally located on the north quays, close to the Millennium Bridge over the River Liffey, this contemporary hotel is within walking distance of theatres, the main shopping areas and the financial district. When it opened in 1998 it was a first for Dublin, with striking 'east meets west' interiors created by the internationally renowned designer, John Rocha, and the same team oversaw a recent development programme with the addition of 48 new bedrooms and extensive conference and meeting facilities - designed around a calm Courtyard Garden, which makes an attractive venue for receptions, or pre-dinner drinks. Stylish public areas include the Café Bar - just the place for a cappuccino or cocktails - and there's a spa, offering holistic and relaxation treatments. Simple, cool bedroom design - the essence of orderly thinking - contrasts pleasingly with the more flamboyant style of public areas, and there is a welcome emphasis on comfort (Frette linen, Aveda toiletries, air conditioning); all rooms have complimentary broadband, Apple Mac plasma screen with keyboard, wireless mouse and surround sound, iPod docking stations and CD players, safe and mini-bar. Exceptionally friendly and helpful staff make every effort to provide the best possible service for guests, and complimentary room upgrades to studios and suites are given when available. Conferences (240). Not suitable for children. Pets permitted by arrangement. **Rooms 138** (12 suites, 6 junior suites, 38 shower only, 5 for disabled, 80 no smoking). Lift. Room service (24 hours). Room rate €340 (SC incl). No private parking (arrangement with nearby car park). Closed 23-27 Dec. **Halo:** This popular restaurant is next to the riverside entrance of the hotel, allowing diners a view over the river and the busy thoroughfare on the quays. The décor sends mixed messages (minimalist oriental stools set beside Georgian style claw-footed tables), but it is a relaxed, informal space and, under head chef Richie Wilson, there has been a change of cooking style; he is serving well thought out and accomplished modern dishes and, in particular, his fish dishes are excellent - examples recently enjoyed by the Guide included an excellent dish of king scallops with shallot purée and smoked bacon, all topped with delicious pea foam. Menus are not too long, and top quality ingredients are a feature; breads are all home made, and a signature dish of Irish Hereford beef with sautéed forest mushrooms, seared foie gras & tarragon mousse, indicates the sophisticated style. All the little niceties of a special meal are observed but without too much formality. A walk-in wine cellar is an unusual feature, where you can browse and take your pick (although no half bottles). As elsewhere in the hotel, good service is a feature: all male staff are dressed in black, and are very courteous and knowledgeable. The wine list includes a good number available by the glass, and four half bottles. **Seats 110** (private room, 22). Air conditioning. D daily 6-10.30pm; à la carte; house wine from €23.50. Amex, Diners, MasterCard, Visa, Laser, Switch. **Directions:** Located on the quays in the city centre beside the Millennium Bridge.

Dublin 1
Panem
CAFÉ
Ha'penny Bridge House 21 Lower Ormond Quay Dublin 1
Tel: 01 872 8510

Ann Murphy and Raffaele Cavallo's little bakery and café has been delighting discerning Dubliners - and providing a refuge from the thundering traffic along the quays outside - since 1996. Although tiny, it just oozes Italian chic - not surprisingly, perhaps, as Ann's Italian architect husband designed the interior - and was way ahead of its time in seeing potential north of the Liffey. Italian and French food is prepared on the premises from 3 am each day: melt-in-the-mouth croissants with savoury and sweet fillings, chocolate-filled brioches, traditional and fruit breads, filled foccacia breads are just a few of the temptations on offer. No cost is spared in sourcing the finest ingredients (Panem bread is baked freshly each day using organic flour) and special dietary needs are considered too: soups, for example, are usually suitable for vegans and hand-made biscuits - almond & hazelnut perhaps - for coeliacs. They import their own 100% arabica torrisi coffee from Sicily and hot chocolate is a speciality, made with the best Belgian dark chocolate. Simply superb. Open Mon-Fri, 8-6, Sat, 9-6 & Sun, 10-4.30. Closed 24 Dec-8 Jan. **No Credit Cards. Directions:** North quays, opposite Millennium Bridge. ◊

Dublin 1
Soup Dragon
CAFÉ
168 Capel Street Dublin 1 **Tel: 01 872 3277**
www.soupdragon.com

Although it may not be as inexpensive as you hope, this little place offers a stylish way to have a hot meal on a budget: a daily choice of soups and stews is available in three different sizes, with a medium portion and a selection of delicious home-made breads and a piece of fruit. Some change daily, while others stay on the menu for a week or a season. Typically there may be dahl (Indian lentil), potato & leek or carrot & coriander soup; or try something more substantial like beef chilli or a very fine Thai chicken curry from the blackboard menu. In line with their healthy philosophy, breakfasts offer a range of freshly squeezed drinks (Red Dragon: strawberry, raspberry and cranberry or home-made lemon & lime lemonade) and smoothies, all made to order so they taste fresh and vibrant. Desserts include old favourites like rice pudding (served with cream) and a range of unusual home-made ice creams. Food to go is also available, and a nice touch - they send customers on their way with a complimentary piece of fruit. * Also at 16-17 Ormonde Quay. **Seats 10.** Open Mon-Fri 8-5.30 & Sat 11-5. Closed Sun, bank hols, Christmas. [Opening times not confirmed at time of going to press.] **No Credit Cards. Directions:** Bridge at Capel Street. ◊

Dublin 1
The Vaults
BAR/RESTAURANT
Harbourmaster Place IFSC Dublin 1 **Tel: 01 605 4700**
info@thevaults.ie www.thevaults.ie

These ten soaring vaulted chambers underneath Connolly Station were built in the mid-19th century to support the railway and have since found many uses, including the storage of Jameson whiskey. In 2002 Michael Martin - previously best known as head chef of the Clarence Hotel restaurant, The Tea

Room - opened it as a multi-purpose venue. The atmosphere is intimate and welcoming and the vaults, which have been treated individually in styles ranging from sleek contemporary to neo-classical, also include some high tech audio visual equipment. Head chef Fraser O'Donnell ensures that everything is made from scratch - mainly grills, pizzas and pastas and his food is skilfully executed and beautifully presented. This place encapsulates the dramatic changes taking place north of the Liffey: simply stunning. Children welcome until 8pm. **Seats 180** (private room 90). (All spaces available to hire, for business or pleasure). Reservations accepted. Food served Mon-Fri 12-8, Sat 1-8. Various menus - lunch, afternoon/evening, Saturday brunch and Sunday roast - à la carte. Vegetarian dishes on main menu. SC 10%. House wine €19. Late night bar & club Fri/Sat to 02.30. Closed Sun, 24-30 Dec, Good Fri, Bank Hols. Amex, MasterCard, Visa, Laser. **Directions:** Under Connolly station; last stop on Luas red line.

Dublin 1
RESTAURANT

The Winding Stair

40 Lower Ormond Quay Dublin 1 **Tel: 01 872 7320**
www.winding-stair.com

This much-loved café and bookshop overlooking the Ha'penny Bridge re-opened in 2006 after a long closure and, to everybody's delight, it has turned out to be better than ever. Although now a proper restaurant with gleaming wine glasses and a fine new La Marzocco coffee machine, something of the old café atmosphere is still to be found in the wooden floorboards, bentwood chairs and simple tables - and, under the direction of Elaine Murphy, good management will ensure that you'll also find friendly staff. The talented young chef, Aine Maguire, is confirming early promise and succeeding in making a mark by sourcing the best possible ingredients and allowing sound cooking and simplicity to take its course. There's plenty of 'the organic and real' on menus that could include superb starters such as an Irish charcuterie plate (Connemara dry cured lamb and beef, salamis from the Gubbeen smokehouse in County Cork, accompanied by home made chutney & capers), and main dishes including outstanding renditions of classics such as bacon and cabbage with parsley sauce, and great seafood - and specials, such as undyed smoked haddock with a delicious white cheddar mash and onions. To finish, there's an excellent Irish farmhouse cheese selection and delicious seasonal desserts which, like the rest of the menu, are very fairly priced. An unusually interesting wine list is clearly put together by enthusiasts, and sourced from a variety of quality suppliers, and you could finish with a superb ristretto, pulled by someone who knows how to use the coffee machine. The Winding Stair is that rarity among Irish restaurants, serving simple, high quality food, and it has a lovely ambience. Aided by nostalgia, it also has loads of personality and has earned a loyal following - book a window table for a view of the river. Children welcome; **Seats 100;** L&D served daily, 12.30-3.30, 6-10.30pm (to 9.30pm Sun); a la carte; house wine from €24. Closed 25-26 Dec, Bank Hols. Amex, Diners, MasterCard, Visa, Laser. **Directions:** Beside Ha'penny Bridge.

Dublin 1
HOTEL

Wynns Hotel

35/39 Lower Abbey Street Dublin 1 **Tel: 01 874 5131**
info@wynnshotel.ie www.wynnshotel.ie

Traditionally a country people's hotel in Dublin city centre, this affordable, three-star hotel is just off O'Connell Street, with the Luas stopping just outside its door. There's a friendly welcome at reception, and they are accommodating, easily taking things like an early check-in in their stride. Rooms have recently been refurbished, are very comfortable for the price, with spotless bathrooms. The revamped dining room is bright and airy, with attentive staff and good, sensible food, which is also good value and the bar also serves good coffee, and plates of food if you wish. While you may have to queue for breakfast if you come later, it's worth the wait, with very efficient service, good tea - and lovely eggs Benedict, and properly grilled rashers. The clientele is likely to be a mixture of continental families, Parish Priests up from the country, sisters on a shopping spree, elderly aunts and young ones on their first date. Visitors are surprised to find a place like this. No glitz, just a very comfortable stay - the perfect hideaway, without breaking the bank. Complimentary valet parking. B&B about €65pps. MasterCard, Visa, Laser. **Directions:** Just off O'Connell Street. ◊

DUBLIN 2

Dublin 2 is the heart of Dublin's tourist region with more pubs, restaurants, clubs and attractions than any other part of town. This is the home to Temple Bar (see entry), Trinity College, the shopping of Grafton Street and peaceful park walks in St. Stephen's Green and the Iveagh Garden. **Papaya** (Ely Place, 01 676 0044) is a Thai restaurant serving all the usual Thai dishes, plus a few more unusual ones. **Chatham Brasserie** (Chatham Street, 01 679 0055) just off Grafton Street is a handy place to take a break from shopping with indoor and outdoor seating with a slightly French elegance offering wholesome, satisfying fare, served by friendly (mainly French) staff. Beside the St. Stephen's Green shopping centre **Wagamama** noodle bar (South King Street; 01 478 2152) is a noisy place full of groovy young things, who find it cool - both for the food and the interior. It is a huge basement canteen which is simple and functional - not a place for those who seek comfort or privacy - but strikingly designed with high ceilings and kids love it. All food served in Wagamama noodle bars is GMO free, portions are generous and the value is good. **Five** on South Anne Street (01 672 8555) attracted praise for its stylishness when it arrived on the scene in 2007, although the the kitchen hadn't settled at the time of our visit; **Bóbó's**, on Wexford Street (01 4005750; www.bobos.ie) has become something of a cult of late - with gourmet burgers all the rage, this retro neighbourhood restaurant serving fun food based on fresh local ingredients has really taken off; quoting Mark Twain 'Sacred cows make the best hamburgers' they say they take their grub seriously but not themselves. A lot of people really like that. For a great Lebanese experience head to St Andrew's Street - **The Cedar Tree** (01 677 2121) is one of Dublin's oldest restaurants (here since 1986) and now also home to **Byblos /The Mezze House** (01 679 1517) which not only serves good food but there's belly dancing too, making for an unusual evening's entertainment. Also in St Andrew Street, another of Ireland's longest-established restaurants, the ever-reliable Italian **Le Caprice** (01 679 4050) and across Dame Street, another great blast from the past is the gloriously unchanging **Nicos** Italian restaurant (01 677 3062). And yet one more well-established place for lovers of Italian food to think about is **Il Posto** (01 679 4769), handily situated on the Grafton Street corner of St. Stephen's Green. Budget accommodation with above average facilities is available in the **Quality Hotel** (Sir John Rogerson's Quay; 01 643 9500), which with a swimming pool and gym offers excellent value for money for business or pleasure guests within a short walk of the main city centre attractions. Visitors requiring accommodation near Dublin Castle might consider the **Parliament Hotel** (01 670 8777; www.parliamenthotel.ie). Theatre packages for shows at nearby Olympia or Gaeity Theatre are offered.

DUBLIN 2 PUBS

Renowned for its pubs, Dublin is the home of Guinness - and of course, to countless famous literary, theatrical and artistic personalities. A good few of them spent many an hour in Dublin's pubs enjoying the legendary Irish banter over a pint of the black stuff, and these connections have added to the romance and intrigue of many of Dublin's finest drinking houses. We've chosen a selection of the finest 'must visit' establishments that represent the very best of Dublin pubs, and we've ordered them in the form of a convenient pub crawl. Alternatively they are all within a short walking distance of central areas such as Grafton Street: Sláinte! Just off the Eastern end of College Green across from the bottom of Trinity College is one of Dublin's oldest and best-loved pubs, **John Mulligan's 'wine & spirit merchant'** (Poolbeg Street; 01 677 5582) is mercifully un-renovated and likely to stay that way - dark, with no decor (as such) and no music, it's just the way so many pubs used to be. The only difference is that it's now so fashionable that it gets very crowded (and noisy) after 6pm - better to drop in during the day and see what it's really like. **The Palace Bar** (Fleet Street; 01 671 7388) is on the eastern edge of Temple Bar and has had strong connections with writers and journalists for many a decade. Its unspoilt frosted glass and mahogany are impressive enough but the special feature is the famous sky-lighted snug, which is really more of a back room. Many would cite The Palace as their favourite Dublin pub. **The International Bar** (Wicklow Street; 01 677 9250) is just a minute's walk towards Georges Street from Grafton Street and this unspoilt Victorian bar makes a great meeting place - not a food spot, but good for chat and music. Across from the International Bar, **The Old Stand** (Exchequer Street; 01 677 7220) is a fine traditional pub (a sister establishment to **Davy Byrnes**, see entry) that occupies a prominent position on the corner of Exchequer Street and St. Andrew's Street and lays claim to being "possibly the oldest public house in Ireland"! Named after the Old Stand at the Lansdowne Road rugby grounds, it has a loyal following amongst the local business community, notably from the 'rag trade' area around South William Street, and also attracts a good mixture of rugby fans and visitors, who enjoy the atmosphere. They offer no-nonsense traditional bar food (12.15-9 daily), but its warm and friendly atmosphere is the main attraction. **The Stag's Head** (Dame Court, 01 679 3701) is between Dame Street and Exchequer Streets, is an impressive establishment that has retained its

original late-Victorian decor and is one of the city's finest pubs. It can get very busy at times but this lovely pub is still worth a visit. Round the corner on George's Street **The Long Hall Bar** (South Great George's Street; 01 475 1590) is one of Dublin's finest bars: a wonderful old pub, it has magnificent plasterwork ceilings, traditional mahogany bar and Victorian lighting. Just off the top end of Grafton Street, **Neary's** (Chatham Street; 01 677 8596) is an unspoilt Edwardian pub just off the top end of Grafton Street which has been in the present ownership for over half a century and is popular at all times of day - handy for lunch or as a meeting place in the early evening and full of buzz later when a post-theatre crowd, including actors from the nearby Gaiety Theatre, will probably be amongst the late night throng in the downstairs bar. Traditional values assert themselves through gleaming brass, well-polished mahogany and classics like smoked salmon and mixed meat salads amongst the bar fare. A few steps down the road, just off the west side of Grafton Street, **McDaids** (Harry Street) was established in 1779 and more recently achieved fame as one of the great literary pubs - and its association with Brendan Behan, especially, brings a steady trail of pilgrims from all over the world to this traditional premises just beside the Westbury Hotel. Dubliners, however, tend to be immune to this kind of thing and drink there because it's a good pub - and, although its character is safe, it's not a place set in aspic either, as a younger crowd has been attracted by recent changes. A mere skip across Grafton Street takes you to **Kehoe's** (South Anne Street; 01 677 8312), which is one of Dublin's best, unspoilt traditional pubs. Kehoe's changed hands relatively recently and added another floor upstairs, but without damaging the character of the original bar. Very busy in the evening - try it for a quieter daytime pint instead. A short walk to the north is **The Bailey** (Duke Street; 01 670 4939), a famous Victorian pub just off the eastern side of Grafton Street that has a special place in the history of Dublin life - literary, social, political - and attracts many a pilgrim seeking the ghosts of great personalities who have frequented this spot down through the years. Although it's now more of a busy lunchtime spot and after-work watering hole for local business people and shoppers. Heading back up towards St. Stephen's Green just beyond the Shelbourne Hotel is **O'Donoghue's** (Merrion Row, 01 676 2807) which has long been the Dublin mecca for visitors in search of a lively evening with traditional music - live music every night is a major claim to fame - but a visit to this famous pub at quieter times can be rewarding too. Further up the road is **Toners** (Lower Baggot Street; 01 676 3090) which is one of the few authentic old pubs left in Dublin and is definitely worth a visit (or two). Among many other claims to fame, it is said to be the only pub ever frequented by the poet W.B. Yeats. Across from Toners, **Doheny & Nesbitt** (Lower Baggot Street; 01 676 2945) is another great Dublin institution, but there the similarity ends. This Victorian pub has traditionally attracted a wide spectrum of Dublin society - politicians, economists, lawyers, business names, political and financial journalists - all with a view to get across, or some new scandal to divulge, so a visit here can often be unexpectedly rewarding. Although it has been greatly extended recently and is now in essence a superpub, it has at its heart the original, very professionally run bar with an attractive Victorian ambience and a traditional emphasis on drinking and conversation. Newly opened as the Guide goes to press, **The Lincoln Inn** (01 676 2978) has been a favourity haunt for staff and students at nearby Trinity College for may a year.
WWW.IRELAND-GUIDE.COM FOR ALL THE BEST PLACES TO EAT, DRINK & STAY

Dublin 2
RESTAURANT

Acapulco Mexican Restaurant
7 South Great Georges St. Dublin 2 **Tel: 01 677 1085**
acapulcoireland@yahoo.co.uk

You'll find reliable Tex-Mex fare at this bright, cheap and notably cheerful place on the edge of Temple Bar. Recently refurbished in warm tones of red, pinks and green, the decor matches the food which is authentic Mexican - nachos with salsa & guacamole, enchiladas, burrito, sizzling fajitas - and good coffee. **Seats 70.** Air con; children welcome; Open 7 days: L 12-4pm (Sun 2-4pm), D 4-10.30pm (Fri/Sat to11pm). Affordable wines, from €18.50. 10% SC on parties of 6+. Amex, MasterCard, Visa, Laser. **Directions:** Bottom of South Gt George's St (Dame Street end).

Dublin 2
HOTEL

Alexander Hotel
Merrion Square Dublin 2 **Tel: 01 607 3700**
alexanderres@ocallaghanhotels.ie www.ocallaghanhotels.ie

Very well situated at the lower end of Merrion Square, within a stone's throw of Dáil Éireann (Government Buildings), the National Art Gallery and History Museum as well as the city's premier shopping area, this large modern hotel is remarkable for classic design that blends into the surrounding Georgian area. In contrast to its subdued public face, the interior is strikingly contemporary and colourful, both in public areas and bedrooms, all of which have been refurbished recently to a very high standard, in restful soft white, cream and brown colour combinations, and have good in-room amenities. Housekeeping is immaculate throughout the hotel. Perhaps its most positive attribute, however, is the exceptionally friendly and helpful attitude of the hotel's staff who, under the supervision of General Manager Declan Fitzgerald, immediately make guests feel at home and take a genuine interest in their comfort during their stay. Meals are offered at the hotel's Caravaggio's Restaurant and a bar menu at Winners contemporary cocktail bar. Conference/banqueting (400/400). Business centre. Secretarial services. Video conferencing. Gym. Children welcome (Under 2s free in parents' room; cots available). No pets. **Rooms 102** (4 suites, 40 no-smoking, 2 for disabled). Lift. B&B about €105. Room-only rate about €295 (max. 2 guests). Open all year. Amex, Diners, MasterCard, Visa **Directions:** Off Merrion Square.

Dublin 2
RESTAURANT

Avoca Café

11-13 Suffolk St. Dublin 2 **Tel: 01 672 6019**
info@avoca.ie www.avoca.ie

City sister to the famous craftshop and café with its flagship store in Kilmacanogue, County Wicklow (see entry), this large centrally located shop is a favourite daytime dining venue for discerning Dubliners. The restaurant (which is up rather a lot of stairs, where queues of devotees wait patiently at lunchtime) has low-key style and an emphasis on creative, healthy cooking that is common to all the Avoca establishments. Chic little menus speak volumes - together with careful cooking, meticulously sourced ingredients like Hederman mussels, Gubbeen bacon and Hicks sausages lift dishes such as smoked fish platter, organic bacon panini and bangers & mash out of the ordinary. All this sits happily alongside the home baking for which they are famous - much of which can be bought downstairs in their extensive delicatessen. Licensed. Meals daily, in shop hours. **Seats 100;** toilets wheelchair accessible; opening hours: 10am-5.30pm Mon-Sat (hot food served until 4.30pm Mon-Fri), 11am-5pm Sun; à la carte. Bookings accepted but not required. SC 10%. Closed 25/26 December, 1 Jan. Amex, Diners, MasterCard, Visa. **Directions:** Turn left into Suffolk St. from the bottom of Grafton St.

Dublin 2
RESTAURANT

Aya Food Bar

49/52 Clarendon Street Dublin 2 **Tel: 01 677 1544**
mail@aya.ie www.aya.ie

This contemporary Japanese restaurant was Dublin's first conveyor sushi bar, restaurant and food hall - it's owned by the Hoashi family, who established Dublin's first authentic Japanese restaurant. Wall-to-wall style is the order of the day - the menu includes a wide range of authentic Japanese sushi, Asian and Japanese tapas, tempura and teriyaki dishes and additions with broader Asian flavours to tempt a range of customers, and you will even find desserts on the conveyer. The sushi conveyor belt has stools and booths for communal diners, as well as restaurant seating for the à la carte. The early dinner ('Twilite Special') offers very good value. Some products are available to take away. Children welcome before 7pm. **Seats 65** (sushi bar & restaurant). Air conditioning. Open daily - Sushi Bar: 12.30-10 (to 11 Fri/Sat); Restaurant: L 12.30-3 (Sat to 4, Sun from 2pm), D 5-10 (Sat to 11, Sun to 9). Set L €19; Set D €30, Early D €18.95 5-7. Also à la carte. House wine from €22. SC 12.5%. Closed 25-26 Dec. Amex, MasterCard, Visa, Laser. **Directions:** Directly behind Brown Thomas off Wicklow Street.

Dublin 2
RESTAURANT

Balzac

35 Dawson Street Dublin 2
Tel: 01 677 4444

Balzac is the latest incarnation in the distinctive building on Dawson Street, which formerly housed La Stampa and, with its grand Belle Epoque entrance, it never fails to impress. It has now been revisited by former head chef, Paul Flynn, whose consultant's stamp of assiduously thought out, refined Bistro cooking defines the new menu. Both the bar and the wonderful dining room, with its magnificent ceiling, have been fitted and furnished with a view to casual luxury, in keeping with the cuisine. Black tables with linen runners and napkins, simple stainless cutlery and glasses, white ware, subdued lighting, mirrors and the formidable flower pot centrepiece on a wooden floor coalesce to create a cosmopolitan ambience, added to by the multinational waiting staff. The menu is a delightful, uncomplicated read, offering starters like oysters mignonette, caramelised onion tart with Corleggy cheese, and assiette of charcuterie. Innovatively, a section is devoted to dishes available as starters or main courses and priced accordingly dishes like grilled field mushrooms with rocket and parmesan, warm carpaccio of lamb with spiced aubergines, and roast whole prawns with saffron cream dressing. The list of main courses is comprehensive, catering for carnivores and vegetarians with dishes such as crispy crubeens & colcannon, spaghetti Balzac, grilled hake with black pudding, raisins and pine nuts; house specialities include Fondue of Shellfish for two persons (€120) and rib roast of beef carved in the room (€25 per person); roasts are a big thing on Sundays, when a selection of roasts is offered along with other options on the Sunday lunch menu and special side dishes include potatoes roast in duck fat. The dessert menu offers plenty of treats plus the unusual option of soft cream cheese with herbs and warm croûtons - and different, too, is the basket of warm Madeleines as petits fours. The wine list at the back of the menu is short, pragmatic and representative of old and new worlds. The food at Balzac is a celebration of quality ingredients, served in one of Ireland's finest dining rooms and - despite some inconsistency in both cooking and service, experienced by the Guide during Balzac's first months - the experience is sure to be enjoyable. And, aside from the dining experience, there is also plenty of entertainment to be found in the bar, where internationally renowned mixologist Alan Kavanagh shakes up a little magic each evening. *Balzac is part of the La Stampa complex, overlooking the Mansion House in central Dublin. In addition to Balzac, the complex includes accommodation, a spa, **Tiger Bec's** restaurant and **Sam Sara Café Bar**. Unsuitable for children after 8pm. **Seats 200** (private room, 70); reservations recommended; L daily, 12-3pm, set L €28.50; D Mon-Sat, 6-11pm, early bird D, €28, 6-7.30pm, set D €50, also a la carte. Sun open all day, 1-8pm. Closed D 24 Dec, 25-27 Dec, Good Fri. Amex, MasterCard, Visa, Laser. **Directions:** Opposite the Mansion House on Dawson Street.

Dublin 2
RESTAURANT
♨ ☆

Bang Café

11 Merrion Row Dublin 2 **Tel: 01 676 0898**
www.bangrestaurant.com

Stylishly minimalist, with natural tones of dark wood and pale beige leather complementing simple white linen and glassware, this smart restaurant is well-located just yards from the Shelbourne Hotel. It is on two levels with a bar in the basement; upstairs, unstressed chefs can be seen at work in one of the open kitchens: an air of calm, relaxed and friendly professionalism prevails. Head chef Lorcan Cribben, who is the current Commissioner-General for the Irish branch of Euro-Toques, the chef's organisation that is committed to defending quality local and artisan ingredients, (Paul Bocuse's 'building blocks of good food'). Here, as would be expected, carefully sourced ingredients are the foundation for menus that offer innovative, modern food: a starter terrine of free range chicken with foie gras, and organic vegetable piccalilli is typical and well-balanced main course options include a signature dish of bangers & mash (made with Hicks sausages), which is also on the menu at the newer Clarendon Café Bar (see entry); also great fish dishes (seared scallops are especially popular), using fresh fish from Bantry, in West Cork. Tempting desserts include several fruity finales (Scandinavian iced berries are a speciality) as well as the ever-popular dark chocolate treats, or there's an Irish farmhouse cheese selection. Attention to detail is the keynote throughout and skilful cooking combined with generous servings and professional service, ensures an enjoyable dining experience and value for money (especially at lunch time). **Seats 99** (private room, 36); reservations required; air conditioning; L&D Mon-Sat 12.30-3pm, 6-10.30pm; à la carte L&D. House wine €21. 12.5% sc on parties of 6+. Closed Sun, bank hols, 25 Dec-3 Jan. Amex, MasterCard, Visa, Laser. **Directions:** Just past Shelbourne Hotel, off St Stephen's Green. ◈

Dublin 2
RESTAURANT/WINE BAR
Ⓝ

Bar Pintxo

12 Eustace Street Temple Bar , Dublin 2
Tel 01 672 8590

This new sister establishment to The Port House on South William Street follows the familiar formula of simple, well cooked hearty tapas served in atmospheric surroundings, with lashings of Spanish and Portuguese wine. Large streetside windows draped in tall curtains give an air of intrigue to the passer by; on entering you are greeted with a lively buzz and character a-plenty. Exposed brick walls, white sanded wooden floors and rack upon rack of wine bottles set the tone, whilst the open kitchen and impressive wine bar provide the action. A classy worn feel is provided in old wooden leather covered chairs and shiny black tables, with the ground floor room providing a brighter dining experience than the cellar room, which offers a more intimate, candlelit ambience. Friendly staff are quick to seat customers and provide a menu of around two dozen dishes divided into hot and cold plates of tapas, in the Spanish and Basque style. You'll find the familiar dishes of patatas bravas, calamari, tortilla and paella, but there is also something for the more adventurous such as Galician octopus or seared foie gras. This is simple, uncomplicated food with big flavours, served in a smart cheerful style, for very acceptable prices. An extensive exclusively Spanish and Portuguese wine list includes an interesting selection of sherries. Some bottles are available by the carafe or glass, and a nice touch is to offer bottles being sold at a lower off licence price for those who want to take something home. Spanish and Basque beers are also offered. No reservations taken; children welcome before 8pm; free broadband wi/fi; air conditioning. **Seats 75;** SC discretionary. Closed 25 Dec. MasterCard, Visa, Laser **Directions:** Centre of Temple Bar, off Main Street opposite Farringtons.

Dublin 2
CAFÉ/RESTAURANT

Bewley's - Café Bar Deli
Bewleys Building 78-79 Grafton Street Dublin 2 **Tel: 01 672 7719**
info@mackerel.ie www.sherland.ie

Established in 1840, Bewley's Café had a special place in the affection of Irish people. Bewleys on Grafton Street was always a great meeting place for everyone, whether native Dubliners or visitors to the capital 'up from the country'. It changed hands amid much public debate in 2005 but, despite renovations, it has somehow retained its unique atmosphere together with some outstanding architectural features, notably the Harry Clarke stained glass windows. The popular Café-Bar-Deli chain has taken over most of the seating area now, but the coffee shop at the front remains, and also the in-house theatre (phone for details). **Cafe Bar Deli: Seats 350** open for food all day 8am-11pm. Closed 25/6 Dec, Bank Hols. Amex, MasterCard, Visa, Laser. **Directions:** Halfway up Dublin's premier shopping street. ◊

Dublin 2
RESTAURANT/WINE BAR

Bleu Bistro Moderne
Dawson St. Dublin 2 **Tel: 01 676 7015**
www.bleu.ie

A younger sister to Eamonn O'Reilly's excellent flagship restaurant One Pico (see entry), this modern bistro is now known generally as 'Bleu' or even 'Blue.' Smartly laid tables are rather close together and hard surfaces make for a good bit of noise which adversely affects the dining ambience. But the food is based on carefully sourced quality ingredients, and pleasingly presented on plain white plates. Although recent experience by the Guide suggests there may be inconsistency in the kitchen, the food is generally cooked with skill; dishes of smoked haddock, risotto of broad beans with poached egg and hollandaise, and pan roasted chicken with lasagne of butternut squash, morels and asparagus attracted particular praise on recent visits. Portions may be on the small side, which can make value on the plate seem less than it looks on the menu, and more cheerful service would make people more inclined to return. Long opening hours allow for a very nice little afternoon menu, which could make an enjoyable late lunch or early evening meal and there is an outdoor seating area for fine weather. Good wine list, with a dozen or so wines by the glass. **Seats 60** (outdoor seating 14). Reservations advised. Air conditioning. Open all day Mon-Sat 9am-midnight, L 12-5, D 5-12, Sun - L 12-4, D 5-10; Set L 2/3 course about €21.50/25. Early D about €29 (5-7.30), Set D about €20, also á la carte L&D. House wine from about €22. Closed bank hols. Amex, MasterCard, Visa, Laser. Directions: At top of Dawson St. off St. Stephen's Green. **Directions:** At top of Dawson St. off St. Stephen's Green. ◊

Dublin 2
HOTEL/RESTAURANT

Brooks Hotel & Francescas Restaurant
Drury Street Dublin 2 **Tel: 01 670 4000**
reservations@brookshotel.ie www.sinnotthotels.com

One of Dublin's most desirable addresses, especially for business guests, the Sinnott family's discreetly luxurious hotel is a gem of a place - an oasis of calm just a couple of minutes walk from Grafton Street. A ground floor bar, lounge and restaurant all link together, making an extensive public area that is quietly impressive on arrival - the style is a pleasing combination of traditional with contemporary touches, using a variety of woods, some marble, wonderful fabrics and modern paintings - and, while a grand piano adds gravitas, there's a welcome emphasis on comfort (especially in the residents' lounge, where spare reading glasses are thoughtfully supplied). Efficient service ensures you are in your room promptly, usually with the help of Conor, the concierge, who never forgets a face or a name. All bedrooms have exceptionally good amenities, including a pillow menu (choice of five types) and well-designed bathrooms with power showers as well as full baths (some also have tile screen TV), and many other features. Boardrooms offer state-of-the-art facilities for meetings and small conferences, and there is a 26-seater screening room. Fitness suite & sauna. Children welcome (under 2 free in parents' room; cots available without charge, baby sitting arranged). No pets. **Rooms 98** (1 suite, 2 junior suites, 3 executive, 87 no-smoking, 5 semi-invalid). Lift. Air conditioning throughout. 24 hr room service. B&B €160pps, ss €100. *Special breaks offered - details on application. Arrangement with car park. Open all year. **Francescas Restaurant:** Pre-dinner drinks are served in a lovely little cocktail bar, **Jasmine**, and the restaurant has a youthful contemporary look, and a welcoming ambience - an open plan kitchen has well positioned mirrors allowing head chef Patrick McLarnon and his team to be seen at work. Tables are elegantly appointed with classic linen cloths and napkins, and waiting staff, smartly attired in black, look after customers with warmth and professionalism. Patrick sources ingredients with great care (wild salmon, organic chicken, dry aged steak, wild boar sausage), his cooking is generally imaginative - and there's a strong emphasis on fish and seafood. Unusual meat dishes may include a starter of McGeough's air-dried Connemara lamb (subject to availability) and a main course of pan-fried Finnebrogue venison. Finish, perhaps, with a zingy home-made lemon tart served with a delicious strawberry or raspberry sorbet and a classy individually packed infusion, or coffee. A nice wine selection includes good quality wines available by the glass. The early dinner offers good value, and breakfast offers a wide variety of juices, cereals and nuts, yoghurt, pastries, meat, cheeses and fruit. A good range of hot dishes includes pancakes with maple syrup, kippers with poached egg and full Irish breakfast as you like it, although service can be slow. [*Informal meals also available 10 am-11.30 daily.] **Seats 30.** Reservations advised. Children welcome. Air conditioning.Toilets wheelchair accessible. D daily, 6-9.30 (Fri/Sat to 10). Early D €18.50 (6-7); also à la carte & vegetarian menus. Closed to non-residents 24/25th December. Amex, MasterCard, Visa, Laser. **Directions:** Near St Stephen's Green, between Grafton and South Great Georges Streets; opposite Drury Street car park.

Dublin 2
HOTEL/RESTAURANT

Brownes Hotel

22 St Stephen's Green Dublin 2 **Tel: 01 638 3939**
info@brownesdublin.com www.brownesdublin.com

Stylish conversion of this fine period house makes an impressive and exceptionally well-located small hotel. Up a short flight of granite steps, through reception, there is a small drawing room furnished with antiques and fresh flowers - the house has the atmosphere of a private home about it. The present owners, the Stein Group, have invested heavily in refurbishment of the premises, including the spacious accommodation. **Brownes Restaurant:** This is one of Dublin's loveliest dining rooms yet, despite good food and a great location, it seems to be something of a well-kept secret and when other well-known restaurants nearby are impossible to get into, there may well be spare tables here. The menu and food are appealing and well presented, although they do perhaps lack the 'wow' factor. But the ambience is lovely and the cooking sound, backed up by professional staff. Small conference/banqueting (24/70). Children welcome (under 6 free in parents' room, cot available without charge). No pets. **Rooms 12** (2 suites). Lift. 24 hour room service. B&B about €200 pps. *Short breaks / golfing breaks offered. L Sun-Fri & D daily. Closed Christmas/New Year. Amex, Diners, MasterCard, Visa, Laser. **Directions:** St. Stephen's Green North, between Kildare & Dawson Streets. ◊

Dublin 2
HOTEL/RESTAURANT

Buswells Hotel

23 Molesworth Street Dublin 2 **Tel: 01 614 6500**
buswells@quinn-hotels.com www.quinn-hotels.com

Home from home to Ireland's politicians, this row of 18th century townhouses has been an hotel since 1921. The location would be hard to beat and it's reasonably priced for the area; it remains a slightly old-fashioned hotel of character and it's a haven for politicians at the Dail (parliament) across the road and there's a special buzz in the bar, where food is served throughout the day and evening. Recent renovations made no fundamental changes and accommodation is comfortable in the traditional style, with the best rooms overlooking Kildare Street or Molesworth Street. Good range of services for conferences, meetings and private dining. Conference/banqueting (85/50). Business centre, secretarial services, video conferencing. Children welcome (Under 3s free in parents' room; cots available free of charge). No pets. **Rooms 67** (2 junior suites, 6 single, 7 shower only, 52 no smoking, 1 for disabled). Lift. B&B €140pps, ss €45. 24 hr room service, Lift. **Trumans:** This elegant, well-appointed restaurant has a separate entrance from Kildare Street, or access from the hotel, and it offers a pleasing ambience and quite extensive menus featuring both modern and simpler dishes: corn fed chicken with bacon parmesan croquettes is a speciality. A good wine list includes half a dozen house wines, a page of fine wines and a strong selection of half bottles. Children welcome. **Seats 60** (private room, 50). Reservations advised. L 12-2.30 (carvery), D 5.30-9.45 (Sun from 6pm). Set D €42, also à la carte. House wine €19.95. SC discretionary. Closed 25-26 Dec. Amex, Diners, MasterCard, Visa, Laser. **Directions:** Close to Dail Eireann, 5 minutes walk from Grafton Street.

Dublin 2
CAFÉ

Butlers Chocolate Café

24 Wicklow Street Dublin 2 **Tel: 01 671 0599**
chocolate@butlers.ie www.butlerschocolates.com

Butlers Irish Handmade Chocolates combine coffee-drinking with complimentary chocolates - an over-simplification, as the range of drinks at this stylish little café also includes hot chocolate as well as lattes, cappuccinos and mochas and chocolate cakes and croissants are also available. But all drinks do come with a complimentary handmade chocolate on the side - and boxed or personally selected loose chocolates, caramels, fudges and fondants are also available for sale. Open 7 days: Mon-Fri 8am-7pm, Sat 9am-7pm, Sun 11am-6pm. Closed 25-26 Dec, Easter Sun & Mon. Also at: 51 Grafton Street (Tel: 01 671 0599); 9 Chatham Street (Tel: 01 672 6333); 18 Nassau Street (Tel: 01 671 0772), 31 Henry Street (Tel 01 874 7419); Heuston Station; Dundrum Shopping Centre; Dublin Airport; 30 Oliver Plunkett St, Cork; 40 William St, Galway. All of the above have similar opening times to the Wicklow Street branch, except Nassau St, Grafton St & Henry St open at 7.30 am on weekdays. Amex, MasterCard, Visa, Laser. **Directions:** 5 city centre locations & Dublin Airport.

Dublin 2
RESTAURANT

Café Bar Deli

13 South Gt George's Street Dublin 2 **Tel: 01 677 1646**
georgesstreet@cafebardeli.ie www.cafebardeli.ie

Despite its obvious contemporary appeal - paper place mat menus set the tone by kicking off with home-made breads and marinated olives - the friendly ghosts of the old Bewleys Café are still alive and well in this inspired reincarnation of this much-loved establishment. Tables are old café style, with bentwood chairs, the original fireplace and a traditional brass railing remain, but a smartly striped awning over the large street window signals the real nature of the place. Imaginative salads are packed with colourful, flavoursome treats with pizza and pasta menus continuing in the same tone, including daily specials. Spelt bread is available, all pasta dishes can be made with gluten/wheat free pasta and a dedicated children's menu was introduced in 2007. A sensibly limited wine list combines quality and style with value; service is friendly and efficient and prices remarkably moderate - an attractive formula for an informal outing. Branches at: Ranelagh, Dublin 6 (Tel 01 496 1886); Cork (Bodega); and Sligo (Garavogue). Children welcome; air conditioning. **Seats 160;** open 7 days: Mon-Sat, 12.30-11; Sun 2-10pm; A la carte. House wine €23 (litre). No reservations. Closed 25-27 Dec, Good Fri. Amex, MasterCard, Visa, Laser. **Directions:** Next door to the Globe Bar.

Dublin 2
CAFÉ/PUB

Café en Seine

40 Dawson Street Dublin 2 **Tel: 01 677 4567**
cafeenseine@capitalbars.com www.capitalbars.com

The first of the continental style café-bars to open in Dublin, Café en Seine is still ahead of the fashion - the interior is stunning, in an opulent art deco style reminiscent of turn-of-the-century Paris. Not so much a bar as a series of bars (your mobile phone could be your most useful accessory if you arrange to meet somebody here), the soaring interior is truly awe-inspiring with a 3-storey atrium culminating in beautiful glass-panelled ceilings, forty foot trees, enormous art nouveau glass lanterns, and statues and a 19th century French hotel lift among its many amazing features. No expense has been spared in ensuring the quality of design, materials and crafts-manship necessary to create this beautiful Aladdin's cave of a bar. Lush ferns create a deliciously decadent atmosphere and the judicious mixture of old and new which make it a true original - and its many 'bars within bars' create intimate spaces that are a far cry from the impersonality of the superpub. Appealing food is a feature too: there's a sociable combination platter serving four people and hot dishes like steak sandwiches, scampi and quiches with salads are popular; everything is spotlessly clean and, while simple, the food is really tasty. An informal range of contemporary dishes is available over lunchtime every day, also light bites all day - and there's a popular Jazz Brunch every Sunday. Little wonder that so many people of all ages still see it as the coolest place in town. Small al fresco covered section at front seats about 30. Lunch daily, 12-3; (Sun brunch 1-4). D daily: Sun-Wed, 5-9; Thu-Sat, 5-10. Wheelchair access. Bar open 10.30am-2.30am daily. Carvery lunch 12-3. Snack menu 4-10. Closed 25-26 Dec & Good Fri. Amex, MasterCard, Visa, Laser. **Directions:** Upper Dawson Street, on right walking towards St Stephen's Green (St Stephen's Green car park is very close). ◊

Dublin 2
RESTAURANT

Café Mao
2-3 Chatham Row Dublin 2
Tel 01 670 4899

téite bia This popular and well located Asian fusion restaurant has recently reopened after a refurbishment, but retains the same general layout and simple colourful décor, including their trademark oversized Andy Warhol style portraits. The menu is slightly expanded to include more vegetarian options as well as a few light salads; however the established favourites such as the chilli squid, Nasi Goreng, and the Thai green curry (vegetable or chicken) are as good as ever. Soups change regularly and, with their garlic and lemongrass naan, provide a filling snack. There is a good selection of genuine Asian beers (any of which complement the generally non-region specific cuisine), and an excellent English cider, as well as a number of cocktails and smoothies, and a small selection of wines by the glass. On the Guide's most recent visit the restaurant was untypically quiet but, as word of the reopening gets about, it is sure to regain its fashionable and convivial atmosphere. Café Mao still provides great value and very quick service and, while the specific dishes may not be completely true to the region's traditional cuisine, the flavours and use of ingredients certainly represents the potential of Asian food in general. At the time of visiting reservations were accepted for large groups only, but individual reservations will normally be taken. Fully wheelchair accessible. Children welcome. **Seats 110.** Air conditioning. Open Mon-Thur 12-8.30, Fri-Sat 12-11pm, Sun 1-10pm. Menu à la carte. SC discretionary. MasterCard, Visa, Laser. **Directions:** City centre - just off Grafton Street at the Stephen's Green end.

Dublin 2
RESTAURANT

Caife Úna
46 Kildare St. Dublin 2 **Tel: 01 670 6087**
caifeuna@hotmail.com www.caifeuna.com

Una NicGabhann's restaurant is an exceptionally friendly, welcoming place and holds an unusual trump card in that it's bilingual. You don't have to speak Irish to eat here, but it's encouraged and many people will find that hearing the language in use, even in Dublin, adds a lot to a meal out. It's a semi-basement and, with a bare floor, and simple wooden tables and chairs - quite sparse, but warmed by the soft pinks of old brickwork. The menu is short and walks a tightrope between traditional Irish home cooking and more contemporary fare, but it will probably include Irish Stew, comfort food like roast chicken with black pudding mash and less usual ingredients like ling, once a staple food in Irish coastal areas. Admirable details include home-made brown bread and, at its best, offers good Irish home cooking with an international flavour, and is reasonably priced. Free broadband WI/Fi. **Seats 40** (outdoors, 2); children welcome before 8pm; food served daily 11am-10pm (close at 5pm Mon); house wine about €18.50. Closed Sun & Bank Hols. MasterCard, Visa, Laser. **Directions:** Turn off Nassau St. and is the second business on the right - basement. ◊

Dublin 2
RESTAURANT
♛

Chez Max
1 Palace Street Dublin 2
Tel: 01 633 7215

Everyone loves Max Delaloubie's friendly brasserie, an almost too-perfect reproduction of 1940s' Paris, opening onto a cobbled street at the entrance to Dublin Castle. The food, too, has that ring of Parisian authenticity - rillettes, frogs' legs, anduoillette (tripe sausage with potato salad & wholegrain mustard) and early concern amongst devotees that such dishes may not survive in this essentially conservative city seem so far to be unfounded. And there is plenty there for everyone including lots of less contentious treats like Croque

Monsieur and Croque Madame, Salade Parisienne, good pastries and a range of classic home-made desserts. Meanwhile, the proprietor continues to make people welcome and wannabe Parisians of every generation can groove to music that stretches from Henri Krein, Brassens and Piaf to St Etienne. The shortish wine list offers few surprises, but overall both wine and food offer very good value for money. **Seats 66** (outdoor, 25) reservations recommended; children welcome; open for breakfast from 7.30; tea/ coffee and pastries served all day; L & D daily 12-3.30 and 5.30-10.30 (to 10 on Sun); House wine €22.50. Closed 25 Dec, 1 Jan. MasterCard, Visa, Laser. **Directions:** On the right of the Dame St. entrance to Dublin Castle.

Dublin 2
RESTAURANT

Chili Club

1 Anne's Lane South Anne Street Dublin 2
Tel: 01 677 3721

This cosy restaurant, in a laneway just off Grafton Street, has great charm; it was Dublin's first authentic Thai restaurant and is still as popular as ever a decade later. Owned and managed by Patricia Kenna, who personally supervises a friendly and efficient staff, it is small and intimate, with beautiful crockery and genuine Thai art and furniture. Supot Boonchouy, who has been head chef since 1996, prepares a fine range of genuine Thai dishes which are not 'tamed' too much to suit Irish tastes. Set lunch and early evening menus offer especially good value. Children welcome. **Seats 40** (private room, 16) L Mon-Fri 12.30-2.30, D daily 6-11. Set L €14. Early D from €14 (6-7pm), Set D €30. A la carte also available. House wine €20. SC discretionary (10% on parties 6+. Closed L Sat & Sun, 25-28 Dec, 1 Jan. Diners, MasterCard, Visa, Laser. **Directions:** Off Grafton Street.

Dublin 2
HOTEL/BAR/RESTAURANT

The Clarence Hotel, Tea Room Restaurant & The Octagon Bar

6-8 Wellington Quay Dublin 2 **Tel: 01 407 0800**
reservations@theclarence.ie www.theclarence.ie

Dating back to 1852, this hotel has long had a special place in the hearts of Irish people - especially the clergy and the many who regarded it as a home from home when 'up from the country' for business or shopping in Dublin - largely because of its convenience to Heuston Station. Since the early '90s, however, it has achieved cult status through its owners - Bono and The Edge of U2 - who have completely refurbished the hotel, sparing no expense to reflect the the hotel's original arts and crafts style whenever possible. Now, however, a dramatic redevelopment and expansion of the hotel is planned in association with UK architects Foster & Partners, who are responsible for many of the world's most remarkable modern buildings; the proposed development will create a new landmark for the city, and include restoration of the quayside facade. Meanwhile, accommodation currently offers a combination of contemporary comfort and period style, with all the expected amenities including mini-bar, private safe, complimentary broadband and temperature control panels. Public areas include the club like, oak-panelled **Octagon Bar**, which is a popular Temple Bar meeting place, and The Study, a quieter room with an open fire. Parking is available in several multi-storey carparks within walking distance; valet parking available for guests. Conference/banqueting (60/70); video conferencing on request; Secretarial service; Laptop-sized safe in rooms. Beauty treatments, massage, Therapy @ The Clarence (also available to non-residents). Children welcome (Under 12s free in parents' room, cots available without charge, baby sitting arranged). No pets. **Rooms 49** (5 suites, incl 1 penthouse; 21 executive, 4 family rooms, 6 no smoking, 1 for disabled). Lift. 24 hr room service, Turndown service. Room rate €340; SC discretionary. **The Tea Room:** The restaurant, which has its own entrance in Essex Street, is a high-ceilinged room furnished in the light oak which is a feature throughout the hotel. Pristine white linen, designer cutlery and glasses, high windows softened by the filtered damson tones of pavement awnings, all combine to create an impressive dining room; there is no separate reception area for the restaurant so you will be shown straight to your table. Head chef Mathieu Melin took the helm in the spring of 2007, and all the signs are that the kitchen continues to be a happy ship. An à la carte menu is the backbone of the food offering but the recent introduction of keenly-priced Market Menus at both lunch (daily) and dinner (Sun-Thu) has been a stroke of genius - at lunch time, there's even an 'In-N-Out' guarantee that groups of up to four can have a 2-course Market Menu lunch in 45 minutes flat. The Market Menus have really livened up the dining scene at The

Clarence, and Mathieu Melin shows his versatility in creating dishes for this menu. His combination plates ('a combination of 5 small dishes') offered as starter and as dessert are worth travelling for; excellent home-made breads with pesto are also superb. A well-chosen, if expensive, wine list includes a selection of very good wines by the glass, and wine service is knowledgeable. *Lighter menus are also available in the hotel - an informal Evening Menu, for example, and Afternoon Tea; as well as a light à la carte and a number of classic main courses, The Octagon Bar Menu offers a great cocktail menu. **Seats 90.** Toilets wheelchair accessible. L Sun-Fri 12.30-2.30, D daily 7-10.30 (Sun to 9.30). Special Market Menu - L €26 12.30-2.30pm (Sun-Fri); D €39 (Sun-Thurs 7-8pm); also a la carte L & D. House wine from €26. SC 12.5% on groups 8+. Octagon Bar Menu,12-10pm daily. Closed L Sat and 24 Dec-27 Dec. Amex, Diners, MasterCard, Visa. **Directions:** Overlooking the River Liffey at Wellington Quay, southside, in Temple Bar.

Dublin 2
CAFÉ/BAR

Clarendon Café Bar

32 Clarendon Street Dublin 2 **Tel: 01 679 2909**
www.clarendon.ie

A sister to Bang Café (see entry), the Stokes brothers' stylish contemporary café-bar just off Grafton Street has a chic exterior with a large glass frontage and some simple little aluminium tables and chairs outside. It's a big place, with bars spread over several storeys, but subtle decor - dark wooden floors, pale walls, chrome bars, comfortable wicker chairs - soft background music, and a warm and friendly welcome create a lovely ambience and there's a very nice buzz about it. And, as in Bang, there's a commitment to interesting food, promised on menus that name suppliers and are not over-extensive yet offer a wide range of tempting dishes: starters might include seafood like smoked haddock and cod fish cakes, or seared scallops with chorizo and roasted red pepper, for example, then there are pannini for busy lunch times (and sandwiches made to order), and mains like corn-fed chicken & chive mash with smoked bacon lardons, all scrumptious bangers & mash with a piquant shallot & mustard jus. Great char-grilled steaks are served with classic béarnaise & fries and, sensibly, there's an accurate description of the cooking, e.g. 'rare; very red, cool centre' etc, which avoids confusing orders and makes life a lot easier in the kitchen too. The wine list is short, but makes up in interest anything it may lack in length - and an exceptional choice is offered by the glass. One of the best modern bars in Ireland. Open 10-11. Food served: Mon-Thu 12-3 / 5-9.30pm, Fri-Sun, 12-6pm. No reservations. Air conditioning. Toilets wheelchair accessible. A la carte. Wines from €15.50. SC 12.5% on groups 6+. Closed 25 Dec, Good Fri. Amex, MasterCard, Visa, Laser. **Directions:** From St Stephen's Green, walking down Grafton Street - 1st street on left, 100yards.

Dublin 2
HOTEL/RESTAURANT

Conrad Dublin & Alex Restaurant

Earlsfort Terrace Dublin 2 **Tel: 01 602 8900**
dublininfo@conradhotels.com www.conraddublin.com

Situated directly opposite the National Concert Hall and just a stroll away from St Stephen's Green, this fine city centre hotel celebrated its twentieth anniversary in 2005 with the completion of a major refurbishment programme, and it was the Guide's Business Hotel of the Year in 2006. This is an extremely comfortable place to stay - friendly staff are well-trained and helpful, and many of the pleasantly contemporary guestrooms enjoy views of the piazza below and across the city; nice touches include providing an umbrella in each room - and also a laminated jogging map of the area with one- and three-mile routes outlined. The Conrad has particular appeal for business guests, as all of the bedrooms also well-designed to double as an efficient office, with ergonomic workstation, broadband, dataports, international powerpoints and at least three direct dial telephones with voice-mail - and the hotel also has extensive state-of-the-art conference and meeting facilities, a fitness centre and underground parking. Public areas include a raised lounge, which makes an ideal meeting place, and the popular **Alfie Byrne's Pub**, which is home to locals and visitors alike and opens on to a sheltered terrace.

Conference/banqueting (320/280). Executive boardroom (12). Business centre; secretarial services; video conferencing; free broadband wi/fi; laptop-sized safe in bedrooms. Underground carpark (100). Children welcome (under 18s free in parents' room, cots available, baby sitting arranged). **Rooms 192** (16 suites, 7 junior suites, 165 no-smoking, 1 for disabled). Lift. 24 hr room service. Turndown service. B&B €235 pps, no SC. Open all year. **Alex:** Chef Brian Meehan leads the kitchen team at The Conrad's seafood restaurant, Alex. The decor is contemporary classic - a bright open plan room, with Elizabeth Cope paintings and low music, has polished tables with crisp white runners, and smart modern place settings - and menus are divided into choices from Land or Sea. Fish choices are quite extensive, balanced by a handful of meat and vegetarian choices. Delicious home-made breads (including a lovely Guinness bread) begin your meal and, although the tone is international, there may be some dishes with an Irish slant - the aim is to offer seasonal dishes based on top quality ingredients and cooked simply, using as little added fat and salt as possible. Sometimes special culinary events are arranged. Attentive service from friendly staff helps ensure that dining here is an enjoyable experience. **Seats 92**; air conditioning, children welcome, live jazz on Saturday eve. B 7-9.30am; L 12.30-2.30pm (from 1pm Sun), D 5.30-9.30pm daily. Set L €30, set 3 course Sun L €40 (inc glass of champagne); early D €30, 5.30-7pm; set 4 course D €40; house wine from €26. Restaurant closed D 25 Dec, L 26 Dec. Amex, Diners, MasterCard, Visa, Laser. **Directions:** On the south-eastern corner of St Stephen's Green, opposite the National Concert Hall.

Dublin 2   Cookes Restaurant
RESTAURANT   14 South William Street Dublin 2 **Tel: 01 679 0536**
cookes1@eircom.net www.cookesrestaurant.com

Cookes has one of the most pleasant locations of any Dublin restaurant, and was among the first to offer tables outside, on the pedestrianised street under the trademark dark green awning. Johnny Cooke is a great chef and was probably also the first to present the real essence of The Med to Dublin diners. The restaurant may not have quite the cachet it once had but, as always, the very best ingredients provide the basis for stylish food including fresh fish, and you can expect a really good steak, although you may have difficulty in getting the chef to agree if you like yours well done. Begin, perhaps, with an antipasto platter to share; main course platters are also available, including a Seafood Array that requires a week's notice and includes sea urchins, abalone, and palourde clams. Cookes is known for its breads, and desserts and cheeses are usually worth leaving room for. Service is very friendly (some might feel it over-familiar), and wine service can be outstanding. Avoid the upstairs room unless you are in a large group - eat downstairs, or preferably outside, and try and get a table from which to 'people-watch', especially in the afternoon. **Seats 100** (outdoor seating 40). Unsuitable for children under 8 yrs; air conditioning. L & D daily; L 12-4.30, D 6-10, Value L&D avail €24 (Value D 6-7pm). House wine €26; SC 12.5% on groups 6+. MasterCard, Visa, Laser. **Directions:** On corner of Castle Market and South William Street.

Dublin 2   Coopers Restaurant
RESTAURANT   62 Lr. Leeson Street Dublin 2 **Tel: 01 676 8615**
info@coopersrestaurant.ie www.coopersrestaurant.ie

Situated near Leeson Street Bridge in an attractive old cut-stone coach house, this restaurant offers a lot of the old favourites. Prawns pil pil, Caesar salad and beef tomato & mozzarella salad are typical starters, for example, and you may expect steaks various ways, lamb cutlets, a fish dish of the day and a vegetarian pasta dish. The restaurant is on two levels and, although the decor might not win any prizes, the natural stone walls and the character of the building give it a pleasing atmosphere for enjoying their mid-range food. In summer, especially, it is a place worth knowing about for the outdoor seating, which is comfortably set up with plants around and an awning to protect diners from extremes of weather; a pleasant spot to enjoy the light lunch menu (€15), perhaps, or the early evening menu (from €20). Toilets & public areas wheelchair accessible. **Seats 130** (outdoors, 30, private room up to 80); children welcome; L Mon-Fri, 12-3, Set L €18.50/€22.50 2/3 course; D Mon-Sat, 5.30-"late," early D €20/24.50, 5.30-7; set D 37.95; also a la carte L&D; house wine €19.50; 10% SC on groups 8+. Closed L Sat & L Sun, 25-27 Dec, Good Fri. Amex, Diners, MasterCard, Visa, Laser. **Directions:** Just before Leeson St. bridge coming from town centre.

Dublin 2   Cornucopia
RESTAURANT   19 Wicklow Street Dublin 2 **Tel: 01 677 7583**
cornucopia@eircom.net

You don't have to be vegetarian to enjoy this established wholefood restaurant, which is well located for a wholesome re-charge if you're shopping around Grafton Street. Originally a wholefood store with a few tables at the back and, although it has now been a dedicated restaurant for some time, a waft of that unmistakable aroma remains. It may give out mixed messages in various ways - the smart red and gold frontage and pavement screen seem inviting in a mainstream way, but the atmosphere is actually quite student / alternative. It is very informal, especially during the day (when window seats are well placed for people watching), and regulars like it for its simple wholesomeness, redolent of home cooking. Vegetarian breakfasts are a speciality and all ingredients are organic, as far as possible. Yeast-free, dairy-free, gluten-free and wheat-free diets catered for and no processed or GM foods are used. Organic wines too. **Seats 48.** Mon-Sat 8.30am-8pm (Thu to 9pm), Sun 12-7. All à la carte (menus change daily); organic house wine about €16 (large glass about €3.95). Closed 25-27 Dec, 1 Jan, Easter Sun/Mon, Oct Bank Hol Sun/Mon. MasterCard, Visa, Laser. **Directions:** Off Grafton St. turn at Brown Thomas. ◇

Dublin 2	# Da Pino
RESTAURANT	38-40 Parliament Street Dublin 2
	Tel: 01 671 9308

Just across the road from Dublin Castle, this busy youthful Italian/Spanish restaurant is always full - and no wonder, as they serve cheerful, informal, well cooked food that does not make too many concessions to trendiness and is sold at very reasonable prices. Paella is a speciality and the pizzas, which are especially good, are prepared in full view of customers. Children welcome. **Seats 75.** Open 12-11.30 daily. À la carte. Wine from €15.90. Closed Christmas & Good Fri. Amex, Diners, MasterCard, Visa, Laser. **Directions:** Opposite Dublin Castle. ◇

Dublin 2	# Darwins
RESTAURANT	16 Aungier Street Dublin 2 **Tel: 01 475 7511**
	darwinsrestaurant@eircom.net

Proprietor Michael Smith's own butchers shop supplies certified organic meats to this restaurant in an area known for its butchers but not, until recently, so much as a dining destination. But, together with a strong team, Michael has opened up a whole new area for Dublin's discerning diners. Flavoursome cooking that pleases the eye as much as the taste buds combines sophistication with generosity, making the most of well-sourced ingredients, including excellent vegetables and delicious fish. Given Michael's background, you may expect excellent meats - especially great steaks - but it may be more of a surprise to find that vegetarians are so well looked after, and that one of the house specialities is a delicious vegetarian risotto of wild mushrooms and sun-dried tomato. Finish with a choice of gorgeous puddings - a well-made classic lemon tart perhaps - or mature farmhouse cheeses (attractively presented plated with fresh fruit and oatcakes) and a wack of irresistible Illy coffee. Good, reasonably priced house wines set the tone for a fair wine list - with interesting food, great service and competitive pricing too, it is no surprise that this restaurant is doing well. **Seats 50;** Air conditioning; Children welcome before 7; D Mon-Sat, 5.30 to 11; Early D daily 5-7 about €19.50; also à la carte. Closed Sun, 25-26 Dec & Bank Hols. Amex, MasterCard, Visa, Laser. **Directions:** Opposite Carmelite Church. ◇

Dublin 2	# The Davenport Hotel
HOTEL	Merrion Square Dublin 2 **Tel: 01 607 3900**
♛ ⌂	davenportres@ocallaghanhotels.ie www.ocallaghenhotels.ie

féile bia On Merrion Square, close to the National Gallery, the Dáil (Parliament Buildings) and Trinity College, this striking hotel is fronted by the impressive 1863 facade of the Alfred Jones designed Merrion Hall, which was restored as part of the hotel building project in the early '90s. Inside, the architectural theme is continued in the naming of rooms - Lanyon's Restaurant, for example, honours the designer of Queen's University Belfast, and the Gandon Suite is named after the designer of some of Dublin's finest buildings, including the Custom House. The hotel, which is equally suited to leisure and business guests, has been imaginatively designed to combine interest and comfort, with warm, vibrant colour schemes and a pleasing mixture of old and new in both public areas and accommodation. Bedrooms are furnished to a high standard with orthopaedic beds, air conditioning, voicemail, modem lines, personal safes and turndown service in addition to the more usual amenities - all also have ample desk space, while the suites also have fax and laser printer. Above all, perhaps, The Davenport is known for the warmth and helpfulness of its staff, and it makes a very comfortable base within walking distance of shops and galleries; it is the flagship property for a small group of centrally located hotels, including the Alexander Hotel (just off Merrion Square) and the Stephen's Green Hotel (corner of St Stephen's Green and Harcourt Street). Conference/banqueting (380/400). Business centre. Gym. Children welcome (Under 2s free in parents' room; cots available, baby sitting arranged). No pets. **Rooms 115** (2 suites, 10 junior suites). Lift. 24 hr room service. B&B about €97.50pps. Open all year. Amex, Diners, MasterCard, Visa. **Directions:** Just off Merrion Square. ◈

Dublin 2
PUB

Davy Byrnes

21 Duke Street Dublin 2 **Tel: 01 677 5217**
www.davybyrnes.com

Just off Grafton Street, Davy Byrnes is one of Dublin's most famous pubs - references in Joyce's Ulysses mean it is very much on the tourist circuit. Despite all this fame it remains a genuine, well-run place and is equally popular with Dubliners, who find it a handy meeting place. But a modern gastro-pub this is not - the bar food offered is quite traditional, providing 'a good feed' at reasonable prices. Irish stew is the house speciality and oysters with brown bread & butter, beef & Guinness pie and deep-fried plaice with tartare sauce are all typical, and there's always a list of daily specials like sautéed lambs liver with bacon & mushroom sauce, pheasant in season - and, in deference to the Joycean connections, there's also a Bloomsday Special (gorgonzola and burgundy). Half a dozen wines are available by the glass, and about twice that number by the bottle. Not suitable for children under 7. Outside eating area. Bar food served daily, 12.30-9 (winter to 5). House wine €17.95. Eoin Scott - Irish roots, trad and contemporary songs 9-11pm Sun-Tue. Closed 25-26 Dec & Good Fri. MasterCard, Visa, Laser. **Directions:** 100 yards from Grafton Street.

Dublin 2
RESTAURANT

Dax Restaurant

23 Upper Pembroke Street Dublin 2 **Tel: 01 676 1494**
olivier@dax.ie www.dax.ie

Olivier Meisonnave named this appealing restaurant after his home town in Les Landes, and it was the culmination of a longheld ambition. Flagged floors, light-toned walls and pale upholstery set off simple contemporary darkwood furniture, and it all adds up to a tone of relaxed contemporary elegance. Specialties like sautéed foie gras with apple and whole roasted seabass with herbs, feature on frequently changed menus that offer a carefully judged selection of dishes that can make up a standard 3-course meal, or be ordered as a light plate to enjoy with wine - a growing trend in Dublin at the moment, and a welcome one. Charcuterie and tapas style plates serve as starters or stand-alone dishes, and you'll also find substantial main courses (including a good steak), classic puddings and exceptional cheeses. An outstanding, mainly French, wine offering includes many great wines, a fair selection of affordable bottles, a carefully chosen choice of half bottles, and many by the glass. **Seats 65** (Private room seats 14); No suitable for children under 8 yrs. No wheelchair access. Air con. Reservations recommended. Open Tue-Sat, L 12.30-2.30; D 6-10.30, Set L €26, Early 3 course D €32, 6-7pm, Tue-Thurs; also á la carte. SC 12.5% on groups 6+. Closed Sun, Mon, 25 Dec - 4 Jan. Amex, MasterCard, Visa, Laser. **Directions:** On Upper Pembroke Street.

Dublin 2
RESTAURANT
Diep Le Shaker
55 Pembroke Lane Dublin 2 **Tel: 01 661 1829**
info@diep.net www.diep.net

This fashionable two-storey restaurant is elegantly appointed, with comfortable high-back chairs, good linen and fine glasses and, with sunny yellow walls and a long skylight along one side of the upper floor creating a bright atmosphere, the ambience is always lively. This is a restaurant with many fans and, and at its best, the cooking is excellent; a team of Thai chefs has developed a new menu of Royal Thai Cuisine: signature dishes include Lab Gai (spicy minced chicken salad), seafood dishes like Gaeng Goong Maprow Oon (red tiger prawn curry) and Pla Thod Kratiem Prik Thai (crispy whole sea bass). Service is invariably charming and solicitous. Not suitable for children after 9 pm. Air conditioning. Toilets wheelchair accessible. Jazz Tue & Wed night. **Seats 120.** Reservations accepted. L Mon-Thu 12.15-2.30 (Fri 12-5.30), D Mon-Wed 6.15-10.30, D Thu-Sat 6.15-11.15. L & D à la carte. House wine from about €21. SC 12.5% on parties 6+. Closed L Sat, Sun, bank hols, 25-29 Dec. Amex, MasterCard, Visa, Laser. **Directions:** First lane on left off Pembroke Street. ◇

Dublin 2
RESTAURANT
Dobbins Wine Bistro
15 Stephens Lane Dublin 2 **Tel: 01 661 9536**
dobbinsbistro@gmail.com

téile bia This restaurant hidden away near Merrion Square is something of a Dublin institution, run since 1978 by the late John O'Byrne and manager Patrick Walsh. Recently a major revamp transformed the restaurant - gone are the famous old Nissen hut and sawdust-strewn floors of old, here instead is a sleek modern look with smart leather banquettes and chairs, and contemporary lighting. But fans were glad to find that the fundamentals remain in place. A visit to this unique oasis has always been a treat for great hospitality, food which was consistently delicious in a style that showed an awareness of current trends without slavishly following them, and a love of wine. Now, while old hands may miss the cosiness of the previous Dobbins, the hospitality and professionalism has not changed and, although the presentation may be slicker, the cooking should still please. Ingredients are sourced with care, and reflect the locality: Dublin Bay prawns (not the ubiquitous tiger prawns found in so many establishments that should know better), and pork that is served with crackling indicate the philosophy and you'll find good value here too. Children welcome. Air conditioning. **Seats 120** (private room, 40). L Mon-Fri 12.30-2.30, D Tue-Sat 7.30-10.30. Set L about €24.50, D à la carte. House wine from €20. SC discretionary. Closed L Sat, all Sun, D Mon, bank hols, Christmas week. Amex, Diners, MasterCard, Visa, Laser. **Directions:** Between Lower & Upper Mount Street. ◇

Dublin 2
RESTAURANT
The Dome Restaurant
St Stephens Green Shopping Centre St Stephens Green Dublin 2
Tel: 01 478 1287

téile bia At the top of the shopping centre, this bright, airy daytime restaurant has a lot going for it before you take a bite: beautiful views over St Stephen's Green, a friendly atmosphere, fresh flowers - and sometimes even live background music. There's a self-service section and salad bar plus a blackboard describing dishes. Everything on display is very appetising and friendly chefs are at hand behind the counter to assist your choices. The food style is basically French and Mediterranean, also a full breakfast which is served from 8 am, and afternoon meals every day. Main courses like steak Wellington, braised lamb shank and cod au gratin should tempt the most determined sandwich muncher - and there are lovely desserts supplied by the **Mardi Cake Shop**, next door. Children are made very welcome too, with high chairs, changing facilities and bottle warming available. Great value for money too. Children welcome. **Seats 200.** Air conditioning. Open Mon-Sat, 8-6 (Sun 10-6, Thu to 8). A la carte. Wines (1/4 bottles) from €5.20. SC discretionary. Closed 25-26 Dec. MasterCard, Visa, Laser. **Directions:** Top floor of St. Stephen's Green Shopping Centre. ◇

Dublin 2
RESTAURANT
🍴 € Ⓔ

Dunne & Crescenzi

14 & 16 South Frederick Street Dublin 2 **Tel: 01 677 3815**
dunneandcrescenzi@hotmail.com www.dunneandcrescenzi.com

féile bia Always a delight for its unpretentiousness and the simple good food it offers at reasonable prices, this Italian restaurant and deli is very near the Nassau Street entrance to Trinity College, and the first of what is a small family chain of restaurants in and around the city. It's the perfect place to shop for genuine Italian ingredients - risotto rice, pasta, oils, vinegars, olives, cooked meats, cheeses, wines and much more - and a great example of how less can be more. How good to sit down with a glass of wine (house wine is reasonably priced, and bottles on sale can be opened for a small corkage charge) and, maybe, a plate of antipasti - with wafer-thin Parma ham, perhaps, several salamis, peppers preserved in olive oil, olives and a slice of toasted ciabatta drizzled with extra virgin olive oil... There are even some little tables on the pavement, if you're lucky enough to get them on a sunny day. Indoors or out, expect to queue: this place has a loyal following. **Seats 60** (outdoor, 20). Air conditioning. Open Mon-Sat 8-11, Sun L only 12-6. Á la carte; wine from about €12. Amex, MasterCard, Visa, Laser.
Directions: Off Nassau Street, between Kilkenny and Blarney stores. ◇

Dublin 2
RESTAURANT
🍴 Ⓔ

Eden

Meeting House Square Temple Bar Dublin 2 **Tel: 01 670 5372**
eden@edenrestaurant.ie www.edenrestaurant.ie

A highlight of the Temple Bar area, this spacious two-storey restaurant was designed by Tom de Paor and has its own outdoor terrace on the square - and terrace tables have the best seats for the free movies screened on the square on Saturdays in summer; modern, with lots of greenery and hanging baskets, there's an open kitchen which adds to the buzz and a fresh, contemporary house style provides quite extensive seasonal menus that make use of organic produce where possible, in updated classics which suit the restaurant well. Head chef Michael Durkan's menus are clear and to the point: specialities include a deliciously simple starter of smokies (smoked haddock with spring onion, crème fraîche and melted cheddar cheese), and down to earth dishes like beef & Guinness stew, and belly of pork. Organic beef is a feature - an excellent chargrilled sirloin with red onion, chips and a classic béarnaise sauce, perhaps - and vegetables, which always include a vegetable of the day, are exceptionally varied and imaginative. A three-course pre-theatre menu is great value. A well-balanced and fairly priced wine list includes bubblies and cocktails, and half a dozen wines by the glass. Great food and atmosphere, efficient service and good value too - Eden continues to fly the flag for Temple Bar. Children welcome before 8pm. **Seats 96** (private room, 12-30; outdoor seating, 32). Air conditioning. L daily,12.30-3 (Sun 12-3). D daily 6-10.30 (to 10 Sun). Set L €26, Early Bird D €25 (6-7, Sun-Thu), also à la carte. House wine from €23. SC 12.5% on groups 6+. Closed bank hols, 25 Dec - 2 Jan. Amex, Diners, MasterCard, Visa, Laser.
Directions: Next to the Irish Film Theatre, opposite Diceman's Corner.

Ely HQ

Dublin 2
RESTAURANT/WINE BAR

Hanover Quay Docklands Dublin 2 **Tel: 01 633 9986**
hq@elywinebar.com www.elywinebar.ie

téile bia This, the third and most recent of Erik and Michelle Robson's wine bar/cafés, is south of the river in the new Hanover Quay area of the city, which is nearing completion. On a corner site, it's an angular premises with huge windows and, with hard lines, drum lamp shades, canteen style tables and (a few) large flower motifs on soft furnishings, there's a slightly retro-60s side to the décor. It has a young, stylish feel to it, a strong cocktail menu, the great wine list that has become the trademark of the Ely group, and large eating areas on two levels, ground floor and downstairs. Smartly presented menus offer a choice of about a dozen starters and main courses, with the familiar emphasis on well-sourced ingredients but with a rather more sophisticated tone and higher prices than the other Ely menus. Good service is a strong point and this looks set to be a real winner in this fast-maturing and attractive area of the city. Free broadband wi/fi; children welcome before 7pm (high chair, baby changing facilities); toilets wheelchair accessible. **Seats 200** (private room, 45; outdoors, 80); air conditioning. L daily 12-3pm (to 4.30pm Sun); D daily 5.30-10.30pm (to 10pm Sun). SC 12.5% on groups 6+. Closed Christmas week. Amex, Diners, MasterCard, Visa, Laser. **Directions:** On the South Quays - Hanover Quay is off Sir John Rogerson's Quay.

Ely Winebar & Café

Dublin 2
RESTAURANT/WINE BAR

22 Ely Place Dublin 2 **Tel: 01 676 8986**
elywine@eircom.net www.elywinebar.ie

téile bia In an imaginatively renovated Georgian townhouse just off St Stephen's Green, the was the first of Erik and Michelle Robson's 'series' of Ely wine bar/ cafés; it first opened in 1999 and, since then, they have built on their commitment to offer some of the greatest and most interesting wines from around the world - earning an unrivalled reputation for their unique list and, especially, for the quality and range of wines offered by the glass. And the exceptional wine offering is backed up by other specialities including a list of premium beers; on the food side, organic produce, notably pork, beef and lamb from the family farm in County Clare, is a special feature - and you will not only find premium cuts, but also products like home-made sausages and mince, which make all the difference to simple dishes like sausages and mash or beefburgers. Two much bigger sister establishments, 'ely chq' and 'ely hq', opened in the IFSC and on Hanover Quay in 2006 and 2007 respectively (see entries). **Seats 100.** Children welcome before 7pm. Open Mon-Sat 12 noon-12.30 am. L 12-3 (1-4 Sat), D 6-10.30 (to 11 Fri/Sat). Bar open to midnight. Wines from EUR26. SC 12.5% on groups of 6+. Closed Sun, Christmas week, bank hols. Amex, Diners, MasterCard, Visa, Laser. **Directions:** Junction of Baggot Street/Merrion Street off St. Stephen's Green.

Fallon & Byrne

Dublin 2
RESTAURANT

11-17 Exchequer Street Dublin 2 **Tel: 01 472 1000**
www.fallonandbyrne.com

This chic, contemporary French restaurant could easily be missed given its location above their ground floor speciality grocery and food market (which simply begs you to browse). But once up the flight of stairs or lift, professionalism prevails as diners are swiftly greeted at the door and escorted to their table. Except for large flower arrangements displayed against the rear wall, decoration is minimal - high ceilings, white walls, no paintings but, oddly, it doesn't feel stark, but has that special French bistro ambience. Two islands of comfortable leather seating dominate the central area, surrounded by simply laid darkwood tables and chairs. There's a definite buzz to this bright and airy restaurant and a bar along one end provides a reception area where you can have a drink (if you can find a free stool) while waiting for your table - an agreeable interlude, as you watch the attentive staff at work. At your table, breads, butter and water are presented, along with appealing menus offering a refreshingly simple and well balanced choice. Authentic French bistro cooking is what's on offer here: a deliciously sweet French onion soup, for example, or seared foie gras with cinnamon brioche, or summer truffle brulée to start, followed by main courses with an equally French tone such as a lean and succulent loin of rabbit with fig & onion tart, morel mousse & cherry sauce. Even the long and mysterious trek to the toilets on the top floor (not an unusual experience in this area) will not dent enthusiasm for this place, with its simple and well executed menu, great tasting food, professional staff and good value. Fallon & Byrne, downstairs: Surrounded by bottles on the walls, you are in the cellar - clever idea; popular with the post-work crowd, who love the atmosphere and affordable menu - light bites (cheeseboard, salads, patés, olives) are also offered, and you can choose from the bottles around you (corkage €10). Before leaving, spend a little time looking around what has become Dublin's favourite food store - you are unlikely to leave empty-handed. **Directions:** Central Dublin, just off lower end of Grafton Street. ◊

Dublin 2 # Fire
RESTAURANT The Mansion House Dawson Street Dublin 2 **Tel: 01 676 7200**
enquiries@mansionhouse.ie www.mansionhouse.ie

The Mansion House has been the official residence of the Lord Mayor of Dublin since 1715 - the only mayoral residence in Ireland, it is older than any mayoral residence in Britain. A very large room previously known as The Supper Room is now used as a restaurant - the room itself is of sufficient interest to be worth a look even if you haven't time to eat, although the unusual Celtic themed contemporary décor of the current occupant, 'Fire', is unexpected in this graceful old room. The central feature that inspires the name is a huge wood-burning stove which also influences the menus, as most of the food is cooked in it; what you may expect here is an emphasis on quality ingredients and simple char-grilled dishes such as a speciality 'Tuscan' lamb cutlets (marinated in olive oil with rosemary and lemon, then char-grilled and served with roast aubergine, hummus and gremolata), char-grilled chicken and good steaks. Desserts tend to be a high point, service is smart and a fairly priced wine list includes above-average quality house wines at under-average prices. D Mon-Sat, 5.30-10pm, Sat, Jazz L, 1-4pm. Closed Sun. ◊

Dublin 2 # Fitzers Restaurant
RESTAURANT 51 Dawson Street Dublin 2 **Tel: 01 677 1155**
eat@fitzers.ie www.fitzers.ie

A very popular meeting place after work or when shopping in town, Fitzers offers reliable Cal-Ital influenced cooking in a smart contemporary setting, and has a heated al fresco dining area on the pavement. **Seats 90;** Open daily 11am-11pm; Early D €17.95, 5-7pm; set D €40; house wine €22; SC 12.5% on parties 6+. Closed Dec 25/26, Good Friday. Amex, Diners, MasterCard, Visa, Laser. Also at: *Temple Bar Square, Tel: 01-679 0440(12-11 daily, cl 25 Dec & Good Fri) *National Gallery, Merrion Square Tel: 01-663 3500 Mon-Sat 9.30-5, Sun 12-4.30, closed Gallery Opening days). **Directions:** Halfway up Dawson Street, on the right heading towards St Stephen's Green.

Dublin 2 # The Fitzwilliam Hotel
HOTEL St Stephens Green Dublin 2 **Tel: 01 478 7000**
enq@fitzwilliamhotel.com www.fitzwilliamhotel.com

If a comfortable city centre base is what you're after, you won't get more central than this stylish contemporary hotel, and, behind the deceptively low-key frontage, lies an impressively sleek interior created by Sir Terence Conran's design group: public areas combine elegant minimalism with luxury fabrics and finishes, notably leather upholstery and a fine pewter counter in the bar, which is a chic place to meet in the Grafton Street area. In addition to the hotel's premier restaurant, Thornton's (see separate entry), breakfast, lunch and dinner are served daily in their chic informal restaurant Citron, on the mezzanine level, which is popular with Dubliners escaping from the retail experience. Some of the bedrooms overlook the Green and, while quite compact for a luxury hotel, all are finished to a high standard with air-conditioning, safe, broadband, stereo CD player and minibar, and care has been lavished on the bathrooms too, including designer toiletries. There's an in-house hair & beauty salon, Free Spirit, and the hotel has a great hidden asset - Ireland's largest roof garden. Conference/banqueting (80/60). 3 conference rooms. Secretarial services. Children welcome; (under12s free in parents' room; cots available free of charge). 24 hour room service. **Rooms 128** (2 suites, 128 executive, 90 no-smoking, 4 for disabled). Lift. B&B about €160pps. No service charge. Open all year. Amex, Diners, MasterCard, Visa, Laser. ◊

SOUTH GREAT GEORGE'S STREET AREA

South Great Georges Street is on the edge of Temple Bar, on the south side of Dame Street. It is an interesting street, with many busy pubs and restaurants of all ethnic cuisines and sizes, and it attracts weary shoppers from nearby Grafton Street and early evening revellers. One of the first ethnic restaurants in the area is at the Dame Street end of Georges Street is the **Good World Chinese Restaurant** (South Great Georges Street; 01 677 5373), it prides itself on an especially full range of genuine Chinese dishes; it is popular with the local Chinese community - who especially appreciate the high standard of their Dim Sum. Directly across the street, **Yamamori Noodles** (South Georges Street; 01 475 5001) is a great buzzy place for family outings, offering good value speedy cooking with lots of flavour, generous portions and oodles of atmosphere too. A couple of doors up **Brasserie Sixty6** (South Great Georges Street; 01 400 5878) is a large high-ceilinged restaurant with unfussy modern décor - well known for a whole wall of mis-matched plates that lend warmth and informality, it aims to offer something different from the standard fare with a bill that won't break the bank.

WWW.IRELAND-GUIDE.COM FOR THE BEST PLACES TO EAT, DRINK & STAY

Dublin 2
RESTAURANT

Gotham Café

8 South Anne Street Dublin 2
Tel: 01 679 5266

This lively, youthful café-restaurant just off Grafton Street does quality informal food at reasonable prices and is specially noted for its gourmet pizzas - try the Central Park, for example, a Greek style vegetarian pizza with black olives, red onion & fresh tomato on a bed of spinach with feta & mozzarella cheeses and fresh hummus, which is just one of a choice of sixteen tempting toppings. Other specialities include Caesar salad, baby calzone and Asian chicken noodle salad There's a good choice of pastas too - and it's a great place for brunch on Sundays and bank holidays; consistent quality at fair prices. As part of a recent major renovation, a baby-changing facility has been created and a children's menu has been introduced too. Light breakfasts, including home-baked muffins, are now offered, from 10.30am [*A sister outlet, **The Independent Pizza Company**, is at 28 Lr Drumcondra Road, Dublin 9]. Children welcome. Air conditioning. **Seats 65** (outdoor seating, 10). Open daily: Sun-Thu 12 -11, Fri-Sat 12-12; (L 12-5, D 5-12). A la carte. House wine about €17.50. SC discretionary (10% on parties of 6+). Closed 25-26 Dec & Good Fri. Amex, MasterCard, Visa, Laser. **Directions:** Just off Grafton Street.

Dublin 2
HOTEL

The Grafton Capital

Stephens Street Lower Dublin 2 **Tel: 01 648 1100**
info@graftoncapital-hotel.com www.capital-hotels.com

In a prime city centre location just a couple of minutes walk from Grafton Street, this attractive hotel offers well furnished rooms and good amenities at prices which are not unreasonable for the area. Rooms are also available for small conferences, meetings and interviews. The popular 'Break for the Border' night club next door is in common ownership with the hotel. Small conferences (22). Business centre. Wheelchair access. Parking by arrangement with nearby carpark. Children welcome (Under 12s free in parents' room; cots available; baby sitting arranged). No Pets. **Rooms 75** (3 junior suites, 19 no-smoking, 4 for disabled). Lift. B&B about €100pps, ss €40. Short breaks offered. Closed 24-26 Dec. Amex, Diners, MasterCard, Visa, Laser. **Directions:** Near St. Stephen's Green (opposite Drury Street carpark). ◊

Dublin 2
GUESTHOUSE

Harrington Hall

69/70 Harcourt Street Dublin 2 **Tel: 01 475 3497**
harringtonhall@eircom.net www.harringtonhall.com

Conveniently located close to St Stephen's Green and within comfortable walking distance of the city's premier shopping areas, Trinity College and the National Concert Hall, Henry King's fine family-run guesthouse was once the home of a former Lord Mayor of Dublin and has been sympathetically and elegantly refurbished, retaining many original features. Echoes of Georgian splendour remain in the ornamental ceilings and fireplaces of the well-proportioned ground and first floor rooms, which include a peaceful drawing room with an open peat fire. Although there are some smaller, more practical bedrooms at the back, the main guestrooms are beautiful and relaxing with sound-proofed windows, ceiling fans and lovely marbled bathrooms. Service can be a little reserved but housekeeping is a strong point, and good breakfasts are served in a sunny yellow room with pictures of Dublin streetscapes to ensure a bright start to your day. All round this is a welcome alternative to a city-centre hotel, offering good value, handy to the Luas (tram), and with the huge advantage of free parking behind the building; luggage can be stored for guests arriving before check-in time (2pm). Small conferences (12). Children welcome (under 3s free in parents' room, cot available without charge). Parking (10). **Rooms 28** (2 junior suites, 3 shower only, 6 executive, 2 Family Rooms, all no smoking). Lift. 24 hour room service. B&B about €86.50, ss €20. Open all year. Free wi/fi. Amex, Diners, MasterCard, Visa, Laser. **Directions:** Off southwest corner of St. Stephen's Green (one-way system approaches from Adelaide Road). ◇

Dublin 2
HOTEL

Hilton Dublin

Charlemont Place Dublin 2 **Tel: 01 402 9988**
allan.myhill@hilton.com www.dublin.hilton.com

féile bia Overlooking the Grand Canal, this modern hotel is just a few minutes walk from the city centre and caters well for the business guest. Each double-glazed bedroom provides a worktop with modem point, swivel satellite TV and individual heater as well as the usual facilities. A buffet-style breakfast is served in the well-appointed **Waterfront Restaurant**. Conference/banqueting (350/270). Underground carpark. Children welcome (Under 12s free in parents' room; cots available). No pets. Lift. **Rooms 189** (78 no-smoking, 8 for disabled). Room rate from about €110 (max. 2 guests). Weekend specials from €176. Open all year. Amex, MasterCard, Visa. **Directions:** Off Fitzwilliam Square. ◇

Dublin 2
RESTAURANT

Hô Sen

6 Cope Street Temple Bar Dublin 2 **Tel: 01 671 8181**
timcostigan@hotmail.com www.hosen.ie

Ireland's first authentic Vietnamese restaurant, Hô Sen was our Ethnic Restaurant of the Year for 2006; the chefs are trained in Vietnam and take pride in bringing their cuisine to this pleasingly simple restaurant - and in introducing this lighter, clear-flavoured Asian cooking style at prices which are very reasonable by Dublin standards, and especially for Temple Bar where restaurants are often over-priced. Dimmed lights and candles create an appealing atmosphere from the street and, with comfortably-spaced tables, gentle background jazz and chopsticks supplied as well as western cutlery, the scene is set for an interesting evening. Vietnamese cooking has a reputation for being among the healthiest in the world and, although the familiar Asian styles feature - fresh herb flavours of coriander and lemongrass are dominant, and there is a light touch to both the flavours and the cooking. An extensive menu is shorter than it seems, as it includes many variations on a theme, and dishes are explained quite clearly. Specialities include Cá Kho Tô, a hotpot made with your choice of fish from the catch of the day, in which a generous amount of fish is cooked in a rich-flavoured 'pork marinade' with mushrooms, ginger root, lemongrass and a mixture of Vietnamese herbs and spices, including chilli. Choosing an appropriate wine might be a little problematic - perhaps beer or tea would be a better choice. Although the presentation isn't fancy, everything is appetising, and service is lovely - pleasant, helpful and efficient. And, as the cooking here is as exciting as the welcome is warm, this place is a little gem - and its growing popularity is a reassuring sign that Dubliners appreciate quality and value when they find it. **Seats 120** (private room available seats 20). L Thu-Sun 12.30-2.30 (3 Sun); D Tue-Sat 5-10.30 (9 Sun), Early Bird D about €16.95 (5-6.30). Wines from €16.95. Closed Mon, 17 Mar, 25 Dec. MasterCard, Visa, Laser. **Directions:** In Temple Bar, behind the Central Bank. ◇

Holiday Inn Dublin

Dublin 2
HOTEL/RESTAURANT
98-107 Pearse Street Dublin 2 **Tel: 01 670 3666**
info@holidayinndublin.ie www.holidayinndublincitycentre.ie

The Holiday Inn brand may possibly summon up the wrong images for independent travellers, but this centrally located hotel is not only a convenient place for visitors to stay, but has earned a particularly good reputation on several counts as a venue for business meetings and conferences (parking available), for food that is well above the standard expected from a mid-range hotel, and for its helpful staff. The accommodation offers all that would be expected (plus a gym for residents' use). Conferences/Banqueting (400), secure car parking, business centre, gym. **Rooms 101;** room rate from about €120 to €150 at weekends, open all year. **The Green Bistro:** This pleasant two-tier restaurant has tasteful décor, simple darkwood furniture and an outside area under a canopy where you can eat or just have a drink. It offers good straightforward fare in a central location until 10:30pm - appealing food, freshly cooked to order, includes pizza, pasta, fish and (excellent) steaks and is good value. Live music Sunday. 12.5% service charge for groups of 6 or more. MasterCard, Visa, Laser. **Directions:** Eastern end of Pearse Street. ◊

Hugo's

Dublin 2
WINE BAR/RESTAURANT
6 Merrion Row Dublin 2
Tel 01 6765955

A new Dublin sister for Gina Murphy and Padraig McLoughlin's impressive bar and restaurant in Tullamore, The Wolftrap (see entry), this recently opened wine bar and restaurant is easily recognised by its bright turquoise façade. The interior is more restrained but atmospheric, with rich wallpaper and plenty of mirrors and wine bottles on display; a downstairs area is similarl in style and has additional tables, with less formal seating towards the front. Hugo's has already become popular with style-conscious Dubliners and can be a busy place in the evenings, making for a convivial atmosphere - and friendly staff contribute to this ambience. As would be expected the wine list is extensive and well balanced between classics and more unusual offerings, with bottles ranging in price from €20 to €300; a larger selection of wines by the glass would be welcome, although those that are available are a good representation of the range available. A varied menu incudes some authentically French dishes such as frogs legs and moules frites, but the appeal of Hugo's is mainly as a wine bar, and the menu includes plenty of small/starter dishes that would be ideal if you wanted to nibble at some thing while just visiting for a few glasses of wine. Service may be slighty disorganised but staff are friendly. Open: L Mon-Fri 12-5 (Sat & Sun Brunch 11-4p); D daily, 5-11. All major cards. **Directions:** just off the Baggot Street corner of St. Stephen's. ◊

Il Primo Restaurant

Dublin 2
RESTAURANT
16 Montague Street Dublin 2 **Tel: 01 478 3373**
info@ilprimo.ie www.ilprimo.ie

This long established Italian restaurant has recently reopened with chef Anita Thoma and front of house man John Farrell now the new owners. They've spruced up the restaurant into a smart continental style, but the old fashioned warmth remains - and the giant picture window, where customers can see and be seen, is still the most striking feature. The ever-friendly John Farrell welcomes Italianophiles into the tiny downstairs dining area, which looks through the service bar area to the kitchen. More seating is available upstairs in two other dining rooms, though downstairs is the popular choice with regulars. Il Primo specialises in rustic Italian food, matched by mostly Tuscan wines. The wine list has long been famed and is rightly renowned, with wine imported directly from the wineries offering some unique treats as well as good prices. The menu includes some of the restaurant's old favourites, such as seafood lasagne, along with some new ones - Barolo-braised oxtail with pappardelle, for example; pasta is home-made and the effort shows in the quality. Main courses are divided into a remarkable range of risottos (you may well find the best risotto in Ireland here), creative pastas and gourmet pizza. The many simple dishes often have a curious twist and are evidence of Anita Thoma's wide repertory of rustic Italian food. Il Primo's casually stylish atmosphere makes it a perfect venue for the casual foodie as well as those looking for a treat without formality. Separate dining/function rooms available (30);

reservations recommended at weekend; children welcome; air conditioning. **Seats 80.** L Mon-Sat, 12.30-3, D daily 6-11 (Sun to 10); à la carte. House wines from €25 per litre. No SC (12.5% for groups 5+). Closed L Sun. Amex, Diners, MasterCard, Visa, Laser. **Directions:** 5 mins from St. Stephen's Green between Harcourt Street & Wexford Street.

Dublin 2
RESTAURANT

Imperial Chinese Restaurant

12A Wicklow Street Dublin 2 **Tel: 01 677 2580**

imperial@hotmail.com

Mrs Cheung's long-established city centre restaurant has enjoyed enduring popularity with Dubliners and has also a clear vote of confidence from the local Chinese community, who flock here for the Dim Sum at lunchtime - a good selection of these delectable Cantonese specialities is available between 12.30 and 5.30 daily: beef tripe is very enjoyable and Fried Seafood Noodles also attract regular praise: lots of succulent prawns, scallops and squid with Pak Choi. Crispy aromatic duck is another speciality from a wide-ranging selection of Chinese dishes. *Imperial Chinese was our Ethnic Restaurant of the Year in 1999. Children welcome. **Seats 180.** Private room available. Open daily 12.30-11.30 (L12.30-2.10 Mon-Sat). Set L about €12, Set D about €30. Also à la carte. House wine about €17. SC 10%. Closed 25-26 Dec. Amex, MasterCard, Visa, Laser. **Directions:** On Wicklow Street near Brown Thomas. ◊

Dublin 2
RESTAURANT

Jacobs Ladder

4 Nassau Street Dublin 2 **Tel: 01 670 3865**

dining@jacobsladder.ie www.jacobsladder.ie

féile bia Adrian and Bernie Roche's smart contemporary restaurant is up a couple of flights of stairs and has a fine view, overlooking the playing fields of Trinity College. The decor is on the minimalist side with a wooden floor and paintings for sale; good-sized tables with classic white linen and comfortable high-back chairs bode well. Adrian's cooking style is creative modern Irish and, while there is a slight leaning towards fish, his wide ranging seasonal menus always include some less usual meat dishes: steamed loin of rabbit - and imaginative vegetarian dishes. Several menus are offered - set menus at lunch and dinner, an à la carte and a Tasting Menu - and, although service can sometimes be a little slow, Adrian is a talented and dedicated chef, and the food is cooked to order. Dinner begins with a complimentary amuse-bouche - a tasty demi tasse of vegetable cream soup perhaps and excellent home-made breads; beautifully presented starters might include a house speciality of cep brulée (with its mousse, potato tuile & sautéed ceps) or roast quail, with eggs en cocotte, followed by main courses; panache of seafood, with basil gnocchi & summer vegetables or roast breast of duck served with fondant potatoes, braised small lettuce, white pudding and foie gras apple jus. This is complicated fare, but well executed. Classic desserts may be based on fruit grown by the family, and are worth leaving room for, or there are Irish farmhouse cheeses. A meal here should always be enjoyable and the set menus offer good value; however, if you order from the à la carte where starters are €14.50-18.50 and mains around €33 - this becomes an expensive restaurant and the slow service needs to be addressed. A very nicely balanced and selected wine list includes six good house wines. Children welcome. **Seats 80** (private room, 50). L Tue-Sat 12.30-2.30; D Tue-Sat, 6-10; Set D €44; Tasting menu €80, also à la carte. House wine from €21. No SC. Closed Sun & Mon, 25 Dec - 6 Jan, 17 Mar, Good Friday & 1 week Aug. Amex, Diners, MasterCard, Visa, Laser. **Directions:** City centre overlooking Trinity College.

Dublin 2   # Jaipur
RESTAURANT   41-46 South Great Georges Street Dublin 2 **Tel: 01 677 0999**
info@jaipur.ie   www.jaipur.ie

téite bia This custom-built restaurant is named after the "Jewel of Rajasthan" and offers a contemporary image of ethnic dining. It's a cool and spacious place, with a large modern spiral staircase leading up to an area that can be used for private parties, with the main restaurant below it. Modern decor and warm colours send the right messages and it is a pleasing space. Head chef Kaushick Roy uses mostly Irish ingredients, while importing fresh and dried spices directly, and his menus offer an attractive combination of traditional and more creative dishes. Service is attentive and discreet. Jaipur was the first ethnic restaurant in Ireland to devise a wine list suited to spicy foods. * There is a possibility that Jaipur may relocate to a new city centre premises during 2008. **Seats 125** (private room, 50). D daily, 5.30-11.30. Early D €22, 5-7pm; also A la carte. House wine from €18. Air con. Closed 25-26 Dec. * Also at: 21 Castle Street Dalkey, Co.Dublin, Tel: 01 285 0552; 5 St.James' Terrace, Malahide, Co.Dublin, Tel: 01 845 5455. Amex, MasterCard, Visa, Laser. **Directions:** At the corner of Sth Great Georges St. and Lower Stephens St.

Dublin 2   # Kilkenny Restaurant & Café
CAFÉ/RESTAURANT   5-6 Nassau Street Dublin 2 **Tel: 01 677 7075**
info@kilkennyshop.com

téite bia Situated on the first floor of the shop now known simply as Kilkenny, with a clear view into the grounds of Trinity College, the Kilkenny Restaurant is one of the most pleasant places in Dublin to have a casual bite to eat - and the experience lives up to anticipation: ingredients are fresh and additive-free (as are all the products on sale in the shop's Food Hall) and everything has a home-cooked flavour. Salads, quiches, casseroles, home-baked breads and cakes are the Kilkenny Restaurant specialities, and they are reliably good. They also do an excellent breakfast: fresh orange juice to start and then variations combinations of the traditional fare. [Kilkenny was the Dublin winner of our Irish Breakfast Awards in 2003.] A range of Kilkenny preserves and dressings - all made and labelled on the premises - is available in the shop. Air conditioning. Children welcome. **Seats 190.** Open Mon-Sat, 8.30-5.30 (Thu to 7), Sun 11-5.30. Breakfast to 11.15, lunch 11.30-3. A la carte. Licensed. Air conditioning. Closed 25-26 Dec, 1 Jan, Easter Sun. Amex, Diners, MasterCard, Visa, Laser. **Directions:** Opposite TCD playing fields.

Dublin 2   # L'Ecrivain
RESTAURANT   109a Lower Baggot Street Dublin 2 **Tel: 01 661 1919**
sallyanne@lecrivain.com   www.lecrivain.com

téite bia Derry and Sallyanne Clarke's acclaimed city centre restaurant is the destination of choice for many of Dublin's most discerning diners, and equally popular with the social set. On two levels - spacious and very dashing, it has lots of pale wood and smoky mirrors, and the main seating level includes a conservatory complete with awning which also acts as an airy and comfortable smoking area. Lovely elegant table settings promise seriously good food, and the cooking style - classic French with contemporary flair and a strong leaning towards modern Irish cooking - remains consistent, although new ideas are constantly incorporated and the list of specialities keeps growing. Specialities change seasonally but dishes which this kitchen has made its own include a starter of baked rock oysters with York cabbage & crispy cured bacon, with a Guinness sabayon, a fine modern interpretation of traditional Irish themes - perhaps followed by a main course of loin & rack of spring lamb with organic leeks, aubergine schnitzel and lamb sweetbreads. Menus offered by Derry Clarke and Chef de Cuisine Stephen Gibson include set menus at lunch at dinner, an à la carte and a Tasting Menu (€120) that is available to whole tables only, between 7 and 8.30pm. Whatever the time and menu, all the thoughtful little touches of a special meal abound - and there are some major ones too, like the very welcome policy of adding the price of your wine after the 10% service charge has been added to your bill, instead of charging on the total as most other restaurants do: this is an expensive restaurant but a gesture like this endears it to customers who happily dig deep into their pockets for the pleasure of eating here. Seafood, lamb, beef and game, in season, are all well represented, but menus often include neglected ingredients like rabbit, which is always appealingly served, and vegetarian dishes are handled with style. Pastry chef Joyce O'Sullivan's wonderful puddings are presented with panache and might include Black Forest Gateau fondant (cherry ice cream with cherry & white chocolate mousse), or toffee apple semi freddo; a special wine is suggested for each dish on the dessert menu and an extensive tea and coffee menu is offered. Presentation is impressive but not ostentatious, and attention to detail - garnishes designed individually to enhance each dish, careful selection of plates, delicious home-made breads and splendid farmhouse cheeses - is invariably faultless. Lunch, as usual in top rank restaurants, offers outstanding value. Sommelier Martina Delaney is renowned for her fine, constantly changing wine list, and her warmth and enthusiasm when helping guests with their wine selection; the list, which includes an impressive selection available by the bottle, half bottle or glass, also offers many special bottles a tempting range of champagnes and digestifs. [L'Ecrivain was the winner of our Wine Award in 2002.] **Seats 104** (private room, 20. outdoor seating, 22). Children welcome before 9pm; air con. L Mon-Fri 12.30-2, D Mon-Sat 7-10.30, Set L 2/3 course, €30/45. Set D €75 (Vegetarian Menu about €50). Tasting Menu €120. House wine from €30. SC discretionary. Closed L Sat, all Sun, Christmas & New Year, Easter, bank hols. Amex, MasterCard, Visa, Laser. **Directions:** 10 minutes walk east of St Stephens Green, opposite Bank of Ireland HQ.

Dublin 2
RESTAURANT

L'Gueuleton
1 Fade Street Dublin 2
Tel: 01 675 3708

This no-frills French restaurant took Dublin by storm when it opened in the autumn of 2004 - so much so that, in a very short time, it became necessary to extend. The format: simple premises and no-nonsense French bistro decor, with tightly packed tables and a few seats at the bar (with views into the kitchen), plus menus that make no distinction between courses and offer a combination of less usual dishes (Catalan snails with fennel and mortea sausage) and the classic (navarin of lamb). A plat du jour on the lunch menu, served with a glass of wine (or coffee or juice) is popular and great value (€15). Add to this great cooking, a short, all French wine list (by Simon Tyrrell), pretty efficient service and terrific value for money - and you have the kind of restaurant that Dubliners had been praying for. The original chef, Troy Maguire, left amidst much publicity in 2007, to set up the new Locks (see entry), but Warren Massey has stepped into the role with aplomb and the kitchen continues to please. The only downside is the continuing no reservations policy. **Seats 75** (outdoor, 20). Open Mon-Sat, L 12.30-3, D 6-10. Closed Sun. A la carte. House wines from €15. No reservations; SC 12.5% on groups 5+. MasterCard, Visa, Laser. **Directions:** At Hogans Bar, off Georges St. ◊

Dublin 2
RESTAURANT/WINE BAR

La Cave Wine Bar & Restaurant
28 South Anne Street Dublin 2 **Tel: 01 679 4409**
lacave@iol.ie   www.lacavewinebar.com

féile bia Margaret and Akim Beskri have run this characterful place just off Grafton Street since 1989 and it's well-known for its cosmopolitan atmosphere, late night opening and lots of chat. An excellent wine list of over 350 bins (predominantly French) includes over 15 bubblies, an exceptional choice of half bottles and a separate list of wines by the glass. With its traditional bistro atmosphere and classic French cooking, it's a great place to take a break from shopping, or for an evening out, or to hold a party. Classic menus with the occasional contemporary twist might include: paté de campagne, moules marinieres, Wicklow lamb cutlets, warm salad of duck livers, and tarte tatin - all indicate the style. A private room upstairs (with bar) is suitable for parties and small functions - Christmas parties are a speciality, but it's ideal for any kind of party, family reunions or even small weddings. Children welcome before 8pm. **Seats 28** (private room, 28). Air conditioning. Open Mon-Sat 12.30-11, Sun 5.30-11. Set L €14.25. Early D €17.25, 4-7pm Set D 2/3+ course €17.25/€32.50. Also à la carte. House wine from €18. SC discretionary. Closed L Sun, 25-26 Dec, Good Fri, L Bank Hols. Amex, Diners, MasterCard, Visa, Laser. **Directions:** Just off Grafton Street.

La Maison des Gourmets

Dublin 2
CAFÉ

15 Castle Market Dublin 2 **Tel: 01 672 7258**
info@la-maison.ie

In a pedestrianised area handy to car parks and away from the hustle and bustle of nearby Grafton Street, this French boulangerie has a smart little café on the first floor and also a couple of outdoor tables on the pavement for fine weather. Home-baked bread is the speciality, made to a very high standard by French bakers who work in front of customers throughout the day, creating a wonderful aroma that wafts through the entire premises. Their award-winning sourdough bread is used as the base for a selection of tartines - French open-style sandwiches served warm - on the lunch menu: baked ham with thyme jus and smoked bacon cream, perhaps, or vegetarian ones like roast aubergine with plum tomato, fresh parmesan & basil pesto. Add to this a couple of delicious soups (typically, French onion with Emmental croûtons), a hot dish like classic beef bourguignon with potato purée, one or two salads - and a simple dessert like strawberries with balsamic reduction and fresh cream - and the result is as tempting a little menu as any discerning luncher could wish for. Portions are on the small side, which suits most lunch time appetites, and service can be a little slow; but everything is very appetising, the atmosphere is chic and you can stock up on bread and croissants from the shop as you leave - just don't think in terms of a quick bite. **Seats 24** (outdoors, 10); air con; children welcome. Open Mon-Sat, 8-5 (L 12-3). A la carte. SC discretionary. House wine about €19. Closed Sun, bank hols, 4 days Christmas. Amex, Diners, MasterCard, Visa, Laser. **Directions:** Pedestrianised area between Georges Street Arcade and Powerscourt Shopping Centre.

La Mère Zou

Dublin 2
RESTAURANT

22 St Stephen's Green Dublin 2 **Tel: 01 661 6669**
info@lamerezou.ie www.lamerezou.ie

Eric Tydgadt's French/Belgian restaurant is situated in a Georgian basement on the north side of the Green. The style is now leaner-lined and fresh, but the essence of the restaurant hasn't changed since it opened in 2000. The reputation of La Mère Zou is based on classic French/Belgian country cooking, as in rillette of pork with toasted baguette or steamed mussels with French fries and prices are reasonable - a policy carried through to the wine list too. The lunch menu - which offers a choice of three dishes on each course - also suggests six or seven more luxurious seafood dishes from the à la carte, or, at the other extreme, they offer a range of Big Plates, with a salad starter and a main course served together on a king size plate. This is one of Dublin's most pleasant and most reliable restaurants with a sister establishment, **La Péniche**, on the Grand Canal (see entry). **Seats 55** (private room, 8, outdoor, 6); children welcome; Live jazz Fri-Sat 9-11; L Mon-Fri, 12-2.30. D 6-10.30 (Sun to 9.30). Early D €24.50 (6-7), Set L €24.50; also à la carte. House wine €21.50. SC discretionary (10% on groups 6+). Closed L Sat, L Sun, 25 Dec - 1st Fri Jan. Amex, Diners, MasterCard, Visa, Laser. **Directions:** Beside Shelbourne Hotel.

Léon Bistro

Dublin 2
RESTAURANT

33 Exchequer Street Dublin 2 **Tel: 01 670 7238**
www.cafeleon.ie

Having successfully recreated a corner of Paris in Dublin with their sophisticated brand of pastry cafés, Léon has now opened its first bistro with décor that's been cleverly devised to create a genuine Gallic ambiance. Choose a table down the back amongst the mismatched chairs, large gilt mirror, showpiece chandelier and distressed panelling and you will soon believe you're somewhere in Montmartre. The menu enhances the illusion with its list of genuine French classics; perhaps a croque madam or omelette for lunch or maybe Toulouse sausage, beef bourguignon or duck confit for dinner. There's a vast choice of authentic dishes and, although the cooking was a little uneven on the Guide's visit, service is relaxed and informal, making this a good spot to meet friends for a glass of wine and laid back meal. And be sure to leave room for dessert: order a classic from the menu or choose from the dazzling pastry display up front, where individual tarts and pastries, all made in-house, ensure a meal here will always end on a high note. Open 8am-11pm Mon-Sat; 10am-10pm Sun. **Directions:** Midway along Exchequer Street. ◈

Dublin 2
RESTAURANT

Les Frères Jacques

74 Dame Street Dublin 2 **Tel: 01 679 4555**
info@lesfreresjacques.com www.lesfreresjacques.com

One of the few genuinely French restaurants in Dublin, Les Frères Jacques opened beside the Olympia Theatre in 1986, well before the development of Temple Bar made the area fashionable. Most of the staff are French, the atmosphere is French - and the cooking is classic French. The decor is soothing - all the better to enjoy seasonal menus that are wide-ranging and well-balanced but - as expected when you notice the lobster tank on entering - there is a strong emphasis on fish and seafood; game also features in season, although there will always be prime meats and poultry also. Lunch at Les Frères Jacques is a treat (and good value) but dinner is a feast. The à la carte offers classics such as west coast oysters (native or rock) and grilled lobster, individually priced, and probably game in season. Finish with cheeses (perhaps including some Irish ones) or a classic dessert like warm thin apple tart (baked to order), with cinnamon ice cream and crème anglaise. The wine list naturally favours France and makes interesting reading. Reservation recommended; children welcome. **Seats 65** (private room, 40). L Mon-Fri, 12.15-2.30; D Mon-Sat, 7-10.30. Set 3 course L €22.50; Set 4 course D €36; also à la carte. House wine €22. SC 12.5%. Pianist on Fri/Sat nights. Closed L Sat, all Sun, 24 Dec-3 Jan. Amex, MasterCard, Visa, Laser. **Directions:** Next to Olympia Theatre. ◇

Dublin 2
HOTEL

Longfields Hotel

10 Lower Fitzwilliam Street Dublin 2 **Tel: 01 676 1367**
info@longfields.ie www.longfields.ie

Located in a Georgian terrace between Fitzwilliam and Merrion Squares, this reasonably priced hotel is more like a well proportioned private house, furnished with antiques in period style - notably in elegant public areas. Comfortable bedrooms are individually furnished, some with four-posters or half-tester beds, although they vary considerably in size as rooms are smaller on the upper floors. Small conferences (22). 24 hour room service. Children welcome (cots available). No pets. Lift. **Rooms 26** (2 junior suites, 19 shower only). B&B about €87.50pps, ss about €47.50 Open all year. Amex, MasterCard, Visa, Laser. **Directions:** On corner of Fitzwilliam Street & Baggot Street. ◇

Dublin 2
BAR

Market Bar & Tapas

Fade Street Dublin 2 **Tel: 01 613 9090**
info@tapas.ie www.tapas.ie

This large bar is located in the Victorian redbrick block best known for the George's Street Market Arcade. It's an attractive space with lofty ceilings, including a mezzanine floor and simple, stylish furnishings - unfortunately the wooden floor and hard surfaces bounce noise around and there's precious little to absorb it. It was an immediate hit with young Dubliners and the food, which is cooked in an open kitchen, has earned The Market Bar a reputation for serving some of the best tapas in Dublin. The menu is loosely Spanish, offering nibbles like olives, smoked almonds and anchovies, and more substantial dishes which can be ordered as small or large portions and include appealing renditions of Spanish classics like tortilla, morcilla inchos and patatas bravas. Allowing a little licence for local tastes, and providing you don't mind eating in a busy bar, this could be a good choice for casual eating while socialising. Toilets wheelchair accessible, bar access via ramp; children welcome before 7pm; air conditioning. Food daily: Mon-Sat 12-10; Sun 4-10. Closed 25-26 Dec, Good Fri. Amex, MasterCard, Visa, Laser. **Directions:** Off Georges St. ◇

Dublin 2
RESTAURANT
📷☆🍴

The Mermaid Café

69-70 Dame Street Dublin 2 **Tel: 01 670 8236**
info@mermaid.ie www.mermaid.ie

Ben Gorman and Mark Harrell's unusual restaurant on the edge of Temple Bar is not large, but every inch of space is used with style in two dining areas and a wine lounge. They celebrated a decade in business in 2005 and they've achieved well-earned recognition for a personal style of hospitality, imaginative French and American-inspired cooking and interesting decor. Innovative, mid-Atlantic, seasonal cooking can be memorable for inspired combinations of flavour, texture and colour - and specialities like New England crab cakes with piquant mayonnaise, the Giant Seafood Casserole (which changes daily depending on availability) and pecan pie are retained on daily-changing menus by popular demand. Vegetables, always used imaginatively, are beautifully integrated into main courses - rump of lamb with roast vegetable & couscous tart, aubergine & cumin purée is a good example. Then delicious desserts, wonderful Irish cheeses (like the deeply flavoured Gabriel and Desmond from West Cork, served with apple chutney) and coffees with crystallised pecan nuts: attention to detail right to the finish. Lunch menus are extremely good value, and Sunday brunch is not to be missed if you are in the area. Wines are imported privately and are exclusive to the restaurant. **Seats 75** (private room, 24). Reservations required. Air conditioning. Toilets wheelchair accessible. L 12.30-2.30 (Sun brunch to 3.30), D 6.00-11 (Sun to 9). Set L €21.95/25.95 2/3 courses, also á la carte; D á la carte. House wine €22.95. SC discretionary except tables 5+. Closed Christmas, New Year, Good Friday. *Next door, **Gruel** (Tel 01 670 7119), is a quality fast-food bistro (60 seats) under the same management, with a large & loyal following; open Mon-Sat 11-10.30; Sun 11-9. Amex, MasterCard, Visa, Laser. **Directions:** Next door to Olympia Theatre, opposite Dublin Castle.

Dublin 2
HOTEL/RESTAURANT
📷🏛🏛☆

Merrion Hotel

Upper Merrion Street Dublin 2 **Tel: 01 603 0600**
info@merrionhotel.com www.merrionhotel.com

HOTEL OF THE YEAR

Right in the heart of Georgian Dublin, opposite Government Buildings, this luxurious hotel comprises four meticulously restored Grade 1 listed townhouses built in the 1760s and, behind them, a contemporary garden wing overlooks formal land-scaped gardens. Luxurious public areas include two interconnecting drawing rooms with log fires and French windows (giving access to the gardens), which are immensely popular for business meetings or afternoon tea, and an attractive cocktail bar for evening time. Irish fabrics and antiques reflect the architecture and original interiors with rococo plasterwork ceilings and classically proportioned windows - and the hotel owns one of the most important private collections of 20th-century art. Maintenance is immaculate - refurbishment of soft furnishings, for example, is so skilfully effected that it is completely unnoticeable. Discreet, thoughtful service is an outstanding feature of the hotel and staff, under the excellent direction of General Manager Peter MacCann, are exceptionally courteous and helpful - there's a pervading sense of comfort and warmth that's especially welcoming and appealing: every guest is made to feel like a VIP from the moment of arrival - and, passing through the magnificent reception rooms, buzzing with chatter, tinkling china and crackling fires, a sense of immediate calm takes over. In a world of indentikit hotels with bland service, The Merrion feels incredibly special. Beautifully furnished guest rooms and suites have sumptuous bathrooms (all with separate bath and shower) and all the extras expected in a hotel of this calibre, including broadband, cosy bathrobes and bespoke Irish Heather & Moss toiletries. The hotel's Tethra Spa, with its Romanesque styled pool and marble steam room is predictably luxurious, and offers a compact gym and extensive treatment menu using E'Spa products. Dining options match standards elsewhere in the hotel: choose between the elegant vaulted Cellar Restaurant (see below) and Restaurant Patrick Guilbaud (see separate entry), which is also on site. Breakfast is especially noteworthy with exquisite baked goods, an excellent buffet and tempting menu cooked to order. Conference/banqueting (60/50). Broadband wi/fi; garden; fitness room; spa; steam room; swimming pool; guides available for walking. **Rooms 143** (20 suites, 10 junior suites, 80 no smoking, 5 for disabled, ground floor bedrooms suitable for less able). Children welcome (under 2s free in parents' room, cot available free of charge, baby sitting arranged). Air conditioning. Lift. 24 hr room service, B&B €180 pps. Underground valet parking, €20 per night. Open all year. **The Cellar Restaurant:** Warm, friendly staff swiftly seat arriving guests at beautiful classically appointed tables in this elegant vaulted dining-room, and explain Executive Head Chef Eddie Cooney's well-balanced menus, which are changed daily and have a refreshingly straightforward tone. With comfortable furniture and thoughtfully designed lighting and ventilation, this is a very relaxing room - and the philosophy is to source the best ingredients and treat them with respect in a simple style that shows the food to advantage without over-emphasis on display. Seasonality is key and though the kitchen works with many gourmet ingredients it is the signature dish of Merrion fish & chips with mushy peas and tartare sauce which best highlights their respect for clean flavours and quality ingredients.Pair this ethos with a good wine list (which offers an impressive amount of wines by the glass), attentive service, solid cooking and imaginative menus and you have an accessible introduction to The Merrion's high standards. *In fine summer weather the hotel also offers dining outdoors on the terrace. **Seats 86;** air conditioning; children welcome; L Mon-Fri 12.30-2, Set L €24.95; D daily 6-10, early D 6-7 Mon-Thurs €32.50, also à la carte. Sun Brunch 12.30-2.30. **The Cellar Bar:** Much more than an ordinary bar, this atmospheric series of vaulted rooms is everything you could wish for in the bar of an outstanding hotel. In an interesting reverse of the usual procedure, an exciting new wine list offering a remarkable range of wines, sherries, champagnes and dessert wines by the glass or bottle has been the inspiration for new lunch and evening menus devised by the hotel's Executive Head Chef, Eddie Cooney. To the best of our knowledge, this is a new departure for an Irish hotel - changed times indeed. Open all year. Amex, Diners, MasterCard, Visa, Laser. **Directions:** City centre, opposite Government Buildings.

Dublin 2
HOTEL

Mont Clare Hotel

Merrion Square Dublin 2 **Tel: 01 607 3800**
montclareres@ocallaghanhotels.ie www.ocallaghanhotels.ie

féile bia A few doors away from the National Gallery, this well-located and relatively well-priced hotel is in common ownership with the nearby Davenport and Alexander Hotels, and is a popular choice for business guests. The hotel is imaginatively decorated in contemporary style - except the old stained glass and mahogany Gallery Bar, which has retained its original pubby atmosphere. Compact bedrooms are well furnished and comfortable - and executive rooms for business guests have full marbled bathrooms and good amenities, including air conditioning, three direct line phones, a personal safe, ISDN lines and fax - and multi-channel TV with video channel. Business centre; use of gym (at Davenport Hotel). Conference/banqueting. (200). Children welcome (Under 2s free in parents' room; cots available free of charge). No pets. **Rooms 80** (40 no-smoking). Lift. Room rate about €245. Open all year. Amex, Diners, MasterCard, Visa, Laser. **Directions:** Corner of Clare Street, just off Merrion Square. ◊

Dublin 2
RESTAURANT

Montys of Kathmandu

28 Eustace Street Temple Bar Dublin 2 **Tel: 01 670 4911**
montys@eircom.net www.montys.ie

féile bia Shiva Gautham's modest-looking restaurant opposite the Irish Film Centre is the only one in Ireland to specialise in Nepalese cuisine, and the food here is invariably very enjoyable - at agreeably moderate prices. The chefs are all from Nepal and although all the familiar Indian styles are represented- tandoori, curry etc - the emphasis is on Nepalese specialities and varying standard dishes by, for example, using Himalayan spices. The menu is quite extensive and includes a platter of assorted starters which is a good choice for a group of four, allowing time to consider the rest of the menu without rushing; there's also a fair selection of vegetarian dishes, including a traditional Nepali mixed vegetable curry which can be served mild, medium or hot. Friendly and exceptionally helpful staff are perhaps the most outstanding feature of the restaurant service throughout is gently attentive and staff are happy to offer suggestions, or to choose a well balanced meal for you, including specialities like Kachela (a starter of raw minced lamb with garlic, ginger, herbs and spices which is said to be a favourite amongst the Newars in Kathmandu, served with a shot of whiskey) and Momo - these Nepalese dumplings served with a special chutney require 24 hours notice and are 'the most popular dish in Kathmandu'. But you will also find sound renditions of old favourites here, including Chicken Tika Masala: moist pieces of tender boneless chicken cooked in the tandoori, and served in a creamy masala sauce. This can be a really rewarding restaurant and, in addition to an extensive wine list (organised by price) and drinks menu, they even have their own beer, 'Shiva', brewed exclusively for the restaurant. Children welcome. **Seats 60** (private room, 30) L Mon-Sat, 12-2; Set L €20; D daily 6-11.30pm, (Sun to 10.30), Tasting Menu about €50. L&D à la carte available. SC 12.5% on groups 6+. House wine from €18. Closed L Sun, 25-26 Dec, 1 Jan & Good Fri. Amex, MasterCard, Visa, Laser. **Directions:** Temple Bar - opposite the Irish Film Centre(IFC).

Dublin 2
HOTEL

Morgan Hotel
10 Fleet Street Temple Bar Dublin 2
sales@themorgan.com www.themorgan.com

In deepest Temple Bar, this unusual boutique hotel is characterised by clean simple lines and unclut-tered elegance. Bedrooms have 6' beds in light beech, with classic white cotton bed linen and natural throws, while standard bedroom facilities include satellite TV and video, CD/hi-fi system, mini-bar, safe, voicemail and Internet access. Bathrooms in the better rooms are spacious and spare in style, although some less desirable rooms are shower only; some rooms also have a sound-proofing problem and it would be wise to ensure that your room is not over the bar. Staff are very helpful and there are nice touches about the hotel, such as having an umbrella available on loan for the duration of your stay. An excellent buffet breakfast offers lots of fresh fruit as well as yoghurts, muesli, good croissants and other breads, cheeses, charcuterie, good coffee and the usual full fry at €18 per person. The stylish Morgan Bar is open all day and offers an oasis of comfort and relaxation amongst the hustle and bustle of Temple Bar - try an exotic Morgan Mai Tai, perhaps? Casual dining is available in the **Morgan Bar**, where an excellent (and extensive) tapas menu is served all day (12.30pm until 9.30pm). Children welcome (cots available without charge, baby sitting arranged). **Rooms 66** (1 suite, 1 junior suite, 15 executive, 30 shower only, 33 no-smoking). Lift. Room rate €220. Closed Christmas. Amex, Diners, MasterCard, Visa, Laser. **Directions:** Off Westrmoreland Street. ◊

Dublin 2
CAFÉ

Nude Restaurant
21 Suffolk Street Dublin 2 **Tel: 01 672 5577**
niamh@nude.ie www.nude.ie

Nude offers fantastic very fresh food - organic whenever possible - in an ultra-cool, youthful environ-ment. Just off Grafton Street, it's a great place for a healthy breakfast or a quick snack, with plenty of room to sit down at long canteen-style tables. Queue up, order and pay at the till, then collect your food if it's ready or it will be delivered to your table. Just looking at the fresh fruit and vegetables hanging or racked up in the open kitchen should revive you while you wait! A choice of soups all come with with freshly baked breads; there are hot wraps - or try the chill cabinet for salads like Caesar or tomato & mozzarella, and cold wraps or soft bread rolls. Freshly squeezed juices, smoothies and organic Fair Trade coffees, teas and herbal teas are all very popular and the menu caters for vegetar-ians and other dietary requirements. **Seats 40.** Open daily 7.30am-9pm (to 10pm Thurs, 8pm Sun). * Also at: 38 Upper Baggot St 01 668 0551; George's Quay, 01 677 4661; Dublin Airport. MasterCard, Visa, Laser. **Directions:** Near Dublin Tourism office. ◊

Dublin 2
GUESTHOUSE

Number 31
31 Leeson Close Lr Leeson Street Dublin 2 **Tel: 01 676 5011**
number31@iol.ie www.number31.ie

GUESTHOUSE BREAKFAST OF THE YEAR

Formerly the home of leading architect, the late Sam Stephenson, Noel and Deirdre Comer's hospitable 'oasis of tranquillity and greenery' just off St Stephen's Green has recently re-opened after major refurbishment and it makes a relaxing and interesting city centre base, with virtually everything within walking distance in fine weather. You approach the Georgian townhouse from the garden, and the welcome is warm and friendly (tea/coffee and cookies served as your car is being parked in their secure car park); public areas of the house are spacious and very comfortable, and the accommodation is in two different buildings - the elegant Georgian town-house on Fitzwilliam Place (decorated in deep tones) and the beautifully converted coach-house (much brighter), with an interconnecting patio garden. The elegant bedrooms have exceptionally comfortable beds, good bathrooms (except, perhaps, that the lighting could be improved), and nice little extras including complimentary bottled water as well as phones, flat screen TV and

DVD player. And breakfasts, served at communal tables inside, and in the conservatory are a treat to treasure juices, fresh fruit and cereals on display, freshly baked breads and delicious preserves, and lovely hot dishes like kippers, Eggs Benedict or scrambled egg with smoked salmon all cooked to order... it has a homely feel as the kitchen is beside the breakfast room and there is no door, so you can watch as your breakfast is being prepared. Prices are moderate for central Dublin, and this is a lovely place to stay in fact, with its stay-in-all-day atmosphere, you might find it hard to leave. Not suitable for children under 10. No pets. Rooms at the back are quieter. Secure parking. **Rooms 20** (all en-suite & no smoking). B&B from about €75, ss €25. Open all year. Amex, MasterCard, Visa. **Directions:** From St. Stephen's Green on to Baggot Street, turn right on to Pembroke Street and left on to Leeson Street. ◇

Dublin 2
PUB/GUESTHOUSE

O'Neill's Pub & Guesthouse

37 Pearse Steet Dublin 2 **Tel: 01 677 5213**
oneilpub@iol.ie www.oneillsdublin.com

Established in 1885, this centrally located pub on the corner of Pearse Street and Shaw Street is easily recognised by the well-maintained floral baskets that brighten up the street outside. Inside, this cosy bar has kept its Victorian character and charm (two bars have lots of little alcoves and snugs) and serves a good range of reasonably priced home-cooked food - typically steak champignon with red wine sauce, served with French fries and an attractive salad; lamb filo parcels with mint yoghurt and chilli con carne - all good value. (Accommodation is available in en-suite rooms, with breakfast served in a pleasant room above the pub; rather expensive for simple accommodation at about €45 pps midweek - about €60 at weekends - but conveniently located.) Bar food: L 12.30-2.30, D 5.30-8. Closed Christmas & Good Fri. Amex, MasterCard, Visa, Laser. **Directions:** Opposite Pearse Street side of Trinity College. ◇

Dublin 2
PUB

M J O'Neill's Public House

2 Suffolk Street Dublin 2 **Tel: 01 679 3656**
mike@oneillsbar.com www.oneillsbar.com

A striking pub with its own fine clock over the door and an excellent corner location, this large bar has been in the O'Neill family since 1920 and is popular with Dubliners and visitors alike. Students from Trinity and several other colleges nearby home into O'Neill's for its wide range of reasonably priced bar food, which includes a carvery with a choice of five or six roasts and an equal number of other dishes (perhaps including traditional favourites such as Irish Stew) each day; finish off with some home-made rhubarb pie, perhaps. There is also a well-presented sandwich/salad bar. B 10-12; Carvery 12 - 10.15 pm daily (open from 12.30 Sun); also extensive à la carte bar menu; set 3 course L €20; 2/3 course D €15/€20. Live traditional music every Mon night at 9pm. No children after 9pm. Closed 25 Dec, Good Fri. Amex, MasterCard, Visa, Laser. **Directions:** On the corner of Suffolk St and Church Lane, opposite the DublinTourist Centre.

Dublin 2
BAR/RESTAURANT
👑

Odessa Lounge & Grill

13/14 Dame Court Dublin 2 **Tel: 01 670 7634**
info@odessa.ie www.odessa.ie

Tucked away just a few minutes walk from Grafton Street, this has long been a favourite haunt for Dublin's bright young things and was one of the first places in Dublin to do brunch - a smart entrance gives way to a fashionably furnished restaurant and, downstairs, a more clubby room with comfy leather chairs, subdued lighting, and plenty of room to spread out and read the papers in peace is an appealing place to be after a late night on the town. Menus, which were ahead of fashion when Odessa opened in 1994, haven't changed in years yet they still seem fresh and have an emphasis on seasonal ingredients - fresh seafood includes Galway Bay lobster and wild Irish crab, when available, and a summer speciality is glazed rump of lamb with mint crushed potatoes and balsamic jus. Skilful cooking, very good value for the quality of food and style of restaurant, and Irish staff who combine efficiency with good humour make this a great place to dine. *The Odessa Club (www.odessaclub.ie) is a private Members Bar with screening facilities on the second floor, and is affiliated with Societe De Kring (www.kring.nl) in

Amsterdam; wine tasting dinners are held regularly, and Odessa Club members are offered a special rate for accommodation nearby at **Grafton House** (www.graftonguesthouse.com; Tel 01 679 2041), 26/27 South Great George's Street. **Seats 190** (private room, 60). Air conditioning. Sat & Sun open brunch 11.30-4.30; D daily 6-10.30, Early bird D €18.50 (Sun-Fri, 6-7); Set D €28/40 2/4 course. House Wine €20. SC 12.5%. Closed Bank Hols, 25/26 Dec. Amex, MasterCard, Visa, Laser. **Directions:** Just off George's Street / Exchequer Street.

Dublin 2
RESTAURANT

The Old Mill
14 Temple Bar Dublin 2
Tel: 01 671 9262

Long before Temple Bar became trendy, Moroccan chef-patron Lahcen Iouani had a loyal following in the area - since the mid-80s, in fact, when this restaurant delighted discerning Dubliners in an earlier guise as 'Pigalle'. The name change has relevance to local history (you can read all about it on the back of the menu) but other things have thankfully remained the same and Lahcen continues to offer good French cooking at refreshingly modest prices. The place has a homely feeling, like stepping back in time to an old French restaurant - giving good value to the customer is something he feels strongly about. A blackboard menu offers traditional starters like paté de foie de canard and salade niçoise, and classic main courses such as boeuf Bourginonne and sole meunière are unusually well-priced. Vegetarian dishes are offered and there's also a good value early menu. **Seats 50.** Reservations accepted. Air conditioning. Open Mon-Sun, 12.30-11.30; L 12.30-4, D 5-11. Set L about €16.95, value D from 5-7.30pm, also à la carte. House wine from about €19. SC discretionary except on parties of 8+ (12.5%). MasterCard, Visa, Laser. **Directions:** Above Merchants Arch on Temple Bar Square (behind Central Bank). ◈

Dublin 2
RESTAURANT

One Pico Restaurant
5-6 Molesworth Place Schoolhouse Lane Dublin 2 **Tel: 01 676 0300**
www.onepico.com

Quietly located in a laneway near St. Stephen's Green, just a couple of minutes walk from Grafton Street, Eamonn O'Reilly's One Pico is one of Dublin's most popular fine dining restaurants. The surroundings are elegant, with crisp white linen and fine china and glassware, and the cooking is exceptionally good: sophisticated, technically demanding dishes are invariably executed with confidence and flair. The range of menus offered includes lunch and pre-theatre menus which, as usual in restaurants of this calibre, represent great value, an 8-course Tasting Menu, a vegetarian menu (on request), and an à la carte, with about ten quite luxurious dishes offered on each course, plus optional side dishes which should not be necessary as each main course is individually garnished. There is an occasional small nod to Irish traditions, but this is classical French cooking with a modern twist, albeit based for the most part on the very best local ingredients. Specialities include creative seafood dishes - roasted skate wing is accompanied by crisp potato with crab, spinach purée and herb butter, for example - and there are also upbeat versions of traditional meat dishes such as a braised beef daube with roasted vine tomatoes. Eamonn O'Reilly cooks with first class ingredients, turning them into classic dishes with lovely clean flavours, and his own unique style on each dish. To finish, it is difficult to decide between an innovative and delicious cheese menu, or beautifully presented desserts that taste as good as they look - and include refreshing choices like a summer creation of luscious Wexford strawberries with creme patissiere, crisp tartine & strawberry granitaé. This is a fine restaurant and has earned its place among the city's best. *A sister restaurant is **Bleu Bistro Moderne** - see entry. **Seats 85** (private room, 46). Air conditioning. L& D Mon-Sat: L12-3, D 6-11. Set L €30, Early D €38 (6-7.30); Set D €38, Tasting Menu €90, also à la carte. House wine €28. SC discretionary. Closed Sun, bank hols, 24 Dec-5 Jan. Amex, Diners, MasterCard, Visa, Laser. **Directions:** 2 mins walk off St. Stephen's Green/Grafton Street near Government Buildings.

Dublin 2
RESTAURANT

Pasta Fresca

2-4 Chatham Street Dublin 2
Tel: 01 679 2402

This long-established Italian restaurant in the Grafton Street shopping area specialises in fresh pasta, and is known for its consistent standards; their popular all-day menu is based on good home-made pastas, thin-based crispy Neapolitan pizzas, a wide range of interesting salads with well-made dressings. There are plenty of vegetarian dishes on offer - bruschetta rosso, with fresh tomatoes & mozzarella, for example, or fettucine al broccoli - and a speciality pasta salad (with Tuscan beans, sweetcorn, fresh vegetables, shaved Parmesan & house dressing). A shorter list of grills includes fish of the day and several chicken dishes: their own Pollo Pasta Fresca, for example, is well worth trying, chicken breast filled with mozzarella cheese and spinach, wrapped in bacon, served with herby mashed potatoes and salad. Evening menus offer a wider choice and shoppers and diners alike can also buy Italian groceries, fresh pasta and sauces made on the premises from their deli counter. Children welcome. **Seats 150** (outdoors, 20). Air conditioning. Open all day Mon-Sat, 12-12, Sun 1-12. Set L €9.95 (11-5); D also à la carte. House wine from €17.95. SC discretionary. Closed 25 Dec, 1 Jan. Amex, Diners, MasterCard, Visa, Laser. **Directions:** Off top of Grafton Street. ◊

Dublin 2
RESTAURANT/WINE BAR

Pearl Brasserie

20 Merrion Street Upper Dublin 2 **Tel: 01 661 3572**
info@pearl-brasserie.com www.pearl-brasserie.com

Just a few doors away from The Merrion Hotel, Sebastien Masi and Kirsten Batt's stylish basement restaurant has an open peat fire and an aquarium that runs the length of the bar, where aperitifs and a light bar menu are served. The style is contemporary international, with a classic French base and a pleasing emphasis on clean flavours highlighting the high quality of ingredients. Several menus are offered, including an attractive vegetarian menu, and there is a leaning towards towards fish and seafood, which Sebastien cooks with accuracy and flair - a fresh crab meat & guacamole starter is served with tomato & gazpacho & potato galette, for example - and specialities from the land include luscious pan-fried foie gras with toasted brioche and strawberry & rhubarb compôte (and an optional glass of Montbazillac, which is hard to resist); main courses include prime meats - pan-fried fillet beef with fondue of spinach and roquefort croquette potato, is a speciality - and there are less usual luxurious dishes such as squab pigeon Rossini, with pan-fried foie gras and black truffle mashed potato. Desserts are a highlight and include particularly good ices, and coffee is served with home-made chocolates. Charming, efficient and well informed service complements Sebastien Masi's unusual and beautifully presented meals. The wine list is a good match for the food, favouring France and including a good choice of half bottles. *Separate Wine Bar area serving nibbles & light bar menu. Also available for cocktails and apperitif and digestif drinks. Children welcome. **Seats 80** (private area, 10); reservations recommended; air-conditioning. L Mon-Fri 12-2.30, D Mon-Sat 6-10.30. 'Value' L €24, D à la carte; also vegetarian menu. House wine €21. SC discretionary. Closed Sun, bank hols. Amex, MasterCard, Visa, Laser. **Directions:** Opposite Government Buildings, near Merrion Hotel.

Dublin 2
PUB

The Pembroke

31/32 Lower Pembroke Street Dublin 2 **Tel: 01 676 2980**
info@pembroke.ie www.pembroke.ie

There was consternation amongst traditionalists when this fine old pub was given a complete makeover some years ago, creating the bright and trendy bar that it is now - it even has a cyber café in the basement. But, if the cosiness of old has now gone for ever, the spacious new bar that took its place has character of its own and, along with some striking design features (notably lighting), the atrium/ conservatory area at the back brings the whole place to life and there is space for a large number of outdoor tables. Meeting the needs of those who get in to work before the traffic builds up, bar food begins with an impressive breakfast menu offering everything from cereals or muesli to the Full Irish, with all sorts of more sophisticated treats like scrambled egg with smoked salmon. Later menus offer appealing hot dishes and a range of bar snacks. **Seats 200** (private room 60, outdoor seating 80). Food served Mon-Sat, 7.30am-8pm. Closed Sun, Christmas & Good Fri. *Layla Turkish restaurant upstairs, see entry. Amex, Diners, MasterCard, Visa, Laser. **Directions:** Near St Stephen's Green - off Lr Baggot Street.

Dublin 2
RESTAURANT

Peploe's Wine Bistro

16 St Stephen's Green Dublin 2 **Tel: 01 676 3144**
reception@peploes.com www.peploes.com

In the basement of the Georgian terrace than runs along the north side of St Stephen's Green, Peploe's is very handy to both the Grafton Street area and the nearby offices - perfect territory for a laid-back wine bar. The retro décor is reminiscent of a chic 1950s New York brasserie and creates a warm and inviting atmosphere, complete with neat table settings and stylishly-dressed staff. Although the dining room appears cramped, it is comfortable and the service is pleasant and professional. The menu offers a good variety of dishes, if only for an appetiser or two (from a choice of ten starters) to accompany your wine, and the dozen or so main courses are well-balanced between pasta, meat and fish, plus the chef's specials which are notified at the table. A choice of tasty breads gets your meal off to a good start, followed by quite unusual dishes such as carpaccio of veal with aioli, or lightly-crusted Brie which is set off well by marinated Pruneaux d'Agen. An autumn menu might include venison loin, cooked to your taste, girolle mushrooms and balsamic jus while the chef's special is likely to be deliciously fresh fish. A generous apple & blackberry crumble would be enough for two people and delightfully fruity, or you may finish with a choice of French and Irish cheeses, and good coffee. An extensive wine list includes a dozen or more champagnes and about thirty wines by the glass. Service is smart, the atmosphere is great and the cooking has style - all this and a reasonable bill too. **Seats 90.** Reservations required. Air conditioning. Toilets wheelchair accessible. Children welcome. Open 12.30-3.30pm & 6-10.30pm daily; Early D €25, Sun-Wed, 6-8pm; L&D à la carte, (also set D €52.50 for groups 8+ only); house wine €22; SC 12.5% on groups 6+. Closed 24-29 Dec, Good Fri. Amex, MasterCard, Visa, Laser.
Directions: North side of St. Stephen's Green.

Dublin 2
RESTAURANT/WINE BAR

The Port House

64a South William St. Dublin 2 **Tel: 01 677 0298**
info@porthouse.ie www.porthouse.ie

This recent Dublin venture by the team who created **The Porterhouse** (Parliament Street and other branches), bears all their hallmark attention to detail - the wine bottles on high shelves, warm brick walls, remains of an old fireplace, flagged floors and simple mismatched modern furniture make this basement wine bar highly atmospheric, especially when seen in candlelight. But, although that's a great start, there's more to this little place than atmosphere and they deliver well on the food side too, bringing a taste of Spain to South William Street. Menus offer a couple of dozen tapas size items (think 'small starter'), divided into hot and cold 'pinchos'; order a few to share and see how it goes, depending on whether you're just having a drink and a nibble or want the equivalent of a light meal. There are some tempting items on offer, some more familiar than others: nibbles like toasted almonds with paprika, less usual offerings such as foie gras or mini sirloin steaks, and regional Spanish cheeses and tasty renditions of many of the well known tapas classics like calamares rabas (squid in batter), tostas de setas (mushrooms with garlic butter), tortilla (Spanish omelette) and patatas bravas (deep fried potato cubes with tomato sauce). Cooking is good and it's fun. There are some value wines, and also some interesting Basque bottled beers too (the ale and lager are perhaps better than the stout). Not suitable for children under 10 yrs; no reservations accepted. **Seats 50** (private room, 6, outdoors, 6); Air conditioning; Tapas served daily, all day 11-1am (Sun to 11pm); house wine from €3.50 per glass. Closed 25-26 Dec. MasterCard, Visa, Laser. **Directions:** A few doors up from the corner of Exchequer St and South William Street. ◊

Dublin 2
PUB

The Porterhouse

16-18 Parliament Street Temple Bar Dublin 2 **Tel: 01 679 8847**
www.theporterhouse.ie

Dublin's first micro-brewery pub opened in 1996 and, although others have since set up, The Porterhouse was at the cutting edge. Ten different beers are brewed on the premises and connoisseurs can sample a special tasting tray selection of plain porter (a classic light stout), oyster stout (brewed with fresh oysters, the logical development of a perfect partnership), Wrasslers 4X (based on a West Cork recipe from the early 1900s, and said to be Michael Collins' favourite tipple), Porter House Red (an Irish Red Ale with traditional flavour), An Brain Blasta (dangerous to know) and the aptly named Temple Brau. But you don't even have to like beer to love The Porterhouse. The whole concept is an innovative move away from the constraints of the traditional Irish pub and yet it stays in tune with its origins - it is emphatically not just another theme pub. The attention to detail which has gone into the decor and design is a constant source of pleasure to visitors and the food, while definitely not gourmet, is a cut above the usual bar food and, like the pub itself, combines elements of tradition with innovation: Carlingford oysters, Irish stew, beef & Guinness casserole are there, along with the likes of home-made burgers and a good range of salads. This is a real Irish pub in the modern idiom and was a respected winner of our Pub of the Year award in 1999. No children after 9pm. **Seats 50.** Open noon - 11.30 daily (Thu-Sat to 12.30). Bar food served 12-9.30 daily (Sun from 12.30). Closed 25 Dec & Good Fri. [*The original Porterhouse is located on Strand Road on the seafront in Bray, Co. Wicklow and, like its sister pub in Temple Bar, it offers bar food daily from 12.30-9.30. Tel/Fax: 01 286 1839. There is also a Porterhouse in London, at Covent Garden.] MasterCard, Visa.

Dublin 2
RESTAURANT

The Purty Kitchen

34/35 East Essex Street Temple Bar Dublin 2 **Tel 01 6770945**
templebar@purtykitchen.com www.purtykitchen.com

In the heart of Temple Bar, this new sister establishment of the popular Purty Kitchen in Monkstown offers some comfort and respite in a very busy part of the city. It's in a street corner pub with an authentic stone period frontage and, inside, a large high-ceilinged u-shaped room with an impressive bar in the centre, and large front windows which create a pleasing sense of space and lots of natural light. A dark wooden floor and polished darkwood tables and chairs lend character to the relaxed, uncluttered space, and traditional booths offer a little privacy. Extremely friendly staff are quick to make customers feel welcome, swiftly taking drinks orders and offering an extensive bar menu which features a good selection of appetisers, salads, open sandwiches (served on the Purty Kitchen's excellent homemade seed bread), steaks, homemade burgers and chicken; there's a strong emphasis on fish and seafood, including specialities of Purty Seafood Chowder and the Purty Seafood Platter. In addition to a well stocked bar there is also a well-balanced wine list, with some offered by the glass. With its simple tasty food, served in comfortable surroundings and at reasonable prices - plus a packed schedule of late night entertainment during the weekends - this is a very welcome newcomer to Temple Bar. All major credit cards accepted. Open Mon-Wed 12-12.30am; Fri-Sun 12-4am. Food served daily from 12pm until 10.30pm, except Sun when food finishes at 9.30pm. **Directions:** A 10 second walk past the Temple Bar Market Square.

POWERSCOURT TOWNHOUSE CENTRE

South William Street Dublin 2 www.powerscourtcentre.com

Built in 1774 as a Town House for Lord Powerscourt, it was extensively refurbished and opened as a Shopping Centre in 1981. It is right in the middle of the Grafton Street/Georges Street shopping area and, whilst offering interesting shops, Powerscourt Townhouse is also home to a selection of bars, restaurants and cafés, some within a lovely central atrium that can be particularly restful especially when there is a pianist playing. Promising places to drop into for a bite include **Café Fresh** (01 671 9669), well known for its delicious vegetarian and vegan food; **La Corte** (01 633 4477), from the **Dunne & Crescenzi** stable (see entries), provides simple Italian food and great coffee; **Ba Mizu** (01 674 6712) is a stylish bar/restaurant serving an appealing contemporary menu, and **Mimo** (01 679 4160) - a sister establishment - is on the top floor, serving coffee, food and wine in an informal, relaxed and spacious environment. For more information on Powerscourt Townhouse see their website, www.powerscourtcentre.com.

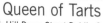

WWW.IRELAND-GUIDE.COM - FOR THE BEST PLACES TO EAT, DRINK & STAY.

Dublin 2
CAFÉ

Queen of Tarts
4 Cork Hill Dame Street Dublin 2
Tel: 01 670 7499

Behind Yvonne and Regina Fallon's quaint traditional shopfront near Dublin Castle lies an equally quaint traditional tea room, with warmly welcoming friendly and efficient staff, and wonderful smells wafting across the room as they struggle to make space for new arrivals to the comfortable, lived-in little room. Yvonne and Regina both trained as pastry chefs, but there's nothing 'cheffy' about the good home baking that you'll find here - the emphasis is on wholesomeness and real flavour. Service begins with breakfast (including a vegetarian cooked breakfast) which is served until the lunch/afternoon menu takes over at noon. Home-made scones, buttermilk brown bread, roast chicken & coriander tartlets, warm plum tarts with cream, chocolate fudge cake, orange chocolate pinwheel cookies and much else besides take their place on a surprisingly extensive menu, which includes some seriously good sandwiches and salads - most people pop in for a snack, but you could just as easily have a 3-course lunch. Inexpensive, consistently excellent food, lovely atmosphere and great service - what more could anyone ask? [*Also at: City Hall, Dame St. Tel 01 672 2925]. **Seats 25.** Air conditioning. Toilets wheelchair accessible. Children welcome. Open daily: Mon-Fri 7.30-7 (L12-7); Sat/Sun 8.30-7. Closed 24 Dec-02 Jan, bank hols. **No Credit Cards. Directions:** Opposite the gates of Dublin Castle. ◇

Dublin 2
RESTAURANT

Relax Café @ Habitat
6-10 Suffolk Street Dublin 2
Tel: 01 677 1433

The admirable aim at this popular mezzanine café is to deliver authentic Irish style food, using organic ingredients where possible. The menu offers a traditional cooked breakfast which happily includes kidneys and home-baked soda bread; French toast and omelettes are also on offer, as are starters, salads and more substantial main courses. Interesting dishes could include baked leek, hazelnut & Gubbeen crêpe; pan-fried Barbary duck breast with kumquat compôte & French beans; and organic pork and leek sausages with scallion champ and sautéed onions. The menu here is always promising and this remains a justifiably popular place to meet for an informal meal. **Seats 54.** Lift. House wines €15, €3.75 glass. No SC. Open all week 9.15 am to 6pm. MasterCard, Visa, Laser. **Directions:** Entrance is by College Green, other entrance Suffolk Street. ◇

Dublin 2
RESTAURANT
◇ ★ ★ ♔

Restaurant Patrick Guilbaud
21 Upper Merrion Street Dublin 2 **Tel: 01 676 4192**
restaurantpatrickguilbaud@eircom.net www.restaurantpatrickguilbaud.net

For a quarter of a century this spacious, elegant French restaurant in a Georgian townhouse adjoining the Merrion Hotel has been the leading fine dining restaurant in Ireland. Approached through a fine drawing room, where drinks are served, the restaurant is a bright, airy room, enhanced by an outstanding collection of Irish art, and opens on to a terrace and landscaped gardens which make a delightful setting for drinks and al fresco dining in summer. Head chef Guillaume Lebrun has presided over this fine kitchen since the restaurant opened and is renowned for exceptional modern classic cuisine, based on the best Irish produce in season: his luxurious, wide-ranging menus include a wonderfully creative 9-course Tasting Menu (€150), themed as 'Sea & Land', perhaps, and celebrating traditional Irish themes with Gallic flair; at the other end of the spectrum, a daily table d'hôte lunch menu offers the best value fine dining in Dublin. Contemporary French cooking at its best, combined with the precision and talents of a team of gifted chefs, produces dishes of dexterity, appeal and flavour: a speciality starter of lobster ravioli, for example, is made from Clogherhead lobster coated in a coconut scented lobster cream and served with hand made free range egg pasta, toasted almonds and lightly curry-flavoured olive oil. The main course house speciality is a magnificent dish of Challan duck (for two people) and, in due course, an assiette of chocolate ends your meal in spectacular fashion, with a plate of no less than five cold and hot chocolate desserts. Consistent excellence is the order of the day: cheeses are supplied by Sheridan's cheesemongers, breads are home-made, and the mostly French wine list includes some great classics, alongside some reasonably-priced offerings. A visit here is always an experience to treasure, each dish a masterpiece of beautiful presentation, contrasting textures and harmonious flavours, all matched by faultless service - under the relaxed supervision of Restaurant Manager Stéphane Robin, service is invariably immaculate, and Patrick Guilbaud himself is usually present to greet guests personally. Every capital city has its great restaurant and this is Dublin's gastronomic heaven: Restaurant Patrick Guilbaud continues to set the standard by which all others are judged. *On the Guide's most recent visit, in summer 2007, the experience was outstanding as usual but the restaurant was about to close for major refurbishment, so some details given here may have changed.* Children welcome. **Seats 80** (private room, The Roderic O'Conor Room is available for up to 25 people). Air conditioning. L & D Tue-Sat 12.30-2.15, D 7.30-10.15. Set L €35/45 for 2/3 courses. Vegetarian Menu (Main courses from €28). 9-course Tasting Menu €150. L&D à la carte available. House wine from about €38. SC discretionary. Closed Sun & Mon, bank hols, Christmas week. Amex, Diners, MasterCard, Visa, Laser. **Directions:** Opposite Government Buildings.

Dublin 2
RESTAURANT

Saagar Indian Restaurant

16 Harcourt Street Dublin 2 **Tel: 01 475 5060 / 5012**
info@saagarindianrestaurants.com www.saagarindianrestaurants.com

Meera and Sunil Kumar's highly-respected basement restaurant just off St Stephen's Green is one of Dublin's longest established Indian restaurants and, although it is an old building with an interesting history (Bram Stoker, author of Dracula, once lived here), it has a contemporary feel, with wooden flooring and restrained decor - and a music system featuring the latest Indian music. It is an hospitable place and you will be warmly welcomed - and probably offered a drink in the little bar while choosing from the menu. The cooking is consistently good, offering a wide range of speciality dishes, all prepared from fresh ingredients and considerably coded with a range of one to four stars to indicate the heat level. Thus Malai Kabab is a safe one-star dish, while traditional Lamb Balti and Lamb Aayish (marinated with exotic spices and cooked in a cognac-flavoured sauce) is a three-star and therefore pretty hot. Beef and pork are not served but this is balanced by a good vegetarian selection, and the side dishes such as Naan breads, which are made to order in the tandoori oven, are excellent. Customer care is a high priority here, and service is always knowledgeable and attentive. The Kumars also have restaurants in Athlone and Mullingar. Children welcome, but not very young babies (under 1), or after 10pm. **Seats 60.** Toilets wheelchair accessible. L Mon-Fri, 12.30-2.30; D 6-11 daily. L&D à la carte available. House wine about €16. SC discretionary. Closed L Sat, L Sun & Christmas week. Amex, Diners, MasterCard, Visa, Laser **Directions:** Opposite Children's Hospital on Harcourt Street (off St. Stephen's Green).

Dublin 2
RESTAURANT

Saba

26 -28 Clarendon Street Dublin 2 **Tel: 01 679 2000**
www.sabadublin.com

The old Rajdoot on Clarendon Street, where many had their first taste of foreign food, has now been taken over by a Thai and Vietnamese restaurant called Saba, meaning 'happy meeting place' in Thai. The décor is black, modern and sophisticated, but staff are friendlier than such backdrops often deliver. There's some real culinary adventure here like the smoked trout mieng kam with ginger, shallots, lime and peanuts, served on betel nut leaves: you roll the mix of highly flavoured fish and spices into a cigar shape using the pungent betel leaves - an exciting marriage of the interesting and unusual with recognisable flavours. You'll find old favourites too such as tempura vegetables with a mustard and lime mayonnaise: a good selection of whole baby carrots, broccoli, asparagus and aubergine with a gentle sheet of crispy batter all well matched with the high tone of the citrus sauce. Main courses include cua lot, soft shell crab with birds eye chilli, galangal root and kaffir lime leaf - with a three star chilli warning. An unusual and interesting main course, it encompasses a cornucopia of flavours and textures, from the strong and sweet to rich and deep. Grilled lobster tail is also available with spinach, yellow beans and brown and red rice: the sweet white meat is given a spicy crust and served with gentler flavours from the rice. Less adventurous diners will be happy to find phad Thai and green chicken curry as well as classic Thai noodle soups such as tuk tuk soup of spicy egg noodles, Vietnamese parsley, chicken and peanuts. Refreshing desserts include plates of sorbets - mango, lychee and strawberry. They also have an interesting list of non-alcoholic drinks perhaps reflecting our changing times. There are now plenty of other places to get authentic cheap and cheerful Vietnamese and Thai food, but this is the smart version and well worth the culinary detour. Wheelchair access to toilets, children welcome before 8pm. **Seats 130;** air con; reservations recommended. Open daily noon-11pm (12 - 10pm Sun); set L €25; set D €29.50; also a la carte L&D; coeliac & vegetarian options available; house wine from €15.95. SC 10% added to groups 6+. Closed 25-26 Dec. Amex, MasterCard, Visa, Laser. **Directions:** Parallel to top of Grafton Street, behind Westbury Hotel.

Dublin 2
RESTAURANT

Salamanca

1 St Andrew's Street Dublin 2
Tel: 01 670 8628

The concept of tapas was new to Dublin when John Harvey opened this atmospheric, informal bar and Spanish restaurant in the heart of Dublin several years ago, and it immediately struck a chord with Dubliners. The entrance is pleasant - past a bar with flowers on the counter - and welcoming staff show you straight to a simple marble-topped table. The menu - which is in Spanish with English explanations - is flexible enough to suit anything from a light lunch to a full dinner and plenty of choices: three tapas plates will make a generous lunch for two. Spanish staples are generally well-handled: langoustines with serrano ham, squid in chilli butter and patatas bravas are all tasty and presentation is simple and traditional. A handy location, tasty food, delightful staff and good value make this place busy at peak times, so be prepared to wait. The wine list includes a range of sherries by the glass, the traditional accompaniment for tapas, and their lovely frothy-topped mocha served in a tall glass is a great reviver. Meals: Mon-Thu, 12 noon-11 pm, Fri & Sat to midnight. Closed Sun. MasterCard, Visa. **Directions:** Near Dublin Tourism. ◊

Dublin 2
RESTAURANT

Shanahan's on the Green

119 St. Stephen's Green Dublin 2 **Tel: 01 407 0939**
sales@shanahans.ie www.shanahans.ie

téile bia This opulent restaurant was Dublin's first dedicated American-style steakhouse - although, as they would be quick to reassure you, their wide-ranging menu also offers plenty of other meats, poultry and seafood. However, the big attraction for many of the hungry diners with deep pockets who head for Shanahan's is their certified Irish Angus beef, which is seasoned and cooked in a special broiler, 1600-1800F, to sear the outside and keep the inside tender and juicy. Steaks range from a 'petit filet' at a mere 8 oz/225g right up to The Shanahan Steak (24 oz/700g), which is a sight to gladden the heart of many a traditionally-minded Irishman - and, more surprisingly perhaps, many of his trendier young friends too. Strange to think that steak was passé such a short time ago. There is much else to enjoy, of course, including a dramatic signature dish of onion strings with blue cheese dressing. The wine list includes many special bottles - with, naturally, a strong presence from the best of Californian producers. Not suitable for children. **Seats 100.** Reservations required. Air conditioning. L Fri only (except for groups), 12.30-2. D daily, 6-10.30. Set L €45; otherwise à la carte. (SC discretionary, but 15% on parties of 6+). House wine €30. Closed Christmas period. Amex, Diners, MasterCard, Visa, Laser. **Directions:** On the west side of St Stephen's Green, beside Royal College of Surgeons.

Dublin 2
HOTEL/RESTAURANT

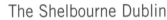

The Shelbourne Dublin
27 St Stephen's Green Dublin 2 **Tel: 01 663 4500**
eimear.ogrady@renaissancehotels.com www.shelbourne.ie

The Irish Constitution was drafted here and the recent brief closure of this opulent 18th-century hotel overlooking St Stephen's Green (Europe's largest garden square) has served as a reminder to Dubliners that it is still central to life in the city today. Ranking among the world's great hotels, it has emerged from its recent restoration and refurbishment with all the old grandeur intact, and the entrance creates an even stronger impression since the lift has been relocated to allow the original staircase to take pride of place once again in the magnificent faux-marble entrance hall - now also enhanced by the creation of a new reception area. The Lord Mayor's Lounge - always a popular meeting place for Afternoon Tea - has had a light hand in the renovation and the famous Horseshoe Bar, renowned as a meeting place for local politicians and theatrical society and nothing short of a Dublin institution, has been taken back to its old Sam Stephenson designed interior. New rooms added at the back of the hotel have increased the accommodation, and all are luxurious - but the older suites, named after famous people who have stayed there in the past, have all been refurbished to bring back the original glamour, and are very much in demand. Dining choices are between the stylish, No. 27 Bar & Lounge, and the opulent Saddle Room (see below). The hotel is much in demand for events and meetings, with a number of restored meeting/private dining and The George Moore Suite, and the state-of-the-art Great Room next door, for larger events. rooms in the main building including The Constitution Room. The Shelbourne Club, a fine leisure complex with 18m swimming pool, sauna, jacuzzi, steam room and much else besides is situated within the hotel complex. Conference/banqueting (500/350). Business centre, Broadband wi/fi, laptop-sized safe in rooms. Gift shop. 24 hour room service. Lift. Pets permitted. **Rooms 265** (19 suites, 18 junior suites, 46 executive, 247 no smoking, 7 for disabled); Children welcome (under 12s free in parents room, cots available free of charge, baby sitting arranged); B&B €192 pps. Open all year. **The Saddle Room:** Although there is no obvious sign over the door, hotel guests will spot this enticing looking restaurant within minutes of entering The Shelbourne's large foyer. The Saddle Room majors in seafood and steaks, with a large open plan kitchen putting the talented team on show for all to see. Divided in two by banquettes, the quieter side of the dining room features dark woods, moody lighting and cosy banquettes, creating a buzzy, clubby atmosphere. Tables, which are quite wide, are dressed with linen, beautiful Riedel glasses and flickering tea lights setting the scene for some serious food. The menu offers lots of interesting choices, with seafood and steak the obvious focus. The Oyster Bar serves four kinds of fresh oysters - it's interesting to order a combination and compare their individual characteristics - while a choice of Irish beef cuts fares well from The Grill. All dishes come with accompaniments, but side orders are usually required to make up a main course, pushing up the price of dining significantly. An extensive and informative wine list is conveniently divided into drinking styles, and the friendly and knowledgeable sommelier helpfully guides guests towards further recommendations. Desserts offer a range of freshly interpreted classics and there's a tempting cheese trolley too. Don't come to this stylish restaurant expecting stiff, formal service; although undeniably five-star, the excellent staff manage a perfect balance of informed and charming service that will only enhance your dining experience. Toilets wheelchair accessible. **Seats 135** (private room, 18); reservations recommended; air con; L&D daily, L 12-2pm, D 6-10pm; a la carte L&D; house wine €30; SC discretionary. Open all year. Amex, Diners, MasterCard, Visa, Laser. Barfood also served 11-9pm daily. **Directions:** Landmark building on north side of St Stephen's Green.

Silk Road Café

Dublin 2
CAFÉ/RESTAURANT

Chester Beatty Library Dublin Castle Dublin 2 **Tel: 01 407 0770**
silkroadcafe@hotmail.com www.silkroadcafe.ie

In a fine location in the heart of the city centre, Dublin Castle provides wonderful gardens and historic architecture which greatly enhance the enjoyment of a visit to this unusual restaurant, which is situated in the clock tower beside the Chester Beatty Library (European Museum of the Year in 2002, and one of the few Dublin museums offering free entry). Middle Eastern, Mediterranean, vegetarian and organic are the themes brought together by Abraham Phelan and his small but dedicated team, who create inspired versions of classics like Greek moussaka, Moroccan cous cous, falafel and spinach & feta pie to the delight of their many returning customers. Fresh organic herbs are used in all dishes and, in line with halal/kosher rules, all dishes are made without the use of pork or beef. Prices are very reasonable. Toilets wheelchair accessible. Children welcome. **Seats 65** (private room 30). Air conditioning. Open Mon-Fri, 10-5; à la carte. No service charge. MasterCard, Visa, Laser. **Directions:** Beside Chester Beatty Library in Dublin Castle.

The South William

Dublin 2
BAR

52 South William Street Dublin 2 **Tel: 01 672 5946**
info@southwilliam.ie www.southwilliam.ie

Opened in January 2007 by brothers Marc and Conor Bereen, with Troy Maguire - who was well known from L'Geuleton at the time - involved as a food consultant, The South William was always going to do something different. A retro style cocktail bar, with plastic seats, and worn leather couches lend the room a laid back kitsch feel, and friendly staff add to the relaxed atmosphere. The food offering was deliberately restricted and kept to a theme - a short menu consists of eight gourmet pies, which reflect traditional Irish staples such as bacon and cabbage or Guinness braised beef shin. The wine list is short too, with a good mix of old and new world at a fair cost, with some offered by the glass, and there is a good selection of imported beers, bottled and on tap. In the evenings, the South William parks away its day time chill and removes the bar stools 'to facilitate the art of dancing' as the lounge bar transforms to a funky night club with its own DJ. **Seats 110.** Open daily (normal bar hours Mon-Wed, to 2.30am Fri/Sat, to 1am Thurs & Sun); food served 12-10pm daily. Amex, MasterCard, Visa, Laser. Closed 25 Dec. **Directions:** On south end of South William Street on same side of street as Powerscourt Town House.

Stauntons on the Green

Dublin 2
GUESTHOUSE

83 St Stephen's Green Dublin 2 **Tel: 01 478 2300**
stauntonsonthegreen@eircom.net www.stauntonsonthegreen.ie

Well-located with views over St Stephen's Green at the front and its own private gardens at the back, this guesthouse - which is in an elegant Georgian terrace on the south of the Green and has fine period reception rooms - offers moderately priced accommodation of a good standard, with all the usual amenities. Maintenance could be a little sharper and front rooms would benefit from sound-proofing from traffic noise, but it's in the heart of the business and banking district and the Grafton Street shopping area is just a stroll across the Green. Meeting rooms are available, with secretarial facilities on request - and there's private parking (valet parking service offered - it would be wise to phone ahead with your time of arrival to arrange this, as there is no parking at the door). Children welcome. No pets. **Rooms 57** (all en-suite, 24 shower only). B&B about €76 pps, ss €20. Closed 24-27 Dec. Amex, Diners, MasterCard, Visa, Laser. **Directions:** On south side of the Green. ◊

Stephen's Green Hotel

Dublin 2
HOTEL

St Stephen's Green Dublin 2 **Tel: 01 607 3600**
stephensgreenres@ocallaghanhotels.ie www.ocallaghanhotels.ie

This striking landmark hotel on a south-western corner site overlooking St Stephen's Green is the newest of the O'Callaghan Hotels group (Alexander, Davenport, Mont Clare - see entries). Public areas include an impressive foyer and, in memory of the writer George Fitzmaurice who used to live here, 'Pie Dish' restaurant and 'Magic Glasses' bar - both named after titles from his work. It's a great location and bedrooms have exceptionally good facilities, particularly for business travellers, including air conditioning, 3 direct line telephones, voice mail and modem line, desk, mini-bar as standard. Small conference/meeting rooms. Business centre. Gym. Children welcome (Under 2s free in parents' room; cots available). No pets. **Rooms 75** (9 suites, including 2 studio terrace suites, 3 penthouse suites, junior suites; 40 no-smoking rooms, 2 for disabled). Lift. 24 hour room service. Room rate about €295, max. 2 guests). Open all year. Amex, Diners, MasterCard, Visa. **Directions:** Corner of Harcourt St. and St. Stephen's Green. ◊

Dublin 2
RESTAURANT

Steps of Rome
1 Chatham Street Dublin 2
Tel: 01 670 5630

One of a cluster of inexpensive little Italian places specialising in pizza around Balfe and Chatham Streets, each with its following, this authentic one-room café just beside Neary's pub is a favourite lunch spot for many discerning Dubliners. A good place to take a break. (Branch at: Ciao Bella Roma, Parliament St.) **Seats 18.** Open 12 noon-11pm Mon-Sat, Sun 1-10pm. House wine about €14. No service charge. **No Credit Cards. Directions:** Just off top of Grafton Street. ◊

TEMPLE BAR

The hub of the action for many visitors, the area others may wish to avoid. Whatever your feelings for the tourist centre of Dublin everybody should visit it once during daytime to judge it for themselves. Street performers and buskers ply their trade in and around Temple Bar Square which can be a great place to sit down and enjoy the atmosphere on a sunny day. There are many interesting places to visit such as the Irish Film Centre that host ever changing exhibitions and Meeting House Square has weekly outdoor cinema screenings in the summer and a Farmers' Market every Wednesday and Saturday. The whole area is full of bars and restaurants and one of the best known and amongst the first new-wave places in the area is the **Elephant & Castle Restaurant** (Temple Bar, 01 679 3121) which is popular for large salads and bowls of chicken wings and its lively atmosphere. While in Meeting House Square, the cheap and cheerful **Il Baccaro** (01-6714597) serves no nonsense Italian cuisine in a most convenient location. For reasonably priced accommodation, **The Principal Hotel** (Fleet Street; 01 670 8122) is conveniently situated in the heart of Temple Bar, within easy walking distance of all the city's main attractions. It is fairly small, allowing an intimate atmosphere and a welcome emphasis on service.

Dublin 2
HOTEL

Temple Bar Hotel
Fleet Street Temple Bar Dublin 2 **Tel: 01 677 3333**
reservations@tbh.ie www.templebarhotel.com

féile bia This pleasant hotel is relatively reasonably priced, and handy for both sides of the river. Spacious reception and lounge areas create a good impression and bedrooms are generally larger than average, almost all with a double and single bed and good amenities. Neat, well-lit bathrooms have over-bath showers and marble wash basin units. Room service menu (6-10pm). No parking, but the hotel has an arrangement with a nearby car park. Conference/banqueting (70/60). Wheelchair access. Children welcome (Under 12s free in parents' room, cots available without charge). No pets. **Rooms 129** (35 no-smoking, 2 for disabled). Lift. B&B about €100pps, ss €60. Closed Christmas. Amex, Diners, MasterCard, Visa, Laser. **Directions:** Near Fleet Street car park. ◊

Thornton's Restaurant

Dublin 2
RESTAURANT

128 St Stephen's Green Dublin 2 **Tel: 01 478 7008**
thorntonsrestaurant@eircom.net www.thorntonsrestaurant.com

With views overlooking St Stephen's Green, Kevin and Muriel Thornton's renowned restaurant is found on the top floor of the Fitzwilliam Hotel. You can take a lift up through the hotel, but it is best approached from its own entrance on the Green: mounting the wide staircase, deep-carpeted in dark blue, conveys a sense of occasion. The rather plain dining room has had a welcome renovation and is now a more stylish space: the square room has been divided by panels of glass over-printed with sepia toned fish scales; Just like the arresting photography hanging on the walls these were shot by Kevin, who is as adept with a camera as a frying pan. The clever revamp has seen the addition of an intimate canapé bar with comfy sofas where diners can drop in for a more relaxed experience. Miniature creations - perhaps foie gras rolled in toasted almonds or goose with aubergine chips - can be individually ordered to accompany some exceptional wines by the glass, such as the celebrated dessert wine, Chateau d'Yquem (€40 per glass).

For those who have come to dine, however, the understated linen-clad tables leave you in no doubt that the food is to be the star here. Given that Kevin Thornton is one of the most talented chef's in the country, lunch, with two courses costing just €35, represents outstanding value. Dinner is a full-on gourmet affair and though the à la carte offers just three choices per course; it's the tasting menus, available as 5, 8 or 14 courses (€85, €125, €180) that really showcase his genius. Kevin Thornton has a perfectionist's eye for detail with a palate to match, and uses only the very best seasonal ingredients. He has a name for generosity with truffles and he will not disappoint: a vegetarian first course of warm white asparagus is served with truffle hollandaise and green asparagus bavarois for example, and among the seafood dishes you will find a luxurious signature dish of sautéed prawns with prawn bisque, and truffle sabayon. Other signature dishes include roast suckling pig, and trotter served with glazed turnip and a light poitin sauce - and variations on these creations appear throughout an 8-course Surprise Menu (€125). Desserts, like a signature warm Valrhona chocolate fondant, and imaginative petit fours, are always exquisite. Although beautifully presented, this is not show-off food - the cooking is never less than sublime and the emphasis is always on flavour. As one would expect for dining at this level, the wine list is extensive, featuring many great marques and a good choice of wines by the glass. Service, under the guidance of Kevin's brother, maître d'Garret Thornton, is formal and never less than polished, although recent visits suggest that there's a need for real presence in the dining room to match the level of passion in the kitchen. Cooking this exceptional will always be the star of the show, but it would be nice to see Thorntons delivering a restaurant experience with a wow factor to match. Reservations required. Children welcome. Air conditioning. **Seats 90.** L Tue-Sat, 12.30-2; D Tue-Sat, 7-10.30pm. L&D a la carte; Tasting Menu also offered, from €95-185 for 5-14 courses. House wine from €27-40. SC discretionary. Closed 1 week over Christmas. Amex, Diners, MasterCard, Visa, Laser. *Canapé Bar open from 1pm to midnight. **Directions:** On St Stephen's Green (corner at top of Grafton Street); entrance beside Fitzwilliam Hotel.

Town Bar & Grill

Dublin 2
RESTAURANT

21 Kildare Street Dublin 2 **Tel: 01 662 4800**
reservations@townbarandgrill.com www.townbarandgrill.com

Ronan Ryan and Temple Garner's New York/Italian style restaurant beneath Mitchell's wine merchants is very much 'town'. A delicate hand with the decor - warm floor tiles, gentle lighting and smart but not overly-formal white-clothed tables with promising wine glasses - creates a welcoming tone on arrival in the L-shaped basement, and professional staff are quick to offer the choice of a drink at the bar or menus at your table. Starters are likely to include a really excellent antipasti plate and dishes rarely seen elsewhere, such as rabbit fricassée, while house versions of classics like Italian sausage amatriaciana, with gnocchi or pappardelle, appear among main courses which will also offer several interesting fish dishes and, in season, game such as crown of pheasant. An Irish and Italian cheeseboard is offered and moreish desserts may include classics like Town tiramisu; combinations are sometimes unusual, and flavours are delicious. Interested, well-informed staff add greatly to the enjoyment of a meal here, and the cooking is generally confident and accurate, set off handsomely by simple presentation on plain white plates. Prices are fair for the high quality of food and service offered, with lunch and pre-theatre menus offering very good value. There is also - perhaps uniquely in a city centre restaurant of this calibre - a special children's menu, offering healthy low-salt and low-sugar 'real' food such as char-grilled chicken breast bruschetta with buffalo mozzarella & tomato salsa, and home-made fish fingers with oven roasted chips. Sunday lunch, available as a one-, two- or three-course menu, offers a well-balanced choice that, while more adventurous than the usual Sunday lunch, includes the elements of tradition. The wine list offers many interesting selections, and some very special bottles, notably from Tuscany and the Napa Valley; a good choice is available by the glass. *A sister restaurant '**South Bar & Grill**' opened at Beacon South Quarter, Sandyford, in summer 2007 (see entry). Free Broadband wi/fi; Children welcome. **Seats 80.** Air conditioning. Open daily: L 12-5.30, D 5.30-11 (to 10 on Sun); set L €26.95; pre-theatre menu €29.95, Mon-Thurs 5.30-7.15; Set 3 course D €55.95, also à la carte. House wine €22.50. Pianist Thu-Sat from 8pm, Jazz on Sun from 8. SC 10% on groups 5+. Closed 25 Dec, Good Fri. Amex, MasterCard, Visa, Laser. **Directions:** Opposite side door of Shelbourne, under Mitchell's wine shop.

Dublin 2
HOTEL

Trinity Capital Hotel

Pearse Street Dublin 2 **Tel: 01 648 1000**
info@trinitycapital-hotel.com www.capital-hotels.com

A stylish hotel right beside the headquarters of Dublin's city centre fire brigade (inspiring the name 'Fireworks' for its unusual club-style bar) and opposite Trinity College. Very centrally located for business and leisure, the hotel is within easy walking distance of all the main city centre attractions on both sides of the Liffey and the lobby wine and coffee bar make handy meeting places. Rooms have a safe, interactive TV, phone, data ports, hair dryer, trouser press, tea/coffee trays, comfortable beds and good bathrooms -junior suites suites have jacuzzi baths, hi-fi system and mini-bar. The Siena Restaurant offers an above-average experience for an hotel dining room, providing an appealing alternative for guests who prefer to dine in (D daily, 6-9.30). Guests have free admission to all the bars and clubs in the city centre owned by Capital Bars, including the adjacent Fireworks night club. Conference/banqueting 40/80. Meeting rooms; secretarial services. Children welcome (under 12s free in parents' room; cots available without charge, baby sitting arranged). **Rooms 82** (4 suites, 4 junior suites, 24 no-smoking, 3 shower only. Lift. 24 hour room service. B&B about €106.50 pps, ss €30. (Room only, about €199). Amex, Diners, MasterCard, Visa, Laser. **Directions:** City centre. ◈

Dublin 2
GUESTHOUSE

Trinity Lodge

12 South Frederick Street Dublin 2 **Tel: 01 617 0900**
trinitylodge@eircom.net www.trinitylodge.com

This well-signed and attractively maintained guesthouse offers excellent location and a high standard of accommodation at a reasonable price, just yards away from Trinity College. As is the way with Georgian buildings, rooms get smaller towards the top so the most spacious accommodation is on lower floors. The reception area is a little tight, but guest rooms have air conditioning and are stylishly furnished in keeping with the age of the building, and most have bath and shower; as it is a listed building it is not permissible to install a lift, a point worth bearing in mind if stairs could be a problem. An extensive breakfast is served in a bright, boldly decorated basement and, although no dinner is offered, there are numerous good restaurants nearby. *The addition of 6 new bedrooms is planned at the time of going to press, also extension of the restaurant. Outdoor terrace. No private parking (multi-storey carparks nearby). Air-conditioned rooms have a safe, direct-dial phone, tea/coffee making facilities, multi-channel TV, trouser press and iron. Children welcome (under 5 free in parents' room; cots available); free broadband wi/fi; no pets. **Rooms 16** (6 family, 1 ground floor, all shower only and no-smoking). Room service (limited hours). B&B €80pps. Closed 23-27 Dec. Amex, Diners, MasterCard, Visa, Laser. **Directions:** Off Nassau Street, near Trinity College.

Dublin 2
RESTAURANT

Trocadero Restaurant

3/4 St Andrew Street Dublin 2 **Tel: 01 677 5545**
www.trocadero.ie

The Dublin theatrical restaurant par excellence with deep blood-red walls and gold-trimmed stage curtains, black and white pictures of the celebrities who've passed through the place dimly lit, intimate tables with individual beaded lampshades and snug, cosy seating, the 'Troc' is one of Dublin's longest-established restaurants and has presided over St. Andrew Street since 1956. It has atmosphere in spades, with food and service to match. Comforting menus reminiscent of the '70s offer starters like French onion soup, deep-fried brie, chicken liver pâté and avocado prawn Marie Rose, followed by ever-popular grills - fillet steak (with Cashel Blue cheese perhaps), Wicklow rack of lamb and sole on the bone are the mainstays of the menu, also wild Irish salmon and Dublin Bay Prawns from Clogherhead, naturally all with a sprinkling of freshly chopped parsley. Desserts include apple and cinnamon strudel and wicked chocolate and Baileys slice, and a better-value wine list will be hard to find. There's privacy too - sound-absorbing banquettes and curtains allow you to hear everything at your own table with just a pleasing murmur in the background. Lovely friendly service too: magic. * A new bar was added in 2007. **Seats 110.** Air conditioning. Children welcome (up to 9pm). D Mon-Sat, 5-12. Pre-theatre D 5-7pm €25, but table to be vacated by 7.45pm - also à la carte,. House wine from about €19. Closed Sun, 25 Dec - 2 Jan, Good Fri. Amex, Diners, MasterCard, Visa, Laser. **Directions:** Beside Dublin Tourism Centre.

Dublin 2   Tulsi Restaurant
RESTAURANT   17a Lr Baggot Street Dublin 2 **Tel: 01 676 4578**
sharmin@gofree.indigo.ie   www.tulsi-indian.com

One of a small chain of authentic Indian restaurants, this bustling place has a compact reception area leading into an elegant restaurant with echoes of the Raj in the decor. Tables are set up with plate warmers, fresh flowers, sauces and pickles and service is brisk. There's a slight leaning towards Punjabi style cooking, with its use of nuts and fruit in sauces, but also tandoori, tikka, biryani, balti and an extensive vegetarian menu. A selection of naan breads is offered and the food quality overall is consistently high; this, together with good value, make booking at both lunch and dinner advisable. Indian beer available. **Seats 64** (outdoor,8). L Mon-Sat, 12-2.30, D daily, 6-11. Set L €10.95. Set D €25, also à la carte. House wine €17.50. Closed L Sun, L bank hols; 25-26 Dec, Good Fri. * Tulsi has a number of branches, including: 4 Olive Mount Terrace, Dundrum Road, Dundrum (01 260 1940); Lr Charles St., Castlebar, Co Mayo (Tel: 094 25066); Buttermilk Way, Middle St., Galway Tel: 092-564831). Sister restaurants 'Shanai Indian' at Cornelscourt S.C. and Old Bray Road, Foxrock, Co Dublin. Amex, Diners, MasterCard, Visa, Laser. **Directions:** 2 minutes walk east from St. Stephen's Green (Shelbourne Hotel side).

Dublin 2   Unicorn Restaurant
RESTAURANT   12B Merrion Court off Merrion Row Dublin 2 **Tel: 01 676 2182**
www.unicornrestaurant.com

In a lovely, secluded location just off a busy street near St. Stephen's Green, this informal and perennially fashionable restaurant is famous for its antipasto bar, piano bar and exceptionally friendly staff. It's particularly charming in summer, as the doors open out on to a terrace which is used for al fresco dining in fine weather - and the Number Five piano bar, which extends to two floors, is also a great attraction for after-dinner relaxation with live music (Wed-Sat 9pm-3am). Aside from their wonderful display of antipasto, an extensive menu based on Irish ingredients (suppliers are listed) is offered, including signature dishes such as risotto funghi porcini (which is not available on Monday), and involtini 'saltimbocca style' - pockets of veal stuffed with Parma ham, mozzarella and sage, braised in white wine and lemon sauce; good regional and modern Italian food, efficient service and great atmosphere all partially explain The Unicorn's enduring success - another element is the constant quest for further improvement. There is always something new going on - the 'Unicorn Foodstore' round the corner, on Merrion Row, is a relatively recent addition to the enterprise, for example, also the Unicorn Antipasto/Tapas Bar - and there is now a bar menu in the piano bar, which is a fair indication of the popularity of this buzzing restaurant. Many of the Italian wines listed are exclusive to The Unicorn: uniquely, in Ireland, they stock the full collection of Angelo Gaja wines and also the Pio Cesare range. Not suitable for children after 9pm. **Seats 80** (private room 30; outdoor 30). Reservations required. Air conditioning. Open Mon-Sat, L12.30-4.30, D 6-11 (Fri/Sat to 11.30), Fri open all day. A la carte. House wine about €23. SC discretionary. Closed Sun, bank hols, 25 Dec-2 Jan. Amex, Diners, MasterCard, Visa, Laser. **Directions:** Just off Stephen's Green, towards Baggot St. ◇

Venu Brasserie

Dublin 2
RESTAURANT

Annes Lane Dublin 2 **Tel: 01 670 6755**
www.venu.ie

Following in the footsteps of a father who has run the best restaurant in Ireland for a quarter of a century can't be easy but Charles Guilbaud's big new restaurant has now taken its own place in the city. It is situated in the basement of an office building, and aims to offer good, simple food at fair prices. Whether or not you like the décor - some find it depressingly canteen-like, while others see the plainness of the rather boxy wooden furniture and red leather banquettes as the height of cool - you're bound to love the affordable all-day menus and a concise, fairly priced wine list that includes four well-chosen house wines. Although by no means an exclusively French menu, head chef Sebastien Geber offers many dishes that will bring back the best kind of memories: think gratinated onion soup with croutons (a vegetarian variation of the classic, no less), and vegetarians might also think green leaf salad with roasted vegetables. Several starters are also available as main courses - duck leg confit, with Lyonnaise potatoes, for example. Main courses tread a carefully chosen path, offering a great choice from steak & chips or traditional fish & chips, to spicy dishes like grilled lamb skewers with cumin & coriander spices and the luxury of grilled Irish lobster. This is good simple food, and desserts like bread and butter pudding or home-made ice creams mainly follow in the same vein, although there are some surprises too. Together with long opening hours and smart service, the great cooking and value here will earn many happy fans for Venu. Toilets wheelchair accessible. Children welcome. **Seats 120;** air conditioning. Open L Thu-Sat, D daily, 4.30-11pm; set L 12-5pm, €20; also a la carte; House wine €19.50. Closed L Sun-Wed, 25/26 Dec, 1 Jan, Easter. Amex, MasterCard, Visa, Laser. **Directions:** From Grafton Street on to South Anne street, take 1st right.

The Westbury Hotel

Dublin 2
HOTEL/RESTAURANT

Grafton Street Dublin 2 **Tel: 01 679 1122**
westbury@jurysdoyle.com www.jurysdoyle.com

Possibly the most conveniently situated of all the central Dublin hotels, the Westbury is a very small stone's throw from the city's premier shopping street and has all the benefits of luxury hotels - notably free valet parking - to offset any practical disadvantages of acess to the location. Unashamedly sumptuous, the hotel's public areas drip with chandeliers and have accessories to match - like the grand piano on The Terrace, a popular first floor meeting place for afternoon tea, and frequently used for fashion shows. Accommodation is similarly luxurious, with bedrooms that include penthouse suites and a high proportion of suites, junior suites and executive rooms. With conference facilities to match its quality of accommodation and service, the hotel is understandably popular with business and corporate guests, but it also makes a great base for a leisure break in the city. Laundry/dry cleaning. Fitness Room. Conference/banqueting (220/220). Business centre. Secretarial services, video conferencing, broadband wi/fi. Children welcome (cots available free of charge; baby sitting arranged). No pets. **Rooms 205** (14 suites, 4 junior suites, 25 executive rooms, 155 no-smoking, 3 for disabled). 24 hr room service. Lifts. B&B from €252 pps. SC 15%. Car park. Open all year. **Restaurants:** After a drink in one of the hotel's bars - the first floor Terrace bar and the Sandbank Bistro, an informal seafood restaurant and bar accessible from the back of the building - the Russell Room offers classic dining, with some global cuisine and modern Irish influences. **Russell Room: Seats 120;** children welcome; air conditioning. SC 15%. L daily, 12.30-2.30; D daily 6.30-10.30 (Sun to 9.30). Set L €34, Set D 2/3 course €35/€55, also à la carte. House wine from €25. Open all year. Amex, Diners, MasterCard, Visa, Laser. **Directions:** City centre, off Grafton Street; near Stephens Green.

Dublin 2
HOTEL/RESTAURANT

The Westin Dublin

Westmoreland Street Dublin 2 **Tel: 01 645 1000**
reservations.dublin@westin.com www.westin.com/dublin

Two Victorian landmark buildings provided the starting point for this impressive hotel, and part of the former Allied Irish Bank was glassed over to create a dramatic lounging area, **The Atrium**, which has a huge palm tree feature and bedroom windows giving onto it like a courtyard (effective, although rather airless). The magnificent Banking Hall now makes a stunning conference and banqueting room, and the adjacent Teller Room is an unusual circular boardroom - while the vaults have found a new lease of life as **The Mint**, a bar with its own access from College Street. It's an intriguing building, especially for those who remember its former commercial life, and it has many special features including the business traveller's 'Westin Guest Office', designed to combine the efficiency and technology of a modern office with the comfort of a luxurious bedroom, and the so-called 'Heavenly Bed' designed by Westin and 'worlds apart from any other bed'. A split-level penthouse suite has views over Trinity College (and a private exercise area). Very limited parking (some valet parking available, if arranged at the time of booking accommodation). Fitness room. Conferences/Banqueting (250/170); business centre, secretarial services, video conferencing, free broadband wi/fi. **Rooms 163** (17 suites, 7 junior suites, 19 for disabled). Lift. 24 hour room service. Room rate about €359 (max 2 guests). Children welcome (under 17s free in parents room, €45 for roll away bed, cot available at no charge, baby sitting arranged). **The Exchange:** An elegant, spacious room in 1930s style, the restaurant continues the banking theme and, with a welcome emphasis on comfort, it simply oozes luxury. Everything about it, from the classily understated decor in tones of cream and brown to the generous-sized, well-spaced tables and large carver chairs says expensive but worth it. And, in the Guide's experience, that promise generally follows through on to the plate in well-executed menus - a fairly contemporary style, and confident, unfussy cooking endear this restaurant to visitors and discerning Dublin diners alike. Friendly service from knowledgeable young waiting staff. There is live music on Saturday night and at Sunday Brunch, which is quite an institution and, like the pre-theatre dinner menu, offers good value. **Seats 70.** Breakfast daily 6.30-10, L Mon-Fri 12-2.30, D Tue-Sat 6-10, Early D €22, 6-7pm. Sun Brunch 12-4.30, €42.50; live music (jazz) Sat D & Sun brunch; house wine €30. Restaurant closed L Sat, D Sun, Mon. Hotel open all year. Amex, Diners, MasterCard, Visa, Laser. **Directions:** On Westmoreland Street, opposite Trinity College.

DUBLIN 3

CLONTARF / FAIRVIEW

Fairview and its more fashionable shoreside neighbour, Clontarf, are a few miles from central Dublin and convenient to attractions such as the Croke Park stadium; championship golf at the Royal Dublin Golf Club, walking, bird watching, kite surfing and many other activities on Bull Island, a large island in Dublin Bay. There are also sites of historical significance such as the Casino at Marino and Fairview Crescent, a former home of Bram Stoker, author of Dracula. In Fairview, casual dining is available at **Ristorante da Enzo** (01 855 5274), a basic little restaurant known for its warm and friendly staff, great food and atmosphere - and terrific value. A little further out, Clontarf is an affluent suburb, with all the shops, pubs, restaurants and cafés to be expected in such an area. **Picasso** (01 853 1120) is an popular local Italian restaurant near the seafront on Vernon Avenue.
WWW.IRELAND-GUIDE.COM FOR THE BEST PLACES TO EAT, DRINK & STAY.

Dublin 3
RESTAURANT

Canters Restaurant

9 Fairview Strand Fairview Dublin 3 **Tel: 01 833 3681**
info@canters.ie www.canters.ie

This chic addition to urban Northside Dublin dining is a sister restaurant to well-established Washerwoman's Hill Restaurant in Glasnevin (see entry) and it strikes a happy balance between the needs of those who simply want to 'eat out' and those who feel the need for a smarter dining experience. Starters offer a nod to older tastes with some modern twists such as garlic mushrooms with goats cheese crumble and sun dried tomato pesto as well as the ever popular carpaccio of beef with parmesan cheese and rocket. Main courses tend towards the traditional and hearty but lighter, more contemporary options include good pasta dishes, such as porcini ravioli with roast butternut squash, sage butter, pine nuts & parmesan shavings. Ever-popular steaks are here -T-bone steak and sirloin steaks, along with rump of lamb, or fillet of pork wrapped in streaky bacon with baby leeks and an apple jus; and fish can include modern dishes like salmon with wilted spinach and a sundried tomato & prawn cream sauce. Desserts feature old favourites such as sticky toffee pudding with butterscotch sauce and a cappuccino and chocolate chip mousse. Canters have structured their menu to appeal to the diversity of their local clientele, but this is definitely a notch above your usual neighbourhood restaurant. Broadband wi/fi; children welcome; toilets wheelchair accessible. **Seats 90** (outdoor, 8; private room, to 56); air con; reservation recommended. Open L daily, 12-3 (Sun L 1.30-3.30pm); set L €19; D daily from 5.30-10pm (to 9 pm Sun); early D €26, Mon-Thu, 5.30-7.30pm; also a la carte. Average starter €8, average main course €19, average dessert €6.50, house wines €17. SC of 10% for groups 7+. MasterCard, Visa, Laser. **Directions:** In the heart of Fairview, opposite Centra.

Dublin 3
HOTEL/RESTAURANT

Clontarf Castle Hotel

Castle Avenue Clontarf Dublin 3 **Tel: 01 833 2321**
info@clontarfcastle.ie www.clontarfcastle.ie

This historic 17th century castle is located near the coast, and convenient to both the airport and city centre. Although is a pity that the extensive grounds were given over to development some years ago so that special sense of space has been lost, the hotel itself has been sensitively developed with each new development or update imaginatively incorporated into the old castle structure, retaining the historic atmosphere; some rooms, including the restaurant and the old bar, have original features and the atrium linking the old castle to the hotel is an impressive architectural feature. Recent major refurbishment and upgrade has resulted in a very stylish blend of the contemporary and traditional in all areas which, together with the hotel's longstanding reputation for professional and caring service, makes the Castle a seriously desirable venue for events of all kinds, both personal and corporate. The hotel is understandably popular with the business community, and their extensive conference and meeting facilities have yet again been upgraded, to provide the latest technology for the benefit of anything from a single business guest to a conference for 600 - and experienced, unobtrusive service to match. Luxurious, warmly decorated bedrooms are also furnished with great style, and equally well equipped for leisure and business guests with wireless broadband, voicemail and US electrical sockets in addition to the many other amenities found in a hotel of this standard. Bathrooms are well designed, and all south-facing rooms have air conditioning. Off duty, or for informal meetings, the hotel has two bars - the chic **Indigo Lounge** and, for traditionalists, **Knights Bar** - and dining in will be no hardship either (see restaurant, below). Well-trained and friendly staff greatly contribute to the atmosphere and comfort of a visit here, and the recent investment has ensured that the hotel remains at the cutting edge for business guests. Conference/banqueting (600/400). Business centre; secretarial services; broadband wi/fi; laptop-sized safes in bedrooms. Children welcome (Under 12 free in parents' room; cots available free of charge, baby sitting arranged). No pets. **Rooms 111** (3 suites, 2 junior suites, 7 executive rooms, 97 no-smoking, 2 for disabled, 9 ground floor). Lift. 24 hr room service. Turn down service. B&B €100 pps, ss €80. **Restaurant:** Despite the labyrinth of narrow hotel corridors, **Fahrenheit Grill**, once reached, is a large, spacious restaurant comprising three interconnecting rooms. Décor is immediately striking, and aside from one room with an impressively high ceiling and old wooden beams, is modern and glamorous. Bold colours, dark wood furniture, black chandeliers, graphic banquettes and gold panelling all add up to create a chic, comfortable dining space. The menu is quite extensive, with steaks from the grill the focal point; several cuts of dry-aged Irish beef are offered, all having hung for 21 days. Seafood is dominant too, with the signature Dublin Bay Prawn cocktail especially good. Vegetables have been given real consideration, and the exciting Mediterranean mix, served in gleaming copper pans, deserves serious attention. Service is genuinely friendly and professional, and despite a limited wine list Fahrenheit Grill makes for a truly enjoyable dining experience. D Mon-Sat, 6.30-10.30 (Sun 6.30-10); L Sun only, 12.30-2.30. Set D 2/3 course, €50/€60; house wine €20. Bar food available in Knights Bar all day, every day. Hotel closed 25 Dec.* There is a sister hotel, the Crowne Plaza, at Dublin Airport. Amex, MasterCard, Visa, Laser. **Directions:** Take M1 from Dublin

Airport, take a left on to Collins Avenue, continue to T junction, take left on to Howth Road. At second set of lights, take a right on to Castle Avenue, continue to roundabout, take right into hotel.

Dublin 3   Hemmingways
CAFÉ/WINE BAR   Vernon Avenue Clontarf Dublin 3
   **Tel: 01 833 3338**

This unusual establishment has counterparts in one or two fishing ports in the west and south-west of Ireland but with the possible exception of Cavistons in Dun Laoghaire - there is nothing remotely like it in the Dublin area. Essentially it is a fish shop that will also cook up fresh fish for you as selected from the counter: at present the 'restaurant' is a casual space with seating on high stools along a counter on one wall, better suited to 2 or 3 people eating rather than groups. The Hemmingways offering of informal seafood and tapas together with its wet fish bar is proving so popular that there are plans afoot to develop the business to full seafood restaurant catering for up to 40, with wine and tapas bar. Meanwhile, it's a fun place to enjoy fresh fish. **Seats 12** (bar stool style); Open daily from 12.30 - 8pm (to 9pm Fri/Sat); House wine €19. Closed Sun, 25 Dec. MasterCard, Visa, Laser. **Directions:** On the seafront in Clontarf, next to the Butler's Pantry.

Dublin 3   Jurys Croke Park Hotel
HOTEL   Jones's Road Dublin 3 **Tel: 01 871 4444**
crokepark@jurysdoyle.com www.jurysdoyle.com

The first major hotel to be built in this area, Jurys brought much-needed facilities and is very useful for business visitors, and fans attending events at Croke Park stadium. The design is pleasant and very practical, with extensive public areas including a very large foyer/reception with good seating arrangements and several sections conducive to quiet conversation - and a vast bar has a predictably large screen. An inner courtyard comes into its own in sunny weather, and a there's a gym for guests' use. A room card key is required to operate the lift (which can be annoying, but is a useful security measure), and accommodation is well-equipped with everything required by the business traveller; light sleepers should request a quietly-located room as some overlook the railway line, which may be disturbing. Staff make up in cheerfulness and willingness anything they lack in experience, and food in the hotel's Sideline Bistro is a step above the standard normally expected in hotels. Fully wheelchair accessible. Conferences/Banqueting; Business centre, secretarial services, laptop-sized safes in bedrooms; Fitness room. **Rooms 232** (2 suites, 35 executive, 10 shower only, 5 family rooms, 4 ground floor, 12 for disabled); room rate from €104 per night; 24 hr room service; lift; turndown service. Children welcome (cot available; baby sitting arranged); no pets. Open all year. Amex, Diners, MasterCard, Visa, Laser. **Directions:** From North Circular Road turn left onto Jones's Road, cross The Royal Canal and Jurys Croke Park Hotel is on your left.

Dublin 3   Kinara Restaurant
RESTAURANT   318 Clontarf Road Dublin 3 **Tel: 01 833 6759**
info@kinara.ie www.kinara.ie

This smart two-storey restaurant specialising in authentic Pakistani and Northern Indian cuisine enjoys a scenic location overlooking Bull Island - and is now firmly established as the area's leading ethnic restaurant. Fine views are a feature at lunch time or on fine summer evenings, and there's a cosy upstairs bar with Indian cookbooks to inspire guests waiting for a table or relaxing after dinner. A warm welcome from the dashing Sudanese doorman, Muhammad, ensures a good start, and the restaurant has a very pleasant ambience, with soft lighting, antiques, interesting paintings, the gentlest of background music and streamlined table settings. The menu begins with an introduction to the cuisine, explaining the four fundamental flavours known collectively as 'pisawa masala' - tomato, garlic, ginger and onions - and their uses. Each dish is clearly described, including starters like kakeragh (local crab claws with garlic, yoghurt, spices and a tandoori masala sauce) and main courses such as the luxurious Sumandari Badsha (lobster tails with cashew nuts, pineapple, chilli and spices). There is a declared commitment to local produce - notably organic beef, lamb and chicken - and a section of the menu devoted to organic and 'lighter fare' main courses (typically Loki Mushroom, a vegetarian dish of courgettes and mushrooms in a light spicy yoghurt sauce). The kitchen team have over 80 years experience between them and the quality of both food and cooking is exemplary: dishes have distinct character and depth of flavour, and everything is appetisingly presented with regard for colour, texture and temperature - and fine food is backed up by attentive, professional service under the supervision of restaurant manager, Anwar Gul, and fair prices. Care and attention marks every aspect of this comfortable and attractive restaurant, earning it a loyal following. *Kinara was the Guide's Ethnic Restaurant of the Year in 2004. **Seats 77** (private room 20). Air conditioning. Children welcome. L Thu, Fri & Sun, 12.30-2.45; D daily, 6-11.30. Set L €14.95; early D €19.95 (Mon-Thu, 5.30-7.30pm); also à la carte L&D. House wine about €18.50. Closed 25-26 Dec, 1 Jan. Amex, MasterCard, Visa, Laser. **Directions:** 3km (1.5 m) north of city centre on coast road to Howth (opposite wooden bridge).

DUBLIN 4

Dublin 4
GUESTHOUSE

Aberdeen Lodge

53 Park Avenue Ballsbridge Dublin 4 **Tel: 01 283 8155**
aberdeen@iol.ie www.halpinsprivatehotels.com

Centrally located (close to the Sydney Parade DART station) yet away from the heavy traffic of nearby Merrion Road, this handsome period house in a pleasant leafy street offers all the advantages of a hotel at guesthouse prices. Elegantly furnished executive bedrooms and four-poster suites have air conditioning and all the little comforts expected by the discerning traveller, including a drawing room with comfortable chairs and plenty to read, and a secluded garden where guests can relax in fine weather. Staff are extremely pleasant and helpful (tea and biscuits offered on arrival), housekeeping is immaculate - and, although there is no restaurant, a Drawing Room menu offers a light menu (with wine list), and you can also look forward to a particularly good breakfast - fresh and stewed fruits, home-made preserves, freshly-baked breads and muffins, big jugs of juice and hot dishes cooked to order - including delicious scrambled eggs and smoked salmon, kippers and buttermilk pancakes with maple syrup, as well as numerous variations on the traditional Irish breakfast. Guests may join residents for breakfast - a useful service for early morning meetings - and the spa at the nearby sister property, Merrion Hall (see entry), is available for guests' use. [Aberdeen Lodge was the Dublin winner of our Irish Breakfast Awards in 2004.] Boardroom, business and fitness facilities for business guests - and mature secluded gardens. Small conferences/banqueting (50/40). Children welcome. No pets. **Rooms 17** (2 suites, 6 executive rooms, all no-smoking). 24 hour room service. B&B €75 pps, ss €35. Residents' meals available: D (Drawing Room Menu) €22 + all-day menu. House wines from €30. Open all year. Amex, Diners, MasterCard, Visa, Laser. **Directions:** Minutes from the city centre by DART or by car, take the Merrion Road towards Sydney Parade DART station and then first left into Park Avenue.

Dublin 4
HOTEL

Ariel House

50-54 Lansdowne Road Ballsbridge Dublin 4 **Tel: 01 668 5512**
reservations@ariel-house.net www.ariel-house.net

This fine family-run establishment occupies three seamlessly adjoined Victorian houses beside the famous old rugby ground in leafy Ballsbridge. It makes a good impression from the outset, with tarmacadamed parking (plus extra parking to the rear), gardens laid out in lawn and shrubbery, making a pleasant place to sit with a book on a summer's day, and a sweep of granite steps leading up to the entrance. Inside, you'll find an elegant hallway, reception and a bay-windowed residents' lounge with antique furnishings, open gas fire, TV and a supply of daily newspapers. The 37 bedrooms are spread throughout the three storeys, including some at garden level, and at the time of the Guide's early summer visit in 2007 a major refurbishment programme was discreetly under way; this has since been completed, and the house re-launched with some fanfare. Bedrooms offering a combination of period décor and modern comforts (all have TV and tea/coffee making facilities) vary in size - deluxe rooms and junior suites have four-posters and brass beds, and special attention is paid to the quality of beds in all rooms; bathrooms vary, standard rooms having compact, tiled bathrooms with bath and shower, heated towel rail, toiletries and hairdryer. Breakfast, served in an extended conservatory overlooking the garden, is a most pleasant experience: attentive staff, fresh flowers on white linen table cloths, clematis trailing outside the window and carefully cooked full Irish fry as well as an array of fruit and cereals. Under the management of Jennie McKeown, a daughter of the house and a professionally trained young hotelier, this is a well-run establishment. Children welcome (under 6s free in parents' room, cots available free of charge); free broadband wi/fi; parking (25). **Rooms 37** (3 junior suites, 10 executive, 3 family, 1 shower only, 10 ground floor, all no smoking). B&B €60 pps or €99-150 for a single room. MasterCard, Visa, Laser. **Directions:** On Lansdowne Road off Ballsbridge.

Dublin 4   Baan Thai
RESTAURANT   16 Merrion Road Ballsbridge Dublin 4
                                                                                                    Tel: 01 660 8833

Delicious aromas and oriental music greet you as you climb the stairs to Lek and Eamon Lancaster's well-appointed first floor restaurant opposite the RDS. Friendly staff, Thai furniture and woodcarvings create an authentic oriental feeling and intimate atmosphere - and, as many of the staff are Thai, it's almost like being in Thailand. A wide-ranging menu includes various set menus that provide a useful introduction to the cuisine (or speed up choices for groups) as well as an à la carte. The essential fragrance and spiciness of Thai cuisine is very much in evidence throughout and there's Thai beer as well as a fairly extensive wine list. [*Also at: Leopardstown, 01 293 6996]. **Seats 64** (private room, 24); children welcome; air con. L Wed-Fri only; set L €10, 1 course. D daily 6-11, (to 11.30pm Fri & Sat); set 3 course D €30. MasterCard, Visa, Laser. Closed 24-26 Dec. **Directions:** Beside Paddy Cullen's pub in Ballsbridge.

Dublin 4   Bahay Kubo
RESTAURANT   14 Bath Avenue Sandymount Dublin 4
                                                                                                    Tel: 01 660 5572

Don't be put off by trains rumbling overhead as you approach this unusual Filipino restaurant - once you get upstairs past the rather worn carpeted entrance and stairway, you will find yourself in a modern room with a spacious and welcoming atmosphere. Friendly staff seat new guests immediately and bring iced water with menus that are well organised with explanations about the Filipino dishes. Several set menus are offered and an à la carte which is, by oriental standards, quite restrained; anyone who likes Chinese food should enjoy the Filipino versions, which are similar but with generally fresher flavours of lemongrass, ginger, chilli and coconut; no MSG is used and soups are refreshingly free of cornstarch. As in some other oriental cuisines, the weakness is in the dessert menu, so make the most of the excellent savoury dishes instead. Service is attentive, making up in willingness anything it may occasionally lack in training. **Seats 80.** Reservations required. D Tue-Sat, 6-11 (Sun 5-10), L Thu & Fri, 12-2.30. Set Menu from about €29, also à la carte Live music Thu & Sat. Closed Mon Amex, MasterCard, Visa, Laser. **Directions:** Above Lansdowne Bar, at railway bridge. ◇

BALLSBRIDGE HOTELS
www.D4hotels.com

The former JurysDoyle hotels in Ballsbridge, recently sold for development, have re-opened under new management pending planning decisions on the sites. The **Ballsbridge Inn** and **Ballsbridge Towers** (previously Jurys Hotel Ballsbridge and The Towers) offer quality accommodation in a wonderful location; this is a room only operation with a lobby area and Food Hall serving continental style breakfast and day food. A full restaurant is available at its adjacent sister property **Ballsbridge Court** (see below). Full bar facilities from 5pm. Room rates: Ballsbridge Inn €105; Ballsbridge Towers €135. Ballsbridge Court (formerly the Berkely Court Hotel), offers fine accommodation with a good standard of service, and its wonderful bar loved by locals. Ballsbridge Court has a full restaurant/brasserie, open from 7am-11pm. Rooms €135.00

Dublin 4
RESTAURANT

Bella Cuba Restaurant

11 Ballsbridge Terrace Dublin 4 **Tel: 01 660 5539**
info@bella-cuba.com www.bella-cuba.com

téite bía Juan Carlos & Larissa Jimenez's bright, warm-toned restaurant is decorated with dramatic murals by a Cuban designer, providing a uniquely Cuban atmosphere - and Juan Carlos's cooking demonstrates the Spanish, Caribbean and South American influences on Cuba's food. Most dishes are slow cooked, with very little deep frying, and the flavours are of aromatic spices and herbs - predominantly garlic, cumin, oregano and bay. Informative menus give the names of dishes in two languages, with a full description of each, and it's well worth a visit to experience something genuinely different: begin with a famous Cuban cocktail like a Daiquiri or Mojito and then try a speciality of Caribbean rack of lamb or red snapper with coconut cream. The wine list, which offers a choice fairly balanced between the old and new, includes a pair of Cuban bottles. The early evening 'Value Menu' allows you to choose from a limited selection on the à la carte. Not suitable for children after 7pm. **Seats 30.** D daily, 5 - 11 (to 10.30 Sun). L Thu & Fri, 12-3. Value L about €10.50, Early D about €25 (5-7). Also à la carte. House wine about €19.50. SC discretionary. Closed Christmas. Amex, MasterCard, Visa, Laser. **Directions:** Middle of Ballsbridge. ◇

Dublin 4
RESTAURANT

Berman & Wallace

Belfield Office Park Beaver Row Clonskeagh Dublin 4 **Tel: 01 219 6252**
bermanandwallace@eircom.net www.bermanandwallace.com

téite bía This smart pavilion-style restaurant, in a courtyard surrounded by office buildings, supplies the local business community with wide-ranging high quality brasserie-style daytime food. Choose from such all-time favourites as Irish Stew, fish and chips, bangers and mash (made with Hicks sausages) and baguettes filled with chargrilled steak and garlic mayonnaise, to pasta dishes, lamb passanda, chicken piri-piri with herb risotto and a great deal more. There are also several revitalising or detoxing juices and smoothies for the diet conscious, and there is a daily health lunch special on offer. Wines by the glass or by bottle. Parking for 20 cars. **Seats 80** (outdoor 20). Open Mon-Fri, 7.30-3. Closed Sat/Sun, Christmas, Easter, bank hols. Amex, MasterCard, Visa, Laser. **Directions:** From Donnybrook, turn at Bus Station up Beaver Road towards Clonskeagh. Turn left at second set of lights into business park and follow signs.

Dublin 4
HOTEL

Bewleys Hotel

Merrion Road Ballsbridge Dublin 4 **Tel: 01 668 1111**
ballsbridge@bewleyshotels.com www.bewleyshotels.com

This modern hotel is cleverly designed to incorporate a landmark period building next to the RDS (entrance by car is on Simmonscourt Road, via Merrion Road or Anglesea Road; underground carpark). Bedrooms are spacious and well-equipped with ISDN lines, iron/trouser press, tea/coffee facilities and safe, making a good base for business or leisure visits. Like its sister hotels at Newlands Cross, Leopardstown and Dublin Airport, you get a lot of comfort here at a very reasonable cost. *Restaurant: See entry for O'Connells in Ballsbridge. No pets; garden; parking; business centre; free broadband. **Rooms 304** (10 shower only, 64 family rooms, 254 no smoking, 12 for disabled, 50 ground floor). Lift; limited room service. Room rate €109; children welcome (under 16s free in parents room, baby sitting arranged, cots available free of charge). Closed 24-26 Dec. Amex, Diners, MasterCard, Visa, Laser. **Directions:** At junction of Simmonscourt and Merrion Road.

Dublin 4
RESTAURANT

Brownes

18 Sandymount Green Sandymount Dublin 4
Tel: 01 269 7316

The energetic proprietor, Peter Bark, has moved this restaurant up a rung or two recently and it is now not only a good daytime café and neighbourhood restaurant in the evening, but it attracts diners from beyond the area too. During the day you'll find gourmet sandwiches, (crayfish tails; rare beef, horseradish and rocket) and, by night, simple, classical French-inspired food. Décor is minimal, with good paintings by local artists and simple bentwood chairs, but Cathal Brugha Street trained chef Neil Hawley cooks things like a mean moules marinière (starter or main - nice fat mussels in a wine and cream sauce), and great meats including aged sirloin (crusty on the outside and pink within, served with chunky, crispy 'real' chips) and pan-fried rack of lamb, served on a bed of flageolet beans, with tasty, slightly waxy, continental style new potatoes. Finish with a well-made traditional dessert (crème brulée, crumble) or excellent home-made ice creams and sorbets. BYO wine - a small corkage charge is levied "unless you offer us a glass of something nice". Coffee could be the weak point, so call for the (surprisingly modest) bill and have it at home. **Seats 22;** about €32-35 for 3 courses. ◇

Dublin 4   # Butlers Town House
GUESTHOUSE

44 Lansdowne Road Ballsbridge Dublin 4 **Tel: 01 667 4022**
info@butlers-hotel.com   www.butlers-hotel.com

On a corner site in Dublin's 'embassy belt' and close to the Lansdowne Road stadium, this large townhouse/guesthouse has been extensively refurbished and luxuriously decorated in a Victorian country house style and is a small hotel in all but name. Public rooms include a comfortable drawing room and an attractive conservatory-style dining room where breakfast is served; an attractive all-day menu is also offered. Rooms are individually decorated and furnished to a high standard, some with four-poster beds. Private parking (15). Wheelchair accessible. Not suitable for children. No pets. **Rooms 19** (3 superior, 1 disabled, all no smoking). 24 hr room service. Turndown service offered. B&B about €95, ss €45; no SC. Closed 21 Dec-5 Jan. Amex, Diners, MasterCard, Visa, Laser, **Directions:** Corner of Lansdowne Road and Shelbourne Road. ◇

Dublin 4   # Canal Bank Café
RESTAURANT

146 Upper Leeson Street Dublin 4 **Tel: 01 664 2135**
info@tribeca.ie   www.canalbankcafe.com

Trevor Browne and Gerard Foote's well-known almost-canalside restaurant is designed to meet the current demand for quality informal food or 'everyday dining', but the philosophy is to use only the best ingredients - organic beef and lamb, free-range chicken and a wide variety of fresh fish daily. The menu is user-friendly, divided mainly by types of dish - starters like crispy fried calamari with lemon mayonnaise, big salads (Caesar, niçoise) and, for those who need a real feed, steaks various ways and specialities like Brooklyn meatloaf with spinach, onion gravy & mashed potatoes, and there's also a good sprinkling of vegetarian dishes. A carefully selected, compact wine list includes a good choice of house wines - and a range of brunch cocktails too.] Children welcome. **Seats 65.** Air conditioning. Open 10am-11pm daily (from 11am Sun). A la carte. House wine €18.95. SC 10% on parties of 6+. Closed 24-28 Dec & Good Fri. Amex, Diners, MasterCard, Visa, Laser. **Directions:** Ballsbridge side of the canal on Leeson Street.

Dublin 4   # The Courtyard Restaurant & Piano Bar
RESTAURANT

1 Belmont Avenue Donnybrook Dublin 4 **Tel: 01 283 0407**
info@thecourtyardcafe.ie   www.thecourtyardcafe.ie

Set well back from the road and approached through the courtyard that inspired the name, this popular neighbourhood restaurant is a relaxed spot with some style, where good food combines attractively with reasonable prices and a pleasing ambience. It's not a place that visitors are likely to find by chance, but useful to know about, especially as they are open from late afternoon every day so you can enjoy a leisurely early evening meal before going on to a concert or the theatre in town. Piano in the evening. **Seats 170** (private room, 70, outdoors, 40); air conditioning; children welcome; D Mon-Sat, 5.30-10.30 (Sun 5-9); L Sun only, 5-9; Early D about €20, 5.30-7; Sun L about €25; House wine €18-20. SC 10%. Closed 25 Dec, Good Fri. Amex, Diners, MasterCard, Visa, Laser. **Directions:** Behind Madigans pub. ◇

Dublin 4   # Donnybrook Fair Café
RESTAURANT

89a Morehampton Road Donnybrook Dublin 4 **Tel: 01 614 4849**
donnybrookfaircafe@hotmail.com   www.donnybrookfair.ie

The sleek looks of the exterior of Dublin's chicest supermarket, Donnybrook Fair, are matched by some equally sleek products on the shelves: fine food produce from across the globe jostles with local producers' goods as well as delectable treats from the fish and deli counters. Up a spiral stairway from the shop floor you'll find Donnybrook Fair Café, a bright and airy space where the menu features plenty of old reliables, with starters including simple soups and salads, chicken and liver paté, while main courses include rack of lamb, home-made burgers, rib-eye steak and a wide selection of fish. Desserts will please lovers of golden oldies such as chocolate brownie cake, vanilla crème brûlée and mandarin cheesecake. The eclectic wine list contains plenty of moderately priced wines, as well as more expensive wines by the glass. Although it sometimes struggles to keep up with the high end produce found below, this smart café remains a popular place to meet for a bite. Children welcome. **Seats** 80 (private room, 25); air conditioning; reservations accepted; food served all day, Mon-Sat, 8am - 9.30pm (L 12-3, D 5.30-9.30); Sun brunch only, 12-4pm; set Sun set meal €23.95; early D €23.95, Sun-Fri, 5.30-7pm, also a la carte L&D; house wine from €19; SC on groups of 10+. Closed Sun eve, Christmas. MasterCard, Visa, Laser. **Directions:** City side of Donnybrook village, AIB on corner.

Dunne & Crescenzi

Dublin 4
RESTAURANT

11 Seafort Avenue Sandymount Dublin 4 **Tel: 01 667 3252**
dunneandcrescenzi@hotmail.com www.dunneandcrescenzi.com

féile bía Genuine Italian fare is what you'll find at this small restaurant, a younger branch of the well-known Dublin 2 establishment (see entry). Like its older sister, it's a quality ingredients-led place with tightly packed tables, an extensive Italian wine list and a menu that dispenses with the idea of courses, offering instead a selection of charcuterie plates, panini and other light dishes like insalata caprese, and some hot dishes so you can have a light bite or a full meal as appetite dictates. House wine about €14. MasterCard, Visa, Laser. **Directions:** Next to O'Reilly's pub. ◇

Dylan Hotel Dublin

Dublin 4
HOTEL/RESTAURANT

Eastmoreland Place Dublin 4 **Tel: 01 660 3000**
justask@dylan.ie www.dylan.ie

It feels as if it's in a peaceful backwater, yet this splendid Victorian building is just yards from one of Dublin's busiest city centre roads. Arrival at the gates of Dylan is an experience in itself, especially in the evening, when it is magically lit by old fashioned lamps outside the main entrance, where doormen greet you. A modern wing sits comfortably with the original building and the lobby offers a foretaste of the edgy design beyond: leather padded walls, over-sized floral motifs and tactile wallpaper along with ultra-modern seating and creative lighting are just some of the quirky elements that create an atmosphere of decadent elegance. The edgy look continues in the individually designed bedrooms, which are fitted to a very high specification. Standard rooms are laptop compatible and include a plasma screen TV, MP3 players, safes, cordless phones with voicemail and speakerphone, customised 7th Heaven Beds, Frette linen, air conditioning, under floor heated bathrooms, power showers, robes & slippers, Etro toiletries, mini bar and twice daily housekeeping. Even the most demanding international traveller would be hard pressed to complain at this five star boutique hotel. Not suitable for children. Business centre, secretarial services, free broadband wi/fi. **Rooms** 44 (6 suites, 38 executive, 15 shower only, 1 disabled, all no smoking); Lift; 24hr room service. B&B from €395 per room for Dylan Luxury (€275 off peak, other rooms discounted depending on availability), Dylan Style €440, Dylan Experience €690, one Dylan Signature Suite €800. Lifts. Non-smoking hotel. Open all year except 25-26 Dec. **The Still:** This strangely named bright, white dining room is filled with no less then nine glittering chandeliers, luxurious cream and white chairs, wildly curved furnishings, a pale padded wall and a baby grand piano. The ambience is lavish 1940s Hollywood decadence and there are always plenty of big Irish names to be spotted here. Head chef Padraig Hayden was previously at One Pico and his classical discipline shows in menus that are indulgent, but always deliver. Specialities that are faultless, in the Guide's experience, include fresh lasagne with Dublin Bay prawns, white leek, salsify and roasted scallops; and roasted venison with pureed parsnip and root vegetable terrine. The dessert menu includes some very dressy versions of classics - including pear tatin with Poire William ice cream, spun sugar, and vanilla syrup, perhaps. An extensive wine list leans heavily towards classic super stars, with prices to match, although there is plenty of choice at more accessible prices. Attentive service is a hallmark of this smart hotel - doors are held open for guests, and highly knowledgeable waiting staff explain each course. A champagne cocktail will set you back about €20 but this is not a place people visit to count the pennies: Dylan is very much a place to be seen, so the prices match the opulent stage setting. **Restaurant: Seats** 44 (private room, 12, outdoors, 20); air conditioning; L daily, 12.30-2.30pm, D daily 6-10.30pm (to 11pm Thu-Sat); set 3 course L €38, also a la carte L&D. Average starter €21, main courses €35, desserts €15. Tasting Menu of 8 courses €110. House wine from €20.95. SC discretionary. Amex, Mastercard, Visa, Laser. **Directions:** Just off Upper Baggot Street before St. Marys Road.

Dublin 4
CAFÉ/RESTAURANT

Expresso Bar Café

1 St Mary's Road Ballsbridge Dublin 4
Tel: 01 660 0585

Great flavour-packed food, good value and efficient service invariably pleases the loyal following at Ann-Marie Nohl's clean-lined informal restaurant, which is renowned for carefully sourced ingredients that make a flavour statement on the plate. An all-morning breakfast menu offers many of the classics, often with a twist: thus a simple poached egg on toast comes with crispy bacon and relish, porridge is a class act topped with toasted almonds and honey, and French toast comes with bacon, or winter berries and syrup. Lunch and dinner menus tend to favour an international style, but the same high standards apply: whether it's a Dublin Bay Prawn pil pil with Chilli, coriander, char-grilled lime and crusty toast, or grilled balsamic chicken with a peach and baby spinach salad, or a vegetarian pasta such as fettucine with black olive, rocket, sundried tomato tapenade & oven roasted vine tomatoes, it's the quality of the ingredients and cooking that make the food here special. Wines on display add to the atmosphere, and an informative and well-chosen wine list offers half a dozen by the glass, and a pair of half bottles. Weekend brunch is a must. Not suitable for children after 5pm. Air conditioning. **Seats 60** (outdoor, 14). Open Mon-Fri, 7.30am-9.15pm (B'fst 7.30- 9.30; all day menu to 9.30pm), Sat 9am-9.15pm, Sun brunch 10am-5pm. Closed D Sun, 25 Dec, 1 Jan, Good Friday. MasterCard, Visa, Laser. **Directions:** Opposite Dylan Hotel, off Upper Baggot Street.

Dublin 4
HOTEL/RESTAURANT

Four Seasons Hotel

Simmonscourt Road Dublin 4 **Tel: 01 665 4000**
reservations.dublin@fourseasons.com www.fourseasons.com/dublin

téile bia Set in its own gardens on a section of the Royal Dublin Society's 42-acre show grounds, this luxurious hotel enjoys a magnificent site, allowing a sense of spaciousness while also being convenient to the city centre - the scale is generous throughout and there are views of the Wicklow Mountains or Dublin Bay from many of the sumptuous suites and guest rooms. A foyer in the grand tradition is flanked by two bars - the traditional wood-panelled Lobby Bar and the newer Ice, which is deliciously contemporary, and very popular with Dubliners. Accommodation is predictably luxurious and, with a full range of up-to-the-minute amenities, the air-conditioned rooms are designed to appeal equally to leisure and business guests. A choice of pillows (down and non-allergenic foam) is provided as standard, the large marbled bathrooms have separate bath and shower, and many other desirable features - and there's great emphasis on service, with twice daily housekeeping service, overnight laundry and dry cleaning, one hour pressing and complimentary overnight shoe shine: everything, in short, that the immaculate traveller requires. But the Spa in the lower level of the hotel is perhaps its most outstanding feature, offering every treatment imaginable - and a naturally lit 14m lap pool and adjacent jacuzzi pool, overlooking an outdoor sunken garden. Outstanding conference and meeting facilities make the hotel ideal for corporate events, business meetings and parties in groups of anything up to 550. Conferences/Banqueting (550/450), business centre, secretarial services, video conferencing (on request), broadband wi/fi. Children welcome (under 18s free in parents' room, cot available free of charge, baby sitting arranged). **Rooms 196** (16 suites, 26 junior suites, 178 no-smoking, 13 for disabled). 24 hr room service, Lift, Turndown service. Room rate €315 (max. 3 guests). No SC. Open all year. **Seasons Restaurant:** This spacious, classically-appointed restaurant overlooks a leafy courtyard and no expense has been spared on the traditional 'grand hotel' decor and, whether or not it is to your taste, this is an extremely comfortable restaurant and the service is usually exemplary. Executive Head Chef Terry White's contemporary international menus have their base in classical French cooking and offer a wide-ranging choice of luxurious dishes, with a considerate guide to dishes suitable for vegetarians, 'healthier fare' and dishes containing nuts. An unusual speciality dish to try is an Irish scallop tasting, prepared with Parmesan with creamy spicy sauce, jalapeno salsa or natural, with caviar. An extensive hors d'oeuvre buffet of hot and cold dishes has become a favourite feature of late, and a 7-course Tasting Menu is offered. The standard of cooking is high and, while it may not rival the city's top independent restaurants as a cutting edge dining experience, this is a fine hotel restaurant with outstanding service - and a good pricing policy ensures value for money, given the luxurious surroundings. Sommelier Simon Keegan's excellent wine list includes some very good wines by the glass. *Informal menus are also available at varying times in The Café (daily), and in Ice Bar (Tue-Sat); Afternoon Tea, served daily in the Lobby Lounge, includes an extensive menu of classic teas and infusions. Air conditioning. **Seats 90** (private room, 12). Breakfast 7-11 daily, L 12.30-2.30 daily, D 6.30-9.30 daily. Set L from €35; à la carte also available D. House wine from €33. Amex, Diners, MasterCard, Visa. **Directions:** Located on the RDS Grounds on corner of Merrion and Simmonscourt Roads. ◇

The French Paradox

Dublin 4
RESTAURANT/WINE BAR

53 Shelbourne Road Ballsbridge Dublin 4 **Tel: 01 660 4068**
pch@chapeauwines.com   www.thefrenchparadox.com

On a busy road near the RDS, this inspired and stylish operation brings an extra dimension (and a whiff of the south of France) to the concept of wine and food in Dublin. French Paradox combines a wine shop, a large and atmospheric ground floor wine bar (where weekly wine tastings are held) and a dining room on the first floor, which gains atmosphere from the irresistible charcuterie on display close beside the tables. The main emphasis is on the wide range of wines available by the glass - perhaps 65 wines, kept in perfect condition once open using a wine sommelier, with inert gas. Pierre and Tanya Chapeau are renowned for their directly imported wines and food is, in theory, secondary here; but, although the choice is deliberately limited (a small à la carte offers a concise range of dishes, as single or shared charcuterie plates), the quality is exceptional and although the hot dinner dishes may be less successful - everyone just loves specialities like the foie gras, the smoked duck salad and the 'Bill Hogan', made with the renowned thermophilic cheeses from west Cork... and sitting outside on a sunny summer day, enjoying a plate of charcuterie with any one of the dozens of wines available by the glass, you could be lunching in the south of France. Classic desserts - tarte tatin, chocolate terrine, crème brulée - and excellent coffees to finish. Wines offered change regularly (the list is always growing), and food can be purchased from the deli-counter to take home. Not suitable for children after 7pm. **Seats 25** (+25 in tasting room, +12 outside). Air conditioning. Toilets wheelchair accessible. L&D Mon-Thu, 12-3 & 6-9.30; open all day Fri & Sat, 12-9.30. Set L €16.95; value D €25, 6-8.30pm. A la carte. House wines (6) change monthly, from €19. Closed Sun (except for "Rugby Match" Sundays), Christmas, Bank Hols. Amex, MasterCard, Visa, Laser. **Directions:** Opposite Ballsbridge Post Office.

Furama Restaurant

Dublin 4
RESTAURANT

G/F Eirepage House Donnybrook Dublin 4 **Tel: 01 283 0522**
info@furama.ie   www.furama.ie

ETHNIC RESTAURANT OF THE YEAR

In the sleek black interior of Rodney Mak's long-established restaurant, Freddy Lee, who has been head chef since the restaurant opened in 1989, produces terrific food with an authenticity which is unusual in Ireland. The waiter stationed beside the entrance opens the door and welcomes customers on arrival, setting the tone for excellent service that is as friendly as it is technically correct. With the dining room reached over a curving bridge and water features, the quietly elegant interior is free of the hanging lanterns and oriental kitsch that mark out so many Chinese restaurants. Customers here are largely locals and faithful regulars drawn here by the reliably authentic take on classic Chinese dishes, which include faultless crispy duck, dim sum fried or steamed, and excellent seafood dishes like the seared scallops with ginger, spring onion and soy glaze beautifully presented in their shells. Although Chinese restaurants are notoriously weak in the dessert department, Furama's banana fritters are an exception, presented piping hot in feathery batter with toasted sesame seeds, a pool of caramel syrup and a scoop of vanilla ice cream; it is also extremely good value as desserts including the excellent fritters are only €3-3.50, yet a side dish of mangetout with oyster sauce is charged at €6.50. House wines at €20 are also available by the glass, which is useful; more expensive wines on the list favour expense account diners, running to the €40-60 level. This restaurant is highly recommended for its consistency over the years, both in quality of food and impeccable service. A Special Chinese Menu can be arranged for banqueting with one week's notice (up to 30 people) and outside catering is also available. Parking. **Seats 70.** Mon-Fri: L 12.30-2pm, D 6pm-11.30pm, Sat D only 6pm-11.30pm, Sun open 1.30pm-11pm; D Various set menus from about €35. A la carte available. House wine from about €19. Air conditioning. SC 10%. Closed Sat L, 24-26 Dec & Good Fri. Amex, Diners, MasterCard, Visa, Laser. **Directions:** Opposite Bective Rugby Ground in Donnybrook, near town side of Donnybrook Bridge. ◇

Dublin 4   Glenogra House
GUESTHOUSE   64 Merrion Road Ballsbride Dublin 4 **Tel: 01 668 3661**
                                            info@glenogra.com www.glenogra.com

Conveniently located for the RDS and within 3 minutes walk of the Sandymount DART station, this well known guesthouse is run by the owners, Peter and Veronica Donohoe, who are doing an excellent job. The public areas have all been refurbished and, from the minute you arrive there is a great sense of welcome and hospitality - lovely fresh flowers in the large hall, someone to carry your bags to your room and explain the facilities, the security of knowing there is safe parking. The bedrooms are not furnished in the latest style - expect to find darkwood furniture, fringed lampshades and little dressing table mirrors - but they are comfortable and clean, and offer some welcome extras, including smart white bathrobes and portable radios. Moreover, you'll get a really good breakfast, with plenty of choice, (including scrambled egg with smoked salmon) leaf tea and exceptionally delicious home-made muesli. Children welcome (under 10s free in parents' room, cots available free of charge). Free broadband wi/fi, no pets. **Rooms 13** (2 shower only, 1 family room, all no-smoking). B&B €59.50 pps, ss €30. Closed 22 Dec - 10 Jan. Amex, Diners, MasterCard, Visa, Laser. **Directions:** Opposite Four Seasons Hotel, RDS.

Dublin 4   Grand Canal Hotel
HOTEL   Grand Canal Street Dublin 4 **Tel: 01 646 1000**
                                     reservations@grandcanalhotel.com www.grandcanalhotel.com

Smartly maintained and with a secure car park, this business hotel located in the up-and-coming Grand Canal area is ideal for anyone requiring fairly priced quality accommodation within walking distance of Dublin city centre and the Ballsbridge area. Reception is friendly and efficient, and public areas are bright, clean and relaxing. The top floor is dedicated to executive rooms, but all rooms are spacious and have hospitality tray, cable TV, WiFi, direct dial telephone, iron, and hairdryer; bathrooms have large baths and quality towels and the standard of housekeeping is good. A fairly standard but well-presented buffet breakfast is served in a pleasant breakfast room. The hotel has a range of meeting rooms, and food of various kinds is available in different areas during the day and evening; the useful Canal Express Bar was opening at the time of the Guide's 2007 visit - it serves coffee and snacks for people in a hurry, whether hotel guests or popping in off the street. Conferences/Banqueting (140/120); free parking for guests; broadband wi/fi; Children welcome (under 3s free in parents' room, cot available free of charge, baby sitting arranged); **Rooms 142** (31 executive, 18 family, 6 for disabled); 24 hr room service; Lift; B&B €55 pps, single €95. Closed 22-28 Dec. Amex, Diners, MasterCard, Visa, Laser. **Directions:** Beside the north end of the Grand Canal on Grand Canal Street.

Dublin 4   Herbert Park Hotel
HOTEL   Ballsbridge Dublin 4 **Tel: 01 667 2200**
                                     reservations@herbertparkhotel.ie www.herbertparkhotel.ie

This large, privately-owned contemporary hotel is attractively located in an 'urban plaza' near the RDS and the public park after which it is named. It is approached over a little bridge, which leads to an underground carpark and, ultimately, to a chic lower ground foyer and the lift up to the main lobby.

Public areas on the ground floor are impressively light and spacious, with excellent light meals and drinks provided by efficient waiting staff. The bright and modern style is also repeated in the bedrooms, which have views over Ballsbridge and Herbert Park and are stylishly designed and well-finished, with a high standard of amenities. A good breakfast is served in the Pavilion Restaurant, a bright, elegant, contemporary room which overlooks a garden terrace (where tables can be set up in fine weather. Team building, jazz events, golf packages and special breaks are all offered. A good choice for the business guest or corporate events as well as private guests, this hotel is reasonably priced for the standard of accommodation and facilities offered, and staff are efficient, enthusiastic and warm. Conference/banqueting (120/220). Business centre, video conferencing, broadband wi/fi, laptop-sized safes in bedrooms. Fitness room, garden, newsagent. Children welcome (under 2 free in parents' room, cots available free of charge, baby sitting arranged, playground). No pets. **Rooms 153** (2 suites, 40 executive rooms, 138 no-smoking, 8 for disabled). Lift. 24 hr room service. Turndown service. B&B €120pps. SS €120. No SC. Open all year. **Restaurant: Seats 200.** Breakfast 8-10 (Sat & Sun to 10.30, Sun from 8); L 12.30-2.30; D daily 5.30-9.30. Set L €30 (Buffet Sun L €39.50); D à la carte. House wine €23.50. Amex, Diners, MasterCard, Visa. **Directions:** In Ballsbridge, shortly before RDS heading out of city.

Dublin 4
RESTAURANT

Itsa4

6a Sandymount Green Sandymount Dublin 4 **Tel: 01 219 4676**
itsa4@itsabagel.com www.itsabagel.com

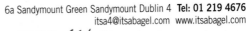 This smart contemporary place has a 'New York Diner' feel, appropriate given the American connections of Domini and Peaches Kemp, the talented and hard-working sisters who are already well known for the 'Itsa Bagel' cafés - but this is a fully-fledged restaurant and not an extension of the bagel concept. Quality ingredient-led menus have a strong emphasis on provenance and no obvious distinction between starters and main courses; you might start, for example, with a platter of Terry Butterly's excellent pale smoked salmon, served in a portion generous enough to serve two easily, or perhaps a portion of potato skins with cheddar, dry-cured bacon and a sour cream dip as another nibbling option to share. The daily pasta dishes are invariably excellent and specialities include superb dry-aged rib-eye beef, which is served with a gorgeously rich béarnaise sauce and great vegetables (from Gold River Farm, in Co Wicklow); the house 'organic' chips (which are unpeeled) have instigated debate as many feel that they have 'more flavour but less crispness' than regular chips. As is often the case in the organic debate, it is the organic/traditional farming question rather than the variety (or even its locality) that comes under scrutiny - given the correct variety, organic chips will be just as crisp as any other. Excellent desserts include gorgeous home-made ice creams and sorbets, and perfectly matured Sheridans cheese is served simply on a wooden platter with warm biscuits and grapes. Java Republic organic Fairtrade coffees are good (and served with excellent breakfasts too - try the eggs Benedict), service is friendly and efficient, and there's an interesting well-priced wine list which includes unusual bottles from specialist suppliers. Toilets wheelchair accessible. Free broadband wi/fi. Children welcome before 8.45pm (high chair, children's menu, baby changing facilities). **Seats 55** (outdoor, 10); air conditioning; L & D Tue-Sun: Tue-Sat, 12-4 and 6-10; Sun 11-4 and 5-9; set 2/3 course D., €22/25; house wine €17. Closed Mon (except Bank Hols); 25-26 Dec, Good Fri, Easter Sun. MasterCard, Visa, Laser. **Directions:** On Sandymount Green.

Dublin 4
RESTAURANT

Kites Restaurant

15-17 Ballsbridge Terrace Ballsbridge Dublin 4 **Tel: 01 660 7415**
kites@eircom.net

Lots of natural light with white painted walls, dark wooden fittings and a rich, dark carpet create a good first impression at this split-level Ballsbridge restaurant, and a mix of diners gives the place a nice buzz. The cuisine is a combination of Cantonese, Szechuan, Peking and Thai - predominantly Cantonese - and menus range from the standard set meals to a decent list of specials. For the indecisive, a house platter of appetisers makes a good beginning, offering a selection of spring rolls, wontons, sesame prawn toasts, spare ribs along with some more unusual additions. Duckling and seafood are specialities: half a crispy aromatic duck comes with fresh steaming pancakes, while a combination dish of salt & pepper jumbo king prawns and a stir-fry chicken is interesting. Stir-fried

Georgina Campbell's Ireland

lamb with ginger & spring onion (one of the few Peking dishes) is to be recommended. Courteous, good humoured and charming service adds considerably to the experience. **Seats 100** (private room, 40). Air conditioning. L daily 12.30-2, D daily 6.30-11.30. Set L €19,50, set D €34; also à la carte. House wine from €22. SC 10%. Closed 25-26 Dec. Good Fri. Amex, Diners, MasterCard, Visa, Laser. **Directions:** In the heart of Ballsbridge. ◇

Dublin 4
RESTAURANT

La Péniche

Grand Canal Mespil Road Dublin 4 **Tel: 087 790 0077**
info@lapeniche.ie www.lapeniche.ie

Dining afloat is an attraction in many European cities but, until recently, Dublin has remained stubbornly out of the loop, so perhaps it should come as no surprise that it is Eric Tydagt and his team at the popular French/Belgian restaurant 'La Mere Zou' who finally introduced the city to this entertaining experience. The barge is smartly got up with red velvet couches and seat covers, and gleaming varnished tables complete with a small lamp and button to call for service. It's quite a squeeze when fully booked, but that's all part of the fun. The menu is based on authentic French bistro dishes, and the idea is that you can have a full four-course meal, a simple charcuterie plate or just a dessert with coffee. Typical sharing dishes include Galway Oysters, a platter of duck rillette, saucisson, paté de campagne & cured ham), and a similar plate offering a combination of charcuterie and cheese. Homely hot dishes range from good soups and rustic classics such as flavoursome Toulouse sausage with basil pesto mash, to a prawn & smoked fish pie, with white wine sauce & pomme purée. There's a special too, and vegetarians can look forward to classic salads and hot dishes like mushroom vol-au-vent with mixed salad. The atmosphere is helped along by very friendly and helpful service and, as well as a good choice of (mainly French) wines, there's a small list of French beers and ciders. On Thursdays dinner is even more fun, eaten under way as La Péniche cruises the canal. The barge is a great place for a party, and can be hired exclusively, with live music if requested. All round it's a hugely entertaining addition to the Dublin dining scene, and adds a new dimension to the city. *La Péniche was our Atmospheric Restaurant of the Year in 2007. Children welcome. **Seats 44** (outdoors, 40); L Tue-Fri, 12-3pm; D Tue-Sat, 6-10.30pm; Sun L only, 2pm-5pm; set L €35; also a la carte L&D. SC 10% on groups 6+. Closed Mon, 1 Jan - 15 Jan. MasterCard, Visa, Laser. **Directions:** Boat on Grand Canal - Mespil Road.

Dublin 4
RESTAURANT

The Lobster Pot

9 Ballsbridge Terrace Ballsbridge Dublin 4 **Tel: 01 660 9170**
www.thelobsterpot.ie

On the first floor of a redbrick Ballsbridge terrace, conspicuously located near the Herbert Park Hotel - and just a few minutes walk from all the major Ballsbridge hotels - this long-established restaurant has lost none of its charm or quality over the years. The whole team - owner Tommy Crean, restaurant manager (and sommelier) John Rigby and head chef Don McGuinness - have been working here together since 1980 and the system is running very sweetly. How good it is to see old favourites like dressed Kilmore Quay crab, home-made chicken liver paté and fresh prawn bisque on the menu, along with fresh prawns mornay and many other old friends, including kidneys turbigo and game in season. The menu is a treat to read but there's also a daily fish tray display for specials - dishes are explained and diners are encouraged to choose their own combinations. All this and wonderfully old-fashioned service too, including advice from John Rigby on the best wine to match your meal. If only there were more places like this - long may it last. D Mon-Sat, 6.30-9.30. House wine about €22.50. SC 12.5%. Closed Sun, 24 Dec-4 Jan, bank hols. Amex, Diners, MasterCard, Visa, Laser. **Directions:** In the heart of Ballsbridge adjacent to the US Embassy. ◇

Marble Hall

Dublin 4
B&B

81 Marlborough Road Donnybrook Dublin 4 **Tel: 01 497 7350**
marblehall@eircom.net www.marblehall.net

B&B BREAKFAST OF THE YEAR

First time visitors have no idea of the delights that lie ahead as they arrive at Shelagh Conway's wonderful B&B, which is discreetly situated in a redbrick Georgian terrace, with no signage just a neatly presented frontage, with a pair of parking spaces at the front and granite steps leading up to the door. But this warm and welcoming place will quickly work its charm. Shelagh herself is always on hand to look after guests, and her house is a gem. Everything is immaculate, with polished wooden floors and beautiful ceiling cornices throughout the ground floor; a little sitting room at the front of the house has a white marble fireplace and period armchairs - there's a TV/DVD player here for guests' use, along with a collection of DVDs, books and magazines. The period bedrooms are large and bright, with big comfortable beds, plenty of pillows, books, mineral water, television and hairdryer and a spruce little shower room. Double doors from the sitting room open on to a lovely breakfast room with round and oval tables, and antique lace cloths; here, although there are only three rooms, Shelagh sets up a sideboard of delicious things including fresh fruits, pineapple, perhaps compôtes of fresh and dried fruits, muesli, cereals and yoghurt, home-baked bread and honey, which guests can help themselves to while she is prearing delicious hot dishes including Cashel Blue pancakes with crispy bacon and grilled mushrooms as well as a perfectly cooked and well-presented version of the traditional Irish breakfast. This is Irish hospitality at its best and very hard to leave. No wheelchair access. Own parking (4). **Rooms 3** (all non-smoking and en-suite); B&B €45-50 pps, ss€15. Closed 1 Dec-6 Jan. MasterCard, Visa, Laser. **Directions:** Located between Donnybrook and Ranelagh.

Merrion Hall

Dublin 4
GUESTHOUSE

54 Merrion Road Ballsbridge Dublin 4 **Tel: 01 668 1426**
merrionhall@iol.ie www.halpinsprivatehotels.com

This adapted Edwardian property opposite the RDS is one of the small group of privately owned Halpin guesthouses; handy to the DART (suburban rail), it makes a good base for business or leisure. New rooms have recently been completed, almost doubling the original accommodation, and all rooms are comfortably furnished with period furniture (some have 4-posters), fine original windows, TV, and bathrobes - and bathrooms are well-appointed, with in-bath jacuzzi and quality cosmetics. There's a well-stocked library, a comfortable big drawing room, and a fine, airy, spacious, basement dining room and outside patio, with tables set up in summer. In common with other Halpin establishments, good breakfasts are served here - an attractive buffet and well-presented fry. This is a very comfortable guest house and, although some rooms are susceptible to the late night/early morning rumble of the nearby DART, and jacuzzis in neighbouring bathrooms, it runs smoothly, without any sign of pressure from the extra rooms. Off-street parking at the back. Small conference/private parties (50/50). Garden. Children welcome (under 2s free in parents' room, cots available free of charge). No pets. **Rooms 34** (8 junior suites,10 executive, 4 family rooms, 4 ground floor, 2 for disabled, all no smoking). Lift. 24 hr service. Turndown service. B&B €75 pps, ss €35. Drawing Room/room service menu available 7am-9pm daily; set D €22; house wine €25. Open all year. Amex, Diners, MasterCard, Visa. **Directions:** Opposite the RDS in Ballsbridge.

Merrion Inn

Dublin 4
PUB

188 Merrion Road Dublin 4 **Tel: 01 269 3816**
themerrioninn@gmail.com

The McCormacks are a great pub family (see separate entry for their Mounttown establishment) and this attractive contemporary pub on the main road between Dublin and Dun Laoghaire makes a handy meeting place. It is a spacious place on two floors, with various quiet sections on the ground floor and an attractive covered outdoor section at the back to relax in relative peace, away from the busy bars. What you can expect to get here is above average pub fare: a hot and cold buffet is served at lunch time and there's a well balanced dinner menu with vegetarian and gluten free dishes marked up. Main course choices offer quite an extensive range of popular dishes salads, chicken dishes, omelettes, bangers & mash, several fish dishes, steaks various ways - then there are home-made desserts, which change daily. There's a large function room with bar upstairs, and a partially covered heated patio area is available for smokers. Toilets wheelchair accessible; children welcome before 9pm. **Seats 200** (private room, 70); Bar food served daily 12-10 (L12-3, D 3.30-10). Buffet / à la carte. House wine from €14.95. Closed 25 Dec & Good Fri. Amex, Diners, MasterCard, Visa, Laser. **Directions:** Opposite St. Vincent's Hospital.

Dublin 4
HOTEL

Mespil Hotel
Mespil Road Dublin 4 **Tel: 01 488 4600**
reservations@leehotels.com www.mespil.com

This fine modern hotel enjoys an excellent location in the Georgian area of the city, overlooking the Grand Canal and within walking distance of St Stephen's Green and all the city centre attractions in fine weather. Public areas are spacious and elegant in an easy contemporary style, and bright, generously-sized bedrooms are comfortably furnished with good amenities including fax/modem connection and voicemail. Dining options include the 200-seater **Glaze Restaurant**, which is open for lunch and dinner daily and offers a well-balanced choice of traditional and contemporary fare based on carefully sourced ingredients at fair prices, and the Terrace Bar, where lunch and light snacks are served. The hotel takes pride in the friendliness and efficiency of the staff and is moderately priced for the area; special breaks offer especially good value. Small meeting and seminars (35). Children welcome (Under 12s free in parents' room, cots available free of charge, baby sitting arranged). No pets. **Rooms 255** (15 for disabled). Lift. Room service (limited hours). Room rate €155 (max. 3 guests). Closed 24-26 Dec. Amex, MasterCard, Visa, Laser. **Directions:** On the Grand Canal at Baggot St. Bridge.

Dublin 4
HOTEL

The Montrose Hotel
Stillorgan Road Dublin 4 **Tel: 01 269 3311**
info@montrose.ie www.montrose.ie

This south-city hotel, which is conveniently located near the University College campus and the RTÉ studios, has recently undergone extensive refurbishment, and changed ownership; most rooms are now offered to executive standard, and there is also some wheelchair friendly accommodation. All rooms have quite good facilities (direct dial phone, multi-channel TV, tea/coffee-making facilities and trouser press/iron), also 12 hour room service and laundry/dry cleaning services. Executive rooms also have a modem line and complimentary newspaper and business magazines. The hotel's Belfield Restaurant is open for lunch and dinner every day and offers traditional food such as roasts, sole on the bone and roast duck (pianist on Fridays). Although conference facilities are not extensive (max. 70 delegates), there's a business centre, seven meeting rooms and free parking, making this an attractive venue for small events. Children welcome (under 12s free in parents' room, cots available free of charge). **Rooms 180** (3 suites, 36 executive). Lift, limited room service. B&B from €101pps, ss about €74; weekend specials available. Open all year. Amex, Diners, MasterCard, Visa, Laser. **Directions:** On Stillorgan dual carriageway near RTE studios, opposite UCD campus.

Dublin 4
HOTEL

Mount Herbert Hotel
Herbert Road Sandymount Dublin 4 **Tel: 01 668 4321**
info@mountherberthotel.ie www.mountherberthotel.ie

Close to Lansdowne Road DART station and the RDS, this sprawling hotel is made up of a number of interconnecting houses and offers comfortable, well-priced accommodation with easy access to the city centre. It has been upgraded and refurbished many times over the years, and has good business and conference facilities; rooms are quite simple and on the small side, but its many regular guests like it for its friendliness and good value - and, with the uncertainty surrounding the future of other hotels in the area, many new guests will doubtless come to see it as a home from home in the near future. **Rooms 172.** Room rate from €69 to €220. MasterCard, Visa, Laser. **Directions:** On Herbert Rd, near Ballsbridge and Lansdowne Rd.

O'Connells Restaurant

Dublin 4
RESTAURANT

Bewleys Hotel Merrion Road Dublin 4 **Tel: 01 647 3304**
info@oconnellsballsbridge.com www.oconnellsballsbridge.com

téile bia Located in a large semi-basement under Bewley's Hotel, this remarkable restaurant strives to provide quality ingredient-driven modern Irish cooking - simple food, with natural flavours, often emphasised by cooking in a special wood-fired oven. It has dark wood-panelled walls, and floor to ceiling windows overlooking a courtyard used for al fresco dining; atmosphere has always been a problem here, and if there's an off-day with the food, people really notice the surroundings. The restaurant is run by Tom O'Connell, a brother of Darina Allen, of Ballymaloe Cookery School, and of Rory O'Connell, previously of Ballymaloe House, who visits regularly and works closely with the kitchen team. Rosemary Kearney, author of 'Healthy Gluten Free Eating', is also a consultant, and O'Connell's is probably Ireland's most coeliac-friendly restaurant, offering home-baked gluten-free bread and a dinner menu that is almost entirely gluten-free. Menus are a hymn to quality ingredients, stating that pork, beef, eggs and catering supplies are sourced using Bord Bia's Quality Assurance Schemes, and also naming a number of individual artisan producers and suppliers, often in dishes that have become house specialities. Fish is from Castletownbere, specially aged Slaney beef comes from Wexford, organic pork is from Tipperary and Gold River Farm in Co Wicklow supply vegetables; Irish farmhouse cheese, matured on the premises, is served with home-made biscuits and classic desserts include (genuinely) home-made ice creams - a nice idea here is to offer two little desserts from a choice of eight: just the job after a filling meal. A highly informative wine list is offered, which includes a value-for-money selection (8 white, 7 red). This remains an unique restaurant, offering meals based on the very highest quality ingredients, at very moderate prices; the lunch offering, which includes a superior sort of carvery, is especially good value, and speedy too. Fully wheelchair accessible. **Seats 180** (summer courtyard, 60). Air conditioning. Buffet L daily 12.30-2.30 (Sun to 4). D daily 6-10 (Sun to 9.30). Sun Buffet & Early D (6-7) about €19.75. Set D about €28.50. Also à la carte D available. SC 10%. House wines from €20. Closed eve 24- eve 27 Dec. Amex, Diners, MasterCard, Visa, Laser. **Directions:** Off Merrion Road at Simmonscourt Road, opposite the Four Seasons Hotel. ◇

Ocean Bar

Dublin 4
BAR

Charlotte Quay Dock Ringsend Road Dublin 4 **Tel:** 01 668 8862
info@oceanbar.ie www.oceanbar.ie

Dramatically situated on the water's edge with lots of glass on two sides, and extensive outdoor patio seating to take advantage of views over the Grand Canal Basin, Ocean has great atmosphere and makes an excellent meeting place for people of all ages. Great location, friendliness of the staff, and comfortable lounging couches all make it a great place to relax - and a particularly good choice for visitors to the city. There's a choice of several bars and dining areas and, while menus offering a wide range of contemporary favourites may not contain many surprises, care is taken on sourcing ingredients, pleasant food is freshly prepared and competently cooked. Tables are laid with simple cutlery, paper napkins - and food is served modern bistro style on big white plates. The Sunday jazz brunches are a particular success. Function rooms are available too, one on the ground floor next to the bar and two downstairs. Conference/banqueting. Children welcome. Children welcome. **Seats 180** (private room, 80; outdoor seating, 80). Air conditioning. Toilets wheelchair accessible. Food served daily, 12 -10. House wine €21. Closed 25 Dec, Good Fri. Amex, MasterCard, Visa, Laser. **Directions:** On Pearse Street/Ringsend Road bridge (Grand Canal Basin). ◇

Orchid Szechuan Chinese Restaurant

Dublin 4
RESTAURANT

120 Pembroke Road Dublin 4
Tel: 01 660 0629

This long established restaurant has a faithful following - not surprisingly, as the food is high quality, and provides for both conservative and adventurous tastes, whilst the service is admirably efficient and friendly. Once you have braved the entrance (which can be a little off-putting) the interior is warm, welcoming and typically Chinese with smoky mirrors and black-painted walls decorated with simple floral designs. Fresh flowers and linen napkins set the tone for clearly presented menus that offer many

Szechuan specialities but also some Cantonese and even a few Thai dishes. Try the light and crispy deep-fried scallops, served with a simple light soy dip, and follow with Yin-yang Prawn two prawn dishes (one hot and spicy, the other a mild fresh flavoured stirfry) served side-by-side, both delicious and pretty or popular roast duck in plum sauce, prettily garnished with an orchid. 'House dinners' are good-value; one is dedicated entirely to Dim Sum, which is served in the evening here and includes some eight dishes as well as jasmine tea or (very good) coffee. The wine list is on the pricey side, but offers a good choice. **Directions:** On Pembroke Road. ◇

Dublin 4
GUESTHOUSE
🍴 Ⓔ

Pembroke Townhouse

90 Pembroke Road Ballsbridge Dublin 4 **Tel: 01 660 0277**
info@pembroketownhouse.ie www.pembroketownhouse.ie

féile bia Conveniently located close to the RDS and Lansdowne Road, this fine guesthouse has all the amenities usually expected of an hotel. There's a drawing room and study for residents' use and the comfortably furnished rooms, which are individually designed, have recently been re-decorated; all have a safe and facilities for business guests (wi-fi is available in all areas), as well as direct dial phone, cable television, tea/coffee facilities and trouser press (but no tea / coffee making facilities). Breakfast is the only meal served, but it offers a full buffet and less usual dishes like sautéed lambs liver served on a bed of sautéed onions and topped with bacon, as well as the traditional cooked breakfast. When arriving by car, it is best to go the carpark at the back, as you can then take a lift with your luggage (avoiding heavy traffic and steep steps to the front door). Private parking at rear. **Rooms 48** (1 suite, 2 family, 3 shower only, 2 disabled, 38 no smoking). Lift. Limited room service. B&B €65-95 pps, single €95. *High Speed WI-FI Internet access is available in all areas of the Pembroke Townhouse. Amex, Diners, MasterCard, Visa, Laser. **Directions:** Pembroke Road leads on to Baggot St. On the right hand side going towards town.

Dublin 4
RESTAURANT
🍴 Ⓔ 🍽

Poulot's Restaurant

Mulberry Gardens Donnybrook Dublin 4
Tel: 01 269 3300

féile bia Lorna Jean and Jean Michel Poulot's restaurant is tucked away down a laneway and easy to miss. The L-shaped dining-room overlooks a pretty courtyard garden, floodlit at night, and the decor is simple - a warm neutral scheme opens the area up and creates a sense of space. Jean Michel brought with him a reputation for his time at Halo at the Morrison and, before that, at a number of other important kitchens including Ballylickey Manor in County Cork, where Lorna Jean was also working at the time. Jean Michel's menus offer detailed descriptions of a range of luxurious dishes, including French classics like seared duck foie gras (served with brioche and a fig compôte) and more unusual specialities such as a fennel and Parmesan risotto with yellow fin tuna and shellfish cream; among the main course specialities you will find a very refined loin of venison - little cylinders of tender, lean meat, served with celeriac cream, wild mushrooms and a game jus flavoured with juniper and black pepper. Classic desserts include an excellent crème brulée, and Valrhona chocolate fondant - served, perhaps, with a superb hazelnut ice cream. Presentation on huge white plates is dramatic and, like the oversized menus, acts as a reminder that this is definitely fine dining, and not for those days when you're in the mood for something simple. The atmosphere, however, is relaxed, helped by service which has retained an old-style professionalism. An extensive wine list is Lorna Jean's special interest and, although it naturally leans towards France, it offers a careful selection from all over the world. * Cookery and wine courses available, details from the restaurant. Toilets wheelchair accessible. Children welcome. Air conditioning. **Seats 70.** Open Mon-Sat, L12-3, D 7-10.30. Closed Sun, Mon; Bank Hols. Amex, Diners, MasterCard, Visa, Laser. **Directions:** From city, first left after Victoria Avenue; to city, right turn opposite Ulster Bank in Donnybrook.

Dublin 4
HOTEL/RESTAURANT

Radisson SAS St Helen's Hotel

Stillorgan Road Dublin 4 **Tel: 01 218 6000**
info.dublin@radissonsas.com www.dublin.radissonsas.com

 Set in formal gardens just south of Dublin's city centre, with views across Dublin Bay to Howth Head, the fine 18th century house at the heart of this impressive hotel was once a private residence. Careful restoration and imaginative modernisation have created interesting public areas, including the Orangerie Bar and a pillared ballroom with minstrels' gallery and grand piano. Bedrooms, in a modern four-storey block adjoining the main building, all have garden views (some of the best rooms also have balconies) and air conditioning, and are well-equipped for business guests. Accommodation is comfortably furnished to a high standard in contemporary style, although some rooms (and bathrooms) are less spacious than might be expected in a recent development. Conference/banqueting (350/220); also St Helen's Pavilion (600/800) in summer. Business centre, video conferencing, free broadband wi/fi. Fitness centre; beauty salon. Garden. Ample parking. Children welcome (under 18s free in parents' room, cots available without charge, baby sitting arranged). **Rooms 151** (25 suites, 70 no-smoking, 8 for disabled). 24 hr room service, Lift, Turndown service. Room rate from €170 (max. 3 guests). Open all year. **Talavera:** In four interconnecting rooms in the lower ground floor, this informal Italian restaurant is decorated in warm Mediterranean colours and, with smart wooden tables dressed with slips, modern cutlery, fresh flowers and Bristol blue water glasses, it is atmospheric when candle-lit at night. A well-balanced menu offers a balanced choice of dishes inspired by tradition and tailored to the modern palate. Good cooking is matched by a good atmosphere and caring service from friendly, efficient staff. The wine list offers a strong selection of regional Italian bottles to match the food. *Lighter menus are also offered all day in the Orangerie Bar and Ballroom Lounge. **Seats 140.** Air conditioning, toilets wheelchair accessible. D daily 6-10.30. Set menus from €35; also a la carte. Amex, Diners, MasterCard, Visa, Laser. **Directions:** Just 5.5km (3 miles) south from the city centre, on N11. ◇

Dublin 4
RESTAURANT

Roly's Bistro

7 Ballsbridge Terrace Ballsbridge Dublin 4 **Tel: 01 668 2611**
ireland@rolysbistro.ie www.rolysbistro.ie

 This bustling Ballsbridge bistro has been a hit since the day it opened. Chef-patron Colin O'Daly (one of Ireland's most highly regarded chefs) and head chef Paul Cartwright present imaginative, reasonably priced seasonal menus at lunch and an early dinner, and also an evening à la carte menu - and the chef's art is not confined to the plate: Colin's paintings adorn the walls and the menu card has a delightful reproduction of his "Sensitive study of a young dancer in morning light". A lively interpretation of classical French cooking gives more than a passing nod to Irish traditions, world cuisines and contemporary styles, and carefully sourced ingredients are the sound foundation for cooking that rarely disappoints. Breads, from the in-house bakery, may include sliced yeast loaves, bacon & onion, tomato and pesto flavours, gluten-free bread and brown soda. Many specialities have evolved over the years: Dublin Bay Prawns are always in demand (and may be served Neuberg, a speciality that comes with a tian of mixed long grain and wild rice), and an upbeat version of traditional Kerry lamb pie is another favourite. Service is usually efficient although staff can seem under pressure, and high demand can sometimes lead to a rush to turn around tables too quickly; but everyone loves the buzz, and Roly's has always given value for money - they offer a good range of wines at an accessible price. Offering quality with good value has been the philosophy of the restaurant from the outset; this it continues to do well on the whole, and the set menus - notably the pre-theatre - offer particularly good value. **Seats 220.** Air conditioning. L daily 12-2.45 (to 3 Sun), D daily 6-10; Set L €20.95; Early D 2/3 course €22.95/€25.95 (Mon-Thu, 6-6.45), Set D €42; L&D also à la carte. SC10%. Closed Good Fri & 25-27 Dec inc. Amex, Diners, MasterCard, Visa, Laser. **Directions:** Heart of Ballsbridge, across the road from the American Embassy.

Dublin 4
HOTEL/RESTAURANT

Schoolhouse Hotel

2-8 Northumberland Road Ballsbridge Dublin 4 **Tel: 01 667 5014**
reservations@schoolhousehotel.com www.schoolhousehotel.com

Dating back to its opening in 1861 as a school, this canalside building at Mount Street Bridge has seen many changes, and it is now one of Dublin's trendiest small hotels - and an ideal place to stay while exploring Dublin. A huge amount of business goes through the hotel and can show signs of wear and tear, but the spacious individually decorated bedrooms (all named after Irish writers) are well appointed, with king size beds, very good fabrics, air conditioning, power showers and the usual amenities expected of a quality hotel; breakfast is very good too, with hot dishes like the full Irish or French toast equally well cooked. Head chef Kevin Arundel has earned an enviable reputation for smart cooking in both **The Inkwell Bar** which is always a-buzz with young business people of the area - and the restaurant, **Canteen**, where his signature dish is seared scallops with black pudding, spiced apple purée and roasting juices, and many people head here specially to try it; local lobster with cajun spiced butter, herb salad & chips is another favourite. Kevin is very much a hands-on chef and this shows in happy customers whether he is cooking for the extensive bar menu with all its popular dishes (bagels, baguettes, sambos, soups, burgers, steaks, pasta etc), or the more substantial dishes on the evening menu (monkfish, duck, fillet steak, scallops), he delivers quality at a competitive price. Small conference/banqueting (18/85). Wheelchair accessible. Parking. Children welcome (Under 5s free in parents room; cots available with no charge). No pets. Lift. **Rooms 31** (30 no-smoking, 10 ground floor, 2 for disabled). B&B from about €99 pps, SS €66. SC discretionary. Closed 24-26 Dec. Amex, Diners, MasterCard, Visa. **Directions:** Southbound from Trinity College, at the end of Mount St. across the Grand Canal.

Dublin 4
GUESTHOUSE

Waterloo House

8-10 Waterloo Road Ballsbridge Dublin 4 **Tel: 01 660 1888**
info@waterloohouse.ie www.waterloohouse.ie

Evelyn Corcoran's pair of Georgian townhouses make a luxurious and reasonably priced base in a quiet location, which is very convenient to the city centre and also Lansdowne Road (rugby), RDS (equestrian & exhibitions) and some of the city's most famous restaurants. Excellent breakfasts are a high point of any stay. Equally attractive to the business or leisure traveller. Conservatory & Garden. Wheelchair access. Own parking. Children welcome (under 4 free in parents' room, cot available). No pets. Garden. **Rooms 17** (1 disabled). Lift. B&B about €60 pps, ss about €20. Closed Christmas. MasterCard, Visa, Laser. **Directions:** South on Stephens Green on Merrion Row for 1 mile. First turn right after Baggot Street Bridge. ◇

DUBLIN 5

RAHENY is a pleasant suburb with some excellent amenities including St. Anne's Park, once home to the Guinness family; this is one of the finest parks in North Dublin - stretching from Raheny village down to the coast at Bull Island, and then along to the edges of Clontarf, it has extensive parkland walks, famous rose gardens and playing fields. A protected Victorian red brick stable yard (1885) has recently been renovated and converted into artists' studios, a gallery and the **Rose Café** (087 671 7791), which overlooks the park and offers wholesome home-made fare; it is situated in a spacious (if very bright and, perhaps, hot) first floor conservatory, and also has some tables out in the courtyard in fine weather. There is an artisan food market here every Saturday, and there is a monthly arts & crafts market (on a Sunday). At the Kilbarrack end of Raheny, just off the coast road to Howth, **Il Fornaio** (01 832 0277) is a great little restaurant/bakery serving simple, ingredient-led authentic Italian food in casual surroundings; their pizzas are renowned and it's the ideal place to pick up the makings of a picnic.

WWW.IRELAND-GUIDE.COM - FOR THE BEST PLACES TO EAT, DRINK & STAY

DUBLIN 6

Dublin 6 is a mostly residential sector of the city and is made up of well known vibrant suburbs such as Rathmines, Rathgar, Templeogue and Terenure. **Diep Noodle Bar** (www.diep.net; 01 497 6550) is a younger sister to Diep le Shaker off Fitzwilliam Square in Ranelagh. It is a colourful little place quickly gained a reputation as the in place for discerning young things to meet. It has a great atmosphere, chic, clean-lined decor and - as if a mixture of Thai and Vietnamese food weren't fashionable enough - a cocktail bar too. While the entrance to the buzzing restaurant **Ouzo** (Sandford Road, Ranelagh; 01 491 2253) is not obvious as it's somewhat concealed beside the doors to McSorley's pub, once discovered however, you'll find yourself in a one-off restaurant. Fresh, well cooked food that is served at very reasonable prices together with willing, friendly service that reflects genuine (but today not always observed) 'old-fashioned' Irish hospitality, and you have an unusual restaurant for these times. * Also at 11, Upper Baggot Street, Dublin 4 (Tel 01 667 3279).
WWW.IRELAND-GUIDE.COM FOR ALL THE BEST PLACES TO EAT, DRINK & STAY

Dublin 6
RESTAURANT

Antica Venezia
97 Ashfield Road Ranelagh Dublin 6
Tel: 01 497 4112

A real throw-back in time and refreshingly so: this entirely Italian-run restaurant has a classic Italian 70's interior with stained wooden floors and ceiling beams, Venetian trompe-l'oeil scenes on the walls and candlewax-dripped Chianti bottles on every table. The food is also traditional Italian, with a menu that could easily date back to the Seventies too: old-fashioned favourites like stuffed mushrooms and antipasto misto of Italian meats are followed by classics like chicken breast with mushroom and white wine sauce, salmon with lemon butter sauce, pork with marsala sauce and a choice of pasta dishes and pizzas, with predictable but good desserts such as banoffi, tiramisu and cassata as well as a selection of ice creams. Consistently good food, with service that is laid back but attentive - a perfect recipe for a popular neighbourhood restaurant. **Seats 45.** Reservations advised. Air conditioning. Children welcome. D daily, 5-11, L Fri only 12-2.30. A la carte. House wine €18.50. SC discretionary, but 10% on parties of 6+. MasterCard, Visa, Laser. ◊

Dublin 6
RESTAURANT

Bijou Bistro
47 Highfiield Road Rathgar Dublin 6 **Tel: 01 496 1518**
bijourestaurant@eircom.net

A distinctly French atmosphere prevails at this neighbourhood restaurant and, despite recent developments which have virtually doubled its size, it is still advisable to book a table. It's appealingly decorated in a gently modern style, with soft neutral tones and good lighting, and the well-tried system of casual dining is offered in a comfortably furnished area on the ground floor and there's a more formal restaurant upstairs. Well made breads accompany an innovative menu with a dozen or so choices on each course and several fish specialities each evening (typically chargrilled loin of swordfish with chive mash and spiced chickpea salsa); other specialities include risotto of spiced cajun chicken with parmesan herb salad, while more traditional tastes will welcome dishes like pork fillet with sage & bacon potato cake, cooked with accuracy and style - and served on plates decorated with a colourful art deco flourish. Finish with classic desserts or an Irish cheese selection with muscat grapes. A good wine list, plus a couple of weekly specials. Children welcome. **Seats about 100** (private room, 14). Air conditioning. Times on application. SC discretionary. Closed Christmas/ New Year. Amex, Diners, MasterCard, Visa, Laser. **Directions:** Rathgar crossroads. ◊

Dublin 6
RESTAURANT
Ⓝ 🖼

Eatery 120
120 Ranelagh Road Dublin 6
Tel: 01 470 4120

With its impressive picture window and stylish dark frame, the front of Eatery 120 looks like an old fashioned Spanish deli and the interior is a comfortable mix of cushioned banquettes, bistro chairs and clusters of moon lamps giving it a New York feel with a touch of continental style. Although only recently opened at the time of our visit, there was already a real buzz about it and some dishes really shone and, if the awful name can be overlooked, this is a neighbourhood restaurant which should draw diners from beyond the catchment area. It is one of a new breed of restaurants serving up well sourced but unfussy food, with the occasional adventurous item for more jaded palates: quirky starters include sardines on toast as well as slow roasted beetroot and goats' cheese salad, while main courses include a healthy array of fish with some interesting accompaniments; old favourites find a place here too - confit of Barbary duck legs with madeira jus, for example, and 12 oz rib-eye steak béarnaise. Desserts tend to be crowd pleasers such as fresh fruit and meringue or rhubarb crumble, though there's some adventure to be found in the excellent Crozier Blue cheese with spiced pear. Sticky wine lovers will be please to find the Hungarian Tokaji Aszú (5 Puttonyos) on offer. Reservations recommended; air conditioning. **Seats 90** (private room to 60, outdoors 12). L Tue to Sun 12-3 (from 11am Sun); D Tue to Sun 5.30–10pm (to 8.30pm Sun); early D €22.95, 5.30-6.45pm. Wine from €19. SC 12.5% on parties of 6+. Closed Mon, 25-26 Dec. Amex, Diners, MasterCard, Visa, Laser. **Directions:** Heading from town, less than 5 minutes from Ranelagh triangle.

Dublin 6
RESTAURANT

Mint

47 Ranelagh Village Dublin 6 **Tel: 01 497 8655**
info@mintrestaurant.ie www.mintrestaurant.ie

Having built up his experience in the Michelin-starred kitchens of Paul Rankin, Conrad Gallagher, John Burton-Race and Tom Aikens, a young Dylan McGrath returned to Dublin recently to cook in Mint. It wasn't long before canny diners recognised his immense talent and fresh take on cooking, making Mint one of the hottest spots in Dublin today. Despite being a small restaurant, it's classy and understated and is cleverly designed to maximise on space. There's no room for a reception area - which is a pity - but friendly staff will seat you at your stylish, white-clothed table and allow you to linger over aperitifs before offering the menu. Before ordering you'll be presented with a showcase of amuse-bouches that can't fail to excite you or alert you to the kitchen's impressive capabilities. Those who love fine dining without the pomp will enjoy Mint's atmosphere - cool jazz, leather banquettes, dark woods and the most beautiful tableware, much of it bespoke from an Irish ceramicist based in London. Despite the laid-back feel, service is polished and professional to complement the skilful cooking. With just an à la carte dinner menu - starters range from €27-40, mains €35-48 - the option of a seven-course tasting menu of €105 is surprisingly good value. A signature starter of scallops includes warm skate & balsamic terrine, glazed slices of duck, shallot rings & rosemary; Dylan's signature lamb dish features chickpeas, aubergine purée, dried tomato petals and buckler sorrel salad. Given the sheer brilliance, creativity and originality of the cooking, and considering the little extras like amuse bouches, exquisite breads, pre-desserts and petit fours, you'll leave Mint feeling your money was well spent. A pricey wine list offers little under €35. Wheelchair accessible. Children welcome, but not suitable after 8pm. **Seats 45.** Reservations advised. L Fri, 12.30-2.30; D Tue-Sun, 6.30-10.00. Wines from €34. Closed Sun, Mon, bank holidays. Amex, MasterCard, Visa, Laser. **Directions:** Centre of Ranelagh Village. ◊

Dublin 6
RESTAURANT

Poppadom Indian Restaurant

91a Rathgar Road Dublin 6 **Tel: 01 490 2383**
www.poppadom.ie

Behind a neat but unremarkable frontage in a row of modern shops lies Poppadum, a colourful and airy new wave Indian restaurant, with linen-clad tables, comfortable chairs and a bar. The aim here is to demonstrate the diversity of Indian cooking and offer some appealingly unusual dishes. Complimentary poppadoms with fresh chutney dips are brought before menus which offer regional specialities including a starter of Karwari Prawns - deep-fried jumbo prawns marinated in ginger, garlic, yoghurt, garam masala and barbecued in the tandoor - and main courses ranging in heat, including chicken and lamb specialities. Vegetarians have plenty of dishes available as main courses or side orders, and variations like garlic, onion & coriander naan and lime rice offer a subtle change from the norm. Food presentation is contemporary and service solicitous. Make a point of trying the masala tea, made with leaf tea and cardamom pods. A sound wine list helpfully provides advice on the styles that partner spicy food well. Children welcome. **Seats 48;** reservations advised; air conditioning. D daily, 6-12. A la carte. Wines from €19. SC discretionary. Closed 25 Dec. Amex, MasterCard, Visa, Laser. **Directions:** A minute away on the same side as Comans Pub, Rathgar.

TriBeCa

Dublin 6
RESTAURANT

65 Ranelagh Village Dublin 6
Tel: 01 497 4174

An outpost of the Canal Bank Café (see entry), this bright and airy New York style restaurant was a hit from the start for its good fast food and relaxed, casual feel, with decor and wooden floors and tables. Carefully sourced burgers (made from 100% organic beef), salads, omelettes and chicken wings take their place beside the fusion inspired dishes that keep the more adventurous diners happy. It's not cheap, but it is wholesome fare - and portions are generous so it works out as quite good value for money. Children welcome. *Wine Upstairs, a wine bar offering carefully selected wines and also some equally carefully chosen food to go with them - charcuterie plates, and a couple of hot special each night - opened on the first floor in 2007. Children welcome. Seats 70 (outside seating 16). Reservations advised. Air conditioning. Toilets wheelchair accessible. Open daily, 12-11. Set L about €9.50/15 (12-5); otherwise à la carte, plus daily blackboard specials. House wine about €17.50. Closed Dec 24-26, Good Fri. MasterCard, Visa, Laser. **Directions:** Heading southbound from city centre, halfway along Ranelagh main street, on right. ◊

Vermilion

Dublin 6W
RESTAURANT

94-96 Terenure Road North Terenure Dublin 6W. **Tel: 01 499 1400**
mail@vermilion.ie www.vermilion.ie

This purpose-built restaurant is on the first floor above the Terenure Inn pub and the decor - a contemporary, smart interior in soft primary colours - reflects an innovative food philosophy, which offers colourful, beautifully presented and updated versions of many Indian favourites. Interesting nibbles are provided, and the menu includes specialities from Kerala, Tamil-Nadu and Goa, and pride is clearly taken in the quality of ingredients and cooking. Each summer, from June to September, Vermilion hosts an Indian Summer Festival, following a culinary trail around India - complete with Bollywood movie clips and belly dancing. Although the menu gives detailed explanations, this is not a traditional Indian restaurant, so don't expect the usual, familiar experience of 'popular' Indian food. Service is friendly and solicitous. The restaurant recently introduced a new loyalty card, offer up to 15% credit back to returning customers. Seats 90. Reservations advised. Air conditioning. D daily 5.30-11 (to 10pm Sun), L Sun only, 2-5pm; set Sun L €25 (in winter only). Early D €20/24 daily, 5-30-7pm (to 6.30 Fri/Sat); also à la carte; House wine from €19.50. SC 10% on groups 6+. Live Jazz Thurs nights (Sept - May only). Closed 25-26 Dec, Good Fri. Amex, Diners, MasterCard, Visa, Laser. **Directions:** 200 yards from Terenure crossroads.

DUBLIN 7

Dublin 7 is in the north inner city on the banks of the River Liffey and is within walking distance of all of the major sites and attractions in Dublin. It includes the well known city centre neighbourhoods of Smithfield and the Four Courts which are both next to the River Liffey. Tourist attractions include the aforementioned Four Courts and the Jameson Distillery and whiskey tour is a 'must visit' while in the city. Comfortable budget accommodation is available in the **Comfort Inn** (Smithfield Plaza, 01 490 8200). Also in Smithfield, **The Old Jameson Distillery** (01 807 2355 ; www.whiskeytours.com) has a bar and restaurant, open to the public daily.
WWW.IRELAND-GUIDE.COM FOR ALL THE BEST PLACES TO EAT, DRINK & STAY

Hanley at the Bar

Dublin 7
RESTAURANT

The Distillery Building May Lane Dublin 7
Tel: 01 878 0104

Well known caterer Claire Hanley's smart daytime restaurant near the Jameson Distillery has always been popular with the lawyers from the nearby Law Library and the Four Courts, but was otherwise a well-kept secret until this area began its recent phase of rapid development. High stools at the bar provide a comfortable perch if you are waiting for a table (it gets very busy at lunch time), but it's worth a little patience as you may expect good contemporary cooking in very chic surroundings. ◊

The Hole in the Wall

Dublin 7
RESTAURANT/PUB

Blackhorse Avenue Phoenix Park Dublin 7
Tel: 01 838 9491

PJ McCaffrey's remarkable pub beside the Phoenix Park is named in honour of a tradition which existed here for around a hundred years - the practice of serving drinks through a hole in the wall of the Phoenix Park to members of the army garrison stationed nearby. Today the Hole in the Wall also claims to be the longest pub in Ireland - and it is certainly one of the most interesting. They have always offered food too - a bar menu available throughout the afternoon and evening - but with the arrival of Damien Grey, who will be well known to viewers of RTE's 'The Restaurant', a while ago, the bar has been well and truly raised. With a new dining room opened in 2007, it's now as much a restaurant as a pub and the house speciality these days is free-range chicken breast with butternut squash, artichokes, shitake mushrooms & beurre blanc, it's a far cry from the Beef & Guinness Pie, Dublin Coddle, and Irish Stew of old. Even fish and chips are fresh cod with duck fat chips There's also a new wine shop in the pub, source of the extensive wine list offered in the restaurant. Children welcome Piano Fri & Sat night. Wheelchair access to toilets. Parking. Bar menu served daily (2-10). Closed 25 Dec & Good Fri. Amex, MasterCard, Visa, Laser. **Directions:** Beside Phoenix Park.

Rhodes D7

Dublin 7
RESTAURANT

The Capel Building Mary's Abbey Dublin 7 **Tel: 01 804 4444**
info@rhodesD7.com www.rhodesd7.com

féile bia Despite debate amongst Dubliners as to whether Gary Rhodes was ill-advised to open here in 2006, in a part of town which is only just beginning to blossom, it appears to be thriving. The restaurant is set back from the street a little allowing for tables at a terrace along the front, which is perfect for smokers although the space is tight for comfort and ease of service. Inside, the basic structure is modern but the designers have gone for a mixum-gatherum of styles which does little for the atmosphere: the interior is dominated by some specially commissioned and very colourful large modern paintings which you will love or loathe but, with an antique table here, trellis-back chairs there, modern table settings, and some vaguely old-fashioned light fittings, it doesn't add up to a 'look'. But it is on the food, wine and service - that Rhodes is judged and, although, essentially a franchise - Gary Rhodes was upfront from the start that he would not personally be cooking - head chef Paul Hargraves worked with him as sous chef for six years before coming to Dublin, and his cooking is impressive. The menu is well-judged, offering plenty of choice from a dozen or so appealing starters and main courses including specialities such as haddock rarebit and gammon steak. Decent wines from an interesting list should certainly please, with a good choice by the glass. Based on a UK prototype, some feel that there's an 'Englishness' which seems stilted in Dublin but the Rhodes menus have been adapted carefully and there's a genuine commitment to using Irish produce where possible. The cooking is generally excellent and, although service was inconsistent in the early days, this is becoming a favourite with Dubliners. Children welcome; Toilets wheelchair accessible. **Seat 248** (private room, 50, outdoors, 50); air conditioning pianist playing various times. Food served Mon-Sat, 12-10.15pm (closed Mon D), set 2 course L €17.50; also a la carte L&D. Closed all Sun & Mon D, Bank Hols. Amex, MasterCard, Visa, Laser **Directions:** Junction of Capel St. and Mary's Abbey.

Seven

Dublin 7
RESTAURANT

73 Manor Street Dublin 7
Tel: 01 633 4092

Tightly packed with darkwood tables and dark leather highback chairs, this smart little restaurant is in a redbrick corner building in Stoneybatter, a pleasant residential area near the Phoenix Park Aside from likely association with the address, the theme that inspired the name is the seven wonders of the world - illustrated in light boxes mounted on the wall, and also runs through the menu, which is sensibly restricted to seven starters and seven main courses. What draws people to this little spot is good simple food, i.e. carefully sourced quality ingredients and well-cooked unfussy food: begin with smoked haddock chowder with mussels and bacon, perhaps, or a simple tasty starter of crisp calamari with a mixed leaf and sesame soy dressing. Choices are well-balanced including fish and vegetarian dishes, but the most popular main course by far is a really good rib eye steak, perfectly caramelised on the outside and juicy inside, served with delicious mash and green beans. Flavour and texture combinations are carefully judged; this is particularly noticeable in the choice of accompaniments for each dish and therein lies the reason the food here is so delicious. Seven was an immediate hit with local residents, and the combination of small size and big popularity means there will be more than one sitting and your best chance of getting in without a reservation, on any day of the week, will be to arrive very early. **Seats 38.** L Mon-Fri 12-2.30; D Mon-Fri 6-9.30, Sat 5.30-9.30. Closed Sun. ◇

DUBLIN 8

Dublin 8 is the only postcode that crosses the River Liffey and is made up of areas on both sides of the river, at the western edges of the city centre. The best known areas/attractions in Dublin 8 for the visitor to Dublin are the Guinness Brewery, Kilmainham Gaol, The Irish Museum of Modern Art, Christchurch Cathedral, St. Patrick's Cathedral and the Phoenix Park. Heuston Station (serving the West and South West of Ireland) is also in Dublin 8. The atmospheric **Havana Tapas Bar** (Grantham Street ; 01 476 0046) is only just in Dublin 8 and has a newer branch down the road in South Great George's Street, Dublin 2 (01 400 5990). **The Brazen Head** (Lower Bridge Street; 01 677 9549) is Dublin's (possibly Ireland's) oldest pub and was built on the site of a tavern dating back to the 12th century - and it's still going strong. Full of genuine character, this friendly, well-run pub has lots of different levels and dark corners. Food is wholesome and middle-of-the-road at reasonable prices - visitors will be pleased to find traditional favourites like Irish stew. Live music nightly in the Music Lounge. **The Chorus Café** (Fishamble Street; 01 616 7088) is a small restaurant with a big heart. It is a bright and friendly little place is near the site of the first performance of Handel's Messiah, hence the name - and some features of the decor. Interesting breakfasts are followed by an all-day procession of good things. It is a useful daytime place to know about if you're visiting anywhere in the Christchurch area. **The Guinness Brewery** (St. James Gate; 01 471 4261) is home to the modern glass-walled Gravity Bar which serves the most spectacular pint of Guinness in Dublin - indeed, in all Ireland from its unique position atop the impressive Guinness Storehouse, a handsome 1904 building. The Guinness Museum tells the story - using fascinating high tech exhibits - of the famous company's 250-plus years in business. It also includes (on Level 5) the traditional Brewery Bar, serving nourishing Irish fare (seafood chowder, beef & Guinness stew). NB: you have to pay in to use these bars. Down the road is Royal Hospital Kilmainham and the Irish Museum of Modern Art which is also home to the self service **Grass Roots Café** (01 612 9900) which is a pleasant place for an informal meal, whether or not you are visiting the museum - it has good parking facilities and the spacious room, which is attractively located overlooking a garden area, has a pleasingly cool modern ambience. Food quality and presentation is good (large white plates), cafeteria style service is efficient - and it's a handier choice for a quick lunch than city centre venues, perhaps. Across the River Liffey **Nancy Hands** (Parkgate Street; 01 677 0149) is a newish pub with an old feel, but far from being a theme pub. It's a characterful place for a drink and the selection stocked is unusually extensive. Food was an important aspect of Nancy Hands from the outset and, on the whole, it is well done with menus successfully straddling the divide between traditional bar food (seafood chowder, steaks; lunchtime carvery) and lighter international fare. A couple of doors along, **Ryan's of Parkgate Street** (01 677 6097) is one of Ireland's finest and best-loved original Victorian pubs, with magnificent stained glass, original mahogany bar fixtures and an outstanding collection of antique mirrors all contributing to its unique atmosphere. Bar food is available every day except Sunday and, upstairs, there's a small restaurant, **FXB at Ryans**, serving food which is a step up from bar meals. For good budget accommodation try **Jurys Inn Christchurch** (01 454 0000) which is within walking distance of the main city centre areas on both sides of the Liffey and close to Dublin Castle and events in Temple Bar; large multi-storey car park at the rear has access to the hotel. New to the area and opening as the Guide goes to press are two more luxurious options, **Hilton Dublin Kilmainham** (01 420 1800; www.hilton.co.uk/dublinkilmainham) on the Inchicore Road - convenient to Heuston Station and the main road south (N4) - and **Radisson SAS Royal Hotel** (junction of Golden Lane and Chancery Lane; 011 218 5626; www.royal.dublin.radissonsas.com) within walking distance of Trinity College and the Grafton Street area.

WWW.IRELAND-GUIDE.COM FOR ALL THE BEST PLACES TO EAT, DRINK & STAY

Dublin 8
CAFÉ/RESTAURANT

Bar Italia Café

Lr Exchange Street Essex Quay Dublin 8 **Tel: 01 679 5128**
acrobat_ltd@yahoo.it www.baritalia.ie

In a modern office block on the edge of Temple Bar and close to the Civic Offices known disparagingly to Dubliners as 'The Bunkers', this little Italian trattoria style restaurant has floor-to-ceiling glass to make the most of a splendid view across the Liffey towards the magnificent Four Courts - and there's plenty of space outside to enjoy lunch 'al fresco' when the weather's right. Attentive Italian waiters quickly seat new arrivals, service throughout is quick and professional and the banter lends a relaxed atmosphere - matched by colourful, flavoursome food, simply presented. The minestrone soup can be memorable, panini and pasta dishes are the business, and it's a place worth seeking out for their espressos alone. And it's great value too. **Seats 25.** Outdoor seating. Open every day: Mon-Fri, 8-6, Sat 9-6, Sun 12-6. A la carte. Closed Christmas/New Year. Also at: Bar Italia, 26 Lower Ormond Quay, Dublin, 1 (Tel 01 874 1000). MasterCard, Visa. **Directions:** South quays, west end of Temple Bar (near Dublin Corporation head office). ◊

Dublin 8
CAFÉ
Ⓝ

The Cake Café

The Daintree Building Pleasants Place (behind Camden Street) Dublin 8
Tel: 01478 9394

A love of traditional food and recognition of the environmental impact of their business are the driving forces behind this paradise for cake lovers. But don't be fooled by the name, they've plenty of quality savouries too. A homely atmosphere is created with flower print table cloths, and dainty higgledy piggledy crockery and the open kitchen means you can watch staff merrily baking away. The cookies and cream with cardamom panna cotta and the 'adult jelly & icecream' made with wine and home-made ice cream are trademark products and expertly made with quality ingredients. As is the lemon curd cake, chocolate brownie and there's a wonderful array of beverages to go with the cakes from iced latte to sweet spiced milk, extra rich Valhrona hot chocolate and twenty different teas including liquorice mint. A substantial lunch, or breakfast, can be had too including, terrine of Cashel Blue cheese with hazelnut and crème fraiche; Portuguese sardines on toast with black pepper and lemon juice; or something simple from the breakfast menu like toast with proper butter and their own brown sugar marmalade. But their own beans on toast are a marvel, made from scratch with cannellini beans, sausage and tomato, served on hot buttered toast. Faultless. They hope to open in the evenings in the summer months. **Seats 16** inside and 25 outside, Average main course €6, average dessert €4, house wines €19.10, €5.20 glass. No SC. Open 8.30am to 5.30pm Mon Fri, Sat 9-6, Closed Sun. MasterCard, Visa, Laser. **Directions:** Behind Daintree Shop on Camden Street.

Dublin 8
CAFÉ

Gallic Kitchen

49 Francis Street Dublin 8 **Tel: 01 454 4912**
galkit@iol.ie

This little spot in Dublin's "antique" district has been delighting locals and visitors alike for some years now. Patissière Sarah Webb is renowned for quality baking (quiches, roulades, plaits, tartlets, wraps) and also salads and delicious little numbers to have with coffee. A judicious selection from an extensive range is offered to eat in the shop: sourcing is immaculate, cooking skilful and prices reasonable, so you may have to queue. Outside catering offered (with staff if required). Open Mon-Sat, 9-4.30. *Sarah also has a stall at several markets: Temple Bar (Sat, 9-5); Dun Laoghaire (Thu, 10.30-5); Leopardstown (Fri, 11-5); Laragh, Co Wicklow (one Sun each month). MasterCard, Visa, Laser. ◊

Dublin 8
RESTAURANT

Locks Restaurant

1 Windsor Terrace Portobello Dublin 8 **Tel: 01 454 3391**
info@locksrestaurant.ie www.locksrestaurant.ie

It's a risk opening a new restaurant on the site of a well-loved former restaurant, and keeping the same name. Yet Locks' new incarnation, under co-owners Kelvin Rynhart and Teresa Carr (formerly of Bang Café) and chef co-proprietor Troy Maguire (of L'Gueuleton) succeeds in outshining the old Dublin haunt, asserting itself as a choicer, more relevant take on Dublin dining. The ground floor dining room is brighter and buzzier than before, though the upstairs room, despite being coolly revamped, lacks the buzz of downstairs. Large feature windows overlook the canal, allowing diners watch the world go by in sheer comfort. Whitewashed tongue and groove walls create a relaxed Scandinavian ambiance while dark parquet floors and ochre bucket seats add a sophisticated city vibe. The food is best described as bistro de luxe, featuring rustic French classics with gourmet accents. Luxurious ingredients, including truffles, foie gras and single estate chocolate are expertly handled alongside choice artisan produce from Ireland and the continent. Fans of L'Gueuleton will spot old favourites like snails and Troy's signature black pudding and apple tarte tatin. Portions verge on the large side, leaving little room for dessert, which is a shame, as the short selection is strikingly original with several savoury elements creeping on to the plates. The open fronted kitchen allows diners to view the action, and a small bar area is popular for an aperitif or browsing the menu. The young, hip floor staff, gathered from some of Dublin's coolest eating places (including quite a few from L'Gueuleton), provide lively, informed service, as well as being well versed in the intricacies of the menu. They can offer help with the wine list too, which is broad and interesting but would benefit from added tasting notes. These minor gripes aside, Locks offers exciting, good value dining in vibrant surroundings and is already a huge success. Children welcome. **Seats 80** (private rooms, 12/24). L Mon-Fri,12-3; D Mon-Sat, 6-11, L&D a la carte. Reservations accepted. Closed L Sat, all Sun, bank hols, Christmas week. Amex, Diners, MasterCard, Visa, Laser. **Directions:** Half way between Portobello and Harold's Cross Bridges.

Dublin 8
RESTAURANT/BAR

The Lord Edward

23 Christchurch Place Dublin 8 **Tel: 01 454 2420**
ledward@indigo.ie www.lordedward.ie

Dublin's oldest seafood restaurant/bar spans three floors of a tall, narrow building overlooking Christchurch Cathedral. Traditional in a decidedly old-fashioned way, The Lord Edward provides a complete contrast to the current wave of trendy restaurants that has taken over Dublin recently, which is just the way a lot of people like it. If you enjoy seafood and like old-fashioned cooking with plenty of butter and cream (as nature intended) and without too many concessions to the contemporary style of presentation either, then this could be the place for you. While certainly caught in a time warp, the range of fish and seafood dishes offered is second to none (sole is offered in no less than nine classic dishes, for example), and the fish cookery is excellent, with simplest choices almost invariably the best. There are a few non-seafood options - traditional dishes like Irish stew, perhaps, or corned beef and cabbage - and desserts also favour the classics. This place is a one-off - long may it last. Bar food is also available Mon-Fri, 12-2.30. Children welcome. **Seats 40.** L Mon-Fri, 12.30-2.30, D Mon-Sat 6-10.15. 5 course D €35; also à la carte. House wine from €20. Reservations required; SC 12.5% on groups 8+. Closed L Sat and all Sun, 24 Dec-2 Jan, bank hols. Amex, Diners, MasterCard, Visa, Laser. **Directions:** Opposite Christchurch Cathedral.

Dublin 8
RESTAURANT

Nonna Valentina

1-2 Portobello Road Dublin 8 **Tel: 01 454 9866**
acrobat_ltd@yahoo.it www.dunneandcrescenzi.com

A recent addition to the Dunne and Crescenzi group of restaurants, this attractively located two-storey restaurant is named after Stefano Crescenzi's grandmother and enjoys a pleasant outlook over the Grand Canal. Simple rooms with hardwood flooring and white clothed tables are given a sense of occasion by neat chandeliers and smart chair covers but, although this is at the fine dining end of the restaurants in the group, the main emphasis is on immaculately sourced ingredients, great service and the buzz created by rooms full of happy diners. Concise menus in Italian and English may include old favourites like bruschetta, buffalo mozzarella or breseola. Specialities include delicious home-made pastas, deeply-flavoured sauces, and a short choice of main courses including a perfectly cooked organic fillet steak, poultry and game. And sweet-toothed diners would do well to leave a little room for delicious home-made desserts. All this plus excellent coffee, a short, carefully selected wine list, great service and very fair prices. **Seats 60** (private room, 20); Air con; Food served all day 12-11; set L €22.50; early D €22.50, 5-7pm, also á la carte; House wine about €18. Closed 25 Dec. Amex, MasterCard, Visa, Laser. **Directions:** On the banks of the canal.

Dublin 8
CAFÉ
Ⓝ

The Phoenix Cafe

Ashtown Castle The Phoenix Park Visitors Centre Dublin 8
Tel: 01 677 0090

Hidden away next to the Áras an Uachtaráin Visitor Centre, you'll find the Phoenix Café. The modern building is sympathetic to the lush green surroundings and the first floor has a dramatic double height roof, floor to ceiling windows and a quirky antler chandelier. The vast majority of ingredients are organically sourced and café fare includes a wide range of hearty quiches, soups and a daily hot special. Salads change regularly but could include carrot with pumpkin and black onion seed, or broccoli and cauliflower, as well as leaf salads and potato salads. Dainty cakes can include lemon drizzle cake, hummingbird cake, flourless chocolate cake and muffins, always including flour-free options. Real care is taken in the preparation of the food and this, combined with the sylvan setting, makes The Phoenix Café a real hidden treasure. **Seats 80** inside, 70 outside. Main course with three salads €9.50, hot daily special €10.50, desserts €2.80 to €4. Lunch only 7 days. Open Summer 10 -5, Winter 10 4. Closed 10 days over Christmas. No SC. **No credit cards. Directions:** Watch out for a small turning off the roundabout for Áras an Uachtaráin and the American Ambassador's residence. Follow directions for Visitor Centre for the Áras. ◇

DUBLIN 9

The Botanic Gardens (Botanic Road; 01 804 0300; www.botanicgardens.ie; open 9am daily) are in Glasnevin and provide a great (free!) morning or afternoon out for visitors to Dublin. They are only a few minutes bus or taxi ride from the city centre and guided tours are available at various times of the day. Further out from the city is DCU (Dublin College University) which is home to Ireland's newest and most exciting multi-venue performance space - **The Helix** (Collins Avenue, Glasnevin; 01 700 7000; www.thehelix.ie). The Helix is a multi-venue arts centre that comprises three auditoria serving a mixture of high quality music, drama and entertainment. Since its opening in 2002 by President Mary McAleese, The Helix has generated an impressive reputation for staging cutting edge and diverse theatre and music. If you have worked up a thirst at the gardens or fancy a pint after a show then the **John Kavanagh 'GraveDiggers' Pub** (Prospect Square, Glasnevin; 01 830 7978) lays claim to being the oldest family pub in Dublin - it was established in 1833 and the current family are the 6th generation in the business. Known as 'The Gravediggers' because of its location next to the Glasnevin cemetery and its associated folk history, this is a genuine Victorian bar, totally unspoilt - and it has a reputation for serving one of the best pints in Dublin. No music, "piped or otherwise". Theme pub owners eat your hearts out. **Porterhouse North** (Cross Guns Bridge, Glasnevin; 01 830 9922; www.porterhousebrewco.com) is a large white canalside building that was originally a garage and has been redeveloped to retain some of the original art deco features. Inside it is a very trendy pub with a buzzy atmosphere giving it obvious youth appeal. Menus offer a range of popular dishes but, although interesting as a bar, it's not really a food place (perhaps with the exception of pizzas), more a place to drop in for a drink. The nearby **Independent Pizza Company** (Lr Drumcondra Road; 01 830 2044) is a sister restaurant of the popular Gotham Café just off Grafton Street (see entry), and the menu includes many of the Gotham favourites, so you can expect

to find designer salads and contemporary pasta dishes, for example, alongside the excellent range of gourmet pizzas for which they are best known. Family-friendly (crayons, colouring books provided) and a handy place for a meal on the way to the airport. Lunchtime specials are good value and there's a good drinks menu, including speciality coffees.
WWW.IRELAND-GUIDE.COM FOR ALL THE BEST PLACES TO EAT, DRINK & STAY

Andersons Food Hall & Café

Dublin 9
CAFÉ/WINE BAR

3 The Rise Glasnevin Dublin 9 **Tel: 01 837 8394**
info@andersons.ie www.andersons.ie

Previously a butchers shop, with its original 1930s' tiled floor, high ceiling and façade, Noel Delaney and Patricia van der Velde's wonderful delicatessen, wine shop and continental style café is quietly situated on a side road, so the unexpected sight of jaunty aluminium chairs and tables outside - and a glimpse of many wine bottles lining the walls behind the elegant shopfront - should gladden the hearts of first-time visitors sweeping around the corner from Griffith Avenue. Oak fittings have been used throughout, including the wine displays, and the chic little marble-topped tables used for lighter bites suit the old shop well - in the extension behind, there are larger tables and space for groups to eat in comfort. Now, where cuts of meat were once displayed, there's a wonderful selection of charcuterie and cheese from Ireland and the continent, with the choice of an Irish or Iberian plate offering a delicious selection of produce, all served with speciality breads. A short blackboard menu of hot dishes and specials, plus a daily soup, a range of salads, gourmet sandwiches, wraps, hot panini, pastries and classic café desserts complement the charcuterie and cheese which have the gravitas to balance the collection of wines lining the walls - and, in addition to the wine list, which changes regularly, you can choose any bottle to have with your food at a very modest corkage charge. There's also an extensive drinks menu, offering speciality coffees and teas, and some unusual beverages, like Lorina French lemonade. A weekend breakfast menu offers all kinds of treats including smoked salmon and scrambled eggs, and a number of dishes uses various Hicks sausages - Hicks wine & garlic sausage, for example, served on ciabatta with tomato, smoked applewood cheddar & sweet pepper relish. * Also at: **Andersons Crêperie** (01 830 5171), Carlingford Road, Drumcondra, Dublin 9, where the speciality is buckwheat pancakes, but they also offer charcuterie, cheeses etc. **Seats 45** (outside seating 18); No reservations, children welcome (childrens menu, high chair, baby changing facilities), toilets wheelchair accessible. Open Mon-Sat, 9-7 (to 8.30 Thu-Sat), Sun 10-7); last food orders half an hour before closing. 14 House Wines (€17.95-€24.95) & 160 wines available from the wine shop at €6 corkage. Closed 1 week over Christmas, Good Fri & Easter Sun. MasterCard, Visa, Laser. **Directions:** Off Griffith Avenue, near junction with Mobhi Road.

Egans House

Dublin 9
GUESTHOUSE

7-9 Iona Park Glasnevin Dublin 9 **Tel: 01 830 5283**
info@eganshouse.com www.eganshouse.com

Within walking distance of the Botanic Gardens and convenient to an amazing number of places - the airport, north Dublin golf clubs, Dublin City University, The Helix (DCU Performing Arts complex), Dublin port and the city centre - the Finn's family-run guesthouse offers comfortable, well-maintained accommodation at a reasonable price. All rooms are en-suite, with full bath, phone, tea/coffee trays. Work desk, internet access, safe. Wine licence. Parking. Children welcome (Under 3s free in parents' room; cots available). No pets. Garden. **Rooms 23** (22 shower only, 14 no-smoking, 13 ground floor, 4 family rooms). B&B €60, No SS. Closed 22-28 Dec. MasterCard, Visa, Laser. **Directions:** North of city centre - Dorset Street - St. Alphonsus Road- Iona Park.

The Maples House Hotel

Dublin 9
HOTEL/RESTAURANT

79-81 Iona Road Glasnevin Dublin 9 **Tel: 01 830 4227**
info@mapleshotel.com www.mapleshotel.com

Conveniently located near the Botanic Gardens and Dublin City University, this neat double-fronted Victorian redbrick hotel is well lit, with flags to help you find it in a largely residential street. Although by no means a smart boutique or designer hotel, it offers the kind of reliability and comfort that is welcome in a suburban setting. Cosy fires (log effect, but still cheering) and a relaxed atmosphere, plus the spacious bar and rather attractive ground floor restaurant all make the visitor feel welcome. Accommodation is spotlessly clean and comfortable, and rooms have not only the traditional facilities of tea and coffee making equipment and hair dryer, but also flat screen televisions and the computer connections that today's traveller requires. All bedrooms have a neat en suite shower room, and the area is generally quiet, so you should be sure of a good night's sleep. The large hotel bar attracts non-residents and the restaurant, complete with fire, serves modern Irish food in a most pleasant setting, with white linen and modern crockery and glassware, plus a decent wine list and attentive service from pleasant staff, makes a meal here a relaxing experience. B&B about €60-90 pps. MasterCard, Visa, Laser. ◇

Dublin 9
RESTAURANT

The Washerwoman's Hill Restaurant

60a Glasnevin Hill Glasnevin Dublin 9 **Tel: 01 837 9199**
info@washerwoman.ie www.washerwoman.ie

féile bia Convenient to the Botanic Gardens and the airport area, first impressions of the outside of this popular neighbourhood restaurant may be a little dusty but a prompt welcome and the offer of a choice of tables should help new arrivals warm to it. Traditional, slightly country kitchen in style, this charming restaurant is quite dimly-lit and cosy, with simply-laid darkwood tables and local artwork displayed on the walls. Well-balanced traditional table d'hôte and à la carte menus offer the popular dishes, sometimes with a contemporary twist, and the cooking style is quite homely. Some suppliers are listed on the menu and special diets can be accommodated. The ambience on the ground floor is warmer and more relaxed than a first floor room, which has rather gimmicky decor. [*A sister restaurant, **Canters**, is in Fairview (see entry)] Children welcome (not after 10pm). **Seats 70** (private rom, 35). Air conditioning. L Sun-Fri 12.30-3.30 (Sun 1.30-4); D daily 6-10. Set L about €20, Set Sun L about €26, early D about €26 (6-8). Set D about €35; also à la carte. House wine about €17.50. Closed Sat L. 25-26 Dec, Good Fri. **Directions:** Past Bon Secours hospital, opposite the Met Office.

DUBLIN 14

Dublin 14
RESTAURANT

Indian Brasserie

Main Street Rathfarnham Dublin 14
Tel: 01 492 0261

For anyone who has been to India, finding a truly authentic restaurant which offers a similar experience is not easy: Samir Sapru's Indian Brasserie comes close. It is just a minute's walk from Rathfarnham Castle, at the Butterfield Avenue end of the village, and the water feature at the entrance is instantly therapeutic. This is carried through by the warmth of the reception, and the restaurant, which has functional seating and a comfortable atmosphere, is run as a buffet; it offers freshly prepared wholesome food, aiming to make it the nearest to home cooking that can be achieved in a restaurant. The selection usually includes around eight starters, five or six salads and seven or eight main courses, with each dish individually prepared from scratch and the selection worked out so that all the dishes complement each other. Breads - which are baked quickly at a very high temperature - are cooked to order. The hospitality is intended to make each guest feel as if they are visiting a private house - customers are encouraged to try a little of everything that has been prepared on the night. The Indian Brasserie has earned a loyal clientèle, and also offers a takeaway service. Fully wheelchair accessible; children welcome (high chair, children's menu). **Seats 70.** D daily 5-10 (to 11pm Sat). L Sun only 12.30-3pm. Early D, €20, Mon-Fri, 5-7pm; set 2/3 course D €23.50/€29; also a la carte; set Sun L €20. House wine about €15. SC 10% on groups 8+. Closed Good Fri, 25-27 Dec. Amex, MasterCard, Visa. **Directions:** At the Butterfield Avenue end of Rathfarnham village.

Dublin 14
CHARACTER PUB

The Yellow House

1 Willbrook Road Rathfarnham Dublin 14
Tel: 01 493 2994

Named after the unusual shade of the bricks with which it is built, the landmark pub of Rathfarnham makes a perfect rendezvous, with no chance of confusion. The tall and rather forbidding exterior gives little hint of the warmth inside, where pictures and old decorative items relevant to local history repay closer examination. (Traditional bar food is served in the lounge and there's a restaurant upstairs serving evening meals and Sunday lunch.) Closed 25-6 Dec & Good Fri. Amex, Diners, MasterCard, Visa, Laser. **Directions:** Prominent corner building in Rathfarnham Village.

DUBLIN 15

Dublin 15
COUNTRY HOUSE

Ashbrook House

River Road Ashtown Castleknock Dublin 15 **Tel: 01 838 5660**
evemitchell@hotmail.com

Although it is only about a 15 minute drive from the airport outside rush hour (and a similar distance from the city centre), Eve Mitchell's lovely Georgian country house is in a countryside location beside the Tolka River. Set in 10 acres of grounds, with a grass tennis court, walled garden and many garden paths to wander, it is also just beside the Phoenix Park and within a few minutes' drive of seven golf courses. There are two magnificent drawing rooms, and the large beautifully furnished bedrooms are very comfortable, with phone, tea/coffee facilities and en-suite power showers; two family rooms have a single bed as well as doubles. TV lounge. Children welcome (baby sitting arranged) No pets. No smoking house. B&B about €45 pps. Single supplement about €15. Closed Christmas/New Year. MasterCard, Visa, Laser. **Directions:** Off N3, 15 minutes from airport; similar distance from city centre. ◊

Dublin 15
HOTEL

Castleknock Hotel & Country Club

Porterstown Road Castleknock Dublin 15 **Tel: 01 640 6300**
reservations@chcc.ie www.towerhotelgroup.com

This new hotel just outside Castleknock Village is a welcome addition to the limited accommodation and amenities in the area. With its own golf course, extensive conference facilities and countryside views, it makes a pleasant base for both business and leisure guests. Spacious, comfortably furnished bedrooms are not over-decorated and have cable TV, radio, telephone with voice mail, high speed internet access, in room safe, tea/coffee facilities and trouser press as standard, and bathrooms have separate shower and bath. Non-smoking bedrooms are available on request (subject to availability), and there are also a number of interconnecting rooms for families. The hotel offers formal dining in The Park restaurant, and an informal option in The Brasserie, where breakfast is also served. Conferences/Banqueting, golf, leisure centre. Ample parking. **Rooms 144;** B&B from €75 pps. Closed 24-26 Dec. MasterCard, Visa, Laser. ◊

Dublin 15
RESTAURANT

Cilantro

Above Brady's Pub Old Navan Road Castleknock Dublin 15
Tel: 01 824 3443

Brady's Inn - a large but pleasant pub - is a local landmark in Castleknock, and above it you will find this very agreeable owner-run Indian restaurant. Modern, clean lined and smartly decorated, with black leather fireside seating in the reception area, and generous white-clothed tables set up with crisp linen napkins, generous fine wine glasses and fresh flowers, it creates a good first impression - enhanced by a warm welcome from friendly Indian staff. A balanced wine list (including some Indian beers) and menus are promptly presented, and aperitifs follow swiftly. Poppodums and an array of chutneys make tasty nibbles to begin with, while looking through menus that offer a wide range of dishes, including many of the traditional favourites, but also less known dishes. Tandoori specialities feature on the main course choices, and a mixed tandoori dish brings together pieces of lamb, chicken and beef, cooked over charcoal in the tandoor. Various creamier dishes are offered too, plus tempting naan breads and an unusual range of side vegetables. To finish, try a refreshing lassi (a traditional, slightly salty, mixture of yoghurt and water). Sister establishments: Tulsi (Galway, Dublin), Kasturi. **Seats 90;** D daily 5-11.30pm. MasterCard, Visa, Laser. **Directions:** Over Brady's Pub. ◊

Dublin 15
RESTAURANT

La Mora

Luttrellstown Castle Resort Castleknock Dublin 15 **Tel: 01 860 9500**
lamora@luttrellstown.ie www.luttrellstown.ie

La Mora is the formal restaurant at Luttrellstown Castle Resort's clubhouse and its first floor location affords diners delightful views across the golf course to the mountains in the distance. The clubhouse is a handsome stone and wood-clad building that draws on mountain lodges for inspiration. This log cabin theme is wonderfully executed inside with heavy beams, walls clad in honeyed wood and a soothing palette of moody greys, browns and reds that draws on Ralph Lauren's distinctive interiors look. Non-members are welcome and diners can linger in the stylish Clubhouse Bar before moving to La Mora, the gorgeous restaurant that's a sophisticated mix of wood-clad walls, gigantic canvasses and muted furnishings. The large, bright room is especially family-friendly by day and justifiably popular for Sunday lunch with large tables, plenty of room and a good children's menu. While weekend lunch offers favourites like rack of lamb or roast rib eye, dinner menus might feature more unusual dishes like West Cork lobster salad or Thai baked sea bass; cooking is impressive, exact and beautifully presented. On the Guide's visit, we experienced distracted service and felt the restaurant to be understaffed; nevertheless La Mora (Italian for blackberry) provides extremely good food in a remarkable setting and a visit here is sure to be enjoyable. *Luttrellstown Castle Hotel & Resort is due to re-open at some stage in 2008 following an extensive refurbishment programme. See website for details (www.luttrellstown.ie). **Directions:** In Luttrellstown golf club.

Dublin 15   The Twelfth Lock
HOTEL/BAR/RESTAURANT   Castleknock Marina The Royal Canal Castleknock Dublin 15
Tel: **01 860 7400** info@twelfthlock.com www.twelfthlock.com

The Twelfth Lock is a fine bar, with a warm, friendly atmosphere and views out over the picturesque Royal Canal. The main bar is modern, light and airy, with a variety of high and low wooden tables dotted around, and a fine fire that would warm up the coldest evening - and, there's also a sizeable heated deck with views out over the canal. Interesting bar menus offer a good range of quality, informal fare such as lamb chops or grilled salmon steak, with good vegetarian choices also. Attentive staff cope well even when the bar is busy. *The Bar Bistro offers a slightly more formal evening dining experience, Wednesday-Saturday only. **Accommodation:** The ten guest rooms are on the lower ground floor and a little dark, but furnished to a high standard. Children are welcome, but not allowed in bar after 7pm. **Rooms 10** (1 disabled). Lift. Room service (limited hours). Room rate about €115 (with breakfast); weekend rates available. Bar Meals Mon-Thurs, 12 noon-9:30pm; Fri-Sun 12 noon-8:30pm. Outside eating. Wheelchair accessible. **Bar Bistro** open Wed-Sat from 7pm(to 11:30am midweek, 12:30am Fri & Sat). Amex, MasterCard, Visa, Laser. **Directions:** On Royal Canal, at Twelfth Lock near Brady's Castleknock Inn Pub. ◇

DUBLIN 16

Dublin 16   DUNDRUM SHOPPING CENTRE
Dundrum Shopping Centre has attracted a lot of restaurants, mostly casual - including **Milano**, **Café Mimo** (at House of Fraser) - and, at the time of going to press Roly Saul is due to re-locate here from Dun Laoghaire to open his latest venture **Roly Saul The Restaurant** (www.roly.ie).

Dublin 16   Café Mao
RESTAURANT   The Mill Pond Civic Square Dundrum Shopping Centre Dublin 16
Tel: **01 296 2802** dundrum@cafemao.com www.cafemao.com

This modern, airy two storey restaurant is a younger sister of the well known Café Mao restaurants in Dublin. Conveniently located in a restaurant piazza to the rear of the shopping centre, it's a handy place for an après shop bite. The atmosphere is bright and buzzy, and interesting food is based on seasonal ingredients; the standard of cooking is consistently good, offering simple, tasty food that is served quickly and at a reasonable price. Chilli squid, Nasi Goreng and Malaysian chicken are established favourites, vegetarians might try a starter of Jakarta salad followed by Thai green vegetable curry. Chilli strength is considerately indicated on the menu, also vegetarian and low fat dishes, dishes containing nuts. A compact but wide-ranging drinks menu includes cocktails, fresh juices and smoothies, a range of coffees and teas and speciality beers as well as wines. Café Mao Dundrum Shopping Centre offers healthy food, good value and friendly efficient service. Fully wheelchair accessible; Children welcome; **Seats 130** (outdoor, 50); serving food daily 12.00-23.00 and Sun 12.00-10.00; Value L €9.95, value D €15, 5-7pm; set 2/3 course D €24/€28; House Wine €18. Closed 25/26 Dec. **Directions:** At the back of Dundrum Shopping Centre next to the Old Mill Pond.

Harvey Nichol's First Floor Restaurant

Dublin 16
RESTAURANT
☆

Dundrum Shopping Centre Sandyford Road Dublin 16 **Tel: 01 291 0488**
www.harveynichols.com

Before the arrival of Harvey Nichols in Ireland the concept of fine dining in a department store was quite alien to most Dubliners, but the First Floor Restaurant & Bar at Harvey Nichols has a separate entrance and express lift so, having whizzed up, most find that the scene has been set pretty impressively. The interior - designed by French interior architect Christian Biecher - is contemporary cool, with vibrant pinks taking the lead in the popular bar (where in-house mixologists are at hand to create the perfect cocktail...) and a combination of warm, plummy pinks and yellows linking into the restaurant too, where glass walls, high-backed couches and banquettes are balanced by slouchy leather carver chairs and crisp, white-clothed classic modern table settings. Head chef Thomas Haughton arrived at Dundrum via a lot of prestigious kitchens, most recently Luttrellstown Castle, so his modern classic cooking should come as no surprise. Dishes on a typical dinner menu could include luxurious starters such as carpaccio of Wagyu beef with parmesan mousse and crisp onion tempura, or a rillette of fragrant crab with tartare of avocado and tomato and thyme milkshake, and main courses like pot roasted belly of pork with caramelised parsnip and turnip purée or pan seared seabass with fennel confit, sauce vierge and black olive tapenade. Despite the hype, the clean-flavoured cooking is outstanding and, although portions aren't huge, this sophisticated restaurant offers one of south Dublin's most exciting dining experiences. The wine list is impressive too offering treats for the connoisseur as well as a choice of eight good, well-priced house wines. Good value can also be found through a variety of inventive promotions which include pre-theatre dining, themed gourmet evenings and special value cocktail and wine events. Toilets wheelchair accessible; Children welcome before 9pm. **Seats 80** (private room, 12); air conditioning; L daily, 12-3; Set L about €25, set Sun L about €27.50; D Mon-Sat, 6-10, value D about €25, 6-7.30pm, Set D about €30, also a la carte D; House wine about €18; SC 12.5%. Closed Sun D and 25/26 Dec. Amex, Diners, MasterCard, Visa, Laser.
Directions: Above Harvey Nichol's department store in the Dundrum Shopping Centre. ◇

IMI Residence

Dublin 16
HOTEL
Ⓝ

Sandyford Road Dublin 16 **Tel: 01 207 5900**
reservations@imi.ie www.imi.ie/accommodation

Within easy access of the M50, (Sandyford Industrial Estate exit), 1 km from the Luas stop at Balally and on local bus route to Dundrum less than ten minutes away, the residence is on spacious grounds surrounded by trees with lots of parking. It is a residence rather than an hotel, rather like upmarket university campus accommodation. The reception area is typical of the facility: modern, minimalist, high-ceilinged, high-windowed, with bare concrete walls covered here and there with modern paintings and wall hangings. There is a definite business air about the place - lots of light and no frills, yet good uncomplicated service by efficient, friendly staff. Comfortable bedrooms are decorated in smart, muted tones (blue/grey carpet, cream walls), with work space, TV, telephone and internet lines. Particularly neat, well maintained shower rooms have black and blue tiles and full length mirror. Only a continental, self service breakfast is offered, with good coffee. The residence is an ideal base for the business traveller and its understated operation should appeal to a wider category of cost-conscious visitors to Dublin. Conferences (300); broadband; wheelchair friendly; laptop-sized safes in bedrooms; children welcome (under 6s free in parents' room, cot available free of charge). **Rooms 50** (all shower only, executive and no smoking, 25 ground floor, 2 for disabled); limited room service, Lift. B&B is excellent value at €65 per room. **Directions:** Entrance where Clonard Road meets Sandyford Road at traffic lights.

L'Officina by Dunne & Crescenzi

Dublin 16
RESTAURANT
Ⓝ

Dundrum Shopping Centre Dundrum Dublin 16 **Tel: 01 216 6764**
dunneandcrescenzi@hotmail.com www.dunneandcrescenzi.com

Located in an informal dining piazza to the rear of Dundrum Shopping Centre, this younger sister to the well-known Dunne & Crescenzi restaurants offers al fresco dining alongside the fountains in the Old Mill Pond. Decorated in tune with the style of food service - simple, no-fuss, efficient - there's a buzzy atmosphere, and an impressive display of wine contrasts with the simplicity of paper place mats and minimal table settings. Italian staff are quick to greet and seat arriving guests; menus and wine list are promptly presented, along with an outline of the mouthwatering daily specials. Impeccably sourced ingredients form the backbone of healthy menus at L'Officina, where the use of artisan products is proudly highlighted and there are plenty of simple classic Italian dishes on offer such as Caprese salad, panini, or minestrone soup. Menus also include platters that are particularly good for sharing and sampling several dishes. Evening menus are a little more extensive, including fish and organic fillet of beef, and plenty of choice for vegetarians. Finish with a treat from a selection of home-made desserts, partnered with some of Ireland's finest coffee. All round, L'Officina offers great quality at a fair price and the staff are terrific. **Directions:** At the rear of the shopping centre - next to the fountain. ◇

DUBLIN 18

Bordering onto Stillorgan (sometimes Dublin 4, or Co Dublin) and Blackrock (Co Dublin), Dublin 18 is a chameleon area, with edges a little blurred and, it seems, sometimes shifting... But one thing is certain, and it's that the burgeoning business parks have ensured the choice of interesting places to eat and comfortable places to lay your head are on the increase: a lively business area, it now has the 352 bedroom **Bewleys Hotel Leopardstown** (01 293 5000; www.bewleyshotels.com), for example, offering a high level of comfort (and links to the airport) for as little as €89; and also the newer, design-led 82-room contemporary **Beacon Hotel** (see entry).
WWW.IRELAND-GUIDE.COM FOR GREAT PLACES TO EAT, DRINK & STAY

Dublin 18   The Beacon Hotel
HOTEL   Beacon Court Sandyford Business Region Dublin 18
Ⓝ   **Tel: 01 291 5000**

In burgeoning south county Dublin, Sandyford has become the focus for extensive development, and the Beacon Hotel is a most welcome facility. Located within sight of the M50 motorway, five minutes walk from the Luas tramline, (15 minutes to the city centre) and about 20 minutes by car to the ferry at Dun Laoghaire it looks no different to the neighbouring glass/concrete exteriors of a private hospital and office block but that is just on the outside: internally the hotel is a model of cutting edge design. Although it resembles its sister hotel, The Morgan in Temple Bar (see entry), The Beacon is bolder, more designer led. The open plan, light-filled foyer has the appeal of an art gallery with elegant cande-labras, moulded wall sculpture and bizarre seating arrangements as exemplified by a cleverly adapted four poster bed. It is unashamedly a business hotel with several air-conditioned meeting rooms equipped to the highest standards, also free underground parking for guests, accessible by lift from the lobby. Bedrooms are ultra modern, a happy amalgam of provocative lighting, both over and under the bed, beds set playfully at an angle and crimson velour "headboards"; pristine bathrooms are behind sliding, opaque glass doors, emphasising the streamlined experience, and housekeeping overall is excellent There is a ground floor bar and a Thai Restaurant which doubles as breakfast room - break-fast, as in the Morgan, is expensive at €19.95 but not at all as well done here. Sunday Brunch at The Beacon features a jazz band and well known local artists. Reception is cool and uninvolved- and, despite the sexy ambience, it is not a place for lingering; very few guests are in the bar at night and breakfasts are devoured in minutes. **Directions:** In the heart of the Sandyford business region. ◇

Dublin 18   Bistro One
RESTAURANT   3 Brighton Road Foxrock Village Dublin 18 **Tel: 01 289 7711**
                                                          bistroone@eircom.net

féile bia This popular neighbourhood restaurant can get very busy but there is a bar on the way in, where guests are greeted and set up in comfort, and the attitude throughout is laid back yet not without care. Ingredients are carefully sourced - fresh produce comes from organic farmers' markets, cheeses from Sheridan's cheesemongers, smoked fish from Frank Hederman. Seasonal menus - which considerately indicate dishes containing nuts or nut oil - offer eight or ten tempting choices per course. Starters will almost certainly include the ever-popular Bistro One's salad with pancetta, rocket & pine nuts - while the pasta and risotto selection can be starter or main course as preferred: typically, spaghetti with organic meatballs & fresh basil, perhaps, or Carnaroli risotto with green pea and organic mint. Main courses include classics - in seafood dishes and organic meats. There are generous side vegetables and a choice of French and Irish cheese; home-made ice creams or classic puddings to finish. Children welcome. **Seats 75.** D Tue-Sat 6-10.30, L 12-2.30. A la carte. House wine €22. SC 10%. Closed Sun, Mon & 25 Dec - 2 Jan. MasterCard, Visa, Laser. **Directions:** Southbound on N11, first right after Foxrock church. ◇

Dublin 18   The Gables Restaurant
RESTAURANT   The Gables Foxrock Village Dublin 18 **Tel: 01 289 2174**
                              value@mccabeswines.ie www.mccabeswines.ie

This imaginative venture by McCabes Wines, whose shop is part of the restaurant, offers a wine experience in addition to brunches and stylish contemporary food. The wine list offers quality wines at an unusually low mark-up - and you can have any wine from about 800 available in the shop at a moderate corkage charge. The list, which is organised by grape variety, offers a good range of wines by the glass - and a novel 'try before you buy' offer: you taste a wine before ordering it and, if you like it, you can add it to your bill and have a case put into your car (at a very favourable price) while dining at The Gables: easy peasy. Head chef Chris Allen came to the Gables with experience at some impressive English restaurants, including Harrods and The Ivy, under his belt and is now doing a good job here. Modern food with an international tone is offered in congenial surroundings, and service is prompt and efficient. **Seats 70** (outdoor, 20). Open 8am-10pm daily (Sun 10-9). L 12.30-4 (Sun brunch 10-4.30); D 6-9.30 (Sun 5.30-9). Á la carte. House wine from €18. SC discretionary. Closed 25 Dec, Good Fri. Amex, Diners, MasterCard, Visa, Laser. **Directions:** Travelling into the city on N11, turn off left for Foxrock Village.

Dublin 18
RESTAURANT
⬤ⒺⓃ

South Bar and Restaurant

Unit a8 Beacon South Quarter Sandyford Dublin 18 **Tel: 01 293 4050**
reservations@south.ie www.south.ie

Building on the success of their hugely popular Town Bar and Grill, Ronan Ryan and Temple Garner have brought their brand of smart, contemporary dining to the suburbs. This time they're serving classic bistro fare in a dining room so slick you'll forget you've just driven through an industrial estate to get here. Externally the green copper cladding and curving glass hint at the visual treat indoors: a dramatic sweeping staircase, huge slabs of bespoke terrazzo flooring, a cascade of silver pendant lights and a giant glass wall that floods the basement with natural light. While the ground floor dining room is spacious and handsome, it's the versatile basement room that's most atmospheric and unique. For Sunday lunch, request a table at the foot of the stairs where you can watch generations of families and smart young couples arrive and depart; by night cosy-up in a banquette across the room, where you'll enjoy moody lighting and views of the chic horseshoe-shaped cocktail bar. Comfy seats, large tables, fresh buds and crisp linen make it a sophisticated but relaxed affair. Menus featuring modern classics, simply cooked and attractively presented, have wide appeal. Favourites like beer battered fish, Caprese salad, pork belly or the house burger, use the choicest ingredients and, as you'd expect, everything, from the bread to the tartar sauce and ice cream, is home-made. Portions are filling but sensible, allowing room for the excellent desserts, should you wish. Given the quality of the cooking, food here is good value. Choose from the interesting selection of house wines (the house champagne is especially affordable) and you'll keep your bill agreeably low. South's staff are friendly, obliging and efficient, making dining here a very pleasant experience. A pianist plays for Sunday lunch, and there's live music on offer Thursday to Saturday nights too, lending extra buzz to this impressive, atmospheric new restaurant. Toilets wheelchair accessible; Children welcome (high chair childrens menu, baby changing facilities). **Seats 200** (private dining 55), free parking (40 cars), live music (jazz Fri/Sat night, modern piano Sun L). Open 7 days; food served 12-11pm (to 10pm Sun). L 12-4 daily, D 6-11 daily (to 10pm Sun). Early D €29.95, Sun-Thur, 5.45-7pm; set 3 course D €49.95. SC 10% on groups 5+. Closed Good Fri, 25 Dec. Amex, Diners, MasterCard, Visa, Laser. **Directions:** N11 Stillorgan dual carriageway South, right at Newtownpark Avenue junction. At roundabout take 3rd exit, left at T junction.

Dublin 18
HOTEL/RESTAURANT

Stillorgan Park Hotel

Stillorgan Road Stillorgan Dublin 18 **Tel: 01 200 1800**
sales@stillorganpark.com www.stillorganpark.com

féile bía This fine hotel is a sister establishment to the famous Talbot Hotel in Wexford; improvements have been made in recent years and it is furnished in a lively modern style throughout. Public areas include the stylish reception and lounge areas, and bedrooms - some with views of Dublin Bay - are spacious, attractively decorated, with well-finished bathrooms. Ample free parking is an attraction and good facilities for business guests include work space and fax/modem lines in rooms. A regular airport coach service leaves from the front door. Conference/banqueting (500/370); business centre; video conferencing, free broadband wi/fi. Children welcome (under 12s free in parents' room, cots available without charge, baby sitting arranged). Fitness room, day spa, steam room. **Rooms 150** (8 junior suites, 132 executive rooms, 129 no-smoking, 6 for disabled) Lift. B&B from €65 pps, ss €44. No SC.

The Purple Sage Restaurant: An attractive, informal restaurant and welcoming staff. Menus are appealing in a fairly contemporary style, including imaginative vegetarian cooking and healthy options, which have always been a feature. Toilets wheelchair accessible; children welcome (high chair, children's menu, baby changing facilities). **Seats 120;** reservations recommended; air conditioning. L Mon-Fri, 12.45-2.30; D Mon-Sat, 5.45-9.30; Sun L 12.30-3.30pm. Set L €26; set Sun L €26; early D €25.50, Mon-Sat 5.45-7.30pm, Set D €37.50; à la carte D also available; house wine €22; no SC. Amex, Diners, MasterCard, Visa, Laser. **Directions:** Situated on main N11 dual carriageway.

DUBLIN 22

R R R

Dublin 22, on the western edges of the city, is a busy commercial area known mainly for its industrial estates and business parks - and the huge Liffey Valley Shopping Centre. Hotels which service the needs of the area well include the landmark **Red Cow Moran Hotel** on the Naas Road (01 459 3650; www.moranhotels.com), with outstanding conference facilities; **Bewleys Hotel Newlands Cross** (01 464 0140; www.bewleyshotels.com), offering a lot of space and comfort at a modest price; and the newer **Clarion Hotel Liffey Valley** (01 625 8000; www.clarionhotelliffeyvalley.com), cleverly disguised as a warehouse but actually quite stylish within. On the Naas Road, at Kingswood, the new **Comfort Inn Citywest** (1850 605 705; www.comfortinns.ie) offers good accommodation and facilities for a budget hotel, and is well located for business travellers. The most recent addition to the area is the **Louis Fitzgerald Hotel** (01 403 3300; www.louisfitzgeraldhotel.com).
WWW.IRELAND-GUIDE.COM FOR THE BEST PLACES TO EAT, DRINK & STAY

Dublin 22
RESTAURANT/BAR
N R R R

Kingswood Country House

Kingswood Naas Road Clondalkin Dublin 22 **Tel: 01 459 5250**
info@kingswoodcountryhouse.ie www.kingswoodcountryhouse.ie

In an unlikely location on the grounds of the Comfort Inn Hotel just off the busy Naas Road, this delightful Georgian property was long seen as an oasis of civilised hopsitality in an area known for industrial parks and heavy traffic and, after major restyling, has recently reopened as part of the Thomas Read bar and restaurant group. While its distance from the city centre might discourage casual visits, it is easy to find - and ideal for travellers arriving from, or leaving for, the south and west of Ireland. Downstairs in the newer part of the building - which opens onto a patio area and small landscaped garden with water features - a comfortable contemporary bar with TV screens serves a reasonable selection of bar food every day (useful for the nearby the nearby Citywest Business Park) but due to its location the bar is quiet in the afternoon, making an ideal stop ideal for a time-pressed getaway. A small glass atrium connects this to the older part of the building where, downstairs, a lounge/drawing room is comfortably furnished in a more traditional style than the bar, and the excellent Josef's Restaurant is upstairs. **Josef's Restaurant:** Situated upstairs in the 280 year old house, the restaurant (which is named after the famous tenor, Josef Locke, who once lived here) is divided into four comfortably furnished areas, one of which is entirely self-contained, giving it an intimate feel - and a contemporary take on lighting gives the low ceilinged attic a spacious feel. The menu offers a broad selection of dishes, including a good choice of seafood, poultry and vegetarian dishes, and plenty of side orders. The style is mainly traditional and the cooking is accomplished - on the Guide's visit a dish of pot-roasted Kildare lamb with a sweet potato purée and rosemary & garlic port was particularly enjoyable. Well-made desserts also tend to be classical and there is a good cheese board offered too. The wine list leans towards old world classics, although the six new world house wines for €20 offer excellent value. Service is professional and friendly and this is certain to become a popular dining destination. **Seats 70;** toilets wheelchair accessible; children welcome before 8pm; Josefs open for L&D, Tue-Sat, 12.30-2.30 & 6-10 (to 10.30pm Sat); Sun L only, 12-4pm; set L €25; early D €21, 5-7pm; bar open all day for food, 12-8pm. Restaurant closed Sun D, Mon. MasterCard, Visa, Laser. **Directions:** Kingswood exit off N7 Naas Road - 3km (1.5 miles) past Newlands Cross heading south.

DUBLIN 24

Tallaght is one of the fastest developing areas of western Dublin and lies at the foot of the Dublin - Wicklow mountains. Particularly well known for its shopping centre and its Luas (tram) line, making travelling to the city centre very easy. The stylish **Plaza Hotel** (Belgard Road; 01 462 4200; www.plazahotel.ie) serves the area well, with secure underground parking and extensive conference and banqueting facilities.
WWW.IRELAND-GUIDE.COM FOR THE BEST PLACES TO EAT, DRINK & STAY

COUNTY DUBLIN

Dublin County is divided into the three administrative "sub-counties" of Dun Laoghaire-Rathdown to the southeast, South Dublin to the southwest, and the large territory of Fingal to the north. However, although these regions are among the most populous and economically active in all Ireland, the notion of Greater Dublin being in four administrative parts is only slowly taking root - for instance, all postal addresses still either have a Dublin city numbered code, or else they're simply County Dublin.

Inevitably, it is in the countryside and towns in the Greater Dublin Region that some of the pressures of the success of the Irish economy are most evident. But although Dubliners of town and county alike will happily accept that they're part of a thrusting modern city, equally they'll cheerfully adhere to the old Irish saying that when God made time, He made a lot of it. Those with long family associations with the county certainly have this approach. But as the region has also experienced the greatest population changes in recent years, it has its own multinational dynamism.

The traditionally relaxed approach is good news for the visitor, for it means that if you feel that the frenetic pace of Dublin city is just a mite overpowering, you will very quickly find that nearby, in what used to be - and for many folk still is - County Dublin, there continue to be oases of a much more easy-going way of life waiting to be discovered.

Admittedly, the fact that the handsome Dublin Mountains overlook the city in spectacular style means that, even up in the nearby hills, you can be well aware of the city's buzz. But if you want to find a vigorous contrast between modern style and classical elegance, you can find it in an unusual form at Dun Laoghaire's remarkable harbour, where one of the world's most modern ferryports is in interesting synergy with one of the world's largest Victorian artificial harbours.

A showcase marina within the haven, expensively built so that its style matches the harbour's classic elegance, has steadily developed, while the harbour area of Dun Laoghaire town beside it continues to be improve in quality and vitality.

Northward beyond the city into Fingal, despite the proximity of the airport you'll quickly discover an away-from-it-all sort of place of estuary towns, extensive farming, pleasant parkland, fishing and sailing ports, and offshore islands alive with seabirds. The large island of Lambay – a nature reserve – has Ireland and the world's newest gannetry, an offshoot of the previous global front-runner, the gannetry on the stack rock at Ireland's Eye eight kilometres to the south. This was established (almost within city limits, another world first) back in 1989, and served as a reminder that the gannet is not a seagull – it's a pelican.

Fingal is an easygoing environment of leisurely pace in which it's thought very bad form to hasten over meals in restaurants where portion control is either unknown, or merely in its infancy. It's interesting to note that connoisseurs of this intriguing region reckon that one of its long established features, the

Georgina Campbell's Ireland

Dublin-Belfast mainline railway first used in 1838, effectively creates a "land island" on the Donabate-Portrane peninsula, as there are only two road crossings into this sandy territory with its four golf courses. Add in the legendary Portmarnock links just across the estuary, and this is golfing heaven.

Local Attractions & Information

Balbriggan/Skerries, Ardgillan Castle	01 849 2212
Blackrock, Deepwell House & Gardens	01 288 7407
Donabate, Newbridge House, Park & Traditional Farm	01 843 6534
Dun Laoghaire, Farm Market (Harbour Plaza, Thurs 10.30am-4pm)	087 611 5016
Dun Laoghaire, Harbour Office (24 hours)	01 280 1130
Dun Laoghaire, National Maritime Museum, Haigh Terrace	01 280 0969
Dun Laoghaire, Tourist Information	1850 230 330
Leopardstown Racecourse	01 289 3607
Leopardstown, Farm Market (Fri 11am-7pm)	087 611 5016
Malahide, Malahide Castle & Demesne	01 846 2184
Malahide, Fry Model Railway (Malahide Castle)	01 846 3779
Malahide, Talbot Botanic Gardens (Malahide Castle)	01 846 2456
Malahide, Coffee shop (Malahide Castle)	01 846 3027
Naul (Fingal), Seamus Ennis Centre (Traditional Music)	01 802 0898
Rathfarnham, Marlay Demesne Gardens	01 493 7372
Sandycove, James Joyce Museum (Martello Tower)	01 280 9265
Sandyford, Fernhill Gardens (Himalayan species)	01 295 6000
Skerries, Skerries Mills - Working Windmills, Craft and Visitor Centre	01 849 5208
Tallaght, Community Arts Centre, Old Blessington Road	01 462 1501

Blackrock
RESTAURANT

Dali's Restaurant

63-65 Main Street Blackrock Co Dublin
Tel: 01 278 0660

Just across the road from the Library, this appealing restaurant has a loyal local clientèle and a reputation beyond the immediate area. There's a chic little bar just inside the door and a gently contemporary dining area, up a few steps, beyond. Menus are appealingly light and colourful, including some unusual dishes, a first course of potted rabbit terrine with toasted sourdough and apricot & mustard pickle, perhaps, or baby spinach with marinated girolles, garlic & truffle croutons, hard-boiled duck egg and pecorino shavings and there's an emphasis on fresh seafood. Daily fish specials are offered and, at lunchtime, might include excellent main courses like poached smoked coley with spring onion mash, poached egg & spinach hollandaise, or linguini with black clams. Dinner menus also offer plenty of seafood, such as roast fillet of monkfish, seared scallops and seared tuna, whilst meat lovers will enjoy panfried magret duck breast, roast guinea fowl or rack of lamb. Desserts are more than tempting - steamed peach pudding with almond ice cream, frozen strawberry and champagne terrine or warm chocolate and hazelnut pudding are all typical. There is also an excellent cheese board offering a selection of Irish and French. Good value for money, and honest cooking based on quality ingredients, has them beating a path to the door, so booking is essential, especially at weekends. Set lunch menus offer a choice of four or five dishes on each course and are particularly good value. Professional, efficient service and a good wine list complete an appealing package. Children welcome. Air conditioning. **Seats 65.** L Tue-Sat, 12-3, Sun L, 12.30-3.30pm; D Tue-Sat 6-10pm. Set L from about €15. A la carte L&D available; house wine about €20, sc discretionary except 10% on parties of 6+. Closed D Sun, all Mon, 25-27 Dec. Amex, Diners, MasterCard, Visa, Laser. **Directions:** Opposite Blackrock Library. ◊

Tonic

Blackrock
CAFÉ/BAR

5 Temple Road Blackrock Village Co Dublin **Tel: 01 288 7671**
mail@tonic.ie www.tonic.ie

This smart designer bar brings some welcome style to Blackrock village with its cool walnut woodwork, cube chairs, cream leather banquettes and artwork for sale on exhibition - all of which, plus a big screen upstairs, have made it the in place for the trendy young crowd. Informal menus are offered through the day - brunch, daytime and evening bistro - and there's a patio area for al fresco dining in fine weather; however, perhaps it's more a place to drop into for a drink in stylish surroundings. Toilets wheelchair accessible. **Seats 100.** Open 12am-12pm; food served all day 12-11, L12-4, D 4-11. Closed 25 Dec & Good Fri. Amex, MasterCard, Visa, Laser. **Directions:** Centre of Blackrock village. ◇

Daniel Finnegan

Dalkey
PUB

2 Sorrento Road Dalkey Co Dublin
Tel: 01 285 8505

This is a pub of great character and is much-loved by locals and visitors alike. It's comfortable and cosy, with wood panelling and traditional Irish seating in 'snugs', and the large extension built a few years ago has now 'blended in'. Food is served at lunchtime only - a full hot bar lunch, including starters such as baked Dalkey crab, brie fritters with apple coulis and main courses like roast stuffed pork steak, honey roast half duck and grilled cod steak, followed by traditional desserts like apple pie and lemon cheesecake. The fresh fish (from the harbour nearby) is excellent, the vegetables predictable but tasty and good value. No reservations - get there early to avoid a long wait. Carpark nearby. Bar food 12.30-3pm Mon-Sat. Closed 25 Dec, Good Fri & & New Year. Amex, Diners, MasterCard, Visa, Laser. **Directions:** Near Dalkey DART station. ◇

IN

Dalkey
WINE BAR

115-117 Coliemore Road Dalkey Co Dublin **Tel: 01 275 0007**
info@indalkey.ie www.indalkey.ie

This stylish contemporary café-bar in the centre of Dalkey has retained a special niche, offering something rather different from pubs and restaurants in the area. The atmosphere is relaxed and what you get here is informal dining in comfortable, pleasant surroundings: menus are offered for breakfast and lunch (including a 'mini' lunch of soup, warm open sandwich & small fried, at €7.95) as well as dinner, and there's a separate children's menu. Regular dishes range from the ubiquitous steak, and bistro dishes like lamb shank (deliciously tender) to crisp confit of duck; specialities include Kimchee prawns - fish is purchased daily from local markets - and an interesting (possibly unique) house speciality is home-raised Irish bison! Drinks include a fairly priced cocktail menu and there are some organic wines. **Seats 80** (+15 outdoors; private room 40); toilets wheelchair accessible; children welcome (high chair, children's menu, baby changing facilities); live piano jazz classics Thu - Sun 10pm-1am. Open 10 am-11pm (Fri & Sat to 1.30). Bar meals daily: 10-11. Meals Daily - L 12-4, D 5-10. Value L €7.95; value D Thu-Sun, 7-10pm, €19.95; set 2/3 course D €15.95/€21.95. Á la Carte L&D also available. Amex, Diners, MasterCard, Visa, Laser. **Directions:** At the end of Dalkey's main street, across from AIB bank.

Jaipur Restaurant

Dalkey
RESTAURANT

20 Castle Street Dalkey Co Dublin **Tel: 01 285 0552**
info@jaipur.ie www.jaipur.ie

féile bia This stylish south County Dublin branch of a small chain of highly-regarded progressive Indian restaurants (see entries under Dublin 2 and Malahide) is well-established as a favourite in the area. The trademark modern decor is a refreshing change from traditional Indian restaurants - warm colours send the right messages and it is a pleasing space. Menus offer an attractive combination of traditional and more creative dishes; Jaipur Jugalbandi, an assortment of five appetisers is a good choice for a group settling for a meal, to avoid indecision. Fresh and dried spices are directly imported but proprietor Asheesh Dewan and long-serving head chef Mahipal Rana are keen to make the most of Irish ingredients, notably organic Wicklow lamb braised in yoghurt and spices and speciality seafood dishes. Jaipur is a fine restaurant - and was the first ethnic restaurant in Ireland to

Georgina Campbell's Ireland

devise a wine list especially suited to spicy foods. Service is attentive and discreet. **Seats 70**; Air con; D daily, 5-11; Early D €22, 5-7; Set D from €30, also à la carte. House wine €18. Closed 25 Dec Amex, MasterCard, Visa, Laser. **Directions:** On Dalkey's main street.

Dalkey
RESTAURANT

Nosh

111 Coliemore Road Dalkey Co Dublin **Tel: 01 284 0666**
comments@nosh.ie www.nosh.ie

téite bia Samantha and Sacha Farrell's bright, contemporary restaurant is next to the famous Club Bar and, with its clean lines and lightwood furniture, no-nonsense menus and quality ingredients, it has a special place in the Dalkey dining scene. Paidraig Murphy took over as head chef in 2007 and continues the house style; his contemporary seasonal menus have a slight bias towards fish and vegetarian food, and change throughout the day: their great weekend brunch menu, which includes traditional Irish and buttermilk pancakes and a wide range of coffees and other drinks is very popular. For lunch there's some overlap from dishes on the Brunch menu and a dozen or so other choices, ranging up to the "Posh Nosh" daily special. In the evening, you might begin with a prawn starter and proceed to beer battered cod with home-made chips (a house speciality). Vegetarians are well looked after with dishes such as sweetcorn fritters with mixed bean ragoût. Desserts are home-made and there's a limited but well-chosen wine list, with a few half bottles. Not suitable for children after 8pm; wheelchair accessible; air conditioning. **Seats 45.** L Tue-Fri, 12-4 (Sat & Sun, Brunch 12-4); D Tue-Sun 6-10; value D €23, 6-7.45pm; also a la carte. House wine €19.50. Closed Mon, bank hols. MasterCard, Visa, Laser. **Directions:** End of Dalkey town, take left.

Dalkey
RESTAURANT/PUB

The Queen's Bar & Restaurant

12 Castle Street Dalkey Co Dublin **Tel: 01 285 4569**
queens@clubi.ie

The oldest pub in Dalkey, and also one of the oldest in Ireland, The Queen's was originally licensed to 'dispense liquor' as far back as 1745, and renovations and improvements in recent years have been done with due respect for the age and character of the premises. It's attractively done up, with dark wood, little alcoves and a raised level breaking up the space, and there's also a small section outside at the front to go if the weather's fine. Good bar fare is available and the more contemporary Queen's Restaurant is busy, but worth a wait: good food includes Shepherd's Pie and Lamb Shank among the house specials; there's a good selection of pastas and pizzas or try steak, chicken and burgers from the grill. A late evening drink in the outside front section is quiet and relaxed; earlier, it's lively, particularly in summer. Wheelchair accessible. **Restaurant Seats 70**; D daily from 6pm; early D 6-7.30. Bar menu Mon-Fri, 12-4 & 5-7.30; Sat 12-4; Sun 12.30-3.45. Closed 25 Dec & Good Fri. Amex, Diners, MasterCard, Visa, Laser. **Directions:** Centre of town, beside Heritage Centre. ◇

Dalkey
RESTAURANT

Ragazzi

109 Coliemore Road Dalkey Co Dublin **Tel: 01 284 7280**

Possibly Dublin's buzziest little bistro, this is the pizza place where everyone goes to have their spirits lifted by theatrical Italian waiters and great value. Lovely pastas, luscious bruschettas - but best of all the pizzas, renowned for their thin, crisp bases and scrumptious toppings. But it's the atmosphere that counts - every town should have a place like this. D served daily, 5.30-10.30pm. ◇

Dalkey
RESTAURANT

Thai House Restaurant

21 Railway Road Dalkey Co Dublin **Tel: 01 284 7304**
tony@thaihouse.ie www.thaihouse.ie

Established in 1997, Tony Ecock's bustling two-storey restaurant has earned a loyal following and head chef Wilai Khruekhcai has maintained a reputation for including dishes that do not pander too much to the western palate. In typical oriental style, a number of set menus are offered and there is also an extensive à la carte which offers a wider choice. After an aperitif in the wine bar/reception area, begin, perhaps, with the Thai House Special Starter Pack, a sampling plate of six starters, well-balanced in flavour and texture and including some vegetarian options; service can be under pressure at times, so it is a good plan to get your starters ordered promptly. After this you can relax and consider the options including authentic Thai soups and main courses which include a range of curries - a speciality is fresh monkfish dumplings in green curry sauce - and vegetarian dishes are listed separately. Groups of four can share a dessert platter. The wine list includes a page of house favourites and a Thai beer. Not suitable for children after 8pm. Air conditioning. **Seats 34.** D Tue-Sun. Closed Mon. Amex, Diners, MasterCard, Visa, Laser. **Directions:** 100 metres from Dalkey DART Station. ◇

Dublin Airport
HOTEL/RESTAURANT

Carlton Hotel Dublin Airport

Parkway House Old Airport Road Co Dublin **Tel: 01 866 7500**
info@carltondublinairport.com www.carltondublinairport.com

féile bia Although not actually in the airport complex, this purpose-built 4 star hotel is very close to it, and convenient to the M1 and M50 motorways and it is worth special consideration as, unlike most other hotels in the area, it aims to provide a dining experience (see Clouds restaurant below), rather than just offering food. Just 200 metres from the entrance to the airport, it's a new hotel and is especially suited to the business traveller and for conferences and meetings; the bedrooms and suites all have oversized beds and bathrobes, clothes press and complimentary broadband. There are 19 conference rooms (catering for up to 550 theatre style), fully-equipped with all the necessary ancillary technology including wired and wireless broadband, telephone and video conferencing and air conditioning.There is secure parking for 250 cars, and a shuttle to the airport door every 10 minutes. Conference/Banquets (500/300); Business centre, secretarial services, laptop-sized safes in bedrooms, free broadband wi/fi. **Rooms 100** (1 suite, 6 junior suites, 20 executive, 10 family, 13 ground floor, 7 for disabled); children welcome (under 12s free in parents' room, cots available free of charge); lift; all day room service. **Clouds at the Carlton:** The Carlton Hotel may be an ordinary looking building from the exterior but few locations can rival the stunning views from their rooftop restaurant. The dining room is decorated in a modern yet warm style which allows the dramatic views and smart clientèle to take centre stage. The highly regarded chef Patsy McGuirk has been a consultant since opening, and it shows in many ways, including detail; your meal begins with an amuse bouche (perhaps a tiny cup of celeriac soup with white truffle oil), for example, setting a high culinary tone from the outset. Menus are simply written and tend to be conservative, drawing on classic French and Irish influences - and rightly reflecting the coastal location with dishes such as Howth seafood chowder or delicious chilled crab cocktail with a Bloody Mary jelly. Main courses are smart versions of old favourites such as grilled fillet of Irish beef with button onions, wild mushroom ragout and chive mash, or (a well known Patsy McGuirk speciality) roast crispy duckling Grand Marnier with a potato and herb stuffing - and the unmissable Dover sole, simply served with parsley and lemon butter. Stylish desserts might include a gingerbread parfait with a sweet port wine reduction, and you'll find a good selection of Irish cheeses. An interesting wine list includes ten wines of the month and about a dozen half bottles. Besides good food and a panoramic view of the city, this aptly named restaurant also boasts one of the capital's highest smoking areas, with dramatic views of landing aircraft. Above-average informal fare is available elsewhere in the hotel, and includes a children's menu. **Seats 120** (private room, 60; outdoors, 40); pianist on Saturday evenings; children welcome before 8pm. D daily 6.30-9.30pm (6-9 on Sun), L Sun only, 12-3pm; set Sun L €29; house wine from €24.50; SC 10% on groups 8+; closed 24-26 Dec. Amex, MasterCard, Visa, Laser. **Directions:** Close to Dublin airport on the Swords/Santry road: M50 exit 4 (Ballymun) or M1 - Santry exit.

Dublin Airport
HOTEL

Clarion Hotel Dublin Airport

Dublin Airport Co Dublin **Tel: 01 808 0500**
info@clarionhoteldublinairport.com www.clarionhoteldublinairport.com

féile bia This large, comfortable hotel is right at the airport and has recently undergone extensive refurbishment. It makes an ideal meeting place and there is complimentary wifi in the lobby, bar and restaurant. Bedrooms all have TV and pay movies, and mini-bar; guests may use the ALSAA Leisure Complex swimming pool, gymnasium and sauna free of charge. Well-equipped meeting rooms/conference suites available for groups of up to 300. Courtesy bus to and from the airport terminal (24 hr). In line with other Clarion hotels, Kudos bar and restaurant offers lively informal food in attractive surroundings. Parking. Children welcome (Under 12s free in parents' room; cots available without charge). Wheelchair accessible. **Rooms 248** (15 executive rooms, 4 family rooms, 2 for disabled). Lift. 24 hour room service. Room rate about €250. Closed 24-25 Dec. Amex, Diners, MasterCard, Visa, Laser. **Directions:** In airport complex, on the right when entering airport. ◇

Dublin Airport
HOTEL

Radisson SAS Hotel Dublin Airport

Dublin Airport Co Dublin **Tel: 01 844 6000**
res@dubairport-gsh.com www.greatsouthernhotels.com

féile bia This spacious modern hotel in the airport complex is just two minutes drive from the main terminal building (with a coach service available). Rooms are all double-glazed and include a high proportion of executive rooms. It's a good choice for business guests and, should your flight be delayed, the large bar and restaurant on the ground floor could be a welcome place to pass the time. Conference/banqueting (450/300); video conferencing; business centre; secretarial service. Children welcome (under 10s free in parents' room; cots available free of charge). **Rooms 229** (2 suites, 3 junior suites, 116 executive rooms, 184 no-smoking, 2 rooms for disabled, 2 family rooms) Lifts. Room service (24 hr). Room rate about €270 (1 or 2 guests). Closed 24-25 Dec. Amex, Diners, MasterCard, Visa, Laser. **Directions:** Situated in airport complex. ◈

DUBLIN AIRPORT AREA

A number of new hotels have sprung up around Dublin airport recently, but they are not always as close as you might expect. **The Clarion** and **Radisson SAS** hotels are on site (see entries), and the following are in the locality. Budget accommodation is available at the **Tulip Inn** (01 895 7777; www.tulipinndublinairport.ie), and **Travelodge** (01 807 9400; www.travelodge.ie). Nearby hotels offering more extensive facilities and a higher level of service include: **Bewleys Hotel** (01 871 1000; www.bewleyshotels.com), **Carlton Dublin Airport Hotel** (see entry), **Crowne Plaza Hotel** (01 862 8888; www.cpdublin-airport.com), and **Hilton Dublin Airport** (01 866 1800; www.hilton.co.uk/dublinairport). **Roganstown Golf & Country Club Hotel** and **Belcamp Hutchinson** country house are also convenient to the airport (see entries). The nearest town is Swords, where you will find **Wrights cafe bar** (01 840 6760; bar food available) and **The Old Boro Pub** (01 895 7685), both centrally located, and you could eat at **Indie Spice** restaurant (01 807 7999; www.indiespicecafe.com), or the owner-chef run **Cookers** (01 8409911) in an area of the town known as Applewood Village. The attractive coastal town of Malahide is also convenient to Dublin airport, and offers a wide range of restaurants and bars (see entries). **WWW.IRELAND-GUIDE.COM FOR THE BEST PLACES TO EAT, DRINK & STAY**

DUN LAOGHAIRE

Dún Laoghaire is a seaside town and ferry port situated some 12 km south of Dublin city centre. The name derives from its founder, Laoghaire, a 5th century High King of Ireland, who chose the site as a sea base from which to carry out raids on Britain and France. The harbour is notable for its two granite piers - one of which is the busiest pier for leisure walking in Ireland - and is home to four yacht clubs. On the way into Dun Laoghaire, tucked away on Monkstown Crescent, is **Seagreen** (Tel: 0 1 2020130 www.seagreen.ie) a treasure trove store with modern furniture, distinctive artwork, fine fashion labels, luxury gifts - and **Ellen's Tea Rooms,** where a French chef cooks delicious homemade daytime food. And, nearby in Glasthule, **The Eagle House** (Glasthule Road; 01 280 4740) is a fine traditional establishment that is full of interest and a great local. The interior is dark, but has a fascinating collection of model boats, ships and other nautical bric-à-brac and is arranged in comfortably sized alcoves and 'snugs' on different levels. Bar meals, available at lunchtime and in the evening, can be very good. **WWW.IRELAND-GUIDE.COM FOR THE BEST PLACES TO EAT, DRINK & STAY**

Dun Laoghaire
RESTAURANT
😊 Ⓔ Ⓝ

Alexis Bar & Grill

17-18 Patrick Street Dun Laoghaire Co Dublin **Tel: 01 280 8872**
info@alexis.ie www.alexis.ie

Tucked away on Patrick Street, off Dun Laoghaire's main drag, huge glass windows allow passers-by a promising glimpse inside Alexis, the bright bistro owned by respected Dublin chef Alan O'Reilly and his brother Pat, and named after the great French chef and humanitarian Alexis Soyer, who visited Ireland in the mid-19th century and created the soup kitchens which provided wholesome food for the needy during the Famine. A warm, friendly welcome demonstrates the customer-friendly ethos of this southside newcomer, which has generously spaced tables, comfy banquettes and bentwood seats, delightful service and a menu which is as notable for very fair pricing as for its appeal to the tastebuds. An open kitchen runs along the back wall of the large open dining room, while a long tongue and groove bar makes a chic focal point, dispensing drinks and coffees. Much of the cooking is rustic French and Italian in origin and the menu doesn't differentiate between starters and mains (small portions of many dishes can be ordered). Admirable pride in quality ingredients is seen first in a menu that lists the provenance of key produce and that promise follows through on the plate in flavoursome, precise cooking: food is handsomely presented with meat and seafood dishes all expertly cooked and wonderfully fresh. A keenly priced wine list offers 12 wines by the glass. Great cooking, interested staff, attention to detail and (all too unusually for the Dublin area) great value make this an especially welcome addition to the Dun Laoghaire scene. Reservations required; toilets wheelchair accessible; children welcome; air conditioning. **Seats 90.** L

Tue-Fri 12.30-2.30, Sun 12.30-3; D Tue-Sun 5-10pm. L&D à la carte; house wine €20. Closed Mon, Bank Hols. MasterCard, Visa, Laser. **Directions:** Coming from Dun Laoghaire harbour - straight up Marine Road on to Patrick Street.

Dun Laoghaire
RESTAURANT/WINE BAR

Bodega Wine & Tapas

Pavilion Centre Dun Laoghaire Co Dublin
Tel: 01 284 2982

Formerly the Forty Foot bar and restaurant, this ultra-modern two-storey premises in the Pavilion Centre has recently changed hands, and is now part of the Jay Bourke/Stephen Pile empire - of the Eden, Market Bar and Café Bar Deli fame in partnership with Thomas Read. Although only open since July 2007, experienced chefs from Eden quickly succeeded in making this one of Dun Laoghaire's most popular venues. Seating is designed to impress, with huge windows allowing views over the harbour and Dublin Bay. The bar area has comfortable sofas around the central polished wood bar and you can eat in any part of the room, although the dining area at one end is the most comfortable option and has tables simply laid with good linen and cutlery and handsome, plain glasses. The outdoor terrace, particularly on a warm day, is a delight. The best of the Market Bar menu has been imported: Fish Pie, with smoked salmon, coley and haddock; chorizo stew with potatoes and peppers; and calamari with chilli mayo, accompanied by a basket of bread, are typical of the colourful, tasty and good value food offered. The tapas menu here has become the fashionable food of this area and, with attentive and well-informed staff and a pleasing ambience, it's not at all surprising that this place is so popular. Wines are international and reasonably priced. Toilets wheelchair accessible; Children welcome before 9pm (high chair, baby changing facilities); Bookings only available for groups 8+. Broadband wi/fi. **Seats 150** (private room, 100, outdoors, 60). Food is available daily from midday until 10pm (to 9pm Sun). Pub: normal hours, late bar Saturday and Sunday. Sc 10% on groups 8+. Closed 25 Dec, Good Fri. MasterCard, Visa. **Directions:** At Pavilion Centre.

Dun Laoghaire
RESTAURANT

Café Mao

The Pavilion Dun Laoghaire Co Dublin **Tel: 01 2148090**
dunlaoghaire@cafemao.com www.cafemao.com

This large, informal contemporary café-restaurant near the harbour is a sister of Café Mao at Dundrum Shopping Centre (see entry). It is run on the same lines, with the philosophy of providing simple, quick and healthy food, with youthful appeal, at a reasonable price - and there's always a good buzz. Dishes with nuts are highlighted on the menu, also chilli strength, low fat and vegetarian dishes. There are house specialities including Nasi Goreng, Malaysian chicken and five spiced chicken; daily specials are particularly good value, and there's a daily cake selection - e.g. cappuccino with walnut gateau, toffee & apple gateau, pecan pie & Mississippi mud pie - and an interesting drinks menu. It's a good place for brunch, with tables outside for fine weather. **Seats 120;** fully wheelchair accessible; children welcome until 7pm; large parties welcome. Open daily 12 - 11 (to 10 Sun); Early D about €15 5-7; Bookings accepted. Closed 25 Dec, Good Fri. MasterCard, Visa, Laser. **Directions:** Dun Laoghaire seafront, near station. ◊

Dun Laoghaire
RESTAURANT

Cavistons Seafood Restaurant

59 Glasthule Road Dun Laoghaire Co Dublin **Tel: 01 280 9245**
info@cavistons.com www.cavistons.com

Caviston's of Sandycove has long been a mecca for lovers of good food - here you will find everything that is wonderful, from organic vegetables to farmhouse cheeses, cooked meats to specialist oils and other exotic items. But it was always for fish and shellfish that Cavistons were especially renowned - even providing a collection of well-thumbed recipe books for on-the-spot reference. At their little restaurant next door, they serve an imaginative range of healthy seafood dishes influenced by various traditions and all washed down by a glass or two from a very tempting little wine list. Cavistons food is simple, colourful, perfectly cooked - it speaks volumes for how good seafood can be. Start with Cavistons smoked salmon plate, perhaps, or tasty panfried crab and sweetcorn cakes with red pepper mayonnaise, then follow with seared king scallops with a saffron and basil sauce - or a more traditional panfried haddock fillet with tartare sauce. Gorgeous desserts include timeless favourites like chocolate brownies with chocolate sauce & cream, or you can finish with a selection of Cavistons cheeses (they sell a great range in the shop). Don't expect bargain basement prices though - this may be a small lunch time restaurant but the prime ingredients are costly - and it's a class act. Children welcome. **Seats 28.** L 3 sittings: Tue-Fri - 12, 1.30 and 3pm, Sat 12, 1.45, 3.15pm A la carte. SC discretionary. Closed Sun, Mon & Christmas/New Year. Amex, Diners, MasterCard, Visa, Laser. **Directions:** Between Dun Laoghaire and Dalkey, 5 mins. walk from Glasthule DART station. ◇

Dun Laoghaire
RESTAURANT
Ⓝ

The Gastropub Company

6-7 Marine Road Dun Laoghaire Co Dublin **Tel: 01 214 5772**
info@thegastropub.ie www.thegastropubcompany.com

This new pub on Marine Road is one of Dun Laoghaire's busiest and its covered terrace is very lively during the day. The interior is spacious and welcoming, with wood - all of which is salvage - the primary feature: Floorboards came from 300-year-old beams that supported the Dublin docks before steel came along; the mahogany bar top is from a school laboratory - look hard enough and you can still see some scratched initials. The mirrored back bar also has a long history - it comes from the refurbished Hill 16 pub near Croke Park. There's a dedicated restaurant space at the back, opposite the open kitchen, where not only are the chefs working hard, but obviously enjoying what they do. The à la carte menu includes fish soup, goat's cheese tart or fried lamb's liver to start; to follow there's Wicklow lamb shank, slow cooked pork belly or rare steak for mains, as well as burgers and fried fish. Delicious desserts might include poached pear with ice cream, glazed lemon tart or sticky toffee pudding. Service is friendly, with just the right amount of attention, and the wine list includes a good selection available by the glass (and there's an Orange Muscat to accompany desserts). Alternatively, you can buy wine in the shop next door and pay just €8 corkage. Sunday lunch is unusual - a whole roast chicken, accompanied by the usual trimmings, is brought to the table and you carve it yourself. A good atmosphere and reasonable prices makes this a very family-friendly restaurant. MasterCard. **Directions:** On Marine Road, opposite the Pavilion. ◇

Dun Laoghaire
PUB

P. McCormack & Sons

67 Lr Mounttown Rd Dun Laoghaire Co Dublin
Tel: 01 280 5519

This fine pub (and 'emporium') has been run by the McCormack family since 1960. It's one of the neatest pubs around, especially now that the trees and shrubbery between the car park and an imaginative conservatory extension at the back of the pub have grown, so the car park is no longer visible. There is also nicely designed outdoor eating/drinking space between the car park and the conservatory; divided into two small areas, with large rectangular marble-topped tables and outdoor heaters, it is an appealing area. The main part of this well-run pub is full of traditional character, and bar food cooked to order includes fresh fish available on the day as well as classics like home-made hamburger (with mixed leaf salad, fries & a choice of toppings), hot sandwiches and salads. Evening menus offer tasty light dishes like warm crispy bacon and croûton salad, and steak sandwiches alongside more substantial dishes including a fish special, a 10 oz sirloin steak or pasta dishes with fresh parmesan. Not suitable for children after 9pm. Toilets wheelchair accessible. Bar food daily, 12-3 & 4-10. Closed 25 Dec, Good Fri. Amex, Diners, MasterCard, Visa, Laser. **Directions:** Near Dun Laoghaire at Monkstown end.

Dun Laoghaire
RESTAURANT
Ⓦ Ⓔ Ⓕ

Rasam

18-19 Glasthule Road Dun Laoghaire Co Dublin **Tel: 01 230 0600**
info@rasam.ie www.rasam.ie

Above The Eagle pub in Glasthule, this is an appealing restaurant, impressively decorated in dark teak, with traditional Balinese furnishings and generous, well-spaced tables. Rasam offers something different from other Indian restaurants, as the cuisine is lighter and more varied - the menu is laid out like a wine list, with the name of the dish and a brief (but clear) description, and the name of the region it comes from alongside the price. Two head chefs are from Bengali and Kerala regions, so the food reflects that as well as other regions. You might begin with samosas which are delightfully served; main courses might include a relatively simple Kori Gassi, which is a long-established dish at Rasam - chicken is simmered in a spicy masala of brown onions and tomatoes, and other meats are well represented - Pork Sobotel, is an aromatic example. Shakahari Thali, is a memorable mixture of five lentils, cooked with spinach and other vegetables, tempered with spice. Many special ingredients are used in the cooking here, including rare herbs and spices unique to the restaurant, all ground freshly each day. Everything is made on the premises - great accompaniments include delicious naan bread and chapatti, and there is an extensive range of side dishes. Indian restaurants are not known for their desserts but, in addition to some western dishes like millefeuille of strawberries & almonds and baked alaska, there's an interesting 'Falooda' kulfi with saffron & pistachio, which is served on a bed of sandalwood syrup - and an otherwise classic crème brulée is 'easternised' with rose petal flavouring. An extensive wine and drinks menu is thoughtfully selected for compatibility with Indian food, and solicitous staff ensure that everything is as it should be. All round, for a great Indian dining experience, Rasam has earned its place right at the top of the league. *Rasam was our Ethnic Restaurant of the Year, 2007. Children welcome. **Seats 75.** Reservations required; D daily, 5.30-11.30 (Sun to 11); Early D €21.95, 5.30-6.30, Set 4 course D €44.95, also a la carte. Closed 25-26 Dec, Good Fri. MasterCard, Visa, Laser. **Directions:** Over The Eagle pub.

Dun Laoghaire
RESTAURANT
Ⓝ

Real Gourmet Burger

The Pavilion Dun Laoghaire Co Dublin **Tel: 01 284 6568**
info@realgourmetburger.ie www.realgourmetburger.ie

With burgers the coming thing on the casual dining scene at the moment, smart informal restaurants specialising in this much-maligned dish are among the most noticeable new arrivals in Dublin this year. And, with its handsome lean lined room and speciality organic burgers, this recent arrival has opened up the quality options for eating out casually in the Dun Laoghaire area, especially for families looking for quality. The range of burgers offered includes beef, lamb, venison and chicken and there are options for vegetarians and children, plus simple side orders of salad or chips. All burgers are cooked medium or well done, due to health regulations which is fine for some, especially chicken, but this requirement is always a disappointment for those who like to sink their teeth into a real beef-burger that's pink and juicy in the middle No fault of the restaurant, however, and they're doing a great job. Service is an especially high point here too, and it's very family-friendly. **Directions:** In the Pavilion in Dun Laoghaire. ◊

Dun Laoghaire
HOTEL

Rochestown Lodge Hotel

Rochestown Avenue Dun Laoghaire Co Dublin **Tel: 01 285 3555**
info@rochestownlodge.com www.rochestownhotel.com

Well set back from the busy road, this modern hotel has a café-bar alongside it with tables outside, giving it a welcoming feeling and, although tables may seem rather close to the parking area, there should not be not too many cars at the door as there is an underground car park. A large, stylishly furnished reception area sets the tone for bright, spacious public areas and comfortable guestrooms - which offer a range of options from family rooms to junior and executive suites, and with power showers and internet access, they are well set up for business guests. Good leisure facilities include an air conditioned gym, 15m heated pool, hydro therapy pool, steam room and sauna - and a luxurious new spa, 'Replenish', which offers a unique range of therapies. There's an intimate Snug bar, and menus in the minimalist café-bar offer a variety of steaks and a balanced range of seafood, poultry and meats. Underground parking (complimentary); wheelchair accessible. **Rooms 90.** Standard B&B room rack rate €140 per night. Café Bar food opened Mon-Fri, 5.30-9.30pm, Sat, 12-3pm & 5.30-9.30pm, Sun 12-9.30pm. Replenish Spa opening hours. Mon-Fri, 10am-8pm, Sat 9am-6pm, Sun 10am-6pm. ◊

Dun Laoghaire
HOTEL
Ⓝ

Royal Marine Hotel

Marine Road Dun Laoghaire Co Dublin
Tel: 01 280 1911

Having been closed for some four years, the Royal Marine Hotel in Dun Laoghaire re-opened its doors to the public shortly before we went to press. The original Victorian building has been restored to its former glory, and The Dun Laoghaire Historical Society are very happy with all the refurbishments. New buildings on each side house conference facilities on the right, and very comfortable accommodation on the left. About a third (82) of the bedrooms are in the original building, the rest in the new area; all are air conditioned, spacious and comfortable, with double quilted mattress and flat screen tv among the features. Many of the rooms have wonderful views over the harbour and Dublin Bay, the 52 executive suites have balconies and there are family rooms available (connecting doors). Now styled as a conference, destination and leisure spa, it boasts some very welcome new facilities, combining well with the traditional warmth and friendliness that has always been present in this landmark hotel. The hotel has a restaurant, The Dune and two bars - the bright and airy Pavilion at the front and the Hardy, with a good cocktail menu, at the back. At the time of the Guide's visit, the hotel had only recently re-opened and was still a work in progress; the food side of the operation, in particular, seemed to be having teething problems and it would not be fair to make a judgment until they have settled in. The main entrance has traditionally been from Marine Road but, when all outside work is completed, a new entrance from the coast road will sweep past the landscaped gardens and band-stand to the imposing main hotel porch. A spa, with 9 treatment rooms, a hydrotherapy bath and a hammam is planned. Conference/banqueting 800/550. **Rooms 228.** Amex, Diners, MasterCard, Visa, Laser. **Directions:** Town centre, 200 yards from ferry terminal. ◇

Dun Laoghaire | **Tribes**
RESTAURANT | 57a Glasthule Road Glasthule Dun Laoghaire Co Dublin
Tel: 01 236 5971

Proprietor-chef Karl Whelan aims to offer top quality at reasonable prices at this appealing neighbour-hood restaurant, something that attracted attention from the outset. It's a pleasing restaurant, modern but not too sharp-edged, with comfortable high-backed leather chairs and warm-toned lampshades over some of the tables, softening the lighting. Lunch menus offer wholesome down to earth dishes like baked fish with colcannon or steak sandwiches, and homely puddings; on evening menus, the tone gears up and it becomes a more elegant experience, with more refined cooking and a sense of occa-sion. Staff are pleasant, helpful and efficient, it's an enjoyable place to be and prices are reasonable which is just what a good neighbourhood restaurant should be. An asset to the area. *Valaparaiso (01 280 1992), a popular Spanish/Mediterranean restaurant over Goggins pub in Monkstown, is a sister restaurant. Children welcome; **Seats 60** (outdoors, 10); air conditioning; L Mon-Sun, 12.30-4pm, D Mon-Sun, 5.30-10 (from 6pm Sat); house wine €19; SC 10%. Closed 25-26 Dec, 1 Jan, Good Fri. Amex, MasterCard, Visa, Laser. **Directions:** Just past Dun Laoghaire heading South. ◇

Glencullen | **Johnnie Fox's Pub**
CHARACTER PUB | Glencullen Co Dublin **Tel: 01 295 8911**
info@jfp.ie www.jfp.ie

Nestling in an attractive wooded hamlet in the Dublin Mountains, south of Dublin city, this popular pub dates back to the eighteenth century and has numerous claims to fame, including the fact that Daniel O'Connell was once a regular, apparently, and it's "undoubtedly" the highest pub in the land. A warm, friendly and generally well run place, just about equally famous for its food, the "Famous Seafood Kitchen", which can be enjoyable, and its music "Famous Hooley Nights" (booking advisable). Unlike so many superficially similar pubs, it's also real. Kitsch, perhaps, but the rickety old furniture is real, the dust is real and there is a turf or log fire at every turn. It's a pleasant place to drop into at quieter times too, if you're walking in the hills or just loafing around, and Dubliners find it an amusing place to take visitors from abroad. Recommended as an unusual outing rather than a meal out, but reservations are recommended if you wish to eat. Own parking. Children welcome (under supervision, not after 7.30pm). Traditional Irish music and dancing. Reservations recommended for food. Own parking. Children welcome (under supervision, not after 7.30pm). Traditional Irish music and dancing. **Seats 352** (private room, 55, outdoor 60). Open daily, food 12.30-9.30; all menus à la carte, house wine 19.50. No SC. Closed 24-25 Dec & Good Fri. Amex, Diners, MasterCard, Visa, Laser. **Directions:** In Dublin Mountains, 30 minutes drive from Dublin city centre. 5 mins from junction 15 of M50.

HOWTH

The fishing port of Howth is easily accessible by DART from Dublin, and is an interesting place to wander around. The fish shops along the west pier attract a loyal clientèle, and for many a year it's been a tradi-tion to come out from town after work on a Thursday to buy fish for the fast day on Friday - while that is largely a thing of the past, the shops still stay open later on Thursday evenings, which gives the place a special buzz in summer, when people stay on for a walk around the harbour or a bite to eat before going home. There is a lengthy beach that stretches as far as Sutton and there is also a spectacular cliff top walk around the peninsula that overlooks Dublin Bay - this should not be missed on a fine day (at the top of the hill the popular **Summit Inn** (01 832 4615) provides a good stop off point for a drink and/or

a bite to eat). The area is also well known as being home to Ireland's largest public golfing complex in Deer Park; this is also home to a castle and a lovely hill walk amongst the famous Rhodendron gardens, the spectacular sea and coastal views from the top are breathtaking and you can even see as far as the Mountains of Mourne in Northern Ireland on a clear day. A **Farmers' & Fishermen's Market** is held on the pier every Sunday, and there are several interesting food shops around the village too: up in the village, **Baily Wines** (01 832 2394) is not only an interesting owner-run wine shop but also offers a carefully selected choice of deli products, including some of the finest Irish artisan foods. Then up beside the church, there's **Main Street Flowers & Country Market** (01 839 5575) for flowers, fresh produce and some specialist groceries. On the harbour front, is **Casa Pasta** (01 839 3823), known for its great atmosphere and inexpensive food appealing to all age groups. There are a few ethnic restaurants: **Lemongrass** (01 832 4443) above the impressive and popular **Findlaters Bar**, the long-established **El Paso** (01 832 3334) and a stylish Indian, **The Village Restaurant** (01 832 0444), which are all on the front. Also on the harbour front you will find the **Waterside Bar** and the more traditional **Wheelhouse Restaurant** (01 839 0555) which is known for its steaks. Up in Howth village **Ella** (seen entry) is a chic restaurant/wine bar and **Cibo** (01 839 6344) offers ingredients-led all day food. For accommodation: the village centre **Baily Hotel** (01 832 2691; www.baily.com) is under energetic young management and has been re-styled as a boutique hotel (the cool **Bá Mizu** next door is attached to the hotel).
WWW.IRELAND-GUIDE.COM FOR THE BEST PLACES TO EAT, DRINK & STAY

Howth   Abbey Tavern
RESTAURANT/PUB   Abbey Street Howth Co Dublin **Tel: 01 839 0307**
                                              info@abbeytavern.ie www.abbeytavern.ie

Just 50 yards up from the harbour, part of this famous pub dates back to the 15th century, when it was built as a seminary for the local monks. Currently owned by James and Eithne Scott-Lennon, this well-run and immaculately maintained pub retains authentic features including open turf fires, original stone walls, flagged floors and gas lights. In 1960 the Abbey started to lay on entertainment and this has brought the tavern its fame: the format is a traditional 5-course dinner followed by traditional Irish music. It's on every night but booking is essential, especially in high season. Daytime food is offered in the bar but, in the Guide's recent experience, the evening meals served upstairs in The Abbot are better. This atmospheric dining room is one of Dublin's longest-established restaurants, dating right back to 1956 and, with open fires and natural stone walls, it has character and a welcoming ambience; fresh fish is a speciality, but menus are not long and everything offered should be wholesome and enjoyable in a homely style that suits the surroundings. **Seats 70** (private room, 40). Reservations required. Air conditioning. L&D 12-3 / 7-10 Tue-Sat, (Bar Sun L 12.30 - 4); Set D 2/3 course €33/38, also à la carte, house wine €18. SC discretionary. Children welcome; carpark on harbour. Restaurant closed Sun, Mon; establishment closed 25 Dec & Good Fri. Amex, Diners, MasterCard, Visa, Laser. **Directions:** 15km (9 m) from Dublin, in the centre of Howth. ◇

Howth   Aqua Restaurant
RESTAURANT   1 West Pier Howth Co Dublin **Tel: 01 8320 690 / 1850 34 64 64**
                                                dine@aqua.ie www.aqua.ie

Previously a yacht club, this is now a fine contemporary restaurant with plenty of window tables to take advantage of sea views westwards, towards Malahide, and take in the island of Ireland's Eye to the north. What was once a snooker room is now a characterful bar with a unique blend of original features and modern additions - with an open fire and comfortable seating, it has retained a cosy, clubby atmosphere and is a lovely place to relax before or after your meal. The restaurant is a large, bright room with white-clothed tables set up smartly, comfortable highback chairs and subtle decor inspired by the history of the building and maritime themes constantly evolving, it is a source of pleasure to regular guests who frequently notice small changes. The kitchen is behind a glass screen, so you can see head chef Tom Walsh and his team of chefs at work, adding to the interest of a meal. The style of cooking is strong, simple and modern; given the location, seafood is the natural choice but rib-eye beef is also a speciality. Menus offer a pleasing repertoire - deep-fried calamari on spiced tomato sauce with warm pesto; a starter salad of rocket with red onion, crisp Parma ham & fresh parmesan shavings topped with poached egg & sweet balsamic dressing; Aqua Fish & Chips; good pasta dishes and, although choices are restricted, the lunch and early dinner menus offer very good value and are understandably popular with the loyal local clientèle, who also love the jazz lunch on Sundays. The waterside location, well-sourced ingredients, good cooking and service all make dining at Aqua a pleasure; à la carte menus are pricey, but offer much wider choice of dishes - the value of the set menus keeps people going back. **Seats 80.** L Tue-Sun, 12.30-3pm (to 4pm Sun); D Tue-Sun 5.30-10.30, Sun 6.30-9.30; L Sun. Early D €29.95 (5.30-7), Set Sun L €29.95. Also à la carte. Live jazz Sun L. House wine €21.95, SC 10% on groups 6+. Closed Mon L, 25-26 Dec, Good Fri. Amex, MasterCard, Visa, Laser * Wheelchair accessible from summer 07. **Directions:** Left along pier after Howth DART Station.

Howth Deep

RESTAURANT 12 West Pier Howth Co Dublin

 **Tel 01 806 3921**

Housed in a handsome stone building on Howth's West Pier, Deep is a fresh dining space that's bright, modern and cosy. The original dining room, with its sloping tongue and groove ceiling and large mirrors is simple and atmospheric while the adjoining room next door is newer, showier and shinier. The menu has a seafood bias, with a mix of imported and local fish and shellfish, all simply and attractively prepared. Excellent signature dishes, like wafer thin calamari with lime aioli or fish and chips using Tiger Beer batter, deserve their regular billings on the appealing menu. Desserts are the usual suspects and are written on a blackboard that staff have to drag around the restaurant somewhat cumbersomely. Staff could be better informed, and service a little tighter, but Deep's cooking and relaxed atmosphere ensures diners a pleasant experience. **Seats 90** (private room; 40); children welcome before 6pm; air conditioning. Open for L&D Tue-Sun, L 12.30-4pm, D 5.30pm-9.30pm (last sitting). Early D €29.95, Tue-Sat 5.30-6.30 pm (to 7pm Tue-Thurs); house wine €19.95; SC 10% on groups 6+. Closed Mon (open Bank Hol Mons), Good Fri, 25-26 Dec. MasterCard, Visa, Laser. **Directions:** Left along pier after Howth DART Station.

Howth Ella

RESTAURANT/WINE BAR 7 Main Street Howth Co Dublin

Tel 01 839 6264

Aoife Healy's chic little restaurant and wine bar is in the centre of Howth village, just across from the Baily Hotel, and it has a loyal following of local diners who enjoy the relaxed, intimate atmosphere, consistently good cooking and very obliging staff who always want to be sure that everyone is enjoying their meal to the full. Although plenty of seafood is offered (and seafood cooking is accomplished) Ella offers a good range of other foods - perhaps more so than other restaurants in the area; Pork Fillet wrapped in Prosciutto, with Calvados jus is atypically tempting example. Cooking is kept pleasingly simple and there's an emphasis on fresh local foods, with suppliers credited on the menu of (fish and seafood from Wrights of Howth, Dorans & Nicky's Plaice, and meats and poultry from Ray Collier butchers, just a couple of doors away). Long opening hours make this a great neighbourhood restaurant, and an early dinner menu offers especially good value. Not suitable for children after 8pm. **Seats 32.** Reservations accepted. Toilets wheelchair accessible. Open Mon- Sat L 12.45-2.45; D 6-10. Set L €17, early D €25 (6-7). Also à la carte. Closed Sun, 1 Jan - 10 Jan. MasterCard, Visa, Laser. **Directions:** On the main street - opposite the Baily Hotel.

Howth King Sitric Fish Restaurant & Accommodation

RESTAURANT WITH ROOMS East Pier Howth Co Dublin **Tel: 01 832 5235**

info@kingsitric.ie www.kingsitric.ie

Named after an 11th century Norse King of Dublin who had close links with Howth, Aidan and Joan MacManus' striking harbourside establishment is one of Dublin's longest established fine dining restaurants. The bright and airy first floor restaurant takes full advantage of the harbour views, especially enjoyable on summer evenings. From this East Pier site, chef-patron Aidan can keep an eye on his lobster pots on one side and the fishing boats coming into harbour on the other. Informative notes on menu covers state the restaurant's commitment to local quality produce - and gives a listing of Irish fish in six languages. Specialities worth travelling for include a luscious red velvet crab bisque, and classics such as sole meunière and Dublin lawyer. In winter, lovers of game are well looked after and farmhouse cheeses and desserts are always worth leaving room for. Aidan MacManus oversees one of the country's finest wine lists, with strengths in Chablis, Burgundy and Alsace, with the special feature of a temperature controlled wine cellar on the ground floor. The house wine is outstanding for both quality and value, and a perfect match for delicious fish cooking. Aidan and Joan MacManus work hard to keep fine dining prices accessible - lunch is especially good value, also their Special Value Menu (D Mon-Thu, no time restriction). The King Sitric was the Guide's Seafood Restaurant of the Year in 2006, and received the Wine List of the Year Award in 2001; the restaurant operates a Food & Wine Club off-season. Banqueting (65). **Seats 65** (private room, 28). Air conditioning. L Mon-Sat,12.30-2.15; D Mon-Sat, 6.30-10. Set L from €30. 'Value' D €35/40 (Mon-Thu evening all year, no time restrictions); 4-course Set D €55; also à la carte; house wine from €23; SC discretionary (12.5% parties 8+). Restaurant closed Sun, bank hols. **Accommodation:** There are eight lovely rooms, all with sea views and individually designed bathrooms. **Rooms 8** (2 superior, 1 family room, 3 ground floor, all no-smoking). B&B from €72.50 pps, ss €32.50; children welcome (under 12s free in parents' room, cots available free of charge; baby sitting arranged); limited room service. Amex, MasterCard, Visa, Laser. **Directions:** Far end of the harbour front, facing the east pier.

Howth
RESTAURANT

The Oar House

8 West Pier Howth Co Dublin
Tel 01 839 4562

Although only open a year, the nautically-themed interior of The Oar House - an old smoke house on Howth's West Pier - has a lived-in feel that makes you believe it's been sating diners for decades. A sister restaurant to the ever-popular Casa Pasta on the harbour front, the corrugated roof, fishing nets, buoys, old sailing masts and instruments give it an atmosphere that's at once vibrant and welcoming. Tables are dressed with paper cloths and the casual vibe makes it extremely relaxing and child-friendly. A vast menu features every manner of seafood, from chowder to shellfish to fish pie (many of which can be ordered as tapas) and is supplemented by a long list of daily specials written up on big boards. From grilled sardines to baked monkfish, or maybe succulent scampi to seafood platters everything is simply and cleverly prepared in the bustling open kitchen. Caring service, big portions, good desserts and a choice setting make this place a real treasure for fish fans. Children welcome (high chair; baby changing facilities); parking outside on pier. **Seats 50** (outdoors, 20); reservations recommended; open all day 12.30-10.30 (to 10pm Sun). Value L €22, 3-6pm; house wine €19. Closed Good Fri, 25 Dec. Amex, MasterCard, Visa, Laser. **Directions:** On the West Pier next to Doran's fish shop

---

Howth/Sutton Area
HOTEL

Marine Hotel

Sutton Cross **Tel: 01 839 0000**
info@marinehotel.ie www.marinehotel.ie

Well-located on the sea side of a busy junction, this attractive hotel has ample car parking in front and a lawn reaching down to the foreshore at the rear. Public areas give a good impression: a smart foyer and adjacent bar, an informal conservatory style seating area overlooking the garden and a well-appointed restaurant. Bedrooms, some of which have sea views, have recently been refurbished. A popular venue for conferences and social gatherings, especially weddings, the Marine is also the only hotel in this area providing for the business guest. Business centre; secretarial services. Conference/banqueting (200/190). Golf nearby. Garden. Children welcome (under 3 free in parents' room; cots available without charge). No pets. **Rooms 48** (1 junior suite, 6 shower only, 31 executive rooms, 12 no-smoking, 2 disabled). Lift. Limited room service. B&B about €90 pps, ss about €30. Meridian Restaurant: L&D daily; bar meals available, 5-8pm daily. Closed 25-26 Dec. Amex, Diners, MasterCard, Visa, Laser. **Directions:** Take coast road towards Howth from city at Sutton Cross. ◊

Killiney
HOTEL

Fitzpatrick Castle Hotel Dublin

Killiney Co Dublin **Tel: 01 230 5400**
jenna.shortall@fitzpatricks.com www.fitzpatrickshotels.com

Located in the fashionable suburb of Killiney, this imposing castellated mansion overlooking Dublin Bay dates back to 1741. It is surrounded by landscaped gardens and, despite its size and grand style, has a relaxed atmosphere. Spacious bedrooms combine old-world charm with modern facilities, and a fitness centre has a 22 metre pool, jacuzzi, spa and relaxation deck. Although perhaps best known as a leading conference and function venue, Fitzpatrick's also caters especially well for business guests and 'The Crown Club', on the 5th floor functions as a 'hotel within a hotel', offering pre-arranged private transfer from the airport and a wide range of facilities for business guests. Five championship golf courses, including Druid's Glen, are nearby. Garden. Lift. **Rooms 113.** Room rate about €130. Closed 24-26 Dec. Amex, Diners, MasterCard, Visa, Laser. **Directions:** Take M50 from the airport, follow signs for Dun Laoghaire ferry port; south to Dalkey - top of Killiney hill. ◊

Leixlip
HOTEL/RESTAURANT
R R R

Becketts Country House Hotel

Cooldrinagh House Leixlip Co Dublin
Tel: 01 624 7040

A handsome house on the County Dublin side of the river that divides Leixlip, this house was once the home of Samuel Beckett's mother and it is now an unusual hotel, offering a personalised service for business guests: from the moment you arrive, a butler looks after all your needs, whether it be dining, laundry, limousine facilities or tailored requirements for meetings or conferences. Imaginatively converted to its present use, luxurious accommodation includes four boardroom suites and six executive suites, all furnished to a high standard in a lively contemporary style. All have a workstation equipped for computers, including modem/Internet connection and audio visual equipment, private fax machines etc. are also available on request. Public areas, including a bar and an attractive modern restaurant, have a far less business-like atmosphere. Cooldrinagh House overlooks the Eddie Hackett-designed Leixlip golf course, for which golf tee-off times may be booked in advance. Conference/banqueting (350/250) Business centre/secretarial services. Golf. Wheelchair accessible. No pets. **Rooms 10** (4 suites, 6 executive rooms) B&B from about €75. Open all year except Christmas. **Restaurant:** Atmosphere is the trump card in this stylish restaurant, with its stone walls, old wooden floors and soft lighting - and an exceptionally warm and genuine welcome. Pristine white tablecloths, gleaming silverware and glasses, and candlelit tables create a romantic atmosphere. Arriving guests are shown to their table promptly, and menus quickly follow, along with a basket of home-made breads. The à la carte - which is very expensive - is available every night (the signature dish is Beckett's Aromatic Duck, with sultana, ginger & sage stuffing, and classic orange sauce), but it is worth getting here in time for the early dinner, which offers great value. An impressive range of wines (seen across the back wall as you enter the restaurant) is another attractive feature - and all this, plus the warm and efficient service that is part of the charm at Beckett's, ensures a strong local following, so booking is advisable. **Seats 130.** L Mon-Fri 12.30-2.15 & Sun 12.30-6; D daily: Early D Mon-Fri 6-7.30, €27.50; a la carte D daily 6-10. Closed L Sat. Amex, Diners, MasterCard, Visa. **Directions:** Take N4, turn off at Spa Hotel, next left after Springfield Hotel. ◇

Lucan
PUB
N R R R

Courtney's Pub

1 Main Street Lucan Village Co Dublin **Tel: 01 628 0351**
info@courtneyslounge.com www.courtneyslounge.com

The thatched roof, old-fashioned windows and hanging baskets of Courtney's Bar attract customers in and inside is every bit as pleasant. Comfortable seating, an optional dining area and friendly staff make eating here a pleasure. Bar food includes steak sandwich, golfer's grill as well as a selection of salads including a very good Cajun Chicken Caesar. It's all reasonably priced and available from 12.30pm to 9pm. Outdoors at the back, there is a pretty terrace on two levels, within sound if not sight of the Griffeen river. Upstairs is a popular restaurant, Dukes (as in John Wayne), with dishes such as beef, monkfish and duck. ◇

Lucan
HOTEL
R R R

Finnstown Country House Hotel

Newcastle Road Lucan Co Dublin **Tel: 01 601 0700**
manager@finnstown-hotel.ie www.finnstown-hotel.ie

Approached by a long tree-lined driveway, this fine old manor house is set in 45 acres of woodland and (despite a large, blocky extension), is full of charm. It may not be immediately obvious where the hotel reception is, but an open fire in the foyer sets a welcoming tone and all of the large, well-proportioned reception rooms - drawing room, restaurant, bar - are elegantly furnished in a traditional style well-suited to the house. Although quite grand, there is a comfortable lived-in feeling throughout. Bedrooms vary and include some studio suites, with a small fridge and toaster in addition to the standard tea/coffee making facilities; although most rooms have good facilities including full bathrooms (with bath and shower), some are a little dated, and the view can be disappointing if you are looking over the extension - and light sleepers should ensure a quiet room is allocated if there is a wedding or other function taking place. Residential golf breaks are a speciality. Conference/banqueting (300). Leisure centre; swimming pool; tennis. Children welcome (Under 3s free in parents' room; cots available without charge, baby sitting arranged). Pets permitted. Parking (200). Wheelchair accessible. *The hotel came into new ownership just before the guide went to press, so changes may be expected. **Rooms 77** (28 executive, 20 family, 10 no-smoking, 1 for disabled). B&B €65, ss €45. Limited room service. Closed Christmas. **The Dining Room:** As in the rest of the house, the decor of this comfortable room, is pleasantly quirky - and, with good lighting and piano playing, the atmosphere is relaxing. Rather small tables are nicely set up with fresh flowers, and menus are not over-ambitious, offering about five choices on each course; most are familiar but there are may be some surprises, and what arrives on the plate is far from the average hotel meal: quality ingredients are used and down to earth cooking has the emphasis on flavour - and food is attractively presented without ostentation, all making for an enjoyable meal that is also good value for money. **Seats 100** (private room, 30). L daily 12.30-2.30pm (Sun 1-6pm); D Mon-Sat 7.30-9.30; set L €29.95. set D, €42. L&D also à la carte. House wine €21.50. House closed Christmas. *Long term accommodation also available in apartment suites. Amex, Diners, MasterCard, Visa, Laser. **Directions:** Off main Dublin-Galway Road (N4): take exit for Newcastle off dual carriageway.

Lucan   # La Banca
RESTAURANT   Main Street Lucan Village Co Dublin **Tel: 01 628 2400**
`R` `R` `R`   www.labanca.ie

This pleasant neighbourhood restaurant off Lucan's winding main street is well positioned near the Italian Embassy. Moving swiftly through the dark and distinctly tatty entrance area, you will be pleasantly surprised by a bright, modern and well presented restaurant, where arriving guests are welcomed by friendly Italian staff who show you to your table promptly and present a comprehensive Italian menu, good bread and gorgeous garlic infused olive oil. A wide choice of antipasti dishes includes a delicious shared plate, a sociable choice if dining out with friends. Main course choices include all the Italian staples, including pasta dishes like cannelloni alla carne and pizzas. Fish is also well represented in perfectly cooked sea bass and swordfish. As is often the case in Italian restaurants, service is good, with friendly Italian waiters always ready to be of assistance. *The Vault Bar is a small downstairs area (you have to brave the dark entrance area again to reach it or the toilets); it opens on Friday & Saturday nights and is available for private parties. Live music in Vault Bar Fri-Sat night. Opening hours Tue-Sat 4-10.30pm, Sun 2-9.30pm. ◊

`R`   # MALAHIDE

The attractive coastal town of Malahide is only 15 minutes from the airport, and about 25 minutes into Dublin city by frequent direct trains (DART). There's no shortage of things to do: championship golf includes two courses in **Portmarnock**, the Christy O'Connor-designed **Roganstown GC** in nearby Swords, and **The Island at Donabate**, and there's good walking at Malahide and Portmarnock beaches, and **Malahide Castle** (01 846 2184), where you'll also find the **Fry Model Railway** and and tea rooms, there is extensive parkland and the **Talbot Botanic Gardens** - and the castle hosts concerts in the summer months. Plentiful accommodation includes the ever-growing **Grand Hotel** (01 845 0000; www.thegrand.ie), with every facility; there's quality shopping too and a **Farmers' Market** every Saturday - and the town is alive with bars, cafés and restaurants. In New Street, **Gibneys** pub (01 845 0863) is a first port of call for many; this characterful place has a large beer garden at the back and offers contemporary bar food and an interesting wine selection (including a blackboard menu by the glass); next door is their award-winning wine shop & off-licence. In a first floor premises on The Green, and overlooking the marina area, the relaxed **Ciao Ristorante** (01 845 1233) can claim one of the best views in town - rivalled perhaps by **Cruzzo Bar & Restaurant** (01 845 0602; www.cruzzo.ie): right at the marina, it's a stylish venue on two levels and, although both food and service have their ups and downs, it can be very enjoyable - and the location always gives a sense of occasion. The highly-regarded Indian restaurant **Kinara** (see entry) is also planning to open in Malahide soon.

WWW.IRELAND-GUIDE.COM FOR THE BEST PLACES TO EAT, DRINK & STAY

Malahide   # Bon Appetit
RESTAURANT/CAFÉ   9 St James Terrace Malahide Co Dublin **Tel: 01 8450 314**
                                   info@bonappetit.ie www.bonappetit.ie

 After training in many of London's top Michelin-starred restaurants, talented young chef Oliver Dunne returned to Ireland to make his name at Mint in Ranelagh. After three years there he made the move to Malahide in 2006 to take over the renowned Bon Appetit from Patsy McGuirk, one of Ireland's most accomplished chefs. Following a complete refit of the four-storey Georgian building, in a terrace close to the sea, Dunne has chosen the first floor for his fine dining restaurant. A sensual palette of muted metallics and moody greens creates a real sense of luxury in two classically proportioned adjoining rooms. Silk lined walls, contemporary chandeliers, cream carver chairs, huge mirrors, fresh flowers and generous linen-draped tables all set the tone for Dunne's inspired cuisine. Favouring luxury ingredients like quail, guinea fowl, foie gras and duck perhaps alongside turbot, lobster, Dublin Bay prawns and scallops, each dish is paired with cleverly considered accompaniments. Cooking is highly sophisticated, each plate served as a tiny work of art, with Dunne using classic touches like an amuse bouche, pre-dessert and petit fours to further showcase his originality. The wine list is lengthy, with some value to be found, and service here is formal, but warm and relaxing. The chic ground floor cocktail bar is a nice space for digestifs, or a pleasant way to kick start an evening in one of Dublin's most exciting new restaurants. Downstairs, **Café Bon** is an informal but equally stylish operation in the basement, with longer opening hours. Here head chef Andy Turner turns out smart modern dishes - quail and black pudding with poached egg on top, foie gras parfait, upscale steaks; it's much more accessible than the fine dining restaurant and the early bird offers good value. **Bon Appetit:** Children welcome (high chair); pianist at the weekend, air conditioning. **Seats 100** (private room, 40); D daily 6-10.30pm (to 9.30 Sun); L Sun only, 12-3.30pm; early D €25 6-7pm; set 2/3 course D, €35/42; Gourmet Menu €85; also a la carte; house wine €22; SC 10% on groups 8+. Closed 1st week Jan, 1st two weeks Aug. Amex, Diners, MasterCard, Visa, Laser. **Directions:** Coming from Dublin go through the lights in the centre of Malahide and turn left into St James's Terrace at Malahide Garda Station.

Malahide   Cape Greko
RESTAURANT   Unit 1 First Floor New Street Malahide Co Dublin **Tel: 01 845 6288**
R   info@capegreko.ie www.capegreko.ie

This friendly first floor restaurant offers a genuinely relaxed big Greek Cypriot experience and it's a fun, good value place for a group outing. It's a simple room decorated in cool blue and white to match the Greek flag that takes pride of place over the wine rack, with high-backed lightwood chairs and tables simply laid. You can be sure of a warm welcome, and friendly staff are quick to take orders from menus that offer a good selection of the classics - tzatsiki, hummus with pitta bread, grilled halloumi with tomato & onion salad and calamari. Favourites from the main courses include lamb kleftiko (meltingly tender slow cooked lamb shank), or chicken kebabs served with tzatsiki. A range of side orders includes a Mediterranean salad, along with other staples such as couscous and roasted peppers, but it's worth checking whether you need to order extras as some dishes are very generous. There is live music on Friday nights too, which makes it a real night out. *A second branch is in Bray (01 286 0006). Children welcome before 9pm. **Seats 54;** reservation recommended. D Mon-Thu, 5-midnight, Fri-Sun, 12.30 - midnight (Sun to 10pm). Set 2 course L €13.50; value D €19.95, 5-7pm daily (to 6.30pm Sat). MasterCard, Visa, Laser. **Directions:** At the corner of New Street above Marios Pizzas.

Malahide   Jaipur Restaurant
RESTAURANT   St James Terrace Malahide Co Dublin **Tel: 01 845 5455**
R   malahide@jaipur.ie www.jaipur.ie

This chic new-wave Indian restaurant is one of four Jaipurs - the others are in Dublin 2, Dalkey and Greystones (see entries); it's in the basement of a fine Georgian terrace and, although Malahide is particularly well-served with interesting eating places, it has earned a loyal following. Cooking is crisp and modern - a contemporary take on traditional Indian food; head chef Kuldip Kumar came from the 5* Imperial Hotel in New Delhi and it shows in colourful, well-flavoured dishes that have a lot of eye appeal. Vegetarian choices are particularly appealing, old favourites like tandoori prawns take well to the contemporary treatment and even desserts - not usually a strength in ethnic restaurants - are worth leaving room for. **Seats 80;** air conditioning; D daily, 5-11. Early D, €22 (5-7pm). Set menus €25-45 (incl 4-course Tasting Menu), also a la carte. House wine from €18. Closed 25-26 Dec. Amex, MasterCard, Visa, Laser. **Directions:** In Georgian terrace facing the tennis club in Malahide.

Malahide   Siam Thai Restaurant
RESTAURANT   1 The Green Malahide Co Dublin **Tel: 01 845 4698**
R   siam@eircom.net www.siamthai.ie

One of Dublin's longest-established Thai restaurants, the popular Siam Thai has smart blue-covered heated terrace at the front and a spacious interior, with a full bar; the back is subtly lit and ideal for private parties, and the front area has pleasant views out over the marina. A typically warm Thai welcome gets guests into the mood, and there is a pianist on some nights, which adds to the atmosphere. Menus offer many of the Thai classics on an extensive à la carte as well as the set menus, so it is wise to order an aperitif and allow plenty of time to decide - or the indecisive might begin with Siam Combination Appetisers, followed perhaps by main courses of Tiger prawns or duck. Outstandingly friendly staff are knowledgeable and efficient. Children welcome. Air conditioning. Live music (piano or live Thai band) most nights. **Seats 120** (private room, 45, outdoor, 30); L daily 11.30-5; D daily 5-12. Early D €21 (5-7.30 Sun-Thu); Set D €32/36 2/3 coure; à la carte also available. House wine €20. Closed 25-26 Dec. Amex, Diners, MasterCard, Visa, Laser. **Directions:** In Malahide village, near marina overlooking the green. ◇

Malahide   ## Silks
RESTAURANT   5 The Mall Malahide Co Dublin
R   **Tel: 01 845 3331**

This smart Chinese restaurant is spacious, modern and airy, with cheerful decor, and staff who are friendly and helpful, to match. The long menu is predictable, offering all the familiar set menus and dishes - the sizzlers and sweet & sours are there, along with Peking duck with pancakes, spiced chicken, and shared starter platters (spring rolls, chicken satay, spare ribs, wontons) followed, perhaps, by Garlic Prawn, Sweet & Sour Chicken, Duck Cantonese Style and Beef with Green Peppers, along with side dishes like Yung Chow Fried Rice. Desserts are unsurprising: banana fritters with an above average vanilla ice cream, perhaps, or a simple bowl of lychees. Silks may not be the first port of call for those seeking genuinely authentic chinese cuisine - there is a sense that the cooking has been 'dumbed down' for the Irish palate - but this has never been an issue with the loyal customers of this enormously popular neighbourhood restaurant, who have always enjoyed the busy atmosphere and friendly service. Reservations are essential as this restaurant is busy every night of the week. **Seats 90** (private room 20). Air conditioning. D daily: Mon-Sat 6-12.30. Sun 5-11. A la carte. **Directions:** Opposite Garda Station. ◇

Malahide Area   ## Belcamp Hutchinson
COUNTRY HOUSE   Carrs Lane Malahide Road Balgriffin Dublin 17 **Tel: 01 846 0843**
                         belcamphutchinson@eircom.net www.belcamphutchinson.com

Dating back to 1786, this impressive house just outside Malahide takes its name from the original owner, Francis Hely-Hutchinson, 3rd Earl of Donoughmore. It is set in large grounds, with interesting gardens, giving it a very away-from-it-all country atmosphere - yet Belcamp Hutchinson is only about half an hour from Dublin city centre (off peak) and 15 minutes to the airport. The present owners, Doreen Gleeson and Karl Waldburg, have renovated the house sensitively: high ceilinged, graciously proportioned rooms have retained many of their original features and are furnished and decorated in keeping with their age. Bedrooms are very comfortable, with thoughtfully appointed bathrooms and views over the gardens and countryside. Although its convenient location makes this an ideal place to stay on arrival or when leaving Ireland, a one-night stay won't do justice to this lovely and hospitable place. No dinner is served, but the restaurants (and good shopping) of Malahide are nearby. Walled garden; maze. Golf, equestrian, walking, garden visits, tennis and sailing are all nearby. Not suitable for children under 10. Pets welcome. **Rooms 8** (all with full bath & overbath shower). B&B €75 pps, no ss. Garden. Closed 20 Dec-1 Feb. MasterCard, Visa, Laser. **Directions:** From city centre, take Malahide Road; past Campions pub, 1st lane on left (sign on right pointing up lane).

Monkstown
CAFÉ/PUB

The Purty Kitchen

3-5 Old Dunleary Road Monkstown Co Dublin **Tel: 01 284 3576**
info@purtykitchen.com www.purtykitchen.com

Established in 1728 - making it the second oldest pub in Dublin (after The Brazen Head) and the oldest in Dun Laoghaire - this attractive old place has seen some changes, but its essential character remains, with dark wooden floors, good lighting, large mirrors and a good buzz. It's well set up for enjoyment of the bar food for which it has earned a fine reputation, with shiny dark wooden tables (a candle on each) and inviting menus which still have some old favourites like the famous Purty Seafood Chowder and traditional Mussels Marinière. But, although best known for seafood - and a wide range is offered, including Prawn and Crayfish Pil Pil, Caribbean style Crab Cakes and tender calamari and Pacific Rock Oysters. Head chef Jacqueline Foster has brought her American experiences to the kitchen: butcher's block selections include chargrilled fillet steak, North Star short ribs and Hereford Beef Burger. Lovely fresh food with a home-cooked flavour, presented attractively on different shaped plates, make this an unusually enjoyable informal dining experience. A list of House Favourites also includes some dishes that have stood the test of (considerable) time, such as a traditional breakfast, home-made beef burgers and seafood quiche, all at reasonable prices. A garden terrace offers a pleasing outdoor alternative in fine weather, and the Food & Wine Emporium next door specialises in artisan Irish foods. Restaurant D two sittings 7pm & 9pm, reservations advisable. No reservations in bar but names taken when you arrive and you can wait at the bar. *A new Purty Kitchen has now opened in Temple Bar (see entry). A la carte menu available Mon-Fri 12-9.45, Sat-Sun, 12.30-9.45. Veg menu also available. Purty Kitchen Food & Wine Emporium open every day (pub hours). Toilets wheelchair accessible. House wine from about €16.50 (€4.50 per glass). Live music Tue & Fri evenings. Closed 25 Dec, Good Friday. Amex, Diners, MasterCard, Visa, Laser. **Directions:** On left approaching Dun Laoghaire from Dublin by the coast road.

Mount Merrion
RESTAURANT

Michael's Food & Wine

57 Deerpark Road Mount Merrion Co Dublin
Tel: 01 278 0377

In fine weather, a few tables for alfresco dining set a welcoming tone outside Michael and Mary Lowe's wine shop, Italian deli and little trattoria style restaurant. You'll notice bottles of wine in view as you arrive and, in the shop, find the walls lined from floor to ceiling with Michael's collection of specially imported Italian wine; a table displaying speciality foods (pastas, Italian sauces etc) takes centre stage and a deli counter at the back of the shop offers charcuterie, great cheeses, olives, and other treats to take home. At the back, a small room is simply furnished with wooden tables and chairs and small candles, and a blackboard notice sums up the philosophy of this little place very well: "No salt or sugar added, 99% ingredients & 1% skill"! A blackboard menu offers a small selection of dishes (some available in two sizes) including a must-try and totally delicious antipasta dish with bruschetta, sun blushed tomatoes, salami, prosciutto, red and green pesto, olives, a pair of handmade Italian cheeses and a choice of salads. Main dishes normally include a hot special such as pizzaiola - mozzarella, aubergine, bruschetta, red pesto, regato and parmesan, and vegetarians will also enjoy the 'veggie snack' of focaccia, courgette, aubergine, pesto, red peppers, mozzarella, layered and served with fresh rocket leaves wrapped in a slice of roasted aubergine. Tempting desserts are displayed in a glass cabinet in the wine shop where you may may choose a bottle to enjoy with your meal for a corkage fee of about €5.75 and, on bottles over €30, there is no corkage charge. The quality of ingredients used and generous portions make for very good value, and friendly service and advice is always at hand. Cheese & Wine night on Wednesdays, 7pm onwards. **Seats 24;** D Thurs-Fri, 7-9.30pm, L Sat only 12-3pm. MasterCard, Visa, Laser. **Directions:** Situated off Fosters Avenue on Deerpark Road just passed Kiely's of Mount Merrion.

Portmarnock
HOTEL/RESTAURANT

Portmarnock Hotel & Golf Links

Strand Road Portmarnock Co Dublin **Tel: 01 846 0611**
sales@portmarnock.com www.portmarnock.com

Originally owned by the Jameson family of whiskey fame, Portmarnock Hotel and Golf Links enjoys a wonderful beachside position overlooking the islands of Lambay and Ireland's Eye. Convenient to the airport, and only eleven miles from Dublin city centre, the hotel seems to offer the best of every world - the peace and convenience of the location and a magnificent 18-hole Bernhard Langer-designed links course. A recent extension has added a new wing to the hotel and, although this obstructs the views once enjoyed from the fine dining restaurant, it does afford them to many of the 40 new bedrooms. Décor in the original hotel and old house is a little tired and dated looking in places, and this is most obvious where the existing hotel joins up with the new accommodation. Patterned carpets, fussy wallpaper and loud colours give way to a more sophisticated palette of soft greys and dark woods. While all accommodation is imaginatively designed and furnished to a high standard of comfort, with good bathrooms, the new bedrooms are superior in many ways. The new rooms have unusual sea green colouring with bespoke headboards featuring enlarged images of grainy sand. The cool green colour scheme and contemporary styling are extremely appealing, so it's worth requesting a new room when booking. The Jameson Bar, in the old house, has character and there's also an informal Links Bar and Restaurant next to the golf shop (12-10 daily). Conference/banqueting (350/250) Business centre. Golf (18). Oceana, health & beauty: gym, sauna, steam rooms & a wide range of treatments. Children welcome (under 4 free in parents' room, cots available without charge, baby sitting arranged). No pets. Garden. **Rooms 98.** Lift. 24 hour room service. B&B about €157.50 pps, ss about €75. Open all year. **Osborne Restaurant:** Named after the artist Walter Osborne, who painted many of his most famous pictures in the area including the view from the Jameson house, the restaurant is in a semi-basement overlooking gardens at the side of the hotel. First-time visitors may not find it easily, so inquire at reception. Though extremely comfortable with well-appointed tables, the restaurant's décor is now quite dated; when it first opened in 1996 it was an important addition to a sparse north Dublin dining scene, and a succession of distinguished chefs put this formal dining room firmly on the map. Now it is less a culinary destination and more a fine dining option for resident guests and a 'special occasion' restaurant for local residents - but those who have not eaten here for some time will be agreeably surprised by the good food currently offered. Menus feature imaginative combinations attractively presented, with about six dishes on each course, and fish features strongly, reflecting the coastal location. Sophisticated starters might include monkfish carpaccio, foie gras terrine or pan-seared scallops, all priced around €13. Main courses range from €23 to €30: brill might be served with watermelon and squid; crayfish tails with sweetbreads, beetroot and artichokes. Traditionalists will enjoy a good steak with hand cut chips and, perhaps, a pint of beer from the bar. Desserts are especially good, with the dessert platter a showcase for the talented pastry chef's creations. Though the extensive wine list is confusing and difficult to follow there are plans afoot to scale down the variety and tidy things up. Service is friendly and not overly formal, making this a relaxed, comfortable space to dine. Air conditioning. **Seats 80** (private room, 20). D only Tue-Sat, 7-10. Set D from €47, Tasting Menu from €50-60. A la carte available; house wine from €19.85; SC discretionary. Closed Sun, Mon. Links Brasserie open 12-10 daily. Amex, MasterCard, Visa, Laser. **Directions:** On the coast in Portmarnock. ◊

Saggart
RESTAURANT

Avoca Café Rathcoole

Naas Road Saggart Co Dublin **Tel: 01 257 1800**
rathcoole@shop.avoca.ie www.avoca.ie

Although it's right on a busy road and lacks the pretty setting associated with Avoca shops outside the city, this purpose-built lifestyle emporium is airy and colourful, with all the by now famous Avoca sections offering lovely shopping areas that are ideal for gifts and showcasing the best of Irish goods. A large enticing food hall with plenty of natural light looks out onto newly landscaped gardens, and upstairs there are two restaurants; **The Birdcage** which is self-service and the **Egg Café** (for reservations 01 257 1810) with table service. They share a large outdoor terrace, which will be very popular when the weather allows - and has lovely views of the Dublin Mountains. It tends to be very busy, but friendly staff and lovely food will compensate for any delays; as in the other Avoca cafés, you will be spoiled for choice of wholesome dishes from the well-designed self-service counters. A perfect place to stop for delicious food, with ample parking. **Seats 100;** Open daily 9.30-6pm (to 8pm Thurs). **Directions:** By edge of Naas Road, just west of Citywest campus.

Saggart

HOTEL

R R R

Citywest Hotel Conference Leisure & Golf Resort

Saggart Co Dublin **Tel: 01 401 0500**

info@citywesthotel.com www.citywesthotel.com

Only about 25 minutes from the city centre and Dublin airport (traffic permitting), this large hotel was planned with the needs of the rapidly expanding western edge of the capital in mind. It is set in its own estate, which includes two 18-hole golf courses and a comprehensive leisure centre with a large deck level swimming pool and a wide range of health and beauty facilities. The other big attraction is the hotel's banqueting, conference and meeting facilities, which include a convention centre catering for 4,000 delegates, making Citywest one of the largest venues in the country. All round, a valuable amenity for West Dublin. Conference/banqueting (4,000/2,000); secretarial services, video-conferencing. Leisure centre, swimming pool. Hairdressing/beauty salon. Children welcome (under 6 free in parents' room, cots available free of charge). **Restaurant:** L Mon-Fri, D daily. **Rooms 892** (19 suites, 759 no smoking). Lift, room service 24 hr. B&B about €75 pps, ss €30. Open all year. Amex, Diners, MasterCard, Visa, Laser. **Directions:** Off Naas Road - N7 (from Dublin, take left after Independent printers & follow road for about a mile. ◊

SKERRIES

So far remarkably unspoilt, Skerries is not completely undeveloped but its essential atmosphere has remained unchanged for decades (perhaps because it does not yet have marina and all its attendant development) and it makes a refreshing break from the hurly-burly of Dublin city. The harbour is renowned for its fishing, notably Dublin Bay prawns (langoustine), and the surrounding area is famous for market gardening, so it has always been a good place for a very substantial bite to eat - and there are several pubs of character along the harbour front to enjoy a pint before your meal - or the **Coast Inn**, just across the road from the **Red Bank** (see entry), does a great line in cocktails. **Olive Coffee & Wine** (see entry) is a very attractive little place accross from Gerry's Supermarket, there are a couple of ethnic restaurants, and **Russell's** (01 849 2450) is a friendly neighbourhood restaurant. While in the area, allow time to visit **Skerries Mills** (working windmills (Tel: 01 849 5208)) and take a stroll in **Ardgillan Castle and Victorian Gardens** (Tel: 01 849 2212) nearby at Balbriggan which has a great children's playground, (both also have tea rooms). There are many testing golf courses in the area and there are plenty of coastal and parkland walks.

WWW.IRELAND-GUIDE.COM FOR THE BEST PLACES TO EAT, DRINK & STAY

Skerries

CAFÉ/WINE BAR

Ⓝ

Olive

86a Strand Street Skerries Co Dublin **Tel: 01 849 0310**

info@olive.ie www.olive.ie

Peter and Deirdre Dorrity's charming specialist food shop and café is in the centre of Skerries with a wide pavement at the front that allows space for an outside seating area - making a very pleasant place to enjoy a bite to eat while people-watching in fine weather. The shop sells a carefully selected range of artisan produce from Ireland and abroad, including their own home-made range of hummus, basil pesto, olive tapenade and sweet Harissa pepper oil; a range of unusual salads is also freshly prepared for the shop and all these items make regular appearances on the café menu, along with other good things including home-made soups, panini and home-baked cookies. In July and August, they also open as a wine bar in the evening at weekends, offering simple fare like platters of meats and farmhouse cheeses. All this, and keen, knowledgeable staff too. Toilets wheelchair accessible; children welcome (high chair). **Seats 30** (outdoors, 18). Open daily 9.30-7pm; house wine €17.50. Closed Christmas. MasterCard, Visa, Laser. **Directions:** Turn right at monument in town, on the right.

Skerries
RESTAURANT/GUESTHOUSE

Red Bank House & Restaurant

5-7 Church Street Skerries Co Dublin **Tel: 01 849 1005**
sales@redbank.ie www.redbank.ie

Golfing breaks are a speciality at Terry McCoy's renowned restaurant with accommodation in the characterful fishing port of Skerries. The restaurant is in a converted banking premises, which adds to the atmosphere (even the old vault has its uses - as a wine cellar) and Terry is an avid supporter of local produce, with fresh seafood from Skerries harbour providing the backbone of his menu. Menus, written in Terry's inimitable style, are a joy to read and a statement at the end reads: "All items on the menu are sourced from Irish producers and suppliers. There are too many items for us to list all ingredients after each dish but you can take my word for it, we use local Irish because it's the freshest & so the best." Dishes conceived and cooked with generosity have names of local relevance - grilled goat's cheese St. Patrick, for example, is a reminder that the saint once lived on Church Island off Skerries - and dishes suitable for vegetarians are marked on the menu. The dessert trolley is legendary - a large space should be left if you fancy pudding. An informative, fairly priced wine list includes a wide selection of house wines, and a good choice of half bottles - and the early dinner and Sunday lunch menus offer great value. **Seats 60** (private room,10). D Mon-Sat, 6.30-9.45; L Sun only, 12.30-4.30. Set Sun L €33/35; Set D €50/55. A la carte also available; house wines from €24.50; no sc. Children welcome (high chair). Closed D Sun and L Mon-Sat. Restaurant only closed 24-27 Dec. **Accommodation:** 18 fine, comfortably furnished guest rooms have all the amenities normally expected of an hotel. Facilities for private parties (50). Gourmet Golf breaks - up to 40 golf courses within 20 minutes drive. While in the area, allow time to visit Skerries Mills (working windmills (Tel: 01 849 5208)) and the beautifully located Ardgillan Castle and Victorian Gardens (Tel: 01 849 2212) nearby, where there are tea rooms. Free broadband; Children under 4 free in parents' room (cots available free of charge). Pets permitted in certain areas. **Rooms 18** (all superior & no-smoking, ground floor bedroom, 1 for disabled). B&B €60 pps, ss €15 (DB&B rate is good value at €90 pps). Accommodation open all year. Amex, Diners, MasterCard, Visa, Laser.
Directions: Opposite AIB Bank in Skerries.

Skerries
BAR/RESTAURANT

Stoop Your Head

Harbour Road Skerries Co Dublin
Tel: 01 849 2085

After a quiet off-season drink a few doors along at Joe May's, there can be no greater pleasure in north Dublin than to slip into 'Stoops' for some of Andy Davies' mainly seafood cooking. 'Fresh, simple and wholesome' is how he describes his food, and who could want any more than that? If it's busy you may have to wait at the little bar - where you can opt to eat if you like, or have a look at the menu while waiting for a table (they seem to turn over fairly fast). The surroundings are simple - chunky wooden tables, closely packed - and the menu is not elaborate but there is plenty to choose from, and there are blackboard specials every day too; what could be more delightful than starters of dressed crab, or moules marinière - or perhaps a classic fresh prawn Marie Rose, as Dublin Bay prawns (langoustines) are landed in Skerries and a speciality; like the crab claws, they are offered as starters or main courses, in irresistible garlic butter. You don't have to eat seafood here - there are other choices like Asian chicken salad, or pasta dishes or even fillet steak medallions - but it would be a pity to miss it. Super fresh and deliciously simple, it's a treat. Toilets wheelchair accessible. **Seats 50** (outdoor seating, 20); air con; no reservations. Children welcome (high chair, children's menu, baby changing facilities). L & D daily: L 12-3, D 5.30-9.30 (Sun D 4-8). House wine about €17. Closed 25 Dec & Good Fri. MasterCard, Visa, Laser.
Directions: On the harbour front in Skerries.

Stillorgan
RESTAURANT

Beaufield Mews Restaurant & Gardens

Woodlands Avenue Stillorgan Co Dublin **Tel: 01 288 0375**
info@beaufieldmews.com www.beaufieldmews.com

Dublin's oldest restaurant is located in a characterful 18th century coachhouse and stables - surrounded by beautiful mature gardens where guests can have an aperitif on the lawn before dinner, or take coffee afterwards, as the gardens are lit up at night. With its mature trees, spacious surroundings and old-fashioned feeling about the buildings and gardens, you could be forgiven for thinking you have been mysteriously transported to the country - there's even an antique shop where guests are encouraged to have a browse before dining (Open 3-9pm). In 2007 the Cox family who have owned and run Beaufield Mews for over 50 years surprised everyone by doing a revamp, changing the traditional, old-fashioned restaurant into a sophisticated contemporary one, with modern décor and furnishings. But, as original features like wooden beams, old heavy latch doors and bare brick walls have been retained, the end result isn't too much of a shock and the concensus is that it still has plenty of character and menus, although updated, also remain in tune with the old Beaufield Mews that so many people know and love. The gardens are a very special feature, and growing more precious to city dwellers all the time; a large outdoor patio area over-looking the gardens allows guests to relax with an aperitif or an after-dinner coffee in fine weather, and drink in the atmosphere. Good wine list. Not suitable for children after 6.30pm. **Seats 200** (private room, 60; outdoor seating, 20). D Tue-Sat, 6.30-10; L Sun only, 12.30-2.30 (Sun L €23.95). Early D €23.50 (Tue-Thur, 6.30-7.30); D à la carte. SC 12.5% Closed Mon, bank hols, Good Fri. Amex, Diners, MasterCard, Visa, Laser. **Directions:** 4 miles from city centre, off Stillorgan dual carriageway.

Stillorgan
RESTAURANT

China Sichuan Restaurant

4 Lower Kilmacud Road Stillorgan Co Dublin
Tel: 01 288 0882

Despite well-publicised plans to move to a new location in nearby Sandyford, this Dublin favourite remains in its original unprepossessing setting of a suburban shopping centre, cheek by jowl with a late night convenience store and buzzing, even on weekday nights, with fans of the authentic Chinese cuisine. With smiling welcomes and friendly accommodating service, the Hui family have been presiding over what many rate as the best Chinese restaurant in the country for over 20 years. Old favourites like the tea-smoked duck, sizzling and shredded dishes and three styles of dumpling are still there along with an impressive range of seafood which includes scallops, squid and cuttlefish. Star dessert is the plate of toffee banana fritters, sent piping hot from the kitchen to the table, where the accomplished waiters deftly dip each toffee coated morsel into iced water and arrange the crisp fritter alongside vanilla ice cream. Brisk lunchtime business features a well-priced table d'hôte and fast service while the evening attracts a more leisurely mix of regular diners, celebratory groups and a fair representation of suits entertaining out-of-towners. Well selected wine list with a good price range. Children welcome. Children welcome. **Seats 100** (outdoor, 20). Reservations required. Air conditioning. L daily 12.30-2.30 (from 1pm Sun). D daily 6-10.30. Set L about €16 (Sun €17), Set D about €36; à la carte available; house wine about €20; SC10%. Closed L Sat, 25-27 Dec & Good Fri. Amex, MasterCard, Visa, Laser. **Directions:** On Kilmacud Road, above shops.

Swords
HOTEL/RESTAURANT

Roganstown Golf & Country Club Hotel

The Naul Road Swords Co Dublin **Tel: 01 843 3118**
info@roganstown.com www.roganstown.com

Set in a 300 acre estate in north county Dublin and built around the original Roganstown House, this is primarily a golf hotel but its convenience to Dublin airport and the city make it an attractive destination for travellers who wish to avoid the big airport hotels, business guests and those seeking a weekend break from the capital without a long drive. It is a pleasant, well-managed hotel with a friendly can-do attitude, and very comfortable accommodation in well-appointed modern rooms which overlook the championship golf course, a Japanese-styled courtyard or mature front gardens; rooms, which are uncluttered and work well, have good facilities including a laptop safe, direct dial telephone, internet access, satellite TV, minibar, hairdryer, iron and ironing board, and tea & coffee making facilities. The hotel has earned a reputation for good food, both in the comfortable O'Callaghans Bar, and **McLoughlins Restaurant**, which offers fine dining in very pleasant surroundings and attracts diners from a wide area. Head chef Lewis Bannerman has been with the hotel since it opened, and he successfully balances the requirements of different kinds of guests. While not cutting edge, his food is imaginative and skilfully prepared, and the dining experience here is always enjoyable. Conference facilities include the wheelchair accessible Aungier Suite which has state-of-the-art facilities, its own bar and splendid views of the golf course, which is also ideal for banqueting, and can be subdivided into smaller groups as desired. An additional two dedicated boardrooms can each accommodate up to 16 delegates. For golf lovers, the Christy O'Connor Junior-designed golf course will be an exciting challenge. Conferences/banqueting (300/240), business centre, free Broadband wi/fi. Children welcome (cots avail free of charge, baby sitting arranged). Golf (18), leisure centre with 'pool, day spa, beauty salon. **Rooms 52** (3 shower only, 16 executive, 1 junior suite, 43 no smoking, 20 groundfloor, 3 for disabled); Room service limited hours; Lift. B&B €85-137.50 pps, ss €40. Midweek specials offered. Closed 24-26 Dec. Helipad. Amex, Diners, MasterCard, Visa, Laser. **Directions:** Take Ashbourne road from Swords village, take right turn for Naul, 500m on the left.

COUNTY CARLOW

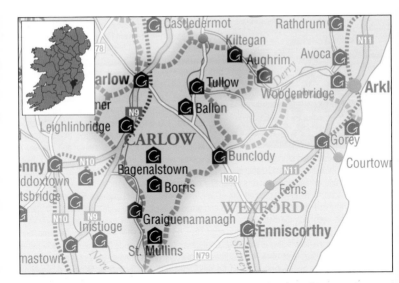

Carlow's character and charm is within easy reach of Dublin, and the metropolitan commuter spread is present, yet also kept at bay with a lively sense of place. Although it is Ireland's second smallest county, it confidently incorporates such wonderful varieties of scenery that it has been memorably commented that the Creator was in fine form when He made Carlow. Whether you're lingering along the gentle meanderings of the waterway of the River Barrow, or enjoying the upper valley of the River Slaney while savouring the soaring outlines of the Blackstairs Mountains as they sweep upwards to the 793 m peak of Mount Leinster, this gallant little area will soon have you in thrall.

There's history a-plenty if you wish to seek it out. But for those who prefer to live in the present, the county town of Carlow itself fairly buzzes with student life and the energetic trade of a market centre which is also home to a micro-brewery that, among other admirable products, is the source of the award-winning O'Hara's Stout. A more leisurely pace can be enjoyed at riverside villages such as Leighlinbridge and Bagenalstown. Leighlinbridge - pronounced "Lochlinbridge" – has for many years been Carlow's most community-conscious riverside village, the holder of a Tidy Towns Gold Medal and an Entente Floriale winner. There are also welcome improvements taking place to fulfill Bagenalstown's potential as a proper miniature river port, while the hidden hillside village of Borris is an enchantment in itself.

Local Attractions & Information

Carlow Eigse – Arts Festival (June)	059 914 0491
Carlow Town Tourist Information	059 917 0776
Carlow County Carlow Rural Tourism	059 913 0411 / 913 0446
Carlow Craft Brewery Micro-brewery	059 913 4356
Tullow Altamont Gardens	059 915 9444

Bagenalstown
COUNTRY HOUSE

Kilgraney House

Borris Road Bagenalstown Co Carlow **Tel: 059 977 5283**
info@kilgraneyhouse.com www.kilgraneyhouse.com

In a lovely site overlooking the Barrow Valley, Bryan Leech and Martin Marley's charming late Georgian house - which (encouragingly) takes its name from the Irish 'cill greíne', meaning 'sunny hill or wood' - is set in extensive wooded grounds. It is a serene and restful place with beautiful walks, and Altamont gardens nearby; Bryan and Martin have a great love of gardens - a recent project has been the development of their monastic herb gardens, and the kitchen garden provides plenty of good things for Bryan to transform into delicious dinners. His cooking style is creative and contemporary, making full use of local and artisan produce. Six-course menus begin with an amuse bouche and, although there are various influences at work, there's a leaning towards Japan, notably in specialities like their own home-smoked duck and a very beautiful dish of wild Slaney salmon wrapped in nori and wasabi. Your breakfast next morning will showcase local foods, including cheeses, more traditionally. But it is for the sheer sense of style pervading the house that it is most famous - Bryan and Martin's enjoyment in its restoration and furnishing is abundantly clear: elegant, yes, but with a great sense of fun too. Dinner can be shared with other guests at a communal table, or served at separate tables; a short, informative wine list is chosen with care - and non-residents are welcome by reservation. An Aroma Spa offers a range of therapies and massages, for both men and women, including pregnancy treatments. Self-catering accommodation is also available, in two courtyard suites, the gate lodge and a recently restored cottage. Herbal treatment room (massage & aromatherapy); hot tub. Small conferences. Not suitable for children under 12. **Rooms 8** (2 suites, 3 shower only, 1 ground floor, all no smoking). No pets. B&B about €85, ss about about €35. D (non-residents welcome by reservation), 8 pm. Set 6-course D about €50. (Vegetarian meals or other special dietary requirements on request.) Wines from about €20. Closed Mon-Tue and mid Nov-Feb. Helipad. Amex, MasterCard, Visa, Laser. **Directions:** Just off the R705, halfway between Bagenalstown and Borris. ◇

Bagenalstown
COUNTRY HOUSE

Lorum Old Rectory

Kilgraney Bagenalstown Co Carlow **Tel: 059 977 5282**
enquiry@lorum.com www.lorum.com

Bobbie Smith's mid-Victorian cut stone granite rectory was built for the Rev. William Smyth-King in 1864, and it now makes a warm and welcoming family home. Elegant and homely, there's a library as well as a lovely drawing room where guests can gather around the fire and relax; spacious accommodation includes one particularly impressive guest room with a four-poster and all rooms are very comfortable, with big beds, phones and tea/coffee trays. But it is Bobbie Smith's easy hospitality that keeps bringing guests back: Bobbie, who is a member of the international chefs' association, Euro-Toques, is committed to using local produce and suppliers whenever possible and is renowned for delicious home cooking using mainly organic and home-grown ingredients; rack of local lamb is a speciality, cooked with a honey, mustard & rosemary glaze, and residents have dinner at a long mahogany table, where wonderful breakfasts are also served. This relaxed place was the Guide's Pet Friendly Establishment in 2000 and guests are still welcome to bring their own dogs, by arrangement. This area makes an ideal base for exploring the lush south-east of Ireland, and is close to many places of interest, including medieval Kilkenny, Altamont Gardens, New Ross (where river cruises are available, and you can see the famine ship Dunbrody), Kildare's National Stud and Japanese Gardens. Also close by is Gowran Park racecourse and activities such as golf and a riding school (offering both outdoor and indoor tuition). Dinner must be booked by 3 pm; a concise, well priced wine list with tasting notes is offered. Private parties/small conferences (10). Cycling. Own parking. Garden. Not suitable for children under 10 years. **Rooms 5** (all en-suite, all shower only and no smoking). B&B from €75 pps, ss €20. Dinner for residents by arrangement(8pm) €45. Closed Dec/Jan/Feb. Amex, MasterCard, Visa, Laser. **Directions:** Midway between Borris & Bagenalstown on the R705.

Ballon
HOTEL/RESTAURANT

Ballykealey Manor Hotel

Ballon Co Carlow **Tel: 059 915 9288**

ballykealeymanor@eircom.net www.ballykealeymanorhotel.com

Seat of the Lecky family for three centuries, the present house was designed by Thomas A Cobden, built in the 1830s as a wedding present. Gothic arches and Tudor chimney stacks add unique character, and the house is set in well-maintained grounds and promising first impressions are well founded. Owners Edward and Karen Egan completely refurbished the hotel when they took over some years ago and new rooms recently added do not detract from the original house. Bold decorative touches in the entrance hall set a confident tone that is carried through into spacious reception rooms, furnished in an elegant mixture of contemporary style and period features, combining comfort with a friendly atmosphere. Individually designed bedrooms are luxuriously furnished, decorated in keeping with the character of the house and have all the expected amenities. **The Oak Room** This aptly-named restaurant is in what was previously the drawing room and library, and retains many original features including 10 foot solid oak dividing doors, hand-carved oak bookcases and fine cornices and mouldings, a handsome setting for enjoyable food. Conferences/banqueting (20-260). Wheelchair access; children welcome (under 6 free in parents' room, cot available without charge). Pets by arrangement. **Rooms 12** (1 junior suite, 4 shower only, 2 non-smoking). B&B about €70pps, ss about €20; no SC. Closed 24 Dec. **Seats 32** (private room 32). D daily, 7-9.30; L Sun only 12.30-3.30. D A la carte, Set Sun L €25.50. House wines €18. A la carte bar menu available 12.30-9.30. Closed 24 Dec. MasterCard, Visa, Laser. **Directions:** 10 miles from Carlow on the N80. ◇

Ballon
RESTAURANT

The Forge Restaurant

Kilbride Cross Ballon Co Carlow **Tel: 059 915 9939**

theforgekilbride@eircom.net

'The Forge for home baking and local produce' is their motto and it sums up nicely the appeal of Mary Jordan's unpretentious daytime restaurant. Off the road but handy to it and with ample parking, the granite building dates back to the 1700s and it makes a great place to break a journey for a wholesome bite. Mary takes pride in sourcing local ingredients and her menus offer simple home cooking fresh scones and jam, home-made vegetable soup, ploughman's sandwiches and comforting hot lunch time favourites like baked ham or roast beef, and of course tea and coffee. There is also a tourist information point as well as local art and craft work for sale. Walkers are welcome and packed meals supplied on request. All round, a great little place for a break and known for its consistency. Wheelchair friendly. Children welcome. Parking. **Seats 60** (outdoor, 30, private room, 14. Open 9.30-5 daily (Sun to 3.30), L 12.45-2.30 (Sun to 3.30). Late opening by arrangement; Set 3 course L about €15.95, set Sun L about €18.30, also A la carte. House wine €18.50. Closed 10 days at Christmas. MasterCard, Visa, Laser. **Directions:** Off the N80, between Ballon and Bunclody.

Ballon
COUNTRY HOUSE

Sherwood Park House

Kilbride Ballon Co Carlow **Tel:** 059 915 9117

info@sherwoodparkhouse.ie www.sherwoodparkhouse.ie

Built around 1700 by a Mr Arthur Baillie, this delightful Georgian farmhouse next to the famous Altamont Gardens is listed by Maurice Craig, the foremost authority on Ireland's architectural history, and beautifully located, with sweeping views over the countryside. Patrick and Maureen Owens, who have welcomed guests here since 1991, accurately describe it as "an accessible country retreat for anyone who enjoys candlelit dinners, brass and canopy beds, and the relaxing experience of eating out while staying in". Spacious accommodation is furnished in period style and thoughtful in the details that count - and Maureen takes pride in offering guests real home cooking based on the best of local produce, including "best locally produced Carlow beef and lamb, from Ballon Meats" and fish from Kilmore Quay. As well as having Altamont Gardens on the doorstep (just 5 minutes away on foot), there's a lovely garden on site and it's a good area for walking - and fishing the Slaney. Dinner is available by arrangement and is mainly for residents, although non-residents are welcome when there is room - it is served at 8pm and guests are welcome to bring their own wine and any other drinks. (Please remember to give advance notice if you would like dinner.)

Children welcome (under 3s free in parents' room; no cot available). Pets permitted by arrangement. Garden. D €40 (BYO wine); non-residents welcome by reservation. **Rooms 5** (all en-suite & no smoking). B&B €50 pps, ss €10. Amex, MasterCard, Visa, Laser. **Directions:** Signed from the junction of the N80 and N81.

Borris
PUB
🅝 🆁

M O'Shea
M O'Shea Borris Co Carlow
Tel: 059 97 73106

Halfway up the steep main street of Borris, this unspoilt old-world grocery-pub is well worth a visit. The old grocery section at the front links into a modern-day shop next door - a very practical arrangement that brings past and present together in a delightful way. Conversions and extensions towards the back allow for several larger rooms, where food can be served or music sessions held, and there's a paved area at the back for fine weather. Absolutely charming. Sandwiches, weekday lunches available. Music every fortnight or so: "it's a bit random". Closed 25 Dec & Good Fri. ◇

Borris
HOTEL
🅦 🆁

The Step House Hotel
66 Main Street Borris Co Carlow **Tel: 059 977 3209**
cait@thestephouse.com www.thestephouse.com

Stylishly decorated and furnished in period style, with antiques throughout, the original section of James and Cait Coady's attractive old house has well-proportioned reception rooms including a fine dining room (previously used for breakfast) and a matching drawing room that overlooks the back garden. Comfortable, elegant bedrooms include one with a four-poster and all are furnished to a high standard with smart shower rooms, TV and tea/coffee facilities. *At the time of going to press, The Coadys (who also own one of Ireland's finest classic pubs, Tynans Bridge Bar, in Kilkenny city) are due to re-open following a major redevelopment that will see The Step House becoming a fully fledged hotel and restaurant. MasterCard, Visa, Laser. **Directions:** From main Carlow-Kilkenny road, take turning to Bagenalstown. 16km (10 miles) to Borris. ◇

🆁

CARLOW

Situated on the banks of the river Barrow about 80km from Dublin, Carlow (www.carlowtourism.com) is a friendly, bustling student town with good local transport and shopping facilities, plenty of sporting activities, banks, hotels and bars. The name Carlow is derived from the old Irish place name Ceatharloch, meaning 'four lakes' and today it is a youthful town, with a large student population attending the local Institute of Technology - recent growth has seen the population rise to about 20,000, approximately 4,000 of which are students. The countryside around the town is attractive, with many pretty towns and villages, scenic routes and places of historic interest to visit. Although not renowned as a dining destination in recent years, the characterful old restaurant **The Beams** (059 913 1824) once drew diners from a wide area but is now open only on Saturday nights - the town has a number of good informal eating places notably the long-established **Lennon's Café Bar** (see below) and a couple of new arrivals, including the popular **Rattlebag Café** (059 913 9568) on Barrack Street - an ideal place to drop into for a snack (home baking is delicious), or maybe something more substantial, and **Cobdens Wine Bar** (059 914 6821, open Thu-Sun at time of going to press) on College Street, serving a wide variety of wines (including many by the glass) and an interesting short menu including salami plates and cheese plates, sourced from Carlow farmers' market. **Hennessy's Fine Foods** (059 913 2849) on Dublin Street, is a great deli and café, open all day Mon-Sat and now serving wonderful dinners on Sat.

Carlow
GUESTHOUSE

Barrowville Townhouse
Kilkenny Road Carlow Co Carlow **Tel:** 059 914 3324
barrowvilletownhouse@eircom.net www.barrowvillehouse.com

Dermot and Anna Smyth's exceptionally comfortable guesthouse is just a few minutes walk from the town centre and has long been a favourite with discerning visitors to the area. It is a fine period house set in lovely gardens, and there is also a particularly pleasant and comfortable residents' drawing room, with an open fire and plenty to read. The house is immaculately maintained and bedrooms - which inevitably vary in size and character due to the age of the building - are comfortable and stylishly furnished with a mixture of antiques and fitted furniture, as well as direct dial phones, tea/coffee trays and television, and thoughtfully designed, well-finished bathrooms. Maintaining the tradition of the house under previous ownership, very good breakfasts are served in a handsome conservatory (complete with a large vine) overlooking the peaceful back garden. Garden. Private parking (10). Not suitable for children. No pets.
Rooms 7 (2 shower only, all no-smoking). B&B €55pps, ss €20. Closed 24-26 Dec. Amex, MasterCard, Visa, Laser. **Directions:** South side of Carlow town on the N9.

Carlow
PUB

Lennon's Café Bar
121 Tullow Street Carlow Co Carlow
Tel: 059 913 1575 lennonscafebar@eircom.net

Sinéad Byrne runs this attractive modern café-bar with her husband, Liam, and their stylish contemporary design and deliciously healthy, reasonably priced food is a hit with both locals and visitors to the town. In a manner reminiscent of that great Kerry speciality, the pub that gradually develops into a restaurant at the back without actually having a dedicated restaurant area, the design of the bar - which has a striking metal spiral staircase at the back - helps the atmosphere to shift into café gear as you move through it. Simple, uncluttered tables and speedy service of jugs of iced water bode well for menus that include a host of wholesome dishes: home-made soups; open sandwiches (on freshly-baked home-made bread); ciabattas, wraps, some very tempting salads (fresh salmon with home-made fresh herb mayo perhaps) and a range of hot specials like steak & kidney pie topped with pastry & served with champ, or cod & mussel bake. Dishes suitable for vegetarians are highlighted, gluten-free bread is available for coeliacs and everything is really wholesome and freshly made to order from top quality ingredients (some local sources are named on the menu). Home-made desserts too - hazelnut meringue roulade with raspberry sauce, perhaps, or hot apple crumble. This well-balanced good home cooking won our Happy Heart Eat Out Award for 2003. Children welcome; Toilets wheelchair accessible. Breakfast Mon-Sat 10-11am; L Mon-Fri,12-3pm, Sat 12-4pm; D Thu-Fri 5.30-9pm; a la carte menu.Closed 25 Dec, Good Fri. MasterCard, Visa, Laser. **Directions:** At Junction of Tullow Street & Potato Market.

Clonegal
RESTAURANT

Sha-Roe Bistro
Main Street Clonegal Co Carlow **Tel: 053 937 5636**
sha-roebistro@hotmail.com

Away from the main road to anywhere, the delightfully pretty and well-preserved village of Clonegal on the borders of Wexford and Carlow is now home to one of our best young chefs, Henry Stone, and his partner Stephanie Barrillier and, in a fine 18th century building, their small but beautifully appointed restaurant promises a dining experience well worth a detour. A lovely sitting room acts as reception area, and simple décor throughout - warm cream walls, pale wooden floors, plain darkwood tables, comfortable chairs, the warm glow of night lights - provides a pleasing backdrop for rather good paintings, which are for sale. Original features include a huge open stone fireplace, now with a wood burning stove, and a pretty courtyard provides a retreat for smokers, or for dining in fine weather. Behind the warm welcome lies a professional efficiency that allows guests to relax and feel confident that everything will run smoothly. Menus based on seasonal foods might begin with lightly-seared scallops, or a smoked duck breast spring roll with crisp vegetables. Of the main courses, beef - matured for seven weeks - is a delight, also a gorgeously tender rump of Wexford lamb and an exceptional main course speciality Henry developed when he was head chef at nearby Marlfield House, is slow roasted pork belly with Savoy cabbage and pear chutney - it is worth a journey to sample this dish alone. Seafood such as cod with pea purée & mash will also be offered, also an appealing vegetarian dish such as creamed polenta with Portobello mushroom & rocket. Many of the tempting desserts feature seasonal fruits, or you may want to try the local cheese plate. Suppliers are credited on the menu and a short but well chosen wine list includes a good fairly-priced house selection as well as a number of wines by the glass. This is a serious kitchen and is earning a well-deserved reputation for faultless cooking, excellent service and superb value. Space is limited so reservations are essential especially in summer.* After Sunday lunch, a visit to historical Huntington Castle (just around the corner) might be recommended. Not suitable for children after 8pm. **Seats 25.** D Wed-Sat, 6.30-9.30, a la carte; L Sun only, 12.30-3.30, set Sun L €30; house wine €19.50. Closed Sun D, Mon, Tue and Jan. MasterCard, Visa, Laser. **Directions:** Off N80 Enniscorthy-Carlow road, 8 km from Bunclody, on Main St.

Leighlinbridge
HOTEL/BAR/RESTAURANT

The Lord Bagenal Hotel

Main Street Leighlinbridge Co Carlow
Tel: 059 972 1668 info@lordbagenal.com www.lordbagenal.com

The Lord Bagenal is beautifully situated on the River Barrow, with a fine harbour and marina right beside the inn and a pleasant riverside walk nearby. Although now a large hotel rather than the pub that is fondly remembered by many regular patrons, proprietors James and Mary Kehoe have taken care to retain some of the best features of the old building - notably the old end bar, with its open fire and comfortably traditional air - while incorporating new ideas. (A novel - and highly practical one - is a supervised indoor playroom, which is in the bar but behind glass so that, in time-honoured fashion, offspring can be seen and not heard). Bar meals include a lunchtime carvery/buffet which draws local diners from a wide area, but it is the new fine dining restaurant that will be of interest to visitors - and fortunately there is no need to travel far after dinner, as the bedrooms are just a few yards away. A large marbled foyer with a raised seating area and a fine selection of James Keogh's art collection, features a lovely circular stairway with toughened glass steps leading to accommodation that includes the spacious new deluxe riverside rooms with views over the river, bridge and marina. All are comfortably furnished in a modern hotel style with phones, TV and tea/coffee facilities, while the new ones have extra features including flat screen TV and impressive bathrooms with roll tops baths. Golf & equestrian nearby; fishing boats for hire. Marina (30 berths). Conferences/ banqueting (500/280). Garden, fishing, walking. Children welcome (under 3s free in parents' room, cot available free of charge, baby sitting arranged; playroom). No pets. **Rooms 39** (all en-suite, 1 for disabled). Lift, all day room service; B&B from €65 pps, ss €45.* Special breaks offered. **Waterfront Restaurant:** The new restaurant is in a bright, high-ceilinged room opening on to a large covered deck area overlooking the marina and river. Set up smartly with generous well-spaced tables dressed classically in white linen, it has a partially open kitchen where diners can catch a glimpse of head chef George Keogh and his team at work - his style is contemporary, using well-sourced foods, which he combines in an interesting and flavoursome way. Although only recently open at the time of the Guide's visit (and, perhaps, a little early for specialities of the house to have developed), dishes attracting favourable mention included a lovely starter of breast of quail with wild mushroom risotto and salsify crisps, and a main course of confit belly of pork with apple, white asparagus and colcannon mash. George's good cooking, aligned with the renowned Lord Bagenal wine list and a very pleasing setting, makes a combination to savour and this restaurant deserves to succeed. **Seats 90.** D daily 6-10 (to 9pm Sun); à la carte. House wine €18. Bar food 12-10 daily. Closed 25 Dec. Amex, Diners, MasterCard, Visa, Laser. **Directions:** Just off the main N9 Dublin/Waterford Road in Leighlinbridge. 12km (8 m) Carlow/32 km (20 m) Kilkenny.

Leighlinbridge   # Mulberry's Restaurant

CAFÉ

Arboretum Garden Centre Kilkenny Road Leighlinbridge Co Carlow
Tel: **059 972 1558**   arboretum@eircom.net   www.arboretum.ie

This pleasant self-service restaurant is in the garden centre at the Arboretum offers an attractive selection of wholesome, freshly-prepared food. Tables are simply set up, but every second table has fresh flowers; in addition to a blackboard menu, a self-service counter presents an appetising display of salads and quick-serve dishes - everything is fresh and home-made with good ingredients, and there's a nice flair in the desserts (banoffi pie is a house speciality). Not really a wine place, but there's wine by the glass from the fridge, and a few quarter bottles, also fruit drinks (including apple juice) and minerals. A good place to break a journey, as there's a pleasant ambience and a browse around is relaxing. Ample parking (150). Wheelchair friendly. Children welcome. Wine licence. Open 9-5 Mon-Sat, Sun 11-5. Closed 25 Dec & 1 Jan. Amex, Diners, MasterCard, Visa, Laser. **Directions:** From Carlow, take N9 towards Leighlinbridge.

St Mullins   # Mulvarra House

B&B

St Mullins Graiguenamanagh Co Carlow
Tel: **051 424 936**   info@mulvarra.com   www.mulvarra.com

Noreen Ardill's friendly and well-maintained modern house is in a stunning location overlooking the River Barrow above the ancient and picturesque little harbour of St Mullins and, although it may seem unremarkable from the road, this relaxing place is full of surprises. Comfortably furnished bedrooms have balconies to take full advantage of views of the romantic Barrow Valley, for example, and not only is there the luxury of (limited) room service, but even a range of treatments (massage, mud wraps, refresher facials) to help guests unwind from the stresses of everyday life and make the most of this magical place. Noreen - a keen self-taught cook - prepares dinners for residents to enjoy in the dining room which also overlooks the river: quality produce, much of it local, is used in home-made soups, seafood paté, fresh Barrow salmon, stuffed loin of pork and Baileys bread & butter pudding, all of which are well-established favourites, although menus are varied to suit guests' preferences. Genuinely hospitable and reasonably priced, this is a tranquil place where the host wants guests to relax and make the most of every moment. Special breaks offered. Walking; fishing; treatments/mini spa (must be pre-booked). Pets permitted by arrangement. Garden. Children welcome (under 3s free in parents' room; cot available without charge; baby sitting arranged). Room service (limited hours). Rooms 5 (all en-suite & no-smoking, 1 family room). B&B €40, ss €10. Residents D nightly, €30 (7.30pm, by reservation). House wine €20. Closed Mid Dec-Mid Jan. MasterCard, Visa, Laser. **Directions:** 7km (4.5 m) from Graiguenamanagh; take R702 from Borris, turn right in Glynn; signposted from Glynn.

Tullow   # Ballyderrin House

CAFÉ/B&B

Shillelagh Road Tullow Co Carlow
Tel: **059 915 2742**   ballyderrinhouse@eircom.net   www.ballyderrin.com

The Holligan family offer comfortable B&B accommodation at their home near Carlow and, with Pamela Holligan's well known cookery school on site, good food is sure to be part of the experience. Set on two acres and comfortably close to the capital for short breaks, there is plenty to do in the area including fishing in the River Slaney, golfing at the nearby championship course at Mount Wolseley Hilton, horse riding and visiting gardens, including Altamont, which is very close. Dogs permitted outside; Children welcome (under 5s free in parents' room, cots available free of charge). **Rooms 4** (2 executive, 2 family, all shower only and no smoking). B&B €35 pps, ss €20; 25% discount for children. Closed 25-26 Dec. MasterCard, Visa, Laser. **Directions:** From Tullow take R725 towards Shillelagh. About 1/4 mile from town on left hand side (well signed).

Mount Wolseley Hilton Hotel

Tullow
HOTEL/RESTAURANT

Tullow Co Carlow **Tel: 059 915 1674**
www.mountwolseley.ie

In a lovely area of green and gently rolling hills and river valleys, the immaculate exterior of this modern hotel attached to the Christy O'Connor-designed championship course creates a good impression on arrival, a feeling quickly reinforced by friendly, helpful staff who set a welcoming tone that is noticeable throughout the hotel. You don't have to be a golfer to enjoy a visit here - the hotel also has special appeal for spa-lovers and it makes an attractive venue for weddings and other events but it must help, as this is a picturesque and varied course to play. The hotel is only an hour and a half from Dublin and, with spacious public areas, well finished accommodation and plenty of activities on offer both in the area and on site, it is understandably popular as a short break destination. Conferences/Banqueting (750/550); Business centre, video conferencing, laptop-sized safes in bedrooms. Archery, clay pigeon shooting, cookery classes, garden visits nearby, golf (18), leisure centre (fitness room, pool, sauna, jacuzzi, steam room, spa), tennis, walking. Heli Pad. **Rooms 143** (3 suites, 3 junior suites, 4 executive, 4 family, 60 no smoking). Lift; 24 hr room service. Children welcome (cot available free of charge, baby sitting arranged, playground, play room); dogs permitted by arrangement. **Fredericks Restaurant** Named after Frederick York Wolseley, the original owner of the estate, the restaurant is in an airy dining room where smartly appointed tables with crisp white linen and fresh flowers provide an appropriate background for imaginative contemporary cooking backed up by helpful, well-informed service. Ever-popular braised shank of lamb is a speciality and the food standard is much higher than is usual in hotels. The set dinner menus offer very good value. **Seats 180** (private room, 70, outdoors, 30); air conditioning; L daily, 12-3pm; D 6-9.30pm. Open all year. MasterCard, Visa, Laser. **Directions:** N7 from Dublin, left in Castledermot for Tullow. Take left at bridge, then right.

Rathwood

Tullow
CAFÉ

Rath Tullow Co Carlow **Tel: 059 915 6285**
info@rathwood.com www.rathwood.com

féile bia This award-winning garden centre and shopping emporium near Tullow is a good place for a journey break (or even a day out) as, in addition to an exceptionally wide range of quality goods for garden and home (including classy gift items), there is good wholesome food available all day. Going well beyond what might be expected in a garden centre café, an extensive deli menu is offered, using all fresh local Irish produce in, for example, an open sandwich of roast chicken on homemade brown bread. And there are more substantial meals too, with lovely home-made desserts including a moreish lemon mousse cake - a useful place to know about. Country walks. Outdoor play area. **Seats 56** (+50 in conservatory); wheelchair friendly; children welcome (high chair, childrens' menu, baby changing facilities). Open 7 days: Mon-Sat 9.30am-5pm (including bank hols); Sun 11-5; L daily 12.30-2.30 (to 5 Sun); set 3 course L €18.45; Sun L €19.50; house wine (half bottle) €9.95. MasterCard, Visa, Laser. **Directions:** Just over an hour from Dublin, take Blessington or Naas to Tullow road - well signed on R725 to Shillelagh.

COUNTY CAVAN

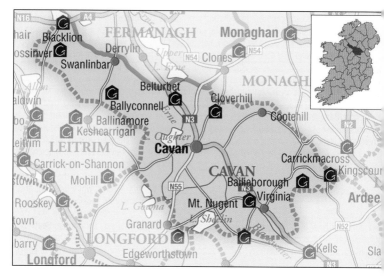

This is one of Ireland's most watery counties. It's classic drumlin country, interwoven with more lakes than they know what to do with. But the very fact that the meandering waterways dictate the way of the roads means that much of Cavan is hidden. In today's intrusive world, this is a virtue. It is a place best discovered by the discerning visitor. Much of it has quiet and utterly rural charm, seemingly remote. But it isn't so very far from Belfast or Dublin, and modern Cavan is noted for an economic vibrancy and entrepreneurial flair typical of modern Ireland.

Yet if you take your time wandering through this green and silver land - particularly if travelling at the leisurely pace of the deservedly renowned Shannon-Erne Waterway which has joined Ireland's two greatest lake and river systems - then you'll become aware that this is a place of rewardingly gentle pleasures. And you'll have time to discover that it does have its own mountain, or at least it shares the 667 m peak of Cuilcagh with neighbouring Fermanagh.

No ordinary mountain, this - it has underground streams which eventually become the headwaters of the lordly River Shannon, while 47 kms to the southeast is the source of the River Erne near Bellanagh – it eventually flows northwest, so Ireland's greatest rivers are closely interwined, yet only connected by canal.

Cavan is much more extensive than is popularly imagined, for in the northeast it has Shercock with its own miniature lake district, while in its southeast it takes in all of Lough Ramor at the charming lakeside village of Virginia. It also shares Lough Sheelin, that place of legend for the angler, with Westmeath and Meath, while in the far northwest its rugged scenery hints at Donegal. And always throughout its drumlin heartlands you can find many little Cavan lakes which, should the fancy take you, can be called your own at least for the day that's in it.

Local Attractions & Information

Bailieboro Tourism Information	042 966 6666
Ballyjamesduff Cavan County Museum	049 854 4070
Ballyjamesduff International Pork Festival (June)	049 854 4242 / 087 632 0042
Belturbet Tourist Office	049 952 2044
Cavan Town Cavan Crystal	049 433 1800
Cavan Town Tourist Information	049 433 1942
Cootehill Maudabawn Cultural Centre	049 555 9504
Cavan Cavan Equestrian Centre	049 433 2017
Mullagh Lakeview Gardens	046 924 2480
Shannon-Erne Waterway (Ballinamore-Ballyconnell)	071 964 5124

Bailieborough
CAFÉ
R

Planet Earth Café

Lower Main Street Bailieborough Co Cavan
Tel: 042 966 5490 diane@planet-earth.ie www.planet-earth.ie

Small is indeed beautiful at this little health food shop, bakery & café, where they rise at 5 am to bake their range of breads and cakes freshly each day and produce great gourmet foods on site. As word has spread, it has become a destination for foodies who are likely to find themselves anywhere near the area. Foccacia bread is a speciality and delicious salads, pasta dishes and outstanding desserts are the hallmarks of exceptionally honest, flavoursome food - and not only is Fairtrade coffee served, but Fairtrade gifts are on sale too. Lucky people of Bailieborough! **Seats 21;** open Tue-Sat, 9-5pm, wine licence. Closed Sun, Mon. ◊

Ballyconnell
PUB/RESTAURANT
R

Angler's Rest

Main Street Ballyconnell Co Cavan
Tel: 049 952 6391

Golf, fishing, walking and cycling are among the pursuits that attract visitors to this lovely lakeland area and Francis McGoldrick's characterful pub makes a welcoming and moderately priced base for a relaxing stay. The premises have been greatly extended recently but the philosophy remains the same: staff are hospitable, the bar has spirit and accommodation is both comfortable and reasonably priced - a real inn, in fact. There's a pleasantly informal restaurant and, as the proprietors are also the chefs, you can be sure of consistency in the kitchen. Live music some evenings (inquire for further details.) Children welcome; cot available free of charge. Garden; pool table. B&B offered, about €35 pps, ss €15. Bar Food served daily, L 12.30-3 pm, D 6-9pm. Closed 25 Dec & Good Fri. Mastercard, Visa. **Directions:** On N3, main street in Ballyconnell village. ◊

Ballyconnell
RESTAURANT
R

Pól O'D Restaurant

Main Street Ballyconnell Co Cavan
Tel: 049 952 6228 polod@oceanfree.net\

Paul and Geraldine's O'Dowd's popular restaurant on the main street consists of two cottagey ground floor rooms - each with the country character of stripped pine, old brick and stonework - and a newer dining room upstairs, with white table linen and candlelight, which has added a pleasing space and comfort. Diners travel from far and wide to eat here, and the atmosphere of the place plus the warm welcome (and good service) you'll get from Geraldine and her team are as strong a draw as Paul's wholesome cooking. A 3-course dinner menu offers a choice of about ten dishes on each course, with starters ranging from predictable (but tasty) mushroom soup to an unusual dish of roast quail with a local speciality, boxty (potato pancake), and main courses offering everything from ever-popular fillet steak or lamb cutlets to a seafood selection or a simple vegetarian option. Country generosity is the name of the game here - you get a good selection of side vegetables as well as a big portion of the main dish and the same applies to desserts. Children welcome. Wheelchair accessible. **Seats 50.** Open Wed-Sat 6.30-9.30; Wed-Sat. Set 2/3 course D €39.50, early menu €25 (5-6.30), also à la carte; house wine €20. Bookings strongly recommended. Closed Sun-Tue. Amex, MasterCard, Visa, Laser. **Directions:** On main street of Ballyconnell village.

Ballyconnell
HOTEL
R

Slieve Russell Hotel & Country Club

Ballyconnell Co Cavan **Tel: 049 952 6444**
slieve-russell@quinn-hotels.com www.quinnhotels.com

Close to the attractive town of Ballyconnell, this vast flagship of the Sean Quinn Group is set amongst 300 acres of landscaped grounds and, in the foyer, seating areas are arranged around marble colonnades and a central staircase, flanked on either side by a bar and two restaurants. Although all this invariably takes first-time visitors by surprise, it is very much the centre of the local community. Recent developments include the addition of a new conference centre, the Ciúin Spa & Wellness Centre, also 60 superior rooms and two presidential suites and all bedrooms have extra large beds, spacious marble bathrooms and pleasant country views. Dining choices are offered between the traditional, Conall Cearnach Restaurant and the newer continental/Asian style contemporary restaurant, Setanta - but it is the outstanding leisure facilities that attract the numbers, notably a championship golf course and Country Club. Off-season value breaks. Children under 3 free in parents' room, cot available free of charge; crèche, playroom; baby sitting arranged. Conference/banqueting (1200/600); secretarial services, video conferencing, broadband wi-fi. Leisure centre (swimming pool, jacuzzi, fitness room, steam room, spa with treatment centre and hairidresser). Golf (18 & 9), tennis, garden, walking, equestrian nearby. Shop. No pets. **Rooms 219** (2 presidential suites, 20 suites, 53 executive; 85 family, 8 single, 2 for disabled). Children welcome (under 3s free in parents' room, cots available); Lift. 24-hr room service; turn-down service. B&B from €135 pps high season, single €185. Helipad. Open all year. Amex, Diners, MasterCard, Visa, Laser. **Directions:** Take N3 from Dublin to Cavan, proceed to Belturbet then Ballyconnell.

BELTURBET

BELTURBET is a bustling, unspoilt little town on the River Erne. An excellent base for exploring the river and the Shannon-Erne Canal, cruisers can be hired in Belturbet and the area attracts anglers for the variety of catch to be had in the local waters. Of the many pubs and restaurants in the town, **Cassidy's pub** (049-9522559) is a gem, a classic Irish roadside bar situated just beside the river; and, across the bridge in the main part of town, the old **Erne Bistro** has recently re-opened under new management and is now known as **The Lawn Restaurant & Lounge** (049 952 2443).

Belturbet
RESTAURANT/GUESTHOUSE
R

International Fishing Centre
Loughdooley Belturbet Co Cavan **Tel: 049 952 2616**
michelneuville@eircom.net www.angling-holidays.com

At this lovely waterside location, the Neuville family offers residential fishing holidays; the restaurant is not open to the public in the usual way, but people on boating holidays may come in off the river when there is room - there are pontoons at the bottom of the garden and, weather permitting, terrace dining is an appealing option. Several fine wooden 'cabins' offer accommodation for up to six and each have a deck overlooking the river, making an attractive destination for a family holiday whether fishing or not. The centre is like a little corner of France, with all signage in French, including the menus which are clearly displayed and offer a range of traditional dishes, many of them from Alsace - and great value: a no-choice 4-course dinner at 7pm is only about €18, and a later menu offering several choices is about €25. A compact French wine selection is also keenly priced, making for a refreshingly reasonable bill. Charmant. **Rooms 18** (B&B about €45 pps en-suite, standard €40; details of cabins for groups available on request). Restaurant seats 35. Max preferred table size 10. (Private Room, 8, outdoor seating, 12). Set D 7-9pm daily, €18 & €25. House wine from €16. No s.c. Closed 1 Dec-1 Mar. MasterCard, Visa. ◊

Belturbet
RESTAURANT
N R

Le Rendezvous
Main Street Belturbet Co Cavan
Tel: 049 952 2443

Although not at all special in appearance, either outside or in, this small restaurant which opened in November 2006, is a valuable addition to the eating options in Belturbet, bringing a genuine French dining experience to the town centre. Chef patron, Christophe Grellier, who comes from the Vendée region of France, is friendly and informal, and the surroundings have a French feeling in their simplicity. Except for an atmospheric set of large framed black and white vintage photos with classic French themes, the décor is plain, with lemon walls, comfortable leather dining chairs and darkwood tables simply set, bistro style, with good cutlery laid on raspberry pink paper napkins (replaced between courses), and tea lights providing some atmosphere when the daylight dwindles. The music is also French - authentic and pleasant, if at times a bit too loud, perhaps- and the well-trained French staff have lots of personality. Add to that the French patron, a Belgian commis chef and a menu that features classics of French cooking such as boeuf bourguignon, poulet bordelaise and crème brulée and you have something rather special going on here. The décor may have been been done on a shoe string, but there's nothing budget about the food - the emphasis is firmly on quality (suppliers credited), and portions are generous too. Expect excellent renditions of classics like braised lamb shank and steaks (with really good sauces), at least one seafood dish and delicious desserts and a good choice of wine by the glass too. **Seats 30** (60 when upstairs open). D daily, from 5.30: Mon-Thu to 9.30; Fri & Sat to10pm, Sun to 9pm. L Sun only, 12.30-2.30. A la carte; also early 3-course D 5.30-7.30, €20. **Directions:** On the left as you drive from Enniskillen. ◊

Belturbet
PUB/RESTAURANT/B&B
R

Seven Horseshoes
Belturbet Co Cavan
Tel: 049 952 2166

Although officially an hotel, the heart of this friendly place at the centre of town is the bar, which is full of character, with an unusual wattle hurdle ceiling, plenty of local history, an open fire for cold days and the pleasingly dim atmosphere that makes Irish pubs so relaxing. This makes it very popular with boating folk, who also head up from the river for hearty home cooking served in the bar at reasonable prices: steaks, mixed grills, lamb cutlets and pan-fried plaice are the order of the day. Just right for appetites fired up by plenty of fresh air. There is a more formal dining option available upstairs, where an à la carte menu offers popular dishes like chicken & sweetcorn soup, Caesar salad, steaks and roast duckling all well-cooked and pleasantly presented, with some imaginative touches. Accommodation is offered in simple, comfortably appointed modern en-suite rooms. Bar food available daily: L 12.30-3 (Sun 1-4), evenings 5-9. Restaurant D daily, L Sun only (carvery). Set D €25/30, also a la carte, **Rooms 10** (1 executive, 1 family room); children welcome (under 5s free in parents' room, cot available free of charge, baby sitting arranged); B&B €50pps; ss €10; no pets. Boat trips nearby, fly fishing, coarse fishing nearby, golf nearby, snooker, walking. Amex, MasterCard, Visa, Laser. **Directions:** Town centre.

Blacklion
RESTAURANT WITH ROOMS

MacNean House & Bistro
Main Street Blacklion Co Cavan
Tel: 071 985 3022

It's been all-change in Neven Maguire's renowned County Cavan establishment over the last year or so. Having rounded the previous one off neatly with their Christmas wedding, he and his bride Amelda headed off for a much-deserved honeymoon and holiday of a lifetime, leaving the builders to move in and transform MacNean House from the modest restaurant with rooms that we had all grown to love, into a spacious place of understated elegance with, of course, a power house of a new kitchen to match. The prospect of a meal here has long brought devotees from all over Ireland, and beyond a fact recently acknowledged by Cavan County Council who, in an unusual and timely act, presented him with a special award for his culinary achievements and for promoting tourism in the area. Despite his demands outside the kitchen, Neven shows no sign of being distracted and his cooking continues to astonish and delight: perfectly judged food, that makes the most of meticulously locally sourced ingredients (proudly credited on the menu), is invariably an experience to treasure. Menus include a 10-course Tasting Menu (with fish and vegetarian variations available), great value Dinner Menus, and a keenly priced Sunday lunch. The 'new' restaurant has a small bar which, together with elegant high-backed chairs, immaculate linen and restrained creamy white crockery, all create the right ambience for full enjoyment of Neven's exquisite food. Main dishes are interspersed with all the treats that are part of the dining experience in the grandest restaurants - meals begin with a gorgeous assortment of yeast breads and dipping oil, and there will also be pre-starters, pre-desserts and superb petits fours. Of the growing number of specialities, caramelised pork belly with foie gras is an outstanding example and desserts have always been a particular passion for Neven, so it's a must to leave room for one of his skilfully crafted confections. This is outstanding cooking, served with charm and it offers exceptionally good value. An accessible wine list leans towards France and includes a dozen house wines (all €20), and eight half bottles. As we have said many a time, genuine enthusiasm for good food combined with exceptional creativity, skill and hospitality mark this restaurant out as nothing short of a national treasure. **Accommodation:** The new rooms now offer accommodation to match the restaurant. Restrained, thoughtfully furnished and very comfortable, they make this the short break destination par excellence - the only problem here is getting a booking, especially at weekends, so take a midweek break if you can. **Seats 40.** D Thu-Sun (Wed-Sun in high season) 7-9.30pm; L Sun only, 12.30-3.30, €29; set D € 45; Gourmet D €55; vegetarian menu €35; also à la carte. House Wine from €20. Service discretionary. **Accommodation: Rooms 10** (all en-suite and no smoking), €70 pps. Tea/coffee tray & TV in rooms. Children welcome; cot available free of charge. Pets allowed by arrangement. Establishment closed 23 Dec - 1 Feb. MasterCard, Visa, Laser. **Directions:** On N17, main Belfast-Sligo road.

Cavan
HOTEL/RESTAURANT

Cavan Crystal Hotel
Dublin Road Cavan Co Cavan **Tel: 049 436 0600**
info@cavancrystalhotel.com www.cavancrystalhotel.com

This impressive modern hotel on the Dublin side of Cavan town is a great asset to the area, bringing a health and fitness club, conference and banqueting facilities and a focal point for local activities. In common ownership with the adjacent Cavan Crystal Showroom and Visitor

Centre, it can offer guests the opportunity to tour the crystal factory - and even to cut your own crystal. The striking contemporary design is not immediately obvious from the outside, but the tone is set in the foyer and public areas, including a three-storey atrium area which provides an impressive setting for the hotel's Atrium Bar. Bedrooms are stylish and comfortable and, in addition to all the usual facilities, bathrobes, complimentary bottled water & newspaper plus iron & ironing board are in all rooms as standard. In addition to a pool and good leisure facilities in the Zest Health & Fitness Club, there's also an award-winning beauty salon and hair salon. Conference/banqueting (500/350); business centre, secretarial services, video conferencing. Leisure centre (swimming pool, sauna, jacuzzi, steam room, gym, treatment rooms, hair dressing). **Rooms 85** (3 suites incl. 1 Presidential, 66 executive; 2 family rooms, smoking rooms on request; 9 ground floor, 6 for disabled); Children welcome (under 4s free in parents' room, cots available free of charge, baby sitting). Lift; All day room service. B&B €90 pps, ss €25. Closed 24 & 25 Dec. **Opus One Restaurant:** The restaurant is on the first floor, off the central atrium area, and has a smart but comfortable feeling, created by native Irish wood and mellow brickwork combined with contemporary furnishings. Chef Dave Fitzgibbon has been with the hotel since 2003 and, cutting a bit of a culinary dash, he balances traditional dishes with some epicurean adventures. Creativity abounds and the ever-popular steak is upgraded to become grilled 'rib eye steak with a shallot and bacon dumpling, confit of pearl onion, café de Paris butter and veal jus' - a dish that will satisfy most, traditionalist or not. Other specialities include a starter of baked goat's cheese and pumpkin seed tartlet with white onion mousseline and beetroot ice, and creative vegetarian options are always on the menu. An accessible wine list from the old and new world is mostly priced around the €24 mark but there are some real treats on offer too, as well as a very good half-bottle selection. Friendly staff are well trained and informed, making dinner at Opus One a pleasure - though be warned that the lunch menu is quite different. **Seats 100;** reservations recommended; air con; children welcome before 9pm. D Mon-Sun, 6-10; L daily 12.30-3.30. Set Sun L €25; set 2/3 course D €28/€45, also a la carte L&D. Service discretionary. Amex, MasterCard, Visa, Laser. **Directions:** On N3, a few minutes from town centre in Dublin direction.

Cavan
RESTAURANT
Ⓝ Ⓡ

The Oak Room Restaurant

Main Street Cavan Co Cavan
Tel: 049 437 1414 www.theoakroom.ie

Voted Baileys Euro-Toques Young Chef of the Year in 1997 and with a CV that features stints at Dromoland Castle and Thorntons, chef-proprietor Norbert Neylon is well versed in the nuances of fine cuisine. He opened the original Oak Room restaurant in the Cavan Crystal Heritage Centre in 2001 and built up a reputation that brought diners coming from far beyond the immediate area to sample his excellent cooking in its relaxing ambience - but the restaurant was destroyed by fire two years later. In 2006, The Oak Room reopened, this time in this upstairs location in Cavan town, over his father-in-law's pub. The restaurant has a separate entrance, and the second and third floor dining rooms are modestly decorated with bare wood tables, cream walls, oak floors, warm lighting and an eclectic mix of art. Norbert's preference for local ingredients sees his suppliers listed on a menu that endeavours to strike a tricky balance between gourmet cooking and hearty portions. While not all dishes succeed, and combinations can be heavy, the food is ambitious and imaginative. Service, under the direction of June Neylon, is friendly and informal - and, although the dining room can be noisy when busy at weekends, this is a pleasant, inviting environment. **Seats 70.** Reservations recommended; not suitable for children; air conditioning. D Tue-Sat, 5.30-9.30. Early D €26, 5.30-7.30pm; set 4 course D €46; also à la carte. House wine from €21. SC discretionary. Closed Sun & Mon, 24-26 Dec. Amex, MasterCard, Visa Laser. **Directions:** Main St. Cavan town, above Smith & Wilson pub.

Cavan
RESTAURANT
Ⓡ

The Side Door

Drumalee Cross Cootehill Road Cavan Co Cavan
Tel: 049 433 1819 bookings@chuig.com

féile bia A younger sister restaurant to two successful and admirably consistent restaurants in Navan (The Loft) and Kells (The Ground Floor), The Side Door is based on the same principles of accessibility (good quality international food at a fair price), funky surroundings that make for an informal atmosphere that appeals equally to different age groups - and well-trained staff, who greet guests promptly on arrival and provide watchful service throughout. All fresh meat and poultry used is Irish and fully traceable - good to know when you're tucking into tasty meals that include popular starters like spicy chicken wings, and old main course favourites like char-grilled steaks and home-made burgers. Popular dishes from around the world include pastas, pizzas and a good selection of salads; specialities include vegetarian dishes - a Green Thai curry, perhaps - and there's a daily specials board, including fish specials. **Seats 90.** D daily 5.30 -10.30 (Sat to 11.30, Sun 4-9), early D about €18.50 (Tue-Sat, 5.30-7.30), otherwise à la carte; L Sun only,12.30-4. House wine about €17.95. 10% SC. Closed Mon; 25 & 26 Dec, Sun hours on Bank Hols. MasterCard, Visa, Laser. **Directions:** On the Cootehill Road, 1km from Cavan town, above the Orchard Bar. ◇

Cavan Area
HOTEL/RESTAURANT

Radisson SAS Farnham Estate Hotel

Farnham Estate Cavan Co Cavan **Tel: 049 437 7700**
info.farnham@radissonsas.com www.farnhamestate.com

A winding driveway through lush parkland and a maturing golf course brings you to the dramatic entrance of Farnham Estate Hotel: the reception is in a giant glass atrium linking the classical building dating from 1810 to the striking 21st century extension impressive by any standards although, after set-down, residents are asked to park several hundred metres from the entrance and use a cour-tesy bus which, while it leaves the front of the house clear of parking, may be less than amusing in bad weather. While not universally admired, most visitors see the hotel as an inspired marriage of the ancient and modern, and it has a warm, friendly atmosphere. There are three stunning drawing rooms in the house itself, and The Wine Goose Cellar Bar is atmospherically situated underground, in tunnels. The old house also has eight suites which have been cleverly restored with a sensitive eye to the past and some real modern flair: tradi-tional fabrics cover exotic seats and old-fashioned shapes are given quirky colours and patterns, an idea which has been overdone in Ireland recently, but this is an early example and it was achieved with a sure eye and quality materials. Rooms in the extension are sleek, modern and comfortable with walk-in showers and bath tubs, and all rooms have wireless high-speed internet access, robes, irons, hairdryer, mini bar, coffee making facilities, simple heat control and complicated interactive flat screen TV & radio. The 1,250 acre estate has a private lake for fishing, seven kilometres of walks and a partially constructed 18-hole golf course (due to be open in mid-2008). The health spa offers nine-teen treatment rooms, a thermal suite, a relaxation room, an indoor-outdoor infinity pool and its own restaurant. This is an appealing venue for business, conferences and weddings - The Redwood Suite, which has ten meeting rooms, can take up to 380 delegates theatre-style or seat 220 for a function. Conferences/Banqueting (380/220); business centre, video conferencing; free broadband wi/fi; laptop-sized safes in bedrooms. Archery, clay pigeon shooting, fly fishing, equestrian nearby, golf (18), fitness room, swimming pool, steam room, spa (treatment rooms, hair dressing). Heli Pad. **Rooms 158** (8 suites in the old house, 4 new suites, 120 no smoking, 50 ground floor, 8 for disabled.) Children welcome (under 17s free in parents' room, cots available free of charge, baby sitting arranged). Lifts; 24 hr room service; no pets. B&B €110pps, ss €85. **Botanica Restaurant:** Beside the Botanica Bar on the upper level of the impressive lobby/atrium area, smart casual is the tone in this spacious dining room overlooking the lawns around the old house. Breakfast, lunch and dinner are all served here and in its evening guise it's the most sophisticated of several enjoyable dining experiences offered at the hotel, all of which, including The Pear Tree Restaurant at the Health Spa, have botanical themes inspired by the estate's abundant plant life. A private dining area, The Lemon Tree, is ideal for groups of up to 35 in the Botanica Restaurant, and there's another private dining area called The Potting Shed located within the kitchen itself, where a small party of a dozen or so can watch the chefs and be part of the action. Menus offer many of the old favourites like steak and crispy duckling, albeit dressed up for dinner, and also a sprinkling of less usual choices an organic barley & vegetable broth, for example, or saddle of rabbit with cepes. While sophisticated the cooking is not unduly complicated, and flavour-some food and friendly staff make for an enjoyable dining experience. A well-balanced wine list offers half a dozen house wines, a similar number of half bottles, a pair of each of organic and de-alcoholled wines, and plenty to choose from under €30. Botanica Restaurant: **Seats 180** (private room, 40); Children welcome; L served daily 12.30-3, D served daily 7-9.30. Set L €30, Gourmet D €55, D also á la carte. House wine €22. Open all year. Amex, MasterCard, Visa, Laser. **Directions:** From Dublin, N3 to Cavan town, then take the Killeshandra Road for 3km to the gates of the estate. The hotel is a 1.7km drive from the gates.

Cloverhill
RESTAURANT WITH ROOMS
🏆☆🍽️ R

The Olde Post Inn

Cloverhill Co Cavan **Tel: 047 55555**
gearoidlynch@eircom.net www.theoldepostinn.com

Gearoid and Tara Lynch's restaurant is in an old stone building in a neatly landscaped garden which served as a post office until 1974 and, since then, has made an attractive and popular inn. Gearoid is a talented chef and, with Tara managing front of house with efficiency and charm, they make a good team - since taking over in 2002 they have earned a reputation beyond the immediate area for fine food and genuine hospitality. There's a pleasant rural atmosphere about the place, with a bar to enjoy your pre/post-prandial drinks and an old-world style throughout, with dark beams and simple wooden furniture - but, comfortably rustic as it may seem (and all the more welcome as the continuing rush to shiny modernism threatens to sweep away the oddly characterful throughout Ireland), that is far from the case in the kitchen, and elegantly-appointed tables with crisp white linen and gleaming glasses give a hint of the treats to come. Gearoid's route to Cloverhill has included time in some fine establishments - at least one of which lives on here, in a house speciality: 'Le Coq Hardi' chicken breast (stuffed with potato, apple, bacon & herbs, wrapped in bacon and served with an Irish whiskey sauce). A committed Euro-Toques chef, Gearoid sources ingredients with great care and shows respect for regional and seasonal foods, and the excellent cooking is made all the more enjoyable by the friendly, helpful local staff. The Olde Post Inn was our Newcomer of the Year in 2004. Ample parking. **Seats 80** (private room, 25); children welcome (high chair, baby changing facilities) toilets wheelchair accessible. D Tue-Sun, 6.30-9.30 (Sun to 8.30), L Sun only, 12.30-3. Set D about €53, also à la carte, Gourmet Menu €75. Set Sun L €28. Closed Mon. **Accommodation:** While not especially luxurious or large, the seven en-suite rooms at the inn are convenient for diners who don't wish to travel far from the dinner table, and most have full baths. Children welcome, under 4s free in parents' room, baby sitting can be arranged, cot available free of charge. No pets. **Rooms 7** (2 shower only, 1 family room, all no smoking), B&B €50 pps, ss €10. Closed 24-27 Dec. Amex, MasterCard, Visa, Laser. **Directions:** 9km (6 m) north of Cavan town: take N54 at Butlersbridge, 2.5km (2 m) on right in Cloverhill village.

Kingscourt
HOTEL

Cabra Castle Hotel & Golf Club

Kingscourt Co Cavan **Tel: 042 966 7030**
sales@cabracastle.com www.cabracastle.com

Renamed Cabra Castle in the early 19th century, this impressive hotel is set amidst 100 acres of grounds, with lovely views over the Cavan countryside. Although initially imposing, with its large public rooms and antique furnishings, the atmosphere is relaxing. The bedrooms vary in size and outlook, but all are comfortable and individually decorated; accommodation includes some ground floor rooms suitable for less able guests and, in addition to rooms in the main building, newer rooms in an extension are particularly suitable for families. There are also some romantic beamed rooms in a converted courtyard, providing modern comforts without sacrificing character. The combination of formal background and easy ambience make this a good venue for private and business functions; it is popular for both weddings and conferences (250/500 respectively). Business centre; broadband wi/fi. A tennis court, beauty salon and helipad have all been added recently; Equestrian, fishing and garden visits nearby. Golf (9), walking, massage, hair dressing, boutique. Off-season value breaks. Children welcome (under 2s free in parents' room, cots available without charge, baby sitting arranged); pets permitted by arrangement. **Rooms 86** (2 suite, 2 junior suites, 26 shower only, 4 family rooms, 40 no smoking, 1 for disabled). All day room service (7am-10pm). B&B €118pps, ss €25. Closed at Christmas. Amex, MasterCard, Visa, Laser. **Directions:** Dublin - N2 - Navan - R162 - Kingscourt.

Kingscourt
CHARACTER PUB

Gartlans Pub

Main Street Kingscourt Co Cavan
Tel: 042 966 7436

This pretty thatched pub is a delightfully unspoilt example of the kind of grocery/pub that used to be so typical of Ireland, especially in country areas. Few enough of them remain, now that the theme pub has moved in, but this one is real, with plenty of local news items around the walls, a serving hatch where simple groceries can be bought, all served with genuine warmth and hospitality. The Gartlans have been here since 1911 and they have achieved the remarkable feat of appearing to make time stand still. Closed 25 Dec & Good Fri. **Directions:** On the main street in Kingscourt village. ◇

Mountnugent

FARMHOUSE

R

Ross House

Mountnugent Co Cavan **Tel: 049 854 0218**
rosshouse@eircom.net www.ross-house.com

In mature grounds on the shores of Lough Sheelin, Peter and Ursula Harkort's characterful old house enjoys an excellent location and offers a good standard of accommodation at a modest price. Bedrooms, which are distinctly continental in style, have telephone, TV and tea/coffee trays and some unusual features: three have their own conservatories, four have fireplaces (help yourself to logs from the shed) and most have unusual continental style showers. Peace and relaxation are the great attraction, and there's a fine choice of activities at hand: a pier offers boats (and engines) for fishermen to explore the lake, there's safe bathing from a sandy beach, and also tennis. Ross House is also an equestrian centre, with all facilities including riding lessons, cross country riding, shows and breeding, outdoor arena and warm-up area and the most recent addtion, for 2008, an indoor arena. Ulla cooks for everyone, making packed lunches, sandwiches, high tea and a 4-course dinner (€22; wine list from about €11). Equestrian, fishing (fly fishing & Coarse), tennis. Children welcome (playground, cot available, €5); pets permitted. **Rooms 6** (all en-suite & shower only). B&B €38 pps, ss €10. SC discretionary. MasterCard, Visa, Laser. **Directions:** From Dublin Airport: M50, then N3 to Navan-Kells-Mountnugent. 5 Km from Mountnugent, signposted.

R

VIRGINIA

This attractive town is on the the northern side of beautiful Lough Ramor, which has wooded shores and a great reputation for coarse fishing. It makes a good base for a fishing holiday, or simply exploring an attractive and unspoilt part of the country. For travellers between Northern Ireland and Dublin it's the ideal spot to take a break - up at **The Park Hotel** (049 854 6100), perhaps, which has character and very friendly staff and is set in well-maintained parkland and its own golf course and you can get a bite in the bar then take a stroll along the shore. In the village, the preferred choice for many discerning diners is **The Cinnamon Stick** (049 854 8692) which is a clean-lined coffee shop where they do a mean Illy coffee and serve wholesome home-made food. Another option, in a waterside position right on the Dublin road, is the **Lakeside Manor Hotel** (049 854 8200; www.lakesidemanor.ie) which has been earning compliments for good food lately - but don't expect a manor house.

COUNTY CLARE

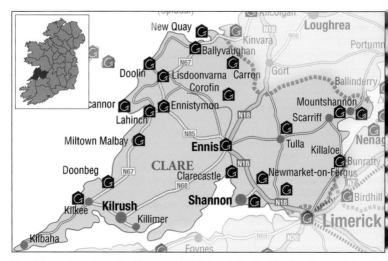

Clare is impressive, a larger-than-life county which is bounded by the Atlantic to the west, Galway Bay to the north, the River Shannon with Lough Derg to the east, and the Shannon Estuary to the south. Yet it's typical of Clare that, even with its boundaries marked on such a grand scale, there is always something extra added.

Thus the Atlantic coasts includes the astonishing and majestic Cliffs of Moher. Close under them in dangerous water is the majestic breaker known as Aileens, the surfer's Nirvana. Less challenging nearby, but still at the top of world standards, is one of Ireland's greatest surfing beaches nearby at Lahinch, which is also a golfer's paradise. As for that Galway Bay coastline, it is where The Burren, the fantastical North Clare moonscape of limestone which is home to so much unexpectedly exotic flora, comes plunging spectacularly towards the sea around the attractive village of Ballyvaughan.

To the eastward, Lough Derg is one of Ireland's most handsome lakes, but even amidst its generous beauty, we find that Clare has claimed one of the most scenic lake coastlines of all. As for the Shannon Estuary, well, Ireland may have many estuaries, but needless to say the lordly Shannon has far and away the biggest estuary of all. It is the port of call for the largest freight ships visiting Ireland, and on its northern shore is Shannon Airport. Yet the Estuary is also home to a numerous and remarkable friendly dolphin population, with Kilrush the most popular port for dolphin-watching.

The county town of Ennis has seen steady expansion, yet it is managing itself so well within its new bypass that it is the holder of a Gold Medal in the National Tidy Towns competition. Places like Ennistymon, Milltown Malbay, Corofin and Mountshannon - they all have a very human and friendly dimension. For this is a county where the human spirit defines itself as being very human indeed, in the midst of scenic effects which at times seem to border on the supernatural.

Local Attractions & Information

Ballyvaughan Aillwee Cave	065 707 7036
Bunratty Bunratty Castle & Folk Park, C/O Shannon Heritage Centre	061 360 788
Cliffs of Moher Tourist Information	065 708 1171
Corofin Clare Heritage Centre	065 683 7955
Ennis Tourist Centre	065 682 8366
Killimer Killimer-Tarbert Ferry	065 905 3124
Kilrush Kilrush Heritage Centre	065 905 1577
Kilrush Scattery Island Interpretive Centre	065 905 2139
Kilrush Vandeleur Walled Garden	065 905 1760
Quin Craggaunowen (Celts & Living Past), C/O Shannon Heritage Centre	061 360 788
Quin Knappogue Castle, C/O Shannon Heritage Centre	061 360 788
Shannon Airport Tourist Information	061 471 664

BALLYVAUGHAN

This attractive little port is best known for its major attraction, the Aillwee Cave, but its seafood comes a close second - and, as it is in a leafy valley with a wide range of amenities close at hand, it makes a comfortable base for exploring the Burren. The Burren is a unique rocky landscape well known for the rare flowers and fauna that grow in profusion over the limestone pavements. Ballyvaughan is surrounded by megalithic tombs such as Poulnabrone dolmen, celtic ring forts, medieval churches and castles. The area is a haven for walkers and, in particular, hill walkers. Hotel accommodation is available in the village at **Hylands Burren Hotel** (065 707 7037; www.hylandsburren.com), who offer all day food (speciality: seafood) and off-season breaks. Of the pubs, the traditional **Monks Bar** (065 707 7059), on the pier, has open fires and, at its best, a name for good seafood, while those with a yen for a real old pub of character should drop in for a jar at nearby **O'Loughlins**, family-run for generations. New to the village is **The Soda Parlour Coffee House and Crêperie** (Wed-Sun 10-5): nice menu of sweet and savoury crepes at fair prices plus enticing ice cream (sundae style). Outside Ballyvaughan (3km from the village on Lisdoonvarna Corkscrew Hill road), Cathleen Connole's **Burren Wine and Food** (065 707 7046), is a long-established wine and fine food shop which now opens for lunch, May-Sep; a delightful mother and daughter operation, it offers herbs and saladings from their own garden, local cheese etc. (including a magnificent St. Tola Feta cheese) plus excellent pizzas using local products. **WWW-IRELAND-GUIDE.COM FOR THE BEST PLACES TO EAT, DRINK & STAY**

Ballyvaughan
CAFÉ

Aillwee Cave

Ballyvaughan Co Clare **Tel: 065 707 7036**
info@aillweecave.ie   www.aillweecave.ie

Visitors to this 2-million-year-old cave will see more than the amazing illuminated tunnels and waterfalls, for there is also much of interest to food lovers. Cheese-making demonstrations show how the local Burren Gold cheese is made and, even if the process is in a quiet phase at the time of a visit, there is still plenty to see - and buy, thanks to a well-stocked food shop; free tastings of the cheeses and home-made fudge are available here, and other goodies to take home, including home-made preserves. Just inside the entrance to the cave there is a souvenir shop with a good book section (including travel and cookery books of Irish interest), and a café serving inexpensive, wholesome fare - typically baked potatoes with Burren Gold cheese. Fast food (coffee, panini etc) is also available - and there is now a garden centre as well as a mountain trail "guaranteed to work up an appetite". *The Liscannor Rock Shop is a sister enterprise. Children welcome. Café **Seats 60.** Wheelchair access (to building only, not the cave). Meals all day Mon-Sun (10-6.30). Closed mornings in Dec; Christmas. Diners, MasterCard, Visa, Laser. **Directions:** 4.5 km (3 miles) south of Ballyvaughan. ◈

Ballyvaughan
GUESTHOUSE

Drumcreehy House

Ballyvaughan Co Clare **Tel: 065 707 7377**
info@drumcreehyhouse.com   www.drumcreehyhouse.com

Just along the road beyond the Whitethorn restaurant and craftshop, Armin and Bernadette Grefkes' attractive purpose-built guesthouse makes a comfortable and moderately-priced base for a break in this lovely area and is a delightful place to stay. The furnishing style is a mixture of old and new with antiques and newer country furnishings blending well; front bedrooms have sea views across Galway Bay while those at the back have a pleasant outlook over the Burren - and all have phones and television. There's also a comfortable sitting room with an open fire available for guests' use and everything is spotless and full of character. A very good breakfast includes local cheese, from Annaliese Bartelink in Kilnaboy, gravadlax, smoked salmon and unsusual hot dishes such as herrings with horseradish sauce as well as the more usual options. Free broadband wi/fi. Beach nearby (10 minute walk). Garden. **Rooms 10** (all en-suite & no smoking, 2 family, 2 ground floor). Children welcome (cot available without charge, baby sitting arranged); Pets permitted. B&B €55 pps, ss €16. Closed 24-26 Dec. MasterCard, Visa, Laser. **Directions:** 2 km (1 mile) outside Ballyvaughan village - N67 in Galway direction; house on right.

Ballyvaughan
RESTAURANT/COUNTRY HOUSE

Gregans Castle Hotel

Ballyvaughan The Burren Co Clare **Tel: 065 707 7005**
stay@gregans.ie www.gregans.ie

Gregans Castle has a long and interesting history, going back to a tower house, or small castle, which was built by the O'Loughlen clan (the region's principal tribe) between the 10th and 17th centuries and is still intact. The present house dates from the late 18th century and has been added to many times; it was opened as a country house hotel in 1976 by Peter and Moira Haden who (true to the traditions of the house) continued to develop and improve it, together with their son Simon, who is now Managing Director. The exterior is a little stark, in keeping with the lunar landscape of the surrounding Burren but, once inside, all is warmth, comfort and hospitality. It is a place with a uniquely serene atmosphere. Peace and quiet are the dominant themes: spacious rooms with lovely countryside views are luxuriously furnished with understated style by Simon's wife Freddie - and deliberately left without the worldly interference of television. Yet this luxurious hotel is not too formal or at all intimidating; non-residents are welcome to drop in for lunch or afternoon tea in the Corkscrew Bar - named after a nearby hill road which, incidentally, provides the most scenic approach to Ballyvaughan. In fine weather guests can sit out beside the Celtic Cross rose garden and watch patches of sun and shade chasing across the hills. In the morning, allow time to enjoy an excellent breakfast - a delicious buffet set up with fresh juices and fruits, organic cereals, freshly baked bread, home-made preserves and local produce including Burren Smokehouse organic smoked salmon, Burren Gold organic cheese and Limerick ham; the menu of hot dishes reads very simply - but the secret is in the quality ingredients, which sing with flavour. Small Conferences/Banqueting (15/65); free broadband wi/fi. Croquet, cycling, falconry, gardens, walking, wine courses. Golf and garden visits nearby. Children welcome (no concessions, but cot available, €15, baby sitting arranged). No pets. All day room service. No Pets. **Rooms 21** (3 premier suites, 3 junior suites, 7 ground floor) B&B €117.50 pps; ss €75. No SC. **The Dining Room** is decorated in a rich country house style and elegantly furnished in keeping with the rest of the house. Most tables have lovely views over the Burren (where there can be very special light effects as the sun sets over Galway Bay on summer evenings) and dinner is often accompanied by a pianist or, more unusually, a hammer dulcimer. A commitment to using local and organic produce, when available, is stated on the menu - all fish is caught locally around Galway Bay, and Burren lamb and beef come from local butchers. Head chef Adrian O'Farrell's wide-ranging menus reflect this philosophy in fresh, colourful dishes that blend traditional values and contemporary style - in a speciality starter of home cured gravadlax, for example, a main course of slow braised shank of Burren lamb, and delicious desserts may include their Irish Mist Mousse (which features in the Blue Book Recipe Collection, 'Irish Country House Cooking'), and there is always a fine selection of local cheeses, with home-made biscuits. The wine list is an interesting read and includes an impressive selection of organic and biodynamic wines, leading off with the Spanish house wines. Dinner is a treat at Gregans Castle, but they also offer an attractive short à la carte lunch menu (served in The Corkscrew Bar) and delicious Afternoon Teas too. **Seats 50** (Private Room, 34). Unsuitable for children under 8 years after 6.30pm. D daily, 6.30-8.30; À la Carte. House wines from €24. Service charge discretionary. Short à la carte lunch is available in the Corkscrew Bar, 12-2.30 daily. Afternoon Tea, 3-5 daily. Hotel closed 1 Nov-13 Feb. MasterCard, Visa, Laser. **Directions:** On N67, 5km south of Ballyvaughan.

Ballyvaughan
GUESTHOUSE

Rusheen Lodge

Knocknagrough Ballyvaughan Co Clare **Tel: 065 707 7092**
rusheen@iol.ie www.rusheenlodge.com

John and Rita McGann swapped houses with their daughter Karen, who now runs Rusheen Lodge to the high standards for which it is well known, and they live next door so there's no shortage of experienced hands nearby for very busy times - and, as it was John McGann's father, Jacko McGann, who discovered the Aillwee Cave, an immense network of caverns and waterfalls under the Burren which is now a major attraction in the area, the McGanns understand better than most the popularity of

Ballyvaughan as a visitor destination. Fresh flowers in both the house and garden create a riot of colour in contrast to the overall green-greyness of the surrounding Burren, suggesting an oasis in a wilderness - which is just what Rusheen Lodge aims to provide. Constant refurbishment is the policy here and a 3-room executive suite introduced in 2002 has proved popular; all of the generously proportioned, well-appointed bedrooms have phones, tea/coffee trays, TV, trouser press and good bathrooms. All this, plus spacious public rooms, good food and warm hospitality make Rusheen Lodge a particularly pleasant place to stay. While evening meals are not provided, the pubs and restaurants of Ballyvaughan are only a few minutes' walk and breakfast - whether traditional Irish or continental - is a major feature of a stay. Children welcome (under 3s free in parents' room, cot available without charge, baby sitting arranged). No pets. Garden. **Rooms 9** (2 suites, 1 executive, 2 family, 3 ground floor, all no-smoking). B&B €50pps, ss€20. Closed mid Nov-mid Feb. MasterCard, Visa, Laser. **Directions:** 0.75 km from Ballyvaughan village on the N67, Lisdoonvarna road.

BUNRATTY

With its famous medieval Castle and Folk Park, Bunratty attracts vast numbers of visitors and there is plenty of competition here when it comes to accommodation, restaurants and, of course, entertainment: of the hotels, the best known are the **Bunratty Castle Hotel** (061 478700; www.bunrattycastlehotel.com), a modern hotel on a rise overlooking Bunratty Castle and Folk Park which is attractively designed to reflect its Georgian origins, and the **Bunratty Shannon Shamrock Hotel** (061 361177; www.dghotels.com) which was built in the 1960s at the time when the castle was restored; it has good conference and leisure facilities and offers special breaks. **Avoca Handweavers** (061 364029) also have an outlet at Bunratty and, with wholesome daytime café food available, this can be a good place to break a journey.

WWW.IRELAND-GUIDE.COM FOR THE BEST PLACES TO EAT, DRINK & STAY

Bunratty
CHARACTER PUB/RESTAURANT

Durty Nelly's
Bunratty Co Clare
Tel: 061 364 861   www.durtynellys.ie

Although often seriously over-crowded with tourists in summer, this famous and genuinely characterful old pub in the shadow of Bunratty Castle somehow manages to provide cheerful service and above-average food to the great numbers who pass through its doors. All-day fare is served downstairs in the bar (all day, noon-11pm) and the Oyster Restaurant (lunch and dinner); upstairs there is a more exclusive restaurant, The Loft, open in the evening only (Mon-Sat, 6-10). Both areas offer à la carte menus. Closed 25 Dec, Good Fri. Amex, MasterCard, Visa, Laser. **Directions:** Beside Bunratty Castle.

Bunratty
RESTAURANT

The Red Door Restaurant
Bunratty House Hill Road Bunratty Co Clare
Tel: 061 466 993   www.thereddoorrestaurant.com

This semi-basement restaurant is at the back of the Bunratty estate, overlooking Bunratty Park and the castle; as you drive through tall iron gates and up the drive to Bunratty House, you can't miss the banner signs proclaiming that you've arrived at The Red Door Restaurant This hospitable and characterful restaurant's will to please quickly attracted a loyal following. There's a bar as you enter, with sofas to relax in and views across the park, and the labyrinth of small rooms in the downstairs restaurant are well furnished, with red and cream brick walls subtly lit, and comfortable leather dining chairs, creating an intimate, relaxed ambience. The Early Bird menu offers hearty main courses such as roast stuffed pork steak; the dinner menu is more ambitious and a note informs diners that the beef is raised nearby and sourced from a local butcher. A short wine list, grouped by country, is reasonably priced. D Tue-Sun, 5.30-10; L Sun only, 12.30-3.30. Closed Mon. **Directions:** Behind Bunratty Castle, at Bunratty House enter tall tall iron gates & follow signs. ◇

Carron
CAFÉ

Burren Perfumery Tea Rooms

Carron Co Clare Tel: **065 708 9102**
burrenperfumery@eircom.net www.burrenperfumery.com

When touring Clare you will be pleased to find this charming spot - the perfumery is beautifully laid out, with a herb garden (where many native plants are grown - and later used in the organic herbal teas), pleasing old buildings and lovely biodynamic scents. The little tea rooms are beside the distillation room, where essential oils are extracted in a traditional still, and open on to a courtyard opposite the perfumery shop. Although small and simple, the tea rooms are pretty, with floral waxed tablecloths, fresh flowers and odd cups and saucers all creating a happy mismatch of pastels - and what they do is of high quality, made freshly on the premises, and uses local organic produce. At lunch time there might be summer minestrone & herbs soup with brown bread, or salad plates - a home-made organic goat's cheese & spinach quiche served with mixed salad - or, from a range of traditional home baking, you might just have a lavender flower muffin. There are all kinds of teas and tisanes, also natural juices - and coffee is served in individual cafetières. In July & August, Sunday lunch is offered, with special dishes available (booking required), and organic wines are now offered by the glass (€3.20-3.50) or bottle (€18-22). Children welcome (high chair); **Seats 20,** open daily 10-4.15 (to 5 on Sun), Apr-Sep. Set 2 course L €15. Organic wine €18 a bottle or €3.20-3.50 per glass. [Perfumery open daily 9am-5pm all year (except Christmas); high season (Jun-Sep) open to 7pm.] MasterCard, Visa, Laser. **Directions:** In the Burren, east of Gort - off R480 & N67.

Corofin
FARMHOUSE

Fergus View

Kilnaboy Corofin Co Clare Tel: **065 683 7606**
deckell@indigo.ie www.fergusview.com

Mary Kelleher runs a very hospitable house and the care taken to ensure guests enjoy their visit to the full is apparent in her attention to detail. Locally sourced quality foods and home-grown fruits, vegetables and herbs are showcased in interesting breakfasts that include home-made yoghurt, freshly squeezed juice, home-made muesli, Anneliese Bartelink's excellent local Poulcoin cheeses and a wide range of teas as well as cooked breakfasts with free range eggs. Although a little on the small side, in order to include en-suite facilities, bedrooms are comfortable and thoughtfully furnished. As well as a comfortable sitting room, there is a relaxing conservatory which opens on to the garden and has extensive views. There's also a lovely stone cottage next door, Tigh Eamon, which has been charmingly converted for self-catering accommodation. *No evening meals, but Mary will direct you to the best local choices. Children welcome (cot available, €12). Walking. Garden. No pets. **Rooms 6** (5 en-suite,1 shower only,1 with private bathroom, all no-smoking). B&B €38 pps; ss €15. Closed end Oct-March. **No Credit Cards. Directions:** Follow R476 to Corofin -2 miles north, on Kilfenora Road.

DOOLIN

Most famous for its music, and as a ferry port for visits to the nearby Aran Islands, Doolin also makes a good base for exploring the area, or a journey break when touring the Burren. Useful places to know about include the **Doolin Crafts Gallery** (Tel 065 707 4309), which is just outside Doolin, beside the cemetery, and in new ownership; it has a pleasant café and garden as well as a shop selling quality crafts and home-made fare. Also on the edge of Doolin - at the top of the hill - the **Aran View House Hotel** (065 707 4061; www.aranview.com) is a family-run hotel with dramatic sea views across to the islands; new to the town, for those who prefer contemporary design, is the new 'boutique' **Tir gan Ean House Hotel** (065 707 5726; www.tirganean.ie). In the village, the friendly **O'Connors Pub** (065 7074168) is renowned for its traditional Irish music and also offers good food and, although it's looking a bit scruffy these days, everyone loves Deirdre Clancy & Niall Sheedy's **Doolin Café** (065 824 505460), which is open for lunch and dinner every day in summer.

WWW.IRELAND-GUIDE.COM FOR THE BEST PLACES TO EAT, DRINK & STAY

Doolin
COUNTRY HOUSE/RESTAURANT

Ballinalacken Castle Country House & Restaurant

Doolin Co Clare **Tel: 065 707 4025**
ballinalackencastle@eircom.net ballinalackencastle.com

Well away from the bustle of Lisdoonvarna, with wonderful views of the Atlantic and the West coast, Declan O'Callaghan's unusual property is easily identified from afar by the 15th century castle standing on it. With its welcoming fire, well-proportioned public rooms and antique furnishings, the house has retained a Victorian country house atmosphere, and comfortable accommodation includes two recently renovated suites - one with panoramic views, the other an historic room with a fireplace. Children welcome (under 2s free in parents' room, cot available without charge, baby sitting arranged). Pets permitted by arrangement. Clay pigeon shooting and walking. Equestrian, fishing (fly, coarse & sea angling), hunting/shooting and scuba diving all nearby. **Rooms 12** (1 suite, 1 junior suite, 3 executive, 1 room shower only, 2 family; all no-smoking). B&B €80pps, SS €80. Limited room service. Closed 1 Nov-mid Apr. **Restaurant:** Michael Foley, previously of Dromoland Castle, is the chef and this traditional restaurant provides a fine setting for his modern cooking, founded on the best local produce. Menus offer a good choice of local seafood, well-made soups, and interesting vegetarian options and well-balanced flavours and accurate cooking make the most of prime ingredients like local scallops and Burren lamb. Good coffee rounds off the evening nicely, and excellent service is provided by pleasant staff. **Seats 32** (private room, 14); open to non-residents; reservations recommended; children welcome. D Wed-Mon, 7-8.45pm; set 3 course D €40, also A la carte. House wine €21; Service discretionary. Restaurant closed Tue. Amex, MasterCard, Visa. **Directions:** Coast road, R477 North of Doolin Village.

Doolin
COUNTRY HOUSE
Ⓝ

Ballyvara House

Doolin Co Clare **Tel: 065 707 4467**
info@ballyvarahouse.ie www.ballyvarahouse.ie

This large guesthouse just outside Doolin village is smartly presented, and offers hotel standard accommodation. Public areas are impressively spacious and comfortable, and amenities for guests' use include a library and residents' bar (with wine licence), and a games room with pool table. Two suites have king size mahogany sleigh beds and a private lounge area, and the other stylishly furnished bedrooms include double, triple and family rooms, with queen size beds as standard where there is a double; some rooms have balconies, and all have well equipped bathrooms with spa or Jacuzzi bath, power showers and heated towel rails. Good in-room facilities include TV/radio, tea/coffee facilities, hairdryer, direct dial telephone, alarm clock and ironing facilities. An extensive breakfast menu is offered, and served in a bright and attractive room - or in your room if preferred. Outside there's a private courtyard garden and an outdoor sitting patio (for smokers), also plenty for children, including a multi-purpose astro turf playing court - lined for soccer, basketball and tennis - a play area, and even resident donkeys and ponies. The atmosphere may seem a little impersonal, but perhaps that goes with the territory when you get hotel standard accommodation. No dinner but guests are referred to Tir gan Ean Hotel in Doolin, which is in common same ownership. Children welcome (under 3s free in parents' room, cot available free of charge, baby sitting arranged, playground). Pool table, tennis, garden, walking. Equestrian, garden visits and golf nearby. **Rooms 11** (all en-suite, 2 suites, 2 family, 1 shower only, 5 ground floor, 1 for disabled); limited room service; B&B €100pps; ss €40. Closed Oct-Apr. Amex, MasterCard, Visa, Laser. **Directions:** In Doolin take the left at Fitzpatrick's Bar; up hill; 0.5 mile on left.

Doolin
RESTAURANT/GUESTHOUSE

Cullinan's Seafood Restaurant & Guesthouse

Doolin Co Clare **Tel: 065 707 4183**
cullinans@eircom.net www.cullinansdoolin.com

Proprietor-chef James Cullinan and wife Carol have earned a loyal following at their comfortable dining room overlooking the Aille river. Along with an à la carte, menus include an attractive early dinner offering great value with three or four choices (including vegetarian dishes) on each course. Menus showcase locally sourced seafood, including Burren smoked salmon, Doolin crabmeat and Aran scallops, in modern Irish cooking with a French influence and carnivores are well looked after too, with a duo of Clare lamb cutlet and loin among the specialities. To finish, there are tempting home-made desserts or farmhouse cheeses. Quite an en extensive wine list favours France and includes a good choice of half bottles. Children welcome. **Seats 25** D Thu-Tue, 6-9. A la carte; 2/3 course early D €24/30 (6-7pm). House wines €20. SC discretionary. Closed Wed & 25-26 Dec. **Accommodation:** Warm hospitality, comfortable beds and a tasty breakfast make this a good place to stay, at a reasonable price. Children welcome (under 3s free in parents' room, cot available without charge). Garden. No pets. **Rooms 8** (3 shower only, 2 family rooms, 3 ground floor, all no-smoking); all day room service. B&B €50 ss €20. Closed Christmas. MasterCard, Visa, Laser. **Directions:** Centre of Doolin.

Doolin
RESTAURANT

Roadford House Restaurant

Killagh Doolin Co Clare **Tel: 065 707 5050**
roadfordhouse@eircom.net www.roadfordrestaurant.com

Located close to the buzzy village of Doolin, Frank and Marion Sheedy's smart contemporary restaurant is an oasis of calm - a place where everything is operated in a personal and highly professional manner. A well-maintained exterior with attractive planting and plenty of parking makes a good impression from the start, and the restaurant is comfortable, with well-chosen modern table settings hinting at the stylish cooking that Frank has in store. Marion Sheedy is a skilled hostess and offers a warm and professional welcome, setting the tone for what is to come - fine dining at very fair prices. The menu, in the modern Irish style, emphasises the very best local food prepared in an imaginative way: superb Burren lamb and tender beef, sparkling fresh seafood (including seared scallops, perhaps), local cheese, unusual vegetarian options, seasonal vegetables, and to round off the meal, delicious desserts. Everything comes to the table freshly cooked and in prime condition, and details, such as really good breads, are excellent - Frank Sheedy has a happy knack of choosing delightful accompaniments to his carefully sourced ingredients and he cooks with confidence and skill. You will dine in style. The wine list is fairly short but well chosen to match the food, and keenly priced. **Seats 34;** reservations recommended; children welcome before 7pm (high chair); D served Tue-Sun (high season, call to check low season), 6-9.30pm. Sun L winter months only, 12-3pm. Early D €30, 6-6.45pm, also a la carte. House wine €19; SC 10% on groups 8+. Closed Mon (except Easter weekend), 24-26 Dec, 7 Jan to end Feb. MasterCard, Visa, Laser. Accommodation also available. **Directions:** In centre of village take slip road opposite Mc Dermotts pub, 50m up on right hand side.

Doolin
RESTAURANT

Stone Cutters Kitchen

Luogh North Doolin Co Clare **Tel: 065 707 5962**
stonecutterskitchen@eircom.net www.stonecutterskitchen.com

Karen Courtney and Myles Duffy's traditional thatched cottage between Doolin and the Cliffs of Moher is well-signed and, judging by the way they were packing 'em in on the day the Guide came to call, finding that cosy traditional surroundings and Myles's good home cooking are just what families want when they're out and about in the area. A blackboard proclaims the specials of the day in addition to the main menu, and you can expect sound renditions of old favourites like fish pie, home-made fresh fish & chips, beef & Guinness stew, also very good home baking. A useful place to know about. Wheelchair friendly; children welcome (high chair, children's menu, baby changing facilities, play ground). **Seats 70** (outdoor, 24, private room, to 26); reservations recommended; house wine €14.95. Food served 12.30-9.30pm daily Jun-Sept and Easter, weekends only Easter-Jun. Closed end Sept - Easter. Amex, Diners, MasterCard, Visa, Laser. **Directions:** 1.6km (1 mile) north of the Cliffs of Moher on the R478 opposite Doolin Pottery.

Doonbeg
RESORT/RESTAURANT

Doonbeg Lodge

Doonbeg Co Clare **Tel: 065 905 5602**
reservations@doonbeggolfclub.com www.doonbeggolfclub.com

At Doonbeg Golf Club on Doughmore Bay, The Lodge offers very luxurious accommodation - and, although it is a private club, there is limited visitor access to both golf and accommodation when available. The contrast between the wild landscape of Clare, the brooding sea and the luxurious interiors of The Lodge lends a distinctly romantic tone to the hotel, which is on first approach appropriately reminiscent of a baronial Scottish castle, although closer inspection reveals a cluster of more intimate buildings and, in acknowledgment of Irish tradition, all are slated-roofed and built in local stone. It has an Irish 'great house' feel with an American opulence - 'a relaxed country house atmosphere with an unparalleled level of the service' is the aim and, with the apparent ease born of long experience,

House Manager Bernie Merry (previously at nearby Moy House, Lahinch) ensures the atmosphere is always warm and service professional. And then there is the White Horses Spa, designed by the US-based Irish designer Clodagh: offering every possible kind of pampering, the design is inspired by the local environment (the walls of the fitness room, for example, feature a continuous image of the beach at Doonbeg) and non-golfers, especially, could pass many an agreeable hour here. **Restaurants:** Good food is a very high priority at The Lodge, and there are three choices: **Darby's** is for everybody, a great spacious pub-like bar where you can have good food like fish and chips, prawn salads, and steaks. Meals are also offered in the **Members' Bar**, where the ambience is elegant yet clubby - and fine dining is offered in **The Long Rooms**, an intimate restaurant with its own bar, antique mirrors and a great bay window looking on to the ocean. Much-lauded American chef Tom Colicchio, the force behind New York City's Grammercy Tavern, is a consultant, and the kitchen team is led by Aidan McGrath who set the bar high from the outset and has earned a reputation for this restaurant far beyond the golfing community. Spa; golf shop. Accommodation from €210-390 per courtyard room (ocean and river view available at greater cost). Amex, MasterCard, Visa, Laser. **Directions:** North side of Doonbeg village, off the main Lahinch/Kilkee road. ◊

Doonbeg
BAR/RESTAURANT/B&B

Morrissey's Seafood Bar & Grill

Doonbeg Co Clare **Tel: 065 905 5304**
info@morrisseysdoonbeg.com www.morrisseysdoonbeg.com

This attractive family-run bar in Doonbeg village has upped the ante over the last couple of years and it is now run by Hugh Morrissey, an energetic member of the upcoming generation. While retaining some of the charm of the old bar, he has given this lively seafood bar & grill a refreshing new look, with an extension on to the River Cree and a lovely decking area overlooking the river, which has brought excellent views and light to the dining room. The interior is all darkwood floors, cream walls and burgundy leather, a nice contrast to a collection of paintings and photographs, both new and old, of the village and local coastline. Simply presented menus are just the right length with dishes such as seafood chowder, Carrigaholt crab claws and Atlantic jumbo prawns for starters along with main fish courses such as home-made scampi sauce or fresh fillet of salmon with warm baby potato salad. Main offerings from the grill include an Angus sirloin steak, whilst in winter, specialities include roasted monk fish and meat casseroles. Cooking is good, and well-trained staff are friendly and efficient. **Accommodation:** Seven bedrooms are bright and pristine, with good facilities - phone, ISDN, TV, iron/trouser press. The difficulty here is getting a booking, as the rooms are understandably in great demand. Children welcome (under 3s free in parents room, cot available at no cost) **Rooms 7** (all en-suite, 2 Executive, 1 Junior Suite, all no smoking); B&B about €50, SS €20. **Restaurant:** No reservations accepted. **Seats 70** (private room, 30; outdoor dining for 30); toilets wheelchair accessible; children welcome before 10pm; L 12-2.30; D 6-9.30; House Wine about €18. Closed Mon and Nov, Jan, Feb. MasterCard, Visa, Laser. ◊

ENNIS

The county town - and the main road junction of County Clare - Ennis has a venerable history, dating back to 1241 when Ennis Abbey was founded by Donough Cairbeach O'Brien for the Franciscans. It became a famous seat of learning so it is appropriate that this characterful old town with winding streets is equally notable for its progressiveness in some areas of enterprise. Comfortable hotels in the area include the **Best Western West County Hotel** (065 682 8421; www.bestwestern.ie) which is a short walk from the centre of town and known for its exceptional business and conference facilities; also a short distance from the town centre, **Auburn Lodge** (065 682 1247) is a pleasant owner-managed hotel, with traditional music in the bar every night. **The Woodstock Hotel & Golf Club** (065 684 6600; www.woodstockhotel.com) is predominantly a golfing hotel located a few km outside Ennis; it is built around a 19th century manor house on around 200 acres, now mostly utilised by the golf course; **Halpino's Restaurant**, previously on the High Street, is now at Woodstock Hotel - and has been replaced in the town centre by **Zucchini** (see entry). For lovers of Indian food, **Kasturi** (065 684 8065), next to ESB on Carmody Street, offers authentic cooking and friendly service.
WWW.IRELAND-GUIDE.COM FOR THE BEST PLACES TO EAT, DRINK & STAY

Ennis
FARMHOUSE

Newpark House

Ennis Co Clare **Tel: 065 682 1233**
newparkhouse.ennis@eircom.net www.newparkhouse.com

Strange as it may seem to find an authentic farmhouse in a country setting within easy walking distance of Ennis, the Barron family home is a genuine exception. This 300 year old house is of great historic interest and has large homely rooms furnished with old family furniture, and a quiet atmosphere. Bedrooms vary in size and character, but are comfortable and full of interest. The en-suite bathrooms also vary considerably, and first-time guests may need a fairly independent spirit in order to get into the ways of the house as information is not always forthcoming. However, regular guests adore the place and its exceptionally convenient location makes it a useful base for touring the area, following country pursuits (golf, horse riding, fishing, walking) or genealogy - there's a lot of useful material in the house and the Barrons can give advice on researching your roots. Children welcome (under 4s free in parents' room, cot available free of charge, baby sitting arranged); pets permitted by arrangement. **Rooms 6** (all en-suite & no smoking, 1 shower only; 1 family room). B&B €55 pps, ss €10. Closed 1 Nov-Easter. MasterCard, Visa, Laser. **Directions:** 1 mile outside Ennis; R352, turn right at Roselevan Arms.

Ennis
HOTEL/RESTAURANT

Old Ground Hotel

O'Connell Street Ennis Co Clare **Tel: 065 682 8127**
sales@oldparkhotel.ie www.flynnhotels.com

This ivy-clad former manor house dates back to the 18th century and, set in its own gardens, creates an oasis of calm in the bustling centre of Ennis. The Old Ground was bought by the Flynn family in 1995 and has been imaginatively extended and renovated by them in a way that is commendably sensitive to the age and importance of the building. Despite the difficulties of dealing with very thick walls in an old building, major improvements were made to existing banqueting/conference facilities in the mid '90s, and extra storeys have since been added to provide fine new rooms; as the famous ivy-clad frontage continues to thrive, the external changes are barely noticeable to the casual observer, and major refurbishment has also taken place throughout the interior of the hotel, including all the older bedrooms. However guests may find some of the older bedrooms and bathrooms rather cramped, especially when occupied by two people. A traditional style bar, Poet's Corner (bar menu 12-9) features traditional music on some nights. *Town Hall Café (see entry), is an informal contemporary restaurant in an historic building adjacent to the hotel. Children welcome (under 2 free in parents' room, cot available without charge, baby sitting arranged). Conference/banqueting (130/200). No pets. Garden. **Rooms 114** (12 suites, 6 junior suites, 50 executive rooms, 20 no-smoking, 1 for disabled.) Lift. 24 hour room service; turndown service. B&B €85pps; ss €32. Closed 24-26 Dec. **O'Brien Room Restaurant:** The hotel's formal dining room is at the front of the hotel and has warmth and charm, in an elegant old-fashioned style. Today's kitchen team has been part of the hotel for many years, and they take pride in using local produce in enduring speciality dishes such as Burren lamb with rosemary & honey glaze or fillets of turbot with lemon & chive beurre blanc, followed by homely desserts like seasonal fruit crumbles. **Seats 65** (private room, 70). Toilets wheelchair accessible. Air conditioning. L&D daily: L12-2.30, D 6.30-9.15. Closed 25-26 Dec. Amex, Diners, MasterCard, Visa, Laser. **Directions:** Town centre.

Ennis
HOTEL/RESTAURANT

Temple Gate Hotel

The Square Ennis Co Clare **Tel: 065 682 3300**
info@templegatehotel.com www.templegatehotel.com

This family-owned hotel was built in the mid '90s on the site of a 19th century convent, to a design that retains the older features including a church. Existing Gothic themes have been successfully blended into the new throughout the hotel, creating a striking modern building which has relevance to its surroundings in the heart of a medieval town, and succeeds in providing the comfort and convenience demanded by today's travellers, at a reasonable price. 'Preachers' pub offers a bar menu (10-9.30 daily) and traditional music every weekend - and the shops and many famous music pubs of the town centre are just a short walk across a cobble-stoned courtyard. Conference/banqueting (190/160). 24hr room service. **Rooms 73** (2 suites, 39 no smoking, 3 family rooms, 13 ground floor). Lift. B&B €89 pps, ss €35. **Restaurant: JM's Bistro** is located in a lovely high ceilinged room with lots of character. With comfortable seating and professional, attentive and friendly service, it's a relaxing place to linger after an active day and the hustle and bustle of the town. International influences are seen in starters such as woodland risotto (with mushrooms & black pudding), Thai fish cakes or local seafood chowder. Main courses may include a speciality of prime oven-roasted monkfish on spring onion colcannon, or Burren rack of lamb with fresh herb crust and tomato & mint chutney. An attractive dining-in option for residents, and an enjoyable experience for all. Toilets wheelchair accessible; children welcome (high chair, children's menu, baby changing facilities). Open daily, 7am-9.45pm, L 12.45-3 & D 7-9.45 (to 9.15 Sun); set L €19.95, set D €35. Closed 25-26 Dec. Amex, Diners, MasterCard, Visa, Laser. **Directions:** Town centre location - In Ennis, follow signs to tourist office: hotel is beside it.

Ennis
RESTAURANT

Town Hall Café

O'Connell Street Ennis Co Clare **Tel: 065 682 8127**
oghotel@iol.ie www.flynnhotels.com

Adjacent to (and part of) The Old Ground Hotel, the Town Hall Café has a separate street entrance and a contemporary feel. The old town hall has been well restored and the restaurant is in an impressive high-ceilinged room with sensitive spare decor - large art works which will be loved or loathed, big plant pots and simple table settings allow the room to speak for itself. Daytime menus offer a mixture of modern bistro-style dishes and tea-room fare, now with more emphasis on casual fare wraps, open sandwiches etc - just what people need to re-charge during a day's shopping, it seems. In the evening, it all moves up a notch or two, when a small à la carte menu is offered. Desserts from a daily selection. Reservations recommended except for snacks. **Seats 80.** Open from 10am daily: L 10-4.45pm, D 6-9.30pm. House wines from €17. Closed 24-26 Dec. Amex, Diners, MasterCard, Visa, Laser. **Directions:** On main street of Ennis town. ⚐

Ennis
RESTAURANT
Ⓝ 🍴

Zucchini Restaurant

7 High Street Ennis Co Clare **Tel: 065 686 6566**
reservations@zucchini.ie www.zucchini.ie

This first floor restaurant is spacious, comfortable and attractively designed, and hung with paintings by local artists. It's a friendly, buzzy restaurant that is popular with the locals and is a pleasant place to dine. The menu offers the standard international dishes so familiar in Ireland today, featuring local seafood, local beef and lamb, etc, and also vegetarian options, but what makes it different is that owner-chef Colm Chawke takes pride in showcasing local produce and he is a good chef, so the quality ingredients he seeks our are treated with respect an have real flavour. Pricing is fair and the early dinner menu offers good value. Slow service can let the kitchen down, unfortunately; although the staff are charming, service can be slow and lacking in professional expertise. In addition to a fairly short but well chosen and fairly priced wine menu, a full bar and beer menu is also available and there is a pleasant, spacious lounge area dedicated for aperitifs and after dinner drinks. **Seats 80.** Children welcome before 8pm (high chair, children's menu); air conditioning. D daily, 5-9.30pm. Early D €24.50, 5-7pm, also à la carte; house wine from €19.50. Closed 3 days Christmas. **Directions:** Located in Ennis town centre.

Ennistymon
RESTAURANT WITH ROOMS

Byrnes Restaurant & Accommodation

Main Street Ennistymon Co Clare **Tel: 065 707 1080**
byrnesennistymon@eircom.net www.byrnes-ennistymon.com

Located in a fine period house at the top of this old market town, Byrnes is a stylish high-ceilinged restaurant with views of Ennistymon's famous cascading river from the airy restaurant and an extensive outdoor dining area at the rear of the house. The Byrne family offer genuine hospitality and this, when wedded to contemporary style and ambitious standards of food, should ensure that a visit here will not disappoint. The surroundings stylish, airy and yet cosy, with gentle music are conducive to relaxation, and a warm welcome from Richard Byrne gets guests off to a good start. Mary Byrne is a skilful chef and everything is freshly cooked to order - her fairly short but well-balanced menu offers contemporary Irish cuisine with an emphasis on fresh local seafood and local meat, and there are always interesting vegetarian options. Gravad lax is something of a signature dish and makes an excellent starter with home baked bread; fish dishes are simple in style but very good to eat, and tender lamb shank may be served with delicious cabbage flavoured with bacon. Leave room for desserts such as a more-ish chocolate cake and delicious home made ice creams. Prices are reasonable for the quality with an early bird and Dinner/B&B deals offering especially good value. A short but well chosen wine list includes plenty of half bottles and wine by the glass. Air conditioning. Not suitable for children after 8 pm. **Seats 55** (outdoor, 40, private room, 15). L in summer months only, 12-2.30pm. D, Mon-Sat, 6.30-9.30pm; Set D about €35, also à la carte. House wines from €20. Closed Sun (except bank hol weekends), Christmas, Nov and Feb. Phone to check opening at lunch time and off season. ****Accommodation** is offered in six spacious, elegant, comfortable, hotel standard bedrooms (all en suite) individually furnished and decorated in fine period style. However it should be noted that rooms are on the 3rd floor and there is no lift. **Rooms 6** (all en suite, 3 family rooms). B&B €50 pps, ss €10. MasterCard, Visa, Laser. Call ahead to check opening times Nov-Feb as they may be closed. **Directions:** Large, prominent building at the head of the main street.

Ennistymon
RESTAURANT

Holywell Italian Café

Ennistymon Co Clare **Tel: 065 707 7322**
info@holywell.net www.holywell.net

In the centre of Ennistymon, this is one of four descendants of the much-loved Italian café, previously at Ballyvaughan (the others are at Fanore, Lahinch and Galway). You enter a tiny hall and there is a corridor-bar, with two spacious rooms to the right and left. It's a comfortable place to eat - the familiar Tyrolean-style interior has been reproduced, and both rooms have large windows letting in plenty of light - and wines offered by the glass are generous. However, although the food is still all vegetarian, specialising in simple dishes like pastas and pizzas, the philosophy of 'simple excellence' seems to have slipped a little. Nonetheless, it is a useful place to know about, with long opening hours in summer. Open 11am-11pm daily. Phone to check opening off season. MasterCard, Visa. ◊

Fanore
RESTAURANT

Italian Trattoria

Craggagh Fanore Co Clare
Tel: 065 707 6971

Another of the four descendants of the well-known vegetarian Italian café, previously at Ballyvaughan, the menu here has also moved away from the trademark pizzas, towards a more balanced trattoria menu - and it includes meat. Although there is still a strong leaning towards vegetarians, the minestrone now includes diced beef, the antipasti plate includes stuffed Parma ham rolls and chicken liver paté, and home-made pasta is offered with seafood bolognese sauce - and you can even have a grilled meats plate. Home-made ices are a speciality. It's a relaxed place, with wonderful views at sunset. Staff are friendly and efficient, there's a short, well-selected list of Italian wines (also beers and minerals), and coffees - and the long opening hours (11am-11pm in summer) make this a useful place to know about. Open in the summer only. ◊

KILFENORA

One of the most famous music centres in the west of Ireland, traditional Irish music and set dancing at **Vaughan's Pub** (Tel: 065 708 8004; www.vaughanspub.com) and (previously thatched) barn attract visitors from all over the world; it's been in the family since about 1800 and serves traditional Irish food (seafood chowder, bacon & cabbage, beef & Guinness stew) based on local ingredients. Discerning travellers looking for a snack head for the nearby **Visitor Centre**, which does a very nice line in good home baking.
WWW.IRELAND-GUIDE.COM FOR THE BEST PLACES TO EAT, DRINK & STAY

KILKEE

Aside from its appeal as a base for golfing holidays, Kilkee is a traditional family holiday destination located on the Atlantic coast facing a lovely beach which slopes very gently into the Bay - many would say there is nowhere else to be during the long Irish summer holidays. Kilkee is for walkers too. The walk along the coastline to the Diamond Rocks is one of the most breathtaking and exhilarating in Ireland and the local cliffs rival that of the famous Cliffs of Moher, but without the entrance fee and the large crowds. Other local attractions include Scuba Diving, Fishing, Horse Riding and Dolphin Watching. If staying in a large impersonal hotel is not your thing, consider **Halpins Townhouse Hotel** (065 905 6032; www.halpinsprivatehotels.com) where the Halpin family adapted the original Victorian building to provide en-suite bathrooms which means that bedrooms are neat rather than spacious, but they are comfortable and well-appointed. There's a characterful basement bar with an open fire and a restaurant called Vittles. Alternatively the **Stella Maris Hotel** (065 905 6455; www.stellamarishotel.com) is a long established family-run hotel with a warm and friendly atmosphere that has recently been refurbished.
WWW.IRELAND-GUIDE.COM FOR THE BEST PLACES TO EAT, DRINK & STAY

Kilkee
RESTAURANT

Murphy Blacks

The Square Kilkee Co Clare **Tel: 065 905 6854**
www.murphyblacks@hotmail.com

Although the restaurant is quite modern, it is in a Victorian building and proprietors Cillian Murphy and Mary Redmond have retained period features to keep the authentic atmosphere of the existing pub. Cillian is an ex-fishing skipper who ensures the freshest fish possible and the effort that goes into ensuring the best from suppliers shows, in succulent, well-flavoured food. He is in charge of front of house and Mary is the chef - a winning combination that has earned Murphy Blacks a reputation well beyond the immediate area. Menus have a leaning towards seafood, and specialities include crab tartlet, a delicious prawn tempura with chilli dip and a superb main course of cannelloni of plaice. But meat eaters are well catered for too, with classics like rack of lamb and steaks, and there is always a vegetarian choice. Desserts are home-made and the selection changes monthly. A balanced, accessibly priced wine list includes eight half bottles. **Seats 36** (outdoors, 12); D Mon-Sat, 6-9pm. Closed Sun. Reservations advised. MasterCard, Visa, Laser.

Kilkee | # The Strand Restaurant & Guesthouse
RESTAURANT/GUESTHOUSE | Strand Line Kilkee Co Clare **Tel: 065 905 6177**
| thestrandkilkee@eircom.net www.thestrandkilkee.com

This long-established seafront restaurant has been in family ownership for 130 years, and is now run by Johnny Redmond, who is the chef, and his wife Caroline. An unassuming yellow exterior gives little hint of the friendly welcome, buzzing atmosphere and wonderful views that await guests who can begin with an aperitif in the small bar/lounge looking out over Kilkee Bay and the Atlantic beyond. In the split level restaurant, a gentle colour scheme and simply laid tables allow the view to take centre stage, and floor to ceiling windows right along one side ensure a view for all tables. Menus - mainly seafood, plus favourites such as fillet steak, rack of lamb and a vegetarian dish - arrive promptly at your table, along with delicious home baked breads and a jug of water, and there's a tempting list of daily specials for seafood lovers a big bowl of Atlantic Mussels to start, perhaps, then baked John Dory, whole seabass or Dover sole. Finish with a home-made dessert such as apple & rhubarb crumble or hazlenut toffee meringues (deliciously chewy)... Friendly, efficient service, great cooking and apparently effortless management by Johnny and Caroline make dining here a very enjoyable experience. **Accommodation:** Six individually decorated en-suite bedrooms, some with sea views, offer comfortable accommodation above the restaurant. More rooms are planned in 2008. **Restaurant:** Children welcome (high chair, children's menu); **Seats 46** (outdoor, 12); reservation recommended; D 6-9.30pm, a la carte. SC 10% on groups 6+. Closed Dec-Mar (open 2 weeks over Christmas). **Rooms 6** (all en-suite, 5 shower only); children welcome (under 3s free in parents' room, cot available free of charge). B&B €46 pps, ss about €10. Closed Jan & Feb. MasterCard, Visa, Laser. **Directions:** On the waterfront in Kilkee.

KILLALOE / BALLINA

At the southern end of Lough Derg - a handsome inland sea set in an attractive blend of mountain and hillside, woodland and farm - Killaloe straddles the Shannon with two townships - Ballina in Tipperary on the east bank, and Killaloe in Clare, with the ancient cathedral across the river to the west. However, while it's all usually known as Killaloe (Co Clare), establishments of interest to the Guide happen to be on the east (Tipperary) side of the river. The aptly named **Lakeside Hotel** (061 376122; www.lakeside-killaloe.com) is popular for its location and facilities, while **Liam O'Riain's** (061 376722) is a traditional unspoilt pub. Then there's Gooser's, an attractive almost-riverside pub; it gets very busy in summer but makes a pleasant off-season stop and, at its best, the food can be enjoyable. (See also entry for **Cherry Tree Restaurant**.)

WWW.IRELAND-GUIDE.COM FOR THE BEST PLACES TO EAT, DRINK & STAY

Killaloe | # Cherry Tree Restaurant
RESTAURANT | Lakeside Ballina Killaloe Co Clare **Tel: 061 375 688**
| www.cherrytreerestaurant.ie

Harry McKeogh's impressive modern restaurant is a favourite weekend destination for discerning Limerick residents, who enjoy the waterside location and consistently excellent contemporary cooking. A high-ceilinged room with well-spaced, classically appointed tables and River Shannon views makes for a fine restaurant although its exceptional spaciousness can make it seem a little short on atmosphere and some added factor, such as a host with a big personality, is perhaps needed to bring it fully to life. All is well in the kitchen, however, and as you arrive, you will notice Chef de Cuisine Mark Anderson and his team at work, and Harry or one of his staff will show you to a small reception area nearby or straight to your table. Mark, who was our Chef of the Year in 2006 is committed to using the best local ingredients, many of them organic. These special foods and their suppliers are highlighted on simply worded seasonal menus offering a well-balanced choice of dishes - perhaps three on each course on the set menu, five on the à la carte - peppered with luxurious ingredients like truffles, foie gras, crab and diver caught scallops. But simpler foods have always been just as good here - the Cherry Tree's salads are legendary, for example, and an outstanding ingredient that has inspired more than one speciality dish is their superb beef, especially perfectly cooked dry-aged steak - and the Comeragh Mountains 'black-faced' lamb has also provided the base for outstanding dishes. Excellent puddings, each with a suggested dessert wine to accompany, might include a seasonal raspberry panna cotta with raspberry sorbet: perfection. There's a fine Irish farmhouse cheese plate too, and an interesting, carefully chosen wine list includes seven half bottles. Set menus - especially Sunday lunch - offer outstanding value, and a dedicated Children's Menu has been introduced, with three delicious choices on each course. **Seats 60** (private room, 10). Toilets wheelchair accessible. Children welcome until 7pm (children's menu). D 6-10 Tue-Sat. Set D €48; also à la carte; Sun L 12.30-3, Sun L €29; house wine €18.50. Closed Sun D, Mon, 24-26 Dec, last week Jan, 1st week Feb. Amex, MasterCard, Visa, Laser. **Directions:** At Molly's Pub in Ballina turn down towards the Lakeside Hotel, the Cherry Tree Restaurant is just before the hotel, on the left.

LAHINCH

This bustling seaside resort is especially popular with lovers of the great outdoors - one of Ireland's greatest surfing beaches is here, on Liscannor Bay, and it is equally renowned for golf. A long sandy beach and Seaworld, a leisure complex, also attract family holidaymakers. **The Atlantic Hotel** on Main Street (065 708-1049) is a good place to go for an informal bite to eat, and those who prefer to stay in large hotels will find all facilities at the centrally located 4* **Lahinch Golf & Leisure Hotel** (065 7081100; www.lahinchgolfhotel.com). **O'Looney's Bar** a long-established surfers' bar on the promenade, in common ownership with **Moy House** (see entry) has undergone major redevelopment and is about to reopen as the Guide goes to press: O'Looney's Bar and Waves Restaurant may seem plain from the street, but inside it is magic, with wonderful views of the prominade and the sea - and amazing decor by US based Irish designer Clodagh. Chef Cedric Bottarlini is working closely with Antoin O'Looney, and the fine dining room upstairs looks set to become a very desireable seafood destination.

Lahinch
RESTAURANT

Barrtra Seafood Restaurant

Lahinch Co Clare **Tel: 065 708 1280**
barrtra@hotmail.com www.barrtra.com

Views of Liscannor Bay from Paul and Theresa O'Brien's traditional, whitewashed cottage on the cliffs just outside Lahinch can be magic on a fine evening - and pleasingly simple décor, large windows and a conservatory allow them to take centre stage. Local seafood is the other star attraction - Barrtra was our Seafood Restaurant of the Year in 2002 - and Theresa's excellent, unfussy cooking continues to make the most of a wide range of fish, while also offering a choice for those with other preferences.

Several menus are offered in high season, starting with their famous 5 O'clock Menu which is a real snip - giving value has always been a priority here and local seafood is all offered at customer-kindly prices; lobster is a speciality, when available, and is very reasonably priced - on the dinner menu it only attracts a small supplement. Otherwise expect dishes like the richly flavoured Barrtra fisherman's broth, hot smoked mackerel with potato salad and wholegrain mustard mayonnaise, and perfectly cooked fish with excellent sauces; exact timing and perfect judgement of flavourings enhances the fish, while always allowing it to be "itself". Vegetarian dishes are highlighted on menus, and vegetables generally are another strong point (note the large polytunnel), a deliciously flavoursome combination that will include beautiful Clare potatoes is served on a platter. Paul is a great host, managing front of house with easy hospitality, and is responsible for an interesting and keenly priced wine list, which includes a wide choice of house wines and half bottles, several sherries and a beer menu. Quality and outstanding value are the hallmarks of this great little restaurant - and recent visits by the Guide confirms that it remains as delightful as ever. Children welcome before 6.30pm. **Seats 40.** D only, Tue-Sun (also Mon Jul & Aug) 5-10pm. Early D (3-course) 5-6.30, €28; set 6-course D €40; also à la carte. House wines from €20. s.c. discretionary. Closed Mon (except Jul-Aug) & Jan-Feb. Phone to check opening hours off season. MasterCard, Visa, Laser. **Directions:** 3.5 miles south of Lahinch N67.

Lahinch
COUNTRY HOUSE

Moy House

Lahinch Co Clare **Tel: 065 708 2800**
moyhouse@eircom.net www.moyhouse.com

This stunning house just outside Lahinch was our Country House of the Year in 2003 and, although many new properties have opened since then, it remains one of Ireland's most appealing (and luxurious) country houses. It's on a wooded 15 acre site on the river Moy and enjoys a commanding position overlooking Lahinch Bay, with clear coastal views and, although it appears to be quite a small, low building as you approach, its hillside position allows for a lower floor on the sea side - a side entrance below has direct access to the dining room and conservatory, and the lower bedrooms use the narrow spiral staircase which joins the two floors internally. A large drawing room on the entrance level has an open fire and honesty bar, where guests are free to enjoy aperitifs before going down to dine, or to relax after dinner. Decor, in rich country house tones, uses rugs and beautiful heavy fabrics to great advantage and bedrooms, which all have sea views, are wonderfully spacious and luxuriously appointed, and lovely bathrooms have underfloor heating; one extra-luxurious suite has a private conservatory overlooking the Atlantic. Bedrooms have recently been refurbished in a gently contemporary style, giving the house a new freshness, and this has also been applied in the dining room (also with a conservatory, allowing lovely views for everyone) where a 4-course residents' dinner and breakfast are served at separate tables. There's a short but interesting wine list, all round, this lovely house offers a unique experience. Children welcome (cot available at no charge; baby sitting arranged). **Rooms 9** (3 shower only, 2 family rooms, 1 suite, 1 for disabled, all no smoking) B&B about €125 pps, ss €40. D 7-8.45 (residents only, reservations required), about €50. House wine about €24. Closed Jan. Helipad. Amex, Diners, MasterCard, Visa, Laser. **Directions:** On the sea side of the Miltown Malbay road outside Lahinch. ◊

Lahinch
HOTEL/RESTAURANT

Vaughan Lodge

Ennistymon Road Lahinch Co Clare **Tel: 065 708 1111**
info@vaughanlodge.ie www.vaughanlodge.ie

Michael and Maria Vaughan's hotel - purpose-built to high specifications, mainly with the comfort of golfers in mind - offers peace and relaxation within easy walking distance of the town centre. They see it as a 'designer country house hotel' and that is a fair description, especially given their own hospitality, which is a combination of genuine warmth and professional expertise. Pleasing contemporary design combines with quality materials and a great sense of space in large, clean-lined bedrooms and public areas - including a clubby bar with leather easy chairs and sofas which golfers, in particular, are sure to enjoy; the ambience throughout is of a comfortable gentleman's club. A drying room is available for golfers' or walkers' wet clothing. Children welcome (under 12 free in parents' room; cot available without charge). No pets. **Rooms 22** (1 junior suite, 4 executive, 6 ground floor, 1 shower only, all no smoking); B&B €115 pps, ss €40. All day room service. Lift. Ample parking space. **Restaurant:** Run as a stand-alone restaurant specialising in seafood, this is a large, spacious room and dark polished wood tables, crisp linen runners and elegant table settings set the tone for head chef, Carol O'Brien's fine cooking. Refreshingly, her menus are to the point and written in clear, accurate English; although there is an emphasis on fresh local seafood, interesting artisan foods from area feature strongly, some of them from named producers - Connemara oak-smoked lamb, St Tola goats cheese, excellent Burren lamb and beef. All are used in an interesting modern Irish style as, for example, in mussel and chorizo risotto, McGeough's air-dried lamb with fig chutney, or monkfish with a fresh pea purée. The five course meal is excellent value and is presented in a series of beautifully cooked dishes including a palate-tingling sorbet, fabulous desserts, and a well chosen cheese plate. The wide-ranging wine list (grouped by price) includes a strong house selection and plenty of half bottles - and sound advice on making your choice too. Carol O'Brien is a confident chef who is producing top quality food, which - together with excellent hospitality and service - makes

Georgina Campbell's Ireland

this one of the best dining experiences in Co Clare. **Seats 60.** D daily Tue-Sun 6.30-9.30; set D €40. House wine €23. SC 10% on groups 8+. Closed Mon, Nov - Mar. Amex, Diners, MasterCard, Visa, Laser. **Directions:** On N85 just at the edge of Lahinch on the left.

Liscannor
CHARACTER PUB/RESTAURANT

Vaughans Anchor Inn
Main Street Liscannor Co Clare
Tel: 065 708 1548

The Vaughan family's traditional bar has great character, with open fires and lots of memorabilia - it was our Pub of the Year in 2006 and it's just the place for some seriously good seafood at fair prices, either in the bar or in a newer restaurant area at the back. Although famed locally for their seafood platters (and they are delicious - and great value) there's much more to the menu than that: Denis Vaughan is a creative chef who cooks everything to order and patience is quite reasonably requested on this score, as it gets very busy and everything really is fresh - they offer about twenty varieties of fish, and the menu may even be changed in mid-stream because there's something new coming up off the boats. However, you don't have to eat seafood to eat well here - vegetarian options are offered and they do excellent steaks too. Cooking combines old-fashioned generosity with some contemporary (and, in some cases, sophisticated) twists: succulent fresh salmon, for example, may be a pan seared fillet with mussel, pea and fresh herb risotto & shell fish oil, while perfectly seared scallops may come with buttered samphire, smoked haddock & spring onion potato cake with truffled white wine & caviar butter. It's understandably very popular and they don't take bookings so, get there early - lunch time (when some more casual dishes, like open sandwiches, are also offered) might be worth a gamble but, if you want to have a reasonably quiet dinner without a long wait, get there before seven o'clock. Good bread, good service - and great value. Toilets wheelchair accessible; children welcome before 9pm (high chair, children's menu). **Seats 106.** Food served 12-9.30 daily; house wine €17. Accommodation also available. Closed 25 Dec. (Open Good Fri for food, but bar closed.) MasterCard, Visa, Laser. **Directions:** 2.5 miles from Lahinch on Clifs of Moher route.

Lisdoonvarna
HOTEL/RESTAURANT

Sheedys Country House Hotel & Restaurant
Lisdoonvarna Co Clare **Tel: 065 707 4026**
info@sheedys.com www.sheedys.com

HOST OF THE YEAR

John and Martina Sheedy run one of the west of Ireland's best-loved small hotels - it offers some of the most luxurious accommodation and the best food in the area, yet it still has the warm ambience and friendly hands-on management which make a hotel special. The sunny foyer has a comfortable seating area - and an open fire for chillier days - and cosy bar is just the place to snuggle down with an after dinner drink and explore the rather fine range of interesting Irish Whiskeys including Midleton Rare. All the bedrooms are spacious and individually designed to a high standard with generous beds, quality materials and elegant, quietly soothing colours; comfort is the priority, so bathrooms have power showers as well as full baths and there are bathrobes, luxury toiletries and CD music systems, in addition to the usual room facilities. Fine food and warm hospitality remain constant qualities however - and an original feature has already enhanced the exterior in a way that is as useful as it is pleasing to the eye: the gardens in front of the hotel have been developed to include a rose garden, fruit trees, and also a potager (formal vegetable and herb garden), which supplies leeks, Swiss chard, beetroot and cabbage to the kitchen: a delightful and practical feature. Not suitable for children, except babies (cot available free of charge). No pets. **Rooms 11** (3 junior suites, 2 with separate bath & shower, 1 for disabled, all no smoking). B&B €70 pps, ss €25. A recently introduced DB&B rate offers exceptional value at €120 pps. **Restaurant:** The combination of John Sheedy's fine cooking and Martina's warmth and efficiency front of house make Sheedy's a must-visit destination for discerning visitors to the area. A stylishly subdued olive-grey, curtainless dining room with plain candle-lit tables provides an unusual setting for carefully-presented meals that showcase local products, especially seafood; amuse-bouches sent out from the kitchen while you are choosing your dinner (delicious little bites likes parsnip crisps, semi-dried tomatoes and black olives in spiced oil) sharpen the anticipation of delights to come. And everything on John's well-balanced menus just seems so appetising. His cooking style reflects a pride in carefully sourced local foods and pleasing combinations of classic and modern Irish. Savour interesting dishes made from sparkling fresh seafood, tender and uniquely flavoured lamb and beef, and local farmhouse cheeses from the Burren: everything is cooked to order, every dish is beautifully presented, and vegetarian dishes are equally appealing. Finish with a gorgeous speciality dessert such as home-made ice cream or old-fashioned lemon posset with fresh fruit - rhubarb, perhaps, or raspberries - and crisp shortbread. Under Martina's direction, the service is gently paced, professional and unobtrusive and a carefully selected wine list complements the cooking at prices that are very fair for the quality provided. The same high standards apply at breakfast when an extensive menu is on offer: delicious fresh fruit compôtes and juices; great home-made bread and pancakes; a cheese plate, a fresh fish dish, as well as classic Burren smoked salmon with scrambled eggs. Not suitable for children after 7.30pm. **Seats 25.** D daily, 7-8.30. A la carte. House wine €19.50. SC discretionary. MasterCard, Visa, Laser. **Directions:** 200 metres from square of town on road to Sulphur Wells.

Miltown Malbay

GUESTHOUSE/RESTAURANT

The Admiralty Lodge

Spanish Point Miltown Malbay Co Clare **Tel: 065 708 5007**

info@admiralty.ie www.admiralty.ie

Golfers - and, outside the main holiday season when holidaymakers are staying in the adjacent campsites, anyone who seeks peace - will love this luxurious guesthouse and restaurant just minutes away from Spanish Point Links Course, and very convenient to Doonbeg and Lahinch. A sweeping entrance leads to the smartly maintained building - there's an old 1830s lodge in there somewhere, with various extensions in different finishes creating the rather pleasing impression of a cluster of buildings. The exterior can seem a little bleak (it is hard to soften buildings with greenery in west Clare) - but, once inside, a large reception area with matt cream marble floors, mahogany desk, deep purple chaise longue and two huge elephant feet plants set the tone, and a spacious air of luxury takes over. Smart, comfortable and restful public areas continue in the same vein and large, airy bedrooms have a similar sense of style and generosity, with king size four-posters and sumptuous marbled bathrooms with bath and power shower, flat screen TV and stereo. Children welcome (under 3s free in parents' room). Pets by arrangement. Garden, walking. Golf nearby. **Rooms 12** (1 superior, all no smoking, 1 ground floor, 1 disabled). Air conditioning. Room service (all day). Turndown service. B&B €100pps, ss €60. Closed Nov-Mar. **Piano Room:** The restaurant is a long, warmly decorated room with beautiful Waterford crystal chandeliers, a grand piano, and French doors leading to a large garden. Immaculate table settings set the tone for a classic/modern menu which is interesting in its simplicity and matches the style of cooking which is well thought out, with the main ingredient complemented by imaginative accompaniments. Complimentary pre-starters and really good breads arrive very promptly and very professional formal service is provided by (mainly) French staff, who are knowledgeable about the food. Everything is perfectly cooked and elegantly presented - creative desserts, especially, are stunning to look at and a pleasure to savour. Although the seasonal aspect of the location tends to mean that chefs change from year to year, the standard of this restaurant has been consistently excellent from the outset, and it attracts diners from a wide area. An early bird menu offers particularly good value. **Seats 55** (private room, 30); air conditioning; toilets wheelchair accessible. Pianist weekends or nightly in summer. D Tue-Sun 6.30-9.30 (Mon residents only); Lounge Menu L daily, 12-3 (except Sun). Early D €30 (6-7), Set D €39. House wine €24. SC discretionary. Restaurant closed Sun L; also on Mon night (except for residents). Helipad. Amex, MasterCard, Visa, Laser. **Directions:** From Ennis take Lahinch road into Miltown Malbay, on to Spanish Point. ◇

Miltown Malbay
RESTAURANT/B&B

Berry Lodge Restaurant & Cookery School

Annagh Miltown Malbay Co Clare **Tel: 065 708 702.**
info@berrylodge.com www.berrylodge.com

Near the coast of west Clare, between Kilkee and Lahinch, this Victorian country house has been run by Rita Meade as a restaurant with accommodation since 1994 and, more recently, as a cookery school. The restaurant, which is open for dinner every night in high season and is available for small private functions, has an informal country style with pine furniture and a conservatory at the back of the house, overlooking the garden. Wide-ranging menus offer local seafood and exceptional meats from a local butcher, whilst a particular talent with poultry provides a speciality of slow roast spiced duckling with Guinness honey & orange sauce & red onion marmalade. *Golf breaks available (transfer available to Lahinch or Doonbeg Golf Clubs). **Seats 40.** D daily 7-9, by reservation. Set D €34/40, 2/3 courses. House wines €20. SC discretionary. **Accommodation:** Neat en-suite bedrooms are furnished with an attractive country mixture of old and new. Children welcome. No pets. **Rooms 5** (all shower only). B&B €44 pps, ss about €12. House Closed 1 Jan-Easter. MasterCard, Visa, Laser. **Directions:** N87 from Ennis to Inagh, R460 to Miltown Malbay, N67 to Berry Lodge over Annagh Bridge, second left, first right to Berry Lodge.

Miltown Malbay
RESTAURANT

Black Oak

Rineen Miltown Malbay Co Clare
Tel: 065 708 440

Set on a hillside with views over Liscannor Bay, Tom & Bernie Hamilton's large modern house may not look like a restaurant, but it is well-established and very comfortable, with plenty of sofas and chairs in the smallish reception area. The warm-toned dining room has well-spaced, well-appointed tables, fresh flowers, good linen and glasses an attractive setting for Bernie's good cooking. Her moderately priced menus offer a fair choice, with starters like St Tola goat cheese, crab in filo pastry and mussels in wine, and main courses such as rack of lamb and the house speciality of Seafood Pot (a selection of fish cooked in a tomato, leek, saffron & garlic sauce and served in its own pot) well-presented with a selection of side vegetables. Desserts tend towards the classics - lemon tart, variations on crème brûlée. This restaurant delivers what it promises: good fresh food, with a high level of comfort and service at reasonable prices - booking is essential. Not suitable for children under 13; air conditioning; reservation recommended. **Seats 65** (Max table size, 10). D Tue-Sun, 6-10 pm. Set 5 course D €39. Closed Mon & Christmas-April. MasterCard, Visa. **Directions:** 7 km outside Lahinch village on the Miltown road.

MOUNTSHANNON

The lakeside village of Mountshannon prospers in a sunny south-facing position. It is an attractive relaxed village with plenty to recommend it: **Keane's pub** (061-927214) is a good traditional bar lounge and shop, An Cupán Caifé (061-927275) is an attractive little cottage restaurant (now being run by Dagmar Hilty once again, fans will be glad to hear) and the friendly **Mount Shannon Hotel** (061-927162) where chef Noel Lyons, formerly of the very popular Noel's restaurant in the village, cooks for The Harbour Restaurant; the hotel offers weekend music and bar food daily –an open fire is a welcome sight here in chilly weather.

New Quay
HISTORIC HOUSE

Mount Vernon

Flaggy Shore New Quay Co Clare **Tel: 065 707 8126**
mtvernon@eircom.net www.hidden-ireland.com/mountvernon

Set back from the flag-stone shore and looking on to the cliffs of Aughinish, you enter another place at Mount Vernon, a magical country house whose owners, Mark Helmore and Aly Raftery, seem to have a special empathy with it. Named after George Washington's residence in Virginia, it was built in the 18th century for his friend Colonel William Presse of Roxborough, who served in the American War of Independence. The three tall cypress trees in the walled garden are thought to be a gift from George. At the end of the 19th century it became the summer home of Sir Hugh Lane, the noted art collector, and then to his aunt Lady Augusta Gregory of Coole Park, County Galway. Many of the leaders of Ireland's cultural renaissance stayed and worked here, including WB Yeats, AE (George Russell), Sean O'Casey, Synge and GB Shaw. The lovely reception rooms have fine antique furniture, paintings and batiks and painted panels from Sir William Gregory's' time as Governor of Ceylon; three fireplaces were designed and built by the Pre-Raphelite painter Augustus John. The bedrooms are spacious and interesting with views to the sea, or the wonderfully tended gardens, which include lovely walled gardens to the side that provide a sheltered place to sit out in the sunshine. (And don't forget to ask about the cobweb clearing walks.) There is a leisurely feel here and meals are an event with drinks and conversation at 7.30 and dinner at 8.00pm. There's an emphasis on organic and local foods, especially seafood like crab, lobster, salmon and monkfish in summer, moving towards game and other meats in the cooler months. Although conveniently located, only 20 miles from Galway city, this is a world apart. Golf links at Lahinch and Doonbeg are within comfortable driving distance. Guided walks on the Burren available locally. Not suitable for children under 12. Equestrian, fly fishing, golf and hunting/shooting all nearby. **Rooms 5** (4 en-suite, 1 with private bathroom, all no smoking); B&B €120 pps, ss €30. Residents D 8pm nightly, €55, must be booked by noon on the previous day, house wine €22. Closed 1 Jan-1 Apr. MasterCard, Visa, Laser. **Directions:** New Quay is between Kinvara and Ballyvaughan.

NEWMARKET-ON-FERGUS/SHANNON

Useful places to know about in the Shannon / Newmarket-on-Fergus / Dromoland area include several hotels which are right at Shannon airport: **Oakwood Arms Hotel** (Tel 061 361500; www.oakwood arms.com) is a neat owner-managed hotel with good facilities, including conference facilities; **Shannon Court Hotel** (previously Quality Hotel Shannon, Tel 061 364 588; www.irishcourthotels.com) offers modern accommodation at a reasonable price; the **Rezidor Park Inn** formerly known as the Great Southern Hotel Shannon Airport (061 471122; www.rezidorparkinn.com) is directly accessible from the main terminal building at Shannon Airport, and is in an unexpectedly lovely location overlooking the estuary and, with its views and rather gracious atmosphere, it retains a little of the old romance of flight.
WWW.IRELAND-GUIDE.COM FOR THE BEST PLACES TO EAT, DRINK & STAY

Newmarket-on-Fergus
COUNTRY HOUSE/RESTAURANT

Carrygerry House

Newmarket-on-Fergus Co Clare **Tel: 061 360500**
info@carrygerryhouse.com   www.carrygerryhouse.com

Only 10 minutes from Shannon airport and in a beautiful rural setting, Carrygerry is a lovely residence dating back to 1793. It overlooks the Shannon and Fergus estuaries and, peacefully surrounded by woodlands, gardens and pastures, seems very distant from an international airport. A young couple, Niall and Gillian Ennis, took over as proprietors in the summer of 2003 and the ambience is very pleasant, with spacious, comfortable reception rooms, open fires and an hospitable atmosphere. Bedrooms in the main house are quite spacious and traditionally furnished in line with the rest of the house, while those in the coach yard are more modern but in need of refurbishment; although planned for 2007 this had not been completed at the time of going to press and we recommend guests to check when making inquiries about accommodation. Conference/banqueting (80/94). Children welcome (under 3s free in parents' room, cot available without charge, baby sitting arranged); No pets. **Rooms 11** (3 shower-only, 1 family room, all no-smoking). B&B €75 pps, ss €40. House closed 23-26 Dec. Amex, MasterCard, Visa, Laser. **Restaurant:** The restaurant, which is open to non-residents, is shared between the dining room and a conservatory on the front of the house, overlooking gardens. Set up classically with white cloths, decent glasses and fresh flowers, it's a pleasant spot to enjoy food cooked to order by Niall Ennis. He is a good chef, who changes menus monthly and takes pride in using local ingredients in season - a main course of sea bass with white wine sauce was enjoyed on a recent visit, not only for its generous quantity of perfectly cooked fish but because the fillets were grouped around a good mound of spinach and ruby chard - very buttery, and with a touch of balsamic: delicious. Good breads, some appealing dishes not often found on other menus - a starter of home-made gravadlax salmon, for example - and excellent local meats as, perhaps, in herb & Dijon mustard crusted rack of Clare lamb. Vegetarian dishes available on request. Attractive surroundings, real food and pleasant, friendly service make for an enjoyable outing - and a good breakfast is served here too. **Seats 45** (private room, 12), not suitable for children after 8pm; D Tue-Sat, 6.30-9.30pm; set 2/3 course D, €35/€40; house wine €19. Restaurant closed Sun, Mon. **Directions:** Very close to Shannon airport, on old Newmarket-on-Fergus road.

Newmarket-on-Fergus
HOTEL/RESTAURANT/CASTLE

Dromoland Castle Hotel

Newmarket-on-Fergus Co Clare **Tel: 061 368 144**
sales@dromoland.ie www.dromoland.ie

The ancestral home of the O'Briens, barons of Inchiquin and direct descendants of Brian Boru, High King of Ireland, this is one of the few Irish estates tracing its history back to Gaelic royal families, and it is now one of Ireland's grandest hotels, and one of the best-loved. Today's visitor will be keenly aware of this sense of history yet find it a relaxing hotel, where the grandeur of the surroundings - the castle itself, its lakes and parkland and magnificent furnishings - enhances the pleasure for guests, without overpowering. It is an enchanting place, where wide corridors lined with oak panelling are hung with ancient portraits and scented with the haunting aroma of wood smoke, and it has all the crystal chandeliers and massive antiques to be expected in a real Irish castle. Guest rooms and suites vary in size and appointments, but are generally spacious, have all been refurbished recently and have luxurious bathrooms. The Brian Boru International Centre can accommodate almost any type of gathering, including exhibitions, conferences and banquets. Conference/banqueting (450/300); business centre; secretarial services on request. Leisure centre (indoor pool, sauna, jacuzzi, masseuse, beauty salon, hairdressing); Spa; championship golf (18); tennis, cycling, walking, clay pigeon shooting, croquet, fly fishing, garden, snooker, pool table. Gift shop, boutique. No pets. Children welcome (under 12's free in parents' room, cot available free of charge, baby sitting arranged). **Rooms 98** (6 suites, 8 junior suites, 13 executive, 49 separate bath & shower, all no smoking, 1 disabled). Lift. 24 hr room service. Room rate €443 (max 2 guests), SC inc. Breaks offered. Closed 24-26 Dec. **Earl of Thomond Restaurant:** Dining here is a treat by any standards - it is a magnificent room, with crystal, gilding and rich fabrics, and has a lovely view over the lake and golf course. Outstanding food and service match the surroundings, and then some: begin with an aperitif in the Library Bar, overlooking the eighth green, before moving through to beautifully presented tables and gentle background music provided by a traditional Irish harpist. David McCann, who has been doing a superb job as executive head chef since 1994, presents a table d'hôte menu, a vegetarian menu, and an à la carte offering a wonderful selection of luxurious dishes. The table d'hôte is more down-to-earth - a little less glamorous than the carte but with the same quality of ingredients and cooking; although the style is basically classic French some dishes highlight local ingredients and are more Irish in tone. Delicious desserts include a number of variations on classics and there's an excellent range of Irish farmhouse cheeses. Lunch is only served in the Earl of Thomond Restaurant on Sunday, when an appealing menu offers a wide choice of interesting dishes - often including a special Dromoland version of Irish Stew. The cooking here is invariably superb, and excellent service, under the direction of restaurant manager Tony Frisby, is a match for the food. The wine list - about 250 wines, predominantly French - is under constant review. (House wines from about €27). The breakfast menu includes a number of specialities - buttermilk pancakes with lemon & maple syrup, Limerick ham with mushrooms, poached eggs, toast & cheddar cheese - as well as a well-laden buffet, and the traditional Irish cooked breakfast. A 15% service charge is added to all prices. **Seats 90** (private room 70). D daily, 7-9, L Sun only 12.30-1.30; Set Sun L €40; Set D €65; Vegetarian menu €56; à la carte D also available. *The Gallery Menu offers a lighter choice of less formal dishes throughout the day (11.30-6.30), including Afternoon Tea. *Beside the castle, the Dromoland Golf and Country Club incorporates an 18-hole parkland course, a gym, a Health Clinic offering specialist treatments, also the Green Room Bar and Fig Tree Restaurant (6.30-9.30), which provide informal alternatives to facilities in the castle, including excellent food (9am-9.30pm). Closed 24-26 Dec. Helipad. Amex, Diners, MasterCard, Visa, Laser. **Directions:** 26km (17 m) from Limerick, 11km (8 m) from Shannon. Take N18 to Dromoland interchange; exit & follow signage.

QUIN

Quin is an historic village about 15 km from Ennis, and is home to a heritage site, **Craggaunowen** (061 530 788; open daily in summer); telling how the Celts arrived and lived in Ireland, it includes replicas of dwellings and forts, and the ancient castle is also an attraction. A major feature is the Brendan Boat built by Tim Severin who sailed from Ireland to Greenland, re-enacting the voyage of St. Brendan, reputed to have discovered America centuries before Columbus. **The Gallery Restaurant** (065 682 5789; www.thegalleryquin.com) is located on the Main Street opposite Quin Abbey and operated by owner-chef Gerry Walsh, who takes pride in showcasing local produce (D Tue-Sun, also L Sun). **Zion Coffee House & Restaurant** (065 682 5417;www.zion.ie) is a more casual restaurant beside the Abbey, offering good breakfasts and lunches, and light refreshments throughout the day - also popular locally for informal evening meals.

WWW.IRELAND-GUIDE.COM FOR THE BEST PLACES TO EAT, DRINK & STAY

Scariff
RESTAURANT

Mac Ruaidhri's

The Square Scariff Co Clare **Tel: 061 921 999**
info@macruaidhris.com www.macruaidhris.com

On the square at the top of this hilly little country town you'll find MacRuaidhri's, a neatly presented and attractive restaurant run by local man Manus Rodgers and talented head chef Peter Martin. Expect a warm welcome, good service and a concise, keenly priced early dinner at this pleasant restaurant and a wide range of choices on a later menu. Specialities include seafood, and roast rack of Burren lamb. Reservations advised. Children welcome; Toilets wheelchair accessible. **Seats 60** (outdoors, 6); reservations required; air conditioning; D Wed-Sat. 6-9.15 (open Tue D Jul-Sep), Sun L only, 12-2.30; house wine €19. Closed Sun D, Mon, and Tue in winter. MasterCard, Visa, Laser. **Directions:** From Ennis follow signs for Tulla/Scariff until Bodyke village, turn right, 5km (3 miles), going straight through Tuamgraney. On Scariff square. ◊

Tulla
RESTAURANT

Flappers Restaurant

Main Street Tulla Co Clare
Tel: 065 683 5711

The most remarkable thing about Jim and Patricia McInerney's small split-level restaurant in the village of Tulla is that it has been consistently enjoyable over such a long period. Patricia is the chef, and the dishes she sends out from the kitchen are a daily testament to her imagination, insistence on good ingredients and attention to detail. The room is simple - refreshingly free of decoration, except for a pair of striking pictures and fresh flowers on the tables but there's always a prompt welcome and tables (which are covered in classic white linen in the evening) are nicely spaced. Lunchtime draws on hearty, good value home cooked food from a simple menu. In the evening there's a fairly priced à la carte menu offering a well-balanced choice of dishes which are a little out of the ordinary, with specialities including a starter salad of fresh crabmeat with coriander, chilli & lime and a main course of roast rack of lamb with scallion mash and (a rarity in Irish restaurants) fresh mint sauce; fish and vegetarian dishes are equally good, and delicious genuinely home-made desserts (something else we would like to see more often) might include simple treats like crushed meringues with fresh fruit & passion fruit purée. Service is confident and pleasant, and a well-chosen wine list offers some good bottles at reasonable prices - and there's even a take-away service, a boon to self-catering holidaymakers. **Seats 40.** Air conditioning; wheelchair access to toilets. B Mon-Fri 9.30am-noon, L Mon-Sat 12-3pm, D Fri-Sat, 7-9.15pm. A la carte; house wine about €17; SC discretionary (except 10% on groups of 8+). Closed Sun, bank hols; 2 weeks Nov & Jan. MasterCard, Visa, Laser. **Directions:** Main street Tulla village, 10 miles from Ennis. ◊

CORK CITY

It is Cork, of all Ireland's cities, which most warmly gives the impression of being a place at comfor with itself, for it's the heart of a land flowing in milk and honey. Cork is all about the good things i life. While it may be stretching things a little to assert that the southern capital has a Mediterranea atmosphere, there's no doubting its Continental and cosmopolitan flavour, and the Cork people relaxed enjoyment of it all.

The central thoroughfare of St Patrick's Street is comfortably revitalised in a handsome and mainl pedestrianised style which is continued in the bustling urban network radiating from it. This fine thor oughfare was a river channel until 1783, as the earliest parts of Cork city were built on islands wher the River Lee meets the sea. But for more than two centuries now, it has been Cork's main street, affec tionately known to generations of Corkonians as "Pana". Designed by Catalan architect Beth Gali, th regeneration project brought a flavour of Barcelona's Ramblas to a city which responded with enthu siasm and pride.

Oliver Plunkett Street has received the same improvement, and Grand Parade has responded to creat a city centre with attractive pedestrian priorities. As we head into 2008, the potential of the Port c Cork area in the city for sympathetic re-development is being actively progressed.

Cork's unique qualities, and its people's appreciation of natural produce, make it a favoured destina tion for connoisseurs. Trading in life's more agreeable commodities has always been what Cork and it legendary merchant princes were all about. At one time, the city was known as the butter capital c Europe, and it continues to be unrivalled for the ready availability of superbly fresh produce, seen a its best in the famous English Market where Grand Parade meets Patrick Street, while the Cork Fre Choice Consumer Group (021 7330178) meets each month to promote the cause of quality food.

The way in which sea and land intertwine throughout the wonderfully sheltered natural harbour, an through the lively old city itself, has encouraged waterborne trade and a sea-minded outlook. Thu today Cork is at the heart of Ireland's most dynamically nautical area, a place world-renowned for it energetic interaction with the sea, whether for business or pleasure.

In the city itself, we find two Irish stouts being brewed - Murphy's and Beamish. Each has its ow distinctive flavour, each in turn is different from Dublin's Guinness, and it is one of life's pleasures in a characterful Cork pub - to discuss and compare their merits while savouring the Cork people' delightful line in deflationary and quirky humour.

Local Attractions & Information

Cork Airport	021 431 3031
Cork Arts Society	021 427 7749
Cork City Gaol	021 430 5022
Cork-European Capital of Culture	021 455 2005
Cork Farmers Market Cornmarket Street (Sats 9am-1pm)	021 733 0178
Cork Tourist Information	021 425 5100
Guinness Cork Jazz Festival (late October)	021 421 5170
Cork International Choral Festival (April/May)	021 421 5125
Cork International Film Festival (October)	021 427 1711
Cork Public Museum	021 427 0679
Crawford Gallery, Emmett Place	021 480 5042
English Market (covered, with specialty food stalls), corner between Grand Parade & Patrick Street	021 427 4407
Firkin Crane Dance Centre Shandon	021 450 7487
Frank O'Connor House (Writers Centre) 84 Douglas Street	021 431 2955
Glucksman Gallery, UCC	021 490 1844
Good Food In Cork (Consumer Group) – Cork Free Choice	021 733 0178
Opera House	021 427 0022
Railway Station	021 450 4888
Tig Fili Arts Centre & Publishers, MacCreddin Street	021 450 9274
Triskel Arts Centre Tobin Street, off Sth Main Street	021 427 2022

CORK CITY

There is a good choice of budget accommodation available in Cork that will suit the leisure and business guest, including; the T**ravelodge Hotel** (Frankfield Road; 021 431 0722) near Cork Airport; **Jurys Inn** (Andersons Quay; 021 494 3000) is in a very convenient central location with all the features that Jurys Inns are well known for: room prices include comfortable en-suite accommodation for up to two adults & two children (including a sofa bed) and there is space for a cot (which can be supplied by arrangement). **The Quality Hotel** (John Redmond Street; 021 452 9200), also in the city centre, has above average facilities including a good leisure centre (gym, pool, sauna and Jacuzzi); dedicated meeting rooms for up to 100 delegates are serviced by a dedicated conference porter. For quick, quality Pan-Asian food noodle lovers could head for the local branch of the UK-based **Wagamama** (South Main Street; 021 427 8872) chain; it offers healthy, inexpensive meals, including an extensive choice of meat, seafood and vegetarian dishes, all cooked to order and promptly served. For those a little more comfort on a budget **Milano** (Oliver Plunkett Street; 021 427 3106) might be a good option; like its Dublin sister restaurant (see entry) it specialises in providing good moderately priced Italian food - mainly, but not exclusively, authentic pizzas and pastas - in stylish surroundings. It's family-friendly and consistency and good service are their strong points; they're happy to cater for large parties, drinks receptions etc too; live jazz on Wednesday nights.
WWW.IRELAND-GUIDE.COM FOR THE BEST PLACES TO EAT, DRINK & STAY

Cork City
RESTAURANT

Amicus

14 A French Church Street Cork Co Cork
Tel: 021 427 6455

Tucked into a small space in Cork's Huguenot district, Ursula and Robert Hales' restaurant looks interesting from the (pedestrianised) street and has some tables outside in fine weather. It's bright and modern, with large prints and paintings on the walls - and, although small and tightly packed with tables (which adds to the sense of buzz), well placed mirrors give an impression of space. Arriving guests are promptly seated and offered quite extensive laminated menus featuring popular international dishes: salads, bruschetta, gourmet sandwiches and wraps, pastas on the daytime menu with some overlap on to the evening menu which offers more substantial dishes, notably seafood. Real, uncomplicated food, fair pricing and a youthful atmosphere add up to an attractive package which is clearly popular with locals and visitors alike. Service, under Ursula's direction is efficient, with children made welcome. **Seats 40** (outside seating, 26). Open Mon-Sat 8am-10.30/11pm, Sun 12-10pm; L 12-6pm, D 6-10pm (till 11pm Fri/Sat); house wine about €15. Closed 25-26 Dec. MasterCard, Visa, Laser. **Directions:** Just off the centre Patrick Street, between the Modern & the Ulster Bank. ◈

Cork City
RESTAURANT

Bangkok 93 - A Taste of Thailand

8 Bridge Street Cork Co Cork **Tel: 021 450 5404**
maryan@iol.ie

Cork city's longest established restaurant specialising in Thai cuisine, Mary Anne and Jim Ryan's restaurant started off in 1993 as 'A Taste of Thailand' and soon earned a loyal following that kept it busy all the time. Recently, having completed a major refurbishment - and not content with a complete makeover of the décor - they re-opened with a new name too, hence BANKOK 93 - A Taste of Thailand. Jim trained in Thailand and Australia, and freshness and authenticity are the key words here: everything is cooked to order with no artificial colours, flavours or additives used, and fresh ingredients are all Irish, except for exotics, and mainly come from the English Market. Many dishes are offered with a number of variations, including vegetarian options, but other special dietary requirements (vegan, diabetic etc) can also be catered for. The new menus are quite extensive but organised in a user-friendly way by style - curry, grills and stir-fries, noodles and so on - and, for the undecided, there are a couple of the familiar banquet meals, offering a balanced selection of dishes on each course for groups of four or six. House specialities include traditional Thai curries, Thai beef salad and Pad Thai noodles, but the range offered is wide and some European dishes are offered too. Making everything to order (mild, medium or hot to suit personal preference, or giving you 'fresh chillies on the side' so you can adjust your own meal to taste), sound cooking and attractive presentation add up to an appealing package: good food, service and value explain this restaurant's enduring popularity. The wine list offers a balanced choice of world wines, including some half and quarter bottles, also beers including Singha and Tiger. **Seats 50** (private room, 8); children welcome (high chair); air conditioning. L Mon-Sat, 12.30-2pm; D Mon-Sun, 6-11pm (5.30-10.30pm Sun); Early D €22 (6-7 pm); Set menus ('banquets') for min. 4 persons from €29.50, otherwise à la carte. House wine from €21.50 (beers, including Thai beers, available). Closed 24-26 Dec. MasterCard, Visa, Laser. **Directions:** 1 minute walk from city centre.

Cork City — # Bodéga

CAFÉ/BAR

46-47 Cornmarket Street Cork Co Cork **Tel: 021 427 2878**
info@bodega.ie www.bodega.ie

Outdoor tables with overhead canopies alongside the entire front of this old warehouse building make for an inviting entrance. Inside, a large open space with high ceilings and old mirrors resembles a large Amsterdam brown-café, with people of all ages sitting down. There is a laid-back, relaxed atmosphere without any pressures to order or finish one's meal. Food is not ambitious, but is made well: the lunch menu may offer soup and sandwiches, a lamb casserole or a vegetarian pasta dish. Dinner may range from quesadillas to steaks (and a choice of simple desserts) whilst Sunday welcomes a relaxed brunch menu. There is also a healthy option and children's menu. Friendly staff, moderate prices and a relaxing atmosphere make Bodéga a prime place for everyone to chill out. Parking in the area is not difficult after 6.30pm. **Seats 80** (private room, 50). Open all day, 12-9: Daytime food, Mon-Sat 12-5 (L12-3); also Sat & Sun brunch. D Wed-Sun 5 -10.30. Set L from about €7.50; set D about €18.50. Also à la carte. House wine €14.50; quarter bottles, €4.30. Establishment closed 25 Dec, Good Fri. Amex, Diners, MasterCard, Visa, Laser. **Directions:** 2 minutes from Grand Parade in the historic Irish Market. ◈

Cork City — # Boqueria

PUB/WINE BAR

6 Bridge St. Cork Co Cork **Tel: 021 455 9049**
tapas@boqueriasixbridgest.com

Located in an attractive former pub in an old building, this welcoming place caused quite a stir when it first opened, and is now an established part of the Cork dining scene. A long, narrow premises with upholstered bar stools and comfortable seating at tables towards the back, the character of the original bar was retained, and improved with a new black marble topped bar, wine racks and large, unframed modern oil paintings. The menu offers a mixture of genuine Spanish tapas dishes along with some Irish variations, such as smoked salmon, black pudding and Irish cheeses. Some of these little dishes are cold plates such as charcuterie or smoked fish, dependent on well-sourced artisan/organic products, whilst others are freshly cooked and served hot. Many of the familiars are here - tortilla espana, patatas bravas, plus lots of interesting hybrids too. There's a full licence, and a list of about 40 Spanish wines includes quarter bottles, and sherries by the glass. Not suitable for children after 7pm. **Seats 40;** air conditioning; food served Mon-Sat, 8.30am - 11pm, Sun 5.30pm-10pm; house wine €19.50. Closed Good Fri, 24-25 Dec. MasterCard, Visa, Laser. **Directions:** Between Patrick St. and MacCurtain St. on Bridge St. ◈

Cork City — # Café Gusto

CAFÉ

3 Washington Street Cork Co Cork **Tel: 021 425 4440**
info@cafegusto.com www.cafegusto.com

Big ideas are at work in this little designer coffee bar near Singer's Corner, which specialises in gourmet rolls, wraps and salads, either to go or to eat on the premises. The brainchild of Marianne Delaney, former manager of The Exchange on George's Quay, and her Ballymaloe-trained partner Denis O'Mullane, who take pride in sourcing the very best quality ingredients - small is indeed beautiful here, where coffee is made by baristas trained to master standard, using 100% arabica beans from the Java Roasting Company. The same philosophy applies to the food in this tiny café, in a short menu ranging from Simply Cheddar (freshly baked Italian bread filled with Dubliner cheese, beef tomato, white onion & Ballymaloe relish) to The Flying Bacon (filled with chicken, bacon, Emmenthal, honey Dijon, lettuce & tomato). Food prices are not much more than supermarket sandwiches and the extensive range of coffees, teas, herbal teas etc is keenly priced too. A breakfast menu lays the emphasis on healthy options. Great value, popular local meeting place - if only there were more like this. *There's another café beside the Clarion Hotel on Lapps Quay, and a sister restaurant Liberty Grill, on Washington Street (see entry). Air conditioned. **Seats 20.** Open Mon-Sat, 7.45 am-6pm. Closed Sun, bank hols. **No Credit Cards. Directions:** On corner of Washington Street & Grand Parade.

Café Paradiso

Cork City
RESTAURANT

16 Lancaster Quay Western Road Cork Co Cork **Tel: 021 427 7939**
info@cafeparadiso.ie www.cafeparadiso.ie

Denis Cotter and Bridget Healy's ground-breaking vegetarian restaurant produces such exciting mainstream cooking that even the most committed of carnivores admit to relishing every mouthful and it attracts devotees from all over Ireland - and beyond. House specialities that people are happy to cross the country for include delicious deep-fried courgette flowers with a fresh goats cheese & pinenut stuffing, olive & caper aoili and basil courgettes, which is a brilliant example of the cooking style at this colourful little restaurant. It's a modest, slightly bohemian place with a busy atmosphere and, although it may have a persistently well-worn look these days there is plenty to compensate for any downside in the surroundings and staff, under the direction of Bridget Healy, are not only friendly and helpful but obviously enthusiastic about their work. Seasonal menus based on the best organic produce available are topped up by daily specials, which might include potato gnocchi or a vegetable risotto, followed by a seasonal dessert. A well-priced global wine list features an exceptional choice in New Zealand wines (from Bridget's home country) and a number of organic wines; carafes of New Zealand wines represent quality at a fair price. The cooking is never less than stunning - and significantly, in this era of "cheffy" food and big egos, the creator of this wonderful food describes himself simply as "owner cook"; many of Denis Cotter's creations are featured in his acclaimed books: Café Paradiso Cookbook and Café Paradiso Seasons. Café Paradiso may be small and a little tired around the edges, but it still packs a mighty punch. ***Accommodation:** three rooms are available over the restaurant for dinner guests, at a room rate of about €160. **Seats 45** (outdoor seating, 6). Toilets wheelchair accessible. L Tue-Sat, 12-3, D Tue-Sat 6.30-10.30. A la carte. House wines from €22. Service discretionary. Closed Sun, Mon, Christmas week. Amex, MasterCard, Visa, Laser. **Directions:** On Western Road, opposite Jurys Hotel. ◇

Citrus Restaurant

Cork City
RESTAURANT

Barrycourt House East Douglas Village Cork Co Cork
Tel: 021 436 1613

Harold Lynch and Beth Haughton's restaurant is a lovely bright space, with windows on two sides and simple uncluttered tables - not a lot to absorb the sound of happy people enjoying Harold's cooking, but there's a good buzz. The style is international but as much as possible is based on local produce: meats and fish come from the English Market. Harold's menus read simply and are full of things you'd love to try - and a plate of anti-pasti makes a good start with your aperitif, while making the main choices. Starters might include a mildly spicy fish soup with rouille and there will usually be one or two tempting vegetarian dishes and updated classics such as salmon & potato cakes; excellent raw materials are generally allowed to speak for themselves. Tempting desserts tend to be variations on favourite themes and a well-chosen wine list is short but sweet. Service, under Beth's supervision, is charming and efficient. **Seats 60.** Toilets wheelchair accessible. Children welcome before 9pm. Mon-Sat: L12-3.30, D 5.30-10, Sun D only, 5-9. House wine €18.50. SC discretionary. Closed L Sun, Christmas Day. Amex, MasterCard, Visa, Laser. **Directions:** Through Douglas village, 1st left after Bully's Restaurant. ◇

Clarion Hotel Cork

Cork City
HOTEL

Lapps Quay Cork Co Cork **Tel: 021 422 4900**
info@clarionhotelcorkcity.com www.clarionhotelsireland.com

féile bia Those who like contemporary hotels and enjoy the buzz of the city centre will love the Clarion. In a brilliant central location with a wide terrace and boardwalk along the River Lee, this striking hotel embodies many of the best features of other recently built Clarion hotels and has excellent amenities including state-of-the-art conference facilities, spa, swimming pool, and gym. The entrance foyer is highly dramatic, with an atrium soaring right up to a glass roof, and rooms are arranged off galleries, which overlook the foyer; well-appointed accommodation includes riverside suites and a penthouse suite. A choice of dining is offered: Sinergie, a brasserie style restaurant, offers an international menu, good cooking and attentive service, while the Kudos bar provides an informal alternative and serves Asian fusion food to 10pm (weekends to 8pm). Conferences/Banqueting (350/270), business centre, free broadband wi/fi, secretarial services. Leisure centre with pool, fitness room, sauna, steam room, jacuzzi; beauty salon. **Rooms 191** (2 suites, 10 for disabled, 5 family, 95 no smoking); limited room service; Lift, children welcome (under 12s free in parents' room, cots available at no charge, baby sitting arranged). B&B €125pps, ss€125. Closed 24-27 Dec. Amex, Diners, MasterCard, Visa, Laser. **Directions:** Corner of Clontarf St. and Lapps Quay. Diagonally across from City Hall.

Cork City
HOTEL
N

Cork International Airport Hotel

Cork Airport Cork Co Cork **Tel: 021 454 9800**
info@corkairporthotel.com www.corkinternationalairporthotel.com

Linked by a covered walkway leading to the door of the new Cork Airport terminal, this recently opened hotel could not be handier for the time-pressed traveller. More than just convenient, however, it also has style and even humour - the aviation theme that pervades the hotel extends to the rooms, which are available in Economy, Business and First Class categories. Facilities are tailored to travellers' needs and include a Pullman Lounge where the business traveller can book a seat, take a shower, check emails, read in comfort and have a bite to eat - and an on-site spa is due to open shortly after the Guide goes to press. Special features include free Wifi throughout the hotel, and breakfast from 3.30am. Conference/ banqueting (400). Park & Fly packages available. **Rooms 150.** Room rate about €110 (1-2 guests). Amex, MasterCard, Visa. **Directions:** Situated opposite the new Cork Airport terminal. ◇

Cork
BAR/RESTAURANT
⬛ E N

The Cornstore Wine Bar & Grill

Cornmarket Street Cork
Tel 021 427 4777

In the buzzy Coal Quay renewal area, this new sister establishment to the highly regarded Aubars in Limerick (see entry) is in a stylishly converted two-storey granite mill building. Colourful Spanish tiles in the reception area lead to an expanse of polished wooden floors cleverly divided into areas of alcoves, flexible table and chair seating and more intimate booths, as well as a bar counter popular with singletons in for a quick drink or snack. Lobster is something of a speciality here, appearing as a starter with warm lemon butter; whole or half with hollandaise, pea purée and divine house chips as a main course, or the trencherman's surf & turf option of medallion of beef with half lobster and béarnaise sauce. Silky duck liver paté with Cumberland sauce is a popular starter, as is the generous fresh prawn cocktail served in a crushed ice coupe with proper Marie Rose sauce. For sharing there is a freshly baked country loaf served with tapenade, hummus, and pesto for dipping, and a range of stone-baked pizzas come straight from special ovens. The Cornstore's premium steaks are 100% Irish beef, hung 21-28 days - and choices range from the 10oz rib-eye to a 16oz T-bone. A short but irresistible list of homemade desserts features treats like pecan tart with mocha ice cream, crème brulée with shortbread biscuit and a different chocolate dessert each day - the molten-centred chocolate fudge cake is worth a detour. A well-balanced wine list leans towards the New Word, and features 20 wines by the glass (€4.50-€11) including a great value house pinot grigio at €4.50. Although only open a few weeks at the time of going to press, The Cornstore has quickly become one of Cork's hotspots, attracting customers with top class food, value for money and sharp service that manages to be both friendly and efficient. L&D daily 12-4pm and 5-10.30pm. MasterCard, Visa, Laser. **Directions:** City centre - on Cornmarket Street.

Cork City
RESTAURANT
⬛ €

Crawford Gallery Café

Emmet Place Cork Co Cork **Tel: 021 427 4415**
crawfordinfo@eircom.net www.ballymaloe.ie

An excellent collection of 18th- and 19th-century landscapes is housed in this fine 1724 building and its large modern extension. And this is also home to the Crawford Gallery Café, one of Cork city's favourite informal eating places, which is managed by Isaac Allen, grandson of Myrtle and the late Ivan Allen, founders of Ballymaloe House - and, by a remarkable coincidence, also a descendant of Arthur Hill, architect of a previous extension to the gallery, completed in 1884. Menus in this striking blue and white room reflect the Ballymaloe philosophy that food is precious and should be handled carefully, so Isaac Allen's freshly prepared dishes are made from natural local ingredients, and he also offers Ballymaloe breads and many of the other dishes familiar to Ballymaloe fans. Except for a few specialities too popular to take off (such as their spinach & mushroom pancakes), the menu changes weekly but the style - a balanced mixture of timeless country house fare and contemporary international dishes featuring carefully sourced meats, fish from Ballycotton and the freshest of seasonal vegetables - remains reassuringly constant. Substantial dishes, such as classic sirloin steak and chips, with béarnaise sauce - or a big vegetarian option like Mediterranean bean stew with coriander & basmati rice - are great for a real meal, and the home-made pickles, relishes, chutneys and preserves are delicious details. And, for a lighter bite, the home baking is outstanding. A short well-balanced wine list offers some half bottles. Conference/banqueting: available for private parties, corporate entertaining, lectures etc in evenings; details on application. **Seats 60.** No reservations. Toilets wheelchair accessible. Open Mon-Fri, 10am-4.30pm, Sat, 9.30am-4pm, L 12.30-2.30. Set L €20; also à la carte. House wine €17.50. Service discretionary. Closed Sun, 24 Dec-7 Jan, bank hols. Amex, MasterCard, Visa, Laser. **Directions:** City centre, next to Opera House. ◇

Cork City
PUB

Dan Lowrey's Tavern
13 McCurtain Street Cork Co Cork
Tel: 021 4505071

This characterful pub beside the Everyman Palace Theatre was established in 1875 and is named after its founder. Long before the arrival of the "theme pub", Lowrey's was famous for having windows which originated from Kilkenny Cathedral, but it also has many of its own original features, including a fine mahogany bar. It has been run by Anthony and Catherine O'Riordan since 1995 and Catherine oversees the kitchen herself, so it's a good place for an inexpensive home-cooked meal - popular dishes like home-made quiche or lasagne served with salad or fries, for example, or seafood bake, filled with salmon, monkfish & cod, topped with creamed potatoes and toasted breadcrumbs. It's popular with local business people at lunch time. Not suitable for children after 9pm. **Seats 30** (plus outdoor seating for 10) L & D daily: 12-3.30 & 7-9, Sun L 12.30-5 €12.50. (Sandwiches available all day). Closed 25 Dec & Good Fri. **No Credit Cards. Directions:** Next to Metropole Gresham Hotel, across from Isaacs Restaurant. ◇

ENGLISH MARKET

It is hard to imagine a visit to Cork without at the very least a quick browse through the English Market and - although it is most famous for its huge range of fresh food stalls selling everything from wet fish, and almost forgotten vegetables to cheeses, freshly baked breads and, these days, imported produce like olives - there's a growing choice of places to top up the browser's energy levels along the way. The premier spot is **Farmgate Café** on the first floor (see entry), but a growing number of stalls are offering nourishment on the go: Mary Rose's **Café Central** stall is well-known to regulars - she used to sell pork & bacon there but converted it to a coffee stall about 5 years ago, and now does a roaring trade in croissants, coffees and confectionery. Then **Fruit Boost** came along, serving fresh juices, soon followed by **The Sandwich Stall**, which serves filled rolls & coffee. And, more recently, there is **Joup** (www.joup.org), offering more substantial fare, including breakfast and lunches (mainly soups & salads) and also coffee & other beverages during the day.
WWW.IRELAND-GUIDE.COM FOR THE BEST PLACES TO EAT, DRINK & STAY

Cork City
CAFÉ

Farmgate Café
English Market Cork Co Cork **Tel: 021 427 8134**
knh@eircom.net

téite bia A sister restaurant to the Farmgate Country Store and Restaurant in Midleton, Kay Harte's Farmgate Café shares the same commitment to serving fresh, local food - and, as it is located in the gallery above the English Market, where ingredients are purchased daily, it doesn't come much fresher or more local than this. The atmosphere is lively and busy, as people come and go from the market below, giving a great sense of being at the heart of things. With its classic black and white tiles, simple wooden furniture and interesting art work there's a combination of style and a comfortably down to earth atmosphere which suits the wholesome food they serve. Having highlighted the freshness of local ingredients for some time in dishes that were a mixture of modern and traditional, Kay Harte and her team now offer regional dishes using the food they buy in the market, and have introduced lesser known foods such as corned mutton to their menus alongside famous old Cork ones with a special market connection, like tripe & drisheen and corned beef & champ with green cabbage. Menus depend on what is available in the English Market each day, including "oysters to your table from the fish stall" and other fish - used, for example, in a chowder that is ever-popular with market regulars. And, however simple, everything is perfectly cooked - including superb breakfasts. Either full cooked or continental breakfast is offered, with self-service or table service available. All this and delicious home-baked cakes, breads and desserts too; whether as a bite to accompany a coffee, or to finish off a meal, a wonderfully home-made seasonal sweet is always a treat. This is an interesting and lively place to enjoy good food - and it's great value for money. * Farmgate Café was the winner of our Irish Breakfast Awards in 2007. **Seats 110.** Meals Mon-Sat, from 8.30am - 5pm: B'fast 8.30-10.30, L 12-4. Licensed. Closed Sun, bank hols, Dec 25-3 Jan. Diners, MasterCard, Visa, Laser. **Directions:** English Market - off Oliver Plunkett Street and Grand Parade. ◇

Cork City
RESTAURANT

Fenns Quay Restaurant

5 Sheares Street Cork Co Cork **Tel: 021 427 9527**
www.fennsquay.ie

Situated in a 250-year old listed building, this is a bright, busy restaurant with a welcoming atmosphere and simple decor enlivened by striking modern paintings. Both lunch and dinner menus offer plenty of interesting choices, including a number of vegetarian options (highlighted) and daily specials, including seafood sourced daily from the nearby English Market. Carefully sourced ingredients are local where possible (including meat from the owners' own business, which is a point of pride) presented in a pleasing bistro style. Specialities include char-grilled fillet steak "Wellie Style", an enduring favourite which comes with house cut potato chips. An interesting wine list offers variety at reasonable prices, with several by the glass - good value is a feature of both food and drink. A very comfortable outdoor seating area makes a pleasant extension to the restaurant, and recent refurbishments have enabled wheelchair access to the restaurant but not to toilets, unfortunately, as it is a listed building. Air conditioning. Children welcome. On street parking can be difficult during the day, but is easy to find after 6.30. **Seats 60** (outdoor seating, 10). Open all day Mon-Sat 10am-10pm; L 12.30-3, D 6-10. L Deal €10 (12.30-5), also à la carte; set 2/3 course D, €22.50/27.50; à la carte also available. House wine €17.95. SC 10% on groups 6+. Closed Sun, 25 Dec, bank hols. Amex, MasterCard, Visa, Laser. **Directions:** Central city - 2 minutes from the Courthouse.

Cork City
RESTAURANT WITH ROOMS

Flemings Restaurant

Silver Grange House Tivoli Cork Co Cork **Tel: 021 482 1621**
info@flemingsrestaurant.ie www.flemingsrestaurant.ie

Clearly signed off the main Cork-Dublin road, this large Georgian family house is home to Michael and Eileen Fleming's excellent restaurant with rooms. On a hillside overlooking the river, the house is set in large grounds, including a kitchen garden, which provides fruit, vegetables and herbs for the restaurant during the summer. It is a big property to maintain and the entrance can seem a little run down, but this is quickly forgotten when you enter the light, airy double dining room, which is decorated in an elegant low-key style that highlights its fine proportions, while well-appointed linen-clad tables provide a fine setting for Michael Fleming's classical, modern French cooking. Seasonal table d'hôte and à la carte menus offer a wonderful choice of classics, occasionally influenced by current international trends but, even where local ingredients feature strongly, the main thrust of the cooking style is classical French - as in a superb speciality starter of pan-fried foie gras de canard with Timoleague black pudding & glazed apple. Less usual choices might include Roast Loin of Venison with Poached Pear, an imaginative combination and beautifully presented. Desserts may include a deep apple pie served with home-made ice cream - and a selection of cheese is served traditionally, with biscuits and fruits. Michael's cooking is invariably excellent, presentation elegant, and service both attentive and knowledgeable. A great antidote to the sameness of modern multicultural restaurants - a visit to a classic restaurant like this is a treat to treasure. Good wine list - and good value all round. *A converted basement into a comfortable bar/lounge seats up to 70. Banqueting (90). **Seats 80** (private room 30; outside seating, 30). Children welcome. L&D daily, 12.30-3, 6.30-10; reservations not necessary. Set L €28.50, D à la carte. House wine about €22. SC discretionary. **Accommodation:** There are four spacious en-suite rooms, comfortably furnished in a style appropriate to the age of the house (B&B €55 pps, ss €33). Closed 24-27 Dec. Amex, MasterCard, Visa, Laser. **Directions:** Off main Cork-Dublin route, 4km from city centre.

Cork City
HOTEL

Gresham Metropole Hotel & Leisure Centre

MacCurtain Street Cork Co Cork **Tel: 021 4508122**
info@gresham-metropolehotel.com www.gresham-hotels.com

This imposing city-centre hotel next door to the Everyman Palace Theatre and backing on to the River Lee, celebrated its centenary in 1998. Always popular with those connected with the arts and entertainment industry, there are many displays (photos and press cuttings) of stars past and present in the public areas and the atmospheric, traditionally-styled Met Tavern. Many of the hotel's original features remain, including the marble facade, exterior carved stonework and plaster ceilings. Recent refurbishment has greatly improved the bedrooms, most of which now combine a period feel with modern facilities, and care has been taken to bring previously neglected areas back to their former elegance by, for example, correcting ceiling heights which had been changed in previous 'improvements'. Conference and meeting facilities have air conditioning and natural daylight. (450). Children welcome (under 2 free in parents' room, cot available without charge, baby sitting arranged). No pets. Arrangement with nearby car park. **Rooms 113** (2 junior suites, 44 executive rooms,10 shower only, 55 no-smoking, 1 for disabled). B&B about €127.50pps. Open all year. Amex, Diners, MasterCard, Visa, Laser. **Directions:** City centre hotel. ◊

Cork City
HOTEL/RESTAURANT

Hayfield Manor Hotel

Perrott Avenue College Road Cork Co Cork **Tel: 021 484 5900**
enquiries@hayfieldmanor.ie www.hayfieldmanor.ie

Set in two acres of gardens near University College Cork, the city's premier hotel provides every comfort and a remarkable level of privacy and seclusion, just a mile from the city centre. Although quite new, it has the feel of a large period house, and is managed with warmth and discreet efficiency. Public areas include a choice of restaurants, both excellent of their type - the formal Orchids, which overlooks gardens at the back, and the newer smart-casual Perrotts - and a redesigned bar that skilfully links the contrasting traditional and contemporary styles of the interior. Spacious suites and guest rooms vary in decor, are beautifully furnished with antiques and have generous marbled bathrooms, all with separate bath and shower. On-site amenities include the unusual new Beautique spa, with indoor pool, and treatment rooms furnished with antiques. *Hayfield Manor was our Hotel of the Year in 2006. Conferences/Banqueting (110/120); business centre, secretarial service; free broadband wi/fi. 24 hr room service. Lift. Turndown service. Garden, golf nearby, leisure centre (fitness room, pool, jacuzzi); spa (treatment rooms, massage, hairdressing). **Rooms 88.** (4 suites, 4 interconnecting, 4 for disabled); children welcome (under 12s free in parents' room, cot available free of charge, baby sitting arranged). Lift. B&B €140, ss €65. **Orchids:** Since the refurbishment of Hayfield's Bar - a judicious blend of traditional and contemporary, resulting in the cosy atmosphere of a traditional bar, with chic modern touches - it has become an appealing place for an aperitif before going in to this fine dining restaurant, which overlooks the walled garden at the back of the hotel and has recently been completely refurbished in an elegant contemporary style that works well with the old style of the building. Well spaced tables are very comfortably arranged in three sections, with the main area opening on to the garden, and a raised section beside it. Emphasising the relative formality - Orchids is normally an evening restaurant, although open for lunch when there is demand - tables are set up classically, with pristine white linen and gleaming glasses. Head chef Graeme Campbell bases his menus on local produce where possible, and continues the tradition of fairly classical cuisine with an occasional contemporary twist for which this restaurant is well known, and a meal here is always enhanced by professional and caring service. **Perrotts:** In a conservatory area at the front of the hotel, this smart and relaxing contemporary restaurant offers an informal alternative to dining in Orchids. Open for lunch and dinner daily, it has a bright and airy atmosphere and plenty of greenery, and quickly became established as a favoured destination with discerning Corkonians who enjoy the ambience and stylish bistro cooking. The choice of dishes offered is wide, ranging from updated classics, to international lunchtime favourites like Perrotts home-made burger with bacon and Emmenthal cheese, spicy guacomole and tomato relish dip, and hand-cut chips. Stylish surroundings, varied menus, confident cooking and helpful, attentive service make for a very enjoyable dining experience. **Orchids: Seats 90;** children welcome; air conditioning. D daily, 7-10. Set D €45/55, 2/3 course, also à la carte. House wine from €31.75. SC in restaurant of 10% on parties of 10+. Perrotts Restaurant, 12.15-2.30 & 6-10 daily. Amex, Diners, MasterCard, Visa, Laser. **Directions:** Opposite University College Cork - signed off College Road.

Cork City
HOTEL/RESTAURANT

Hotel Isaacs & Greenes Restaurant

48 MacCurtain Street Cork Co Cork **Tel: 021 450 0011**
greenes@isaacs.ie www.isaacscork.com

Opposite the Everyman Palace Theatre and approached through a cobbled courtyard, this attractive hotel offers comfort in spacious rooms at a fairly reasonable price. Recent major renovations have made this a much more confident and comfortable hotel. New windows have reduced traffic noise, the fourteen new superior rooms are quietly impressive and have set the standard for refurbishment of all the existing bedrooms, which is now complete. A few of the rooms at the back have a charming outlook on to the waterfall, which is a feature from the restaurant. Small Conferences (50); broadband wi/fi; secretarial services available (from reception), video conferencing by arrangement. Children welcome (under 3 free in parents room, cot available free of charge, baby sitting arranged). All day room service. Car park nearby. No pets. Garden (courtyard). Self-catering apartments available (open all year). **Rooms 47** (14 executive, 4 shower-only, 37 no-smoking, 2 for disabled). Lift. Room service (all day). B&B €75 pps, ss €25. Closed 24-27 Dec. **Greenes:** Despite being next door to the well-known Isaacs restaurant (with the confusion of the hotel's similar name) Greenes is well-established as a successful stand-alone restaurant and has earned a following. The approach from the street is attractive, under a limestone arch to a narrow courtyard with a waterfall - which is floodlit at night, making an unusual feature when seen from the restaurant. The reception and the two restaurant areas have character and the atmosphere is definitely 'independent restaurant' rather than 'hotel dining room'. Head chef Frederic Desormeaux's menus are quite adventurous, offering modern renditions of classic dishes, sometimes with a French slant and often based on local ingredients, especially seafood. Starters might include air dried smoked Connemara lamb on salad leaves, with fresh figs, beetroot dressing & balsamic reduction, while main courses include classics like pan-fried T-bone steak with home-made chips as well as more unusual dishes pan-fried cod on a cassoulet of cannelloni beans with chorizo, cherry tomatoes & roast garlic aioli, perhaps. Seasonal fruits feature strongly among the desserts (a dessert platter for two to share is an option) or, unusually, you can have a selection of Tipperary cheeses, with chutney, home-made biscuits and a shot glass of port. Accurate cooking, attractive presentation and friendly, helpful service - plus a lively atmosphere and quite reasonable prices - should ensure an enjoyable meal. The early dinner menu is especially good value. Outdoor dining in heated courtyard; Barbecues in summer. Children welcome (high chair, childrens menu). **Seats 100** (private room, 36, outdoor, 30). L Mon-Sun, 12.30-3 (to 4pm Sun); D daily 6-10 (Sun & Bank hols to 9.30). Value L €15; early D €30 (6-7pm); set 2/3 course D €35/45; also à la carte. Set Sun L €30. House wine from about €18. SC10% on groups 10+. Closed 24-27 Dec. Amex, Diners, MasterCard, Visa, Laser. **Directions:** City centre - 400 m down MacCurtain Street, on left; entrance opposite Everyman Palace Theatre, through cobblestone archway.

Cork City
CAFÉ

Idaho.Café

19 Caroline Street Cork Co Cork
Tel: 021 427 6376

This friendly and well-located little café hits the spot for discerning shoppers, who appreciate Mairead Jacob's wholesome food - this is that rare treat, good home cooking based on the best of ingredients. The day begins with breakfast, and a very good breakfast it is too: everything from lovely hot porridge with brown sugar and cream to warm Danish pastries, muffins, or Belgian waffles with organic maple syrup and the option of crispy bacon. You can choose from this menu up to noon, when they ease into lunch, with tasty little numbers like a house special of gratinated potato gnocchi with smoky bacon & sage or, equally typical of the treats in store, crispy duck, spring onion and Irish brie quesadillas or shepherdess's pie (using organic beef). But best of all perhaps, as baking is a speciality, are the 'Sweet Fix' temptations which are just ideal for that quick morning coffee or afternoon tea break - the coeliac-friendly 'orange almond' cake has developed a following, and there's a wide of range hot and cold drinks, including 'Hippy' specialist teas. Dishes which are vegetarian, or can be adapted for vegetarians, are highlighted on the menu at this great little place. Great service, and great value too: full marks. **Seats 30.** Toilets not wheelchair accessible. Children welcome. Open Mon-Thu, 8.30-5, Fri/Sat 8.30-6pm; B'fst 8.30-12, L 12-4.30. House wine from €16.50 or from 2.95 a glass, specialist beers from about €3.75. Closed Sun, Bank Holidays, 24-26 Dec. **No Credit Cards. Directions:** Directly behind Brown Thomas, Cork. ◊

Cork City
HOTEL

Imperial Hotel

South Mall Cork Co Cork **Tel: 021 427 4040**
info@imperialhotelcork.ie www.flynnhotels.com

This thriving hotel in Cork's main commercial and banking centre dates back to 1813 and has a colourful history - Michael Collins spent his last night here, no less, and that suite now bears his name. However, it's the convenient location - near the river and just a couple of minutes walk from the Patrick Street shopping area - that has always made this hotel so popular for business and pleasure, also the free car parking available for residents. It has been run by the Flynn family (of the Old Ground Hotel in Ennis, Co Clare) since 1998, and they have recently completed a major renovation and refurbishment of the hotel, which has brought new life to its fine old public areas and transformed others: the popular Pembroke Restaurant, is now a more spacious and stylish contemporary restaurant, allowing for changing moods throughout the day, for example, and Souths Bar has retained its character alongside the introduction of updated furnishings. As well as upgrading existing bedrooms, new superior rooms have been added and also a stunning 2-bedroom penthouse suite with wraparound balcony and views over the city. Most recently, the Escape Lifestyle & Salon Spa and has opened the first of its kind in Ireland. Live jazz in the bar on Friday nights is popular with guests and locals alike. Attractive weekend and off-season rates are offered. Conference/banqueting (280/220). Private car park. Children welcome (cots available without charge). No pets. **Rooms 130** (20 suites, 20 executive, 8 shower-only, 2 for disabled). Lift. 24 hour room service. B&B about €87.50 pps, ss €45. Closed 24-27 Dec. Amex, Diners, MasterCard, Visa, Laser. **Directions:** City centre location. ◊

Cork City
RESTAURANT

Isaacs Restaurant

48 MacCurtain Street Cork Co Cork
Tel: 021 450 3805

In 1992 Michael and Catherine Ryan, together with partner/head chef Canice Sharkey, opened this large, atmospheric modern restaurant in an 18th-century warehouse and it immediately struck a chord with people tired of having to choose between fine dining and fast food, and became a trend-setter in the modern Irish food movement. The combination of international influences and reassuring Irish traditions was ahead of its time, and it quickly gained a following of people who enjoyed both the informal atmosphere, and the freshness of approach in Canice Sharkey's kitchen. In a quiet, low-key way, this restaurant has played a leading role in the culinary revolution that has overtaken Ireland over the last decade or two. Their original blend of Irish and international themes, together with a policy of providing quality food and good value in an informal, relaxed ambience has attracted endless imitations. Ingredients are carefully sourced, the cooking is consistently accomplished and menus are freshened by occasional inspired introductions (a plate of tapas, for example, which can be a starter or a lovely light lunch). A list of about seven specials changes twice daily, and most dishes are available with little oil and no dairy produce, on request. The service is terrific too, and a visit here is always great fun. The wine list - which is considerately arranged by style ('dry, light and fresh', 'full bodied' etc) follows a similar philosophy, offering a good combination of classics and more unusual bottles, at accessible prices, and Isaacs coffee is organic and Fair Trade. Toilets wheelchair accessible; Children wlecome (high chair, baby changing facilities). **Seats 120.** L Mon-Sat 12.30-2.30, D daily 6-10 (Sun to 9). Short à la carte and daily blackboard specials; vegetarian dishes highlighted. House wine from €20. Service discretionary. Closed - L Sun, Christmas week, L Bank Holidays. Amex, Diners, MasterCard, Visa, Laser. **Directions:** 5 minutes from Patrick Street; opposite Gresham Metropole Hotel.

Cork City
RESTAURANT

Ivory Tower

The Exchange Builldings Princes Street Cork Co Cork
Tel: 021 4274665

Seamus O'Connell, one of Ireland's most original culinary talents, runs this unusual restaurant upstairs in an early Victorian commercial building; the entrance to the dowdy building is uninspiring but as you arrive in the high-ceilinged room with its slightly faded decor, eclectic ornaments and modern paintings, you will receive a warm and friendly welcome, and soon be impressed by the efficient service and outstanding food and cooking. The surroundings are basic, slightly bohemian, but no resources are spared when it comes to sourcing the very best quality ingredients (all local and organic or wild, including game in season). Creative menus and excellent details like delicious home-baked breads and imaginative presentation are the hallmarks of The Ivory Tower - and vegetarian dishes interesting enough to tempt hardened carnivores are always a feature. Varied international menus change frequently and will certainly contain some surprises. Typical but not necessarily available - would be starters like a perfectly light battered tempura of squash, shiitake & pepper, or a selection of nigri sushi, followed by a middle course of sorbet perhaps. Among the main courses, you will find seasonal treats such as salmon on samphire, also fillet steak teriyaki perhaps, and unusual vegetarian dishes like gnocchi with truffle, girolles, asparagus & parmesan. To finish there are indulgences like dark chocolate silk cake with liquorice & coffee, exotic fruits, and cheeses served with fresh figs. An interesting wine list offers fair value for a restaurant of this calibre. Not suitable for children under 5. Private room available. **Seats 35.** L Tue-Sat, 12-3, D Tue-Sat, 6.30-10 (Tue is Sushi Night). 5-course D about €60; Surprise Menu about €75. House wine from about €18. SC discretionary. Closed Mon-Wed. Amex, MasterCard, Visa, Laser. **Directions:** Corner of Princes/Oliver Plunkett street.

Cork City
RESTAURANT

Jacobs On The Mall

30A South Mall Cork Co Cork **Tel: 021 425 1530**
info@jacobsonthemall.com www.jacobsonthemall.com

Its location in the former Turkish baths creates a highly unusual and atmospheric contemporary dining space for what many would regard as Cork's leading restaurant. Head Chef Mercy Fenton does a consistently excellent job: modern European cooking is the promise and, with close attention to sourcing the best ingredients allied to outstanding cooking skills, the results are commendably simple and always pleasing in terms of balance and flavour. Details like home-made breads are good, and fresh local and organic produce makes its mark in the simplest of dishes, like delicious mixed leaf salads; similarly a house speciality of free range chicken stuffed with Gubbeen, savoy cabbage and bacon, with a thyme jus that presents an upbeat dish based on traditional Irish themes. Reflecting the availability of local produce, lunch and dinner menus change daily and are sensibly brief - with seafood and vegetables in season especially strong points: a simple meal of Ballycotton crab salad, and sirloin steak with lyonnaise potatoes could be memorable, for example. Creativity with deliciously wholesome and colourful ingredients, accurate cooking, stylish presentation and efficient yet relaxed service all add up to an outstanding dining experience. Finish on a high note - with a delectable falling chocolate cake, with vanilla ice cream, perhaps, or farmhouse cheeses, which are always so good in Cork, served here with fruit and home-made oatcakes. An interesting and fairly priced drinks list includes cocktails, and a wide choice of spirits and after dinner drinks; the wide-ranging wine list includes many interesting bottles, some organic wines and a good choice of half bottles and wines by the glass. Children welcome. Special diets willingly accommodated with advance notice. *Development under way at the time of going to press will see Jacobs extended to become a 37-bedroom boutique hotel, Jacobs Mill (www.jacobsmill.com) in the near future. Toilets wheelchair accessible; children welcome; special diets willingly accommodated with advance notice. **Seats 130** (Private room, 50, with own bar); air conditioning. L Mon-Sat 12.30-2.30, D Mon-Sat 6.30-10pm. A la carte. House wines from €22; sc10% (excl L). Closed Sun, 25/26 Dec, L on bank hols. Amex, Diners, MasterCard, Visa, Laser.
Directions: Beside Bank of Ireland, at the Grand Parade end of the South Mall.

Cork City
RESTAURANT

Jacques Restaurant

Phoenix Street Cork Co Cork **Tel: 021 427 7387**
jacquesrestaurant@eircom.net www.jacquesrestaurant.ie

NATURAL FOOD AWARD

An integral part of Cork life since 1982, sisters Eithne and Jacqueline Barry's delightful restaurant has changed with the years, evolving from quite a traditional place to a smart contemporary space. But, while the surroundings may go through periodic re-makes, the fundamentals of warm hospitality and great food never waiver and that is the reason why many would cite Jacques as their favourite Cork restaurant. There is always a personal welcome and, together with Eileen Carey, who has been in the kitchen with Jacque Barry since 1986, this team has always a put high value on the provenance and quality of the food that provides the building blocks for their delicious meals - and, appropriately, Jacque is now leader of the Cork Slow Food Convivium. Menus are based on carefully sourced ingredients from a network of suppliers built up over many years and, together with skill and judgement in the kitchen, this shows particularly as they have the confidence to keep things simple and allow the food to speak for itself. You could start your meal in delectably civilised fashion with a half bottle of Manzanilla, served with nuts and olives, while considering choices from menus that are refreshingly short, which allows this skilled team to concentrate on the delicious cooking that is their forte. There are also daily specials, which may include unusual items - lam's tongue with mustard & breadcrumbs, with a fresh beetroot & carrot slaw, for example. Some of the moreish starters may also be available as a main course, and there are numerous wonderful speciality dishes, with a focus on fresh fish, such as hake simply cooked on or off the bone - typically served with hollandaise

& sprouting broccoli & champ; delicious desserts or Irish cheeses are offered to finish. An interesting, informative wine list matches the food, and includes some organic wines, a wine of the month and a good choice of half bottles. Consistently good cooking in stylish, relaxed surroundings, genuinely hospitable service, and excellent value are among the things that make Jacques special. The early dinner menu offers particularly good value. Children welcome. **Seats 62**; air conditioning. An interesting, fairly priced wine list includes some organic wines and about ten half bottles. Open D only Mon-Fri 6-10. Early D, 6-7pm, €21.90; also à la carte D. House wine about €20. SC discretionary. Closed Sat, Sun, Bank Hols, 24 Dec - 27 Dec. Amex, MasterCard, Visa, Laser. **Directions:** City centre, near G.P.O.

Jurys Cork Hotel

Cork City
HOTEL
Ⓝ

Western Road Cork Co Cork **Tel: 021 425 2700**
cork@jurysdoyle.com www.jurysdoyle.com

Following complete redevelopment of their original riverside site on Western Road, Jurys Cork Hotel has re-opened and is no doubt set to become one of the most popular Cork hotels again, especially perhaps for business guests. Well-located, it is beside the university and within comfortable walking distance of the city centre in good weather, and also handy for those who wish to make a neat exit westwards on leaving. It has a range of meeting rooms and a dedicated executive floor and lounge on the penthouse floor; executive extras include complimentary continental breakfast and drinks and canapés in the evening as well as turndown service, daily newspapers and business magazines. Jurys always had a reputation for its lively bar and The Weir Bar, which is designed to take advantage of the riverside setting and has a decking area, looks set to continue the tradition; informal dining is available in the Weir Bistro. Bedrooms have been finished to a high specification with air conditioning, 25" LCD TV, work desk, laptop safe, 'fair price minibar' as standard, and smart bathrooms all have separate bath and power shower and classy toiletries. A leisure centre with 18m swimming pool, sauna, spa bath etc is open, and a spa will follow. Business centre; complimentary broadband throughout the hotel. Laundry/drycleaning. Complimentary guest parking. **Rooms 182.** Room rate from €119 to €275. Open all year. **Directions:** Shortly before University College Cork. ◊

Kingsley Hotel

Cork City
HOTEL/RESTAURANT

Victoria Cross Cork Co Cork **Tel: 021 480 0500**
info@kingsleyhotel.com www.kingsleyhotel.com

Possibly the most attractively located hotel in the city, the Kingsley is conveniently situated alongside the River Lee, just minutes from both Cork airport and the city centre and has always been especially appealing to business visitors, for whom it quickly becomes a home from home. Major investment over the last two years has enlarged and upgraded the hotel yet remarkably it has retained the sense of intimacy and homely atmosphere that has been a special feature from the outset. A large, comfortably furnished foyer has a welcoming feel to it, with staff always on hand to assist guests - and there is a comfortable lounge/informal restaurant area a few steps up from it (and overlooking the weir) which, like the River Bar beside it, makes a good meeting place. A caring atmosphere is noticeable throughout the hotel, from the moment guests are greeted on arrival, and accommodation is personally decorated and well-planned to make a good home from home. Spacious rooms offer traditional comfort with a contemporary edge, and are designed with care: air conditioning, work station with complimentary broadband, interactive TV, personal safe, trouser press with ironing board, same day laundry and all of the small extras that make a difference. Executive suites at the back of the hotel include a room suitable for private entertaining or meetings (and especially luxurious bathrooms) and have river views and an impressive 750 square metre 2-bedroom Presidential Suite built over two floors; with its own hot tub balcony, and spacious living area on the penthouse level, it is Cork's premier suite. The hotel's Business & Conference Centre is a top venue for small and medium sized meetings has also been upgraded (see hotel website for full details). Good health and fitness facilities include the Yauvana holistic lifestyle spa, with exclusive Indian treatments. Conference/banqueting (230/200); business centre, broadband, secretarial services; video conferencing, on request; 24 hour room service. Leisure centre (recently refurbished & gym equipment renewed), swimming pool; treatment rooms, beauty salon. Children welcome (under 12s free in parents' room; cot available without charge, baby sitting arranged). Garden. Riverside walks. Pets permitted by arrangement. Parking. **Rooms 131** (71 separate bath & shower, 4 suites, 6 for disabled, all no smoking). Air conditioning. Lift. B&B €80 pps, ss

€65. Open all year. **Otters Restaurant:** This lovely restaurant is on two levels, so different that it almost seems like two restaurants: the upper level is bright and airy and, overlooking the river and linear park with fishermen and joggers out on a summer's day, it has a wonderful ambience; the lower, which is darker, with more closely spaced tables, might be cosier in winter. As elsewhere in the hotel, attention from friendly staff is outstanding right from the beginning, when you are escorted courteously to your table luxuriously set up with crisp linen, smartly polished cutlery and glassware; bread (made in-house) is brought immediately, together with chilled butter and iced water. Appealing menus may include starters like bruschetta of goat's cheese and crab mayonnaise and fresh fish also features among the main courses, typically seared cod, garnished with roast cherry tomatoes and rocket salad. The cooking can sometimes be a little uneven, but desserts are likely to be the highlight of a meal here: an orange & polenta cake with berry compôte and an elegant layered chocolate mousse both attracted special praise on a recent visit. And, with its elegant setting and such attentive staff, a meal here should always be enjoyable. **Seats 140** (private room 20). L & D daily: L 12.30-3, D 5.30-10 (Sun 6-10). Set L €30; Early Bird D 5.30-7.30 €26. set D €50; D also à la carte. House wine from around €17. SC discretionary. *Lounge and bar food also available through the day. Open all year. Amex, Diners, MasterCard, Visa, Laser. **Directions:** On main N25 Killarney road by Victoria Cross.

Cork City
GUESTHOUSE

Lancaster Lodge

Lancaster Quay Western Road Cork Co Cork **Tel: 021 425 1125**
info@lancasterlodge.com www.lancasterlodge.com

This modern purpose-built guesthouse is just beside the newly re-opened Jurys Hotel and, as there is still major construction work going on in the area, guests arriving by car can easily miss the turn into the carpark from the one-way street and, to enter by a side street (also one way), have to loop back past the university entrance and back around the cathedral. Once you have arrived safely, however, there is secure parking in the grounds. This is a place that was built to offer hotel quality accommodation at a moderate price, and it is comparable to a budget hotel; public areas are not grand but prompt, friendly reception should help to offset any poor impression given by the difficulties of the surrounding area, and there is bottled water on each floor, newspapers in the breakfast room and generally pleasing surroundings throughout, including original art works. Spacious guest rooms which include 9 new ones - are furnished to a high standard (with free broadband, safes, 12 channel TV, trouser press, tea/coffee facilities and room service as well as the more usual facilities) and the bathrooms, some with jacuzzi baths, are well-designed. Efficient double glazing helps to offset traffic and construction noise in rooms at the front (if you do not need to open windows), but rooms at the back may be a better option. Breakfast is served in a bright contemporary dining room. Judging by a summer 2007 visit, the surrounding construction work seems to have taken its toll on morale here recently, but it remains a useful address and should be back on form when the area has been tidied up. Small conferences (20); wheelchair friendly; children welcome (under 5s free in parents' room, cot available, baby sitting arranged, high chair); dogs permitted by arrangement. Free secure parking. 24 hour reception. **Rooms 48** (2 executive rooms, 5 shower only, 2 family, 3 ground floor, 2 for disabled, all no smoking). Lift; limited room service. B&B from €70 pps. ss €35 Closed 23-28 Dec. Amex, Diners, MasterCard, Visa, Laser. **Directions:** Opposite Café Paradiso.

Cork City
RESTAURANT

Les Gourmandises Restaurant

17 Cook Street Cork Co Cork **Tel: 021 425 1959**
www.lesgourmandises.ie

Just off South Mall, this little restaurant feels like an outpost of France - the menu at the entrance will draw you in, and you'll be glad you noticed it. It's run by Patrick and Soizic Kiely - both formerly of Restaurant Patrick Guilbaud but, although that says a lot about the key standards, this is far more reminiscent of family-run restaurants in France. There's nothing flash about the quiet style of this restaurant: a small reception area is cleverly arranged to make three compact seating areas with a bar, fresh flowers and stylish cushions; the welcome is cordial without being effusive, and the team under Soizic's guidance go about their business with quiet competence. The long, narrow, high-ceilinged room, formerly a Turkish bath, is a restrained, modern white space, with comfortable subdued lighting and low key music. The menu is not overlong, but changes daily to accommodate the day's market; there is usually a seafood platter, which varies and may contain 5 or so elements, each treated differently and with appropriate sauces/garnishes, arranged to please the eye as well as the palate. Outstanding dishes may include a 'crab sandwich' starter, of spanking fresh crab with remoulade sauce, layered in three tiers with toasted brioche & fresh dill. Presentation is stylish, and great attention is given to the marriage of complementary flavours - a tiny pink lamb rack, for example, comes with rosemary and black olive tapenade - and careful seasoning. To finish, there may be upbeat classic seasonal desserts and a good French & Irish cheese selection, and lovely coffee. The wine list is not long but very well chosen, with some real finds including the house wines. Terrific food and good value: this is one of the hidden treasures you'd like to keep a secret lest it become too popular. Children over 6 welcome. **Seats 30.** L Fri only (also all of the week before Christmas), 12-2. D Tue-Sat, 6-9.30. Early D, 2/3 course: about €27.50/31.50. Also à la carte. House wine about €22. Closed Sun, Mon; Mar, Sep. MasterCard, Visa, Laser. **Directions:** City centre - access to Cook Street from South Mall. ◊

Cork City   Liberty Grill
RESTAURANT   32 Washington Street Cork Co Cork **Tel: 021 427 1049**
                                            dine@libertygrillcork.com www.libertygrillcork.com

Liberty Grill is a sister establishment to Café Gusto (Washington Street & Lapps Quay, see entry), so you may expect the same food philosophy based on quality ingredients, where possible organic and locally sourced. It's situated on the renovated ground floor of an early Victorian block, with menus displayed on a lectern outside the door, and it's an attractive room, with some exposed stonework, darkwood floor and modern designer chairs. Lighting is well designed, and a brilliant white ceiling also reflects light, giving it a bright and spacious atmosphere. Comfortably spaced tables are set up bistro style and a youthful clientele creates a buzz. Separate menus are offered for brunch, lunch and dinner. The extensive brunch menu is very appealing, especially if you are staying 'room only' in the area. Lunch and dinner menus major in a choice of burgers, steaks (including a vegetarian option) and salads, and fresh fish from the English Market. A small wine list is offered. Liberty Grill offers real, tasty food and good value in pleasant surroundings. Children welcome before 9pm. **Seats 50.** Open Mon-Fri 8am-9pm, Sat 8-10. A la carte. House wine €16. Closed Sun, Bank Hols, 1st week in Aug. Amex, MasterCard, Visa, Laser. **Directions:** On Washington Street in block between North Main Street and Courthouse.

Cork City   Lotamore House
GUESTHOUSE   Tivoli Cork Co Cork **Tel: 021 482 2344**
                                                 lotamore@iol.ie www.lotamorehouse.com

Sidney and Geri McElhinney's large period house is set in mature gardens and, although not overly grand, it was built on a generous scale. The approach and exterior maintenance is a little off-putting (although work was in progress on the driveway on our summer 2007 visit), but it is a large and comfortable house and many regular guests prefer it to staying in an hotel. Some refurbishment was undertaken in 2006 and the spacious, airy rooms have air conditioning, phones, TV and trouser press (tea/coffee trays on request), and they're comfortably furnished, with room for an extra bed or cot; all have full bathrooms. A large drawing room has plenty of armchairs and an open fire and, although only breakfast and light meals are offered, Fleming's Restaurant (see entry) is next door. Meetings/Small conferences by arrangement (25). Children welcome (cot available). Own parking. **Rooms 19** (All no-smoking, 1 family room). Garden. No pets. B&B €65 pps, ss €20. Closed 22 Dec-5 Jan. MasterCard, Visa, Laser. **Directions:** On N8, 10 minutes drive from Cork City. ◊

Cork City
HOTEL

Maryborough Hotel & Spa

Maryborough Hill Douglas Cork Co Cork **Tel: 021 436 5555**
info@maryborough.ie www.maryborough.com

This hotel, which is quietly situated on the south of the city and very convenient to Cork airport and the Jack Lynch Tunnel, has a fine country house at its heart and is set in its own gardens. The main entrance is via the original flight of steps up to the old front door and as a conventional reception area would intrude on the beautifully proportioned entrance hall, guests are welcomed at a discreetly positioned desk just inside the front door. The original house has many fine features and is furnished in period style with antiques; spacious public areas now extend from it, right across to the new accommodation wing through the Garden Room, a spacious contemporary lounge furnished with smart leather sofas. The new section of the hotel - which is modern and blends comfortably with the trees and gardens surrounding it - includes excellent leisure facilities, the main bar and restaurant, and guest accommodation. Guest rooms and suites are exceptionally attractive in terms of design - simple, modern, bright, utilising Irish crafts: rooms are generously-sized, with a pleasantly leafy outlook and good amenities; compact, well-lit bathrooms have plenty of marbled shelf space, environmentally friendly toiletries, very small baths and towels, and suggestions on saving water by avoiding unnecessary laundry. Conference/banqueting (500/400); business centre, secretarial services, video conferencing, free broadband wi/fi, laptop-sized safes in bedrooms. Leisure centre (swimming pool, jacuzzi, sauna, steam room); beauty salon; Spa. Children welcome (under 2s free in parents room, cots available without charge, baby sitting arranged). No pets. **Rooms 93** (2 suites, 3 junior suites, 88 executive rooms, 37 no-smoking, 8 for disabled). Lift. 24 hour room service. B&B €85 pps, ss €25. Closed 24-26 Dec.
Zings: Creative use of lighting separates areas within this design-led dining area without physical divisions - and the tables are considerably spot lit (ideal for lone diners who wish to read). Gerry Allen, who has been head chef since the hotel opened in 1997 and has earned a local following, offers European cuisine with Mediterranean flavours on quite extensive menus. Although international influences dominate, local produce is used - pretty desserts that are worth leaving room for include a commendable number of choices using seasonal fruits, for example, and local farmhouse cheeses are also a strong option. A good selection of house wines is offered, also an unusually wide choice of half bottles, all moderately priced. Not suitable for children after 7pm. **Seats 120.** Air conditioning. L daily 12.30-2.30, D 6.30-9.30. Set L €30, D à la carte. House wines from €25. SC discretionary. Amex, Diners, MasterCard, Visa, Laser. **Directions:** Near Douglas village & adjacent to Douglas Golf Club; signed from roundabout where Rochestown Road meets Carrigaline Road.

Cork City
HOTEL

The Montenotte Hotel

Montenotte Co Cork **Tel: 021 453 0050**
reservations@themontenottehotel.com www.themontenottehotel.com

Previously the Country Club Hotel, the 'new' Montenotte is perched high over the city in a fashionable residential area, and it offers a pleasant alternative to city centre accommodation. Public rooms include The Vista Bar and Merchants Bistro, both with city views of Cork; lunch (carvery) and light evening food is available in the bar, and the stylish Merchants Bistro offers contemporary cooking in the evening. Bright en-suite bedrooms are not especially large, but have all the facilities expected of a modern hotel, including tea & coffee facilities and complimentary wi-fi internet access. Good leisure facilities include a gym, 18m swimming pool, sauna, steamroom and Jacuzzi. For longer stays, The City Suites 2 bedroom apartments offer all the services of a hotel, with more space and privacy. **Rooms 108.** B&B from €139 per double room, or €99 single. **Directions:** From Patrick's Street in the City Centre cross Patrick's Bridge and travel along McCurtain Street. At the lights, take a left turn up Summerhill North to St. Luke's Cross, at the St. Luke's Cross junction turn right to proceed along the Middle Glanmire Road. The Montenotte Hotel is on your right just after the first bend in the road. ◈

Cork City
RESTAURANT

Nakon Thai Restaurant

Tramway House Douglas Village Cork Co Cork **Tel: 021 436 9900**
www.nakonthai.com

Efficient reception by smiling staff gets guests off to a good start at this smart restaurant in Douglas village. The aim is to provide traditional Thai cuisine in a relaxed and friendly atmosphere and several menus offer wide range of dishes, including all the popular Thai dishes - house specialities include hot & sour prawn soup - but also some lesser-known dishes. Everything is freshly cooked, without any artificial flavourings or MSG and, although the flavours typical of Thai cuisine - coriander, lime, chilli, saltiness - seem to have been tamed somewhat, authentic dishes always meet with approval. A simple dessert selection includes exotic Thai fruit salad for a refreshing finish. An informative fairly priced wine list deserves investigation (a gewurtztraminer partners Thai food exceptionally well, for example); imported Thai beers are also available. Children welcome. **Seats 42.** Air conditioning. D daily: Mon-Sat 5.30-11, Sun 5-10. Set menus from about €19.50; à la carte also available. House wine from €17.95. SC discretionary. Closed 24-28 Dec, Good Fri. Amex, Diners, MasterCard, Visa, Laser. **Directions:** Douglas Village opposite Rugby Club. ◇

Cork City
HOTEL

Radisson SAS Hotel & Spa Cork

Ditchley House Little Island Cork Co Cork **Tel: 021 429 7000**
info.cork@radissonsas.com www.radissonsas.com

Situated just east of Cork city, adjacent to an industrial estate, the location of this hotel is not attractive but it is near the Jack Lynch Tunnel, which gives easy access to the airport, and it is set in landscaped gardens. It follows the familiar Radisson practice of adding a well-designed modern build to an old property, with stylish contemporary interiors including spacious public areas. Designed to appeal to both leisure and business guests, the large Banks Bar is equally suitable for a relaxing drink and casual food, or for business meetings, and The Island Grillroom offers a more intimate dining area. Accommodation is to the usual high standard for new Radisson hotels, offering very comfortable rooms. In addition to other facilities expected of a hotel of this standard, WiFi internet access is complementary throughout the hotel. 'The Retreat' leisure facilities include a Spa, with nine treatment rooms and a relaxation suite, and a Fitness Centre with hydrotherapy pool and state of the art gymnasium. Conference/banqueting (450). **Rooms 129.** B&B from €60-80 pps. Open all year. **Directions:** Signed off main Cork-Midleton road. ◇

Cork City
HOTEL

Radisson SAS Hotel Cork Airport

Cork Airport Cork Co Cork **Tel: 021 494 7500**
res@corkairport-gsh.com www.gshotels.com

Formerly the Great Southern, this stylish modern hotel is very handily located, close to the terminal. Ideal for a first or last night's stay, it's also a useful meeting place and is well equipped for business guests. It aims to provide a tranquil haven for travellers amid the hustle and bustle of a busy airport; its success can be judged by its popularity with a discerning local clientèle as well as travellers passing through. Rooms have voice mail, fax/modem lines, desk space and TV with in-house movie channel as well as more usual facilities like radio, hair dryer, tea/coffee trays and trouser press. Leisure centre. Parking (150). Business centre. Conference/banqueting (100). **Rooms 81** (81 executive, 38 no smoking, 4 disabled). Lift. Room rate about €95-115 for a double or twin. Amex, MasterCard, Visa, Laser. **Directions:** Off Cork-Kinsale road; situated within airport complex. ◇

Cork City
HOTEL

Rochestown Park Hotel

Rochestown Road Douglas Cork Co Cork **Tel: 021 489 0800**
info@rochestownpark.com www.rochestownpark.com

téite bia Formerly home to the Lord Mayors of Cork, this attractive hotel stands in lovely grounds and the original parts of the building feature gracious, well-proportioned public rooms. Guest rooms are furnished to a high standard with all the comforts - including air conditioning and safe in executive rooms - as well as the usual conveniences, making this popular for business guests. Facilities include a fine leisure centre with a swimming pool, sauna, steam room and computerised gymnasium, as well as a Thalasso Therapy centre. Although they rarely get the credit for it, this was the first thalassotherapy centre in an Irish hotel and predated the current fashion for spas by many years. The hotel's conference and meeting facilities are very highly regarded. Conference/banqueting (700/440); free broadband wi/fi. Children welcome (under 6 free in parents' room; cots available free of charge, baby sitting arranged, creche). Leisure centre (swimming pool, sauna, fitness room, massage, spa), beauty salon. Garden. Parking (500). No pets. **Rooms 163** (1 suite, 3 junior suites, 90 executive rooms, 25 no smoking, 23 ground floor, 5 for disabled). Lift. 24 hour room service. B&B about €70 pps, ss €25. SC 12.5%. Thalassotherapy breaks offered, also short breaks (W/E: 2B&B/1D €135). Long stay self-catering available. Open all year except Christmas. L&D daily 12.30-2.30 & 6-10 (Sun 5.30-8pm). Bar menu 10-9 daily. SC 12.5%. Amex, Diners, MasterCard, Visa, Laser. **Directions:** Second left after Jack Lynch Tunnel, heading in Rochestown direction.

Cork City
HOTEL

Silver Springs Moran Hotel

Tivoli Cork Co Cork **Tel: 021 450 7533**
www.moranhotels.com

téile bía A sister hotel of the Red Cow Moran Hotel in Dublin, this landmark hotel is situated in 25 acres of landscaped gardens about five minutes drive from the city centre; built on a steeply sloping site just above the main Cork-Dublin road, it has the natural advantage of views across Cork harbour from many public areas and bedrooms. Thanks to a major makeover (including modernisation of all bedrooms), which was overseen by John Duffy Design and completed without the hotel closing at any time, it has shaken off its blocky 1960s concrete image and this stylish "new" hotel is once again an attractive choice for discerning travellers and the business community. Conferences/Banqueting (1,500/1,050); business centre, secretarial services, video conferencing, broadband wi/fi. A well-equipped leisure centre with a 25-metre pool (sauna, jacuzzi, steam room, massage, beauty salon). Children welcome (under 5s free in parents' room, cot available free of charge, baby sitting arranged). **Rooms 109** (5 suites, 2 mini-suites, 29 executive rooms, 16 no-smoking rooms and 5 for disabled). B&B about €70 pps, ss €30. Closed 25-26 Dec. Amex, Diners, MasterCard, Visa, Laser. **Directions:** At the Tivoli flyover above the main Cork Dublin road and clearly signed off it. (From Cork, take first left then right at the flyover.)

Cork City
RESTAURANT

Star Anise

4 Bridge Street Cork Co Cork **Tel: 021 455 1635**
staranise@eircom.net www.staranise-cork.com

A smartly painted frontage and cool frosted glass windows create a good impression on arrival at this chic contemporary restaurant - a feeling quickly confirmed by an attractive interior, with clean-lined modern table settings (linen napkins, gleaming glasses), mellow lighting, judiciously placed plants and some very attractive paintings and prints. Virginie Sarrazin's welcome is speedy, and the hospitality is genuine: a choice of table (if available), and tempting menus promptly presented. Proprietor-chef Lambros Lambrou's pleasingly seasonal, accurately described menus are well-balanced - with imaginative choices for vegetarians, and also some daily specials - and the reading is made all the more enjoyable by the arrival of a complimentary amuse-bouche and speedily delivered bread. Speciality dishes tend to favour seafood - Mediterranean fish stew, for example, and carnivores will love the slow cooked lamb, with classic desserts to finish. Imaginative food, sassy service, and an interesting wine list too; wines by the glass chalked up on a board start at about €5 and include a sparkling wine. Children welcome (high chair). **Seats 35.** Air conditioning. L & D Tue-Sat, 12-2.30; D, 6-10. Early D €22.95, 6-7pm; also A la carte. House wine from €21. SC 10% on groups 6+. Open all year. Diners, MasterCard, Visa, Laser. **Directions:** Between Patrick's Bridge and McCurtain Street.

Cork City
RESTAURANT
Ⓝ

Table

Brown Thomas Dept. Store 18-21 Patrick Street Cork City Co Cork
Tel: 021 427 5106 table@itsabagel.com www.itsabagel.com

A younger cousin of sisters Peaches and Domini Kemp's highly regarded Dublin restaurants Itsabagel and Itsa4, Table is a stylish daytime restaurant on the second floor of Brown Thomas Cork, the chicest store in town. With smart modern décor contrasting with a neo-classical background, it's an appropriate setting for sassy food with a basic respect for tradition: the Kemps are renowned for their commitment to quality and meals here are based on local and organic products as much as possible, also fair trade tea and coffee. Breakfast, lunch and early supper menus are offered, with snacks (oatmeal & raisin cookies, chocolate brownies, freshly baked scones or any of their gorgeous desserts) in between, and special diets are catered for with dishes suitable for vegetarian, gluten-free, low fat and low salt diets all of which may sound a bit 'worthy', but it's not like that at all. Fresh, colourful and tasty, this is classic Kemp fare and Itsabagel/Itsa4 fans will find many familiar dishes, including steak sandwiches and great salads - mixed leaves with Ardsallagh goat's cheese, perhaps, along with candied nuts, roasted red peppers and balsamic dressing. There's a junior menu too, offering things like home-made burger with hand-cut fries or penne with cream and roast cherry tomatoes, and lovely pressed juices or fresh orange juice to go with it and, of course, adults can choose from a nice little wine list, including a quartet of bubblies. Children welcome (high chair, childrens' menu). **Seats 52;** air conditioning. Food served Mon-Sat, 9am-6.30pm, L 11.30-4pm; Sun L only, 12-6pm. Open same hours as BT. Visa, Laser. **Directions:** 2nd floor, Brown Thomas, Patrick Street.

COUNTY CORK

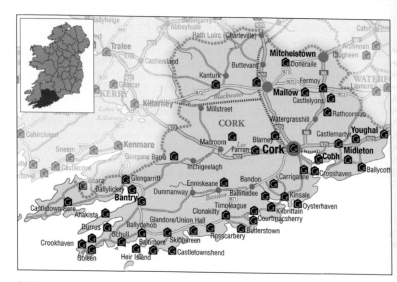

Cork is Ireland's largest county, and its individualistic people take pride in this distinction as they savour the variety of their territory, which ranges from the rich farmlands of the east to the handsome coastline of West Cork, where the light of the famous Fastnet Rock swings across tumbling ocean and spray-tossed headland.

In this extensive county, the towns and villages have their own distinctive character. In the west, their spirit is preserved in the vigour of the landscape. By contrast, East Cork's impressive farming country, radiating towards the ancient estuary port of Youghal, is invitingly prosperous.

The spectacularly located township of Cobh - facing south over Cork Harbour - asserts its own identity, with a renewed sense of its remarkable maritime heritage being expressed in events such as a Sea Shanty Festival, while the town's direct link with the Titanic – Cobh was the ill-fated liner's last port of call – is also commemorated in many ways.

Different again in character is Kinsale, a bustling sailing/fishing port which is home to many intriguing old buildings, yet is a place which is vibrantly modern in outlook, and it has long been seen as Ireland's gourmet capital.

The county is a repository of the good things of life, a treasure chest of the finest farm produce, and the very best of seafood, brought to market by skilled specialists. As Ireland's most southerly county, Cork enjoys the mildest climate of all, and it's a place where they work to live, rather than live to work. So the arts of living are seen at their most skilled in County Cork, and they are practised in a huge territory of such variety that it is difficult to grasp it all, even if you devote your entire vacation to this one county.

Local Attractions & Information

Ballydehob Nature Art Centre	028 37323
Bantry Bantry House	027 50047
Bantry Murphy's International Mussel Fair (May), C/O Westlodge Hotel	027 50360
Bantry Tourism Information	027 50229
Blarney Blarney Castle	021 4385252
Cape Clear Island International Storytelling Festival (early September)	028 39157 / 087 971 1223
Carrigtwohill Fota Estate (Wildlife Park, Arboretum)	021 481 2728
Castletownbere Mill Cove Gallery (May to September)	027 70393
Castletownroche Annes Grove (gardens)	022 26145
Clonakilty Lisselan Estate Gardens	023 33249

Cobh The Queenstown Story	021 481 3591
Cobh Sirius Arts Centre	021 481 3790
Cork Airport	021 431 3131
Glanmire Dunkathel House	021 482 1014
Glanmire Riverstown House	021 482 1205
Glengarriff Garinish Island	027 63040
Kinsale Gourmet Festival (early October), c/o Jack Walsh	021 477 9900
Kinsale Charles Fort	021 477 2263
Kinsale Desmond Castle	021 477 4855
Kinsale Tourism Information	021 477 2234
Macroom Brierly Gap Cultural Centre	026 42421 / 41764
Mallow Cork Racecourse	022 50207
Midleton Farm Market Sats 9am-1.30pm	021 463 1096 / John Potter Cogan 021 463 1096
Midleton Jameson Heritage Centre	021 461 3594
Millstreet Country Park	029 70810
Mizen Head Mizen Vision Signal Station	028 35115 / 35225
Shanagarry Ballymaloe Cookery School Gardens	021 464 6785
Schull Ferries to Sherkin, Cape Clear and Fastnet	028 28278
Schull Schull Planetarium	028 28552
Skibbereen Tourism Information	028 21766
Skibbereen West Cork Arts Centre	028 22090
Slow Food Ireland (c/o Glenilen Farm, Drimoleague)	028 31179 / 086 814 1091
Youghal Myrtle Grove	024 92274

Ahakista
FARMHOUSE

Hillcrest House

Ahakista Durrus Bantry Co Cork **Tel: 027 67045**
hillcrestfarm@ahakista.com   www.ahakista.com

Hospitality comes first at this working farm over-looking Dunmanus Bay, where Agnes Hegarty's guests - including walkers, who revel in the 55 mile "Sheep's Head Way" - are welcomed with a cup of tea and home-baked scones on arrival. It is a traditional farmhouse with some recent additions, and makes a comfortable base for exploring the area, or a traditional family holiday - there's a swing and a donkey on the farm, rooms are big enough for an extra child's bed and it's only five minutes' walk to the beach. There's a sitting room for guests, with television and an open fire, and bedrooms - either recently refurbished or in a new extension - have power showers or bath, very comfortable beds, electric blankets, hair dryers, tea/coffee making facilities and clock radios. Two new rooms are on the ground-floor, with direct access to a sheltered patio, and parking close by. Fine cooked-to-order breakfasts will set you up for the day, and moderately priced evening meals are available if required - although there are plenty of good restaurants nearby, also pubs with traditional Irish music. Hillcrest House was our Farmhouse of the Year in 2001. Children welcome (under 3s free in parents' room, cot available without charge). **Rooms 4** (3 en-suite & no-smoking, 3 shower only, 1 with private bathroom) B&B €34 pps. Evening meals by arrangement (7 pm; €24); light meals also available. *Self-catering cottage and farmhouse also available, all year - details on the website. Closed 1 Nov - 1 Mar. MasterCard, Visa, Laser. **Directions:** 3 km from Bantry, take N71 and turn off for Durrus, then Ahakista - 0.25km to Hillcrest.

Ahakista
PUB

The Tin Pub

Ahakista Durrus Bantry Co Cork **Tel: 027 67337**
mail@tinpub.com   www.tinpub.com

Tom Harrington runs one of the most relaxed bars in the country: known affectionately as "the tin pub" because of its corrugated iron roof, it has a lovely rambling country garden going down to the water at the back, where children are very welcome to burn off excess energy. Other than succumbing to the telephone a year or two ago after years of resistance, it's a place that just doesn't change. Music sessions Sunday and Tuesdays; also 'Boutique Concerts' see events page on their website for details (includes big names, e.g. Mary Coughlan, Mundy, Ronnie Drew) Normal pub hours don't apply in this part of the world but they're open from 12 noon in summer and evenings all year (open Mon-Fri 5, Sat 4, Sun 3 - bar food available any time), except 25 Dec & Good Fri. **Directions:** Sheeps Head direction, from Durrus. ◇

Ballycotton
HOTEL/RESTAURANT

Bayview Hote

Ballycotton Co Cork **Tel: 021 464 674**
res@thebayviewhotel.com www.thebayviewhotel.con

John and Carmel O'Briens' fine hotel overlooking Ballycotton Harbour enjoys a magnificent location on the seaside of the road with a path down through its own gardens to the beach. The O'Briens completely rebuilt the hotel in the 1990s, keeping the building in sympathy with the traditional style and scale of the surrounding buildings and harbour, and its immaculate grounds classy cream paintwork and smart black railing create an excellent first impression. Traditional homely public areas include a pleasant bar with clubby leather furniture, a cosy atmosphere - and friendly staff. Accommodation is comfortable and rooms are regularly refurbished; although they vary according to their position in the building, th bedrooms all have sea views. Small conferences/banqueting (40/90). Children welcome (under 12 free in parents' room, cot available without charge, baby sitting arranged). No pets. Garden, tennis, fishing walking. **Rooms 35** (2 suites, 5 no-smoking rooms, 5 ground floor). B&B €95pps, ss€32. Lift, all da room service, turndown service. Closed Nov-Apr. **Capricho at the Bayview:** Head chef Ciaran Scully ha been at the Bayview since 1996 and his creative cooking has earned a loyal following. The restaurar is smartly furnished, with a nice traditional feel, and the best tables have lovely harbour and sea views Ciaran is a committed chef and Féile Bia member, who takes pride in sourcing the finest ingredients and gives a page of his menu over to crediting both local produce and suppliers. Although base squarely on local produce, the cooking is classic French and there are contemporary international over tones and also some retro dishes and an element of fun, too. Unusual speciality dishes in the repertoir include three variations of 'Fishy, Fishy, Fishy', one of which is a trio of timbale of crabmeat, ketal coated prawns, and slivers of Shanagarry smoked salmon with citrus dressing; another, based on braise pigs cheek and Gubbeen sausage, is called 'Three Little Pigs'. Vegetarian dishes are not always liste on the menu, so you may have to ask for a special dish to be made to order. Delicious desserts ma include a refreshing terrine of orange, pink grapefruit and raspberries, with honey crisps and gooseberr ice cream, and a selection of farmhouse cheeses is served with a terrine of dried figs and crab apple jelly. In fine weather, light meals may be served in the garden. An informative wine list includes a goo choice of half bottles. Children welcome (high chair, childrens menu). **Seats 45** (private room 28) D 7 9 daily, L Sun only, 1-2. D à la carte. Wines from about €23. (Bar meals available daily 12.30-6). Amex Diners, MasterCard, Visa, Laser. *The nearby **Garryvoe Hotel** is in the same family ownership and ha recently undergone impressive redevelopment; its beachside location makes it a popular base for famil holidays (see website above for details.) **Directions:** At Castlemartyr, on the N25, turn on to the R63 in the direction of Garryvoe - Shanagarry - Ballycotton.

Ballydehob
RESTAURANT

Annie's Restauran

Main Street Ballydehob Co Cor
Tel: 028 3729.

Anne and Dano Barry have been running the famous restaurant since 1983 - and, for many, visit to West Cork is unthinkable without a mea here. Extending into the building next door a whil ago allowed them to upgrade the whole restaurar so all facilities, including disabled toilets, are o the ground floor - but it's still the same Annie's just a bit bigger. Annie is a great host, welcomin everybody personally, handing out menus - an then sending guests over to Levis' famous old pu across the road for an aperitif. Then she come over, takes orders and returns to collect people when their meals are ready - there has never been roor for waiting around until tables are ready, so this famous arrangement works extremely well. As to th ood at Annie's, there's great emphasis on local ingredients and everything is freshly made on the day: wild smoked salmon comes from Sally Barnes nearby at Castletownshend; fresh fish is delivered every night; meat comes from the local butcher; their famous roast boned duck is from nearby Skeaghanore Farm; their west Cork farmhouse cheeses include one of Ireland's most renowned cheeses, Gubbeen (made by Annie's sister-in-law, Giana Ferguson), smoked foods come from the Gubbeen Smokehouse, and all the breads, ice creams and desserts for the restaurant are made on the premises. Cooking by Dano, or Annie herself - is simple and wholesome, the nearest to really good home cooking you could ever hope to find in a restaurant. Prices are very fair - the 4-course dinner menu is priced by choice of main courses and there's a carefully chosen wine list, with plenty of bottles under €30; annual tasting sessions decide on the six wines selected as House Wines for the year - interesting choices, and great value too. Not suitable for children after 9 pm. Toilets wheelchair accessible. Air conditioning. **Seats 45.** D Tue-Sat 6.30-10, Set D €36/47 2/3 courses, à la carte also offered. House wines €20. SC Discretionary. Closed Sun, Mon & 14 Oct - 1 Dec. MasterCard, Visa, Laser. **Directions:** Streetside, midway through village.

Ballydehob
CHARACTER PUB

Levis' Bar

Corner House Main Street Ballydehob Co Cork
Tel: 028 37118

The Levis sisters ran this 150-year-old bar and grocery for as long as anyone can remember - sadly, Julia died in 2006 but, with help from younger members of the family, Nell is still welcoming visitors as hospitably as ever. It is a characterful and delightfully friendly place, whether you are just in for a casual drink or using the pub as the unofficial 'reception' area for Annie's restaurant across the road (see entry for Annie's above). Closed 25 Dec & Good Fri. **Directions:** Main street, opposite Annie's. ◇

Ballylickey
GUESTHOUSE

Ballylickey House

Ballylickey Bantry Bay Co Cork **Tel: 027 50071**
ballymh@eircom.net www.ballylickeymanorhouse.com

Built some 300 years ago by Lord Kenmare as a shooting lodge, and home to the Franco-Irish Graves family for five generations, this fine house enjoys a romantic setting overlooking Bantry Bay, with moors and hills behind. Many will remember it when it was run as a country house by the present owner's parents, George and Christiane Graves, and known as Ballylickey Manor; since George and Christiane's retirement their son Paco now operates it along simpler lines, offering bed and breakfast in both the main house and a number of cottages and chalets in the wonderful gardens which were laid out many years ago by Paco's grandmother, Kitty. Guests with a literary turn of mind will be interested to know that the poet Robert Graves was a great-great uncle of Paco's, and visited the house on many occasions. Garden, outdoor heated swimming pool, walking, fishing. Children welcome (under 4s free in parents' room, cot available). Pets allowed in some areas by arrangement. Private parking. **Rooms 11** (2 suites, 1 junior suites, 5 executive, 3 single, 6 ground floor, all no smoking). B&B from €90 pps, ss €20. Closed Nov-Mar. **Directions:** On N71 between Bantry & Glengariff.

Ballylickey
HOTEL/RESTAURANT

Seaview House Hotel

Ballylickey Bantry Co Cork **Tel: 027 50462**
info@seaviewhousehotel.com www.seaviewhousehotel.com

A warm welcome and personal supervision are the hallmarks of Kathleen O'Sullivan's restful country house hotel close to Ballylickey Bridge. Public rooms, which are spacious and well-proportioned, include a graciously decorated drawing room and a cocktail bar, both overlooking lovely gardens at the front of the house, and with outdoor seating for fine weather, also a cosy library and television room. Rooms vary, as is the way with old houses, and the most luxurious accommodation is in junior suites in a new wing; but many rooms have sea views, all are generously sized and individually decorated (six have just been refurbished) and most have good bathrooms. Family furniture and antiques enhance the hotel, and standards of maintenance and housekeeping are consistently outstanding. Garden. Children welcome (under 4s free in parents room, cot available, baby sitting arranged). Pets permitted in some areas by arrangement. **Rooms 25** (6 junior suites, 2 family rooms, 5 ground floor rooms, 1 shower only, 2 for disabled, all no smoking). No lift. B&B €95 pps, ss €25. **Restaurant:** Overlooking the garden, with views over Bantry Bay, the restaurant is elegant and well-appointed with antiques, fresh flowers and plenty of privacy. Set five-course dinner menus change daily and offer a wide choice on all courses; the style is country house cooking, with the emphasis firmly on local produce, especially seafood, in dishes like simple fresh Bantry Bay crab salad with Marie Rose sauce, or roast rack of lamb with rosemary. Choose from classic desserts or local cheeses to finish and then tea or coffee and petits fours may be served out of doors on fine summer evenings. A carefully selected and informative, wine list offers an extensive range of well chosen house wines, a generous choice of half bottles - and many treats. Service, as elsewhere in the hotel, is caring and professional. **Seats 50.** Children welcome (high chair, childrens menu). Toilets wheelchair accessible. D 6.45-9 daily, L Sun only 12.45-1.30; Set D €30/40, 2/3 courses. House wines from €20. 10% sc. Hotel closed mid Nov-mid Mar. Amex, MasterCard, Visa, Laser. **Directions:** 10 mins drive from Bantry, on N71 to Glengarriff.

BALTIMORE AREA

Baltimore village has strong associations with the sea and sailing, diving, angling and kayaking are among some of the most popular activities here. If you prefer to stay on dry land, there are some lovely walks in the area and beautiful gardens to visit as well as golf, horseriding and much more. Although it still retains its unique laid-back holiday atmosphere, it's all change in Baltimore village as we go to press - and it's mostly down to Youen Jacob, who set up his famous Breton restaurant **Chez Youen** (028 20136; www.youenjacob.com) here in 1979, and his sons; between them they now have several establishments around the square in the village and, at the time of the Guide's summer 2007 visit two of them - Baltimore Bay Guesthouse and The Waterfront pub - had been partially demolished and were well on the way to becoming a new hotel, **The Waterfront** (028 20600; www.waterfronthotel.ie). The Waterfront includes a pub, two restaurants and accommodation some new rooms, plus the existing ones in the previous Baltimore Guest House. Also on the square, **La Jolie Brise Pizza & Grill** (028 20600) is run by Youen Jacob Jnr. and Pascal Jacob; this cheerful continental-style café spills out on to the pavement and will also be accessible from The Waterfront, despite the slight change of name continues to provide holiday-makers with inexpensive, all-day meals (seafood as well as pizza) to be washed down with moderately priced wines (except, perhaps, at breakfast time). Around the corner **Chez Youen** is still doing what it does best: simple but dramatic presentation of seafood in the shell this is a pricey affair (a shellfish platter costs €60) but different from other places, and Youen's wine list is also unusual - he imports a wide range of wines directly from France (see his website for full details). This may seem very like a Jacob takeover of Baltimore but, although it was certainly a village with the heart torn out of it for the 2007 season, the feeling is that it will be good for the town in the long run, giving this pleasing place a new lease of life once it is complete. Just a 10-minute trip ferry from Baltimore harbour, **SHERKIN ISLAND** is a small island 5.5 km long and 2.5 km wide, with a population of only a hundred or so and three lovely safe beaches. There is an hotel on the island, **The Islanders Rest** (Tel 028 20116; www.islandersrest.ie), and **Horseshoe Cottage** (see entry) is an interesting and hospitable place to stay. Those taking the ferry to the island for the day will find **The Jolly Roger Tavern** (028 20598) useful to know about, for a bite to eat, and for music too.
WWW.IRELAND-GUIDE.COM FOR THE BEST PLACES TO EAT, DRINK & STAY

Baltimore	Baltimore Harbour Hotel
HOTEL	Baltimore Co Cork **Tel: 028 20361**
	info@baltimoreharbourhotel.ie www.baltimoreharbourhotel.ie

Quietly located off the road, just a couple of minutes' walk from the village/harbour area, this privately owned hotel enjoys a lovely position overlooking Roaring Water Bay and is well located for exploring the area. Having been extensively redesigned in recent years, the hotel is now the centre of a compact complex that offers various types of accommodation - cleverly designed to include a traditional arch and a leisure centre. Modern furnishings, with plenty of light wood, create a sense of space in public areas, and all rooms are comfortably furnished, with neat bathrooms and sea views. The hotel's Clipper Restaurant caters for a wide range of tastes, and offers a children's menu. Public areas include a bright semi-conservatory Garden Room. *Although on the market at the time of going to press, the hotel is likely to be sold as a going concern. Children are well looked after - there's a playroom, a children's club in school holidays and under 5s are free in parents' room (cots available without charge, baby sitting arranged). Off-season breaks are good value. No pets. Lift. **Rooms 64.** B&B about €84 pps, ss about €25. *Various packages and short breaks are offered; details on application. Closed Christmas-New Year. Amex, Diners, MasterCard, Visa. **Directions:** Signposted on the right as you enter Baltimore on the R595 from Skibbereen.

Baltimore
CHARACTER PUB

Bushe's Bar

The Square Baltimore Co Cork **Tel: 028 20125**
tom@bushesbar.com www.bushesbar.com

Everyone, especially visiting and local sailors, feels at home in this famous old bar. It's choc-a-bloc with genuine maritime artefacts such as charts, tide tables, ships' clocks, compasses, lanterns, pennants et al - but it's the Bushe family's hospitality that makes it really special. Since Richard and Eileen took on the bar in 1973, it's been "home from home" for regular visitors to Baltimore, for whom a late morning call is de rigeur (in order to collect the ordered newspapers that are rolled up and stacked in the bar window each day).

Now, it's in the safe hands of the next generation - Tom, Aidan and Marion Bushe - so all is humming nicely. Simple, homely bar food starts early in the day with tea and coffee from 9.30, moving on to Marion's home-made soups and a range of sandwiches including home-cooked meats, salmon, smoked mackerel or - the most popular by far - open crab sandwiches (when available), served with home-baked brown bread. Although, like all pubs, it can get a little scruffy at busy times, this is a terrific pub, at any time of year, and was a very worthy recipient of our Pub of the Year Award in 2000. Children welcome before 9pm. Bar food served 9.30am-8pm daily (12.30-8 Sun). Bar closed 25 Dec & Good Fri. Amex, MasterCard, Visa, Laser. **Directions:** In the middle of Baltimore, on the square overlooking the harbour.

Baltimore
HOTEL

Casey's of Baltimore

Baltimore Co Cork **Tel: 028 20197**
info@caseysofbaltimore.com www.caseysofbaltimore.com

The Casey family's striking dark green hotel is just outside Baltimore and enjoys dramatic views over Roaring Water Bay to the islands beyond. It has been ingeniously developed over the years to add more accommodation and extend the ground floor public areas towards the back, taking advantage of the view over well-kept gardens - including a kitchen garden that supplies seasonal produce to the kitchen towards the sea. Some bedrooms also have wonderful views and, although they may seem a little dated, rooms are quite comfortably furnished, with all the usual facilities, and compact bathrooms have full bath and shower. Friendly staff create a relaxed atmosphere and, as well as a spacious restaurant with sea views, there are well-organised outdoor eating areas for bar food in fine weather; local seafood is the speciality, of course, but menus always offer other choices, including at least one vegetarian dish. Small conferences/banqueting (35/80). Incentive packages; short breaks. Children welcome (under 3s free in parents' room, cots available without charge, high chair, childresn menu, baby changing facilities), but not in public areas after 7 pm. No pets. **Rooms 14** (1 shower only, 4 ground floor) B&B €87.50 pps, ss €20. Bar meals daily 12.30-3 & 6.30-9. **Restaurant Seats 80:** Air conditioning. L & D daily: L12.30-3, D 6.30-9. Set L (Sun) €25. à la carte L&D also available; house wine from €19; service discretionary. Closed 20-27 Dec. Amex, Diners, MasterCard, Visa, Laser. **Directions:** From Cork take the N71 to Skibbereen & then R595 to Baltimore; on right entering the village.

Baltimore
RESTAURANT

Customs House

Baltimore Co Cork **Tel: 028 20200**
www.thecustomshouse.com

Gillian Oliva and her American husband Billy (who is the chef) have been running this well known restaurant since 2006, and it continues to please with good cooking and value. You ring the doorbell to go into the restaurant which is in two interconnecting rooms and has a classy and relaxed feeling, with very low music, a subtle shade of yellow on the walls, oil paintings, venetian blinds and floorboards painted rather funkily with (sound-absorbent) red rubber. There's delicious home-made ciabatta bread on the table, water is brought without asking (efficient service is a strong point here) and two menus are offered: a very short menu offering just two dishes on each course, including a vegetarian option, for €35 and one with more choice for €45. Local seafood is dominant, of course - a seafood tapas plate is a speciality starter, and Dover sole on the bone is an ever-popular main course - but you'll also find alternatives including dry aged Hereford beef and roast breast of local Skeaghanore duck, an all-Irish cheese selection may offer lesser known cheeses such as Ardagh Castle and Crozier Blue as well as some of the more famous local ones. Pride is taken in both the ingredients (local, where possible) and the cooking here; upbeat classic desserts and breads - are all home-made. The wine list offers a fair choice and includes some half bottles and pudding wines, but none by the glass, and you can round off your meal with artisan hand-roasted coffee, or one of a choice of Dilmaha teas. **Seats 34.** D, 7-11. Set D €40; not suitable for children under 13. Opening times & days vary, please call in advance off season. Closed Oct-Apr. **No Credit Cards. Directions:** Beside the Garda Station 50 metres from the pier.

Baltimore
CAFÉ

Glebe House Gardens

Glebe Gardens Baltimore Co Cork **Tel: 028 20232**
glebegardens@eircom.net www.glebegardens.com

Jean and Peter Perry's wonderful gardens just outside Baltimore attract a growing number of visitors each year and they have a delightful café for those in need of a restorative bite; it's all very wholesome - and they generously allow you to bring your own picnic too, if preferred. The menu is sensibly short but the food, using organically grown ingredients from the garden and from named local craft suppliers, is unpretentious, and cooked (to order) to a very high standard indeed. For example, you might try a four fish chowder, accompanied by delicious home-made brown bread and the lightest, fluffiest white scone you are likely to find anywhere followed, perhaps, by a scrumptious three cheese (Irish farmhouse) and tomato tart accompanied by a delicately dressed salad from the garden. Other possibilities include smoked mackerel pate with a green salad, breads and toasts, or a children's lunch, of Rosscarbery sausage with pea & potato mash - and all this at a surprisingly reasonable cost. Simply delicious. Gardens open weekends Easter-June and Wed-Sun Jun-Aug. **Directions:** Off Skibbereen-Baltimore road: entrance directly opposite 'Baltimore' sign as you enter the village. ◇

Baltimore
RESTAURANT

The Mews

Baltimore Co Cork
Tel: 028 20390

Owner-chef Denis Connolly's hospitable and atmospheric restaurant is a romantic spot, with white linen-clad candlelit tables and strategically placed plants, stone walls and an adjacent conservatory that is bright and fresh for early dining, turning into an equally romantic setting as candle light as darkness falls. Menus are contemporary and the cooking is based on carefully sourced fresh ingredients in generous and light dishes inspired by international influences. Freshly-baked breads and tapenade get the evening off to a good start, and starters like a house seafood chowder, or a grilled pear, watercress & walnut salad should not disappoint. Main courses will include more than one seafood dish, a vegetarian choice - such as a filo basket filled with Moroccan spiced vegetables - and a variation on traditional themes, such as fillet steak with roast tomatoes, garlic, parmesan and onion marmalade. Desserts include home-made ice creams, or you could finish with an open cheese plate and freshly brewed coffee. **Seats 32** (outdoors, 4). D Mon-Sat, 6-10pm; à la carte. House wine €21.95. Closed Sun, Oct-May. **No Credit Cards. Directions:** In village of Baltimore (signed in laneway just before the harbour).

Baltimore
CAFÉ/RESTAURANT WITH ROOMS/WINE BAR

Rolf's

Baltimore Co Cork Tel: **028 20289**
info@rolfsholidays.eu www.rolfsholidays.eu

The Haffner family have been at this delightful place for over 25 years, and the complex which began as a holiday hostel and is now styled 'country house' - has been extensively upgraded so that, in addition to self-catering accommodation with character and their popular restaurant and wine bar, all of their guest rooms are now en-suite. Although not a country house in the conventional sense, it certainly has a great deal to offer, including a lovely garden terrace with a sea view which is available for fine weather. The café is open during the day and serves an à la carte lunch, with a more extensive dinner menu offered in the Restaurant 'Café Art', which has a dedicated local following and delights visitors with its great food and atmosphere. Refreshingly, Euro-Toques chef-owner Johannes Haffner's wide-ranging menus include quite a few classics and retro dishes (beef stroganoff made with vodka is a speciality), and all baked goods and desserts are home-made - and he uses as much home-grown, organic and local produce as possible. A well-chosen wine list includes a range of champagne cocktails and aperitifs, and many treats among the main listing including an unusually good choice of half bottles - and many wines not listed are available by the glass in the Wine Bar. **Accommodation:** Children welcome (cot available free of charge). **Rooms 14** (all en-suite, all shower only, all no smoking). €40-50 pps; ss €10-20. Three self catering holiday cottages also available. Pets permitted by arrangement. Garden. Walking. **Restaurant: Seats 60** (also outdoor 40). Toilets wheelchair accessible. B 8.30-11, L 12-2.30, D 6-9.30 (to 9 off-season). A la carte. House wine from €20. Open all week. Reservations advised. Closed 24-26 Dec. MasterCard, Visa, Laser. **Directions:** On Baltimore Hill, 10 minute walk from village.

Baltimore
B&B

Slipway

The Cove Baltimore Co Cork Tel: **028 20134**
theslipway@hotmail.com www.theslipway.com

Quietly located away from the bustle around the square, but within easy walking distance of several excellent restaurants, Wilmie Owen's unusual house has uninterrupted views of the harbour and distant seascape from all the bedrooms, and also the first floor breakfast room, which has a balcony (a delightful room but, unfortunately, not available to guests, except at breakfast time). There's a lovely garden and a self-catering cottage is also available for weekly rental (sleeps 2); details on application. Not suitable for children under 12; no pets. Garden. **Rooms 4** (all shower only & no-smoking, 1 family room, 2 ground floor). B&B €39 pps, ss €16/€31 low/high season. Closed Nov-Mar officially, but phone to check, open over New Years. **No Credit Cards. Directions:** Through Baltimore village, to the Cove, 500 metres.

Baltimore Area
B&B

Horseshoe Cottage

Sherkin Island Baltimore Co Cork Tel: **028 20598**
joe@gannetsway.com www.gannetsway.com

Joe and Fiona Aston offer an authentic experience at their beautifully located island B&B, which is open for most of the year. Although small, it is well laid out, with a pretty sheltered garden that not only pleases the eye but also supplies organic vegetables for the table, and there's a comfortable sitting room with lots of books and games. There are three en suite bedrooms, all simply but comfortably furnished with good quality beds and linen, and tea and coffee making facilities. Fiona cooks dinner for guests - fresh fish, local meat, and soups and salads feature and, of course, seasonal vegetables from the kitchen garden too. The day begins with a hearty breakfast of fresh fruit or fruit compôte, home-baked bread and, again, the best of local/artisan food including smoked salmon and scrambled eggs and fresh fish. And this is a B&B with a difference, as Fiona offers various therapies to guests and Joe has a 45' schooner, the Anna M, which he uses to take guests out on fishing/sight-seeing trips of Roaring Water Bay, mainly for dolphin and whale-watching. **Rooms 3.** B&B €35pps, €38 in Jul/Aug. **Directions:** On Sherkin Island within easy walking distance of pier and pubs, yet in a quiet position facing south above Horseshoe Bay.

Baltimore Area
RESTAURANT

Island Cottage

Heir Island Skibbereen Co Cork **Tel: 028 38102**
www.islandcottage.com

Just a short ferry ride from the mainland yet light years away from the "real" world, this place is unique. Hardly a likely location for a restaurant run by two people who have trained and worked in some of Europe's most prestigious establishments - but, since 1990, that is exactly what John Desmond and Ellmary Fenton have been doing at Island Cottage. Everything about it is different from other restaurants, including the booking policy: a basic advance booking for at least six people must be in place before other smaller groups of 2 to 4 can be accepted - not later than 3pm on the day; changes to group numbers require 24 hours notice and a booking deposit per head is required to reserve a table (you post a cheque or postal order). The no-choice 5-course menu depends on the availability of the fresh local, organic (where possible) and wild island ingredients of that day, which might include salmon, shrimp and crab. A typical menu might be: marinated salmon on a bed of mayonnaise, with homemade brown bread; roast duck leg (made using hand-reared ducks "of exceptional quality" from Ballydehob) with béarnaise sauce & roast potatoes with rosemary; green salad with a little Gubbeen cheese; hot lemon soufflé; filter coffee. Off season cookery courses offered; also cottages for rent - details from the restaurant. **Seats 24** (max table size 10; be prepared to share a table). Set Menu - no choice, no exceptions D €40. Wed-Sun, 8.15-11.45 pm; one sitting served at group pace. Wine from €20. Off-season: groups of 16-24 by arrangement. Closed Sun- Tue, and mid Sep-mid Jun (please phone to check off season opening days/times). **No credit cards.** *Off season cookery courses available. **Directions:** From Skibbereen, on Ballydehob road, turn left at Church Cross, signposted Hare Island and Cunnamore. Narrow winding road, past school, church, Minihan's Bar. Continue to end of road, Cunnamore car park. Ferry (blue boat) departs Cunnamore pier at 7.55 returns at 11.55 (journey: 4 minutes.) For ferry, contact John Moore / Richard Pyburn Tel: 086 809 2447.

Bandon
B&B

Kilbrogan House

Bandon Co Cork **Tel: 023 44935**
fitz@kilbrogan.com www.kilbrogan.com

This elegant three-storey Georgian townhouse, built in 1818, faces out on to Kilbrogan Hill, a quiet, mostly residential street in Bandon town. In 1992 brother and sister Catherine and David Fitzmaurice bought it in a dilapidated state and, following sympathetic restoration, opened as a guesthouse in 2004. You get the feeling that this listed house has changed little since it was built. At the back, a large lawn is surrounded by shrubs and tall trees and the stables behind the house, which have been converted into holiday flats rented out by the owners, add to the olde worlde atmosphere. Inside, a large hall is welcoming, with a polished wooden floor and a curving staircase leading up to bedrooms and a first floor sitting room a piano - there is also a drawing room on the ground floor for guests' use, and a conservatory half way up the stairs at the back of the house. Some of the bedrooms look out on to Kilbrogan Hill and the hills beyond the rooftops, others on to the gravel parking area and the lawn and trees at the back; all have mod cons such as flat-screen TV, broadband internet connection and hairdryer, but are elegantly furnished with antiques (including very comfortable beds with lovely starched cotton sheets), and interesting prints decorate the walls; well appointed bathrooms have full bath and power shower, and heated towel rails. Blue and white check cotton napkins and tablecloth on the breakfast table give a cheerful country feel, and David is a trained chef, so you can look forward to a delicious cooked breakfast. This is a lovely place to stay, and a great asset to the area. Not suitable for children under 12 yrs; Broadband. **Rooms 4** (all no smoking); B&B €50 pps, ss €10. Closed Dec, Jan. *Self catering also available, rates on application. Amex, MasterCard, Visa, Laser. **Directions:** Turn right at Methodist church, follow signs for Macroom, bear left at Post Office. Take 1st right 200yards up hill on right. ◇

Bandon
RESTAURANT/PUB

The Poachers Inn

Clonakilty Road Bandon Co Cork **Tel: 023 41159**
mclaughlinbc@hotmail.com

Barry and Catherine McLoughlin opened this roadside bar and restaurant just outside Bandon shortly after our 2007 guide went to press. It's a typical pub with a cosy ambience, dark wood, hunting prints, a fireplace corner with leather sofas, and other seating divided between banquettes and high tables with bar stools. But, although this place may be unremarkable in appearance, the kitchen is turning out wonderfully flavourful dishes based on fresh local seafood. Already, they have earned a great reputation in the locality for their fine food and hospitality - Barry is the chef and, once guests learn that he was previously at Fishy Fishy Café and Casino House (widely recognised as two of the finest restaurants in an area well known for its good food), expectations are immediately raised. And there should be no cause for disappointment here as top quality ingredients are deftly handled although very much a bar, the seafood is restaurant quality, both in taste and contemporary presentation on smart white plates. Crispy crab and prawn cakes come with spicy mango and plum salsa, and deep dish seafood pie is comfort food of the first order; dishes like West Cork seafood chowder at about €6.50, and fresh crab-meat open sandwiches at around €10.95, are popular with the many family groups who are attracted to this spot. Steak, a chicken dish and a vegetarian choice is also offered for non-fish eaters, and desserts are of the homely, mostly served hot-sticky toffee pudding, bread and butter pudding, and apple cinnamon & walnut crumble are all typical. Catherine manages front of house and service under her direction is informal, but pleasant and efficient. Wines are served by the glass from a dispenser, a choice of four or five each red and white, also a rosé. This new venture is a great asset to the area, and cookery courses are planned for 2008. Free broadband wi/fi; Toilets wheelchair accessible; Children welcome before 9pm (high chair). Pub food served daily, 12-7.30pm (to 7pm Sun). **Restaurant: seats 50** (outdoors, 10), reservations required, air conditioning, D Thurs-Sat only, 7-10pm; L Sun only, 12-3.30pm; house wine from €19. Restaurant closed Sun D & Mon-Wed, house closed 25 Dec. MasterCard, Visa, Laser. **Directions:** On the main West Cork road heading out of Bandon, right hand side.

Bandon Area
CAFÉ

Blue Geranium Café

Hosfords Garden Centre Cappa Enniskeane Co Cork **Tel: 023 39159**
john@hosfordsgardencentre.ie www.hosfordsgardencentre.ie

Garden lovers travel from all over Ireland to visit Hosfords, which is one of the country's best garden centres and specalises in geraniums hence the name of their attractive new cafe, which opened in June 2007 and is proving popular with locals as well as garden centre customers. It's a large airy glasshouse-style space with modern pale wood, and large tubs of palms and tree ferns used as dividers; large sliding doors open on to an inviting outdoor patio area where tables and chairs are set up, and a children's playground alongside. The setting is attractive seasonal flowers such as a bunch of sweet peas on every table and the food, although self-service, is good quality. Typical of the best type of food now expected at lifestyle shopping outlets and top garden centres, with prices to match, you can expect to find dishes like quiche and salad (€10.50), chicken pie with mash (€13.50), and home-bakes such as freshly baked scones with jam and butter (€2.75). Staff take the self-service aspect of the operation a little too literally at times - no help appears to be available for elderly or incapacitated visitors taking food to their tables. Open Tue-Sat 10-5, Sun 12.30-5. Closed Mon. **Directions:** On the Bandon-Clonakilty road (N71). ◇

BANTRY

Delightfully situated at the head of Bantry Bay, this historic town has much to offer the visitor - notably the mid-18th century Bantry House, which is still a family home; set in lovely grounds and gardens, it houses the French Armada Museum. The Beara peninsula is to the northwest, with Sheep's Head also nearby, on the peninsula south of Bantry Bay and all have many spectacular walks. Rowing, sailing and golf are popular past times for visitors to the area. Several hotels in the town include the (very) large new **Maritime Hotel, Spa & Suites** (023 20126) along the quay below Bantry House; smart and modern, it was only partially open at the time of our visit attractive features include a first floor restaurant well-positioned to take advantage of the view. The long-established **Westlodge Hotel** (027 50360; www.westlodgehotel.ie) on the edge of the town has extensive amenities, making it a weather-proof base for a family holiday; by contrast, the offering is modest at the O'Callaghan family's **Bantry Bay Hotel** (027 50062; www.bantrybayhotel.net) on Wolfe Tone Square, but there is warm family hospitality to compensate.

WWW.IRELAND-GUIDE.COM FOR THE BEST PLACES TO EAT, DRINK & STAY

Bantry
BAR/RESTAURANT

O'Connor's Seafood Restaurant

The Square Bantry Co Cork **Tel: 027 50221**
oconnorseafood@eircom.net www.oconnorseafood.com

Peter and Anne O'Brien run this long-established seafood restaurant right on the main square (site of Friday markets and the annual early-May mussel festival) and, although no longer directly in the O'Connor family, there's actually a very old family connection as Anne's great-grandmother was the original owner of the bar licence back in 1914 - which makes for pretty good continuity by any standards. In 2006 Peter and Anne decided it was time to make some changes, and the whole place was completely refurbished - emerging with the modern, but very comfortable look it has today. And, other than that, they were careful to retain the things that make this place special - the same staff, the same food and, best of all, the same fair prices. So, you will still find the lobster and oyster fish tank sending all the right messages and Bantry Bay mussels, cooked all ways, remain a speciality - try their Mussels in Murphy's Stout (steamed in stout and cream), followed perhaps by lobster (when in season), and served with an abundance of fresh vegetables. There's a fair choice of non-fish dishes available too, all using local produce - roast rack of local lamb is another speciality (served with a port & thyme jus), also crispy roast Skeaghanore duck, with ginger & orange sauce. At lunchtime there's a more casual menu offered, including hot or open sandwiches (fresh local crab and mayo smoked salmon & Durrus cheese) as well as a range of Bantry Bay mussels dishes and hearty fare such as O'Connor's Seafood Pie or sirloin steak. Children welcome before 8 pm (high chair). **Seats 48.** Air conditioning. L 12.15-3, D 6-10 (Sun to 9). Early D €28 (6-7pm); Set D 2/3 course €26/28.50. Also à la carte. House wine €18.50. SC discretionary. Closed 25 Dec, Bank Hols, Sun Oct-May, but telephone to confirm opening times off-season. MasterCard, Visa, Laser. **Directions:** Town centre; prominent location on square.

Bantry
CAFÉ/SHOP/BAKERY

Organico

2 Gelngarriff Road Bantry Co Cork **Tel: 027 51391**
info@organico.ie www.organico.ie

Hannah and Rachel Dare's vegetarian café is situated above the Organico bakery and food shop, near the centre of the town. In a spacious room (with internet connection) they offer tasty snacks, breads and cakes from the bakery, and lunches including splendid salads. Rachel, a Ballymaloe-trained cook, is the force behind the menu, which is based on organic vegetables, salads, pulses, (spelt) flours and raw cane sugar - and even the milk in the Fair Trade organic latte is organic too. Local free range and artsisan foods also feature farmhouse cheeses, butter, eggs and, for the non-vegetarian, the most interesting fact is that dishes such as minestrone soup, which are usually dependent on a good meat stock, are full of flavour. And yes, even their little wine list is organic. The staff are pleasant and efficient, and it's good value for money - well worth a visit. Children welcome (high chair, childrens menu); broadband wi/fi. **Seats 50.** Open Mon-Sat, 9.30-5.30pm. L 12-3.30pm. House wine €19.95. Closed Sun, Bank Hols, 24 Dec - 15 Jan. Amex, MasterCard, Visa, Laser. **Directions:** On road from Main Square to Glengarriff, 3 mins walk from tourist office.

Bantry
CHARACTER PUB

The Snug
The Quay Bantry Co Cork
Tel: 027 50057

Maurice and Colette O'Donovans' well-named bar is a cosy and welcoming place, bustling with life and ideal for a wholesome bite at moderate prices. Maurice is the chef and takes pride in using local produce and giving value for money; his menus feature a wide range of popular dishes, many of which are in the house style. At lunch time, home-made soups and favourites like deep-fried mushrooms with garlic mayonnaise top the bill and are followed by a range of open sandwiches, panini, baguettes and fourly baps and specials such as roast lamb or goujons of fresh haddock. More extensive evening menus offer dressier dishes as well, including starters like Bantry Bay prawn cocktail or oak smoked salmon salad, and a good choice of main courses including steaks, home-made beefburgers and local Skeaghamore duck with orange sauce as well as a number of fish dishes - including Bantry Bay mussels, of course. This wholesome fare, together with good value, keeps 'em coming back for more.. Children welcome (but not after 9pm). Food served daily, 10.30am-9pm (Sun 12.30-9). Closed 25 Dec & Good Fri. MasterCard, Visa, Laser. **Directions:** Beside Garda Station, on the quay as you enter Bantry.

Bantry Area
RESTAURANT WITH ROOMS

Larchwood House Restaurant
Pearsons Bridge Bantry Co Cork
Tel: 027 66181

The gardens are a special point of interest here, complementing the restaurant, which is in a relatively modern house with both the traditionally-furnished lounge and dining room enjoying lovely garden views. Sheila Vaughan, a Euro-Toques chef, presents seasonal dinner menus: warm duck salad with ginger, quite traditional main courses such as loin of lamb with lemon and mint, and classical desserts like lemon ice cream or warm chocolate cake with caramel sauce - good cooking and, while the pace is leisurely, the view of the garden is a treat. This is a haven for garden lovers, who often make it a base when visiting the many gardens in the locality; here, the Ouvane River flows through the three acre woodland garden, which includes an island accessible via a footbridge and stepping stones all created by Aidan Vaughan. B&B accommodation is also offered, €40 pps, no ss. Gardens open Mon-Fri 9am-5pm, also several Sundays in June (phone to check dates). **Seats 25.** D Mon-Sat, 7-9.30. Set D €45. House wine €23. SC discretionary. Closed Sun & Christmas week; limited openings in winter, please call ahead to check. Amex, Diners, MasterCard, Visa. Laser. **Directions:** Take the Kealkil Road off N71 at Ballylickey; after 2 miles signed just before the bridge.

BEARA PENINSULA

Aside from Castletownbere (see entry), a tour around the scenic BEARA PENINSULA has remarkably few places where you might be tempted to stop for a bite except for **Mossie's Ulusker House** at Adrigole (see entry) - stay overnight. At Bunaw on Kilmacallogue Harbour, at the northern end of the Healy Pass, **Teddy O'Sullivan's** is a pleasantly traditional and hospitable pub offering good simple food (try a big bowl of the mussels the area is famous for); at **Derreen Gardens**, nearby at Lauragh, there is also a café serving teas or, further west at the village of Ardgroom, look out for **The Village Inn**, a well-maintained and friendly traditional pub serving home-cooked food. Should hunger strike way out west at Allihies, **O'Neill's pub** offers bar food (and a restaurant upstairs Thu-Sun evenings; 027 73008) and there's even simple Failte Ireland approved accommodation at Mary O'Sullivan's **Seaview B&B** (027 73004).
WWW.IRELAND-GUIDE.COM FOR THE BEST PLACES TO EAT, DRINK & STAY

Beara Area
B&B

Mossies at Ulusker House
Trafrask Adrigole Beara Co Cork **Tel: 027 60606**
mossies@eircom.net www.mossiesrestaurant.com

Mossies is situated in lovely gardens just outside the village of Ardrigole and, having been lovingly restored by current owners David and Lorna Ramshaw, this old house now makes a wonderful place to stay, with elegant and stylish public rooms and very comfortable bedrooms. More than just a B&B, this is really a country house experience and guests are offered the opportunity to dine in. This you would be very wise to do, as Lorna is an accomplished cook and offers a fine dining dinner, using locally sourced ingredients, beautifully presented on the plate. As this peninsula offers the visitor so little in the way of comfort and style, Mossie's is a place to be cherished. Booking ahead strongly advised. Garden, walking, watersports (scuba diving nearby). Children welcome (under 3s free in parents room); **Rooms 4** (all en-suite, 3 shower only, all no smoking); limited room service; dogs permitted by arrangement. Residents D daily, 6-9pm (from 7pm Sun); set D €19-21; house wine from €19; Childrens high chair and menu. Closed Jan. MasterCard, Visa, Laser. **Directions:** Well signed on Glengarriff to Castletownbere road.

Blarney
GUESTHOUSE

Ashlee Lodge

Tower Blarney Co Cork **Tel: 021 438 5346**
info@ashleelodge.com www.ashleelodge.com

Anne and John O'Leary's luxurious purpose-built guesthouse is just a couple of miles outside Blarney and within very easy striking distance of Cork city. (A bus from the city will drop you outside their door.) Everything is immaculate, beginning with the impressive reception area with highly polished floor and well-kept plants and fresh flowers in all the public areas, including the breakfast room. Bedrooms may not have views, but the exceptionally high level of comfort more than compensates: spacious, stylishly decorated rooms have king size beds and all the latest technology - wide screen TV, radio and CD unit, direct dial phones with modem access, personal safe and individually controlled air conditioning - as well as tea/coffee facilities, trouser press, hairdryer and (just the thing for padding along to the hot tub on the first floor) bathrobes and towelling slippers. But the most outstanding feature of Ashlee Lodge is the O'Learys themselves, who are exceptionally helpful hosts and genuinely wish to assist guests in every way possible - notably with local knowledge of all kinds, especially the many golf courses nearby; they arrange tee times, provide transport to and from golf courses and generally act as facilitators. They take great pride in giving a breakfast to remember too - an impressive buffet is beautifully laid out with lots of juices, cereals and fresh fruits in season, then there are freshly-baked breads, real honeycomb on every table, and a wide range of hot dishes including fish of the day, all impeccably cooked to order - and prettily presented too. Everything is pristine and the only small downside is that the hard flooring used throughout the house can be noisy. *Dinner is sometimes available, by arrangement - Anne is the chef, and she offers an appealing choice of about five starters and half a dozen main courses There's also a choice of 14 wines, all available by the glass and preserved by 'La Verre de Vin' system. Spa with Hot tub, massage. Free broadband wi/fi, garden, fishing nearby. Golf breaks. **Rooms 10** (4 suites, 1 shower only, 6 ground floor, 1 for disabled, all no smoking). B&B €70 pps, ss €25. D daily, 6-8.30pm. Closed 20 Dec - 31 Jan. Amex, MasterCard, Visa, Laser. **Directions:** Located on R 617 Blarney-Killarney road: from Blarney village take road past Blarney Park Hotel, signed Killarney, for approx 2km; turn left at filling station - Ashlee Lodge is on left about 0.5km further on.

Blarney
CHARACTER PUB

Blairs Inn

Cloghroe Blarney Co Cork **Tel: 021 438 1470**
blair@eircom.net www.blairsinn.ie

John and Anne Blair's pretty riverside pub is in a quiet, wooded setting. Sitting in the garden in summer, you might see trout rising in the Owennageara river, while winter offers welcoming fires in this comfortingly traditional country pub. It's a lovely place to drop into for a drink and they offer food in both the bar and a restaurant area. Outdoor seating is provided in a covered patio area, with bar. Children welcome before 7pm. **Seats 45** (restaurant/bar) & 100 in garden. Bar menu 12.30-9.30 daily. Restaurant L 12.30-4, D 6.30-9.30. A la carte. House wine €21. Service discretionary. Live traditional music Mon, 9.30pm, Jun-Sept. Closed 25 Dec & Good Fri. Amex, Diners, MasterCard, Visa, Laser. **Directions:** 5 minutes from Blarney village, on the R579.

BLARNEY

Blarney, 5 miles (8km) north of Cork city, is world famous for its castle and the Blarney Stone, with its traditional power of conferring eloquence on those who kiss it... Although it attracts a lot of tourists, its convenience to the city also also make it a good base for business visitors. **The Blarney Park Hotel**

(021 438 5281) has excellent facilities for business and leisure, and is a popular conference centre; those who prefer a smaller but lively establishment may like the **Muskerry Arms** (021 438 5200), a traditional pub and guesthouse with traditional music in the bar each evening.
WWW.IRELAND-GUIDE.COM FOR THE BEST PLACES TO EAT, DRINK & STAY

Blarney	Blarney Castle Hotel
HOTEL	Village Green Blarney Co Cork **Tel: 021 438 5116**
	info@blarneycastlehotel.com www.blarneycastlehotel.com

This attractive family-run hotel overlooks the village green in the centre of Blarney, beside the castle. It has been in the Forrest family since 1837 but, with the exception of the restaurant, reception area and a very characterful old bar, they completely rebuilt the hotel a few years ago. The new accommodation includes spacious, bright bedrooms with excellent views and all have a double and single bed, wide screen TV, tea/coffee-making; and well-finished bathrooms. Helpful, friendly staff create a welcoming atmosphere and prices are reasonable. The adjacent Lemon Tree Restaurant may not carry through the anticipated Mediterranean theme, but offers meals that are above the standard expected in hotel dining rooms and staff are very hospitable. Short breaks available all year. Golfing breaks offered; numerous golf courses nearby, transport etc arranged for guests. Children welcome (under 5 free in parents' room, cot available without charge, baby sitting arranged.) Pool table. Private parking. **Rooms 13** (1 junior suite,1 shower only, all no smoking). No lift. B&B about €60 pps, ss €20. [Meals: The Lemon Tree Restaurant: D 6.30-9.30. Bar food 12-9.30 daily.] Closed 24-25 Dec. Amex, MasterCard, Visa, Laser. **Directions:** Centre of Blarney, on village green (next to Blarney castle entrance). ◇

BUTLERSTOWN

Butlerstown is a pretty pastel-painted village, with lovely views across farmland to Dunworley and the sea beyond. At **Atlantic Sunset B&B** (Dunworley, 023 40115) Mary Holland provides comfortable accommodation and a genuinely warm welcome in her neat modern house with views down to the sea near sandy beaches and a coastal walk. The house is wheelchair accessible and the ground floor rooms are suitable for less able guests. **O'Neill's Pub** (023 40228) is as pleasant and hospitable a place as could be found to enjoy the local view - or to admire the traditional mahogany bar and pictures that make old pubs like this such a pleasure to be in. O'Neill's is now a popular stopping off point for the "Seven Heads Millennium Coastal Walk" so it may be useful to know that children (and well-behaved pets) are welcome.
WWW.IRELAND-GUIDE.COM FOR THE BEST PLACES TO EAT, DRINK & STAY

Carrigaline	Carrigaline Court Hotel & Leisure Centre
HOTEL/RESTAURANT	Main Street Carrigaline Co Cork **Tel: 021 485 2100**
	reception@carrigcourt.com www.carrigcourt.com

This conveniently-located modern hotel offers hands-on management and attentive staff that really make the difference. Fresh primrose yellow paintwork creates a good first impression which is carried through into bright, spacious public areas - and interesting contemporary furniture is an attractive feature throughout, notably in the pleasing new Collins Bar which was completely redesigned in 2007; emphasising the hotel's position at the heart of the community, there are large plasma screens for major sporting events, and traditional Irish music sessions (local players) are held here on Monday nights. Accommodation includes several suites, and all bedrooms are attractively decorated and well-equipped for business guests with work desks, ISDN lines and safes as well as the more usual amenities - and luxurious marbled bathrooms. Conference/banqueting facilities (350/220), also smaller meeting rooms; secretarial services; free broadband wi/fi. Leisure centre (swimming pool, jacuzzi, sauna, steam room, massage), beauty salon. Children welcome (under 12s free in parents' room, cot available without charge, baby sitting arranged). Weekend offers and golf breaks offered. No pets. **Rooms 88** (2 suites, 1 junior suite, 2 family, 1 for disabled). Lift. 24 hour room service. Turndown service offered. B&B €93 pps, ss €20. Closed 25-26 Dec. **The Bistro:** Three separate smartly set up dining spaces offer a choice of atmosphere and ensure a more intimate ambience for quieter times. Friendly staff offer a prompt welcome, and the menu à la carte, plus specials - is wide-ranging and affordable. Michael Kelly, head chef since 2007, offers menus with a slightly more international tone than previously; but careful sourcing has always been the policy here and even if, for example, the starter plate of meats is Spanish (excellent local artisan products are available,) there is still occasional mention of local produce. Bantry Bay mussels feature, for example, and a warm salad of wild mushrooms & rocket leaves comes with a shaving of the superb west Cork cheese,

Georgina Campbell's Ireland

Gabriel. Main courses are strong on seafood, but there's also a wider choice, including char-grilled steaks with classic accompaniments. Prettily presented desserts might include a meringue roulade with praline Baileys filling, or there's a platter of local farmhouses cheeses. Reliable food, efficient service and a pleasing ambience make for an enjoyable meal - and good value for money keeps people coming back. Well-chosen wine list. Air conditioning. Toilets wheelchair accessible. Children welcome (high chair, childrens menu, baby changing facilities). **Seats 150** (private room, 50). D Mon-Sat 6-9.45pm, D Sun 6-8.45pm, L Sun only 12.30-2.15pm. Set D €40, also à la carte; set Sun L €25. House wine from €16.95. Closed 25-26 Dec. Amex, Diners, MasterCard, Visa, Laser. **Directions:** Follow South Link Road and then follow signs for Carrigaline.

Carrigaline
GUESTHOUSE

Glenwood House

Ballinrea Road Carrigaline Co Cork **Tel: 021 437 3878**
info@glenwoodguesthouse.com www.glenwoodguesthouse.com

This well-respected guesthouse is in purpose-built premises, very conveniently located for Cork Airport and the ferry and set in gardens, where guests can relax in fine weather. Comfortable, well-furnished rooms (including five newer ones recently added, and one designed for disabled guests) have all the amenities normally expected of hotels, including ISDN lines, TV with video channel, trouser press/iron, tea/coffee facilities and well-designed bathrooms. Breakfast has always been a strong point - fresh fruits and juices, cheeses, home-made breads and preserves as well as hot dishes (available from 7am for business guests, until 10 am for those taking a leisurely break). A guest sitting room with an open fire makes a cosy retreat on dark winter evenings. Children welcome (Under 5s free in parents' room, cot available without charge). Free broadband wi/fi. No pets. Garden. **Rooms 15** (3 shower only, 1 for disabled, 13 no smoking, all ground floor). Room service (limited hours). B&B €50pps, ss €9. Private parking (15). Closed mid Dec-mid Jan. MasterCard, Visa, Laser. **Directions:** Entering Carrigaline from Cork, turn right at Ballinrea roundabout.

Castlemartyr
HOTEL/RESTAURANT

Capella Castlemartyr

Castlemartyr Co Cork **Tel: 021 464 4050**
reservations.castlemartyr@capellahotels.com www.capellacastlemartyr.com

Built around a 17th century manor house and the ruins of an adjacent castle that belonged to the Knights Templar and dates back to 1210, this new 5* hotel promises to open up East Cork to an appreciative new international audience. The entrance has been moved from the impressive old gates in the centre of Castlemartyr village to a safer location around the corner on the Ballycotton road, but anything lost in old-world grand is gained in the sweeping approach that skirts the partially completed 18-hole Ron Kirby-designed golf course, and gives a hint of the lush variety to be found in the 220-acre estate. The driveway leads around the ancient castle to the beautiful entrance of the old house which was once owned by Sir Walter Raleigh (who later sold it to the Earl of Cork, Richard Boyle) and includes among its special features a stunning ballroom, declared 'the best room in Ireland' by the renowned 18th century travel chronicler Arthur Young, and now fully restored. Eleven of the hotel's 109 guestrooms and suites are in the old house and the rest are in a new section alongside it which is uncompromisingly modern, yet sits surprisingly comfortably beside the elegance of the old. The Capella philosophy is to combine luxurious amenities with individualised service - how many hotels can boast a personal assistant who can arrange everything from outings with a local fisherman, to visiting a nearby beekeeper, or organising private musical performances in the gardens or readings by well known authors! It may all have a slightly fairytale air to it, but an emphasis on service is always appreciated, and for a large hotel to gear activities towards individual preferences in this way is actually recognition of the importance of the genuine hospitality traditionally offered by smaller establishments. In true country house style, guests can even take the hotel's resident dogs - a beautiful pair of setters called Earl and Countess - for walks on the estate. **Accommodation** is predictably luxurious - the rooms are huge, ranging from a mere 500 sq ft to a Presidential Suite of over 3,000 sq ft and they sport correspondingly enormous beds and all the expected technological bells and whistles, including a central computer system that controls all the room functions from the bedside. Conferences/Banqueting; business centre, free broadband wi/fi secretarial services, video conferencing, laptop-sized safes in bedrooms. Archery, clay pigeon shooting, croquet, cycling, falconry, garden, golf (18 when complete), leisure centre (swimming pool, fitness room, jacuzzi, sauna, steam room), destination spa, beauty salon (masseuse, hair dressing), walking, wine courses. Equestrian and fishing (fly, coarse, sea angling) nearby. Children welcome (cot available free of charge, baby sitting arranged). **Rooms 109**; Lift; 24 hr room service; B&B €270pps. Heli-Pad. **Dining:** Given its location in an area internationally renowned for the range and quality of its produce, there is a welcome emphasis on cooking that is driven by availability of seasonal produce; this applies in all areas from the Spa Café at the 24,400 sq ft Auriga Spa to the Bell Tower fine dining restaurant, and it will be interesting to see how head chef Laurence Agnew's daily-changed menus and, indeed, the entire dining experience work out alongside other highly regarded establishments in the area. A room that promises to become very popular with local guests as well as residents is the Knights Bar - complete with restored rococo ceiling, baby grand piano and martini trolley service, it's the place for afternoon tea with home-made scones and jam and, later on perhaps, sampling a few tipples from the trolley. *In addition to the accommodation and amenities offered at the hotel, the Castlemartyr Resort offers guests the option of staying at the 42 contemporary Golf Lodges (built within the old walled garden, and with direct access to the golf course) and 10 cottagey Mews Residences in the 'Old Bawn' area of the castle, both of which have been open for business since early August 2007 (see www.castlemartyrresort.ie for details). The 18-hole championship golf course and Castlemartyr Golf Club (with pro shop and all services) will be fully open early in 2008, while the first 9-holes have been available for play since late summer 2007. **Bell Tower Restaurant:** Children welcome (high chair, children's menu); **Seats 60** (private room, 8); air conditioning; L daily, 12-2.30pm; D daily, 6-9.30pm; set 2/3 course D, €65/75; gourmet D, €90. Open all year. Amex, Diners, MasterCard, Visa, Laser. **Directions:** On main N25 from Cork.

CASTLETOWNBERE

Although it is currently rather run down and could be described as a "place that time forgot", there are signs of regeneration in the fishing port of Castletownbere and it makes a good base for exploring the beautiful south-western tip of the Beara peninsula. Berehaven is a safe anchorage for yachts and is ideal for watersports, from sea angling to windsurfing. The area is also ideal for land-based outdoor activities with golfing, hiking, biking and hill walking all available nearby. The 5* **Dunboy Castle Hotel** (01 631 6000; www.dunboycastlehotel.com) was under construction on the 40-acre waterside site of the original castle south-west of the town at the time of our summer 2007 visit and it will undoubtedly bring a new focus to the area when it opens; "an amazing neo-gothic folly" is how one observer described it and it will be interesting to see how the original castle is incorporated into the later design. Whether staying nearby or visiting Castletownbere for the day, visitors need food: in addition to **McCarthy's** (see entry) you could try **John Patricks Butcher & Restaurant**, a quirky, inexpensive place where you'll find wholesome lunches for walkers (simple Irish food - bacon and cabbage, Irish stew, steaks); **Gallagher's** offers generous fare too, including excellent home-made cakes. Also, Ciannit Walker's interesting food shop **Taste at the Pier** (027 71842; not actually at the pier at all, but just off the square) has plans to introduce a daytime café. If you need something in the evening, you might try **Cottage Heights Seafood Restaurant** (027 71743; www.cottage-heights.com), on an elevated site at Derrymiham - or **The Old Bakery** (027 70869), which is well recommended locally; mainly seafood, as you'd expect, and reasonably priced.

WWW.IRELAND-GUIDE.COM FOR THE BEST PLACES TO EAT, DRINK & STAY

Castletownshend
BAR/RESTAURANT

Mary Ann's Bar & Restaurant

Castletownshend Skibbereen Co Cork **Tel: 028 36146**
maryanns@eircom.net www.maryannsbarrestaurant.com

SEAFOOD BAR OF THE YEAR

Mention Castletownshend and the chances are that the next words will be 'Mary Ann's', as this welcoming landmark has been the source of happy memories for many a visitor to this picturesque west Cork village over the years. (For those who have come up the hill with a real sailor's appetite from the little quay, the sight of its gleaming bar seen through the open door is one to treasure.) The pub is as old as it looks, going back to 1846, and has been in the energetic and hospitable ownership of Fergus and Patricia O'Mahony since 1988; they have loved it and maintained it well (the last time we visited, Fergus was up a ladder beside the front door with a paintbrush in his hand), but any refurbishments at Mary Ann's have left its original character intact. The O'Mahonys have built up a great reputation for food in both the bar and the restaurant, which is split between an upstairs dining room and The Vine Room at the back, which can be used for private parties; alongside it there is a garden which has been fitted with a retractable awning over the tables, allowing for all-weather dining. Seafood is the star, of course, in both bar and restaurant and it comes in many guises, usually along with some of the lovely home-baked brown bread which is one of the house specialities. Another is the Platter of Castlehaven Bay Shellfish and Seafood - a sight to behold, and usually including langoustine, crab meat, crab claws, and both fresh and smoked salmon. Much of the menu depends on the catch of the day, although there are also good steaks and roasts, served with delicious local potatoes and seasonal vegetables. Desserts are good too, but local West Cork cheeses are an excellent option that may prove too difficult to resist. One of the most appealing things about Mary Ann's is that such a wide choice is available in the bar as well as the restaurant and that includes daily blackboard specials, which may offer real treats like lobster thermidor or lobster mayonnaise. Some bar food indeed! The O'Mahonys also have a very successful art gallery on the first floor. **Restaurant Seats 30** (outside, 100, private room 30). Toilets wheelchair accessible. Children welcome. D daily in summer, 6-9; L 12-2.30. A la carte. House wine from €18.95. SC discretionary. *Bar food 12-2.30 & 6-9 daily. Closed Mon Nov-Mar, 25 Dec, Good Fri & 3 weeks Jan. Amex, MasterCard, Visa, Laser. **Directions:** Five miles from Skibbereen, on lower main street.

CLONAKILTY

Clonakilty is a quaint town of narrow streets, brightly coloured houses and hanging baskets. For visitors to the area there are several safe beaches nearby, walks in the countryside and local attractions such as **The West Cork Model Railway Village, Lisselan Estate Gardens** (023 33249) and **Lios-na-gCon Ringfort.** The unlikely product that Clonakilty is most famous for today is black pudding - specifically, Edward Twomey's delicious grainy black pudding. It is now available from every supermarket and good food store throughout the country and, of course, you can buy it (and many other excellent meats) from their fine butchers shop, in Pearse Street. - a good choice if you are in self-catering accommodation in the area. You will, of course, find local black pudding on every breakfast menu in the area - including, no doubt, the traditional **Emmet Hotel** (023 33394; www.emmethotel.com), which is situated on a lovely Georgian Square and has a separate restaurant, **O'Keeffe's** attached (see entry); and **Quality Hotel & Leisure Centre** (Tel: 023 36400; www.choicehotelsireland.ie), which is a little out of the town and, with good facilities and activities for children, is an extremely popular destination for family holidays and short breaks. At the time of going to press we have been informed that Elain McCarthy, proprietor of the popular **Malt House Granary Restaurant** (023 34355) is taking leave of absence and the restaurant is to be leased for at least a year.

WWW.IRELAND-GUIDE.COM FOR THE BEST PLACES TO EAT, DRINK & STAY

Clonakilty   # An Sugan
BAR/RESTAURANT   41 Wolfe Tone Street Clonakilty Co Cork **Tel: 023 33498**
                                                    ansugan4@eircom.net www.ansugan.com

 The O'Crowley family has owned this characterful bar and restaurant since 1980: it's always been a friendly, well-run place and, although it can be very busy at times, their reputation for good food is generally well-deserved. Menus change daily and are very strong on seafood - specialities include Union Hall smoked salmon parfait, baked crab An Sugan, and seafood basket while daily fish specials could include a choice of ten, ranging from cod on a bed of champ to lobster An Sugan (fresh lobster flamed in a brandy & tomato sauce). If you're not in the mood for seafood you might try a terrine of the famous Clonakilty puddings or a prime Hereford sirloin steak. Lunch menus are shorter and simpler, but also offer a wide choice of seafood - and some traditional comfort food, like bacon & cabbage. A new private dining room is available for 2008. No private parking. **Seats 42.** Food served 12-9.30 daily; L12-4.30, D 5-9.30. Set Sun L €28, Set D €30/35, also A la carte. House wine from €18. Service discretionary. Restaurant reservations advised. Closed 25/26 Dec & Good Fri. MasterCard, Visa, Laser. **Directions:** From Cork, on the left hand side as you enter Clonakilty.

Clonakilty   # Dunmore House Hotel
HOTEL   Muckross Clonakilty Co Cork **Tel: 023 33352**
                            dunmorehousehotel@eircom.net www.dunmorehotel.com

The magnificent coastal location of the O'Donovan family's hotel has been used to advantage to provide sea views for all bedrooms and to allow guests access to their own stretch of foreshore. Comfortable public areas include a traditional bar and lounges, whilst the contemporary dining room is light, bright, and home to a fine collection of paintings. Bedrooms are furnished to a high standard and make a comfortable base for the numerous outdoor leisure activities in the area, including the hotel's own nine hole golf course, free to residents; packed lunches available on request. Hands-on owner-management, a high standard of maintenance and housekeeping, and professional, friendly staff make this a pleasing hotel. Conference/banqueting 200/250. Wheelchair accessible. Children welcome (under 3 free in parents' room, cot available without charge; junior evening meal 5.30-6.30). Golf, fishing, walking. Dogs allowed in some areas. **Rooms 23** (2 junior suites, 4 shower only, 1 for disabled). B&B about €75 pps, ss €10. Bar food available all day (12-8.30). **Restaurant Seats 80.** Toilets wheelchair accessible. Air conditioning D daily, 7-8.30 (c. €40), L Sun only, 1-2.30 (c. €25). Closed Christmas; 19 Jan-11 Mar. Amex, Diners, MasterCard, Visa, Laser. **Directions:** 4 km from Clonakilty town, well signed. ◈

Clonakilty
RESTAURANT
◍ ☆ Ⓔ ◭

Gleeson's

3 Connolly Street Clonakilty Co Cork **Tel: 023 21834**
reservations@gleesons.ie www.gleesons.ie

Robert and Alex Gleeson's fine restaurant has a discreet, smartly-maintained frontage and rather mysterious interior, with dark woods and deep, rich tones in furnishings which exude quality and include many original touches (such as beautifully simple slate place mats). Robert's cooking style is modern French and his experience in famous kitchens - The Dorchester, for example - should give an idea of what to expect. His menus, which offer about seven choices on each course on the à la carte and three on the early dinner menu, are not over-elaborate but this is emphatically fine dining albeit with a pleasingly relaxed tone that makes it feel welcoming and accessible to all. Local produce, like Skeaghanore duck, from Ballydehob, is show-cased in dishes such as a starter terrine of ballontine of Skeaghanore duck & foie gras, served with celeriac remoulade & mango chutney - or you might try an gently updated classic main course of roast loin of monkfish wrapped in Parma ham served with creamed savoy cabbage and pan-roasted cocotte potatoes. Vegetarian dishes are imaginative (tian of Mediterranean vegetables with buttered spinach, polenta, black bean salsa & red pepper sauce perhaps) and classical desserts include delicious home-made ice creams (a speciality of the house), or local farmhouse cheeses, served with home-made crackers, are a tempting alternative. Precise cooking and perfectly balanced flavours characterise the cooking throughout and a meal is a restorative experience; classically trained chefs are an increasingly rare treasure these days and cooking of this calibre is a joy, especially when accompanied by pleasing surroundings and friendly professional service, as it is here. This fine restaurant has deservedly earned a loyal following, and reservations are strongly recommended. Prices are fair throughout and the early dinner menu offers outstanding value. A carefully selected, wide-ranging and very informative wine list kicks off with champagnes and champagne cocktails and a lovely selection of wines by the glass; the main list is arranged by style, with tasting notes and the half bottle selection is well chosen. Not suit-able for children under 7 yrs. **Seats 45.** D Tue-Sat, 6-9.30. Set 3 course D with coffee €35 (all eve Tue-Thu, 6-7pm Fri-Sat); also à la carte. House wine from €19.50. SC discretionary. Closed Sun (except bank hol weekends) & Mon; 24-26 Dec, 3 weeks Jan/Feb. Amex, MasterCard, Visa, Laser. **Directions:** Town centre; next door to Scannel's Pub.

Clonakilty
CAFÉ
◍ Ⓔ

Harts Coffee Shop

8 Ashe Street Clonakilty Co Cork **Tel: 023 35583**
hartscoffeeshop@gmail.com

 For nearly a decade, good home cooking has been the attraction at Aileen Hart and Tony O'Mahoney's friendly coffee shop in the town centre, and the consistently high standard they have maintained over that time has regulars making a beeline for this welcoming spot as soon as they hit town. A nifty little menu offers all kinds of healthy meals - ranging from a breakfast ciabatta with bacon, eggs & cheese, through warm baguettes (peppered steak strips, perhaps, with lettuce and mayo), sandwiches toasted and cool -

all served with side salad & home-made vinaigrette dressing - to specials such as an Irish cheese plate with a choice of crackers or bread. A Specials board suggests additions to the regular menu - soups (vegetables, perhaps, or pea & mint) based on home-made stocks, which are also used in traditional stews (beef & Beamish, perhaps), available in regular or large portions. But best of all, perhaps, is the choice of home-baked scones just like your granny used to make, served with home-made jam, and tarts - everything from a vegetarian quiche to an old-fashioned apple tart served with cream - and cakes ranging from healthy carrot cake to gooey orange chocolate drizzle cake. Simple, wholesome, home-made: just lovely! Great selection of drinks too, including freshly squeezed juices teas and Green bean coffees. Wine licence. **Seats 30.** Children welcome. Open Mon-Sat, 10-5. Closed 3 weeks Christmas, Sun & Mon. **No Credit Cards. Directions:** Clonakilty town centre.

Clonakilty
HOTEL/RESTAURANT

The Lodge & Spa at Inchydoney Island

Inchydoney Island Clonakilty Co Cork **Tel: 023 33143**
reservations@inchydoneyisland.com www.inchydoneyisland.com

This hotel enjoys great views over the two 'Blue Flag' beaches at Inchydoney, which bring crowds to the area in summer, so many guests will prefer this as an off-season destination. The building is architecturally uninspired, but it has mellowed as landscaping of the large carpark on the seaward side matures - and once inside the hotel, that pampered feeling soon takes over. Dramatic artworks in the spacious foyer are impressive, and other public areas include a large, comfortably furnished first-floor residents' lounge and library, with a piano, extensive sea views, and a soothing atmosphere. Most of the generously sized bedrooms have sea views and all are furnished and decorated in an uncluttered contemporary style, with air conditioning, safe and all the more usual amenities. The exceptional health and leisure facilities that make this a special destination for many returning guests include a superb Thalasso-therapy Spa, which offers a range of special treatments and makes Inchydoney a particularly attractive place for an off-season break. Special breaks are a major attraction - fishing, equestrian, golf, therapies - and its romantic location ensures its popularity for weddings. Conferences/banqueting (300/250); secretarial services. Self-catering apartments available (with full use of hotel facilities). Thalassotherapy spa (24 treatment rooms); beauty salon; swimming pool; walking; snooker, pool table. Children welcome (under 3s free in parents' room, cots available for €15, baby sitting arranged). **Rooms 67** (3 suites, 1 junior suite,2 for disabled). Lift; 24 hr room service. B&B €180, ss €45. SC10%. Open all year except Christmas. **Gulfstream Restaurant:** Located on the first floor, with panoramic sea views from the window tables, this elegant restaurant offers fine dining in a broadly Mediterranean style. Fresh local produce, organic where possible, features on seasonal menus that always include imaginative vegetarian options - and willingly caters for any other special dietary requirements. Lighter dishes for spa guests are also offered, with nutritional information outlined. **Seats 70** (private room 250). Non-residents welcome by reservation. Children welcome. Toilets wheelchair accessible. Air conditioning. D 6.30-9.45; Set 5 course D €60, also à la carte. House wine €20. SC10%. [*Informal/ bar meals also available 11-9 daily.] Amex, MasterCard, Visa, Laser. **Directions:** N71 from Cork to Clonakilty, then causeway to Inchydoney.

Clonakilty
RESTAURANT

O'Keeffe's of Clonakilty

Emmet Square Clonakilty Co Cork **Tel: 023 33394**
emmethotel@eircom.net www.emmethotel.com

Marie O'Keeffe's well-regarded restaurant is hidden away in the centre of Clonakilty, on a lovely serene Georgian square that contrasts unexpectedly with the hustle and bustle of the nearby streets - a most attractive location, although parking is likely to be difficult in high season. Although located in separate premises next door, O'Keeffe's also has direct access from the Emmet Hotel (www.emmethotelcom) and bookings are made through the hotel. The restaurant overlooks the square and, with bold decor that is unexpected in an old house, it has plenty of atmosphere. Marie O'Keeffe's reputation for creative modern cooking is well established in the area, and she is well known for her commitment to using seasonal local produce, much of it organic, when possible. Seafood tends to take the starring role on her concise, moderately priced menus, which are topped up with daily specials depending on the best produce available on the day; local meats and poultry always feature too, of course; breast of chicken stuffed with Clonakilty black pudding is a house speciality, served with a mustard mash and chicken jus. Several imaginative vegetarian dishes are offered (spelt lasagne with goat's cheese, semi-sundried tomatoes, spinach & ricotta is a speciality that is also suitable for coeliacs) and, given notice, other special dietary requirements can be met. A courtyard garden is pleasant for al fresco dining in fine weather; Sunday lunch is available in the restaurant, otherwise bar lunches are provided in the hotel. **Seats 50** (outdoor seating, 40). Reservations advised. Children welcome. D daily, 6.30-9.30; à la carte. House wine €17.40. SC discretionary. Bar L daily 12.30-2.30 with bar menu from 12-10pm (in the hotel). Restaurant closed 25 Dec. Amex, Diners, MasterCard, Visa, Laser, Switch. **Directions:** In the centre of Clonakilty - turn left into Emmet Square at the Catholic Church.

Clonakilty
BAR/RESTAURANT

Richy's Bar & Bistro

Wolfe Tone St. Clonakilty Co Cork **Tel: 023 21852**
richysbarandbistro@eircom.net www.richysbarandbistro.com

 Situated in the centre of Clonakilty, close to a little park, Richy Virahsawmy's bar and bistro is one of those relaxed places where today's specials are chalked up on a blackboard and where you'll find a real cross-section of people. It's spacious and appealingly furnished with smart window blinds and wooden floors giving a clean, modern feeling, softened by warm yellow walls and paintings well lit in little recessed alcoves. Well-spaced tables, banquettes along one wall and a bar in one of the two eating areas create a comfortable setting for food that ranges widely around the Mediterranean, with a leaning towards Spain - and locally sourced ingredients may include less usual food like samphire, as well as local lamb and fish. A thoughtfully selected, clear and reasonably priced wine list is organised by style and includes an interesting house selection (9, all available by the glass, and other drinks are available from the bar, which is handy for families with young children). A great place to know about, especially when on a family holiday. * Richy has published a cookbook, West Cork Fusion; and he also has plans to open in Cork city. **Seats 70** (outdoors, 16). Children welcome before 9pm (high chair, childrens menu). Open daily; Summer 12 - 10pm; winter, 5-10pm. Early D Mon-Thu, 5-7, €25; also a la carte. House wine €19.95. Closed 25 Dec. Amex, MasterCard, Visa, Laser. **Directions:** Next to tourist office.

Clonakilty Area
BAR/RESTAURANT

Deasy's Harbour Bar & Seafood Restaurant

Ring Village Clonakilty Co Cork
Tel: 023 35741

Just across the road from the water in the pretty village of Ring, this former pub has a decking area at the front and large windows taking advantage of the view of Clonakilty Bay and the boats moored nearby. Inside, brick walls are decorated with nautical bric-a-brac - fishing net, a ship's wheel, wooden model ships and there are coffee table books on marine themes to browse; with all this, and candlelight as well as sea views, it's an atmospheric setting for fine seafood. Simply set tables keep the focus on menus which are a little international in style (no house or local specialities mentioned), but offer a wide range of seafood including less usual varieties such as shark, as well as fairly classic prime fish dishes - monkfish medallions wrapped in prosciutto with seared scallops and dill creme fraîche, perhaps. Piquant dips and sauces are out of the ordinary, adding a new dimension to familiar dishes - grilled John Dory fillets may come with a spicy local beetroot relish & celeriac purée for example. Other than seafood, there are some token offerings of meat or poultry for carnivores, and vegetarians are always offered an interesting alternative. Good cooking is also seen in tasty vegetables and delicious desserts, and details like lovely breads and thoughtful presentation. With an informal relaxed atmosphere, interesting food and a lovely setting, this has become a popular spot so book well ahead, especially in high season. Service can show signs of pressure at busy times, but friendly staff are always good humoured and helpful. Not suitable for children after 7pm. **Seats 50;** D Wed-Sat 6-9.30; L Sun only, 1-3; set Sun L €28; house wine €20. Closed Sun D, Mon, Tue and 24-26 Dec. MasterCard, Visa, Laser. **Directions:** 2km outside Clonakilty.

Cobh
Knockeven House

COUNTRY HOUSE

Rushbrooke Cobh Co Cork **Tel: 021 481 1778**
info@knockevenhouse.com www.knockevenhouse.com

Clearly signed on the outskirts of Cobh, and at the end of a long winding driveway overhung by tall trees, you will find John and Pam Mulhaire's large and peacefully situated 1840s house. Its rather plain exterior, tarmac parking area and low-maintenance garden give no hint of the luxurious interior which is revealed when the front door opens on to a huge hall, where a deep red carpet and dramatic flower arrangement set on an antique desk set the tone for a house that offers guests the best of every world: lavish decor and facilities worthy of a top-class hotel, along with great hospitality, and reasonable prices. The Mulhaires have lived here for 20 years, but only opened for guests in 2004 - Pam is very chatty, relaxed and friendly, a natural hostess who treats her guests to tea and home-made scones on a silver tray on arrival, and on request at any time. An impressive drawing room has plenty of comfortable seating and an open fire and, like the rest of the house, the bedrooms are also decorated with sumptuous good taste (although lovers of old houses may be disappointed by the practical PVC double-glazed windows). Accommodation is very comfortable, with generous beds and immaculate en-suite bathrooms that have power showers (no full bath) and many thoughtful details, including pristine white bathrobes and Molton Brown toiletries. A good breakfast served on white Villeroy & Boch china, with pristine white cotton napkins includes a delicious fresh fruit salad, fresh orange juice, good-quality cereals, yoghurts, ham and cheese as well as a sound rendition of the traditional hot breakfast. This is an exceptionally comfortable place to stay and, although no dinner is offered, the restaurants of Midleton (or Monkstown, just across the ferry) are not too far away. Children welcome (cot available). **Rooms 4** (all en-suite and no smoking); limited room service. B&B €60pps, single about €75. MasterCard, Visa, Laser. **Directions:** On the outskirts of Cobh.

Cobh
Sheraton Fota Island Golf Resort & Spa

HOTEL

Fota Island Cobh Co Cork **Tel: 021 467 3000**
reservations.fota@sheraton.com www.sheraton.com/cork

A beautiful long tree-lined driveway, with glimpses of the water to the right, has always been the entrance to Fota Island Golf Club and in no way prepares first time visitors for what awaits around the last corner: whilst the recently planted trees will eventually soften this controversial building, it is easy to see why there was such local opposition to the development. However, as is often the case with new developments, things look different once you get inside. Guests are welcomed at the door, then you move through a large lobby/reception that opens into a spacious high-ceilinged area, with warm lighting, an open fire and lots of comfy seating. Off this, a bar looks over lawns to the front, with a decking area for fine weather; this comfortable and appealing room has an open fire which is shared with the adjacent restaurant - also overlooking the grounds, it's a clean-lined room, with classic white linen softened by warm lighting. Accommodation is luxurious, with a high proportion of suites and superior rooms, and many rooms enjoying panoramic views over woodlands or golf course; all are spacious and extremely comfortable, with huge beds and big flat screen tv, in addition to the usual facilities, and beautiful bathrooms have double-ended bath with head rests and separate walk-in shower. Good food has been a feature in all areas of the hotel since it opened and dining choices include the Fota Restaurant, offering a smart option for all-day meals, The Cove seafood grill room for evening dining, and The Amber Bar for light meals at any time. Complimentary wireless internet available in all public areas. *The Island Spa is a big attraction, another is golf - it can sometimes be difficult to get enough tee times at the adjacent Fota Island Golf Club, but it is hoped that the new 9-hole course will allow more flexibility. Championship golf course (18), spa, fitness room, swimming pool. Fly fishing, sea angling and equestrian nearby. Children welcome (cots available at no charge, baby sitting arranged); Conferences/Banqueting (400/280), business centre, secretarial services, Free Broadband. **Rooms 131** (8 suites, 8 junior suites, 40 executive); B&B room rate about €165; 24 hr room service; Lift. Open all year. **Restaurant: Seats 80** (outdoor, 30), serves food daily, 12.30-10.30; "The Cove" seafood grill room, seats 40, open Tue-Sat, 7pm-10pm; Barfood served 12.30-8 daily. Helipad. Amex, Diners, MasterCard, Visa, Laser. **Directions:** N25 east from Cork. Approx. 8 km (5m) later take a left and follow signs for Fota island. ◇

CROSSHAVEN

On the west side of Cork Harbour, 17 km from Cork city, Crosshaven is a favourite seaside resort for Cork people and an important yachting centre. The seasonal nature of the town means that restaurants tend to come and go but there are several pubs of character including **Cronin's** (see entry), where the Cronin family has a reputation for good seafood, and **The Moonduster Inn** (021 483 1610; www.moondusterinn.com), which also has an attractive first floor restaurant with views cross the water to Currabinny.

WWW.IRELAND-GUIDE.COM FOR THE BEST PLACES TO EAT, DRINK & STAY

Crosshaven
CHARACTER PUB

Cronin's Pub

Crosshaven Co Cork **Tel: 021 483 1829**
info@croninspub.com www.croninspub.com

The Cronin family's Victorian pub on the harbour front has oodles of character and, with its walls and high shelves crammed with maritime memorabilia, it serves as a sort of unofficial exhibition of local history. It has always had a good reputation for food, especially seafood, and now there's an enthusiastic new generation at work here, with Joeleen Cronin front of house and her brother Dennis (who is Ballymaloe-trained) as part of the kitchen team. While still feeling their way at the time of the Guide's visit, they are doing a good job with both the bar food and an evening restaurant, **The Shore Thing**. The restaurant is in a narrow high-ceilinged room off a passageway behind the bar and, although comfortable once seated, it is a little tightly-packed but there are plans to extend the restaurant area into part of the bar currently occupied by a pool table, which will be an improvement. Table presentation is plain and simple, and the mainly seafood menu is sensibly short; good ingredients are mainly sourced locally, cooking is good and presentation unfussy. The popular lunchtime bar menu is more extensive and includes quite a lot of pub food staples as well as seafood. Ample free parking in public carpark across the road. Bar food served Mon-Fri, 11.45-2.45pm, Sat, 11.45-3.30pm. Restaurant closed Sun, Mon & Jan. Amex, Diners, MasterCard, Visa, Laser. **Directions:** Straight into village, at car park.

Doneraile
HISTORIC HOUSE

Creagh House

Main Street Doneraile Co Cork **Tel: 022 24433**
info@creaghhouse.ie www.creaghhouse.ie

Michael O'Sullivan and Laura O'Mahony left a perfectly normal home to take on this Regency townhouse in need of renovation in 2000; since then, they have been giving it enormous amounts of TLC on an ongoing basis and their efforts are now beginning to pay off, as it is reaching its full glory. A listed building, with notable historical and literary connections, stately reception rooms and huge bedrooms, its principal rooms are among the largest from this period outside Dublin, and have beautiful restored plasterwork. Yet it is a relaxed family home and place of work (Michael and Laura both have offices in restored outbuildings), and this hospitable couple have clearly thrived on the challenge of restoration. Accommodation is wonderful, in vast rooms with huge antique furniture, crisp linen on comfortable beds, little extras (bowls of fruit, bottled water, tea/coffee/hot chocolate making facilities), and bathrooms to match - bath and separate shower, and big, soft towels. All modern partitions have been removed to restore the original scale, and 19th century furniture is used throughout, with 18th and 19th century prints and modern paintings. Anyone interested in architecture and/or history is in for a treat when staying here and Doneraile is well-placed for exploring a wide area - Cork, Cashel, Lismore and Killarney are all within an hour's drive. Garden lovers will be fascinated by the 2-acre walled garden behind Creagh House, which is under restoration ("black topsoil four feet deep!") and the house is beside Doneraile Court, which has 600 acres of estate parkland, free to the public. Golf nearby. Children welcome (under 3s free in parents room, cot available free of charge). No pets. Garden. **Rooms 3** (all en suite, with separate bath and shower, all no smoking). Residents' supper (2-course dinner, €30) available with 24 hours notice. B&B €100-120 pps, no ss. Closed Oct-Mar. Amex, MasterCard, Visa. **Directions:** Take N20 (Limerick road) from Mallow - 12.5km (8 m).

Durrus
RESTAURANT WITH ROOMS

Blairs Cove House

Durrus Bantry Co Cork **Tel:** 027 61127
blairscove@eircom.net www.blairscove.ie

Philippe and Sabine de Mey's beautiful property enjoys a stunning waterside location at the head of Dunmanus Bay. Additions over the years have enlarged the restaurant considerably - including an elegant conservatory overlooking a courtyard garden but the original room is unchanged and very atmospheric: lofty, stone-walled and black-beamed, with a magnificent chandelier as a central feature, gilt-framed family portraits on the walls, and lots of candles. Philippe and Sabine still offer accommodation (see below), but the restaurant has now been leased and is run independently by Gaby and Elk Stubner, restaurant manager and chef, respectively. There are no obvious changes - an enormous central buffet still displays a large hors d'oeuvre selection featuring lots of seafood and interesting salads, and the grand piano is used as before, to display an array of desserts The style of cooking remains the same too, with the main courses including meats, char-grilled at a wood-fired grill at one end of the restaurant and a good choice of fresh fish and seafood and a selection of local farmhouse cheeses is offered in addition to the dessert display. **Accommodation:** The accommodation is still run by Philippe and Sabine de Mey. Four suites/small apartments, offered for self-catering or B&B, are furnished in very different but equally dashing styles and there is also a cottage in the grounds. Children welcome (under 2s free in parents' room, cot available free of charge). B&B €115 pps, ss €30; no SC. Amex, Diners, MasterCard, Visa. Restaurant **Seats 70** (private room, 40). Reservations required. L Sun only, 1-3pm; set Sun L €29. D Tue-Sat, 7-9.30pm. Set D €46/56, 2/3 course; house wine €20, SC discretionary. Closed Sun D (except bank hol weekends), Mon & 7 Jan - 14 Feb. **Directions:** 3km (1.5 m) outside Durrus on Mizen Head Road, blue gate on right hand side.

Durrus
B&B

Carbery Cottage Guest Lodge

Durrus Bantry West Cork Co Cork **Tel:** 027 61368
carberycottage@eircom.net www.carbery-cottage-guest-lodge.net

With well-maintained gardens, plenty of parking and beautiful views, this purpose-built B&B and adjoining self-catering cottage creates a great first impression and a warm welcome extends to your four-legged friends too, with kennels provided, and large grassed penned areas for dogs to run. Owners Mike Hegarty and Julia Bird will be known to many as previous owners of the unique Tin Pub at Ahakista, and they have brought the unique laid-back charm associated with it to this venture, which offers a home from home with all sorts of hospitable gestures such as a well-stocked drinks fridge where you replace what you take, or use it to store your own. A very comfortable guest sitting room has lots of books, DVDs and games, and there's a sheltered patio for guests; tea and coffee is always available in the dining room where residents' evening meals are served at a big wooden table: seafood dinners are a speciality but the menu also includes other choices including home-made soup (served with freshly baked yeast bread) and steak, perhaps, or a casserole, and various home-made puddings. Bedrooms are spacious, simply furnished and modern - not the height of luxury, but very comfortable; two are en-suite with separate bath and shower, the third has a similar bathroom across the corridor. Full breakfasts are available all morning, and packed lunches can be arranged. This is a real can-do place, and would make a wonderfully relaxed holiday base. Fishing nearby, walking, short breaks, free broadband WI/Fi, dogs very welcome. Children welcome (under 12's free in parents' room). **Rooms 3** (2 en-suite, 1 with private bathroom, 2 family rooms, 1 ground floor, 1 partially equipped for disabled). B&B €40 pps, no ss. Open all year. Residents D, Mon-Sat, 6-8, €30. *Self catering also avail. **No Credit Cards. Directions:** Between Durrus and Ahakista.

Durrus
CAFÉ

Good Things Café

Ahakista Road Durrus Co Cork **Tel: 027 61426**
info@thegoodthingscafe.com www.thegoodthingscafe.com

Great ingredients-led contemporary cooking is the magnet that draws those in the know to Carmel Somers' simple little café-restaurant just outside Durrus village. Well-placed to make the most of fine West Cork produce, she also sells specialist foods from Ireland and abroad and a few books including the great little guide to local producers of Good Food in Cork, produced by Myrtle Allen and Caroline Workman. The daytime café menu offers a concise list including great salads, West Cork fish soup, West Cork Ploughmans (a trio of local cheeses served with an onion cassis compôte), Durrus cheese, spinach & nutmeg pizza... then there are irresistible desserts to choose from a display. Dinner brings a more formal menu, with a choice of four on each course, and will feature some of the daytime treats along with main courses like turbot with dill sauce with wilted spinach and local spuds, or beef fillet with pesto. Service is prompt and attentive from the moment a choice of breads and iced water is brought to your table to the arrival of home-made chocolate truffles with your coffee. Ingredients are invariably superb and, at its best, a meal here can be memorable; this place is a one-off and it is well worth planning a stop when travelling in West Cork, especially during the day, when the bright atmosphere and white café furniture seems more appropriate. An interesting, well-priced wine list includes seven well-chosen house wines, and a good choice of half bottles. *Cookery classes also available; details from the restaurant. **Carmel plans to move into new premises in 2008, so keep an eye on her website. Toilets wheelchair accessible; ample parking. Children welcome. **Seats 40** (plus 10 outdoor in fine weather). In summer, open all day (11-9) Wed-Mon (daily in Aug & during Bantry Music Festival), L 12.30-3; D (7-9). A la carte. House wine about €18. Closed Tue and Sep-Easter. Reservations advised for dinner; a call to check times is wise, especially off-season. MasterCard, Visa, Laser. **Directions:** From Durrus village, take Ahakista/Kilcrohane Rd.

Farnanes
PUB

Thady Inn

Farnanes Co Cork
Tel: 021 733 6379

Formerly a barracks for British soldiers, this small pub is set well back from the road and the present owners, Den and Martha O'Flaherty, have kept it simple, just as the previous generation did for 30 years before them. They offer a small menu and do a limited number of well-known dishes well: egg mayonnaise, smoked salmon, home-cooked chicken, ham or tongue salad and - the dish that has really made their reputation - great steaks, served with perfectly cooked crispy chips - rounded off with homely apple tart and cream. A good place to break a journey - it's refreshing to visit a pub that hasn't been done up and concentrates on the business of being an inn - looking after wayfarers well. Open 10.30am-12.30am; food available from 5pm daily (last orders 10pm). **No Credit Cards. Directions:** Off N22 between Macroom and Cork.

Farran
COUNTRY HOUSE

Farran House

Farran Co Cork **Tel: 021 733 1215**
info@farranhouse.com www.farranhouse.com

Set in 12 acres of mature beech woodland and rhododendron gardens in the rolling hills of the Lee Valley, Patricia Wiese and John Kehely's impressive house was built in the mid-18th century, although its present elegant Italianate style only dates back to 1863. It is beautifully situated with views over the medieval castle and abbey of Kilcrea, and its location west of Cork city makes this a good base for exploring Cork and Kerry. Since 1993 Patricia and John have painstakingly restored the house to its former glory and, although there are some contemporary touches as well as antiques, none of its original character has been lost - there's a fine drawing room for guests' use (complete with grand piano) and a billiard room with full-size table. Despite its considerable size, there are just four bedrooms - all exceptionally spacious and decorated with style; dinner is offered on most nights, by prior arrangement, and a speciality is home-produced lamb, bred and raised at Farran House. The house is available all year for private rental by groups and this is, perhaps, its most attractive use. Broadband. Games room. Office facilities. Golf nearby (six 18-hole courses within 20 km). Children welcome (under 8s free in parents' room, cot available without charge). No pets. Garden. **Rooms 4** (all en-suite, 2 with separate bath & shower; all no smoking); B&B €99 pps, ss €30 (advance bookings only - 10% discount on 3 night stays; off-season rates reduced); residents D daily, 7.30pm, €45 (24 hours notice; not available Sun or Mon, but Thady Inn (021 733 6379) nearby does good meals). Self-catering coach house (4-6 people, from €500 pw); house also available for self-catering (groups of 8-9, from about €3,500 pw). Closed 1 Nov-31 Mar. MasterCard, Visa, Laser. **Directions:** Just off N22 between Macroom & Cork: heading west, 8km (5 miles) after Ballincollig, turn right to Farran village, up hill, 1st gate on left.

FERMOY

If you need to break a journey in Fermoy, head for Jason & Fiona Hogan's **Munchies Eating House** (Tel: 025 33653), on Lower Patrick Street- this simple café has an old-fashioned style, but food is carefully-sourced (including produce from their own organic plot) and freshly cooked with care - and they have a great coffee and tea menu. Open all day Mon-Sat (9-5). Or, if you are in the mood for something spicier, you might try Brendan and Tina Moher's authentic **Thai Lanna** (025 30900) on McCurtain Street: everything is cooked to order by native Thai chefs and Nina, who is head chef, previously had her own restaurant in Thailand and teaches Thai cooking in Ireland. Open for dinner every evening and lunch Thu & Fri. For the sporting tourist, Fermoy's main attraction is the excellent salmon fishing on the Blackwater, and angling for trout in several of the tributary streams.
WWW.IRELAND-GUIDE.COM FOR THE BEST PLACES TO EAT, DRINK & STAY

Fermoy
RESTAURANT
R

La Bigoudenne
28 MacCurtain Street Fermoy Co Cork
Tel: 025 32832

At this little piece of France in the main street of a County Cork town, Noelle and Rodolphe Semeria's hospitality is matched only by their food, which specialises in Breton dishes, especially crêpes - both savoury (made with buckwheat flour) and sweet (with wheat flour). They run a special pancake evening once a month or so, on a Saturday night. But they do all sorts of other things too, like salads that you only seem to get in France, soup of the day served with 1/4 baguette & butter, a plat du jour and lovely French pastries. Opening times are a little complicated, but it's worth taking the trouble to work them out as it's a lovely spot - and even the bill is a pleasant surprise. **Seats 36.** D Tue-Fri, 5.45-9.30, D Sat-Sun, 6.45-9.30: Early D Tue-Thu 5.45-7 (about €21), later D €35 & à la carte; L Thu only, 12.30-3.30. Set D €35, also à la carte. House wine €16.80. Closed Mon & 1-15 Oct. Amex, MasterCard, Visa. **Directions:** On the main street, opposite ESB. ◇

Fermoy Area
COUNTRY HOUSE

Ballyvolane House
Castlelyons Fermoy Co Cork **Tel: 025 36349**
info@ballyvolanehouse.ie www.ballyvolanehouse.ie

The Greene family's gracious mansion is surrounded by its own farmland, magnificent wooded grounds, a trout lake and formal terraced gardens - garden lovers will find a stay here especially rewarding. The Italianate style of the present house - including a remarkable pillared hall with a baby grand piano and open fire - dates from the mid-19th century when modifications were made to the original house of 1728. Jeremy and the late Merrie Green first welcomed guests to their home in 1983, and is now run by their son Justin and his wife Jenny; Justin has management experience in top hotels and they are an extremely hospitable couple, committed to ensuring that the standards of hospitality, comfort and food for which this lovely house is renowned will be maintained. Elegantly furnished and extremely comfortable, it has big log fires, and roomy bedrooms furnished with family antiques look out over beautiful grounds. Ballyvolane has private salmon fishing on 8km of the great River Blackwater, with a wide variety of pring and summer beats, so it is logical that delicious food should be another high point at Ballyvolane, where memorable modern Irish dinners are served in style at separate tables or around a long mahogany table, depending on the occasion. An Australian chef, Peter Briody, took over the kitchen in 2007 but the house style remains country house, and all ingredients are home grown or sourced from the local area, and organic where possible: wholesome house specialities include wild garlic soup, roast rib of McGrath's Hereford beef with béarnaise sauce, and carrageen moss pudding with walled garden rhubarb. A carefully chosen, evocative and very informative wine list complements the food; among the treats in store you'll find a clutch of lovely house wines (including an organic red), half a dozen champagnes, and a good choice of dessert wines. A lovely relaxed guest Drawing Room at the back of the house has recently been restored (and looks as if it has always been that way), and five extra 'retreat' bedrooms are under construction in one of the walled gardens at the time of going to press. There is much of interest in the area, making this an excellent base for a peaceful and very relaxing break. A self-catering cottage is also available. French is spoken. Conferences/Banqueting (50). Children welcome (under 3s free in parents' room, cot available, free of charge). Pets permitted in some areas. Garden, croquet, fishing, walking, cycling. Free Broadband wi/fi. **Rooms 6** (all en-suite, 1 shower only, 1 ground floor, 1 for disabled, all no smoking). B&B €85 ps ss €30. D daily at 8pm, non residents also welcome (all by reservation); 3/4 course D €45/60. House wine from €24. Closed 24 Dec - 1 Jan. Amex, Diners, MasterCard, Visa, Laser. **Directions:** Turn right off main Dublin-Cork road N8 just south of Rathcormac (signed Midleton), following house signs on to R628.

GLANDORE / UNION HALL

The attractive village of GLANDORE is beautifully situated in a sheltered location overlooking Glandore Harbour and its guardian rocks, Adam and Eve. The all year population is small and it will never be a place for mass tourism but there is comfortable accommodation to be found at guesthouses in the area and at the family-run **Marine Hotel** (see entry), right beside the little harbour in the village; the hotel has undergone reconstruction recently, and has now re-opened. And the same family also own the beautifully located period house, **The Rectory** (028 33072; www.rectoryglandore.com), which is used mainly for weddings and private functions but is occasionally open as a restaurant as well, if not booked to capacity. Glandore is also fortunate in its pubs, which have different characters and are all special in their own way: **The Glandore Inn**, for example, acts as unofficial clubhouse for the local sailing community (and serves sound food), while the old-fashioned **Casey's** (at the 'top of the town') only opens in the evenings and is a place for impromptu sessions and late-night craic. Across the bridge, in UNION HALL, **Dinty's Bar** (028 33373) does good bar meals, and there is comfortable B&B accommodation to be found at **Shearwater** (028 33178), with sea views from all rooms.
WWW.IRELAND-GUIDE.COM FOR THE BEST PLACES TO EAT, DRINK & STAY

Glandore
PUB

Hayes' Bar

The Square Glandore Co Cork **Tel: 028 33214**
dchayes@tinet.ie www.hayesbar.ie

Hayes Bar is beautifully located overlooking the harbour and has outdoor tables - and Ada Hayes' famous bar food. The soup reminds you of the kind your granny used to make and the sandwiches are stupendous. Everything that goes to make Hayes' special - including the wines and crockery collected on Declan and Ada's frequent trips abroad - has to be seen to be believed; their travels also affect the menu, inspiring favourites like Croque Monsieur and there's a tapas menu, offering Manchego cheese, Serrano ham, chorizo Pamplona and so on, with fino sherry and Spanish wines and beer. Wine is Declan's particular passion and Hayes' offers some unexpected treats, by the glass as well as the bottle, at refreshingly reasonable prices. Great reading too, including a lot of background on the wines in stock - and you can now see some of Declan's paintings exhibited, from June to August. By any standards, Hayes' is an outstanding bar. Meals 12-5, Jun-Aug; Tapas Menu 6-9; weekends only off-season. Closed weekdays Sep-May except Christmas & Easter. **No Credit Cards. Directions:** The Square, Glandore. ◇

Glandore
HOTEL/RESTAURANT
Ⓝ

The Marine

The Pier Front Glandore Co Cork **Tel: 028 33366**
info@themarine.ie www.themarine.ie

After a long closure (many wondered if it would ever re-open as an hotel at all), the O'Brien family's hotel down beside the harbour emerged from its crysalis-like redevelopment just in time for the 2007 season and it is just as bright and beautiful as anyone could have wished. The 'new' Marine is a compact yet very complete complex, with 18 lovely 2- and 3-bedroom self-catering houses in addition to a totally revamped bar, an impressive new first floor restaurant and 11 of the original rooms also refurbished - in the pretty creeper-clad block across the car park. The family also own The Rectory (see Glandore round-up above), and they have always had a reputation for good food and hospitality, so the re-opening of the hotel is a real boost to the village. Although it has changed so much, the old hotel was not completely demolished and returning guests will find something strangely familiar about it, especially in the stylish new bar which is totally different and yet retains the same friendly atmosphere, and helpful staff. The bar menu (which is neither extensive nor revealing) offers wholesome fare and the surroundings looking out at the harbour from the circular feature bar, perhaps, or sitting out on the deck are relaxing. **Restaurant:** This fine high-ceilinged first floor room is tiered to take full advantage of the harbour and sea views, and stylishly furnished in warm tones, with comfortable contemporary seating and uncovered wooden tables set up attractively for smart-casual dining. Proprietor Shane O'Brien is heading up the kitchen team and the aim is to present simple food with a bit of a twist to give a sense of occasion. Menus are well-balanced but local seafood tops the bill, of course Union Hall smoked mackerel pate with apple & lime salad and toast, perhaps, followed by Glandore Bay fish pie with organic mixed salad - and there's a vegetarian option on both the main menu and a separate children's menu. Popular desserts to finish include fruit crumbles, chocolate cake, bread & butter pudding or, perhaps, Rosscarbery strawberries in a tuile basket. An informative wine list is organised by style. Toilets wheelchair accessible; children welcome before 9 pm (high chair, childrens menu, baby changing facilities). **Seats 90;** reservations recommended. L Sun only, 12.30-3pm. D daily, 6-8.30pm. Amex, MasterCard, Visa, Laser. **Directions:** On the pier front in Glandore. ◊

Glanmire
RESTAURANT

The Barn Restaurant

Glanmire Co Cork
Tel: 021 486 6211

This long-established neighbourhood restaurant has a devoted local clientèle who love the good French/Irish cooking and professional service. An attractive entrance conservatory leads to a comfortable lounge/reception area, where the welcome is warm and you can choose from menus which offer a good choice of quite traditional dishes - starters like home-smoked salmon or chef's duck & chicken liver patés and main courses of roast farmyard duckling, steaks various ways, and fresh seafood are all typical. This large restaurant is divided up into several comfortable dining areas, with well-spaced tables attractively set up with fresh flowers. Everything is cooked to order, with the emphasis on flavour and wholesomeness - and professional, attentive service; all round a reassuringly old-style approach. Vegetarians are well looked after, saucing and presentation are good, and accompaniments are carefully selected. Sunday lunch is very popular and menus are similar in style. Car park. Reservations advised (essential at weekends). **Seats about 160.** D daily, 6-9.30, L Sun only 12.30-2.30. Set D about €36, Set Sun L about €22. House wine about €22. Closed Ash Wed & Good Fri. Amex, Diners, Visa, Laser. **Directions:** On the edge of Cork city, on the old Youghal road at Glanmire. ◊

GLENGARRIFF

Famous for its mild Gulf Stream climate and lush growth - especially on nearby Garinish Island, with its beautiful gardens - Glengarriff has been a popular tourist destination since Victorian times and a little of that atmosphere still exists today. The rather grand looking **Eccles Hotel** (027 63319 www.eccleshotel.com) overlooks the harbour and is perhaps most obviously associated with that era (although it actually dates as far back as 1745), while the smaller, moderately priced and very hospitable family-run **Casey's Hotel** (027 63010) nearby, was established in 1884 and has been run by the same family ever since. The new kid on the block is the **Glengarriff Park Hotel** (027 63000; www.glengarriffpark.com), a smartly presented modern hotel with a nice traditional bar and quite decent bistro-style food available during the day and evening in their Blue Pool Bistro.
WWW.IRELAND-GUIDE.COM FOR THE BEST PLACES TO EAT, DRINK & STAY

Goleen
RESTAURANT WITH ROOMS

The Heron's Cove

The Harbour Goleen Co Cork **Tel: 028 35225**
info@heroncove.ie www.heronscove.com

  When the tide is in and the sun is out there can be few prettier locations than Sue Hill's restaurant overlooking Goleen harbour. The Heron's Cove philosophy is to use only the best of fresh, local ingredients and in summer there's a natural leaning towards seafood - typically in wholesome starters like plump, perfectly cooked Bantry Bay moules marinières or, more unusually, West Cork smoked sprats. Main course specialities include fillet of John Dory in a caper butter sauce. If you're not in a fishy mood, there might be Goleen lamb cutlets (served on a bed of champ, with rosemary jus, perhaps) or crispy roast Skeaghanore duckling, and there's always at least one vegetarian dish. More-ish desserts include the Heron's Cove signature dessert, a baked chocolate & vanilla cheesecake, and a wide selection of home-made ice creams - passion fruit, blackcurrant, blackberry, rum & Michigan cherry (to name a few of the less usual ones). Great ingredients, cooking which is generally pleasing, and friendly attentive service should make for an enjoyable meal - and, considering the quality of ingredients, fairly priced. An unusual Wine on the Rack system offers a great selection of interesting, well-priced wines that change through the season - they are listed but the idea is that you can browse through the bottles and make your own selection. Children welcome. **Seats 30;** D daily in summer, 7-9 (bookings essential Oct-Mar); à la carte. House wine €22.50. SC discretionary. Closed Christmas & New Year. **Accommodation:** Comfortable, if slightly dated, en-suite rooms are offered (refurbishment likely for 2008 season), some with private balconies, have satellite TV, phones, tea/coffee-making facilities and hair dryers. Garden. **Rooms 5** (4 shower only, all no smoking, 1 family room). B&B €55 pps, ss €35. Children welcome (under 5s free in parents' room, cot available free of charge). Open for dinner, bed & breakfast all year except Christmas/New Year, but it is always advisable to book, especially off-season. Amex, Diners, MasterCard, Visa, Laser. **Directions:** Turn left in middle of Goleen to the harbour, 300 m from village.

Goleen Area
FARMHOUSE

Fortview House

Gurtyowen Toormore Goleen Co Cork **Tel: 028 35324**
fortviewhousegoleen@eircom.net www.fortviewhousegoleen.com

Violet & Richard Connell's remarkable roadside farmhouse in the hills behind Goleen is immaculate. It is beautifully furnished, with country pine and antiques, brass and iron beds in en-suite bedrooms (that are all individually decorated) and with all sorts of thoughtful little details to surprise and delight. Richard is a magic man when it comes to building - his work around the house includes a lovely conservatory dining room, finished with great attention to detail. For her part, Violet loves cooking, and provides guests with a great choice at breakfast - juices, fruit compotes, organic yoghurts and local honey, local kippers and much more. Violet's idea of a 'standard Irish breakfast' is Caherbeg free range bacon & sausages and Clonakilty black & white pudding with tomato and egg, and you can have lots of other cooked treats too, including scrambled egg and smoked salmon *Self-catering cottages also available. Children under 2 free in parents' room. No pets. Garden. **Rooms 5** (4 shower only, 1 family room, 3 ground floor, all no smoking). B&B €50 pps, no ss. Closed 1 Nov-1 Mar. **No Credit Cards. Directions:** 2 km from Toormore on main Durrus-Bantry road (R591).

Gougane Barra

Gougane Barra
HOTEL/RESTAURANT

Gougane Barra Hotel

Gougane Barra Macroom Co Cork **Tel: 026 47069**
gouganebarrahotel@eircom.net www.gouganebarra.com

In one of the most peaceful and beautiful locations in Ireland, this delightfully old-fashioned family-run hotel is set in a Forest Park overlooking Gougane Barra Lake (famous for its monastic settlements). The Lucey family has run the hotel since 1937, offering simple, comfortable accommodation as a restful base for walking holidays - rooms are comfortable and have recently been given a gentle upgrade but not over-modernised; all look out on to the lake or mountain, and there are quiet public rooms also recently refurbished and now slightly more upbeat - where guests like to read. There has been very little real change over the years, and that's just the way people like it but, since Neil Lucey and his wife Katy took over management of the hotel from Neil's parents in 2005, their energy has brought a fresh approach. Walking holidays will remain an important part of the business, but there's now a new cultural edge too as Neil opened a little theatre in the hotel and they host a production each summer. And, while the spirit of the place will thankfully remain unchanged, the many improvements made recently include a stronger emphasis on food, and visitors are encouraged to drop in for informal meals - Katy's delicious bar menus include specialities like a moreish warm chicken salad, the superb house chowder which she brought from her father's kitchen in Lahinch, where her parents ran Mr Eamon's famous restaurant for many years - and her lovely rich walnut and treacle bread. It's a good place to bear in mind for afternoon tea too, a cup of tea with a freshly baked sultana scone, local strawberry jam and whipped cream goes down a treat when you're out and about. More formal meals, including breakfast, are served in the lakeside dining room which has also been gently upgraded to match Katy's good cooking. A carefully selected wine list complements the menus; informative and to the point, it includes well-chosen house wines, a good choice of half bottles and a cocktail menu. This is a magical place - as ever, the monks chose well. Intimate family weddings welcome (65). Shop. Garden, walking. No pets. Children welcome (under 11s free in parents' room, cots available at no charge). **Rooms 26** (all en-suite & no smoking, 8 shower only, 1 family room, 8 ground floor, all no smoking). B&B €70 pps, No SS. **Restaurant: Seats 70;** L&D daily, 12.30-3 (Sun, 12.45-2.30) and 6-8.30pm (Sun to 8.45); set Sun L €27, early D €27, 5.30-7pm; set 3 course D €40; house wine from €17.50. Closed 20 Oct - 7 Apr. Amex, MasterCard, Visa, Laser. **Directions:** Situated in Gougane Barra National Forest; well signposted.

Kilbrittain
RESTAURANT

Casino House

Coolmain Bay Kilbrittain Co Cork **Tel: 023 49944**
chouse@eircom.net

Kerrin and Michael Relja's delightful restaurant is just a few miles west of Kinsale and it is well worth the effort of getting here, as it is one of the best in an area which takes great pride in the excellence of its food. It's a lovely old house and it has an unusually cool continental style in the decor, but Kerrin's hospitality is warm - and Michael's food is consistently excellent, in wide-ranging seasonal menus based on the finest local ingredients: Ummera smoked organic salmon, fresh seafood from nearby fishing ports (don't miss his wonderful speciality lobster risotto) and Ballydehob duck all feature - a starter dish of four variations of duck is another speciality. Tempting vegetarian dishes are often listed ahead of the other main courses and nightly specials will include extra seafood dishes, all with individual vegetable garnishes and deliciously simple seasonal side vegetables. Variations on classic desserts are delicious (a delectable rhubarb & shortbread tartlet, with white chocolate & hazelnut crème and almond ice cream, for example) and local cheeses are always tempting in this area... An al fresco early summer dinner, or Sunday lunch, can be an especially memorable experience. Casino House was our Restaurant of the Year in 2005. *Casino Cottage: sleeps two €85 per night (or €155 for 2 nights), everything provided except breakfast - which can be supplied if needed. Longer stays discounted;

weekly & winter rates available. **Seats 35** (private room 22; outdoor dining 16). D Thu-Tue, 7-9, L Sun only,1-3; all à la carte; house wine from €20.90. Closed Wed, and 1 Jan-17 Mar. Amex, MasterCard, Visa, Laser. **Directions:** On R600 between Kinsale and Timoleague. ◇

Kilbrittain
FARMHOUSE

The Glen Country House
The Glen Kilbrittain Co Cork **Tel: 023 49862**
info@glencountryhouse.com www.glencountryhouse.com

Although classified (correctly) as a farmhouse, Guy and Diana Scott's home is an elegant period house and they have recently renovated it to a high standard for guests. It is quietly located in a beautiful area, and the four large double bedrooms have lovely views across Courtmacsherry Bay. There's even a family suite (consisting of a double room and children's room, with interconnecting bathroom) and guests have the use of a comfortable sitting room, and a dining room where breakfasts are served - a buffet with fresh and poached seasonal fruits, freshly squeezed orange juice, organic muesli and organic yoghurt, and a menu of hot dishes including bacon produced locally from free range pigs and eggs from their own hens. It's a relaxed place, where dogs are welcome to join the two house spaniels (guests' horses are welcome too!) and, although there are no dinners, evening meals and baby sitting are offered for children, allowing parents to go out to one of the excellent local restaurants - Casino House and Dillon's of Timoleague are nearby. Unusually, the Scotts produce their own fuel (oats) for heating the house and water. Free broadband wi/fi. Children welcome (under 4s free in parents' room, cot available without charge, baby sitting arranged). Garden. Pets permitted outdoors. **Rooms 5** (all en-suite & no smoking, 4 shower only, 1 family room). B&B €65 pps, ss €10. Closed Nov-Easter. Heli-pad. *Self catering apartment also available, sleeps 4. MasterCard, Visa, Laser. **Directions:** Signposted off the R600, midway between Kinsale and Clonakilty.

Kilbrittain
BAR/RESTAURANT

féile bia

The Pink Elephant
Harbour View Kilbrittain Co Cork **Tel: 023 49608**
info@pinkelephant.ie www.pinkelephant.ie

This low pink bungalow-style building is on a superb elevated site overlooking the sea and across the bay to Courtmacsherry and, as it is open for lunch as well as dinner in summer, it is a very useful place to know about. Picnic tables overlook a lawn towards the sea, or you can eat inside in a large room with a piano, which has been painted exuberantly in swirling shades of pink, and is put to good use in the evening when one of the staff tinkles the ivories and sings, along with one of the waitresses. Delicious food includes outstandingly good home-made bread, and menus naturally favour local seafood - lunch dishes are marked up on a blackboard in the bar (another lists wines available by the glass), and might include an excellent Provençal fish soup, or sausage and mash. Evening dishes depend on 'whatever the fishermen drop in', with prime seafood like lobster and brill offered if you're lucky. An unusual, informative and evocative wine list is illustrated with labels, and includes a pair of Fairtrade wines and a good choice of half bottles and dessert wines among many treats. Service is laid-back but efficient and charming. Children welcome before 9pm (high chair, childrens menui); toilets wheelchair accessible. **Seats 80** (outdoors, 30); pianist in the evening; L daily 12-2.30 (Sun from 12.30), D daily 6-9, L&D a la carte; house wine from €20. Open 7 days in summer, phone for opening times in winter. MasterCard, Visa, Laser. **Directions:** On R600 coast road near Kilbrittain.

KINSALE

One of Ireland's prettiest towns, Kinsale sits at the mouth of the River Bandon and has the old-world charm of narrow winding streets and medieval ruins tucked in around Georgian terraces - all contrasting with the busy fishing harbour and marina of today. It has excellent leisure activities including yachting, sea angling, and golf - most notably the **Old Head of Kinsale Golf Club** - for culture lovers the town also has several art galleries. It was known several decades ago as the 'gourmet capital of Ireland' and, while that claim would now be hotly disputed by several other contenders, it is on the up and up again, offering a remarkable variety of good restaurants and an exceptionally active programme of culinary activities- and, less widely recognised but of equal interest to the visitor, some of the best accommodation in the country. In the town, **The White Lady Hotel** (021 477 2737) offers moderately priced accommodation and a restaurant with pizzas, pastas and burgers as well as fresh seafood and steaks - a good choice for families. Kinsale also got its first Eastern European restaurant recently, when **Jolas** (18/19 Lr O'Connell Street; 021 4773322) came to town; Jola, previously of Kensington's 'Wodka', has brought the flavours of Russia, Lithuania, Poland and Hungary to West Cork and is open for lunch and dinner. Outside the town, **Innishannon House Hotel** (Tel 021 477 5121; www.innishannon-hotel.ie) is a romantic riverside 'petit chateau' style house in lovely gardens and - also in the Innishannon direction - the recently restored 13-bedroom **Ballinacurra House** (087 2867443; www.ballinacurra.com) is a luxurious venue, available for private parties, small weddings, golfing groups and corporate events. The town's many pubs offer a judicious mixture of music and food - especially seafood; across the bridge, towards the west, Castle Park has a sandy south-facing beach and **The Dock Bar** (Tel: 021 477 2522) is a friendly pub.

WWW.IRELAND-GUIDE.COM FOR THE BEST PLACES TO EAT, DRINK & STAY

Kinsale
HOTEL

Actons Hotel

Pier Road Kinsale Co Cork **Tel: 021 477 9900**
information@actonshotelkinsale.com www.actonshotelkinsale.com

Overlooking the harbour and standing in its own grounds, this attractive quayside establishment is Kinsale's most famous hotel, dating back to 1946 when it was created from several substantial period houses. It has changed a lot since then, and has recently undergone extensive renovations that include a new look modern bar, Waterfront Bar & Bistro, and a contemporary makeover for the restaurant, as well as refurbishment of bedrooms. A Health & Fitness Club offers a new swimming pool with separate children's pool, hot tub, sauna, steam room and whirlpool spa; there's also a gym, aerobics room, solarium and treatment facilities. Good conference/banqueting facilities too (300/250). Children welcome (under 4 free in parents' room, cots available without charge, baby sitting arranged.) No pets. Wheelchair access. Lift. Garden. **Rooms 73** (2 junior suites, 14 executive, 1 shower only, 2 for disabled, 50 no smoking). B&B €100 pps, ss €40 (wide range of special breaks available). **Captain's Table Restaurant**, L&D daily (speciality: the 'Derek Davis' steamed local seafood platter). Bar food available daily, 12-9.30. Closed 24-26 Dec, all Jan. Amex, MasterCard, Visa, Laser. **Directions:** On the waterfront, short walk from town centre. ◇

Kinsale
GUESTHOUSE

Blindgate House

Blindgate Kinsale Co Cork **Tel: 021 477 7858**
info@blindgatehouse.com www.blindgatehouse.com

Maeve Coakley's purpose-built guesthouse is set quietly in its own gardens high up over the town and, with spacious rooms, uncluttered lines and a generally modern, bright and airy atmosphere, Blindgate makes a refreshing contrast to the more traditional styles that prevail locally. All bedrooms are carefully furnished with elegant modern simplicity, have full en-suite bathrooms and good facilities including fax/modem sockets as well as phones, satellite TV, tea/coffee trays and trouser press. Maeve is an hospitable host - and well-known in Kinsale for her skills in the kitchen, so breakfast here is a high priority: there's a buffet displaying all sorts of good things including organic muesli, fresh fruits and juices, farmhouse cheese and yoghurts, as well as a menu of hot dishes featuring, of course, the full Irish Breakfast alongside catch of the day and other specialities - so make sure you allow time to enjoy this treat to the full. Broadband. Children over 7 welcome (baby sitting arranged). No pets. Garden. **Rooms 11** (all en-suite & no smoking, 5 ground floor, 2 for disabled); room service (all day). B&B €72.50 pps, no ss. Closed late Dec-mid Mar. Amex, MasterCard, Visa, Laser. **Directions:** From Fishy Fishy Café: take left up the hill, keeping left after St Multose Church. Blindgate House is after St Joseph's Primary School, on the left.

Kinsale
HOTEL/RESTAURANT

The Blue Haven Hotel

3/4 Pearse Street Kinsale Co Cork **Tel: 021 477 2209**
info@bluehavenkinsale.com www.bluehavenkinsale.com

féile bia This famous hotel has an attractive exterior, with its name emblazoned in blue and white stained glass above the entrance and flags hanging from poles, giving it a cosmopolitan look. Under new ownership since 2004, proprietor Ciaran Fitzgerald continues to do everything possible to restore its previously great reputation. Due to the nature of the building, public areas are quite compact, but a major refurbishment programme has seen a complete redesign of the bar, which now has a much more open contemporary feeling, and the lower deck of the restaurant, to create a cocktail lounge incorporating a residents' lounge where afternoon tea can be served during the day. All the bedrooms have double glazing to offset the street noise that is inevitable in a central location and, although not large, both the rooms and their neat bathrooms make up in thoughtful planning anything they lack in spaciousness - and there is extra accommodation available a few doors away at **The Old Bank House** (see entry), which is now in common ownership. Conferences/Banqueting (80/70); free broadband wi/fi. Children welcome (unders 8s free in parents' room, cots available, baby sitting arranged). No pets. Street parking. **Rooms 17** (4 shower only, 3 single, 17 no smoking). B&B €100, ss €40. **Restaurant:** The restaurant can be accessed from the hotel or by a separate entrance, under-lying the sense of it being more than an hotel dining room. The decor is restful, lifted by interesting features such as a five-foot silver candelabra in one corner and a piano in another. Each table has a single flower and nightlight, giving a pleasant soft atmosphere, and simple but quite pleasing table settings. A lobster tank at the entrance to the restaurant sets the tone for menus that have the emphasis on seafood, balanced by steak, chicken and vegetarian dishes - and there is a separate chil-dren's menu. Cooking is sound, care is taken with presentation, and an extensive wine list and good service add to the pleasure of a meal here. **Seats 60.** L & D daily, set L €27.50, set D €45, à la carte also available. House wine from €20; sc 10%. Closed 25 Dec. Amex, Diners, MasterCard, Visa, Laser. **Directions:** In the centre of town.

Kinsale
B&B

Chart House

6 Denis Quay Kinsale Co Cork **Tel: 021 477 4568**
charthouse@eircom.net www.charthouse-kinsale.com

Billy and Mary O'Connor offer very appealing accommodation at this delightful 200 year old house, which they have completely renovated, with attention to period details. Beautifully furnished bedrooms have orthopaedic mattresses, phone, TV, hair dryer and a trouser press with iron; tea and coffee are served by the fire in a cosy reception/sitting room, and an imaginative breakfast menu is served communally on a fine William IV dining room suite. Not suitable for children. No pets. **Rooms 4.** (2 suites with jacuzzi baths, 2 shower only, all no-smoking). B&B from €60 pps (depending on room), single occupancy 75%; single room €50. Closed Christmas week. Amex, MasterCard, Visa, Laser. **Directions:** On Pier Road between Actons and Trident Hotels, turn right after Actons, last house on right.

Kinsale
RESTAURANT/WINE BAR

Crackpots Restaurant

3 Cork Street Kinsale Co Cork **Tel: 021 477 2847**
crackpts@iol.ie www.crackpots.ie

Carole Norman's attractive and unusual restaurant has a lot going for it - not only can you drop in for a glass of wine at the bar, as well as the usual meals, but all the pottery used in the restaurant is made on the premises so, if you take a fancy to the tableware or any of the deco-rative pieces on the walls, you can buy that too. Menus are imaginative and considerate, with attractive options for vegetarians, and many of the specialities are seafood, notably shellfish: lobster, moules marinière, crab toes (in a coconut & lemongrass sauce), seared scallops, and whole sautéed prawns in their shells, and old favourites like chowder and smoked salmon are sure to make an appearance. If you feel like a change from fish there might be organic roast duck, or a classic fillet steak on the evening menu. Children welcome before 9pm (high chair). **Seats 55.** Air conditioning. L Sun only, 12-3pm; D Mon-Sat 6-10. Early D €25 (6-7); otherwise à la carte, house wines €20. Closed month of Jan. Amex, MasterCard, Visa, Laser. **Directions:** Between Garda Station and Wine Museum.

Kinsale
PUB

Dalton's

3 Market Street Kinsale Co Cork **Tel: 021 477 7957**
fedalton@eircom.net

Frances and Colm Dalton's cheerful little red-painted town-centre bar has a characterful, traditional-look interior with green & white floor tiles and lots of wood - and is well worth seeking out for good home cooking. It's a friendly spot and they make a good team - Colm is chef, while Frances is the baker - providing wholesome lunches which are more restaurant meals than usual bar food, five days a week. While there's plenty of choice, the menu is sensibly limited to eight or nine dishes, plus a couple of specials each day; there's an understandable emphasis on seafood - steamed mussels, crab cakes, smoked salmon with home-baked brown bread, warm seafood salad - and a sprinkling of other dishes. Good quality, fresh ingredients and real home cooking make for some delicious flavours - and desserts (apple & black-berry crumble perhaps) are all home-made. A short wine list offers a number of wines by the glass, and an above-average choice of quarter bottles. Outside lunchtime, Daltons operates normally, as a bar. **Seats 30.** L Mon-Fri 12.30-4; house wine €21. Closed 25 Dec, Good Fri. **No credit cards. Directions:** Entering Kinsale from Cork, straight on past Blue haven Hotel, left at end; Daltons on left, opposite Market Place.

Kinsale
CAFÉ/RESTAURANT

Fishy Fishy Café
Crowley's Quay Kinsale Co Cork
Tel: 021 470 0415

Martin and Marie Shanahan's Fishy Fishy Café mark two is a very big restaurant, by West Cork standards, yet they've been full to capacity at peak times ever since opening in 2006, and they have kept the original Fishy Fishy (which has a wet fish bar) open too. The new premises was previously an art gallery and now has an atmospheric interior on two levels. It makes a design statement from the outset, with wooden gates opening onto a decking path leading to the front door - a bit like a zen garden, it is fitted into a neat rectangle with rounded beach stones filling the gaps. The interior is bright, airy and stylishly simple, with a smart bar, unpretentious café-style darkwood furniture and plenty of doors opening out on to the patio and balcony. A large paved outdoor seating area is enclosed by a hedge and, when it's warm enough to eat outside, is set up mainly with aluminium chairs and tables and seriously business-like parasols, giving it a continental air of dedication to the comfortable enjoyment of good food. The Shanahans' reputation for offering the widest possible range and freshest of fish is unrivalled throughout Ireland, and shellfish lovers might be lucky enough to feast on a lunch of oysters, mussels and perhaps even Christy Turley's crab cocktail - Christy is a local food hero, a third generation Kinsale fisherman who supplies much of Fishy Fishy's catch. Prices are very fair for the quality offered, and that includes the wine. Fishy Fishy is almost as famous for its celebrity spangled queues as for the fabulous fish and, true to their original style, no reservations are accepted. Fishy Fishy Café was our Seafood Restaurant of the Year in 2007. **Seats 150** (private room, 40, outdoors, 60); no reservations accepted; air conditioning; children welcome; open daily 12-4.30; a la carte menu. Closed Christmas 3 days. **No credit cards.**

Kinsale
CAFÉ

Fishy Fishy Cafe @ The Gourmet Store
Guardwell Kinsale Co Cork
Tel: 021 477 4453

This delightful fish shop, delicatessen and restaurant is a mecca for gourmets in and around Kinsale and was our Seafood Restaurant of the Year in 2001. Although all sorts of other delicacies are on offer, seafood is the serious business here - and, as well as the range of dishes offered on the menu and a specials board, you can ask to have any of the fresh fish on display cooked to your liking. Not that you'd feel the need to stray beyond the menu, in fact, as it makes up in interest and quality anything it might lack in length - and vegetarian dishes available on request. [See also entry for the new Fishy Fishy]. Not suitable for children under 7. Wheelchair accessible. No reservations. **Seats 36.** Tue-Sat 12-3.45; à la carte; house wines from about €18. Closed Sun & Mon, 3 days Christmas. **No Credit Cards. Directions:** Opposite St Multose church, next to Garda station.

Kinsale
GUESTHOUSE

Friar's Lodge
Friar's Street Kinsale Co Cork **Tel: 021 477 7384**
mtierney@indigo.ie www.friars-lodge.com

Maureen Tierney's friendly and exceptionally comfortable purpose-built guesthouse is very professionally operated, and offers an attractive alternative to hotel accommodation in the centre of Kinsale - it even has private parking, and there is a drying room for wet golfing gear. The style is a pleasing combination of traditional and modern and the spacious guest rooms have well-designed bathrooms - most with full bath and shower; as well as the more usual facilities, rooms also have computer/internet connection, safe and TV with DVD. Guests have use of an elegantly furnished sitting room with an open fire and, although evening meals are not offered, a good breakfast is served in a pleasant dining room. This is a very pleasing place to stay and offers good value too, in comparison with hotels. Children welcome (under 5s free in parents' room, cot available free of charge). **Bedrooms 18** (2 executive, 2 shower only, 2 family rooms, 16 no smoking); lift; limited room service; B&B €65 pps, ss €15. Closed 22-27 Dec. MasterCard, Visa, Laser. **Directions:** Centre of Kinsale, next to parish church.

Kinsale
GUESTHOUSE

Harbour Lodge

Scilly Kinsale Co Cork **Tel: 021 477 2376**
relax@harbourlodge.ie www.harbourlodge.ie

This waterfront guesthouse is extremely comfortable and the position, away from the bustle of the town centre, is lovely and peaceful; some bedrooms have balconies overlooking the marina, and there's a large conservatory "orangerie" for the leisurely observation of comings and goings in the harbour, also a sitting room with an open fire for chilly days. Thoughtfully furnished bedrooms have top of the range beds and luxurious bathrooms, and an extensive breakfast is served in the conservatory. The proprietors have recently acquired The Spinnaker restaurant, which is next door, and guests will be able access it directly through the garden. Walking, cycling. Golf and many other activities nearby. Special breaks offered. Children welcome. Garden. **Rooms 9** (1 suite, 1 family room, 1 shower only, all no smoking). B&B from €99 pps. Open all year. Amex, Diners, MasterCard, Visa, Laser. **Directions:** Scilly waterfront: 1km (0.5 mile) from town centre, beside The Spinnaker. ◊

Kinsale
PUB/RESTAURANT

Jim Edwards

Short Quay Kinsale Co Cork **Tel: 021 477 2541**
info@jimedwardskinsale.com www.jimedwardskinsale.com

This characterful old place in the heart of Kinsale is known for its atmosphere and the consistent quality of the hearty food served in both bar and restaurant. Its authentic cosy pub atmosphere is embellished with electric "oil" lamps above some of the tables, and the décor - a polished wood floor with inset patterned tiles, mustard and maroon colour scheme, and curios on display - works really well, for a relaxed pub atmosphere. Seafood is the speciality, but there's plenty to please everyone on all menus, from spicy chicken wings, or crab claws in garlic butter to sirloin steak, on the extensive bar menu and lunch menu - and then the treats of scampi or fresh lobster or rack of lamb on the a la carte; everything is carefully prepared and really tasty. Smartly dressed staff are very professional and efficient, and it's good value. Children welcome. **Seats 70;** food served daily 12.30-10pm; L 12.30-3.30 (to 3pm Sun), set Sun L €24.90; D 6-10pm; Set 2/3 course D, €16/22, also a la carte L&D; house wine €21. Amex, MasterCard, Visa, Laser. **Directions:** Town centre. ◊

Kinsale
RESTAURANT

Le Bistro

Main Street Kinsale Co Cork **Tel: 021 477 7117**
eat@lebistrokinsale.com www.lebistrokinsale.com

Jean-Marc Tsai and Jacqui St John-Jones' popular town centre premises is embellished by murals by local artist Sheila Kern and, in this lively and attractive 'Paris bistro style' restaurant, Jean-Marc offers a unique mélange of classic French and Asian food in the evening, and French bistro style for lunch. Jean-Marc is one of Ireland's great chefs and all who remember the fine dining experience at Chez Jean-Marc, or his superb Asian food at the Chow House will be delighted with his current venture: Vietnamese spring rolls, maquereau au vin blanc, 'trou normand' (apple sorbet with calvados), it's all here, on daily-changing menus. Jean-Marc is always in the kitchen and Jacqui is always out at the front, otherwise they are closed. The wine list changes every three months, and offers organic and chemical-free wines - also imported French beers. Off season, Asian nights (Vietnamese, Chinese and Thai) are held on Sundays, for local residents. Gorgeous food, great service, good value - and an enjoyable ambience: this place has it all. **Seats**

60. Children welcome before 8pm. D Daily 6 - 10, Early Bird D €20 before 7.30. House Wine from €19.50. Closed Feb and Tue, Oct-Jun. MasterCard, Visa, Laser. **Directions:** In the centre of Kinsale, corner of Market St and Main St.

Kinsale
RESTAURANT

Man Friday

Scilly Kinsale Co Cork **Tel: 021 477 2260**
www.man-friday.net

High up over the harbour, Philip Horgan's popular, characterful restaurant is housed in a series of rooms, and it has a garden terrace, which makes a nice spot for drinks and coffee in fine weather. Philip presents seasonal à la carte menus that major on seafood but offer plenty else besides, including several vegetarian choices and ever-popular duck, steak and lamb. While geared to fairly traditional tastes, the cooking is generally sound and can include imaginative ideas - and there's usually a good buzz, which adds hugely to the enjoyment of a meal. Simple, well-made desserts include good ice creams. Service is, for the most part, cheerful and efficient and, unlike many other restaurants in the area, which are seasonal, Man Friday is open in the winter. **Seats 130** (private room, 40). Not accessible to wheelchairs. D Mon-Sat, 6.45-10; gourmet D about €40; also à la carte, house wine from about €20; sc discretionary. Closed Sun, Dec 24-26. Amex, MasterCard, Visa, Laser. **Directions:** Overlooking the inner harbour, at Scilly. ◇

Kinsale
RESTAURANT

Max's Wine Bar

48 Main Street Kinsale Co Cork
Tel: 021 477 2443

Run by a young couple, Olivier and Anne Marie Queva - the chef and restaurant manager respectively - Max's has a loyal following in the locality, and it's a happy find for visitors too. Returning visitors will remember it as a more cottagey place, with mirror-varnished tables and a pretty conservatory out at the back, but it closed for major refurbishment recently, and now has a new layout that allowed for a new kitchen and better use of space. Although the style is smarter, and more contemporary, something of the spirit of the old Max's lives on - and the food is as good as ever, so everyone is happy. Olivier's seasonal menus change regularly and offer a pleasing balance of luxurious ingredients and the more homely; seafood from the pier - langoustines and oysters (in season), mussels, or black sole is the main feature, with a balance of meats and poultry (roast rack of Irish lamb is a consistent favourite), and appealing vegetarian dishes offered too. An informative wine list offers a range of house wines (available by the glass), an above average choice of half bottles and a range of aperitifs, dessert wines and ports. Not suitable for children after 7pm. **Seats 30.** L Wed-Mon,12.30-3 (Sun 1-3), D Wed-Mon, 6.30-10. Set L/Early D (6.30-7.30) €21.90; also à la carte; house wine €18.50, SC discretionary. Closed Tue; 31 Oct-1 Mar. Amex, MasterCard, Visa, Laser. **Directions:** Street behind the petrol station on pier.

Kinsale
GUESTHOUSE

The Old Bank House

11 Pearse Street Kinsale Co Cork **Tel: 021 477 4075**
info@oldbankhousekinsale.com www.oldbankhousekinsale.com

This fine townhouse in the centre of Kinsale is in common ownership with the Blue Haven Hotel, and is a great asset to it. It has an elegant residents' sitting room, a well-appointed breakfast room and very comfortable, spacious bedrooms with good amenities, and quality materials - all rooms are furnished with antiques and decorated to the same impeccable standard, with lovely bathrooms. Children welcome (under 1s free in parents' room, cot €20, baby sitting arranged); free broadband wi/fi. Golf-friendly: tee-off times, hire of clubs, transport to course, golf tuition can all be arranged; golf storage room. **Rooms 17** (1 suite, 1 junior suites, 2 family rooms, all no smoking). Lift. Room service (all day). B&B €90 pps, ss€90. Closed 23-28 Dec. Amex, MasterCard, Visa, Laser. **Directions:** In the heart of Kinsale, next to the Post Office.

Kinsale
B&B

The Old Presbytery

43 Cork Street Kinsale Co Cork **Tel: 021 477 2027**
info@oldpres.com www.oldpres.com

This old house in the centre of the town has provided excellent accommodation for many years and the current owners, Philip and Noreen McEvoy have kept up this tradition well. Bed and breakfast is offered in the original bedrooms, which have character - stripped pine country furniture and antique beds which have been refurbished, and the McEvoys have also added three self-catering suites, each with two en-suite bedrooms, sitting room, kitchenette and an extra bathroom. The new rooms are well-proportioned and furnished in the same style and to the same high standard; they can be taken on a nightly basis (minimum stay 2 nights), sleeping up to six adults. The top suite has an additional lounge area leading from a spiral staircase, with magnificent views over the town and harbour. C h i l d r e n welcome (cot available without charge); free broadband wi/fi. **Rooms 6** (3 suites, 2 shower only, 2 family rooms, 1 ground floor, all no-smoking). B&B €80 pps, ss €80. Self-catering apartments, from €170 per night (min 2 nights). Closed 1 Dec-mid Feb. Amex, MasterCard, Visa, Laser. **Directions:** Follow signs for Desmond Castle - in same street.

Kinsale
GUESTHOUSE

Perryville House

Long Quay Kinsale Co Cork **Tel: 021 477 2731**
sales@perryville.iol.ie www.perryvillehouse.com

One of the prettiest houses in Kinsale, Laura Corcoran's characterful house on the harbour front has been renovated to an exceptionally high standard and provides excellent accommodation only 15 minutes from the Old Head of Kinsale golf links. Gracious public rooms are beautifully furnished, as if for a private home. Spacious, individually decorated bedrooms vary in size and outlook (ones at the front are most appealing, but the back is quieter) and all have extra large beds and thoughtful extras such as fresh flowers, complimentary mineral water, quality toiletries, robes and slippers. The suites have exceptionally luxurious bathrooms although all are well-appointed. Breakfasts include home-baked breads and local cheeses; morning coffee and afternoon tea are available to residents in the drawing room and there is a wine licence. No smoking establishment. Own parking. Not suitable for children. No pets. **Rooms 26** (5 junior suites, 8 superior, all no-smoking). B&B from €100 pps, No SC. Closed Nov-1Apr. *Wireless internet throughout the house. Amex, MasterCard, Visa, Laser. **Directions:** Central location, on right as you enter Kinsale from Cork, overlooking marina. ◇

Kinsale
PUB/RESTAURANT

The Spaniard Inn

Scilly Kinsale Co Cork **Tel: 021 477 2436**
info@thespaniard.ie www.thespaniard.ie

Who could fail to be charmed by The Spaniard, that characterful and friendly old pub perched high up above Scilly? Although probably best known for music (nightly), it offers bar food all year round and there's a restaurant in season. Popular traditional fare (Spaniard seafood chowder, smoked salmon platter, Oysterhaven mussels and oysters) for which The Spaniard is well known is served informally in the bar alongside more contemporary dishes. Evening meals in the restaurant - which has its own separate bar - are more extensive. Live trad music, Mon/Wed/Sat. Bar meals: L 12.30-3 (to 5.30 Fri/Sat/Sun); Restaurant D: 6-10 (from 6.30, Sun). Early D, €25 6-7pm.House wine, €20. Closed 25 Dec & Good Fri, (restaurant also closes 2 weeks Nov & Jan). Amex, MasterCard, Visa, Laser. **Directions:** At Scilly, about 0.5 kilometre south-east of Kinsale, overlooking the town.

Kinsale
RESTAURANT

Toddies Restaurant

Kinsale Brewery The Glen Kinsale Co Cork **Tel: 021 477 7769**
toddies@eircom.net www.toddieskinsale.com

Pearse and Mary O'Sullivan's bustling down town restaurant and bar was our Atmospheric Restaurant of the Year in 2006. The address may give the impression that it is 'out of town' but if you walk down Pearse Street (away from the harbour) and turn right at the T junction, you'll see their sign across the road, outside a fine limestone archway. It's above the Kinsale Brewery, with whom there is a strong working relationship as they pump their Kinsale lager, wheat beer and stout directly up to Toddies bar. From the courtyard, exterior stairs lead

up to the restaurant, pausing at the large and stylish al fresco dining area provided by two terraces before arrival at the bar and a smart split-level dining room. It's an exciting enterprise, and there's a growing fan club who love not only Pearse's fine modern Irish cooking, but also the inside-or-out table arrangements, great service by Mary and her bubbly staff, and the whole atmosphere of the place. Seafood is, of course, the star and fresh lobster risotto is one of many speciality dishes that had already established Toddies as a leading restaurant in the area - but Pearse's high regard for local meats (and many other local products, including West Cork cheeses), ensures a balanced choice. **Seats 36** (terrace, 60). Children welcome. D daily 5-10.30 (from 6.30 Sat & Sun). Gourmet menu €50, also á la carte. House wine from €25.50. SC 10% on groups 10+. Closed 15 Jan-end Feb. *Guests can eat at the bar, or in the restaurant. MasterCard, Visa, Laser. **Directions:** Drive to the end of Pearse St., take right turn, Toddies is second on the left through limestone arch and into courtyard.

Kinsale
HOTEL

Trident Hotel

Worlds End Kinsale Co Cork **Tel: 021 477 9300**
info@tridenthotel.com www.tridenthotel.com

This blocky, concrete-and-glass 1960s waterfront hotel enjoys an exceptional location and, under the watchful management of Hal McElroy, has long been a well-run, hospitable and comfortable place to stay. Recent development has now seen major changes including - most importantly from the guest comfort point of view - the addition of 30 new front-facing executive rooms, all with king size beds and air conditioning as standard, and separate bath and shower. Older bedrooms are also fairly spacious and comfortable,

with phone, TV and tea/coffee trays (iron and board available on request), and small but adequate bathrooms. The genuinely pubby Wharf Tavern is so far unchanged, and remains one of the town's most popular good meeting places. Conference/banqueting (220/200); video-conferencing on request. Sauna, gym, steam room, jacuzzi. Children welcome (under 3 free in parents room, cot available without charge, baby sitting arranged). No pets. Lift. **Rooms 66** (2 suites, 2 wheelchair accessible). B&B €95 pps, ss €33; no SC. **Restaurant: Pier One:** The restaurant, which has been refurbished and re-named, is well-located on the first floor with views over the harbour, which also makes it an exceptionally pleasant room for breakfast. The food is good and especially welcome in winter, when many of the smaller restaurants are closed. **Seats 80** (private room, 40). D daily, 6.30-9, L Sun only 1- 2.30. Set Sun L €23; Set D €28, D also à la carte; Bistro menu avail 4-9; Bar Menu 12-9. House wine from €19. SC discretionary. Toilets wheelchair accessible. Amex, MasterCard, Visa, Laser. **Directions:** Take the R600 from Cork to Kinsale - the hotel is at the end of the Pier Road.

Kinsale
RESTAURANT

The Vintage Restaurant

50 Main Street Kinsale Co Cork **Tel: 021 477 2502**
vintagerestaurant@eircom.net www.vintagerestaurant.ie

This is one of Kinsale's oldest and most famous restaurants, and proprietors Diana and Frank Ferguson are on a mission to move away from its recent 'expensive exclusivity', providing a relaxed place to dine, with accessibly priced tasty food. The cottage charm has been retained, however - old stonework and ancient oak beams, soft furnishing and table linen, with a cosy atmosphere. Chef Par Karpf offers menus that are much shorter and to the point, with an emphasis on fish, although you will find appealing old favourites for non-fish eaters, such as dry-aged steak, and roast duck, all at a fair price. Good quality ingredients are prepared with care, skilfully cooked and attractively presented. Everything - including the quality of service is professional without being over fussy. A shortish wine list offers some treats, but only the house wine by the glass. Toilets wheelchair accessible; not suitable for children after 8pm (high chair). **Seats 52** (private room 20). L Sun only (and Bank Hol Mon), 12.30-4pm. D Tue-Sun, 6-10; à la carte. House wine from €23. Closed Mon & Jan-Feb. Amex, MasterCard, Visa, Laser. **Directions:** From the Post Office, turn left at the Bank of Ireland - restaurant is on the right.

Kinsale Area
BAR/RESTAURANT

The Bulman

Summercove Kinsale Co Cork **Tel: 021 477 2131**
info@thebulman.com www.thebulman.com

Uniquely situated on the outskirts of Kinsale - it looks across towards the town and has a sunny western aspect - The Bulman is a characterful maritime bar. It's a great place to be in fine weather, when you can wander out to the seafront and sit on the wall beside the carpark, and it's cosy in winter when you can sip local beer from the Kinsale Brewery beside the fire in the downstairs bar. The first floor restaurant specialises in seafood, much of it locally caught, including less usual fish like sea bream. Portions are generous and you may wish the style could be a little simpler, but the overall dining experience should be enjoyable. Own carpark. **Seats 50.** (Phone for food service times). Closed 25 Dec & Good Fri. Not suitable for children under 12. Toilets wheelchair accessible, restaurant upstairs isn't. Restaurant: seats 51; L Mon-Sat, 12.30-3pm, Sun L only, 1-4pm, D Tue-Sat, 6-9.30pm; earlybird menu 6-7pm, about €21.95/25.95 2/3 course, also a la carte; house wine about €20. Bar food also available Mon-Sat, 12.30-3pm. Restaurant closed D Sun & Mon. Amex, MasterCard, Visa, Laser. **Directions:** Beside Charles Fort, short distance from Kinsale. ◇

Kinsale Area
HOTEL

Carlton Kinsale Hotel & Spa

Rathmore Road Kinsale Co Cork **Tel: 021 470 6000**
info@carltonkinsalehotel.com www.carltonkinsalehotel.com

Entering through woodland down a narrow winding driveway with occasional passing places, first-time guests get no hint of what lies ahead and even on arrival at set-down (and a rather confusing parking arrangement), the hotel presents an inscrutable, blocky exterior. But, on entering the lofty foyer backed by a wall of glass - all is revealed, as you catch your first view through to the sea beyond; and, when drawn over to the doors that open out on to a large decking area, even the weariest or most curmudgeonly check-in could hardly fail to be won over (on a fine day at least) by the beauty of Oysterhaven Bay. Although many will feel that the hotel itself does little to enhance its surroundings, it is well-designed to ensure that guests get the maximum benefit when looking out; the bright décor (intended to echo the colourful West Cork streetscapes perhaps?) won't be to everyone's taste, but it should be easy to let that go, as the view is the main focus in all of the public areas, including the aptly named Oysterhaven View restaurant on the second floor. Accommodation, in more restful tones, includes suites, sea view rooms and deluxe rooms, the latter overlooking gardens, and with doors opening on to private terraces to compensate for the lack of a view; all rooms are very comfortably furnished, with all the usual amenities, and separate bath and shower, although oddly for a new hotel, most rooms have only standard 4' 6" double beds. The hotels's C Spa, plus swimming pool, sauna and gym among other leisure facilities, will make this a popular short break destination, especially off-season, and there is a regular complimentary bus for transfers to Kinsale. Free broadband wi/fi. Spa, leisure centre with 'pool, fitness room, garden. **Rooms 70** (2 suites, 34 executive, 20 family rooms, 24 ground floor, 6 for disabled). Children welcome (under 3s free in parents room, baby sitting arranged); Lift; 24 hr room service; B&B €96 pps, ss €55. Closed 23-27 Dec. Helipad. **Directions:** 5km from Kinsale town centre. R600 (main Cork-Kinsale road), east of Kinsale. ◇

Kinsale Area
COUNTRY HOUSE

Glebe Country House

Ballinadee nr Kinsale Bandon Co Cork **Tel: 021 477 8294**
glebehse@indigo.ie www.glebecountryhouse.com

Set in two acres of beautiful, well-tended gardens (including a productive kitchen garden), this charming old rectory near Kinsale has a lovely wisteria at the front door and it is a place full of interest. The building dates back to 1690 (Church records provide interesting details: it was built for £250; repairs and alterations followed at various dates, and the present house was completed in 1857 at a cost of £1,160). More recently, under the hospitable ownership of Gill Good, this classically proportioned house has been providing a restful retreat for guests since 1989, and everybody loves it for its genuine country house feeling and relaxing atmosphere. Spacious reception rooms have the feeling of a large family home, and generous, stylishly decorated bedrooms have good bathrooms, phones and tea/coffee making facilities. The Rose Room, on the ground floor, has French doors to the garden. A 4-course candle-lit dinner for residents, much of it supplied by the garden, is served at a communal table (please book by noon) and,

although unlicensed, guests are encouraged to bring their own wine. Breakfasts are also delicious, and this can be a hard place to drag yourself away from in the morning although there are many things to do nearby, including golf, and it is well placed for exploring the area. The whole house may be rented by parties by arrangement and several self-catering apartments are also available. Children welcome (under 10s free in parents' room, cots available without charge, baby sitting arranged.) Pets permitted. **Rooms 4** (2 shower only, all no-smoking), B&B €55 pps, ss €15. Residents' D Mon-Sat, €35, at 8pm (please book by noon). No D on Sun. BYO wine. Closed Christmas. Diners, MasterCard, Visa, Laser. **Directions:** Take N71 west from Cork to Innishannon Bridge, follow signs for Ballinadee 9km (6 miles). After village sign, veer left, 2nd on the right.

Macroom
HOTEL

The Castle Hotel & Leisure Centre

Macroom Co Cork **Tel: 026 41074**
castlehotel@eircom.net www.castlehotel.ie

In the ownership of the Buckley family since 1952, this well-managed hotel is ideally located for touring the scenic south-west and is equally attractive to business and leisure guests. Major recent developments have added superior executive bedrooms and suites, an extensive new foyer and reception area, an impressive new bar and the more contemporary 'B's' Restaurant. Extensive leisure facilities include a fine swimming pool (with children's pool, spa and massage pool), steam room, solarium and gym. Special breaks are offered, including golf specials (tee times reserved at Macroom's 18-hole course). Friendly staff take pride in making guests feel at home. Children welcome (under 3s free in parents' room, cots available without charge; playroom; baby sitting arranged). Conference/banqueting (150). No pets. **Rooms 60.** B&B €75 about pps, ss €25. Food available 9.30am-9pm. ('B's' Restaurant 12-3 & 6-8.45; 'Next Door Café' 9.30-5.30; bar food 12-9.30) Closed 24-28 Dec. Amex, MasterCard, Visa, Laser. **Directions:** On N22, midway between Cork & Killarney. ◊

Macroom
BAR/RESTAURANT

The Mills Inn

Ballyvourney Macroom Co Cork **Tel: 026 45237**
millinn@eircom.net www.millinn.ie

One of Ireland's oldest inns, The Mills Inn is in a Gaeltacht (Irish-speaking) area and dates back to 1755. It was traditionally used to break the journey from Cork to Killarney - and still makes a great stopping place as the food is good and freshly cooked all day - but is now clearly popular with locals as well as travellers. New owners took over in 2003 and they are continuing to develop the premises while retaining its old-world charm and a genuine sense of hospitality. Accommodation is also offered; comfortable rooms have a strong sense of style. **Rooms 13** (some shower only, 1 for disabled). B&B about €45pps, no ss. Amex, Diners, MasterCard, Visa, Laser. **Directions:** On N22, 20 minutes from Killarney. ◊

Mallow
COUNTRY HOUSE/RESTAURANT

Longueville House Hotel

Mallow Co Cork **Tel: 022 47156**

info@longuevillehouse.ie   www.longuevillehouse.ie

When Michael and Jane O'Callaghan opened Longueville House to guests in 1967, it was one of the first Irish country houses to do so. Its history is wonderfully romantic, "the history of Ireland in miniature", and it is a story with a happy ending: having lost their lands in the Cromwellian Confiscation (1652-57), the O'Callaghans took up ownership again some 300 years later. The present house, a particularly elegant Georgian mansion of pleasingly human proportions, dates from 1720, (with wings added in 1800 and the lovely Turner conservatory - which has been completely renovated - in 1862), and overlooks the ruins of their original home, Dromineen Castle. Very much a family enterprise, Longueville is now run by Michael and Jane's son William O'Callaghan, who is the chef, and his wife Aisling, who manages front of house. The location, overlooking the famous River Blackwater, is lovely. The river, farm and garden supply fresh salmon in season, the famous Longueville lamb, and all the fruit and vegetables. In years when the weather is kind, the estate's crowning glory is their own house wine, a light refreshing white, "Coisreal Longueville" - wine has always been Michael O'Callaghan's great love, and he now uses their abundant apple supply to make apple brandy too. Public rooms include a bar and drawing room, both elegantly furnished with beautiful fabrics and family antiques, and accommodation is equally sumptuous; although - as is usual with old houses - bedrooms vary according to their position, they are generally spacious, superbly comfortable and stylishly decorated to the highest standards. Dining here is always a treat (see below) and breakfast is also very special, offering a wonderful array of local and home-cooked foods, both from the buffet and cooked to order; Longueville was the National Winner of our Irish Breakfast Awards in 2003, and it's worth calling in even if you can't stay overnight - what a way to break a journey! As well as being one of the finest leisure destinations in the country, the large cellar/basement area of the house has been developed as a conference centre, with back-up services available. The house is also available for small residential weddings throughout the year. Conference/banqueting (50/120), secretarial services, free broadband wi/fi. Children welcome (under 2s free in parents' room, cot available free of charge, baby sitting arranged). No pets. Garden, walking, hunting/shooting, fly fishing, clay pigeon shooting. Equestrian, golf and garden visits nearby. (Shooting weekends available in winter; telephone for details). **Rooms 20.** (6 junior suites, 1 superior, 3 family, 2 single, 2 shower only; all no-smoking). B&B €130pps, ss €32. Closed early Jan-mid Mar. **Presidents Restaurant:** Named after the family collection of specially commissioned portraits of all Ireland's past presidents (which made for a seriously masculine collection until Ireland's first woman president, Mary Robinson, broke the pattern) this is the main dining room and opens into the beautifully renovated Turner conservatory, which makes a wonderfully romantic setting in candlelight; there is a smaller room alongside the main restaurant, and also the Chinese Room, which is suitable for private parties. William O'Callaghan is an accomplished chef, and home- and locally-produced food is at the heart of all his cooking, in starters like house smoked salmon, or salad of crab with dry cured Longueville ham; main courses of Longueville lamb and home-reared pork; and desserts such as a croustade of caramelised apple with Longueville apple brandy ice cream - and it is hard to resist the local farmhouse cheeses. Delicious home-made chocolates and petits fours come with the coffee and as elsewhere in the house service, under Aisling O'Callaghan's direction, is outstanding. Menus have been shortened and simplified recently, allowing William more direct control in the kitchen - an improvement which makes for a more intimate, and even more enjoyable dining experience. A fine wine list offering many treats has particular strength in the classic French regions and includes a half a dozen champagnes, and a good choice of dessert wines and half bottles; it includes many wines imported directly by Michael O'Callaghan. Children welcome (high chair, childrens menu). **Seats 84** (private room 12). D daily, 6.30-9; Set 2/3 course D €40/60, Menu Gourmand €85; light meals 12.30-5 daily. House wine €30, SC 10% added to parties of 8+. Restaurant closed Mon& Tues in Nov and early Dec. House closed 7 Jan - 16 Mar. Amex, MasterCard, Visa, Laser. **Directions:** 5km (3 m) west of Mallow via N72 to Killarney.

MIDLETON

Midleton is a busy market town and home of the **Jameson Heritage Centre** at the **Old Midleton Distillery** (021 461 3594; www.whiskeytours.ie), where you can find out all you every wanted to know about Irish whiskey, and get a bite to eat too. The first choice for accommodation in the town centre is **Midleton Park Hotel & Spa** (021 463 5100; www.mildletonpark.com), with all facilities, and food lovers will enjoy the **Farmers' Market** on Saturday mornings (one of the best in the country). This demand for daytime food in this busy shopping town is reflected in the number of restaurants offering all-day menus including **Ryans on the Mall** (021 463 9960) on Riverside Way, which offers whole some moderately priced food including things like home-made chicken goujons for children and is useful to know about for visitors with a young family in tow. Midleton is well-placed for visiting Cork city, and also exploring the whole of East Cork, including Cobh (last port of call for the Titanic), **Fota Wildlife Park & Arboretum** and Youghal, famed for its connections with Sir Walter Raleigh. The pretty fishing village of Ballycotton merits a visit, and offers good coastal walking.

WWW.IRELAND-GUIDE.COM FOR THE BEST PLACES TO EAT, DRINK & STAY

Midleton	Farmgate
RESTAURANT	The Coolbawn Midleton Co Cork
Tel: 021 463 2771

téile bia This unique shop and restaurant has been drawing people to Midleton in growing numbers since 1985 and it's a great credit to sisters Maróg O'Brien and Kay Harte. Kay now runs the younger version at the English Market in Cork, while Maróg looks after Midleton. The shop at the front is full of wonderful local produce - organic fruit and vegetables, cheeses honey - and their own super home baking, while the evocatively decorated, comfortable restaurant at the back, with its old pine furniture and modern sculpture, is regularly transformed from bustling daytime café to sophisticated evening restaurant (or Friday and Saturday) complete with string quartet. A tempting display of fresh home bakes is the first thing to catch your eye or entering and, as would be expected from the fresh produce or sale in the shop, wholesome vegetables and salads are always irresistible too. Maróg O'Brien is a founder and stall holder of the hugely successful Midleton Farmers' Market, which is held on Saturday mornings. *Farmgate was the winner of our Natural Food Award in 2007. Open Mon-Sat, 9-5pm, L 12-4, D Thu-Sat, 6.45 - 9.30pm. Closed Sun, Bank Hols, 24 Dec-3 Jan. MasterCard, Visa, Laser. **Directions:** Town centre. ◇

Midleton	Finíns
BAR/RESTAURANT	75 Main Street Midleton Co Cork
Tel: 021 463 1878

Finín O'Sullivan's thriving bar and restaurant in the centre of the town has long been a popular place for locals to meet for a drink and to eat some good wholesome food. The entrance is bright and cheery, painted in pillarbox red and white, and the theme is continued inside, where black topped tables are simply set up with the basics needed for a meal. This attractive, no-nonsense place offers a wide range of popular home-made dishes, mostly based on local produce notably fresh seafood from Ballycotton and harbour steaks, also old favourites like a well-made Irish Stew; evening menus are more extensive and include some more specialities including roast duckling. Good short wine list. Bar food available Mon-Sat 10.30am-10pm, specials available noon-6.30pm; Restaurant D Mon-Sat, 7-9.45pm. Bar menu à la carte; set D €40. House wine €18. Closed Sun, bank hols. **Directions:** Town centre.

Fire & Ice Café

Midleton
CAFÉ

The Courtyard 8 Main Street Midleton Co Cork **Tel: 021 463 9682**
fireandice@eircom.net www.fireandicecafe.ie

Anyone who remembers the original Fire and Ice, which was a must-visit place in Clifden several years ago, will make a point of heading straight for Gary Masterson and Winnie Lynch's café, which is located in a courtyard just off the main street and away from the traffic - you turn off through big gates and the café is in view. It's a simple place without pretensions, but it's Gary's food that's attracting a growing fan club. He's a great chef and, although international in tone (panini, pizza, cous cous, bruschetta, noodles), his informal, weekly-changed menus reflect the seasonal availability of local produce seafood from Ballycotton, East Cork meats, organic (non-imported) salads and vegetables, and artisan products like Ardsallagh goat's cheese from Carrigtwohill. Although not long, menus offer great range of informal brunch/lunch style dishes (omelettes, kedgeree, great warm salads, pasta dishes) and a few heartier ones, notably East Cork steaks. Vegetarian dishes have strong appeal and special diets are catered for - goat and soy milk are offered for hot drinks. As well as managing front of house Winnie, who is also a chef, whips up delicious cakes and tarts for desserts and snacks. Magic. Toilets wheelchair accessible; children welcome (high chair); **Seats 50** (outdoor, 9). Food served Mon-Sat, 9-5pm, L 12-3.30pm; no reservations accepted; house wine €18. Closed Sun, bank hols, 2 weeks Jan. **No credit cards. Directions:** Off Main Street.

Loughcarrig House

Midleton
COUNTRY HOUSE

Midleton Co Cork **Tel: 021 463 1952**
info@loughcarrig.com www.loughcarrig.com

Bird-watching and sea angling are major interests at Brian and Cheryl Byrne's relaxed and quietly situated country house, which is in a beautiful shore side location. Comfortable rooms have tea/coffee making facilities and there's a pleasantly hospitable atmosphere. Children welcome (under 2s free in parents' room). Pets permitted by arrangement. Sea fishing, walking, Garden. **Rooms 4** (all en-suite. shower only & no smoking). Closed 16 Dec-16 Jan. B&B €40 pps, ss €10. SC discretionary. **No Credit Cards. Directions:** From roundabout at Midleton on N25, take Whitegate Road for 2 miles.

O'Donovan's

Midleton
RESTAURANT

58 Main Street Midleton Co Cork
Tel: 021 463 1255

An attractive limestone-fronted building on the main street, Pat O'Donovan's highly-regarded restaurant blends traditional and modern decor - some features have been retained from its previous use as a pub, tables are elegantly set up with classic white linen tablecloths and napkins, and original modern oil paintings adorn the walls. But the most interesting feature is Ian Cronin's hand-written mouthwateringly promising menu which, with a choice of 10 starters, and 7 main courses and desserts, offers a varied and adventurous meal and excellent value. Nothing but the best ingredients are allowed in this kitchen, and they are locally sourced where possible - fish comes from Ballycotton, mussels from Rossmore and scallops (when available) from Castletownbere. The cooking is excellent, and some dishes enjoyed on a recent visit will give the flavour - penne with wild mushroom and bacon to start, followed by a main course of salmon wrapped with Parma ham and a delicious dessert of clafoutis with ice cream: all perfectly cooked well presented and full of flavour. Efficient, informative staff ensure that guests will enjoy their meal to the full, and there's a good wine list includes some interesting, unusual wines, and a fair choice of half bottles. An early dinner menu offers outstanding value at about €25 for three courses. **Seats 60.** D Mon-Sat, 6-9.30. A la Carte; house wine about €21. Closed Sun. MasterCard, Visa, Laser. **Directions:** Travelling eastwards, at eastern end of Main Street, on right-hand side - oppositre entrance to Midleton Distillery. ◇

Midleton
RESTAURANT

Raymond's Restaurant

Distillery Walk Midleton Co Cork **Tel: 021 463 5235**
raymondsrestaurant@eircom.net

Attractively situated on the quieter short stretch of road leading up to the gates of the Old Midleton Distillery, and opposite the river and a small park, this smart modern restaurant is an appealing place and especially convenient for visitors to the distillery. Proprietor-chef Raymond Whyte is originally from the area and, after travelling and gaining experience abroad and at several highly-regarded establishments within Ireland, he settled here and opened his own restaurant in 2003. The style is broadly French/Mediterranean, but he takes pride in sourcing local produce for the kitchen, including seafood from Ballycotton, and meats from local farms and the cooking is good. Children welcome before 6.30pm (high chair, childrens menu). **Seats 55;** reservations recommended; L served daily, 12-3pm; D served Tue-Sat, 5-10pm; open all day Sun, 12-9pm. Early bird D, €28, 5.30-7pm; then a la carte; house wine €20. Closed Mon D & Bank Hol Mons. Amex, MasterCard, Visa, Laser. **Directions:** On Distillery Walk.

Midleton Area
GUESTHOUSE/RESTAURANT

Ballymaloe House

Shanagarry Midleton Co Cork **Tel: 021 465 2531**
res@ballymaloe.ie www.ballymaloe.com

Ireland's most famous country house, Ballymaloe was one of the first to open its doors to guests when Myrtle and her husband, the late Ivan Allen, opened The Yeats Room restaurant in 1964. Accommodation followed in 1967 and since then a unique network of family enterprises has developed around Ballymaloe House - including not only the farmlands and gardens that supply so much of the kitchen produce, but also a craft and kitchenware shop, a company producing chutneys and sauce, the Crawford Gallery Café in Cork city, and Darina Allen's internationally acclaimed cookery school. Yet, despite the fame, Ballymaloe is still most remarkable for its unspoilt charm: Myrtle - now rightly receiving international recognition for a lifetime's work "recapturing forgotten flavours, and preserving those that may soon die"- is ably assisted by her children, and now their families too. The house, modestly described as "a large family farmhouse", is indeed at the centre of the family's 400 acre farm, but with over thirty bedrooms is a very large house indeed, and one with a gracious nature. The intensely restorative atmosphere of Ballymaloe is remarkable and, although there are those who would say that the cooking is 'too homely', there are few greater pleasures than a fine Ballymaloe dinner followed by a good night's sleep in one of their thoughtfully furnished country bedrooms - including, incidentally, Ireland's most ancient hotel room which is in the Gate House: a tiny one up (twin bedroom, with little iron beds) and one down (full bathroom and entrance foyer), in the original medieval wall of the old house: delightful and highly romantic! Ground floor courtyard rooms are suitable for wheelchairs. Conferences/banqueting (60/120). Children welcome (cot available; baby sitting arranged). Pets allowed by arrangement. Outdoor swimming pool, tennis, walking, golf (nearby). Gardens. Shop. **Rooms 33** (5 ground floor, 1 disabled, 4 shower only, all no smoking). B&B €160pps, ss €25. SC discretionary. Room service (limited hours) No lift. Self-catering accommodation also available (details from Hazel Allen). **Restaurant:** The restaurant is in a series of domestic-sized dining rooms and guests are called to their tables from the conservatory or drawing room, where aperitifs are served. A food philosophy centred on using only the highest quality ingredients is central to everything done at Ballymaloe, where much of the produce comes from their own farm and gardens, and the rest comes from leading local producers. Jason Fahey has been head chef at Ballymaloe since 2004 and continues the house tradition of presenting simple, uncomplicated food in the 'good country cooking' style, which allows the exceptional quality of the ingredients to speak for themselves. This is seen particularly at Sunday lunchtime when - apart from the huge range of dishes offered, - the homely roasts and delicious vegetables are as near to home cooking you are ever likely to find in a restaurant, and what a joy that is. Then things move up a number of notches in the evening, when daily 7-course dinner menus, offer more sophisticated dishes, including vegetarian options, but there is still a refreshing homeliness to the tone which, despite very professional cooking and service, is perhaps more like a dinner party than a smart restaurant experience. Ballymaloe brown bread, a selection of their own pate and terrines served with brioche and home-made chutney, a tart of locally smoked fish with tomato & chive beurre blanc, superb roast belly of pork with crispy crackling and apple sauce, Irish farmhouse cheeses with home-made biscuits and an irresistible dessert trolley that includes country sweets like rhubarb compôte, and home-made vanilla ice cream are typical of simple dishes that invariably delight. The teamwork at Ballymaloe is outstanding and a meal here is a treat of the highest order. Finish with coffee or tea and home-made petits fours, served in the drawing room - before retiring contentedly to bed. Children welcome at lunchtime, but the restaurant is not suitable for children under 7 after 7pm. (Children's high tea is served at 5.30.) Buffet meals only on Sundays. **Seats 110.** Not suitable for children under 7yrs, or after 7pm. L daily 1-1.15pm (to 1.30pm Sun), D daily 7-9.15pm (Sun 7.50-8.30pm); Set D €70, Set L about €38. House wine from €22. Service discretionary. Reservations essential. House closed 23-26 Dec, 2 weeks Jan. Helipad. *Self Catering Accommodation also available. Amex, Diners, MasterCard, Visa, Laser. **Directions:** Take signs to Ballycotton from N 25. Situated between Cloyne & Shanagarry.

Midleton Area
CAFÉ

Ballymaloe Shop Café

Ballymaloe House Shanagarry Co Cork **Tel: 021 465 2032**
ballymaloeshop@eircom.net

At the back of Wendy Whelan's magnificent crafts, kitchenware and gift shop at Ballymaloe House, there is a very nice little family-run café selling wholesome home-bakes and just the kind of light, nourishing fare that is needed to sustain you through a shopping expedition that may well be taking longer than you had planned. So take the weight off your feet, settle down with an aromatic cup of coffee or a glass of wine, or home-made lemonade - and a taste of this delicious home cooking. A simple menu of salads, light lunches, cakes and biscuits is offered - savoury bakes like goat's cheese, potato & mint tart, perhaps, and sweet treats such as chocolate tart, and pistachio macaroons. Everything is based on locally sourced fresh ingredients as far as possible, including smoked seafood from Frank Hederman in Cobh, local organic salads, Bill Casey's Shanagarry smoked salmon, and Gubbeen smoked bacon. * Wendy has a charming self-catering cottage, Rockcliffe House, in Ballycotton; details from the shop. Open 10-5 daily, L 12.30-4. House wine €4.50 per glass. Closed 23-27 Dec. Amex, MasterCard, Visa, Laser. **Directions:** 3.5km (2 m) beyond Cloyne on Ballycotton road. ◊

Midleton Area
COUNTRY HOUSE/RESTAURANT

Barnabrow Country House

Barnabrow Cloyne Midleton Co Cork **Tel: 021 465 2534**
barnabrow@eircom.net www.barnabrowhouse.com

Geraldine Kidd's sensitive conversion of an imposing seventeenth century house provides stunning views of Ballycotton, and the decor is commendably restrained. Innovative African wooden furniture is a point of interest and spacious, comfortable bedrooms are stylishly decorated. Some bedrooms are in converted buildings at the back of the house, with breakfast served in the main dining room, at a communal table. Barnabrow can cater for weddings (for which there is great demand) and other functions (up to 150) as well as normal private dining. Derek Stewart has been cooking at the Trinity Rooms Restaurant since 2005 and continues the philosophy and cooking style that has earned a fine reputation. Children welcome (under 1s free in parents' room, cots available, free of charge, baby sitting arranged). Pets permitted in some areas. Conference/banqueting (60/150). **Rooms 19** (17 shower only, 2 family, all no smoking). B&B €90pps, ss €25. D 7-9 Thu-Sun, L Sun Only 1-2.30; D à la carte; Set Sun L €27; value D €35, 5.30-7pm; set 3 course D €50. House wine from €22; service discretionary (10% on parties of 10+). Restaurant closed Mon-Wed; house closed 23-27 Dec. Diners, MasterCard, Visa, Laser. **Directions:** From Cork N25 to Midleton roundabout, right for Ballinacurra, left for Cloyne, then on to Ballycotton road for 1.5 miles.

Mitchelstown
CAFÉ
R

O'Callaghan's Delicatessen, Bakery & Café

19/20 Lower Cork Street Mitchelstown Co Cork **Tel: 025 24657**
ocalhansdeli@eircom.net www.ocallaghans.ie

féile bia The ideal place to break a journey, O'Callaghans have an impressive deli and bakery as well as tasty fare for a snack or full meal in the café. This is the place to stock up with delicious home-baked breads and cakes, home-made jams and chutneys - and, best of all perhaps, there's a range of home-made frozen meals. They do a range of seasonal specialities too, including wedding confectionery and Christmas treats, made to order. There's also a great home-made gluten free range, offering everything from soda breads, to sweet and savoury tarts. For smokers, and anyone who prefers to eat out of doors, there is a sun deck which has a covered area. To avoid the busy main street, park around the corner on the road to the creamery - or, coming from Dublin, parking is also available on the new square (on right after second set of lights); but remember the square is not available for parking on Thursday - market day.   Restaurant **Seats 140** (outdoor 20). Food served Mon-Sat, 8.30 am- 5 pm; L 12.30-5pm. Closed Sun, bank hols, 24-27 Dec. Amex, Diners, MasterCard, Visa, Laser. **Directions:** On main street, right side heading towards Dublin.

Monkstown
BAR/RESTAURANT/GUESTHOUSE

The Bosun

The Pier Monkstown Co Cork **Tel: 021 484 2172**
info@thebosun.ie www.thebosun.ie

Nicky and Patricia Moynihan's waterside establishment close to the both the car ferry across to Cobh and the Ringaskiddy ferries (France and Wales) has grown a lot over the years, with the restaurant and accommodation becoming increasingly important. Bar food is still taken seriously, however; although including kangaroo among the starters may seem odd (the air miles don't bear thinking about), seafood takes pride of place and afternoon/evening bar menus include everything from chowder or garlic mussels through to real Dingle Bay scampi and chips, although serious main courses for carnivores such as beef with brandy & peppercorn sauce and beef & Guinness casserole are also available. Next to the bar, a well-appointed restaurant provides a more formal setting for wide-ranging table d'hôte and à la carte menus - and also Sunday lunch, which is especially popular. Again seafood is the speciality, ranging from popular starters such as crab claws or oysters worked into imaginative dishes, and main courses that include steaks and local duckling as well as seafood every which way, from grilled sole on the bone to medallions of marinated monkfish. There's always a choice for vegetarians, and vegetables are generous and carefully cooked. Finish with home-made ices, perhaps, or a selection of Irish farmhouse cheeses. Not suitable for children after 7pm. **Restaurant Seats 80** (max table size 12). Private room 30. Air conditioning. Toilets wheelchair accessible. D daily 6.30-9, L Sun 12-2.30, Set D €47.50, Set Sun L €29.50; à la carte also available; house wine about €22, sc discretionary. Bar food available daily 12-9). Closed 24-26 Dec, Good Fri. **Accommodation:** Bedrooms are quite simple but have everything required (phone, TV, tea/coffee trays); those at the front have harbour views but are simpler only, while those at the back are quieter and have the advantage of a full bathroom. Fota Island Golf Course is only 12 minutes away, also Fota House and Wildlife Centre. **Rooms 15** (9 shower only, all no smoking). Lift. B&B €60 pps, ss €7. Children welcome (under 5s free in parents' room, cot available without charge). No pets. Closed 24-26 Dec, Good Friday. Amex, Diners, MasterCard, Visa, Laser. **Directions:** On sea front, beside the Cobh ferry and near Ringaskiddy port ferry.

Oysterhaven
RESTAURANT

Finders Inn

Nohoval Oysterhaven Co Cork **Tel: 021 477 0737**
www.findersinn.com

Very popular with local people (but perhaps harder for visitors to find) the McDonnell family's well-named old-world bar and restaurant is in a row of traditional cottages east of Oysterhaven, en route from Crosshaven to Kinsale. It can look uncared for from the road, but it's a very charming place, packed with antiques and, because of the nature of the building, broken up naturally into a number of dining areas. Seafood stars, of course - smoked salmon, Oysterhaven oysters, bisques, chowders, scallops and lobster are all here, but there are a few other specialities too, including steaks, lamb and tender crisp-skinned duckling, and the cooking, by brothers Rory and Cormac McDonnell, is excellent. Good desserts, caring service under the supervision of a third brother, Donough, and a great atmosphere - well worth taking the trouble to find. Not suitable for children under 7, or older after 10 pm. **Seats 90** (private room, 70). D Tue-Sun, 7-9.30pm; L Sun only, 2-7pm. A la carte; sc discretionary. Toilets wheelchair accessible. Closed Mon; Christmas week. MasterCard, Visa, Laser. **Directions:** From Cork, take Kinsale direction; at Carrigaline, go straight through main street then turn right, following R611 to Ballyfeard; about 700 metres beyond Ballyfeard, go straight for Nohoval (rather than bearing right on R611 for Belgooly).

Oysterhaven
RESTAURANT

Oz-Haven Restaurant

Oysterhaven Co Cork **Tel: 021 477 0974**
www.ozhaven.com

In a delightful waterside location at the head of Oysterhaven creek, the colourful exterior of Australian Paul Greer's cottage restaurant warns guests to expect something out of the ordinary. There's a great sense of fun (including a giant fish tank with two huge Amazon fish) and, despite its modernism, the wacky decor works surprisingly well with the old building. The restaurant is divided between three separate areas, well-spaced tables have comfortable high-back carver chairs and are simply laid in contemporary style, with generous wine glasses and white plates. The best of local ingredients - Oysterhaven mussels and oysters, Gubbeen cheese, local meats - are to be found alongside less likely ones, such as crocodile and kangaroo (Paul is Australian after all). Oz-Haven continues to present food with a difference, in entertaining surroundings, and friendly service is under Paul's personal direction. **Seats 55** (private room 25, outside dining 25). Toilets wheelchair accessible. Children welcome. D Mon-Sat, 7-9.30; L Sun & bank hols, 1-5. Set Sun L €26.95; set D €39.95 (value D €29.95 all eve Wed-Fri, Sept-May); gourmet menu €65, also à la carte. House wine €19.95. Closed Mon, Tue (except in Summer), 24-26 Dec. Amex, MasterCard, Visa, Laser. **Directions:** 30 min from Cork city, turn left for Oysterhaven just before Kinsale.

Rathcormac
CAFÉ

Posh Nosh
Riversdale Rathcormac Co Cork
Tel: 025 37595

This upmarket deli, specialist food shop and café is a good place to take a break on a journey, serving a good range of in-house home baking, salads and hot dishes of the day, also good coffee. And, if you'd like to stock up while you're here, the food shop sells quality French and Italian imports and Irish artisanal and speciality foods such as Ditty's biscuits, farmhouse cheeses and preserves, and local free range eggs. You can eat in or take away and the delicious hot meals to go are clearly popular with the locals. Open all day, Tue-Sat. **Directions:** Just through Rathcormac village, heading south towards Cork on N8 Dublin-Cork road; on side turning, facing Murphy's pub.

Rosscarbery
HOTEL

Celtic Ross Hotel, Conference and Leisure Centre
Rosscarbery Co Cork **Tel: 023 48722**
reservations@celticross.com www.celticrosshotel.com

This modern hotel is close to the sea, overlooking Rosscarbery Bay (although not on the sea side of the road), and well placed as a base for touring west Cork; the facilities in the leisure centre offer alternative activities for family holidays if the weather should disappoint. It's an attractive building with an unusual tower feature containing a bog oak, which is quite dramatic; public areas are spacious, and the bedrooms - many of which have sea views - have all the usual facilities. However, although currently in the hands of a proactive management team who aim to raise and maintain standards, shortage of accommodation in the area means that this hotel is always busy, and a fair degree of wear and tear is to be expected. Short breaks brochure available. Leisure centre (swimming pool, therapies). Children welcome (under 4s free in parents' room, cots available free of charge, baby sitting arranged). Conference/banqueting (150). No pets. **Rooms 66** (1 shower only, 3 for disabled, 10 no smoking). Wheelchair access. Lift. B&B from about €55 to €110 pps, ss about €25. Self-catering available with use of hotel leisure facilities. **Directions:** Take N71 from Cork City, 10 minutes drive west of Clonakilty.

Rosscarbery
RESTAURANT

O'Callaghan-Walshe
The Square Rosscarbery Co Cork **Tel: 023 48125**
funfish@indigo.ie

Well off the busy main West Cork road, this unique restaurant is on the square of the old village of Rosscarbery and has a previous commercial history that's almost tangible. Exposed stone walls, old fishing nets and glass floats, mismatched furniture, shelves of wine bottles and candlelight all contribute to its unique atmosphere - which is well-matched by proprietor-host Sean Kearney's larger-than-life personality. Then there's the exceptional freshness and quality of the seafood - steaks theoretically share the billing, but West Cork seafood 'bought off the boats at auction' steals the scene. Martina O'Donovan's menus change daily but specialities to look out for include the famous Rosscarbery Pacific oysters, of course, also a superb West Cork Seafood Platter, char-grilled prime fish such as turbot, and grilled whole lobster. Ultra-freshness, attention to detail in breads and accompaniments - and a huge dose of personality - all add up to make this place a delight. O'Callaghan-Walshe was the Guide's Atmospheric

Georgina Campbell's Ireland

Restaurant of the Year for 2004. An interesting wine list includes a good choice of half bottles. Not suitable for children after 7 pm. **Seats 40.** D Tue-Sun 6.30-9.15. D à la carte, house wine about €20, sc discretionary. Closed Mon, open weekends only in winter (a phone call to check is advised). MasterCard, Visa, Laser. **Directions:** Main square in Rosscarbery village. ◇

Rosscarbery
CAFÉ

Pilgrim's Rest
The Square Rosscarbery Co Cork
Tel: 023 31796

A charming café just across the square from O'Callaghan-Walshe, The Pilgrim's Rest gives out all the right vibes (delicious Illy coffee and lovely home-bakes) and is well worth checking out for a journey break. Off season menus are quite restricted - just coffee and cakes in winter - but there is much more choice of wholesome light meals in summer. Open 6 days in summer, Tue, 12-5pm, Wed-Sun, 10-5pm; more limited opening off season, please call ahead to confirm. Closed Mon. MasterCard, Visa. **Directions:** Off N71, on main square of Rosscarbery village. ◇

Schull
GUESTHOUSE

Corthna Lodge Country House
Air Hill Schull Co Cork **Tel: 028 28517**
info@corthna-lodge.net www.corthna-lodge.net

Situated up the hill from Schull, commanding countryside and sea views, Martin and Andrea Mueller's roomy modern house just outside the town is one of the best located places to stay in the area. Although fairly compact, bedrooms are comfortable with good amenities, and there's plenty of space for guests to sit around and relax - both indoors, in a pleasant and comfortably furnished sitting room and outdoors, on a terrace overlooking the lovely garden towards the islands of Roaring Water Bay. House computer available for guests' internet access; unusually, there's also a gym, a hot tub, a barbecue area - and a putting green. Children over 5 welcome. **Rooms 6** (all shower only & no smoking). B&B €42.50-47.50 pps, ss €22.50, triple room €115-125. Closed 15 Oct-15 April. MasterCard, Visa, Laser. **Directions:** Through village, up hill, first left, first right - house is signposted. ◇

Schull
RESTAURANT
♛ 🏉

Grove House
Colla Road Schull Co Cork **Tel: 028 28067**
katarinarunske@eircom.net www.grovehouseschull.com

Overlooking Schull Harbour, this beautifully restored period house offers quality, relaxed surroundings and great food just a few minutes walk from the main street, and is now run by Katarina Runske, her mother Catherine Noren (previously at Dunworley Cottage, Butlerstown) and family. The approach is still less than immaculate but landscaping has matured a little and slight untidiness around the house is not typical of the interior, where housekeeping is exemplary. There is plenty of parking, and a terrace overlooking the harbour and all the activity on the pier is set up attractively with garden furniture and parasols, so you can relax with a glass of wine or lunch. It is a pleasing house, and any period features have been retained in well-proportioned reception rooms. Katarina also teaches piano so there is music in the house, with a grand piano in the green room. A lovely dining room, set up stylishly with simple contemporary linen and cutlery, the restaurant has earned a following for unique ingredients-led cooking with a distinctive Swedish flavour, and is now regarded as the best place to dine in the area. About seven choices are offered on each course at dinner, and there are nightly seafood specials. The house signature dish - herrings three ways - is sure to be among the starters, and main courses will include other firm favourites like local duck in plum & red wine sauce, and Swedish meatballs. Puddings are a highlight, also local cheeses - and excellent home-made breads may include an unusual light rye style brown, and a white yeast loaf. Katarina is 'wine mad' and her informative list is extensive for a small place - you can sense the enjoyment she has had in making the selection, which includes real some treats, and wine service is also helpful. Restaurant L 12.30-3.30, D 6.30-10.30; house wine €17.50 closed L Sun - Open weekend only off season, but can be opened on request. Accommodation also available all year. Amex, MasterCard, Visa, Laser. **Directions:** On right beyond Church of Ireland Colla Road, 4 mins walk from village.

Harbour View Hotel

Schull
HOTEL
N

Main Street Schull Co Cork **Tel: 028 28101**
enquiries@harbourviewhotelschull.com www.harbourviewhotelschull.com

This attractive new family-run hotel overlooking Schull harbour replaces the old East End Hotel, and is a real asset to the town. The exterior is traditional - cheerfully painted in true West Cork style and with colourful window boxes on the upper window ledges and the interior has hit a nice level of contemporary style, which is smart and up to date but not making too obvious a statement. The hotel does not look very big from the outside and the main public areas, including the bar and restaurant, are just a comfortable size for a small town, so the extent of the amenities may come as a surprise - these include an impressive leisure centre with a swimming pool, gym and beauty rooms, which are all open to the local community as well as residents, and friendly, welcoming staff are on hand to deal with inquiries. The accommodation is a big change for the area too, as stylish and very comfortable bedrooms have been given a lot of TLC, including specially made local furniture, which is unusual and gives the rooms a feeling of being special; smart bathrooms all have a full bath too. Prices are very reasonable for the standard offered. **Rooms 30.** Leisure centre (swimming pool, gym, beauty salon). B&B €60-80 pps, ss €15. 50% reduction for children. **Directions:** Overlooking the harbour - on the right as you enter Schull from Ballydehob direction. MasterCard, Visa, Laser. ◇

Hillside House B&B

Schull
B&B
N

Hillside Schull Co Cork **Tel: (028) 282248**
mmacf@oceanfree.net

Disregard the dull exterior of this warm and welcoming B&B just outside Schull - it has great views over the bay, is well away from any village noise and will make a homely and moderately-priced base for a stay in the area. The décor is a little dated too, but offset by good paintings, interesting old furniture and top rate beds. Everything works and the breakfast is good, with home-made breads and jams, plenty of fruit and the option of fish as well as the full Irish. And your hosts are generous with local information too - just what people need on holiday. Children welcome (under 3s free in parents' room, cot available free of charge); **Rooms 3.** B&B €35pps, ss€5. Closed Oct-May. **No credit cards.** **Directions:** Turn right at side of church coming from Skibbereen.

Stanley House

Schull
B&B

Schull Co Cork **Tel: 028 28425**
stanleyhouse@eircom.net www.stanley-house.net

Nancy Brosnan's modern house provides a West Cork home from home for her many returning guests. Compact bedrooms are comfortably furnished with tea/coffee making facilities and there's a pleasant conservatory running along the back of the house, with wonderful sea views over a field where guests can watch Nancy's growing herd of deer and sometimes see foxes come out to play at dusk. Good breakfasts too. Children welcome (under 3s free in parents' room, cots available without charge). No pets. Garden. **Rooms 4** (all shower only, all no-smoking, 2 ground floor). B&B €34pps, ss €12.50. Closed 31 Oct-1 Mar. MasterCard, Visa, Laser. **Directions:** At top of main street. follow signs for Stanley House.

T J Newman's / Newman's West

Schull
CHARACTER PUB/CAFÉ/WINE BAR

Main Street Schull Co Cork **Tel: 028 27776**
info@tjnewmans.com www.tjnewmans.com

Just up the hill from the harbour, this characterful and delightfully old-fashioned little pub has been a special home-from-home for regular visitors, especially sailors up from the harbour, as long as anyone can remember. The premises was bought by John and Bride D'Alton in 2003 but, although Kitty Newman is missed, the old bar remains much as it always has been and remains the most popular pub in the town. However, the D'Altons' café/winebar, Newman's West, which replaced the old off-cence, has very successfully introduced a new flavour to the informal dining options in Schull. Offering lovely food and great value in immaculate premises, they have a second first-floor room that doubles as an art gallery, and provide newspapers for a leisurely browse over an excellent cup of coffee. A cleverly thought out menu offers all sorts of tempting bits and pieces, notably the Newman's West Gourmet Choice and delicious desserts. Every tourist town should have a place like this. Broadband wi/fi. Children welcome. **Seats 50.** Toilets wheelchair accessible. Food served all day 9-12 (Sun, 10am-11pm). House wines (16), €15.90 (€4.50 per glass). Closed 25 Dec, Good Fri. **No Credit cards. Directions:** Main West Cork route to Mizen Head.

Schull Area
COUNTRY HOUSE

Rock Cottage

Barnatonicane Schull Co Cork **Tel: 028 35538**
rockcottage@eircom.net www.rockcottage.ie

Garden-lovers, especially, will thrill to the surroundings of Barbara Klotzer's beautiful slate-clad Georgian hunting lodge near Schull, which is on a south-facing slope away from the sea, nearby at Dunmanus Bay. A fascinating combination of well-tended lawns and riotous flower beds, the rocky outcrop which inspired its name - and even great estate trees in the 17 acres of parkland (complete with peacefully grazing sheep) that have survived from an earlier period of its history - create a unique setting. The whole of the main house has been redecorated recently but it has always been known for its style and comfort, with welcoming open fires and bright bedrooms which - although not especially large - are thoughtfully furnished to allow little seating areas as well as the usual amenities such as tea/coffee making facilities, and en-suite power showers. There's a sheltered courtyard behind the house and also some appealing self-catering accommodation, in converted stables. And Barbara is an accomplished chef - so you can look forward to a dinner based on the best of local produce, with starters like fresh crab salad or warm Ardsallagh goat's cheese, main courses of Rock Cottage's own rack of lamb, or even lobster or seafood platters, beautiful vegetables and classic desserts like home-baked vanilla cheesecake or strawberry fool. Extensive breakfast choices include a Healthy Breakfast and a Fish Breakfast as well as traditional Irish and continental combinations - just make your choice before 8pm the night before. Barbara also offers laundry facilities - very useful when touring around. Not suitable for children under 10. No pets. garden. walking. **Rooms 3** (all en-suite, 2 shower only, all no smoking). B&B from €65 pps, ss €30. Breakfast, 8.30-9.30 (order by 8pm the night before). Residents D Mon-Sat, €45, at 7.30pm; house wine €18. No D on Sun. Open all year. MasterCard, Visa, Laser. **Directions:** From Schull, 10km, at Toormore, turn into R591 after 2km. Sign on left.

Skibbereen
RESTAURANT

Kalbo's Bistro

48 North Street Skibbereen Co Cork
Tel: 028 21515

After a decade in business, Siobhan O'Callaghan and Anthony Boyle continue to do a great job at this bright, buzzy town-centre restaurant. It's not a smart place, but there has always been an air of quality about it - staff are quick and helpful and Siobhan's simple food is wholesome and flavoursome in a light contemporary style - lovely home-made soups, pastas, tarts, ciabattas, and scrumptious salads at lunchtime and more serious dishes of local seafood, rack of lamb, steaks and so on in the evening. Specialities include home-made burgers, that come with a choice of toppings, also local Skeaghanore duck - on a bed of parsnip mash, perhaps, with redcurrant, port & orange sauce - and vegetarian options are imaginative. The dishes are popular, but this is real food; consistently delicious, it is well sourced, accurately cooked, appetisingly presented - and has real flavour. A short but interesting wine list includes a pair of organic wines and four half bottles. Whether for a quick lunchtime bite or a more leisurely meal, Kalbo's is a great choice - and good value too. **Seats 42.** Open daily in summer: L Mon-Sat, 12-3, D Mon-Sat, 6.30-9.30. A la carte; house wine €17.95, sc discretionary. Closed Sun; 24-28 Dec & Good Fri. Amex, Diners, MasterCard, Visa, Laser. **Directions:** In town centre.

Skibbereen
HOTEL

West Cork Hotel

Ilen Street Skibbereen Co Cork **Tel: 028 21277**
info@westcorkhotel.com www.westcorkhotel.com

This welcoming hotel enjoys a pleasant riverside site beside the bridge, on the western side of the town. It came into new ownership in 2007 and, in addition to recent refurbishment which had been completed with some style, the function room has been extended and is now a very pleasant room with river views. The main entrance is currently from the street (the main through road) and is quite small, but the hotel opens up behind the foyer, to reveal a bright and airy bar along the river side of the hotel, and a modern restaurant, where breakfast is served to residents, as well as main meals. Bedrooms are not especially large, but they are comfortably furnished in a neutral contemporary style and have all the necessary amenities (phone, tea/coffee tray, TV) and neat, well-designed en-suite bathrooms, so this would make a good base from which to explore this beautiful area. Unless there is further redevelopment along the river, rooms at the back should be quieter and have a pleasant outlook over trees and river. Garden. Private parking. **Rooms 30** (7 junior suites, 4 shower only). Closed 22-28 Dec. Amex, Diners, MasterCard, Visa, Laser. **Directions:** Follow signs N71 to Bantry through Skibbereen. ◇

Timoleague
RESTAURANT

Dillon's
Mill Street Timoleague Co Cork
Tel: 023 46390

In the '90s, Dillon's traditional shopfront on the main street in Timoleague was a welcome sight for anyone needing a good food stop when heading west from Cork and, although they don't do daytime food any more, it's still something of an oasis in this area. The dining experience has moved up a few gears since then, but the informal café-style restaurant is much the same and, although Isabelle Dillon isn't in the kitchen herself these days, she's very much in evidence front of house. Vivien Toop is the chef now, but the philosophy of using the best local produce and making everything on the premises remains constant breads, pasta and desserts are all home-made. Vivien's interesting menus offer about half a dozen choices on each course, and they change frequently, although some specialities (or variations) are always likely - de-boned roasted quail is a favourite, for example, and may be stuffed with bacon, almonds, prunes & raisins and served with a Muscat sauce. A well-chosen wine list is organised by style, and includes some interesting half bottles. This is an unusual restaurant and the slightly bohemian décor and background jazz make for an atmospheric outing. **Seats 30**; not suitable for children under 7 yrs after 7pm. Open for D Thu-Sun, 6.30pm-9.30pm; à la carte. Closed Mon-Wed (open Bank Hol Mon); first 2 weeks Mar, first 2 weeks Oct. Reservations recommended. **No credit cards. Directions:** On main street of village. On M71.

YOUGHAL

Famous for its associations with Sir Walter Raleigh, Youghal is an historic town on the estuary of the Blackwater, and was once the second largest port in Europe, the many historic buildings and monuments within its walls have seen its designation as an Irish Heritage Port. Today, thanks to a recently opened by-pass, the town is more accessible for leisurely visits and it is well worth lingering a little to take in the historical walking tour which visits a number of diversely interesting old buildings, including the famous 1777 Clock Gate over the main street. **Old Imperial Hotel with Coachhouse Bar & Restaurant** (024 92435; www.theoldimperialhotel.com): at the front of this recently renovated town centre hotel is a wonderful old-world bar, previously known as D.McCarthy; while the rest of the hotel provides the usual facilities, this is a lovely little low-ceilinged bar of great character, with an open fire and a long history to tell - it's worth calling here for this alone. On the western end of the town, the popular **Tides Restaurant** (024 93127; www.tidesrestaurant.ie) is a useful place to know about, not least for its long opening hours; accommodation is also available. Fishing in the River Blackwater (noted for salmon, trout and excellent coarse fish), golf, angling, pitch and putt and yachting are just some of the activities that are located either near or in the town. There is also a fine 5km blue flag beach.

WWW.IRELAND-GUIDE.COM FOR THE BEST PLACES TO EAT, DRINK & STAY

Youghal
RESTAURANT WITH ROOMS

Aherne's Seafood Restaurant & Accommodation
163 North Main Street Youghal Co Cork **Tel: 024 92424**
ahernes@eircom.net www.ahernes.com

Now in its third generation of family ownership, one of the most remarkable features of Aherne's is the warmth of the FitzGibbon family's hospitality and their enormous enthusiasm for the business which, since 1993, has included some fine accommodation. But it is for its food - and, especially, the ultra-fresh seafood that comes straight from the fishing boats in Youghal harbour - that Aherne's is best known. While John FitzGibbon supervises the front of house, his brother David reigns over a busy kitchen. Bar food tends towards simplicity, and is all the better for that - oysters, chowder, Yawl Bay smoked salmon and oysters make for great snacks or starters (all served with the renowned moist dark brown yeast bread), and you'll find at least half a dozen delicious hot seafood main course dishes like baked cod wrapped in bacon and gorgeous prawns in garlic butter - its sheer freshness tells the story. Restaurant meals are naturally more ambitious and include some token meat dishes - rack of lamb with a rosemary jus or mint sauce, char-grilled fillet steak with mushrooms and shallot jus or pepper sauce - although seafood is still the undisputed star of the show. Specialities like pan-fried scallops with spinach, bacon & cream, or fresh crab salad can make memorable starters, for example, and who could resist a main course of hot buttered Youghal Bay lobster? These are, in a sense, simple dishes yet they have plenty of glamour too. It is well worth planning a journey around a bar meal at Aherne's - or, if time permits, a relaxed evening meal followed by a restful night in their very comfortable accommodation. A wine list strong on classic French regions offers a good selection of half bottles and half a dozen champagnes. **Seats 60** (private room, 20). Toilets wheelchair accessible. D 6.30-9.30 daily; fixed price 2-course set D €35; 3-course €45; also à la carte; house wine €22, sc discretionary. *Bar food daily, 12-10. **Accommodation:** The stylish rooms at Aherne's are generously sized and individually decorated to a high standard; all are furnished with antiques and have full bathrooms. Excellent breakfasts are served in a warm and elegantly furnished residents' dining room. Studio apartments are also available, equipped to give the option of self-catering if required. Conference room (20). Safe & fax available at reception; free broadband wi/fi. Children welcome (under 5s free in parents' room, cot available without charge, baby sitting arranged). Pets permitted in certain areas. **Rooms 13** (4 junior suites, 2 family rooms, 3 ground floor, 1 for disabled). B&B €105 pps, ss €25. Wheelchair access. Closed 24-28 Dec. Amex, MasterCard, Visa. **Directions:** on N25, main route from Cork-Waterford.

Youghal
FARMHOUSE

Ballymakeigh House

Killeagh Youghal Co Cork **Tel: 024 95184**
ballymakeigh@eircom.net www.ballymakeighhouse.com

Set at the heart of a dairy farm, this attractive old house is immaculately maintained and run by Euro Toques chef and cookery writer, Margaret Browne, who provides a high standard of comfort, food and hospitality in one of the most outstanding establishments of its type in Ireland. The house is warm and homely with plenty of space for guests, who are welcome to use the garden and visit the farmyard. Bedrooms are full of unique character and equally comfortable, founded on excellent hospitality. Margaret Browne has a national reputation for her cooking (and is the author of a successful cookery book); an impressive dinner menu is offered every night, and non-residents are very welcome in the restaurant. Garden, walking. Off-season value breaks, special interest breaks. Self-catering accommodation is also available nearby, in a restored Victorian house. Children welcome (under 3 free in parents' room, cot available free of charge). Pets allowed in some areas by arrangement. **Rooms 6** (all en-suite & no smoking, 3 shower only, 1 family room). B&B €65 pps, ss €10. D daily, 7-8pm, residents only; Set D €40-45; house wine from €20; SC discretionary. House closed Nov 1-Feb 1. MasterCard, Visa, Laser. **Directions:** Off N25 between Youghal & Killeagh (signed at Old Thatch pub).

COUNTY DONEGAL

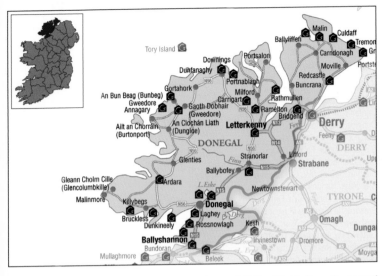

Golden eagles are no mere flight of fancy in Donegal. Glenveagh National Park in the northern part of the county is the focal point of a programme for the re-introduction of this magnificent bird to Ireland – it was last seen here in 1912. The first six Scottish-born chicks of the new wave were released at Glenveagh in June 2001. By the end of 2004, 15 adult birds were soaring over Donegal, with a further nine sightings to the south in Sligo and Leitrim. Over a five year period, 50 birds have been released, and the high expectations of success for the project began to be fulfilled with the first chick hatched and fledged in 2007.

Travel at sea level is also an increasingly significant element in visits to Donegal, one of Ireland's most spectacularly beautiful counties. It is much-indented by the sea, but the introduction of local car ferry services is shortening journeys and adding interest. The ferry between Greencastle and Magilligan across the narrow entrance to Lough Foyle has become deservedly popular, and another car ferry – between Buncrana and Rathmullan across Lough Swilly – adds to the travel options, albeit at a more leisurely pace.

For many folk, particularly those from Northern Ireland, Donegal is the holiday county par excellence. But in recent years, despite the international fluctuations of trading conditions, there has been growth of modern industries and the re-structuring of the fishing, particularly at the developing harbour of Killybegs, home port for the largest fishing vessels. This Donegal entrepreneurial spirit has led to a more balanced economy, with the pace being set by the county town of Letterkenny, where the population has increased by 50% since 1991. More recently, Letterkenny has become home to an impressive Arts Centre, a masterpiece of modern architecture.

But much and all as Donegal county is increasingly a place where people live and make a living, nevertheless it is still a place of nature on the grand scale, where the landscape is challenged by the winds and weather of the Atlantic Ocean if given the slighest chance. Yet at communities like Bundoran and Rossnowlagh, where splendid beaches face straight into the Atlantic, enthusiastic surfers have demonstrated that even the most demanding weather can have its sporting uses.

For most folk, however, it is the contrast between raw nature and homely comfort which is central to Donegal's enduring attraction. For here, in some of Ireland's most rugged territory, you will find many sheltered and hospitable places whose amenities are emphasised by the challenging nature of their broader environment. And needless to say, that environment is simply startlingly utterly beautiful as well.

Local Attractions & Information

Arranmore Ferry Burtonport-Arranmore	074 952 0532
Buncrana Lough Swilly Ferry	074 938 1901
Buncrana National Knitting Centre	074 936 2355
Bundoran Tourism Information	071 984 1350
Churchill Glebe House & Gallery (Derek Hill)	074 913 7071
Donegal Airport Carrickfin	074 954 8232
Donegal Highlands Hillwalking/Irish Language (adults)	074 973 0248
Donegal Town Donegal Castle	074 972 2405
Donegal Town Tourism information	074 972 1148
Donegal Town Waterbus Cruises	074 972 1148
Dunfanaghy Workhouse Visitor Centre	074 913 6540
Dungloe, Mary from Dungloe Int. Festival (July/August)	074 952 1254
Dungloe Tourism Information	074 952 1297
Glencolumbcille Folk Museum	074 973 0017
Glencolumbcille Tourism Information	074 973 0017
Glenties Patrick Mac Gill Summer School (August)	074 954 6101
Glenveagh National Park (Castle, gardens, parkland)	074 913 7090
Greencastle Lough Foyle Ferry	074 938 1901
Greencastle Maritime Museum	074 938 1363
Inishowen Inishowen Tourism (Carndonagh)	074 937 4933
Letterkenny An Grianan Theatre	074 912 0777
Letterkenny Regional Cultural Centre	074 912 9186
Letterkenny Earagail Arts Festival	074 916 8800
Letterkenny County Museum	074 912 4613
Letterkenny Newmills Watermill	074 912 5115
Letterkenny North West Tourism	074 912 1160
Lifford Cavanacor Historic House	074 914 1143
Rathmullan Lough Swilly Ferry	074 938 1901
Tory Island Ferry	074 953 1320 / 953 1340 / 913 5061

Annagry
RESTAURANT WITH ROOMS

Danny Minnie's Restaurant
Annagry Co Donegal **Tel: 074 954 8201**
www.dannyminnies.com

The O'Donnell family has run Danny Minnie's since 1962, and a visit is always a special treat. There's nothing about the exterior as seen from the road to prepare first-time visitors for the atmosphere of this remarkable restaurant: hidden behind a frontage of overgrown creepers a surprise: once through the door you are suddenly surrounded by antiques and elegantly appointed candle-lit tables and on summer evenings there may even be a harpist playing. The menu is presented in both Irish and English, and Brian O'Donnell's cooking matches the surroundings well - fine, with imaginative saucing, but not at all pompous. On the wide-ranging à la carte menu, seafood stars in the main courses - lobster and other shellfish, availability permitting - and there is also a strong selection of meats including Donegal mountain lamb, typically served with honey, garlic and rosemary gravy, and Donegal beef, served various ways including classic Beef Wellington. Vegetables are a strength and gorgeous desserts, such as cardamom and lime pannacotta with a refreshing rhubarb and strawberry compôte, can be relied on to create an appropriately delicious finale. And the staff are lovely too - attentive waitresses provide warm and friendly service. There's nowhere quite like Danny Minnie's, winner of the Guide's Atmospheric Restaurant of the Year in 2000. Not suitable for children after 9pm. Reservations required. Seats 80. D Mon-Sat, 6.30-9.30pm. Set D €50; also à la carte; house wine about €25; no sc. (Phone ahead to check opening hours, especially off peak season) Closed Sun D, 25/26 Dec, Good Fri & early week off season. [Accommodation is also offered in seven non-smoking rooms, five of them en-suite, two family rooms; B&B €65pps, ss€10]. MasterCard, Visa, Laser. **Directions:** R259 off N56 - follow Airport signs.

Ardara
CHARACTER PUB

Nancy's Bar
Front Street Ardara Co Donegal
Tel: 074 954 1187

This famous pub, in the village renowned for its tweeds and handknits, is a cosy, welcoming place in its seventh generation of family ownership, with five or six small rooms packed with bric à brac and plenty of tables and chairs for the comfortable consumption of wholesome home-made food, especially seafood. Famed equally for a great pint of Guinness and the house chowder - maybe try it with a "Louis Armstrong" (smoked salmon on brown bread topped with grilled cheese) and finish with an Irish coffee. Or there's "Charlie's Supper", a speciality of prawns and smoked salmon warmed in a chilli & garlic sauce. Things moved up a notch or two here in 2007, when another bar area was opened, and also an outdoor seating area with an awning giving more room to enjoy everything this delightful pub has to offer. Great live music too. Children welcome before 9pm (high chair, baby changing facilities). Bar food served daily 12-9, from Easter to September. Wheelchair access to toilets. Closed 25 Dec & Good Fri. **No Credit Cards. Directions:** In Ardara village; half an hours drive from Donegal Town.

Ardara
COUNTRY HOUSE/RESTAURANT

Woodhill House
Woodhill Ardara Co Donegal **Tel: 074 954 1112**
yates@iol.ie www.woodhillhouse.com

Formerly the home of Ireland's last commercial whaling family, John and Nancy Yates' large house is on the edge of the village, overlooking the Donegal Highlands, and their years of restoration work are now bearing fruit. They offer accommodation in recently converted outbuildings, overlooking the gardens as well as the main house, and rooms are all en-suite, but vary greatly in position, size and character so it is advisable to discuss your requirements when booking. The new garden rooms are slightly dearer but they are very spacious and appealingly furnished, with good en-suite bathrooms. There's also a bar and restaurant (it is popular locally - booking recommended) offering quite tradi-tional food based on local ingredients at reasonable prices: specialities include Donegal mountain lamb, and carrageen pudding. The gradual restoration of the gardens is perhaps Nancy's greatest achievement, and renovations on both the main house and outbuildings are still on-going. Small conferences/ private parties (50). Children welcome (under 5s free in parents' room, cot available without charge). Pets permitted in some areas. **Rooms 14** (6 shower-only, 1 family room, 4 ground floor, 1 for disabled). B&B €60 pps, ss €10. **Restaurant:** Seats 50 (private room, 15). Children welcome. Reservations accepted. D 6.30-10pm daily, Set D €39.50; house wine €20; sc discre-tionary. Bar open normal hours (no food). House closed 20-27 Dec. Amex, Diners, MasterCard, Visa, Laser. **Directions:** 500m from Ardara village.

Ballybofey
HOTEL

Jackson's Hotel
Ballybofey Co Donegal **Tel: 074 913 1021**
info@jacksons-hotel.ie www.jacksons-hotel.ie

This attractive family-run hotel is set in its own gardens and enjoys a tranquil position alongside the River Finn. A welcoming open fire in the spacious, elegantly furnished foyer creates a good first impression, a feeling followed through in other public areas including the restau-rant, overlooking the garden. Recent development has seen the addition of 50 new rooms as well as a large conference centre, meeting rooms, and an underground carpark. All bedrooms are furnished to a high standard, and are comfortable with telephones, tea/coffee trays and TV/DVD - the best have river views. Conference/banqueting (1,400/550); business centre, ISDN lines, secretarial services. Leisure centre (22m pool), hot tub, jacuzzi. Snooker, pool table. Children welcome (under 2 free in parents' room, cots available without charge, baby sitting arranged, playroom). Special breaks offer good value. Horse-riding, golf, fishing and bike hire all nearby. Pets permitted in some areas. Garden. **Rooms 89** (2 suites, 5 executive rooms, 50 no smoking, 10 disabled, 10 family rooms). Wheelchair access. Lift. 24 hour room service. B&B about €80 pps, ss about €20. *Food available all day (9am-10.30pm); Restaurant: D 6-9.15 daily, Sun L 12.30-4. Open all year. Amex, Diners, MasterCard, Visa, Laser. **Directions:** Beside the river, in the centre of town. ◊

Ballybofey
HOTEL

Kee's Hotel
Stranorlar Ballybofey Co Donegal **Tel: 074 913 1018**
info@keeshotel.ie www.keeshotel.ie

This centrally located, all-year hotel has been in the Kee family since 1892. Spacious public areas allow plenty of areas for guests to relax, and good food is offered in the pleasantly informal Old Gallery bistro where daily-changing menus are based on the best of local produce. Rooms at the back have views of the Blue Stack Mountains and all bedrooms are regularly refurbished and have good bathrooms. Residents have direct access to a fine leisure centre, with swimming pool. Golf and fishing nearby. Conference/banqueting (200/250). Children welcome (under 3s free in their parents' room; cots and high chairs available, baby sitting arranged). Special breaks offered by the hotel, and offering very good value, include golfing holidays, bank holiday breakaways and a novel "Post Christmas Recovery Break". No pets. **Rooms 53** (32 executive rooms, 23 family, 39 no smoking, 1 for disabled). Lift. Room service (24 hr). B&B about €90 pps, ss €15. Children welcome. Toilets wheelchair accessible. Seats 120; food served 12.30-10pm. SC discretionary. [Informal bistro style meals served in the Old Gallery, 12.30-3 and 5.30-9.30 daily.] Amex, Diners, MasterCard, Visa, Laser. **Directions:** On the main street in the village of Stranorlar.

Ballyliffin
HOTEL/RESTAURANT

Ballyliffin Lodge and Spa
Shore Road Ballyliffin Co Donegal **Tel: 074 937 8200**
info@ballyliffinlodge.com www.ballyliffinlodge.com

This impressive hotel in Ballyliffin village is a great asset to the area - with a beautiful view, space and comfort. Public areas include a traditional bar, Mamie Pat's, and the spacious guest rooms are finished to a high standard with many extras. General Manager Cecil Doherty, who is also a joint-proprietor of the hotel, has considered every detail including excellent on-site leisure facilities, with swimming pool and spa treatments. Discounts are available for hotel guests at Ballyliffin GC, and short breaks are offered. The

hotel also accepts wedding parties (remember the Donegal catch-phrase is 'up here it's different'). Conference/banqueting 500/400; secretarial service. Children welcome (under 5 free in parents' room, free cot available). **Rooms 40** (12 junior suites, 4 superior, 4 disabled, all no smoking). B&B €90 pps, ss €20. Lift. Room service (limited hours). Open all year except 25 Dec & Good Fri. **Holly Tree Restaurant:** There is a classic and intimate feel to this rather small exclusive room: head chef Kwanghi Chan is well known in Ireland for his accomplished modern European cuisine; he and his team produce classic dishes, sometimes with an Asian twist - and people travel specially to eat here. You can choose between the set dinner, and an à la carte; which includes some unusual appetisers and a speciality of fresh whole fish; desserts are also very good, notably a gorgeous steamed lemon pudding. A well thought out wine list includes plenty of half bottles, and service is excellent. Children welcome. **Seats 55,** reservations required, toilets accessible for wheelchairs, air conditioning, vegetarian menu available. D daily, 6.30-9.30. L Sun only, 12.30-4. Set D €40, Set Sun L €18. D also a la carte. Bar meals, 12.30-9 daily. House Wine €18. Closed 25 Dec, Good Friday. Residents can get a discount on local golf. Helipad. Amex, Diners, MasterCard, Visa, Laser. **Directions:** In Ballyliffin village (signed).

BALLYSHANNON

On the southern shores of Donegal Bay, Ballyshannon is the gateway to County Donegal and is one of the oldest towns in Ireland, having been made a Borough by Royal Charter in 1613. The poet William Allingham was born here - his father was a ship-owner and merchant - and it is also the birthplace of Rory Gallagher, the rock guitarist. Hungry visitors might head for the friendly family-run Italian restaurant **Soprano's** (Tel: 071 985 1415) on Main Street, which is open for both lunch and dinner, offers good value and is very family-friendly; or the appealingly elegant new restaurant/café/wine bar **Nirvana** (071 9822369) on the Mall, which is open for light food during the day as well as offering lunch and dinner menus.
WWW.IRELAND-GUIDE.COM FOR THE BEST PLACES TO EAT, DRINK & STAY

Bridgend
BAR/RESTAURANT

Harry's Bar & Restaurant
Bridgend Co Donegal **Tel: 074 936 8444**
info@harrys.ie www.harrys.ie

The Doherty family's friendly bar and restaurant is a useful place to know about when travelling in the Derry/Inishowen area as they offer quality food through the day, and the family-friendly atmosphere, carefully sourced food and good value ensures a local following. Wide-ranging menus are offered but they're best known for their dry-aged Donegal steaks, and seafood from Greencastle both in the bar, during the day, and the restaurant at night. **Seats 110.** Toilets wheelchair accessible; Children welcome (high chair, childrens menu, baby changing facilities); Free broadband wi/fi. L&D Mon-Sat 12.15-4pm, 4-9pm; Sun L 12.15-3.30pm, D 4.30-9pm; set Sun L €21; house wine €17. Various live music at weekends, see website for details. Open all year. Amex, MasterCard, Visa, Laser. **Directions:** At junction of Buncrana-Derry and Letterkenny-Derry roads, about 19km (12 m) north of Letterkenny, 5km (3) miles from Derry.

Bruckless
FARMHOUSE

Bruckless House
Bruckless Co Donegal **Tel: 074 973 7071**
bruc@bruckless.com www.bruckless.com

Clive and Joan Evans' lovely 18th-century house and Connemara pony stud farm is set in 18 acres of woodland and gardens overlooking Bruckless Bay - an ideal place for people who enjoy quiet countryside and pursuits like walking, horse-riding and fishing. The gardens are not too formal but beautifully designed, extensive and well-maintained - they really enhance a visit here, as does the waterside location: guests have direct access to the foreshore at the bottom of the garden. Family furniture collected through a Hong Kong connection adds an unexpected dimension to elegant reception rooms that have views over the front lawns towards the sea, and the generous, comfortably furnished bedrooms. Accommodation includes two single rooms and there is a shared bathroom - although the house is large, the guest bedrooms are close together, so they are ideal for a family or a group travelling together. Enjoyed home-produced eggs at breakfast, which is the only meal served - guests are directed to local restaurants in the evening. Self-catering accommodation is also available all year, in a two-bedroomed gatelodge. Garden, equestrian, walking, fishing. **Rooms 4** (2 en-suite, 2 single, all no-smoking) B&B €60pps, no ss. Weekly rates also offered. Pets permitted in certain areas. *A two-bedroom Gate Lodge, sleeping four, is available for self-catering. Closed 1 Oct-31 Mar. Amex, MasterCard, Visa. **Directions:** On N56, 12 miles west of Donegal.

Bunbeg
HOTEL

Ostan Gweedore
Bunbeg Co Donegal **Tel: 074 953 1177**
reservations@ostangweedore.com www.ostangweedore.com

Although its blocky 1970s' architectural style may not be to today's taste, Ostan Gweedore was built to make the most of the location - and this it does exceptionally well. Spacious public areas, including the aptly named Ocean Restaurant and the Library Bar ("the most westerly reading room on the Atlantic seaboard") have superb views over the shoreline and Mount Errigal - as does the Sundowner Wine & Tapas Bar, which offers a wide range of wines by the glass and a menu of small tapas-style dishes to nibble while you watch the sun sinking in the west. The hotel takes pride in the restaurant - extensive menus offer a wide range of dishes based mainly on local produce, especially seafood and Donegal mountain lamb - and it has a strong local following. Most of the bedrooms have panoramic sea views, and although some may seem a little dated, they are all comfortable. It's a very relaxing place and in high season is ideal for families, with its wonderful beach and outdoor activities, including tennis, pitch & putt and day visits to nearby islands Tory, Gola and Arranmore. If you enjoy fresh air and exercise, ask at reception for the booklet Walks in the Bunbeg Area, which was specially commissioned by the hotel and details a variety of planned walks and cycle paths in the locality. Wet days are looked after too, with excellent indoor leisure facilities including a 19-metre swimming pool, Jacuzzi and gym, supervised by qualified staff, and a new health and beauty spa which offers all the current pamper treatments. *Donegal Airport, Carrickfin is nearby. This romantic setting is predictably popular for weddings; conferences/banqueting 300/350); broadband wi/fi. Leisure centre; spa. Fishing and golf (9 hole) available locally. **Rooms 34** (3 suites, 6 family rooms, 1 ground floor, 1 for disabled). B&B €85 pps,

ss €20. Children welcome (Under 5s free in parents' room at managements discretion, cot availabl
without charge, baby sitting arranged). **Ocean Restaurant:** D daily, 7-8.45, à la carte; Sundown
Tapas bar: 7pm-9.30pm daily. Closed Nov-Feb (open for New Years). Amex, MasterCard, Visa, Lase
Directions: From Letterkenny, take coast road past hospital.

BUNCRANA / INISHOWEN

Only a short distance from Derry City, BUNCRANA is a popular seaside resort on the eastern shore
Lough Swilly, and is the gateway to the INISHOWEN PENINSULA which extends between Loug
Swilly and Lough Foyle and is a favourite destination for golfers and walkers. It is a beautiful, main
mountainous area and Ireland's most northerly point, Malin Head, is at its tip; a 100-mile (161 kn
circular scenic drive known as the 'Inis Eoghain 100' is signposted around the peninsula and make
a lovely outing on a good day. There are stopping places en-route **McGrory's of Culdaff** (see entry)
often the most convenient and, in Buncrana, **The Beach House Bar & Restaurant** (074 936 1050
www.thebeachhouse.ie) is an attractive informal restaurant near the ferry which links Buncrana wit
Rathmullan on the western shore of Lough Swilly in summer. This pleasing place operates long hou
in season and has lovely views across the lough.
WWW.IRELAND-GUIDE.COM FOR THE BEST PLACES TO EAT, DRINK & STAY

BUNDORAN

A popular seaside resort on the southern shore of Donegal Bay, Bundoran looks across to the hills c
Donegal in the north and is backed by the Sligo-Leitrim mountains to the south. Of the many hote
in and around the town, the best located by far is the **Great Northern Hotel** (071 984 1204
www.greatnorthernhotel.com) which is situated at the centre of an 18-hole championship golf cours
overlooking Donegal Bay; it also offers a new conference centre and good leisure facilities, And, if yo
enjoy traditional pubs, make a point of calling in at **Brennans / Criterion Bar** on Main Street - it's a
fine an unspoilt Irish pub as you'll find anywhere: "no television, just conversation".
WWW.IRELAND-GUIDE.COM FOR THE BEST PLACES TO EAT, DRINK & STAY

BURTONPORT

BURTONPORT (Ailt an Chorrain) is a small fishing port and sea angling centre in The Rosses
renowned for its catches of salmon, lobster and crab in the summer months - fresh seafood whic
(along with many other varieties) finds its way on to menus in family-run pubs such as **Skippers Taver**
(074 954 2234) and **The Lobster Pot** (074 954 2012) both of which have a national reputation fo
fresh home-cooked food and warm hospitality. Just off the town, the island of Arranmore has now go
an hotel, **Arranmore House Hotel** (074 952 0918; www.arranmorehousehotel.ie), which is open a
year; the island is accessible by frequent car ferries.
WWW.IRELAND-GUIDE.COM FOR THE BEST PLACES TO EAT, DRINK & STAY

Carrigart | The Olde Glen Ba
CHARACTER PUB/RESTAURANT | Glen Carrigart Co Donega
 | **Tel: 074 915 513**

PUB OF THE YEA

Just the sort of old pub advertising people dream
about, the McLaughlin family's bar looks as it mus
have a hundred, maybe two hundred years ago
Low ceilings, ancient weathered bar and furniture
fires in winter, a big old room and then anothe
behind. Then it got so popular they built on
further room, which is very light and bright, wit
paintings on the walls and this is also for drinkin
and sitting while you wait for a table to become
available in **The Restaurant:** A dynamic youn
couple, Thomas & Maretta McLaughlin, run i
although working like mad all the time, Thomas has a word for everyone and is funny and relaxed an
Maretta's the bubbly, glamorous and friendly wife who is front of house. Between them they've mad
such a roaring success of the place that they have to have two sittings every evening, and then go o
beyond the summer proper into the end of October, as there are lots of golfers in the Rosapenna are
until then. After that they do meals at weekends, maybe taking a break mid-winter. Why is it s

opular? Because it provides just what you want: delicious, fresh, imaginative dishes served in an easy tmosphere, in a very basic but well thought out setting. And what might you eat? Tempura prawns, erhaps, served with a sweet chilli dipping sauce, and lovely halibut with dauphinoise potatoes, plaice ith crab sauce and also local Hereford beefsteaks; good vegetables, local, meat and all fish brought n nearby. All this and a good wine list, great service and good value too. No wonder it's popular. hildren welcome before 9pm; toilets wheelchair accessible; **Seats 50**; D Tue-Sun, 6-9pm; house wine 16.50; SC discretionary. Closed Mon (May-Sept) and occasional weekends. MasterCard, Visa, Laser. **irections:** 5 minutes from Carrigart village.

Culdaff

HOTEL/BAR/RESTAURANT

McGrory's of Culdaff

Culdaff Inishowen Co Donegal **Tel: 074 93 79104**

info@mcgrorys.ie   www.mcgrorys.ie

féile bia In an area that has so much to offer, in terms of natural beauty and activities like golf, angling and walking, McGrory's would make an ideal base. An inn in the true sense of the word, offering rest and refreshment to travellers, this north-western institution was established in 1924 nd remains in the active care of the McGrory family, who set great store by the traditions of hospi- ality and personal care while also keeping an eye on changing tastes and the requirements of a ast-moving society. It is now a pleasing combination of old and new which is easy on the eye, and ncludes an evening restaurant as well as the bar where informal meals are served. Accommodation is offered in comfortable bedrooms that vary in size and outlook but are attractively furnished in a classic contemporary style; all have well-planned bathrooms and all the necessary amenities (phone, ea/coffee tray, TV). For anyone touring the Inishowen peninsula this is a logical place to take a break, s popular bar food is available throughout the day. But it is probably for music that McGrory's is most amous - as well as traditional sessions in The Front Bar on Tuesday and Friday nights, Mac's Backroom Bar (constructed on the site of the old outhouses of McGrory's shop) is a major venue for ve shows featuring international names. (Live music Wednesday and Saturday; events listings on the web.) Conference/banqueting (100/150). Special interest/off season breaks offered (midweek; weekend; golf - special rates with Ballyliffin Golf Club, early breakfast arranged.) Children welcome under 4 free in parents' room; cot available free of charge, baby sitting arranged). No pets. **Rooms 7** (all en-suite, 4 shower only, 4 family rooms, 17 no smoking). Lift. Room service (limited hours). B&B about €55-65, ss €10. Restaurant: D Tue-Sun, L Sun. Bar meals daily, 12.30-8.30. Car park. Restaurant closed Mon; establishment closed 24-26 Dec. Amex, MasterCard, Visa, Laser. **Directions:** On R238 around Inishowen Peninsula. ◊

DONEGAL TOWN

Donegal Town was originally a plantation town and is now best known as the main centre for the tweed ndustry and crafts. A visit to the area would be unthinkable without calling into Magee's on The Diamond where there are hand loom weaving demonstrations; wholesome fare is available at the in- tore restaurant, **The Weavers Loft**, and also at **The Blueberry Tea Room** (074 972 2933), just off The Diamond, on Castle Street. **The Craft Village**, on the edge of the town, is well worth a visit and there's a very nice little coffee shop, **Aroma** (see entry), serving good home cooking, notably baking. **WWW.IRELAND-GUIDE.COM FOR THE BEST PLACES TO EAT, DRINK & STAY**

Donegal

GUESTHOUSE

Ⓝ

Ard na Bréatha

Drumrooske Middle Donegal Town Co Donegal **Tel: 074 972 2288**

info@ardnabreatha.com   www.ardnabreatha.com

Although it is in a slightly surprising location in a mainly residential area on the edge of the town, Theresa and Albert Morrow's welcoming guesthouse is tucked into a quiet corner and has a pleasant view out over their attractive garden to the countryside beyond. It is, as they say on their brochure, 'a place worth finding' and guests who have done so are clearly delighted. Theresa is a caring hostess, the house is planned with care to allow for everything possible that will help people to relax (including a proper bar with bar stools and an open fire), and there is a very happy atmosphere. Accommodation s in a separate building, just a few steps from the house; simple country style rooms are bright and comfortable, and all have phone, TV and full bath with shower. A lot of care also goes into breakfast, which is a very laid back affair, with all the treats people like to spoil themselves with on holiday, and a flexible attitude to timing. When there is demand, the Morrows also operate a fully-fledged restau- ant in the evening - tables are classically set up with white linen, and Albert offers a full dinner menu with about five choices on each course; ingredients are locally sourced and organic where possible, and specialities include Donegal rack of lamb and sirloin of Irish Angus beef. Well chosen wine list too. Many guests opt to dine in on the first evening of their stay and never feel the need to go out fo the rest of their stay, and it's easy to see why. Small conferences/banqueting (20/45); free broadban wi/fi. Children welcome (under 3s free in parents' room, cot available, baby sitting arranged); whee chair accessible; **Rooms 6** (1 family room, 3 ground floor, all no smoking); all day room service; dog permitted; B&B €49pps, ss €15. Closed 15 Nov - 15 Jan. MasterCard, Visa, Laser. **Directions:** Hous is 1.5km (1 mile) from Donegal town. Take Killybegs road from Donegal town centre. First road to righ for Lough Eske, continue to Vivo shop, take a right and go straight on.

Donegal   Aroma
CAFÉ   The Craft Village Donegal Co Donegal **Tel: 074 972 322.**
👑 €   paddyrast@eircom.ne

Tom Dooley's smart little café at the Craft Village just outside Donegal Town has won a lot of friend for its warm and friendly atmosphere and excellent freshly cooked food that offers much more tha would be expected of a coffee shop. Tempting cakes, desserts and breads are all homemade and che Arturo de Alba Gonzalez's menus include a frequently-changed blackboard, offering cooked-to-orde dishes like real vegetable soups, fried polenta, prosciutto, garlic mushrooms and mixed leaves or whit wine risotto with chargrilled chicken and seared asparagus, also salads like smoked chicken & avocad and, for the hungry young Mexican, chimichangas. Ingredients are impeccably sourced and everythin, looks and tastes delicious - the quality of the food and good cooking both show on the plate. Service under Tom's supervision is knowledgeable and efficient - with good espresso coffee and an extensiv tea menu to go with the great home bakes, this makes a good daytime stop. And, although the coffe shop is small, there's a large outdoor eating area for fine weather. Children welcome. **Seats 3** (outdoors, 16); open Mon-Sat, 9.30am-5.30pm (L 12-4); set L €17.50; SC disc. Closed Sur MasterCard, Visa, Laser. **Directions:** 1.6km (1m) outside town on old Ballyshannon road.

Donegal   Saint Ernan's House
HISTORIC HOUSE   Donegal Co Donegal **Tel: 074 972 106**
👑 🏛 👁   res@sainternans.com www.sainternans.com

Set on its own wooded island, connected to th mainland by a causeway built after the famine b tenants as a gesture of thanks to a caring landlord Brian and Carmel O'Dowd's lovely Victorian countr house on the edge of Donegal Town is remarkabl for its sense of utter tranquillity. This atmosphere is due, in part, to its unique location - and also, on imagines, to the kindly ghosts who seem to resid here, especially the spirit of John Hamilton, tha young landlord who built the house in 1826. Tha other-worldliness remains, and there is an almos tangible sense of serenity about the place that makes it the perfect retreat from the stresses of moder life. The spacious public rooms have log fires and antique furniture - plenty of space for guests to reac or simply to relax in front of the fire - and the individually decorated bedrooms echo that restfulness as in all old houses, they vary in size and position but most also have lovely views and all are furnishe to a high standard with antiques, and have good amenities including (surprisingly perhaps) televisior Many guests would see no need to leave the island during their stay, but there is much to do and se in the area: the craft shops of Donegal Town are almost on the doorstep, for example, and Glenveag National Park is just a short scenic drive away. The dining experience at Saint Ernans follows the sam philosophy of quiet relaxation and is only for resident guests; simple country house-style dinner menu offer two or three choices on each course and are based on local produce, with vegetarian dishes o request. Not suitable for children under 6 yrs. **Rooms 6** (3 suites, 1 ground floor, all no smoking). B& €120 pps, ss €40. D Residents Only. Seats 16, D 7-8 daily, Set D €52 (semi-à la carte, priced b course); house wine €27. Closed end Oct-mid Apr. MasterCard, Visa, Laser. **Directions:** 1.5 mile sout of Donegal Town on R267.

Downings   Rosapenna Hotel & Golf Resor
HOTEL   Downings Co Donegal **Tel: 074 915 530**
                                                        rosapenna@eircom.net www.rosapenna.i

Discerning golfers may think they've died and gone to heaven when staying at Frank and Hilary Casey' fine hotel on the shores of Sheephaven Bay. Although large and impressive, with comfortable an exceptionally spacious public areas and guest rooms that have been thoughtfully designed down to th very last detail, it is a very hospitable and relaxing place to stay. And, of course, as virtually every guest is bound to be a golfer, residents make up a sociable community of golfers, either in the hotel, or at the superb new golf pavilion. The restaurant is open to non-residents but, in practice, it is usually filled to capacity by hotel guests. Golf breaks offered. Golf (18), residents' green fees €30, angling, snooker, indoor 'pool, tennis. Children welcome (baby sitting arranged, cots available at no charge). **Rooms 53** (1 suite, 5 junior suites, 4 family rooms, 3 shower only, 27 ground floor, all no smoking); all day room service; pets permitted in some area by prior arrangement. B&B €90pps, ss €20. **Restaurant: seats 100;** D daily 7.15-8.30, children welcome, reservations required. Hotel closed end Oct-mid Mar. Amex, Diners, MasterCard, Visa, Laser. **Directions:** 36km (23m) northwest of Letterkenny, R425 to Carrigart then 2.5km. ◇

DUNFANAGHY

Many people will have a soft spot for this traditional holiday area, often recalling family holidays spent at the famous old **Arnold's Hotel** (074 913 6208; www.arnoldshotel.com), which has been in the same family for three generations and is still a very comfortable, laid-back place to stay. Nearby at Marble Hill Strand the **Shandon Hotel** (074 913 6137; www.shandonhotel.com) overlooks Sheephaven Bay, and most of the comfortable bedrooms have sea views; within walking distance of the beach and with a children's play centre it's a popular family holiday destination and, with good food and the recently added Spa & Wellness Centre, it appeals to all age groups. A little place that visitors will enjoy in the centre of the village is **Muck'n'Muffins** (074 913 6780), where you'll find a pottery studio on the ground floor and, upstairs, a coffee shop and wine bar overlooking the pretty garden centre next door as well as the pier and the sea view across to Horn Head. The local Killyhoey Beach features on many of the 18 holes at the scenic **Dunfanaghy Golf Club** and Dunfanaghy makes an ideal base for touring Horn Head and the northern peninsulas. While in the locality the **Dunfanaghy Workhouse Visitor Centre** (074 913 6504) is worth a visit, it is a famine centre in the town that remembers the 19th century famine which ravaged Ireland. The only place in Ireland where the corncrake can be heard in its natural habitat, Dunfanaghy is also a major centre for brown trout anglers and special interest holidays.

WWW.IRELAND-GUIDE.COM FOR THE BEST PLACES TO EAT, DRINK & STAY

Dunfanaghy
RESTAURANT WITH ROOMS
👐 ☆ 👁 🅔

The Mill Restaurant
Figart Dunfanaghy Letterkenny Co Donegal **Tel: 074 913 6985**
themillrestaurant@oceanfree.net   www.themillrestaurant.com

Beautifully located on the shore of the New Lake, which is a special area of conservation, the mill was the home of Susan Alcorn's grandfather and, as they are a family of accomplished painters, the walls are hung with wonderful water colours. Susan and her husband Derek, who is the chef, have earned a dedicated following here, as the location is superb, the welcome warm and the cooking both imaginative and assured - and they also offer very good value. The dining room is on two levels, with plenty of windows framing the views, fresh flowers on the tables, soft lighting and some well-placed antiques - a room of character and atmosphere. Menus are based firmly on the best ingredients, local where possible, and change every 4-6 weeks. While based on the classics, the house style is very much its own boss and perhaps the most enjoyable aspect of Derek Alcorn's cooking is that he createshis perfectly judged dishes complete with their complementary accompaniments, rather than main dishes with token vegetables on the side. Sometimes the ingredients may be unusual or under-used, as in a starter of pan-fried Horn Head mackerel with rhubarb, baby potato, beetroot and organic leaf salad but the originality is more in the way ingredients are combined, and in the detail, than in the choice of main ingredients. House specialties include an unusual upside down fish pie, which is filled with all manner of good things - lobster, crab claws and john dory in a brandy cream sauce and gorgeous desserts might include a seasonal fruit crumble tart with custard & ginger ice cream, as well as a good Irish cheese plate. But the overall experience here is much more than the sum of its parts and, under Susan's direction, the hospitality and service is exemplary too. Overnight guests will also have a delicious breakfast to look forwards to a lovely buffet of fruits, juices, cereals etc, hot dishes cooked perfectly to order and all the little treats of home-baked breads and preserves. Children welcome. **Seats 50.** Air conditioning. D Tue-Sun 7-9pm, Set D €39; house wine €18; sc discretionary. Closed Mon, mid Dec-mid Mar. **Accommodation**

is offered in six individually decorated rooms. The decor is simple but stylish, with good beds and some antique pieces, and there's also a lovely little sitting room off the dining room, with an open fire, and comfy big chairs and sofas to relax in. Children welcome (under 5s free in parents' room, cot available without charge). Free broadband wi/fi; no pets; garden; walking; cycling. **Rooms 6** (all en-suite & no-smoking, 2 shower only). B&B €50 pps, ss €20. Establishment closed mid Dec - mid Mar. Amex, MasterCard, Visa, Laser. **Directions:** N56 from Letterkenny to Dunfanaghy. 1km (1/2 m) outside Dunfanaghy on Falcarragh road on right hand side at the lake.

Dunfanaghy area
BAR/RESTAURANT

The Cove

Port na Blagh Dunfanaghy Co Donegal
Tel: 074 913 6300

Set well back from the road with plenty of parking at the front but no garden or landscaping to soften the approach, this two storey building can look a little bleak on arrival but any negative impression is quickly forgotten once inside Peter Byrne and Siobhan Sweeney's warm and welcoming restaurant. Peter shows arriving guests up to the first floor bar, where the luckiest guests will get seats at a corner table with big windows on both sides and views over the harbour. Waiting here for your table is no hardship, but orders taken from Siobhan's down-to-earth à la carte menu, offering nine or ten choices on each course you'll be whisked away downstairs again, to an atmospheric dining room with a big open fire, lots of wood and good art on the walls. Specialities here include a really good house chowder served with home-baked brown bread and, along with a well-judged range of favourites, you'll find some less usual dishes too, such as crispy fried whitebait and whole boned quail. Main courses include a fair amount of seafood; pan-seared scallops served with a fino sherry & balsamic jus and organic mixed leaf salad is a house speciality but you'll also find delicious meat dishes such as slow cooked belly of pork, or shank of lamb, and imaginative vegetarian dishes too. Quite an extensive, informative wine list is broadly organised by price (Everyday Wines/Fine Wines) and offers plenty to encourage you to linger on a little after dinner. Toilets wheelchair accessible; not suitable for children under 10 yrs after 6.30pm; **Seats 42;** reservations recommended; D Tue-Sun (& Bank Hol Mons), 5.30-9.30pm, early bird D, 2/3 course, €20/25; also à la carte; house wine €18. Closed Mon (except Bank Hols) and Jan - 16 Mar. Diners, MasterCard, Visa, Laser. **Directions:** On the main Creeslough-Dunfanaghy road (N56) in Portnablagh, overlooking the harbour.

Dunkineely
HOTEL/RESTAURANT

Castle Murray House Hotel

St. John's Point Dunkineely Co Donegal **Tel: 074 973 7022**
info@castlemurray.com www.castlemurray.com

Martin and Marguerite Howley's beautifully located clifftop hotel has wonderful sea and coastal views over the ruined castle after which it is named. It is a comfortable and relaxing place to stay, with a little bar, a residents' sitting room and a large terrace that can be covered with an awning in a good summer, so meals may be served outside. Bedrooms have a mixture of modern and older pieces that give each room its own character, and are gradually being refurbished; most have sea views and all are quite large with a double and single bed, refurbished bathrooms (some with full bath) and facilities including digital TV as well as phone and tea/coffee trays. A sunny area on the sheltered flat roof at the back of the building has direct access from some bedrooms. Lovely breakfasts are served in the restaurant, and there's an appealing bar menu. Banqueting (60). Children welcome (cots available, baby sitting arranged). Pets permitted by arrangement. Garden. Walking. Off-season value breaks. **Rooms 10** (6 shower only, all no smoking). B&B €70pps, ss €20. **The restaurant** is on the seaward corner of the hotel overlooking the sea and the castle (which is floodlit at night), and an open fire makes for real warmth in this dramatic location, even in winter. Remy Dupuy, who has been head chef since 1994, works alongside Marguerite Howley and there is a consistent house style, with a strong emphasis on local produce. Menus are well priced and there is plenty to choose from, including vegetarian dishes. Seafood is the speciality of the house in the summer months - Remy has dedicated fishermen who fish lobster, monk, scallops and other fish for him. Mouthwatering menus open with starters like prawns & monkfish in garlic butter, and also offer a duo of Inver & Bruckless Bay oysters - and non-fishy treats like pan-fried foie gras; main courses choices are extensive, including less usual dishes like stuffed rabbit saddle with black pudding & Calvados, roast pheasant (in season)

and at least one vegetarian option as well as seafood dishes - and it's good value too, even the supplement for lobster, from McSwynes Bay, is very reasonable. In winter, when seafood is less plentiful, there are more red meats, poultry and game. Service, under the direction of restaurant manager Jorg Demmerer, is friendly and accommodating - and the wonderful location, helpful staff and interesting food make this a place people keep coming back to. The wine list leans towards the Old World, particularly France, and offers good house wines, some non-alcoholic wines, an extensive selection of champagnes and plenty of half bottles. **Seats 60** (outdoors, 20). Not suitable for children after 8pm. D daily 6.30-9.30 (to 8.30 Sun), L Sun only 1.30-3.30; D from €50.00; Set Sun L €30; house wine €21; No SC. Bar menu also available - phone to check times; also wise to check restaurant times off season. Hotel closed mid Jan-mid Feb. MasterCard, Visa, Laser. **Directions:** Situated on the N56, 8km from Killybegs, 20 km from Donegal Town on the coast road to St Johns Point; first left outside Dunkineely village.

GLENVEAGH NATIONAL PARK

Glenveagh National Park (Tel: 074 9137090; www.heritageireland.ie) is open to visitors all year, although visitor facilities are seasonal (mid March-early November). The Victorian castle, which is the focal point for visitors to the Park, was donated to the State by the last private owner, Henry Plummer McIlhenny, together with most of its contents - and the gardens are among the most interesting in Ireland, with many unusual and rare plants displayed in a series of garden rooms - the Pleasure Grounds, the Walled Garden, the Italian Garden and so on; garden tours are given regularly by experienced gardeners, but guests are also free to wander freely. The Interpretative Centre includes a restaurant, but there's a treat in store if you go to the **Tea Rooms** at the castle itself; they are in an attractive stone courtyard attached to the castle and specialise in excellent home baking.
WWW.IRELAND-GUIDE.COM FOR THE BEST PLACES TO EAT, DRINK & STAY

GREENCASTLE

The ruins of the castle this "typical" Donegal holiday village and commercial fishing port was named after still stand on a rock overlooking the entrance to Lough Foyle. There is an 18-hole golf course and an excellent bathing beach locally, and a maritime museum in the village close to the place where the Greencastle - Magilligan ferry leaves from the harbour. The **Inishowen Maritime Museum** is an interesting place to visit - it runs multiple themes and exhibitions of a maritime nature from Easter until October. The **Harbourside Café** (074 938 1835) is a nice little café next to the maritime museum that is open all day in summer and offers lots of tasty little bites - sandwiches, plain, toasted and gourmet sandwiches, plus homely bakes (scones, muffins and tray bakes, which change daily). Freshly squeezed orange juice is a tempting option on the drinks list - and there's delicious Illy coffee too. Overlooks the ferry, so you can be sure not to miss it.
WWW.IRELAND-GUIDE.COM FOR THE BEST PLACES TO EAT, DRINK & STAY

Greencastle
BAR/RESTAURANT

Kealys Seafood Bar
The Harbour Greencastle Co Donegal **Tel: 074 938 1010**
kealys@iol.ie

The ferry between the fishing port of Greencastle and Magilligan Point in Northern Ireland brings many new visitors to an area that used to seem quite remote - and those in the know plan their journeys around a meal at Kealys excellent seafood restaurant. It's a low-key little place where simplicity has always been valued and, even if it's just to pop in for a daytime bowl of Tricia Kealy's Greencastle chowder and some home-baked brown bread, don't miss the opportunity of a visit to Kealys - if we did an award for seafood chowder, Kealys would take the prize! The approach to seafood is creative and balanced, seen in dishes which are modern in tone but also echo traditional Irish themes, and in which delicious local organic vegetables are used with fish to make the most of both resources. Typical dishes might include baked fillet of hake on braised fennel with a tomato & saffron butter sauce and, perhaps, a classic Irish partnership of baked salmon with a wholegrain mustard crust served on Irish spring cabbage and bacon. There will be at least one meat or poultry dish offered every day and there's always an imaginative vegetarian dish too - Gubbeen cheese & almond fritters, on a seasonal salad with honey & mustard dressing, for example. Breads are a speciality - you might find that one of them makes a

Georgina Campbell's Ireland

perfect partner for one of the range of Irish farmhouse cheeses. Service is smart and friendly - and a compact but appealing wine list offers good value, and includes a small selection of half and quarter bottles. Toilets wheelchair accessible; children welcome until 9pm. **Seats 65.** L Tue-Sun high season and Sat-Sun low season, 12.30-2.45pm; D Tue-Sun high season, Fri- Sun low season, 7-9.30pm (Sun to 8.30pm); Set D €35, also à la carte. House wine €15. Bar food served 12.30-3pm daily. Closed Mon, 2 weeks Nov, 25 Dec, Good Friday. Amex, MasterCard, Visa, Laser. **Directions:** On the harbour at Greencastle, 20 miles north of Derry City.

KILLYBEGS

Killybegs is Ireland's premier deep sea fishing port and a popular sea angling centre. For comfortable modern town centre accommodation try the well-established **Bayview Hotel** (074 973 1950; www.bayviewhotel.ie), with swimming pool and leisure centre, or the stylish newer **Tara Hotel** (074 974 1700;www.tarahotel.ie). Dining options in the area include the 200-year old farmhouse restaurant, **Kitty Kellys** (074 973 1925; www.kittykellys.com), outside the town at Largy, which has special appeal for traditionalists - in both ambience and food.
WWW.IRELAND-GUIDE.COM FOR THE BEST PLACES TO EAT, DRINK & STAY

Kincasslagh
CHARACTER PUB

Iggy's Bar
Kincasslagh Co Donegal
Tel: 074 954 3112

Just a short walk up from the harbour - it's also called the Atlantic Bar - Ann and Iggy Murray have run this delightfully unspoilt pub since 1986 and it's an all year home-from-home for many a visitor. The television isn't usually on unless there's a match and Ann makes lovely simple food for the bar, mainly seafood - home-made soups, delicious crab sandwiches and Rombouts filter coffee. Children welcome. Bar open 10-12.30 daily, light food available 12-6, Mon-Sat. No food on Sundays. Closed 25 Dec & Good Friday. **No Credit Cards. Directions:** On the corner of the Main Street, where the road turns off to the harbour.

Laghey
COUNTRY HOUSE

Coxtown Manor
Laghey Co Donegal **Tel: 074 973 4575**
coxtownmanor@oddpost.com www.coxtownmanor.com
HIDEAWAY OF THE YEAR

Just a short drive from the county town, this welcoming late Georgian house set in its own parkland is in a lovely, peaceful area close to Donegal Bay. Belgian proprietor, Edward Dewael - who fell for the property some years ago and is still in the process of upgrading it - personally ensures that everything possible is done to make guests feel at home. A pleasant wood-panelled bar with an open fire is well-stocked, notably with Belgian beers and a great selection of digestifs to accompany your after dinner coffee - and it extends into a pleasant conservatory on one side and a comfortable drawing room, also with open fire on the other. Accommodation is divided between a recently converted coach house at the back where the new bedrooms are very spacious, with plenty of room for golf gear and large items of luggage, and have excellent bathrooms to match - yet many guests still prefer the older rooms in the main house, for their character; some have countryside views and open fireplaces (turf, firelighters and matches supplied!) and they are large, comfortable and well-proportioned, with updated bathrooms, robes and Gilchrist & Soames toiletries. Children welcome (under 16 free in parents' room; cot available without charge, baby-sitting arranged). Walking; garden. No pets. **Rooms 9** (2 junior suites, all en-suite, 1 shower only, 5 no smoking, 2 ground floor). B&B €85 pps, ss €29. Breakfast buffet 8-10am; (cooked options include delicious Fermanagh dry-cured black bacon.) **Dining Room:** Although dinner is now mainly for residents, the elegant and well-appointed period dining room is very much the heart of the house and is - like the food served here - attractive yet not too formal. Friendly staff promptly offer aperitifs and menus which are priced by course and offer mostly classic dishes with an emphasis on seafood (scallops from Donegal Bay, clams and mussels from Lissadell, for example), also Thornhill duck and local Charolais beef - a sound foundation for proficient cooking: starters will certainly include at least one shellfish dish (trio of Donegal Bay lobster, North Sea shrimps and prawns on filo pastry, perhaps); main course choices are also likely to favour seafood, but may also include less usual dishes like squab pigeon alongside Donegal lamb (with thyme jus). The produce is mostly local - and of superb quality - but the style is Belgian, offering a different experience from other dining options in the area. Belgian chocolate features strongly on the dessert menu but there are lighter options. Good food and lovely service from friendly, well-trained staff ensure that a meal here will be a special experience. Restaurant open to non-residents by reservation when there is room. **Seats 30.** D Tue-Sun, 7-9pm; set D €50. House wine €22.50. Restaurant closed Sun, Mon, house closed Nov, 6 Jan-6 Feb. Amex, MasterCard, Visa, Laser. **Directions:** Main sign on N15 between Ballyshannon & Donegal Town.

LETTERKENNY

The Letterkenny area - including Rathmullan and Ramelton - provides a good central location for exploring the county; a ferry between Rathmullan and Bundoran operates in summer (45 minutes). Originally a fishing village, which developed on the banks of Lough Swilly, Letterkenny town is now one of the largest and most densely-populated towns in Donegal - and one of the fastest-growing towns in Ireland. The **Donegal County Museum** is in the town and you will also find some great wholesome home-cooked and organic food amidst the gorgeous smell of herbs and spices in **Simple Simon's** (Oliver Plunkett Road; 074 912 2382 - opposite the library - other branches in Donegal Town and Glenties), it is just the spot for lovers of herbal teas and home-made soups; while on Lower Main Street **The Yellow Pepper** (074 912 4133) is a bright and homely family-friendly restaurant located in an old shirt factory, offering wholesome food including home-grown vegetables, and cheerful service. For those who need accommodation in an hotel with leisure facilities, the new **Clanree Hotel** (074 912 4369; www.clan-reehotel.com) is a good choice, conveniently situated on the edge of town. For moderately-priced town centre hotel accommodation, try the **Letterkenny Court Hotel** (Main Street; 074 912 2977; www.letterkennycourthotel.com), or the new **Ramada Encore** (074 912 3100; www.encoreletterkenny.com), 5 minutes outside Letterkenny towards Ramelton. Travellers passing through the area who wish to avoid the town can get a bite at **The Silver Tassie Hotel** (074 912 5619; www.heblaneygroup.com), where bar food is available throughout the afternoon and evening.

WWW.IRELAND-GUIDE.COM FOR THE BEST PLACES TO EAT, DRINK & STAY

Castle Grove Country House Hotel

Letterkenny
HOTEL/RESTAURANT

Letterkenny Co Donegal **Tel: 074 915 1118**
reservations@castlegrove.com www.castlegrove.com

Parkland designed by "Capability" Brown in the mid-18th century creates a wonderful setting for Raymond and Mary Sweeney's lovely period house overlooking the lough. Castlegrove is undoubtedly the first choice for discerning visitors to the area, especially executives with business in Letterkenny; it is, as Mary Sweeney says, an oasis of tranquillity. Constant improvement is the policy and recent years have seen a number of additions, always carefully designed and furnished with antiques to feel like part of the main house. The original walled garden is under restoration as part of an on-going development of the gardens which will continue for several years. Public rooms include two gracious drawing rooms, each with an open fire, and a proper bar. Bedrooms are spacious and elegantly furnished to a high standard with antiques and, where practical, bathrooms have walk-in showers as well as full bath. Good breakfasts include a choice of fish as well as traditional Irish breakfast, home-made breads and preserves. Mary Sweeney's personal supervision ensures an exceptionally high standard of maintenance and housekeeping and staff are friendly and helpful. Two boats belonging to the house are available for fishing on Lough Swilly and there is a special arrangement with three nearby golf clubs. Conference/banqueting (25/50). House available for private use (family occasions, board meetings etc) Not suitable for children under 12. No pets. **Rooms 14** (1 suite, 2 junior suites, 2 shower only, 2 disabled, all no-smoking) B&B about €80 pps, no ss. *Weekends/ short breaks available. Open all year except Christmas. **The Green Room:** This large room is in a recent extension, but furnished in keeping with the original house, with generous classically appointed, well-spaced tables. Carefully sourced specialist and local ingredients are used: many of the herbs, vegetables and soft fruits are home grown, the seafood - such as Swilly oysters - is local, and local meats are regularly used. Since Peter Cheesman joined as head chef in 2007, the cooking is creative and yet simplified in style and full of flavour which makes for some very enjoyable dishes; examples which attracted particular praise on a recent visit included two lamb dishes - a starter of Connemara air-dried lamb with sheep's cheese, beetroot pickles, beet shoots and baby beetroot, and a superb main course of County Wexford lamb neck fillet with slow cooked confit shoulder, parsnip purée, roast shallots & rosemary gravy. These dishes are much simpler on the plate than they sound, and absolutely delicious. Good desserts are a little on the rich side but irresistible - a warm rhubarb and apricot crumble is crunchy and juicy, and comes with crème anglaise and lovely vanilla ice cream. Not suitable for children under 10 after 7pm. **Seats 50** (private room, 15). B'fst 8-10 daily, L 12.30-2 Mon-Sat, D 6.30-9 daily. Reservations required. Closed L Sun; 23-29 Dec. Amex, Diners, MasterCard, Visa, Laser. Directions: R245 off main road to Letterkenny. ◇

Letterkenny
RESTAURANT

Lemon Tree Restaurant

39 Lower Main Street Letterkenny Co Donegal
Tel: 074 912 5788

féile bia With its pretty lemon canopies, lemon painted and tiled frontage and colourful hanging flower baskets, this popular family-run restaurant in the centre of Letterkenny is easy to find. Inside it is warm and welcoming, with terracotta tiles, wooden furniture and peach sponged walls lending warmth, and an open kitchen adding buzz as you can watch brothers, Gary and Christopher Molloy at work. The restaurant is Féile Bia certified and all meats are Irish sourced; fresh fish is a special feature and unusually these days - everything is made freshly on site, including all breads, pastries, pastas and desserts. The house style is a mixture of traditional Irish and French classic, influenced by country house cooking: a wide choice of starters might include hand made ravioli of Irish cheeses with roast vegetables and a fresh pepper coulis and, among the dozen or so main courses, there may be an unusual tasting plate of grilled fish. An early dinner menu offers good value and includes home-baked pizzas as well as a wide selection of seafood, poultry and meats. (***The Oak Tree**, on Port Road, is sister restaurant in the town and offers the same menu, but adds a bistro style menu during the day). Children welcome; **Seats 40;** reservations recommended. Open for D daily from 5-10pm (to 9.30pm Sun); L Sun only, 1-2.30pm. Closed Good Fri, 24-26 Dec. MasterCard, Visa, Laser. **Directions:** Centre of town.

Letterkenny
HOTEL

Radisson SAS Hotel Letterkenny

The Loop Road Letterkenny Co Donegal **Tel: 074 919 4444**
martina.gallagher@radissonsas.com www.radissonsas.com

féile bia This fine modern hotel on the edge of Letterkenny town is well-placed for short breaks in one of Ireland's most beautiful areas, and within easy walking distance of the town; although it has been surrounded by building sites, new shops and other amenities have now opened nearby (Marks & Spencer is a useful landmark just opposite the entrance). It is a pleasing contemporary building: an atrium lobby with maple panelling and leather furniture lends a great sense of space and sets a smart tone for the rest of the hotel. There's a mix of suites and rooms, all featuring modern facilities and very nice bathrooms - Business Class rooms also have a desk area with broadband. The hotel's **TriBeCca Restaurant** was an immediate success; an early dinner menu offers great value and breakfast, which is also served here, is well above the usual hotel offering. Under the watchful eye of General Manager Ray Hingston, this is a well-managed hotel, and a pleasant place to stay. Children welcome (cot available free of charge). No pets. Golf, gardens, walking, wind surfing etc nearby. Parking (200). Business centre. Conference/banqueting (450/300). Leisure centre (17m swimming pool, steam room, sauna.) **Rooms 114** (1 suite, 2 junior suites, 3 shower only, 6 disabled.) Lift. 24 hr room service. B&B about €74.50, ss €14.50. TriBeCa: Seats 80. D Tue-Sat, 6-9.30; L Sun only 12.30-3. Set D about €32.50, also à la carte; Set Sun L about €21.50. House wine about €21. SC discretionary. Bar meals available 12.30-8 daily. Amex, MasterCard, Visa, Laser. **Directions:** Drive to Letterkenny town, turn left at Tourist Office - hotel on right. ◇

Lough Eske
HOTEL/RESTAURANT

Harvey's Point Country Hotel

Lough Eske Donegal Co Donegal **Tel: 074 972 2208**
info@harveyspoint.com www.harveyspoint.com

Blessed with one of Ireland's most beautiful locations, on the shores of Lough Eske, this well-managed hotel was first opened by the Gysling family in the late 1980s, with chalet-style buildings linked by covered walkways and pergolas creating a distinctly alpine atmosphere reminiscent of their native Switzerland - a style that suited the site well, with the open low-level design allowing views of the lough and mountains from most areas of the hotel. Other than its location, the most outstanding feature of this hotel has always been the friendliness and helpfulness of the staff, and that is still its great strength. Otherwise, guests re-visiting today will find many changes, and a far more luxurious establishment: rooms in the new 40-room extension may not all have a lake view - but acres of space, six foot beds and a circular bath the size of a small swimming pool will please many guests. However, the older rooms - which are tucked away in front of the extension, along the ground floor corridor - may be of more interest to those in the know; although less luxurious, they are very comfortable and will appeal if you would enjoy being closer to the countryside, with access to the lough. * A spa and swimming pool are planned for 2008/9, also a new conference venue. Conference/banqueting 300/400; video conferencing. Treatment rooms (hair, beauty, holistic). Not very suitable for children (no facilities). Pets permitted. Garden. **Rooms 42** (4 suites, 38 junior suites, 20 ground floor, 2 disabled). Lift. Turndown service. Open all year. **Restaurant:** The bar and restaurant areas are still their old selves: a welcoming log fire sets the tone in the bar, where menus are promptly offered by friendly staff, and in the restaurant - a large room, extending right down to the foreshore - elegantly appointed tables are set up to take advantage of the beautiful view across the lough and, perhaps, the hotel's pet geese coming in at feeding time. Paul Montgomery has been head chef since 2006 and he offers a number of menus, including a Celtic Trail dinner menu, with dishes inspired by all the Celtic regions, and the Green Garden Trail, for vegetarians; also a simpler but attractive Cuisine Art lunch menu. His classically toned menus offer an extensive choice and look a little complicated, but the cooking is assured and well up to the theatrical nuances of the fine dining experience laid on by attentive and well-trained restaurant staff. The restaurant is also open for lunch, every day except Saturday, and Room Service and Bar Snack menus are also offered. **Seats 100** (private room, 50). Air conditioning. Toilets wheelchair accessible. L 12.30-2.30pm (Sun 12-4) & D daily 6.30-9.30pm. Set D €55; Set L €35; house wine from €19.50; no SC. Off season (Nov-Mar), closed D Sun, all Mon & Tue. MasterCard, Visa, Laser. * A bar menu is also served daily, 12-5.30pm. MasterCard, Visa, Laser. **Directions:** N15 /N56 from Donegal Town - take signs for Lough Eske & hotel. (6km from Donegal Town.)

Lough Eske
B&B

Rhu-Gorse

Lough Eske Co Donegal **Tel: 074 972 1685**
rhugorse@iol.ie www.lougheske.com

Beautifully located, with stunning views over Lough Eske (and windows built to take full advantage of them), Grainne McGettigan's modern house may not be not architecturally outstanding but it has some very special attributes, notably the warmth and hospitality of Grainne herself, and a lovely room with picture windows and a big fireplace, where guests can relax. Bedrooms and bathrooms are all ship-shape and residents can have afternoon tea as well as breakfast, although not evening meals; however Harvey's Point is very close (see entry), and Donegal town is only a short drive. Animals are central to Rhu-Gorse, which is named after a much-loved pedigree dog bred by Grainne's father-in-law (a descendant now follows her around everywhere), and one of her special interests is breeding horses: not your average B&B, but a comfort-able, hospitable and very interesting base for a walking holiday or touring the area. Golf nearby. Children welcome (under 3s free in parents' room). Pets allowed in some areas. Garden. **Rooms 3** (2 shower only, 1 family room, all no smoking). B&B about €40, ss €10. Closed 31 Oct-31 Mar. MasterCard, Visa, Laser. **Directions:** Take N15 /N56 from Donegal Town. Take signs for Lough Eske & Harvey's Point Hotel. Pick up signs for Rhu-Gorse. ◊

Malin
HOTEL

Malin Hotel

Malin Co Donegal **Tel: 074 937 0606**
info@malinhotel.ie www.malinhotel.ie

féile bia Patrick and Fiona Loughrey's attractive hotel has been extensively upgraded since they took it over in 2003, and extended to provide four new bedrooms and a lift. The bar is a popular meeting place, and neat bedrooms have phones, tea/coffee and TV; the older rooms have been re-designed and, along with their bathrooms, completely refurbished. While some rooms are not very large, they are inviting and comfortable - offering a friendly and moderately priced base for exploring this beautiful area. The hotel's **Jack Yeats Restaurant** is earning a good reputation; however food hours are variable due to the seasonality of the business (bar meals usually all day from 12 noon in high summer, with dinner daily from 6pm); the midweek dinner menu (Wed-Fri, 6 -9.15) offers great value.

Conference/banqueting (200/300); free broadband wi/fi; secretarial services. Walking. Children welcome (under 4s free in parents' room, cot available free of charge, baby sitting arranged). No pets. **Rooms 18** (1 suite, 7 executive, 11 shower only, 1 family room, 1 for disabled, all no smoking). Lift. Limited room service. B&B €65 pps, ss €10. Closed 25 Dec. MasterCard, Visa, Laser. **Directions:** Overlooking the village green in Malin town.

Moville Area
HOTEL
🏨 Ⓝ

Carlton Redcastle Hotel & Spa

Redcastle Moville Inishowen Co Donegal **Tel: 074 938 5555**
info@carltonredcastle.ie www.carltonredcastle.ie

Beautifully located overlooking Lough Foyle, on the shore side of the scenic route that runs up the eastern coast of the Inishowen peninsula, this 4* hotel is near the traditional holiday town of Moville yet, surrounded by extensive grounds and its own 9-hole parkland golf course, it's in a world of its own. Popular with locals as well as people on leisure breaks, it can be very busy as weekends but midweek short breaks offer good value and a much calmer atmosphere. It's an attractive hotel, with spacious public areas and good amenities, and the restaurant (Waters Edge) and Thalasso Spa, in particular, make full use of the lovely waterside location. Bedrooms and suites, which have wonderful views, are smartly decorated and finished to a high standard. **Rooms 93.** B&B about €70-135pps, suites from €180. Midweek breaks offered. Open all year except Christmas. Helipad. MasterCard, Visa, Laser. **Directions:** From Letterkenny or Derry, R238 to Moville - Inisowen Paninsula.

Ramelton
COUNTRY HOUSE

Ardeen

Ramelton Co Donegal **Tel: 074 915 1243**
ardeenbandb@eircom.net www.ardeenhouse.com

Overlooking Lough Swilly, and set in its own grounds on the edge of the heritage town of Ramelton, Anne Campbell's mid-nineteenth century house is well-located for touring Donegal and Glenveagh National Park. It is not too grand and has the comfortable atmosphere of a family home - the drawing room and dining room are both furnished with antiques and have open fires, making this a very warm and comfortable place to return to after a day out. Individually decorated bedrooms with views over the lough or nearby hills all have their own character and are charmingly furnished (Anne is very handy with a sewing machine and time available in the winter is well used for guests' comfort). No dinners, but Anne can recommend pubs and restaurants nearby. Children welcome (under 2s free in parents' room, cots available free of charge). Garden, tennis. No pets. *Self-catering also available in the 'Old Stables'; details on request. **Rooms 5** (4 en-suite with shower, 1 twin has private bathroom, all no smoking, 1 family room). B&B €35 (standard); en-suite €40 pps, ss €10. Closed Oct-Easter. MasterCard, Visa. **Directions:** Follow river to Town Hall, turn right; 1st house on right.

Ramelton
COUNTRY HOUSE

Frewin

Rectory Road Ramelton Co Donegal **Tel: 074 915 1246**
flaxmill@indigo.ie www.frewinhouse.com

Thomas and Regina Coyle restored this large Victorian house with the greatest attention to period detail and guests have the opportunity to drink in the atmosphere on arrival while having a cup of tea in the little book-lined library, where the old parish safe is still set in the wall. Bedrooms vary, as is the way in old houses, but they are all beautifully furnished with antiques, and snowy white bedlinen - and a robe provided in case of night-time forays along the corridor (one bathroom is private, but not en-suite). A delicious breakfast, including freshly baked breads warm from the oven, is taken communally at a long polished table. This beautiful house is most unusual, notably because Thomas Coyle specialises in restoring old buildings and is a collector by nature - much of his collection finds a place in the house, some is for sale in an outbuilding at the back. Not suitable for children under 8. No pets. Garden. **Rooms 4** (3 shower only, 1 with private bath, 1 family room, all no smoking). B&B about €75-80, ss about €15. D about €35 (by arrangement). Closed 23 Dec-1 Jan. MasterCard, Visa. **Directions:** Take R245 from Letterkenny. Travel 7 miles approx and take right turn on approach to Ramelton. Located 400 yards on right. ◇

RATHMULLAN

An attractive small town on Lough Swilly, Rathmullan makes a good base for exploring the Fanad peninsula and as a ferry runs between the little harbour and Buncrana in summer (mid May to September; from Buncrana every 1 hr 20 mins from 9am-7.40pm; from Rathmullan every 1 hr 20 mins from 9.40am - 8.10pm), the Inishowen peninsula, Derry city and the north Antrim coast are also cessible. Long sandy beaches and availability of holiday homes and other accommodation make it popular choice for family holidays, and Portsalon golf club - one of Ireland's oldest golf clubs, unded in 1891 - is just a few miles up the coast.

An Bonnán Buí

athmullan
ESTAURANT

Pier Road Rathmullan Co Donegal **Tel: 074 915 8453**
bonnanbui@yahoo.ie   www.bonnanbui.com

cked into a side street in Rathmullan village, Martin Kelly and Monica Santos' informal restaunt has real draw-you-in appeal from the road, with its attractive frontage, and the warm friendly mosphere inside is equally pleasing to summer visitors and locals alike. Menus offer familiar Irish d Mediterranean influenced food, but Monica is Brazilian so - uniquely in this region - you will so find authentic South American cooking here. Open Thu-Sun, 5.30-9.30; Sun 1-5 (L & light eals/snacks). **Directions:** In Rathmullan village, on the road opposite the pier; on left when going vay from the sea. ◇

Fort Royal Hotel

athmullan
OTEL/RESTAURANT

Rathmullan Co Donegal **Tel: 074 91 58100**
fortroyal@eircom.net   www.fortroyalhotel.com

verlooking the sea, and with direct access to a sandy beach, the Fletcher family's attractive Victorian tel is set in 19 acres of lawn and woodland above Lough Swilly - and has perhaps the best location any establishment in the area. It's a comfortable, quiet base for family holidays or visiting places of cal interest, including Glenveagh National Park and Glebe House, the late artist Derek Hill's former me. Public rooms are spacious, well-proportioned and comfortably furnished in country house style, th big armchairs and open fires. Well-appointed bedrooms (all en-suite) are designed for relaxation d enjoy a pleasant outlook over wooded grounds. Croquet, tennis, golf, pitch & putt are available on e premises, and activities such as riding and fishing are nearby. It's an ideal place for those seeking quiet break, and many will like it all the better because it doesn't offer too much in the way of facilies. Special interest breaks offered. (A 3-day mid-week golf package includes a round of golf at osapenna and one at Portsalon) Children welcome (under 4 free in parents' room, cot available thout charge, baby sitting arranged). Pets permitted. Garden.* Three attractive self-catering cottages e available in the hotel grounds; details on application. **Rooms 15** (all en-suite & no smoking). hildren welcome (under 5s free in parents' room, cot available without charge, babysitting arranged). ets permitted in some area. Garden. B&B €95pps, ss €35. Hotel closed Nov-Mar. **Restaurant:** This tractive traditional dining room overlooking lawns and woodland is well-appointed, with crisp white nen and fresh flowers. Much of the food at Fort Royal comes from the hotel's own walled gardens d is cooked by Tim Fletcher, who has been head chef since 1995 and proprietor since 2000. His ghtly dinner menus offer about five classic choices on each course, considerably priced to allow two-three-course options. Tea or coffee is served in the lounge afterwards - or, on fine evenings, you ould take it outside and enjoy the view down over the lough. Staff are very pleasant and helpful. An formative, fairly priced wine list offers several dessert wines and half a dozen well-chosen half ottles. **Seats 50.** Not suitable for children under 10. D daily, 7.30-9 (Sun D is a cold buffet). Set D 45. House wine €16.50. *Light lunches may be available in the bar or at tables in the garden, 12-daily. Phone ahead to check availability. Amex, Diners, MasterCard, Visa, Laser. **Directions:** amelton road from Letterkenny, straight on to Rathmullan. ◇

Rathmullan House

athmullan
OUNTRY HOUSE/RESTAURANT

Rathmullan Co Donegal **Tel: 074 915 8188**
info@rathmullanhouse.com   www.rathmullanhouse.com

Set in lovely gardens on the shores of Lough Swilly, this gracious nineteenth century house is fairly grand, with public areas which include three elegant drawing rooms, but it's not too formal - and there's a cellar bar which can be very relaxed. It was built as a summer house by the Batt banking family of Belfast in the 1800s, and has been run as a country house hotel since 1961 by the Wheeler family. Recently, under the energetic management of William and Mark Wheeler, and Mark's wife, Mary, an impressive extension was completed to a design that is in sympathy with the surroundings. Here they have ten very desirable, individually decorated bedrooms, and The Gallery, a state of the art conference facility for up to 80 delegates. Bedrooms in the original house vary in size, decor, outlook and cost, but all are comfortably furnished in traditional country house style. Donegal has an other-worldliness that is increasingly hard to capture in the traditional family holiday areas and, although now larger Rathmullan House still retains a laid-back charm and that special sense of place - and it is greatly to their credit that the Wheeler family have developed their business (and extended the season) without compromising the essential character of this lovely place.* Rathmullan House was our Country House of the Year in 2007. Conference/banqueting (80). Swimming pool, steam room, tennis. Children welcome; (free under 12 months, cot €15, baby sitting arranged). Pets permitted by arrangement Pets permitted by arrangement (special pet-friendly room available). Gardens. **Rooms 32** (21 with separate bath & shower, 9 ground floor, 1 for disabled). B&B €140 pps, ss €45, SC 10%. **The Weeping Elm:** The dining room was revamped and extended in the recent renovations, but the famous tented ceiling (designed by the late Liam McCormick, well known for his striking Donegal churches) has been retained. It is a pleasing room that makes the most of the garden outlook - including a formal garden beside the extension, which is maturing nicely - and provides a fine setting for Tommy Tuhkanen's modern Irish cooking, as well as the tremendous breakfasts for which Rathmullan is justly famous. Cooking here is upbeat traditional and meticulously-sourced menus are based on the very best of local and artisan foods - and fresh produce from their own restored walled garden. There are many beautifully conceived combination dishes, and you can look forward to specialities like Fanad Head crab plate, assiette of Pat Patton's Rathmullan lamb, with loin, braised shoulder, kidney and mini shepherd's pie, with rosemary gravy, roast carrots fennel and, perhaps, a fine farmhouse cheese selection or a refreshing compôte of garden fruits with carrageen pudding. (Both cheeses and carrageen are equally at home as part of the legendary Rathmullan breakfast too.) And a particularly attractive feature of Rathmullan is the Children's Menu - a proper little person's version of the adult menu, with lots of choices and no concessions to 'popular' fare, this is education on a plate. Like everything else here, the wine list is meticulously sourced and informative - unusually, the alcohol content is given along with other details; it also includes half a dozen organic & bio-dynamic wines, lots of lovely bubblies, a wide choice of half bottles and a section dedicated to wines selected to complement the menu, some of them available by the glass. All this plus caring service and a beautiful location.. Rathmullan is in peak form. **Seats 100** (private room, 30); D daily 7-8.45 (to 9.30 Fri/Sat); Set €50/55, 2/3 courses; house wine from €22; SC 10%. *Informal meals are available in Batts Bar & Café and the Cellar Bar: L, 1-2.30pm daily; Early D is also available in The Cellar Bar, 5-8pm daily in summer. Children welcome before 8pm (children's menu, high chair and baby changing facilities available). Closed 7 Jan-9 Feb. Amex, MasterCard, Visa, Laser. **Directions:** Letterkenny to Ramelton - turn right to Rathmullan at the bridge, through village and turn right to hotel.

Rathmullan
RESTAURANT WITH ROOMS

The Water's Edge

Rathmullan Co Donegal **Tel: 074 915 818**
thewatersedge@eircom.net www.thewatersedge.

Neil and Mandy Blaney's large bar and restaurant with rooms is a brand new conversion of an old building and really lives up to its name as diners in the vast dining room on the edge of Lough Swilly can gaze out at one of the finest views to be had anywhere. Arriving guests get a warm welcome and although everything is gleaming glass, light polished wood and shiny steel, carpeted floors keep the noise down and soft lighting from walls and overhead beams soften the atmosphere. Tables are set up simply but attractively, and almost all tables have a view; menus offer a range of dishes divided even between meat and fish (Donegal sirloin steak or roast tail of monkfish), with something imaginative for vegetarians. A well-balanced wine list offers good value. **Accommodation:** Well-appointed room complete with flat screen television offer fine views, and the spacious en-suite bathrooms have (small full baths. A welcome place to stay in this lovely area. Banqueting, 120. Children welcome (under 10 free in parents' room, cot available free of charge); **Rooms 10** (2 suites, 3 ground floor, 1 for disabled all no smoking); B&B €75 pps, ss €35. Closed 25 Dec. MasterCard, Visa, Laser. **Directions:** On your right as you enter Rathmullan from the Letterkenny direction.

Rossnowlagh
HOTEL/RESTAURANT

Sand House Hotel

Rossnowlagh Co Donegal **Tel: 071 985 1777**
info@sandhouse.ie www.sandhouse.ie

féile bia Perched on the edge of a stunning sandy beach two miles long, the Britton family's famous hotel lost its trademark crenellated roof-line a few years ago, but emerged with an elegant new look, reminiscent of a French chateau. Wonderful sea views and easy access to the beach have always been the great attractions of The Sand House, which started life as a fishing lodge in the 1830s and completed its latest metamorphosis with a new floor of bedrooms, a panoramic lift (with the best view in the house), a new boardroom and marine beauty spa. Existing bedrooms were also refurbished; all are very comfortable, with excellent bathrooms - and everyone can enjoy the sea view from the sun deck. Things that never change here include the welcoming fire in the foyer, exceptional housekeeping - and the excellent hospitality. Golf is a major attraction for guests at The Sand House, which is a member of The Emerald Triangle (three strategically placed establishments offering great golf experiences: the other two are Rathsallagh, Co Wicklow, and Glenlo Abbey, Co Galway, see entries). Also partners in 'Play 3 Great Golf Courses in Ireland's North-West' (Donegal GC, Bundoran, Castle Hume). Spa; fishing, cycling, tennis, walking, tennis on site; horse riding, boating and many other activities available nearby. Details on application. Conferences (100). Children welcome (under 5s free in parents' room, cots available without charge, baby sitting arranged). Pets permitted by arrangement. **Rooms 50** (1 suite, 2 junior suites, 5 executive, 5 shower only, 25 no-smoking, 1 disabled). Lift. 24 hour room service. B&B €100pps, no ss. SC discretionary. Closed Dec & Jan. **Seashell Restaurant:** The restaurant is rather unexpectedly at the front of the hotel but is well-appointed, in keeping with the rest of the hotel. John McGarrigle, who has been with the hotel since 2000, presents seasonal 5-course dinner menus, changed daily; fresh seafood and locally sourced lamb and beef (also game, in season) provide the foundation for a traditional repertoire, with interesting side dishes an unusual strength. Finish with a choice of Irish cheeses or hotel-style desserts - if you ask very nicely you might be able to have them up in the conservatory, overlooking the sea. Staff are helpful and attentive. Good choice of wines by the glass. *Soup and sandwiches are also available in the bar at lunchtime, every day except Sunday. **Seats 80.** Children welcome. D daily 7-8.30, L Sun only, 1-2.30. Set Sun L €30; set D €50; house wines from €20. SC discretionary. Closed Dec & Jan. Amex, MasterCard, Visa, Laser. **Directions:** Coast road from Ballyshannon to Donegal Town.

Rossnowlagh Area
GUESTHOUSE

Heron's Cove

Creevy Rossnowlagh Co Donegal **Tel: 071 982 2070**
info@heronscove.ie www.heronscove.ie

For those who prefer to stay at a smaller place with a more intimate atmosphere, Seoirse and Maeve O'Toole's fine 10-bedroom guesthouse at the picturesque little harbour of Creevy Pier has offered a comfortable and hospitable base at a moderate price since opening in 2006, and could be just the ticket. Close to Rossnowlagh beach, and just 10 minutes drive from Donegal Golf Club at Murvagh, it has easy access to many other activities too, including sea angling, surfing and hillwalking; guests also have complimentary use of leisure facilities at the Mill Park Hotel in Donegal Town. The family also operates a restaurant specialising in steak and seafood at Heron's Cove, which is open to non-residents. Short breaks offered. Free broadband wi/fi. **Rooms 10** (6 shower only, all no smoking); children welcome (under 3s free in parents room, cot available free of charge). B&B €75, ss €23. Closed 23-27 Dec, 3 weeks Jan. MasterCard, Visa, Laser. **Directions:** At roundabout on Donegal town side of Ballyshannon Bypass (N15), follow sign for Rossnowlagh (R231), approx 3km (2 miles) from that roundabout.

TORY ISLAND

The Gaeltacht (Irish-speaking) island of Tory lies eight miles off the north-west corner of Donegal and, in spite of its exposed position, has been inhabited for four thousand years. Perhaps not surprisingly, this other-worldly island managed quite well without an hotel until recently, but once Patrick and Berney Doohan's **Ostan Thoraig** (074 913 5920) was built in 1994 it quickly became the centre of the island's social activities - or, to be more precise, **The People's Bar** in the hotel quickly became the centre. The hotel is beside the little harbour where the ferries bring in visitors from mainland port. Although simple, it provides comfortable en-suite accommodation with telephone and television. The hotel is open from Easter to October. A special feature of the island is its 'school' of primitive art (founded with the support of well-known artist the late Derek Hill of nearby **Glebe House and Gallery** Church Hill). It even has a king as a founder member: the present King of the Tory is Patsy Dan Rogers who has exhibited his colourful primitive paintings of the island throughout the British Isles and America. A tiny gallery on Tory provides exhibition space for the current group of island artists. Tory accessible by ferry (subject to weather conditions) from several mainland ports: telephone 074 91 1320 for details, or ask at the hotel.

WWW.IRELAND-GUIDE.COM FOR THE BEST PLACES TO EAT, DRINK & STAY

Tremone
FARMHOUSE

Trean House

Tremone Lecamy Inishowen Co Donegal **Tel: 074 936 712**
treanhouse@oceanfree.net www.treanhouse.co

Way out on the Inishowen peninsula, Joyce and Mervyn Norris's farmhouse is tucked into a sheltered corner in stone-walled countryside beside the sea. Surrounded by a large garden with mature trees and welcoming flowers, it is a substantial house and offers a comfortable base for a relaxing away-from-it all holiday in a homely atmosphere. Guests have the use of a cosy sitting room with an open fire and simple country bedrooms have everything that is needed - the only room without an en-suite shower room has a private bathroom nearby - and, if any other guest prefers a bath, it can be used by arrangement. Joyce's home cooking is another attraction - she makes breakfasts that will really set you up for the day; no dinners but Joyce will advise on the best places to eat in the evening. Children welcome (under 3s free in parents' room, cot available without charge). Pets permitted in some areas by arrangement. Garden. **Rooms 4** (all en-suite, 1 with bath & separate shower, 3 shower only & all no smoking). B&B €32, ss €12. No SC. Open all year except Christmas. MasterCard, Visa. **Directions** From Moville follow R238 5kms, turn right & follow house signs.

COUNTY GALWAY

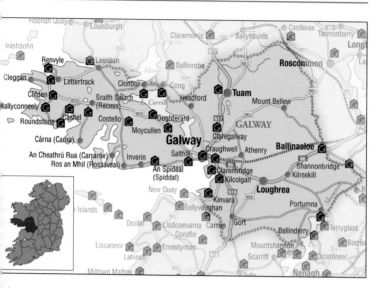

alway surpasses many other parts of Ireland in the spectacular variety and charm of its many scenic utes. But it also has more to offer in the way of slightly offbeat expeditions and experiences, in addi- on to all the usual visual attractions of Ireland's Atlantic seaboard.

isiting the Aran Islands across the mouth of Galway Bay, for instance, can be done by air as well as y sea. However, as the much-visited Aran Islands have shown, the presence of an air service doesn't eem to lessen the popularity of the ferries, and people often seem to think that you haven't properly sited an island unless you go there by boat. Then, too, there are many coastal boat trips, including n informative seaborne tour from Killary Harbour on the county's northwest coast, Ireland's only enuine fjord, while Lough Corrib is also served by miniature cruise liners.

s for sport ashore, the Galway Races at the end of July have developed into a six day meeting which firmly established as Ireland's premier summer horse racing event, while the Ballinasloe iternational Horse Fair in the Autumn is simply unique. It dates back more than 280 years.

his has to be Ireland's most generous county, for in effect you get two counties for the price of one. iey're neatly divided by the handsome sweep of island-studded Lough Corrib, with the big country of iany mountains to the west, and rolling farmland to the east. As a bonus, where the Corrib tumbles into alway Bay, we find one of Ireland's - indeed, one of Europe's - most vibrant cities. Galway is a bustling ace which cheerfully sees itself as being linked to Spain and the great world beyond the Atlantic.

he theme of double value asserts itself in other ways. As Autumn ripeness makes its presence lt, the county and city provide not one, but two, Oyster Festivals. Once September has ushered the traditional oyster season, Galway's long and distinguished connection with the splendid ivalve mollusc is celebrated first with the Clarenbridge Oyster Festival on the southeast shore of alway Bay, and then a week or so later, right in the heart of the city with the International Galway yster Festival itself.

ough Corrib is both a geographical and psychological divide. East of it, there's flatter country, home hunting packs of mythic lore. West of the Corrib - which used itself to be a major throughfare, and now as ever a place of angling renown - you're very quickly into the high ground and moorland which weep up to the Twelve Bens and other splendid peaks, wonderful mountains which enthusiasts would aim as the most beautiful in all Ireland.

neir heavily indented coastline means this region is Connemara, the Land of the Sea, where earth, ck and ocean intermix in one of Ireland's most extraordinary landscapes. Beyond, to the south, the ran Islands are a place apart, yet they too are part of the Galway mix in this fantastical county which as its own magical light coming in over the sea. And yet, all its extraordinary variety happens within ery manageable distances – Galway is a universe within one day's drive.

Georgina Campbell's Ireland

Local Attractions & Information

GALWAY CITY

Arts Centre 47 Dominick Street	091 565 88€
Galway Airport	091 755 56⁹
Galway Arts Festival (July)	091 565 88€
Galway Crystal Heritage Centre	091 757 31¹
Galway Races (late July/early August, Sept & Oct)	091 753 87(
Galway International Oyster Festival (late September)	091 527 282 / 522 066 / 587 99²
Kenny's Bookshops & Art Galleries High Street	091 562 73⁹
O'Brien Shipping (Aran Island Ferries)	091 568 90⁷
Tourist Information	091 537 70(
Town Hall Theatre	091 569 755 / 569 77⁷

CO GALWAY

Aran Islands Heritage Centre	099 61 35⁵
Aran Islands Ferries from Rossaveal	091 568 903 / 561 76⁷
Aran Islands Flights from Inverin Airport	091 593 03⁴
Aughrim Battle of Aughrim Centre	090 967 393⁹
Ballinasloe International Horse Fair (Sept/Oct)	090 964 345²
Clarenbridge Oyster Festival (September)	091 796 34²
Clifden Connemara Pony Show (mid August)	095 21 86²
Clifden Connemara Safari - Walking & Islands	095 21 07³
Gort Thoor Ballylee (Yeats' Tower)	091 631 43⁶
Inishbofin Arts Festival (Biennial, September)	095 45 90⁴
Inishbofin Ferries (Cleggan)	095 44 64²
Killary Cruises on Connemara Lady	091 566 736 / 1800 415 15.
Kinvara Dungaire Castle C/O Shannon Heritage Centre	061 360 78⁸
Letterfrack Connemara Bog Week (May)	095 43 44.
Letterfrack Connemara Sea Week (October)	095 43 44.
Letterfrack Kylemore Abbey & Gardens	095 41 14⁶
Loughrea Dartfield Horse Museum	091 843 96⁶
Roundstone Roundstone Arts Week (July)	095 35 83.
Roundstone Traditional bodhran makers	095 35 80⁶
Tuam Little Mill (last intact cornmill in area)	093 24 141 / 087 412 120

GALWAY

Galway is a vibrant, youthful city with an international reputation for exceptional foods - notably th€ native Irish oysters, which are a speciality of the Clarenbridge area and celebrated at the annu. Oyster Festival there in September. The area is renowned for its seafood, especially shellfish, an speciality produce of all kinds - including local cheeses, fruit and vegetables, and specialities tha do the rounds of other markets around the country - is on sale at the famous city centre **Saturda Market** (beside St Nicholas Church; all day Sat & also Sun afternoon). Restaurants in the area shov case local produce, and - although there is at present no major dining destination here - there ar many good places to eat in both city and county. In addition to the establishments described, it ma be useful to know about the following: Mike and Breda Guilfoyle's hospitable guesthouse **Ardaw House** (College Road; 091 568 833) is convenient to the university and just a few minutes walk fro Eyre Square; accommodation is comfortably furnished, with good amenities. **Westwood House Hot** (091 521 442; www.westwoodhousehotel.com)is on the edge of the city and set back from the roa - the N59 for Clifden; this well-managed hotel has recently completed a major upgrade and offers very good standard of accommodation for business or leisure at fair prices. For budget accommod. tion, consider the city centre **Jurys Inn** (Quay Street; 091 566 444;www.jurysinn.com) which is in superb riverside location beside **Spanish Arch**, and adjacent to the multistorey carpark. East of the cit on the Tuam road, **Travelodge** (091 781 400; www.travelodge.ie) offers simple, clean, budget accon modation without service. Interesting restaurants in Galway are numerous, but some offering different experience from those described separately include the highly regarded Japanese restaura **Kappa-Ya** on Middle Street Mews; the ever-popular **Da Tang Noodle House** (091 788638) on Midd Street and **Viña Mara Restaurant & Wine Bar** (091 561 610; www.vinamara.com), also on Midd reet, which brings a flavour of Spain to the city and specialises in seafood. **Martine's Quay Street ine Bar** (091 091 565 662; www.winebar.ie), which is in the same family ownership as the famous cDonagh's fish shop and restaurant, also on Quay Street. Good daytime cafés abound: **Budding afé** (091 588821) is an unusual little place at the back of Heneghan's Flower Shop on Sea Road; r soup, sandwiches, good home baking, salads and desserts in an unfussy atmosphere, **Antons** ather Griffin Road; 091 582 067) has been feeding a loyal lunch time trade for many years, so it's ist the kind of place visitors need to know about. **Cobblestone Café** (091 56727) on Kirwan's Lane just the spot for vegetarians; **Delight Gourmet Food Bar** (091 567823) on Upper Abbeygate Street sts delicious Illy coffee, smoothies and imaginative sandwiches among many options; **Revive Coffee Rejuice** (Eyre Street; 091 533 779) is a popular day-time rendezvous offering a wide choice of uality snacks etc, based on fresh produce, cooked simply and served at tables, or at a counter - or a covered courtyard with hanging baskets of flowers at the back. **The Bridge Mills** (Dominick treet; 091 566231) has been leased by the **Holywell Italian Café** 'chain', formerly of Ballyvaughan; ey offer a simple package of pizzas and half a dozen pasta dishes with limited starters and desserts reasonable prices. For good Indian food, **Tulsi**, on Buttermilk Walk, Middle Street (091 564 31;www.tulsiindian.com) is a sister restaurant of the reliable Dublin restaurant of the same name; nd, for style and informal fare (pizzas, pastas etc) at a reasonable price, head for **Milano** on Middle treet (091 568 488). Lovers of traditional Irish pubs should head for **Tigh Neachtain** (Cross Street; 91 568 820) or **Naughton's** which is one of Galway's oldest pubs; quite unspoilt, it has great charm, n open fire and a friendly atmosphere - and the pint is good too. But perhaps the nicest thing of all the way an impromptu traditional music session can get going at the drop of a hat. (**Ard Bia** restaurant is on the first floor - see entry).

WW.IRELAND-GUIDE.COM FOR THE BEST PLACES TO EAT, DRINK & STAY

---

ialway City	# Abalone Restaurant
ESTAURANT	53 Dominick Street Galway Co Galway
	Tel: 091 534 895

Round the corner from the Bridge Mills, an off-the-street entrance with a tiny porch leads to Alan Villiams' smartly appointed little restaurant: gently minimalist décor, subdued lighting and gentle ackground music set a romantic tone and tables are promisingly set up with spotless white linen and imple glassware. A small dispense bar doubles as reception desk, where arriving guests are greeted nd quickly settled in with menus and an aperitif. Alan Williams is a dedicated chef and, while his nenu may be short and conventional, he is a good cook with a clear idea of what he wants to achieve, xplaining his popularity with a loyal local clientèle. An amuse bouche starts the ball rolling, then tarters may include a good clam chowder and mains of chargrilled veal cutlet or scallops wrapped in moked applewood bacon. Pleasing desserts might include a wild berry crème brulée or a well-made hocolate mousse. Good coffee to finish. Service is brisk and enthusiastic, and a very short but (apart rom Australia), representative wine list includes a couple of half bottles. **Seats 20;** D Mon-Sat, 6-.0pm; house wine €17.50; 10% sc on parties 8+. Closed Sun. MasterCard, Visa. ◊

---

ialway City	# Ard Bia
RESTAURANT	2 Quay Street Galway Co Galway **Tel: 091 539 897**
	ardbia@gmail.com www.ardbia.com

Ard Bia, literally High Food, is an appropriate moniker for this tiny restaurant upstairs over Naughton's ub on Quay Street. Open from 10am, it offers good sandwiches and day-long hot and cold specials ncluding a generous Ard Bia hamburger and veggie burger; speciality teas are offered, and juices are reshly squeezed at the bar counter, with good daily soups - and a small selection of home-baked fare. The room itself is an awkward space, long and narrow, but plain wooden tables are cleverly arranged to allow views over busy Quay Street; in summer there are a couple of tables outside on the street. Evenings bring a short, interesting menu, well executed; there can be delays at dinner time due to nigh demand, and there is little waiting space. Under Aoibheann MacNamara's direction, the food this ustling is usually reliable, although service can be patchy under pressure. *Nimmo's (see entry) is now under the same management. Children welcome. **Seats 40;** air conditioning; open daily - Mon-Sat, 10-10.30pm (closed 5-6, no D Mon close at 5pm): L 12-4, D 6-10.30; Sun 12-10pm; menus a la carte; house wine €18; SC10% on groups 6+. Closed Mon D; 25/26 Dec. MasterCard, Visa, Laser. **Directions:** Above Tigh Neachtains pub.

Galway City
HOTEL

The Ardilaun Hote

Taylors Hill Galway Co Galway **Tel: 091 521 43**
info@theardilaunhotel.ie www.theardilaunhotel.

This famous old hotel dates back about 1840 and has been in the owner ship of the Ryan family for over 40 years. Recent renovations have extended the hotel considerabl but without losing its gentle old-style atmosphere Everything about the hotel confirms the feeling a well-run establishment and, with space and light added to the welcoming lobby/reception area, th convenient meeting place is a pleasant spot to s for a drink or a sandwich and, as ever, friendly sta make a good impression from the outset. Some the spacious, traditionally furnished public areas overlook gardens at the back, including the dinir room which is still the elegant room of old, with fine windows views and access to the garder Bedrooms are traditionally furnished to a high standard and regularly refurbished. It is a popula wedding and conference venue, and excellent in-house leisure facilities include snooker and a leisur centre with 18m swimming pool. Off-season and special interest breaks are offered an enjoyabl prospect at an hotel that has character an a relaxed atosphere. Conference/banqueting (600/380 business centre; broadband wi/fi. Children welcome (under 3s free in parents' room, cots availabl without charge, baby sitting arranged). Pets permitted in some areas. Gardens. Leisure centre (fitnes room, swimming pool, jacuzzi, sauna, steam room); beauty salon. **Rooms 125** (4 suites, 3 junie suites, 32 executive rooms, 17 family, 9 shower only, 106 no-smoking, 8 groundfloor, 3 for disabled Lift, 24 hr room service. B&B €150 pps, ss €25. No SC. Closed 22-27 Dec. Amex, Diners MasterCard, Visa, Laser. **Directions:** 1 mile west of city centre (towards Salthill).

Galway City
HOTEL

Courtyard by Marriot

Headford Point Headford Road Galway Co Galway **Tel: 091 513 20**
www.marriott.ie/gwyc

Located at Headford Point, well positioned for easy access to north County Galway and within walkin distance of Eyre Square and Shop Street in fine weather, this is the first Courtyard by Marriott in th West of Ireland and, unlike so many of the new hotels that have opened all over Ireland in the last fe years, it is a handsome building and an asset to an undistinguished area of the city. Aimed mainly a the business market, it has a large welcoming reception area with feature fireplace and plenty of varie seating, which makes a pleasant common area to meet people or work (complimentary WiFi) Comfortable unfussy rooms have a large desk and an ergonomic chair, conveniently placed lightin and electrical outlets for working in comfort. All rooms also have a safe, mini fridge, tea/coffee makin facilities, ironing facilities and pay per view movies. Facilities which will have equal appeal to th leisure market include the hotel's Absolute Spa and a fitness suite featuring state-of-the-art cardi vascular equipment and secure underground car parking. **The Olive Tree Bistro** offers popular Iris cuisine with a contemporary & Mediterannean influence. Breakfast offers a choice of healthy buffet o freshly prepared hot dishes cooked to order. Steam room, sauna, fitness room. Children welcom (under 16s free in parents' room, cot available); **Rooms 90;** B&B €75 pps, ss€45; 24hr room service lift. Open all year. Amex, MasterCard, Visa, Laser. **Directions:** Off N84 on way into Galway.

Galway City
RESTAURANT

Da Roberta

169 Upper Salthill Galway Co Galway
Tel: 091 585 808

Roberta and Sandro Pieri see their tightly-packed little restaurant in Salthill as 'a piece of Italy' - and they convey this so successfully that queues regularly form at the door. Sunny, yellow walls are hung with still life prints and posters of "Touring Club Italiano", tables sport linen cloths with peach paper covers it's child-friendly and buzzes with the chatter of happy diners. Roberta smiles as she takes orders, Sandr moves from table to table with bottles of wine exchanging wry banter with customers as he pours wine stuffing corks in his pocket. The menu offers many familiar Italian dishes such as prosciutto and salad leaves with soft cheese and pizzas with thin, crisp bases and a good choice of toppings. Bought-ir desserts come with good coffee and an appropriate all-Italian wine list and also offers Italian beer. So what you get here is charming hospitality, an authentic Italian atmosphere and good value - a great recipe for success. *Nearby, **Osteria da Roberta**, is run by the same family (open Mon-Sat 5-11, Sun 12.30 11). **Seats 46.** Open daily 12.30-11. A la carte. House wine about €18.50. Reservations required Amex, MasterCard, Visa, Laser. **Directions:** Central Salthill, opposite the Church. ◊

Galway City
HOTEL/RESTAURANT

The G Hotel

Wellpark Galway Co Galway **Tel: 091 865 200**
info@monogramhotels.ie www.monogramhotels.ie

An unimpressive facade gives no indication of the stunning interior of this new hotel which is, somewhat unexpectedly, virtually on the Ffrench roundabout and beside a large furniture retailer (valet parking is available): internationally renowned milliner Phillip Treacy, a native of Galway, was given carte blanche to indulge his quirky creativity by owner, Galwayman Gerry Barrett, and he has given the western capital a stunning new hotel. Eyecatching colour combinations, lighting, furniture, carpets, fireplaces make the public rooms both comfortable and delightfully varied. What might have been an intimidating (all black) lobby and reception area, is cleverly enlivened by a wall-mounted, exotic fish tank featuring the strangest creatures: sea horses, born and bred in Connemara. Accommodation is luxurious, as would be expected and this is a fun place that brings a smile to people's faces. Boardroom/Banqueting (20/65), theatre facility next door for 40-150; media centre, broadband, secretarial services; Spa; Golf & equestrian nearby. Wheelchair accessible. **Rooms 101** (3 suites, 26 junior suites, all others deluxe or superior); children welcome (baby sitting arranged); rooms from €200. Helipad. **Restaurant:** The stylish restaurant, brainchild of London restaurateur Laura Santini, offers refined Italian cooking far removed from the cucina rustica one might expect from a high street trattoria. It's a kind of hybrid of international hotel cuisine with Italian undertones and, although it does not reach the dizzy, stylish standards of the rest of the hotel, the theatrical surroundings in combination with competence in the kitchen and agreeable service should make for an enjoyable experience. **Seats 70.** Amex, MasterCard, Visa, Laser. **Directions:** From Oranmore - N6 for Galway East, at Skerrit roundabout take Dublin Road. Proceed to the Ffrench roundabout, take the 4th exit: the g is located immediately on the left. ◇

Galway City
HOTEL

Galway Bay Hotel

The Promenade Salthill Galway Co Galway **Tel: 091 520 520**
info@galwaybayhotel.com www.galwaybayhotel.com

This well-named hotel has clear views over Galway Bay to the distant hills of County Clare from public rooms on the upper ground floor as well as many of the spacious, well-equipped bedrooms - which have all been lavishly re-furbished recently - and the rooftop garden. The large marbled foyer and adjacent public areas are very spacious and, although equally attractive for business or leisure, it's a highly regarded conference centre and a good choice for business guests - as well as the usual facilities, all rooms have modem points and interactive TV for messages, Internet and preview of the bill. Off-season and special interest breaks are offered - details on application. Conference/banqueting (1000/350). Leisure centre, swimming pool, gym; beauty salon. Children welcome (under 2s free in parents' room, cot available free of charge, baby sitting arranged; creche, playroom) Rooftop garden. Ample parking (inc underground). No pets. **Rooms 153** (4 suites, 2 junior suites, 2 executive, 50 no smoking, 13 ground floor, 2 for disabled). Lifts. B&B €125 pps, ss €25. Open all year. Amex, MasterCard, Visa, Laser. **Directions:** Located on Salthill Road beside Leisureland, overlooking Galway Bay.

Galway City
HOTEL/RESTAURANT

Glenlo Abbey Hotel

Bushypark Galway Co Galway **Tel: 091 526 666**
info@glenloabbey.ie www.glenlo.com

féile bia Originally an eighteenth century residence, Glenlo Abbey is just two and a half miles from Galway city yet, beautifully located on a 138-acre estate, with its own golf course and Pavilion, it offers all the advantages of the country. Although it is not a very big hotel, the scale is generous: public rooms are impressive, and large, well-furnished bedrooms have good amenities and marbled bathrooms. The old Abbey has been restored for meetings and private dining, with business services to back up meetings and conferences. For indoor relaxation, the Oak Cellar Bar serves light food and, in addition to the classical River Room Restaurant - a lovely bright room with tables tiered to take full advantage of lovely views over Lough Corrib and the surrounding countryside. Conference/banqueting 160/120; business centre, secretarial services, video conferencing, free broadband wi/fi. Golf (9 & 18 hole); fishing, equestrian, cycling, walking. Children welcome (under 2s free in parents' room, cot available, baby sitting arranged). No pets. Garden. Boutique. **Rooms 46** (4 suites, 2 junior suite, 2 executive, 17 ground floor, 1 for disabled, all no-smoking). Wheelchair access. Lift. 24 hr room service. Room rate from €280 (max 2 guests). Ample parking. Helipad. Open all year except Christmas. **Pullman Restaurant:** This is the restaurant of choice at Glenlo Abbey - perhaps the country's most novel dinner venue, it was our Atmospheric Restaurant of the Year in 2005: four carriages, two of them from the original Orient Express that featured in scenes from "Murder on the Orient Express", filmed in 1974. Adapting it to restaurant use has been achieved brilliantly, with no expense spared in maintaining the special features of a luxurious train. There is a lounge/bar area leading to an open dining carriage and two private 'coupes' compartments, each seating up to six. Background 'clackity-clack' and hooting noises lend an authenticity to the experience and the romance is sustained by discreetly piped music of the 1940s and 50s. The view from the windows is of a coiffeured golf course, Lough Corrib and Connemara hills in the distance. Welcome by smart staff is pleasant, service throughout exemplary. Tables are set up as on a train, with silver cutlery, simple glassware and white linen (although napkins are paper); the food is suitably inclined to Asian influences and, while not cutting edge, it is very enjoyable. In line with the fun of the theme, you could begin your meal with a Pullman Summer Salad - and even end it with Poirot's Pie (apple tart); more typically, try an excellent 'Assiette of Oriental Appetisers' including sushi, sashimi, prawn tempura, smoked salmon, and mini spring roll, soy sauce and wasabi - and follow with a main course of 'Beijing Kao Ya', deliciously crisp-skinned roast half duck with a home-made barbecue & pomegranate sauce. Short, well-chosen wine list. Recommended as much for its unique, special occasion experience as for the fare - but the cooking is reliable and a visit is always enjoyable. **Seats 66;** open for D daily 7-9.30. River Room Restaurant: Seats 60. D daily 7-10; á la carte; house wine €25. House closed 24-27 Dec. Amex, Diners, MasterCard, Visa, Laser. **Directions:** 4 km from Galway on N59 in the Clifden direction.

Galway City
CAFÉ

Goya's

2/3 Kirwans Lane Galway Co Galway **Tel: 091 567010**
info@goyas.ie www.goyas.ie

If only for a cup of cappuccino or hot chocolate and a wedge of chocolate cake, or a slice of quiche, a restorative visit to this delightful contemporary bakery and café is a must on any visit to Galway. There's something very promising about the cardboard cake boxes stacked up in preparation near the door, the staff are super, there's a great buzz and the food is simply terrific. What's more, you don't even have to be in Galway to enjoy Emer Murray's terrific baking - contact Goya's for her seasonal mail-order catalogues "Fabulous Festive Fancies" (Christmas cakes, plum pudding, mince pies etc) and "Easter Delights" (simnel cake and others); wedding cakes also available. If you're wondering where to start, why not try a speciality Goyas, 3-layer chocolate gateau cake. **Seats 56** (outdoor, 20), wheelchair accessible. Open all day Mon-Sat (L 12.30-3). MasterCard, Visa, Laser. **Directions:** Behind McDonaghs Fish Shop, off Quay Street. ◈

Galway City
HOTEL

Harbour Hotel

New Docks Road Galway Co Galway **Tel: 091 569466**
info@harbour.ie www.harbour.ie

This contemporary style hotel is conveniently situated at the heart of the city and offers comfortable, if expensive, accommodation with secure parking adjacent. Functional bedrooms with all the usual facilities (TV, trouser press) and well-fitted bathrooms have recently been refurbished and, although the hotel is still relatively new, an extension has already been added, to provide extra dining space, a separate breakfast room and a residents' lounge: a clear indication of Galway's current popularity as a holiday destination. Conference/banqueting 100/80; secretarial services, free broadband wi/fi. Spa, fitness room, steam room, sauna, jacuzzi, massage. Children welcome (under 16s free in parents' room, cot available without charge, baby sitting arranged). No pets.

ooms 96 (14 executive, 4 for disabled, 55 no smoking). 24 hr room service, Lift. B&B €99 pps, s €60. Open all year except Christmas. Amex, Diners, MasterCard, Visa, Laser. **Directions:** Beside e docks in Galway, 5 mins from Eyre Square.

Galway City
&B

The Heron's Rest B&B

Longwalk Spanish Arch Galway Co Galway **Tel: 091 539 574**
theheronsrest@gmail.com www.theheronsrest.com

The name of Sorcha Molloy's delightful B&B is far from fanciful when looking for it along the Longwalk, you may well find it signed by a visiting heron sitting on a car roof at her door. The location must be the best of anywhere you could stay in Galway - right in the centre of the city just seaward of Spanish Arch and with every-thing within easy walking distance, yet quietly situated with views across the river and out to sea. And it is a charming house, with lots of TLC lavished on the sweet waterside rooms, and a lot of care in everything Sorcha does, right down to the choice of natural toiletries and environmentally-friendly cleaning and laundry prod-ucts. Breakfast is served in the kitchen and, to streamline the cooking and serving in the compact space available, she asks guests to order from a surprisingly extensive choice and choose a time, the night before. The menu is typically generous, offering 8 or 9 hot dishes (ranging from French toast with grilled banana, bacon & maple syrup to traditional potato farls with smoked almon, rocket & sour cream) along with fresh baked bread or muffins, fresh orange juice, fruit salad nd cheeses and a range of teas (including herbal teas) and espresso coffee. And, although there are o evening meals, afternoon tea and gourmet picnic baskets are both available on request and some f the city's most interesting restaurants, including Nimmo's and Sheridans on the Docks, are just a tone's throw away. Magic. Free broadband wi/fi; masseuse. **Rooms 2** (en-suite, 1 shower only, 1 family oom); limited room service. Children welcome (under 3s free in parents' room). B&B €75 pps. No vening meals but afternoon tea and gourmet picnic baskets are available on request. Closed Dec-Apr. mex, MasterCard, Visa, Laser. **Directions:** On the Longwalk, near Spanish Arch.

Galway City
HOTEL

Hotel Meyrick

Eyre Square Galway Co Galway **Tel: 091 564 041**
reshm@monogramhotels.ie www.hotelmeyrick.ie

ormerly the Great Southern, this historic railway hotel overlooking Eyre Square right in the centre of alway was built in 1845 and has always had a special place in the hearts of Galway people, who were ad to see the name change when it came into the Monogram Hotels group in 2006 - it is now a sister stablishment to the famous **g Hotel** in Galway and the **d Hotel** in Drogheda (see entries). Prior to the ale, a major refurbishment programme had been undertaken, intended mainly to reinstate the randeur and elegance of its 19th century heyday; this had been partially achieved, most notably in he public areas, where marble flooring, high ceilings, chandeliers and rich fabrics all contributed to e-creating the grandeur of old. However, this was all changed shortly before the Guide went to press, nd a modern approach has been adopted instead. Since the takeover, further investment has also een re-styling of the main restaurant overlooking Eyre Square, The Oyster Grill Restaurant, and the round floor Oyster Bar and the opening of a stylish new late night lounge TOSH. Accommodation has lso had a makeover - the wide corridors (designed so that ladies in hooped dresses could pass without nconvenience) remain, and are especially impressive in these days of compact modern buildings and, lthough standard rooms have been treated in a simple modern style, the best have period detail and re now superior rooms and junior suites - spacious and decorated in keeping with their stature, with athrooms to match, and there are opulent 'level 5' suites, with access to an executive lounge. The otel's Square Spa & Health Club is on the top storey, with panoramic views over Galway city and arbour from the rooftop hot tub which, it has to be said, are interesting rather than scenic. Conference/banqueting (300); business centre. Leisure centre, indoor swimming pool. Children under 2 free in parents' room, cots available without charge, baby sitting arranged. No pets. 24 hour room ervice. **Rooms 99** (13 suites, 8 junior suites, 36 executive, 46 no-smoking, 2 for disabled). Lift. B&B bout €140 pps, ss €30. Closed 23-27 Dec. Amex, Diners, MasterCard, Visa, Laser. **Directions:** In eart of the city overlooking Eyre Square.

Galway City
HOTEL

The House Hote

Spanish Parade Galway Co Galway **Tel: 091 538 90**
info@thehousehotel.ie www.thehousehotel.

Cat lovers will immediately feel at home in this new hotel nea Spanish Arch with cat motifs everywhere and a brochure image (a chilled out ginger enjoying the best sofa, it's easy to see that th smart establishment is homely at heart. But you don't have to b feline-friendly to appreciate the excellent facilities and man thoughtful touches which aim to make this your Galway 'hom away from home'. Even the names of the public areas are reminder of this aim - The Parlour Bar & Grill; The Relax Loung The Den and, like home, the furniture doesn't all match. Althoug styled 'boutique' - and all rooms are individually designed - th hotel is bigger than it seems, with a range of accommodatio options including comfy, classy and four suites overlooking Galwa harbour; all have a high comfort factor including triple glaze windows, air conditioning, minibar, LCD TV (with on deman movies, music and internet), laptop safe, complimentary broac band and bathrobe & slippers and a complimentary hotel umbrella

All have smart en-suite bathrooms too, although about half have shower only (rain dance shower hea to compensate for lack of a good soak). There's free internet access throughout the hotel, and othe services include in-room spa treatments by Absolute Spa, and same day laundry and dry cleanin service just like home really. **Rooms 40**; lift, 24 hr room service; Children welcome (cots available fre of charge, baby sitting arranged); B&B €110pps, ss€45. Closed 25-26 Dec. Amex, MasterCard, Visa Laser. **Directions:** A block away from the Spanish Arch.

Galway City
BAR/RESTAURANT/GUESTHOUSE

The Huntsman Inr

164 College Road Galway Co Galway **Tel: 091 562 84**
info@huntsmaninn.com www.huntsmaninn.cor

Within walking distance of the city centre and easily accessible by car, this busy spot looks like a prett row of houses and, with its colourful hanging baskets, the façade cleverly disguises a large interio Contemporary décor and muted colours complement an airy atmosphere, and it's a relaxed, comfortabl place for flavoursome food at a reasonable price. Friendly, efficient staff, simple table settings an uncomplicated menus reflect a refreshingly down to earth philosophy. A varied menu offers reliabl favourites such as Huntsman fish cakes, char-grilled steak burger or chicken Caesar salad, and a shoi dessert menu concludes with Illy coffee; everything is cooked with care and well presented, this is a vei busy place and they manage the numbers well. The New World dominates a compact fairly priced win list, which matches the food well. **Accommodation:** The 12 smart, contemporary en-suite bedrooms offe all the usual conveniences plus satellite TV and computer facilities and a good breakfast. Childre welcome (under 10s free in parents' room, cots available free of charge). Lift. **Rooms 12** (2 suites, shower only, 6 no smoking). B&B €60pps, ss €20. Live music (Fri & Sat); broadband wi/fi. **Restaurar seats 200** (outdoors, 50); air conditioning; toilets wheelchair accessible; children welcome before 9pr (high chair, childrens' menu, baby changing facilities); L daily 12.15-3, D daily 5.30-9.30. Bar foo served daily, 12.30-9.30pm. Live Funky Jazz on Thurs from 6.45 pm. Closed Good Fri, 23 Dec - 29 Dec Amex, MasterCard, Visa, Laser. **Directions:** Follow signs for Galway East, just before Eyre Square.

Galway City
RESTAURANT

K C Blake

10 Quay Street Galway Co Galway **Tel: 091 56182**

K C Blakes is named after a stone Tower House, of a type built sometime between 1440 and 1640 which stands as an example of the medieval stone architecture of the ancient city of Galway and th Caseys' restaurant, with all its sleek black designer style and contemporary chic, could not present . stronger contrast to such a building. Proprietor-chef John Casey sources ingredients for K C Blake with care and cooks with skill in wide-ranging menus that offer something for every taste: traditiona Irish (beef and Guinness stew), modern Irish (pan-fried scallops and black pudding), classical Frenc (sole meunière) to global cuisine (a huge choice here - oriental duck with warm pancakes stuffed wit cucumber and spring onion). Professional service, creative cooking and smart surroundings make fc quite a sense of occasion - yet this remarkably consistent operation is aimed at a wide market an fairly priced. The upstairs dining room is a more cheerful choice - unless you prefer a people-watching window table downstairs. D daily, 5-10pm. Closed 25 Dec. Amex, MasterCard, Visa. **Directions:** Cit centre, near Spanish Arch. ◊

Galway City
COUNTRY HOUSE

Killeen House

Bushy Park Galway Co Galway **Tel: 091 524 179**
killeenhouse@ireland.com www.killeenhousegalway.com

Catherine Doyle's delightful, spacious 1840s house enjoys the best of both worlds: it's on the Clifden road just on the edge of Galway city yet, with 25 acres of private grounds and gardens reaching right down to the shores of Lough Corrib, offers all the advantages of the country, too. Catherine's thoughtful hospitality and meticulous standards make a stay here very special, beginning with tea on arrival, served on a beautifully arranged tray with fine linen and polished silver - a house speciality extending to the usually mundane tray provided in your bedroom. Guest rooms are luxuriously and individually furnished, each in a different period, e.g. Regency, Edwardian and (most fun this one) Art Nouveau; the bedding is exquisite, bathrooms are lovely and there are many small touches to make you feel at home. And, although the menu is not exceptionally extensive, breakfast is a delight. Not suitable for children under 12. Garden; walking; broadband wi/fi. No pets. *Killeen House was our Guesthouse of the Year in 2003. **Rooms 6** (1 shower only,1 ground floor). Lift. B&B €90pps, ss €50. Closed 24-27 Dec. Amex, Diners, MasterCard, Visa. **Directions:** On N59 between Galway city and Moycullen village.

Galway City
RESTAURANT

Kirwan's Lane Restaurant

Kirwans Lane Galway Co Galway **Tel: 091 568 266**
clic@eircom.net

A stylish modern restaurant in common ownership with O'Grady's of Barna (see entry), Kirwan's Lane is a little oasis just off one of Galway's main shopping thoroughfares - on a fine day you can sit outside, and take time to breathe in the salt air away from the bustle of the city. Indoors the airy two-storey restaurant is presented stylishly: with Georgia O'Keeffe-influenced oil paintings on white walls and quiet jazz hanging in the air. Smartly appointed tables have their white damask covered with paper tablecloths at lunchtime, when specials may include seafood risotto and fried fillets of plaice, or salads and other lighter dishes. Or you can choose from a well-judged à la carte that is not over-extensive, but takes on board the tastes of vegetarians and meat-eaters as well as having a strong showing of fish and shellfish. Outstanding breads set the tone for what is to come - adventurous modern Irish cooking: goat's cheese and beetroot risotto, perhaps, or crisp calamari in tempura batter on a bed of wilted pak choi, or organic salmon paired with a mixture of new potatoes, tomatoes and chorizo... Finish with a tempting pudding or home-made ice cream and really good coffee. With good cooking backed up by a relaxed ambience, attentive service, and an interesting wine list with well-chosen house wines, this is a pleasant place to eat. Children welcome. No parking (multi-storey carpark nearby). **Seats 90** (private room 60, outdoor seating 20). Air conditioning. L& D daily: L12.30-2.30, D 6-10. Set D about €42.50, also à la carte. House wine €19.50. Closed 24-29 Dec. Amex, MasterCard, Visa, Laser.
Directions: Just off Cross Street and Quay Street. ◇

Galway City
RESTAURANT

The Malt House Restaurant

Olde Malt Mall High Street Galway Co Galway **Tel: 091 567 866**
fergus@themalthouse.ie www.malt-house.com

This old restaurant and bar in a quiet, flower-filled courtyard off High Street is a cosy oasis, away from the often frenetic buzz of modern Galway. It has character - enhanced by low lighting, candles, background jazz and the sound of happy diners at night - and is well-managed, with bar and waiting staff coping seamlessly, even at the busiest of times. Informal meals are served in the bar, and the restaurant is comfortably set up with well-spaced tables smartly dressed in white and maroon (the Galway colours). Brendan Keane, who has been head chef since 1997, offers several menus and, although fairly traditional, there are occasional contemporary notes; and the restaurant is developing areas of speciality - beginning, perhaps, with the range of cocktails offered as aperitifs in the bar, then in menus which demonstrate a desire to offer a genuine choice from the usual line-up, including gluten-free dishes and vegetarian choices. Native Galway oysters are properly served, with a small salad and excellent breads; other good dishes include oven roasted duck breast, classic Dover sole on the bone, and a feathery chocolate fondant. Service is swift and attentive - and wine buffs will enjoy mulling over a wide-ranging list, presented by grape variety, with extensive notes; there are some bargains to be had. In addition to the main dinner menus, there is an evening bar menu, a lunch menu that extends through the afternoon and a pre-theatre menu that offers outstanding value. This is a relaxed, consistent restaurant, where people come to have a good time. **Seats 100** (private room, 20; also outdoor dining for 30). Children welcome. Air conditioning. Food served all day Mon-Sat: L 12-5, Set L €24.50 (value L €10.95). D 5-10, early bird €19.90 (5-7pm) Also à la carte L&D available, house wine from €19.90; no SC. Closed Sun, Bank Hols & Dec 25-Jan 2. Amex, MasterCard, Visa, Laser. **Directions:** Located in a courtyard just off High Street. ◊

Galway City
RESTAURANT/WINE BAR

Nimmo's Restaurant & Wine Bar
Spanish Arch Galway Co Galway **Tel: 091 561 114**
ardbia@gmail.com www.nimmos.ie

Under the new ownership of Aoibheann MacNamara of Ard Bia (see entry), this long-established riverside restaurant, adjacent to the historical Spanish Arch and the new Galway Museum, has been transformed. Nimmo's is now, in fact, two restaurants, one downstairs serving casual mid-priced meals in a wine bar atmosphere and a more sophisticated, higher priced restaurant upstairs, each with its own menu served from separate kitchens. The simple squat stone building is in the old Claddagh area of the city, but the former ramshackle appeal of the place has been replaced by a spare modernity: bare wooden floors, off-white painted walls, generously spaced tables and chairs in the same colour with Aoibheann's trademark quirky art choices apparent here and there. Light, air and the relaxed ambience (including unexceptional table settings with paper napkins) do not hide the seriousness of the operation, however, the food here is very good. New Zealand chef Jessica Murphy oversees both kitchens but it is upstairs where she displays her unique talent to best advantage. The sensibly short blackboard menu favours fresh fish and seafood over meat dishes, all carefully prepared and well presented (all the more pity that the blackboard list is marred by misspellings.) Some dishes, such as a very successful boudin of guinea fowl and black pudding, are original and others, such as roasted turbot with braised potatoes and a lovely light beurre blanc, are more familiar but, whatever your choice, you will be rewarded by cooking of a high order by a dedicated, imaginative chef who has a wonderful way with charcuterie and seafood. Prices are not unreasonable for food of this quality (main courses €17-35, with lobster and black sole at the higher end) and it is complemented by an interesting wine list compiled by Simon Tyrrell (with no explanatory notes, however). Children welcome; **Seats 80** (private room, 30, outdoors, 10); reservations required; Upstairs restaurant: D only Thu, Fri & Sat 6.30- 10.30pm. Downstairs at Nimmo's: D Tue-Sun, 7-11pm.House wine from €20. Closed Mon, Bank Hols, 25-26 Dec. MasterCard, Visa. **Directions:** Harbour front, beside Spanish Arch. ◊

Galway City
RESTAURANT

Oscar's Restaurant Galway
Dominick Street Galway Co Galway **Tel: 091 582 180**
oscarsgalway@eircom.net www.oscarsgalway.com

This is a love-it-or-loathe-it place: the decor is wildly wacky, with overloud jazz and dim lighting giving it a night clubby atmosphere - but few would question Michael O'Meara's position as Galway's most innovative chef. The menu, in an old-fashioned wine list cover, is extensive: cooking influences are eclectic, including those of Indonesia, Malaysia and the East, although some dishes are quite European in style (roast rabbit with apricots) or even traditional Irish (fish cakes in an oatmeal crust). Food is sourced with care, and suppliers are credited on menus; some ingredients are unusual in Irish restaurants - starters might include a warm salad of lamb sweetbreads, for example. Staff are very interested and attentive - and, while first-time guests find it difficult to know what to make of the place initially, all the signs indicate something serious going on in the kitchen. The cooking is very good, flavours are delicious and less adventurous diners can rely on a really good steak, or rack of Connemara lamb (served boulangère perhaps, with a wild crab apple reduction). Portions are large, including desserts which tend more towards the classics: nectarines poached with star anise and cinnamon, with a raspberry compôte and vanilla ice cream, perhaps. Good service, under the supervision of restaurant manager, Sinead Hughes, who is responsible for the wine list, which favours Europe, but also has some choice also from Australia, Chile and California. Despite the wackiness of the room and presentation, this is a reliable restaurant and everything on Oscar's extensive menu is prepared and cooked to order - and Michael O'Meara's expressive, confident cooking has deservedly earned a following in Galway. **Seats 45.** D Mon-Fri, 7-9.45pm (from 6pm Sat). D à la carte. House wines from about €19.50. Closed Sun (except Bank Hol weekends when they close Mon instead). MasterCard, Visa, Laser. **Directions:** 2 minutes across bridge from Jurys.

Galway City
HOTEL

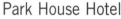

Park House Hotel

Forster Street Eyre Square Galway Co Galway **Tel: 091 564 924**
parkhousehotel@eircom.net www.parkhousehotel.ie

This hotel just off Eyre Square has the individuality that comes with owner-management and provides an exceptionally friendly and comfortable haven from the bustle of Galway, which seems to be constantly in celebration. Warmly decorated public areas include a well-run bar with lots of cosy corners where you can sink into a deep armchair and relax, and a choice of dining options - The Park for formal dining, and The Blue Room for informal meals. Guest rooms are spacious, very comfortably furnished and well-equipped for business travellers, with a desk, internet access and safe; generous, well-planned bathrooms are quite luxurious, with ample storage space and Molton Brown toiletries. Good breakfasts include a buffet selection (with a delicious fresh fruit salad), plus a choice of hot dishes, including fish. And you know you're in Galway when you find oysters on the room service menu... If you want a thoroughly Irish welcome in the heart of Galway, you could not do better than stay at this cosy and central hotel: the prices are very reasonable - and private parking for residents is a real plus. **Park Room Restaurant** (D & L Mon-Sat 12-3/6-9.30, D&L Sun 12.30-9); bar food L&D daily 12-9.30. Children welcome (under 12s free in parents' room, cots available free of charge). No pets. **Rooms 84** (5 junior suites, 3 for disabled, 3 family rooms). Lift. All day room service. B&B about €115 pps, ss about €115. Closed 24-26 Dec. Amex, MasterCard, Visa, Laser. **Directions:** Located adjacent to Eyre Square. ◈

Galway City
HOTEL

Radisson SAS Hotel & Spa

Lough Atalia Road Galway Co Galway **Tel: 091 538300**
sales.galway@radissonsas.com www.radissonhotelgalway.com

féile bia Ideally situated on the waterfront, overlooking Lough Atalia, this fine contemporary hotel is more central than its scenic location might suggest, as the shops and restaurants off Eyre Square are only a few minutes walk. An impressive foyer with unusual sculptures, audacious greenery and a glass-walled lift raise the spirits, and attractive public areas include the Veranda Lounge and a pleasant room in a sunny position looking over the roman-style leisure centre towards Lough Atalia. Guest rooms are furnished to a very high standard throughout with excellent bathrooms and facilities; luxurious 'Level 5' suites have superb views, individual terraces and much else besides - all of which, plus services such as 3-hour express laundry, make this the ideal business accommodation. [Radisson SAS Hotel Galway was our Business Hotel of the Year for 2005]. Excellent facilities for conferences and meetings are matched by outstanding leisure facilities, including a destination spa, Spirit One, which offers a range of beauty treatments, pamper programmes and spa break packages (details on application). Friendly, helpful staff are a great asset in every area of the hotel. Children welcome (under 16s free in parents' room; cot available without charge, baby sitting arranged) Conference/banqueting (1000/570). Video-conferencing, business centre, secretarial services, free broadband wi/fi. Leisure centre (17m pool, children's pool, gym, sauna, steam bath, Jacuzzi, outdoor hot tub); spa, beauty salon. No pets. Underground car park. Helipad. **Rooms 261** (2 suites, 2 junior suite, 16 executive, 9 family, 13 for disabled.) Lift. 24hr rooms service. B&B €120pps, ss €100. **Restaurant Marinas:** The dining experience in this large split-level restaurant has an understandably Scandinavian tone (including a buffet option), but decor in blues and browns is inspired by Lough Atalia and there is a sense of style and confidence about the room that is reflected in capable, friendly service. An extensive à la carte menu is international in style and flavours, although non-fish eaters will find enduring favourites like chargrilled beef fillet, rack of lamb, and a vegetarian dish such as couscous stuffed bell peppers. Although there is little mention of local produce, wheat free and vegetarian dishes are highlighted, and also healthy eating options for guests attending Spirit One spa. But Marinas also offers the less usual option of a Scandinavian style buffet, which is an attractive choice if you are dining early, while everything is fresh. The best thing about the buffet is the varied selection of marinated salads and vegetables, cold meats, smoked fish, served with a wide choice of condiments and dressings; although some dishes will deteriorate while keeping hot, the buffet is good value and an enjoyable experience in such pleasant surroundings. The wine list is well thought out and includes about a dozen wines by the glass and nine half bottles - a boon for business guests dining alone. The restaurant works equally well next morning for its famous Scandinavian buffet breakfast. *The Atrium Bar Menu has a more Irish tone, and offers an informal dining option, including a very reasonably priced 4-course buffet lunch. **Seats 220** (private room 80). Air conditioning. Toilets wheelchair accessible. Children welcome (high chair, childrens menu, baby changing facilities). D daily, 6-10.30pm, L Sun only, 12.30-3. D à la carte. House wines from €24. Guests dining in the hotel are entitled to a 35% discount on usual rates in the underground car park. Bar food also available daily. Amex, Diners, MasterCard, Visa, Laser. **Directions:** By lane from Lough Atalia, 3 minutes walk from bus & train station.

Galway City
PUB

Sheridan's on the Dock

Galway Docks Galway Co Galway
Tel: 091 564 905

A lovely stone building on the corner of the docks nearest the city, this is one of Galway's oldest pubs dating back to at least 1882, when the writer Padraic O'Conaire was born there. A sailor's pub, it still has local clientele and is now owned by the Sheridans of cheese fame, and managed by Seamus Sheridan. It has been completely refurbished with black slate floors, white walls, pine tables, little stools and moss green window seats. It is a pub with - according to Seamus - the cheapest pint in Galway, the biggest selection of beers and the biggest selection of wines (40 to date). Added to this is the best Honduras coffee and a small menu of some of the foods from their shop in the city, with plans for a restaurant upstairs. A short menu might include a ham hock, chorizo & bean stew, a smoked seafood board, and of course, a fine cheese board. *Also at: **Sheridans Shop & The Winebar**, 14-16 Churchyard Street (091 564832; opposite St Nicholas' Church), where wine classes, readings, private parties and events can be held. Food served: 4.30-9.30pm Mon-Fri, from 12.30 Sat. Closed Sun. *Plans for extended opening hours at time of going to press. Amex, Diners, MasterCard, Visa, Laser. **Directions:** On the docks. ◇

Aran Islands
B&B/CAFÉ/RESTAURANT

An Dún

Inis Meain Aran Islands Co Galway **Tel: 099 73047**
anduninismeain@eircom.net www.inismeainaccommodation.com

A short jump from Inis Mor, this interesting island is the most traditional of the group - very few cars, wonderful walks, and some people still wearing traditional clothes; by contrast the Inis Meain Knitting Co. factory and showroom offers great bargains on unique products only to be found in specialist outlets in Milan and Japan. At the foot of Dun Conchubhar (Connor's Fort) is Teresa and Padraic Faherty's restaurant and B&B, An Dún, which was the home of Padraig's grandfather and was the first restaurant on the island when it opened in 1989. In 2000 it was refurbished and extended to include en-suite bedrooms (modern, well fitted out, comfortable, great views), a new dining room and a mini-spa; Teresa is qualified in aromatherapy and can arrange packages for the new spa, especially off-season. More recently a neat garden has been added along the side of the house, which is almost next door to Synge's cottage, and their small shop has become a café/snack bar where seafood chowder, leek & potato soup, Aran smoked salmon and soda bread feature; this leads on to a deck in front, which adds to the atmosphere of leisure. The island's pretty traditional pub is just five minutes' walk. Mini-spa (sauna, steam shower, massage); aromatherapy. Shop. Children welcome (under 3s free in parents' room, cot available without charge). No Pets. Garden. Walking, cycling. **Rooms 5** (all en-suite, shower only and no smoking; 2 ground floor). B&B €50, ss €5-15 (advance booking only in winter). **Restaurant:** There are two dining rooms - the inner one is original and cottagey, while a modern extension has wooden floors and windows on two sides, with wonderful sea and mountain views. The style and atmosphere is homely and everything Teresa serves is made on the premises - some of the best traditional food on the islands is to be found here. Local foods star: fish straight from currachs, their own floury Inis Meain potatoes, fertilised in the traditional manner, with seaweed; scones, crumbles and tarts using local fruits. Specialities include fish dishes like home-made chowder or a trio of ultra-fresh mackerel, pollock and salmon on a lemony apricot sauce, and on cool days there will be stews, and home-cooked roasts of lamb, beef and gammon. interesting desserts like Baileys or brandy carrageen or blackberry tart. A short wine list includes a Concannon, from the Livermore vineyard in California, which has local connections. Children welcome (high chair). **Seats 40** (outdoor seating 10). Reservations required (non-residents welcome). Wheelchair accessible toilets. L 12-3.30pm; D daily in summer, 6.30-9.30. Set D available for residents, €25, otherwise à la carte. House wine €18. Open all year except 1 week Oct & 1 week Jan. MasterCard, Visa, Laser. **Directions:** Centre of island, near church.

Aran Islands
CAFÉ

Fisherman's Cottage
Inishere Aran Islands Co Galway **Tel: 099 75073**
foodwise@eircom.net www.southaran.com

Inis Oirr, the smallest and most easterly of the Aran Islands is a tranquil place, perfect for quiet contemplation and relaxed walks and swimming in crystal clear waters. At the south end of the island and a 5 minute walk along the sea from the pier, you arrive at Maria and Enda Conneely's Fisherman's Cottage, a lovely white and blue cottage with half door, set among interesting herb and flower gardens. A pretty blue, green and white theme makes the dining room bright, and the conservatory has the same colour scheme, with lovely views of the bay. Enda and Maria are Slow Food members and feel that it is important that the food we eat does not have to travel too far, especially food that can be produced locally, so they try to use organically produced foods as well as locally caught wild fish and other produce from the Island - the aim is to do what they can to provide tasty local food that is unique to the island. Enda, a native of South Aran, has studied widely, including medicinal cooking in Switzerland, and cooking at the Cordon Vert Vegetarian School in Manchester, and Maria has studied Shiatsu and Macrobiotics, so the food reflects their love for a natural healthy lifestyle. Next door to the café, they have built another cottage style South Aran Centre. Yoga, cookery and Irish/English language classes are planned here - for further information contact Maria and Enda. Not suitable for children; broadband wi/fi; cookery classes. **Seats 54** (private room, 20, outdoors, 35); L&D Tue-Sun, 10-4pm and 7-9pm; house wine €18-24. Closed Mon, Nov-Mar. MasterCard, Visa, Laser. **Directions:** Turn right at the pier and 400 metres further on.

Aran Islands
RESTAURANT

Inis Meáin Restaurant
Inis Meain Aran Islands Co Galway **Tel: 086 826 6026**
post@inismeain.com www.inismeain.com

NEWCOMER OF THE YEAR

Inis Meain is the middle island of the group, and is the most tranquil and least visited; it is just 3 miles across and supports 150 inhabitants who appreciate this unique and special place. Ruairi de Blacam is a native of the island and a chef; he and his wife, Marie-Therese, who is from Cork and has a business and fashion background, decided to create a business on the island that would allow them live in this peaceful landscape of terraced limestone and traditional culture. Old traditions of farming, sport, and music are a large part of daily life here, and they are true to this in creating a haven of fine food and a peaceful place for rest. The long, low cut-stone building, designed by de Blacam & Meagher architects, blends into the surrounding limestone landscape. The dining space and kitchen are almost one and diners are given a view of the open simple kitchen, or an amazing panoramic 90% view of the island, sea and sky. The room is modern and spare; a great black and white photograph of a fisherman easing a periwinkle out of a shell, with a pint of stout beside him, gives real feeling to the whole place. The ingredients used are mainly sourced on the island: lobster and crab are caught by fishermen who use the local currachs; potatoes and vegetables grown in small fields are fertilized by seaweed from the shore. Ruairi's food is simple and beautifully cooked crab salad with aioli (freshest crab imaginable); foie gras and chicken liver paté; roast chicken with roasted carrots and fennel, and local potatoes in their skins (chicken sourced from a farmer in Ballyhaunis - tastes like mother's, and with no added flavours.. scrumptious). Catch of the day might very well be ling, once a staple food in these parts, simply fried with tiny mace-doine of red and yellow peppers sprinkled on top. Finish, perhaps, with a perfect crème brulée or a gloriously ordinary apple tart and just be glad you found this place. Unsuitable for children; Restaurant & toilets wheelchair accessible. Free broadband wi/fi. **Seats 30** (private room, 20, outdoors, 20). L Wed-Sun, 12.30-2.30; D Wed-Sat, 7.30-9.30; house wine €18. Closed Sun D, Mon, Tues, Nov-Feb. MasterCard, Visa, Laser. *B&B also available. MasterCard, Visa, Laser. **Directions:** After passing only pub on your left take next right then take first left to the restaurant.

Aran Islands
GUESTHOUSE

Kilmurvey House

Kilronan Inis Mor Aran Islands Co Galway **Tel: 099 61218**
kilmurveyhouse@eircom.net www.kilmurveyhouse.com

Treasa Joyce's 150-year old stone house stands out as a beacon at the foot of the island's most famous attraction, Dun Aonghasa. It's a fine house and well kept, with a neatly manicured front garden and a walled vegetable garden at the back. It's steeped in history and has a large high-ceilinged hall and wide stairs giving a feeling of spacious grandeur. The spacious bedrooms are stylish and beautifully finished, with great views of fields, Dun Aengus and sea; four new rooms (and a conference room) were added in 2007 and two of the biggest rooms have king sized beds. Residents' dinners are based on home-grown, local produce - guests love Treasa's baked cod, which she makes with an herb pesto crust or a tapenade, or beef and Guinness casserole on cool evenings - and there is a short, but well-chosen, wine list. Comfortable accommodation, good food, and warm hospitality make this an ideal place to stay. Conferences (60). Children welcome (under 5s free in parents' room, cots available free of charge, high chair). No pets. Garden; walking. **Rooms 12** (all en-suite, 4 shower only, 2 family, all no smoking), B&B €50, ss €15. Residents' D: €30, 7pm, by arrangement - please check when booking. House wine €22. Closed 31 Oct-1 Apr.* **Café An Sunda Caoch** (The Blind Sound) is a café at the Dun Aonghusa visitor centre, run independently by Treasa Joyce, which serves delicious home-made food - soups, cakes (don't miss the gorgeous fruit cake) sandwiches - every day in summer, 11am-5pm. MasterCard, Visa, Laser. **Directions:** 7km (4.5 m) from Kilronan (take minibus from harbour, or rent bicycles).

Aran Islands
RESTAURANT/HOSTEL

Mainistir House

Inis Mor Aran Islands Co Galway **Tel: 099 61169**
mainistirhouse@eircom.net www.mainistirhousearan.com

It's over fifteen years since Joel d'Anjou opened this long single storey whitewashed building on a hill overlooking Galway Bay as a hostel and restaurant, and it is still the most talked about place on the islands. Despite the hostel atmosphere, Mainistir House provides guesthouse comfort at a hostel rate. But you don't even have to be staying here to experience Joel's famous 'Vaguely Vegetarian Buffet' (changes daily) which is served nightly and written on a blackboard. Six large tables are set up with checked cloths and everyone is served a starter - say a delicious lentil soup - then there are half a dozen dishes displayed on a big round table: prunes with onions & apple; tomato salad with pesto dressing & soft Boursin cheese; rice bulgur pilaf & canellini beans in a ragu sauce & vegetable stir fry of cabbage, red peppers, carrots and mint are all possible, and delicious desserts are offered as extra. Service is prompt (and colourful), this is great food - and this fun and funky restaurant continues to give amazing value. Bring your own wine. Christmas and New Year packages available. **Restaurant Seats 45.** D daily, 8pm. Set Menu €15. BYO wine. **Accommodation:** (8 private rooms plus hostel accommodation for up to 70; all no smoking). B&B about €22.50pps, ss €7.50 (includes a simple breakfast of porridge/cereals & freshly baked bread each morning). MasterCard, Visa. **Directions:** 1 mile along the main road from the harbour. ◇

Aran Islands
B&B/RESTAURANT

Man Of Aran Cottages

Kilmurvey Inis Mor Aran Islands Co Galway **Tel: 099 61301**
manofaran@eircom.net www.manofarancottage.com

Despite its fame - this is where the film Man of Aran was made - Joe and Maura Wolfe make visiting their home a genuine and personal experience. The cottage is right beside the sea and Kilmurvey beach, surrounded by wild flowers, and Joe has somehow managed to make a productive garden in this exposed location, so their meals - for residents only - usually include his organically grown vegetables (even artichokes and asparagus), salads, nasturtium flowers and young nettle leaves as well as Maura's home-made soups, stews and freshly-baked bread and cakes. Dinner is served in the little restaurant but there are benches in the garden, with stunning views across the sea towards the mountains, where you can enjoy an aperitif, or even eat outside on fine summer evenings. The three little bedrooms are basic but full of quaint, cottagey charm and they're very comfortable, although only one is en-suite. Breakfast will probably be a well cooked full-Irish - made special by Joe's beautifully sweet home-grown cherry tomatoes if you are lucky - although they'll do something different if you like. Packed lunches are available too. Children welcome (under 4s free in parents room, cot available). No pets. Garden, walking. **Rooms 3** (1 en-suite, all no smoking). B&B €40, ss €10. Closed Nov-Feb. **No Credit Cards. Directions:** Mini bus or cycle from Kilronan, 6.5km (4 m).

Aran Islands
RESTAURANT/WINE BAR

O'Malley's @ Bay View

The Pier Kilronan Inishmor Aran Islands Co Galway
Tel: 099 61041

The O'Malley brothers, who have earned a special reputation for their great cooking in Pier House Restaurant (see entry) have taken on a new challenge at Bay View which, like Pier House, occupies a very prominent position on the pier. As you approach by boat you'll see the large two-storey white building, with wooden benches on the terrace. Now totally refurbished, it has been converted to make a smart modern wine and tapas bar. There are three golden painted rooms with original coving and high ceilings, including a bright mirror-backed wine bar in the first room; paintings adorning the walls are for sale at the time of our visit, shortly after the restaurant opened in July 2007, the large and beautiful works were by local artists Cyril and Finuala Flaherty, and Jackie Rowantree. The main food offering is tapas (calamari with sweet chilli sauce for example, and prosciutto roll, stuffed with rocket and cottage cheese, pizzas and gourmet burgers and wine by the bottle or glass (6) - but a full Irish breakfast is served till 5pm, and main courses include pan-fried mackerel with chorizo and potato salad, or Moroccan tagine with cinnamon and coriander couscous. Desserts like baked raspberry cheesecake with raspberry purée or chocolate tarte and rhubarb compôte alone should tempt the hundreds of day trippers to sample the food of these two passionate well travelled and brilliant cooks. Open 10 am till 10pm. MasterCard, Visa, Laser. **Directions:** Large two-storey white building on the pier in Kilronan.

Aran Islands
HOTEL

Ostán Oileain Árainn - Aran Islands Hotel

Kilronan Inishmor Aran Islands Co Galway **Tel: 099 61104**
info@aranislandshotel.com www.aranislandshotel.com

Just a short walk from the pier, this small cut stone hotel overlooking Kileany Bay and Kilronan harbour has a homely appearance and it marks a change for the Aran Islands in that it is the islands' first regular modern hotel (it could be described as luxurious), and will operate throughout the year. The most popular spot in the hotel is **Paitin Jack's** with open stone fireplace, low ceilings, and a two tier layout; this bar often has traditional music played on one level and bar food served on the higher level. The dining room is also low ceilinged, and finished in wood and stone, with a view of the bay from 3 long small windows at one end; a communal balcony running along the front of the hotel will be decked with suitable sea hardy shrubs, and should be interesting and fun if you are in a holiday mood. Accommodation is very comfortable and five of the 22 en-suite bedrooms have good views of bay and harbour; bedrooms are really cosy, with shades of gold, yellow and red, which would tempt you to holiday on the island even in winter time. There is a lift, power showers, seven TV channels, direct dial telephone, iron, hair-dryer, and tea/coffee stand, all contributing to a modern island. Head chef Declan

Brannigan, who is from Dublin and has married an islander, loves this new challenge; his food is modern Irish and he offers an à la carte, set dinner and an extensive bar food menu, which is available from 5pm to 11.30 pm during the season. Wheelchair friendly; free broadband wi/fi; cycling, walking; Children welcome (under 5s free in parents' room, cots available free of charge, baby sitting arranged). **Rooms 22** (2 shower only, 5 single, 3 ground floor, 2 for disabled, 20 no smoking). Lift, Limited room service; B&B €55-115 pps, ss €25. Closed Dec 20-28. Diners, MasterCard, Visa, Laser. **Directions:** In Kilronan, Inishmore Island.

Aran Islands
RESTAURANT/GUESTHOUSE

Pier House Guest House

Kilronan Inishmor Aran Islands Co Galway **Tel: 099 61417**
pierh@iol.ie

In a new building, right on the pier where the boats arrive, Maura & Padraig Joyce run this large well-kept guesthouse. As you walk from the ferry you will be offered tours of the island (mini-bus or pony and trap) or invited to hire one of the thousand or so bikes available on the island. Kilronan is the action centre of the island and Pier House is around the corner from pubs, cafés, a supermarket and the local hall; the attractive beach is round the next corner. While perhaps less charterful than some of the older houses, rooms are comfortable, with more facilities than most island accommodation (TV and phones as well as communal tea/coffee making facilities downstairs to use at any time) and views over sea and hills, and flag-stoned fields at the back. There's also a large residents' lounge and the house generally is comfortable and well-run. The restaurant is currently leased (see entry). *Four attractive self-catering apartments are also offered. Children welcome (under 5s free in parents' room). **Rooms 10** (all en-suite & no smoking, 1 ground floor). B&B €60 pps, ss €20. MasterCard, Visa, Laser. **Directions:** Galway to Rosamhil then Ferry, 30 minutes to Island.

Aran Islands
RESTAURANT

Pier House Restaurant

Kilronan Inis Mor Aran Islands Co Galway **Tel: 099 61811**
info@aranrestaurant.com www.pierhouserestaurant.com

Brothers Damien and Ronan O'Malley run this fine restaurant beside the pier, and it would be hard to imagine a better location for an island restaurant, as it so close to the ferry and all the life of Kilronan village, with beautiful views across the harbour. The setting is very relaxing and, with seating equally divided between inside and outdoor tables, it's a good place to be, whatever the weather. The cooking is modern Irish in style and, naturally enough, features locally caught fresh fish and seafood, with plenty of other choices - including an imaginative vegetarian dish, and meat such as braised Connemara lamb shank. Good home-made breads and delicious desserts are excellent. An extensive drinks menu offers spirits and beer as well as a wine list. The brothers have earned a loyal following and Pier House Restaurant is regarded by locals as 'the' place for a special evening out and since the opening of their newer place nearby, **O'Malleys @ Bay View** (see entry) food at The Pier House Restaurant continues to impress. **Seats 44** (+outdoor 40, private room 12); Children welcome until 8; Open Daily L 12-5, D 6-10. Set Value D Sun-Thu €32, also a la carte. House wine €19. Closed mid Oct - mid Mar. MasterCard, Visa, Laser. **Directions:** Overlooking pier and bay, 50 metres from the ferry point.

Aran Islands
B&B

Radharc An Chlair

Castle Village Inis Oirr Aran Islands Co Galway **Tel: 099 75019**
bridpoil@eircom.net

Brid Poil's welcoming dormer house looks over the Cliffs of Moher, with views of Galway Bay on the left, and has had a great reputation for many years - she came over from Clare twenty years ago when she married Peadar and thought this would be a nice thing to do. Her many regular guests clearly agree - when the ferry from Doolin started, all Clare came over and are still coming so you need to book a month ahead. A keen cook, Brid's philosophy is 'simple and in season' which should be the mantra of all on the islands: roast beef, baked ham with carrots and cabbage or hake baked with onion and bay leaf are among her most popular dishes, also Darina's bread and butter pudding. Brid only makes dinner for guests by arrangement, and there are treats for breakfast too, including prune and apricot compôtes, freshly baked scones, and home-made grapefruit marmalade. Children welcome (under 5s free in parents' room); free broadband wi/fi. No pets. Garden; walking. **Rooms 6** (5 shower only, 1 bath, 2 ground floor, all no smoking). B&B €35 pps, ss €10. Residents D by arrangement. **No Credit Cards**. **Directions:** At Castle Village, overlooking Cliffs of Moher.

Aran Islands
B&B/RESTAURANT

Tig Congaile

Moore Village Inis Meain Aran Islands Co Galway **Tel: 099 73085**
bbinismeain@eircom.net

Arriving on Inis Meain by boat, you will see Tigh Congaile on the hill above the little port. It is a lovely pale primrose painted, green-silled house with a perfectly manicured lawn surrounding it, and it's just a 3-minute walk from the pier or the beach. Vilma Conneely worked in banking in California, met and married Padric, came back home with him and opened Tigh Congaile 15 years ago; so, on arrival, you are offered freshly brewed Guatemalan coffee to enjoy in the large dining room, which has a wonderful view and is hung with the work of local artists, displayed for sale. An all day/evening menu on the wall is ideal for the non-stop visitors coming on to the island from the various ferries. Vilma specialises in organic and sea vegetables, and uses as much seafood as she can get locally and from Galway - she is lauded quietly by many of the marine biologists in UCG for her interest in this, and her wonderful Sea Vegetable Soup is a speciality known well beyond the islands. Accommodation is in minimalist rooms with modern style wooden floor, comfortable beds and neat en-suite facilities - everything is immaculately clean and, of course, every room has a view to die for. If sitting outside on a fine day, the peace and the view make this the best spot on the island. Conference/meetings (45). **Seats 45.** Toilets wheelchair accessible. L&D daily, 11-4pm, 7-9pm; reservations required. A la carte. House wine about €16. Children welcome (high chair, childrens menu, under 2s free in parents' room, cot available free of charge). **Rooms 7** (all shower only, ground floor & no smoking, 1 family); B&B €38, ss €7. Fishing, cycling, walking, garden. Closed Oct-Easter. MasterCard, Visa, Laser. **Directions:** Five minutes walk from the pier.

R

BALLINASLOE

Hayden's Hotel (090 964 2347; www.lynchotels.com) has been welcoming guests since 1803 and is still very much the centre of local activities. For lunch and evening meals, try the surprisingly named **Kariba's Restaurant** (090 964 4830) on Society Street, which provides honest food at fair prices and is well-supported by local people; a useful place to break a journey as food is available all day Mon-Sat. **Tohers** (090 964 4848) is an attractive traditional bar and restaurant on Dunlo Street which was closed for renovations at the time of the Guide's last visit. Call in advance if you plan visiting. A new hotel, **The Carlton Shearwater** (www.carlton.ie) opened at Marina Point, shortly before the Guide went to press. In line with other Carlton hotels, it offers a high standard of comfort and facilities.

WWW.IRELAND-GUIDE.COM FOR THE BEST PLACES TO EAT, DRINK & STAY

Ballinasloe Area
COUNTRY HOUSE

Ballinderry Park

Kilconnell Ballinasloe Co Galway **Tel: 090 968 6796**
george@ballinderrypark.com www.ballinderrypark.com

At the end of a winding track, a smallish but perfectly proportioned early Georgian house comes into view. Recently rescued from dereliction, the house always demands more to be done, but George Gossip and his wife Susie have worked wonders, creating a comfortable home out of a ruin. All the interior walls are clad in panelling - not reclaimed, but new and designed by George. The effect is of timeless elegance and the palette of colours used in the various rooms is strikingly beautiful, especially the intense blue of the dining room. The bedrooms (two doubles with en-suite bathrooms, plus one twin room with shower only) are spacious, with comfortable beds and lots of light. While there are some eccentricities, these only add to the special nature of a stay at Ballinderry Park. The books and photographs, old framed silhouettes and antique maps that one finds throughout the house clearly speak of the owners' own taste, rather than that of some interior designer. In the evening, guests are invited to help themselves to a drink from a well-stocked cupboard then sit beside the log fire to peruse an interesting wine list that is both short and remarkably good value. George is not only a thoughtful host but well known in Ireland as a terrific cook, who seeks out the best ingredients (notably game, in season) and dreams up meals that are imaginative but don't strive for effect. And he will send you on your way with a wonderful breakfast as a warm memory of your stay. And, before you leave the area, there is a particularly fine ruined abbey awaiting your attention in nearby Kilconnell village. Children welcome (under 3s free in parents'

room, cots available free of charge). Cookery classes, fly fishing, walking, special interest breaks on site; Golf and hunting nearby. Dogs permitted in certain areas by arrangement. **Rooms 4** (2 shower only, all no smoking); B&B €95 pps, ss €20. Residents' D at 8pm, €48; house wine from €23. Closed 1 Nov - 31 Mar - but will open over winter for groups. Amex, MasterCard, Visa, Laser. **Directions:** R348 from Ballinasloe, through Kilconnell, take left for Cappataggle, immediately left & continue until road turns into one avenue.

Ballyconneely
COUNTRY HOUSE

Emlaghmore Lodge
Ballyconneely Co Galway **Tel: 095 23529**
info@emlaghmore.com www.emlaghmore.com

Built in 1862 as a small fishing lodge, Nicholas Tinne's magically located house is situated halfway between Roundstone and the 18-hole links golf course at Ballyconneely, in a Special Area of Conservation. It has been in the Tinne family for over 75 years and is quite a modest house in some ways, but it is comfortably furnished in keeping with its age. It feels gloriously remote and has its own river running through the garden with fly fishing, yet it is only a few hundred yards from sandy beaches and there are good pubs and restaurants nearby too. Nick also cooks dinner for residents: seafood treats and local meat prevail. Not suitable for children. No pets. Golf, pony trekking & windsurfing nearby. Walking, fly fishing, garden. *Self-catering cottage also available nearby. **Rooms 4** (2 en-suite, 1 shower only; 2 with private bathrooms; all no smoking). B&B €80, ss €40. Residents D, €50 at 8.30pm (please book by 10am.). House wine €15. Closed 1 Nov-Easter. MasterCard, Visa. **Directions:** Turn inland off coast road 100 metres on Roundstone side of Callow Bridge. 10 km (6 m) from Roundstone, 4km (2.5m) from Ballyconneely.

Ballyconneely
HOTEL/RESTAURANT

Mannin Bay Hotel
Ballyconneely Co Galway **Tel: 095 23120**
info@manninbay.com www.manninbay.com

Formerly known as Erriseask House, this famous small hotel re-opened after major renovations and refurbishment in 2007, as Mannin Bay Hotel. The size and style of the building may set off alarm bells on the approach but, although the old house is initially unrecognisable, the stunningly beautiful setting is unchanged and, somehow, a little of the spirit of the old Erriseask remains, perhaps partly because the name is still there, carved in slate at the entrance The existing rooms and suites are still there too, now refurbished, and a further twelve two-bedroom studios, complete with living room, have been added; aimed mainly at the golf market they are very comfortable and appealingly decorated in a soothing neutral style that allows the views to take centre stage. The bar has been redesigned and now integrates more closely with a new, and larger restaurant. Fully wheelchair accessible. Banqueting. Equestrian, sea angling and golf all nearby. Lawn bowls, croquet, tennis, walking on site. Children welcome (under 6s free in parents' room, cot available free of charge, baby sitting arranged). **Rooms 24.** Lift; limited room service. B&B €100pps, no ss. **Restaurant:** Despite the rudimentary modern exterior and relatively bald grounds surrounding the hotel (a landscaping operation is underway), the restaurant is decidedly cosy and inviting. The long room has several windows overlooking the coast, but many face out on to the soulless car park, which is a shame given the beauty of this area. Nevertheless the upholstered seats, well-spaced tables and windows hung with heavy beige drapes make this a pleasant place to linger over dinner. With chef Richard Hart having learned his trade at Gleneagles Hotel in Scotland and Roscoff in Belfast, the food is quite elaborate; Connemara produce like crab, oysters and lamb all feature prominently, paired with seasonal produce, and beautifully presented. It was early days when the Guide visited and, although friendly, service was a little patchy. Once fully settled down, this promises to be a valuable addition to the local dining scene. **Seats 55** (outdoors, 20); reservations recommended; D daily, 6.30-9.15pm, set D €49.95; also a la carte; house wine from €18.50. House closed 5 Jan - 1 March. MasterCard, Visa Laser. **Directions:** 8km (5 miles) from Clifden town adjacent to Connemara Golf Links.

Barna
PUB

Donnelly's of Barna

Barna Co Galway
Tel: 091 592 487

Although Barna has recently become so built up, Donnelly's of Barna is still a landmark at the cross-roads, where a little road leads down to the little harbour. Established in 1892, this seafood restaurant and bar, serves food all day and always seems to be busy. It is a comfortable old world pub with little snugs, comfy corners and bric à brac as well as a more formal dining area. The same bar menu is served throughout the house, and the atmosphere is a casual friendly pub rather than formal dining. The menu offers a lot of seafood starters like moules marinière or pan-fried crab claws, and main courses of haddock mornay and fillet of salmon are all regulars - balanced by other favourites like oven roast duckling and sirloin steak. Although not inexpensive, the combination of good cooking, friendly attentive service and a relaxing ambience make this good value. Desserts - home-made chocolate brownie with vanilla ice cream & raspberry sauce and passion fruit crème brulee among them - are enticing and the wine list is not too pricey. ◊

Barna
RESTAURANT

O'Grady's on the Pier

Sea Point Barna Co Galway **Tel: 091 592223**
www.ogradysonthepier.com

SEAFOOD RESTAURANT OF THE YEAR

In a stunning position, with views over the harbour and beach to distant mountains, Michael O'Grady's charming seafood restaurant is popular among Galway diners. It is a lovely spot on a fine summer's day, with pretty blue and yellow tables set up outside the restaurant, and old boats around the harbour adding to the atmosphere. Inside, a low key interior with simple table settings and nautical and seafood-related décor has character; there are some contemporary elements (especially on the first floor), but tradition has also been allowed its place - the old fireplace has been retained, for example, which bodes well for cosy sessions in wild weather - and Michael's aim is for his seafood to be "simply prepared and very fresh as my father did it years ago". This he and his team are doing very well, although world cuisine is given a little space too, notably among the daily blackboard specials. Interesting dinner menus offer a wonderful choice plus daily specials. Recent visits have found this charming place on top form - the cooking skill and style is impressive, and attentive, helpful staff back up the kitchen well, ensuring that the laid back atmosphere is genuinely relaxing. Special dishes include a main course special Tasting Trio of Seafood, composed of seared king scallops, pan-fried fillet of sea bass, and grilled fillet of sea-trout. The cooking is skilfully judged, and one of the most delicious seafood dishes you are likely to encounter anywhere. (Ever innovative, Michael was winner of our Creative Seafood Dish Award in 2001.) There's always some choice for non-seafood eaters, and desserts are delicious too - if you can find room. Service, under the direction of the host, is attentive, and there's an extensive wine list. Children welcome. **Seats 95** (private room 25, outdoor seating 25). Air-conditioning. D daily 6-10, L Sun only 12.30-2.45. Set Sun L about €25, D à la carte; house wine €18.50. Closed Christmas week. Amex, MasterCard, Visa, Laser. **Directions:** 4 miles west of Galway city on the Spiddal Road. ◊

Barna
HOTEL

The Twelve Hotel

Barna Village Co Galway **Tel: 091 597 000**
enquire@thetwelvehotel.ie www.thetwelvehotel.ie

Named after Connemara's famous Twelve Bens mountains, this new hotel has brought contemporary fashions to an area known until recently for its quiet, traditional style. It replaces a long-established hotel and the site has been well-used to create a sense of ample space, even though the building is right on the corner of two roads in Barna village, now a cramped suburb of Galway. You arrive through a small but quirky reception area, or directly from the car park through a covered seating area to the bar, which is a fine space with couch/seating and fire, and bookshelves full of books including children's. The earthy mix of black tables, clay/brown walls and wooden flooring is relaxing, and the sense of informality is emphasised by central raised counter-style tables and tall stools set up for parties up to ten as well as a spread of tables at normal height. The bar menu offers the usual fare - soups, burgers, fish & chips, pizzas and more interesting items such as a Tapas Platter for two consisting of lamb sausage, crostini, prawns and Kalamata olives with feta cheese: interesting, tasty and nicely presented at €16.90 for two. The dark tones continue among the 48 bedrooms with subtle alterations of lighting and materials to make rooms distinctive from each other. Some have their own cocktail bar. Large gilt-framed, old-fashioned mirrors are a feature on the corridors; leaning against the walls rather than attached to them - many of us have done this at home for years, for all the wrong reasons, but this is one of the year's most noticeable design statements in hotels. Fully wheelchair accessible. Conferencing/Banqueting (120/90); free broadband wi/fi. secretarial services, video conferencing. Children welcome (under 5s free in parents' room, cots available free of charge, baby sitting arranged). Lift, all day room service. **Rooms 48** (25 suites, 12 executive, 8 shower only, 22 family, 3 for disabled, all no smoking). B&B €75 pps, ss€30. **West At The Twelve:** The first floor restaurant, also predominantly black, has a variety of booths with leather banquettes seating, mood lighting from ceiling lights and fat table candles. The focus is on wine, with wines visible on temperature-controlled racks behind glass and a champagne bar within the room. Well chosen wines are listed by grape variety, 'with' and 'without skins' and ranges wide, with detailed notes and added pages of aperitifs, vodkas, whiskies (including a recipe for hot whisky), after dinner drinks. The straightforward simplicity of the menu is appealing it is reasonably priced and with no cheffy descriptions; food is well presented and service is attentive, although staff tend to be inexperienced. This is a restaurant with aspirations to do something a little different, and do it well - it may take some time to settle down. **Seats 120** (private room 96; outdoors, 10); children welcome before 7pm; air conditioning; pianist at weekends; D Wed-Sun 6.30-10pm (6-9pm Sun); early D €20, 6-7pm only; set 2/3 course D €20/26, gourmet menu €65 also a la carte. L Sun only, 12-4; set Sun L €20. House wine €22. Closed Mon, Tue. Amex, Diners, MasterCard, Visa, Laser. **Directions:** At the crossroads in Barna Village.

Cashel
COUNTRY HOUSE/RESTAURANT

Cashel House Hotel

Cashel Connemara Co Galway **Tel: 095 3100**
res@cashel-house-hotel.com www.cashel-house-hotel.com

Dermot and Kay McEvilly were among the pioneers of the Irish country house movement when they opened Cashel House as a hotel in 1968. The following year General and Madame de Gaulle chose to stay for two weeks, an historic visit of which the McEvillys are justly proud - look out for the photographs and other memorabilia in the hall. The de Gaulle visit meant immediate recognition for the hotel, but it did even more for Ireland by putting the Gallic seal of approval on Irish hospitality and food. The beautiful gardens, which run down to a private foreshore, contribute greatly to the atmosphere, and the accommodation includes especially comfortable ground floor garden suites, which are also suitable for less able guests (wheel chair accessible, but no special grab rails etc in bathrooms). Relaxed hospitality combined with professionalism have earned an international reputation for this outstanding hotel and its qualities are perhaps best seen in details - log fires that burn throughout the year, day rooms furnished with antiques and filled with fresh flowers from the garden, rooms that are individually decorated with many thoughtful touches. Service (with all day room service, including all meals) is impeccable, and delicious breakfasts include a wonderful buffet display of home-made and local produce (Cashel House was the Connaught winner of our Irish Breakfast Awards in 2001). Conference/banqueting (15/80). Children welcome; cot available (€10); baby sitting arranged; playroom. Pets permitted in some areas. Walking, tennis. Gardens (open to the public). Well-located for local horse shows (Justice Connemara Pony & Irish Sport Horse Stud Farm is located within the hotel grounds; guests may view). * Self catering accommodation is also available nearby; details on application. **Rooms 32** (13 suites, family rooms, 6 ground floor, 1 shower only). B&B €135pps, no ss; SC12.5%. **Restaurant:** A large conservatory extension makes the most of the outlook on to the lovely gardens around this well appointed split-level restaurant, which is open to non-residents. Although ably assisted by well-trained staff, including Arturo Amit who has been head chef since 2003, Dermot McEvilly has overseen the kitchen personally since the hotel opened, providing a rare consistency of style in five course dinners that showcase local produce, notably seafood. Despite occasional world influences - a plate of warm Cleggan mussels with tomato chilli and garlic, for example - the tone is classic: roast Connemara lamb is an enduring favourite and there is an emphasis on home-grown fruit and vegetables, including some fine vegetarian dishes and homely desserts, such as rhubarb or apple tart, or strawberries and cream - then farmhouse cheeses come with home-baked biscuits. The personal supervision of Kay McEvilly and restaurant manager Ray Doorley ensures exceptionally caring service.

and an extensive and informative wine list includes many special bottles for the connoisseur - yet there are also plenty of well-chosen, more accessible wines (under about €30), and a good choice of half bottles. *A short à la carte bar lunch menu offers interesting snacks and sandwiches, but also delicious hot meals, including Irish stew or even lobster if desired; afternoon teas are also served daily in the bar. (Bar L12.30-2.30, Afternoon Tea 2.30-5). **Restaurant Seats 85.** D daily 7-9, L 12-2.30. Set D €55. Set Sun L €30; also à la carte. House wine €25. 12.5% s.c. Closed 2 Jan-2 Feb. Amex, MasterCard, Visa, Laser. **Directions:** South off N59 (Galway-Clifden road), 1 mile west of Recess turn left.

Cashel
HOTEL/RESTAURANT

Zetland Country House

Cashel Bay Cashel Co Galway **Tel:** 095 31111
zetland@iol.ie www.zetland.com

Originally built as a sporting lodge in the early 19th century, Zetland House is on an elevated site, with views over Cashel Bay and still makes a good base for fishing holidays. This is a charming and hospitable small hotel, with a light and airy atmosphere and an elegance bordering on luxury, in both its spacious antique-furnished public areas and bedrooms which are individually decorated in a relaxed country house style, and include two lovely newer rooms, more recently opened. The gardens surrounding the house are very lovely too, underlining the peaceful atmosphere of the house. Its unusual name dates from the time when the Shetland Islands were under Norwegian rule and known as the Zetlands - the Earl of Zetland (Lord Viceroy 1888-1890) was a frequent visitor here, hence the name. Conference/banqueting (30/75). Tennis, cycling, walking, snooker. Children welcome (cot available, €10; baby sitting arranged). Pets permitted by arrangement in certain areas. Garden. **Rooms 20** (6 executive, 2 family, 1 shower only, 3 ground floor, all no smoking) B&B €120pps, ss €45. **Restaurant:** Like the rest of this lovely hotel, the dining room is bright, spacious and elegant. Decorated in soft, pretty shades of pale yellow and peach that contrast well with antique furniture - including a fine sideboard where plates and silver are displayed - the restaurant is in a prime position for enjoying the view and makes a wonderful place to watch the light fading over the mountains and the sea. A warm welcome and quietly efficient service from staff who are clearly happy in their work greatly enhances the pleasure of dining here. The kitchen makes good use of the vegetables and herbs grown in the hotel garden, along with the best of local produce, notably lobster - and also game in season. From a menu offering about five equally enticing dishes on each course, a typical meal might be deep fried langoustine wanton with tomato fondue, rocket salad, passionfruit sorbet with szechuan pepper and rack of Connemara of lamb (served, perhaps, with a caraway, cherry tomato &aubergine tart, and rosemary jus); finish with Irish cheeses, or a classic dessert such as chocolate fondant, or home-made ices and sorbets. Excellent breakfasts are also served in the restaurant - home-made preserves are an especially delicious feature. **Seats 45;** non residents welcome by reservation; children welcome. D daily 7-9; gourmet D €56. *Snack lunches available, 12-2 daily; restaurant SC 12.5%; house wine €29. Amex, Diners, MasterCard, Visa, Laser. **Directions:** N59 from Galway. Turn left after Recess.

CLAREGALWAY

Just north-east of Galway on the junction of the N17 and N18 roads, Claregalway is now a fast-growing satellite town for Galway city. Business guests visiting the area will find all the required facilities at the large **Claregalway Hotel** (091 738300; www.claregalwayhotel.ie), or at the smaller more intimate hotel, **The Arches** (www.arches-hotel.com). Only 10km from the city, the town is very convenient to Galway airport. The ruins of a Franciscan abbey built by John de Cogan in 1290 were one of the most beautiful of its kind in the country; the church consists of nave, choir, north aisle and transept, surmounted by a graceful tower, of which parts remain in good state of preservation. The area is also notable as the origin of the Irish ancestors (Patrick Lynch) of Che Guevara.
WWW.IRELAND-GUIDE.COM FOR THE BEST PLACES TO EAT, DRINK & STAY

The Old School House Restaurant

Clarinbridge
RESTAURANT

Clarinbridge Co Galway **Tel: 091 796 898**
www.oldschoolhouserestaurant.com

Although it is beside the main road, Kenneth Connolly's old schoolhouse restaurant is behind a high wall in its own garden, so it has a pleasantly rural feel. The dining room is spacious and full of character: bright and tall-windowed, with quality china and linen napkins, interesting prints on the walls - and welcoming staff, who offer menus promptly. The choice offered is wide and well-organised: seafood is predictably strong, but there will also be some attractive steak and poultry dishes, and several creative vegetarian options and it is good to see a children's menu offered. A pleasingly simple cooking style is based on carefully sourced quality Irish produce, with generous portions that are appealingly presented. To finish, the well-chosen Irish cheeseboard is a good bet. A fairly priced wine list offers a wide range of styles. Efficient service, from knowledgeable and attentive staff, adds to the pleasure of a meal here. **Seats 60** (private room, 30, outdoor, 16). Toilets wheelchair accessible. D Tue-Sun, 6.30-10; L Sun only 12.30-2.30. Early D about €25, 6.30-7.30. D à la carte. Set Sun L, about €24 (children's menu €10). House wine about €18.50. Closed Mon, 24-27 Dec, 31 Dec-3 Jan. Amex, MasterCard, Visa, Laser. **Directions:** 9km (6 miles) from Galway city, on N18 Galway-Limerick road. ◇

CLIFDEN

The main town of Connemara, Clifden nestles on the edge of the Atlantic with a dramatic backdrop of mountains. Although it has been somewhat over-developed recently, it remains an excellent base for exploring this exceptionally scenic area; the quality of food and accommodation available in and around the town is very high, and there is plenty to do: walking, horse riding, and bathing are all on the doorstep, the **Connemara Garden Trail** is relaxing and educational, and the island of Inishbofin (see entries) can be visited by ferry from Cleggan. For those who require a leisure centre and/or conference facilities, **The Clifden Station House Hotel** (095 21699; www.clifdenstationhouse.com) is built on the site on the old railway station and has everything required; the complex also includes a railway museum and a range of upmarket shops and boutiques. Outside the town, the beautifully located **Rock Glen Country House Hotel** (095 21035;www.rockglenhotel.com) offers space and a peaceful atmosphere. **WWW.IRELAND-GUIDE.COM FOR THE BEST PLACES TO EAT, DRINK & STAY**

Abbeyglen Castle Hotel

Clifden
HOTEL

Sky Road Clifden Co Galway **Tel: 095 21201**
info@abbeyglen.ie www.abbeyglen.ie

Set romantically in its own parkland valley overlooking Clifden and the sea, Abbeyglen is family-owned and run in a very hands-on fashion by Paul and Brian Hughes. It's a place that has won a lot of friends over the years and it's easy to see why: from the minute arriving guests meet Gilbert the parrot at reception, it's clear that this place is different; it's big and comfortable and laid-back - and there's a charming generosity of spirit about the place. Complimentary afternoon tea for residents is a particularly hospitable speciality, served in a spacious drawing room or in front of an open peat fire in the relaxing bar, where many a late night is spent. A major building programme saw the addition of six new superior rooms - and the refurbishment of the large existing bedrooms. Not suitable for children. No pets. Garden, tennis, pitch and putt, snooker, sauna, walking. Wheelchair accessible. Lift. Helipad. **Rooms 45** (25 superior, 20 standard, all en-suite). Room service (limited hours). B&B €101pps, ss €30. 12.5% s.c. Closed 6 Jan-1 Feb Amex, Diners, MasterCard, Visa, Laser. **Directions:** About 300 metres out of Clifden on the Sky Road, on the left.

Ardagh Hotel & Restaurant

Clifden
HOTEL/RESTAURANT

Ballyconneely Road Clifden Co Galway **Tel: 095 21384**
ardaghhotel@eircom.net www.ardaghhotel.com

Beautifully located, overlooking Ardbear Bay, Stéphane and Monique Bauvet's family-run hotel is well known for quiet hospitality, low-key comfort and good food. Public areas have style, in a relaxed homely way: turf fires, comfortable armchairs, classic country colours, and a plant-filled conservatory area upstairs are pleasing to the eye and indicate that peaceful relaxation is the aim here. Bedrooms vary according to their position but are well-furnished with all the amenities required for a comfortable stay. (Not all have sea views - single rooms are at the back, with a pleasant countryside outlook). Bedrooms include some extra large rooms, especially suitable for families. Children welcome (cot available without charge, baby sitting arranged). Pets permitted. Garden, walking; snooker, pool table. **Rooms 17** (2 suites, 4 shower only, 2 family rooms, all no smoking). Room service (all day). B&B €87.50 pps, ss €30.* Short / off-season breaks available. **Restaurant:** This long-established restaurant is a well-appointed light-filled room on the first floor, with stunning sea and mountain views - and a warm reception is sure to set the tone for an enjoyable evening. Monique Bauvet's menus are wide-ranging: an excellent choice of local seafood may include oysters, mussels, scallops, organic salmon, crab, lobster, and a variety of fish including black (Dover) sole, and there will be a fair choice of meats too, including local lamb - a roast rack, perhaps, with roasted celeriac mash and a rosemary & thyme jus - along with some poultry and at least one imaginative vegetarian choice. Cooking is reliable and delicious home-made breads, well-flavoured soups (including the creamy house chowder), organic vegetables, home-grown salads and home-made ice creams are among the details that stand out, and there is also a good cheese selection, served with grapes, celery and crackers. Home-made petits fours will follow with your coffee (or tea/tisane). Relaxed service, under the direction of Stéphane Bauvet, contributes to an atmosphere of confident professionalism that greatly enhances a meal here. A fairly priced wine list strong on old world wines, especially Bordeaux and Burgundy, also has an interesting choice from South Africa and offers eight half bottles. **Seats 60.** D 7.15-9.30pm daily (Sun D 7.30-9.15), Set D €50, à la carte also available; house wine €22; sc discretionary. Closed Nov-Mar. Amex, Diners, MasterCard, Visa, Laser. **Directions:** 3 km outside Clifden on Ballyconneely Road.

Clifden
HOTEL/RESTAURANT
Ⓝ

Foyles Hotel

Main Street Clifden Co Galway **Tel: 095 21801**
info@foyleshotel.com www.foyleshotel.com

This handsome 19th century hotel in Clifden town centre has played a central role in the hospitality of the area for many a year - proprietor Eddie Foyle is related to a number of key players including brothers Paddy and Billy (Quay House and Dolphin Beach), and the hotel was their family home. Today, with design-led modern hotels appearing in virtually every part of Ireland, hotels like Foyles are becoming a rarity - and, one suspects, something that will seem increasingly precious with each passing year. Stepping in off the street into the old-fashioned foyer/lounge - a comfortable space with well worn settees, gas fire, fussy florid carpet and a bavarian-style wooden staircase leading to bedrooms is like stepping back in time, and it is a very calming experience. Upstairs, the hotel's Victorian origins are seen in pleasingly wide corridors (hooped dresses were in fashion at the time), and large, well-proportioned rooms - which are comfortably old-fashioned, with good beds and modern bathrooms. And, true to its roots, you'll find hands-on family management, and interested service from pleasant staff who are happy to help guests to get the most from their visit to the area. **Rooms 25.** B&B about €45-65 pps. Closed 7 Jan-1 March. **Marconi Restaurant:** Welcoming window views of tables set up with white linen cloths and napkins, candles and pretty floral bouquets in old cups-as-vases are visible from the public footpath - and may well attract you in to this popular restaurant, which is accessible from the street or through the hotel. Barely audible jazz plays in a quirkily attractive and comfortable Frenchy room displaying memorabilia and artefacts - the Marconi connection with the town, Alcock & Brown's remarkable trans-Atlantic flight and landing near Clifden and, right in the middle of the restaurant, a redundant merchant navy compass. Look out for the zany painting depicting famous former visitors to the hotel in chef's uniform - you may recognise Winston Churchill and Seamus Heaney, and perhaps be tempted to guess the identity of others. Warm, relaxed staff present an extensive à la carte menu offering plenty of local seafood (mussels steamed in chilli & coconut broth; crabmeat terrine with smoked salmon; lovely, simple fried fillets of lemon sole in parsley butter), balanced by meat dishes such as lamb shank with mustard mash or pork fillet with pear & apple crisps, and at least one vegetarian dish. The cooking may be a little uneven but excellent raw materials are used and it is very good value, especially the early dinner - 3 courses from the à la carte for €24.95; available to 6.45pm only. A conservative, well-priced wine list includes 6 half bottles and a choice of house wines, unusually including a Rosé d'Anjou. Open from 6 to 9pm daily. Early D €24.95, also à la carte. **Directions:** On the Main Street in centre of Clifden. ◇

Clifden
RESTAURANT

G's Restaurant

The Square Market St Clifden Co Galway **Tel: 095 22323**
gsrestaurant@hotmail.com

Formerly known as The Spice Club, this well-established restaurant has a striking black and maroon shopfront set back from a corner of the square (and with menus clearly displayed outside), and is popular with discerning locals in the know. A small reception area leads to a long restaurant with well

Georgina Campbell's Ireland

spaced tables and maroon, black and cream painted walls decorated with mirrors and oriental print; while not very atmospheric, a window at one end overlooks the estuary - and, once your food arrives, it will take centre stage, notably due to excellent seafood cooking: lovely appetisers of deep-fried mini Thai fish cakes, perhaps, or tasty crab lasagne (a house speciality), and main courses like crisp pan-fried sea bass, or scallops seared to perfection with a butter sauce flavoured with smoked bacon. The à la carte menu is supplemented by a list of daily specials, desserts include refreshing fruity options, and there's a well-priced list of about two dozen wines. Children welcome (high chair, childrens menu). **Seats 56** (outdoors, 8). L daily July & Aug only, 12-3pm; D daily in summer, 6-10pm. SC 10% on groups 6+. Closed 25/26 Dec, 2 weeks Jan & Mon-Wed low season. Ringing to check opening times off season is highly recommended. MasterCard, Visa, Laser. **Directions:** In centre of Clifden.

Clifden
COUNTRY HOUSE

Mallmore Country House
Ballyconneely Road Clifden Co Galway **Tel: 095 21460**
www.mallmore.com

Alan and Kathleen Hardman's restored Georgian home near Clifden is set peacefully in 35 acres of woodland grounds. Connemara ponies are bred here, and the grounds are teeming with wildlife. The house has a warm and welcoming atmosphere, and there's a lovely drawing room for guests' use with an open turf fire and a beautiful sea view out over the gardens. Accommodation is spacious - individually decorated rooms in period style have superb views, and en-suite shower rooms. Tea and coffee is available all day, and the Hardmans take great pride in sending their guests off for the day with a really good breakfast, served in a formal dining room. **Rooms 6** (all en-suite); broadband wi/fi available; B&B €35-40 pps. **Directions:** 1.5 km from Clifden; signed off Ballyconneely road. ◇

Clifden
RESTAURANT

Mitchell's Restaurant
Market Street Clifden Connemara Co Galway
Tel: 095 21867

 This attractive and well-managed family-run restaurant offers efficient, welcoming service and very agreeable "good home cooking" all day, every day throughout a long season - and they have been doing so, with admirable consistency, since 1991. An all-day menu offers a wide range of lightish fare - everything from sandwiches and wraps to seafood chowder; the international flavours are there but how refreshing it is to find old friends like deep-fried Gubbeen cheese and bacon & cabbage there amongst the home-made spicy fish cakes and fresh crab salad with home-made brown bread. There's some overlap on to an à la carte evening menu, which offers a judicious selection from the snack menu but the choice is much wider and includes half a dozen appealing meat and poultry dishes and a vegetarian dish of the day as well as eight or nine seafood dishes and a choice of main course salads. This is a very fair place, offering honest food at honest prices. **Seats 70.** Air conditioning. Not suitable for children after 6 pm. Open daily, 12-10; set 3 course D about €27.50; also à la carte. House wine from about €18.50. Closed Nov-Feb. Amex, Diners, MasterCard, Visa, Laser. **Directions:** Next to SuperValu supermarket. ◇

Clifden
GUESTHOUSE

The Quay House
Beach Road Clifden Co Galway **Tel: 095 21369**
thequay@iol.ie www.thequayhouse.com

 In a lovely location - right on the harbour, with pretty water views when the tide is in - The Quay House is the oldest building in Clifden and was built around 1820. Since then it has had a surprisingly varied usage: it was originally the harbourmaster's house, then a convent, then a monastery; it was converted into a hotel at the turn of the century and finally, since 1993, has been relishing its most enjoyable phase as a guesthouse, in the incomparable hands of long-time hoteliers, Paddy and Julia Foyle. It's a fine house, with spacious rooms - including a stylishly homely drawing room with an open fire. And the accommodation is exceptionally comfortable, in airy, wittily decorated and sumptuously furnished rooms that include not only two wheelchair-friendly rooms, but also seven newer studio rooms, with small fitted kitchens, balconies overlooking the harbour and, as in the original rooms, all have excellent bathrooms with full bath and shower. Breakfast is served in a charming conservatory, decorated with a collection

of silver domes and trailing Virginia creeper criss-crossing the room on strings, and it is simply superb - treats include a buffet laid out to tempt you as you enter. Orders for your tea or coffee are taken even before you sit down at a table beautifully set up with individual jugs of freshly squeezed orange juice. Hot dishes, such as a perfectly cooked traditional Irish or scrambled eggs with smoked salmon are all served with crisp toast, and fresh top-ups of tea and coffee. Although officially closed in winter it is always worth inquiring. *The Quay House was our Guesthouse of the Year for 2006, and also the national winner of the Irish Breakfast Awards. Children welcome (under 12 free in parents' room, cots available without charge). No pets. Garden. Walking. **Rooms 14** (all with full bathrooms, 2 ground floor, all no smoking, 1 for disabled). B&B from €75pps, ss €40. Closed Nov-mid Mar. MasterCard, Visa, Laser. **Directions:** 2 minutes from town centre, overlooking Clifden harbour - follow signs to the Beach Road.

Clifden
B&B

Sea Mist House

Clifden Connemara Co Galway **Tel: 095 21441**
sgriffin@eircom.net www.seamisthouse.com

Sheila Griffin's attractive house was built in 1825, using local quarried stone. Major renovations undertaken over the last few years have retained its character while adding modern comforts, allowing her to offer stylish and comfortable accommodation. A recently added conservatory has made a lovely, spacious room overlooking the garden, where guests can relax - and fruit from the garden is used in spiced fruit compôtes and preserves which appear at breakfast along with home-made breads, American-style pancakes with fresh fruit salsa and scrambled eggs with smoked salmon and a special of the day which brings an element of surprise to the menu each morning. The cottage garden adjacent to the house has been developing over the years and is now reaching maturity - guests are welcome to wander through it and soak in the tranquil atmosphere. There are also many other gardens to visit nearby (the Connemara Garden Trail). Private parking (3). No pets. Garden. **Rooms 4** (all shower only & no-smoking, 1 family room). B&B €58pps, ss €20. Closed Christmas, also mid-week off season. MasterCard, Visa, Laser. **Directions:** Left at square, a little down on right.

Clifden
CAFÉ

Two Dog Café

1 Church Hill Clifden Co Galway **Tel: 095 22186**
kennel@twodogcafe.ie www.twodogcafe.ie

Freshly painted a burnt orange colour with royal blue windows and door, this smashing little café just off the square in Clifden is a gem, combining home-made cakes, gourmet sandwiches and aromatic Illy coffees and other quality drinks with charming service, a laid-back newspaper-reading atmosphere and an Internet cafe upstairs. Ingredients are carefully sourced, using fresh local produce where possible (often from the local farmers' market), and everything is freshly made on the premises. They do several imaginative soups and a wide range of gourmet sandwiches, wraps, panini and quiches - just the sort of thing for a light daytime bite. Try their Chinese roast duck wrap with hoi-sin sauce, cucumber and scallions, or Mediterranean couscous salad or perhaps a chicken caesar salad - with romaine lettuce, smoked chicken, bacon, parmesan, home-made croutons and a freshly-prepared caesar dressing. But, luscious as all the wholesome savoury choices may be, it's really the display of home bakes that proves irresistible to any with the slightest hint of a sweet tooth. Scones, brownies, pan-roasted pear cake, lemon drizzle cake, orange & almond cake (flourless - ideal for coeliacs), carrot cake and light and tasty raspberry cake are all light and delicious... Just like granny used to make - magic! A must for daytime visitors to Clifden. Children welcome. **Seats 28.** Open daytime 10.30-5 (Sun, Aug only 12.30-4). No reservations. Closed Sun all year except Aug, Mon Dec- May & all Nov, last week in Apr. MasterCard, Visa. **Directions:** Behind the Alcock & Brown Hotel in Market Square.

Ballykine House

Clonbur
FARMHOUSE

Clonbur Co Galway **Tel: 094 954 6150**
ballykine@eircom.net www.ballykinehouse-clonbur-cong.com

Comfortable accommodation and Ann Lambe's warm hospitality make this an appealing base for a peaceful holiday. There are guided forest walks from the house, angling on Lough Corrib, an equestrian centre (at nearby Ashford Castle) and bikes for hire locally. It's also well-placed for touring Connemara. Moderately priced rooms have TV, tea/coffee making facilities and hairdryers. No evening meals but the pubs and restaurants of Clonbur are all within walking distance, and so is Ashford Castle. On fine evenings guests often like to walk to the pub or restaurant of their choice and get a lift back later. There's plenty of comfortable seating in the sitting room and conservatory for lounging and chatting, also a library room for visitors, pool table - and a drying room for anglers. Garden. **Rooms 5** (4 with en-suite shower; 1 with private bath, restricted use), B&B about €30, ss €10. Closed 1 Nov-17 Mar. **No Credit Cards. Directions:** 3 km from Cong, on Cong/Clonbur Rd - R345. ◈

Fairhill House Hotel

Clonbur
HOTEL
Ⓝ

Main Street Clonbur Co Galway **Tel: 094 954 6176**
fairhillhouse@eircom.net www.fairhillhouse.com

The Lynch family's friendly Victorian hotel in the centre of the pretty village of Clonbur dates back to 1830 and has recently been sympathetically refurbished, bringing it up to the standards demanded by today's travellers without spoiling its character. Accommodation is simple, but very comfortable for a country hotel. The new decor is gentle on the eye, most rooms have both single and double beds and all bathrooms have a full bath; many a swankier place pays less attention to these important basics. The heart of the hotel is the cosy bar, also accessible directly from the road, which has an open fire, lots of memorabilia and a sense that a lot of good nights are enjoyed here. A large restaurant at the back of the hotel also doubles as a small function room for local events. This would make a very pleasant base for a break in this exceptionally beautiful area. **Rooms 20.** B&B from about €45 pps. Open all year except Christmas. **Directions:** Main Street, Clonbur.

John J. Burke & Sons

Clonbur
PUB/RESTAURANT

Mount Gable House Clonbur Co Galway **Tel: 094 9546175**
tibhurca@eircom.net www.burkes-clonbur.com

Everybody loves Burke's pub - this characterful old family-run pub is one of this attractive village's greatest assets, well known for both food and music. It's a friendly, welcoming place no matter when you might drop in and very much the heart of the community and sporting activities - and the business of feeding people with good traditional meals is taken seriously both in the bar, during the day, and the more formal dining area overlooking the garden towards Mount Gable at the back of the pub in the evening. Bar meals are quite traditional - egg mayonnaise, spicy wedges, roasts, home-made lasagne, apple tart. There's a much wider range offered in the evening: starters like baked mussels or venison sausage, for example, followed by the likes of steaks, rack of lamb and fish from sea and river. Irish stew is a speciality - a unique version, using prime cuts of locally farmed lamb with herb dumplings and the friendly relaxed style (the food is kept refreshingly simple), with traditional music and dancing later in the evening, wins a lot of friends. Booking for the restaurant is essential in high season. Bar meals 9.30am-5pm daily (except 23-28 Dec & 31 Dec); D daily 6.30-8.30. Closed 25 Dec, Good Fri. MasterCard, Visa, Laser. **Directions:** 30 miles north of Galway city, between Lough Corrib & Lough Mask. ◈

St. Clerans Country House

Craughwell
COUNTRY HOUSE/RESTAURANT
🏰 ☆ 🏛 👁 🍷 Ⓡ

Craughwell Co Galway **Tel: 091 846 555**
info@stclerans.com www.stclerans.com

Once the home of the film director John Huston, St Clerans is a magnificent 18th century manor house on 45 acres of gardens and grounds, beautifully located in rolling countryside. It was carefully restored some years ago by previous owner, the American entertainer Merv Griffin, and decorated with no expense spared to make a sumptuous, hedonistically luxurious country retreat and restaurant. There's a great sense of fun about the furnishing and everything is of the best possible quality; reception rooms include a magnificently flamboyant drawing room and spacious bedrooms that are individually decorated and have peaceful garden and countryside views; most are done in what might best be described as an upbeat country house style, while others - particularly those on the lower ground floor, including John Huston's own favourite room, which opens out on to a terrace with steps up to the garden - are restrained, almost subdued, in atmosphere. All are spacious, with luxuriously appointed bathrooms (one has its original shower only) and a wonderful away-from-it-all feeling. Housekeeping is immaculate, and there has been a discernible sense of purposeful new management on recent visits by the Guide. Banqueting (40), free broadband wi/fi. Equestrian, fishing, golf and hunting nearby. Croquet, walking. **Rooms 12** (6 junior suites, 6 executive. 1 shower only, 4 gound floor). B&B €200 pps, no ss. Children under 11 years free in parents room; cots available free of charge; baby sitting arranged. Closed 24-26 Dec. **Restaurant:** The restaurant, which is open to non-residents by reservation, provides an elegant setting for cooking by Japanese head chef Hisashi Kumagai (Kuma). The room has lovely views of pastoral east Galway, including a fine tree which dominates a near meadow, and is floodlit at night; it is an impressive room and appointments are quite classical, with plain white linen-clad tables, fine glassware, silver, and china and gold candle holders. Aperitifs are served in the drawing room by a turf fire, to muted strains of Chopin and Beethoven (but not from the grand piano that suits the room so well). 4-course set dinner menus, printed on parchment-like paper tied with ribbon, offer a choice of 4 or 5 dishes on each course. Kuma is an accomplished chef, ingredients are always the very best and his food is beautifully presented: Kinvara smoked organic salmon is served with citrus argan oil, Reggiano parmesan cheese and mesclum mixed salad to make a starter that is as healthy as it is beautiful, and an equally exceptional main course dish is roulade of roasted loin of lamb with sundried tomato & pesto. Desserts might include an unusual crème de menthe, dark chocolate & green tea mousse with Franjelico white chocolate sauce. The wine list offers some treats and is under constant revision; it includes a good choice of half bottles. Service by local staff is charming and attentive and, overall, local diners are fortunate to have this rare gem within striking distance of Galway city. **Seats 30.** D 7-9pm daily, €65; house wine from €25. SC discretionary. Closed 24-26 Dec. Amex, MasterCard, Visa, Laser. **Directions:** 4km (2 miles) off N6 between Loughrea and Craughwell.

Furbo
HOTEL/RESTAURANT

Connemara Coast Hotel
Furbo Co Galway **Tel: 091 592 108**
info@connemaracoast.ie www.sinnotthotels.com

This beautifully located hotel is an attractive building which makes the best possible use of the site without intruding on the surroundings: set on the sea side of the road, in its own extensive grounds, it is hard to credit that Galway city is only a 10 minute drive away. An impressive foyer decorated with fresh flowers sets the tone on entering, and spacious public areas include a mezzanine and library, and a pleasant patio area on the sea side of the hotel. Facilities are particularly good too - a fine bar, two restaurants, a children's playroom and a leisure centre among them - and a policy of constant refurbishment and upgrading ensures that the hotel always has a warm, well-cared for atmosphere; 30 new bedrooms opened in 2007 and an ongoing programme of upgrades is continuing throughout the older rooms. This most likeable of hotels is understandably popular for conferences - the facilities and service are both excellent (the conference centre has also been refurbished), and the location is magic. A range of special breaks is offered both here and at its fine sister hotel, **Brooks Hotel**, in Dublin (details on application). Conference/banqueting (400/300); free broadband wi/fi; secretarial services, video conferencing. Children welcome (under 3s free in parents' room; cots available without charge, baby sitting arranged; playroom). Leisure centre (swimming pool, jacuzzi, fitness room, sauna, steam room); masseuse; pool table, tennis, walking. **Rooms 142** (1 suite, 10 executive rooms, 7 ground floor, 25 family rooms, 1 for disabled, 132 no smoking). B&B €120pps, ss €40. 24 hr room service. Lift. **Restaurant:** Assisted by staggered dining times that allow the kitchen to present every dish at its best, the hotel succeeds in serving very good food in the two dining rooms, where welcoming details such as proper butter curls and good nutty breads make a good first impression. Appealing menus are changed every day (a boon for regular diners and guests staying for several nights), and they credit both the head chef, Ulriche Hoeche, and also Patrick Kelly, who is the restaurant manager and sommelier. Ulriche offers a wide range of dishes, notably local seafood - braised monkfish is a speciality and local meats are often represented by roast rack of Connemara lamb. **Gallery Restaurant: Seats 50;** D 7-9.30pm daily (children welcome), set D €40; informal D, Daly's 7-9.30pm daily; bar food daily 12.30-6.30 (1-4 Sat/Sun). Open all year. Amex, MasterCard, Visa, Laser. Heli-Pad. **Directions:** 9km (6m) from Galway city on Spiddal road.

Headford
COUNTRY HOUSE

Lisdonagh House

Caherlistrane nr Headford Co Galway **Tel: 093 3116**
cooke@lisdonagh.com www.lisdonagh.com

Situated about 15 minutes drive north of Galway city in the heart of hunting and fishing country
Lisdonagh House enjoys beautiful views overlooking Lake Hackett. It is a lovely property, with large
well-proportioned reception rooms, and very comfortable bedrooms decorated in period style, with
impressive marbled bathrooms to match. A five-course dinner menu is served in a handsome dining
room, and offers fish and meat, although a vegetarian main course would be available on request; a
pleasant breakfast is also served in the dining room. Children welcome. Pets permitted in some areas.
Equestrian, fishing, walking, cycling. *Two villas in the courtyard are also available, either for self
catering or fully serviced. The main house can be rented exclusively for private functions. Small
conferences (50). Dogs permitted in certain areas. Boat trips, hunting/shooting and coarse fishing on
site; golf and garden visits nearby. Children welcome (under 2s free in parents' room, cots available
free of charge, baby sitting arranged, creche). **Rooms 9** (2 shower only, 1 family room, 4 ground floor
all no smoking). B&B from €90-140 pps, ss about €30. 5 course residents' dinner, €49 is served
between 7 and 9pm. House wine €29. Closed 1 Nov-1 May. Amex, MasterCard, Visa, Laser.
Directions: N17 to within 7km (4 m) of Tuam, R333 to Caherlistrane.

Inishbofin
HOTEL/RESTAURANT

The Dolphin Hotel & Restaurant

Inishbofin Co Galway **Tel: 095 4599**
info@dolphinhotel.ie www.dolphinhotel.ie

Brother and sister, Pat and Catherine Coyne opened The Dolphin Restaurant here in 2000
and it quickly gained a following so there was delightment all round when, in 2006, it was
developed as a small hotel. Set in landscaped grounds, is a wonderful addition to this beautiful
unspoilt island. The building is a modern mix of slatted wood and brick and, in tune with the island's
interest in the environment, solar panels and under floor heating have been installed. There are
eleven large, bright bedrooms, with thick deep blue carpets, walnut furniture, great beds, TV and tea
making facilities; all are en-suite and some with a bath. Upstairs rooms have sea and mountain views,
and three special ground floor rooms have their own private sundeck on to the garden. One bedroom
has disabled access; dining and lounge areas also have disabled access. Public areas include two
dining rooms, which can be joined to accommodate parties of up to 100, with a deck for alfresco
dining. There is a lovely resident's lounge, also with access to decking, with great views. Banqueting
(100). Walking, live music (trad.). Boat trips, angling, cycling and scuba diving all nearby. Children
welcome (under 3s free in parents' room, cot available at no charge, baby sitting arranged). **Rooms
11** (8 shower only, 1 for disabled, all no smoking); B&B about €50-60 pps. **Restaurant:** Menus
change throughout the day at this versatile restaurant, which continues to be a great asset to the
island. Catherine cooks great food and has started to grow her own organic vegetables and herbs. At
lunchtime - which considerably runs all afternoon - there's a range of drinks to comfort or refresh,
depending on the weather, then made to order club or open sandwiches, or simple hot meals.
Evening menus are more substantial - rack of lamb or fish of the day. **Seats 100** (outdoor seating,
20). Open daily in summer: L 12-5; D 7-9.30. à la carte; house wine from €17.95. Establishment
closed Nov-Mar. MasterCard, Visa, Laser. **Directions:** Travel from Galway to Clifden and on to Cleggan
Pier where boat leaves to Inishbofin Island. ◇

Inishbofin
HOTEL

Doonmore Hotel

Inishbofin Island Co Galway **Tel: 095 45804 / 14**
info@doonmorehotel.com www.doonmorehotel.com

The Doonmore Hotel was built on the site of the Murray family farmhouse in 1968; overlooking the
sea and sand dunes, with geraniums along the front lounge, it looks more like a traditional guesthouse
than a hotel, and offers old fashioned comfort. Traditional music is played regularly, and on cold days
there are peat fires in the low-ceilinged sitting room and lounge. It is a very family-friendly place with
a baby listening service in bedrooms, along with the usual facilities. 'Murray's' is well known for wholesome cooking - home baking, local produce like Connemara lamb and fresh seafood. There are fine
sandy beaches on hand and there's a fitness room, cycling, sea angling, boat trips, scuba diving and
walking. Small conferences/banqueting (40/80). Children welcome (under 3s free in parents' room,
cots available at no charge, baby sitting arranged); toilets wheelchair accessible; broadband wi/fi.
Rooms 20 (15 shower only, 5 family rooms, 16 ground floor); B&B about €60-65 pps, ss €10.
Restaurant seats 45 and opens daily to residents & non-residents, 12-9pm. Establishment closed Oct-
Mar. Heli-pad. Amex, MasterCard, Visa, Laser. **Directions:** Ferry from Cleggan. ◇

Inishbofin House Day's Hotel & Marine Spa

Inishbofin
HOTEL

Inishbofin Island Co Galway **Tel: 095 45809**
info@inishbofinhouse.com www.inishbofinhouse.com

For many years, the Day family's modest hotel on Bofin pier has been the first port of call for many visitors to the island and anyone returning after a few years will now be surprised to find a large luxury hotel overlooking the inner harbour. Public areas include a large bright high-roofed entrance lobby and lounge with Spanish tiles, a smart and stylish bar and a dining room, on two levels, with great views to the sea and mountains. On the first floor a truly lovely library/lounge with balconies off it is totally constructed in glass, allowing excellent panoramic views, and the luxurious bedrooms all have bath and shower. The Day family also operate a bar beside the pier (food available in summer). Banqueting (180). Spa, beauty salon. Children welcome (cot available, baby sitting arranged). No pets. Garden. **Rooms 34** (2 with separate bath & shower, 2 disabled, all no smoking). Lift. Room service (limited hours). Closed Jan-Feb. Visa, Laser. **Directions:** Ferries to the island run regularly from Cleggan, with ticket offices in Clifden (regular buses between Clifden and Cleggan) and also at Kings of Cleggan. For bookings and enquiries, phone: 095 44642 or 095 21520. Credit card bookings are accepted. ◊

Moran's Oyster Cottage

Kilcolgan
CHARACTER PUB/RESTAURANT

The Weir Kilcolgan Co Galway **Tel: 091 796 113**
moranstheweir@eircom.net www.moransoystercottage.com

This is just the kind of Irish pub that people everywhere dream about. It's as pretty as a picture, with a well-kept thatched roof and a lovely waterside location (with plenty of seats outside where you can while away the time and watch the swans floating by). People from throughout the country beat a path here at every available opportunity for their wonderful local seafood, including lobster, but especially the native oysters (from their own oyster beds) which are in season from September to April (farmed Gigas oysters are on the menu all year). Then there's chowder and smoked salmon and seafood cocktail and mussels, delicious crab salads - and lobster, with boiled potatoes & garlic butter. Private conference room. The wine list is not over-extensive, but carefully selected, informative and fairly priced. Morans was the Guide's Seafood Pub of the Year in 1999. **Seats 100** (private rooms, 8 and 12; outdoor seating, 50/60). Air conditioning. Toilets wheelchair accessible. Meals 12 noon -10pm daily. House wine from about €18. Closed 3 days Christmas & Good Fri. Amex, MasterCard, Visa, Laser. **Directions:** Just off the Galway-Limerick road, signed between Clarenbridge and Kilcolgan.

Keogh's Bar & Restaurant

Kinvara
BAR/RESTAURANT

Main Street Kinvara Co Galway **Tel: 091 637 145**
mikeogh@eircom.net www.kinvara.com/keoghs

Michael Keogh took over this old pub in the picturesque village of Kinvara in 1996 and refurbished it, creating a cosy bar with an open fire and a restaurant with character behind it, with wooden floors and benches and oilcloth-covered tables - and a large fireplace with a traditional black stove. The food is modern Irish bar meals, served by charming international staff, and there are tables outside in summer. Local seafood is the main speciality - an informal bite of fine, creamy, fishy chowder for example, or steamed mussels (both come with home-made brown bread), or more serious main courses like cod fillet with beurre nantais or pan-fried monkfish Provençal. There are plenty of other choices too, including warm goat's cheese salad, or rack of Kinvara lamb; homely desserts might include a freshly-baked apple and rhubarb crumble. Children welcome, air conditioning. **Seats 50** (outdoor seating, 18). Weekly music sessions in summer. Food available daily 9.30am-10pm (Sun from 12), B 9.30, L 12.30-5, D 6-10. A la carte. House wine from €15.95. Reservations accepted. Closed 25 Dec, Good Fri. Amex, MasterCard, Visa, Laser. **Directions:** Kinvara village - on the coast road to Doolin, 19km (12 m) from Galway. ◊

The Pier Head Bar & Restaurant

Kinvara
PUBRESTAURANT

The Quay Kinvara Co Galway **Tel: 091 638188**

Mike Burke's well-known harbourside establishment has lots of maritime character and views out over the harbour to Dunguaire Castle. You'll find seafood like fat, tasty mussels in moules marinière, with a milky onion and wine broth, and pan-fried skate, which is rarely seen on restaurant menus. Lobster is a speciality - served in the shell with garlic butter and a side salad - and something else they take pride in is top of the range steak, using local beef (totally traceable), which is slaughtered and butchered specially. And there's also music, all year: bands on Friday & Saturday nights usually, also traditional on Sunday afternoon. (Phone ahead to check availability). Children welcome. **Seats 100** (private room 50). D Mon-Sat, 5-9.30pm; a la carte; house wine about €15. Closed 25 Dec & Good Fri. Diners, MasterCard, Visa, Laser. **Directions:** Kinvara harbour front. ◇

LEENANE

There can be few more spectacular locations for a village than Leenane, which is tucked into the shoreline at the head of Ireland's only deepwater fjord, backed by dramatic mountains. In the village you will find the delightful little Blackberry Café (see entry) and, just along the shore, is the **Leenane Hotel** (095 42249; www.leenanehotel.com), which is a relatively budget-conscious cousin establishment to Rosleague Manor at Letterfrack (see entry). And not far away - an eight mile scenic drive northwest of Leenane, on the Louisbourg road, is the **Delphi Mountain Resort & Spa** (095 42208; www.delphiadventureholidays.ie); it has recently changed ownership and is closed for major refurbishment at the time of going to press, re-opening in 2008 - details will be on their website; the adventure centre operating from the same site remains open.

WWW.IRELAND-GUIDE.COM FOR THE BEST PLACES TO EAT, DRINK & STAY

Leenane
CAFÉ

Blackberry Café & Coffee Shop

Leenane Co Galway
Tel: 095 42240

Sean and Mary Hamilton's lovely little restaurant is just what the weary traveller hopes to happen on when touring or walking in this beautiful area. They're open through the afternoon and evening every day during the summer, serving home-made soups and chowders with home-baked bread, substantial snacks such as fish cakes and mussels, and delicious desserts like rhubarb tart and lemon meringue pie with cream. Extra dishes such as hot smoked trout and a chicken main course might be added to the menu in the evening, but the secret of the Blackberry Café's appeal is that they don't try to do too much at once and everything is freshly made each day. **Seats 40.** Open 12-4.30 and 6-9 daily in high season. A la carte. House wine about €15 (1/4 bottles also available). Closed Tue in shoulder seasons. Closed end Sep-Easter. Visa, Laser. **Directions:** On main street, opposite car park. ◇

Leenane
COUNTRY HOUSE

Delphi Lodge

Leenane Co Galway **Tel: 095 42222**
stay@delphilodge.ie www.delphilodge.ie

féile bia One of Ireland's most famous sporting lodges, Delphi Lodge was built in the early 19th-century by the Marquis of Sligo, and is magnificently located in an unspoilt valley, surrounded by the region's highest mountains (with the high rainfall so dear to fisherfolk). Owned since 1986 by Peter Mantle - who has restored and extended the original building in period style - the lodge is large and impressive in an informal, understated way, with antiques, fishing gear and a catholic collection of reading matter, creating a stylish yet relaxed atmosphere. The guest rooms are all quite different, but they have lovely lake and mountain views, good bathrooms, and are very comfortably furnished. Dinner, for residents only, is taken house-party style at a long oak table - traditionally presided over by the person lucky enough to catch the day's biggest salmon. The set menu begins with an amuse-bouche ('Tongue Tickler'), of Irish goat's cheese beignets with beetroot salad, perhaps, and has earned a reputation for good cooking that reaches far beyond the valley; current house specialities delighting the happy fisherfolk are classic dishes like langoustine bisque, bouillabaisse and rib of beef - and there are sometimes unusual ingredients like the nephrops from Killary Bay, which might come with warmed rocket butter. Coffee and home-made chocolates round off the feast in the Piano Room, where, perhaps, the good company of other guests may keep you from your bed. The famous Delphi Fishery is the main attraction, but many people come for other country pursuits, painting, or just peace and quiet. A billiard table, the library and a serious wine list (great bottles at a very modest mark-up) can get visitors through a lot of wet days. * Delphi Lodge was our Country House of the Year in 2006. Small conferences/banqueting

(20/28); Free broadband wi/fi. Fly fishing, hunting/shooting, cycling, snooker, walking. Sea angling, golf and garden visits nearby. **Rooms 12** (all executive standard). B&B €100 pps, ss €30. Residents D 8pm; D €50; 8 well-chosen house wines, all €23; SC discretionary. Closed 20 Dec - mid Jan. MasterCard, Visa, Laser. Heli-pad. **Directions:** 8 miles northwest of Leenane on the Louisburgh road.

Letterfrack
CAFÉ

Avoca Café Letterfrack

Letterfrack Co Galway **Tel: 095 41058**
www.avoca.ie

A very useful place to know about when you are exploring this beautiful area wholesome light meals and refreshments in the well known Avoca style, albeit on a smaller scale, and lovely clothing and crafts to buy too. Open daily Mar 15-Jan 15, 9am-6pm. **Directions:** On main Clifden-Westport road overlooking Ballinakill Bay at Letterfrack, Connemara.

Letterfrack
RESTAURANT

Kylemore Abbey Restaurant & Tea House

Kylemore Letterfrack Co Galway **Tel: 095 41155**
info@kylemoreabbey.ie www.kylemoreabbey.ie

Providing you are tolerant of tour buses and high season crowds, this dramatically located Abbey offers a surprising range of things to see: a brief stroll from the abbey along the wooded shore leads to the Gothic church, a fascinating miniature replica of Norwich cathedral, for example, then there's a fine craft shop in a neat modern building beside the carpark and also a daytime self-service restaurant, where everything is made on the premises, including traditional meals like beef & Guinness casserole and Irish stew. Big bowls of the nuns' home-made jams are set up at the till, for visitors to help themselves - beside them are neatly labelled jars to buy and take home. A short distance away, the nuns also run a farm and a restored walled garden, which supplies produce to the Garden Tea House. **Seats 240.** Meals daily 9.30-5.30. Closed Christmas Day & Good Fri. (The Garden Tea House, in the restored walled garden, is open Easter-Hallowe'en, 10.30-5.) Amex, MasterCard, Visa, Laser. **Directions:** 2 miles from Letterfrack, on the N59 from Galway. ◊

Letterfrack
RESTAURANT

Pangur Bán Restaurant

Letterfrack Co Galway **Tel: 095 41243**
pban@indigo.ie www.pangurban.com

John Walsh's pretty, whitewashed roadside cottage has a tiny front garden and a large carpark at the back; you enter into a reception / bar area which is unexpectedly bright and airy, with a raised wooden ceiling although, with whitewashed walls and an old fireplace, it retains its natural cottagey character, and table settings are appropriately simple. A relaxing meal with John's good home cooking and service to match is the aim, and this is achieved well. Local produce including game, in season - is used whenever possible in dishes that vary widely in style from quite traditional dishes like braised Galway lamb shanks, to those with international influences, such as a speciality dish of Vietnamese crab with papaya & pink grapefruit. But leave some room for a little indulgence from a wide choice of desserts, ranging from home-made ice creams to rhubarb fool. A nice wine list includes a pair of half bottles, a couple of bubblies, wines by the glass and a few beers. *Cookery classes at weekends off-season. **Seats 45** (private room, 22). D Tue-Sun, 6-9.30; set 2/3 course D €20.50/€25.50, also A la carte. L Sun only, 12-3pm. House wine €18.95. SC 12.5% on groups 8+. Closed Mon, Jan & Feb (A phone call to check opening times any time except high season is advised.) MasterCard, Visa, Laser. **Directions:** In Letterfrack village.

Letterfrack
COUNTRY HOUSE

Rosleague Manor Hotel

Letterfrack Co Galway **Tel: 095 41101**
info@rosleague.com www.rosleague.com

This lovely, graciously proportioned, pink-washed Regency house looks out over a tidal inlet through gardens planted with rare shrubs and plants. Although the area also offers plenty of energetic pursuits, there is a deep sense of peace at Rosleague and it's hard to imagine any better place to recharge the soul. The hotel changed hands within the Foyle family a few years ago and its energetic young owner-manager, Mark Foyle, is gradually working his way through a major renovation programme: the conservatory bar, restaurant and a number of bedrooms (and their bathrooms) have now been refurbished (two were actually demolished and re-built) and some have four-poster beds; and the gardens (already extensive, and listed in the Connemara Garden Trail) have been further developed to make new paths and establish a wild flower meadow. This is a very pleasant, peaceful place to stay and, with a choice of two lovely drawing rooms with log fires, as well as the bar, guests have plenty of space. And the restaurant - a lovely classical dining room, with mahogany furniture and a fine collection of plates on the walls - is open to non-residents by reservation. Head chef Pascal Marinot, who has been at Rosleague since 2000, offers a daily-changing dinner menu in a quite traditional style - starters like oysters with shallot vinegar & lemon, or home-made chicken liver paté with cranberry sauce & Melba toast, a soup course, and straightforward main courses such as black sole on the bone. For dessert, Rosleague chocolate mousse is an inherited speciality - going back to Mark's uncle, Paddy Foyle's, time in the kitchen. Small Conferences/Banqueting (16/85). Children welcome (under 4s free in parents' room, cot available free of charge, baby sitting arranged) Garden, tennis, fishing, walking. Pets permitted. **Rooms 20** (4 junior suites, 3 family, 2 ground floor). B&B €125pps, ss €35. **Restaurant Seats 50** (Private Room seats 12). D 7.30-9 daily, non-residents welcome by reservation; Set D €48. House wine €21. Closed mid Nov-mid Mar. Amex, MasterCard, Visa, Laser. **Directions:** On N59 main road, 11km (7 miles) north-west of Clifden.

Moycullen
RESTAURANT

White Gables Restaurant

Moycullen Village Moycullen Co Galway **Tel: 091 555 744**
info@whitegables.com www.whitegables.com

féile bia Kevin and Ann Dunne have been running this attractive cottagey restaurant on the main street of Moycullen since 1991, and it's now on many a regular diner's list of favourites. Arriving guests can have an aperitif in the bar before heading into the restaurant, where open stonework, low lighting and candlelight create a soothing atmosphere. Kevin sources ingredients with care and offers weekly-changing dinner and à la carte menus, with daily specials, and a set Sunday lunch which is in great demand. Cooking is consistently good in a refreshingly traditional style and features local meats including Connemara lamb (including the speciality smoked lamb) and excellent beef from the famous butchers McGeoughs of Oughterard; fresh fish and seafood, including lobster thermidor, is another speciality and many a guest wouldn't dream of ordering anything but the roast half duckling à l'orange. Good desserts and friendly, efficient service all help make this one of the area's most popular restaurants. An interesting wine list includes some classics and well-chosen house wines. **Seats 45.** Children welcome. Air conditioning. D Tue-Sat, 7-10; L Sun only, 12.30-3. Set D €44.50 (5 course), also à la carte; Set Sun L €26.50. House wine €22.50; sc discretionary. Closed Mon & 23 Dec-14 Feb. Amex, Diners, MasterCard, Visa, Laser. **Directions:** On N59 in Moycullen village, 11km (8 m) from Galway city.

ORANMORE

Between Galway city and Athenry, first impressions of Oranmore are that it is dominated by the N6 and the **Quality Hotel & Leisure Centre** (091 792244; www.qualityhotelgalway.com) is right on the roundabout, so you can't miss it - has outstanding family facilities and is a popular place for business meetings. But there are two other newer hotels (**Ramada Encore** and **The Coach House Hotel**, 091 788367, which opened on Main Street just before the Guide went to press). Oranmore itself is a pleasant place and it has the friendly **Mary's Tea Rooms** for breakfasts and scones etc and a number of good ethnic restaurants including the beautifully appointed **Asian Fusion / Royal Villa Restaurant** (091-790823), which replaced the longstanding Royal Villa in Galway city and offers an interesting mix of well-executed Chinese, Thai and Japanese cuisine in lovely surroundings (good wine list; and good puddings too, not usually a strong point in Asian restaurants).
WWW.IRELAND-GUIDE.COM FOR THE BEST PLACES TO EAT, DRINK & STAY

OUGHTERARD

Oughterard is a charming riverside village, famous for various things, depending on your point of view: it is known as the Gateway to Connemara, renowned for its fishing and for McGeough's butchers, who make the most wonderful air-dried meats, and other specialities well worth seeking out. On the Galway side of the village, **Brigit's Garden** (see entry) at Roscahill is an interesting place to visit, and their tea rooms specialise in home-baking while, in the village itself, **Sweeney's Oughterard House** (091 552 207; www.sweeneys-hotel.com) is a famous old-world hotel. There is also a restaurant **The Yew Tree** (091 866 986) on the main street, which is open all day, 9am-6pm, Mon-Sat and serves good home-cooked food - also including delicious home baking.

Corrib Wave Guesthouse

ughterard
JESTHOUSE

Portcarron Oughterard Co Galway **Tel: 091 552 147**
cwh@gofree.indigo.ie www.corribwave.com

fisherman's dream, Michael and Maria Healy's unpretentious waterside guesthouse offers warm, mily hospitality, comfortable accommodation, an open turf fire to relax by and real home cooking. rooms have phone, tea/coffee-making, TV, radio and a double and single bed; some are suitable for milies. Maria cooks dinner for guests - fresh trout and salmon from the lake, Irish stew, bacon & bbage - just the kind of thing people want. Best of all at Corrib Wave is the location - utter peace d tranquillity. Golf and horse riding nearby and everything to do with fishing organised for you. ildren welcome. Fly fishing; garden; walking. **Rooms 10** (all en-suite, 4 shower only, 2 family, 5 und floor, all no smoking). B&B €40, ss €15. Breakfast 8-9.30. Residents D 7.30pm. Closed 1 c-1 Feb. MasterCard, Visa. **Directions:** From Galway, signed from N59, 1 km before Oughterard.

Currarevagh House

ughterard
UNTRY HOUSE

Glann Road Oughterard Co Galway **Tel: 091 552 312**
mail@currarevagh.com www.currarevagh.com

Tranquillity, trout and tea in the drawing room - these are the things that draw guests back to the Hodgson family's gracious, but not luxurious early Victorian manor overlooking Lough Corrib. Currarevagh, which was built in 1846 as a wedding present for Harry Hodgson's great, great, great grandfather, is set in 150 acres of woodlands and gardens, with sporting rights over 5,000 acres. Guests have been welcomed here since 1890 (almost certainly making Currarevagh Ireland's oldest guesthouse, certainly the longest in contin-

us family membership) and the present owners, Harry and June Hodgson, are founder members of the sh Country Houses and Restaurants Association ('Ireland's Blue Book'), now joined by their son Henry. t, while the emphasis is on old-fashioned service and hospitality, the Hodgsons are adamant that the mosphere should be more like a private house party than an hotel, and their restful rituals underline e differences: the day begins with a breakfast worthy of its Edwardian origins, laid out on the sideboard the dining room; lunch may be one of the renowned picnic hampers required by sporting folk. Then re's afternoon tea, followed by a leisurely dinner. Fishing is the ruling passion, of course - notably wn trout, pike, perch and salmon - but there are plenty of other country pursuits to assist in building an appetite again for Henry's dinners, all based on fresh local produce. His 5-course dinner menus ght begin with a salad of James McGeough's air-dried lamb, then a crab and watercress soup, followed medallions of pork and finally a dessert such as chocolate truffle, and Irish cheeses; there is no choice t menus are changed daily and there is quite an extensive, fairly priced wine list. Children welcome nder 2s free in parents room, cot available at no charge). Pets permitted. Garden, walking, tennis, arse fishing, pool table. Sea angling, equestrian and golf nearby. **Rooms 15** (all en-suite, 2 shower only, family room, 2 single, 6 no smoking). B&B €104pps, ss €35 or single room €90-104. No SC. 4 urse D €45, at 8pm (non-residents welcome by reservation). Wines from €19.50. Closed mid Oct-ar (house available for private hire in winter). MasterCard, Visa, Laser. **Directions:** Take N59 to ghterard. Turn right in village square and follow Glann Road for 6.5km (4 m).

Ross Lake House Hotel

ughterard
OTEL

Rosscahill Oughterard Co Galway **Tel: 091 550 109**
rosslake@iol.ie www. rosslakehotel.com

uietly located in six acres of beautiful gardens, this charming country house was built in 1850 and now a protected building. The current owners, Henry and Elaine Reid, bought the property in 1981 d have gradually refurbished it, so the hotel now offers luxurious accommodation in spacious rooms d suites, all individually furnished with antiques - including some with four-poster beds. While aciously-proportioned and impressively furnished, hands-on management and the warm interest of e proprietors and their staff ensure a welcoming and surprisingly homely atmosphere. Weddings are speciality, especially off season (banqueting, 200). Short breaks offered. Children welcome (under free in parents' room, cot available without charge). No pets. Garden. Tennis. Walking, cycling, hing. **Rooms 13** (1 suite, 1 junior suite, 3 superior, 1 shower only, 1 family room, 3 ground floor, no smoking) B&B about €85, ss €30. D 7-8.30 daily, L Sun 1.45-5. Closed 1 Nov-15 Mar. Amex, asterCard, Visa, Laser. **Directions:** Signed off Galway-Oughterard road.

Oughterard Area
CAFÉ

Brigit's Garden Caf[é]

Pollagh Roscahill Co Galway **Tel: 091 550 9[..]**
info@galwaygarden.com www.galwaygarden.c[..]

Jenny Beale's beautiful themed garden ne[..]
Oughterard reflects the Celtic festivals and, [..]
addition to woodland trails, a ring fort and a sto[..]
chamber has a café that is worth a visit in its o[wn]
right. A pine-ceilinged modern room that also a[..]
as reception/shop has a small kitchen open to vi[ew]
at one end, and is set up with tables covered in o[..]
fashioned oil cloth; everything's very simple, w[ith]
plain white crockery and stainless cutlery a[nd]
paper serviettes and, in fine weather, there [..]
seating outside too. A short (vegetarian) blackbo[ard]
menu offers a daily soup - chunky, wholesome vegetable with thyme, perhaps - a meal in itself w[ith]
brown bread & butter, and a special such as home-grown chard and blue cheese pasta. Lovely toast[ed]
sandwiches are generously filled with salad and a choice of fillings (egg mayonnaise, goat's cheese[..]
herb, hummus & olive, cheese & scallion), and great home bakes include delicious scones with ja[m]
& cream, a luscious, walnut & apricot carrot cake, which is nutty and moist. Good coffee, tea[..]
tisanes, and soft drinks like cranberry or lemon juice - just the kind of place you need to know ab[out]
when exploring the area. Good toilets too, including baby changing facilities and environmental[ly]
friendly waste disposal including reed bed sewage treatment. **Seats 50** (+35 outdoors). Toile[t]
wheelchair accessible. Children welcome; children's playground. Open 11-5 daily (Sun 12-5). Clos[ed]
Oct - mid Apr. MasterCard, Visa, Laser. **Directions:** Just off the N59 between Moycullen a[nd]
Oughterard.

Portumna
RESTAURANT

Dyson's Restaura[nt]

Patrick Street Portumna Co Galw[ay]
Tel 0909 7423[..]

John and Heather Dyson's long-awaited restaurant in the centre of Portumna opened to a wa[rm]
welcome from enthusiastic local diners just before the guide went to press. Behind a smart mar[ble]
frontage, it's an attractive premises on two floors, with a few tables in the ground floor reception a[rea]
- used mainly for early dinners and anyone who finds stairs difficult - and the main dining room [on]
the first floor, with a pleasant decked area off it for use in fine weather. The interior is bright a[nd]
uncluttered - pale wood floor, darkwood tables, comfortable upholstered chairs in brown or crea[m]
leather and good modern seascapes on the walls - and the simplicity is effective. John, who had exp[e]
rience in some distinguished kitchens abroad before settling here, takes pride in sourcing the best[..]
ingredients locally where possible, with an emphasis on organic foods and fish brought in daily fr[om]
Galway; his menus offer about half a dozen starters (typically including seared scallops on a saffr[on]
risotto; galantine of quail spiked with raisins, served with a salad with quail eggs and walnuts), a[nd]
10 main courses - which sensibly include four steak options as well as more adventurous choices l[ike]
duck breast with Chinese five spices, chillies & pineapple, and roast halibut with spinach [..]
hollandaise. Portions are generous (as are the well-made sauces - it might be an idea to ask for sauc[e]
on the side), so you may have to plan ahead to save room for desserts like molten chocolate puddin[g]
crème brulée with caramelised plums or lemon meringue pie. A short but well assembled wine list a[lso]
emphasises organic production and the house wines are great value. Good food, pleasing surroundin[gs]
and friendly service make for an enjoyable outing and this new restaurant promises to be a great ass[et]
to the area. **Seats 50.** D Wed-Sun, 5-10. A la carte; starters €5-15; main courses €20-25 desse[rt]
€6. Major credit cards. **Directions:** Town centre, a couple of doors from the Post Office.

Portumna
HOTEL

Shannon Oaks Hotel & Country Clu[b]

St. Josephs Rd Portumna Co Galway **Tel: 090 974 17[..]**
sales@shannonoaks.ie www.shannonoaks[..]

Situated near the shores of Lough Derg and adjacent to the 17th century Portumna Castle and esta[te]
this spacious privately-owned hotel is quite impressive on arrival - a large lobby has a polished wood[..]
floor, faux-marble pillaring and ample seating in contemporary style, while other public rooms inclu[de]
a warm-toned restaurant, which can be opened out in summer, and a cosy, pub-like bar with [..]
informal mezzanine restaurant. It's a good choice for business and corporate events - bedrooms ha[ve]

conditioning as standard, and conference and meeting facilities are designed for groups of all sizes, th full back-up services. Off-duty delegates will find plenty to do too: a fine leisure centre on-site s an air-conditioned gymnasium as well as a swimming pool and ancillary services, and nearby activ- es include river cruising, fishing, golf, horseriding, cycling and clay pigeon shooting. Portumna stle, with restored kitchen gardens, is worth a visit. Conference/banqueting (300/350); secretarial rvices. Leisure centre (swimming pool, fitness room, jacuzzi, sauna, steam room); beauty salon; lking. Children welcome (under 5s free in parents' room, cot available free of charge, baby sitting anged, playground). No pets. **Rooms 68** (3 suites, some no smoking, 2 for disabled). B&B €80 pps; about €30. 24 hr rooms service, Lift. Amex, Diners, MasterCard, Visa, Laser. **Directions:** Situated St Joseph Road,Portuma.

---

ecess

TEL/RESTAURANT

Ballynahinch Castle Hotel

Recess Co Galway **Tel: 095 31006**
bhinch@iol.ie   www.ballynahinch-castle.com

Renowned as a fishing hotel, this crenellated Victorian mansion enjoys a most romantic position in 450 acres of ancient woodland and gardens on the banks of the Ballynahinch River. It is impressive in scale and relaxed in atmosphere - a magic combination, which, together with a high level of comfort and friendliness (and an invigorating mixture of residents and locals in the bar at night), combine to bring people back. The tone is set in the foyer, with its huge stone fireplace and ever-burning log fire (which is a cosy place to enjoy ternoon tea) and the many necessary renovations and extensions through the years have been under- ken with great attention to period detail, a policy also carried through successfully in furnishing both blic areas and bedrooms, many of which have lovely views over the river. A stay here is always a storative treat - especially if you have one of the rooms on the top floor which have just been refur- shed in a lovely gentle ever-so-slightly-modernised classic style with bathrooms to match. And, after restful night's sleep, a Ballynahinch breakfast will give you a good start ahead of a day's fishing, lderness walks on the estate, or simply touring the area. (Ballynahinch was the Connaught winner our Irish Breakfast Awards in 2002.) Fishing: 3 miles of private fly fishing for Atlantic salmon, sea ut and brown trout. Landscaped gardens and wilderness walks on 450 acres; members of nnemara Garden Trail; cycling, tennis. Golf nearby. Small conferences (12). welcome (under 3s free parents' room; cots available without charge, baby sitting arranged). No pets. **Rooms 40** (3 suites, l with separate bath & shower, All no smoking) No lift. 24 hr room service. B&B €125 pps, ss €30, : 10%. Short/special interest/off season breaks offered - details on application. **Owenmore estaurant:** This bright and elegant room has the classic atmosphere of a splendidly old-fashioned ning room, and is carefully organised to allow as many tables as possible to enjoy its uniquely beau- ful river setting, where you can watch happy fisherfolk claiming the last of the fading daylight on the cks below. Daily dinner menus have plenty of fine local produce to call on - wild salmon, of course, so sea fish, Connemara lamb and prime Irish beef (supplied by the renowned butcher, McGeough's Oughterard) - a great basis for specialities with enduring popularity like poached wild Atlantic lmon, baked Connemara lamb cutlets and lobster. Vegetarians are well looked after too - home-made asta is a speciality, papardelle served with artichoke hearts, garlic and Parmesan cheese, perhaps. taff are hospitable and relaxed, and a thoughtfully assembled wine list offers an unusual range of ouse wines and a good choice of half bottles. *Excellent meals are also served in the hotel's charac- rful bar - a mighty high-ceilinged room with a huge fireplace, and many mementoes of the pleasures rod and hunt. An informal alternative to the Owenmore experience - and a great place for non-resi- ents to drop into for a bite when touring Connemara. Owenmore Restaurant open daily, D 6.30-9 (Set €49+10%sc), house wines from €24.70. Bar meals 12.30-3 & 6.30-9 daily. SC 10%. Closed hristmas & Feb. Amex, Diners, MasterCard, Visa, Laser. **Directions:** N59 from Galway - Clifden; left ter Recess (Roundstone road), 6 km.

Recess
HOTEL/RESTAURANT

Lough Inagh Lodge
Recess Connemara Co Galway **Tel: 095 3470**
inagh@iol.ie www.loughinaghlodgehotel.

Maire O'Connor's former sporting lodge on the shores of Lough Inagh makes a delightful small hotel, with a country house atmosphere. It has large, well-proportioned rooms, interesting period detail and lovely fireplaces with welcoming log fires, as well as all the modern comforts. Public areas include two drawing rooms, each with an open fire, and a very appealing bar with a big turf fire and its own back door and tiled floor for wet fishing gear. Bedrooms, which include one recently added room and several with four-posters, are all well-appointed and unusually spacious, with views of lake and countryside. Walk-in dressing rooms lead to well-planned bathrooms and tea/coffee-making facilities are available in rooms on request. While it has special appeal to sportsmen, Lough Inagh makes a good base for touring Connemara and is only 42 miles from Galway; in addition to fishing, golf, pony trekking and garden visits are all nearby. Off-season breaks offer especially good value. Small conferences/banqueting (15/50). Children welcome (under 3s free in parents' room, cots available without charge). Pets permitted. Garden, walking, cycling, fly fishing. Equestrian, sea angling, garden visits and hunting/shooting all nearby. **Rooms 13** (5 junior suites, 1 family, 10 no smoking, 4 ground floor) room service (24 hr). B&B €140 pps, ss €20. **Finisglen Room:** This handsome dining room has deep green walls and graceful spoonback Victorian mahogany chairs, and non-residents are welcome for dinner by reservation. Fiona Joyce has been head chef since 2002, and the food in both the restaurant and the bar is excellent; alongside the popular dishes like smoked salmon, pan-fried steaks, lobster (when available) you may find less usual choices including starters of grilled fish sausage, or air-dried Connemara lamb. Desserts, including a wide range of ices, are home-made, service friendly, and portions generous. The wine list includes a fair range of half bottles, some non-alcoholic wines and, unusually, a rosé among the house wines. *Tempting bar menus are also offered for lunch, dinner and afternoon tea. **Seats 36;** L 12.30-4; D daily 6.45-9pm (reservations required). Set D €49; also a la Carte. House wine €22; Bar meals 12.30-4 & 6.30-9pm daily. SC10%. Closed mid Dec-mid Mar. Amex, Diners, MasterCard, Visa, Laser. **Directions:** From Galway city travel on N59 for 64km (40 m).Take rght N344 after Recess; 5km (3 m) on right.

Renvyle
HOTEL

Renvyle House Hotel
Renvyle Co Galway **Tel: 095 4351**
info@renvyle.com www.renvyle.com

In one of the country's most appealing remote and beautiful areas, this famous Lutyens-esque house has a romantic and fascinating history, having been home to people as diverse as a Gaelic chieftain and Oliver St John Gogarty - and it became one of Ireland's earliest country house hotels, in 1883. In good weather it is best approached via a stunning scenic drive along a mountain road with views down into a blue green sea of unparalleled clarity. Once reached, the hotel seems to be snuggling down for shelter and although it has limited views, there is a shift of emphasis to the comforts within, a feeling reinforced by the cosy atmosphere of the original building, with its dark beams, rug strewn floors and open fire - and a snug conservatory where guests can survey the garden, and the landscape beyond. Photographs and mementoes recording visits from the many famous people who have stayed here - Augustus John, Lady Gregory, Yeats and Churchill among them - keep guests happily occupied for hours, but there is plenty to distract you from this enjoyable activity, including a heated outdoor swimming pool, tennis, trout fishing, golf (9 hole), and croquet - while the surrounding area offers more challenging activities including archaeological expeditions, horse riding, hill walking, scuba diving and sea fishing. Just loafing around is perhaps what guests are best at here, however, and there's little need to do much else. The hotel's bar food is excellent too - all this, plus the scent of a turf fire and a comfortable armchair, can be magic. The grounds and gardens around the hotel are a special point of interest a

Renvyle, and come as a delightful contrast to the magnificently rugged surrounding scenery. Special breaks (midweek, weekend and bank holiday) are very good value and Renvyle makes an excellent conference venue. Conference/banqueting (200); secretarial services. Children welcome (under 2s free in parents' room, cots available without charge; crèche (seasonal), playroom, children's playground, children's tea, baby sitting arranged). Pets permitted by arrangement. Archery, all-weather tennis court, clay pigeon shooting, croquet, lawn bowls, fly fishing, sea angling, snooker. **Rooms 68** (4 suites, 40 no smoking, 1 for disabled, 6 family rooms). B&B €119, no ss, no SC. **Restaurant:** Whilst bar lunches and light meals in the conservatory are very enjoyable during the day (and this is a great place to plan a break when touring the area), dinner at Renyle is an occasion to be relished. The large dining room which is cannily organised with a window along one side where parents can see their children in the supervised playroom next door is formally appointed and there is a pianist at the grand piano every night, adding to the sense of occasion. General Manager Ronnie Counihan is always on hand to chat with guests, and head chef Tim O'Sullivan looks after the inner man admirably. His menus feature local seafood and Connemara produce, including Renvyle rack of lamb, local lobster and vegetables in season and not only is his cooking spot on but he has written a cookery book, so you can try out his recipes at home.*Renvyle House was selected for a Féile Bia Award in 2006. Restaurant open 7-9 daily (Set D €45). Bar meals 11-5 daily (excl 25 Dec, Good Fri). Closed 1-21 Dec & 7 Jan - 8 Feb. Helipad. Amex, Diners, MasterCard, Visa, Laser. **Directions:** 18km (12 miles) north of Clifden. ◊

ROUNDSTONE

This charming village is clustered around its traditional stone-built harbour, so seafood is very much the speciality in every bar and restaurant. The Conneely family's **Eldons Hotel** (095 35933; www.connemara.net) is a comfortable family-run hotel with its own seafood restaurant, **Beola**, next door, and there is also the Vaughan family's **Roundstone House Hotel** (095 35864; www.irishcountry-hotels.com). Both have a well-earned reputation with locals and visitors alike - and both offer golf and sea angling breaks.

WWW.IRELAND-GUIDE.COM - THE BEST PLACES TO EAT, DRINK & STAY

Roundstone
CHARACTER PUB/RESTAURANT

O'Dowd's Bar

Roundstone Co Galway **Tel: 095 35809**
odowds@indigo.ie www.odowdsbar.com

The O'Dowd family have been welcoming visitors to this much-loved pub over-looking the harbour for longer than most people care to remember - and, although there are some new developments from time to time, the old bar is always the same. It's one of those simple places, with the comfort of an open fire and good pint, where people congregate in total relaxation - if they can get in (it can be very busy in the summer months). A reasonably priced bar menu majoring in seafood offers sustenance or, for more formal meals, the restaurant next door does the honours: seafood chowder, mussels, crabmeat etc; Connemara lamb; blackberry & apple pie. **Seats** 36. Children welcome before 8pm (high chair, children's menu). Meals 12-10 daily (to 9.30 in pub). Reservations required in restaurant. Á la carte. House wine from €18.50. SC 10% on parties of 6+. Self-catering accommodation available - details on application. Closed 25 Dec. Amex, MasterCard, Visa, Laser. **Directions:** On harbour front in Roundstone village.

Roundstone Area
B&B

The Anglers Return

Toombeola Roundstone Connemara Co Galway **Tel: 095 31091**
info@anglersreturn.com www.anglersreturn.com

This charming and unusual house near Roundstone was built as a sporting lodge in the eighteenth century and, true to its name, fishing remains a major attraction to this day. But you don't have to be a fisherperson to warm to the special charms of The Anglers Return: peace and tranquillity, the opportunity to slow down in a quiet, caring atmosphere in this most beautiful area - this is its particular appeal. The house is set in three acres of natural gardens (open every day in spring and summer; best in late spring) and makes good base for the Connemara Garden Trail - and, of course, for painting holidays. Bedrooms are bright and comfortably furnished in a fresh country house style, although only one is en-suite (the other four share two bathrooms between them); this is not a major problem and the overall level of comfort is high. However, bathroom arrangements are gradually being improved - one now features a restored Victorian ball & claw cast-iron bath. As well as fishing, there is golf nearby, and riding and boat trips can be arranged for guests - and there are maps and information for walkers too. No television, but instead there are lots of books to read - and tea or snacks are available at any time during the day or evening, (out in the secluded back garden in fine weather, or beside the fire in the soothing drawing room, perhaps); dinner is available for groups staying several days, otherwise bookings can be made in nearby restaurants. Breakfast will include freshly baked breads, home-made yoghurts, marmalade and jams, and freshly picked herb teas from the garden - and you are even invited to collect your own egg. Not suitable for children. Walking, fishing, garden. **Rooms 5** (1 en-suite, 4 with shared bathrooms; all no smoking). B&B €48, ss by arrangement. *Special interest breaks offered (painting, walking); details on application. Closed 1 Dec-28 Feb. **No Credit Cards. Directions:** From Galway, N59 Clifden road; turn left onto R341 Roundstone road for 6.5km (4 m); house is on the left.

Tuam
BAR/RESTAURANT

Finns Restaurant
Milltown Tuam Co Galway **Tel: 093 51327**
johnfinn.indigo.ie

John and Lucy Finn's attractive restaurant is on the river, in a charming little award-winning tidy town a few miles north of Tuam - a welcome sight for hungry travellers between Galway and Sligo. John cooks an eclectic mix of international and traditional dishes - reasonably priced and served in a relaxed atmosphere. The cooking is sound, it's good value for money and the small village setting - where everyone seems to know someone at another table - makes a welcome change from busy towns. On the down side, bookings are not accepted, which is a major disadvantage when diners may travel especially to eat here and then have the inconvenience of a long wait for a table. Children welcome. **Seat 80** (Private room, 14). No reservations. D Tue-Sun, 5-9pm. A la carte; house wines from about €16 Service discretionary. Closed 3 days Christmas & Easter. Children welcome. MasterCard, Visa, Laser **Directions:** 8 miles from Tuam, main N17 to Sligo. ◇

COUNTY KERRY

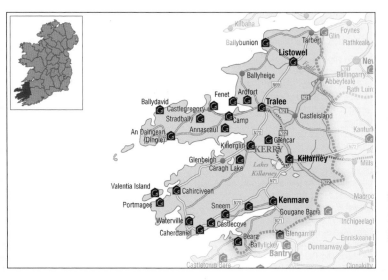

It's something special, being Kerry. This magnificent county in the far southwest has Ireland's highest and most varied mountains, and certain favoured areas also have our longest-lived citizens. Then, too, it's a region which has long been a global pioneer in the hospitality business - in 2004, the scenically-blessed town of Killarney celebrated 250 years in the forefront of Irish tourism, while its most senior hotel, the Great Southern, celebrated its own 150th anniversary.

So visitors inevitably arrive with high expectations. Kerry, however, can face the challenge. This magnificent county really is the Kingdom of Kerry. Everything is king size. For not only has Kerry mountains galore - more than anywhere else in Ireland - but there's a rare quality to Carrantuohill, the highest of all.

By international standards, this loftiest peak of MacGillicuddy's Reeks (try pronouncing it "mackil-cuddy") may not seem particularly notable at just 1038 m. But when you sense its mysterious heights in the clouds above a countryside of astonishing beauty, its relative elevation is definitely world league. And all Kerry's mountains sweep oceanwards towards a handsome coastline which rings the changes between sheltered inlets and storm tossed offshore islands. Visually, Kerry has everything.

But these days, spectacular scenery isn't enough on its own. Like other leading visitor destinations, Kerry is well aware of the need to provide accessible entertainment and an increasing choice of places with cultural and historical interest. Here too, the Kingdom can oblige. And it can also oblige those with sporting interests. On September 16th 2007 on the hallowed turf of Croke Park in Dublin, Kerry won their 34th annual All-Ireland Football Championship in convincing style against Cork.

The oldest fossil footprints in the Northern Hemisphere are in Kerry, and they're about 350 million years old. You'll find them way down west, on Valentia Island, and they're reckoned one of the seven wonders of Ireland. In much more modern times, the Antarctic explorer Tom Crean was from Kerry. He came from the little village of Annascaul on the majestic Dingle Peninsula, and when he had finished with adventuring, he returned to Annascaul and opened the South Pole Inn.

The town of Killarney, among the lakes and mountains where they're re-establishing the enormous white-tailed sea eagle, has long been a magnet for visitors, but Killarney is determined not simply to rest on its laurels after more than a Quarter Millennium as Ireland's premier tourist destination, for it was in 1754 that its attractions were first internationally promoted. Meanwhile, on the more immediate question of keeping the place clean, Killarney scored well in the latest national Tidy Town contest, announced in September 2007 – it came in with a Gold Medal.

So too Kenmare in recent years. Across the purple mountains from Killarney, the lovely little town of Kenmare in South Kerry is both a gourmet focus, and another excellent touring centre. As one of the prettiest places in Ireland, Kenmare puts the emphasis on civic pride,

In the far northeast of this large county, Listowel – famed for its writers and its Race Week in September – has the restored Lartigue Monorail, another award-winning attraction. It's unique. And if you want to know how unique, well, you'll just have to go and see for yourself.

Local Attractions & Information

Beaufort Hotel Dunloe Castle Gardens	064 44 111
Castleisland Crag Cave	066 714 1244
Dingle Ocean World	066 915 2111
Dunquin Great Blasket Centre	066 915 6444 / 915 6371
Farranfore Kerry International Airport	066 976 4644
Kenmare Walking Festivals	064 41 034
Kenmare Heritage Centre	064 41 233
Killarney Muckross House, Gardens & Traditional Farm	064 31 440
Killarney Tourism Information	064 31 633
Killorglin Kerry Woollen Mills	064 44 122
Killorglin Puck Fair (ancient festival), mid-August	066 976 2366
Listowel St John's Art Centre	068 22 566
Listowel Writers' Week (June)	068 21 074
Tralee Kerry County Museum	066 712 7777
Tralee Rose of Tralee Festival (late August)	066 712 3227
Tralee Siamsa Tire Arts Centre	066 712 3055
Valentia Island The Skellig Experience	066 947 6306
Valentia Island Valentia Heritage (Knightstown)	066 947 6411
Waterville Craft Market	066 947 4212

Ardfert
PUB

Kate Browne's Pub
Ardfert Co Kerry
Tel: 066 713 4055 / 4030

Situated on the main road but with parking to the side, this friendly and attractive pub has an old world ambience, with roughly plastered walls and country pine. The main dining area is a large, bright and airy room with an unusual slate bar and an old solid fuel stove, and another eating area off the main bar has an inviting open fire which makes guests feel at home. This is not a place to expect cutting edge cooking, but you'll find wholesome fare at all times of day, and with generous portions. Local seafood features in popular dishes like chowder (with excellent home-baked bread), prawn cocktail made with fresh prawns, which is very often not the case, and baked mussels, as well as main course fish dishes; but a wide ranging menu is offered to suit all tastes and the restaurant is very popular with families - a special children's menu is available too. Toilets wheelchair accessible; children welcome (high chair, children's menu, baby changing facilities); **Seats 100** (outdoors, 20, private room, 50); food served daily, 12-10pm; house wine €20. Closed 25 Dec, Good Fri. Amex, Diners, MasterCard, Visa, Laser. **Directions:** 5 km north of Tralee, on the left as you enter Ardfert.

Ballybunion
GUESTHOUSE/BAR/RESTAURANT

Harty-Costello Townhouse Bar & Restaurant
Main Street Ballybunion Co Kerry **Tel: 068 27129**
hartycostello@eircom.net www.hartycostellos.com

Although styled a townhouse, Davnet and Jackie Hourigan's welcoming town centre establishment is really an inn, encompassing all the elements of hospitality within its neatly painted and flower bedecked yellow walls. The spacious bedrooms have television, phones, tea & coffee-making facilities and hair dryer, and also comfortable chairs and curtains thoughtfully fitted with blackout linings to keep out intrusively early light in summer. All bedrooms, and the residents' lounge, were completely refurbished recently and, while practical elements of the old rooms were sensibly retained, the style is now more contemporary and uncluttered. There's a choice of three bars and an evening restaurant where seafood is the speciality, complemented by an extensive wine list. It all adds up to a relaxing and hospitable base for a golfing holiday, or for touring the south-west. Golfing breaks and short breaks are offered: details on application. Walking; broadband wi/fi; children welcome (under 12s free in parents' room, cot available); no pets. **Rooms 8** (all en-suite and no smoking). B&B €70 pps, ss €20.

Room service (all day). Meals available Mon-Sat, 12-4 (bar); 6.30-9.30 (restaurant). No food on Sun; establishment closed 30 Oct-30 Mar. Amex, MasterCard, Visa, Laser. **Directions:** 50 miles from Limerick N69; 40 miles from Killarney.

Ballybunion
COUNTRY HOUSE/RESTAURANT/PUB

Iragh Ti Connor

Main Street Ballybunion Co Kerry **Tel: 068 27112**
iraghticonnor@eircom.net www.golfballybunion.com

The name, which translates as "the inheritance of O'Connor", says it all: what John and Joan O'Connor inherited was a 19th century pub, and thanks to their scrupulous attention to detail, their inheritance has now been transformed into a fine establishment. The rooms are all generous and have been carefully refurbished and furnished with antiques, and bathrooms with cast-iron tubs and power showers. Public areas are also furnished with style and individuality and, in to addition good bar food in the character old pub, there's a fine dining restaurant with a well-deserved reputation for good cooking. Golfing holidays are a serious attraction and this is one of the best places for discerning golfers to stay. Free broadband; Children welcome (under 3s free in parents' room, cot available without charge). Small conferences (60). Garden. No pets. **Rooms 17** (2 junior suites, 15 superior rooms, all no smoking). B&B €95 pps, ss €60. No SC. *Golf breaks offered, with tee times arranged at Ballybunion Old Course. Closed Dec & Jan. Amex, MasterCard, Visa, Laser. **Directions:** Top of main street, opposite statue of Bill Clinton. ◇

Ballybunion
GUESTHOUSE

Teach de Broc

Links Road Ballybunion Co Kerry **Tel: 068 27581**
info@ballybuniongolf.com www.ballybuniongolf.com

You don't have to play golf to appreciate this highly popular guesthouse, but it certainly must help as it is almost within the boundaries of the famous Ballybunion links. Aoife and Seamus Brock offer an extremely high standard of comfort, with satellite television in all rooms, and there is a commitment to constant upgrading and improvement: fairly recent additions include a new guest lounge and a wine/coffee bar, more fine bedrooms, and an electric massage chair for easing golfers' aches and pains after a long day on the links. Yet, however comfortable and well-located this exceptional guesthouse may be, it's the laid-back and genuinely hospitable atmosphere created by this energetic and dedicated couple that really gets them coming back for more. Always keen to provide the best possible service for the discerning golfer, an excellent breakfast is served from 6am, with freshly baked scones and croissants among the good things offered. The wine bar idea, originally intended to offer just a light bite, has developed a little each year; home-made gourmet pizzas are the speciality of the house - and the light evening meals available to residents proved such a popular alternative to going into town to eat that it's now become 'Strollers Bistro' and offers an à la carte menu, with a choice of half a dozen starters and main courses like rack of Kerry lamb and chargrilled sirloin steak as well as the original pizza menu. Home-made desserts may include a speciality chocolate fondant, and an Irish cheeseboard comes with a glass of port. Wine licence. *Stay & Play golf breaks offered; details on application. Masseuse on call. Laundry service; horse riding nearby; own parking; garden. Not suitable for children; no pets. Broadband wi/fi (no charge). Masseuse on call. Laundry service; horse riding nearby; own parking; garden. Not suitable for children; no pets. **Rooms 14** (all en-suite, 4 with separate bath & shower, 2 shower only, all no-smoking, 1 for disabled). Lift. Turndown service. All day room service. B&B €80pps, ss €50. Closed 1 Nov - 15 Mar. MasterCard, Visa, Laser. Heli-pad. **Directions:** Directly opposite entrance to Ballybunion Golf Club.

Caherdaniel
HOTEL/RESTAURANT

Derrynane Hotel

Caherdaniel Co Kerry **Tel: 066 947 5136**
info@derrynane.com www.derrynane.com

If only for its superb location, this unassuming 1960s-style hotel would be well worth a visit, but there is much more on offer. The accommodation is quite modest but very comfortable and the food is good - and, under the excellent management of Mary O'Connor and her well-trained staff, this hospitable, family-friendly place provides a welcome home from home for many a contented guest. Activity holidays are a big draw - there are beautiful beaches, excellent fishing, Waterville Golf Course offers special rates at certain times - and the hotel has published its own walking brochure. Don't leave the area without visiting Daniel O'Connell's beautiful house at Derrynane or the amazing Ballinskelligs chocolate factory. *Derrynane Hotel was our Family Hotel of the Year in 2005. Children welcome (under 4s free in parents' room, cots available without charge, baby sitting arranged; playroom) Heated outdoor swimming pool, tennis, pool table, fitness room, steam room, walking, garden. Equestrian and fishing (coarse, sea angling) nearby. **Rooms 70** (all en-suite, 15 family rooms, 32 ground floor, 50 no smoking). Room rate from €95. *Special breaks offered: details on application. Closed Oct-Easter. **Restaurant:** Overlooking the heated outdoor swimming pool and the hotel's gardens, the restaurant enjoys stunning sea views - be sure to ask for a table by the window, as the view is a major part of the experience. While not a fine dining experience, good food has always been a feature of the hotel and there is a commitment to high quality ingredients, local where possible. The 4-course dinner menus offer a good choice of simply presented popular dishes like smoked salmon, chicken liver mousse, Kerry lamb or beef, and duckling - and a very reasonably priced children's menu is offered. Attentive staff do everything possible to make a meal here a pleasant experience - and a helpful wine list is clearly presented. *A light bar menu is also available every day, 11am-9pm. **Seats 100.** D 6.30-9 daily, Set D €42. Also à la carte, sc discretionary. House wine €19.90. *All day salad bar available for light meals. Hotel closed Oct- Easter. Amex, Diners, MasterCard, Visa, Laser. **Directions:** Midway on Ring of Kerry.

Caherdaniel
COUNTRY HOUSE

Iskeroon

Caherdaniel Co Kerry **Tel: 066 947 5119**
info@iskeroon.com www.iskeroon.com

Geraldine Burkitt and David Hare's beautiful old house is in a secluded position overlooking Derrynane Harbour, and the effort taken to get there makes it all the more restful once settled in. All three of the comfortable and interestingly decorated bedrooms overlook the harbour and the islands of Deenish and Scarriff and each has its own private bathroom just across a corridor. The private pier at the bottom of the garden joins an old Mass Path which, by a happy chance, leads not only to the beach but also to Keating's pub (known as Bridie's) where a bit of banter and, perhaps, some good seafood is also to be had in the evenings, although it's wise to check on this beforehand. In keeping with the caring philosophy of this lovely house, solar panels were installed to heat the water. Free Broadband wi/fi. Unsuitable for children. No pets. Fishing (fly, coarse, sea angling), walking and scuba diving nearby. Garden. *Self-catering studio apartment for two also available. **Rooms 3** (all with private bathrooms, all no smoking). B&B €75 pps, ss €75. Closed Sep-May. MasterCard, Visa, Laser. **Directions:** Between Caherdaniel and Waterville (N70), turn off at the Scariff Inn, signed to Bunavalla Pier. Go to the pier and left through "private" gate; cross beach and enter through white gate posts.

CAHIRCIVEEN

Cahirciveen is a small market town half way round the Ring of Kerry; situated on the River Feale, at the foot of Benetee mountain, it overlooks Valentia Harbour and is the shopping centre of South Kerry - traditional fair days are still held on the street. Attractions of interest include the **Heritage Centre** -

situated in the old Royal Irish Constabulary Barracks adjacent to the town centre - which has craft workshops, an audio-visual display and archaeological remains on view. As well as **QCs**, in the town (see entry), handy places to take a break on the Ring of Kerry include **O'Neills 'The Point Bar'** (066 947 2165) at Renard Point, just beside the car ferry to Valentia island: Michael & Bridie O'Neill's immaculately maintained pub is well-known for its fresh seafood (phone ahead to check times). On the main Ring of Kerry road, it is useful to know about Pat Golden's family-run "one stop shop" the **Quarry Restaurant** (066 947 7601; www.patscraftshop.com): not only will you get good home cooking here, but there's also a post office and foodstore, filling station, tourist information point, bureau de change, a fine craft shop, with quality Irish clothing and gift items - and the unique 'Golden Mile Nature Walk'. New to the town and due to open shortly after the Guide goes to press, **The Watermarque Hotel** (066 947 2222; www.watermarquehotel.ie) will bring welcome facilities, including a spa.

WWW.IRELAND-GUIDE.COM FOR THE BEST PLACES TO EAT, DRINK & STAY

Cahirciveen   # QC's Seafood Bar & Restaurant

BAR/RESTAURANT   3 Main Street Cahirciveen Co Kerry **Tel: 066 947 2244**

info@qcbar.com   www.qcbar.com

Kate and Andrew Cooke's sensitively renovated bar and restaurant has some great original features that give it character, including a rugged stone wall and an enormous fireplace. The bar counter is also over a century old and there are numerous pictures of local interest and nautical antiques, reflecting Andrew's special love affair with the sea (he runs a yacht charter service* as well as the bar). The sea is fundamental here anyway, as local fish is the main feature, supplied by the family company, Quinlan's Kerry Fish at Renard's Point. There's a big Spanish influence here, so expect delicious chargrills, with lots of olive oil and garlic: fresh crab claws and crabmeat are a speciality, also sizzling prawns, and pan-seared baby squid. Menus are flexible - any of the starters can be served in a main course size, and, although it undoubtedly helps to like seafood, there are plenty of other choices. Main courses include excellent meats to balance up all that ultra-fresh seafood especially rack of Kerry lamb and char-grilled fillet steak (supplied by a local butcher). The most pleasing aspect of the food is its immediacy - everything is ultra-fresh, simply prepared and full of zest and, given the quality, it is also good value. At the back of the restaurant, there's a charming sheltered outdoor dining area and landscaped garden, carved from the hillside by their own sheer willpower - and, as Andrew is quick to point out, a hired digger. [*For yacht charter information, see www.YachtCharterKerry.com] An interesting wine list leans strongly towards Spain, especially the reds, although house wines are from France & Chile; it is good to see sherry listed as a mainstream wine rather than relegated to aperitif status. Children welcome. **Seats 50** (outdoors, 40). Meals: L 12.30-2.30 in Summer (Jun-Aug) only (closed Sun L); D 6-30-9.30pm, 7 days in Jul-Aug, 6 days shoulder season (closed Mon), Winter Thu-Sun. Closed 25 Dec, Good Fri; annual closure 8 Jan - mid Feb. Minimum credit card charge, €25. MasterCard, Visa, Laser. **Directions:** In the centre of Caherciveen.

Caragh Lake   # Carrig House Country House & Restaurant

COUNTRY HOUSE/RESTAURANT   Caragh Lake Killorglin Co Kerry **Tel: 066 976 9100**

info@carrighouse.com   www.carrighouse.com

At the heart of Frank and Mary Slattery's sensitively extended Victorian house lies a hunting lodge once owned by Lord Brocket - and he chose well, as it is very attractive and handsomely set in fine gardens with the lake and mountains providing a dramatic backdrop. The house is welcoming and well-maintained, with friendly staff (Frank himself carries the luggage to your room) and a relaxed atmosphere, notably in a series of sitting rooms where you can chat beside the fire or have a drink before dinner. This is a place where you can lose yourself for hours with a book, or playing chess, cards or board games in the games room, or boating out on the lake. Some of the large, airy bedrooms have their own patios, and all are furnished with antiques, and have generous, well-designed bathrooms with bath and shower - an impressive Presidential Suite has a sitting room with panoramic views across the lake to the Magillicuddy Reeks, two separate dressing rooms and jacuzzi bath. The extensive gardens are of great interest - a map is available, and personalised tours can be arranged. Not suitable for children under 8 except small babies (under 1 free of charge, cot available, baby sitting arranged). Dogs allowed in some areas. Swimming (lake), fishing (ghillie & boat available), walking, garden, croquet. **Rooms 16** (1 suite, 1 junior suite, 3 no smoking) B&B about €80 pps, ss €50. Closed Dec-Feb. **Lakeside Restaurant:** Beautifully situated overlooking the lake, the restaurant is a fine room with well-spaced tables and a relaxed atmosphere. Open to the public as well as resident guests, extensive menus offer a balanced choice, with fresh Kerry seafood and Kerry lamb the main specialities, also a vegetarian option available. **Seats 55** (private room, 15) Outdoor dining for 20. D daily, 7-9. Extensive à la carte. House wine about €25. SC discretionary. Non-residents welcome (booking essential). Establishment closed Dec-Feb. Diners, MasterCard, Visa, Laser. **Directions:** Left after 2.5 miles on Killorglin/Glenbeigh Road N70 (Ring of Kerry), then turn sharp right at Caragh Lake School (1.5 miles), half a mile on the left. ◇

Caragh Lake
HOTEL

Hotel Ard na Sidhe

Caragh Lake Killorglin Co Kerry **Tel: 066 976 9105**
hotelsales@liebherr.com www.killarneyhotels.ie

Set in woodland and among award-winning gardens, this peaceful Victorian retreat is in a beautiful mountain location overlooking Caragh Lake. Decorated throughout in a soothing country house style, very comfortable antique-filled day rooms provide plenty of lounging space for quiet indoor relaxation and a terrace for fine weather all with wonderful views. Bedrooms shared between the main house and some with private patios in the garden house are spacious and elegantly furnished in traditional style, with excellent en-suite bathrooms. This is a sister hotel to the **Hotel Europe** and **Dunloe Castle** (see entries), whose leisure facilities are also available to guests. Dooks, Waterville, Killeen and Mahony's Point golf courses are all within easy reach. **Rooms 18** (3 suites,1 family room, 5 ground floor, 6 no smoking). Children welcome (Under 2s free in parents' room; cots available free of charge). No pets. B&B €75 pps (ss €75), SC included. Limited room service. **Fairyhill Restaurant:** Like the rest of the hotel, the dining room has intimacy and character and, after a fireside drink and a look through the menu, this is a delightful place to spend an hour or two. There's an emphasis on local ingredients and updated interpretations of traditional Irish themes on menus that may offer aromatic Kerry mountain lamb, and may include several fish dishes, although there is a stronger emphasis on meats than is usual in the area. Finish with imaginative desserts, or the Irish cheese plate. Coffee and petits fours can be served beside the drawing room fire. Non-residents are welcome by reservation. Seats 32 (private room, 10, outdoors, 16). D only, 7-8.30pm, usually closed on Mon; hotel closed mid Oct- May. Amex, Diners, MasterCard, Visa, Laser. **Directions:** Off N70 Ring of Kerry road, signed 5 km west of Killorglin.

Castlegregory
PUB

Spillanes

Fahamore Maharees Castlegregory Co Kerry **Tel: 066 713 9125**
marilynspillane@tinet.ie www.spillanesbar.com

It's a long way down from the main road to reach the Maharees, but many would make the journey just for a visit to Marilyn and Michael Spillane's great traditional pub - they work hard at both the food and hospitality, and have earned loyal following as a result. There's a tempting display of salads and desserts to choose from and seafood stars on the menu, such as mussels, crab claws and scampi made from Dingle prawns. And there's plenty for meat-lovers too, such as chargrilled steaks and chicken dishes (in the evening), some vegetarian dishes and some with child-appeal too. The pub is full of character and it can get very busy at times, which can mean a queue to be seated - and this sometimes puts the service under pressure so that tables are not cleared as thoroughly as one might like.   *Self-catering accommodation also offered, in two new 2-bedroom apartments opposite the pub (beside beach); each sleeps 5. Toilets wheelchair accessible; children welcome (high chair, children's menu, baby changing facilities). Meals daily in high season, 1-9.30 (Sun 2-9); low season from 6pm. Closed Nov-Mar. MasterCard, Visa, Laser. **Directions:** Dingle Peninsula, 3.5 miles north of Castlegregory, between Bandon and Tralee bays.

DINGLE PENINSULA ANNASCAUL & CASTLEGREGORY

he Dingle peninsula, dividing the bays of Tralee and Dingle, is one of the most popular leisure desti-
ations in Ireland for both visitors and residents, who enjoy it for many reason including the rugged
enery, history, away from it all atmosphere, outdoor activities music and good accommodation, food
d drink and, despite its remote location it is an all-year destination. The area is particularly good for
alking, hill walking and diving and dolphin watching (see **Dingle Town**, below). **Annascaul** on the
uthern side of the peninsula is a much-photographed village and features on many postcards and
avel guides, mainly because of the brilliantly colourful and humorous frontage painted on to his pub
v the late **Dan Foley**. It was also the birthplace of the Antarctic explorer **Tom Crean**, who was part of
obert Scott's ill-fated attempts to reach the South Pole; **The South Pole Inn** (066 915 7388;
ww.southpoleinn.ie) at the lower end of the street is named in honour of Crean and his connections
ith the great Irish explorer Sir Ernest Shackleton. On retiring in 1920, Crean returned to Annascaul,
arried and ran the South Pole Inn with his wife; today, it is a delightful, well-run pub, full of fasci-
ating Shackleton and Crean memorabilia. **Castlegregory** is directly across from Annascaul, on the
orthern side of the Dingle Peninsula; it is the only real village in a large and unspoilt area, which gives
special appeal to those who prefer a quiet destination, especially outside the main holiday season.
orth of Castlegregory, **The Maharees Peninsula** is famous for its long sandy beaches and clean water,
aking it popular for family holidays, and there is a group of islands off the peninsula, known simply
"The Maharees". Activities offered in the area (bookable through **Castlegregory Visitor Centre**, 066
139422) include golf, horseriding, cycling, fishing, windsurfing and, especially, diving. Waterworld
ve centre is located at Pat & Ronnie **Fitzgibbon's Harbour House Guesthouse & Islands Restaurant**
66 713 9292; www.maharees.ie) at Scraggane Pier; they run diving courses (and their facilities
clude a swimming pool) and, aside from offering comfortable accommodation (8 rooms), this is a
eful place to know about when touring as the restaurant is open to non-residents and they are usually
en for lunch as well as dinner (a phone call is advised). Further west, underneath Mount Brandon
d shortly before the road runs out at Brandon Point, **Mullallys Bar** (066 7138154), in the hamlet
Brandon, is as pleasant a traditional pub as you'll find anywhere, neat as a new pin and with a
elcoming fire and good food offered.

NGLE PENINSULA: Dingle Town / Ventry / Slea Head Areas: The main town in Kerry's most
rtherly peninsula, Dingle is a lively all-year destination renowned for its music, crafts, fishing and,
r over twenty years, for its most famous inhabitant, **Funghie** the friendly dolphin who is the area's
st-loved resident and shows every sign of enjoying the attention of the many visitors who go out by
at from the harbour every day to watch him. This **Gaeltacht** (Irish speaking area) is of great histor-
al interest, and there are many ancient remains, especially in the **Ventry / Slea Head / Ballyferriter**
ea west of the town. In Dingle Town, **Goat Street Café** (066 915 2770), on the main street, does
vely zesty food, including delicious sandwiches (also to take away), and **Global Village** (066 915
325) on Main Street offers daily-changed menus cooked by proprietor-chef Martin Bealin; on the
rbour, overlooking the marina, the café **Cassidys on the Pier** (066 915 2952) serves interesting
od all day in summer, beginning with breakfast, and a seriously tempting evening menu at certain
nes. **West of Dingle: The Stone House** is a restaurant inspired by the Gallarus Oratory, just across
e road; this extraordinary grey building even has a stone roof - and fortunately for the hungry visitor,
od food too; well-balanced evening menus offer a wide choice, daily lunch menus are on a black-
ard. Near Smerwick Harbour, and on the Kerry Way walking route, **Tig Bhric** (066 915 6325;
ww.tigbhric.com) is beside the early Christian monastic settlement Riasc (7 miles west of Dingle);
s a delightful bar, B&B and shop offering lovely home-made soups and sandwiches in the daytime,
d dinner every evening except Friday - when there is traditional music. Nearby, the **Smerwick
arbour Hotel** (066 915 6470; www.smerwickhotel.com) offers all the usual facilities and makes an
usual conference venue. **Tig Áine** (Tel: 066 9156214; www.tigaine.com) in Ballyferriter is a recent
dition to the area overlooking Clogher Strand that offers good food, pleasant service and the most
ectacular views.

WW.IRELAND-GUIDE.COM FOR THE BEST PLACES TO EAT, DRINK & STAY

ingle
AR/RESTAURANT

Ashes Seafood Bar

Main Street Dingle Co Kerry **Tel: 066 915 0989**
ashesbar@eircom.net www.jamesashes.com

This old pub in the centre of Dingle has a smart traditional frontage, and lots of warm
mahogany that makes for a warm and cosy feeling in the friendly bar. The pub goes back to
349 and is now owned by Sean and Anna Roche, who specialise in seafood. Menus offer a lot of
ats like lobster, langoustine (Dublin Bay prawns) and scallops, but they also include a wide range

of other fish and seafood, some appealing choices for non-fish eaters, including homely traditiona dishes like beef & Guinness stew and braised shank of lamb. Evening menus are more extensive an include more of the luxurious choices and separate vegetarian and children's menus are offered too Good cooking, great staff and a relaxed atmosphere make this an excellent choice for informal dining A compact and otherwise informative wine list gives no vintages; four house wines and two half bottle are offered. Toilets wheelchair accessible; Children welcome (high chair, children's menu, bab changing facilities). **Seats 50;** L&D Mon-Sat, 12-3 & 6-9; Set L €13; à la carte; house wine €19 Closed Sun, 25 Dec, Good Fri. MasterCard, Visa, Laser. **Directions:** Lower Main Street, Dingle.

Dingle
GUESTHOUSE

Bambury's Guesthouse

Mail Road Dingle Co Kerry **Tel: 066 915 124**
info@bamburysguesthouse.com www.bamburysguesthouse.com

téile bia Just a couple of minutes walk from the centre of Dingle, Jimmy and Bernie Bambury's wel run, purpose-built guesthouse has spacious modern rooms with tea/coffee trays, phone satellite TV, hair dryer and complimentary mineral water. Bernie Bambury's breakfasts include griddl cakes with fresh fruit and honey a house speciality and vegetarian breakfasts are offered by arrange ment. Not suitable for children under 4; no pets. Own parking. **Rooms 12** (all shower only & n smoking, 1 family, 3 ground floor) B&B €60, ss €20. Open all year. MasterCard, Visa, Lase **Directions:** On N86, on the left after the Shell garage, on entering Dingle.

Dingle
GUESTHOUSE

Castlewood House

The Wood Dingle Co Kerry **Tel: 066 915 278**
castlewoodhouse@eircom.net www.castlewooddingle.com

This luxurious new purpose-built guesthouse c the western edge of Dingle town is run by Brian an Helen Heaton - Brian's parents, Nuala an Cameron, run the well-established Heaton's gues house next door and a little gate connects the tw Although it is on the land side of the road, th house is built on a rise and, from the many room with sea views, all you are aware of is the vie across Dingle Bay. The scale is generou throughout: public rooms include an impressiv dining room where a good breakfast is served, an a drawing room with views across the bay for guests' use. Guest rooms are spacious and individual decorated to a very high standard, with smart bathrooms and a lot of attention to detail. Free broa band wi/fi; masseuse. **Rooms 12** (2 junior suites, 3 family, 1 for disabled, 4 ground floor, all n smoking). Children under 2 free in parents' room (cots available free of charge). Lift. Limited roo service. B&B €75 pps, ss €21. Closed Dec-mid Feb (open few days over New Years day). MasterCar Visa, Laser. **Directions:** Take Milltown road from Dingle, located around 500m from town centre on th right.

Dingle
RESTAURANT

The Chart House

The Mall Dingle Co Kerry **Tel: 066 915 225**
charthse@iol.ie www.charthousedingle.co

FEILE BIA AWAR

téile bia Even in an area so well-endowed wi good eating places, Jim McCarthy attractive stone-built restaurant is outstandin There's a smart little bar just inside the door where Jim, the perfect host, always seems to meeting, seating and seamlessly ensuring th everyone is well looked after and generally having good time. And head chef Noel Enright leads talented kitchen team: his menus are based on t best of fully traceable local ingredients, sometim in dishes with an international tone - a supe speciality starter of Annascaul black pudding is wrapped in filo pastry and served with apple and da chutney and hollandaise sauce, other dishes are just gently updated - rack of Kerry mountain lam

r example, may be accompanied by a fondant potato, redcurrant and rosemary jus; accurate, confi-
nt cooking lends these traditional foods a new character, and a large selection - perhaps half a dozen
more - of simple, perfectly cooked side vegetables are the ideal complement. Seafood is well repre-
nted, of course, and mainstream vegetarian dishes have wide appeal. Desserts include classics like
basket of home-made ice creams, or luscious lemon-scented pannacotta. But those with a savoury
oth will still feel that the smart money is on the Irish cheeses, which are cannily offered with a glass
vintage port and served with delicious home-made oat biscuits and two varieties of grapes. Terrific
ospitality, top class ingredients and gimmick-free creative cooking all add up to a great restaurant,
hich is also moderately priced especially if you choose dishes marked as selected for the 'Value
enu'. An interesting wine list includes South African wines imported directly, and has helpful tasting
ptes as well as a clear layout of country of origin and vintages - and, of course, there's always a
nateau MacCarthy in stock. *Jim McCarthy was our Host of the Year in 2003. Toilets wheelchair
ccessible; children welcome, **Seats 45;** air conditioning. D 6.30-10, daily in summer (Jun-Sep),
stricted opening in winter - please phone ahead to check; all evening value D €35, also à la carte.
C discretionary. House wine €19.50. Closed 6 Jan-13 Feb. MasterCard, Visa, Laser. **Directions:** Left
the roundabout as you enter the town.

---

ingle
OTEL

Dingle Benners Hotel

Main Street Dingle Co Kerry **Tel: 066 915 1638**
info@dinglebenners.com www.dinglebenners.com

his 300-year old centrally-located hotel makes a very comfortable base within comfortable walking
stance of the whole of Dingle town. Public areas include a streetside bar which has a lot more
ersonality than would be expected of an hotel (food available from 12 noon daily) and a large, bright,
ning room towards the back of the building. Bedrooms in the older part of the hotel have a lot of
haracter (some have four-posters) but the spacious newer bedrooms at the back of the hotel are
uieter, and convenient to the car park. Golf nearby. Private parking (50). Banqueting (100). Children
elcome (under 3 free in parents' room, cot available without charge, baby sitting arranged). No pets.
ooms 52 (33 superior, 9 no smoking, 4 suitable for less able guests). Lift. B&B €107 pps, ss €25.
Short breaks offer good value - details on application. Closed 18-26 Dec. Amex, Diners, MasterCard,
sa, Laser. **Directions:** Town centre, half way up Main Street on left beside Bank of Ireland.

---

ingle
OTEL

Dingle Skellig Hotel

Dingle Co Kerry **Tel: 066 915 0200**
reservations@dingleskellig.com www.dingleskellig.com

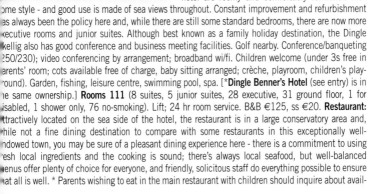

téile bia It may be modest-looking from the road,
but this 1960s hotel enjoys a superb
shoreside location on the edge of the town and has
won many friends over the years. It is a well-run,
family-friendly hotel, with organised entertainment
for children - and an attractive feature of the hotel
is their policy of dedicating floors for family use to
avoid disturbing those without children. There is a
good leisure centre, also a health and beauty
centre, the Peninsula Spa. Public areas in the
hotel are roomy and comfortably furnished with
ome style - and good use is made of sea views throughout. Constant improvement and refurbishment
as always been the policy here and, while there are still some standard bedrooms, there are now more
xecutive rooms and junior suites. Although best known as a family holiday destination, the Dingle
kellig also has good conference and business meeting facilities. Golf nearby. Conference/banqueting
250/230); video conferencing by arrangement; broadband wi/fi. Children welcome (under 3s free in
arents' room; cots available free of charge, baby sitting arranged; crèche, playroom, children's play-
round). Garden, fishing, leisure centre, swimming pool, spa. [*Dingle Benner's Hotel (see entry) is in
he same ownership.] **Rooms 111** (8 suites, 5 junior suites, 28 executive, 31 ground floor, 1 for
isabled, 1 shower only, 76 no-smoking). Lift; 24 hr room service. B&B €125, ss €20. **Restaurant:**
ttractively located on the sea side of the hotel, the restaurant is in a large conservatory area and,
hile not a fine dining destination to compare with some restaurants in this exceptionally well-
ndowed town, you may be sure of a pleasant dining experience here - there is a commitment to using
esh local ingredients and the cooking is sound; there's always local seafood, but well-balanced
enus offer plenty of choice for everyone, and friendly, solicitous staff do everything possible to ensure
at all is well. * Parents wishing to eat in the main restaurant with children should inquire about avail-

able times for family dining. D daily in summer, 7-9; set 2/3 course D, €38.50/45. Bar meals als available, 12.30-9pm. *Short breaks (e.g. golf, spa, off-season) offer good value; details on applica tion. Self-catering also available, in the hotel's Dingle Marina Cottages. Hotel open weekends only winter (Nov-mid Feb); closed 17-27 Dec. Amex, Diners, MasterCard, Visa, Laser. Heli-pad. **Direction** On the sea side of the road as you approach Dingle from Tralee & Killarney.

Dingle   Doyle's Seafood Restaurant & Townhouse

RESTAURANT WITH ROOMS   5 John Street Dingle Co Kerry **Tel: 066 915 117**

cdoyles@iol.ie   www.doylesofdingle.co

Originally a small pub built in 1790, Doyle was established as a restaurant over a quart of a century ago - and was one of the first in a town which is no renowned for good eating places. Currently in the hospitab hands of Charlotte Cluskey and her son John, it's a cosy, chara terful place with an old kitchen range and natural materials - ston floor, a real wooden bar and high stools - which all create a relaxe country atmosphere. Local seafood is the main attractio including lobster and oysters. However, there are one or tw concessions to non-seafood eaters such as Kerry mountain lam done various ways or traditional beef & Guinness stew, and vege tarian dishes are available. Puddings are nice and traditional there's a selection of farmhouse cheeses to finish. Good accom modation is also offered. **Seats 46;** air conditioning; D on Mon-Sat 6-10. Early D €25/30 (6-7.15pm), 2/3 course set €25/30, also à la carte; house wine €19.95; no sc. Restaura closed Sun. B&B €76 pps, ss €64. Establishment closed 7 Jan-15 Mar. Amex, Diners, MasterCar Visa, Laser. **Directions:** On entering Dingle, take third exit from roundabout into The Mall; turn rig into John Street.

Dingle   Greenmount House

GUESTHOUSE   Upper John Street Dingle Co Kerry **Tel: 066 915 141**

info@greenmount-house.com   www.greenmount-house.co

Just five minutes walk from the centre of Dingle John and Mary Curran have run one of Ireland finest guesthouses since the mid-70s. It's a exceptionally comfortable place to stay, quiet located on the hillside, with private parking an uninterrupted views across the town and harbour the mountains across the bay. The spacious, we appointed bedrooms are mainly junior suites wit generous seating areas and particularly goo amenities, including fridges as well as tea/coffee making trays, phone and TV (and, in most case also their own entrance and balcony); all bathrooms have recently been upgraded and a hot tu installed. The older part of the house was demolished in 2006 and has since been rebuilt to provic five new superior rooms just about to open at the time of our summer 2007 visit, they will add furthe to the appeal of this outstanding guesthouse. There's also a comfortable residents' sitting room wit an open fire, and a conservatory overlooking the harbour, where wonderful breakfasts are serve Greenmount won our Irish Breakfast Award for the Munster region, in 2001, and it has always been point of pride: the aroma of home baking is one of the things that gives this house a special warmth and all the preserves are home-made too; there's a wonderful buffet - laden down with all kinds fresh and poached fruits, juices, yogurts, cheeses, freshly baked breads - as well as an extensive choic of hot dishes, including the traditional full Irish breakfast. The wonder is that anyone ever leaves th place of a morning at all. Children welcome (cot available free of charge, baby sitting arranged Broadband wi/fi; no pets; Garden, walking. Parking (15). **Rooms 14** (10 junior suites, 3 shower onl 2 ground floor, all no smoking). B&B €85pps, ss €45, SC discretionary. Closed Dec 15-27 MasterCard, Visa, Laser. **Directions:** Turn right and right again on entering Dingle.

Dingle
RESTAURANT

The Half Door

John Street Dingle Co Kerry **Tel: 066 915 1600** halfdoor@iol.ie

Denis and Teresa O'Connor's cottagey restaurant is one of the prettiest and consistently popular in town, and well-known for great seafood. Menus go with the seasons but whatever is available is perfectly cooked and generously served without over-presentation. An outstanding speciality of the house is the seafood platter, available hot or cold as either a starter or main course with (depending on availability of individual items) lobster, oysters, Dublin Bay prawns, scallops, crab claws and mussels (attractively presented with garlic or lemon butter). Good traditional puddings or Irish farmhouse cheeses to follow. **Seats 50.** Air conditioning. D Mon-Sat, 6-10. Early D 6-6.30 only; later, à la carte. Closed Sun; Christmas. MasterCard, Visa. **Directions:** On John Street. ◇

Dingle
GUESTHOUSE

Heaton's House

The Wood Dingle Co Kerry **Tel: 066 915 2288**
heatons@iol.ie www.heatonsdingle.com

Cameron and Nuala Heaton's fine purpose-built guesthouse is set in well-maintained gardens just across the road from the water and, although convenient to the town, it's beyond the hustle and bustle of the busy streets. An impressive foyer-lounge area sets the tone on arrival and spacious, regularly refurbished, bedrooms confirm first impressions: all have bathrooms finished to a very high standard and phones, TV and hospitality trays - and the junior suites and superior rooms are not only luxurious, but also very stylish. Getting guests off to a good start each day is a point of honour and breakfast includes an extensive buffet (everything from fresh juices to cold meats and Irish cheeses) as well as a full hot breakfast menu. *See also **Castlewood House**, which is in the same family ownership. Fishing, walking, garden. Not suitable for children under 8. No pets. **Rooms 16** (2 junior suites, 5 superior, 2 family rooms, 5 ground floor, 1 for disabled, all no smoking). B&B €69 pps, ss €32. Room service (limited hours). Closed 1 Dec-26 Dec. MasterCard, Visa, Laser. **Directions:** 600 metres beyond marina, at front of town.

Dingle
BAR/RESTAURANT

Lord Baker's Restaurant & Bar

Dingle Co Kerry **Tel: 066 915 1277**
info@lordbakers.ie www.lordbakers.ie

Believed to be the oldest pub in Dingle, this business was established in 1890 by a Tom Baker. A popular businessman in the area, a colourful orator, member of Kerry County Council and a director of the Tralee-Dingle Railway, he was known locally as "Lord Baker" and as such is now immortalised in John Moriarty's excellent bar and restaurant in the centre of Dingle. A welcoming turf fire burns in the front bar, where bar food such as chowder and home-baked bread or crab claws in garlic butter is served. At the back, there's a more sophisticated dining set-up in the restaurant proper (and, beyond it, a walled garden). Seafood (notably lobster from their own tank) stars, of course, and speciality dishes include monkfish wrapped in bacon, with garlic cream sauce, and pan-fried sole on the bone with lemon butter; but there's also a good choice of other dishes using local mountain lamb (roast rack or braised shank, perhaps), also Kerry beef, chicken, and local duckling, all well-cooked and served in an atmosphere of great hospitality. In addition to the main menu there are chef's specials each evening and an unusual house speciality features on the dessert menu: traditional plum pudding with brandy sauce! Sunday lunch in the restaurant is a particularly popular event and very well done (booking strongly advised); on other days, the lunchtime bar menu, plus one or two daily specials such as a roast, can be taken in the restaurant. An informative wine list includes a Connoisseur's Selection of fen wines. John is an excellent host, caring and watchful - no detail escapes his notice, ensuring that every guest in Dingle's largest restaurant will leave contented. **Seats 120.** L Fri-Wed, 12.30-2; D Fri-Wed, 6-10. Set D about €24, also à la carte; light lunch, €10. House wine about €22. Rest. closed Thurs, house closed 24-26 Dec. Amex, MasterCard, Visa, Laser. **Directions:** Town centre.

Dingle
GUESTHOUSE

Milltown House

Dingle Co Kerry **Tel: 066 915 1372**
info@milltownhousedingle.com www.milltownhousedingle.com

The Kerry family's attractive guesthouse on the western side of Dingle is set in immaculate gardens running down to the water's edge and enjoys beautiful views of the harbour and distant mountains. Day rooms include an informal reception room, a comfortably furnished sitting room and a conservatory breakfast room overlooking the garden - breakfast is quite an event, offering everything from fresh juices and fruit, through cold meats and cheeses, freshly baked breads and an extensive cooked breakfast menu. The bedrooms all very comfortable and thoughtfully furnished with phone, TV with video channel, tea/coffee making facilities and iron/trouser press - include two with private patios. Constant upgrading is the policy here: a number of rooms have recently been increased in size and a new lounge, with sea and mountain views, was added to the front of the house. Not suitable for children under 10. No pets. Garden. **Rooms 10** (6 junior suites, all with full bath en-suite, all no smoking, 3 ground floor). B&B €80 pps, ss €50. Room service (limited hours). Closed 28 Oct-27 Apr. Amex, MasterCard, Visa, Laser. **Directions:** West through Dingle town, 0.75 miles from town centre.

Dingle
CAFÉ

Murphy's Ice Cream & Café

Strand Street Dingle Co Kerry **Tel: 066 915 2477**
dingle@murphysicecream.ie www.murphysicecream.ie

Many would make the trek to Dingle solely for the pleasure of tucking into one of the treats on offer at this cheerful blue and white fronted café down near the harbour. The Murphy brothers, Kieran and Séan, have been making ice cream with fresh Kerry milk and cream here since 2000 and have earned a national reputation in the meantime - now they supply a network of discerning restaurants and specialist outlets around the country and have a second café in Killarney. The café is unusual in that it only offers coffees and ice cream (the full range of flavours which is growing all the time), scooped in time-honoured fashion from a freezer cabinet in the shop and available in little tubs to take away if you like, milk shakes and and ice cream desserts (sundaes, banana split). The only exception to this rule is German baker Wiebke Murphy's collection of superb utterly irresistible gateaux, which are displayed in a cabinet and would be very difficult to ignore. There's also a Murphy's Ice Cream cake the perfect party piece, and some of the Murphy's own favourite chocolates. Toilets wheelchair accessible; Children welcome; **Seats 25** (outdoors, 8). Open 7 days a week - high season, 11-10pm; low season, 11-6.30pm. Closed Jan. **No credit cards. Directions:** Town Centre.

Dingle
B&B

Number Fifty Five

55 John Street Dingle Co Kerry **Tel: 066 915 2378**
stelladoyledingle@gmail.com www.stelladoyle.com

Stella Doyle's charming B&B in the centre of Dingle offers accommodation with character - and a high level of comfort at a very affordable price. Although the frontage seems small from the road, it is larger than it looks: the two guest bedrooms are on the ground floor and delightfully furnished in a fresh country house style, with television and full bathrooms (bath and power shower). But there is a surprise in store when you go upstairs to the first floor and find a light and spacious open plan living room, which has great style and, like the rest of the house, is furnished with antiques and original art. There's a large seating area at one end and, at the other, a dining area with large windows looking out to fields at the back of the house; here Stella, who spent most of her working life as a chef, serves delicious breakfasts for guests; no menu - 'anything you like, really'. Guests are welcomed to this hospitable haven with a cup of tea on arrival - and breakfast is sure to send them happily on their way. Not suitable for children. No pets. **Rooms 2** (both en-suite with full bath & no smoking). B&B €37.50 pps, ss €18.50. Closed 30 Sep-mid Apr. **No Credit Cards. Directions:** At main road roundabout, turn right up the mall; turn right up John Street - the house is at the top on the left side.

Dingle
RESTAURANT

Out of the Blue

Waterside Dingle Co Kerry **Tel: 066 915 0811**
timmason@eircom.net www.outoftheblue.ie

Tim Mason's deli and seafood restaurant is an absolute delight. Discerning locals know how lucky they are to have such an exciting little place on their doorstep and it's just the kind of place that visitors dream of finding - it is not unusual to find a different language spoken at every table. You can't miss the brightly-painted exterior from the road, an attractive decked area encloses the outside seating area and, once you get inside, it is obvious that this is a highly focused operation, where only the best will do: there's a little wine bar at the front and, in the simple room at the back (slightly extended in 2007, which added a couple of extra tables and makes it much more comfortable), seriously delicious seafood cookery is the order of the day for those lucky enough to get a table. Everything depends on the fresh fish supply from the boats that day and if there's no fresh fish, they don't open. Head chef Seamus MacDonald cooks wonderful classics, some-times with a modern twist - examples might include Glenbeigh mussels 'marinières', traditional French-style soups (with home-made brown bread), Dublin Bay prawns (langoustines) with garlic butter, perhaps, or sweet chilli sauce, and there may be less usual fish like pollock. Lobster is more expensive than it was but still reasonably priced in comparison with some other restaurants, and you may sometimes be offered crayfish, which is a rarity on Irish menus - and this is reflected in the price; either might be cooked 'en casserole' with cognac, or chargrilled with thyme & olive oil, then served with garlic butter. A short but skilfully assembled wine list - largely sourced by restaurant manager Irene Grobbelaar and Tim's brother, Ben Mason, of the Wicklow Wine Company complements the food perfectly, and has a dozen fish named in five languages on the back: this place is a little gem. *Tim has plans for another restaurant in Dingle - watch www.ireland-guide.com for details. Children welcome before 8pm. **Seats 34** (+ 24 outdoors); air conditioning. L & D Thu-Tue, L 12.30-3pm, D 6.30-9.30pm (Sun 6-8.30). Reservations accepted (required for D). A la carte. House wines from €18. Closed Wed ('usually'), also days when fresh fish is unavailable & mid Nov-early Mar. MasterCard, Visa, Laser. **Directions:** Opposite the pier on Dingle harbour.

Dingle
GUESTHOUSE

Pax House

Upper John Street Dingle Co Kerry **Tel: 066 915 1518**
paxhouse@iol.ie www.pax-house.com

Just half a mile out of Dingle, this modern house enjoys what may well be the finest view in the area and it is also one of the most comfortable and relaxing places to stay. John O'Farrell took over as proprietor in 2007 and, although no major changes were necessary, he has re-decorated throughout. Thoughtfully furnished bedrooms have every amenity, including a fridge and safe, and most of the well-finished bathrooms have full bath; two suites have their own terraces where guests can lounge around and enjoy that stupendous view. Breakfast is an enjoyable event with lots of home-made goodies; it is served in a bright and airy dining room overlooking the bay and with a terrace outside it for fine weather and there's a cosy sitting room with a fire for guests' use too. Children welcome (under 3s free in parents room, cots available at no charge). Pets permitted by arrangement. Garden, walking. **Rooms 13** (3 superior, 5 shower only, 1 family room, 6 ground floor, all no-smoking). B&B €70 pps, €30 ss. Wine licence. Closed 1 Nov-1Apr. MasterCard, Visa, Laser. **Directions:** Turn off at sign on N86. ◈

Gorman's Clifftop House & Restaurant

Dingle Area
GUESTHOUSE/RESTAURANT

Glaise Bheag Ballydavid Dingle Co Kerry **Tel: 066 915 5162**
info@gormans-clifftophouse.com www.gormans-clifftophouse.com

Beautifully situated near Smerwick Harbour on the Slea Head scenic drive and Dingle Way walking route, Sile and Vincent Gorman's guesthouse is, as they say themselves "just a great place to relax and unwind". Natural materials and warm colours are a feature throughout the house, and open fires create a welcoming laid-back atmosphere. The bedrooms are attractively furnished in a pleasing country style with thoughtfully finished bathrooms and include some on the ground floor with easy access from the parking area; four superior rooms have jacuzzi baths and other extra facilities but all are very comfortable. The Gormans are knowledgeable and helpful hosts too, advising guests on everything they need to know in the area. Breakfast - an excellent buffet with hot dishes cooked to order - is a treat that will set you up for the day. *Gorman's was our Guesthouse of the Year in 2002. Children welcome (under 3s free in parents' room, cot available free of charge). No pets. Garden, cycling, walking. **Rooms 9** (2 junior suites, 2 superior, 1 for less able, 1 shower only, all no smoking). B&B about €85 pps, ss €35. Short breaks offered - details on application. **Restaurant:** With large windows commanding superb sea views, this is a wonderful place to enjoy Vincent Gorman's good cooking. Begin with a fresh seafood chowder, perhaps - or an attractive speciality of potato cake & Annascaul black pudding sandwich with mushroom & bacon sauce, main courses include several seafood dishes (roast fillet of monkfish with roasted peppers, balsamic vinegar & olive oil dressing is a speciality) and the ever-popular sirloin steak; vegetarian choices are always given too. Desserts, including home-made ice creams and a wicked chocolate nemesis, are a strong point too, or you can finish with an Irish cheese plate. Sile, who is a warm and solicitous host, supervises front of house. An interesting and informative wine list offers plenty of good choices for all pockets and includes organic house wines and eight well chosen half bottles. **Seats 35.** D Mon-Sat, 7-9pm. Set D €32/38.50. House wine from €18.50. Restaurant closed Sun. House open Oct-Mar by reservation only; Closed 1 Jan-10 Feb. MasterCard, Visa, Laser. **Directions:** 12.5km (8 m) from roundabout west of Dingle Town - sign posted An Fheothanach. Keep left at V. ◇

The Old Pier

Dingle Area
RESTAURANT/GUESTHOUSE

Feothanach Ballydavid Co Kerry **Tel: 066 915 5242**
info@oldpier.com www.oldpier.com

Situated on the edge of the world overlooking the Atlantic and the Blasket Islands, Padraig and Jacqui O'Connor's friendly restaurant is so popular with locals that there are two sittings for dinner - and the importance of punctuality is stressed: arriving for the first sitting at 6.30, you may well find the restaurant already choc-a-block with people. Extensive menus are strong on local seafood which may include lobster, black sole, and prawns (langoustine) when available. There's a house chowder, mixed fish dishes based on the available catch, succulent bakes such as fresh cod in breadcrumbs and also good steaks and local lamb dishes. Good cooking, together with generous portions, moderate prices and efficient, good-humoured service have all earned a following for this big-hearted restaurant. **Accommodation:** The five pine-furnished en-suite rooms are offered in various combinations (single, twin, double, family) and have tea/coffee facilities, hair dryer and sea or mountain views. Special offers apply all year round. Children welcome (under 10s free in parents' rooms, cot available free of charge, baby sitting arranged); **Rooms 5** (1 family room, all en-suite, shower only and no smoking). Pets permitted by arrangement. **Restaurant: Seats 38** (private room, 10, outdoors, 20); reservations required; D served daily, 6.30pm & 8.30 pm; set 5 course D about €32.95; house wine from €13.95. Restaurant closed Nov-Mar, accommodation open all year. MasterCard, Visa, Laser. **Directions:** 11.5km (8m) west of Dingle.

The Tankard

Fenit
BAR/RESTAURANT

Kilfenora Fenit Tralee Co Kerry **Tel: 066 713 6164**
tankard@eircom.net

Easily spotted on the seaward side of the road from Tralee, this bright yellow pub and restaurant has a great reputation, especially for seafood. An imaginative bar menu, which overlaps to some extent with the restaurant à la carte, is available from lunchtime to late evening, serving a good range of food. Seafood chowder with delicious hi-fibre home-made brown bread, salads like smoky 'Boxty' (smoked salmon with potato cake & salad), cold seafood dishes such as fresh crab and apple salad (a house speciality) and hot snacks including steamed mussels Tankard-style, and plenty of non-seafood dishes too, including warm chicken salad, home-made burgers, pastas and sandwiches. Toilets wheelchair accessible. Children welcome (high chair, children's menu, baby changing facilities). **Seats 130.** D daily 6-10, L daily, 12-4. Set Sun L €22, D à la carte. House wines from about €18; sc discretionary *Bar meals daily, 2-10pm. Closed Good Fri. Amex, Diners, MasterCard, Visa, Laser. **Directions:** 5 miles from Tralee on Spa/Fenit road.

Fenit
PUB/RESTAURANT WITH ROOMS

West End Bar & Restaurant

Fenit Tralee Co Kerry **Tel: 066 713 6246**
westend@hotmail.com

The O'Keeffes have been in business here since 1885, and the present pub - which is exactly seven minutes walk from the marina - was built by chef Bryan O'Keeffe's grandmother, in 1925. Good food is available in both the cosy bar and the restaurant, which has earned a sound reputation in the area and includes an attractive conservatory dining area at the harbour end of the building. Bryan is a member of the Panel of Chefs of Ireland and his style is "classic French with Irish popular cuisine", with seafood and meats billed equally as specialities. Hand-written menus offer over a dozen starters ranging from Tralee Bay seafood chowder, to classic mussels 'Ernie Evans' style, and main courses also include old favourites - steaks, half roast duckling - and a very wide range of seafood dishes, leading off with lobster or grilled black (Dover) sole on the bone. Simple, moderately priced accommodation is offered in ten en-suite rooms (B&B €35, no ss). Bar/restaurant Meals 5.30-10pm daily in season. A la carte; house wines from €19.50. Phone ahead to check food service off-season. Closed Jan-Mar. MasterCard, Visa, Laser. **Directions:** 11km (7 miles) from Tralee, well signposted.

KENMARE

Renowned for its fine restaurants and outstanding accommodation (the range and quality is exceptional for a town of its size), The Heritage Town of Kenmare (Neidín/ 'little nest') is pleasingly designed and ideally sized for comfortable browsing of its quality shops and galleries. It also has a full complement of characterful pubs, and makes an excellent base for exploring both south Kerry and the near parts of west Cork. At **Prego** (Henry Street, 064 42350), Gerry O'Shea's team offer a wide range of tasty dishes throughout the day beginning with a lovely breakfast menu; their formula using best local produce in simple, casual food with an Italian slant has been so successful that they've extended both menu and opening hours (now 9am-10.30pm in season) and opened a second restaurant, **Bácús** (see entry). Just across the bridge, the Arthur family's spacious country house **Sallyport House** (064 42066; www.sallyporthouse.com) is in a quiet and convenient location overlooking the harbour, with a garden and mountain views at the rear. A little further out, on the Castletownbere road, Peter & Amanda Mallinson offer comfortable, moderately priced accommodation at their Killaha East home, **Sheen View Guesthouse** (064 42817; www.sheenview.com). High up at the famous Moll's Gap viewing point on the Ring of Kerry, **Avoca Handweavers** (064 34720; www.avoca.ie) is an outpost of the County Wicklow weaving company, selling its fine range of clothing and crafts - and offering wholesome and appealing home-made fare with that amazing view, to sustain the weary sightseer (10-5 daily mid-Mar-mid-Nov).
WWW.IRELAND-GUIDE.COM FOR THE BEST PLACES TO EAT, DRINK & STAY

Kenmare
RESTAURANT

An Leath Phingin Eile

35 Main Street Kenmare Co Kerry
Tel: 064 41559

Mayo's loss has been Kerry's gain, now that Eddie and Gaelen Malcolmson, formerly of the lovely Linenmill Restaurant in Westport, have opened here in the premises previously occupied by the veteran Kenmare restaurant An Leath Phingin. The building has a lot going for it in terms of atmosphere on two floors with lots of wood and open stone in view, it has a warm and welcoming feeling even on a wet night. The back room was changed to allow for more seating and the tables are close - but not too close for comfort and friendly, well-briefed waiting staff work under Gaelen's direction to make a visit here a real pleasure. Eddie is a fine classical chef in the modern European style, and his wide-ranging menus offer a balanced choice of eight dishes on each course, based mainly on local ingredients including Billy Clifford's oganic produce; you'll find plenty of treats including starters like a perfect twice-baked crab soufflé with hazelnut crust & a crab & tomato bisque, and main courses such as char-grilled fillet of Irish Angus beef with polenta cake, button mushrooms and red wine jus.

Desserts might include home-made ices and sorbets, and perhaps a just-set vanilla pannacotta with fresh raspberries & confit orange zest, or there are local Knockatee cheeses with home-made caraway biscuits. A carefully selected wine list includes eight interesting house wines (one of the reds is Massaya from Lebanon, another is Moillard organic pinot noir), offering excellent value at €18-24, and all available by the ½ litre or by the bottle, and there are lovely dessert wines too. Children welcome (high chair). **Seats 35** (private room, 16); D only Wed-Mon, 6-10. A la carte. House wine from €18. Closed Tue high season; month of March; Christmas week; call ahead to check opening times off season. MasterCard, Visa, Laser. **Directions:** Town centre.

Kenmare
RESTAURANT
N

Bácús Bistro

Main Street Kenmare Co Kerry **Tel: 064 48300**
www.bacuskenmare.com

In a small room along the 'restaurant mile' at the top of Main Street, Gerry O'Shea opened this little sister restaurant to the deservedly popular Prego in 2006 and it was an immediate success. It's open all day and is equally known for good casual food through the day, including excellent breakfasts, and for bistro-style evening meals. As at Prego, fresh, local and organic ingredients are the starting point for everything they do and the cooking is good and its popularity is simply explained: generous food, well served in a good atmosphere and very keenly priced. What more could you want? Children welcome; toilets wheelchair accessible. **Seats 36** (outdoors, 8); Food served daily, all day, 9am-10pm; L 12-4, D 6-10pm; à la carte; house wine €16.95. Amex, MasterCard, Visa, Laser. **Directions:** Top of Main Street Kenmare, on left hand side.

Kenmare
HOTEL

Brook Lane Hotel

Kenmare Co Kerry **Tel: 064 42077**
info@brooklanehotel.com www.brooklanehotel.com

Situated just outside Kenmare on the Ring of Kerry Road (take the turn off for Sneem), this smart boutique hotel is sleek and modern, offering all the flair and comfort of a custom-built hotel but with the service and intimacy of the very best kind of B&B. Public areas include the smart-casual Casey's Bar & Bistro, and a fine dining restaurant, open for dinner and Sunday lunch. The very comfortable bedrooms are decorated in soothing warm neutrals in a clean and contemporary style; business guests will find plenty of workspace. Brook Lane offers comfort, excellent service, and great value for money - so booking well in advance is advised. Conferences/Banqueting (50/100), secretarial services, free Broadband wi/fi. Cycling, equestrian, fly fishing, sea angling, garden visits and golf all nearby. Children welcome (under 4s free in parents' room, cots available free of charge, baby sitting arranged). **Rooms 20** (1 junior suite, 8 executive, 2 family rooms, 9 ground floor, 1 for disabled, all no smoking); 24 hr room service; air conditioning Lift; B&B about €75 pps, ss €25. Special/off-season offers available. Casey's Bar & Bistro: meals 12.30-9.30 daily; live music in bar at certain times. Restaurant D 6.30-9.30 daily, L Sun only 12.20-3.30. Closed 24-26 Dec. MasterCard, Visa, Laser. **Directions:** A short walk from the centre of town.

Kenmare
RESTAURANT

D'Arcy's Oyster Bar & Grill

Main Street Kenmare Co Kerry **Tel: 064 41589**
keatingrestaurants@ownmail.net www.darcys.ie

Situated at the top of Main Street opposite the Landsdowne Hotel, this well known restaurant was previously a bank and is now owned by John and Georgina Keating, who specialise in local seafood, particularly oysters. A bank interior always lends a bit of gravitas and, with timeless jazz, understated décor and crisp white linen, it provides a pleasingly neutral setting. Service is professional in tone and well laid out menus are promptly presented, offering a wide range of oyster dishes, also other fish and seafood, some meats such as rack of Kerry lamb and rib-eye steak, and vegetarian dishes too. Desserts tend towards the classic summer pudding, crème brulée, hot chocolate fondant. The cooking was a little uneven on the Guide's most recent visit, but the offering at D'Arcy's is different from other restaurants and its focus on oysters is interesting. Restaurant not suitable for children under 7. **Seats 60.** Serving food Tue-Sun 12-10 May-Sept, Thu-Sun 6-10 Oct-Apr; à la carte. House wine €19.50; sc discretionary. Closed Mon in summer, Mon-Wed Oct-Apr & mid Jan 7- mid Feb. MasterCard, Visa, Laser. **Directions:** Top of Main Street on left.

The Horseshoe

Kenmare
BAR/RESTAURANT

3 Main St Kenmare Co Kerry **Tel: 064 41553**
thehorseshoe@eircom.net www.neidin.net/horseshoe

Everyone loves the atmosphere at this pleasingly old-fashioned bar and restaurant at the bottom of Main Street; it is a cosy place and has always been known for unpretentious and wholesome good food, served in the informal oil-cloth-tabled restaurant at the back, with an open fire and original cattle stall divisions. Paul Bevan took over as proprietor in 2006, after many years in the previous ownership, so fans were reassured to find that it's in safe hands and chef Ron Murphy is serving up pleasing meals of steaks, rump of lamb and prime fish including black sole and all sauces used are fresh and are home-made. This cosy bar is especially attractive when visiting out of season, and it's open all year. Children welcome before 10pm. **Seats 35;** air conditioning. Open for D Mon-Sun, 5-10pm; à la carte. 12.5% SC on groups 10+. Open all year. MasterCard, Visa, Laser. **Directions:** Centre of Kenmare.

Jam

Kenmare
CAFÉ

6 Henry St Kenmare Co Kerry **Tel: 064 41591**
info@jam.ie www.jam.ie

James Mulchrone's delightful bakery and café has been a great success since the day it opened in March 2001 and, unlikely as this may seem in a town that has some of the best eating places in Ireland, it brought something new and very welcome. Affordable prices, friendly service and an in-house bakery have proved a winning combination; everything is made on the premises using the best of local produce and you can pop into the self-service café for a bite at any time all day. To give a flavour of the wide range offered, lovely main course choices include salmon & spinach baked in pastry with horseradish and a selection of quiches. If you're planning a day out, they have all you could want for a delicious picnic here, including a wide range of sandwiches and salads, terrines and all sorts of irresistible cakes and biscuits. The café menu changes daily and party platters and celebration cakes are made to order (48 hours notice required for special orders). The stated aim is "to provide fresh, quality, imaginative food at affordable prices in nice surroundings"; this they are doing very well both here and at their Killarney branch. A new bakery was due to open in Kenmare at the time of going to press. *Also at: 77 High Street, Killarney; Tel: 064 31441. Seats 55; air conditioning. Open Mon-Sat, 8am-6pm; house wine €4.75 per glass. Closed Sun, 4 days Christmas. MasterCard, Visa, Laser. **Directions:** Lower Henry Street on the left.

Lime Tree Restaurant

Kenmare
RESTAURANT

Shelburne Street Kenmare Co Kerry **Tel: 064 41225**
limetree@limetreerestaurant.com www.limetreerestaurant.com

Tony and Alex Daly's atmospheric restaurant is entering into its fifteenth year and remains one of the most consistently popular dining choices in the area. It's in an attractive cut stone building built in 1832 and set well back from the road: an open log fire, exposed stone walls, original wall panelling and a minstrels' gallery (which provides an upper eating area) all give character to the interior - and there is a contemporary art gallery on the first floor, which adds an extra dimension to a visit here; fine original artwork in the restaurant gives a hint of what may be for sale. A la carte menus offer plenty of choice, plus daily specials (including vegetarian options) - a little less emphasis on local seafood than might be expected but that allows for a wider choice and, among several fish dishes, a speciality is pan-roasted fish served with boxty potato cake, Kenmare salmon, perhaps, also served with a champagne & mussel velouté. Some dishes have a world cuisine tone, and there are plenty of main stream choices too: Kenmare seafood chowder is an enduring favourite, and an imaginatively updated main course of tenderloin of pork is served with glazed turnip and buttered cabbage, a pork & apple pithviers and cider jus. Desserts tend to be tweaked classics (strawberry shortcake with pistachio ice cream & strawberry syrup) and Munster cheeses are served with water biscuits & pear chutney. Service, under the direction of restaurant manager Maria O'Sullivan, is professional and relaxed; a user-friendly wine list is organised by style ('light, crisp and appealing', 'soft bodied and fruity'...) and includes some interesting bottles. And remember that it might be wise to budget a little extra for dinner here - you could be taking home a modern masterpiece; gallery open from 4pm. Toilet wheelchair accessible. Air conditioning. Not suitable for children after 7 pm. **Seats 60** (private room, 18). D daily 6.30-10; à la carte (average main course about €23). House wine €20; sc discretionary. Closed-Nov-Mar. MasterCard, Visa, Laser. **Directions:** Top of town, next to Park Hotel.

Kenmare | The Lodge
GUESTHOUSE | Killowen Road Kenmare Co Kerry **Tel: 064 41512**
| thelodgekenmare@eircom.net www.thelodgekenmare.com

Rosemarie Quill's large, purpose-built guesthouse is just 3 minutes walk from the centre of town, offers hotel-style accommodation in spacious rooms which have king size beds, everything you could possibly need - including controllable central heating, phone, TV, safe, iron/trouser press and tea/coffee facilities, as well as well-finished bathrooms - at guesthouse prices. There is also plenty of comfortable seating and even a bar. Children welcome (under 3 free in parents' room, cot available without charge). 24 hour room service. No pets. Garden. **Rooms 10** (all en-suite & no smoking; 4 ground floor, 1 disabled). B&B from about €45-55pps, ss about €30. Closed Nov- Mar). MasterCard, Visa. **Directions:** Cork road, 150m from town opposite golf course. ◊

Kenmare | Mulcahys Restaurant
RESTAURANT | 36 Henry Street Kenmare Co Kerry
👑 ☆ | **Tel: 064 42383**

If you are ever tired of finding the same old dishes on every menu, just head for Kenmare and refresh your palate at Bruce Mulcahy's original, efficiently run and friendly contemporary restaurant. A light-filled room is spacious and stylish, with smart modern table settings, funky cutlery and delicious breads on a pretty little bamboo tray. Far from being yet another copy-cat chef playing with world cuisines, Bruce has gone to the source to learn his skills - he learned about fusion food in Thailand, for example, and studied the art of sushi making in Japan; but the secret of this restaurant's great success is that, although many dishes are highly unusual, exciting menus cater for conservative tastes as well as the adventurous palate. All produce used here is certified organic, and vegetarians get a dish of the day on the blackboard. Dishes especially enjoyed recently include a warm terrine of scallops and prawns with tomato & red pepper puree and an oyster froth, a magical combination and perfectly cooked; inspired cooking is backed up by charming and knowledgeable staff working under Laura Mulcahy's direction - and, judging by the Guide's 2007 visit on a very busy night, any previous problems with service have been resolved. The early dinner menu is great value - and there's also a magical wine list to match the food. Toilets wheelchair accessible; children welcome before 9pm (high chair). **Seats 45.** D daily, 6-10; set 2/3 course D €30/45, also à la carte. House wines from €21.50. SC 10% on groups 8+. Closed 23-26 Dec. MasterCard, Visa, Laser. **Directions:** Top of Henry Street.

Kenmare | Muxnaw Lodge
COUNTRY HOUSE | Castletownbere Road Kenmare Co Kerry **Tel: 064 41252**
| muxnawlodge@eircom.net www.neidin.net

Within walking distance from town (first right past the double-arched bridge towards Bantry), Hannah Boland's wonderfully cosy and homely house was built in 1801 and enjoys beautiful views across Kenmare Bay. This is very much a home where you can relax in the TV lounge or outside in the sloping gardens (you can even play tennis on the all-weather court). A building programme brought a couple of superior new rooms on stream recently but, while the original ones now seem old-fashioned by comparison, all the bedrooms are tranquil and comfortable, individually furnished with free-standing period pieces and pleasant fabrics - and have cleverly hidden tea/coffee-making facilities. Notice is required by noon if you would like dinner, a typical meal cooked in and on the Aga might be carrot soup, oven-baked salmon and apple pie, but guests are always asked beforehand what they like. Not suitable for children. Garden. **Rooms 5** (all en-suite & no-smoking). B&B €40. Residents D about €20. Closed 24-25 Dec. MasterCard, Visa. **Directions:** 2 minutes drive from Kenmare Town.

Kenmare
BAR/RESTAURANT

P F McCarthys
14 Main Street Kenmare Co Kerry
Tel: 064 41516

This fine establishment, previously known as the Fáilte Bar, goes back to 1913 and is now run by Paul and Breda Walsh, who took over in 2006. The renovated premises now brings natural light into bright rooms - it has a spacious feeling and a dining area separated from the bar by low partitions, topped by wine bottles for privacy. Everyone loves it, whether for a snack lunch or more leisurely dinner. Breda is known for her wholesome, fresh-tasting food: at lunchtime there's an extensive choice of home-made soups, salads, light snacks and a wide range of sandwiches. Evening menus are more selective, offering a full dinner menu, plus daily specials of fresh fish and steak dishes. Ingredients are carefully sourced and there's a home-made flavour to the food, including desserts. There's a great buzz, a friendly atmosphere and efficient service under Paul's direction. **Seats 60.** Outdoor seating available (garden). Toilets wheelchair accessible. Children welcome before 9pm. Food served Mon-Sat 10.30-3 and 5-9. No food on Sun. A la carte; house wine from €18.95; SC discretionary. Closed 25 Dec, Good Fri. MasterCard, Visa, Laser. **Directions:** First Pub/Restaurant on the right hand side as you travel up Main Street. ◊

Kenmare
RESTAURANT

Packie's
Henry Street Kenmare Co Kerry
Tel: 064 41508

 In a town blessed with an exceptional choice of wonderful eating places, the Foley family's buzzy little restaurant has long been a favourite for returning visitors. The long main room has a tiny reception bar with a couple of stools shoehorned into it, and a dividing stone feature wall with foliage-filled gaps in it provides privacy and, along with candlelight, mirrors and framed pictures, makes for a warm, relaxed atmosphere - an impression immediately confirmed by welcoming staff, who are exceptionally friendly and efficient, keeping everyone at the closely packed tables happy throughout the evening. Head chef Martin Hallissey's menus (plus each evening's specials) are based mainly on local ingredients, notably organic produce and fish - and, although there's clear interest in international trends, combinations tend to be based on traditional themes, such as classic Irish stew with fresh herbs, which is a speciality. Close examination of menus will probably reveal more dishes that have stood the test of time than new ones, but what remains impressive is the basic quality of the food, especially local seafood, and the satisfying skill with which simple dishes are cooked, which is very pleasing. And there is no shortage of treats, including, perhaps, real prawn cocktail and roast lobster with garlic or citrus butter (fairly priced at €31.50). Finish with Irish farmhouse cheeses or good desserts, including unusual dishes like lemon posset with shortbread: gorgeous. An interesting and well-priced wine list offers plenty to choose from, with some available by the glass. Children welcome (high chair). Seats 30; air conditioning. D Mon-Sat, 6-10; à la carte. House wine from €18; sc discretionary. Reservations advised. Closed Sun; mid Jan- end Feb. MasterCard, Visa, Laser. **Directions:** Town centre.

Kenmare
HOTEL/RESTAURANT

Park Hotel Kenmare
Kenmare Co Kerry **Tel: 064 41200**
info@parkkenmare.com www.parkkenmare.com

This renowned hotel enjoys a magnificent waterside location in the midst of Ireland's most scenic landscape, with views over gardens to the ever-changing mountains across the bay - yet it's only a short stroll to the Heritage Town of Kenmare. Many travellers from all over the world have found a home from home here since the hotel was built in 1897 by the Great Southern and Western Railway Company as an overnight stop for passengers travelling to Parknasilla, 17 miles away. The current proprietor, Francis Brennan, re-opened the hotel in 1985, and has since earned international acclaim for exceptional standards of service, comfort and cuisine; it is a most hospitable and relaxing place, where a warm welcome and the ever-burning fire in the hall set the tone for a stay in which guests are discreetly pampered by outstandingly friendly and professional staff. And since 2004 that pampering has been taken to new heights in the hotel's deluxe destination spa, Sámas, which translates from the Gaelic as 'indulgence of the senses'. Unlike anything else offered in Ireland, Sámas adjoins the hotel on a wooded knoll and is designed to rejuvenate the body, mind and spirit; there are separate male and female areas (also two day suites for couples) and guests can choose from over forty holistic treatments, designed by a team of professionals to meet individual needs. Lifestyle programmes incorporating spa treatments with other activities in the area - walking on the Kerry Way, golf, fishing, horse trekking - offer a unique way to enjoy the deeply peaceful atmosphere of this luxurious hotel. As for the guest accommodation, spacious suites and bedrooms are individually furnished to the highest standards, with antiques, fine linen and home-baked cookies. And, in line with the excellence which prevails throughout the hotel, the outstanding breakfasts served at the Park start the day in style. [Park Hotel Kenmare was the national winner of our Hotel Breakfast of the Year Award in 2005.] Golf club adjacent (18 hole). Garden, tennis, croquet, cycling, walking, snooker. Destination Spa. Reel Room (12-seater cinema). Horse riding, fishing (fly, coarse, sea), mountain walks and stunning coastal drives are all nearby. *At the time of going to press the hotel is in the midst of building 18 lifestyle apartments and 25m lap pool; due for completion spring 2008. **Rooms 46** (9 suites, 24 junior suites, 8 family, 8 ground floor, 3 disabled, 46 no smoking). Lift. 24 hour room service. Children welcome (under 4s free in parents' room, cots available without charge, baby sitting arranged). No pets (but kennels available on grounds). B&B about €173 pps, (single occupancy €215); off-season holistic retreats offer very good value. Hotel closed late Nov-mid Feb except Christmas/New Year. **Restaurant:** The more contemporary restaurants become the norm in Ireland, the more precious the elegance of this traditional dining room seems - and the views from window tables are simply lovely. Ensuring that the food will match the surroundings is no light matter but a stylishly restrained classicism has characterised this distinguished kitchen under several famous head chefs, and Mark Johnson - who joined the hotel in 2006 - maintains this tradition admirably. A table d'hôte menu that is concise, yet leans towards seafood, including lobster, yet allows sufficient choice; there will always be a vegetarian choice and Kerry lamb and local Skeaghanore duck are also enduring specialities. Superb attention to detail - from the first trio of nibbles offered with aperitifs in the bar, through an intriguing amuse-bouche served at the table, well-made breads, presentation of each dish for inspection on a tray before service, punctilious wine service and finally the theatrical little Irish coffee ritual and petits fours at the end of the meal - all this contributes to a dining experience that is exceptional. The wine list, although favouring the deep-pocketed guest, offers a fair selection in the €30-40 bracket and includes a wine suitable for diabetics. Service is invariably immaculate. A short à la carte lounge menu is available, 12-6pm. Not suitable for children after 7pm. Seats 80 (private room, 30, outdoor dining 20). D, 7-9 daily; Set D menu about €55; gourmet menu about €74; also à la carte. House wine from €37.50; sc discretionary. Amex, MasterCard, Visa, Laser. **Directions:** Top of town.

Kenmare

BAR/RESTAURANT

The Purple Heather

Henry Street Kenmare Co Kerry **Tel: 064 41016**
oconnellgrainne@eircom.net

Open since 1964, Grainne O'Connell's informal restaurant/bar was among the first to establish a reputation for good food in Kenmare, and is a daytime sister restaurant to Packie's. It's a traditional darkwood and burgundy bar that gradually develops into an informal restaurant at the rear, as is the way in many of the best Kerry bars - and what they aim for and achieve, with commendable consistency, is good, simple, home-cooked food. Start with refreshing freshly squeezed orange juice, well-made soups that come with home-baked breads, or salad made of organic greens with balsamic dressing. Main courses include a number of seafood salads, vegetarian salads (cold and warm), pâtés including a delicious smoked salmon pâté plus a range of omelettes, sandwiches and open sandwiches (Cashel Blue cheese and walnut, perhaps, or crabmeat with salad) or Irish farmhouse cheeses (with a glass of L.B.V Offley port if you like). This is a great place, serving wonderfully wholesome food in a relaxed atmosphere - and it's open almost all year. *Grainne O'Connell also has self-catering accommodation available nearby. **Seats 45.** Meals Mon-Sat, 10.45-5.30pm; house wine €19. Closed Sun, Christmas, bank hols. Visa, Laser. **Directions:** Town centre - mid Henry Street (on right following traffic flow).

Sea Shore Farm Guest House

Tubrid Kenmare Co Kerry **Tel: 064 41270**
seashore@eircom.net www.seashorekenmare.com

The O'Sullivans' well-named farm guesthouse is beautifully situated overlooking the Beara peninsula, with field walks through farmland down to the shore - and, despite its peace and privacy, it's also exceptionally conveniently located, just a mile from Kenmare town. Mary Patricia O'Sullivan provides old-fashioned Irish hospitality at its best, with welcoming and efficient reception and spotlessly clean accommodation. A pleasant guest lounge has stunning views and plenty of tourist information and Irish heritage books - and Mary Patricia is herself a veritable mine of local information. Spacious, comfortably furnished bedrooms have the considerate small touches that make all the difference to the comfort of a stay. No dinner is offered but breakfast is a feast of fruit salads, yoghurt, cereals etc as well as a choice of scrambled eggs draped with locally smoked salmon, pancakes or traditional Irish. Garden, walking. *Glen Inchaquin Park is nearby and should not be missed. Free broadband wi/fi. Children welcome (under 2s free in parents' room). Jacuzzi, No pets. **Rooms 6** (all en-suite & no smoking, 4 shower only, 2 family rooms, 2 ground floor, 2 for disabled). B&B €65 pps, ss €20. Closed 15 Nov-1 Mar. MasterCard, Visa. **Directions:** Off Ring of Kerry N70 Kenmare/Sneem road; signposted at junction with N71.

Sheen Falls Lodge

Kenmare Co Kerry **Tel: 064 41600**
info@sheenfallslodge.ie www.sheenfallslodge.ie

féile bia Set in a 300-acre estate just across the river from Kenmare town, this stunning hotel made an immediate impact from the day it opened in April 1991; it has continued to develop and mature most impressively since. The waterside location is beautiful, and welcoming fires always burn in the handsome foyer and in several of the spacious, elegantly furnished reception rooms, including a lounge bar area overlooking the tumbling waterfall. Decor throughout is contemporary classic, offering traditional luxury with a modern lightness of touch and a tendency to understatement that adds up to great style; accommodation in spacious bedrooms - and suites, which include an extremely impressive presidential suite - is luxurious: all rooms have superb amenities, including video/DVD and CD players, beautiful marbled bathrooms and views of the cascading river or Kenmare Bay. Outstanding facilities for both corporate and private guests include state-of-the-art conference facilities, a fine library (with computer/internet), an equestrian centre (treks around the 300-acre estate) and The Queen's Walk (named after Queen Victoria), which takes you through lush woodland. A Health & Fitness Spa includes a pretty 15 metre pool (and an extensive range of treatments) and, alongside it, there's an informal evening bar and bistro, 'Oscars', which has its own separate entrance as well as direct access from the hotel. But it is, above all, the staff who make this luxurious and stylish international hotel the home from home that it quickly becomes for each new guest. *Two luxuriously appointed self-contained two-bedroomed thatched cottages, Little Hay Cottage and Garden Cottage, and a 5-bedroomed house on the estate, are available to rent. Conference/banqueting (120/120); free broadband wi/fi, business centre, secretarial services, video-conferencing. Health & Fitness Spa (swimming pool, jacuzzi, sauna, steam room, treatments, beauty salon); boutique, walking, gardens, croquet, clay pigeon shooting, tennis, cycling. Fishing (coarse, fly) and equestrian nearby. Heli-pad. Children welcome (cots available, €25, baby sitting arranged; playground). No pets. **Rooms 66** (1 presidential suites, 20 suites, 8 junior suites, 14 ground floor rooms, 10 no-smoking bedrooms, 1 disabled). Lift. All day room service; turndown service. Room rate €217.50 pp (max 2 guests). **La Cascade:** This beautifully appointed restaurant is designed in tiers to take full advantage of the waterfalls floodlit at night and providing a dramatic backdrop for an exceptional fine dining experience. Philip Brazil has been head chef since 2005, and continues the high standard of cooking which is the hallmark of this lovely restaurant, backed up by faultless service under the supervision of restaurant manager Adrian Fitzgerald. His menus are not over-extensive yet allow plenty of choice and, whilst there's an understandable leaning towards local seafood - including lobster and crab from Castletownbere perhaps, scallops, Dover sole and turbot - Kerry beef and lamb and local Skeaghanore duck are also enduring specialities; a vegetarian menu is available on request, and also a six-course Tasting Menu. Cooking is consistently impressive and, although local ingredients feature, the tone is classic, with only the smallest occasional nod to Irish cuisine. Speciality desserts include updated classics like chocolate & toffee fondant with vanilla ice cream, or mango crème brulée with mango ragout and blackcurrant granité, and farmhouse cheeses are served with scrumptious parmesan biscuits. The atmospheric wine cellar is a particular point of pride - guests can visit it to choose their own bottle, and port may also be served there after dinner - deep-pocketed wine buffs will enjoy the wine list and should make a point of seeing it well ahead of dining if possible, as it details around 950 wines, with particular strengths in the classic European regions, especially Burgundy and Bordeaux, and a fine collection of ports and dessert wines. *Light lunches and afternoon tea are available in the sun lounge, 12-6 daily, and the informal Oscar's Bistro offers an extensive à la carte dinner menu, including a children's menu, Wed-Sun, 6-10pm. **Restaurant Seats 120** (private room, 20; outdoor seating, 12). Pianist, evenings. Toilets wheelchair accessible. D daily 7-9. Set D €65, gourmet D €95. House wines from €36.80. SC discretionary. Hotel closed Jan 2 - Feb 1. Amex, Diners, MasterCard, Visa, Laser. **Directions:** Take N71 Kenmare (Glengariff road); turn left at Riversdale Hotel.

Kenmare
COUNTRY HOUSE/GUESTHOUSE

Shelburne Lodge

Cork Road Kenmare Co Kerry **Tel: 064 41013**
shelburnekenmare@eircom.net www.shelburnelodge.com

Tom and Maura Foley's fine stone house on the edge of the town is well set back from the road, in its own grounds and lovely gardens. It is the oldest house in Kenmare and has great style and attention to detail; spacious day rooms include an elegant, comfortably furnished drawing room with plenty of seating, an inviting log fire and interesting books for guests to read - it is really lovely, and the feeling is of being a guest in a private country house. Spacious, well-proportioned guest rooms are individually decorated and extremely comfortable; everything (especially beds and bedding) is of the highest quality and, except for the more informal conversion at the back of the house, which is especially suitable for families and has neat shower rooms, the excellent bathrooms all have full bath. But perhaps the best is saved until last, in the large, well-appointed dining room where superb breakfasts are served: tables are prettily laid with linen napkins and the menu offers all kind of treats, beginning with freshly squeezed juices, a choice of fruits (nectarine with strawberries, perhaps) with extras like natural yoghurt, honey and nuts offered too, lovely freshly-baked breads, home-made preserves, leaf tea and strong aromatic coffee, and - as well as various excellent permutations of the full traditional Irish breakfast - there's fresh fish, and Irish farmhouse cheeses too. Simply delicious. [Shelburne Lodge was our Guesthouse of the Year in 2005, and also winner of the Best Guesthouse Breakfast Award.] No evening meals are served, but residents are directed to the family's restaurant, Packie's (see entry). Children welcome (under 2s free in parents' room, cot available without charge). Garden, tennis. Own parking. No pets. **Rooms 10** (3 shower-only, 1 family, 1 ground floor). B&B €80, ss €40. Closed Dec 1-mid Mar. MasterCard, Visa. **Directions:** 500 metres from town centre, on the Cork road R569.

Kenmare
GUESTHOUSE

Virginia's Guesthouse

36 Henry Street Kenmare Co Kerry **Tel: 064 41021**
virginias@eircom.net www.virginias-kenmare.com

Mulcahy's restaurant and Virginia's guesthouse share an entrance, but are run quite separately. Neil and Noreen Harrington are superb hosts and, although the décor in their guestrooms would benefit from updating, they have big comfortable beds and everything you could need including phone, television, safe and tea/coffee trays - and en-suite power showers. And their breakfasts are a point of honour, offering amongst many delights a fresh orange juice cocktail with ginger, melon with feta cheese, a compôte of organic rhubarb with blueberries, natural yogurt, organic porridge (with or without whiskey cream), and banana pancakes along with all the usual egg dishes (free range eggs) and fries, simply delicious. **Rooms 8** (all shower only & no smoking, 1 family); B&B €45-60 pps, ss €15; off-season 3 night specials from €265 per room. MasterCard, Visa, Laser. **Directions:** Top of Henry Street.

KILLARNEY

Known all over the world for its romantic beauty (Lakes of Killarney, Killarney National Park, the Ring of Kerry) the Killarney area has long been a source of inspiration for poets, painters and writers and, despite the commercial tone of the town itself - which has been a centre of tourism since the days of the Victorian Grand Tour - the surroundings are stunning and, with a number of the country's finest hotels in the town and immediate area, it remains an excellent base for exploring the area, or for leisure activities, notably golf. When visiting Muckross House at the National Park, **The Garden Restaurant** (064 314440; www.muckross-house.ie) is open 9-5 daily, all year except Christmas/NewYear, and offers just the kind of good, wholesome food that's welcome, in attractive surroundings. Nearby, in the Muckross area, the Huggard family's **Lake Hotel** (064 31035; www.lakehotel.com) is romantically located right on the lakeshore. And, convenient to the Killarney Golf & Fishing Club, **Sheehan's 19th Green** family-run guesthouse (064 32868; www.the19thgreen-bb.com) offers a moderately priced haven for golfers. **The Quality Hotel** (Cork Road; 064 31555) has exceptional leisure facilities for a budget hotel including an indoor heated pool, sauna, hot tub, steam room and exercise room. The hotel also has a crèche, kids and teens clubs and outdoor activities for kids including miniature golf. For those who want to be in the town centre and like a hotel of character however, the Buckley family's charming and moderately priced **Arbutus Hotel** (064 31037; www.arbutuskillarney.com) on College Street could be the answer. For a casual bite in town, try **Panis Angelicus** (New Street; 064 39648), a stylish contemporary café and bread shop that has a tempting display of freshly baked breads, scones and gateaux and aromas of freshly brewed Italian coffee, or **Murphys Ice Cream** (066 915 2644;www.murphysicecream.ie) on Main Street (see Dingle entry for details).
WWW.IRELAND-GUIDE.COM FOR THE BEST PLACES TO EAT, DRINK & STAY

Killarney
HOTEL/RESTAURANT

Aghadoe Heights Hotel & Spa

Lakes of Killarney Killarney Co Kerry **Tel: 064 31766**
info@aghadoeheights.com www.aghadoeheights.com

A few miles out of town, this famous low-rise hotel, dating from the '60s, enjoys stunning views of the lakes and the mountains beyond and also overlooks Killarney's two 18-hole championship golf courses. It is now one of Ireland's most luxurious hotels and, under the caring management of Pat and Marie Chawke and their welcoming staff, it is a very special place. While the controversial exterior remains a subject of debate, the interior which now includes 24 new junior suites, a palatial glass-fronted two-bedroom penthouse suite and a luxurious spa & wellness centre - is superb. Stylish, contemporary public areas are airy and spacious, with lots of marble, original artwork, and a relaxed, open ambience and, from the foyer, hints of the stunning view that invite exploration - perhaps into the chic bar which links up with a terrace and the swimming pool area (lots of lounging space for sunny days), or up to the first floor open-plan lounge area, where a delicious traditional Afternoon Tea is served (2-5.30pm). Accommodation is seriously luxurious, in spacious rooms with balconies and lake views, large sitting areas, plasma screen televisions, video, DVD (library available) and a host of extras. Bathrooms are equally sumptuous, with separate shower and all the complimentary toiletries you could wish for. The new 10,000 sq ft spa is among Europe's best and offers couples suites, and some unique treatments - including 'Ayervedic Precious Stone therapy' in a custom-built Aromatherapy cabin. But at the heart of all this luxury it is the caring hands-on management of Pat and Marie Chawke who, with their outstanding staff, make everyone feel at home. And you will leave on a high too, as breakfast is another especially strong point. [Aghadoe Heights was our Hotel of the Year in 2005.] Conference/banqueting (80/75); business centre, secretarial services, video conferencing, laptop-sized safes in bedrooms, free broadband wi/fi. Destination Spa. Leisure centre (swimming pool, jacuzzi, steam room, sauna, fitness room), hair salon. Garden, tennis, walking. Children welcome (Under 2s free in parents' room; cot available, €20, baby sitting arranged). Pets may be permitted by prior arrangement. **Rooms 74** (25 suites, 6 junior suites, 10 family rooms, 10 ground floor rooms, 1 disabled, all non smoking). Lift. Turn down service. 24 hour room service. B&B €185 pps, ss €70. Closed 31 Jan-mid Feb. **The Lake Room:** The restaurant is on an upper floor, integrated into an open plan area, with distant views over the lakes and mountains; it is a bright and elegant space, with beautifully appointed tables and fresh flowers providing an appropriate setting for dining in a hotel of this standard. Head chef Gavin Gleeson - with experience at a number of top kitchens, including Dromoland Castle, before he joined the team at Aghadoe

Heights - has developed new menus which continue in the classical tradition of the hotel but with a lighter, more contemporary tone which is more in keeping with the atmosphere today. Gone, at least for the time being, are the great classics, like grilled chateaubriand sauce béarnaise and sole meunière, now replaced by new dishes wild trout with sea urchin sauce, and fashionable confit belly of pork & milk-fed veal, with peach sauce. A pianist sets the scene each evening and, under the direction of Restaurant Manager Padraig Casey, service is solicitous, as ever. An extensive and informative wine list includes a champagne menu, a strong range of classics, a good choice of wines by the glass and plenty of half bottles. **Seats 120** (private room, 75). Reservations accepted. Children welcome before 7pm (high chair, children's menu, baby changing facilities). D daily, 6.30-9.30pm. Set D €70, also à la carte. House wines from €28. 12.5% SC on groups of 10+. *Informal menus also offered in The Heights Lounge and The Terrace Bar & Bistro (from 10am-9.30pm daily in summer). Restaurant closed end Dec-mid Feb. Helipad. Amex, Diners, MasterCard, Visa, Laser. **Directions:** 3.2km (2 m) north of Killarney; signposted off N22.

Killarney

The Brehon

HOTEL

Muckross Road Killarney Co Kerry **Tel: 064 30700**

info@thebrehon.com www.thebrehon.com

féile bia Appropriately enough, as it is so close to the Irish National Entertainment Centre (INEC), everything at this new hotel, conference centre and spa is on a grand scale - and, while the exterior of the vast five-storey building may be overpowering, most would agree that the contemporary interior matches the official description of 'tasteful splendour'. Everything seems larger than life and, although already showing signs of the heavy wear it is subjected to in places - the design, decor and furnishings of the public spaces are striking and feature some interesting modern art and sculpture. This house style continues through bedrooms and suites, which are extremely comfortable, with air-conditioning as well as more usual features, and luxurious marble bathrooms with separate shower and bath. The restaurant is airy and bright, and a wide ranging breakfast menu is offered. The hotel takes pride in its spa: developed by the Banyan Tree Spa, it is Europe's first Angsana spa and based on holistic Asian healing customs. Conference facilities include four meeting rooms and a large function space, which is also available for weddings. Conferences/Banqueting (250/200); broadband wi/fi; business centre. secretarial services; Spa, beauty salon, hairdressing; Leisure Centre (swimming pool, gym, sauna); walking, tennis, cycling; Golf, fishing and equestrian nearby. Children welcome (under 3s free in parents' room, cot available free of charge, baby sitting arranged). **Rooms 125** (5 suites, 5 junior suites, 30 superior, 3 family, 7 for disabled, all no smoking). B&B €145 pps, ss€30. Lift, 24 hr room service. Open all year. *Special interest breaks each Spring & Autumn, contact for details. Amex, MasterCard, Visa, Laser. **Directions:** Located opposite the national park (N71) 1 mile from town centre.

Killarney

Bricín

RESTAURANT

26 High Street Killarney Co Kerry

Tel: 064 34902

Upstairs, over a craft shop (which you will find especially interesting if you like Irish pottery), Paddy & Johnny McGuire's country-style first-floor restaurant has been delighting visitors with its warm atmosphere and down to earth food since 1990. It's a large area, but broken up into "rooms", which creates intimate spaces - and the country mood suits wholesome cooking, in menus offering a good range of popular dishes. Salmon & crab bake is an enduring favourite, for example, and there are traditional dishes like boxty (potato pancakes) which are not seen as often as they should be in Irish restaurants, and are the house speciality here - you can have them with various fillings - chicken, lamb vegetables - and salad. An interesting range of desserts includes good home-made ice creams. This is a welcoming restaurant, and it has an old-fashioned character which is becoming especially attractive as so many others are adopting a contemporary style. An informative wine list offers a wide range in the €20-30 range, but no half bottles. **Seats 29.** Air conditioning. Children welcome. D Mon-Sat, 6-9. Value D about €21 daily 6-7; Set D from about €27; also à la carte. House wine from €20. Closed Sun and Feb. Amex, Diners, MasterCard, Visa, Laser. **Directions:** On the High Street, Killarney. ◇

Killarney
HOTEL/RESTAURANT

Cahernane House Hotel

Muckross Road Killarney Co Kerry **Tel: 064 31895**
info@cahernane.com www.cahernane.com

This family-owned and managed hotel is in a lovely quiet location, convenient to Killarney town yet - thanks to a long tree-lined avenue and parkland which stretches down to the water it has a charmingly otherworldly atmosphere. The original house was built by the Herbert family, Earls of Pembroke, in the 17th century, and accommodation is divided between fine old rooms (including some suites and junior suites) in the main house, and more contemporary rooms in a recent extension; an atrium joining the two sections makes a pleasant conservatory seating area, opening on to the lakeside grounds. The hotel has many attractive features, not least its generous period sitting rooms and open fires, and a characterful cellar bar (spoilt a little by noise and harsh downlighting) with a real old-fashioned wine cellar. Banqueting (80). Free Broadband wi/fi. Children welcome (under 3s free in parents' room, cot available without charge, baby sitting arranged.) No pets. Garden, walking, fishing, tennis. Golf nearby. **Rooms 38** (28 with separate bath & shower, 15 no smoking). B&B about €130 pps, Single from €150. **The Herbert Room Restaurant:** This classically elegant dining room is situated on the lake side of the house and the setting is perfect for fine dining. Classical table d'hôte and à la carte menus are offered - wild mushrooms risotto, and foie gras with asparagus are typical starters, and main courses might include pan-seared duck breast with sweet potato purée, and paupiettes of black sole with saffron beurre blanc. Farmhouse cheeses are offered with plum chutney, as well as delicious desserts. Cooking is good although it can be let down by disorganised service. Breakfast is a highlight, and a quite an extensive bar menu is offered for those who would prefer to eat informally. Restaurant: L & D daily, 12.30-3 & 7-9.30; set L €35, set 5 course D €55; also bar food, noon-9.30pm; house wine €24.* Off-season breaks offered. Closed mid Dec-mid Jan. Amex, Diners, MasterCard, Visa, Laser. **Directions:** Ouskirts of Killarney, off the N71 near Muckross Park. ◇

Killarney
RESTAURANT

Chapter 40

40 New Street Killarney Co Kerry **Tel: 064 71833**
info@chapter40.ie www.chapter40.ie

A fairly recent arrival on the Killarney dining scene, this smart high-ceilinged restaurant feels spacious and is attractively set up, with simple darkwood tables echoing the polished wooden floor, and contrasting cream leather used on high-backed chairs and bar stools. Menus offered are international in style and include an early dinner which is very good value, a wide ranging à la carte and daily specials for all courses. Begin perhaps with the seafood chowder, which is thickened with potato and carrageen moss, and gluten-free, followed perhaps with the seafood plate, which is always good; for dessert, fresh fruit & mixed berry salad with basil sabayon is a favourite. Sharing dishes, like an antipasto platter and duck confit pancakes, gets a meal off to a sociable start and all main courses include vegetables. A lively atmosphere and good honest cooking along with value and friendly service are the reasons for this restaurant's success; as it's always busy, reservations are essential, especially at weekends. Toilets wheelchair accessible; children welcome (high chair, childrens menu, baby changing facilities); **Seats 72** (private room, 16); air conditioning; D Mon-Sat, 5-10pm; à la carte; house wine €19. Closed Sun. Amex, MasterCard, Visa, Laser. **Directions:** A few minutes walk from car park beside the Tourist Office, near Dunnes Stores.

Killarney
HISTORIC HOUSE

Coolclogher House

Mill Road Killarney Co Kerry **Tel: 064 35996**
info@coolclogherhouse.com www.coolclogherhouse.com

Mary and Maurice Harnett's beautiful early Victorian house is just on the edge of Killarney town and yet, tucked away on its 68-acre walled estate, it is an oasis of peace and tranquillity. The house has been extensively restored and has many interesting features, including an original conservatory built around a 170 year-old specimen camellia - when camellias were first introduced to Europe, they were mistakenly thought to be tender plants; it is now quite remarkable to see this large tree growing under glass. It is an impressive yet relaxed house, with well-proportioned, spacious reception rooms stylishly furnished and comfortable for guests, with newspapers, books, fresh flowers - and open fires in inclement weather - while the four large bedrooms have scenic views over gardens, parkland and mountains. Gazing out from this peaceful place, it is easy to forget that the hustle and bustle of Killarney town is just a few minutes' drive away; it could just as well be in another world. Mary and Maurice enjoy sharing their local knowledge with guests to help them get the most of their stay at what they quite reasonably call 'perhaps the most exclusive accommodation available in Killarney'. Not suitable for children under 8. No pets. Garden, walking. Golf, fishing, garden visits nearby. **Rooms 4** (all en-suite, all no smoking). B&B €120, ss €50. *Coolclogher House is also offered as a weekly rental (from €4,500) for special occasions; suits groups of 10-12; staff can be arranged if required. *Golf breaks offered (B&B or rental). MasterCard, Visa, Laser. **Directions:** Leaving Killarney town, take Muckross Road; turn left between Brehon and Gleneagle hotels, onto Mill Lane; gates on right after 1km (0.5 m).

Killarney
RESTAURANT

The Cooperage Restaurant

Old Market Lane Killarney Co Kerry **Tel: 064 37716**
info@cooperagerestaurant.com

This striking contemporary restaurant is conveniently located in a pedestrianised (if somewhat neglected) laneway between Main Street and the Glebe public carpark, and its smart frontage always gives a good impression. There's a welcoming lounge area, and the pleasing surroundings, together with gentle background jazz, create an atmospheric setting for a pleasant dining experience. Clear, fairly priced menus based on quality ingredients offer plenty of choice, including game in season, and there's always a list of specials, including at least one imaginative vegetarian choice and several fish dishes; home-made desserts range from a wholesome fruit crumble to an indulgent chocolate cake. Good service, although no sign of anyone in charge on the Guide's latest visit. With a lively atmosphere, stylish, flavoursome food, and A concise, well priced wine list, this popular restaurant offers good value; reservations are advised. *A branch of The Cooperage was due to open on Castle Street, Tralee at the time of going to press. Toilets wheelchair accessible. **Seats 80.** Air conditioning. Children welcome (high chair, baby changing facilities). L daily, 12.30-3pm; D 5.30-10pm daily. Early D €23 (5.30-7), otherwise à la carte. House wine €17.50. Closed 25 Dec. MasterCard, Visa, Laser. **Directions:** Under the arch at the Old Town Hall, just off Main Street.

Killarney
GUESTHOUSE

Earls Court House

Woodlawn Junction Muckross Road Killarney Co Kerry **Tel: 064 34009**
info@killarney-earlscourt.ie www.killarney-earlscourt.ie

A new frontage has recently been added to Roy and Emer Moynihan's purpose-built guesthouse quite near the town centre but, although there are always changes for the better, including new and/or refurbished rooms, the essential qualities of hospitality, professionalism, comfort and character to be found within remain unchanged. A welcoming open fire burns in the large beautifully furnished foyer which, together with an adjoining guest sitting room, has plenty of comfortable seating for guests - an ideal rendez-vous, or simply a place to relax -

and, as elsewhere in the house, antiques, books, paintings and family photographs are a point of interest and emphasise the personality of this spacious home from home. Emer's personal attention to the details that make for real comfort - and the ever-growing collection of antiques that guarantees individuality for each room - are the hallmarks of the outstanding accommodation offered, which includes a number of rooms with canopy beds. All the bedrooms are well-planned and generously-sized, with double and single beds, well finished bathrooms, phone and satellite TV; tea/coffee-making facilities are available on request. Guests are directed to restaurants in the town for evening meals, but superb breakfasts are served in a newly-refurbished antique-furnished dining room, where guests are looked after with charm and efficiency. Earls Court was our Guesthouse of the Year for 2004. Fully certified for disadvantaged access. Children welcome (under 3s free, cot available without charge, baby sitting arranged). Pets allowed in some areas. Broadband wi/fi. Garden; jacuzzi; walking; golf nearby. Parking. **Rooms 30** (4 suites, 4 family, 2 for disabled, all no smoking). Lift. Room service (limited hours). B&B €65 pps, ss €40. Closed mid Nov-mid Feb. Amex, MasterCard, Visa. **Directions:** Take the first left at the traffic lights on Muckross road (signed), then 3rd premises.

Killarney
RESTAURANT

Gaby's Seafood Restaurant
27 High Street Killarney Co Kerry
Tel: 064 32519

One of Ireland's longest established seafood restaurants, Gaby's has a cosy little bar beside an open fire just inside the door, then several steps lead up to the main dining area, which is cleverly broken up into several sections and - although this is an expensive restaurant - it has a pleasantly informal atmosphere. Chef-proprietor Gert Maes offers well structured seasonal à la carte menus in classic French style and in three languages. This is one of the great Irish kitchens and absolute freshness is clearly the priority; there are specials on every evening and a note on the menu reminds guests that availability depends on daily landings; but there's always plenty else to choose from, with steaks and local lamb among the favourites. Specialities include Atlantic prawns on a bed of tagliatelle in a light garlic sauce and lobster "Gaby": fresh lobster, cognac, wine, cream and spices - cooked to a secret recipe! Lovely desserts include "my mother's recipe" - an old-fashioned apple & raspberry crumble - or you can finish with an Irish cheese selection and freshly brewed coffee. Delicious. An impressive wine list offers about fifteen interesting house wines by the bottle or glass, and many special bottles, although vintages are not always given. Toilets wheelchair accessible. Air conditioning. Children welcome (high chair). **Seats 75.** D only, Mon-Sat 6-10; gourmet menu €50, also à la carte; house wine €25; sc discretionary. Closed Sun (& Mon, Tue - Jan-Mar). Amex, MasterCard, Visa, Laser. **Directions:** On the main street.

Killarney
CAFÉ

Jam
77 High Street Killarney Co Kerry **Tel: 064 31441**
info@jam.ie www.jam.ie

James Mulchrone's delightful bakery and café in Kenmare has been such a success that he opened a second one in Killarney, bringing the same principles of affordable prices, friendly service and real home-made food using the best of local produce (see entry under Kenmare for details). Children welcome. *Jam is planning a move to 'bigger and better' premises early in 2008. Children welcome. **Seats 24.** Air conditioning. Open Mon-Sat, 8am-5pm. menu changes daily. Closed Sun, 4 days Christmas. MasterCard, Visa, Laser. **Directions:** Town centre.

Killarney
GUESTHOUSE

Kathleens Country House
Madams Height Tralee Road Killarney Co Kerry **Tel: 064 32810**
info@kathleens.net www.kathleens.net

When Kathleen O'Regan Sheppard opened here in 1980, she was one of the first to offer what was effectively hotel standard accommodation at guesthouse prices - and, today, this family-run business continues to offer good value, hospitality and comfort. Individually decorated rooms are furnished to a high standard, with orthopaedic beds, phone, TV, and tea/coffee-making facilities, and the fully tiled bathrooms all have bath and shower. An ongoing programme of maintenance and refurbishment ensures that everything is immaculate, including spacious public areas that provide plenty of room for relaxing. Excellent breakfasts are served in an attractive dining room overlooking the garden, setting you up for the day: everything served at breakfast is based on the finest produce, local where possible, and beautifully presented. Kathleen's - which is off the main Tralee road, just a mile from the town centre - is well situated for a wide range of outdoor pursuits and for some of the country's most beautiful scenic drives. Wheelchair access ground floor only. Children welcome (under 3s free in parents' room, baby sitting arranged). Garden, walking. Free broadband wi/fi. **Rooms 17** (all no smoking, 2 ground floor). B&B €65 pps, ss €15. Turndown service offered. Closed 20 Oct-15 Mar. Amex, MasterCard, Visa, Laser. **Directions:** 1.6km (1mile) north of Killarney Town off N22 (Tralee road).

Killarney
GUESTHOUSE

Killarney Lodge

Countess Road Killarney Co Kerry **Tel: 064 36499**
klylodge@iol.ie www.killarneylodge.net

Catherine Treacy's fine purpose-built guesthouse is set in private walled gardens just a couple of minutes walk from the town centre and offers a high standard of accommodation at a fairly moderate rate. Large en-suite air-conditioned bedrooms have all the amenities expected of an hotel room and there are spacious, comfortably furnished public rooms to relax in. Run by a member of one of Killarney's most respected hotelier families, this is a very comfortable place to stay; you will be greeted with complimentary tea and coffee on arrival - and sent off in the morning with a good Irish breakfast, including home-baked breads and scones. A good choice for the business traveller, and short breaks are available in conjunction with Killarney Golf & Fishing Club - accommodation and green fees are offered at preferential rates. Children welcome (under 12s free in parents room; cot available without charge). Free broadband wi/fi. No pets. Garden. Own secure parking. **Rooms 16** (2 junior suites, 2 family, 1 shower only, 6 ground floor, all no smoking). Room service (all day). B&B €70 pps, ss €30; no sc. Closed Nov-Feb. Amex, Diners, MasterCard, Visa, Laser. **Directions:** 2 minutes walk from town centre off Muckross Road.

Killarney
HOTEL/RESTAURANT

Killarney Park Hotel

Kenmare Place Killarney Co Kerry **Tel: 064 35555**
info@killarneyparkhotel.ie www.killarneyparkhotel.ie

féile bia Situated in its own grounds, a short stroll from the town centre, the Treacy family's luxurious, well run hotel is deceptively modern - despite its classical good looks, it is only fifteen years old. However, it has already undergone more than one transformation - indeed, constant improvement is so much a theme here that it is hard to keep up with developments as they occur. The exceptionally welcoming atmosphere strikes you from the moment the doorman first greets you, as you pass through to a series of stylish seating areas, with fires and invitingly grouped sofas and armchairs; the same sense of comfort characterises the Garden Bar and also the quiet Library. Elegant public areas are punctuated by a sweeping staircase that leads to bedrooms luxuriously furnished in two very different styles. Spacious traditional suites have a private entrance hall and an elegant sitting area with a fireplace, creating a real home from home feeling; all the older rooms are also furnished in a similar warm country house style. However, the junior suites offer a dramatically contemporary style - and a new wow factor; thoughtfully and individually designed, they have air conditioning, well-planned bathrooms and the many small details that make a hotel room really comfortable. Housekeeping is impeccable and the staff are committed to looking after guests with warmth and discretion. A stunning health spa offers eight treatment rooms, outdoor hot tub, plunge pool and jacuzzi; the menu of treatments offered is seriously seductive and it may well happen that some guests never feel the need to leave the hotel at all during their stay. [Park Hotel Killarney was our Hotel of the Year in 2002.] *The nearby hotel, **The Ross** (see entry) is a sister hotel. Conference/banqueting (150/150); free broadband wi/fi; secretarial services, video conferencing. Spa. Leisure centre (swimming pool, sauna, plunge pool, jacuzzi, gym). Library; billiard room. Garden, walking, cycling. Children welcome (under 2s free in parents room; cots available without charge, playroom, creche, baby sitting arranged). No Pets. **Rooms 72** (3 suites, 30 junior suites, 3 family rooms, 1 for disabled, all no-smoking). Lift. 24 hour room service. Turndown service. B&B €200 pps, ss €200; no sc. Closed 24-27 Dec. **The Park Restaurant:** This large and opulent room has the essential elements of grandeur - the ornate ceiling, glittering chandeliers - but has been lightened by a contemporary tone in the furnishings. Odran Lucey, who has been head chef since 1999, has earned a reputation for this restaurant as a dining destination in its own right, making it a great asset to this fine hotel. His menus are appealing and, although not overlong, they offer plenty of choice from which to make up a five course dinner or, as dishes are priced individually, make à la carte choices if preferred. The underlying style is classical but this is creative food, cooked with panache. Although the style is broadly international, it's very much food with an Irish flavour - seen in named ingredients like Dingle crabmeat, Kerry lamb and suppliers are credited on the menu. A main course of roast breast of Skeaghanore duck with colcannon cake & poached kumquats demonstrates skilful blending of traditional partnerships and innovative additions, and good judgment comes into play when it comes to a real classic - Dover sole - which is cooked classically, 'meunière'. Courteous service, knowledgeable service and the presence of a pianist, who plays throughout dinner, add to the sense of occasion. A wide-ranging wine list includes many of the classics and, not only a fair choice of half bottles, but also a sommelier's choice of the week, offering half a dozen good wines by the glass. An interesting feature of the restaurant is an open wine cellar, which guests are free to browse. *Odran Lucey is also responsible for the excellent bistro-style food served in The Garden Bar where - as elsewhere in the hotel - children are made very welcome. **Seats 150** (private room, 40). Children welcome (high chair, children's menu, baby changing facilities); reservations required; air conditioning; toilets wheelchair accessible. D daily 7-9.30; Set D €65; also à la carte. House wines from about €28. SC discretionary. *Food is also served in the bar, 12 noon-9pm daily. Hotel closed 24-27 Dec. Amex, MasterCard, Visa, Laser. **Directions:** Located in Killarney town - all access routes lead to town centre.

Killarney
HOTEL

Killarney Plaza Hotel
Kenmare Place Killarney Co Kerry **Tel: 064 21100**
info@killarneyplaza.com   www.killarneyplaza.com

féile bia In seeking to regain the glamour of the grand hotels, this new hotel offers an alternative to the modernism that has taken over in Irish hotels of late. The scale is large, but the proportions are pleasing and, although undoubtedly glitzy - miles of polished marbled floors and a great deal of gold - quality materials have been used and it will age well. Meanwhile, it has a lot to offer: a central location with underground parking; luxurious accommodation at prices which are relatively reasonable; a choice of three very different dining experiences (see separate entry for **Mentons**); good leisure and relaxation facilities, including a Molton Brown Spa. *Short/off-season breaks are available - details on application. Children welcome (under 4s free in parents' room, cot available free of charge, baby sitting arranged). Pets permitted by arrangement. Leisure centre (swimming pool, sauna, steam room, jacuzzi, gym); Spa. Secure parking (125); valet parking. **Rooms 198** (5 suites, 27 executive, 12 disabled, 140 no smoking). Lift. 24 hour room service. Turndown service. B&B €129 pps, ss €40. Restaurant Grand Pey (250); D daily 6-9pm. Open all year. Amex, Diners, MasterCard, Visa, Laser. **Directions:** Town centre.

Killarney
HOTEL

Killarney Royal Hotel
College Street Killarney Co Kerry **Tel: 064 31853**
info@killarneyroyal.ie   www.killarneyroyal.ie

féile bia Another of Killarney's unrivalled collection of fine hotels, this family-owned establishment is a charming older sister to the luxurious Hayfield Manor Hotel in Cork city (see entry). Proprietors Joe and Margaret Scally have recently lavished care and investment on it, resulting in a beautifully furnished hotel in an elegant period style that is totally appropriate to the age and design of the building. No expense was spared on the highest quality of materials and workmanship, air conditioning was installed throughout the hotel and individually designed rooms all have sitting areas and marble bathrooms. But what is most remarkable, perhaps, is the warm and friendly atmosphere that prevails throughout the hotel, conveyed partly through the soft warm tones chosen for furnishing schemes, but also through the attentive attitude of friendly, caring staff. A combination of light contemporary food and heartier fare is offered throughout the day in the informal bar/bistro area, which is a popular meeting place, while the main dining room is more traditional and reservations are required. Conference/banqueting (50/100); secretarial services; free broadband wi/fi; lap top sized safes in bedrooms. Wheelchair accessible. Children welcome (under 7s free in parents room, cots available without charge, baby sitting arranged). Pets permitted by arrangement. No on-site parking (arrangement with nearby car park). **Rooms 29** (5 junior suites, 3 family rooms, 15 no-smoking, 1 disabled). Lift. 24 hour room service. B&B €110 pps, ss €40. Closed 23-26 Dec. Amex, Diners, MasterCard, Visa, Laser. **Directions:** In Killarney town centre on College Street, off the N22.

Killeen House Hotel

Killarney
HOTEL/RESTAURANT

Aghadoe Killarney Co Kerry **Tel: 064 31711**
charming@indigo.ie www.killeenhousehotel.com

Just 10 minutes drive from Killarney town centre and 5 minutes from Killeen and Mahoney's Point golf courses, this early nineteenth century rectory has become Michael and Geraldine Rosney's "charming little hotel". You don't have to be a golfer to stay here but it must help, especially in the pubby little bar, which is run as an "honour" bar with guests' golf balls accepted as tender; most visitors clearly relish the bonhomie, which includes addressing guests by first names. Rooms vary in size but all have full bathrooms (one with jacuzzi) and are freshly-decorated, with phone and satellite TV. There's a comfortable traditional drawing room with an open fire for guests, furnished with a mixture of antiques and newer furniture. The hotel is popular with business guests as well as golfers; secretarial services are available, also all-day room service. **Rooms 23** (all en-suite). B&B about €80 pps, ss €20; sc 10%. **Rozzers:** Resident guests see no need to go out when a good dinner is offered under the same roof as their (very comfortable) beds, and this charming restaurant is also popular locally. You can have an aperitif in the friendly little bar while browsing 5-course dinner menus that offer a wide choice on each course, plus specials each evening. The range offered is well-balanced, allowing for conservative and slightly more adventurous tastes, and some of the more luxurious dishes, such as oysters, chateaubriand steak or lobster, attract a supplement. Although the style is quite hearty - perfect for hungry golfers - some lighter choices on each course will appeal to smaller appetites, and a daily pasta dish and a vegetarian dish is offered. Like the rest of the hotel, the dining has a cosy charm and the owners' hospitality is outstanding. Restaurant is open to non-residents; **Seats 50** (private room, 28); D daily, 6-9.30pm; Set D about €52, house wines from about €22, restaurant sc discretionary. Closed mid Oct-mid April. Amex, Diners, MasterCard, Visa, Laser. **Directions:** 6.5km (4 m) from Killarney town centre - just off Dingle Road. ◊

Lord Kenmare's Restaurant

Killarney
RESTAURANT
Ⓝ

College Street Killarney Co Kerry **Tel: 064 31294**
info@lordkenmares.com www.lordkenmares.com

féile bia This cosy first floor restaurant has elegant black furniture, polished floors, bare tables and blinds a lot of hard surfaces all add up to a good bit of noise, but nobody seems to mind. Barbary duck breast is their stated speciality, served, perhaps, with pineapple, orange & salsa, but this does not do the restaurant justice as menus offer many more appealing dishes - tender whiskey & Calvados braised pork belly, for example, outstanding steaks and (a dish attracting special praise on a recent visit) a beautifully presented hot seafood platter of prawns (of the tiger variety, alas) fresh salmon, monkfish, scallops, crisp fried calamari, mussels & grilled oysters. Good food, together with great service and value ensure that this cheerful place is always packed even on weekdays, when other restaurants may not be busy, there's lots of buzz; so reservations are strongly advised. A la carte. House wine about €20. **Directions:** Town centre, above Murphy's Bar and Squire's Pub. ◊

The Malton

Killarney
HOTEL/RESTAURANT

Town Centre East Avenue Road Killarney Co Kerry **Tel: 064 38000**
res@themalton.com www.themalton.com

féile bia The pillared entrance and ivy-clad facade of this classic Victorian railway hotel still convey a sense of occasion but guests who remember it of old are in for a shock. A change of ownership has brought more than a change of name and, although the building itself is protected, the interior has had a modern makeover. The fine old inner doors have gone (hopefully resting somewhere safe until there is a change of heart) but the welcoming open fire at the entrance remains and still draws guests through to the spacious grandly-pillared foyer, which has had all of its comfortable furnishings removed and now perhaps intentionally feels very like a railway station. However, it is still convenient to Killarney town (and, of course, the station), the gardens remain intact and it was very much a work in progress at the time of the Guide's summer 2007 visit. The bar had been modernised, but with a lighter hand (Malton prints feature), and other areas had so far remained unchanged. Accommodation in the newer section of the hotel was undergoing updating appropriate to its age and, in the original building, the bedroom corridors (built wide enough 'to allow two ladies in hooped dresses to pass comfortably'), still set the tone for generously-proportioned suites and executive rooms, furnished to individual designs; refurbishment in these areas had not been completed at the time of our visit. There are two restaurants: the great gilt-domed **Garden Room Restaurant** is a prime example of Victorian opulence - contrasting with the smaller contemporary restaurant, **Peppers**. Extensive facilties include a leisure centre, spa and tennis - and, belying its central position, the hotel is famously set in 20 acres of landscaped gardens. Conferences/Banqueting (900/750); broadband wi/fi; business Centre, secretarial services. Extensive facilities include a leisure centre, spa and tennis - and, belying ts central position, the hotel is set in 20 acres of landscaped gardens. **Rooms 172** (2 suites, 34 junior suites, 69 superior rooms, family 10, 4 disabled). Lift. 24 hour room service. B&B €140 pps; no SC. Open all year. **Peppers** is the hotel's bistro-style restaurant, the chef has not changed and tables are very much in demand. Situated quietly in a corner position behind the bar and overlooking the gardens, it is dashingly decorated and the ambience, Mediterranean menus, consistently sound cooking and professional service make an appealing combination. It is well established as one of Killarney's leading eating places. **Seats 150.** Children welcome. D Tue-Sat, 6.30-8.30pm; reservations recommended; house wine €24. Amex, Diners, MasterCard, Visa, Laser. **Directions:** In the heart of Killarney town beside Railway Station.

Killarney
RESTAURANT

Mentons @ The Plaza

Killarney Plaza Hotel Kenmare Place Killarney Co Kerry **Tel: 064 21150**
info@mentons.com   www.mentons.com

téte bía Gary Fitzgerald's first-floor restaurant in bustling downtown Killarney has two entrances - one up a rather grand flight of steps from the street (asserting its independence), the other through the hotel (up stairs or on the lift). It's a bright contemporary space on two levels and several areas, with classy modern table settings and quite a luxurious atmosphere - aided by welcoming staff. It appeals to all ages and is a popular lunch spot, when informal menus offer a range of light dishes such as Mentons chicken and bacon Caesar salad, and more substantial choices like Cronin's jumbo herb sausages with roast garlic mash, apple relish and thyme gravy. An early dinner offers good value, and more structured evening menus are sprinkled with house dishes - a layered starter salad, or homemade rustic agnollotti filled with confit duck leg, sundried tomato and sesame dressing, pecorino & rocket - and include local ingredients such as Cromane mussels. Gary Fitzgerald is a good chef, and the Guide's experience at Mentons has always been enjoyable. **Seats 65;** air conditioning. Children welcome. L daily 12.30-4.30, D daily 6-9. Early D 6-6.45pm, €24.95; also à la carte; house wine from €19.90. Closed last 3 weeks Jan. MasterCard, Visa. **Directions:** Killarney town centre - up steps beside main entrance to Plaza Hotel.

Killarney
HOTEL

Randles Court Hotel

Muckross Road Killarney Co Kerry **Tel: 064 35333**
info@randlescourt.com   www.randlescourt.com

This well located, family-owned and managed hotel has been developed around an attractive house originally built in 1906 as a family residence, and extensively refurbished before opening as an hotel in 1992. Despite recent extension (23 new bedrooms) it still has some of the domesticity and warmth of the family home - period features have been retained and public rooms have been comfortably furnished, including a bar, drawing room and restaurant, which give it welcome character. Spacious, comfortable bedrooms are furnished to a high standard, with the usual amenities and well-appointed bathrooms. *The neighbouring **Dromhall Hotel** (064 39300; www.dromhall.com) is a sister establishment and shared leisure facilities, including a 17-metre pool, sauna, steam room, gym and spa/treatment rooms, are accessible from both hotels. Conference/banqueting (80/30); business centre, secretarial service, video conferencing. Children welcome (under 5s free in parents' room, cot available without charge, baby sitting arranged). Underground car park. Pets permitted by arrangement. **Rooms 78.** Lift. 24 hour room service. Turndown service. B&B €100 pps, ss €30, SC inc. **Checkers Restaurant:** D daily, 7-9.30; bar meals 12-6. Special breaks offered - details on application. Closed 22-27 Dec. Amex, Diners, MasterCard, Visa, Laser. **Directions:** 5 mins walk out of Killarney centre on Muckross Road.

Killarney
HOTEL/RESTAURANT

The Ross Hote

Town Centre Killarney Co Kerry **Tel: 064 3185.**
info@theross.ie www.theross.i

Lovers of contemporary style will adore the Treacy family's impressiv new boutique hotel, which replaces their original and much-love property, which was a sort of 'Queen Mother' of the hotel world; a that now remains is the lovely bow-windowed frontage, which sti gives a hint of the warmth that lay behind. Today an assertive design-led experience begins in a highly theatrical reception area where bemused visitors in trainers perch on leather seats in the elec tric-green light of a standard lamp and wonder at it all. Beyond th lobby things calm down but it prepares the first-time guest for funky stay. Accommodation, in the thirty rooms and five suites, i exceptionally comfortably appointed as would be expected, but muc quieter in tone, the style and many of the details will be familiar t guests who know the Treacys' **Killarney Park Hotel** (see entry), jus across the road; some spacious rooms at the front look across to th waiting jarveys with their jaunting cars and horses and two bay windowed suites at the top have views across the town to the Nationa Park but most rooms are notable for comfort rather than outlook. Public areas include the aptly-name and stylish **Lane Café Bar;** with glass all along one wall and funky furnishings, it's the coolest place i Killarney to meet for cocktails and they serve very good bar food and tapas all day. Broadband wi/fi, secre tarial services. Children welcome (under 4s free in parents' room, cot available free of charge); **Room 30** (5 suites, 1 for disabled, all no smoking); B&B €110 pps; Lift; Closed 24-26 Dec. **Cellar One** Undoubtedly the jewel in this stylish hotel's crown, this stunningly theatrical restaurant is on two levels a 20-seater mezzanine and a 4-seater lower dining room and, although a lift is also available, the gran entrance down a curving glass and steel staircase is the stuff that dreams are made of. Everything abou it is larger than life, including the brilliant lime green and shocking pink furnishings (tempered by sob greys and browns of the main stage set); but there is definitely method to this mad creativity as it is n only a delightful place to eat but - except that the head waiter's desk is not handy to arriving guests, whic can cause a small delay on arrival it's an exceptionally well-designed restaurant from the working angle Head chef Ian McMonagle has responsibility for all food operations in the hotel, and his à la carte menu in Cellar One are smart and modern, with strong world influences but also a few classics and plenty c named local ingredients: Cromane mussels, Skeaghanore duck, St Tola goat's cheese all feature, fo example, and a starter plate of charcuterie is served with home-made chutney, and includes Coole cheese as well as five cured meats; a signature main course is Tequila prawn & firecracker rice (two rice flavoured with chilli and vanilla) and Tequila butter but you could also choose the house variation of a old favourite, such as char-grilled fillet of Kerry beef with sautéed wild mushrooms, baby onions & re wine jus. And then you could finish in high retro style with an individual Baked Alaska. The stunnin setting and great cooking is backed up by friendly, professional staff and both food and wine are goo value. A great night out in fact. **Seats 60** (private room, 60); air conditioning; children welcome (hig chair); D served daily, 6.30-9.30pm; à la carte; house wine €28. *Bar food also available daily, 12.30 8pm. Visa. **Directions:** Situated in the town centre on Kenmare Place.

Killarney
RESTAURANT

Treyvaud's Restauran

62 High Street Killarney Co Kerry **Tel: 064 3306** info@treyvaudsrestaurant.com www.treyvaudsrestaurant.cor

Brothers Paul and Mark Treyvaud opened this attrac tive and friendly town-centre restaurant in 2003 and it has earned a well-deserved local following an reputation well beyond the area. The decor is gent contemporary, and daytime menus are careful constructed to allow anything from a tasty little bi to a full blown meal. You could start with a deliciou bowl of French onion soup, perhaps, or seafoo chowder, which come with excellent home-mad bread, and then something from the 'Nibble section of the menu, such as tasty Treyvaud's fis cakes, or one of their speciality Sambos (the Famous Club Sambo); hot main courses include warm salac and Mark's Specials - their beef & Guinness pie with mashed potatoes is one of the best you'll fir anywhere. The dinner menu takes over at 5 o'clock, and includes some items from the day menu - th oups and the speciality fish cakes, for example - plus a wide range of appealing and fairly priced dishes ncluding favourites like braised shank of Kerry lamb, and some less usual (ostrich, for example, which s farmed in Ireland), several seafood choices and at least two for vegetarians (one of which is likely to e a pasta dish). A short mid-range wine list offers a couple of half carafes and half a dozen fine wines. ood cooking, moderate pricing, long opening hours and well-trained staff with a clear desire to send ustomers away happy with their meal have proved a winning formula for this deservedly popular restau- ant. The early dinner and (very popular) Sunday lunch offer especially good value. Children welcome efore 8pm; **Seats 80** (private room, 50). Reservations recommended. Air conditioning. Daily L12-5; D -10.30 (Sun to 10). L & D à la carte (early D 10% discount on food & drink, 5-7pm); also gourmet D 75. Set 4 course Sun L €22.95. House wine €17.95. Closed Mon & Tue off season (Nov-Feb). MasterCard, Visa, Laser. **Directions:** 500 yards up main street, on the left.

Killarney
RESTAURANT

West End House

Lower New Street Killarney Co Kerry
Tel: 064 32271

osef and Edel Fassbenders' unusual restaurant has a somewhat Tyrolean atmosphere and a most nusual history, having once been (most appropriately) one of Ireland's oldest schools of housewifery. oday it ranks as one of the "old guard" in Killarney hospitality terms as it has been serving whole- ome, hearty fare at lunch and dinner without fuss or ostentation for many years and has retained an nviable reputation for reliability and good value. The surroundings are simple but comfortable - a fire- lace set at an attractively high level in the wall at the end of the bar casts warmth across the room, hich can be very welcome on chilly evenings - and Josef's cooking is comfortingly traditional in a trong house style untroubled by fashion. Local produce is used to advantage, typically in good home- nade soups that come with freshly-baked bread (try the West End chowder, a meal in itself, full of hunky pieces of white fish, some mussels and the odd prawn), main courses such as rack of Kerry mb or tender well-hung steaks that taste like good steaks should. (B&B accommodation is also avail- ble.) Open Tue-Sun, 6-9.30pm. Set D & à la carte; starters from about €5, main courses from about 19. Wine from €23. Closed Mon. MasterCard, Visa. **Directions:** Opposite St Mary's Church. ◇

Killarney Area
AR/RESTAURANT

The Beaufort Bar & Restaurant

Beaufort Killarney Co Kerry **Tel: 064 44032**
beaurest@eircom.net www.beaufortbar.com

féile bia In the fourth generation of family ownership, Padraig O'Sullivan's immaculate establish- ment near the Gap of Dunloe is always a pleasure to visit. The old tree at the front was left afely in place during renovations which, together with other original features like the stonework and n open fire, all contribute to the genuine character. The family take pride in running this fine pub nd the upstairs restaurant is a logical extension of the bar business. Head chef Tim Brosnan, who ined the team in 1999, presents quite extensive, well-balanced à la carte and set dinner menus with generous, traditional tone: seafood cocktail, chicken liver paté; roast rack of Kerry lamb); finish with lassic desserts or farmhouse cheeses. Menus are fairly priced, especially Sunday lunch which is very opular and good value. *A short traditional bar menu is now offered, Tue-Thu evenings. Children elcome (high chair, childrens menu, baby changing facilities). **Restaurant Seats 60** (private room, he Kalem Room, seats 20). D Tue-Sat, 6.30-9.30, à la carte; L Sun only, 1-3; Set Sun L €23. House ine €18. SC discretionary. Restaurant closed D Sun, all Mon. MasterCard, Visa, Laser. **Directions:** ollow the N72 to Killorglin. Turn left at Beaufort bridge, first stone building on left in village.

Killarney Area
HOTEL

Hotel Dunloe Castle

Beaufort Killarney Co Kerry **Tel: 064 44111**
hotelsales@liebherr.com www.killarneyhotels.ie

féile bia Sister hotel to the **Hotel Europe**, Fossa and **Ard-na-Sidhe**, Caragh Lake (see entries), this beautifully located hotel is mainly modern (although the original castle is part of the development) and has much in common with the larger Europe: the style is similar, the scale is generous throughout, and standards of mainte- nance and housekeeping are exemplary. Like the Europe, the atmosphere is distinctly continental; some of the exceptionally spacious guest rooms have dining areas, and all have magnificent views, air conditioning and many extras. The surroundin park is renowned for its unique botanical collection, which includes many rare plants. Golf is, c course, a major attraction here and there is an equestrian centre on site, also fishing on the Rive Laune, which is free of charge to residents. Informal meals are offered at The Garden Café, which open all day and caters for everything from light snacks to hearty main courses. For fine dining th hotel's **Oak Room Restaurant** offers a classic à la carte menu, complemented by an extensive, we balanced and informative wine list which along with plenty of treats - includes a good choice of inte esting affordable wines and an exceptional number of half bottles. Conference/banqueting (250/180 Leisure centre (swimming pool, sauna, fitness room); pool table. Garden, fishing, walking, tennis equestrian. Children welcome (under 2s free in parents' room, cot available without charge, bab sitting arranged; playroom, playground). No pets. **Rooms 102** (2 suites, 29 executive, 10 famil rooms, 1 for disabled, 18 ground floor). Lift; 24 hr room service. B&B from €145pps, ss €7 (weekend specials from about €210). Closed 1 Nov- 6 April. Amex, Diners, MasterCard, Visa, Lase **Directions:** Off main Ring of Kerry road.

Killarney Area
HOTEL

Hotel Europe

Fossa Killarney Co Kerry **Tel: 064 7135**
sales@kih.liebherr.com www.killarneyhotels.

Although now around thirty five year old, this impressive hotel was excep tionally well built and has been so well maintaine through the years that it still outshines many a ne top level hotel. Public areas are very large an impressive, and make full use of the hotel wonderful location, and bedrooms follow a simila pattern, with lots of space, quality furnishing beautiful views and balconies all along the lak side of the hotel. Leisure facilities include a 25 metre swimming pool and the hotel adjoins th three Killarney golf courses - Killeen, Mahony's Point and Lackabane - and the two nine hole course Dunloe and Ross, are nearby. The hotel's continental connections show clearly in the style throughou but especially, perhaps, when it comes to food - breakfast, for example, is an impressive hot and col buffet. Housekeeping is exemplary and, perhaps unexpectedly, this is a very family-friendly hote Equestrian, fishing, (indoor) tennis, snooker. Children welcome (under 12s free in parents room, cc available without charge; playroom, playground). No pets. Lift. *At the time of going to press the hote is closed for a €40m renovation of the ground floor and conference centre, and the introduction of 50,000sq ft spa with 21 treatment rooms. The hotel is due to re-open in March 2008 Conferences/Banqueting (550/400); business centre, broadband wi/fi; video conferencing; lap to sized safes in bedrooms. Equestrian, fishing (coarse & fly), tennis, snooker, garden, leisure centr (pool, fitness room, sauna, steam room); Destination Spa. Children welcome (under 12s free in paren room, cot available without charge, baby sitting arranged; playroom, playground). No pets. Lift. **Room 205** (5 suites, 42 junior suites, 19 family, 1 for disabled). B&B from €105 pps, ss €75. No sc. Close Oct -Easter. Amex, Diners, MasterCard, Visa, Laser. **Directions:** On main Ring of Kerry road, N72.

Killarney Area
HOTEL/RESTAURANT

Muckross Park Hotel & Cloisters Sp

Muckross Village Lakes of Killarney Co Kerry **Tel: 064 2340**
info@muckrosspark.com www.muckrosspark.cor

At the heart of this large, well-executed development lies a fine Victorian house and, although th newer areas have an elegant contemporary style, an atmosphere of timeless quality prevai throughout. With a large conference centre, break-out meeting rooms and mediaeval-style banquetir suite, it is a popular choice for business and weddings, but it also makes a convenient and luxuriou base for the independent traveller. It is located within the Killarney National Park, near Muckros House and Garden, handy to all the championship golf courses in the area, and ideally situated fc exploring south Kerry. Beautifully furnished accommodation offers all that would be expected of a hotel of this calibre - ranging from romantic four-poster suites to spacious contemporary rooms, a featuring luxurious fabrics and many extras - and food and service to match. A good breakfast her will set you up for the day, and a particularly attractive feature of the hotel is the warm 'Irishness' the staff. The adjacent Molly Darcy's pub is in common ownership with the hotel. **Restaurants:** Dinin options are between the Blue Pool restaurant (named after the nearby Cloghreen Blue Pool Natur Trail), and the newer GB Shaw's, which is earning a following for fine food and servic

Conferences/Banqueting (300/160); Spa, walking, hillwalking, cycling, holistic healing, yoga, tai-chi; Championship golf and equestrian nearby. **Rooms 69** (6 suites, 42 double/twin bedrooms with separate seating areas that can be combined to create family rooms). B&B from €100 pps in Garden Wing; short breaks from €265pps. MasterCard, Visa, Laser. **Directions:** On main Kenmare/Ring of Kerry road, almost opposite entrance to Muckross House. ◇

Killorglin
RESTAURANT

Nick's Seafood Restaurant & Piano Bar

Lr Bridge Street Killorglin Co Kerry **Tel: 066 976 1219**

info@nicks.ie

This is one of the famous old restaurants of Ireland and Nick Foley's is clearly thriving. It consists of two attractive stone-faced townhouses - one a traditional bar with a piano and some dining tables, where arriving guests can linger over a drink and place their orders, the other the main dining area. With quarry tiles, darkwood furniture, heavily timbered ceiling, wine bottles lining a high shelf around the walls - and piano playing drifting through from the bar - the dining room has great atmosphere. Nick's cooking style of classic French with an Irish accent has earned a special reputation for his way with local seafood and - although there are always other choices, notably prime Kerry beef and lamb - it is for classic seafood dishes like grilled Cromane mussels, and lobster thermidor that his name is synonymous throughout Ireland. And, if you want to see what that much-maligned item 'the speciality seafood plate' is like at its best, make the journey to Nick's. It's unbeatable Irish seafood, and very good value. Desserts are all home-made and changed weekly, and there's a good cheeseboard too. Although it would be a shame to come here without enjoying such exceptional seafood, vegetarians aren't forgotten either and the service is outstanding, and the music and great atmosphere as beguiling as ever. An extensive wine list, hand-picked by Nick and with many bottles imported directly, includes interesting house wines and an unusual choice of half bottles. Children welcome. **Seats 90** (private room, 40). Air conditioning. Live Piano nightly. D Wed-Sun 6.30-9.45 in winter, daily in summer (to 9.30 Sun); 2 sittings at 6.45 and 9.15. Set D €50. Extensive wine list; house wine from €20; sc discretionary. Closed all Nov and 2 weeks Feb, Mon-Tue in Dec-Mar & Christmas. MasterCard, Visa, Laser. **Directions:** On the Ring of Kerry road, 20 km from Killarney.

Killorglin
RESTAURANT/WINE BAR

Sol y Sombra Wine & Tapas Bar

Old Church of Ireland Lower Bridge Street Killorglin Co Kerry
Tel: 066 976 2347 info@solysombra.ie www.solysombra.ie

Atmospheric is one of the things they do best in the Foley family and this new sister restaurant to Nick's (see entry), run by Clíodhna Foley, is no exception. Located in a former Church of Ireland premises just up the hill a little behind Nick's, it's an impressive place with a long bar, several seating areas and loads of character the name means 'sun and shade' and one inspiration for the choice was the way the light from the stained glass windows plays on the interior. The menu very sensibly leads off with a definition of 'tapa' and explains that what's on offer here is actually 'raciónes' which are larger tapas portions, served on or with bread, and perfect for sharing with friends - a good decision that suits Irish tastes and is proving very popular. The food varies with the seasons and is based mainly on local Irish produce, with speciality foods imported from Spain fo authenticity; an extensive range of little dishes is offered, with calamari a la plancha, roquetas de jamón Serrano, piquillo peppers and Spanish black pudding among the specialities. Desserts include one that will definitely put sherry trifle in the shade- a home-made zesty orange ice cream drizzled with medium sweet sherry. The Foleys have been importing wine for many years and their carefully selected, mainly Spanish, list includes a lot of specially imported bottles; you'll also find a good choice of wines by the glass, including three sherries. Live music is also an important feature here - check the website for details. Toilets wheelchair accessible; Children welcome before 9pm (high chair). **Seats 120** (private room, 25, outdoors, 34). D Wed-Mon, 5.30-10.30pm (also closed Mon in winter); house wine from €18. SC disc. Closed Feb, Tue (& Mon in winter). MasterCard, Visa, Laser. **Directions:** On left as you drive through town. Set back from road next to Nick's Restaurant.

Killorglin Area
BAR/RESTAURANT

Jack's Coastguard Station Bar & Seafood Restaurant

Waters Edge Cromane Killorglin Co Kerry

Tel: 066 976 910

Just a stone's throw from the sea at Cromane, where the mussels that the area is famous for are landed, this handsome stone building is smartly maintained and sends out all the right signals from the outset. Entrance is through an attractive traditional bar at the front, then through to a pleasingly bright and well-proportioned dining room overlooking a garden (landscaping was under way at the time of our visit) and sea at the back; well spaced tables are promisingly set up with crisp white linen and gleaming glasses, and, after a warm welcome, menus are promptly presented. Head chef Helen Vickers is well known in the area and her background is classical, including working at the Ryan family's late lamented Arbutus Lodge Hotel in Cork, where some of Ireland's finest food was once served. So it should come as no surprise to find an angel in the kitchen here, weaving her own special magic with a superb range of seafood including hake, black sole, prawns, lobster, plaice on the bone, turbot, and scallops although the ubiquitous tiger prawn finds its way in, even here, in a speciality tempura dish served with a zucchini salad and sweet chilli sauce. But Cromane mussels also star, of course, typically in classic marinière style. The cooking is really excellent and everything beautifully presented with generous servings of delicious fresh vegetables, and irresistible puddings - vanilla crème brulée with almond biscotti comes highly recommended. Pleasant staff are generally knowledgeable about the menu, and a well chosen wine list complements the food. This restaurant is a great asset to the area and it's well worth building a visit into your plans. Booking is strongly advised, especially at weekends. Be prepared for Dublin prices. **Directions:** Waterside in Cromane.

Listowel
BAR/RESTAURANT

Allo's Restaurant, Bar & Bistro

41/43 Church Street Listowel Co Kerry

Tel: 068 2288

Named after the previous owner, Helen Mullane's café-bar seems much older than it is, as the whole interior was reconstructed with salvaged materials (the flooring was once in the London Stock Exchange). It is brilliantly done, with the long, narrow bar divided up in the traditional way, with oilcloth-covered tables, now extending into a restaurant in the house next door. A team of six chefs cook tasty bistro food here. Expect fun, lively combinations of traditional and new Irish cooking with some international influences, based on carefully sourced ingredients. Theme nights are often held. **Seats 50** (private room, 20, outdoor, 20). Open Tue-Sat, 12-9, L12-7, D 7-9 L & D à la carte; also Early D €27.50, 7-9pm Tue-Thurs; House wine €22. Closed Sun & Mon, 25 Dec & Good Fri. D reservations required. Amex, MasterCard, Visa, Laser. **Directions:** Coming into Listowel on the N69, located half way down Church Street on the right hand side (almost opposite Garda Station).

Listowel
HOTEL

Listowel Arms Hotel

Listowel Co Kerry **Tel: 068 2150**

info@listowelarms.com www.listowelarms.com

This much-loved old hotel is rich in history and especially famous as the main venue for the annual Listowel Writers Week. Since 1996 the hotel has been in the energetic and discerning ownership of Kevin O'Callaghan, who has overseen a major extension and overhaul of the whole premises during the last few years and is doing so once again, with the refurbishment of the standard rooms completed in 2007 and work on the lobby and exterior, plus the addition of new bedrooms, planned for 2008. Improvements are invariably done with great sensitivity, bringing greater comfort throughout the hotel without loss of its considerable character. A very attractive banqueting area and bedrooms all overlook the River Feale - and the race course; these areas are at a premium in Listowel Race Week. Non-residents find this a handy place to drop into for a bite in the bar where they serve traditional dishes like braised beef & stout casserole (12.30-9.30) and you can have tea or coffee in the lounge at other times. Conference/banqueting (500/400); video-conferencing, broadband wifi. Wheelchair accessible. Lift. Children welcome (under 5s free in parents' room, cots available without charge). No Pets. All day room service, **Rooms 42** (all en-suite, 2 suites, 10 executive, 1 family). B&B €70 pps, ss €15. (High rates apply to Festival weeks, incl Irish Open & Listowel Race Week.) Closed 25 Dec. Diners, MasterCard, Visa, Laser. **Directions:** In the corner of the historic old square in Listowel town centre.

Portmagee
GUESTHOUSE/PUB

The Moorings
Portmagee Co Kerry **Tel: 066 947 7108**
oorings@iol.ie www.moorings.ie

féile bia Gerard & Patricia Kennedy's popular guesthouse overlooks the harbour and many bedrooms - which are comfortably furnished with phone, TV, tea/coffee making facilities and full bathrooms - have a sea view. Children welcome (under 3 free in parents' room, cot available without charge, baby sitting arranged). No pets. Traditional Irish music. **Rooms 14** (all en-suite, 5 shower only, all no smoking). B&B from €40 pps, ss about €15. The adjacent **Bridge Bar** is a good place to drop in for a bite to eat, especially seafood, when touring this beautiful area - meals are usually available all day, out a phone call to check times is advised. There is also a restaurant, which is open for evening meals and Sunday lunch. Establishment closed 20 Dec- 10 Jan approx. Amex, MasterCard, Visa, Laser. **Directions:** Turn right for Portmagee 3 miles outside Caherciveen on the Waterville Road. ◇

SNEEM

Situated on the Ring of Kerry between Kenmare and Waterville, Sneem is "a knot" in Irish, and this colourful, immaculately kept village is divided in two by the River Sneem, creating an unusual "hourglass" shape ("The Knot in the Ring"). The first week of August sees Sneem at its busiest with the "Welcome Home Festival", in honour of those who emigrated from Ireland. Moderately priced accommodation and stunning views make a good combination at the O'Sullivan family's hospitable **Old Convent House B&B** (064 45181), and **Sacré Coeur** (064 45186), in the village, is the place where locals and holiday home owners dine; it offers good plentiful food and value for money. Of several good pubs in the village, try Garbhagh and Mary Kavanagh's much-photographed bar **D O'Sheas**, on North Square, (064 45515), which has been singled out as the best food enterprise in the Geopark area (Sneem to Kells) for taking sustainable and local development issues on board; as a novel way to put the area on the map, they created five 'Geopark' drinks - and they serve local food where possible: not 'fine' food, but hearty, country food in generous portions and they're open all year. The new **Sneem Hotel** (064 75100; www.sneemhotel.com) opened at Goldens Cove in 2007, bringing much needed extra accommodation and facilities to the area.
WWW.IRELAND-GUIDE.COM FOR THE BEST PLACES TO EAT, DRINK & STAY

Sneem
HOTEL

The Parknasilla Hotel
Parknasilla Sneem Co Kerry **Tel: 064 45122**
info@parknasillahotel.ie www.parknasillahotel.ie

Set in 300 acres of sub-tropical parkland, overlooking Kenmare Bay, this classic Victorian hotel is blessed with one of the most beautiful locations in Ireland. Formerly the Parknasilla Great Southern Hotel, it came into new ownership in 2007 and is currently closed for major renovations; please consult the hotel website for updates. Amex, Diners, MasterCard, Visa, Laser. **Directions:** 25 km west of Kenmare, on Ring of Kerry. ◇

Sneem
GUESTHOUSE

Tahilla Cove Country House
Tahilla Cove Sneem Co Kerry **Tel: 064 45204**
tahillacove@eircom.net www.tahillacove.com

Although it has been much added to over the years and has a blocky annexe in the garden, this family-run guesthouse has an old house in there somewhere. There's a proper bar, with its own entrance and this, together with quite an official looking reception desk just inside the front door, makes it feel more like an hotel than a guesthouse. Yet this is a refreshingly low-key place, with two very special features: the location, which is genuinely waterside; and the owners, James and Deirdre Waterhouse. Tahilla Cove has been in the family since 1948, and run since 1987 by James and Deirdre who have the wisdom to understand why their many regulars love it just the way it is and, apart from regular maintenance, little is allowed to change. Comfort and quiet relaxation are the priorities. All the public rooms have sea views including the dining room and also a large sitting room, with plenty of armchairs and sofas, which opens on to a terrace, overlooking the garden and cove. Accommodation is divided between the ma house and the annexe; rooms vary considerably but all except two have sea views, many have privat balconies, and all are en-suite, with bathrooms of varying sizes and appointments (only one single shower-only). Although dated (this is part of the charm), all are very comfortable and have phone, T hair-dryer and individually controlled heating. Food is prepared personally by James and Deirdre an the dining room (20) is intended mainly for residents, but others are welcome when there is roon simple 5-course menus change daily. It's also a lovely place to drop into for a cup of tea overlookin the little harbour. Garden; walking; fishing. Children welcome (under 2s free in parents' room, c available without charge). Pets allowed in some areas by prior arrangement. **Rooms 9** (1 shower onl 3 family rooms, 3 ground floor, all no smoking). B&B €75 pps, ss €30. D at 7.45; Set D €35; hous wine €19-22. Non-residents' welcome by reservation. Closed for D Tue-Wed; house closed mid Oc Easter. Amex, MasterCard, Visa, Laser. **Directions:** 16km (11 miles) west of Kenmare and 8km (5 n east of Sneem (N70).

TRALEE

Well-situated at the point where the River Lee flows into Tralee Bay, Tralee is the main town of Coun Kerry and is the gateway to the rugged Dingle Peninsula. Although perhaps most famous for the Perc French song The Rose of Tralee - an association celebrated each August at the international Rose c Tralee Festival - this busy commercial centre has much else to offer in and around the town, includin Siamsa Tíre (the National Folk Theatre of Ireland), horse racing, great beaches (with the Jamie Kno Wind Surfing School) and, at nearby Blennerville, an impressive restored windmill there is a restore steam train running between Tralee and Blennerville, which adds to the fun and, quite near the winc mill, you will find **The Station House** (066 714 9980; www.thestationhouse.ie), where casual food i available all day, and fine dining offered at their restaurant **Conway's** (reservations advised). Other loca activities include horse riding, hill walking and historical sites and some of the best golf courses ii Kerry, including Ballybunion and Tralee Golf Courses, are just a short drive from Tralee. **The Gran Hotel** (066 712 1499; www.grandhoteltralee.com) on Denny Street has old world charm and, with it dark mahogany furniture and open fires in cold weather, the atmosphere is cosy; locals in the knov just love this homely hotel for its bar food: everything is freshly prepared and service is quick and eff cient - a good place to enjoy a cheerful and inexpensive meal, and suited to people of all ages (ver popular for families. Another place that visitors will be delighted to find is **Nuala Dawson's** first floc daytime restaurant (066 712 7745) above Heaton's retail store on The Mall, which is a popular plac for discerning locals; lunch is the main business and only food freshly cooked each day is served, s get here early as the choice becomes limited in the afternoon: they do wonderful salads, quiches home-made soups, breads (including gluten-free), cold meats and salmon cooked on the premises anc - best of all beautiful home-made confectionery. Moderately priced accommodation in Tralee is avail able at the **Comfort Inn** (066 712 1877; www.choicehotels.ie), on Castle Street - and, by contras **Ballyseede Castle Hotel** (066 712 5799; www.ballyseedecastle.com), just off the Tralee-Killarne Road (N21), is a very likeable hotel of character with 15th century origins, now in common ownershi with Cabra Castle in Co Cavan (see entry); set in 35 acres of parkland and garden on the edge of the town, it is spacious and comfortable, with quirky features that give a sense of fun.

WWW.IRELAND-GUIDE.COM FOR THE BEST PLACES TO EAT, DRINK & STAY

Tralee

HOTEL/RESTAURANT

R

Ballygarry House Hotel & Spa

Killarney Road Tralee Co Kerry **Tel: 066 712 332**
info@ballygarryhouse.com www.ballygarryhouse.con

This pleasant hotel just outside Tralee presents a neat face to arriving guests and also ha extensive landscaped gardens at the back; recent improvements to the main Tralee Killarney road have worked in the hotel's favour as a slip road has been created, making access much easier and easing traffic noise. Recent refurbishment has brought a more contemporary tone to the furnishing style, with warm colours creating a welcoming atmosphere in the smart public areas Accommodation is very pleasing, with many thoughtful details adding to the comfort of a stay - room overlooking the gardens at the back are particularly attractive and should be quieter. This is ar appealing hotel, with exceptionally friendly and helpful staff, and it is moderately priced for the hig standard offered. It is understandably popular for weddings (conference/banqueting 250/400). Spa Children welcome (free in parents' room up to 12; cot available without charge, baby sitting arranged) Golf nearby. Walking, garden. No pets. **Rooms 64** (1 suite, 5 junior suites, 1 for disabled) Lift. 24 hou room service. Turndown service. Room rate from about €150, no sc. Closed 24-27 Dec. **Brooks:** Thi well appointed restaurant is pleasingly set up towards the back of the hotel and the modern classical food has great appeal. Quite an extensive à la carte menu is offered, based largely on local produce, and its strength is in the presentation of traditional dishes with a successful modern twist. Cooking is sound, presentation attractive - and, best of all, staff are attentive and hospitable. **Seats 80.** D daily 6.30-9.30; L Sun only 12.30-2.30. D à la carte; Set Sun L about €23. House wine from €20. SC discretionary. Bar meals also available 12-9 daily). Amex, MasterCard, Visa, Laser. **Directions:** 1 mile fromTralee, on the Killarney road. ◇

Tralee

HOTEL

[R]

The Brandon Hotel

Princes Street Tralee Co Kerry

Tel: 066 712 3333

Overlooking a park and the famous Siamsa Tíre folk theatre, and close to the Aquadome, Tralee's largest hotel is at the heart of activities throughout the area. Spacious public areas are impressive, and while there are suites and superior rooms available, some of the standard bedrooms are on the small side; however, all have been refurbished or are due for refurbishment shortly, and have direct-dial phone, radio and TV (no tea/coffee-making facilities) and tiled bathrooms. There's a well-equipped leisure centre and good banqueting/conference facilities. Private parking. **Rooms 183.** B&B from about €60 pps. Closed 21-29 Dec. Amex, Diners, MasterCard, Visa. **Directions:** Town centre. ◇

Tralee

GUESTHOUSE

[R]

Brook Manor Lodge

Fenit Road Tralee Co Kerry **Tel: 066 712 0406**

brookmanor@eircom.net www.brookmanorlodge.com

Set back from the road, in 3.5 acres of grounds, Sandra and Jerome Lordan's large purpose-built guesthouse offers immaculate and particularly spacious accommodation. Public rooms and bedrooms are large and very comfortably furnished - bedrooms are elegantly furnished and have generous beds and all the usual modern facilities - TV, phone, trouser press, tea/coffee making, hair dryer and radio/alarm - everything, in short, that the traveller (and, specifically, the golfing traveller) could need. Breakfast is cooked to order from an extensive menu. Children welcome (under 8s free in parents' room, cot available free of charge). Free broadband wi/fi; No pets. **Rooms 8** (1 suite, 1 junior suite, 2 superior rooms, 2 shower only, 2 family rooms, 3 ground floor, all no smoking.) B&B €70 pps; (single supplement applies). Closed 1 Nov - 1 Feb. MasterCard, Visa, Laser. **Directions:** 2 km from town centre on Fenit road.

Tralee

GUESTHOUSE

[R]

Castlemorris House

Ballymullen Tralee Co Kerry **Tel: 066 718 0060**

castlemorris@eircom.net www.castlemorrishouse.com

Tony and Ciara Fields' attractive creeper-clad Georgian house makes a lovely place to stay. They really enjoy sharing their home with guests who, in turn, appreciate the space and comfort they offer and the friendly atmosphere of a family home. Afternoon tea with home-baked cake or scones is offered in the drawing room on arrival (in front of the fire on chilly days), and guests can use this room at any time, to watch television or relax with a book and, in fine weather, there is a pleasant garden to sit in. Bedrooms are spacious and well-furnished to provide comfort with style, breakfast is a speciality. No dinner is offered, but there are restaurants nearby. Garden. Children welcome (under 4s free in parents room, cot available at no charge, baby sitting arranged). No pets. **Rooms 7** (4 shower only, 2 family rooms, all no smoking). B&B €45 pps, ss €10. Closed Christmas. MasterCard, Visa, Laser. **Directions:** On south Ring Road/Killorglin road (Ring of Kerry) leaving Tralee in Dingle direction.

Tralee

HOTEL/RESTAURANT

[R]

féile bia

Meadowlands Hotel

Oakpark Rd Tralee Co Kerry **Tel: 066 718 0444**

info@meadowlandshotel.com www.meadowlandshotel.com

This hotel in a peaceful part of the town is set in 3 acres of grounds and landscaped gardens, yet within walking distance of the town centre. Open since 1998, the high quality of materials and workmanship is now paying off as the building mellows and takes on its own personality - and this, together with caring service from well-trained staff, is ensuring its position as one of the area's leading hotels. The interior layout and design of the hotel are impressive; notably the whole hotel is wheelchair friendly and furniture, commissioned from Irish craft manufacturers, is interesting, well-made and practical. Stylish, well-designed bedrooms are spacious and comfortable, with strikingly original decor - and the suites have jacuzzis. In addition to the main restaurant, An Pota

Stóir, informal meals, including seafood from the proprietor's fishing boats, are available in **Johnny Franks** bar, (12-9 daily). Conference/banqueting (200/180); free broadband wi/fi; business centre. Golf, equestrian, fishing and walking nearby. Garden. Children welcome (under 3s free in parents' room, cots available free of charge, baby sitting arranged). Wheelchair accessible. No pets. **Rooms 58** (2 suites, 10 superior rooms, 25 no smoking, 1 family, 5 ground floor, 2 for disabled). Lift. 24 hour room service. B&B €105 pps, ss €20. Off-season value breaks available. **The Pota Stóir Restaurant** The dining room is finished in timber and decorated in a somewhat rustic style, with fishing and farming memorabilia - making for a relaxed atmosphere, which is complemented by a high standard of service. The hotel has its own fishing boat (operated by the owner), and offers a short, regularly updated menu consisting of local seafood and some excellent non-seafood dishes; the cooking is fairly traditional but the chef is not unwilling to use local foods imaginatively, and to good effect. The welcome is very friendly and efficient and the attention to detail continues throughout the meal - the staff are knowledgeable and take pride in the quality of food served. The wine list is simple but perfectly adequate and is very good value. Probably not ideal for children, with the exception of Sunday lunch, although the staff would be very accommodating in any situation. **Seats 100** (private room 40) air conditioning; pianist Sat D; D Mon-Sat 7-9.30pm, L Sun only 12-2pm; set 3 course D €35; set Sun L €21.95; house wine from €19.50. SC Disc. Restaurant closed Sun D. Closed 24-25 Dec. Amex, MasterCard, Visa, Laser. **Directions:** 1km from Tralee town centre on the N69, but usually accessed by N21/N22: go straight through the last two roundabouts and turn right at each of the next two traffic lights; the hotel is on the right.

Tralee

Oyster Tavern

PUB/RESTAURANT

The Spa Tralee Co Kerry
Tel: 066 713 6102

This well-maintained bar and restaurant halfway between Tralee and the village of Fenit (a busy fishing port and excellent base for sailing), is easily spotted by its large roof sign. The Oyster has a strong local following, due to the convivial atmosphere in the bar and large selection of seafood in the restaurant. The dining room is basically a large extension to the small bar with a view of the mountains across Tralee Bay on fine days. The menu is essentially traditional and everyone should find something to suit their tastes: an extensive seafood menu sits alongside a balanced choice of non-seafood dishes offering prime meat and poultry and a couple of vegetarian dishes. All food is skilfully prepared and the service is both efficient and friendly. Children are welcome and the restaurant is popular with families, particularly for Sunday lunch. There is a fair selection of wines, starting at €20. Bar open usual hours (no food served in the bar). **Seats 140.** D daily, Summer hours 5-10.15pm (Sun from 6), Winter hours 6-9.45pm (Sun to 8.45pm), L Sun only all year, 12.30-2.30. Set Sun L about €20, D à la carte. House wine from €20. *Times not confirmed at time of going to press - a phone call to check is advised. Closed 25 Dec, Good Fri. Diners, MasterCard, Visa, Laser. **Directions:** 4 miles outside Tralee, on the Fenit road.

Tralee

Restaurant David Norris

RESTAURANT

Ivy House Ivy Terrace Tralee Co Kerry **Tel: 066 718 5654**
restaurantdavidnorris@eircom.net

Restaurant David Norris has earned wide recognition as Tralee's leading fine dining restaurant. Although located on the first floor of an unprepossessing modern building, it has a nice little reception area with a sofa and stools at a small bar, and well-spaced tables are dressed with quality linen, plain glasses and white china, relieved by fresh flowers. A Euro-Toques chef, David Norris sources food with care; the ingredients used are organic wherever possible and everything served is hand-made on the premises. The emphasis is on taste, with beautiful yet not over-elaborate presentation - and the aim is to offer the best of food at reasonable prices. This he achieves well: seasonal menus are simply written and, while very promising, are not over-ambitious. About seven choices are offered on each course of an à la carte menu: seafood is well-represented, as would be expected in this area, but the range of foods offered is wide - Kerry beef may top the bill, also local lamb - and imaginative vegetarian dishes have mainstream appeal. Speciality dishes include a starter of crispy duck confit with Parmesan polenta and a chilli-garlic oil and ever-popular braised shank of lamb may come with an unusual parsley &

parsnip purée and gremolata. Classic desserts, which include speciality hand-made ice creams, round off the meal in style, or there are Irish farmhouse cheeses, served with fresh fruit, home-made preserves and biscuits. Thoughtful detail is evident throughout, from the complimentary amuse-bouche that arrives with your aperitif to the home-made fudge served with your tea or coffee. Consistently good cooking, professional service, an informative but sensibly limited wine list and good value for money have all won this fine restaurant many friends - and recent visits by the Guide confirm yet again David Norris's position as the premier restaurant in the area. Children welcome. **Seats 40.** D Tue-Sat 5.30-9.30 (Sat 7-9.30); early D €26.95, Tue-Fri 5.30-7; also à la carte. House wine €19.95; sc discretionary, except 10% (charged on food only) on parties of 10+. Closed Sun, Mon, all bank hols, 1 week Oct, 1 weeks Jan, 1 week Jul. Amex, MasterCard, Visa, Laser. **Directions:** Facing Siamsa Tire, across the road from the Brandon Hotel.

Tralee
BAR/RESTAURANT

Val's Bar & Bistro

Bridge Street Tralee Co Kerry **Tel: 066 712 1559**
vals@ohallorangroup.com

téite bia This is the happening place in Tralee for informal dining and music - stylish, designer-driven, it's all of a piece with tinted windows, dark woods and very dark leather on seats and bar stools - and traditional music most week nights. Differing floor heights are cleverly exploited, and there's a very sociable feature area at the bottom of the stairs up to the bistro, which looks like an enormous three-sided sofa seating about 10 people. Although gloomy if you come in out of bright sunlight, the lighting is subtle and effective once your eyes adjust. Consistent standards, of both bar and the upstairs bistro food, have been maintained even when there have been changes of personnel, so the policy of providing quality and good value is likely to continue. Menus are well-balanced and have youth appeal, and prices are reasonable. The bar menus is also attractive, and the wine list includes eight well-chosen house wines. Bistro **Seats 60** (outdoor seating, 20). Reservations required. Air conditioning. Toilets wheelchair accessible. L Mon-Sat,12.30-2.30; D daily 6.30-9.30 (Sun to 9). Bar meals 5.30-9 daily. [Times not confirmed at time of going to press, a phone call to check is advised.] Closed L Sun, 25 Dec, Good Fri. MasterCard, Visa, Laser. **Directions:** Town centre, beside Abbey carpark. ◇

Tralee Area
RESTAURANT
R

The Phoenix

Shanahill East Castlemaine Co Kerry **Tel: 066 976 6284**
phoenixtyher@hotmail.com www.thephoenixorganic.com

This unusual vegetarian restaurant exudes charm with its rambling gardens - you can choose whether to eat beneath trailing honeysuckle and fairy lights, or inside in the relaxed and cheerful dining area. The menu promises organic wines and the best of local and organic produce: a delicious salad or home-made soup, and interesting mains such as a house speciality of oven-grilled polenta & spinach cake served with goat's cheese crouton & apricot salsa. Dining at the Phoenix is an earthy experience, based on a strong respect for nature: Lucy the cat may sleep on a cushioned seat, and there are three dogs which guests sometimes take for a stroll. Guests are offered an opportunity to explore the natural garden where most of the kitchen produce is picked fresh daily. This is a little gem, with a touch of magic adding an extra dimension to a relaxing evening. *The Phoenix offers accommodation including gypsy caravans and chalet rental, and has ample garden space to pitch a tent; packed lunches and airport transfers are also available. **Seats 25-30.** Open all day in high season. D from €19.50. Closed Oct-Easter (may open by arrangement). Visa. **Directions:** 7km (4 m) west of Castlemaine on the R561 coastal road to Dingle. (N70 from Killarney or Tralee).

Valencia Island
CAFÉ/RESTAURANT
E N

Lighthouse Café

Dohilla Valentia Island Co Kerry
Tel: 066 947 6304

This unusual little restaurant is well signposted from Knightstown although, if travelling by car, the roads becomes ever smaller and windier and you may wonder if the signs have been turned by some mischievous spirit; but no, you are not lost and when you arrive you will even find space for parking. Then you walk up a grassy track, past flowers wild and planted, and a wonderful organic vegetable garden that has been claimed from the land sloping down to the cliffs. The café, a cheerful little building with a blackboard menu at the entrance and a large polytunnel tucked away behind the outdoor seating area, is a simple room set up in no-nonsense style for comfortable eating - there are no frills here, but what you get is exceptional in its simplicity and goodness. It's worth a visit even just for cup of tea, served cheerfully with mismatched crockery to one of the outdoor tables, where you can sit and drink in the stupendous view. But there's plenty more on offer, from home-made soups served with delicious soda bread fresh from the oven to more substantial dishes and home-bakes for after or for tea. And, should you have time afterwards, you'll find the tetrapod trackway just along from the café... This place is magic. Open daily 11am-7pm (to 10pm Fri-Sun). Call to check opening times off season. **Directions:** Follow the signs from Knightstown. ◊

Valentia Island
CAFÉ

Sea Breeze - Knightstown's Coffee Shop

Knightstown Valentia Island Co Kerry **Tel: 087 783 7544**
grainneseabreeze@hotmail.com

Gráinne Houlihan's bright and funky coffee shop in Knightstown village is a great place to break a journey when touring the area. There's outdoor seating at the front for fine days and, inside, there's a pleasingly old-fashioned café with oilcloth-covered tables; aside from terrific coffees, good home cooking is the great strength, especially baking (warm scone with jam, butter & fresh cream, chocolate fudge cake...). You can have something as simple as a mug of soup and some home-made bread, a speciality sandwich, or one of half a dozen substantial savoury platters, including a vegetarian one, and there's a small wine list. At the back, a long corridor down to the loos is decorated with an eclectic collection of old mirrors - an inspired way to brighten up a long corridor. Toilets wheelchair accessible; children welcome (high chair); house wine from €4 per glass; Open weekends from Easter, 12noon-6pm; open daily in high season (June-end Sep). Closed Jan-Easter. **No Credit Cards. Directions:** On right in main street of village, coming from ferry.

Waterville
GUESTHOUSE

Brookhaven House

New Line Road Waterville Co Kerry **Tel: 066 947 4431**
brookhaven@esatclear.ie www.brookhavenhouse.com

Overlooking the Atlantic Ocean and Waterville Championship Golf Course, Mary Clifford's family-run custom-built guesthouse lays the emphasis on comfort and personal service and, although it may seem a little stark from the road, it is set in an attractive garden, which is peaceful and colourful and, when we visited in 2007, work was under way to develop a little river that runs along the length of the garden, to make a feature of it. The spacious en-suite bedrooms are very comfortable and have all the necessary amenities; twin, double and triple rooms are all available, some with seating areas, all with direct dial phone, TV, hairdryer and tea & coffee making facilities and most with lovely views over the bay - so book a room with a view of the sea if possible. And, as Mary is keen to point out, there's more to Waterville than golf - hill walking, watersports, angling and horse riding are all nearby. Free Broadband wi/fi. Drying room. Children welcome (under 5s free in parents room, cot available at no charge). **Rooms 6** (2 junior suites, 1 shower only, 1 family room, 1 ground floor, all no smoking). B&B €60 pps, ss €40. MasterCard, Visa, Laser. **Directions:** Less than 1km from Waterville on the north side.

Waterville
HOTEL/RESTAURANT

Butler Arms Hotel

Waterville Co Kerry **Tel: 066 947 4144**
reservations@butlerarms.com www.butlerarms.com

Peter and Mary Huggard's hotel dominates the seafront at Waterville; it is one of several to have strong links with Charlie Chaplin and is one of Ireland's best-known hotels. Like many hotels that have been owner-run for several generations, it has established a special reputation for its homely atmosphere and good service. Improvements are constantly being made and public areas, including two sitting rooms, a sun lounge and a cocktail bar, spacious and comfortably furnished, while the beamed Fisherman's Bar has a livelier atmosphere and can be a useful place for a break on the Ring of Kerry route. Bedrooms vary from distinctly non-standard rooms in the old part of the hotel (which many regular guests request) to smartly decorated, spacious rooms with neat en-suite bathrooms and uninterrupted sea views in a newer wing. Off-season value breaks; shooting (woodcock, snipe) Nov-Jan. Golf nearby. Garden; fishing; tennis. Snooker. Wheelchair accessible. Own parking. Children welcome (free cot, baby sitting arranged). No pets. **Rooms 40** (12 junior suites, 34 no-smoking rooms, 1 disabled). Lift. Room service (limited hours). Turndown service. B&B from €95 pps, ss about €30. SC discretionary. **Fishermen's Restaurant:** On the sea-side of the old building, the restaurant is relaxing, with a pleasant ambience, well-appointed linen-clad tables and friendly staff

The menu is flexible, priced as a full 5-course meal or à la carte, and offers a wide-ranging selection of dishes - main courses have an understandable leaning towards local seafood, including lobster, but Kerry mountain lamb, beef, and duckling are also likely choices and there will be at least one for vegetarians. The house style is quite traditional and will please those who rate good, well-cooked food (with lots of flavour) above trendy international menus. And do save a little room for delicious home-made desserts - or a trio of Irish cheeses, served with home-made tomato chutney. **Fisherman's Bar:** bar food available daily 12-3 & 6.30-9. **Restaurant Seats 70.** Reservations accepted (non residents welcome). Children welcome. Toilets wheelchair accessible. D daily, 7-9.30. Set D about €45, also à la carte. Hotel closed late Oct-end Mar, except for special bookings. Amex, MasterCard, Visa, Laser. **Directions:** On Ring of Kerry road. ◇

Waterville
B&B/RESTAURANT

The Old Cable House

Milestone Heritage Site Old Cable Station Waterville Co Kerry
Tel: 066 947 4233 interestingstay@iol.ie www.oldcablehouse.com

For those seeking something different from the double-glazed comforts of modern accommodation, Alan and Margaret Brown's Old Cable House has real Victorian character and the added interest of its transatlantic cable history. It is set high above the town to give clear Atlantic views and simply furnished rooms have everything necessary (including en-suite facilities) but with the emphasis on home comfort, Victorian atmosphere and personal warmth; the pine floors, original sash windows and the feeling of spending time in someone's treasured home are the real plus for those who appreciate vernacular architecture. Three disability-friendly rooms were added on the ground floor in 2007, and a restaurant extension is planned at the time of going to press. At present the restaurant is in an informal dining room, with an open fire - is open to non-residents, and offers what the Browns correctly describe as unpretentious good food with character: Alan, who is the chef, lays the emphasis on seafood and locally sourced meats served in an hospitable atmosphere. Waterville Golf Club is on the doorstep, of course, the whole of the Ring of Kerry is very close by, and there are many interesting things to do when staying here. Cycling, fishing, equestrian, golf and walking all nearby. Free broadband wi/fi. **Rooms 13** (4 family, 3 ground floor, 3 for disabled, all no smoking); Pets permitted. Children welcome (under 5s free in parents' room, cot available free of charge, baby sitting arranged; playground); B&B €35 pps. Restaurant seats 32 (high chair, childrens menu); D daily in summer, 6-9.30pm; early D €20, 6-7pm; house wine from €17. Closed 23 Dec-1 Jan. MasterCard, Visa. **Directions:** In Waterville town.

Waterville
RESTAURANT
🏰 👁

Paddyfrogs Restaurant

The New Line Waterville Co Kerry **Tel: 066 947 8766**
paddyfrogs@eircom.net

Sandra Foster and chef Max Lequet's fine restaurant has a well-earned following with locals, golfers and holidaymakers alike, for its upbeat atmosphere and cooking by a chef who respects good ingredients and obviously loves what he is doing. The restaurant was designed by local architect Albert Walsh and is in a lovely situation, right on the shoreline; bright and open, with eye-catching modern decor, it's perfectly suited to the style of food. Menus offer about half a dozen unusually varied choices on each course, with seafood a strength and a short separate vegetarian menu also offered; dishes which illustrate the style include a moreish starter of pan-seared baby squid served with marinated sautéed courgettes, fresh coriander and caper salad and, from a range of main courses that include variations on the ever-popular fillet steak and excellent roast rack of lamb, or a dish of grilled cod fillet on potato & spinach mousseline. Excellent desserts tend toward the classics - a gorgeous dark Belgian chocolate & brandy mousse on an orange & vanilla sauce perhaps, or there's a Paddyfrogs Irish cheese platter, served with delicious accompaniments - including a shot of home-made spicy white wine. A well-balanced wine list includes interesting house wines and at least six half bottles. Toilets wheelchair accessible; children welcome; ample parking. **Seats 60** (private room, 12, outdoors, 20); D daily 6.30-10; Set D about €40, also à la carte or Vegetarian Menu; house wine about €20. Closed Nov-mid Mar. Amex, MasterCard, Visa, Laser. **Directions:** Ring of Kerry - right on the waterfront in Waterville.

Waterville
BAR/RESTAURANT WITH ROOMS

The Smugglers Inn

Cliff Road Waterville Co Kerry **Tel: 066 947 4330**
thesmugglersinn@eircom.net www.the-smugglers-inn.com

Lucille and Henry Hunt's famous clifftop inn enjoys a remarkable location right beside the world famous championship Waterville Golf Links. Gradual refurbishment of the premises has seen big improvements over the last few years, most recently the whole frontage has been upgraded and, together with colourful window boxes, it makes a welcoming first impression. This is an attractive place for a meal in the comfortable bar or, in fine sunny weather, at garden tables that overlook a mile of sandy beach to the sea and mountains beyond. The popular restaurant is in a large conservatory dining area which is shaded to avoid glare, and has magnificent views of the golf links and clubhouse, Ballinskelligs Bay and the McGillycuddy Reeks. Henry Hunt is a talented and dedicated chef, and local ingredients star in cooking which has a classical foundation, but includes modern dishes too, most noticeably on the bar menu. Seafood is the speciality, but non-seafood lovers have plenty of other choices, including Kerry lamb and beef; there area also really good vegetarian dishes and some less usual choices such as saddle of rabbit. Lunch is served every day (the set lunch menu is good value, as is the early dinner), and bar snacks are available throughout the day, making this an ideal place to take a break when on the Ring of Kerry - although a phone call to check availability of food is advisable. **Restaurant/Bar Seats 90.** Children welcome (high chair; children's menu); air conditioning. Restaurant: L 12-3 (to 4 Sun), D 6-9.30; bar food 12-8.30, (snack menu only 3-6 pm). Set Sun L €30. Early D €30 (6-7pm). Set D €41, also à la carte; house wine €18.50. NB - Minimum credit card transaction is €50. **Accommodation** is also offered, in modest but pleasant rooms which have all been recently redecorated; they vary in size, outlook and facilities (one has a balcony) and price, but all are comfortably furnished in a homely style. There's a large first-floor residents' sitting room with sofas and armchairs, books, television and magnificent sea views. Children welcome (under 4s free in parents' room, cots available without charge). Pets allowed in some areas by arrangement. Garden, walking, fishing. **Rooms 14** (9 shower only, 1 family, 3 ground floor). B&B €50, ss €30. Closed Nov-Mar. Amex, Diners, MasterCard, Visa, Laser. **Directions:** Before village of Waterville, on coast road next to Golf Club.

COUNTY KILDARE

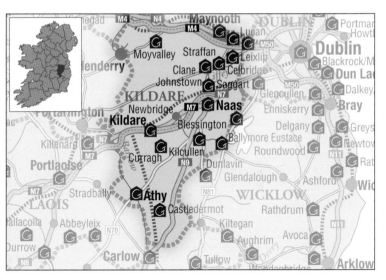

As would be expected of an area which includes the famed racecourses of The Curragh, Punchestown and Naas among its many amenities, Kildare is the horse county par excellence, the boyhood home of Cian O'Connor, Ireland's equestrian Olympic Gold Medallist at Athens in August 2004. The horse is so central and natural a part of Irish life that you'll find significant stud farms in a surprisingly large number of counties. But it is in Kildare that they reach their greatest concentration in the ultimate equine county. Thus it's ironic that, a mere 400 million years ago, Kildare was just a salty ocean where the only creatures remotely equine were the extremely primitive ancestors of sea horses.

But things have been looking up for the horse in County Kildare ever since, and today the lush pastures of the gently sloping Liffey and Barrow valleys provide ideal country for nurturing and training champions. Apart from many famous private farms, the Irish National Stud in Kildare town just beyond the splendid gallops of The Curragh is open for visitors, and it also includes a remarkable Japanese garden, reckoned the best Japanese rock garden in Europe, as well as the Museum of the Horse.

Another cornerstone of Kildare life is golf – the 2006 Ryder Cup between Europe and the US was staged in the county at the K Club, with the home team winning this "most passionate golf experience".

The gradual development of Ireland's motorway network has been particularly beneficial to Kildare, as it has lightened the traffic load through the county's towns. In fact, getting off the main roads is what enjoyment of life in Kildare is all about. The county's proximity to Dublin means that in the most recent population survey, Kildare was second only to neighbouring Meath in its increase, the numbers growing by 21.5% to 164,000. Yet it is surprisingly easy to get away from the traffic, and you'll quickly find areas of rural enchantment and unexpected swathes of relatively untamed nature.

In the northwest of the county is the awe-inspiring Bog of Allen, the largest in Ireland, across whose wide open spaces the early engineers struggled to progress the Grand Canal on its route from the east coast towards the Shannon. Such needs of national transport are intertwined through the county's history. But between the arterial routes, railroads and canals, there is an easier pace of life, and gentle country with it.

A southern leg of the Grand Canal curves away to become the Barrow Navigation, winding it way to Waterford. Beyond Athy, it goes near Kilkea, birthplace of Antarctic explorer Ernest Shackleton, whose growing fame is increasingly celebrated in his native county where his ancestors were involved in building the meeting -house which is now the Quaker Museum in Ballitore.

Local Attractions & Information

Athy Heritage Centre	059 863 3075
Ballitore Quaker Museum & Library	059 862 3344
Carbury Ballindoolin House & Garden	046 973 1430
Celbridge Castletown House	01 628 8252
Curragh The Curragh Racecourse	045 441 205
Edenderry Grange Castle & Gardens	0405 33 316
Kilcock Larchill Arcadian Gardens (follies)	01 628 7354
Kildare (Tully) Irish National Stud	045 521 617 / 521 251
Kildare (Tully) Japanese Gardens	045 522 963
Kildare Tourism Information	045 530 672
Kill Goff's Bloodstock Sales (frequent)	045 877 211
Naas Kildare Failte	045 898 888
Naas Naas Racecourse	045 897 391
Newbridge Riverbank Arts Centre	045 433 480
Punchestown Punchestown Racecourse	045 897 704
Straffan Lodge Park Walled Garden	01 627 3155
Straffan Steam Museum	01 627 3155
Timolin-Moone Irish Pewtermill	0507 24 164

R # ATHY

Athy is pleasantly situated alongside the River Barrow and the Grand Canal, which has three locks in the town, descending to the river. Three hotels have recently opened in the area: **Carlton Abbey Hotel** (059 863 0100; www.carltonabbeyhotel.com) is the most central; it was once a convent and has many original features retained, including an impressive high-ceilinged bar with stained glass windows which is in the old abbey itself. **Bert House Hotel & Leisure** (059 863 2578; www.berthouse.ie) is a reno-vated property in a waterside location nearby at Kilberry; approached by a long drive, it has lots of old world charm and good leisure facilities. **Clanard Court Hotel** (059 864 0666; www.clanardcourt.ie) set in large grounds a mile out side the town, is a popular hotel locally with good business and confer-ence/banqueting facilities. Triona and Brid **Edgar's Gargoyles Café** (059 864 1482)is a useful canalside place to know about, at Grand Canal House beside the bridge; everything is sourced locally where possible and they take pride in good home cooking, offering lunches and casual food featuring home baking throughout the day (Mon-Fri 9-6, Sat & Sun 10-6), with plans for evening opening at the time of going to press.

WWW.IRELAND-GUIDE.COM FOR THE BEST PLACES TO EAT, DRINK & STAY

Athy
COUNTRY HOUSE

Coursetown Country House
Stradbally Road Athy Co Kildare **Tel: 059 863 1101**
www.coursetown.com

Jim and Iris Fox's fine 200-year old house just off the Stradbally road is attached to a large arable farm. The house is welcoming, immaculately maintained and very comfortable, with some unusual attributes, including Jim's natural history library (where guests are welcome to browse) and extensive, well-tended gardens stocked with many interesting plants, including rare herbaceous plants, and old roses and apple trees. Bedrooms vary according to their posi-tion in the house, but all are thoughtfully furnished in a pleasantly homely country house style and have direct dial phones, tea/coffee facilities and hair dryers. Iris takes pride in ensuring that her guests have the comfort of the very best beds and bedding - and the atten-tion to detail in the pristine shower rooms is equally high, with lots of lovely towels and quality toiletries. (A bathroom is also available for anyone who prefers to have a good soak in a tub.) Another special feature is a ground floor room near the front door, which has been specially designed for wheelchair users, with everything completed to the same high standard as the rest of the house. Then there is breakfast - again, nothing is too much trouble and the emphasis is on delicious healthy eating. The wide selection offered includes fresh juices and fruit salad, poached seasonal fruit (plums from the garden, perhaps)

pancakes, French toast with banana & maple syrup, Irish farmhouse cheeses, home-made bread and preserves - and the traditional cooked breakfast includes lovely rashers specially vacuum-packed for Iris by Shiel's butchers in Abbeyleix. Small weddings catered for (20). Not suitable for children under 8 and older children must have their own room. No smoking house. Pets allowed in some areas by arrangement. Garden. **Rooms 4** (all with en-suite shower, all no smoking, 1 for disabled). B&B €60pps, single €80. 10% discount on breaks of 2 nights or more. Closed 3 Nov- 12 Mar. MasterCard, Visa, Laser. **Directions:** Just outside Athy, on R428. Turn off N78 at Athy, or N80 at Stradbally; well signposted.

Ballymore Eustace   ## Ardenode Hotel

HOTEL

Ballymore Eustace Co Kildare **Tel: 045 864 198**

info@ardenodehotel.com   www.ardenodehotel.com

Fitzers Catering (see entry in Dublin 2) took over this small country hotel in 2006. It is not an hotel in the usual sense and customers hoping to drop in for a cup of coffee or a bar lunch will be disappointed but they are open for Sunday lunch and for private functions, mostly weddings. However it is useful to know about this place as they will accommodate guests who are dining at the Ballymore Inn (see entry) and wish to stay nearby, and arrange transport if necessary. Conferences/Banqueting (300/250); tennis court; garden; walking. Children welcome (cots available free of charge, baby sitting arranged); **Rooms 17** (5 shower only, 2 family, all no smoking); B&B €75pps, ss €20. MasterCard, Visa, Laser. **Directions:** From village square take a right at Paddy Murphy's pub, take right after the bridge, follow road and veer to right at fork, located on right.

Ballymore Eustace   ## The Ballymore Inn

RESTAURANT/PUB

Ballymore Eustace Co Kildare **Tel: 045 864 585**

theballymoreinn@eircom.net   www.ballymoreinn.com

It's the fantastic food that draws people to the O'Sullivan family's pub and it's wise to book well ahead to get a taste of the wonderful things this fine country kitchen has to offer. The neatly painted cream and navy exterior, the clipped trees in tubs flanking the front door, the Féile Bia plaque - all bring a sense of anticipation. Hospitality is a strong point at this stylish bar - arriving guests are greeted at a reception area at the door, and you will either be given a table in the front Café Bar area, or you can go through to the 'Back Bar', a big open plan bar with a vibrant atmosphere. There are bar specials and a 'pizza & snack' menu offering home-made soup, delicious salads, warm panetella with various fillings and the famous Ballymore Inn speciality pizzas, based on artisan products and baked in a special pizza oven. An Express Lunch Menu, offers real food for customers in a hurry: a delicious home-made soup, and their renowned Kildare sandwich, or a simple hot dish, and a fish dish of the day (roast fresh cod with stirfry broccoli and bacon & blue cheese sauce, for example); for a more leisurely lunch a full menu is available. Evening Café Bar menus are a little more formal, offering a well-balanced choice, but this is beef country and the inn is renowned for its steaks - chargrilled aged sirloin or fillet - and rack of Slaney lamb is almost equally popular. Nobody understands the importance of careful sourcing better than Georgina O'Sullivan does and, as a matter of course, membership of the Féile Bia programme is highlighted on menus, and producers and suppliers are credited on dishes - and the policy of immaculate sourcing, careful cooking and a relaxed ambience have proved a winning formula. And a concise, customer-friendly wine list includes about ten house wines by the bottle, carafe (50cl) and glass, half a dozen bubblies and ten half bottles. Children welcome to 10pm. **Seats 100** (+16 outside); air conditioning. Reservations advised for Café Bar; Back Bar no reservations. Food served daily, L 12.30-3, D 6-9. House wines from €21.50; sc discretionary. Bar food also served daily 3-9 (Sat/Sun 12.30-9). Closed 25 Dec & Good Fri. Amex, MasterCard, Visa, Laser. **Directions:** From Blessington, take Baltinglass road. After 1.5 miles, turn right to Ballymore Eustace.

Kilkea Castle Hotel

Castledermot
HOTEL/RESTAURANT

Castledermot Co Kildare **Tel: 059 914 5156**
kilkea@iol.ie www.kilkeacastle.ie

The oldest inhabited castle in Ireland, Kilkea dates back to the twelfth century and, as an hotel, has lost none of its elegance and grandeur. Many of the guest rooms have lovely views over the formal gardens and surrounding countryside, and some are splendidly furnished while incorporating modern comforts. Public areas include a hall complete with knights in armour and two pleasant ground floor bars - a cosy back one and a larger one that opens on to a terrace overlooking gardens and a golf course. Some of the bedrooms in the main castle are very romantic making it understandably popular for weddings. The adjoining (architecturally discreet) leisure centre has an indoor swimming pool, saunas, jacuzzi, steam room, well-equipped exercise room and sun bed. Outdoor sports include clay pigeon shooting, archery, tennis and fishing. There is an 18-hole championship golf course with informal meals served in the golf club. Special weekend breaks at the castle are good value. Conferences/banqueting (300/200). Garden. Tennis, Golf (18). Children welcome. No pets. **Rooms 36** (1 suite, 3 junior suites, 8 executive, 2 shower only). 24 hour room service. B&B from about €130 pps, ss about €40. SC 12.5%. Open all year. **De Lacy's:** Named after Hugh de Lacy, who built Kilkea Castle in 1180, this beautiful first-floor restaurant has a real 'castle' atmosphere and magnificent views over the countryside. Large tables sport crisp white linen, and there are fresh flowers and candles on every table. The restaurant overlooks the delightful formal kitchen garden (source of much that appears on the table in summer) and has a bright, airy atmosphere: there is a sense of occasion here. Menus offer a wide choice, with carefully sourced ingredients providing a sound base for enjoyable meals. An updated classic of ever-popular fillet steak is usually on the menu, accompanied by pleasingly simple side dishes. A middle course offers soup or sorbet, and desserts may include old favourites like apple and raisin crumble with ice cream. Afterwards, it is pleasant to take coffee on the terrace in summer and wander around to see the old fruit trees, vegetables and herbs. **Seats 60** (private room 40). L (daily by reservation) 12.30-2, D 7-9.30. Set L about €30. Set D about €55. House wine about €21; sc 12.5%. Toilets wheelchair accessible. Closed 3 days at Christmas. Amex, Diners, MasterCard, Visa, Laser. **Directions:** 3 miles from Castledermot (off M9); signed from village. ◇

CELBRIDGE

Celbridge is attractively situated on the River Liffey 22 kilometres (13 miles) from Dublin and is the third largest town in Kildare. The town is of historical for many reasons, ranging from Celbridge Abbey (and its association with Jonathan Swift) to Castletown House. **Castletown House** (01 628 8252; www.heritageireland.ie) is the largest and most significant Palladian style country house in Ireland and the reason that brings most visitors to Celbridge. It was built in about 1722 for the speaker of the Irish House of Commons, William Conolly (1622-1729) and, in recent history, it was purchased by the Hon. Desmond Guinness in 1967 and, together with the Castletown Foundation (who acquired the house in 1979), he set about preserving the house and restoring the principal rooms. Since 1994 Castletown has been in the care of the State and, following recent conservation work, re-opened to the public in 2007. The café, **CHC at The West Wing** is in the original double-height kitchens of the house and is run by Claire Hanley (see entry for **Hanley At The Bar**, Dublin 7, and www.clairehanley.ie); as well as the usual soups, sandwiches, salads and pasta dishes, you'll find updated versions of the some of the food that would have been familiar on Georgian tables including delicious syllabubs and trifles.
WWW.IRELAND-GUIDE.COM FOR THE BEST PLACES TO EAT, DRINK & STAY

The Village @ Lyon's Demesne - Café la Serre & The Mill

Celbridge
RESTAURANT

The Village Lyon's Demesne Celbridge Co Kildare
Tel: 01 630 3500
info@villageatlyons.com www.villageatlyons.com

This pair of restaurants at the Lyons Demesne is overseen by Irish celebrity chef Richard Corrigan, who is renowned for his dedication to local and artisan foods, and the styles of the fine dining Mill Restaurant, and informal Café La Serre are based on his London success stories, Lindsay House and Bentleys, respectively. These restaurants are the first stage of an unusual project, The Village at Lyons, which will take some time to complete, and is to include some small specialist shops, a cookery chool and accommodation. It is beautifully situated alongside the Grand Canal, the entrance - guarded by stone lions and a new lodge which sports the trademark soft Lyons green - is just beside the 14th lock; approaching along the new driveway you will glimpse proprietor Tony Ryan's beautifully proportioned 1797 Lyons House on a rise to your left, shortly before the restored stone mill buildings appear ahead. The most striking first impression is how well finished the completed sections are, and how well they sit in their imaginatively landscaped setting with delightful little gardens and ever-present water establishing a caring tone that is evident throughout. There's a welcoming scent of woodsmoke on the air as you approach past stone statuary (softened by a scented pink rose) and a bed of box balls, over the little bridge (pausing to admire the mill race below) and in through a massive front door which leads straight into the bar. Known as The Lyons Den (proclaimed in 'antique' stone over the bar one of the few off-key notes in this theatrical and usually well-judged setting), it's a welcoming room with a huge fireplace, plenty of comfortable well-worn leather furniture and a full figure portrait of a lady to welcome arriving guests - something that seems to be de rigeur in these parts. **The Mill** is on the lower ground floor; guests arriving at the front door over the little bridge are greeted and shown to the bar or directly to the restaurant. The first sight of the room from the top of steep steps is dramatic: a fine (very) high-ceilinged dining room, it is classically appointed with crisp white linen and gleaming glasses - and has a range of stunning features including a screen of thinly sliced agate, backlit to show off its complex structure and rich colouring to full advantage and, of course, the mill race itself, which is a sight to behold and thunders magnificently when the windows are opened. Fred Cordonnier joined the team as head chef in 2007 and, under his direction, the cooking is outstanding. His menus are simply worded and not long, perhaps five choices on each course but this allows plenty of choice and the details are excellent: superb breads, a beautiful amuse-bouche of celeriac soup with foie gras tortellini, delicious home-made petis fours. Superb ingredients are taken as read at any establishment connected with Richard Corrigan, and Fred Cordonnier does them full justice in dishes which are well conceived, perfectly cooked and seasoned, and beautifully presented. Service is very professional yet relaxed, and a meal here is a very special experience. Considering the quality, it is not overpriced either (although the wine list is expensive, with nothing under €36), and Sunday lunch is very good value. **Seats 70** (private room, 16); reservations required; air conditioning; D Wed-Sat, 6.30-10pm, L Thu-Sat, 12-2.30pm; Sun, 12-5pm. 2 course set L €35, 3 course set L €55, set D €70, also à la carte D; house wine €33. Closed Mon & Tues, 25-26 Dec, Good Fri. Heli-pad. **Café La Serre**, on the other hand, is a place where guests wandering in can feel at home in a genuinely dressed down sense; this very relaxed and informal space includes a covered courtyard area for the betwixt & betweeners (neither inside nor out), an oyster bar and a high-windowed Turner-style conservatory that offers tables in a bright space alongside the maturing gardens. The menu here is a delightful mix of brunch treats and heartier stuff like Corrigan's fish pie or a superb Tipperary Hereford sirloin steak with béarnaise sauce. The demesne is a delightful venue for private gatherings, including exclusive small weddings - there is a tiny chapel (it has to be seen to be believed), and the accommodation, in luxurious 2-bedroom 'cottages' (complete with Aga in their bespoke kitchens, amongst many other unexpected features), will delight all who stay here. **Seats 80** (outdoors, 20); open Wed-Sun for L&D, L 11-3.30pm, D 6-9.30pm (to 8.30pm Sun); reservations are advisable; house wine €27. Closed Mon & Tues, 25-26 Dec, Good Fri. Heli-pad. Amex, MasterCard, Visa, Laser. **Directions:** Left turn just before bridge in Celbridge village for Ardclough. Follow road for a couple of miles, you will come to a part in the road that has some really tight bends with warning signs. Shortly after that there is a left turn (as signed by a small pale green sign opposite turn). Drive over the hump back bridge and it is immediately on the right with 2 big lions on pillars flanking a gate.

R R R   # CLANE

Clane is a fast-growing small town halfway between Maynooth and Naas; via the motorway which is accessed in Maynooth (about 10 minutes drive), it is about an hour from Dublin city centre at off-peak times. The River Liffey, the Grand Canal and Mondello Racing Circuit, home to Irish Motor Racing, are all close by. The new **Westgrove Hotel & Conference Centre** (045 989900; www.westgrovehotel.com) is on the outskirts, near a small shopping centre; it brings welcome facilities to the town, offering spacious and comfortable accommodation, meeting room, function rooms, and a leisure club, which has a 20 m pool (free to residents) and also an Elemis spa.

WWW.IRELAND-GUIDE.COM FOR THE BEST PLACES TO EAT, DRINK & STAY

Clane

Zest Café

CAFÉ/RESTAURANT

Unit 6/7 Clane Shopping Centre Clane Co Kildare

R R R

Tel: 045 893 22

Mark Condron's well-named lunch-time café and evening restaurant has earned a following for its relaxed atmosphere, friendly staff and fresh home-cooked food. Menus change constantly, but delicious starters might include unusual home-made soups, or classic options like chicken liver terrine. But, for the most part, the style of food is informal, offering a range of interesting pasta dishes, and gourmet pizzas. More serious main courses include good steaks - a 10 oz sirloin, or a chargrilled fillet - several good fish dishes, and imaginative chicken dishes. Lunch menus are much simpler than dinner - vegetable soup and home-made quiche topped with goat's cheese and salad perhaps, or a succulent chicken wrap, but everything is done well here and even the simplest meal is sure to be enjoyable. The wine list is not extensive but offers a surprising range; four wines are available by the glass and there are a couple of half bottles. Children welcome; Toilets wheelchair accessible; **Seats 54;** air conditioning; open Mon-Sat 8.30am-10pm, Sun 2pm-9pm; L&D à la carte; house wine from €18. Amex, MasterCard, Visa, Laser. **Directions:** Off Main Street - turn at AIB, left hand side. ◇

Curragh

Martinstown House

COUNTRY HOUSE

Curragh Co Kildare **Tel: 045 441 26**

info@martinstownhouse.com   www.martinstownhouse.com

Just on the edge of the Curragh, near Punchestown, Naas and The Curragh race courses, this delightful 200-year old house was built by the famous architect Decimus Burton who also designed the lodges in the Phoenix Park, Dublin and is the only known domestic example of this 'Strawberry Hill' gothic architectural style in Ireland. It is on a farm, set in 170 acres of beautifully wooded land, with free range hens, sheep, cattle and horses, an old icehouse and a well-maintained walled kitchen garden that provides vegetables, fruit and flowers for the house in season. It is a lovely family house, with very nicely proportioned rooms - gracious but not too grand - open fires downstairs, and bedrooms that are all different, each with its own special character and very comfortably furnished, with fresh flowers. Meryl Long has welcomed guests to this idyllic setting for many years, aiming to offer them 'a way of life which I knew as a child (but with better bathrooms!), a warm welcome, real fires and good food.' Now Meryl is in the process of handing over the reins to her hotelier son, Edward Booth, and his wife Roisin, who both love the place and the work. A stay here is sure to be enjoyable, with the help of truly hospitable hosts who offers a delicious afternoon tea on arrival - and believe that holidays should be fun, full of interest and with an easy-going atmosphere. Croquet lawn. Golf and equestrian activities nearby. Not suitable for children under 12. No pets. **Rooms 4** (3 en-suite, 1 with private bathrooms, all no smoking) B&B from €95 pps, ss €30. Residents D €55 (by arrangement - book the previous day). House wine about €23. Closed Dec & Jan. Amex, MasterCard, Visa. **Directions:** Kilcullen exit off M9 then N78 towards Athy. Sign at 1st crossroads. ◇

Johnstown

The Morrell Restaurant

RESTAURANT

PGA National Ireland Palmerstown House Johnstown Co Kildare

Tel: 045 906 923

N R R

info@palmerstownhouse.com   www.themorrell.com

This rather grand dining experience at Jim Mansfield's Irish PGA National/Palmerstown House is a surprisingly well kept secret, and it could repay investigation, especially if you are looking for an unusual place for a business outing. Having got off the busy N7, you'll be rewarded by a scenic contrast: an impressive great curved entrance gate, then a bridge, a long winding driveway past a walled garden and paddocks with horses and rolling green fields and a gracious mansion in the distance... The Golf Club is a luxurious modern two storey building with a winding balustrade on each side, balconies, gazebo, water features, and tall lantern lights, surrounded by immaculately tended gardens with wonderful topiary, putting green, and a magnificent golf course. A very spacious lounge bar and casual dining space for golfers is on the ground floor, with amazing views across the 18th green and a man made lake; upstairs, The Morrell restaurant has an unexpectedly old fashioned omfortable feel about it, with dark red walls, cream wainscotting, cream high backed leather chairs, risp white linen and walls covered in all styles of pictures (not originals, alas, they are all in the main ouse). Head Chef Ciaran Cunningham was formerly at The St. Stephens Green Club and the food tyle is traditional fine dining with some nice twists in presentation. Only an à la carte menu is offered, ith starters around €9-12 (a speciality, sauté of Dublin Bay Prawn with tartare of salmon, pickled ucumber and wasabi crème fraiche, perhaps, or twice baked goat's cheese soufflé with warm baby rioche and black olive tapenade); mains €26-31 (maybe a protein-rich treat of seared fillet of prime ish beef, with savoy cabbage and oxtail, beef & oyster pie, or roulade of sole and scallop with a scal-on fondue, spiced apple purée); and desserts, €6, possibly including a delicious pinacolada crème rulee with passion fruit ice cream - and, of course, petits fours with your coffee. Service is attentive nd very friendly, with head waiter Joseph Brennan also ex St. Stephen's Green Club and Peter Hanzlik Prague) from the Citywest hotel. An extensive wine list starts at €25. **Seats 72** (private room 16). D ue-Sat 6-close. House wine from €26. Closed Sun-Mon. Amex, Diners, MasterCard, Visa, Laser. **irections:** Junction 8 of (N7) Naas Road.

Kilcullen
CAFÉ/BAR

Fallons Café & Bar
Main Street Kilcullen Co Kildare
Tel: 045 481 063

Formerly Bernies Bar & Restaurant, this well known premises in the attractive village of Kilcullen was taken over by Brian Fallon (of Fallon & Byrne and Lemongrass, see entries) quite recently, after his much-loved old family hotel, the Red House Inn at Newbridge, was destroyed by fire - and he brought the whole team with him, including chef Rose Brannock, who had made such a success of Café Tomat at The Red House. Following major renovations, the delightful result throughout the building is a mixture of old and new a stylish blend that will be familiar to anyone who knew The Red House - with a very relaxing atmos-here. The neat brown exterior is cheered by colourful window boxes - just a few of the 200 window oxes Brian Fallon bought for the village last summer, a promising sign for first-time visitors, who will lso warm to the welcoming fire and prompt greeting from pleasant staff, who guide you to the restau-ant or to one of several eating areas in the buzzy bar, which is smartly and comfortably set up for ining, with wooden-topped tables and a mixture of aubergine banquettes and painted chairs. Rose Brannock's style is really good, simple bistro food is well-established, and her menus mainly offer a lightly modern taken on old favourites - starters of smoked salmon bruschetta with avocado & tomato alsa, and tiger prawns in batter with sweet chilli sauce are typical, also a main course of roast fillet f hake with baby potatoes and fillet of beef with béarnaise sauce and home-made chunky chips; in hemselves there is nothing remarkable about these dishes but the high quality of ingredients and ooking skill lift them into a special league. Portions are generous, as befits this sporting area, and he value is good. A well chosen list of about 40 wines features top producers and is fairly priced. **irections:** Main street.

Kildare
RESTAURANT

L'Officina by Dunne & Crescenzi
Kildare Retail Village Kildare Town Co Kildare **Tel: 045 535 850**
dunneandcrescenzi@hotmail.com www.dunneandcrescenzi.com

lthough it is in the Kildare Village designer shopping outlet, this outpost of the small chain of high uality Italian restaurants run by Dunne & Crescenzi (see Dublin entries) is the only Italian restaurant n Kildare town and attracts diners who may not necessarily be on a shopping spree at all. Warmly lit nd with lots of wood, the restaurant has a comfortable casual-chic ambience and is well-located vithin the village, with views of the Grey Abbey ruins, giving it a good atmosphere as a dining desti-ation rather than just a place for a quick bite. You may expect the usual Dunne & Crescenzi signatures although simple, the food is based on the best authentic Italian ingredients, and it is consistently igh quality that has earned these restaurants a loyal following. Open throughout the day, you can have anything from a wholesome snack (panini, bruschetta or their famous antipasti) to a relaxed dinner. Mon-Thurs, 10-6pm (to 8pm Thurs), Fri-Sat, 10-10pm, Sun 11-6pm. MasterCard, Visa, Laser. **irections:** Within walking distance of Kildare town, exit 13 M7.

Leixlip — Becketts Country House Hotel

HOTEL/RESTAURANT
R R R

Cooldrinagh House Leixlip Co Kildare
Tel: 01 624 7040

A handsome house on the County Dublin side of the river that divides Leixlip, this house was once the home of Samuel Beckett's mother and it is now an unusual hotel, offering a personalised service for business guests: from the moment you arrive a butler looks after all your needs, whether it be dining, laundry, limousine facilities or tailored requirements for meetings or conferences. Imaginatively converted to its present use, luxurious accommodation includes four boardroom suites and six executive suites, all furnished to a high standard in a lively contemporary style. All have a workstation equipped for computers, including modem/Internet connection and audio visual equipment, private fax machines etc. are also available on request. Public areas, including a bar and an attractive modern restaurant, have a far less business-like atmosphere. Cooldrinagh House overlooks the Eddie Hackett designed Leixlip golf course, for which golf tee-off times may be booked in advance. Conference/banqueting (350/250) Business centre/secretarial services. Golf. Wheelchair accessible. No pets. **Rooms 10** (4 suites, 6 executive rooms) B&B from about €75. Open all year except Christmas. **Restaurant:** Atmosphere is the trump card in this stylish restaurant, with its stone walls, old wooden floors and soft lighting - and an exceptionally warm and genuine welcome. Pristine white tablecloths, gleaming silverware and glasses, and candlelit tables create a romantic atmosphere. Arriving guests are shown to their table promptly, and menus quickly follow, along with a basket of home-made breads. The à la carte - which is very expensive - is available every night (the signature dish is Beckett's Aromatic Duck, with sultana, ginger & sage stuffing, and classic orange sauce), but it is worth getting here in time for the early dinner, which offers great value. An impressive range of wines (seen across the back wall as you enter the restaurant) is another attractive feature - and all this, plus the warm and efficient service that is part of the charm at Beckett's, ensures a strong local following, so booking is advisable. **Seats 130.** L Mon-Fri 12.30-2.15 & Sun 12.30-6; D daily: Early D Mon-Fri 6-7.30, €27.50; à la carte D daily 6-10. Closed L Sat. Amex, Diners, MasterCard, Visa. **Directions:** Take N4, turn off at Spa Hotel, next left after Springfield Hotel. ◇

Leixlip — The Courtyard Hotel

HOTEL
R R

Main Street Leixlip Co Kildare **Tel: 01 629 5100**
info@courtyard.ie www.courtyard.ie

The restored stone walls of the original 18th century building are impressive at this privately owned hotel, which is best entered through an arch from the car park at the back, beside the River Liffey. The reception area is comfortably set up with comfy armchairs and a fireplace and both the Piano Bar and the Riverbank Restaurant - attractive rooms with high arched ceilings and big wooden beams - have views out over the Liffey. Accommodation is warmly furnished in a simple contemporary style and will appeal to business guests, with air conditioning, desk with data/fax lines and Wi-Fi internet; suites have balconies overlooking the gardens and river. Arthur Guinness established his first brewery here in 1759, four years before the world famous St. James' Gate Guinness Brewery, and it seems appropriate that the 'black stuff' should now be served here in the cosy and friendly 'Arthur's Bar'. Conferences/Banqueting (150/150); Free broadband wi/fi; business centre, secretarial services, video conferencing, laptop-sized safes in bedrooms. Children welcome (under 12s free in parents' room, cots available). **Rooms 40** (8 executive, 16 ground floor, 2 disabled); garden; golf, equestrian, fishing and walking nearby. B&B €75pps, no ss. Lift. 24hr room service. Open all year. Amex, Diners, MasterCard, Visa, Laser. **Directions:** Centre of Leixlip.

Leixlip — Leixlip House Hotel

HOTEL/RESTAURANT
R R R

Captains Hill Leixlip Co Kildare **Tel: 01 624 2268**
info@leixliphouse.com www.leixliphouse.com

féile bia Up on a hill overlooking Leixlip village just eight miles from Dublin city centre, this fine Georgian house was built in 1722 and is furnished and decorated to a high standard in period style and, with gleaming antique furniture and gilt-framed mirrors in thick carpeted public rooms decorated in soft country colours, the atmosphere is one of discreet opulence. Bedrooms include two suites furnished with traditional mahogany furniture; the strong, simple deco articularly pleases the many business guests who stay here and there is a welcome emphasis on ervice - all-day room service, nightly turndown service with complimentary mineral water and choco- ates - and a shoe valet service. Hotel guests have complimentary use of a nearby gym. onference/banqueting (100/140). Secretarial services. Children welcome (cot available, baby sitting rranged). No pets. **Rooms 19** (5 executive, 14 shower only, 2 family). B&B from €80 pps, ss €40. **he Bradaun Restaurant:** The commitment to quality evident in the hotel is continued in the restau- ant, a bright, high-ceilinged dining room, elegantly appointed with candles and fresh flowers on ell-spaced tables. Head Chef Brian McCarthy has devised menus that combine imagination, reativity and flair, and food arrives beautifully presented, with wonderful attention to detail. Fish eatures strongly - starters may include stuffed baby calamari, sardine fillets and a mouth-watering eafood cocktail with clams, mussels, smoked salmon, shrimp and crab - and seafood main courses ould be a duo of salmon and hake, a trio of monkfish, scallops and lemon sole and pan-fried John ory. Alternatively, try baked Sneem black pudding with a compôte of rhubarb and fresh berries which nakes an ingenious combination for a starter and meat lovers will be pleased with choices like rack f Wicklow lamb, beef fillet and char-grilled pork fillet stuffed with smoked Gubeen cheese, hazelnut nd sage. Save some appetite for dessert assiette of strawberries in season, iced macaroon parfait, herrimisu (with amarena cherry compôte), glazed lemon tart or vanilla and cardamon panna cotta. A ustomer-friendly wine list offers a wide range of wines by the glass, a dozen Wines of the Month and similar number of half bottles as well as the main listing. Children welcome. **Seats 45.** Food served aily 12-10. D Tue-Sun, 6.30-10 (Sun 12-8pm); Value D €29.50 Tue-Fri 6.30-7.30 (to 10pm Tue- Ved); set Sun L €29.50. Restaurant closed Mon (except for group bookings). Hotel closed 25-26 Dec. mex, Diners, MasterCard, Visa, Laser. **Directions:** Leixlip exit off M4 motorway. Take right in Leixlip illage at traffic lights.

R R R MAYNOOTH

ttractively situated beside the Royal Canal, Maynooth is a busy university town and the centre for the raining of Catholic diocesan clergy in Ireland. The ever-expanding **Glenroyal Hotel** (01 629 0909; ww.glenroyal.ie) has outstanding conference/business and leisure facilities and a branch of the opular Asian restaurant franchise, Lemongrass. Reflecting its youthful population, there are plenty of laces to eat in Maynooth, including a good bar and informal restaurant **No 21 / The Roost** (01 628 843) on Leinster Street (near the harbour. For accommodation in the town, something which is not enerally known is that there are splendid Georgian and Neo-Gothic en-suite rooms at **Maynooth ampus**, which are available for public use - Tel: 01 708 3726 for further details. **WW.IRELAND-GUIDE.COM FOR THE BEST PLACES TO EAT, DRINK & STAY**

laynooth
IOTEL/RESTAURANT
R R R

Carton House Hotel
Maynooth Co Kildare **Tel: 01 505 2000**
reservations@carton.ie www.carton.ie

Previously the residence of the Dukes of Leinster, Carton House is an imposing mansion designed in classic style by the renowned architect Richard Castles, and built around 1740. It is set in one of Ireland's finest country estates - now home to two championship golf courses. No guest could fail to be impressed by the building itself, which is vast yet very elegant - and it has now been skilfully adapted to its new use through a stimulating combination of old and new. It is a natural choice for major corporate events and meetings, and ould make a wonderful venue for special occasions of all kinds - these are, after all, uses that are ot so very far from its previous life of entertainment on a grand scale. Public areas include a whole eries of grand rooms, including The Duke's Study and The Gold Salon, each more impressive than he last, and the old kitchen - with its vast cast-iron stoves still in place - is now a bar, furnished rather urprisingly (but comfortably) in a very modern style. The accommodation has been designed and built n sympathy with the main house; the style is luxurious and contemporary, pleasingly bold in scale and vith some appropriately regal colours - and, of course, rooms have all the little luxuries including robes nd slippers and a minibar, as well as king size beds, LCD screen television, DVD and CD player. Sporting activities are central to Carton House, and are a major attraction at a stylish destination so lose to the capital - as is the hotel's leisure centre which has a full range of beauty and health treat- nents, an 18m pool, children's pool, jacuzzi, sauna & steam room, gym with cardiovascular & strength quipment and a juice bar. There are also two outdoor tennis courts, personal training and a wide range of specific training lessons. Prices are not unreasonable for a hotel of this calibre, and promotiona offers are often attractive. Conferences/Banqueting (multiple rooms available to max. 480), broadban wi/fi; Spa, golf (36); **Rooms 165;** B&B from €140 pps. **The Linden Tree:** The hotel's fine dinin restaurant is a famous and beautiful room overlooking the golf course and gardens, and has bee allowed a more classical style, with pristine white linen and simple, elegant table settings. A visit her will always be worthwhile for the overall experience - at the time of our visit the restaurant was sti finding its feet, but the menus are changing as we go to press. The Linden Tree is mainly an evenin restaurant but it is also open for Sunday lunch which, unexpectedly for an hotel of this calibre, is buffet. * An informal dining option is also available (to members and visitors) in the Clubhouse, whic is some distance from the house in renovated stables. **Seats 160.** Reservations necessary, held for 1 minutes only. D Mon- Sun, 6.30-9.30. A la carte; starters from about €6.50, main courses abou €25, desserts €8.25. SC discretionary. L Sun only, 2-5pm, 3-course buffet. €30. Otherwise lunc for pre-booked groups only. **Directions:** 20 km west of Dublin's city centre (about 30 minutes fro Dublin airport), Carton House is just east of Maynooth and signed from the town. ◇

Moyvalley   Furey's Ba
PUB   Moyvalley Co Kildar
🆁 🆁 🆁   Tel: 046 955 118

Down a slip road off the N4 and insulated from traffic noise by thick hedges, this charming and immac ulately maintained bar and informal restaurant has something of the best kind of Victorian country railwa station about it, with its neat brickwork, jaunty flowers and wooden floors. Although by no means hug a welcoming bar divides informally into cosy sections, and an area towards the back has a stove and view over the Royal Canal giving it the best of every world. Menus posted beside the front doors don't give to much away - soups, sandwiches, steaks, burgers, salads - but references to home-made 'house paté' an 'home-cut chips' hint at the good home cooking for which they are renowned, and one of their famou steaks, with 'all the trimmings' should be just the ticket for whether you're breaking a journey or comir up off a boat. Do call ahead, though, especially if numbers in your party are large, as 'groups can on be fed by arrangement'. Meals Mon-Sat, 12-7.30pm (to 8pm Sat); no food Sun. MasterCard, Visa, Lase **Directions:** Where the road, railway & canal meet between Enfield & Moyvalley. ◇

Moyvalley   Moyvalley Estate
HOTEL/RESTAURANT   Balyna Estate Moyvalley Co Kildare **Tel: 046 955 100**
🄽 🖉 🆁 🆁 🆁   info@moyvalley.com www.moyvalley.co

The long, curving driveway to this new hotel takes you through big open meadows surrounded b mature trees, all part of the 530-acre Balyna Estate, a great mental divider, as you leave behind th busy road (and life) and look forward to the fun or quiet relaxation lying ahead. Although you pass th luxurious 10-bedroom Victorian manor Balyna House first, (available for exclusive use), the hotel uncompromisingly modern. It looks a little stark (and apartments are under construction right oppo site the front door, which seems a strange decision when so much space is available), but it is qui a low building and not unattractive so it should soften with landscaping in due course - the garder around the back of the hotel are interesting, which bodes well. Staff are very friendly and relaxe setting a welcoming tone from the moment you arrive, and an impressively spacious, comfortabl furnished reception area is hung with large atmospheric artwork and has access to the Waterway Restaurant and, up a fine staircase, to the stylish first floor Sundial Bar, where a casual menu offered with large windows overlooking the golf course with plenty of comfortable seating, it's a ve pleasant place to relax and enjoy a bite. Accommodation is mainly in the new hotel, comfortab understated rooms with easy-on-the-eye coffee and cream décor, clean, simple bathrooms an perhaps, access to a patio but, in addition to the ten period rooms in Balyna House (house partie events only), there is some very appealing accommodation in 2- and 3-bedroom units behind the hote in converted outbuildings. These little gems are like tiny townhouses and can be used as hotel roon or for self catering - and only just across a sweetly landscaped courtyard from the hotel. With its love location so near to Dublin, this promises to be a great short break destination and a leisure centre planned for late 2008. Conferences/Banqueting (250/180); free broadband wi/fi; laptop-sized safe in bedrooms; golf (18), archery, clay pigeon shooting, croquet, cycling, fly fishing, garden, walkin Equestrian nearby. Children welcome (under 12s free in parents' room, cot available, baby sittir arranged). **Rooms 64** (2 suites, 6 shower only, 21 ground floor, 2 disabled, all no smoking); Lift, 24l room service; B&B €72.50 pps, ss €35. Closed 25 Dec. Heli-pad. **Waterways Restaurant:** Th pleasing ground floor restaurant is set up in an attractive contemporary style with crisp white linen an comfortable high back chairs, good lighting and gentle music and it opens on to the pretty courtyar where Caribbean barbecues are held on Friday nights in July & August. Quite an extensive à la cart menu offers upbeat versions of many favourites - the house speciality is surf'n'turf and there is choice of four other steaks, served with hand-cut chips, home-made onion rings, mushrooms and bake stuffed tomatoes; other choices are well balanced between fish, meats and poultry, with at least one vegetarian dish included. Sunday lunch is very popular, and an early dinner menu offering a choice of about five dishes on each course, is especially good value. Service is friendly and willing, although a little more training and product knowledge may be needed. A wide-ranging wine list offers several half bottles and some quarter bottles. **Seats 100** (private room, 70, outdoors, 50); children welcome; reservations recommended; air conditioning. Food served daily 12-10pm (from 12.30 Sun); set L €25, set Sun L €25, also L & D à la carte; house wine from €24. Amex, Diners, MasterCard, Visa, Laser. Helipad. **Directions:** Just off the M4 near Enfield.

R **R** **R**   NAAS

Naas is well located for many of the county's sporting activities including horse racing (four courses nearby), golf (five clubs nearby), car racing (Mondello Park) and attractions such as the Wicklow Mountains, The Japanese Gardens and The National Irish Stud. Although the casual visitor may not be especially aware of it, as this bustling town turns its back to its most attractive amenity - Naas is attractively situated on a branch of the Grand Canal and has a proper little harbour. It's a fast-growing place and the youthful new **Osprey House Hotel & Spa** (045 881111; www.osprey.ie), in the Devoy Quarter, provides conference/business and leisure facilities. A wide choice of eating places includes a branch of the popular Dublin restaurant **Pasta Fresca** (045 901542), which is very close to the harbour and, in the town centre, **Lemongrass** (045 482446/871544; www.lemongrass.ie) is behind the Town Hall (just off the main street); this smart modern place is the parent restaurant of a growing chain that now has franchises offering reliable Asian food in many other places and, like **Pasta Fresca**, has the great advantage of long opening hours (about 12.30/1pm-10pm, daily). At the other end of the main street (behind **Lawlors Hotel**, which had just be-opened after renovations at the time of going to press), **The Storehouse** (045 889333) restaurant has character - and if you want real place of character, make a point of dropping into one of Ireland's finest unspoilt old pubs, **Thomas Fletcher** (045 897 328) on the main street, if they are open - it's not a morning place.

WWW.IRELAND-GUIDE.COM FOR THE BEST PLACES TO EAT, DRINK & STAY

Naas   Killashee House Hotel & Villa Spa
HOTEL   Old Killcullen Road Naas Co Kildare **Tel: 045 879 277**
R **R** **R**   reservations@killasheehouse.com   www.killasheehouse.com

Set in an impressive 80 acres of gardens and woodland just outside Naas town, this hotel is approached along an attractive driveway, with striking entrance and lobby areas, and a fine inner courtyard planted with Virginia creeper. A grand staircase leads to a large traditionally furnished lounge on the first floor, with pleasant views and the occasional pianist. Conference and business events are well catered for, and it is a popular wedding venue. Bedrooms, which are well appointed for business guests and have all the usual amenities, include a number of suites, some with four-poster beds. Formal dining is offered at the beautifully appointed main restaurant, **Turners**. On site facilities include the Villa spa and leisure centre, with 25m pool; games room; archery, cycling, walks. *An 18-hole golf course with extensive leisure facilities is under construction. Conference/banqueting (750/700). Business centre; broadband wi/fi; secretarial services, video conferencing. Children welcome (under 4s free in parents' room, cot available without charge, baby sitting arranged). No Pets. Garden, walking, cycling, leisure centre (pool, fitness room), Spa. **Rooms 141** (27 suites, 11 junior suites, 9 shower only, 4 family rooms, 70 no smoking, 6 for disabled). Lift. Room service (24 hrs). B&B from €99 pps, ss €45. Closed 24-25 Dec. MasterCard, Visa, Laser. Helipad. **Directions:** 45 minutes from Dublin on N7 to Naas, then 2km (1.5m) on R448, Kilcullen road.

Naas   La Primavera
RESTAURANT   27 South Main Street Naas Co Kildare **Tel: 045 897 926**
R **R** **R**   info@lap.ie   www.laprimavera.ie

An attractive frontage, with well-maintained hanging baskets in summer, make this town centre restaurant easy to spot - and good first impressions are carried through into a pleasant split-level dining room, and a warm welcome from friendly staff who show arriving guests to simply-laid tables. Menus offer a wide-ranging, fairly contemporary, collection of dishes, including some seafood but mainly showcasing Irish meats - beef, in particular. There are some interesting and unusual dishes offered, and a welcome emphasis on house specialities including starters like a good beef carpaccio, and unusual mains such as house-smoked loin of pork. A speciality 'Charcoal Combo' - fillet steak, smoked pork & rosemary-skewered prawns, demonstrates originality and skill; side orders like crème fraîche mash, and fresh tossed vegetable strips in herbs and olive oil work well. Well-made desserts and good coffee to finish. Well-balanced wine list, although otherwise well-trained staff seem less knowledgeable in this area. All round: imaginative food, good cooking, caring service and good value. **Seats 60.** Reservations accepted. Air conditioning. D daily, 5-10 (Sun to 9.30). Early D about €15 (5-7), otherwise à la carte. House wine about €16. Amex, Diners, Visa, Laser. **Directions:** At traffic lights on Limerick/Kilcullen junction. ◇

Naas

Les Olives

RESTAURANT
R R R

10 South Main Street Naas Co Kildare **Tel: 045 894 788**
lesolives@eircom.net www.lesolivesrestaurant.com

Olivier and Maeve Pauloin-Valory's first floor restaurant has earned a loyal following from a wide area around the town. It's an attractive room, with comfortable seating, neatly appointed tables and a lobster tank all paving the way for a seriously good dining experience. Seafood is a particular attraction, especially oysters and lobsters; in addition to dishes on the main menu - which is in French and English and may include some unusual items, such as roasted rabbit cassolette - daily fish specials are shown on a blackboard, where you may also find some less likely choices, such as kangaroo and, of course, local meats like Kildare beef and lamb. Olivier's good cooking, and friendly, efficient service under Maeve's direction promise a good night out - and the wine list offers a wide range of wines by the glass. A home dining service, 'Les Olives Gourmet Food' is also offered, see website for details. [*Also at: Market Square, Portlaoise (over O'Donoghue's pub); Tel: 057 936 5613). Also planning to open at Whitewater SC, Newbridge.] Beer garden area for smokers. Children welcome. **Seats 60.** Reservations recommended. D Tue-Sat, 6-9.30; D Gourmet Menu €85, also à la carte; L Sun only, set Sun L €28.90. House wines from €19.90; sc discretionary (but10% added for parties of 6+). Closed Sun D, Mon (& Tue after bank hol weekends); Christmas, Good Fri. MasterCard, Visa, Laser. **Directions:** Over Kavanagh's pub, in the centre of Naas.

Newbridge

Keadeen Hotel

HOTEL
R R

Newbridge Co Kildare **Tel: 045 431 666**
info@keadeenhotel.ie www.keadeenhotel.ie

féile bia Centrally located and easily accessible from the M7 motorway, the O'Loughlin family's popular owner-managed hotel is set in ten acres of fine landscaped gardens just south of the town (and quite near the Curragh racecourse). The hotel has been refurbished and generously spacious accommodation is furnished to a high standard. A fine romanesque Health & Fitness Club has an 18-metre swimming pool and aromatherapy room among its attractions, plus a staffed gymnasium. Extensive conference and banqueting facilities (1,000); secretarial services. Video conferencing can be arranged. Leisure centre, swimming pool. Garden. Parking. No Pets. Children welcome (under 3s free in parents rooms; cots available). Weekend specials available. **Rooms 75** (1 suite, 3 junior suites, 20 executive, 1 for disabled) B&B from about €87.50 pps. Weekend specials offered. Closed 24 Dec - 4 Jan. Amex, Diners, MasterCard, Visa. **Directions:** From Dublin take N7 off M50, take sliproad signposted Curragh race course & follow signs for Newbridge. ◇

Straffan

Barberstown Castle

HOTEL/RESTAURANT
🍴🏰📖 R R R

Straffan Co Kildare **Tel: 01 628 8157**
info@barberstowncastle.net www.barberstowncastle.ie

féile bia Steeped in history through three very different historical periods, Barberstown Castle has been occupied continuously for over 400 years. It now includes the original keep in the middle section of the building, a more domestic Elizabethan house (16th century), a 'new' Victorian wing added in the 1830s by Hugh Barton (also associated with nearby Straffan House, now The K Club, with whom it shares golf and leisure facilities) and, most recently, a large new wing added by the current owner, Kenneth Healy, which is built in keeping with its age and style. Some of the individually decorated rooms and suites are in the oldest section, the Castle Keep, but most are more recent - stylish and spacious, some with four-posters. Public areas include two drawing rooms and an elegant bar, and there are big log fires everywhere. Conference/banqueting (200/300); free broadband wi/fi business centre. Garden, walking, archery, clay pigeon shooting. Fly fishing, golf & equestrian nearby. Spa. Children welcome (cot available) No pets. **Rooms 59** (16 junior suites, 17 premier rooms, 21 ground floor, 1 shower only, 3 disabled, all no smoking.) Lift. B&B €120 pps, ss €35. Closed 24-26 Dec. **Castle Restaurant:** Fine dining of character is offered here, and head chef Bertrand Malabat presents a number of menus including a six-course Tasting Menu (served to complete parties only) and a seasonal à la carte with about six choices on each course. The style is classic French with the occasional nod to international fashions; local beef or lamb usually feature, also game in season, and there will be several appealing fish dishes and at least one imaginative vegetarian dish. Finish with a classic sweet like vanilla crème brulée - or a selection of Irish farmhouse cheeses and home-baked breads. Very professional service. Not suitable for children after 8pm. **Seats 100** (private room 32). Reservations advised. D Mon-Sat, 7-9.30; à la carte. House wine about €23.50; sc discretionary (but 10% on parties of 7+). Fine dining restaurant closed Sun, Mon. Light meals are available in the Tea Rooms, 10-8 daily. Closed 24-26 Dec and Jan. Amex, MasterCard, Visa, Laser. **Directions:** West M4 - turn for Straffan exit at Maynooth - follow signs for Naas/Clane.

Straffan
HOTEL/RESTAURANT

K Club - Kildare Hotel & Golf Club
Straffan Co Kildare **Tel: 01 601 7200**
hotel@kclub.ie www.kclub.ie

The origins of Straffan House go back a long way - the history is known as far back as 550 AD - but it was the arrival of the Barton wine family in 1831 that established the tone of today's magnificent building, by giving it a distinctively French elegance. Current owners, the Smurfit Group, opened it as an hotel in 1991. Set in lush countryside, and overlooking formal gardens and its own pair of championship golf courses, the hotel boasts unrivalled opulence. The interior is magnificent, with superb furnishings and a wonderful collection of original paintings by famous artists, including Jack B.Yeats, who has a room devoted to his work. All suites and guest rooms are individually designed in the grand style, with sumptuous bathrooms, superb amenities and great attention to detail. Ahead of the 2006 Ryder Cup, major developments were undertaken by the hotel, including a new bedroom extension, an extension to the Byerley Turk Restaurant, and a spa; further accommodation is to be added in 2008. Although most famous for its golf, the hotel also offers river fishing for salmon and trout and coarse fishing with a choice of five stocked lakes (equipment bait and tackle provided; tuition available). For guests interested in horticulture there is a mapped garden walk, with planting details. On-site amenities include: swimming pool; spa; tennis; walking; fishing; cycling; equestrian. Snooker; pool table. 24 hour concierge; 24 hour room service; twice daily housekeeping. **Rooms 92.** Lift. Room rate from about €280. **The Byerly Turk:** This is the K Club's premier restaurant and, beside it, a pleasantly clubby bar opens on to an elegant terrace with a distinctly French tone - here, on fine summer evenings, guests can consider menus over an aperitif and admire the golf course across the river before heading in to the restaurant, where tall, dramatically draped windows, marble columns, paintings of racehorses, tables laden with crested china, monogrammed white linen, gleaming crystal and silver are all designed to impress. Head Chef Finbar Higgins is commited to using the best of local and estate-grown produce, and all the little touches - a complimentary amuse-bouche, home-made petits fours with the coffee - that make a special dining experience memorable will be in place. He offers a Tasting Menu (€125 per person, served to a full table), based on The Market, The Sea, The Land and The Season, and a wide-ranging à la carte offers many luxurious dishes - a starter of Carlingford Lough oysters with pickled cucumber and sea foam (€26) is typical, for example, and a special main course, 'An beef Tuath', is The Ryder cup signature dish: 2 medallions of Irish beef, shallot and wild mushroom crown, organic carrot with garlic and potato foam, mead sauce (€49). Unusually, there are two dessert menus, a normal one and a special soufflé menu (takes 20 minutes to prepare, €19). Service is professional and friendly - and, given the intertwined history of Straffan House and the Barton family, it is appropriate that the Bordeaux Reserve from Barton and Guestier should be the label chosen for the hotel's house wine. Children welcome. **Seats 115** (private room 14). Air conditioning. Pianist in the evening. D 7-9.30 (Tue-Sat). tasting menu €125; also à la carte. House Wine from about €26; sc discretionary. * **The River Room** is also in the main building and offers an informal dining option, which is especially suitable for families and larger groups. There is no dress code (other than the smart casual rule that applies throughout the hotel) and menus are more like sophisticated bar food. Breakfast is served here and it is also open daily 12-5 and 6-9.45. ***Legends Restaurant** offers stylish European cuisine at the clubhouse of the Arnold Palmer Course, 12.30-9.30 daily. Amex, Diners, MasterCard, Visa, Laser. **Directions:** 29km (18 miles) south west of Dublin airport and city (M50 - N4).

COUNTY KILKENNY

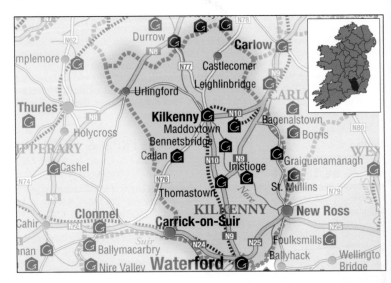

Kilkenny is a land of achingly beautiful valleys where elegant rivers weave their way through a rich countryside spiced by handsome hills. So naturally it's a place whose people care passionately about their county, and the miniature city at its heart. For Kilkenny - the Marble City - is one of Ireland's oldest cities, and proud of it. Its array of ancient buildings is unrivalled. But, by today's standards of population, this gem of a place is scarcely a city at all. Yet it's a city in every other way, with great and justified pride in its corporate status.

Civic pride is at the heart of it, and the city is benefitting from the refurbishment of its ancient quay walls along the River Nore, and the increase in pedestrian zones. Enjoying its reputation as a major centre for civilisation and culture for well over 1500 years, Kilkenny city thrives on a diverse mixture of public debates about conservation, arts festivals, and a comedy festival of international standing.

Rivers define the county. Almost the entire eastern border is marked by the Barrow, which becomes ever more spectacularly lovely as it rolls gently through the beautiful Graiguenamanagh, then thrusts towards the sea at the tiny river port of St Mullins. The southern border is marked by the broad tidal sweep of the Suir, and this fine county is divided diagonally by the meandering of the most beautiful river of all, the Nore.

Invaders inevitably progressed up its tree-lined course past what is now the lovely river village of Inistioge, towards the ancient site of Kilkenny city itself. They quickly became Kilkenny folk in the process, for this is a land to call home.

Local Attractions & Information

Callan Edmund Rice House	056 772 5993
Gowran Gowran Park Racecourse	056 772 6225
Inistioge Woodstock Gardens	056 779 403
Graiguenamanagh Cushendale Woollen Mills	059 972 4118
Kilkenny Kilkenny Castle	056 772 1450
Kilkenny Cat Laughs Comedy Festival (May)	056 776 3416
Kilkenny Rothe House (16c house, exhibitions)	056 772 2893
Kilkenny City Tourist Information	056 77515000
Thomastown Jerpoint Abbey	056 772 4623
Thomastown Kilfane Glen & Waterfall	056 772 4558
Thomastown Mount Juliet Gardens	056 777 3000
Tullaroan Kilkenny GAA Museum	056 776 9202

Bennettsbridge
CAFÉ

Nicholas Mosse Pottery Irish Country Shop

The Mill Bennettsbridge Co Kilkenny **Tel: 056 772 7505**
sales@nicholasmosse.com www.nicholasmosse.com

One of the best reasons to venture out from Kilkenny city to nearby Bennettsbridge is to visit the Nicholas Mosse Pottery in their old mill on the banks of the River Nore. The restored mill is beautifully situated and very spacious, with three floors of pottery, including a large seconds area where some great bargains are to be found, and a 'decorate-it-yourself' studio where you can create something unique to take home. The full range of products is wide, including hand blown glass and table linens, blankets, quilts and knitwear, Clive Nunn furniture and even jewellery from leading craftspeople - as well as acres of the famous sponge-ware. Their café is on the first floor, overlooking the river, and a lovely spot for lunch or teas; good home baking has always been their big thing - including, of course, delicious freshly-baked scones made with the local Mosse's flour, and sold with good coffee or tea. Parking is easy and free and there's a lift in the store, also friendly staff who are always pleased to help. **Seats 40.** Children welcome (high chair, baby changing facilities). Open Mon-Sat 11-4, Sun 1.30-4pm. Closed 24-26 Dec & 1 Jan. Amex, Diners, MasterCard, Visa, Laser. **Directions:** 7km (4 miles) south of Kilkenny, just before bridge turn off.

Callan
COUNTRY HOUSE

Ballaghtobin

Ballaghtobin Callan Co Kilkenny **Tel: 056 772 5227**
catherine@ballaghtobin.com www.ballaghtobin.com

Set in parkland in the middle of a five hundred acre working farm, this immaculately maintained house has been in the Gabbett family for three hundred and fifty years. Graciously proportioned rooms are beautifully furnished and the spacious bedrooms - which Catherine Gabbett has decorated stylishly - all have antique furniture and every comfort, including lovely bathrooms with bath and overbath shower, and tea/coffee trays. The house is surrounded by large gardens, with a hard tennis court, croquet lawn - and even a ruined Norman church - for guests' use. No dinners, but Catherine will direct you to one of several good restaurants within a short drive. Children welcome (under 3s free in parents' room; cot available without charge). Pets allowed by arrangement. Garden, walking, tennis, croquet. Fly fishing, golf and hunting/shooting nearby. **Rooms 3** (all en-suite & no smoking, 2 family rooms). B&B €45 pps, ss €10. Closed Nov-Feb. MasterCard, Visa. MasterCard, Visa. **Directions:** Past Callan Golf Club on left, 4km (2.3 m), bear left; bear left at junction, entrance on left opposite Gate Lodge.

Graiguenamanagh
RESTAURANT/GUESTHOUSE

Waterside

The Quay Graiguenamanagh Co Kilkenny **Tel: 059 97 24246**
info@watersideguesthouse.com www.watersideguesthouse.com

An attractive old stone warehouse on the quayside of this charming village on the River Barrow makes a characterful setting for Brian and Brigid Roberts' well-run restaurant and guesthouse. On fine summer days there are tables outside, and a comfortable reception area leads into the restaurant, where Brigid offers modern European food on varied, enticing menus - in very pleasant waterside surroundings. She uses fresh local produce wherever possible, sometimes including a speciality starter of rare Graiguenamanagh smoked eel. Braised lamb shank with mint jus is a more predictable speciality and, aside from a range of mainstream choices, game might be offered in season and interesting vegetarian choices are always included. Finish with a nice homely dessert such as pineapple, apple & almond pudding with crème anglaise. There's always an Irish cheese plate too, with home-made tomato chutney and a choice of half a dozen ports to accompany. Service is friendly under Brian's supervision - and the wine list, which is extensive, is interesting and fairly priced. The early dinner and Sunday lunch menus offer outstanding value for money. **Seats 42.** Outdoor Dining available in the Summer. D daily, 6.30-9.30pm; L Sun only 12.30-3. Set Sun L €22.50, Early D €22.50 (6.30-7.45). D à la carte. House wine, €19.75. No SC. *In summer there's also a light Daytime Menu available, 11-4. Restaurant open weekends only in winter. **Accommodation:** The rooms are quite simple but comfortable, with direct dial phones, tea/coffee making facilities and TV in all rooms; some rooms at the top of the building are spacious and all overlook the river. Gradual upgrading of the accommodation has been taking place for several years and this is a very pleasant, reasonably priced, place to stay. Book lovers may be interested in weekend book sales at Waterside, which is the home of the Graiguenamanagh Book Festival and booktown project. Hillwalking holidays for small groups are offered. Children welcome (under 3s free in parents' room, cot available without charge, baby sitting arranged). No pets. **Rooms 10** (all shower only & no smoking, 4 family rooms) B&B €49pps, ss €13.50. *Weekend packages/ short breaks from €79 pps. No lift. Closed Jan, 25 Dec. Amex, MasterCard, Visa, Laser. **Directions:** 27km (17 m) south east of Kilkenny on Carlow/Kilkenny border.

Inistioge   # Bassett's at Woodstock
RESTAURANT   Woodstock Gardens Inistioge Co Kilkenny **Tel: 056 775 8820**
                                       info@bassetts.ie www.bassetts.ie

John Bassett grew up in Inistioge and returned with his partner Mijke Jansen to run this scenically located contemporary restaurant at the historic and beautifully restored Woodstock Gardens & Arboretum. In a modern building overlooking the Nore valley, and conveniently situated beside the visitors' carpark, this is not just a 'garden visits café' but a fully fledged restaurant which has become a destination in itself. Assuming you can take your eyes off the magnificent view of the Kilkenny countryside for a moment, you'll first suspect that something special awaits you when you notice saddleback pigs in a small pen near the car park. Mijke and John welcome you personally, and you can have a drink in the little bar or go straight to your table in a room where the view seen through large windows takes centre stage - the other star of the show is chef Emilio Martin Castilla's food, which is really excellent from the first amuse-bouche (carpaccio of beef and foie gras, perhaps, or a mint ravioli) that sets the tone, through to delicious desserts and a cheese plate. On Saturday nights they serve a 9-course menu consisting of small starter-sized portions; you can skip or share courses, but as everyone is served the same course at the same time, there can be gaps of 20 minutes before the next course so a little planning pays off. The highlight was of a recent meal was quail stuffed with cèpes & spring onions, wrapped in smoked pork belly, closely followed by lobster bisque with langoustines and mussels. During the week and for Sunday lunch, an à la carte menu offers all of these tasting dishes served in full portions. The beautiful location, warm atmosphere and delicious food are matched by good service and a short, well-chosen wine list (also wines by the glass suggested to complement each dish). What could be more enjoyable than a drive to one of the most beautiful villages in the South East, and a walk in Woodstock Gardens followed by a memorable meal? **Seats 34** (outdoors, 40); L wed-sun, 12-4 (to 6 on Sun); D Wed-Sat from 7. Closed Mon & Tue. MasterCard, Visa, Laser. **Directions:** Follow signs for Woodstock Gardens.

Inistioge   # The Motte Restaurant
RESTAURANT   Plas Newydd Lodge Inistioge Co Kilkenny **Tel: 056 775 8655**
                                         rodneydoyle@eircom.net

On the edge of the picturesque village of Inistioge, with views of extensive parkland and the River Nore, Rodney & Deirdre Doyle's restaurant is situated in the classically proportioned Plas Newydd Lodge, named in honour of the ladies of Llangollen, who eloped from Inistioge in the late 18th century. Although small in size, this unique country restaurant has great charm. An L shaped room with a Kilkenny marble fireplace and simple, effective decor makes a good setting for Rodney Doyle's accomplished cooking, and many will welcome the slightly retro feel to the menu which offers dishes now seen less often and makes a change from the modern multi-national menu which are currently almost universal. Expect delicious home-made breads, starters like warm duck liver salad with a mustard seed & orange dressing, and main courses such as delicious crispy stuffed duckling, or fillet of beef with their trademark pepper & brandy cream sauce. Menus are sensibly limited, but always include an imaginative vegetarian dish, and classic desserts like strawberry Pavlova or Grand Marnier crème brulée are delicious. Very hospitable service adds to the enjoyment. Small weddings or private parties can be catered for. **Seats 40** (private room 16). Reservations required. Toilets wheelchair accessible. D Wed-Sat 7-9.30 (also Sun of bank hol weekends). Set D €35. House wine €18. SC discretionary (except 12.5% on groups of 6+). Closed Mon, Tue (also Sun, except bank hol weekends); 1 week autumn, 1 week Christmas. Amex, MasterCard, Visa, Laser. **Directions:** Opposite village "name sign" on Kilkenny side of village. ◇

KILKENNY

Kilkenny - Ireland's smallest city both in area and population - is located on the River Nore and is famed for its history and, more recently, for its music, festivals and nightlife. There are many medieval buildings and the city has been referred to for centuries as the "Marble City", for the black stone with distinctive white oyster fossils which was quarried locally and known as Kilkenny Marble or Black Marble; it was exported to all corners of the British Empire and is seen in many of Kilkenny's fine buildings and on the footpaths. Kilkenny hosts the annual **Smithwicks Cat Laughs Comedy festival** in early June when the city becomes the "Comedy Capital of the World", and it also holds a very successful annual **Arts Festival** in late August, when the city is flooded with traditional and foreign music, beautiful paintings and sculptures and much more. For those seeking outdoor activities, this is good walking, golfing (Mount Juliet) and fishing country and there is also horse racing at nearby Gowran Park; however, the sport that the locals live and die by is hurling - Kilkenny are in the top echelons of the game and losing a match is unthinkable. Getting to see a hotly contested hurling match against arch rivals Cork in Nolan Park would be the memory of a lifetime. A rich vein of hospitality runs throughout Kilkenny city and county and, in addition to those selected here, there are numerous places that may be of interest to visitors. **The Newpark Hotel** (056 776 0500; www.newparkhotel.com), for example, is very much at the heart of local activities, and is a popular venue for conferences and meetings; and, in the city centre, **The Hibernian Hotel** (056 777 1888; www.kilkennyhibernianhotel.com)is in an old banking building and has character as well as a degree of luxury. **The Kilkenny Ormonde Hotel** (Ormonde Street; 056 772 3900; www.kilkennyormonde.com) enjoys an outstandingly convenient central location for both business and leisure guests, beside (but not adjacent to) a multi-storey carpark and within walking distance of the whole city. Facilities include a business centre and a leisure centre with pool. *The hotel is embarking on a major upgrade at the time of going to press, to include extending the restaurant. Also in the city, **Café Pierre's** on Parliament Street is popular for its reliable fare and good atmosphere; for details of a variety of other eating places for every budget and occasion, including daytime snacks, the **Kilkenny Good Food Circle Guide** (www.kilkenny tourism.ie) is available from Tourist Information Offices. Outside the city, should your travels take you to the **Callan** area, you may be glad to find the **Old Charter House** (056 775 5902), a village pub offering reliable bar meals and moderately priced accommodation.
WWW.IRELAND-GUIDE.COM FOR THE BEST PLACES TO EAT, DRINK & STAY

Kilkenny
GUESTHOUSE

Butler House

16 Patrick Street Kilkenny Co Kilkenny **Tel: 056 776 5707**
res@butler.ie www.butler.ie

Located close to Kilkenny Castle, this elegant Georgian townhouse was restored by the Irish State Design Agency in the 1970s - and the resulting combination of what was at the time contemporary design with period architecture leads to some interesting discussions. However bedrooms are unusually spacious - some have bow windows overlooking the gardens and Kilkenny Castle - and the accommodation is very adequate, with all the amenities now expected of good guesthouse accommodation. Bathrooms have been refurbished and upgraded, and most rooms now have full bath. Three magnificent bow-windowed reception rooms are available for receptions and dinners. An excellent breakfast is served at the Kilkenny Design Centre (see entry), which is just across the gardens in the refurbished castle stables. Conferences/banqueting (120/70); broadband wi/fi, business centre, secretarial services. Children welcome (under 2s free in parents' room; cot available without charge, baby sitting arranged). Parking (20). Walking, garden. No

Georgina Campbell's Ireland

pets. **Rooms 13** (1 suite, 4 executive, 3 family, 1 shower only). B&B €100 pps, ss €40, sc discretionary. Off-season breaks offered. Closed 23-29 Dec. Amex, Diners, MasterCard, Visa, Laser. **Directions:** City centre, close to Kilkenny Castle.

Kilkenny
HOTEL
R

Hotel Kilkenny

College Road Kilkenny Co Kilkenny **Tel: 056 776 2000**
kilkenny@griffingroup.ie www.griffingroup.ie

Having undergone a major upgrade recently, the Hotel Kilkenny, dubbed 'the four star with flair' begins impressively in the spacious contemporary foyer, which has a very large modern reception desk and relaxed seating areas. Very comfortable accommodation includes the original hundred or so rooms, which have been refurbished in a smart contemporary style that is not too hard edged, and a further 36 newer deluxe rooms. Public areas include a modern bar 'Pure', which has an exceptional speciality drinks menu, and the restaurant, 'Taste', which is a large room on two levels, decorated in a very understated colour palate, it has a 'hotel dining room' atmosphere. The hotel is a popular conference and wedding venue and offers a state-of-the-art conference centre and extensive banqueting facilities. The hotel is set in award winning gardens and has a 5-star Active Health and Fitness club. Ample complimentary car parking. Conference/banqueting 400/380. Children welcome (under 2s free in parents' room; cots available without charge). No pets. **Rooms 103** (24 executive rooms, 5 no smoking, 2 disabled). B&B from about €60 pps. Open all year. Amex, Diners, MasterCard, Visa, Laser. **Directions:** On ring road at Clonmel roundabout exit. ◊

Kilkenny
RESTAURANT
♨ ⊖ € ♀ ♟ R

Kilkenny Design Centre

Castle Yard Kilkenny Co Kilkenny **Tel: 056 772 2118**
info@kilkennydesign.com www.kilkennydesign.com

Situated in what was once the stables and dairy of Kilkenny Castle - and overlooking the craft courtyard - this deservedly popular first floor self-service restaurant is situated above temptations of a different sort, on display in the famous craft shop. Wholesome and consistently delicious fare begins with breakfast for guests staying at Butler House (see entry), as well as non-resident visitors. The room is well-designed to allow attractive and accessible display of wonderful food, all freshly prepared every day: home baking is a strong point, and there is plenty of hot food to choose from as - well seafood chowder with home-made soda bread, for example, and beef & pepper casserole with button mushrooms or a speciality chicken & broccoli crumble with local Lavistown cheese. The lovely crumbly Lavistown cheese is also used in great salads, which are always colourful and full of life - fresh beetroot, asparagus, spinach, red onion, coriander & Lavistown, for example, combine to make a salad worth travelling for, and the selection changes all the time. A short carefully chosen wine list offers seven wines by the bottle or half bottles, and gourmet coffees and herbal teas are offered. Very reasonably priced too - well worth a visit. Toilets wheelchair accessible. Lift. **Seats 150.** Meals daily 11-7. Self service. Closed Sun & banks hols, off-season (Jan-Mar). Amex, Diners, MasterCard, Visa, Laser. **Directions:** Opposite Kilkenny Castle.

Kilkenny
HOTEL
♨ ♀ 👁 R

Kilkenny River Court Hotel

The Bridge John Street Kilkenny Co Kilkenny **Tel: 056 772 3388**
reservations@rivercourthotel.com www.rivercourthotel.com

Beautifully situated in a courtyard just off the narrow, bustling streets of the city centre, with only the River Nore separating it from Kilkenny Castle, this fine hotel enjoys the city's premier location, and has a lovely big riverside terrace area at the front. While equally attractive for business or leisure - bedrooms and public areas are all finished to a high standard and the Health & Leisure Club provides excellent facilities for health, fitness and beauty treatments - the hotel has established a special reputation for conferences and incentive programmes, with state-of-the-art facilities for groups of varying numbers and plenty to do when off duty in the city, as well as outdoor pursuits - golf, fishing, equestrian - nearby. Conference/Banqueting (260/180); free broadband wi/fi. Leisure centre (swimming pool, fitness room, sauna). Children welcome (under 3s free in parents' room, cot available without charge, baby sitting arranged). Limited private parking (access can be a little difficult). Short breaks/special interest breaks offered. **Rooms 90** (2 suites, 20 executive, 4 family, 4 for disabled). Lift. 24hr room service; turndown service. B&B €130pps, ss €40. Closed 24-25 Dec. **Riverside Restaurant:** This aptly named restaurant takes full advantage of the riverside setting and has lovely views of Kilkenny Castle and the River Nore; it is an elegant room, with beautifully appointed tables, silver candlesticks and a grand piano conveying a sense of occasion. The atmosphere is that of a restaurant rather than a hotel dining room, and both the menus and chef Gerard Dunne's good cooking reinforce that impression. A frequently changed dinner menu begins with an amuse-bouche and a choice of popular starters, but main courses are more interesting - a dish of braised breast of duck, carved from the bone and served with wilted Asian greens and clementine & star anis marmalade came in for special praise on a recent visit, for example; side dishes are also excellent, and desserts may include less usual treats like delicious rhubarb syllabub. The early dinner and Sunday lunch menus are particularly good value, and charming service adds to the occasion. **Seats 80** (private room 40, outdoor, 50). D daily 6-9.15, L Sun only 12.30-2.30. Early D €29.95 (6-7pm); Set D €49.95, also à la carte. Set Sun L €29.95. [Food is also served in the Riverview Bar, 12.30-8pm daily.]. Amex, Diners, MasterCard, Visa. **Directions:** Follow city centre signs, directly opposite Kilkenny Castle. Two archways on Dublin side of bridge - use the castle as a landmark.

Kilkenny
GUESTHOUSE

Lacken House

Dublin Road Kilkenny Co Kilkenny **Tel: 056 776 1085**
info@lackenhouse.ie www.lackenhouse.ie

This period house on the edge of Kilkenny city appeals to those who want the comfort of an hotel with the hospitality of a smaller establishment. It was formerly well known as a restaurant but the property changed hands in 2007 and is now operated solely as a guesthouse. It is a very comfortable and convenient place to stay, within walking distance of town and with plenty of private parking although the railway station is also very close. There is a pleasant guest sitting room with an open fire, and the bedrooms vary in size and outlook but all have been extensively refurbished. Excellent breakfasts are served in the restaurant. Children welcome (under 4 free in parents' room, cot available free of charge, baby sitting arranged). No pets. Garden. **Rooms 10** (2 junior suites, 5 power shower only, 2 family rooms, 4 ground floor, all no smoking). B&B €75 pps, ss €25. Closed 24-27 Dec. Amex, MasterCard, Visa, Laser. **Directions:** On N10 Carlow/Dublin Road into Kilkenny City.

Kilkenny
HOTEL

Langton House Hotel

69 John Street Kilkenny Co Kilkenny **Tel: 056 776 5133**
reservations@langtons.ie www.langtons.ie

téite bia Langton's is mainly famous for its maze of bars, with seating areas and restaurants that stretch right through this substantial building to a garden and private car park. Although the fine classic frontage remains, the old traditional bar at the front has been modernised, an outdoor bar and dining area has been added and, beyond the bar, the big Langton Ballroom has also been renovated. Although the hotel reception is small, this is a slightly wacky hotel of some character and good-sized rooms are furnished to a high standard with well-appointed bathrooms, making this a good place to stay if you want to be in the city centre. Langton's also offers a lively middle of the road dining experience - good food without frills, friendly service and good value for money. Conferences/Banqueting (200/250). Private car park. Children welcome (under 5s free in parents room, cot available at no charge, babysitting arranged). **Rooms 30** (2 suites, 4 family rooms, 8 ground floor, 22 no smoking). B&B from €100 pps, ss €25. L & D daily, 12-5.30 & 5.30-10.30. Closed 25 Dec. Amex, MasterCard, Visa, Laser. **Directions:** Town centre.

Kilkenny
GUESTHOUSE

Laragh House

Waterford Road Kilkenny Co Kilkenny **Tel: 056 776 4674**
info@laraghhouse.com www.laraghhouse.com

John and Helen Cooney's modern two-storey white plastered guesthouse was only built in 2005, but is already one of the most popular in the area as it is within walking distance of Kilkenny city centre in fine weather (15 minutes), has off-street parking and, with all the modern amenities, offers a very reasonably priced alternative to an hotel. The eight bedrooms are individually styled, with multi channel TV, direct dial telephone and internet access, and all have whirlpool bath or power showers. There's also a comfortably furnished lounge for guests to relax in, and a smoking area is provided. Broadband wi/fi. Children welcome (under 10s free in parents' room, cots available free of charge). **Rooms 8** (all en-suite & no smoking, 5 shower only, 2 ground floor, 2 disabled); B&B €40-50 pps, ss€10. Limited room service. Closed 24-26 Dec. MasterCard, Visa, Laser. **Directions:** Easily reached from any direction via the city by-pass.

Kilkenny   # Lyrath Estate Hotel - Spa & Convention Centre
HOTEL
🅁

Dublin Road Kilkenny Co Kilkenny **Tel: 056 776 0088**
info@lyrath.com www.lyrath.com

This new hotel is set in 170 acres of mature parklands on the outskirts of Kilkenny city; at its centre is a 17th century house which has been extended to become a large modern hotel with a state-of-the-art conference centre and a spa. It is an unusual hotel and has character; a huge marbled foyer joins the old house and the new extension, and public areas include the comfortable Tupper's Bar and an adjacent conservatory, which offer informal food and open on to a sheltered terrace and interesting gardens at the back, and the large first floor restaurant **Reflections** where breakfast and dinner are served, which overlooks the same area and has picture windows running the length of the room; the old Wine Cellar is open to diners to browse or have an aperitif but it is awkwardly positioned (you have to go through the restaurant and downstairs again) and it is used mainly for functions and groups. Most people opt for a drink in Tupper's or the X Bar, which is on the first floor between Reflections and the hotel's ethnic restaurant, Yindees (see below). Accommodation is spacious and well appointed in a modern classic style; there are several grades of rooms, soothingly decorated in tones of brown and cream - this would be a pleasant place to stay. There are extensive conference and banqueting facilites, also a spa; a leisure centre with swimming pool and gym is planned for 2008. Conferences/Banqueting (1,500/950), 7 board rooms, 3 business centres; Spa; Private club floor. **Rooms 137** (1 penthouse suite, 9 suites, 28 executive). Room rate from €200. **Yindees:** Although not the main restaurant this contemporary Asian restaurant which is oddly located on the first floor, surrounding the vast stairwell and overlooking the lobby, where there may be a pianist adding to the atmosphere, is the most popular dining choice and always has a buzz, although eating in what is effectively a public space is rather strange (choose a table facing back towards the X Bar if possible). The kitchen is open to view, and the menu offers a cross-section of Asian dishes including Japanese, Thai, Chinese, Mongolian, Indonesian and Indian. The food is tasty, staff are well-informed and charming and it's not too expensive. Yindees open Wed-Sat 6-10; Reflections open Mon-Sun 6-9.30 (also breakfast). A la carte. MasterCard, Visa, Laser. **Directions:** Just before Kilkenny on the Dublin/Carlow road. ◇

Kilkenny   # Marble City Bar
PUB
🍺🍸🅁

66 High Street Kilkenny Co Kilkenny **Tel: 056 776 1143**
reservations@langtons.ie www.langtons.ie

féile bia The Langton family's historic bar was re-designed a few years ago by the internationally acclaimed designer, David Collins and, although initially controversial (especially the ultra-modern stained glass window which now graces an otherwise traditional frontage), it is a wonderful space to be in and attracts a varied clientèle. Everyone enjoys the vibrant atmosphere, and the excellent ingredients-led contemporary European bar food: a dish like confit of pork sausages with creamy potatoes and red wine onion gravy or black cherry jus, for example, will probably be based on the superb lean sausages hand-made nearby by Olivia Goodwillie (who also makes Lavistown cheese), and the fresh cod'n'chips in a crispy beer batter will be just in from Dunmore East. More recently the bar has re-invented itself again and the **Marble City Tea Rooms**, below the main bar/restaurant area, offer lighter food like coffees, teas and pastry, 9-7 daily - there's outdoor seating for a couple of dozen people and has access to a lane at the back of the building. Good service, even at busy times; well chosen small wine list. *Tea rooms seating 50 downstairs. Bar food served daily. Food service begins with breakfast, from 10am; main menus from 12 noon-10 pm (Sun: L 12-3; D 5-10). A la carte. House wine about €20

(€5 per glass). Closed 25 Dec & Good Fri. Ample car parking at rear. Amex, Diners, MasterCard, Visa, Laser. **Directions:** Main Street, city centre.

Kilkenny
CAFÉ/RESTAURANT
R

Restaurant Café Sol
William Street Kilkenny Co Kilkenny **Tel: 056 776 4987**
info@cafesolkilkenny.com www.cafesolkilkenny.com

Noel McCarron's popular daytime café and evening restaurant is easy to find, just off the High Street. A small interior porch leads in to a large room warmly decorated in yellow and terracotta giving it a sunny, Mediterranean feeling. The house style is colourful and punchy, showing international influences but based on the best local produce. Daytime menus offer informal dishes like open sandwiches and salads, and some hot dishes. Evening menus offer the more predictable dishes (local beef, of course), but also include some unusual choices - a tasting plate of cured meats and Lavistown cheese. Vegetarians always do well here, too - and the lovely homely desserts are delicious. This is an interesting restaurant, offering something different from the 'sameness' of so many menus, and at reasonable prices. **Seats 45.** Air conditioning. Open all day Mon-Sat, 12-10, Sun 12-9. Set D about €23; Set D for 2 & bottle wine €60. also á la carte. Wines from €18. SC 10% on parties 6+. Closed 25 Dec, 1 Jan. *Free Broadband wi/fi Amex, MasterCard, Visa, Laser. **Directions:** Coming from castle - up High St. - 2nd turn left opposite Town Hall. ◈

Kilkenny
RESTAURANT
R

Rinuccini Restaurant
1 The Parade Kilkenny Co Kilkenny **Tel: 056 776 1575**
info@rinuccini.com www.rinuccini.com

Antonio and Marion Cavaliere's well-known Italian restaurant is in a semi-basement in the impressive terrace opposite Kilkenny Castle and the closely packed tables are an indication of its popularity, with the room quickly filling up. The cooking style is mainly classic Italian, with quite an extensive à la carte evening menu plus a shorter one available as an option at lunchtime. Service is prompt, and food is characterised by freshness of ingredients and a high standard of cooking: excellent minestrone, a superb plate of house antipasti, delicious seafood and memorable pasta, which includes a luxurious house speciality of spaghetti with lobster. Great service and outstanding value for money can be let down by a slightly frantic atmosphere as so many people want to eat at this popular restaurant. Not suitable for children after 8pm. **Seats 105** (private room, 60, also outdoor dining). L daily 12-2.30 (to 3pm Sun), D daily 5.30-10pm (to 9.30pm Sun). Reservations accepted. Early D €27.50 (5.30-7), otherwise à la carte. House wines from €19.95 Accommodation: Seven large, en-suite rooms are offered with air conditioning, and the standard amenities. A breakfast tray is supplied, for you to make up your own continental breakfast in the room. **Rooms 7** (1 junior suite, all shower-only & no-smoking). Amex, Diners, MasterCard, Visa, Laser. **Directions:** Opposite Kilkenny Castle.

Kilkenny
RESTAURANT
R

Swans Chinese
101 High Street The Parade Kilkenny Co Kilkenny **Tel: 056 772 3088**
info@swans.ie www.swansrestaurant.com

Situated on the corner of High Street and Rose Inn street over Ladbrokes bookie office, with the entrance from High Street, Swans has been through a slightly inconsistent period but is now back on form and is once again a very pleasant venue for enjoying well prepared and presented Oriental Cuisine. The room is bright and very relaxing, with red alcoves, comfortable dark brown leather chairs and Chinese wall hangings; charming Chinese waitresses contribute to the ambience and the food has great flavour, bringing nicely served classics like crispy spring rolls, chicken chow mein and szechuan-style dishes to life. With good espressos to finish, this is a useful place to know. Children welcome. **Seats 56;** air conditioning; L Mon-Sat, 12-2.30; L Sun 12.30-5, D daily 5pm-11.30pm; set Sun L €16.50; value D avail 7 days €18.50, also à la carte; house wine €16. Closed 25 Dec, Good Fri. MasterCard, Visa, Laser. **Directions:** Kilkenny centre, 2 mins walk from Kilkenny Castle. ◈

Kilkenny
HOTEL/RESTAURANT

Zuni Restaurant & Townhouse

26 Patrick Street Kilkenny Co Kilkenny **Tel: 056 772 3999**

info@zuni.ie www.zuni.ie

Although Zuni is an hotel ('boutique' style, and offering a more youthful style of accommodation than other comparable establishments), the atmosphere is more restaurant with rooms: an oasis of contemporary chic in this bustling city, it is well established as the in-place for discerning Kilkenny diners. The room is large and airy, overlooking a courtyard (alfresco dining in fine weather) and there's a separate restaurant entrance so you don't have to go through the hotel. Maria Raftery's menus are based on local ingredients but international in tone, with a dish like mixed seafood in saffron broth with seasonal vegetables offered alongside chargrilled Irish sirloin with fresh chips, sautéed mushrooms, onion & grilled tomato. Attractively presented food is always full of flavour: smart salads make tasty starters and Maria, who cooks with panache in view of diners, is a cool and accomplished chef. Menus to note include an early dinner menu which offers a good choice and gives great value for money - and an upbeat contemporary variation on the traditional lunch which packs them in on Sundays. *Zuni Espress, a café nearby, offers coffees and gourmet sandwiches with a global flavour; you can pre-order on 056 779 5899 - just the thing for a picnic lunch, perhaps. Toilets wheelchair accessible. Children Welcome. **Seats 70** (Outdoor seating, 24). (Breakfast); L Tue-Sun 12.30-2.30 (Sun 1-3), D daily 6.30-10 (Sun 6-9). Early D about €25 (6.30-7.30). Otherwise à la carte. House wine from about €22. SC 12.5% added to parties 6+. **Accommodation:** Rooms have direct dial phones, air conditioning, iron/trouser press, TV, tea/coffee-making facilities; the minimalist décor - recently refurbished in pale tones - is difficult to keep immaculate. Breakfast is served in the restaurant. Children welcome (under 12s free in parents' room; cot available without charge, baby sitting arranged). No pets. Private parking, but guests must get the receptionist to open the security bar (best to use the mobile phone, perhaps). **Rooms 13** (8 shower only, 5 no smoking, 1 family room, 1 for disabled, all no smoking). Lift. B&B about €50ps, ss €20. Hotel closed 23-27 Dec. Amex, MasterCard, Visa, Laser. **Directions:** On Patrick Street - leads to Waterford road; 200 yards from Kilkenny Castle. ◇

Maddoxtown
COUNTRY HOUSE

Blanchville House

Dunbell Maddoxtown Co Kilkenny **Tel: 056 772 7197**

mail@blanchville.ie www.blanchville.ie

Monica Phelan's elegant Georgian house is just 5 miles out of Kilkenny city, surrounded by its own farmland and gardens. It's easy to spot - there's a folly in its grounds. It's a very friendly, welcoming place and the house has an airy atmosphere, with matching well-proportioned dining and drawing rooms on either side of the hall, and the pleasant, comfortably furnished bedrooms in period style all overlook attractive countryside. Dinner is available to residents, if pre-arranged, and, like the next morning's excellent breakfast, is taken at the communal mahogany dining table. The Coach Yard has been renovated to make four self-catering coach houses, and the house can also be rented - an ideal arrangement for groups of 12-20 people, for family get-togethers or other special occasions, where guests may have exclusive use of the house and coach yard. More recently, a small spa and holistic centre has been added in the coach yard, with a resident therapist. Blanchville is well-situated for golfers (5 great courses within half an hour's drive, including Mount Juliet). Special breaks offered include art workshop weekends, and bridge breaks. Horse-riding, hunting, fishing, shooting and garden visits nearby. Walking, garden, cycling. Small conferences/private parties (25). Children welcome, under 5s free in parents' room; cot available without charge; baby sitting can be arranged. Pets permitted by arrangement. **Rooms 6** (5 en-suite, 1 with private bathroom, 2 shower only, all non-smoking, 1 family room). B&B €55-60 pps, ss €10. No SC. Turndown service offered. Residents D €50 by prior arrangement only. Closed 1 Nov-1 Mar. Amex, MasterCard, Visa, Laser. **Directions:** From Kilkenny take N10 (Carlow-Dublin road), 1st right 1/2 mile after 'The Pike Pub'. Continue 2 miles to crossroads (Connolly's pub). Take left, large stone entrance 1 mile on left.

Thomastown
COUNTRY HOUSE
R

Ballyduff House

Thomastown Co Kilkenny **Tel: 056 775 8488**
ballydhouse@eircom.net

Set in fine rolling countryside in its own farmland and grounds, Breda Thomas's lovely 18th century house overlooking the River Nore is blessed with an utterly restful location. Breda is a relaxed host who enjoys sharing her home with guests, and offers exceptionally spacious and comfortable accommodation in large period bedrooms with generous bathrooms and beautiful views over the river or gardens. Guests also have the use of large well-proportioned day rooms furnished with family antiques - and many return often, finding this rural retreat a warm and welcoming home from home. Beautiful walks on the estate. Fishing (salmon, trout). Riding, hunting and other country pursuits can be arranged. Garden visits nearby. Children welcome. Pets permitted by arrangement. *Self-catering accommodation also offered at Ballyduff Castle, adjoining Ballyduff House (2-4 bedrooms). Rooms 3. B&B about €60, ss about €10. Open all year. **No Credit Cards. Directions:** 5km (3 m) south of Thomastown. ◇

Thomastown
CAFÉ/RESTAURANT
R

Ethos

Low Street Thomastown Co Kilkenny **Tel: 056 775 4945**
cathal@ethosbistro.com www.ethosbistro.com

Cathal O'Sullivan and (chef) Paul Cullen's attractive restaurant has earned a local following, and its situation on the main street means that visitors find it very easily. It's an inviting spot and the set-up - café by day and bistro by night - is very customer friendly. Paul's lunch menus are casual - soup, salads, sambos, panini, bagels - and a more structured evening menu in a French/Asian style offers half a dozen starters, and about eight main courses. Specialities include seafood dishes like mussels with Thai green curry, or sea bass with chorizo & red pepper - and there will always be good local meats, including Kilkenny beef, but also pork. Duck also features, and vegetarian dishes too - and there's a lovely choice of desserts. Children welcome; toilets wheelchair accessible; **Seats 40** (outdoors, 16); L Mon-Sat, 12-3.30pm, D daily 6.30-9.30pm except Sun & Tue; Sun L only, 12-5pm; house wine about €18; SC 10% on parties 10+. Closed D Sun & Tue, 25 Dec. Amex, MasterCard, Visa, Laser. **Directions:** N9 from Dublin/Waterford - just off Main St. ◇

Thomastown
HOTEL/RESTAURANT
R

Mount Juliet Conrad

Thomastown Co Kilkenny **Tel: 056 777 3000**
mountjulietinfo@conradhotels.com www.mountjuliet.com

féile bia Lying amidst 1500 acres of unspoilt woodland, pasture and formal gardens beside the River Nore, Mount Juliet House is one of Ireland's finest Georgian houses, and one of Europe's greatest country estates. Even today it retains an aura of eighteenth century grandeur, as the elegance of the old house has been painstakingly preserved - and it has a uniquely serene and restful atmosphere. Suites and bedrooms in the main house have period decor with all the comfort of modern facilities and there's additional accommodation in the Club Rooms at Hunters Yard, which is where most of the day-to-day activities of the estate take place, and very close to the main house. There is also self-catering accommodation offered, at the Rose Garden Lodges (close to Hunters Yard) and The Paddocks (at the tenth tee). Mount Juliet is highly respected as a golfing destination, and considerable investment has gone into upgrading the golf course, which now offers an 18-hole putting course in addition to the Jack Nicklaus-designed championship course. But there is much more to this wonderfully relaxing hotel than golf: it is well located for exploring one of Ireland's most beautiful areas and there is no shortage of things to do on the estate - gardens and woodlands to wander, new sports to try, the Spa & Health Club for pampering. The hotel is a top destination for activity breaks - there's an equestrian centre and a spa, and a range of Master Classes is offered in a number of disciplines, including fishing, painting, salsa and wellness. The hotel offers a choice of fine dining in the Lady Helen Dining Room (see below), or an equally attractive contemporary option in the stylish Kendals restaurant at Hunters Yard. Conference/banqueting (140/140). Children welcome (under 12 free sharing with 2 adults, but with extra bed is about €65; cot available €50, baby sitting arranged; children's play area). No pets. Gardens. Equestrian; Angling. Clay pigeon shooting, Archery, Tennis, Croquet, Cycling, Walking, Trails. Spa and Health Club (15m Swimming Pool; Treatments; Hair Dressing). Banqueting (romantic wedding venue, in large marquees set up outside the front of the house, overlooking the river.) **Rooms 58** (2 suites, 8 junior suites, 8 superior, 1 disabled; all no smoking). No Lift. B&B from about €200 pps sc discretionary. Open all year. **Lady Helen Dining Room:** Although grand, this graceful high-ceilinged room, softly decorated in pastel shades and with sweeping views over the grounds, is not forbidding and has a pleasant atmosphere. To match these beautiful surroundings, classic daily dinner menus based on local ingredients are served, including regional Irish farmhouse cheese. Service is efficient and friendly, and there is an extensive international wine list. **Seats 60** (private room 25). Toilets wheelchair accessible. D daily 7-9.30. A la carte. House wine from about €28. *It can be diffi-cult to get a reservation at the Lady Helen Dining Room, especially for non-residents, so booking wel ahead is advised. A very attractive alternative dining option is offered at the newer contemporary restaurant, **Kendals**, which is open for breakfast, & also for dinner (6-10) daily, *Informal dining is available in The Club, Presidents Bar (12am-9pm). Amex, Diners, MasterCard, Visa, Laser. **Directions** M7 from Dublin, then M9 towards Waterford, arriving at Thomastown on the N9 via Carlow and Gowran. (75 miles south of Dublin, 60 miles north of Rosslare). ◇

OUNTY LAOIS

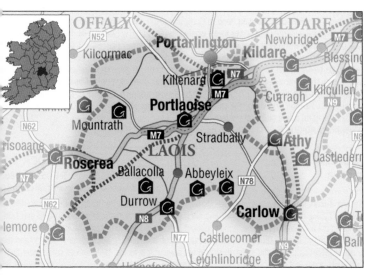

ith its territory traversed by the rail and road links from Dublin to Cork and Limerick, Laois is often mpsed only fleetingly by inter-city travellers. But as with any Irish county, it is a wonderfully warding place to visit as soon as you move off the main roads. For Laois is the setting for Emo Court d Heywood, two of the great gardens of Ireland at their most impressive.

nd it's a salutary place to visit, too. In the eastern part, between Stradbally and Portlaoise, there's e fabulous Rock of Dunamase, that fabulous natural fortress which many occupiers inevitably assumed to be pregnable. Dunamase's remarkably long history of fortifications and defences and sieges and even-al captures has a relevance and a resonance for all times and all peoples and all places.

ut there's much more to Laois than mournful musings on the ultimate vanity of human ambitions. ith its border shared with Carlow along the River Barrow, eastern Laois comfortably reflects Carlow's uiet beauty. To the northwest, we find that Offaly bids strongly to have the Slieve Bloom Mountains ought of as an Offaly hill range, but in fact there's more of the Slieve Blooms in Laois than Offaly, d lovely hills they are too. And though the River Nore may be thought of as quintessential Kilkenny, ng before it gets anywhere near Kilkenny it is quietly building as it meanders across much of Laois, thering strength from the weirdly-named Delour, Tonet, Gully, Erskina and Goul rivers on the way.

long the upper reaches of the Nore in west Laois, the neat little village of Castletown has long been tidy place. Castletown has for the past seventeen years climbed steadily up the rankings in the nnual Tidy Towns contest. Having been the tidiest village in all Ireland in 2001, Castletown repeated e performance and then some in 2002, and at the annual awards ceremony in Dublin Castle, it was nnounced that Castletown was both the tidiest village, and the national overall winner in all cate-ories. This high standard has been maintained, and the most recent National Awards ceremony saw astletown very much in the frame.

ocal Attractions & Information

bbeyleix Abbeyleix Heritage House	057 873 1653
bbeyleix Sensory Gardens	057 873 1325
allinakill Heywood (Lutyens gardens)	0502 33 563
onaghmore Castletown House Open Farm	0505 46 415
onaghmore Donaghmore Workhouse Museum	0505 46 212
mo Emo Court (Gandon house & gardens)	057 862 6573
ortlaois Dunamaise Theatre & Arts Centre	057 866 3356
ortlaois Tourist Information	057 862 1178
lieve Bloom Slieve Bloom Rural Dev. Assoc.	057 913 7299
tradbally National Steam Traction Rally (August)	Joe Degan - jpdegan@eircom.net

R

ABBEYLEI

Abbeyleix takes its name from a 12th century Cistercian abbey and today it is an attractive town w
tree-lined streets. **Café Odhrain** (057 855 7380), a few doors beyond the entrance to the Sens
Garden on the Main Street as you head to Cork, is a clean and pleasant place with efficient frienc
service to break a journey and serves lovely wholesome food all day (about 8-5): fresh & healthy brea
fast (fruits salad with Greek yoghurt, honey & oats; maple syrup pancakes; toasted bagels), pani
hand-cut doorstep sandwiches made to order, salads, home-made soups, hot dish of the day and exc
lent home baking. Apple & rhubarb tarts, scones and jams are delicious, and available to take aw
too. Also on the main street you'll find one of Ireland's best-loved old pubs, **Morrissey's** (0502 3128
it first opened as a grocery in 1775 and, true to the old tradition, 'television, cards and singing a
not allowed'. At the Cork end of the village **Abbeyleix Manor Hotel** (057 873 0111; www.abbeyle.
manorhotel.com) offers practical modern facilities.
WWW.IRELAND-GUIDE.COM FOR THE BEST PLACES TO EAT, DRINK & STAY

Ballacolla
B&B/PUB

Foxrock In

Clough Ballacolla Co Laois **Tel: 057 873 863**
marian@foxrockinn.com www.foxrockinn.co

Sean and Marian Hyland run a very friendly, relaxed little place here for lovers of the country life. H
walking, fishing (coarse and game), golf and pitch & putt are all in the neighbourhood (golf and fishi
packages are a speciality) and they'll make packed lunches to see you through the day. An open fire ar
traditional music (days & times on inquiry) make the pub a welcoming place to come back to and the
is accommodation just up the stairs, in simple but comfortable rooms. Children welcome (under 2s fr
in parents' room, cot available without charge). **Rooms 5** (all en-suite, shower only & no smoking) B&
€45 pps, ss €19. Closed Christmas week & bar closed Good Fri (accommodation open). Visa, Las
Directions: On the R434, which links Durrow (N4) and Borris-in-Ossory (N7). Sign-posted off N7 and N

Durrow
HOTEL/RESTAURANT

Castle Durro

Durrow Co Laois **Tel: 057 873 655**
info@castledurrow.com www.castledurrow.co

Peter and Shelley Stokes' substant
18th century country house midw
between Dublin and Cork is an impressive buildir
with some magnificent period features, and offe
comfort and relaxation with style. A large marble
reception area with fresh flowers gives a welcomir
impression on arrival, and public rooms include
large drawing room/bar, where informal meals a
served (a useful place to break a journey), and
lovely dining room with a gently pastoral outlook
the back of the house (see below). Very spaciou
luxurious accommodation is in high-ceilinged, individually decorated rooms and suites in the ma
house (some with four posters), with views over the surrounding parkland and countryside; some mo
contemporary but equally pleasing ground floor rooms are in a wing - particularly suitable for gues
attending the weddings which have become a speciality, as they are convenient to the banqueting sui
and avoid disturbing other guests. Conference/banqueting (160/170); secretarial services. Childre
welcome (under 5s free in parents' room, cot available without charge, baby sitting arranged, ch
dren's playroom). Pets permitted by arrangement. Spa, garden, walking, tennis (all weather, floodlit
cycling, snooker. Golf, fishing, equestrian all nearby. Hairdressing, beauty salon. **Rooms 24** (10 jun
suites, 3 ground floor, 4 family rooms, all no smoking and with bath & shower). B&B €100 pps,
€40. 24 hr room service. Turn down service. Closed 31 Dec-15 Jan. **Castle Restaurant:** Candles a
lit in the foyer and restaurant at dusk, giving the whole area a lovely romantic feeling. Head chef Dav
Rouse's policy is for careful sourcing of all food, and the quality shows. Fish cookery is especial
impressive and wild Irish venison served with beetroot purée, potato rosti, braised fog, kohlrabi a
aged balsamic vanilla jus - is a speciality in season; it sounds complicated but works well on the plat
A well-balanced cheese plate might include the delicious local Lavistown cheese from Kilkenny. Sta
are very pleasant and helpful. **Seats 60** (private room, 18). Reservations accepted. Toilets wheelcha
accessible. Breakfast 8-10, D daily, 7-8.45 (Sun D, 6-7.45pm). Bar meals also available, 12-7 dail
Set D €50; Bar L à la carte. SC discretionary. House wines €20. Closed 31 Dec-15 Jan. Ame
MasterCard, Visa, Laser. **Directions:** On main Dublin-Cork road, N8, entrance from village green.

Killenard
HOTEL/RESTAURANT

The Heritage Golf & Spa Resort

Killenard Co Laois **Tel: 057 864 5500**
info@theheritage.com www.theheritage.com

téite bia This new luxury hotel and golf resort is set in the Laois countryside, just off the main Dublin-Cork road (N7). It is a very large development and as time progresses the landscaping is softening the hard edges. An impressive atrium sets the tone as you enter the hotel and, with a bifurcated staircase, crystal chandeliers and marbled floors, this lobby is designed to impress; other public areas are spacious and furnished in a similar style. Generous accommodation is in sumptuously furnished suites and guest rooms, which are extremely comfortable - and have beautiful bathrooms with separate shower and free-standing bath - although, surprisingly, some rooms do not have a view. But exceptional leisure facilities are the trump card at this hotel - as well as golf, there is a health club & spa (linked to the hotel by a tunnel), indoor and outdoor bowls, tennis, a 4-mile floodlit walking and jogging track around the golf course - and much more; new facilities are being added all the time. Fine dining is offered in The Arlington Rooom (see below), and an informal option is available at **Sol O'Riens Steakhouse & Italian Restaurant**. Conferences/Banqueting (500/400); business centre, free broadband wi/fi. Children welcome (under 5s free in parents' room, cot available free of charge, baby sitting arranged, playroom). Destination Spa; leisure centre (pool, fitness room, jacuzzi, sauna, steam room); championship golf (18); coarse fishing; walking. **Rooms 98** (3 suites, 10 junior suites, 10 junior suites, 5 family rooms, 5 disabled, 88 no smoking). B&B €162.50 pps, ss €100. Wheelchair Friendly. **Arlington Room Restaurant:** Generous tables, crisp white linen and fine porcelain set the tone for a relaxing experience in this comfortable and well-appointed restaurant. Head chef Mark Kirby offers a wide-ranging 5-course dinner menu which is also priced by course, allowing an element of à la carte flexibility; it includes some less usual dishes such as a starter of pan-fried loin of rabbit on a wild mushroom risotto, with crisp pancetta and thyme jus, and interesting vegetarian choices. The house speciality is grilled brill with prawn risotto, with spinach purée & morel cream, but Irish beef and poultry is also well represented. Excellent home-baked breads are a highlight, also delicious desserts including a hot 'Heritage Soufflé' with your choice of liqueur and, in addition to an Irish farmhouse cheese selection, there's a warm French cheese trio (Roquefort with basil, goat's cheese toast and warm camembert); lovely petits fours and and attentive service add to the occasion. A good, if rather expensive, wine list offers plenty of choice by the glass and several half bottles. **Seats 100** (Private room available seats 45), D daily 7-10 (Sun to 9.30); Set D €65 (Also priced by course). Piano Sat 8-11, air conditioning; House Wine about €23. Children welcome but not after 8. Hotel closed 24-26 Dec. *Food also available in: Greens golf club restaurant (High season 7 days 7-9.30); Sol O'Riens Italian Restaurant & Steakhouse (Wed-Sun 6.30-10) and The Hotel Bar 12-7 daily, includes outdoor seating on patio for 40. 12 Self catering houses available.* **The Heritage Hotel Portlaoise** (see entry) is an older sister to the Killenard hotel in Portlaoise town centre. Hotel closed 24-26 Dec. Amex, MasterCard, Visa, Laser. Heli-pad. **Directions:** M7 exit no. 15 to Killenard.

Mountrath
COUNTRY HOUSE

Roundwood House

Mountrath Co Laois **Tel: 057 873 2120**
roundwood@eircom.net www.roundwoodhouse.com

It is hard to see how anyone could fail to love this unspoilt early Georgian house, which lies secluded in mature woods of lime, beech and chestnut, at the foot of the Slieve Bloom mountains - a sense of history and an appreciation of genuine hospitality are all that is needed to make the most of a stay here, so just relax and share the immense pleasure and satisfaction that Frank and Rosemarie Kennan derive from their years of renovation work. Although unconventional in some ways, the house is extremely comfortable and well heated, and all the bathrooms have been renovated; each bedroom has its particular charm, although it might be wise to check if there is a large group staying, in which case the bedroom above the drawing room may not be the best option. Restoration is an ongoing process and an extraordinary (and historically unique) barn is possibly the next stage; this enterprise defies description, but don't leave Roundwood without seeing it. Children, wh always love the unusual animals and their young in the back yard, are very welcome and Rosemarie do a separate tea for them. Dinner is served at 8 o'clock, at a communal table, and based on the best loc and seasonal ingredients (notably locally reared beef and lamb); Rosemarie's food suits the house - goc home cooking without unnecessary frills - and Frank is an excellent host. An informative and quite exter sive wine list includes a generous choice of half bottles. Free broadband wi/fi. Children welcome (under free in parents' room, cot available without charge; playroom). Garden, croquet, boules, walking - there a mile long walk in the grounds and garden renovation is ongoing. Stabling available at the house; hors riding nearby. Golf nearby. Pets permitted in certain areas. **Rooms 10** (all en-suite, 3 family, 6 no-smokin 2 ground floor). B&B €75 pps, ss €25. No sc. D at 8pm; 5-course set D, €50 (non-residents welcorr by reservation if there is room); please book by noon. House wine €16.50. Dining room closed Sun, b supper available. Establishment closed 25 Dec & month of Jan. Amex, Diners, MasterCard, Visa, Lase **Directions:** On the left, 5km (3 miles) from Mountrath, on R440.

Portaoise
RESTAURANT/DELI

The Kitchen & Foodha

Hynds Square Portlaoise Co Laois **Tel: 057 866 206**
jimkitchen@eircom.n

téite bía Jim Tynan's excellent restaurant and food shop is definite worth a little detour. Delicious home-made food, an ope fire, relaxed atmosphere - a perfect place to break a journey or for special visit. The food hall stocks a wide range of Irish speciality foo products (and many good imported ones as well) and also sells pro ucts made on the premises: home-made terrines and breads fc example (including gluten-free breads - which are also available in th restaurant) lovely home-bakes like Victoria sponges, crumbles ar bread & butter pudding, and home-made chutneys and jams. You ca buy home-made ready meals too and any of the extensive range wines from the shop can be bought for the restaurant without a corkag charge. The restaurant offers a great choice of wholesome far including at least three vegetarian dishes each day - old favourites lik nut roast, perhaps and others like feta cheese tart and broccoli roulade Hereford premium beef is typical of the Irish produce in which suc pride is taken - and self-service lunches come with a wholesome selec tion of vegetables or salads. It's well worth making a special visit here in the autumn, to stock up the home-made and speciality Christmas food. *The restaurant - always notable for its original art - is now off cially home to 'The Tynan Gallery', with regular art exhibitions featuring both local and national artists. **Sea 200** (also outdoor 50+). Open all day Mon-Sat, 9-5.30; L12-2.30. Value L €10.50. A la carte & Vegetaria Menu. House wine from €10.99. Wheelchair access. Closed Sun, 25 Dec-1 Jan. Amex, MasterCard, Visa Laser. **Directions:** In the centre of Portlaoise, beside the Courthouse.

PORTLAOISE

Not a lot of people know this, but the county town of Laois was previously called Marybrough (it wa first established by Queen Mary in 1556 as "the Fort of Maryborough") and was only re-named a 'Portlaoise' in 1922. Today it is a major commercial, retail, and arts centre for the Midlands and ther is much of interest to visitors, including the old jail which is now an arts centre, the ruins of an 80C year old hill-top castle at **Dunamaise**, a large Georgian estate home and surrounding gardens at **Emc** a Georgian square at **Mountmellick**, and especially - the unspoilt **Slieve Bloom Mountains & Fores Park**. In addition to the recommendations below, it may be useful to know that budget accommoda tion is available at the **Comfort Inn** (057 866 6702) on the Abbeyleix road, and other good restaurant in the town include **The Lemon Tree** (057 866 2200) (above Delaney & Sons Bar/The Hare and Houn Bar, and **Palki Indian Restaurant** (057 866 4317) both on Main Street; also, a newcomer to the tow over **O'Donoghue's Pub** on Market Square, is **Les Olives** (057 936 5613; see entry, Naas, Co Kildare,

---

Portlaoise
GUESTHOUSE

Ivyleigh Hous

Bank Place Church Street Portlaoise Co Laois **Tel: 057 862 208**
info@ivyleigh.com www.ivyleigh.cor

This lovely early Georgian house is set back from the road only by a tiny neatly box-hedged forma garden, but has a coachyard (with parking), outhouses and a substantial lawned garden at the back It is a listed building and the present owners, Dinah and Jerry Campion, have restored it immaculate and furnished it beautifully in a style that successfully blends period elements with bold contemporary strokes, giving it great life. Two sitting rooms (one with television) are always available to guests and there's a fine dining room with a large communal table and a smaller one at the window for anyone who prefers to eat separately. Bedrooms are the essence of comfort, spacious, elegant, with working sash windows and everything absolutely top of the range including real linen. Large shower rooms have power showers and many excellent details, although those who would give anything for a bath to soak in will be disappointed. But it is perhaps at breakfast that this superb guesthouse is at its best. An extensive menu shows a commitment to using quality local produce that turns out to be even better than anticipated: imaginative, perfectly cooked and beautifully presented. As well as a full range of fresh juices, fruits, yogurts, cereals and porridge, speciality hot dishes include Cashel Blue cheesecakes - light and delicious, like fritters - served with mushrooms and tomatoes. And through it all Dinah Campion (who must rise at dawn to bake the bread) is charming, efficient and hospitable. This is one of Ireland's best guesthouses, and was Leinster winner of our Irish Breakfast Awards in 2002. No evening meals, but the Campions direct guests to good restaurants nearby. Not suitable for children under 8. No pets. Garden. Golf & garden visits nearby. **Rooms 6** (all shower only & no smoking). B&B €75, ss €20. Closed Christmas period. MasterCard, Visa. **Directions:** Centre of town follow signs for multi-storey car park, 30 metres from carpark.

Portlaoise
RESTAURANT

Kingfisher Restaurant

Old AIB Bank Main Street Portlaoise Co Laois **Tel: 057 866 2500**
www.kingfisherrestaurant.com

Situated in the centre of Portlaoise in the old AIB bank, this atmospheric and highly regarded Indian restaurant specialises in Punjabi cuisine. The welcome from immaculately attired staff is genuinely friendly and the large, high-ceilinged room (the former banking hall), is unusual, with decor portraying the crumbling sandstone walls of an ancient Indian temple. Simple table presentation and long menus may send out warning signals, but poppadoms with dipping sauces see you through the decision-making phase and, once food appears it has the fresh flavours of individual ingredients and authentic spicing creating satisfying combinations - in dishes that vary from creamy styles with almonds, to very spicy dishes with 'angry' green peppers. Tandoori, balti, biryani, 'exquisite' dishes and old favourites like korma, rogan josh, do piaza are all there, but they are skilfully executed, without recourse to elaborate presentation. Food is served with professionalism and charm, and reasonably priced - with a relaxed ambience and people of all ages enjoying themselves, this is a pleasant place to eat. **Seats 75.** L Wed-Fri 12-2.30, à la carte; D daily, 5.30-11.30; Set L menus from €13 per person; set D menus from €29 pp; also à la carte. House wine €16.95. Parking (15). Closed L Sat-Tue; 25 & 26 Dec, Good Fri. Amex, MasterCard, Visa, Laser. **Directions:** Town Centre.

Portlaoise
HOTEL

Portlaoise Heritage Hotel

Portlaoise Co Laois **Tel: 057 867 8588**
info@theheritagehotel.com www.theheritagehotel.com

This very popular hotel is an older sister to the Heritage at Killenard (see entry) and it offers particularly good facilities for conferences and business travellers. Although situated right in the town centre, the hotel's proud boast is that guests never have to leave the premises during their stay, and public areas offer a lot of choices to suit both off duty business/conference guests and leisure guests; there are three dining options, for example - Spago Italian Bistro for informal meals, fine dining at The Fitzmaurice and casual eating at Kellys Foundry Grillhouse, which is a fun place where the speciality is dry aged Irish Hereford beef, cooked on 'Black Rock' (volcanic stone). Accommodation, in several grades of room, is very comfortable and offers all the facilities expected of a good hotel. A dedicated conference wing offers excellent facilities for everything from small meetings to large conferences and events, and there is a fine health & fitness club with 22 m pool, sauna, Jacuzzi, steam room and gym; personal trainer available; beauty therapies. Conferences/Banqueting (500/350), broadband wi/fi, business centre, video conferencing. Leisure centre ('pool, fitness room). Spa (beauty treatments & massage). **Rooms 110** (4 suites, 4 junior suites, 28 executive, 90 no smoking, 4 disabled); Lift; 24 hr room service; Children welcome (under 5s free in parents room, cot available at no charge, baby sitting arranged). Closed 24-27 Dec. Amex, Diners, Visa, Laser. **Directions:** Centre of Portlaoise.

COUNTY LEITRIM

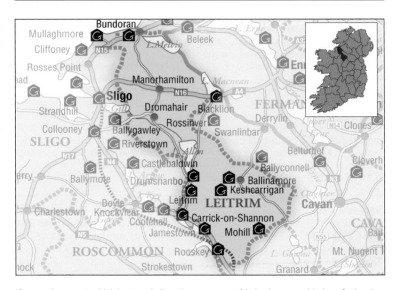

If you seek a county which best symbolises the resurgence of Ireland, you need look no further than Leitrim. In times past, it was known as the Cinderella county. Official statistics admitted that Leitrim did indeed have the poorest soil in all Ireland, in places barely a covering of low fertility. Back in the sad old days of the 1950s, the county's population had fallen to 30,000. It was doubted that it was still a viable administrative entity.

You'd be hard put to visualise those gloomy times now, more than fifty years on. Today, Leitrim prospers. The county town, Carrick-on-Shannon, is one of Ireland's brightest and best, a bustling river port. Admittedly, there are drawbacks. The town's very first traffic lights came into action in the summer of 2004. Formerly, there were no traffic lights in all Leitrim county. Or at least, not on the roads. The modern automated locks on the restored Shannon-Erne Waterway – whose vitality has contributed significantly to Leitrim's new prosperity – may have had their own boat traffic lights since the waterway was reopened in 1994. But it took another ten years before the roads followed suit.

Yet despite the new energy, Leitrim is rightly seen as a pleasantly away-from-it-all sort of place which has many attractions for the determined connoisseur, not least enthusiasts for traditonal music, though "traditional" is scarcely the proper word – in Leitrim, it's vibrantly alive and developing all the time. However, with some of Ireland's better known holiday areas suffering if anything from an excess of popularity, the true trail-blazers may still be able to find the relaxation they seek in Leitrim.

But is it really so remote? Popular perceptions may be at variance with reality. For instance, Leitrim shares the shores of Lough Gill with Sligo, so much so that Yeat's legendary Lake Isle of Innisfree is within an ace of being in Leitrim rather than Sligo of Yeatsian fame. To the northward, we find that more than half of lovely Glencar, popularly perceived as being one of Sligo's finest jewels, is in fact in Leitrim. As for the notion of Leitrim being the ultimate inland and rural county - not so. Leitrim has an Atlantic coastline, albeit of only four kilometres, around Tullaghan.

It's said this administrative quirk is a throwback to the time when the all-powerful bishops of the early church aspired to have ways of travelling to Rome without having to cross the territory of neighbouring clerics. Whatever the reason, it's one of Leitrim's many surprises, which are such that it often happens that when you're touring in the area and find yourself in a beautiful bit of country, a reference to the map produces the information that, yes indeed, you're in Leitrim, a county which also provides most of the land area for Ireland's first Ecotourism 'Green Box'.

Leitrim's significance within this scheme achieved additional recognition when the first An Taisce National Awards were announced. The prize for the most appropriate building in the countryside – a concept which is surely central to An Taisce's very existence – went to Rossinver Organic Centre, whose buildings in North Leitrim near Lough Melvin were designed by Colin Bell

Local Attractions & Information

Ballinamore Shannon-Erne Waterway	1890 924 991
Ballinamore Slieve an Arain Riverbus Cruises	071 964 4079
Carrick-on-Shannon Moonriver Cruises	071 962 1777
Carrick-on-Shannon Tourism Information	071 962 0170
Carrick-on-Shannon Waterways Ireland	071 965 0898
Dromahair Parke's Cas. (restored 17c fortified house)	071 916 4149
Manorhamilton Glens Arts Centre	071 985 5833
Mohill Lough Rynn House and Gardens	071 963 1538
Rossinver The Organic Centre (Ecotourism)	071 985 4338

BALLINAMORE

Ballinamore is a small town beside the Shannon-Erne Waterway, in a lovely area that's great for a family holiday as there's lots to do. Teresa Kennedy's farm guesthouse **Glenview House** (071 9644157), for example, is attractively situated overlooking the waterway, and has a tennis court and an outdoor play area as well as an indoor games room; there's even a little agricultural museum in the outbuildings, and Teresa runs a popular restaurant too. Nearby, also overlooking the canal, **Riversdale Farm Guesthouse** (071 964 4122; www.riversdaleguesthouse.biz) is another homely place to stay, also with lots to do on site - no restaurant, but there's a small leisure complex, with swimming pool and squash - and barges at the bottom of the garden, available for holidays afloat. Nearby in Keeldrin a visit to **Swan Island Open Farm & Davy's Cottage Restaurant** (049 433 3065) is a real treat for all the family with both rare and traditional farm animals to see and feed, and also a children's play area. The farm is open Easter to October and a floating jetty at the farm ensures secure and easy mooring for cruisers; **Davy's Cottage Restaurant** is open year round from 6pm (also lunch on Sundays); there's a friendly bar and the restaurant has an intimate ambience with a homely feeling and lovely simple home-cooked food with real flavour.

WWW.IRELAND-GUIDE.COM FOR THE BEST PLACES TO EAT, DRINK & STAY

CARRICK-ON-SHANNON

R

An ideal location on the River Shannon has resulted in Carrick-on-Shannon becoming one of the most popular destinations for cruise holidays and fishing in Ireland and there is also a golf course on the outskirts of the town. This thriving town is cosmopolitan in its outlook, with a growing range of restaurants and some fascinating shops: the **Market Yard** is a good browsing spot, with an interesting range of little shops and eating places around the central yard. **Vitto's** (071 96 27000) is a bright and airy Italian, casual in style and serving tasty casual food. Beside the bridge, **Cryan's Bar & Restaurant** (Tel: 071-962 0409) is well known for steaks and music. For accommodation, don't overlook **Glencarne Country House** (071-966 7013) which is across the bridge on the Boyle road, with a Co Roscommon postal address, and **Caldra House** (071 962 3040; www.caldrahouse.ie), which is about 2 miles out of town off the R280. **The Dock** (071 9650828; www.thedock.ie) is Carrick's cultural centre - housed in the beautiful 19th Century former Courthouse building, overlooking the River Shannon, it has been wonderfully restored into Leitrim's first integrated centre for the arts, with a 100+ seat performance space, three art galleries, artists' studios, an arts education room; it is also home to **The Leitrim Design House**.

WWW.IRELAND-GUIDE.COM FOR THE BEST PLACES TO EAT, DRINK & STAY

Carrick-on-Shannon
HOTEL
R

Bush Hotel

Carrick-on-Shannon Co Leitrim **Tel: 071 967 1000**
info@bushhotel.com www.bushhotel.com

féile bía One of Ireland's oldest hotels, the Bush is known for its old fashioned hospitality and staff are exceptionally pleasant and helpful. It has undergone considerable refurbishment in recent years and, while rooms will vary in size and comfort, this hotel has personality and the 40 newer rooms are more luxurious. Public areas have character and a pleasing sense of history, and there are two bars, one of which has been given a contemporary make-over and is now a bistro bar. The hotel's pleasant restaurant is notable for its traditional style and courteous service and remains a popular destination. A new conference room offers a full range of business and conference facilities and The Orchard Ballroom makes a bright and inviting venue for large events. Informal meals are available at the self-service coffee shop/carvery, with bar food also offered at lunchtime and in the evening.

Conference/Banqueting (120/400); free broadband wi/fi; business centre, secretarial services. Children welcome (under 2s free in parents' room, cot available without charge). The hotel has a gift shop, tourist information point and bureau de change and can arrange car, bicycle and boat hire and supply fishing tackle and golf clubs. Golf nearby. Tennis; garden. Parking (180). **Rooms 60** (2 suites, 3 family rooms) B&B €89.50pps, single €99.50. *Short breaks offered - details on application. Closed 24-31 Dec. MasterCard, Visa, Laser. **Directions:** Town centre - signed off the N4 bypass.

Carrick-on-Shannon
GUESTHOUSE

Ciúin House

Hartley Carrick-on-Shannon Co Leitrim **Tel: 071 967 1488**
info@ciuinhouse.com www.ciuinhouse.com

Quietly situated on the edge of the town but within comfortable walking distance of all its amenities, Fiona Reynolds' stylish new purpose built guesthouse is effectively a small hotel. Bedrooms are simply but warmly furnished to a high standard and are very well-appointed, with orthopaedic beds and all the in-room facilities expected of an hotel, and some of the pristine bathrooms have Jacuzzi baths. A private sitting room is comfortably furnished with style, and has a gas fire and a surround sound music system and plasma screen multi-channel television for guests' use. An extensive breakfast is served in a bright and airy restaurant, which opens on to a paved area with outside seating in fine weather and is open to the public for breakfast and snacks, lunch and dinner. A high level of comfort and amenities, immaculate housekeeping, hands-on management and an emphasis on genuine hospitality and service all make this a great place to stay. Small conferences/banquets (36). Children welcome (under 3s free in parents' room, cots available free of charge, baby sitting arranged); broadband wi/fi. **Rooms 15** (2 deluxe, 2 family, 2 shower only, 1 ground floor, 1 for disabled). Closed Good Fri, 24-26 Dec. MasterCard, Visa, Laser. **Directions:** From Carrick-on-Shannon take the R280 Letirim road. Follow signs for Cootehall. Left for Hartley at Leitrim Observer offices, signed from road.

Carrick-on-Shannon
COUNTRY HOUSE

Hollywell Country House

Liberty Hill Cortober Carrick-on-Shannon Co Leitrim **Tel: 071 962 1124**
hollywell@esatbiz.com

After many years as hoteliers in the town (and a family tradition of inn-keeping that goes back 200 years), Tom and Rosaleen Maher moved some years ago to this delightful period house on a rise across the bridge, with its own river frontage and beautiful views over the Shannon. It's a lovely, graciously proportioned house, with a relaxed family atmosphere. Tom and Rosaleen have an easy hospitality (not surprisingly, perhaps, as their name derives from the Gaelic "Meachar" meaning hospitable), making guests feel at home very quickly and this, as much as the comfort of the house and its tranquil surroundings, is what makes Hollywell special. Bedrooms are all individually furnished in period style, with tea and coffee making facilities, and delicious breakfasts are worth getting up in good time for: fresh juice, fruits and choice of teas, coffees and herbal teas, freshly-baked bread, home-made preserves, lovely choice of hot dishes - anything from the "full Irish" to Irish pancakes with maple syrup or grilled cheese & tomato with black olive pesto on toast. No evening meals, but Tom and Rosaleen advise guests on the best local choices and there's a comfortable guests' sitting room with an open fire to gather around on your return. A pathway through lovely gardens leads down to the river; fishing (coarse) on site. Lots to do in the area - and advice a-plenty from Tom and Rosaleen on the best places to visit. Not suitable for children under 12. Pets allowed by arrangement. **Rooms 4** (2 junior suites, 2 shower only). B&B about €60 pps, ss about €30. Closed early early Nov- early Feb. Amex, MasterCard, Visa, Laser. **Directions:** From Dublin, cross bridge on N4, keep left at Gings pub. Hollywell entrance is on left up the hill. ◊

Carrick-on-Shannon
HOTEL/RESTAURANT

The Landmark Hotel

Dublin Road Carrick-on-Shannon Co Leitrim **Tel: 071 962 2222**
landmarkhotel@eircom.net www.thelandmarkhotel.com

This aptly named hotel just across the road from the river has a dramatic lobby with a large marble and granite fountain feature - and an imposing cast-iron staircase creates a certain expectation. Bedrooms, many of which have views over the Shannon, are spacious and comfortable, with individual temperature control as well as the more usual amenities (direct dial phone, TV, tea/coffee facilities, trouser press) and well-finished bathrooms. Informal daytime meals are offered in **Aromas Café**, and the balcony dining area previously known as **Ferrari's** (the reason for the name is obvious when you get there) is now more appropriately used as a bar. Conference/banqueting (500/350); secretarial services; broadband wi/fi. Golf nearby. Off-season breaks. Children welcome (under 4s free in parents' room; cots available without charge, baby sitting arranged). No pets. Parking. Heli-pad. **Rooms 60** (2 suites, 6 family rooms, 2 shower only, 2 for disabled). Lift. B&B €109 pps, ss €30. **CJ's Restaurant:** The hotel's fine dining restaurant, CJ's, has earned a local following with discerning diners who enjoy the setting - it is a very elegant room - the welcoming ambience, comfortable surrounds and good cooking. Head chef Brian Aherne's menus offer plenty to choose from - a seafood dish of Dublin Bay prawns in katifi with confit of aubergine, chilli jam and cucumber pickle is a speciality, but the range is wide and you will also find dressed up versions of homely dishes like ever-popular roasted loin of lamb with a brioche herb crust, shepherd's pie, wilted greens & wild garlic. A meal here has all the extra little touches, including an amuse-bouche sent from the chef before your meal, and a complimentary liqueur afterwards, perhaps - and professional service that adds a sense of occasion. This is not an inexpensive restaurant, but it does give good value - and diners have the choice of moving out to the conservatory, to dine there if preferred, and it can be a lovely experience on a fine summer evening. CJ's Restaurant, D 6-10 daily. SC discretionary; closed Sun; Aromas Café, 9-5; Bar food served daily. Hotel closed 25 Dec. Amex, MasterCard, Visa, Laser. **Directions:** On N4, 2 hours from Dublin.

Carrick-on-Shannon
PUB

The Oarsman Bar & Café

Bridge Street Carrick-on-Shannon Co Leitrim **Tel: 071 962 1733**
info@theoarsman.com www.theoarsman.com

This attractive and characterful pub is run by brothers Conor and Ronan Maher, sons of Tom and Rosaleen Maher (see entry for Hollywell), and it will be very clear to anyone who visits that they've inherited "the hotelier's gene": everything is invariably spick-and-span, very welcoming and efficiently run, even at the busiest times. The bar - which is very pleasantly set up in a solidly traditional style with two fires, comfortable seating arrangements for eating the excellent bar meals, and occasional contemporary tastes in the decor - leads off towards a sheltered patio at the back, which makes a spot for a sunny day (and a fully fledged beer garden was due for completion at the time of going to press). Conor and Ronan's sister, Claire, re-joined the team in 2006, and various plans afoot currently include extending the opening hours for bar food, to become more of a gastro-pub. Meanwhile, a strong kitchen team led by Lee Mastin produce consistently excellent food, offered on appealing lunchtime bar menus and more extensive à la carte evening menus offered upstairs. Here you might have a great meal beginning with seared Kilkeel scallops with chorizo sausage, cauliflower purée and tomato & oregano vinaigrette, followed by any one of half a dozen terrific main courses, say rack of Paddy Sheridan's lamb with minted sweet potato, braised celery & rhubarb relish. And, desserts have always been a speciality here, so don't forget to save a space for a wonderful ending. This is one of the country's most pleasant pubs and it just goes on getting better - definitely worth a detour. Free Broadband/WIFI. L & D Tue-Sat 12-3.30 and 6.45-9.45. A la carte. House wine from about €17. Not suitable for children after 9pm. Bar closed 25 Dec, Good Fri. MasterCard, Visa, Laser. **Directions:** Town centre: coming from Dublin direction, turn right just before the bridge.

Carrick-on-Shannon
RESTAURANT
[R]

Shamrat Restaurant
Bridge Street Carrick-on-Shannon Co Leitrim
Tel: 071 965 0934

Although the entrance is small from the street, first-time visitors to this appealing Indian restaurant be surprised to find a spacious L-shaped first floor dining area and enough room for a comfortable reception area at the top of the stairs. Menus are wide-ranging, offering a varied selection of Indian and Bangladeshi dishes; the familiar ones are all there - onion bahjee, chicken tikka or pakora, biryani dishes and perhaps a dozen tandoori specialities. Uncluttered contemporary decor and well-spaced tables with comfortable high-back chairs make a pleasing setting for interesting, authentic and well-cooked food - and attentive service from friendly and helpful staff adds to the enjoyment. Children welcome. L&D daily; Mon-Sat: D 6-11.30; Sun, special family lunch 1-4, à la carte 4-11.30. Set D about €25.95, D also à la carte; Vegetarian Menu about €20.95. House wine about €17.50. Closed 25 Dec. Amex, MasterCard, Visa, Laser. **Directions:** Near the bridge, on right-hand side walking into town.

Carrick-on-Shannon
RESTAURANT
[R]
féile bia

Victoria Hall
Quay Road Carrick-on-Shannon Co Leitrim **Tel: 071 962 0320**
info@victoriahall.ie www.victoriahall.ie

This stylish contemporary restaurant is in an imaginatively restored and converted, almost-waterside Victorian building beside the Rowing Club. Bright, colourful and classy, it has great appeal (chic minimalist table settings, well-spaced tables, good lighting) with a first floor dining space that is especially attractive. The menu offers a wide range of broadly Asian and European dishes, translating into meals that are well-executed and good value - and served by smart, attentive staff. * Associated accommodation is offered at Caldra House, quietly located 2 miles outside the town (096 23040). Children welcome (high chair, childrens menu). **Seats 75.** Reservations accepted. Air conditioning. Toilets wheelchair accessible. Braille menu available. Open daily, 12.30-10. L, 12.30-5, D 5-10. Early D €30, Sun-Thur, 5-7.30pm, also à la carte. Gluten-free menu available. House wine from about €16. SC 10% on groups 8+. Closed 25 Dec, Good Fri. MasterCard, Visa, Laser. **Directions:** On Boathouse Quay, behind the Rowing Club. ◊

Carrick-on-Shannon Area
PUB
[R]

Lynch's Bar/The Sheermore
Kilclare Carrick-on-Shannon Co Leitrim
Tel: 071 964 1029

Well away from the bustle of nearby Carrick-on-Shannon, Padraig and Christina Lynch's friendly traditional bar, grocery and hardware shop on the Shannon-Erne Waterway is known from the road as "The Sheermore" - but presents its much more attractive side to the water. You can sit outside at the back in fine weather and watch the boats going by, or choose between a conservatory overlooking the bridge or a move right into the bar if the weather dictates. This isn't really a food place, but Christina Lynch makes home-made soup every day and cuts sandwiches freshly to order - which can be just the right thing, in the right place. Children welcome. Pets allowed in some areas. Bar food available 12.30-9.30 daily. Wheelchair accessible. Closed 25 Dec, Good Fri. MasterCard, Visa, Laser. **Directions:** 6 miles from Carrick-on-Shannon towards Ballinamore, on the Shannon-Erne Waterway. ◊

Dromohair
RESTAURANT
[N]

Riverbank Restaurant
Dromohair Co Leitrim **Tel: 071 916 4934**
declan@riverbank-restaurant.com www.riverbank-restaurant.com

Formerly Cuisto Perigord, this fine restaurant is now run by returning native John Kelly (the chef), and Cavan man Declan Campbell (restaurant manger). They arrived with some impressive experience under their belts, and John was introduced to cooking by Neven Maguire (see entry for MacNean Bistro) so you can expect refined modern cooking with an emphasis on tiptop ingredients, locally produced where possible - a list of suppliers is included with the menu. The restaurant is in a lovely leafy setting, in what was formerly an orchard, and it's an impressive building, with a big central feature fireplace and lots of character; tables, many of which are windowside, are set up smartly with white cloths and napkins and pleasant and friendly staff are very hospitable. Menus are presented promptly, along with the offer of a drink, and you can choose between an à la carte with six or seven choices per course, plus a couple of unusual vegetarian dishes - feta & basil polenta, for example, with spiced tomato chutney and goat's cheese bruschetta, or roast butternut squash risotto. The set dinner, which is a selection from these, probably including premium dishes like the house speciality of pan-flashed turbot with crab & dill ravioli, ratatouille and asparagus velouté, and will almost certainly include local beef and either a starter or main course of local Thornhill duckling. Desserts tend to be classic with a twist - roasted rhubarb, for example, comes with toasted brioche and walnut ice cream. The wine list includes plenty of bottles at around €25 and under, and there are four half bottles. Sunday lunch offers very good value. Dining here is a very pleasant experience and this restaurant should do well. Children welcome (high chair, childrens menu); **Seats 70** (private room, 30, outdoors, 20); reservations recommended. D Tue-Sun, 6.30-10pm (from 7pm Sun); set D €40; L Sun only, 12.30-3pm; set Sun L €40; house wine €19; SC 10% on groups 10+. Closed Mon, 24-26 Dec. Visa, Laser. **Directions:** 3rd exit for Dromahair from Dublin roundabout in Sligo, follow signs.

Drumshanbo
HOTEL/RESTAURANT
R

Ramada Lough Allen Hotel & Spa

Drumshanbo Co Leitrim **Tel: 071 964 0044**
info@loughallenhotel.com www.loughallenhotel.com

Although signage from the road may be offputting, the interior of this bright and interesting contemporary hotel just outside the characterful village of Drumshanbo will quickly win you over - an attractive foyer area with an open fire and a collection of striking paintings, has glazed doors at the far end - allowing a tantalising glimpse into a high-ceilinged bar; beyond this a clear lake view seen through a wall of glass, with a deck for fine weather. It's also a fine place for a winter trip when, after long walks or a cycle, you can return to the warmth of the fire. **Rushes Restaurant** which, strangely, is not in a waterside position - offers pleasing food, and good bar meals are also served. Accommodation - in spacious, comfortable rooms, furnished in an understated, modern style with fine views - includes some suites and family rooms, and self-catering apartments. Conference/banqueting (220/160). Leisure centre (lakeview swimming pool, hot tub, gym), spa. Children welcome (under 2s free in parents' room, cot available without charge, baby sitting arranged). Garden, walking, cycling, equestrian. No pets. **Rooms 64** (5 junior suites, some family rooms, 4 shower only, 4 for disabled, all no smoking). Lift. 24 hr room service. B&B from €70 pps, ss about €23. Open all year. Amex, Diners, MasterCard, Visa, Laser. **Directions:** 15 km from Carrick-on-Shannon, on Drumshanbo-Sligo road. ◊

Jamestown
RESTAURANT
R

Al Mezza

Jamestown Carrick on Shannon Co Leitrim **Tel: 071 962 5050**
almezza@hotmail.com www.almezza.com

This colourful little Lebanese/Mediterranean restaurant on the edge of the pretty village of Jamestown is run by proprietor-chef Milad Serhan and Dorothy Serhan, who is front of house. It's an unusual little place for a country area, with friendly service as well as good food. Milad's authentic middle eastern menus are quite extensive and it is a good idea, especially on a first visit, to order one of the mezze selections (some of them vegetarian) either as a shared starter, or for a whole meal - this sociable dining style saves a lot of anxious trawling through the menu. For those arriving in Jamestown by boat, it's about half a mile from the quay, but it's a pleasant walk through the village - pavement all the way and past two particularly enticing pubs for a visit in each direction, perhaps. Reservations are not essential, but this is an understandably popular little restaurant and it can be very busy, especially at weekends. Unsuitable for children after 8pm (high chair, childrens menu). **Seats 30** (private room, 20, outdoor +8). Open Wed-Mon 6-10 (to 9.30 Sun). House wine from €16. Closed Tue. Closed New Year. MasterCard, Visa, Laser. **Directions:** On right just before entering Jamestown village.

KESHCARRIGAN

This attractive canalside village has craic and music a-plenty at Des Foley's famous friendly pub **Gertie's** (071 964 2252), which has open fires and plenty of character (and offers food too). Just along the canal a little way, the well known **Canal View House & Restaurant** (071 964 2404), which has its own berthing just across the road, has recently been taken over by the partnership of French duo Vincent Maillard and chef Alexander Jourdan.

WWW.IRELAND-GUIDE.COM FOR THE BEST PLACES TO EAT, DRINK & STAY

Kinlough
RESTAURANT

The Courthouse Restaurant

Main Street Kinlough Co Leitrim **Tel: 071 984 2391**
thecourthouserest@eircom.net www.thecourthouserest.com

In the old courthouse of the attractive village of Kinlough, Piero Melis's little restaurant is a welcoming place and offers good contemporary cooking in the Mediterranean style with some local influences. A wide-ranging menu includes specialities like the perennially popular Linguini di Mare, flat spaghetti with clams and crab in a tomato sauce, and there are always daily specials; other house specialitie include starters like seafood risotto and there is a wide range of main course specialities includin Thornhill duck. Traditional desserts can be selected from a choice of good home-made ice-creams an cakes. Good food and helpful, professional service all encourage return visits. **Seats 40** (private roor 12). D Wed-Mon, 6.30-9.30, L on Sun only 12.30-2.30; set Sun L €21; set 2/3 course D, €28/38 also à la carte. House wines from €18; SC 10% on parties of 6+. Closed - Tue, 2 weeks after Feb 14 Christmas. MasterCard, Visa, Laser. **Directions:** Off main Donegal-Sligo road (N15), 5 km towards Slig from Bundoran. Take turning directly opposite Tullaghan House.

Leitrim
BAR/RESTAURANT
R

The Barge Steakhouse

Leitrim Village Carrick-on-Shannon Co Leitrir
Tel: 071 962 0807

John and Rose Pierce's inviting stone bar and restaurant on the main street begins with a characterful bar with a welcoming open fire at the front and progresses to the restauran and conservatory, with a beer garden at the back. There's a daytime bar menu as well as an à la carte for the restaurant; while there's the occasional nod to fashion, the style is quite traditional offerin starters like garlic mushrooms or prawn cocktail; steaks are the main speciality of the house, and duck ling is also very popular - there are always several fish dishes too, and at least one for vegetarians Freshly prepared food and good value are the reasons for the Barge's popularity and there's a children menu too, and a short wine list. *Marquee available for private functions. Not suitable for childre after 9pm. Toilets wheelchair accessible. **Seats 90** (32 in conservatory; private room 21). Open 12.3C 9.30 daily, L 12.30-6, D 6-9.30 (Sun to 9). A la carte. House wines from about €14. Closed 25 De & Good Fri. MasterCard, Visa, Laser. **Directions:** In Leitrim village: take Drumshambo road out c Carrick-on-Shannon. ◇

Mohill
HOTEL/CASTLE

Lough Rynn Castle Hotel & Estate

Lough Rynn Mohill Co Leitrim **Tel: 071 963 270(**
enquiries@loughrynn.ie www.loughrynn.i

Set amongst 300 acres of rolling countryside historic Lough Rynn Castle has seen major invest ment and a great deal of TLC to restore it to it former glory for its new use as an hotel. Aside fron structural restoration, original furnishings wer located and refurbished before being re-instated ir their former home, and many other luxurious items, including hand-painted silk wallpaper fron Paris, were carefully sourced to complement th property. Approached via a winding wooded road, is now entered through an impressive manne black and gold wrought iron gate, and guests are welcomed at the door. Opulently appointed lounges drawing rooms and a library are remarkably private and intimate for public rooms in an hotel and hav views out over the lawns and lake: a peaceful and comfortable place to read, or have a light lunch o afternoon tea. Bedrooms - ten at present - include luxurious castle rooms offering unique accommo dation, with wonderful views of the estate and surrounding countryside. The aim is to make Lough Rynn a perfect country haven, and no expense or effort has been spared; there is over a square mil of lake, with a marina, and the gardens - which are also of significant historical interest - are unde restoration too, together with the nature trails and lakeside walks. What has been achieved so far i remarkable, but this is still very much a work in progress: new rooms, a leisure centre and spa, and Nick Faldo-designed golf course are all planned for 2008. However, there is plenty to keep visitors occupied here already, including walking, fishing and horse riding. Banqueting (75). Fishing, walking garden; equestrian nearby. Children welcome. **Rooms 10** (including suites and standard & deluxe lak view rooms); Room rate from about €215. Open all year. **Directions:** Signed from Mohill ◇

Rooskey
HOTEL
R

Shannon Key West Hote

The Waters Edge Rooskey Co Leitrim **Tel: 071 963 8800**
info@shannonkeywest.com www.shannonkeywest.con

This well-run riverside hotel on the Leitrim/Roscommon border provides valuable facilities to the are and is open all year making it a particularly good venue for off-season short breaks, meetings an conferences. Comfortably furnished bedrooms have all the usual amenities - direct dial phones, T with video channel, tea & coffee-making facilities and trouser press; two rooms also have fax machines and there is a safe available on request. On-site amenities include a gym, jacuzzi, solarium and steam room (but no swimming pool) and there is plenty to do and see in the area. Reliable bar food also makes this a useful place to bear in mind for breaking a journey. Conference/banqueting (500/360), broadband, secretarial services available; Fitness room, tennis, walking. Children welcome (cots available without charge, baby sitting arranged). **Rooms 40** (17 shower only, 5 family rooms, 15 no smoking, 13 ground floor, 1 for disabled). B&B from about €50 pps, no ss. Amex, MasterCard, Visa, Laser. **Directions:** On N4, main Dublin-Sligo route, midway between Longford and Carrick-on-Shannon. ◇

Rossinver
CAFÉ/RESTAURANT
Ⓝ 🖉

The Grass Roof Café

The Organic Centre Rossinver Co Leitrim **Tel: 071 985 4338**
organiccentre@eircom.net www.theorganiccentre.ie

County Leitrim is at the heart of the 'greening' of Ireland and, as the momentum grows, more and more people are interested in visiting The Organic Centre, either to attend one of the wide variety of courses they offer (free annual booklet available on request), or just to have a look around. The organic display gardens are very interesting, showing how organic food can be grown by everyone, and they include many attractive features including a children's garden with willow sculptures and witches' houses. There's also an Eco-shop stocking all kinds of eco-friendly and ethical products ranging from foods (vegetables, home bakes, Fairtrade) to seeds, books and home products. Inspired by the ultrafresh, seasonal (and, otherwise, often hard to source) produce available to them, the cooks at The Grass Roof Organic Café create great vegetarian meals to feed the staff, people attending workshops and the public. There's even a weekly 'béile gaeilge' (Irish speaking lunch) on Tuesdays and all Irish speakers, even beginners, are very welcome. Tis is an unusual and rewarding place to visit and outside catering is offered too, for 'anything from a picnic to a banquet'. Toilets wheelchair accessible. Children welcome (high chair, baby changing facilities). **Seats 50** (outdoors, 20); Food served daily, 11-5pm. Set 3 course meal, €20; house wine €20-22. Closed 20 Dec-10 Jan. MasterCard, Visa, Laser. **Directions:** 15 mins from Manorhamilton on R282.

COUNTY LIMERICK

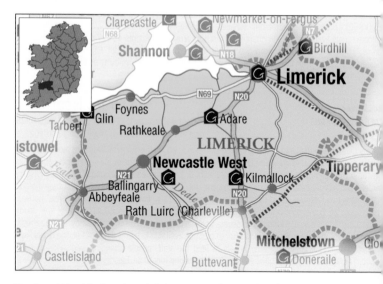

The story of Limerick city and county is in many ways the story of the Shannon Estuary, for in time past it was the convenient access provided by Ireland's largest estuary - it is 80 kilometres in length - which encouraged the development of life along the estuary's sea shores, and into the fresh water of the River Shannon itself.

Today, the area's national and global transport is served by air, sea and land through Shannon International Airport, the increased use of the Estuary through the development of Foynes Port and other deepwater facilities, improvement and restoration of rail links, and a rapidly expanding but inevitably busy road network which is being augmented by a tunnel under the Shannon Estuary immediately seaward of Limerick city.

In Limerick city in recent years, the opening of improved waterway links through the heart of town has seen the welcome regeneration of older urban areas continuing in tandem with the attractive new developments. But significant and all as this is, there's much more to the totality of Limerick county than the city and its waterways.

Inland from the river, the very richness of the countryside soon begins to develop its own dynamic. Eastern Limerick verges into Tipperary's Golden Vale, and the eastern county's Slieve Felim hills, rising to Cullaun at 462 m, reflect the nearby style of Tipperary's Silvermine Mountains.

Southwest of Limerick city, the splendid hunting country and utterly rural atmosphere of the area around the beautiful village of Adare makes it a real effort of imagination to visualise the muddy salt waters of the Shannon Estuary just a few miles away down the meandering River Maigue, yet the Estuary is there nevertheless.

Equally, although the former flying boat port of Foynes - with its evocative Flying Boat Museum well worth a visit - is seeing expansion of the nearby jetty at Aughinish to accommodate the most modern large ships, just a few miles inland we find ourselves in areas totally remote from the sea in country side which lent itself so well to mixed farming that the price of pigs in Dromcolliher (a.k.a Drumcolligher) on the edge of the Mullaghareirk Mountains reputedly used to set the price of pigs throughout Ireland.

The growth of the computer industry in concert with the rapid expansion of the energetic University has given Limerick a new place in Irish life in tandem with its established role as a leading manufacturing centre. The city's vitality and urban renewal makes it an entertaining place to visit, while the eclectic collection on stunning display in the unique Hunt Museum in its handsome waterside setting has a style which other areas of Limerick life are keen to match.

With newfound confidence, Limerick has been paying greater attention to its remarkable heritage of Georgian architecture, with Limerick Civic Trust restoring the Georgian house and garden at 2 Pery Square. It acts as the focal point for an area of classic urban architecture which deserves to be better known.

That said, rugby-mad Limerick still keeps its feet firmly on the ground, and connoisseurs are firmly of the opinion that the best pint of Guinness in all Ireland is to be had in this no-nonsense city, where they insist on being able to choose the temperature of their drink, and refuse to have any truck with modern fads which would attempt to chill the rich multi-flavoured black pint into a state of near-freezing tastelessness aimed at immature palates.

Local Attractions & Information

Adare Heritage Centre	061 396 666
Ballysteen Ballynacourty Gardens	061 396 409
Bruree Heritage Centre and de Valera Museum	063 91 300
Foynes Flying Boat Museum	069 65 416
Glin Glin Castle Pleasure Grounds & Walled Garden	068 34 364
Limerick Belltable Arts Centre, 69 O'Connell St	061 319 866
Limerick Georgian House & Garden, 2 Pery Square	061 314 130
Limerick Hunt Museum, Customs House, Rutland St	061 312 833
Limerick King John's Castle	061 360 788 / 061 411 201 / 202
Limerick Limerick City Art Gallery, Pery Square	061 310 633
Limerick Limerick Museum, John's Square	061 417 826
Limerick Tourism Information	061 317 522
Limerick University of Limerick	061 202 700
Lough Gur Interpretive centre, 3000BC to present	061 385 186
Patrickswell Limerick Racecourse (Greenmount Park)	061 320 000

LIMERICK

Of great historical and strategic importance, Ireland's fourth city is also renowned for its rich cultural tradition, with many excellent museums, galleries and theatres to visit - and Ireland's first purpose-built concert hall. The city also offers a wide range of accommodation, restaurants and pubs, many of them in attractive waterside locations. The famous old restaurant & bar **Moll Darby's** (Tel 061 411522; www.mhm.ie), is on George's Quay, for example, and the wholesome good food served there is pleasing many a visitor these days. Another long-established city centre restaurant with character is **Freddy's Bistro** (061 418749) on Glentworth Street; it's in an atmospheric old stone and brick building, and offers quite straightforward flavoursome food at a reasonable price. A newer restaurant with a pleasing ambience is **Azur** (061 314994) on O'Connell Street, with blue décor to match the name and a French atmosphere (Edith Piaf and a good wine list); the early bird dinner is useful to know about. Also new to the city is branch of the 'almost-nationwide' quality family dining restaurants **Café Bar Deli** (061 485 1865; www.cafebardeli.ie), see Dublin entries. **Poppadom** (061 446644) on Limerick Street is a branch of the Dublin 6 restaurant (see entry), and **Munchy Munchy** (061 313113) is the Chinese where you'll find the city's Chinese residents tucking in. **The Wild Onion** (061 440055; www.wildonioncafe.com) on High Street, is an American-run bakery and café well known for their great simple daytime food, especially breakfasts, and delicious homebakes (closed Sun & Mon). Vegetarians, especially, will enjoy **Ciaran's Café** (061 338787; www.ciarans.ie) on the University of Limerick campus at Castletroy; fresh juices, unusual vegetarian dishes and moreish desserts are on the menu and it has a following beyond the student community. Several smart new hotels have recently opened in the city (see below) and a promising newcomer due to open shortly after we go to press is **No. 1 Pery Square** (061 311182; www.privateireland.com); this fine owner-run townhouse forms part of the Tontine buildings on leafy Pery Square, and will offer 20 bedrooms (including 2 suites), garden, cocktail bar, brasserie dining and 'health & wellness' treatments. For good budget accommodation try the old reliable, **Jurys Inn** (061 207000; www.jurysdoyle.com), on Lower Mallow Street; this no-frills hotel is comfortable and gives a lot for a little - some rooms even have views across the Shannon.

WWW.IRELAND-GUIDE.COM FOR THE BEST PLACES TO EAT, DRINK

Limerick
HOTEL

Absolute Hotel

Sir Harry's Mall Limerick Co Limerick **Tel: 061 463 60**
info@absolutehotel.com www.absolutehotel.com

Located on the far side of the River Shannon where the Abbey River flows into it, this stylish new sister hotel to The House in Galway (see entry) enjoys a great site with a waterside bar and restaurant decked outdoor seating area and views of the hills - and a peaceful situation in what is still a city centre area. A roof garden is also promised although not completed when going to press. Like The House, Absolute is a pleasing combination of an old stone building and contemporary interiors giant blown-up photographs of Limerick in former times make the link, dominating the vast lobby and public areas on all floors. Accommodation is in Comfy (standard), Cosy (deluxe) and Chic (suites) plus three special business suites with boardroom accommodating meetings for up to 12; Comfy rooms are smaller, but there's no shortage of style at any level with standard features including good lighting (although a wall-mounted bed light would be useful), a giant wall-mounted flat screen where you may choose between music, television, pay film and internet; generous storage space; ironing facilities; black-out curtaining; safe; mini-bar and state of-the-art coffee and tea makers. And, for a surprisingly small premium, the larger Cosy rooms also offer free access to the sauna/wellbeing room in the spa as well as internet and movie deals. Fashion led bathrooms are spacious but, with frosted glass door compromising privacy, no bath (only a powe shower with rain dance shower head in all rooms) and a 'Belfast-sink' washbasin, they may not be to everyone's taste. Dining and socialising options are between the very spacious first floor Riverside Restaurant and bar, which overlook the river and leafy bank opposite, with a decking area for sitting out, and the Refuel Café. With its fine location and facilities, complimentary underground car parking and surprisingly reasonable room rates, Absolute represents real value for money for anyone visiting Limerick city. Conference & banqueting; business facilities; spa; same day laundry/dry cleaning **Rooms 102** (includes 3 business suites with boardroom & 12 Chic suites; all rooms shower only). B&E from €45pps. Open all year. All major credit cards. **Directions:** Limerick city centre, on the N7 jus north of the junction between the N7 & N20. ◇

Limerick
BAR/RESTAURANT

Aubars Bar & Restaurant

49-50 Thomas Street Limerick Co Limerick **Tel: 061 31779**
linda@aubars.com www.aubars.com

Padraic Frawley's modern city centre bar and restaurant is on the newly pedestrianised Thoma Street. What was once an old pub is now a dashing contemporary bar and restaurant; the layout i on several levels, with no hard divisions and a mixture of seating in various areas, which is attractive but can lead to confusion between customers coming in to eat rather than have a drink. While the style is uncompromisingly modern, chef Mike Ryan's values are quite traditional, based on soun cooking. Appealing, well-balanced menus change frequently and offer a number of different options for bar food (Aubars) and more structured meals in the casual value dining café/bar (The Grill @ Aubars); rib eye steak with béarnaise sauce, rocket salad & chunky chips is a sound speciality Vegetarians are well looked after, with appealing dishes marked clearly on menus and, all round, a visit here should be an enjoyable experience - and, good value too. **Seats 45** (outdoors, 24). Ope from 8 am; all day brunch menu. L 12-5.30 daily (Sun from 12.30). Set L €15 (12-3); D Mon-Su 5.30-9.30 (to 8.30pm Sun); early D €18.95, Mon-Sat, 5-7pm; A la carte L & D. House wines from €18.95. SC discretionary. Bar meals: 12-8.30 daily. Establishment closed 25 Dec & Good Fri Amex, MasterCard, Visa, Laser. * Live Cuban/Latin music Fri D. **Directions:** Off O'Connell Street second on the left, opposite Brown Thomas. ◇

Limerick
RESTAURANT

Brûlées Restaurant

Corner of Henry St & Mallow St Limerick Co Limerick **Tel: 061 319 931**
brulees@eircom.net

téite bia Donal and Teresa Cooper's restaurant is on a busy corner, with window tables catching a glimpse of the River Shannon and County Clare across the bridge. The interior is well-appointed, with little dining areas on several levels that break groups up nicely, and are elegantly furnished in a simple classic style that makes the most of limited space. For some years this has been the first choice in the city, for discerning local diners and visitors alike. A soothing ambience and nice details - real linen napkins, olives and freshly baked breads to nibble - make a good start, and Teresa's appealing menus show pride in using the best of ingredients, both local and imported; vegetarian dishes are invariably imaginative, also fish and seafood, which will always include daily specials - and which Donal describes to guests very accurately, with prices. Donal's hospitality and thoughtful, professional service are an important part of the experience here, and Teresa's colourful modern Irish cooking is as good as it sounds. Begin, perhaps, with a tian of Skellig crab with avocado carrot & pepper salad and horseradish mayonnaise and, from a balanced choice of main courses, maybe try a speciality dish of fillet steak with Shaws black pudding, champ, carmelised shallots and a choice of four sauces (Cashel Blue cheese, garlic butter, red wine or peppercorn). Side dishes are simple, there's a good cheese selection - and puddings always include, of course, a classic crème brûlée, served with a crunchy brandysnap. Cooking is accurate, presentation is attractive without being fussy and you'll get good value for the high quality of food served- lunch and early dinner menus offer especially good value. An interesting and informative wine list is fairly priced and includes some lovely wines by the glass, also well chosen half bottles. **Seats** 50. L Thu-Fri only, 12.30-2.30; D Mon-Sat, 5-10pm. Early Bird D €30 (5-6.30pm), also à la carte. House wine €20; SC discretionary (12.5% of food on groups of 6+). Closed Sun, Mon; 25 Dec-1 Jan. Amex, Diners, MasterCard, Visa, Laser. **Directions:** On the corner of Henry Street and Lower Mallow Street, near Jurys Inn roundabout.

Limerick
HOTEL

Castletroy Park Hotel

Dublin Road Limerick Co Limerick **Tel: 061 335 566**
sales@castletroy-park.ie www.castletroy-park.ie

téite bia Immaculately maintained gardens, a large and warmly furnished foyer and welcoming staff create a good first impression at this well known hotel near the university. Very popular with business guests and as a conference venue, it also has excellent leisure facilities (including a 1 km jogging track) and, offering a change of scene at the end of the day's business, The Merry Pedlar pub has more character than the usual hotel bar. Public areas are spacious, with plenty of pleasant seating area, and **McLaughlins Restaurant** offers international fine dining in a comfortable well-appointed room with a pleasant outlook. Bedrooms are thoughtfully furnished with the business guest in mind, and regularly re-furbished. Conferences/Banqueting (450/260); free broadband wi/fi; secretarial services; video conferencing. Leisure centre (pool, fitness room, jacuzzi, sauna, steam room); beauty salon Celia Larkin 'Beauty at Blue Door'. Children welcome (under 6s free in parents room, cot available without charge, baby sitting arranged). Conservatory. Garden. **Rooms 107** (7 suites, 5 junior suites, 5 senior suites, 11 executive, 2 shower only, 1 disabled). Lift. 24 hour room service. Turndown service. B&B from €97.50 pps, ss €72.50. No SC. Hotel closed 24-26 Dec. **McLaughlin's Restaurant seats** 90 (private room, 16). Air conditioning. L Mon-Sat, 12.30-2.30, Sun all day, 1.30-8pm; D Mon-Sat 6-10pm. Early D €35, 5.30-7; D also à la carte. Amex, Diners, MasterCard, Visa, Laser. **Directions:** Dublin road, directly opposite the University of Limerick.

Limerick
HOTEL

Clarion Hotel Limerick
Steamboat Quay Limerick Co Limerick **Tel: 061 444 10**
info@clarionhotellimerick.com www.clarionhotelsireland.cor

féile bia This dramatic cigar-shaped 17-store hotel right on the River Shannon water front in the centre of Limerick enjoys panorami views over the city and the Shannon region. Clear lined contemporary elegance is the them throughout and a semi-open plan arrangement c foyer, bars and dining spaces, takes full advantag of the location. Business facilities are excelle and bedrooms - which vary more than usual i hotels due to the unusual shape of the building are offered in several pleasingly simple, moder colour schemes. All rooms have striking maple furniture, air conditioning, and everything that make an hotel room the perfect retreat although, oddly, the lower level of windows is too high to allow yo to savour the view while sitting down; the top two floors offer suites and penthouses for long lets Residents have unlimited use of leisure facilities, and several decked balconies and terraces a different levels encourage guests to enjoy fine weather. Apart from the Malaysian/Thai all-day men offered in the hotel's Kudos Bar, all meals are served in the well-appointed Sinergie Restaurant, a ver attractive contemporary room with river views. Menus are lively and generally well-executed; at its bes a meal here can be a most enjoyable experience. Although this landmark building is easily located gaining access to the hotel can be tricky for those unfamiliar with the city's one-way system; a nearb car park is used by the hotel and it is advisable to get clear instructions before arrival. (There is moderate charge for parking.) Conference/banqueting (180/150). Secretarial services. Golf nearb Video-conferencing. Leisure centre; swimming pool. **Rooms 158.** (3 suites, 80 no smoking, disabled, 5 family rooms). Lift. Room service, limited hours. Children welcome (under 12 free parents' room; cot available without charge). B&B from about €65pps. **Sinergie Restaurant:** L Sur Fri,12.30-2.30; D daily, 7-9.45; (closed L Sat). Set Sun L about €25; Set D about €25; also à carte. **Kudos Bar** serves Asian food, 12-9 daily. Short breaks (inc golfing breaks) offered; details o application. Closed 24-26 Dec Amex, Diners, MasterCard, Visa, Laser. **Directions:** Take Dock Road ex off the Shannon Bridge Roundabout, then first right. ◈

Limerick
RESTAURANT

Copper & Spice
2 Cornmarket Row Limerick Co Limerick **Tel: 061 313 62**
brian@copperandspice.com www.copperandspice.co

Well situated near the restored Milk Market buildings, this attractively named restaurant is brig orange and would be hard to miss. You have to ring a bell to get in, so you are assured of immedia attention from agreeable staff. Indian background music creates atmosphere and the orange theme continued in stylish modern decor and on promptly presented menus, which offer an unusual comb nation of Indian and Thai cuisine; however, there is a stronger leaning towards authentic Indian foo than Thai, with a wide range of vegetarian dishes. This stylish restaurant offers a different experienc from other ethnic restaurants in the city, including home-made ethnic Asian desserts, and gives valu for money. A fairly priced wine list offers a balanced selection of world wines, and Asian beers. * sister restaurant just off the main Dublin-Limerick road is above **The Mill Bar** at Annacotty, in restored mill overlooking the Mulcair River (Tel: 061 338791). Children welcome; toilets wheelcha accessible. **Seats 75;** air conditioning; D daily, 5-10.30. (L Sun, Annacotty branch only, 12.30-4.30 Value D inc. drink €24.50 (5-7); house wine €19; sc 10% on groups 10+. Closed Mon (except Bar Hols), 24-25 Dec, 1 Jan, Good Fri. Amex, MasterCard, Visa, Laser. **Directions:** Near Milk Market buil ings.

Limerick
HOTEL

George Hote
O'Connell Sreet Limerick Co Limerick **Tel: 065 682 300**
reservations@lynchotels.com www.lynchotels.co

This new boutique hotel is right in the heart of Limerick's commercial and shopping centre, and make a very convenient meeting place. It is a warm and welcoming place in a relaxed modern style, and pleasant bar off the lobby has plenty of sofas and easy chairs as well as bar seating and makes a goc place to meet friends when shopping, or sit and read the papers between meetings. Stylish contem porary bedrooms have some nice touches including Egyptian cotton sheets, 26-inch flat screen T d tea & coffee facilities offering choice of teas and coffee. There are no leisure facilties on site but ests have concessional use of the nearby Quay Fitness leisure club, pool and gym at adjacent owley's Quay. The first floor restaurant is casual, looking on to the busy street below and has a realxed mosphere; while there are no surprises on the menu (bruschetta, chicken Ceasar, lamb shank are all pical), it offers very acceptable food and pleasant service. Meeting rooms. Free overnight parking in jacent Howley's Quay multi-storey car park (and favourable rates for business delgates). **Rooms 125.** asterCard, Visa, Laser. Room rate from €99. **Directions:** Town centre, on O'Connell Street. ◇

Hilton Limerick

imerick
OTEL
◑ R

Ennis Road Limerick Co Limerick **Tel: 061 421 800**
reservations.limerick@hilton.com

st across the Sarsfield bridge from the main commercial heart of Limerick, this blocky new seven- orey hotel takes full advantage of views from the upper floors with picture windows, balconies and rraces and has glass-fronted lifts which allow guests with key cards to enjoy the city sights and the stant views of the Galtee Mountains, and are blue-lit at night. Suites with balconies at the top of the tel are especially desirable, but accommodation throughout is pleasant and comfortable, and the nart bathrooms all have bath and shower. Although equally attractive for leisure breaks, the Hilton especially well equipped for business guests - an executive floor has a dedicated lounge, and all oms have laptop safe, high-speed internet access, plus cable and on-demand tv and individual air onditioning. There's a choice of 14 meeting rooms for groups of various sizes, and cutting edge onference technology. Leisure and off duty business guests will all appreciate the Living Well Health lub, which has a 20m pool, plus children's pool, sauna, steam room and Jacuzzi, also a gym and eauty therapy rooms for both men and women. Food is available at either the River Restaurant, or e Terrace Café and Bar, with a large heated terarace. Business centre (staffed). onference/banqueting 500/350 (audio-visual facility is included in the conference fee). **Rooms 165** . Presidential Suite, 18 suites). Room rate from €100. Restaurant: L Mon Fri 12.30 2.30, Sun1-3; Mon Thu 5.30 10, Fri & Sat 6- 11, Sun 9; closed L Sat. Bar open for snacks from 7am Mon-Fri nd 9am Sat & Sun; all-day menu 12 10pm daily. Parking (fee applies). All major credit cards ccepted. **Directions:** In the city centre on the north side of the River Shannon, on the Ennis Road ext to the river. ◇

Limerick Marriott Hotel

imerick
OTEL
◑ R

Henry Street Limerick Co Limerick **Tel: 061 448 700**
www.marriott.com

he new Limerick Marriott is not the largest hotel in the city but it is one of the most luxurious and cores highly where service is concerned. Although starkly modern from the street, the interior is entler with warm colours and a mixture of styles the tone is set in the entrance, where an elegant rass-railed staircase suggestive of old-fashioned hospitality rises from a mainly crisply contemporary bby, and friendly staff immediately do everything possible to make guests feel at home. Mainly aimed t the business guest, spacious warm-toned and very comfortably furnished rooms have high-speed ternet (free wi/fi is available throughout the hotel), a spacious work desk and chair, desk level power ockets, voice mail, safe and complimentary newspaper in addition to all the usual in-room facilities. ther features of the hotel are of equal interest to business and leisure guests, including terraced ardens with views of the city and the River Shannon; Savoy Aqua and fitness club, with swimming ool, Jacuzzi and spa treatments; and the very pleasant Savoy Bar on the ground floor, which reflects he site's previous life as a cinema. **The Savoy Restaurant** is open for breakfast, lunch and dinner and, ith well known chef Tony Schwartz (previously at the renowned Mustard Seed Restaurant at allingarry - see entry) directing the kitchen team, this will be a restaurant to watch. Light food is also vailable throughout the day in the Liszt Lounge. 10 conference, banqueting and private dining suites ccommodating up to 220 guests. Fully serviced business centre. Meeting rooms (10). Swimming ool; spa. Complimentary valet parking (complimentary overnight parking for residents). Pets allowed; ontact hotel for details. Garden. **Rooms 82** (includes 12 business suites). B&B from €80pps. asterCard, Visa, Laser. **Directions:** City centre, on Henry Street. ◇

Lynch South Court Hotel

imerick
OTEL
R

Raheen Roundabout Adare Road Limerick Co Limerick **Tel: 061 487 487**
southcourt@lynchotels.com www.lynchotels.com

eally located for Shannon Airport and the Raheen Industrial Estate, the South Court Hotel presents somewhat daunting exterior, but it caters especially well for business guests. In addition to excellent conference and meeting facilities, comfortable bedrooms are spacious and well equipped. Executi bedrooms have a separate work area providing a 'mini-office' - and 'lifestyle suites' have an in-roo gym, designed by Irish designer Paul Costelloe. Leisure facilities include the 'Polo Lifestyle Clul designed with international rugby player Keith Wood. Paul Costelloe was also involved in the design the stylish café bar, The Cream Room, which is a popular meeting place. Bar lunches are availab every day and the 100-seater Boru's Bistro offers dinner every evening. Conference/banqueti (1250/1000); business centre; video conferencing. Gym, sauna, solarium. Hairdressing. Sho Children welcome (under 2s free in parents' room, cot available without charge, baby sitting arranged No Pets. **Rooms 127** (1 suite, 15 junior suites, 55 executive, 14 no-smoking). Lift. 24-hour roo service. B&B about €80 pps, ss about €26. Amex, Diners, MasterCard, Visa, Laser. **Direction** Located on the main N20 Cork/Killarney road, 20 minutes from Shannon Airport. ◇

Limerick
HOTEL
R

Radisson SAS Hotel & Spa Limeric

Ennis Road Limerick Co Limerick **Tel: 061 456 2(**
sales.limerick@radissonsas.com www.limerick.radissonsas.co

Although just a short drive from the city centre, this hotel enjoys an almost rural settii and views of the Clare mountains. The original building dates back to the 1970s but w. completely revamped recently, and re-opened with an elegant new interior. Public areas, notably tl large open-plan foyer/lounge, have a great a great sense of space and style, with luxurious furnishin Accommodation is also notable for its spaciousness: all rooms are styled deluxe, with the comfort ar amenities that implies, but the spaciousness is the main attraction. A new 'Renaissance' spa h. recently opened in the hotel, with treatment rooms, gym, pool, and outdoor Canadian hot tub amoi the features. Fine conference and business facilities have ample free parking. Conference/banqueti (500/325); free broadband wi/fi, business centre, secretarial services, video conferencing. Destinatic Spa. Leisure centre (indoor swimming pool, steam room, sauna, fitness room). Tennis courts. Childre welcome (cots available; baby sitting arranged). Gardens. Parking. **Rooms 154** (2 suites, 4 juni suites, 14 executive, 4 family, 3 disabled). Lift. 24-hour room service. Turndown service. B&B €72.5 pps, ss €52.50. * Short breaks offered - details on application. **Porters Restaurant:** L 12.30-2.3 daily (from 1pm Sun), D daily, 5.45-9.30pm. Set L €20.50, early D €22.50 (5.45-7pm), set D fro €23.50, also à la carte. Bar food also available daily, 12-9.30pm. Amex, MasterCard, Visa, Lase Heli-pad. **Directions:** On N18, 5 km from Limerick city centre, 20 minutes from Shannon.

Limerick
CAFÉ
N R

The Sage Caf

67/68 Catherine Street Limerick Co Limerick **Tel: 061 409 45**
info@thesagecafe.com www.thesagecafe.co

On most days this centrally located café near the Milk Market has queues of people waiting to lunc on their healthy food, and it's easy to see why. From the green and white striped awning (which ha tables underneath on fine days) to the cool greeny-white of the interior, there is an air of clean, gree calm about the place. It's roomy and light, with some banquette seating around the walls, a fe contemporary oil paintings and wooden tables. They do lovely fresh-flavoured lunch dishes (an eclect collection, including samosas, aromatic Indian dishes and good steaks) and, through the afternoc when the savoury choices will have run out, there will be great home bakes, including scones, ice carrot cake, gooey chocolate cake, baked orange cheesecake, banana and walnut cake and almor cake, maybe served with a dollop of whipped cream and a giant strawberry and there are some glute free choices. Coffee, served in a mug, is good and strong. Children welcome (high chair); toile wheelchair accessible. Food served Mon-Sat, 9-5.30pm; L 12-4pm. Closed Sun, Bank Hol Christmas week. MasterCard, Visa, Laser. **Directions:** Centre of town.

R

ADAR

The chocolate-box village of Adare is not only an interesting and well-located destination in its ow right, but also an excellent place to break a long journey. Useful places to know about in the pret row of cottages along the main street include **The Inn Between** (061 396633), an informal resta rant belonging to **The Dunraven Arms** (see entry) across the road, is a good choice but only ope in summer. **Fitzgeralds Woodlands House Hotel** (Tel 061 605100; www.woodland-hotel.ie) is little way out of the village on the Limerick side; especially popular for weddings and large gath erings, they offer special breaks and have excellent leisure/health facilities including a wide rang of therapies and treatments.
WWW.IRELAND-GUIDE.COM FOR THE BEST PLACES TO EAT, DRINK & STAY

dare
OTEL/RESTAURANT

Adare Manor Hotel & Golf Resort

Adare Co Limerick **Tel: 061 396 566**
reservations@adaremanor.com www.adaremanor.com

The former home of the Earls of Dunraven, this magnificent neo-Gothic mansion is set in 900 acres on the banks of the River Maigue. Its splendid chandeliered drawing room and the glazed cloister of the dining room look over formal box-hedged gardens towards the Robert Trent Jones golf course. Other grand public areas include the Gallery, named after the Palace of Versailles, with its unique 15th century choir stalls and fine stained glass windows. Luxurious bedrooms (21 of them recently refurbished) have dividual hand-carved fireplaces, fine locally-made mahogany furniture, cut-glass table lamps and pressive marble bathrooms with powerful showers over huge bathtubs. Recent additions include a ubhouse in the grounds (complete with full conference facilities) and a "golf village" of two and four droom townhouses which provide a comfortable accommodation option for longer stays, large groups d families; similarly, "The Villas" deluxe serviced residences sleep up to eight guests. nference/banqueting (220/150). Leisure centre, swimming pool, spa treatments; beauty salon; hair-essing. Shop. Golf (18), equestrian; fishing; walking; cycling. Garden. Children welcome (cots ailable without charge, baby sitting arranged). No pets. **Rooms 63** (1 state room, 5 suites, 8 junior ites, 15 ground floor rooms); also townhouses, carriage house & villas (total 246). Lift. 24 hour room rvice. Room rate from about €296. No SC. Open all year. The beautifully appointed **Oak Room** estaurant provides a fine setting for Mark Donohue's modern classical cuisine, which is cooking sed on seasonal produce, including vegetables from the estate's own gardens. Local ingredients ature and Mark recently won the national Féile Bia Chef of the Year competition for his dish of stachio & Herb Wrapped Loin of Slaney Valley Irish Lamb, with Colcannon Mash, Buttered Baby getables, and Shallot & Rosemary. Imaginative vegetarian dishes such as spinach and blue cheese sagne with roast baby beetroot and sweet potato wedges are always offered on the main menu. An course Tasting Menu features favourites from the à la carte and includes some surprises too. A edictably high-end wine list includes some unusual wines (a Pomerol Pétrus 1970, at about 4,450, for example) but there's a sprinkling of affordable bottles, and quite a few by the glass and lf bottle. **Seats 60** D (6.30-9.30) daily; Set D €58.50; 8-course Tasting Menu about €70. House ne from €25; SC discretionary. *More informal bistro style dining is offered all day at the Carriage ouse Restaurant, daily, 7am -10 pm (to 9.30 off season). Open all year. Amex, Diners, MasterCard, sa, Laser. **Directions:** On N21 in Limerick.

---

dare
UESTHOUSE

Carrabawn Guesthouse

Killarney Road Adare Co Limerick **Tel: 061 396067**
carrabawnhouse@eircom.net www.carrabawnhouseadare.com

an area known for high standards, with prices to match, this immaculate owner-run establishment t in large mature gardens provides a moderately-priced alternative to the luxury accommodation arby. Bedrooms are very well maintained with all the amenities required and Bernard and Bridget han have been welcoming guests here since 1984 - many of them return on an annual basis because the high level of comfort and friendly service provided. A good Irish breakfast is served in a conser-tory dining room overlooking lovely gardens, and light evening meals can be provided by arrangement. ildren welcome (cot available without charge). No pets. **Rooms 8** (all shower only & no smoking, 2 mily rooms, 3 ground floor). Room service (limited hours). B&B €50pps, ss €20. Open all year except ristmas. MasterCard, Visa, Laser. **Directions:** On N21, 11km (8 m) south of Limerick.

Adare
HOTEL/RESTAURANT

Dunraven Arms Hote
Adare Co Limerick **Tel: 061 396 6**
reservations@dunravenhotel.com www.dunravenhotel.cc

Established in 1792, the Murp family's large hotel has someh retained the comfortable ambience of a coun inn. A very luxurious inn nevertheless, especia since the recent completion of 12 new jun suites: under the personal management of Bry and Louis Murphy, the furnishing standard superb throughout, with antiques, private dressi rooms and luxurious bathrooms, plus excelle amenities for private and business guests, complemented by an outstanding standard

housekeeping. It's a great base for sporting activities - equestrian holidays are a speciality and bo golf and fishing are available nearby - and also ideal for conferences and private functions, includi weddings (which are held beside the main hotel, with separate catering facilities). The hotel h earned an unrivalled reputation for the quality and value of short breaks offered, and there is ongoing determination to provide personal service and quality in all aspects of its operation whi makes Dunraven Arms an outstanding example of contemporary Irish hospitality at its best. *Dunrav Arms was the our Hotel of the Year in 2004. Conferences/Banqueting (180/250); free broadband w throughout hotel; business centre; secretarial services, laptop-sized safes in bedrooms. Equestria hunting, fishing, shooting, archery and golf nearby. Bike hire; walking. Leisure centre (swimming po steam room, fitness room), beauty salon, massage. Garden. No pets. Children welcome (cots availabl free of charge, baby sitting arranged). **Rooms 86** (6 suites, 24 junior suites, 56 executive, 30 grou floor, 2 family, all no smoking). Lift. 24-hour room service. Turndown service. B&B around €100p no ss. Room-only rate €195. SC12.5%. Open all year. Heli-pad. **Maigue Restaurant:** Named after River Maigue, which flows through the village of Adare, the restaurant is delightfully old fashione more akin to eating in a large country house than in an hotel. Joint head chefs, Colin Greensmith a Shane McGrath, continue the tradition of pride in using the best of local produce. Menus offer balanced selection of about half a dozen dishes on each course and, although particularly renown for their roast rib of beef (carved at your table from a magnificent trolley), other specialities like Ri Maigue salmon and local game in season, especially pheasant, are very popular. Menus are not ov long but may offer some dishes not found elsewhere - a main course of pan-fried calves liver on a b of colcannon with shallots and lardons of bacon, perhaps - and little home-made touches add an ex dimension - farmhouse cheeses are served with home-made biscuits as well as grapes and an ap and date dressing, for example. Service, under the direction of John Shovlin, who has been restaura manager since 1980, is exemplary - as elsewhere in the hotel. A wide-ranging wine list offers so treats for the connoisseur as well as plenty of more accessible wines. Restaurant not suitable for ch dren under 12 after 7pm. **Seats 70** (private room 40). Reservations required. D daily 7-9.30, L S only 12.30-1.30. Set Sun L €27.50, also à la carte; D à la carte. House wine €22, SC 12.5%. [* **Inn Between,** across the road in one of the traditional thatched cottages, is an informal brasserie st restaurant in common ownership with the Dunraven Arms; D Tue-Sat, 6.30-9.30 in summer. *Li bar food (soup and sandwiches) available daily, 12-7.] Amex, MasterCard, Visa, Laser. **Directions:** Fi building on right as you enter the village coming from Limerick (11 miles).

Adare
RESTAURANT

The Wild Geese Restaurar
Rose Cottage Main Street Adare Co Limerick **Tel: 061 3964**
wildgeese@indigo.ie www.thewildgeese

David Foley and Julie Randles' resta rant is in one of the prettiest cottages the prettiest village in Ireland - and, with cons tently good modern Irish cooking and car service, it's an irresistible package. David Foley a fine chef who sources ingredients with car seafood comes from west Cork, there are lo meats, poultry and game in season; everyth comes from a network of small suppliers built over the years. Menus offered include a short 'Value' menu (no time restriction), a semi à la ca which is considerably priced by course, and a separate vegetarian menu, on request. All the niceties of a special meal are observed - delicious home-baked bread (mustard seed, perhaps) is delivered with an amuse-bouche, such as a shot glass of asparagus soup. The cooking style is sophisticated - a luxurious main course example is pan-fried Castletownbere scallops on potato & chive pancakes, with champagne cream sauce, although a more homely rack of Adare lamb with traditional accompaniments such as potato & garlic gratin and rosemary jus is an enduring favourite. Like everything else in your meal, desserts (including ice creams) are freshly made on the premises. Friendly staff and a carefully selected, informative wine list add greatly to the dining experience. Not suitable for children after 7pm. **Seats 60** (private room, 30, outdoor, 10). D Mon-Sat 6.30-10, Sun 6-9 summer only. Earlybird D €30 Sun-Fri, 6-7.30pm; Set D €34/40 (2/3 course), also à la carte & vegetarian menu. House wines €22. Closed Mon (& Sun Oct-Apr). Closed 24 Dec-2 Jan. Amex, Diners, MasterCard, Visa, Laser. **Directions:** From Limerick, at top of Adare village, opposite Dunraven Arms Hotel.

Ballingarry
RESTAURANT/COUNTRY HOUSE

The Mustard Seed at Echo Lodge

Ballingarry Co Limerick **Tel: 069 68508**
mustard@indigo.ie www.mustardseed.ie

COUNTRY HOUSE OF THE YEAR

Dan Mullane's famous restaurant The Mustard Seed started life in Adare in 1985, then moved just ten minutes drive away to Echo Lodge, a spacious Victorian country residence set on seven acres of lovely gardens, with mature trees, shrubberies, kitchen garden and orchard - and very luxurious accommodation. Elegance, comfort and generosity are the hallmarks - seen through decor and furnishings which bear the mark of a seasoned traveller whose eye has found much to delight in while wandering the world. In addition to accommodation in the main house, the conversion of an old schoolhouse in the garden now provides three newer superior suites, a residents' lounge and a small leisure centre with sauna and massage room - this stylish development offers something quite different from the older rooms and is in great demand from regular guests who make Echo Lodge their base for golf and fishing holidays. Small conferences (20); banqueting (70). Children welcome (under 4s free in parents' room, cots available without charge, baby sitting arranged). Pets allowed by arrangement. Garden, walking. Sauna, massage room. **Rooms 16** (2 suites, 4 shower only, 2 family, 2 ground floor, 1 for disabled, all no smoking). Turndown service. B&B €90 pps, ss €30. Special winter breaks offered, depending on availability. Closed Christmas week, 2 wks Feb. **Restaurant:** Food and hospitality are at the heart of Echo Lodge and it is in ensuring a memorable dining experience, most of all, that Dan Mullane's great qualities as a host emerge (he was our Host of the Year in 2001). The evening begins with aperitifs in the Library, prettily served with a tasty amuse-bouche - and this attention to detail is confirmed in the beautiful dining room, where fresh flowers on each table are carefully selected to complement the decor. David Rice took over as head chef in 2007 and continues the house tradition of excellent modern Irish cooking, and the wonderful organic kitchen gardens supply him with much of the produce for the restaurant - do allow time to see them before dinner and, perhaps, hazard a guess as to what will be on the menu - while other ingredients are carefully sourced from organic farms and artisan food producers. Menus are wide-ranging and very seasonal - the components of a delicious salad will be dictated by the leaves and herbs in season. Plum tomatoes and asparagus, in mid-summer perhaps, accompanied by a Parmesan, basil and a balsamic reduction, and the soup course - typically of roast vegetable - is also likely to be influenced by garden produce. Main courses such as an unusual fillet of pork dish (rolled in soft herb and cooked in olive oil, then served with buttered Swiss chard, broad bean risotto, beetroot and cider jus) are based on the best local meats, seafood just up from the south-western fishing ports and seasonal game. Each dish has its own thoughtfully considered garnish and, with such an abundance of garden produce, vegetarians need have no fear of being overlooked - every course features an unusual vegetarian offering. Finish with Irish farmhouse cheeses at their peak of perfection, or gorgeous puddings, which are also likely to be inspired by garden produce. Finally, irresistible home-made petits fours are served with tea or coffee, at the table or in the Library. All absolutely delicious - and, with service that is professional and efficient, yet always relaxed and warm, the hospitality here is truly exceptional. After dinner, take a stroll through the lushly planted pleasure garden; there is even a special route - of just the right length - marked out for smokers. *(The Mustard Seed was selected for our Natural Food Award in 2005, presented in association with Euro-Toques.) An interesting wine list includes an unusually wide range of half bottles, a couple of magnums and a wine of the month. Not suitable for children. **Seats 70** (outdoors, 6). Reservations required; non residents welcome. D 7-9.30 (to 9pm Sun). Earlybird D €40 (Mon-Thurs,7-8); 4-course D, €60. House wine €26. Closed 24-26 Dec, 20 Jan - 9 Feb. Amex, MasterCard, Visa, Laser. **Directions:** From top of Adare village take first turn to left, follow signs to Ballingarry - 11km (8 miles); in village.

Glin
CASTLE

Glin Castle

Glin Co Limerick **Tel: 068 34173**
knight@iol.ie www.glincastle.com

Surrounded by formal gardens and parkland, Glin Castle stands proudly on the south bank of the Shannon; the FitzGeralds, hereditary Knights of Glin, have lived here for 700 years and it is now the home of the 29th Knight and his wife Madame Fitzgerald. The interior is stunning, with beautiful rooms enhanced by decorative plasterwork and magnificent collections of Irish furniture and paintings. But its most attractive feature is that everything is kept just the same as usual for guests, who are magnificently looked after by manager Bob Duff. Guest rooms and suites are decorated in style, with all the modern comforts, plus that indefinable atmosphere created by beautiful old things; accommodation was originally all in suites - huge and luxurious, but not at all intimidating because of the lived-in atmosphere that characterises the whole castle - but there are now "smaller, friendly, rooms with a family atmosphere". And there are many small thoughtfulnesses - the guests' information pack, for example, lists possible outings and itineraries under different interests (gardens, historical etc) and how much time you should allow. When the Knight is at home he will take visitors on a tour of the house and show them all his pictures, furniture and other treasures; interested guests will also relish the opportunity to enjoy the famous gardens, including the 2-acre walled kitchen garden which provide an abundance of seasonal produce for the castle kitchens. There is tennis on site, also an interesting shop - and make sure you fit in a visit to O'Shaughnessy's lovely old pub, just outside the castle walls (see entry). Head chef Seamus Hogan's menus change daily with the seasons, but a favourite dish is roast rack of lamb with puy lentils, wilted spinach & rosemary jus. *Glin Castle was our Country House of the Year in 2005. The garden and house are open to the public at certain times. Small conferences/private parties (20/30). Not suitable for children under 10 except babies (cot available without charge, baby sitting arranged). Pets permitted by arrangement in certain areas. Gardens, walking, tennis. **Rooms 15** (3 suites; all no-smoking). B&B €165pps. Dinner is available by reservation; an attractive menu with about four choices on each course is offered. Dining Room Seats 30. D 7-9.30, Set D €53. House wine from about €25; sc discretionary. Closed 30 Nov - 1 Mar. Amex, Diners, MasterCard, Visa, Laser. **Directions:** 50km (32 miles) west of Limerick on N69, 4 miles east Tarbert Car Ferry; drive up main street of Glin village, turn right at the top of the square.

Glin
CHARACTER PUB

O'Shaughnessy's

Glin Co Limerick
Tel: 068 34115

Not to be missed while in Glin is O'Shaughnessy's pub, just outside the castle walls; one of the finest pubs in Ireland, it is now in its sixth generation of family ownership and precious little has changed in the last hundred years. Open Thu-Tue: Thu & Fri, 10.30-2.30 7 5.30-10.30/11pm; Sat 10.30am-11pm, Sun, 12-3, Mon & Tu€10.30-2.30. Closed Wed. **Directions:** Up into village, take right turn; pub is on your left before the gates to Glin Castle. ◇

KILMALLOCK

In south County Limerick, near the border with County Cork, Kilmallock (Cill Mocheallóg in Irish) is a town of historic and sporting interest in the foothills of the Ballyhoura Mountains. **Deebert House Hotel** (063 31200; www.deeberthousehotel.com) is an early 19th century flour mill that has been under renovation and redevelopment as a 20-bedroom hotel for some time, and is partially open at the time of going to press. Walking holidays are a speciality in 'Ballyhoura country' and this will be a welcome new addition to the accommodation choices in the area.

WWW.IRELAND-GUIDE.COM FOR THE BEST PLACES TO EAT, DRINK & STAY

Kilmallock
FARMHOUSE

Flemingstown House

Kilmallock Co Limerick **Tel: 063 98093**
info@flemingstown.com www.flemingstown.com

Imelda Sheedy King's welcoming farmhouse is on the family's dairy farm just two miles from the medieval village of Kilmallock; well-signed at the entrance, it sits well back from the road up a long drive flanked by fields of grazing cattle, and leading to an immaculately maintained garden in front of the house. The original house dates back to the 18th century and has been sympathetically extended down through the years, to make a large and well-proportioned family home with pleasingly spacious, comfortably furnished reception rooms - and huge bedrooms, furnished with antique furniture and unfussy neutral decor that contrasts well with the dark furniture. En-suite facilities don't include baths, but have power showers - and, like the rest of the house, everything is well maintained and immaculate. Imelda is a great host, offering genuinely warm and welcoming hospitality - and she's also a great cook, as guests discover at a wonderful breakfast spread. The menu offers several choices of prepared fresh seasonal fruit (much of it home-grown, of course), a choice of cereals and, in addition to the "full Irish", you may choose from a range of other hot dishes including kippers, scrambled eggs with smoked salmon, pancakes with fruit, or a platter of cheese. Dinner is also available, by prior arrangement - there's a choice of two or three dishes on each course, including treats like chicken liver paté, Slaney Valley leg of lamb (carved at the table), and apple tart with crème anglaise. This is a lovely place to stay and, aside from the many things to do and see nearby, is well placed to break a journey to or from the south-west. Pets permitted by arrangement. Children over 2 years welcome (2-4 yrs free in parents' room). **Rooms 5** (all shower only & no smoking, 1 family room). B&B €60 pps. ss €10. D €40 (residents only). Packed L on request. Likely to be closed Nov-Mar. MasterCard, Visa. **Directions:** R512 to Kilmallock from Limerick; then towards Fermoy for 3.5km (2 m). House set back from road, on left.

COUNTY LONGFORD

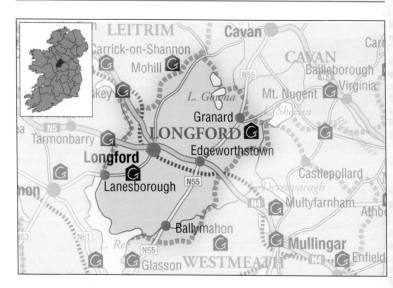

Longford is mostly either gently undulating farming country, or bogland. The higher ground in the north of the county up towards the intricate Lough Gowna rises to no more than 276m in an eminence which romantics might call Carn Clonhugh, but usually it's prosaically known as Corn Hill. The more entertainingly named Molly Hill to the east provides the best views of the lake in an area which arouses passionate patriotism. A few miles to the north is Ballinamuck, scene of the last battle in the Rising of 1798 in a part of Longford renowned for its rebellions against foreign rule.

To the southeast, there is even less pulling of the punches in the name of the little market town in its midst, for Granard - which sounds rather elegant - may be translated as "Ugly Height". Yet this suggests a pleasure in words for their own sake, which is appropriate, for Longford produced the novelist Maria Edgeworth from Edgeworthstown, a.k.a Mostrim, while along towards that fine place Ballymahon and the south of its territory on the Westmeath border, Longford takes in part of the Goldsmith country.

Goldsmith himself would be charmed to know that, six kilometres south of the road between Longford and Edgeworthstown, there's the tiny village of Ardagh, a place of just 75 citizens which is so immaculately maintained that it has been the winner of the Tidiest Village in the Tidy Towns awards. Another award-winner is Newtowncashel in the southwest of the county, atop a hill immediately eastward of Elfeet Bay on northern Lough Ree, where the scenery becomes more varied as County Longford has a lengthy shoreline along the Shannon's middle lake.

West of Longford town at Clondra, the attractive Richmond Harbour is where the Royal Canal - gradually being restored along its scenic route from Dublin - finally reconnnects with the Shannon during 2008, having been closed since 1954. And as for Longford town itself, they're working on it, with an urban regeneration landmark in the restoration of a watermill on the Camlin River, providing the power for the ornamental lamps along the riverside walkway.

Local Attractions & Information

Ardagh Heritage Centre	043 75 277
Ballinamuck 1798 Memorial & Visitor Centre (Community Enterprise Group)	043 24 848
Ballymahon Bog Lane Theatre	0902 32 273
Kenagh Corlea Trackway (Bog Road) Visitor Centre	043 22 386
Longford Backstage Theatre & Arts Centre	043 47 888
Longford Carrigglas Manor (Gandon stableyard, lace museum)	01 6318 402
Longford Tourism Information	043 41 124
Newtowncashel Heritage Centre	043 25 306

Toberphelim House

Granard
FARMHOUSE
R R

Granard Co Longford **Tel: 043 86568**
tober3@eircom.net www.toberphelimhouse.com

Dan and Mary Smyth's Georgian farmhouse is on a rise about half a mile off the road, with lovely views of the surrounding countryside. Very much a working farm, it is an hospitable, easy-going place. There's a guests' sitting room and three bedrooms: two en-suite (shower) with a single and double bed in each and one twin room with a separate private bathroom, all are comfortably furnished and well-maintained. Always improving, the Smyths gave the house a facelift for their 25th wedding anniversary a year or two ago - solid mahogany interior doors, re-tiling the bath and shower-rooms, re-painting the hall, stairs and landing - and an ongoing programme of maintenance continues. Families are welcome and light meals and snacks can usually be arranged. Children welcome. Garden, walking. No pets. **Rooms 3** (2 en-suite shower only, 1 private bathroom, all no smoking). B&B €45 pps, ss €5. Minimum stay 2 nights; prior booking advisable. Closed 20 Sep-1 May. MasterCard, Visa. **Directions:** Take the N55 at the Cavan end of Granard, turn off at the Lir petrol station taking a right at the next junction. The house is situated about 1 km towards Abbeylara, to the left.

Aubergine Gallery Café

Longford
RESTAURANT
R R

1st Floor The White House 17 Ballymahon Street Longford Co Longford
Tel: 043 48633

Brother and sister Stephen and Linda Devlins' popular restaurant, above The White House pub on the main street, is up steep stairs in a smart, light-filled room. It has a lovely curved bar as the focal point as you arrive, with informal seating that allows extra space at lunchtime and is transformed into a reception area in the evening. Lightwood tables and a variety of coloured banquettes and comfortable chairs, together with some interesting artwork, create a vibrant, youthful atmosphere. Stephen Devlin is an accomplished chef and his menus are Irish/Mediterranean with delicious, fresh-flavoured dishes, placing an emphasis on vegetarian dishes. The cooking here is invariably creative, and seafood is well represented too - and some things never change, so a good steak is de rigeur in these parts, as well as delicious poultry. Friendly staff, a warm relaxed atmosphere, stylish cooking and good value explain the success of this popular restaurant. **Seats 45** (+ 20 in lounge area). L Tue-Thu, 12-5, Fri-Sat, 12-4 (Sun open 2-8); D Wed & Thu, 6-8; Fri & Sat, 6-9.30. Set D €32, also à la carte. House wine €16.50. No reservations. Closed all Mon & Tue D, last week May, Dec 24-Jan 2. MasterCard, Visa, Laser. **Directions:** On main street (left as you're heading west), over the old White House pub (entrance on right of ground floor shop). ◇

Viewmount House

Longford
RESTAURANT/COUNTRY HOUSE
R R

Dublin Road Longford Co Longford **Tel: 043 41919**
info@viewmounthouse.com www.viewmounthouse.com

James and Beryl Kearney's lovely 1750s Georgian house just on the edge of Longford town was once owned by Lord Longford, and is set in four acres of beautiful wooded gardens, which are of great interest and designed as a series of rooms. It really is a delightful house and has been sensitively restored with style, combining elements of grandeur with a human scale that makes guests feel very comfortable. Its warmth strikes the first-time visitor immediately on arrival in the hall, which has a welcoming open fire and a graceful white-painted staircase seen against warm red walls. An elegant period drawing room and the six guest bedrooms in the main house all have their particular charm (one is especially large, but all are delightful); but perhaps the handsomest room of all is the unusual vaulted dining room, where an extensive breakfast menu is served. This is a most appealing house, with old wooden floors, rugs, antique furniture - and, most importantly, a great sense of hospitality; and it has grown a lot of late, as the Kearneys have joined the house to restored outbuildings alongside, providing some fine new bedrooms, and a new restaurant which has been created in one of the classic stone outbuildings. The restaurant - opening shortly after the guide goes to press - is a fine room of character, overlooking a Japanese garden with water features. Golf nearby. Children welcome (under 4 free in parents' room). Gardens. No pets. **Rooms 6** (1 suite, 3 bath & shower, 3 shower only, all no smoking). B&B €55, ss €10. *Self-catering also available - details on application. Amex, MasterCard, Visa. **Directions:** From Longford R393 to Ardagh. 11km (7 m), up sliproad to right following signs. Entrance 200m on right.

COUNTY LOUTH

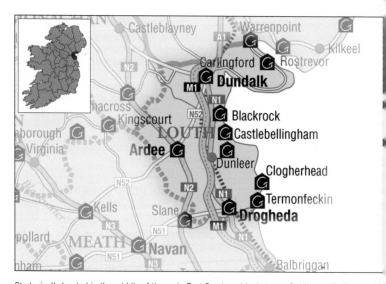

Strategically located in the middle of the main East Coast corridor between Dublin and Belfast, Louth is enthusiastic about the opportunities provided by the opening of the M1 motorway whjch now runs smoothly west of Dundalk. To the south, it crosses to Meath over the River Boyne near Drogheda on a handsome modern structure which is the largest cable-stayed bridge of its type in Ireland, a much admired and award-winning structure designed by Joe O'Donovan. With traffic pressure removed from its other roads, Louth begins to find itself. Though it may be Ireland's smallest county at only 317 square miles (it's just an eighth the size of Cork, the largest), Louth still manages to be two or even three counties in one.

Much of it is fine farmland, and this is celebrated with an annual Cooley Vintage Festival with a tractor world rally which in early August 2007 assembled at least 2,212 vintage tractors from 22 countries – in 2008 they'll be aiming for 2,500. The farmland is at its most productive in the area west of the extensive wildfowl paradise of Dundalk Bay, on whose shores we find the attractive village of Blackrock, one of Ireland's better kept secrets. But as well there are the distinctive uplands in the southwest, whose name of Oriel recalls an ancient princedom which is also remembered in Port Oriel, the busy fishing port at Clogherhead.

In the north of the county, the Cooley Mountains sweep upwards in a style which well matches their better-known neighbours, the Mountains of Mourne, on the other side of the handsome inlet of Carlingford Lough. Its name might suggest that this is a genuine fjord, but it isn't. However, its beauty is such that there's more than enough to be going along with, and on its Louth shore the ancient little port of Carlingford town used to be a best-kept secret. It was a quiet little place imbued with history, but today it is happily prospering both as a recreational harbour for the Dundalk and Newry area, and as a bustling visitor attraction in its own right.

The county's three main townships of Ardee, Dundalk and Drogheda each have their own distinctive style, and all three have been finding fresh vitality in recent years. The historic borough of Drogheda is the main commercial port with its harbour authority adding a new facility across the county border at Bremore in Meath. Drogheda's river valley is crossed by the Boyne Railway Viaduct of 1855 vintage, a remarkable piece of engineering work that it is reckoned one of the seven wonders of Ireland. Dundalk is the county town, and home to the Louth Museum, where a recent acquisition is the riding jacket worn by William of Orange at the Battle of the Boyne in 1690.

Local Attractions & Information

Ardee (Tallanstown) Knockabbey Castle & Gardens	01 6778816
Carlingford Carlingford Adventure Centre	042 9373100
Carlingford Carlingford Sea School	042 9373879

Carlingford Heritage Trust	042 9373888 / 9373454
Carlingford Tourism Information	042 9373033
Castlebellingham Farm Market	0404 43885
Drogheda Beaulieu House and garden	041 9838557
Drogheda Droichead Arts Centre	041 9833946
Drogheda Millmount Museum	041 9833097
Drogheda Highlanes Art Gallery	041 9803311
Drogheda (Tullyallen) Old Mellifont Abbey	041 9826459
Drogheda Tourism Information	041 9837070
Dundalk Louth County Museum	042 9327056
Dundalk Tourism Information	042 9335484
Termonfeckin Irish Countrywomens Assoc. College	041 9822119

Ardee
RESTAURANT
R R

Fuchsia House & The Gables Bar

Dundalk Road Ardee Co Louth **Tel: 041 685 8432**
fuchsiahouse@o2.ie

This attractive restaurant and bar is well set back from the road on the northern edge of Ardee; proprietor chef Sarajit Chanda and his partner Sarah Nic Lochlainn took over here in 2006 after working in well known Dublin restaurants, and transformed the premises to create a smart, uncluttered modern restaurant. Although the greatest strength is authentic Indian cooking, it offers an unusual combination of international, European and Asian cuisine, including Thai and Chinese. You'll find tasty renditions of many popular international dishes - stuffed mushrooms, spicy chicken wings, Caesar salad, burgers various ways and pasta dishes also one or two classic fish dishes, and good steaks. Familiar Indian dishes are offered - curries, tandoori dishes, and excellent vegetarian dishes, all freshly made - and some more unusual ones too, such as lamb in mango sauce (slow-stewed lamb in a fruity, spicy sauce) and palak paneer, a vegetarian dish of spinach with aromatic spices and home-made Indian cottage cheese. Skilful cooking (with authentic spicing), warm hospitality and good value have earned this restaurant a well deserved following. The wine list includes Cobra, among a range of beers. Plenty of parking; fully wheelchair accessible; children welcome (high chair, childrens menu, baby changing facilities). Special dietary needs catered for; full bar; take away available. **Seats 42** (outdoors, 12); L & D, Tue - Sat, 12-2.45 & 6-10.30pm, Sun& Bank Hol Mon, 12-9pm. Mid-week value D, Tue-Thu, 6-close, €24 (inc 1/2bottle of wine). quick L menu €10.50, also a la carte L & D; traditional Sun L €10.50; house wine from €17.50. Closed Mon (apart from Bank Hols), 25-26 Dec. MasterCard, Visa, Laser. **Directions:** On the northern edge of Ardee, on the right heading towards Dundalk. 5 minutes from M1.

Ardee
RESTAURANT
R R

Rolf's Bistro

52 Market Street Ardee Co Louth **Tel: 041 685 7949**
rolfsbistro@eircom.net   www.rolfsbistro.com

Paul and Bernadette Svender's attractive restaurant in the centre of Ardee is a favourite in the town for its pleasing informality, relaxed atmosphere and a refreshing determination to provide quality food and attentive service at affordable prices. The menu, which changes daily, is well-balanced and well-judged. Paul is the chef and his speciality dishes reflect his Swedish background - Scandinavian prawn toast with Swedish caviar, gravad lax and Swedish beef Lindstrom - but he uses local produce a lot and there really is something for everyone here, including seafood, vegetarian dishes, pasta and old favourites like fillet steak. Deft cooking, professional service, a relaxed ambience and fair prices add up to a successful formula and there's an emphasis on comfort - the reception area has squashy sofas, and there's a smoking terrace at the back too. An early dinner menu is particularly good value. **Seats 36.** Toilets wheelchair accessible. Children welcome, but not after 9pm. D Mon-Sat, 5.30-10 (Sat 6-10). Early D about €22 (5.30-7). House wine from about €18. SC discretionary. Closed: Sun; 24-26 Dec. MasterCard, Visa, Laser. **Directions:** Centre of Ardee, opposite SuperValu & Wogan Interiors. Beside Hatch Castle.

Blackrock
RESTAURANT/PUB
R

The Brake

Main Street Blackrock Co Louth
Tel: 042 932 1393

There is little about the neat but plain exterior to prepare first-time visitors for the warmth and country charm of The Brake - all old pine and rural bric-à-brac, it has open fires and friendly staff. It's a great place to stop just for a late afternoon cup of tea but, even better if you're hungry, it has a well-deserved reputation for good bar meals, and not just the usual pub staples, but a very wide choice including proper home-made chicken kiev, and all kinds of seafood especially Dundalk Bay prawns. There are plenty of meat dishes, too, especially steaks, and accompaniments are particularly good, all arranged buffet style, all for a moderate price. Beware of the unusual opening hours though this is a late after-noon into evening place. Not suitable for children under 12. **Seats 120.** Air conditioning. Toilets wheelchair accessible. Bar open 5-11.30. D daily 6-10 (Sun 6-9.30). A la carte; house wine €18; sc discretionary. *The Clermont Arms, a few doors along the front, is in the same family ownership. Closed 25 Dec, Good Fri. MasterCard, Visa, Laser. **Directions:** Turn off the main Dublin-Belfast road 5km (3 m) south of Dundalk.

CARLINGFORD

This delightful medieval village is set amongst spectacular scenery with views across Carlingford Lough to the Mountains of Mourne in County Down. It is a small place and, although off the beaten track, is gradually being 'discovered' so it is best to avoid busy times like festivals, if you want to see it at its best. In the village, the 59-room **Four Seasons Hotel** (042 93 73530; www.4seasonshotel.ie) has good leisure and business facilities, including a leisure centre and function room; it is unconnected with the international brand. The village is very compact and visitors looking around can easily compare the prices, menus and style of the various restaurants and bars: **O'Hares** (042 937 3106) in the centre of the village is a renowned tradition pub/grocery shop and, although it has expanded in recent years (and serves a lot more food than the speciality Carlingford oysters and brown bread of old), the old back bar and open fire remain intact. Around the corner, opposite the pleasantly old-fashioned **McKevitt's Village Hotel** (042 937 3116; www.mckevittshotel.com), **The Oystercatcher Lodge & Bistro** (042 937 3989; www.theoystercatcher.com) offers spacious, clean-lined accommodation; the bistro is run separately and offers a mid-range menu with daily specials emphasising local seafood, notably oysters. Around the corner at the heritage centre the small restaurant **Kingfisher Bistro** (042 937 3716) has a loyal local following; nearby **Food For Thought** (042 938 3838) is a very nice little deli with a few tables perfect for a quick bite or collecting food for a picnic. Back down on Newry Street, **The Baytree Restaurant** (042 938 3848) took over the premises previously occupied by Capitano Correlli just after Guide's 2007 visit and is earning a following - and they have a B&B next door. It might also be of interest to know that the bar and restaurant at **Carlingford Marina** (042 937 3073; www.carlingfordmarina.ie) are open to the public. A little way outside Carlingford - signed off the Dundalk road - **Lilly Finnegans** (042 937 3730) is a pretty, traditional pub (open evenings only). **WWW.IRELAND-GUIDE.COM FOR THE BEST PLACES TO EAT, DRINK & STAY**

Carlingford
GUESTHOUSE

Beaufort House

Ghan Road Carlingford Co Louth **Tel: 042 937 3879**
michaelcaine@beauforthouse.net www.beauforthouse.net

Michael and Glynnis Caine's immaculate property is well-placed to maximise on the attractions of a quiet and beautiful waterside position with wonderful sea and mountain views, while also being just a few minutes walk from Carlingford village. All areas are spacious and furnished to high specifications: hotel standard bedrooms have phone, TV with video channel and tea/coffee making facilities. The Caines were previously restaurateurs, and dinner is available by arrangement for parties of eight or more. (Set D about €40). Associated activities include a sailing school and yacht charter - corporate sailing events (team building and corporate hospitality), including match racing on Carlingford Lough, are a speciality. Golfing can be arranged at any of the five golf courses within 20 minutes' drive. Ample car parking. Small conference/banqueting (20). Children welcome (under 2s free in parents' room). Fishing, cycling, hill walking, bird watching, walking, garden. No pets. **Rooms 5** (2 shower only, 2 family rooms, 1 ground floor, all no smoking). B&B €50 pps, ss €25. D by arrangement only. Closed 25 Dec. MasterCard, Visa, Laser. **Directions:** Approaching from Dundalk, turn right just before the village and harbour; house on shore.

Carlingford
CAFÉ

Georgina's Bakehouse Tearooms

Castle Hill Carlingford Co Louth **Tel: 042 937 3346**
georginastearooms@eircom.net

Georgina Finegan's little daytime restaurant high up in the web of small roads above King John's Castle is well worth seeking out. The bakery has been going for over twenty years now, specialising in meringues and desserts and, since opening the tea rooms in 1997, Georgina has built up a loyal customer base, from far and near. A conservatory and other extra seating has brought some additional space, but the original café is really quite small; but it's cosy and seems just right for simple whole-some fare like soup of the day with a traditional sandwich or ploughman's cheese platter, made with home-made bread. Then there are toasted sandwiches - pastrami and gouda, perhaps, with sweet beet-root - and contemporary snacks like tortilla wraps, with smoked salmon & cream cheese, for example. But many people just drop in for a wedge of old-fashioned lemon meringue pie, or Austrian apple pie, or maybe a slice of carrot cake and a cup of tea - after all, that's where it all started. **Seats 34.** Children welcome. Open daily, 10-5.45 (to 6 Sun). Closed 1 week Sep, Christmas, 1 week Jan. **No Credit Cards. Directions:** Opposite King John's Castle.

Carlingford   # Ghan House
RESTAURANT/COUNTRY HOUSE   Carlingford Co Louth **Tel: 042 937 3682**
ghanhouse@eircom.net   www.ghanhouse.com

Conveniently located just an hour from Dublin or Belfast airports, the Carroll family's 18th century house is attractively situated in its own walled grounds on the edge of Carlingford village, with views across the lough to the Mountains of Mourne. A proper little bar offers a relaxing space where guests can mingle - in a more convivial atmos-phere, perhaps, than beside the drawing room fire, although that too has its moments; it's very pleasant for residents to return to, and especially welcoming for non-residents just coming in for dinner. Accommodation is in four rooms of character in the main house, each with sea or mountain views, and eight newer bedrooms in a separate building, which have been finished to a fairly high stan-dard. And there's even more to it than comfortable accommodation and the delicious meals you will enjoy for dinner or breakfast, as the Carrolls also run a cookery school on the premises. Conference/banqueting (55/85); house available for exclusive use. Garden; walking. Children welcome (under 5s free in parents' room; cots available without charge; baby sitting arranged). No pets. **Rooms 12** (1 shower only, 3 superior, 2 family). B&B Double Room €95 pps, single €75. (Discounts applied on stays of 2 or more nights.) Open all year except Christmas & New Year. **Restaurant:** Dinner is, of course, a high priority at Ghan House. The style is contemporary, based mainly on quality home-grown (vegetable, fruit and herbs), home-made (breads, ice creams, everything that can be made on the premises) and local produce, notably Cooley lamb and beef, dry cured bacon, free range eggs - and seafood: oysters are synonymous with Carlingford (there are also mussels from the lough and lobster from Ballagan, while smoked salmon and crab come from nearby Annagassan). A user-friendly set dinner menu with about five choices on each course is also priced by course, allowing considerable flexibility without having a separate à la carte, and there's a fairly priced wine list. Non-residents are welcome by reservation. **Seats 55** (private room 55). D only, "most days" 7-9.30; Set D €42.50; L Sun only 12.30-3.30, €49.50 (5 course). House wine €18.50; sc discretionary. Children welcome. House closed 24-26 Dec and 31 Dec & 1 Jan. Amex, MasterCard, Visa, Laser. **Directions:** 15 minutes from main Dublin - Belfast Road N1.10 metres after 30 mph sign on left hand side after entering Carlingford from Dundalk direction.

Carlingford   # Magees Bistro
RESTAURANT   Tholsel Street Carlingford Co Louth **Tel: 042 937 3751**
info@mageesbistro.com   www.mageesbistro.com

Right in the heart of Carlingford village, just across the road from O'Hare's pub, this lively restaurant is a first choice for many coming to Carlingford. Its ancient walls with castle windows are a part of the old Heritage town, and the interior is divided into two informal sections with plain wooden tables and chairs, with candlelight adding to the atmosphere. Most tables have views looking into the busy kitchen, and there's a small bar where you can wait for your table if it is not ready. A varied bistro menu includes some unusual choices - half a dozen escargots, for example, and seafood gratin & frogs legs alongside popular dishes like cajun chicken Caesar. Beef and lamb comes from local farms in the Cooley peninsula, and main courses include favourites like a 10oz sirloin steak, chicken supreme and surf & turf, also a lot of local seafood including fresh lobster (good value at around €35), a grilled seafood platter, salmon & cod parcel and various fresh fish of the day specials like John Dory, turbot, monkfish and halibut, all served with baby potatoes and al dente vegetables. Classic desserts to finish - sticky toffee pudding, crème brulée and a delicious vanilla & vodka panna-cotta with marinated balsamic berries are all typical. Well priced wine list, also some draught beers.

With a good atmosphere, good simple cooking and good value it's not hard to see why his restaurant is so popular. Opening hours: L Tue-Fri, 10-3.30pm (from 1pm on Sun), D Tue-Sun 7-9. Closed Sat L and Mon. **Directions:** On the paved street of Tholsel, near the gate tower. ◊

Castlebellingham
BAR/RESTAURANT
🌐 ⓔ ⓝ Ⓡ

McBrides Bar & Restaurant

Main Street Castlebellingham Co Louth
Tel: 042 937 2271

The glossy black exterior of Jim and Barbara Duffy's double-fronted bar and off-licence makes a smart impact on Castlebellingham's busy main street. Inside this historic pub (first opened in 1908) lies a modern, comfortable interior that incorporates plenty of old world character and charm. Locals sip pints at the bar while folks from further afield detour for the excellent lunchtime fare. A genuine gastro-pub with lofty aspirations, the lunch menu might offer specialities like steak and Guinness casserole or a shellfish risotto crammed with fresh Dublin Bay prawns alongside lighter offerings like toasties, salads and soup. Ingredients are well sourced and the cooking is accurate and impressive, suggesting the upstairs restaurant, open in the evenings, has similar appeal. A very welcome addition to the area's dining scene. MasterCard, Visa, Laser. **Directions:** On Main Street in centre of village. ◊

Clogherhead
RESTAURANT
Ⓡ

Little Strand Restaurant

Strand Street Clogherhead Co Louth **Tel: 041 988 1061**
food@littlestrand.com www.littlestrand.com

Catherine Whelahan's popular restaurant is in a neat modern building, on the right hand side as you go through the village of Clogherhead to the beach, set back a little from the road, with steps up to the front door. The fairly large ground floor restaurant is more formally appointed than might be expected for the location and, upstairs, there's an impressive lounge area, used for aperitifs and coffee at busy times. You don't have to be a fish-lover to enjoy a meal here - menus offer a range of meat, vegetarian dishes and local local seafood, brought in to the nearby fishing harbour of Port Oriel, is of course the speciality and very good it is too. House specialities include crab claws in garlic/lemon butter, lobster thermidor and sole on the bone with lemon, lime and dill butter; an exceptional dish is Clogherhead scampi, cooked and served the traditional way with sauce tartare. **Seats 60** (Private room 12-16). Air conditioning. D Wed-Sun (high season) and Bank Holidays, 6pm-"late"; Sun 3-8/8.30pm (depends on demand); à la carte; special value menus offered; house wine about €18, sc discretionary. Closed Mon, Tue (& Wed/Thurs off-season). MasterCard, Visa. **Directions:** 7 miles from Drogheda, 3 miles from Termonfeckin village.

Collon
RESTAURANT WITH ROOMS
🌐 ⓔ Ⓡ Ⓡ

Forge Gallery Restaurant

Church Street Collon Co Louth **Tel: 041 982 6272**
info@forgegallery.ie www.forgegallery.ie

This charming restaurant has been providing good food, hospitality and service for over twenty years now. The building is full of character, and has been furnished and decorated with flair which together with the art exhibitions which are always an interesting feature - makes a fine setting for food that combines country French and New Irish styles. Menus are a little flowery in places (the speciality of the house is Forge Rendezvous of Clogherhead prawns & scallops) but seasonal produce stars, much of it local, especially seafood, but also game in season, vegetables and fruit, and head chef Alan Clarke's cooking is creative and accomplished. This not an inexpensive restaurant (starters on the à la carte rise to €30 for a 'symphony of prawns, claws and smoked salmon rouille', main courses to €40) but there is a shorter, more moderately priced daily menu which is also priced by the course, and Sunday lunch offers very good value. Seafood leaps from the menu but there's plenty else to choose from including great steaks and delicious roast

Aylsebury duckling. A short vegetarian menu is also offered, and there may be a difficult choice between tempting desserts and Irish cheeses. Sound cooking with a contemporary flair, excellent service and an unusual ambience make for enjoyable dining. An interesting wine list includes a wide choice of half bottles. Not suitable for children after 6pm. Private parking (9). **Seats 60.** Air conditioning. Bar. L Sun only, 12.30-4pm. D Tue-Sun, 7-9.30 (Sun 6-8). D à la carte. Set Sun L €30. House wine from €24; sc discretionary (except 10% on parties of 6+). Closed Mon; 24-25 Dec & 2nd week Jan. Amex, Diners, MasterCard, Visa, Laser. **Directions:** On N2, 56km (35 m) from Dublin due north, midway between Slane and Ardee, in centre of village.

Drogheda — # Boyne Valley Hotel & Country Club

HOTEL — Drogheda Co Louth **Tel: 041 983 7737**

R

reservations@boyne-valley-hotel.ie   www.boyne-valley-hotel.ie

Set in large gardens just on the Dublin side of Drogheda town - and handy to the motorway - this substantial hotel has an 18th century mansion at its heart. Graciously proportioned rooms contrast well with later additions, including 34 new rooms added several years ago. Owner-run by Michael and Rosemary McNamara since 1992, it has the personal touch unique to hands-on personal management and is popular with locals, for business and pleasure, as well as making a good base for visitors touring the area. While rooms in the old building have more character, the new ones are finished to the high standard demanded by today's travellers. Fine conference facilities and an excellent leisure centre add greatly to the hotel's attraction. Conference/banqueting (450/450); secretarial services. Leisure centre, indoor swimming pool; beauty salon. All weather tennis; pitch & putt. Garden. Pets allowed by arrangement. **Rooms 72** (1 suite, 13 shower only, 35 no-smoking, 1 disabled). B&B from about €85 pps. Open all year. Amex, Diners, MasterCard, Visa, Laser. **Directions:** On southern edge of Drogheda town. From Dublin turn off M1 to N1 at Julianstown; from Belfast turn off M1 to N1 at Drogheda north. ◇

Drogheda — # D Hotel

HOTEL/RESTAURANT — Scotch Hall Drogheda Co Louth **Tel: 041 987 7700**

R

reservedthed@monogramhotels.ie   www.thed.ie

This cool new hotel is part of an impressive waterfront development in Drogheda, about 30 minutes from Dublin Airport, and is now setting the benchmark for high standards of rejuvenation in the centre of Drogheda. The hotel's contemporary lines contrast pleasingly with the old town, and the interior is bright, clean-lined, spacious and easy on the eye; it has a friendly atmosphere and helpful staff. A huge foyer with some very modern seating divides into the reception/lounge area, and a smart bar and restaurant overlooking the river. Comfortable bedrooms, many with superb views over the river and Drogheda's town centre, all have comfortable chairs and standard amenities. With seven meeting and event suites this is an ideal place to host business meetings, or for private gatherings, and a new function room (300) is planned for 2008. The **'d restaurant'** is well located to take advantage of the river views and, although not matching the ambitious style of the hotel as a whole, the food is good and a meal here should be enjoyable. Conferences Banqueting (100); free broadband wi/fi, business centre, secretarial services. Fully wheelchair accessible. Children welcome (under 12s free in parents room, cots available free of charge, baby sitting arranged); pets permitted in some areas. **Rooms 104** (2 superior, 6 for disabled), 24hr room service; lift; complimentary guest parking. B&B €110. Open all year except Christmas. Amex, MasterCard, Visa, Laser. **Directions:** The entrance to the hotel is c. 300 metres on the left adjacent to the Scotch Hall Shopping Complex.

DUNDALK

The county town of Louth (Ireland's smallest county), Dundalk is in an area rich with historical folk-lore, and is convenient to the Cooley Peninsula and the charming medieval town of Carlingford on the southern shore of Carlingford Lough. Local activities are plentiful and include greyhound and horse racing, swimming, soccer, ice-hockey, walking, salmon & trout fishing, horse riding and golf. Architecturally, Dundalk town was until recently dominated by a massive seven-storey windmill, which begs restoration; however the opening of the new 14-storey **Crowne Plaza Hotel** (042 9335453; www.cpdundalk.ie) just as we go to press has changed all that: with 129 rooms and top floor **Fahrenheit Grill** with views over the Cooley Mountains and Irish Sea, it can be seen from miles around. Good reasonably priced accommodation nearer the ground is available at **Park Inn Dundalk** (042 939 9700; www.dundalkparkinn.ie), which is just north of the town on the Armagh road and also has leisure and conference facilities. In the town centre, the familiar old **Imperial Hotel** (042 933 2241) has undergone extensive renovations and, with secure free parking and a location adjacent to the new shopping centre, The Marshes, it is a convenient place to meet. And also in the town, on the Dublin

road, a colourful garden ablaze with masses of home-raised flowers will lead you to the Meehan family's spick and span B&B, **Rosemount** (042 933 5878).
WWW.IRELAND-GUIDE.COM FOR THE BEST PLACES TO EAT, DRINK & STAY

Dundalk   Ballymascanlon House Hotel
HOTEL
R
Dundalk Co Louth **Tel: 042 935 8200**
info@ballymascanlon.com www.ballymascanlon.com

féile bia Set in 130 acres of parkland, this hotel just north of Dundalk has developed around a large Victorian house. It has been in the Quinn family ownership since 1948 and major improvements have been completed with panache, lifting the hotel into a different class; bright and stylish public areas are furnished and decorated in a warm, comfortably contemporary style, with a homely atmosphere. Spacious and very attractive new bedrooms share the same qualities, with specially commissioned furniture - and, in many cases, views over lovely gardens, the golf course or the attractive old stable yard. A good breakfast is served in the hotel restaurant, which is comfortable but lacks the style of other public areas. Corporate facilities include three versatile meeting rooms, with back up business services available. Impressive leisure facilities include a 20-metre deck level pool and tennis courts. Special interest and off-season deals available. Conference/banqueting (300/250). Leisure centre, swimming pool, Canadian hot tub; golf (18); garden, walking. Children welcome (under 3s free in parents' room; cots available without charge, baby sitting arranged). **Rooms 90** (3 suites, 87 executive rooms, 51 no smoking, 1 for disabled). Lift. Room service (limited hours). B&B €85 pps, ss €30. Open all year. Amex, Diners, MasterCard, Visa, Laser. **Directions:** M1 from Dublin; on the Carlingford road, 5km (3 miles) north of Dundalk. ◇

Dundalk   McKeown's Bar & Lounge
CHARACTER PUB
R
16 Clanbrassil Street Dundalk Co Louth
Tel: 042 933 7938

This well-run pub of character has a great atmosphere and friendly staff - just the place for a pint and welcome reassurance that the great Irish pub is alive and well in Dundalk. Open Mon-Wed, 10.30-11.30; Thu-Sat, 10.30-12.30. Food (soup & freshly made sandwiches) served daily, 10.30-6.30. Closed 25 Dec, Good Fri. **No Credit Cards. Directions:** Town centre - middle of the main street.

Dundalk   Quaglinos at The Century
BAR/RESTAURANT
R
The Century Bar 19 Roden Place Dundalk Co Louth
Tel: 042 933 8567

féile bia Well known restaurateurs Pat and Eileen Kerley run The Century Bar, which is a listed building on a corner site opposite St Patrick's Cathedral, and Quaglino's restaurant. It's a romantic building dating back to 1902, with an ornamental turret on the corner, above the front door - and it has retained many features of historical interest, including the original bar counter and hand carved bar backdrop. The restaurant is above the bar and here Pat Kerley - a committed Euro-Toque chef - takes great pride in the active promotion of Irish cuisine and uses as much local produce as possible, including oysters, lobster and lamb. As in most Louth restaurants, generosity remains the keynote and providing good service with good value is a priority. Quaglino's has always had a strong following and loyal customers (plus many new ones) like this restaurant very much, so reservations are essential. The early dinner menu offers outstanding value. Children welcome. **Seats 30.** D daily, 5-10.30. Early D about €25 (5-7); Gourmet Menu about €45. also à la carte; no SC. House wine about €20. Bar meals Mon-Sat, 12-2.30. Closed 25 Dec, Good Fri. Amex, Diners, MasterCard, Visa, Laser. **Directions:** Just off town centre almost opposite St. Patrick's Cathedral. ◇

Dundalk   Restaurant Number Thirty Two
RESTAURANT
R
32 Chapel Street Dundalk Co Louth **Tel: 042 933 1113**
no.32@ireland.com www.no32.i

Attractively situated in a leafy corner of town near the museum, Susan Heraghty's great little place is the neighbourhood restaurant par excellence and a great asset to Dundalk. It occupies a two-storey corner site, with windows all along one side giving it a sense of space, the smart simplicity of the decor and table settings is appealing, and menus are written in an admirably down-to-earth style - and the same can be said of the prices, notably an exceptional early evening "Express" menu, and the later set menu is not far behind. Menus may include tian of crab & celeriac, grilled lamb burger, and pan seared gurnard with bell pepper escabèche. There has always been a terrific generosity of spirit here in quality of food and service; the later menu is like the Express but with a little more choice and slightly more sophisticated dishes - but prices are still very reasonable. Would that every town in Ireland had a place like this. **Seats 60.** Reservations recommended. Children welcome. D Mon-Sat, 5.30-10. Early 'Express' D €17 (Mon-Thu 5.30-6.30), Set D €26. House wine from €18.95. SC 12.5% on parties 6+. Closed Sun, bank hols. Amex, MasterCard, Visa, Laser. **Directions:** First left turn after courthouse at "home bakery".

Dundalk
RESTAURANT

Rosso Restaurant

5 Roden Place Dundalk Co Louth **Tel: 042 935 6502**
enquiries@rossorestaurant.com www.rossorestaurant.com

Just opposite St Patrick's Cathedral, in Dundalk's new 'dining quarter', this smart contemporary restaurant has decisively positioned itself at the leading edge of local cuisine. The fashionable venue is decked out in minimalist style with striking coffee and cream colour schemes - on arrival one might, perhaps, relax and enjoy an aperitif while reading the menu in the particularly comfy sofas and soft chairs in the open bar and reception area, before continuing to one of the two contemporary, tastefully laid out dining areas consisting of effectively placed light reflecting mirrors, recessed lighting and polished wood tables. Rosso exudes a cheerful lively ambience, especially as the tables fill up. The proprietors are Raymond McArdle, acclaimed executive chef of the Gilhooley family's Nuremore Hotel (see entry) in Co Monaghan, and Louisa Gilhooley, who have assembled a strong team at Rosso; and, now comfortably settled into the role of head chef, Conor Mee uses carefully sourced native produce and cooks with maturity and confidence - and, one detects, much enjoyment. The result is a mix of innovative ideas and re-interpreted classics which excite privileged diners with accomplished dishes such as pressed foie gras, white pudding and confit rabbit terrine served with toasted brioche and pear ginger chutney, or roast lamb and thyme with lamb shank pie, new season turnip mash, spinach, bacon and onions. Typical desserts may include a hot Valhrona chocolate fondant (a little undercooked on a recent visit) with fresh vanilla ice cream. Dinner menus are rather grander and offer more choice than lunch, but the high standard of the cooking and artistic presentation of dishes is a constant factor. A well chosen wine list includes a short choice of wines by the glass, and service is friendly and willing. Children welcome. **Seats 75** (private room, 40); air conditioning; L Tue-Fri, 12.30-2.45; D Tue-Sat, 6-9.45; L&D a la carte; Sun, 12.30-7pm; Value meal Sun all day, 3 courses about €26.50; house wine €20. Closed Sat L, Mon, 25 Dec, 1 Jan. MasterCard, Visa, Laser. **Directions:** Opposite St. Patrick's Cathedral.

Dundalk
BAR

The Spirit Store

George's Quay The Harbour Dundalk Co Louth **Tel: 042 935 2097**
info@spiritstore.ie www.spiritstore.ie

This pub of great character and friendliness is right on the quay, where coasters dock, so you never know what country visiting sailors may come from. But everyone mixes well in the wackily-furnished bars downstairs and - although a youthful place best known for its music (regular events are held in the upstairs bar, often famous names) - people of all ages and backgrounds are welcomed here, even if only for a cup of tea to break a journey. Closed 25 Dec, Good Fri. MasterCard, Visa, Laser. **Directions:** On the quayside, beside the bridge.

Dundalk Area
BAR/RESTAURANT

Fitzpatrick's Bar & Restaurant

Rockmarshall Jenkinstown Dundalk Co Louth **Tel: 042 937 6193**
fitzpatricksbarandrestaurant@eircom.net www.fitzpatricks-restaurant.com

Masses of well-maintained flowers and a neat frontage with fresh paintwork always draw attention to this attractive and well-run establishment. It has plenty of parking and is well organised for the informal but comfortable consumption of food in a series of bar/dining rooms, all with character and much of local interest in pictures and artefacts. Prompt reception, friendly service and traditional home-cooked food (sometimes with a modern twist) at reasonable prices, all add up to an appealing package - and its obvious popularity with locals and visitors alike is well deserved. Well-balanced menus always include a good selection of fresh seafood - a tian of fresh crabmeat to start perhaps, with a purée of apple, avocado & lambs lettuce, main courses like fillet of turbot with chorizo, confit aubergine & roast peppers - and delicious informal meals from the Grill Menu including proper scampi, made with fresh Dublin Bay prawns (langoustine), coated in home-made breadcrumbs and served with tartare sauce. This is not inexpensive food (some main courses may be over €25), but it is real food, and the quantities are generous. It's also a pleasant place to drop into for a cup of tea or coffee - and, a very nice touch, they have a 'Very Important Pet' compound where you can leave your dog while having a meal. Wheelchair friendly; children welcome before 9pm (high chair, childrens menu, baby changing facilities); air conditioning. **Seats 90** (private room 40, outdoors 150). Open daily in summer, otherwise Tue-Sun 12.30 -10pm (Sun 12.30-3.30, 5.30-9pm), L from 12.30, D 6-10. A la carte menus, also vegetarian menu; house wine from €19.95. Closed Mon Oct-Apr (except bank hols), Good Fri, 25 Dec. MasterCard, Visa, Laser. **Directions:** Just north of Dundalk town, take Carlingford road off main Dublin-Belfast road. About 8km (5 m) on left.

Dunleer | Carlito's
RESTAURANT | Main Street Dunleer Co Louth
R | **Tel: 041 686 1366**

People come from miles around to eat at this unassuming Italian restaurant, so it is wise to book well ahead, especially at weekends. Although quite unremarkable from the street, the interior is welcoming, with a comfortable seating area just inside the door where groups can assemble over an aperitif before heading for their table. Tables are simply set (night light, cutlery and a paper napkin) but the welcome is very friendly and you'll quickly be settled into a menu that is well planned to please everyone, regardless of age or the occasion. Expect lovely home-baked bread, real minestrone soup with heaps of flavour, mixed leaf salads with creamy home-made dressing, deliciously crisp thin-based pizzas, a range of pastas and daily specials - such as herb-crusted cod, perfectly cooked and served with local vegetables (choice of boiled or chipped potatoes). Desserts are equally good: real tiramisu, crème brulée with fresh strawberries perhaps, and freshly brewed coffee to finish. Great value too. D Tue-Sat, 6pm-9.30pm, Sun 5-8.30pm. MasterCard, Visa, Laser. **Directions:** On main street.

Termonfeckin | Triple House Restaurant
RESTAURANT | Termonfeckin Co Louth
R | **Tel: 041 982 2616**

The pretty village of Termonfeckin provides a fine setting for Pat Fox's popular restaurant, which is in a 200-year-old converted farmhouse in landscaped gardens surrounded by mature trees. In winter you can settle in front of a log fire in the reception area on cold evenings while pondering the menu over a glass of wine (there's also a conservatory, used for aperitifs in summer). Committed to using the best of local produce, Pat offers wide-ranging menus and daily blackboard seafood extras from nearby Clogherhead including fresh Clogherhead prawns, Annagassan crab, and a dish he entitles, intriguingly, Port Oriel Pot-Pourri. But locally-reared meats feature too, in roast Drogheda smoked loin of pork with a nectarine & Calvados sauce, for example. Specialities include lovely spinach-filled crêpes (baked with cream sauce, tomato sauce and Parmesan) and, for dessert, a chewy meringue dacquoise that varies with the season's fruits. Plated farmhouse cheeses typically include Cashel Blue, Cooleeney and Wexford Cheddar. The wine list reflects Pat's particular interests. Children welcome. **Seats 40.** D Tue-Sun 6.30-9 (to 8.30pm Sun), L Sun only 1-2.30; Set D about €30, à la carte available; early D about €22, 6.30-7.30 only; Set Sun L about €22. House wines about €17-20; sc discretionary. Toilets wheelchair accessible. Closed Mon, Christmas. MasterCard, Visa. **Directions:** 5 miles north east of Drogheda.

COUNTY MAYO

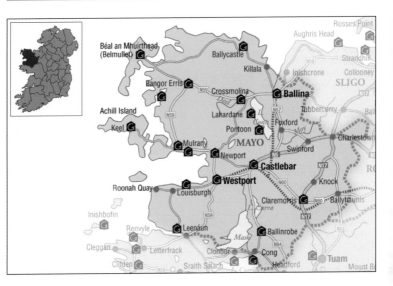

Mayo - far Mayo - might have been a byword for remoteness and declining population in times past. But now it is thriving, with the recent six year Census showed a population increase of 5.3% (to 118,000). However, Mayo is so spacious that it still seems totally uncrowded. And they are a people who enjoy the present as much as savouring the past. No more so than at Westport on Clew Bay, near the famed Holy Mountain of Croagh Patrick. Westport is a neatly planned town which responds to loving care, a winner of Gold Medals in the annual Tidy Towns awards in Ireland, and the Entente Florale in France. Westport House itself is now receiving the TLC, and has been put under an almighty tin roof, an idea which could usefully be used over all Ireland in a wet summer.

Five kilometres east of Mayo's bustling county town of Castlebar, the Museum of Country Life is at Turlough Park House. The first fully-fledged department of the National Museum to be located anywhere outside Dublin, it celebrates Irish country life as lived between 1850 and 1960 in an intriguing display of artefacts which were in regular everyday use, yet now seem almost exotic.

As often, indeed, does Mayo itself - for Mayo is magnificent. All Ireland's counties have their devotees, but enthusiasts for Mayo have a devotion which is pure passion. In their heart of hearts, they feel that this austerely majestic Atlantic-battered territory is somehow more truly Irish than anywhere else. And who could argue with them after experiencing the glories of scenery, sea and sky which this western rampart of Ireland puts on ever-changing display, particularly over Achill Island.

Yet among Mayo's many splendid mountain ranges we find substantial pockets of fertile land, through which there tumble fish-filled streams and rivers. And in the west of the county, the rolling hills of the drumlin country, which run in a virtually continuous band right across Ireland from Strangford Lough, meet the sea again in the island studded wonder of Clew Bay.

Along Mayo's rugged north coast, turf cutting at Ceide Fields near Ballycastle has revealed the oldest intact field and farm system in existence, preserved through being covered in blanket bog 5,000 years ago. An award-winning interpretive centre has been created at the site, and even the most jaded visitor will find fascination and inspiration in the clear view which it provides into Ireland's distant past. A few miles eastward, the charming village of Ballycastle is home to the internationally-respected Ballinglen Arts Foundation, creative home-from-home for artists worldwide.

Nearby, the lively town of Ballina is where the salmon-rich River Moy meets the sea in the broad sweep of Killala Bay. It takes a leap of the imagination to appreciate that the sheltered Moy Valley is in the same county as the spectacularly rugged cliffs of Achill Island. But leaps of the imagination is what Mayo inspires.

Local Attractions & Information

Ballina Street Festival/Arts Week (July) C/O Moy Valley Resources	096 70905
Ballina Tourism Information	096 70848
Westport Tourism Information	098 25711
Ballycastle Ballinglen Arts Foundation	096 43184/43366
Castlebar Linenhall Arts Centre	094 9023733
Castlebar Tourism Information	094 9021207
Castlebar Turlough House (see entry under Turlough)	094 9031773
Ceide Fields Interpretive Centre	096 43325
Clare Island Ferries	098 28288
Foxford Woollen Mills Visitor Centre	094 9256756
Inishkea Island Tours Belmullet	097 85741
Inishturk Island Ferries	098 45541
Killasser(Swinford)Traditional Farm Heritage Centre	094 9252505
Kiltimagh Glore Mill Follain Arts Centre	094 9382184
Knock Interational Airport	094 9367222
Knock Tourism Information	094 9388193
Achill Tourism Information	098 25384
Moy Valley Holidays	096 70905
Turlough Turlough Park House. Museum of Country Life. Open Tuesday to Saturday 10am to 5pm, Sundays 2pm to 5pm, closed Mondays	094 9031755
Westport Clew Bay Archaeological Trail	087 2935207
Westport Westport House & Children's Zoo	098 25 430 / 27 766
Westport Tourism Information	098 25711

ACHILL ISLAND

Achill island is the largest island in Ireland so don't forget to top up with fuel as you're driving on to it; there's a large service station, Lavelle's Esso Garage, on the right - and it is open on Sundays. It is a place of great beauty, with mountains, lakes, valleys, magnificent sea-cliffs, wild moors and spectacular scenery. It has a number of small attractive villages, several unpolluted sandy beaches ideal for bathing, excellent deep sea, shore and lake angling and opportunities for all kinds of outdoor activities. An interesting place that is also useful to know about is Seasamh O'Dalaigh's workshop and gallery, **Dánlann Yawl** (098 36137), at Owenduff (on the right coming from the mainland); it has a teashop during gallery hours, making a pleasant place for a break - and also a 2-bedroom apartment with magnificent views. On the island, the McNamara's family-run **Achill Cliff House Hotel** (098 43400; www.achillcliff.com); quiet, purpose-built, it is especially useful to know about as it is open all year except Christmas.

WWW.IRELAND-GUIDE.COM FOR THE BEST PLACES TO EAT, DRINK & STAY

Achill Dugort
GUESTHOUSE

Gray's Guest House

Dugort Achill Island Co Mayo
Tel: 098 43244

Vi McDowell has been running this legendary guesthouse in the attractive village of Dugort since 1970, and nobody understands better the qualities of peace, quiet and gentle hospitality that have been bringing guests - especially artists and writers - here for the last hundred years. Mrs McDowell is very involved with the cultural life of the island - especially the Desmond Turner Achill Island School of Painting, and the cottage where Nobel prize-winning author Heinrich Böll once lived, which now offers a haven for artists and writers - and is an extraordinarily interested and hospitable hostess. This is an unusual establishment, occupying a series of houses, and each area has a slightly different appeal: there's a large, traditionally furnished sitting room with an open fire, comfortable leather lounge furniture, and several conservatories for quiet reading. Bedrooms and bathrooms vary considerably due to the age and nature of the premises, but the emphasis is on old-fashioned comfort; each of the three houses now has a fitted kitchen with everything you need to rustle up a light lunch, also a washing machine and tumble dryer, and the rooms all have tea & coffee-making trays; there are extra shared bathrooms in addition to en-suite shower facilities and phones for incoming calls. Children are welcome and have an indoor playroom and safe outdoor play area, plus pool and table tennis for older children. Dinner for residents is served in a large, quite formally appointed dining room, where lovely old-fashioned menus offer dishes like smoked mackerel with gooseberry sauce, home-made celery and apple soup, local salmon or a traditional roast, and to finish, blackberry & apple pie with custard; there are several choices on each course and menus change daily. Packed lunches are also available on request. Pets permitted in some areas by arrangement. Children welcome (under 3s free in parents' room). Garden, fishing, walking. Pool table. Wheelchair accessible. Stair lift. **Rooms 14** (13 en-suite, 1 with private bathroom, 13 shower only, 1 family room, 1 ground floor). B&B €55 pps, ss €6, SC discretionary. D 7pm. Set D €32, house wine €18. Closed 24-26 Dec. Personal cheques accepted. **No Credit Cards. Directions:** Castlebar, Westport, Newport, Achill Sound - Dugort!

Achill Keel
CAFÉ

The Beehive
Keel Achill Island Co Mayo
Tel: 098 43134/43018

At their informal restaurant and attractive craft shop in Keel, husband and wife team Michael and Patricia Joyce take pride in the careful preparation and presentation of the best of Achill produce, especially local seafood. Since opening, in 1991, they have extended both the menu and the premises more than once and now offer great all-day self-service food, which you can have indoors, or take out to a patio overlooking Keel beach. Everything is home-made, including delicious soups such as seafood chowder and traditional nettle soup (brotchán neantóg) all served with home-made brown scones. As baking is a speciality, there's always a tempting selection of cakes, bracks, teabreads, fruit tarts, baked desserts and scones with home-made preserves or you can simply have a toasted sandwich, or an Irish farmhouse cheese plate. You may want to allow a little extra time here as the shop is interesting, with quality gift items and clothing lines not found elsewhere. The restaurant is now fully licensed and the Joyces hope to extend opening hours and develop an evening restaurant - details on inquiry. **Seats 100** (outdoor seating, 60; private room, 50). Toilet wheelchair accessible; children welcome (high chair, baby changing facilities). Meals 9.30-6pm daily, Easter-early Nov. A la carte. No sc. Closed Nov-Easter. Amex, Diners, MasterCard, Visa, Laser. **Directions:** Situated in the centre of Keel village overlooking beach and Minuan cliffs.

Achill Keel
RESTAURANT

Ferndale Restaurant
Crumpaun Keel Achill Island Co Mayo **Tel: 098 43908/9**
achillfinedining@eircom.net www.ferndale-achill.com

Stunning views and all-year opening are among the many attractions of Jon Fratschol's unusual restaurant: high over Keel village, it has huge picture windows to make the most of the view and there is, by his own admission, an air of fantasy about the whole place. You would have to look through the menu very carefully to find influences from Jon's Swiss roots, as the Ferndale specialities - a whole page of special dishes - lead off with Mongolian barbeque (a mixture of marinated meats) and a matching page of fish and seafood dishes includes equally unusual creations - but traditionalists will be pleased to know that there are a few more familiar items in there, including fillet steak Ferndale. **Seats 40.** Reservations required. Toilets wheelchair accessible. D daily in summer, 6-10.30; after Hallowe'en open weekends only (Thu-Sun) except fully open over Christmas. A la carte (main courses about €15-25). House wine from about €16. Amex, MasterCard, Visa, Laser. **Directions:** Signed up the hill from Keel village. Take a right at the Annexe Inn, signposted on the left after 400m.

BALLINA

St Muredach's Cathedral is an impressive river bank landmark in Ballina, (gaelic Béal an Átha), which is Mayo's largest town, and has the famous River Moy flowing through it, which creates a particularly pleasant atmosphere. It's a great base for a fishing holiday, or for exploring this beautiful and unspoilt part of the west of Ireland, and there is plenty of good food and accommodation to be found in and around the town, including one of the area's longest-established hotels, the **Downhill House Hotel** (096 21033; www.downhillhouse.ie), which is quietly situated in a riverside location just a short walk from the town centre. And, just across the bridge towards the quay, one of the town's most historic buildings is under development as **The Ice House Hotel** (www.theicehouse.ie). This prestigious boutique hotel is a sister property to the newly opened **Lisloughrey Lodge** at Cong and the highly regarded **Wineport Lodge** in Co Westmeath and (see entries), and is certain to introduce many new visitors to the town.

Ballina
HOTEL

Belleek Castle
Ballina Co Mayo **Tel: 096 22400**
belleekcastlehotel@eircom.net www.belleekcastle.com

Situated just outside Ballina amidst 1,000 acres of woodland and forestry, on the banks of the River Moy, Marshall and Jacqueline Doran's castle was the ancestral home of the Earl of Arran and, with a 16th century armoury, big open fires and massive chandeliers among many quirky features, it now makes an unusual small hotel. This is a wacky place for those who enjoy something out of the ordinary and it would be great fun for a group get together. The Armada Bar is a recreation of the Captains Ward Room from a galleon in the Spanish Armada - partly constructed from timbers salvaged from the galleons of the ill fated Castile Squadron wrecked off County Mayo four centuries ago, it should provide plenty of talking points to pep up your drink. Belleek is as different from a standard modern hotel as it is possible to be, but it manages to combine old world charm with modern comforts - bedrooms will vary according to their position in the house, but the best are bright and spacious, with four-poster beds and views out over the grounds. It makes a romantic wedding venue (the banqueting room is in medieval castle style), and the many activities to choose from nearby include championship golf, walking, surfing, and salmon and trout fishing on site; or, with its informal and friendly ambience, the castle simply makes an unusual base to explore this beautiful area. **Rooms 15.** B&B from about €70 pps, ss €20. MasterCard, Visa, Laser. **Directions:** Follow signs on way into Ballina for Belleek. ◈

Ballina
BAR/RESTAURANT

Crockets on the Quay
Ballina Co Mayo **Tel: 096 75930**
info@crocketsonthequay.ie www.crocketsonthequay.ie

This well-known hostelry is attractively situated on the quay in Ballina, overlooking the River Moy, and it's a surprisingly large premises once you start exploring. It's inviting from the road, with seating outside for fine weather and a very pleasant old-style bar with an open fire (gas, alas) and plenty of pictures and artefacts of local interest giving it a sense of history. Extending behind the traditional bar is a series of contemporary bar areas with trendy low seating and big tables, finishing up with a stylish big bar right at the back, with access to a car park behind the building. Interesting bar meals are served all day by exceptionally friendly, helpful staff and, although the dim lighting seems quite surreal when coming in from the sunshine on a bright summer's day, it's a hospitable place - and it leaps into life at night. **Restaurant:** At the front of the building, overlooking the river, this is a stylish room with a gently modern feel, in quiet warm browns. Well-balanced, interesting menus show pride in local produce and include some unusual ideas alongside well-known dishes. An attractive setting, quality ingredients and some welcome originality make this an interesting place to eat - at its best, the cooking is very enjoyable and friendly staff provide excellent service. Pool table, broadband wi/fi. Not suitable for children after 9pm. Parking (30). **Seats 60** (outdoor seating, 40). Toilets wheelchair accessible. D daily, 5-9.30. Set D €25; also à la carte. House wine €18. Bar menu available daily, 5-9.30. Closed 24-26 Dec, Good Fri. Amex, MasterCard, Visa, Laser. **Directions:** On the edge of Ballina; from town, take main Sligo road, turn left at first traffic lights.

Ballina
WINE BAR
♨ ⊚ ♀ ♈

Gaughans
O'Rahilly Street Ballina Co Mayo **Tel: 096 70096**
edgaug@eircom.net

féile bia This is one of the great old bars of Ireland and has a gentle way of drawing you in, with the menu up in the window and a display of local pottery to arouse the curiosity. It's a fine old-fashioned place, with everything gleaming and a great sense of the pride taken in its care. Michael Gaughan opened the premises as a pub in November 1936 and his son, Edward, took over in 1972. Edward's wife Mary is a great cook and, once they started doing food in 1983 they never looked back; everybody loves the way they un the place and Mary still does all the cooking. Although they sold the pub licence a few years ago and now operate as a wine bar, Mary's specialities have not changed and her good home cooking includes home-made quiche Lorraine with salad, lovely old-fashioned roasts - roast stuffed chicken with vegetables and potatoes, perhaps, or baked gammon, and local seafood, when available smoked salmon all year round, but fresh crab is only served from May to the end of August - such respect for seasonality is rare enough these days, and it is good to see it. There's always a daily special and old favourites like lemon meringue pie and pineapple upside down pudding for dessert. Lighter options on the menu include open smoked salmon or crab sandwich (in season), smoked salmon salad, ploughman's lunch, and it's all great wholesome fare. And, charmingly listed along with the Bewley's tea and coffee, the wine and Irish coffee "Glass of spring water: Free." Now that's style. Children welcome. **Seats 40.** Food served Mon-Sat, 10am-6pm. Closed Sun, bank hols, 25 Dec & Good Fri. Amex, Diners, MasterCard, Visa, Laser. **Directions:** Up to the post office, on the left.

Ballina
HOTEL/RESTAURANT

Mount Falcon Country House Hotel & Estate

Foxford Road Ballina Co Mayo **Tel: 096 74472**
info@mountfalcon.com www.mountfalcon.com

Mount Falcon will be fondly remembered by many for its lovable eccentricity under the previous owner, Connie Aldridge (whose late husband Major Robert Aldridge, a keen archaeologist, helped discover the Ceidhe Fields) and it is now owned by the locally based Maloney brothers, who fell in love with it when visiting in 2002 and bought the estate when they retired. They have since been working on a sensitively executed multi-million euro building and refurbishment plan that included extending the original house and erecting a selection of luxurious courtyard houses and woodland lodges. Mount Falcon is now a 32 bedroom luxury hotel and it is a welcoming place, first seen in a series of ground floor drawing rooms and lounges with comfy sofas, open fires and coffee tables scattered with books and magazines about fishing, hunting and country life in general. Accommodation includes six deluxe rooms on the upper floors of the original house (including two suites, the Wallpool and Connor's Gap, which are named after famous pools on the Mount Falcon Fishery); they have been carefully restored with pitch-pine shutters and floors, original cornices and marble fireplaces whilst integrating all the modern comforts. The other rooms are new and spacious, with custom-designed furniture, television and radio, direct dial phone, personal safe and hairdryer as standard. The estate enjoys more than 2 miles of double bank salmon fishing on the River Moy, and the 100 acres of grounds have been redeveloped and landscaped to incorporate lakeside and woodland walks. Other local activities include championship golf, at nearby Enniscrone Golf Club, and horse riding - and there are many beaches nearby. Conferences/Banqueting (250/180), broadband wi/fi, video conferencing. Spa, leisure centre with indoor 'pool, steam room, sauna, jacuzzi and gym. **Rooms 32** (2 suites, 4 junior suites, 2 for disabled); Children welcome (under 2s free in parents' room, cots available free of charge, baby sitting arranged); Lift; 24 hr room service. B&B €100pps, ss €85. Self catering also available. Helipad. **Restaurant:** Orders are taken while you enjoy an aperitif in the Bolthole Bar, before going through to the classically appointed restaurant, in the original kitchen and storeroom and pantry of the main house; well-spaced tables set up with pristine white line and comfortable chairs set an anticipatory tone for a good dining experience to follow - and, since the arrival of highly regarded head chef Head Chef Phillippe Farineau, you should have a treat in store. His motto of "Irish Produce, French Heart" is used to great effect, as his frequently changed menus are based mainly on locally sourced produce: there is a strong emphasis on seafood - Clew Bay scallops, crabmeat from Broadhaven - and beef and lamb come from Tolans butchers in Ballina. A chef known for finesse, he offers all the little treats of fine dining including a complimentary pre-starter (a little parfait of smoked mackerel, perhaps) as luxurious packaging for a memorable meal that could include local lobster 'Thermidor', and Irish venison. A typical Table d'Hote dinner (€57) offering half a dozen choices on each course might include a crabmeat soufflé or breast of pigeon among the starters, followed perhaps by roast Atlantic halibut with herb crushed potato and confit of fennel or Mayo rack of lamb, and desserts like warm dark chocolate fondant with amaretto icecream - round this off with petit fours and chocolates with tea or coffee and you have a true picture of this fine restaurant. Service is professional and friendly and a very well chosen and informative wine list (perhaps a little overpriced) includes four house wines (€26) and eight half bottles. **Seats 72** (private room 10). L&D daily 12.30-2.30 & 6.30-9.30pm; Sun D only 7-9pm; Closed Sun L. Amex, Diners, MasterCard, Visa, Laser. **Directions:** Just outside Ballina on the N26 to Foxford.

Ballina Area
HISTORIC HOUSE

Enniscoe House

Castlehiill Crossmolina Ballina Co Mayo **Tel: 096 31112**
mail@enniscoe.com www.enniscoe.com

FOOD EXTRA AWARD

In parkland and mature woods on the shores of Lough Conn, Enniscoe can sometimes seem stern and gaunt, as Georgian mansions in the north-west of Ireland tend to be but, with family portraits, crackling log fires, warm hospitality and good home cooking, this hospitable house has great charm. It was built by ancestors of the present owner, Susan Kellett, who settled here in the 1660s, and is a very special place for anglers and other visitors with a natural empathy for the untamed wildness of the area. Large public rooms include a fine drawing room, with interesting period details and plenty of seating, and a more intimate dining room, where Susan's delightfully simple dinners are served. Her menus change daily and make good use of home-grown and local produce in dishes like pan-fried scallops with Madeira dressing and rocket salad and a delicious house speciality of roast free-range pork; homely desserts like rhubarb and orange crumble to finish, and cheeses laid out on the sideboard - as they are again next morning, as part of an excellent breakfast. Traditionally furnished bedrooms are large, very comfortable and, like their en-suite bathrooms, regularly refurbished. There is much of interest around converted outbuildings at the back of the house, including a genealogy centre (The Mayo North Family History Research Centre, Tel: 096 31809), a small agricultural museum with working blacksmith, and conference facilities. The house is surrounded by beautiful woodlands, with a network of paths, and there are restored walled gardens (both ornamental and productive one is run commercially as an organic market garden), which are open to the public and have tea-rooms and a shop. There is brown trout fishing on Lough Conn and other trout and salmon fishing nearby; boats, ghillies, tuition and hire of equipment can be arranged. Small conferences (50). **Rooms 6** (all en-suite & no smoking, 2 family rooms) B&B €98 pps, ss €20. Turndown service. **Restaurant: Seats 20.** D daily, 7.30-8.30pm; reservations accepted; non-residents welcome by reservation. 3-course Set D €48; house wines €16-20. Closed 1 Nov-1 Apr. MasterCard, Visa, Laser. **Directions:** 3km (2 m) south of Crossmolina on R315.

Ballinrobe
HOTEL/RESTAURANT

JJ Gannons Hotel

Main St. Ballinrobe Co Mayo **Tel: 094 954 1008**
info@jjgannons.com www.jjgannons.com

Right in the heart of the thriving town of Ballinrobe, JJ Gannons goes back to 1838 but it's now in the third generation and rather funky from the outside preparing first time visitors for a mainly modern style, which is unusual for the area and reflects the taste of an energetic and very committed young couple, Niki and Jay Gannon, who are developing it as a 'green' hotel. (A geo thermal heating system converts energy from the river, and a wood pellet burner provides back up.) A contemporary bar with a more tradi-tional area at the back caters for all age groups and, impressively, a blackboard offers some twenty wines by the glass. The original eleven bright bedrooms offer a range of standards including a junior suite, and a further 12 bedrooms are planned (as cottage style suites at the river end of the garden); the rooms have been individually furnished with care, and include luxurious touches such as tailor-made linen and goose down duvets to fit the huge (6'6") beds, also velour bathrobes and slippers. Breakfast is served in the bright and airy restaurant, offering freshly squeezed orange juice, pressed apple juice, a JJGannon's smoothie or seasonal fruit kebabs to start you off. With such committed owners, lovely friendly staff and good food, this is a place that's worth a detour. Conferences/Banqueting (50/80), business centre, secre-tarial services, video conferencing, free broadband wi/fi. Fishing, golf and equestrian nearby, walking, massage, short breaks. Children welcome (under 2s free in parents' room, cot available at no charge, free baby monitors, baby sitting arranged). **Rooms 11** (1 suite, 4 junior suites, 1 shower only, 4 family rooms, 1 for disabled, all no smoking); lift; limited room service; B&B €60 pps, ss €15. **Restaurant:** Although it is also used during the day when you can choose between eating in the bar or at a table here, the restau-rant really comes into its own in the evening when well-designed lighting creates a lovely warm ambience as night draws in. Well-appointed tables are smartly clad in white linen and fresh flowers, with comfort-able seating and, as elsewhere in this well-run hotel, staff are welcoming and knowledgeable. Euro-Toques chef Xi Sun offers an appealing à la carte menu with about half a dozen mainly contemporary choices on each course; although here is little specific mention of local ingredients there is a quality tone, and Ballinrobe butcher Martin Jennings is credited with supplying the beef (fillet steaks served with spring onion champ, crispy onion rings & red wine jus, for example). There's an Asian twist to some dishes pot-roasted barbary duck breast with fresh ginger & mint glazed root vegetables and black pepper & orange sauce is a delicious example. Fish is well-represented (a marvellous trio of seabass, salmon and prawns in white wine sauce was enjoyed on a recent visit) and vegetarian dishes are imaginative. Desserts are all home-made and include a daily selection of sorbets and ice creams, served with a fresh fruit compôte. A well-priced, informative wine list includes plenty of wines served by the glass. **Seats 50** (private room, 50, outdoor, 20); air conditioning; reservations recommended; children welcome; L Mon-Sat, 12.30-3.30; D Mon-Sat 6-9.30; Sun, 12.30-9.30; set Sun L €22.50; early D €30, 5-7pm; set 3 course D €50; also a la carte L&D; house wine €20. *Bar food served daily 8am - 9.30pm. Closed 25 Dec. MasterCard, Visa, Laser. **Directions:** Southern Mayo, off N84.

Ballycastle
RESTAURANT

Mary's Bakery & Tea Rooms

Main Street Ballycastle Co Mayo
Tel: 096 43361

Mary Munnelly's homely little restaurant is the perfect place to stop for some tasty home cooking. Baking is the speciality but she does "real meals" as well - a full Irish breakfast, which is just the thing for walkers, home-made soups like mushroom or smoked bacon & potato, and free range chicken dishes. And, if you strike a chilly day, it's very pleasant to get tucked in beside a real fire too. There's also a garden with sea views for fine weather - and home-made chutneys and jams on sale to take home. **Seats 30** (also outdoor seating for 12). Toilets wheelchair accessible. Open 10am-6pm daily in summer (may open later - to 8-ish - in high season; shorter hours off-season); Closed Sun off-season (Oct-Easter), & first 3 weeks Jan. **No Credit Cards. Directions:** From Ballina - Killala - main road to Ballycastle, on way to Ceide Fields.

Ballycastle
PUB

Polke's

Main Street Ballycastle Co Mayo
Tel: 096 43016

This lovely old general merchants and traditional pub is just across the road from Mary's Bakery, and well worth a visit. It was established in 1820 and has remained in the family since then - the present proprietor, Brian Polke, has had responsibility for this national treasure since 1962. Not much has changed it seems: the long, narrow bar behind the shop is completely unspoilt, friendly and a joy to find yourself in. The whole place is immaculate too (including the outside loo in a whitewashed yard at the back), giving the lie to the widely-held view that "character" pubs are, by definition, scruffy. A nice touch of modernity which reflects the close-knit nature of the local community is the collection of pictures donated by artists from the nearby Ballinglen Arts Centre, which are exhibited in the bar and make a fascinating talking point for new arrivals. Open 10am-11.30pm. Closed 25 Dec & Good Fri. **Directions:** On main street.

Ballycastle
HOTEL/RESTAURANT

Stella Maris Country House Hotel

Ballycastle Co Mayo **Tel: 096 43322**
info@stellamarisireland.com www.stellamarisireland.com

Built in 1853 as a coast guard regional headquarters, this fine property on the edge of the wonderfully away-from-it-all village of Ballycastle was later acquired by the Sisters of Mercy, who named it Stella Maris, and it now makes a very special small hotel, restored by proprietors Terence McSweeney and Frances Kelly, who have created a warm and stylish interior where antiques rub shoulders with contemporary pieces. There's a welcome emphasis on comfort throughout public areas, including a cosy bar - but the location is this hotel's major asset and a conservatory built all along the front takes full advantage of it, allowing guests to relax in comfort and warmth while drinking in the majestic views of the surrounding coastline and sea. Accommodation blends understated elegance with comfort in uncluttered rooms that have magnificent views and are furnished with antiques but - with complimentary broadband, modern bathrooms and power showers - offer the best of both worlds. Children welcome (under 4s free in parents' room, cot available free of charge). Walking; fishing. Garden. Equestrian and golf nearby. No pets. **Rooms 12** (1 suites, 6 shower only, 1 ground floor, 1 disabled, all no smoking). B&B €112.50 pps, ss €50. **Restaurant:** Dinner - cooked under Frances' direct supervision - is a very enjoyable experience, based on local ingredients as far as possible, including organic produce from nearby Enniscoe (see entry) and also from the hotel's own new gardens. Strongly seasonal menus are well-balanced and imaginative, without being over-influenced by fashion and the cooking is admirably simple: tian of seasoned crabmeat on tomato concassé with chives and a gazpacho coulis, roast rack of spring Ballycastle lamb with parsnip purée & red wine jus, are typical and there is usually a choice of two fish dishes (vegetarian option on request). Classic desserts include refreshing seasonal fruits - and there will always be an Irish farmhouse cheese plate - then it's back to the conservatory for a digestif... The wine list, while relatively short, has been chosen with care. Residents also have a treat in store each morning, as the Stella Maris breakfast is worth lingering over: lashings of freshly squeezed juice, a beautiful fruit plate, gorgeous freshly-baked brown bread, hand-made preserves and perfect hot food cooked to order, be it a traditional Irish or a special like creamy scrambled eggs with smoked salmon; not a grand display, but exceptionally delicious. Stella Maris was the Connaught winner of our Irish Breakfast Awards in 2004 and was our Hideaway of the Year in 2005. This is indeed a wonderful retreat. Short breaks offered - details on application. Banqueting (40). Restaurant seats 26. Reservations recommended; non-residents welcome. D 7-9 (Mon residents' only), D à la carte, house wine €24. Restaurant closed Mon (to non-residents); hotel closed Oct-Mar. Closed Oct-Apr. MasterCard, Visa, Laser. **Directions:** West of Ballina on R314; 2km (1.5 m) west of Ballycastle.

Belmullet
PUB

An Chéibh

Barrack Street Belmullet Co Mayo
Tel: 097 81007

Situated in the heart of one of Ireland's furthest flung towns, and one almost surrounded by the sea, the Talbot family's friendly An Chéibh ("the anchor") is a very fitting place to find good seafood in a comfortable bar and lounge adorned with nautical memorabilia and local photos of bygone times. Although there's plenty of choice for non-fish eaters, menus are weighted heavily in favour of local seafood, as is the Specials Board, offering seasonal fish such as mackerel or salmon and their Fishermans Platter is legendary, guaranteeing to satisfy the hungriest traveller. There are special set menus on two days in the year Fair Day (15 Aug) and Heritage Day (tbc). Bedrooms are planned for 2008/9. **Seats about 40;** air conditioning; children welcome; food served Mon-Sat, 12.30-9.30 in summer, to 8pm in winter, Sun 1pm-7.30pm; à la carte; house wine about €17.50. Closed Good Fri, 25 Dec. MasterCard, Visa, Laser. **Directions:** Blue pub on the left on main entrance into Belmullet.

Belmullet
HOTEL

Broadhaven Bay Hotel

Ballina Road Belmullet Co Mayo **Tel: 097 20600**
info@broadhavenbay.com www.broadhavenbay.com

This large new hotel enjoys commanding views over Broadhaven Bay and offers not only accommodation but also extensive bar, restaurant and banqueting facilities - all much needed services in the area. Comfortably appointed bedrooms look over the bay to the front and a courtyard to the rear, and all have a safe, tea/coffee making facilities, direct dial phone, iron and plasma tv as standard. Friendly, helpful staff are more than happy to help guests arrange any of the many activities in the area, including championship golf at the world famous Carne Golf Links, canoeing, walking, fishing, diving, cycling and horse riding. With a leisure centre and spa (and even in-house hairdressing), this is a comfortable place to be based when visiting one of the most beautiful parts of Ireland. Conferences/Banqueting (600/500); **Rooms 70,** B&B around €75 pps, ss around €10. **Directions:** On the road into Belmullet. ◊

Castlebar
RESTAURANT
R

An Carraig

Chapel Street Castlebar Co Mayo
Tel: 094 902 6159

Eimar Horan's family-run restaurant in a quiet street just off the town centre has earned a loyal local following. It's an attractive, quite traditional restaurant with cut stone walls and a nautical theme with lots of wood, portholes and an arch that links smaller dining areas and also provides visual interest, and a cosier more intimate atmosphere - a feeling enhanced by gentle lighting and candles. Menus are updated traditional, with steaks and seafood taking the starring roles - many of the old favourites are there, but most will have some kind of twist in the presentation, bringing them up to date. Finish with the shared dessert platter for two. Healthy options are offered and there's willingness to provide for special diets and allergies (advance notice preferred). Good customer care and home cooking is the aim, achieved very successfully - and they give good value too. Guests are even urged to take home a loaf of the home-made bread. **Seats 55.** D Tue-Sun, 6-10pm (Sun 5.30-9.30). Early D €22 (6-7.15); Set D about €28. House wine, about €18. Closed Mon, last 2 weeks Jan. MasterCard, Visa. **Directions:** Town centre, opposite Church of the Holy Rosary. ◊

Castlebar

PUB/CAFE/BAR

Ⓝ Ⓡ

Bar One Gastro Pub

Rush Street Castlebar Co Mayo
Tel: 094 903 4800

In the same family ownership as Dublin's stylish Saba (see entry), Mark and Alan Cadden's new gastropub is the busiest bar food venue in the Castlebar area and that is as it should be as their parents, Mary and Michael, were pioneers of the catering industry west of the Shannon and were for many years owners of the Asgard Bar & Restaurant in Westport. Together with their brother Paul (owner of Saba), it is pleasing to see this generation of Caddens are staying at the forefront of the industry. Bar One is a very modern and well designed bar, with dark timber floors, tables chairs, and with plenty of the square upholstered stools that are currently de rigeur and areas suitable for standing when in for a drink at night. The welcome is warm and friendly, under the watchful eye of Michael, with menus promptly produced and a list of specials explained. The printed menu is wisely compact (3 starters, 10 main courses and 4 desserts): not to be missed is the cod in a crispy beer batter, mushy peas and home-cut fries, and on the Guide's visit an excellent seafood pie was among the daily specials. During the days specials offer 4 or 5 starters and main courses, changed daily, and extras including steaks and prime seafood are added in the evening. Gluten free and vegetarian versions of several dishes are offered, and children are well catered for. At the weekend queues form for the night time D.J. and live music sessions, open till late, so be on time as this is Castlebar's night-time hotspot. Late closing Thursdays to Sunday-2.00a.m. Toilets wheelchair accessible; children welcome (high chair, childrens menu); **Seats 80;** food served all day Mon-Sat, 12-8pm. No food on Sun, Bank Hol Mon. Live music Thurs night. MasterCard, Visa, Laser.

Castlebar

RESTAURANT

◉ € Ⓡ

Café Rua

New Antrim Street Castlebar Co Mayo **Tel: 094 902 3376**
aran@iol.ie

Well located near the Linenhall Arts & Exhibition Centre, you can't miss this attractive little restaurant, with its cheerful red frontage. Ann McMahon set up here over 10 years ago and is still very involved although Aran and Colleen McMahon now look after the day to day running. They are very serious about the food they serve, but the tone is light-hearted - it's not a very large room but pine tables (some covered in red oilcloths) are quite well-spaced and most have a good view of the large blackboard menu that lists all kinds of good things to raise the spirits of weary shoppers and culture vultures. Wholesome, home-made fresh food is the order of the day here, and careful sourcing of ingredients is a point of pride - so pasta dishes are based on the excellent Noodle House pastas from Sligo, Irish farmhouse cheeses and other speciality ingredients are supplied by Sheridans cheesemongers, fish comes from Clarkes of Ballina and pork from Ketterich's of Castlebar. Organic vegetables are supplied by a nearby organic scheme in summer, Macroom stoneground oats go into the porridge that is served with home-made apple compôte in winter - and ingredients for 'the full Irish' (sausages, puddings) come from the renowned butchers, Kellys of Newport. Regular dishes like home-made chicken liver paté, warm chicken salad with garlic mayonnaise and ratatouille crostini are announced on one blackboard, while another gives hot specials like potato & lovage soup, grilled pork chops with carrots, new season potatoes & mushroom à la crème and Cashel Blue potato croquettes with beetroot chutney. There's an interesting drinks menu (wines, juices, hot chocolate with marshmallows) and 'because we know that they love food too', there's also a special children's menu, one of many thoughtful touches. Luscious desserts (rhubarb trifle, for example) and good home bakes too: great little place. Children welcome. **Seats 35.** Open all day Mon Sat, 9.30-5.45pm. Closed Sun; Bank Hols, 1 week at Christmas. MasterCard, Visa, Laser. **Directions:** Near Welcome Inn, opposite Supervalu carpark. ◇

Castlebar
HOTEL
R

Lynch Breaffy House Hotel & Spa

Castlebar Co Mayo **Tel: 094 902 2033**
www.lynchotels.com

This handsome hotel set in its own grounds just outside Castlebar town dates back to 1890 and retains some of its original country house atmosphere, although it can be very busy at times. It has undergone major redevelopment in recent years and its principal attraction is the exceptional sports and leisure facilities it offers. An impressive leisure complex and health spa, Life-Spa and Ku'dos Aqua & Fitness Club, have made the hotel an all-year destination for short breaks: facilities include a gymnasium, 20 metre pool, Café West (for refreshments at the leisure complex), also an exhaustive range of treatments, some of which are not available elsewhere in Ireland. And, with sports facilities that are unique in Ireland, including the Paul McGrath Soccer Academy on site, it now styles itself Breaffy International Sports Hotel. Renovation and considerable refurbishment has also been undertaken recently in public areas and accommodation, and a large number of deluxe bedrooms (including two presidential suites and 20 interconnecting family rooms) have been added recently. Conference/banqueting (500); business centre. Preferential local golf rates. Leisure centre, swimming pool; spa. off-season value breaks. Children welcome (under 2 free in parents' room, cots available without charge, baby sitting arranged). No pets. Garden, walking. **Rooms 125** (10 suites, 40 executive, 10 no smoking, 2 disabled). Lift. 24 hr room service. B&B about €80pps, ss about €26. SC incl. Open all year. Amex, Diners, MasterCard, Visa, Laser. **Directions:** 4km outside Castlebar on the Claremoris Road. ◇

Castlebar area
CAFÉ
R

An Grianán Museum Café

National Museum of Ireland for Country Life Turlough Castlebar Co Mayo
Tel: 094 928 9972 info@leonardcatering.com www.leonardcatering.com

The National Museum of Ireland's Museum of Country Life is a great place to spend an afternoon with the family and, although the grounds would be best enjoyed in the sunshine, it's a useful haven if you happen to strike a bad spell of weather. The old house has some rooms restored to their 19th century glory and a rolling lawn leads down to a large tree-lined lake where, by contrast, the eye is drawn to the straight lines of the large, modern museum; housing three floors of photos and exhibits from the last two centuries. After building up a healthy appetite mooching around the museum, a visit to the courtyard Café in the old house is called for, and it should not disappoint: a short but appealing menu offers a limited choice of wholesome dishes including home bakes such as a freshly made quiche, served with a selection from an excellent salad bar. Children welcome; Toilets wheelchair accessible. **Seats 85** (private room, 40, outdoors, 20); air conditioning; food served during museum opening hours, Tue-Sun, 12-5, L 12-4. Closed Mon and Bank Hols. MasterCard, Visa, Laser. **Directions:** In National Museum of Ireland for Country Life in Turlough, off N5 Castlebar road. ◇

Claremorris
BAR/RESTAURANT

Old Arch Bar & Bistro

James Street Claremorris Co Mayo **Tel: 094 936 2777**
www.theoldarchbistro.com

Fergus and Anne Maxwell's bar and informal restaurant in this recently by-passed town, has an inviting black and white frontage with well-maintained window boxes, and there's a welcoming atmosphere in the comfortable, low-ceilinged reception area and bar. The restaurant is informal and friendly, and staff neatly dressed in black trousers and wine aprons, present large, cheerful dinner menus offering a wide selection of popular dishes, arranged by section offering light dishes, soups & salads, fish & poultry, meat and vegetarian, and there is a separate children's menu. Typical dishes include mussels to start, and perhaps a main of Old Arch chicken supreme. Portions are generous, the cooking is generally good and prices are moderate: ideal for a family-friendly restaurant in a growing town. At lunchtime, sandwiches get a menu of their own, and the main lunch menu changes daily. There's a large garden area too, with gas heaters, barbecue and plenty of seating. Toilets wheelchair accessible; Children welcome before 9pm (high chair, childrens menu, baby changing facilities). **Seats 75** (private room, 55, outdoors, 30); L &D daily: L 12-4, D 6-9 (to 10pm Fri/Sat). House wine €19. Pub food served 12-6pm daily. Closed 25-26 Dec, Good Fri. MasterCard, Visa, Laser. **Directions:** 10km from Knock, on Galway-Sligo/Derry road. Beside railway bridge, on the main street.

Ashford Castle

Cong Co Mayo Tel: **094 954 6003**
ashford@ashford.ie www.ashford.ie

Cong
HOTEL/RESTAURANT/CASTLE

WINE AWARD OF THE YEAR

Ireland's grandest castle hotel, with a history going back to the early 13th century, Ashford is set in 350 acres of beautiful parkland. Grandeur, formality and tranquillity are the essential characteristics, first seen in immaculately maintained grounds and, once inside, in a succession of impressive public rooms that illustrate a long and proud history - panelled walls, oil paintings, suits of armour and magnificent fireplaces. Accommodation varies considerably and each room in some way reflects the special qualities of the hotel. The best guest rooms, and the luxurious suites at the top of the castle - many with magnificent views of Lough Corrib, the River Cong and wooded parkland - are elegantly furnished with period furniture, some with enormous and beautifully appointed bathrooms, others with remarkable architectural features, such as a panelled wooden ceiling discovered behind plasterwork in one of the suites during renovations (and now fully restored). The hotel's exceptional amenities include a neo-classical fitness centre, and sporting activities are detailed in a very handy little pocket book. The castle has three restaurants: **The Connaught Room**, which is mainly for residents, is the jewel in Ashford Castle's culinary crown and one of Ireland's most impressive restaurants; the **George V Dining Room** offers fine dining for larger numbers; the new **Cullen's Cottage**, in the grounds, offers accessible all-day informal dining. In addition The Library and Drawing Room menus offer informal meals including Afternoon Tea. Executive Head Chef, Stefan Matz oversees the cooking for all food operations in the castle, and Cullen's Cottage; since joining the team in 2003, this highly skilled and modest chef has worked wonders to introduce some gentle modernisation of menus, bring the varying dining operations together and ensure high standards in each (see below). Conference/banqueting (110/166); business centre; free broadband wi/fi. Archery, boat trips, clay pigeon shooting, equestrian, walking, garden, fishing (fly & coarse), golf (9), fitness centre, sauna, steam room, massage, beauty salon, hairdressing. Children welcome (under 12s free in parents' room, cot available without charge). No pets. Heli-pad. **Rooms 83** (11 suites, 5 junior suites, 61 executive, 21 ground floor, 6 for disabled, all no smoking). Lift. 24 hour room service. Turn down service. Room rate about €485 (max 2 guests, with breakfast), room only €430; SC 15%. Short/off-season breaks offered - details on application.
The Connaught Room: This small room is one of Ireland's most impressive restaurants. The style is broadly classical French, using the best of local ingredients notably seafood and Connemara lamb, and speciality produce like James McGeough's wonderful cured Connemara lamb from Oughterard. If at least two people (preferably a whole party) are agreed, a seasonal 7-course Menu Dégustation tasting menu is available - and after dinner you will be presented with a souvenir copy of the menu. Attention to detail is superb throughout, and the experience benefits greatly from the personal attendance of Robert Bowe whose constant, caring presence is at the heart of this theatrical experience, complete with perfectly groomed staff and his own unobtrusive commentary on the various dishes as they are served with perfect, silver-domed timing. The wine list is a stunning example of an old-fashioned grand hotel list, and has been Robert Bowe's responsibility for nearly 20 years; during that time he has developed it from 250 listings to over 600, carefully sourced from about 15 suppliers. The Castle's wine programme includes a series of winemaker dinners held each winter (which may involve Irish winemakers from around the world); there also are wines of the month, and recommendations by the glass to accompany individual dishes. **Seats 40** (max table size 14). D only, Thu-Sun, 7-9.30pm; reservations essential (usually residents only); Menu Dégustation 5/7 courses €80/95, also à la carte. The wine list is a stunning example of an old-fashioned, grand hotel list. **George V Dining Room:** Dinner and off-season Sunday lunch are served in this much larger but almost equally opulent dining room, where a combination of fine food and attentive service, under the direction of Maitre d'Hôtel Martin Gibbons, promise an outstanding dining experience. A five-course dinner menu offers a choice of about nine dishes on the first and main courses, including some tempting vegetarian suggestions; the choice is wide, with a suggested wine (by the glass or by the bottle) with each starter and main course. You might begin with the Ashford Castle version of Caesar Salad, and for the main course there's a slight leaning towards seafood, but game will be offered in season, and a speciality that may surprise is the daily roast, served from a carving trolley. Irresistible desserts, or a superb cheese trolley, to finish. Although unarguably expensive, the dining experience at Ashford Castle gives value for money - and the Sunday lunch menu is very reasonable for the quality of food, service and surroundings; it offers

a shortened and somewhat simplified version of the dinner menu, but the same high standards apply. *All meals in the castle are by reservation. *A light daytime menu is available in The Gallery. **Seats 140.** D daily 7-9.30, L Sun only (Oct-May), 1-2pm Set Sun L €39, Set 5 course D €70. A la carte D also available; house wines from €26. SC.15% **Cullen's at The Cottage:** A stone's throw from the Corrib and within sight of the castle, on Ashford's manicured lawns, Cullen's at The Cottage is named after the late Peter Cullen, a much-loved former Maitre D', and offers a completely different experience: mid-priced dining, open to the public, with none of the pomp and ceremony associated with the grandeur of meals served in the castle itself. The kitchen is operated under Stefan Matz's direction but functions independently from the main castle kitchen. Internally the cottage has been transformed, with burgundy coloured banquette seating, plain wood tables, tiled floors, and white walls. The menu, while leaning towards seafood, offers a varied selection of meat and vegetarian dishes, salads and side orders, also a daytime sandwich, pitta and panini section, and coffees, teas and desserts. On a fine summer's day, dining al fresco here has a continental air - and, there's a short fairly priced wine list. Well-trained staff give good service, while appearing to have all the time in the world to chat. **Seats 65** (private room 48, outdoor seating 48). Open 11-9.30 daily (a phone call to check is advised, especially off-season). Reservations accepted. A la carte. Wines from €16. Amex, Diners, MasterCard, Visa, Laser. **Directions:** 48km (30 m) north of Galway on Lough Corrib.

Cong
COUNTRY HOUSE

Ballywarren Country House

Cross Cong Co Mayo **Tel: 094 954 6989**
ballywarrenhouse@gmail.com www.ballywarrenhouse.com

Diane and David Skelton's hospitable country house is in a pleasant rural area of gentle farming countryside just a few minutes' drive east of Cong and Ashford Castle. Large and well-proportioned, it has a welcoming feeling from the minute you arrive through the door into the classic back and white tiled hall. Public rooms are furnished stylishly and include a spacious drawing room with a cosy open fire, and the lovely Garden Room dining room, where dinner is available to guests by arrangement like a dinner party, it's a wholesome 5-course meal based on local ingredients, organic where possible, and all bread and rolls are home-made; a short but surprising wine list includes a choice of six champagnes! An oak staircase leads up to the three charming bedrooms, all with luxurious, well-finished bathrooms. This would make a very comfortable base for a few days spent in the area, the only slight downside is that the road is quite close. Fishing, golf, lake cruising, horse riding, hill walking all nearby. Garden. Children welcome (under 1s free in parents' room, cot available free of charge); **Rooms 3** (all en-suite & no smoking); all-day room service; B&B €74pps, ss €50. Pets permitted in certain areas by prior arrangement. Residents' D at 8pm in the Garden Room; dining room seats 8; set D €38 (4 course); reservation required and should be ordered earlier in the day. House wine €16; No SC. Closed 1 week May, 1 week Oct. Amex, MasterCard, Visa. **Directions:** East of Cong, on the Headford road.

Cong
CAFÉ

Hungry Monk Café

Abbey Street Cong Co Mayo **Tel: 094 954 5842**
robertdevereux@gmail.com www.cong-ireland.com

Poised scenically on the border between Galway and Mayo, Cong is a delightful village in its own right but, thanks to its connections with The Quiet Man - and the interest in Ashford Castle and it surroundings - it is a place where most visitors choose to take a break when exploring the area. And this is where the Hungry Monk comes in - Robert and Susan Devereux's attractive all-day café is just the place to drop in for a wholesome meal or snack, at any time of day. Cottagey and friendly, it has rough walls and brightly coloured mismatched chairs giving it a relaxed and homely feeling, and features the paintings that Robert works on during the winter when the café is closed. There's a great aroma of really good coffee as you arrive - perfect to go with their gorgeous home bakes (chocolate brownie, moist lemon and almond cake with fresh strawberries) or any one of an unusual range of sandwiches (apple, bacon, brie & chutney panini; prawn, rocket leaves with a lemon & black pepper mayo on brown bread) or excellent salads (pear with Cashel Blue cheese, crispy bacon & toasted hazelnuts, with balsamic vinegar & honey dressing, perhaps, or smoked salmon salad). A great little spot. Toilets wheelchair accessible; Children welcome (high chair, childrens menu); **Seats 30;** open Mar-Oct, Mon-Sat, 10-5pm; house wine €4.70 1/4 bottle. Closed Sun (except at bank hol weekends); Nov-Feb. MasterCard, Visa, Laser. **Directions:** Centre of Cong village.

Cong
HOTEL/RESTAURANT

Lisloughrey Lodge
The Quay Cong Co Mayo Tel: **094 954 5400**
lodge@lisloughrey.ie www.lisloughrey.ie

This new hotel enjoys one of the most beautiful locations in Ireland, with views down Lough Corrib and Lisloughrey Quay adding interest in the foreground, with small boats in the harbour and its old stone buildings set against wooded hills. The heart of the hotel is a fine period house on a ten acre site adjacent to Ashford Castle, and with access to its grounds; behind it, new accommodation has been added discreetly in two-bedroom units, built around an attractive landscaped courtyard (where civil wedding ceremonies may be held); to the side, a bright and airy function room is well-designed with direct access to a bar and other public areas, and also to the lawn at the front of the house, making a wonderful setting for weddings and other special occasions. A modern approach has been taken throughout the interior, including the beautiful old house which now sports a fashionable red and matt black colour scheme throughout the main public areas, wooden floors and lots of leather in the bars. The best accommodation is in the old house-one suite has a free-standing copper bath in the room but most rooms are in the new development, accessed by a wide corridor featuring red wall lights and lamps. Bedrooms are not especially large but like those in the otherwise very different sister property, Wineport Lodge in County Westmeath have big, very comfortable beds and tip-top quality pillows and bedding; flat screen TV has the prime position where a mirror would otherwise be, and is well placed for watching a film in bed, and a large wardrobe with trendy padded finish also conceals a good few bells and whistles. Fashion-led bathrooms are spacious but, with a frosted glass door compromising privacy, no bath (only a power shower with rain dance shower head) and a free-flow washbasin (designed to be plugless), they may not be to everyone's taste. Lisloughrey has facilities for business meetings, with the first floor Library in the main house suitable for meetings (or private dinners) of up to 30. Small conferences (30); broadband wi/fi. Treatment rooms, masseuse, walking, boat trips, fishing (trout, salmon), golf & equestrian nearby. **Rooms 50** (22 suites). B&B from €75-125 pps, ss about €50. **Salt Restaurant:** Situated in two rooms on the first floor, with lovely views of the lough and quay, this is one of the most successful areas of the hotel. The red and black scheme is lifted by smart tables classically appointed with crisp white linen and, as the evening draws in, warm lighting softens the atmosphere. Head chef Wade Murphy, like General Manager Marc MacCloskey, came here from Four Seasons hotels, renowned for their high levels of service and here, as elsewhere in the hotel, staff are exceptionally well trained, friendly and helpful. Menus are a little complicated on first reading and may be hard to choose from, but it makes little difference as the cooking is imaginative and accomplished, and dishes are well-conceived - the stylish foie gras cocktail signature dish looks set to be come a modern classic. Wade Murphy is a dedicated and genuine chef, and a meal here is sure to be a special experience. A very good breakfast is served here in the morning too. Amex, MasterCard, Visa, Laser. **Directions:** Just outside Cong, in the Ashford Castle estate.

Foxford
HOTEL

Healys Hotel
Pon toon Foxford Co Mayo Tel: **094 925 6443**
info@healyspon toon.com www.healyspon toon.com

This famous old hotel, loved by fisherfolk, landscape artists and those who seek peace and tranquillity, changed hands in 1998, and there has since been a plan of gradual renovation and refurbishment both indoors and in the gardens, without spoiling the old-fashioned qualities that have earned this hotel its special reputation. Accommodation is modest but comfortable - and also moderately priced. The scale is small and it's an intimate place, and very relaxed; the hotel has lots of information on things to do in the area - including golf at around a dozen nearby courses, fishing, shooting, horse racing, and mountain climbing. The bar has character both here and in the restaurant, the food is above average for a country hotel. Small banqueting facilities (70); garden, fishing. Packed lunches available. Children welcome (under 3s free in parents' room; cots available at no charge, baby sitting arranged). No pets. **Rooms 14** (all shower only & no smoking). B&B €45pps, ss €20.* Bar food available 12.30-9.30 daily; Restaurant L & D daily. Closed 25 Dec. Amex, Diners, MasterCard, Visa, Laser. **Directions:** R310 from Castlebar - 10 min drive; R318 from Foxford to junction R310; R310 from Ballina - 10 min drive.

Lahardane
PUB

Leonard's

Lahardane Ballina Co Mayo
Tel: 096 51003

This unspoilt roadside traditional pub & grocery shop was established in 1897 and the original owners would be proud of it today. If you get hungry, there's always the makings of a picnic on the shelves. Closed 25 Dec & Good Fri.

Lecanvey
BAR

T.Staunton

Lecanvey Westport Co Mayo
Tel: 098 64850/64891

Thérèse Staunton runs this great little pub near the beginning of the ascent to Croagh Patrick - genuinely traditional, with an open fire it has the feeling of a real 'local'. Not really a food place, but home-made soup and sandwiches or plated salads are available every day until 9pm. Occasional traditional music sessions - and frequent impromptu sing-songs. Closed 25 Dec & Good Fri. **No Credit Cards. Directions:** 12.5km (8 m) from Westport on Louisburgh Road.

Mulranny
HOTEL/RESTAURANT

Park Inn Mulranny

Mulranny Westport Co Mayo **Tel: 098 36000**
info@parkinnmulranny.ie www.parkinnmulranny.ie

This landmark hotel, originally built by the Midland Great Western Railways, first opened for business in March 1897 and it became a famous destination during the lifetime of the railway between Westport and Achill Island. Situated on a 42 acre woodland estate, the hotel is now owned by Tom and Kathleen O'Keeffe, who have retained much of its original character and charm while developing a contemporary style. It now has 60 guest bedrooms, and an elegant dining room, modern bar, relaxing lounges and luxurious leisure centre with 20 metre pool - all of which make this an attractive destination for a day out or a holiday. The local blue flag beach, a nearby golf course and wonderful walks will make this a haven for both Irish guests and visitors from other countries. Conference/banqueting (500/300); free broadband wi/fi; business centre. Children welcome (free cot available, baby sitting arranged). No pets. Leisure centre (pool, fitness room, jacuzzi, sauna, steam room); massage; beauty salon; pool table; golf (9), walking. Garden visits, equestrian and fishing nearby. **Rooms 60** (3 superior, 7 shower only, 23 family, 3 disabled, 56 no smoking). B&B €105 pps ss €25. Closed 18-26 Dec. **Nephin Restaurant:** The restaurant is an elegant room and it has the best view, overlooking the Atlantic. It is a formal room, as befits the dining experience offered here, and is set up comfortably but in no way ostentatiously, with good-sized square and round tables, traditional mahogany dining chairs and crisp white linen. Head chef Seamus Commons, who is from Bohola in east Mayo, is well known in Ireland and has worked in some leading restaurants including L'Ecrivain, in Dublin, where he was head chef - now he is back, making his mark in this 'oasis in the west', where he has attracted a following and established the hotel as a destination for food lovers. Menus read well: not over-extensive, but clearly ambitious and offering many unusual ingredients and creative combinations; and - although the Guide's recent experience suggests that the cooking can sometimes be a little inconsistent - they generally deliver on the promise. The Table d'Hôte menu offers three choices on each course and is very good value - and, for a supplement, residents have freedom of the à la carte. Served on wave shape, oval and square plates, presentation is classic but also funky, and all the little niceties of a special meal are observed. Service is excellent and friendly, under the direction of restaurant manager Nick Faujour, and sommelier Nicolas Bonnet's wine list is interesting - and his manner in assisting guests to make the best choice is impressive. **Seats 50;** D daily, 7-9.30pm; set 3 course D, €42.50; also a la carte. Vegetarian menu. **Waterfront Bistro:** Seats 80; food served 12.30-9pm. Bar food also available, 12.30-9pm. Establishment closed 18-26 Dec. MasterCard, Visa, Laser. **Directions:** In Mulranny village on the N59.

Newport
RESTAURANT/COUNTRY HOUSE

Newport House
Newport Co Mayo **Tel: 098 41222**
info@newporthouse.ie www.newporthouse.ie

For two hundred years this distinctive creeper-clad Georgian House overlooking the river and quay, was the home of the O'Donnells, once the Earls of Tir Connell. Today it symbolises all that is best about the Irish country house, and has been especially close to the hearts of fishing people for many years. But, in the caring hands of the current owners, Kieran and Thelma Thompson, and their outstanding staff, the warm hospitality of this wonderful house is accessible to all its guests not least in shared enjoyment of the club-fender cosiness of the little back bar. And, predating the current fashion by several centuries, pure spring water has always been piped into the house for drinking and ice-making. The house has a beautiful central hall, sweeping staircase and gracious drawing room, while bedrooms, like the rest of the house, are furnished in style with antiques and fine paintings. The day's catch is weighed and displayed in the hall - and the fisherman's bar provides the perfect venue for a reconstruction of the day's sport. Newport was our Country House of the Year in 1999, and also selected for our annual Wine Award in 2004. Fishing, garden, walking, snooker. **Rooms 18** (2 with private (non connecting) bathrooms, 2 with bath & separate shower, 4 ground floor, 2 disabled). Children welcome (under 2s free in parents' room; cots available, baby sitting arranged). Limited wheelchair access. Pets allowed in some areas. B&B €164pps, ss €26, no S.C. Closed mid Oct-mid Mar. **Restaurant:** High-ceilinged and elegant, this lovely dining room makes the perfect backdrop for "cooking which reflects the hospitable nature of the house" in fine meals made with home-produced and local foods. Home smoked salmon is a speciality and some of the fruit, vegetables and herbs come from a walled kitchen garden that has been worked since 1720 and was established before the house was built, so that fresh produce would be on stream for the owners when they moved in. John Gavin has been head chef since 1983 and his 5-course menus feature fresh fish, of course - freshwater fish caught on local lakes and rivers, and also several varieties of fish delivered daily from nearby Achill Island; smoked salmon is prepared to a secret recipe, but carnivores will be equally delighted by charcoal grilled local beef or roast spring lamb, and perhaps game in season. To finish, there are Irish farmhouse cheeses with fresh fruit, and classic desserts, often using fruit from the garden. And then there is Kieran's renowned wine list that, for many, adds an extra magic to a meal at Newport. It includes classic French wines about 150 clarets from 1961-1996 vintages, a great collection of white and red burgundies, excellent Rhônes and a good New World collection too. The foundations of this cellar go back many decades to a time when Kieran was himself a guest at Newport; great wines are a passion for him and, while acknowledging that they are irreplaceable, he offers them to guests at far less than their current retail value. Great lists of this scale and quality are almost a thing of the past, so it is a matter of celebration that such a collection should belong to a generous spirit like Kieran, who takes pleasure in allowing others to share his passion. **Seats 38.** L daily, 12-2pm; D daily, 7-9. Set 6 course D €65; house wine from €24. Toilets wheelchair accessible. Non-residents welcome by reservation. House closed 10 Oct-18 Mar. Amex, Diners, MasterCard, Visa, Laser. **Directions:** In village of Newport.

WESTPORT

A great example of good town planning - Westport was designed by the Georgian architect James Wyatt - this charming town has high standards of accommodation and restaurants, making it a very agreeable base. It is a delightful place to spend some time: The Mall, with its lime trees flanking the Carrowbeg River, is especially pleasing to the eye, and nearby Westport House is open to the public in summer and well worth a visit. The famous pilgrimage mountain of Croagh Patrick, known locally as "the Reek" lies some 10km west of the town near the villages of Murrisk and Lecanvey. The mountain presents a striking backdrop to the town and the church on the summit can just be made out with the naked eye from Westport. The town is well known as a sea fishing centre and its annual festival attracts many visitors. Other activities include bathing at many nearby beaches, for golfers there is a championship golf course and 5km north of Westport there is a sailing centre at Glenans, Rosmoney. The Clew Bay Heritage Centre depicts the maritime history of the area and local history and traditions; it also provides a genealogical service. Westport is an ideal base for touring Connemara, Sligo, Galway and Donegal, all of which are within easy driving distance. Along the harbour front there are several pubs and cafes, including **The Creel** (098 26174) a relaxed restaurant that is a good choice for a daytime bite, and - out of town in the same direction, at Rosbeg - **The Shebeen** (098 26528) is an attractive waterside pub with restaurant attached.
WWW.IRELAND-GUIDE.COM FOR THE BEST PLACES TO EAT, DRINK & STAY

Westport
HOTEL/RESTAURANT

Ardmore Country House Hote

The Quay Westport Co Mayo **Tel: 098 2599**
ardmorehotel@eircom.net www.ardmorecountryhouse.cor

Pat and Noreen Hoban's sma family-run hotel is quiet located in immaculately maintained gardens nea Westport harbour, with views over Clew Bay, and offers warm hospitality, very comfortable accom modation and good food. Spacious, individuall decorated guest rooms are all furnished to a ver high standard; the style is luxurious and the rang of facilities - which includes an iron and ironin board and, in many rooms, a separate bath an shower - is impressive. Guests are given the choic of seaview or back of house rooms, allowing for a less expensive option; this also applies to short break offered. An outstandingly good breakfast includes (amongst other equally tempting items) a choice c freshly squeezed juices in generous glasses, fresh fruit (correctly prepared according to type, e skinned grapefruit segments), delicious cafetière coffee, a perfectly-cooked, simple version of 'the fu Irish', and a superb fish plate. Great details too - freshly baked breads, home-made preserves an prompt service. [Ardmore was selected for our Best Hotel Breakfast Award in 2005.] Not suitable fo children. No pets. Garden. **Rooms 13** (all superior; 2 ground floor; all no smoking). Room servic (limited hours); turndown service. B&B €95 pps, ss €35. Closed Jan & Feb. **Restaurant:** A well appointed irregularly shaped room with some useful corners for têtes-à-tête conversations and a se view over the front gardens, the restaurant is the heart of this house; owner-chef Pat Hoban present pleasingly classic menus which make good reading over an aperitif in the comfortable bar and includ a wide range of meat and poultry - but the main emphasis is on local seafood, including shellfish suc as scallops and lobster when available. Accomplished cooking and some imaginative twists in the pres entation add up to a pleasing meal, and service is charming and willing. Not suitable for children **Seats 50.** D 7-9 (daily in summer, Tue-Sat low season); A la carte. House wine €21.50. Closed Su & Mon in low season, all Jan & Feb. Amex, MasterCard, Visa, Laser. **Directions:** 1.5 kms from Westpor town centre, on the coast road.

Westport
HOTEL/RESTAURANT

Carlton Atlantic Coast Hote

The Quay Westport Co Mayo **Tel: 098 29000**
info@atlanticcoasthotel.com www.atlanticcoasthotel.com

Behind the traditional stone façade of an old mill on Westport harbour, this bright moder hotel has spacious public areas combining traditional and contemporary themes and mate rials and creating a smart youthful tone that is continued through to good-sized bedrooms, with goo facilities and stylish Italian bathrooms. Although it may seem like an impersonal city hotel in some ways staff (including those in the excellent leisure centre, and spa) are exceptionally friendly and efficient Conferences/banqueting (160/140). Business centre; secretarial services; video-conferencing. Childre welcome (under 4s free in parents' room, cots available without charge, baby sitting arranged). Leisure centre, swimming pool; spa; fishing; discount at local golf club. Golf breaks; details on application Although slightly reduced from last year, prices remain high, making it worthwhile to shop around however better value off-season/special interest breaks are often available. **Rooms 85** (1 suite, 2 junio suites, 10 superior, 55 no smoking, 3 for disabled). Lift. 24 hr room service. B&B about €135pps, s about €25; SC incl. Closed 22-27 Dec. **Blue Wave Restaurant:** The restaurant is situated right up at the top of the building, which is a good idea, although the view is somewhat restricted by sloping roo windows and the room can be very warm in summer. But the hotel has always taken pride in its food and interesting, well-balanced contemporary menus offer a good choice of imaginative dishes, with a natura leaning towards seafood. Cooking is good and, as elsewhere in the hotel, friendly and helpful service adds to the occasion. Breakfast is also served in the Blue Wave Restaurant - and a very good start to the day it is: a cold buffet selection includes (in addition to the usual fruits and cereals), fresh fruit salad, Greek yoghurt and fruit coulis, a fine continental style choice of cooked meats and cheese, Irish smoked salmon and home-baked breads and pastries - and hot cooked-to-order dishes run to grilled kippers, fresh fish of the day (very nicely cooked) and less hot dishes like pan-fried lambs livers and toasted bagel with cream cheese and Ballina smoked salmon. Children welcome. **Seats 90;** reservations required; air condi tioning. Lift. Toilets wheelchair accessible. D daily, 6.30-9.15. Set D about €36. House wine abou €17.50. SC discretionary. Informal bar menu also offered, 12.30-9 daily. Amex, MasterCard, Visa, Laser **Directions:** Located at Westport harbour, 1 mile from town centre on main Louisburgh and coast road. ◊

Westport
HOTEL

Hotel Westport

Newport Rd Westport Co Mayo **Tel: 098 25122**
reservations@hotelwestport.ie www.hotelwestport.ie

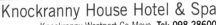

Just a short stroll from Westport town centre this large modern hotel offers excellent facilities for both leisure and business guests, numerous short breaks are offered and the conference and business centre provide a fine venue for corporate events. Constant refurbishment and upgrading is an ongoing feature of this well-managed hotel and, although all bedrooms are well-appointed and have all the usual amenities, 48 rooms and bathrooms are to be enlarged and refurbished in time for the 2008 season. The hotel's extensive leisure facilities include the White Flag Ocean Spirit Spa and there is also a year round Cub's Corner for children (0-3). The whole hotel is unusually wheelchair-friendly, and staff are invariably helpful and friendly which, together with the quiet but almost-central location and outstanding facilities, make this a very pleasant place to stay. Conference/banqueting (500/350); video conferencing; business centre; secretarial services; broadband wi/fi; laptop-sized safes in bedrooms. Leisure centre (swimming pool, fitness room, jacuzzi, sauna, steam room); spa, treatment rooms, hairdressing. Garden. Children welcome (under 3s free in parents' room; cots available without charge; baby sitting arranged; children's playground & playroom). **Rooms 129** (6 suites, 7 for disabled, 86 no smoking, 40 ground floor). Lift. 24 hr room service. B&B €130 pps, ss €20. No SC. Open all year. Amex, Diners, MasterCard, Visa, Laser. **Directions:** From Castlebar Street, turn right on to north mall (do not go over the hump back bridge), then turn on to Newport Road, 1st left and at the end of the road.

Westport
HOTEL/RESTAURANT

Knockranny House Hotel & Spa

Knockranny Westport Co Mayo **Tel: 098 28600**
info@khh.ie www.khh.ie

Set in landscaped grounds on an elevated site overlooking the town, this privately owned Victorian-style hotel opened in 1997. A welcoming open fire and friendly staff at reception create an agreeably warm atmosphere: the foyer sets the tone for a hotel which has been built on a generous scale and is full of contrasts, with spacious public areas balanced by smaller ones - notably the library and drawing room - where guests can relax in more homely surroundings. Bedrooms are also large - the suites have four poster beds and sunken seating areas with views - and most are very comfortable (some with jacuzzi baths). 'Spa Salveo' health spa has nine treatment rooms, swimming pool, gym, and hair salon and, recent development has included a new conference and meeting area. Conferences/Banqueting (600/350); business centre; free broadband wi/fi; laptop-sized safes in bedrooms. Destination Spa. Fitness room, jacuzzi, sauna, steam room, beauty salon. Equestrian and fishing nearby. Children welcome (under 3s free in parents' room, cots available free of charge, baby sitting arranged). **Rooms 97** (9 suites, 41 grand deluxe, 4 junior suites, 3 shower only, all no smoking, 3 family, 4 for disabled.) Lift. 24 hr room service. B&B €125 pps, ss €50. Closed 22-27 Dec. **La Fougère:** Contemporary Irish cooking is offered in the hotel dining room, La Fougère ("the fern"), which is at the front of the hotel, with fine views across the town to Clew Bay and Croagh Patrick. Head chef David O'Donnell's menus are wide-ranging, in a classic/modern style; there is pride in local produce, including the renowned organic Clare Island salmon and Mayo lamb - specialities include a accomplished dish of roast loin of Ballinrobe lamb with cranberry & herb stuffing on aubergine caviar with baby vegetables, potato confit & rosemary jus. Even in a town with plenty of good restaurants to choose from, this is a pleasant place for an outing - there is a sense of the restaurant being well-run, with friendly interaction between staff and guests which adds greatly to the enjoyment of a good meal. A user-friendly wine list blends entertainment and information in various ways; there's a good choice of mid-range wines, and plenty available by the glass. **Seats 150;** children welcome; air conditioning; pianist. D 6.30-9.30. L 1-2.30. Set D €49; Set Sun L €29.50. House wines from €22. SC discretionary. Hotel closed 22-27 Dec. Amex, MasterCard, Visa, Laser. **Directions:** Take N5/N60 from Castlebar. Hotel is on the left just before entering Westport.

Westport
RESTAURANT

Lemon Peel @ The Asgard

The Harbour Westport Co Mayo **Tel: 098 26929**
info@lemonpeel.ie www.lemonpeel.ie

Proprietor-chef Robbie McMenamin recently relocated from Westport town centre to the harbour area, and the move has been a tremendous success. A reception area on the ground floor is a pleasant place to meet, with nautical bric-à-brac and a fire (electric) creating a warm atmosphere, and a wide staircase leads up to the restaurant which has a balcony overlooking the foyer so diners can observe all the comings and goings. The room is bright and airy, with large windows overlooking the harbour area, dark timber floor and solid furniture; friendly staff extend a very warm welcome, adding to the buzz in this busy informal restaurant. The menu is similar in style and content to the successful formula of using good ingredients quite simply (and charging moderate prices) that worked so well in the old restaurant. A wide choice of locally produced foods is offered; Kelly's of Newport black pudding with spiced apple is a particularly enjoyable starter, typically followed by roast lamb steak with rosemary gravy & al dente vegetables, and bread & butter pudding to finish. Nightly specials might include a fish dish like fillet of brill with a crabmeat and creamy mashed potato stuffing, accompanied by a pesto salsa and white wine cream sauce a dish much enjoyed on a recent visit. A short well-balanced wine list includes six house wines, available by the glass. [*Bar food is operated separately, by the Asgard.] **Seats** 60. D only 6-9.30 (Sun 6-9). Early menu about €25 (6-7pm), also à la carte. House wines about €20; SC discretionary. Closed Mon (Telephone off-season to check opening times.) Amex, MasterCard, Visa, Laser. **Directions:** On harbour front, a mile outside Westport on the Louisburgh road. ◇

Westport
CHARACTER PUB

Matt Molloy's Bar

Bridge Street Westport Co Mayo
Tel: 098 26655

If you had to pick one pub in this pretty town, this soothingly dark atmospheric one would do very nicely not least because it is owned by Matt Molloy of The Chieftains, a man who clearly has respect for the real pub: no TV (and no children after 9 pm). Musical memorabilia add to the interest, but there's also the real thing as traditional music is a major feature in the back room or out at the back in fine weather. Matt is often away on tour, but he's a real local when he's back, and takes great pride in this smashing town. It's worth noting that normal pub hours don't apply, this is an afternoon into evening place, not somewhere for morning coffee. Closed 25 Dec & Good Fri. **Directions:** Town centre.

Westport
CAFÉ/RESTAURANT

McCormack's at The Andrew Stone Gallery

Bridge Street Westport Co Mayo
Tel: 098 25619

Go under the archway beside Kate McCormack's sixth generation butcher's shop and up the stairs, where you will find an art gallery on your right and, on your left, this small, unpretentious restaurant with an open counter displaying an array of good things, including home-baked cakes, quiches and patés - the product of generations of family recipes and particularly of Annette McCormack's table. Here, her two daughters, Katrina and Mary Claire, carry on the tradition - and the welcome. Treats especially worth trying include seafood chowder, leek and bacon quiche and, in season, fresh crab on home-made baps. Locally reared meats go into specialities like bacon and cabbage, and a casserole of spring lamb. And don't leave without one of the gloriously home-made desserts. Many of the deli dishes from the shop are on the menu, as well as farmhouse cheeses including the local Carrowholly cheese. Works by local artists hang in the restaurant and adjacent rooms: well worth a visit. **Seats 34.** Children welcome. Open all day Thu-Sat and Mon. Closed Sun & Wed. MasterCard, Visa. **Directions:** Westport town centre - on the main street (the one with the clock tower at the top). ◇

Westport
RESTAURANT
👑 👁

Quay Cottage Restaurant

The Harbour Westport Co Mayo **Tel: 098 26412**
quaycottage@eircom.net ⬤ www.quaycottage.com

Kirstin and Peter MacDonagh have been running this charming stone quayside restaurant just outside Westport since 1984, and it never fails to delight. It's cosy and informal, with scrubbed pine tables and an appropriate maritime decor, which is also reflected in the menu (although there is also much else of interest, including steaks, honey roast duckling and imaginative vegetarian options). But seafood is the star, typically in starters of chowder or garlic grilled oysters and main courses baked fillet of tandoori salmon, served with raita dressing - or bake cod fillet with a pesto & smoked mozzarella crust and tangy lime & champagne sauce. Daily specials are often especially interesting (langoustine, halibut, scallops, lobster for example) and there are nice homely desserts, like rhubarb pie with real custard or a plated farmhouse cheese selection such as Cashel Blue, smoked Gubbeen and an Irish brie, with fresh fruit and biscuits. Freshly-brewed coffee by the cup to finish. There's a great atmosphere in this immaculately maintained restaurant, and Kirstin supervises a friendly front of house team. A fairly priced, well-chosen wine list is informative and includes a number of wines available by the bottle or half bottle. Children welcome. **Seats 80** (private room, 40/15; outdoor seating, 8). Toilets wheelchair accessible (step at front but have a ramp). D 6-10 (Mon-Sat in summer, Tue-Sat in winter). D à la carte; house wine €18.50; SC discretionary (except 10% on parties of 6+). Closed Sun (& Mon in winter), Christmas, all Jan. Amex, MasterCard, Visa, Laser. **Directions:** On the harbour front, at gates to Westport House.

Westport
HOTEL/RESTAURANT
N

Westport Plaza Hotel
Castlebar Street Westport Co Mayo **Tel: 098 51166**
info@westportplazahotel.ie www.westportplazahotel.ie

Adjoining its larger sister property the Castlecourt Hotel, in the centre of Westport, this is a smart, contemporary hotel, with spacious stylishly furnished public areas, including a comfortable bar, and impressive accommodation. Some rooms have balconies overlooking a rooftop garden and, with king size beds, marbled bathrooms with Jacuzzi, air conditioning, plasma screen TV with interactive services, minibar and safe all included as standard, this is a desirable place to stay. Guests have use of the C Club leisure facilities next door, in addition to a new spa due to open on site in time for the 2008 season. Conferences/Banqueting (120/80); business centre; free broadband wi/fi. Leisure centre (pool, fitness room, jacuzzi, steam room); beauty salon, hair dressing. Spa to open winter 07. Equestrian, golf, fishing and garden visits nearby. Children welcome (under 3s free in parents' room, cots available free of charge, baby sitting arranged, creche, playroom). **Rooms 88** (1 suite, 2 junior suites, 5 shower only, 9 family, 5 for disabled); Lift; All day room service. B&B €125pps, ss €35. Open all year. **Restaurant Merlot:** Situated just inside the main entrance and overlooking the busy street, this attractive restaurant has three distinct areas decorated in contrasting styles; all are well appointed with white linen, smart table settings and comfortable chairs, and the welcome from a mainly non-Irish staff is warm and efficient. Menus offer a good variety of modern international dishes, with some local ingredients such as Newport crab, organic Clare Island salmon, named. Food is well presented and enjoyable, although very little time is allowed between courses - this busy restaurant usually does two sittings each night. The wine list includes seven half bottles but none by the glass, only quarter bottles are offered. **Seats 120** (private room, 80); air conditioning; children welcome; reservations required; D daily, 6-9.30pm, set D €39.50; house wine from €22. Open all year. MasterCard, Visa, Laser. **Directions:** Approaching town from the N5, hotel is on the right hand side at first set of traffic lights.

Westport area
BAR/RESTAURANT

The Tavern Bar & Restaurant
Murrisk Westport Co Mayo **Tel: 098 64060**
info@tavernmurrisk.com www.tavernmurrisk.com

Myles and Ruth O'Brien have been running this fine bar and restaurant just outside Westport, at the foot of Croagh Patrick, since 1999 and have built up an enviable reputation. The fine dining restaurant, Upstairs At The Tavern, offers several very attractive menus, including an early dinner, a midweek special, and an à la carte; local seafood from Clew Bay is very much the speciality here, and menus also include named local and artisan foods such as air-dried Connemara lamb and meat from the renowned butchers McGeough's of Oughterard, Chris Smyth's organic leaves and Carrowholly cheeses. Bar menus are quite extensive, with a children's menu as well as a good choice of dishes for full meals, and a range of sandwiches. Traditional Irish music on Wed. Toilets wheelchair accessible. Children welcome (playground, playroom, high chair, childrens menu, baby changing facilities); beer garden; air conditioning; free broadband wi/fi; **Seats 70;** reservations required; D served daily in summer, 6-10pm (D weekends only off-season, although bar food is served daily all year, 12-9.30pm), value D €25 pp Mon-Fri, 6-7.30pm, also a la carte; house wine €17.50. Restaurant closed during the week off-season. Establishment closed Good Fri, 25 Dec. Amex, MasterCard, Visa, Laser. **Directions:** At the foot of Croagh Patrick, 5 mins from Westport.

COUNTY MEATH

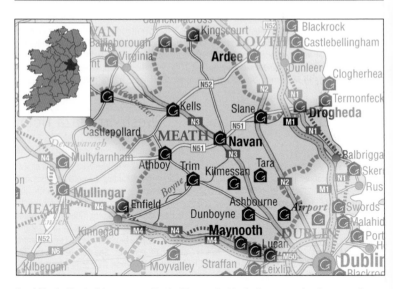

Royal Meath. Meath of the pastures. Meath of the people. Meath of many people... Any recent Census has confirmed what had been expected. The population of Ireland may have increased by 8%, but Meath is the fastest-growing place of all, its increase clocking in at 22.1% and counting.

The numbers aren't huge in today's overcrowded and city-oriented world, perhaps, but nevertheless Meath is a county which finds itself living in interesting times. The proximity of Dublin - with the inevitable pressures of prosperity and population – can be challenging. But it also brings benefits. With an increasingly affluent and discerning population, Meath is able to support a wide variety of hospitable establishments ranging from glossy restaurants of international quality to characterful pubs deep in the heart of the country.

And the inevitable changes – for instance, the need to find ways through the county for new major roads - are projects which you feel Meath can absorb. For this is a county which is comfortable and confident with itself, and rightly so. The evidence of a rich history is everywhere in Meath. But it's a history which sits gently on a county which is enjoying its own contemporary prosperity at a pace which belies the bustle of Dublin just down the road.

And anyone with an interest in the past will find paradise in Meath, for along the Boyne Valley the neolithic tumuli at Knowth, Newgrange and Dowth are awe-inspiring, Newgrange in particular having its remarkable central chamber which is reached by the rays of sun at dawn at the winter solstice.

Just 16 kilometres to the southwest is another place of fascination, the Hill of Tara. Royal Tara was for centuries the cultural and religious capital of pre-Christian Ireland. Its fortunes began to wane with the coming of Christianity, which gradually moved the religious focal point to Armagh, though Tara was a place of national significance until it was finally abandoned in 1022 AD.

Little now remains of the ancient structures, but it is a magical place, for the approach from gently rising eastern flank gives little indication of the wonderful view of the central plain which the hill suddenly provides to the westward. It is truly inspiring, and many Irish people reckon the year is incomplete without a visit to Tara, where the view is to eternity and infinity, and the imagination takes flight.

Local Attractions & Information

Donore Bru na Boinne Visitor Centre	041 988 0300
Dunboyne Hamwood House & Gardens	01 825 5210
Good Food Circle (Meath) c/o	046 907 3426
Kells Grove Gardens & Tropical Bird Sanctuary	046 943 4276
Laytown Sonairte (National Ecology Centre)	041 982 7572

Meath Ashburn Tourism Information	1850 300 789
Navan Navan Racecourse	046 902 1350
Newgrange (inc Dowth & Knowth)	041 988 0300 / 982 4488
Oldcastle Loughcrew Historic Gardens	049 854 1922 / 854 1060
Oldcastle Loughcrew Passage Tombs (3000BC)	049 854 2009
Ratoath Fairyhouse Racecourse	01 825 6167
Summerhill Larchill Arcadian Gardens	01 628 7354
Tara Interpretive Centre	046 942 5903
Trim Butterstream Garden	046 943 6017
Trim Tourism Information	046 943 7227
Trim Trim Castle (restored Norman stronghold)	046 943 8619

ASHBOURNE

Convenient to Dublin airport and on the edge of countryside offering rural activities including horse riding and racing as well as the historical sites of County Meath, this fast-growing town is gradually acquiring much-needed amenities and the recently opened **Marriott Hotel** (see entry) is a welcome addition. Dining options in the town include the popular Chinese restaurant, **EatZen** (01 835 2110; www.eatzen.ie) in the town centre, a stylish modern restaurant that takes pride in presenting authentic Cantonese cuisine - with a twist.

WWW.IRELAND-GUIDE.COM FOR THE BEST PLACES TO EAT, DRINK & STAY

Ashbourne

GUESTHOUSE

R

Broadmeadow Country House & Equestrian Centre

Bullstown Ashbourne Co Meath **Tel: 01 835 2823**

info@irishcountryhouse.com www.irishcountryhouse.com

The Duff family's country guesthouse is also home to a fine equestrian centre; an interest in horses is certainly an advantage here, but this well-located house also makes a good base for other activities in the area. Very much a family business, the house is set well back from the road and surrounded by landscaped gardens. The spacious bedrooms are all en-suite and furnished to hotel standards. Residential riding holidays are a speciality but, as there are 20 golf courses within easy reach, golfing breaks are almost equally popular and the location, close to Dublin airport and a fairly short distance from the city centre, also makes this a convenient venue for meetings and seminars. A short all day menu is available to residents (9am-9pm), with wine or beverages. Small conferences (20). Children welcome (under 5s free in parents' room, cot available without charge, baby sitting arranged). No pets. Garden, tennis, cycling, equestrian. **Rooms 8** (all en-suite, 1 executive with separate bath & shower, 5 with over-bath shower, 2 shower only, 3 family rooms; all no smoking). Room service (all day). B&B €60 pps, ss €20. No SC. *Short breaks offered (equestrian & golf). Closed 23 Dec-2 Jan. MasterCard, Visa, Laser. **Directions:** Off N2 at R125 towards Swords village.

Ashbourne

HOTEL

N R

Marriott Ashbourne

The Rath Ashbourne Co Meath **Tel: 01 835 0800**

info@marriottashbourne.com www.marriottashbourne.com

A good choice for business travellers who need to be near Dublin city and the airport but prefer a less hectic location, this new hotel offers all the amenities and comfort required both on and off duty, with business facilities for meeting and events of all sizes, a high standard of accommodation and plenty to do after hours (including, believe it or not, karaoke in the Red Bar, where red-themed cocktails are a speciality and a bar menu is also available from noon-9pm daily). It is also providing much-needed facilities for the area and the Fitness & Leisure Club is open to local membership. 24 hr room service. Conference, meeting & banqueting facilities; business centre. Fitness & Leisure Club (swimming pool, sauna, steam room, hydrotherapy; gym.) **Rooms 148** (4 suites). Room rate from about €125; special offers/short breaks available. Golf nearby. Ample parking. **Directions:** 23km north of Dublin on main Dublin-Derry road. ◇

Athboy
RESTAURANT/GUESTHOUSE

Frankville House

R

O'Growney St Athboy Co Meath **Tel: 046 943 0028**
degnangeraghty@eircom.net www.bluedoorguesthouse.ie

Degnan and Josephine Geraghty's charming restaurant and guesthouse is in a fine 18th cenury house on the edge of the pretty town of Athboy, offering the grandeur of a large period house and the charm and attention of a smaller guest house. Their soñ Donncha, who is a well known chef, returned to his home town recently to open a restaurant here, and it has brought a new dimension to the town. Like the rest of the house, the bright restaurant is filled with interesting and carefully-chosen antique furniture, making a pleasing setting for the great flavours of Donncha's beautifully presented 7-course Tasting Menu; all ingredients are sourced locally. There is a comfortable lounge for the use of guests, and of the five individually-decorated bedrooms four are en-suite - including a master bedroom - and one has a private bathroom. In addition, an unusual dormitory room downstairs has four bunk beds and access to a showering area with under-floor heating, a boon for families. The Geraghtys enjoy catering for private functions as well as their regular guests and there are small conference/meeting facilities for approximately, with a projector and an organ available if required. There is also a sauna and outside hot-tub. Small conferences/banqueting (30/25). Children welcome (under 8s free in parents' room, cot available free of charge). **Rooms 5** (en-suite); B&B €50pps, ss €10. Restaurant: D Thu-Mon; unsuitable for children under 12 yrs; Seats 25 (private room, 10; outdoors, 8); D at 8pm; 7 course gourmet D €65. Rest closed Tue-Wed. Visa, Laser. **Directions:** North-west of Trim; at end of main street - on edge of town, opposite the church.

R

CLONEE

The Clonee/Dunboyne area is attracting a lot of young families to settle here lately, and acts like a magnet for the growing number of new gardeners - and a good few experienced ones too - who head here to visit the famous **Gardenworks Garden Centre** (01 825 5375), where there is also a café, which is open all day (Mon-Sat, 9.30-5; Sun & bank hols, 12-5). [Also at: Malahide Garden Centre. Tel 01 8450110.] Clonee is also home to the original **EatZen Chinese Restaurant** (01 801 3738) at Unit 1, Clonee Village; see also entry in Ashbourne.
WWW.IRELAND-GUIDE.COM FOR THE BEST PLACES TO EAT, DRINK & STAY

Dunbóyne
RESTAURANT

Caldwell's Restaurant

R

Summerhill Road Dunboyne Co Meath
Tel: 01 801 3866

féile bía In a neat modern building in the centre of Dunboyne, this smart two-storey restaurant is simple and modern in style - clean lines, unfussy table settings; the high-ceilinged ground floor area overlooks a large patio, which gives it a light, bright atmosphere, while tables on the balcony area above have a cosier ambience. Promising menus are refreshingly simply worded and sources highlighted, along with membership of Féile Bia. Set menus offer a choice of three on each course, while the à la carte is wider ranging and dishes sound more luxurious, including seafood specialities and red meats. Desserts tend to be enjoyable variations on classics, with a welcome emphasis on fruits in season. Caldwell's has its heart in the right place - it's great to see the provenance of ingredients given due recognition on a menu - and offers good cooking and a pleasant ambience at fair prices. **Seats 60** (private balcony area 22). Children welcome for Sun L (not after 7.45pm). D Wed-Sat, 5.30-'late'; L Sun only, all day: 1.30-9.30. Early D about €20 (5.30-7); 2-4 course Set D about €20-35. House wine about €19. Closed Mon. Amex, MasterCard, Visa, Laser. **Directions:** Dunboyne village, through lights, 2nd building on left. ◇

Dunboyne
HOTEL

Dunboyne Castle Hotel & Spa

R

Dunboyne Co Meath **Tel: 01 801 3500**
info@dunboynecastlehotel.com www.dunboynecastlehotel.com

Set in 21 acres of woodland and gardens on the Meath-Dublin border, this 18th century mansion opened to widespread acclaim in 2006. It is a stylish development in which the original building, a large 3-storey over basement country house, remains very much the dominant feature in the overall design - the fine interior has been beautifully restored and the two main reception rooms are impressive in scale and have many original features. Most of the accommodation is in the new development and spacious, high-ceilinged rooms and luxuriously furnished reflect the proportions of the old house. This is an extensive development and includes a choice of restaurants, bars, conference and meeting facilities, a dedicated exhibition complex and spa. It is a very popular wedding venue. Conferences/Banqueting (400/300), business centre, video conferencing, free broadband wi/fi

Destination Spa, fitness room; Equestrian and golf nearby. Children welcome (under 12s free in parents' room, cot available at no charge, baby sitting arranged); **Rooms 145** (2 suites, 2 junior suites, 8 executive, 6 shower only, 106 no smoking, 39 ground floor, 8 for disabled); 24 hr room service, Lift; B&B €85 pps, ss €60. Open all year. Amex, MasterCard, Visa, Laser. Heli-pad. **Directions:** N3 into Dunboyne village, left at Slevins pub, few hundred metres down the road on the left.

R R R   ENFIELD

This small town to the west of Dublin is situated on the Royal Canal and was believed to have been on the main road to Tara, seat of the High Kings of Ireland. Since then its history has been continuously interwined with roads, rail and the canal as transport requirements have changed over the years. Today the canal is an attractive feature and, despite its close proximity to the motorway (which has relieved traffic in the town itself), the harbour area has been pleasantly developed as a public park. Nearby at Johnstownbridge, the O'Neill family's 30-room **Hamlet Court Hotel** (046 954 1200; www.thehamlet.ie) has earned a reputation for hands-on management and caring service, and it is especially popular for weddings.

WWW.IRELAND-GUIDE.COM FOR THE BEST PLACES TO EAT, DRINK & STAY

Enfield   Marriott Johnstown House Hotel & Spa
HOTEL   Enfield Co Meath Tel: **046 954 0000**
R R R   info@johnstownhouse.com www.marriottjohnstownhouse.com

téite bia Although close to the motorway, this mainly modern hotel has a carefully restored mid-18th century house at its heart and something of its country house atmosphere lives on. The original house is only a small part of the hotel, but it is the focal point and an unusually fine feature is a drawing room with a ceiling by the Francini brothers, renowned for the beauty and skill of their decorative plasterwork. The hotel has been open for some years but development continues there is now a spa and leisure club and, in addition to rooms in the hotel, 'The Residences' offers additional 2-bedroom duplex accommodation (www.theresidences.ie). The hotel is very attractive for corporate events and business meetings, and has a dedicated outdoor events and corporate activity centre on site (Quest Corporate Events). It is also a pleasing and well-appointed hotel for private guests to stay, and is well located west of Dublin making it a good short break destination or a useful place to break a journey. Conferences/Banqueting (900/400); business centre; free broadband wi/fi; video conferencing. Destination Spa; Leisure centre (fitness room, 'pool, jacuzzi, sauna, steam room); hair dressing; beauty salon. Equestrian and golf nearby. Children welcome (under 12s free in parents' room, cot available free of charge, baby sitting arranged, creche, playroom); **Rooms 126** (7 suites, 4 junior suites, 20 family, 30 ground floor, 4 for disabled); 24hr room service, lift; B&B €100 pps, ss €45. Amex, Diners, MasterCard, Visa, Laser. Heli-pad. **Directions:** Take M4 from Dublin - exit at Enfield.

Kells   The Ground Floor Restaurant
RESTAURANT   Bective Square Kells Co Meath Tel: **046 924 9688**
R   bookings@chuig.com

téite bia A bright and attractive contemporary restaurant in the centre of Kells, The Ground Floor is a sister of The Loft in Navan and has much in common with it: wacky paintings and a youthful buzzy atmosphere, plus interesting, colourful food at accessible prices. Popular dishes from around the world abound in starters like Mexican quesadilla and the Ground Floor Combination, a selection of potato skins, buffalo wings and crostini, with home-made dips. Equally cosmopolitan main courses range from Caesar salads, through sizzling fajitas and home-made burgers and steaks. Interesting daily blackboard specials are often a good bet - and weight-watching options are available for some dishes. Consistent quality and exceptionally pleasant and helpful staff add to the relaxed ambience. The early dinner menu is particularly good value. Children welcome (baby changing facility available). Toilets wheelchair accessible. **Seats 65.** Air conditioning. D Mon-Sat, 5.30-10.30 (to 11 Fri/Sat), Sun 4-9. Early D about €17.50 (Mon-Sat 5.30-7.30 & all day Sun); otherwise à la carte. House wine about €18. SC discretionary except 10% on parties of 4+. Closed 25-26 Dec. MasterCard, Visa, Laser. **Directions:** Centre of Kells on the Athboy/Mullingar Road, in Bective Square. ◈

Kells   Vanilla Pod Restaurant
RESTAURANT   Headfort Arms Hotel Kells Co Meath Tel: **0818 222 800**
R   info@headfortarms.ie www.headfortarms.ie

téite bia Although reached through an entrance just inside the foyer of the Headfort Arms Hotel and in common ownership, The Vanilla Pod is an attractive bistro style restaurant run as an independent entity. In contrast to the hotel, it is very modern, with lots of pale wood, recessed lighting and sleek informal table settings. Efficient staff show you straight to your table to choose from a well-structured contemporary menu, which offers quite a few dishes (including some vegetarian) which can be chosen as a starter or main course. Good quality, carefully sourced ingredients are used, the cooking is sound and service is friendly and knowledgeable. There is an interest in wine - specials are offered from time to time, and there are sometimes wine evenings. **Seats 70.** Air conditioning. D 5.30-9.45, L Sun only, 12-3. Early D about €20 (5.30-7.30), also à la carte; Set Sun L about €25. SC10%. House wine about €18. Closed 25 Dec, Good Fri. Amex, MasterCard, Visa, Laser. **Directions:** On main Dublin-Cavan road, left section of black & white building on right. ◇

Kilmessan
HOTEL/RESTAURANT

R

The Station House Hotel
Kilmessan Co Meath **Tel: 046 902 5239**
info@thestationhousehotel.com   www.thestationhousehotel.com

féile bia The Slattery family's unique establishment is an old railway junction, which was closed in 1963, and all the various buildings were converted to a make an hotel of charm and character. It is an interesting and unusual place to visit, with lovely gardens, and makes a good base for business, or for exploring this fascinating county. It also makes a pretty wedding venue. **Rooms 20.** B&B from about €55pps. Open all year. **The Signal Restaurant:** The chintzy decor, piped Irish music and traditional fare haven't really dated and somehow it all works well, creating a relaxing place with a very warm feeling. The restaurant attracts diners from a wide area - their traditional Sunday lunch is especially renowned. The food is enjoyable in a no nonsense way that is becoming all too rare, portions are generous and it is very family-friendly. Overall a really pleasant little place. **Seats 90.** (Private rooms; outdoor seating, 50). Reservations advised. Children welcome. Toilets wheelchair accessible. L daily 12.30-3 (Sun to 5.30); D daily 7-10.30 (Sun to 9.30). Set D: Mon-Fri about €26; Sat about €50; Sun about €30. A la carte L & D also available, except Sat D. Bar Menu Mon-Sat, 11-6. House wine from about €18. Amex, Diners, MasterCard, Visa, Laser. **Directions:** From Dublin N3 to Dunshaughlin and follow signposts. ◇

NAVAN

Navan is on the banks of the River Boyne, and is the largest town and county town or administrative capital of County Meath. It is famous for its fine furniture and carpets. Navan also hosts an open air market every Friday. The Blackwater river meets the river Boyne on the eastern side of the town at the ancient Poolbeg bridge and there are many beautiful riverside walks. Mahammad Kahlid's attractive, well-maintained and conveniently located **Shahi Tandoori** (Watergate Street; 046 902 8762) is a traditional Indian restaurant with welcoming and hospitable staff, offering good food and service at very fair prices. It is a perfect place to drop into for a break when shopping. 10 minutes drive north of Navan **Scanlons of Kilberry** (046 902 8330; www.scanlonspub.ie) is an old-world pub that has earned a following for its traditional atmosphere and good food, and is especially well-known for great steaks. **The Russell** (046 903 1607), on Ludlow Street just across the road from Bermingham's lovely old bar - is a new restaurant offering an eclectic menu in a very beautiful dining room.
WWW.IRELAND-GUIDE.COM FOR THE BEST PLACES TO EAT, DRINK & STAY

Navan
RESTAURANT

R R

The Loft Restaurant
26 Trimgate Street Navan Co Meath **Tel: 046 907 1755**
bookings@chuig.com

féile bia Older sister to The Ground Floor in Kells, and the newer Side Door in Cavan (see entries), this thriving two-storey restaurant has much in common with them, notably strong modern decor (including some interesting original paintings by the Northern Ireland artist Terry Bradley), exceptionally pleasant, helpful staff and a lively global menu at reasonable prices that lays the emphasis on accessibility: this is a place for all ages and every (or no particular) occasion. The main menu is similar to The Ground Floor, also with daily blackboard specials. Downstairs the "Tapas Bar" serves a range of cold and hot tapas, with wine available by the glass and by the bottle. Children welcome. **Seats 90.** Air conditioning. D daily, 5.30-10.30 (Fri/Sat to 11). Early D €16.50 (Mon-Sat 5.30-7.30, all Sun), otherwise à la carte. House wine about €17.95. 10% sc added to tables of 4+. Closed 25-26 Dec. MasterCard, Visa, Laser. **Directions:** Centre of Navan, corner of Trimgate Street and Railway Street. ◇

Navan
RESTAURANT

N R R

Rendezvous
30 Railway Street Navan Co Meath **Tel: 046 902 9231**
info@rendezvousrestaurant.ie   www.rendezvousrestaurant.ie

Passers-by could easily miss the discreet exterior of Rendezvous (which is in the premises occupied for many years by Hudsons), but inside there's no escaping the statement décor. The frescoed angels, yellow chandeliers, engraved mirror and deep pile carpet may not appeal to everyone's tastes but the menu's wide reaching dishes are designed to please a wide market. Dishes span five continents to offer curries and steak, roasts and seafood, pasta and salads. Despite the perceived lack of focus the Guide found the cooking accurate, portions generous, and the service charming. Given the quality of the food, eating here is great value with their Value Menus for lunch (2 courses with tea/coffee €10) and dinner (3-course s €20) especially well priced. Open Tue-Sun, L 12.30 3; D 5.30-10. Also open bank holiday Mondays. **Directions:** Follow directions to town centre, take right off roundabout, 5th house down on left. ◇

Navan
PUB
R R

Ryan's Bar
22 Trimgate Street Navan Co Meath
Tel: 046 902 1154

This pleasant, well-run and very popular pub makes a good meeting place for a drink or at lunch-time, when contemporary light meals are offered: soups, hot panini bread, wraps (including a vegetarian option) and toasties (honey baked ham, perhaps, with a salad garnish). Apple pie and cream may be predictable but it's enjoyable nonetheless - and there's always a dessert among the daily specials. It's good value, the airy bar makes for a comfortable atmosphere and staff are friendly and efficient. Disc parking. Open from 11.30 am; L Mon-Fri. 12.30-2.30. Closed 25 Dec & Good Fri. MasterCard, Visa, Laser. **Directions:** Main Street Navan.

Navan area
HOTEL/RESTAURANT
😋 ⊙ **R R**

Bellinter House
Navan Co Meath **Tel: 046 903 0900**
info@bellinterhouse.com www.bellinterhouse.com

Not content with creating some of Dublin's most successful informal restaurants - Eden, Odessa, The Market Bar and the Café-Bar-Deli chain among them, Jay Bourke recently entered the world of hoteliers, procuring and overseeing the renovation of this elegant Palladian mansion. Designed by Richard Castle (Carton, Russborough, Powerscourt, Leinster Houses) it's set on the banks of the River Boyne in 12 acres of beautiful parkland, less than an hour from Dublin and Dublin Airport. The interior has been restored with meticulous attention to the architectural integrity of the building, but with an original, contemporary twist. Public rooms include the fanciful Drawing Room tricked out in retro furnishings and commanding soothing views of the river (all day dining is available there, including excellent afternoon tea), the Games Room and Library, the Bellinter Bar (ground floor, perfect for 'pints and cocktails'; bar food available any time) and the cosy Wine Bar in the basement, which is adjacent to the restaurant and offers an interesting, competitively priced wine-list. Outdoors, when the weather permits, the terraces and lawns are ideal for dining al fresco. Accommodation, in 34 individually styled rooms, is divided between the Main House, East and West Wings, and several restored outbuildings. Though all rooms feature luxurious Egyptian cotton sheets, goose down pillows, centrally controlled mood lighting, drinks cabinet and custom-made Italian multi-media 40" plasma screens, the eclectic mix of hand-made and old furniture doesn't always work in harmony. The bathrooms are spacious and beautiful, and while most have a full bath and/or power showers, some are shower only, so it's best to establish which you're being allocated when you book. The certified organic seaweed toiletries are especially nice, and reflect the speciality seaweed baths on offer in the hotel's spa. Teething problems were encountered during the Guide's visit, including staffing problems and careless housekeeping. Though especially popular with young families it's worth noting that babies' bottles can't be prepared in bedrooms and the structure of the old house means buggies must be lifted up and down flights of stairs. The gardens are a point of interest, and the colourful and fun 'pavilion pod' that won Diarmuid Gavin a silver medal at the Chelsea Flower Show has found a new home in the gardens here. Fishing on adjoining Boyne; overlooks Royal Tara Golf Club grounds Spa, massage, indoor 'pool, leisure centre, walking, cycling, fly fishing, pool table. Small Conferences/Banqueting (50/70), secretarial services, free broadband wi/fi; children welcome (cots available, baby sitting arranged, crèche). **Rooms 34** (13 shower only, 1 family room, 10 ground floor); all day room service. B&B room rate €225-380. **Eden Restaurant:** Modelled on the iconic Temple Bar restaurant, Eden, this is an exciting development on the Meath dining scene. Despite the recent departure of chef Eleanor Walsh, the driving force behind the popular Dublin sister restaurant, Bellinter's Eden seems to have been left in very capable hands. The elegant restaurant, in vaulted basement with natural daylight, has well spaced tables, leather swivel chairs and an unusual mustard carpet with discreet graphics that evoke the nearby Hill of Tara. The menu reflects this modern decor, with quality fresh produce used imaginatively in contemporary combinations and an accessible, affordable wine list. Service is friendly and informed, ensuring both residents and non-residents have a relaxing experience. Not suitable for children after 7pm; **Seats 90** (private rooms, 20, outdoors, 20); reservations required; food served all day, 11am-11pm in the drawing room; L Fri-Sun 12-3pm, D daily 6.30-10.30pm; set 2/3 course L Fri-Sun €30/35; early 2/3 course D about €25/30, 5-7pm; also a la carte D; house wine €24. SC 12.5%. Restaurant closed 24-26 Dec. Amex, MasterCard, Visa, Laser. **Directions:** Off N3 near the Hill of Tara. ◇

Navan area
RESTAURANT/PUB

O'Brien's Good Food and Drink House

The Village Johnstown Navan Co Meath
Tel: 046 902 0555

Located in a new development in the centre of Johnstown village, just five minutes' drive from Navan, this popular and fashionable gastro-pub is in the same ownership as Franzini O'Briens Restaurant in Trim, and worth a visit. Wood-panelling, red brick walls and candles on the tables combine to create a modern rustic feel, and the international-style menu has broad appeal, with starters like duck spring rolls, pan-fried black pudding and prawn won tons all well under €10, and main dishes including pizzas, pastas, burgers and chicken dishes under €20, although fresh fish may rise a little above this level. There are tasty vegetarian choices too, including good salads, also appealing side dishes (eg stringy onions, spring onion mash and home-made fries) and a nice dessert menu a light tangy ginger and honeycomb pudding, for example, with crème anglaise. Service is friendly and efficient, and a well-priced wine list offers a balanced range including a house champagne, two dessert wines and some decent wines by the glass. The weekday Early Bird dinner offers particularly good value. Children welcome until 9pm; Toilets wheelchair accessible. **Seats 110** (private room, 60); reservations not necessary; D Mon-Sat 5-10pm; Sun 1-9; Early D about €20, 5.30-7.30; also a la carte and vegetarian menu; SC 10%. Closed Good Fri, 25 Dec. Amex, Diners, MasterCard, Visa, Laser. **Directions:** 1km from Navan on Dublin road.

SLANE

This appealing village is well placed for visiting the historic sites of the area and has a traditional stone-faced 19th century hotel, **The Conyngham Arms** (041 988 4444; www.conynghamarms.com), named after the Conyngham family of Slane Castle, and a remarkable old-world bar, **Boyles Licensed Tea Rooms** (041 982 4195). More recent arrivals include **George's Patisserie**, a neat little deli-café in the centre of the village where chef/proprieter Georg Heise offers a delicious range of desserts and pastries, home-made breads, preserves, jams, chutneys and locally-grown organic fruit and veg - and also a small, interesting selection of wines including organic wines; currently a good place for a snack (Tue-Sat), a bigger café/restaurant is planned. Tankardstown House (041 982 4621; www.tankardstown.ie) is an appealing period property near Slane, opened officially for B&B just before we went to press.
WWW.IRELAND-GUIDE.COM FOR THE BEST PLACES TO EAT, DRINK & STAY

Slane
HOTEL

The Millhouse

The Old Mill Slane Co Meath **Tel: 041 9820723**
info@themillhouse.ie www.themillhouse.ie

Janey Quigley's unusual boutique hotel is scenically located right on the River Boyne and it is quite a place. The riverside setting is very beautiful and it's an interesting place, with big stone mill buildings beside the main house still awaiting development. Inside the hotel, dramatic contemporary décor contrasts with the old building and a series of public rooms draws you through the building as each area links enticingly to the next. The eleven very desirable bedrooms and their bathrooms are all individually designed and, a restaurant opened as we went to press and a spa and swimming pool is planned for 2008. A very desirable venue for weddings and private parties and for short breaks away from the city. Unsuitable for children. Conferences/Banqueting (60/120, or 300 in marquee); free broadband wi/fi. Jacuzzi, sauna, pool table, walking, massage. **Rooms 11** (5 superior, 5 shower only, all no smoking); limited room service; B&B €110pps, ss€90. Visa, Laser. **Directions:** On main N2, on the bridge in Slane.

Tara Area
PUB

O'Connell's

Skryne Nr. Tara Co Meath
Tel: 046 902 5122

Three generations of O'Connells have been caretakers of this wonderfully unspoilt country pub and the present owner, Mary O'Connell, has been delighting customers old and new for well over a decade now.

It's all beautifully simple two little bars with no fancy bits, lots of items of local interest, and a welcoming fire in the grate. What more could anyone want? As for directions: just head for the tower beside the pub, which is visible for miles around. Closed 25 Dec & Good Fri. **No Credit Cards.**

TRIM

Most famous for its enormous Anglo-Norman castle (restored and open to the public) and other medieval monuments, Trim is a small but - thanks to its location only 45km north-west of Dublin - fast-growing town. Well located for visitors interested in the history of the area, it is also becoming a popular short break destination and has recently acquired two new hotels: **Trim Castle Hotel** (046 9483000; www.trimcastle.com) is located shockingly near the castle and its dull, concrete exterior is at odds with the castle walls across the road; however, once inside, it is an exciting new establishment furnished in a contemporary, minimalist style and, in the Guide's (early) experience, with friendly staff serving tasty food. A short distance away and well-signed in the area, **Knightsbrook Hotel and Golf Resort** (see entry). For those who prefer a smaller establishment with hands-on owner management, **Brogan's Bar & Guesthouse** (046 943 1237; www.brogans.ie) is on High Street.

Trim
RESTAURANT

Franzini O'Briens

French's Lane Trim Co Meath
Tel: 046 943 1002

Modern and spacious, this smart and very popular restaurant beside Trim Castle has well-trained staff who greet and seat arriving guests promptly and - by ensuring that everyone settles in comfortably from the start - setting a tone of relaxed efficiency that makes for an enjoyable outing. Space is attractively broken up around a central carpeted square with leather sofas to provide a variety of seating areas and simple, uncluttered table settings are modern and elegantly functional - tall water carafes, finger bowls for nachos and paper napkins. Light-hearted menus offer an excellent range of choices in the international style and, together with an informal, buzzy atmosphere, indicate that this is a place for a good night out. Service is excellent, even at very busy times. Interesting wine list (supplied by Jim Nicholson). *See also **O'Briens Good Food & Drink House**, Navan. **Seats 110.** Reservations accepted. Children welcome before 8.30. Toilets wheelchair accessible. Air conditioning. D Mon-Sat, 6.30-10, Sun: L 1-4, D 4-8.30. Early bird D Mon-Fri 6.30-7.30, €21.95. Also A la carte. House wines from €16.95. SC 10% on groups 4+ Closed Mon off-season (Sept-May), 23-26 Dec, Good Fri. MasterCard, Visa, Laser. **Directions:** Beside Trim Castle.

Trim
HOTEL/RESTAURANT

Knightsbrook Hotel & Golf Resort

Trim Co Meath **Tel: 1850 554 400**
info@knightsbrook.com www.knightsbrook.com

This new hotel in beautiful countryside just outside Trim, makes a luxurious destination for a short golf or leisure break, business conference, or wedding, and is a welcome addition to the options in an area that is convenient to Dublin and also well-placed for visiting the many historical and cultural attractions in County Meath. Palatial public areas are designed to impress and, both here and in the bedrooms, the tone is welcoming with mellow woods and warm-toned furnishings used throughout. Leisure facilities are outstanding, offering a health club with 17m swimming pool and River Spa as well as an 18-hole championship golf course - great for weekenders and also off-duty delegates attending conferences and meetings here. In addition to the hotel accommodation, guests can opt to stay in one of the 3-bedroom holiday homes which are rented out on a weekly-basis. Conference/Banqueting (1,500/700), business centre, secretarial services, video conferencing, broadband wi/fi. Equestrian nearby, fly fishing nearby, golf (18), leisure centre with fitness room and 'pool, spa (beauty salon, massage), tennis, walking. Children welcome (under 3s free in parents' room, cots available at no charge, baby sitting arranged, crèche, playground). **Rooms 131** (4 suites, 8 junior suites, 12 executive, 6 family rooms, 8 for disabled, 80 no smoking); lift; 24 hr room service. B&B €125pps; ss€65. Open all year. Helipad. **The Rococo Restaurant:** While informal dining is available in the Golf Club and bars, this well-appointed high ceilinged room offers the hotel's formal dining experience. Head chef David Molony presents appealing à la carte menus based on locally sourced ingredients, and the cooking is creative and imaginative. A well-selected wine list leans towards the Old World; the hotel operates a wine club, which includes a seven-course tasting menu as part of an evening with a wine maker. A good breakfast is also served in the Rococo restaurant. Amex, MasterCard, Visa, Laser. **Directions:** About a mile from Trim town, on the Dublin Road.

COUNTY MONAGHAN

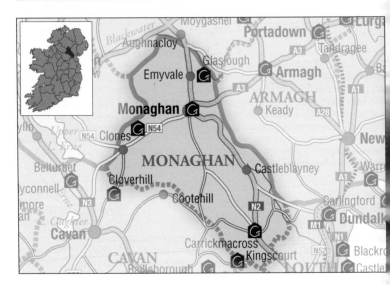

Of all Ireland's counties, it is Monaghan which is most centrally placed in the drumlin belt, that strip of rounded glacial hills which runs right across the country from Strangford Lough in County Down to Clew Bay in Mayo. Monaghan, in fact, is all hills. But as very few of them are over 300 metres above sea level, the county takes its name from Muineachain - "Little Hills". Inevitably, the actively farmed undulating country of the little hills encloses many lakes, and Monaghan in its quiet way is a coarse angler's paradise.

Much of the old Ulster Canal is in Monaghan, while the rest is in Armagh and Tyrone. Once upon a time, it connected Lough Erne to Lough Neagh. It has been derelict for a very long time, but with the success of the restored Shannon-Erne Waterway along the line of the old Ballinamore-Ballyconnel Canal bringing added vitality to Leitrim, Cavan and Fermanagh, the even more ambitious vision of restoring the Ulster Canal is now under way.

Vision of a different sort is the theme at Annaghmakerrig House near the Quaker-named village of Newbliss in west Monaghan. The former home of theatrical producer Tyrone Guthrie, it is a busy centre for writers and artists who can stay there to complete 'work in progress', or defer deadlines in congenial company. The dedicated eccentricity of the area is celebrated at the Flat Lake Cultural Festival around the big house in Hilton Park in August – they hope it will be an annual event, but not everyone has yet returned from the first one in August 2007.

In the east of the county at Castleblayney, there's a particularly attractive lake district with forest park and adventure centre around Lough Mucko. Southwards of Castleblayney, we come to the bustling town of Carrickmacross, still famous for its lace, and a Tidy Towns awardee.

Monaghan's pretty village of Glaslough towards the north of the county is worth a visit, and at Clontibret in northeast Monaghan, there's gold in them thar little hills. Whether or not it's in sufficient quantities to merit mining is a continuing matter of commercial debate, but the fact that it's there at all is another of Monaghan's more intriguing secrets. Another is the county's uncrowded character. It has been confirmed in a recent census, but there seem to be plenty of folk about the place.

Local Attractions & Information

Carrickmacross Carrickmacross Lace Gallery	042 966 2506
Carrickmacross (Kingscourt Rd) Dun a Ri Forest Park	049 433 1942
Castleblayney Lough Muckno Leisure Park	042 46 356
Glaslough Castle Leslie Gardens	047 88 109
Inniskeen Patrick Kavanagh Centre	042 937 8560

Monaghan town Tourism Information	047 81 122
Monaghan town Monaghan County Museum	047 82 928
Monaghan town (Newbliss Rd.) Rossmore Forest Park	047 81 968
Newbliss Annaghmakerrig (Tyrone Guthrie Centre)	047 54 003

Carrickmacross
HOTEL/RESTAURANT

Nuremore Hotel & Country Club
Carrickmacross Co Monaghan **Tel: 042 966 1438**
info@nuremore.com www.nuremore.com

téite bía This fine owner-managed country hotel just south of Carrickmacross is set in a parkland estate, with its own 18-hole golf course, and serves the leisure and business requirements of a wide area very well. As you go over the little bridge ("Beware - ducks crossing") and the immaculately maintained hotel and golf club open up before you, worldly cares seem to recede - this is a place you can get fond of. The hotel invariably gives a good impression on arrival and this sense of care and maintenance is continued throughout. Spacious, comfortably arranged public areas and generous bedrooms with views over the gardens and lakes are regularly refurbished and it would make an excellent base to explore this little known area - and there is plenty to do on site. The superb country club has a full leisure centre and a wide range of related facilities - including a gymnasium and spa - and there are conference and meeting rooms for every size of gathering, with state-of-the-art audio-visual equipment available. Conference/banqueting (600/400); business centre, secretarial services on request, video conferencing; broadband wi/fi. Leisure centre, swimming pool, spa; beauty salon; golf (18), fishing, walking, tennis, garden; snooker. Children welcome (cots available, €13; baby sitting arranged). No pets. Heli-pad. **Rooms 72** (7 junior suites, 11 executive, 5 family, 42 no smoking, 1 disabled). 24 hr room service. B&B €130 pps, ss €50. *Short breaks offered, including spa and golf breaks; details on application. Open all year. **The Restaurant at Nuremore:** The restaurant is to be refurbished shortly after the Guide goes to press but it will retain its pleasant layout, with a couple of steps dividing the window area and inner tables, allowing everybody to enjoy the view over golf course and woodland. This is the leading restaurant in the area, and the head chef, Raymond McArdle, has earned a national reputation for the hotel, which is now on the must-visit destination list for discerning travellers in Ireland. Proprietress Julie Gilhooly has lent every possible support to this talented protegé since his arrival here in 2000, and his spacious, state-of-the art kitchen is the envy of chefs throughout the country. Raymond sources ingredients meticulously, using local produce as much as possible in top rank daily set lunch and dinner menus, a separate vegetarian menu, a 'grown-up' children's menu, and an evening à la carte. Everything, it seems, is similarly impressive and difficult choices must be made on every course. This is exceptional cooking and, under the supervision of restaurant manager Frank Trutet, service is in line with the high standard of food. And there's many a treat in store on the extensive and well-organised wine list, which includes a good house wine selection and a further Sommelier Recommendation in the €30 bracket, an unusually wide choice of dessert wines and half bottles, a fair number of magnums and a menu of Catèrede armagnacs going back to 1920. This is a restaurant offering outstanding value for money, especially at lunch time. *Raymond McArdle was our Chef of the Year in 2005. **Seats 100** (private room, 50). Air conditioning. L Sun-Fri, 12.30-2.30; D daily 6.30-9.30 (Sun to 9). Set L €25 (Set Sun L, €30); Set D €52 (Vegetarian Menu about €25, Children's Menu €17.50); Prestige Menu €80. House wine from €26; sc discretionary. Closed L Sat. Open all year. Amex, Diners, MasterCard, Visa, Laser. **Directions:** Just south of Carrickmacross, 88km (55 m) from Dublin on N2 ot take M1 from Dublin and turn off at Ardee/Derry exit.

Clones
COUNTRY HOUSE

Hilton Par|

Clones Co Monaghan **Tel: 047 5600|**
mail@hiltonpark.ie www.hiltonpark.|

Once described as a "capsule of social history|
because of their collection of family portraits an|
memorabilia going back 250 years or more, Johnn|
and Lucy Madden's wonderful 18th centur|
mansion is set in beautiful countryside, amids|
200 acres of woodland and farmland. With lake|
Pleasure Grounds and a Lovers' Walk to set th|
right tone, the house is magnificent in every sens|
Johnny and Lucy are natural hosts and, as th|
house and its contents go back for so many gene|
ations, there is a strong feeling of being |
privileged family guest as you wander through grandly-proportioned, beautifully furnished rooms. Fou|
posters and all the unselfconscious comforts that make for a very special country house stay are pa|
of the charm, but as visitors from all over the world have found, it's the warmth of Johnny and Lucy|
welcome that lends that extra magic. Formal gardens have been restored and Lucy, an enthusiast|
organic gardener and excellent cook, supplies freshly harvested produce from the walled kitche|
gardens for meals in the house, while other ingredients are carefully sourced from trusted supplier|
Dinner for residents is served in a beautiful dining room overlooking the gardens and lake - and memc|
rable breakfasts are taken downstairs in the Green Room next morning. This is exceptional hospitalit|
with an Irish flavour and, in recognition, Hilton Park was selected for our International Hospitalit|
Award in 1999. Pets allowed in some areas by arrangement. Gardens, boating, fishing (own lake|
walking, cycling. Golf nearby. *Self catering accommodation also available - details on inquiry. *Hilto|
Park is available for group bookings - family celebrations, small weddings and small conferences|
Rooms 6 (all en-suite, with bath & no smoking). B&B €125 pps, ss €40. Not suitable for childre|
under 8 yrs (except babies under 1 free with parents, cot available, 8-14 yrs, 50% disc). Residents |
Tue-Sat, €55 at 8 pm (Fri, 8.30); please give 24 hours notice. Interesting short wine list; house win|
€20/22. SC discretionary. No specific annual closure, but groups only off-season, by arrangemen|
MasterCard, Visa, Laser. **Directions:** 5km (3 m) south of Clones on Scotshouse Road.

Glaslough
HOTEL/HISTORIC HOUSE

Castle Lesli|

Glaslough Co Monaghan **Tel: 047 8810|**
info@castleleslie.com www.castleleslie.cor|

During the three centuries that thi|
extraordinary place has been in th|
Leslie family it has changed remarkably little - an|
its fascinating history has continually intrigued an|
beguiled both Irish and international guests. Mos|
recently the castle ceased operations as an hote|
(guests now stay in the Hunting Lodge), an|
following extensive refurbishment, has re-opene|
as a highly exclusive members club, while retainin|
all of its ancestral charm. The public can no longe|
visit or dine at this incredible property which nov|
caters solely to the whims of its fee paying members (€3000 annual membership per individual o|
couple) although non-members may stay in the castle just once to 'try before they buy'. This privileg|
costs €500 per person (members pay just €300) and includes all drinks and meals, prepared b|
highly acclaimed chef Noel McMeel. Perhaps more accessible is Castle Leslie's Hunting Lodge, |
modern hotel just inside the castle gates that has also enjoyed a vibrant refurbishment. Built aroun|
an atmospheric stable courtyard it is popular with riding enthusiasts participating at Castle Leslie'|
impressive Equestrian Centre, which offers miles of trekking, cross-country rides and jumps on th|
1000-acre estate. The Hunting Lodge features all manner of horsey memorabilia with several of th|
bedrooms designed to especially appeal to horse lovers. A Victorian Spa specialises in organic treat|
ments while Castle Leslie Cookery School, situated in the Castle's restored Victorian kitchens, offers |
choice of evening, one- and two-day courses. Non-residents are welcome to dine at the bar or in the|
hotel's informal brasserie. Conferences/Banqueting (60/48). Children welcome (under 2s free i|
parents' room, cots available free of charge). **Rooms 30** (29 separate bath & shower, 2 family, 1(|
ground floor, all no smoking & equipped for disabled). Lift. B&B €95-115 pps, ss €45. **Snaffle|**

Brasserie: Seats 80; children welcome; D daily; a la carte; L Sun only; house wine €18. Bar food served daily in Conor's Bar. Amex, MasterCard, Visa, Laser. **Directions:** 10 mins from Monaghan Town: Monaghan-Armagh road-Glaslough.

Monaghan
BAR/RESTAURANT

Andy's Bar and Restaurant

12 Market Street Monaghan Co Monaghan **Tel: 047 82277**

www.andysmonaghan.com

téite bia Right in the centre of Monaghan, the Redmond family's bar is furnished and decorated in traditional Victorian style, with a lot of fine mahogany, stained glass and mirrors. Everything is gleaming clean and arranged well for comfort, with high-backed bar seats and plenty of alcoves set up with tables for the comfortable consumption of their good bar food. Substantial bar meals include a range of specials on a blackboard as well as a concise written menu. The restaurant upstairs, which has a pleasingly old-fashioned ambience, offers a much more extensive range of popular and classic dishes, including a good choice of prime fish and steaks various ways. This is good cooking based on quality ingredients and the results are extremely tasty, satisfying - and good value too. Traditional desserts like pavlova and home-made ices are served from a trolley. Members of the Redmond family keep a constant eye on everything, and service is charming and efficient. Bar meals Tue-Sun, 4-10.15. **Restaurant: Seats 50;** D only, Tue-Sun, 4-10.15 (Sun 3.30-10). à la carte; house wine €16.60. Closed Mon, 25 Dec, Good Fri, bank hols & 1-11 Jul. MasterCard, Visa, Laser. **Directions:** Town centre, opposite the Market House.

Monaghan
HOTEL

Hillgrove Hotel

Old Armagh Rd Monaghan Co Monaghan **Tel: 047 81288**

info@hillgrovehotel.com www.hillgrovehotel.com

téite bia Overlooking the town from a fine hillside location, the Hillgrove is the leading hotel in the area; it has recently been smartly refurbished in a pleasing classic contemporary style and offers excellent business and leisure facilities. An impressive foyer sets the tone and the public areas around it are spacious and inviting, including the main bar, PK's, and the Toulouse-Lautrec lounge; the restaurant, Vettriano, offers stylish informality and is open for lunch and dinner every day. All bedrooms are spacious and contemporary, all with pleasant views, a full range of facilities and smart en-suite bathrooms. Staff are friendly and very helpful. Conference/banqueting (1,500/900), business centre, secretarial services, video conferencing, free broadband wi/fi. Leisure centre with 'pool, fitness room, Spa (including beauty salon, massage, hair dressing), garden. **Rooms 87** (2 suites, 2 junior suites, 8 family rooms, 4 for disabled, 18 ground floor, 16 no smoking); Children welcome (under 4s free in parents' room, cot available at no charge, baby sitting arranged, crèche, play room); Lift, 24 hr room service, no pets. B&B from €60 pps, ss €30. Closed 25 Dec. Amex, MasterCard, Visa, Laser. Helipad. **Directions:** Take N2 from Dublin to Monaghan town.

COUNTY OFFALY

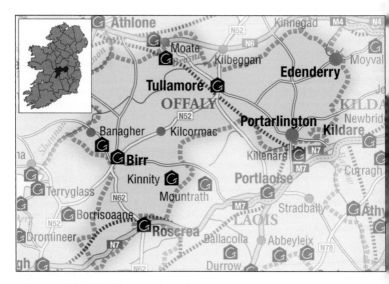

At the heart of the old Ely O'Carroll territory, Offaly is Ireland's most sky-minded county. In the grounds of Birr Castle, there's the Parsons family's famous restored 1845-vintage 1.83m astronomical telescope – rated one of the Seven Wonders of Ireland - through which the 3rd Earl of Rosse observed his discovery of the spiral nebulae. And in Tullamore, there's a thriving amateur Astronomical Society whose members point out that the wide clear skies of Offaly have encouraged the regular observation of heavenly bodies since at least 1057 AD, when astronomy was the province of moon-minded monks.

On a more modern note, the Tullamore Dew Heritage Centre is housed in the restored 1897 canal-side bonded warehouse, which formerly stored the famous local whiskey. The Centre explores Tullamore's distilling, canal and urban history with entertaining style. Style is also the theme of the new County Hall in Tullamore, which has been awarded the An Taisce Sustainable Building accolade.

Back in Birr meanwhile, the restored gardens of Birr Castle are an added attraction. And it's also in the heart of historic hunting country. Offaly is home to the Ormonde, which may not be Ireland's largest or richest hunt, "but it's the oldest and undoubtedly the best." Once upon a time, they invited the neighbouring County Galway Hunt for a shared meet, and afterwards the carousing in Dooly's Hotel in Birr reached such a hectic pitch that the hotel was joyously torched by the visitors. Dooley's was rebuilt to fulfill its central role in Birr, and the hunt from across the Shannon has been known as the Galway Blazers ever since.

The Grand Canal finally reaches the great river at Shannon Harbour in Offaly, after crossing Ireland from Dublin through Tullamore, and on the river itself, waterborne travellers find that Offaly affords the opportunity of visiting Clonmacnoise, where the remains of an ancient monastic university city give pause for thought. In the south of the county, the Slieve Bloom Mountains rise attractively above Offaly's farmland and bogs. These are modest heights, as they attain just 526 m on the peak of Arderin. However, it is their understated charms which particularly appeal, and in the Slieve Blooms we find Ireland's first organised system of gites, the French concept whereby unused farmhouses have been restored to a comfortable standard for self-catering visitor accommodation.

Nestling in a valley of the Slieve Blooms is the unspoilt village of Kinnitty, where Offaly's quality of life is most in evidence. And in the far east of the county, where Offaly marches with Kildare, we find Clonbulloge, top title holder in Offaly in the Tidy Towns awards, a pretty place on the banks of the neat stream known as the Figile River. Yet in Offaly they're not afraid of life's more earthy joys – Annaharvey Farm at Tullamore was the location at the end of September 2007 of that legendary rural showpiece, the National Farming Championship. More than 150,000 people attend. Survive this particular farm-fest, and you can survive anything that the challenge of modern farming has to offer

Local Attractions & Information

Banagher Cloghan Castle (15C Tower House)	057 915 1650
Birr Castle Demesne & Historic Science Centre	057 912 2154
Birr Tourism Information	057 912 0110
Clonmacnoise Visitor & Interpretive Centre	090 967 4195
Edenderry Canal Festival (June)	046 973 2071 / 086 350 3117
Shannonbridge Clonmacnoise & West Offaly Railway	090 967 4114
Slieve Bloom Rural Development Society	057 913 7299
Tullamore Offaly Historical Society	057 912 1421
Tullamore Offaly Tourist Council	057 935 2566
Tullamore Tullamore Dew Heritage Centre	057 932 5016
Tullamore Tourism Information	057 932 5016

BANAGHER

This small town on the western edge of County Offaly sits on the bank of the river Shannon and was originally built to protect a crossing point - impressive fortifications guarding the river crossing are still to be seen. Today, angling and all watersports are attractions; there is a marina and it is a popular stopping place for cruisers on the river, and boats can be hired here. Along the river banks, the Shannon Callows are home to a wealth of wild flowers and bird life, and river buses take visitors along the river to Clonmacnoise, and other places of interest. The town provided a wealth of inspiration for author Anthony Trollope who wrote his first novels here. For those who seek the 'real Ireland' this is an interesting small town to be based, and Pat and Della Horan's small family-run **Brosna Lodge Hotel** (057 915 1350; www.brosnalodge.com) provides the genuine experience, offering good food and genuine hospitality. Good food is also offered at **Flynn's Bar and Restaurant** (0509 51312) where the cosy bar has an open fire, and at **Heidi's Coffee Shop** (0509 52155) -renowned for generous helpings of wholesome food and good value. If a B&B in a quiet and picturesque waterside setting with a pub serving good food only yards away takes your fancy, you won't do better than charming and hospitable **Harbour Master House** (0509 51532) at Shannon Harbour.
WWW.IRELAND-GUIDE.COM FOR THE BEST PLACES TO EAT, DRINK & STAY

Banagher	J.J.Hough
CHARACTER PUB	Main Street Banagher Co Offaly **Tel: 0509 51893**
	johnhough@eircom.net

Hidden behind a thriving vine, which threatens to take over each summer, this charming 250-year old pub is soothingly dark inside making a fine contrast to the cheerful eccentricity of the current owner, Michael Hough. A world famous music pub, it's authentic and unique, family-run and with a wealth of Irish art on the walls. It's a great local and also popular with people from the river cruisers, who come up from the harbour for pints, music and craic - for the last thirty years there's been traditional Irish music here every night from March to November, and on Friday, Saturday & Sunday in winter. Nothing ever changes much here, although they did add a beer garden when the no-smoking law came in. Children and pets welcome. Open 10.30 am - 1 am. No food. Closed 25 Dec & Good Fri.
Directions: Lower Main Street.

BIRR

Birr is a lovely old town steeped in history and it makes a good holiday centre, with plenty to do locally - Birr Castle, with its observatory and magnificently restored gardens to visit, also golfing, fishing, riding and river excursions. The charmingly old-fashioned **Dooly's Hotel** (Tel 0509 20032 www.doolyshotel.com) is one of Ireland's oldest coaching inns, dating back to 1747 and is right on Emmet Square, the centre of Georgian Birr (food served all day); for those who like a little more space, the Georgian **County Arms Hotel** (Tel 0509 20791; www.countyarmshotel.com) is set in its own grounds nearby, with gardens and glasshouses to supply the hotel, and also a leisure centre. There are a number of pleasant cafés in the town including the **Courtyard Café** at Birr Castle, **Emma's Café & Deli** (057 912 5678) on Main Street, and **The Stables** (see entry).
WWW.IRELAND-GUIDE.COM FOR THE BEST PLACES TO EAT, DRINK & STAY

Birr
PUB

The Chestnut

Green Street Birr Co Offaly **Tel: 057 912 201**
clodaghfay@hotmail.com

Clodagh Fay, sister of Caroline Boyd of The Stables (see entry), operates the old Chestnut pub in Birr town, which poured its first pint back in 1823. She refurbished the place beautifully a few years ago with no expense spared on the stylish dark wood interior, slick bar and comfy layout. It is a great place to while away a Sunday afternoon reading the papers by the fire. They serve great cappuccinos and mochacinos along with some of the best Guinness you are likely to find anywhere in the country. Look out for the mouthwatering BBQs they host in the summer - and the full moon market, which takes place on the third Saturday of each month in the courtyard of the pub, stocking everything from organic vegetables to American Indian pottery. (The courtyard is also adjacent to a beautiful secret garden - perfect for long summer evenings.) Open: Mon-Thu, 7pm-closing; Fri from 5pm, Sat & Sun 3pm -closing. Closed 25 Dec, Good Fri. **Directions:** Just off the Main Square, Emmet Square.

Birr
RESTAURANT/GUESTHOUSE

Spinners Town House

Castle Street Birr Co Offaly **Tel: 057 912 167**
spinnerstownhouse@eircom.net www.spinnerstownhouse.com

Conveniently situated near Birr Castle, sympathetic renovation of a row of Georgian townhouses and an old woollen mill, and has created a restaurant and accommodation within the old stone walls, making it an interesting place to stay or have a meal. Several areas are used for dining, including the lobby and drawing room of what was once a substantial private house, which retains its Georgian features, including plasterwork - and red and blue stained glass in the large front door casts lovely shadows on to a wall; some well chosen paintings have been added and, with subdued jazz, a covered terrace and a pretty garden with box hedges and wonderful climbing hydrangeas (and fresh flowers on all the carefully appointed tables), it makes a very attractive dining venue. Early dinner and à la carte menus are offered, with the carte offering a much better choice at a fair price - and showcasing carefully sourced ingredients and good cooking: dishes especially enjoyed on a recent visit by the Guide included an excellent fresh-flavoured starter of crab spring roll with pickled ginger, and a delicious and beautifully presented vegetarian dish of herb-roasted root vegetables with Cashel Blue cheese in puff, served with a red pepper cream sauce but it was a main course of tender herb-rolled lamb with a celeriac purée & salsify crisps that stole the show. And there are lovely puddings too, maybe including a real French lemon tart with unusually good vanilla ice cream. Competent, willing service and well-chosen, good value wines complete an attractive package. *Accommodation is also offered in simple but comfortable bedrooms with en-suite or private showers. **Rooms 13**; B&B from €40pp. Restaurant Open: D Sun, Mon, Wed, Thu 6.30-9; Fri & Sat 6.30-10; L Sun only 12.30-2.30. Closed Tue. A la carte & set menus offered. MasterCard, Visa, Laser. **Directions:** Beside Birr Castle.

Birr
CAFÉ

The Stables Emporium & Tea Rooms

6 Oxmantown Mall Birr Co Offaly **Tel: 057 912 026**
cboyd@indigo.ie www.thestablesrestaurant.com

 The Boyd family's characterful establishment is in a lovely old Georgian house overlooking the tree-lined mall. It was renowned for many years as one of the area's favourite restaurants - now it is run by Caroline Boyd, who has transformed it into a high quality furniture and gift shop, Emporium at the Stables. The store, which is located in the atmospheric old coach house, stocks crystal and glassware, fine furniture, lighting, garden accessories, jewellery and giftware. (Worldwide delivery can be arranged). Better still, in the main house, light lunches, snacks, wine, tea, coffee and delicious desserts are served in the elegant drawing room, complete with open fire and comfortable armchairs also a rather nice little front garden for sitting out in fine weather. Children welcome. Open Tue-Sat, 10.30-5.30 and Sun 1-5.30 (Nov, Dec, Jun, Jul & Aug). Air conditioning. Toilets wheelchair accessible. Closed Dec 25-29. Amex, Diners, MasterCard, Visa, Laser. **Directions:** Town centre, between St Brendan's church & private gates of Birr castle.

Birr
RESTAURANT/PUB

The Thatch Bar & Restaurant

Crinkle Birr Co Offaly
Tel: 057 912 068

This characterful little thatched pub and restaurant just outside Birr shows just how pleasing a genuine, well-run country pub can be. Des Connole, proprietor since 1991, has achieved a well-earned reputation for the immaculate maintenance and atmosphere of the pub, and both bar food and restau rant meals offer generous portions for a reasonable price. Children welcome. Parking. **Seats 50** (private room, 15-20). D 6.30-9.30 daily, Set D about €39, also à la carte; L Sun-12.30 & 2.30; Set Sun L about €22; early evening bar menu Mon-Sat 5-7.30 (except Jul-Aug), à la carte; house wine about €20; SC discretionary. Bar meals Mon-Sat, 12.30-3.30 & 5-7.30. Toilets wheelchair accessible. Restaurant closed D Sun, establishment closed 25 Dec, Good Fri. Diners, MasterCard, Visa, Laser. **Directions:** 1 mile from Birr (Roscrea side).

Kinnitty
COUNTRY HOUSE

Ardmore Country House

The Walk Kinnitty Co Offaly **Tel: 057 913 7009**
info@kinnitty.com www.kinnitty.com

Set back from the road in its own lovely gardens, Christina Byrne's stone-built Victorian house offers old-fashioned comforts: brass beds, turf fires and home-made bread and preserves for breakfast. Bedrooms are deliberately left without amenities, in order to make a visit to Ardmore a real country house experience and encourage guests to spend less time in their rooms and mix with each other - tea is available downstairs at any time. All bedrooms are decorated to a high standard - one with jacuzzi bath - and a ground floor room is wheelchair friendly. Christina runs 1-7 day guided walking breaks in this beautiful and unspoilt area, with dinner in local restaurants, including Kinnitty Castle and Leap Castle - Ireland's most haunted castle (brochure available on request). There's usually a traditional Irish night on Friday nights, at nearby Kinnitty Castle. Children welcome (under 2s free in parents' room, cot available at no charge, baby sitting arranged); pets allowed in certain areas. Children welcome (under 2s free in parents' room, cot available at no charge, baby sitting arranged); pets allowed in certain areas. **Rooms 5** (4 en-suite, 3 shower only, 1 with private bathroom, 1 family room, 1 ground floor, 1 for disabled, all no smoking). B&B €45 pps, ss €10. Closed 23-27 Dec. **No Credit Cards. Directions:** In village of Kinnitty, 9 miles from Birr (R440).

Kinnitty
B&B/RESTAURANT

The Glendine Bistro

Kinnitty Co Offaly
Tel: 057 913 7973

Situated in a charming village at the foot of the Slieve Bloom mountains, the clean-lined simplicity of Percy and Phil Clendennan's attractive contemporary restaurant provides a welcome contrast to other, more traditional, dining options nearby, giving visitors to this unspoilt area a choice of styles. Wide-ranging menus suit the surroundings: this is steak country and prime Hereford beef is sure to feature in steaks various ways, but there are also many more international dishes - barbecued tiger prawns & king scallops with chargrilled peppers, perhaps - and sound cooking is backed up by friendly service. Vegetarian options, typically stir-fries and fresh pasta dishes, are always available. Children welcome. **Seats 60** (private room 15). Air conditioning. D Thu- Sun, 6.30-9. L Sun only, 12.30-2.30. D à la carte. Set Sun L about €20. House wine €18. Closed Mon-Wed; all Jan. **Accommodation:** Bright, comfortably furnished en-suite bedrooms are offered, all with direct dial phones, TV and tea/coffee-making facilities. Children under 8 free in parents' room (cot available without charge). **Rooms 5** (all shower-only & no smoking). Closed Jan. B&B about €32 pps, ss €7. MasterCard, Visa, Laser. **Directions:** 7 miles from Birr, in centre of Kinnitty Village. ◇

Kinnitty
HOTEL

Kinnitty Castle

Kinnitty Co Offaly **Tel: 057 913 7318**
info@kinnittycastle.com www.kinnittycastle.com

Furnished in keeping with its dramatic history and theatrical character, this luxurious Gothic Revival castle in the foothills of the Slieve Bloom Mountains is at the centre of a very large estate with 650 acres of parkland and formal gardens. Public areas include a library bar, Georgian style dining room, Louis XV drawing room and an atmospheric Dungeon Bar where there is traditional music on Friday and Saturday nights all year. Bedrooms are all interesting and comfortable but the best are big and romantic, with stunning views. There are new, atmospheric, medieval-style banqueting/conference facilities and also a small leisure centre. Apart from its olde-worlde character, what makes this hotel special is the helpful staff, who contribute greatly to the overall sense of fun. Tennis, fishing, equestrian, garden. Children welcome. **Rooms 37** (10 suites, 11 junior suites). No lift (long corridors and a lot of stairs). Room rate from about €215. Restaurant: D daily & L Sun. Open all year. Amex, Diners, MasterCard, Visa, Laser. **Directions:** On the R422 - Emo to Birr Road off main N7 Limerick Road.

Shannonbridge

CHARACTER PUB

R

The Village Tavern

Main Street Shannonbridge Co Offaly

Tel: 0905 74112

At J.J. Killeen's wonderful pub and shop weary travellers can be restored, particularly by the house special of hot rum and chocolate - perfect after a damp day on the river. Meanwhile you can also top up on groceries, fishing bait and gas. Music nightly May-September; weekends only off-season. **Directions:** On the main street of Shannonbridge, between Ballinasloe and Cloghan.

R

TULLAMORE

This thriving canalside town is perhaps best known for its most famous product, Tullamore Dew and, while it may no longer be made here, The Tullamore Dew Heritage Centre on the banks of the Grand Canal focuses on the distilling, canal and urban history of the town (tours available daily). Nearby, the splendid Gothic Charleville Forest Castle stands in beautiful parkland - the Charleville oak is one of the biggest and oldest in the country and, botanically, an important survivor of primeval stock. Tullamore is also an ideal base for discovering the Slieve Bloom Mountains, with many beautiful walking and cycling trails, and picnic areas with panoramic views of the surrounding lowlands. Also nearby are the unique 'Lough Boora' parklands; the boglands habitat supports a wide range of flora and fauna and now also hosts some of the most innovative land and environmental sculptures in Ireland - the artists, inspired by the rich natural and industrial legacy of the boglands, have created a series of large-scale sculptures that are now part of the Parklands permanent collection. Tullamore itself offers plenty for visitors, many of whom find it an excellent short break destination with everything in the compact town within walking distance. Well-established restaurants to check out include **Anatolia** (057 932 3669; www.anatolia.ie), on Harbour Street which is open for lunch and dinner, also **Acorn** (057 932 4700) on the same steet which is under renovation at the time of going to press but due to reopen shortly; and the evening Italian restaurant, **Sirroco's** (057 935 2839), which is nearby. Several popular ethnic restaurants include **Shisar** (057 935 1439) on High Street, specialising in Thai/Indian cuisine. More recent arrivals include **Jamies** (see entry) on Harbour Street and an exciting bar and restaurant on William Street, **The Wolftrap** (see entry). The main hotel in the area is the **Tullamore Court** (see entry), but the newer **Days Hotel** (057 932 0350; www.dayshoteltullamore.com) offers a moderately priced alternative likely to be of particular interest to business guests.

WWW.IRELAND-GUIDE.COM FOR THE BEST PLACES TO EAT, DRINK & STAY

Tullamore

RESTAURANT

N

Jamie's Restaurant

Harbour Street Tullamore Co Offaly

Tel 057 935 1269

Just the kind of place that every town needs, Jamies is truly local restaurant: welcoming, full of infectious enthusiasm, with a desire to please and serving good food at reasonable prices. The room is modern but homely, with tables dressed with white linen, and Jamie Owens (who trained at the Adare Manor) runs the show from the kitchen with his mother Jeanette in charge out front ably assisted by daughters Ashling and Jessica. The early bird menu offering a choice of four starters and main courses, then a choice of homemade desserts with tea or coffee is really great value, and a 7oz fillet steak served on champ with a mushroom, whiskey and cream sauce is a real winner. The à la carte menu offers a good selection of dishes, such as black pudding to start, then perhaps veal medallions with madeira, wild mushrooms and cream; the food is well presented and portions are generous. A compact wine list offers 20 wines, including 2 house wines at €18 and, like the food, is well judged and fairly priced. **Seats 40.** D daily, à la Carte 5.30- late, early D €25, 5.30-7.30; L Sun only 12.30-2.30. Major credit cards. **Directions:** Town centre, just across from the canal harbour.

Tullamore

HOTEL

R

Tullamore Court Hotel

O'Moore Street Tullamore Co Offaly **Tel: 057 934 6666**

info@tullamorecourthotel.ie www.tullamorecourthotel.ie

féile bia An attractive building, set back from the road a little and softened by trees, this large modern hotel is welcoming, with an extensive foyer, and bright and cheerful public areas. It serves the local community very well, with an excellent leisure centre and fine banqueting facilities - and has become very popular for short breaks, providing a comfortable and hospitable base within easy walking distance of the whole town. Bedrooms are very pleasantly decorated in an easy modern style, using warm colours and unfussy fabrics - and the staff are exceptionally friendly and helpful. It makes an ideal base for visiting the area and, as the food is generally above the standard expected in hotels, this can be a refreshing place to break a journey. However, the hotel's greatest strength has always been its business and conference facilities and now, with improved state-of-the-art facilities, including nine conference rooms, a business centre, 33 new executive bedrooms (including four suites) and a business centre. Free Broadband, leisure centre, swimming pool, garden. Children welcome (under 4s free in parents room, cot available with no charge, baby sitting arranged). **Rooms** 105 (1 suite, 4 junior suites, 8 family rooms, 90 no smoking, 6 for disabled). Lift. B&B about €105 pps, ss €20. Closed 24-26 Dec. Amex, MasterCard, Visa, Laser. **Directions:** South end of town. ◇

Tullamore
BAR/RESTAURANT
◉♥R
NEW NARRATIVE TO GO IN

The Wolftrap
William Street Tullamore Co Offaly **Tel: 057 932 3374**
info@thewolftrap.ie www.thewolftrap.ie

The brainchild of Gina Murphy and her husband Padraig McLoughlin (previously of the well-known bar and restaurant, Crockets on the Quay, in Ballina, Co Mayo, which is still run by members of the family), this large bar and 'informal fine dining' restaurant is named after a mountain in the nearby Slieve Blooms (the border between Laois and Offaly is at its peak), and occupies a large town centre building near the harbour, which they have renovated and furnished with flair. With its warm atmosphere, long opening hours, imaginative menus and great service, it's the in place - and consistently good cooking (a judicious mixture of traditional and contemporary) invariably hits the spot. **Restaurant:** The stylish first floor restaurant offers an informal but sophisticated experience; it's an impressive and atmospheric room with very high ceilings, clusters of timber wine boxes on high ledges, a magnificent polished timber floor, plenty of wines on display (and 50 wines on the list, including 6 house wines at €18 and six half bottles). Menus, offering a choice of 8 starters, 11 mains and 6 desserts, change every 5-6 weeks but you may expect excellent steaks, a good range of seafood and delicious desserts - a crème brulée with a very tangy mango and passion fruit sorbet stood out on a recent visit. All dishes are cooked to order and everything, including breads and ice creams, is homemade on the premises. As elsewhere in the Wolftrap, staff are very friendly and give excellent service, making this a very good all-round experience - and uit is understandably popular, so reservations are strongly advised, especially at weekends. Traditional music every Tuesday (Padraig is a musician). Late bar with DJ Fri & Sat to 2am. Bar food 7 days, 12-8.30pm (to 8pm Sat). Restaurant D 6.30-10.30 Tue-Sat. House wine €18. Closed Good Fri, 25 Dec. MasterCard, Visa, Laser. **Directions:** In the centre of Tullamore @ the junction of William and Harbour Streets. ◇

Tullamore Area
GUESTHOUSE
R

Annaharvey Farm
Tullamore Co Offaly **Tel: 057 934 3544**
info@annaharveyfarm.ie www.annaharveyfarm.ie

Henry and Lynda Deverell's restored grain barn, with pitch pine floors and beams, open fires and comfortable accommodation, provides a good base for a holiday offering all the pleasures of the outdoor life. Equestrian activities are the main attraction (including tuition in indoor and outdoor arenas), but walking, cycling and golfing also lay their claims - and, for the rest days, major sights including Clonmacnoise and Birr Castle are nearby. Good home cooking has always been a central feature here, and it has developed dramatically since Annaharvey Farm Foods became part of the 'Offaly Delicious' local food producers network and the kitchen, with Rachael Deverell now overseeing the operation, produces even more delicious home-baking and preserves on sale at their Saturday markets. Small conference/banqueting (40/20). Cookery school. Children welcome (under 2 free in parents' room; cot available without charge). No pets. **Rooms 7** (6 shower only, 1 with bath; all no-smoking). B&B about €40pps, ss €15. Meals available for residents only Mon-Sat, about €25 - details on application. Closed Dec & Jan. MasterCard, Visa, Laser. **Directions:** R420 Tullamore - Portarlington. ◇

COUNTY ROSCOMMON

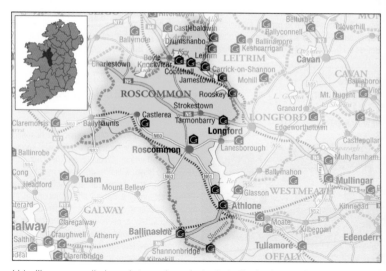

Irish villages are small places, but even by such standards, Keadue in north Roscommon is small indeed. It has just two shops, two pubs, a church and a health centre. The population is barely 150 people. But a third of them seem to be on the local Tidy Towns Committee. They keep their very Irish little village a neat as a new pin, and have celebrated the fact that Keadue (try pronouncing it "Kay-doo") has been the Tidy Towns Gold Medal holder for Roscommon, and for all Ireland.

It could be said that in times past, Roscommon was a county much put upon by the counties about it. Or, put another way, to the casual visitor it seemed that just as Roscommon was on the verge of becoming significant, it became somewhere else. In one notable example - the hotel complex at Hodson's Bay on the western shores of Lough Ree - the location is actually in Roscommon, yet the exigencies of the postal service have given it to Athlone and thereby Westmeath.

But Roscommon is a giving sort of county, for it gave Ireland her first President, Gaelic scholar Douglas Hyde (1860-1949), it was also the birthplace of Oscar Wilde's father, and as well the inimitable songwriter Percy French was a Roscommon man. Like everywhere else in the western half of Ireland, Roscommon suffered grievously from the Great Famine of the late 1840s, and at Strokestown, the handsome market town serving the eastern part of the county, Strokestown Park House has been sympathetically restored to include a Famine Museum. A visit to it will certainly add a thoughtful element to your meal in the restaurant.

Roscommon town itself has a population of 1,500, but it's growing, though the presence of extensive castle ruins and a former gaol tell of a more important past. The gaol was once noted for having a female hangman, today it has shops and a restaurant. Northwestward at Castlerea - headquarters for the County Council - we find Clonalis House, ancestral home of the O'Conor Don, and final resting place of O'Carolan's Harp.

In the north of the county, the town of Boyle near lovely Lough Key with its outstanding Forest Park is a substantial centre, with a population nearing the 2,000 mark. Boyle is thriving, and symbolic of this is the restored King House, a masterpiece from 1730. Reckoned to have been the most important provincial town house in Ireland, it is today filled with exhibits which eloquently evoke the past. Nearby, the impressive riverbank remains of Boyle Abbey, the largest Cistercian foundation in Ireland, date from 1148.

Lough Key is of course on one of the upper reaches of the inland waterways system, and a beautiful part it is too. In fact, all of Roscommon's eastern boundary is defined by the Shannon and its lakes, but as the towns along it tend to identify themselves with the counties on the other side of the river, Roscommon is left looking very thin on facilities. But it has much to intrigue the enquiring visitor. For instance, along the Roscommon shore of Lough Ree near the tiny village of Lecarrow, the remains of a miniature city going back to mediaeval times and beyond can be dimly discerned among the trees down towards Rindown Point. These hints of of an active past serve to emphasise the fact that today, Roscommon moves at a gentler pace than the rest of Ireland.

Local Attractions & Information

Boyle Boyle Abbey (12th C Monastery)	071 966 2604
Boyle Frybrook House (18thC town hse)	079 63 513
Boyle King House (500 years of Irish life)	071 966 3242
Boyle Lough Key Forest Park	071 966 2363 / 967 3122
Boyle Tourism Information	071 966 2145
Castlerea Clonalis House	094 962 0014
Elphin Restored windmill	071 963 5181 / 086 838 2118
Roscommon town Arts Centre	090 662 5824
Roscommon town County Museum	090 662 5613
Roscommon Town Race Course	090 666 3494
Roscommon Town Tourism Information	090 662 6342
Strokestown Park House, Garden & Famine Museum	071 963 3013
Strokestown Roscommon County Genealogy Company	071 963 3380

Carrick-on-Shannon
COUNTRY HOUSE/FARMHOUSE
R

Glencarne House
Ardcarne Carrick-on-Shannon Co Roscommon
Tel: 071 966 7013

On the border between Leitrim and Roscommon - Glencarne House is physically in Leitrim, but the postal address is Roscommon - the Harrington family's large Georgian house is set well back from the road, with a large garden in front and farmland behind, so it is easy to find, yet without intrusion from traffic. Spacious and elegantly furnished with antiques, this is very much a family home and Agnes Harrington has won many awards for hospitality and home-cooked food based on their own farm produce. Good-sized bedrooms all have en-suite bathrooms, and a fine breakfast, cooked to order, will set you up for the day. Garden. Children welcome; pets permitted by arrangement. **Rooms 4** (all en-suite & no smoking). B&B about €45 pps, ss €5. No meals other than breakfast. Closed Nov-Mar. **No Credit Cards. Directions:** On the N4,halfway between Carrick-on-Shannon and Boyle. ◇

Castlecoote
COUNTRY HOUSE

Castlecoote House
Castlecoote Co Roscommon **Tel: 0906 663794**
info@castlecootehouse.com www.castlecootehouse.com

This fine Georgian residence overlooking the beautiful River Suck was built in the enclosure of a medieval castle between 1690 and 1720, and is of historic interest - not least as the birthplace of the Gunning sisters, who became the Duchess of Hamilton (and later, of Argyll) and Countess of Coventry; celebrated for their beauty, portraits of them by Sir Joshua Reynolds hang in the main hall. Having restored the house to its former glory, the present owners, Sarah Lane and Kevin Finnerty, now offer magnificent country house accommodation and they are members of the Ireland West Garden Trail; guided tours of the gardens, which include an orchard of rare apple trees, the towers of the ruined castle, a medieval bridge and even an ice house, are offered by appointment. Snooker, walking, garden, croquet, tennis, trout and coarse fishing on site; equestrian and golf nearby. **Rooms 5,** not suitable for children or wheelchairs. B&B from about €90pps; D by arrangement €49-55 (book previous day). **Directions:** Castlecoote is about 5km southwest of Roscommon, into village, cross bridge, bear right, gates are directly ahead. ◇

Castlerea
COUNTRY HOUSE

Clonalis House
Castlerea Co Roscommon **Tel: 094 962 0014**
clonalis@iol.ie www.clonalis.com

Standing on the land that has been the home of the O'Conors of Connacht for 1,500 years, this 45-room Victorian Italianate mansion may seem a little daunting on arrival, but it's magic - and the hospitable owners, Pyers and Marguerite O'Conor-Nash, clearly enjoy sharing their rich and varied history with guests, who are welcome to browse through their fascinating archive. Amazing heirlooms include a copy of the last Brehon Law judgment (handed down about 1580) and also

Carolan's Harp. Everything is on a huge scale: reception rooms are all very spacious, with lovely old furnishings and many interesting historic details, bedrooms have massive four poster and half tester beds and bathrooms to match and the dining room is particularly impressive, with a richly decorated table to enhance Marguerite's home cooking. Clonalis House is set amid peaceful parklands and is a good base from which to explore counties Roscommon, Galway, Mayo and Sligo. *Two attractive self-catering cottages are also offered, in the courtyard; details on application. A 10% reduction is offered for stays of three or more nights. Horse riding, fishing, shooting and golf (9) are all nearby. Unsuitable for children under 12 years. No pets. **Rooms 4** (3 en-suite, 1 with private bathroom; all no smoking). Garden, walking. B&B €95-110 pps, ss €20. Residents D Tue-Sat, 8pm, about €44 (24 hrs notice required); wines €17. (D not available Sun or Mon.) Closed Oct-Apr. MasterCard, Visa, Laser. **Directions:** N60, west of Castlerea.

Cootehall	Cootehall Bridge Riverside Restaurant
RESTAURANT	Cootehall Boyle Co Roscommon
R	**Tel: 071 966 7173**

Cootehall is one of those places which can't decide which county it is in but, whether it is in Roscommon or Leitrim, this waterside restaurant provides a very complete service and it's the first port of call for many weekenders, as soon as they arrive in the area. After many years under the steward-ship of Manfred Khan, the restaurant changed hands in 2006 and the style is now rustic French/Italian food with Irish influences, although new owner Eric Cahill and his kitchen team have kept some of the old favourites like French onion soup and wiener schnitzel on their menus, which are based mainly on local and organic produce. And Manfred often drops in, as a customer, just to make sure everything is being done right and, judging by the way their good food and value for money have been sending many a customer happy into the night, they're doing a great deal of things absolutely right. And an extension is planned for the 2008 season too. Children welcome (high chair, childrens menu); **Seats 40.** L served Wed-Sat 12-3, Sun L 12.30-5.30; D Wed-Sat 6-9.30. 3 course meal €30-40. Dinner reservations recommended, especially at weekends. House wine €19.50. A phone call to check opening times is recommended, especially off-season. Closed Sun D, Mon, Tues and Nov & Jan. MasterCard, Visa, Laser. **Directions:** Right of the bridge as you approach the village.

Cootehall	M. J. Henry
CHARACTER PUB	Cootehall Boyle Co Roscommon
	Tel: 071 966 7030

The more theme pubs and superpubs there are, the better everyone likes M J Henry's bar, which hasn't changed in at least 30 years and, in true country Irish fashion, is also a food store 'that caters for all your grocery needs'. A visit to Cootehall (the village of well-known writer the late John McGahern) would be unthinkable without checking on this little gem They don't make them like this any more, alas, but this delightful old pub - complete with formica from the most recent renovation - is a gem. Get in beside the fire with a hot whiskey and the world will do you no harm. No bar food, but there is sometimes music. No bar food. Closed 25 Dec & Good Fri. **No Credit Cards. Directions:** 2 miles off N4 Sligo - Dublin road, between Boyle & Carrick-on-Shannon.

Knockvicar	Bruno's Restaurant (formerly Italia)
RESTAURANT	Knockvicar Boyle Co Roscommon **Tel: 071 96 67788**
R	brunoboe@eircom.net

Bruno Boe's beautifully located contemporary (previously known as Italia) restaurant is equally popular with local diners and boating visitors to the marina. The interior is well-designed on two levels to take full advantage of views over the river and Knockvicar marina, and enhanced by decor which is colourful, comfortable and stylishly appointed - fashionable high-back chairs, classy tableware, fine glasses - an unusually cosmopolitan approach for a rural restaurant. Expect a real Italian welcome, authentic Italian cooking - and very fair prices. Service can be slow, but the overall package is so attractive that everybody keeps coming back. Children welcome (high chair, childrens menu); toilets wheelchair accessible. **Seats 70.** D daily 6-10 (to 9.30 Sun), L Sun only 1-4pm. Set Sun L €22; set D €35; also a la carte. House wine about €17. No SC. (reservations required; advisable to ring and check opening hours, especially off-season.) Closed Mon & a few weeks Oct-Nov & Feb. Amex, MasterCard, Visa, Laser. **Directions:** Near Carrick-on-Shannon, on the Knockvicar-Cootehall road.

Knockvicar

B&B/RESTAURANT/PUB

R

Clarendon House Restaurant

Knockvicar Boyle Co Roscommon **Tel:** 071 966 7016
info@clarendon-house.com   www.clarendon-house.com

Greg Bird and Enrico Pastorelli's out of the way pub and restaurant may look ordinary but it's worth getting to, as their mission is to serve honest to goodness locally sourced food like home-made soups, good salads, great steaks and interesting vegetarian dishes. Whether made by Enrico, himself, or the kitchen team, the cooking is good here and everything is created with care. It's a place that is both sophisticated and friendly, which befits lovely Roscommon, and their great Sunday lunch is deservedly especially popular. A charming gazebo that is perfect for small weddings and parties is set up in the gardens in summer and, in winter, the turf stove which divides the bar from the small lounge will have special attraction for locals and visitors alike. **Accommodation:** There are four guest rooms available, and another five in an adjoining house. Banqueting (50); Children welcome; **Seats 38** (private room, 8); D Wed-Mon 5-9pm; set D €23.50/27.50, also a la carte; L Sun only, 12.30-4; set Sun L €19.50; house wine €18. Closed Tues. **Rooms 5.** Children welcome (under 5s free in parents' room, cot available free of charge). Pets permitted by arrangement. B&B €29pps. MasterCard, Visa, Laser. **Directions:** Halfway between Carrick-on-Shannon and Boyle, off N4 Sligo road; take a right towards Keadue; Knockvicar is about 2 miles past post office, on right.

Roscommon

HOTEL

Abbey Hotel & Leisure Centre

Abbeytown Galway Road Roscommon Co Roscommon **Tel:** 090 662 6240
info@abbeyhotel.ie   www.abbeyhotel.ie

The heart of this pleasing hotel is an old manor house and, despite major developments, the atmosphere of the original building still prevails and there's a romantic honeymoon suite with a four-poster in the old house. Big changes have included the addition of a contemporary wing with spacious bedrooms, all designed and decorated to a high standard and with pleasant views. A high level of comfort, together with excellent leisure facilities and good value offered, makes the hotel appealing for short breaks. *Short/golfing breaks offered; details on application. Conference/banqueting (250/300); broadband wi/fi. Leisure centre (20m swimming pool, sauna, steam room, gym, jacuzzi). Children welcome (under 12s free in parents' room; cots available without charge, baby sitting arranged). Garden. No pets. **Rooms 50** (all no smoking, 10 family, 10 ground floor, 4 disabled, 2 shower only). Lift. Room service (limited hours). B&B €120 pps, ss €20. Restaurant & Bar meals daily. House wines from €16.50, no SC. Hotel closed 24-27 Dec. Amex, Diners, MasterCard, Visa, Laser. Heli-pad. **Directions:** N4 to Roscommon, Galway Road; next to the library, on the left.

Roscommon

RESTAURANT WITH ROOMS

N

Gleeson's Townhouse and Restaurant

Market Square Roscommon Co Roscommon **Tel:** 090 662 6954
info@gleesonstownhouse.com   www.gleesonstownhouse.com

féile bia Set right in the heart of Roscommon town, overlooking the square, Mary and Eamonn Gleeson's townhouse and restaurant provides just what every visitor requires a warm welcome, comfortable rooms and first-class food. Over the last 15 years, they have made huge changes to this nineteenth century home. They started out with just a coffee shop and four rooms; today there are 19 ensuite bedrooms, the original coffee shop and a restaurant. Bedrooms are comfortable, with all the usual facilities, including Internet access. There's a junior suite and an excellent executive suite with adjoining sitting-room that would make an ideal base for touring the area. The coffee shop opens for breakfast with home-made scones, bread and cakes, and light lunches include delicious seafood chowder and beef and Guinness stew and lasagne. Small conferences/banqueting (80); free broadband wi/fi; video conferencing. **Rooms 19.** Children welcome (under 3s free in parents' room, 50% discount for under 14s in parents' room, baby sitting arranged, cot available). B&B €55-70 pps, ss €15. **Manse Restaurant:** The Gleesons place great emphasis on food and buy local produce, organic when possible; the weekly Farmers Market is held next door. An excellent residents breakfast is served in the restaurant, until 11.30 - freshly baked breads, croissants and brioche, fresh juices, cereals and porridge served with honey and cream, then hot dishes like the full Irish breakfast or toasted bagel with goat's cheese and onion marmalade. Dinner brings quite an extensive à la carte menu, maybe starting with that famous chowder, packed with fresh fish and served with home-made breads. Follow with Leitrim Organic Farmers beefburger, served with Mossfield garlic herb cheese or Roscommon rack of lamb cooked with an apricot and pine nut crust. Finish with a very moreish tarte tatin, perhaps, or an organic cheeseboard and a good coffee. A good reasonably priced wine list includes some organic wines and a pair of half bottles. Wheelchair access to restaurant & toilets; children welcome (high chair, childrens menu, baby changing facilities); air conditioning. **Seats 55** (private room, 80, outdoors, 30). L&D daily 12-6pm (Sun 12.30-5); 6.30-9pm (Sun 6-9pm); a la carte. Also café open 8am-6pm daily; house wine €16.50. Closed 25-26 Dec. Amex, MasterCard, Visa, Laser. **Directions:** Centre of Roscommon town, on the Square.

The Old Fort

Shannonbridge
RESTAURANT

Shannonbridge Co Roscommon **Tel: 090 967 4973**
info@theoldfortrestaurant.com www.theoldfortrestaurant.com

In a very pleasant site right beside the Shannon, this restaurant is in a restored fort and has oodles of character. The proprietor, Fergal Moran, grew up here and, having fulfilled a lifetime ambition to restore the fort, opened it as a restaurant in 2002. You arrive into a large and welcoming reception area and bar, which has lovely old timbers, a fine bar and comfortable sofas beside an open fire - and an extra dining space, which is useful at busy times or for guests who can't manage the stairs. The main dining room is upstairs and the ambience is lovely, with old wooden floors, well-spaced polished wood tables smartly laid with starched linen napkins and candles. Head chef Brian Maher has been with the restaurant since it opened, and offers several attractive evening menus and great value; the simplest dishes are often best - an excellent steak, cooked as ordered, is very good food which, with attentive service and lovely surroundings, make for a memorable outing. Small weddings. Children welcome. Toilets wheelchair accessible. **Seats 80** (private room, 30). Reservations advised. D Wed-Sun, from 5-9.30 (Sun, in summer only, 5-8); L Sun only 12.30-3. Value D €25 (Wed-Thu, 5-9.30 & Fri-Sat 5-7), Set 2/3 course D €27/40, also à la carte. Set Sun L, €23.50. House wine €18.50. Closed 3 weeks Jan. 1 week Nov. MasterCard, Visa, Laser. **Directions:** Beside the bridge in Shannonbridge.

Keenans Bar & Restaurant

Tarmonbarry
BAR/RESTAURANT

Tarmonbarry (via Clondra) Co Roscommon
Tel: 043 26052 / 26098 info@keenans.ie www.keenans.ie

Just beside the bridge over the Shannon in Tarmonbarry, this well-run bar and restaurant is a favourite watering hole for river folk and makes a great place to break a journey between Dublin and the north-west. The bar is comfortably set up for food and informal meals - mostly quite traditional, but with more international influences in the more expensive evening dishes - are served all day; open sandwiches on home-made wholemeal or soda bread, toasted sandwiches, salads and scones with jam & cream are typical, plus half a dozen daily specials (including specialities such as smoked fish casserole and bacon & cabbage at lunch, perhaps, and more elaborate dishes like roast half duckling). A la carte menus are similar in tone but more extensive - wholesome, hearty fare that pleases all age groups; the steak sandwich (served with onions, chips, garlic butter & home-made horseradish sauce) is not to be missed - while the set dinner menu is a little more formal. Good unpretentious food and cheerful, efficient service keep happy customers coming back. *Shortly after the Guide's 2007 visit a new restaurant opened; both it and the 12 new rooms above it overlook the Shannon. Broadband wi/fi. **Restaurant seats 100.** Food served daily 12.30-8.30; L 12.30-2.30, D 6.30-8.30. D a la carte, Set Sun L €23.95. House wine €18.95. Restaurant closed D Sun. Establishment closed 24/25 Dec, Good Fri. Amex, MasterCard, Visa, Laser. **Directions:** On N5, west of Longford town.

The Purple Onion Bar & Restaurant

Tarmonbarry
RESTAURANT/PUB

Tarmonbarry (via Clondra) Co Roscommon **Tel: 043 59919**
info@purpleonion.ie www.purpleonion.ie

Paul Dempsey and Pauline Roe's roadside pub has an olde world feeling with dark wood, bric-à-brac and prints and, unusually, it doubles as an art gallery, so good original paintings add interest and charm. It can get very busy in the evening, with people waiting for tables, and there may be standing room only; however watchful staff quickly bring menus to arriving diners and, even if you have to read while standing, the choice offered is impressive for a small restaurant, and may include some unusual dishes (grilled sardines, for example), also organic food including salmon and chicken; an early dinner menu is offered, also a separate children's menu and daily changing specials and desserts too. Sensibly, given the clientèle, there's a core of popular dishes, including sirloin and T-bone steaks, but also a fair sprinkling of suggestions to tempt more adventurous diners. Although some may find it dark and cramped (features that tend to go with the territory in old pubs), the restaurant has character and the dining experience overall is enjoyable - the food is interesting and offers something different from other choices in the area, and staff are attentive and genuinely caring. Children welcome before 10pm (high chair, childrens menu). **Seats 55**; air conditioning; L Sun only, 12.30-3.30pm; D Tue-Sun, 5.30-9.30pm (4.30-7.30 Sun). House wine €18.95. Closed Mon, one week Nov. MasterCard, Visa, Laser. **Directions:** On N5, west of Longford town.

COUNTY SLIGO

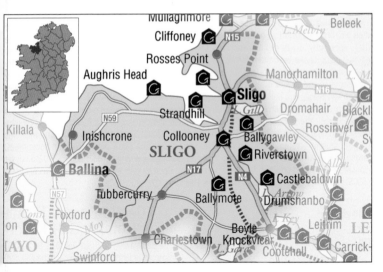

There's a stylish confidence to Sligo which belies its compact area as one of Ireland's smallest counties. Perhaps it's because they know that their place and their way of life have been immortalised through association with two of the outstanding creative talents of modern Ireland, W.B.Yeats and his painter brother Jack. The former's fame seems beyond question, while the latter's star was never higher than it is today.

The town and the county have many associations with Yeats, but few are more remarkable than Lissadell House, the former home of the Gore-Booths. Best known as the family of Constance Gore-Booth - who as Countess Markievicz was much involved with the Easter Rising of 1916 – the Gore-Booths were extraordinary people in several generations, and the sale in 2003 of Lissadell – which is open to the public – was a timely reminder of this, and of Sligo's unique qualities.

But whatever the reason for Sligo's special quality, there's certainly something about it that encourages repeat visits. The town itself is big enough to be reassuring, yet small enough to be comfortable. And the countryside about Sligo town also has lasting appeal. Mankind has been living here with enthusiasm for a very long time indeed, for in recent years it has been demonstrated that some of County Sligo's ancient monuments are amongst the oldest in northwest Europe. Lakes abound, the mountains are magnificent, and there are tumbling rivers a-plenty.

Yet if you wish to get away from the bustle of the regular tourist haunts, Sligo can look after your needs in this as well, for the western part of the county down through the Ox Mountains towards Mayo is an uncrowded region of wide vistas and clear roads.

Local Attractions & Information

Carrowmore Largest Megalithic Cemetry in Ireland	071 916 1534
Drumcliff Drumcliffe Church & Tea Shop/craft shop (Yeats)	071 914 4956
Drumcliff Lissadell House	071 916 3150
Inniscrone Seaweed Bath House	096 36 238
Lissadell House, nr Drumcliff	071 916 3150
Lough Gill Waterbus Cruises	071 916 4266 / 087 259 8869
Sligo Discover Sligo Tours	071 914 7488
Sligo Model Arts & Niland Gallery	071 914 1405
Sligo Abbey (13thC Dominican Friary)	071 914 6406
Sligo Sligo Airport, Strandhill	071 916 8280
Sligo Sligo Art Gallery	071 914 5847
Sligo Tourism Information	071 916 1201
Sligo Yeats Memorial Building, Hyde Bridge	071 914 2693
Strandhill Seaweed Baths, Maritime House	071 916 8686

Aughris Head
PUB/B&B

Beach Bar/Aughris House

Aughris Head Templeboy Co Sligo
Tel: 071 916 6703 / 071 917 6465

The McDermott family's picturesque and beautifully located thatched pub seems too good to be true when you first find it in this quiet and unspoilt place, but there it has been since the 18th century when, apparently, it was a shibín known as Maggie Maye's. Today, after sensitive restoration, it has retained some of the best characteristics of the past and makes a lovely stopping place, with food served in the flag-stoned bar - and access to a beach just a hop across the wall from the car park. Wholesome, home-cooked meals are served here - creamy Atlantic seafood chowder, great steaks, bangers and mash, and delicious home-made desserts too. Bar food daily 1-8 in summer. Phone to check times off-season. **Accommodation:** In a neat bungalow just beside the pub and overlooking the Atlantic Ocean, the McDermotts also offer comfortable, inexpensive, family-friendly B&B accommodation, with neat shower rooms and TV. Complimentary tea and biscuits on arrival. Children welcome (under 2 free in parents' room, cot available, baby sitting arranged); pets allowed in some areas. Garden, scenic walks, sandy beach, boat trips and sea angling arranged. B&B about €30-35, single about €37-40. (Short breaks & family rates available). Open all year. MasterCard, Visa. **Directions:** Off N59 Sligo/Ballina Road, Coast road to Aughris Head/Pier. ◈

Ballygawley
HOTEL
Ⓡ

Castle Dargan Estate
Hotel & Golf Resort

Castle Dargan Estate Ballygawley Co Sligo **Tel: 071 911 8080**
info@castledargan.com www.castledargan.com

Named after the ruins of the ancient castle which remain within its Darren Clarke-designed championship golf course, Castle Dargan House makes a fine centrepiece for this contemporary hotel and is set amongst dramatic scenery on 170 acres of mature woodlands, with uninterrupted views over the countryside and golf course. A lovely period drawing room and meeting room within the original house sets the tone for the well-designed new section across a courtyard to the rear of the old house. A large reception area with high ceilings, warm colour schemes and log fires establish the warm, modern tone that prevails throughout the new areas - the bar is especially striking, featuring a mezzanine level with floor to ceiling windows overlooking a large decking area and the golf course. Alongside is an intimate restaurant, which shares the same views. Accommodation is mainly in the new area - all bedrooms are finished to a high standard, with the usual amenities, and have views of the golf course - but the suites are in the old house and enjoy a special atmosphere. Apartments separately located at the gate of the hotel are also available, each sleeping up to four people. The hotel would make a magnificent wedding venue and the function room, an L shaped room with floor to ceiling windows on two sides and a private bar, is in a prime location on the first floor. Wheelchair friendly. Conferences/Banqueting (400/300), free broadband wi/fi, video conferencing. Championship golf (18), Spa, beauty salon, walking; Hunting/shooting and equestrian nearby. **Rooms 54** (16 junior suites, 4 executive, 14 ground floor, 1 for disabled); Children welcome (under 4s free in parents' room, cot available at no charge, baby sitting arranged); 24 hr rooms service, Lift. B&B €60pps, ss €20. Hall Door Restaurant: seats 60, D daily 6.30-9pm; L Sun only, 12-4pm. Bar food available all day, 10am-9pm. Open all year. Heli-pad. Amex, MasterCard, Visa, Laser. **Directions:** 10 minutes from Sligo town- take the R284 to Ballygawley. There is an alternative access from the Collooney by-pass roundabout via the Dromahair Road.

Ballymote
COUNTRY HOUSE
🐾 🏛 👁

Temple House

Ballinacarrow Ballymote Co Sligo **Tel: 071 918 3329**
enquiry@templehouse.ie www.templehouse.ie

One of Ireland's most unspoilt old houses, this is a unique place - a Georgian mansion situated in 1,000 acres of farm and woodland, overlooking the original lakeside castle which was built by the Knights Templar in 1200 A.D. The Percevals have lived here since 1665 and the house was redesigned and refurbished in 1864 - some of the furnishings date back to that major revamp. Sandy and Deb Perceval first opened the doors of their home to guests in 1981 and it is now managed by their son Roderick and his wife Helena, who are bringing their own brand of energy and enthusiasm to running this amazing house. The whole of the house has retained its old atmosphere and, in addition to central heating, has log fires to cheer the enormous rooms. Spacious bedrooms are furnished with old family furniture and bathrooms are gradually being upgraded. Guests have the use of an elegant sitting room with open fires, and evening meals are served in a very beautiful dining room; Floriane Beguin, previously at Cromleach Lodge, is currently cooking delicious food at Temple House and his meals, based on seasonal produce from the estate and other local suppliers, are a treat to look forward to. There's always an Irish cheeseboard too - and home-made fudge with coffee in the Morning Room. Traditional Irish music and dancing sessions are often held nearby. Fishing (fly & coarse), hunting/shooting, walking, snooker. Golf & garden visits nearby. Free broadband wi/fi available. Children welcome (under 12s 60% discount, babies free in parents' room; cots available at no charge, baby sitting arranged). Pets permitted in some areas. **Rooms 6** (5 en-suite, 2 shower only, 1 with private bathroom, 2 family, all no smoking). B&B from €90 pps, ss €25. Residents 4-course D €42, 7.30pm (book by 1pm, not available Sun); house wine about €17. Children's tea 6.30pm; SC discretionary. *Golf nearby, at Rosses Point, Strandhill and Enniscrone - short breaks available. Closed Dec-Mar. MasterCard, Visa, Laser. Heli-pad. **Directions:** Signposted off N17, 0.5 km south of Ballinacarrow. 11km (7 m) south of N4 junction.

Castlebaldwin — Clevery Mill

RESTAURANT WITH ROOMS/WINE BAR

Castlebaldwin Co Sligo **Tel: 071 912 7424**
cleverymill@eircom.net www.cleverymill.com

This charmingly converted old mill, complete with millwheel, is located in the countryside about 20 minutes' drive from Sligo. From the moment you push open the door of the old stone building, you get a sense of warmth and relaxation. Overnight guests will find six comfortable bedrooms with plenty of character - some rooms have four-poster beds and all are attractively furnished in a country style, with modern en-suite shower rooms. Both residents and people in for a meal will enjoy the old-world country ambience in the bar area or, perhaps, in the smaller snug room adjacent; log fires are an attractive feature and there's a pleasant feeling to the whole building. The main dining room overlooks the old waterwheel and is classically appointed with white linen and full of character; the menu tempts with a wide selection of dishes and lists sources, which are mostly local and organic. **Seats 54;** D Thu-Sun 6.30-9.30, L Sun only 12.30-3.30pm; set Sun L €28; set D about €40. **Rooms 6;** B&B from €75 pps; midweek specials available on request. Closed D Sun, Mon-Wed; house closed Christmas & New Year. MasterCard, Visa, Laser. **Directions:** 14 miles from Sligo, N4 towards Dublin.

Castlebaldwin — Cromleach Lodge

HOTEL/RESTAURANT

Castlebaldwin via Boyle Co Sligo **Tel: 071 916 5155**
info@cromleach.com www.cromleach.com

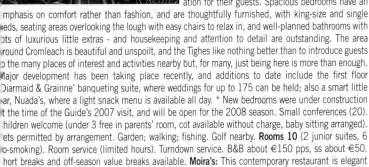

Quietly situated in the hills just above Lough Arrow, Christy and Moira Tighe's very special hotel enjoys one of the finest views in Ireland - and it makes a luxurious retreat for the most discerning of guests. Cromleach is rightly renowned for its exceptionally high standards of both food and accommodation - and, most importantly, the Tighe family and their staff have the magic ingredient of genuine hospitality, doing everything possible to ensure comfort and relaxation for their guests. Spacious bedrooms have an emphasis on comfort rather than fashion, and are thoughtfully furnished, with king-size and single beds, seating areas overlooking the lough with easy chairs to relax in, and well-planned bathrooms with lots of luxurious little extras - and housekeeping and attention to detail are outstanding. The area around Cromleach is beautiful and unspoilt, and the Tighes like nothing better than to introduce guests to the many places of interest and activities nearby but, for many, just being here is more than enough. Major development has been taking place recently, and additions to date include the first floor 'Diarmaid & Grainne' banqueting suite, where weddings for up to 175 can be held; also a smart little bar, Nuada's, where a light snack menu is available all day. * New bedrooms were under construction at the time of the Guide's 2007 visit, and will be open for the 2008 season. Small conferences (20). Children welcome (under 3 free in parents' room, cot available without charge, baby sitting arranged). Pets permitted by arrangement. Garden; walking; fishing. Golf nearby. **Rooms 10** (2 junior suites, 6 no-smoking). Room service (limited hours). Turndown service. B&B about €150 pps, ss about €50. Short breaks and off-season value breaks available. **Moira's:** This contemporary restaurant is elegant and calm - arranged to allow every table to take full advantage of the view, it is decorated in shades of cream and coffee, with black leather high backed chairs and long stylish seating at each end of the room - stripes of lime green, pale mauve, moss green and grey fit beautifully with the voile curtains embroidered in golds and lined in silk. Moira Tighe (who was our Chef of the Year in 2000) remains very involved with the kitchen, and works closely with her team; menus are based on meticulously sourced ingredients - and the many regular guests who have grown attached to Cromleach will be glad to know that the wonderful food has not changed - specialities created by Moira over the years will still feature, along with new dishes, as has always been the case. Everything, from the first little amuse bouche to the last petit four with coffee is a treat - and, as in all aspects of this exceptional place, service is flawless. Children welcome; toilets wheelchair accessible; reservations required. **Seats 60**. Light food served throughout the day. D daily, L Sun only. Menus offered include Residents' Tasting Menu (changed daily); house wines from about €19.95; sc discretionary. Open all year. Amex, MasterCard, Visa, Laser. **Directions:** Signposted from Castlebaldwin on the N4. ◊

Cliffoney
RESTAURANT

The Old Post House

Cliffoney Co Sligo **Tel: 071 917 6771**

theoldposthouse@eircom.net

This attractive stone-faced former post office, with excellent views, is run by Shane McGonigle and his partner Kay Ryan, who have been successfully steering it towards the current carefully balanced blend of popular and more adventurous cooking since taking over here in 2006. Have an aperitif in a small but pleasant reception area, or at your table in a large high-ceilinged dining room with understated modern décor and sweeping coastal views; well balanced menus may include a set menu on some evenings which is very good value and, in summer, lunch and light food is available from noon onwards. There's an emphasis on fish and seafood - often contemporary in style - although you will also find classics like mussels in white wine; main course fish could include Brill or John Dory, while meat dishes can include a sirloin steak or fillet of pork. Stylish presentation adds to the sense of occasion and rather high-end prices are justified by the quality of ingredients and cooking, and friendly service. Sunday lunch is extremely popular and good value, featuring the traditional roast, homely desserts, and seafood. Children welcome. Toilets wheelchair accessible. **Seats 80.** Open from noon daily in summer, for L, lights snacks & D; 'set menu special' €30, also à la carte. off-season phone to check opening hours. Closed Mon (open Bank Hols), Tue, 25 Dec and all of Oct, Nov, Jan. MasterCard, Visa, Laser. **Directions:** On side of main Sligo/Bundoran/Donegal road in the village of Cliffoney. ◊

Collooney
HOTEL/RESTAURANT
R

Markree Castle

Collooney Co Sligo **Tel: 071 916780**

markree@iol.ie www.markreecastle.ie

Sligo's oldest inhabited house has been home to the Cooper family for 350 years. Set in magnificent park and farmland, this is a proper castle, with a huge portico leading to a covered stone stairway that sweeps up to an impressive hall, where an enormous log fire always burns. Everything is on a very large scale, and it is greatly to the credit of the present owners, Charles and Mary Cooper, that they have achieved the present level of renovation and comfort since they took it on in a sad state of disrepair in 1989 - and they have always been generous with the heating. Ground floor reception areas include a comfortably furnished double drawing room with two fireplaces (where light food including afternoon tea is served). There is a lift and also disabled toilets, but the layout of the castle makes it difficult for elderly people or wheelchair users to get around; a phone call ahead to ensure the (very willing) staff are available to help would be wise. The dining room is a very beautiful room and open to non residents for dinner, and lunch on Sunday. There are many idiosyncrasies - in bedrooms, for example - this slightly eccentric place has got real heart; do, however, beware of times when very inexpensive offers are available, as it can be noisy and children are not always kept under control. Horse riding. Conferences/banqueting (50/150). Children welcome (under 4s free in parents' room; cots available). Pets permitted. **Rooms 30** (all en-suite, 5 executive rooms, 1 for disabled; also apartments in the old stables). Lift. B&B from about €90 pps, ss about €10. Non-residents are welcome. (Reservation recommended). Seats 80 (private room, 40) D 7.30-9.30 daily; L 1-2.30 Sun only. Set D about €30. Set Sun L about €18; house wine about €14; no sc. Hotel closed 24-27 Dec. Amex, Diners, MasterCard, Visa. **Directions:** Just off the N4, take the Dromahair exit at Collooney roundabout. ◊

Coopershill House

Riverstown
COUNTRY HOUSE

Riverstown Co Sligo **Tel: 071 916 5108**
ohara@coopershill.com www.coopershill.com

féile bia Undoubtedly one of the most delightful and superbly comfortable Georgian houses in Ireland, this sturdy granite mansion was built to withstand the rigours of a Sligo winter but it's a warm and friendly place. Peacocks wander elegantly on the croquet lawns (and roost in the splendid trees around the house at night) making this lovely place, home of the O'Hara family since it was built in 1774, a particularly perfect country house. In immaculate order from top to bottom, the house not only has the original 18th century furniture but also some fascinating features, notably an unusual Victorian free-standing rolltop bath complete with fully integrated cast-iron shower 'cubicle' and original brass rail and fittings, all in full working order. Luxurious rooms are wonderfully comfortable and have phones and tea/coffee making facilities. Simon O'Hara has now taken over management of the house from his parents, Brian and Lindy, and the house and kitchen run with the seamless hospitality born of long experience.

As well as their own neatly maintained vegetable garden, the O'Haras have a deer farm, so you may well find venison on the dinner menu - medallions, perhaps, with a juniper cream sauce - along with other deliciously wholesome country house cooking. Scallop salad, watercress soup, brill with mustard & tarragon sauce and gooseberry & elderflower ice cream are all typical, served in their lovely dining room where the family silver is used with magnificent insouciance (even at breakfast). A surprisingly extensive wine list offers no less than six house wines - and has many treats in store. Coopershill is well placed for exploring this unspoilt area - and makes a good base for golfers too, with several championship courses, including Rosses Point within easy range. Free broadband wi/fi. Tennis, cycling, boating, fishing, garden, croquet; snooker room. Children welcome (under 2 free in parents' room; cots available without charge, baby sitting arranged). No pets. **Rooms 8** (7 en-suite, 1 shower only, 1 private bathroom, 1 family room, all no smoking). Turndown service. B&B about €129 pps, ss €30. Dining Room Seats 20. D 8.15pm daily (non-residents welcome by reservation); Set D about €57, house wines from €14; sc discretionary.* 10% discount on stays of 3+ days. Closed end Oct-1 Apr. (off-season house parties of 12-16 people welcome.) Amex, Diners, MasterCard, Visa, Laser. **Directions:** Signposted from N4 at Drumfin crossroads. ◇

SLIGO / ROSSES POINT

A fascinating town, with a rich heritage, Sligo has a growing number of hotels: if business and leisure facilities convenient to the town are important, the **Sligo Park Hotel** (Tel 071 916 0291; www.leehotels.com) is a popular choice - this long-established hotel on the edge of the town has good facilities and ample parking; by contrast, the most talked about recent arrival is the shiny new town centre hotel **The Glasshouse** (071 919 4300; www.theglasshouse.ie), also with parking, which will appeal to modernists. There are plenty of popular coffee shops and cafés to sustain a day around the town: informal food, people-watching and entertainment are to be found at **Garavogue & Café Bar Deli** (Tel 071 40100) - a brilliantly located contemporary riverside bar and café with outside seating for fine weather. **Bistro Bianconi** (Tel 071 41744) on O'Connell Street continues to meet the informal family dining market well, and now has outlets in Dublin and Galway. For lovers of Inidan food, a branch of the long-established Dublin restaurant **Poppadom** (Tel 071 914 7171; www.poppadomsligo.com) is a few doors along, and there's another fine Indian restaurant, **Classic Indian** (formerly called Sher-E-Punjab; Tel 071 9147700) on Market Street. Anyone visiting Sligo should make a point of calling into the magnificently traditional **Lyons Department Store**, in business since 1878 and still with its original shopfront; it's a joy to find a quirky owner-run store these days and on, the first floor, they have a café-restaurant serving fresh and wholesome locally-sourced food, Sligo's best kept secret, perhaps. Sligo has a rich cultural heritage and, in the town, the Model Arts & Niland Gallery (see entry - The Atrium Café) is especially worth visiting; there are many associations with the poet W.B. Yeats and his brother, the painter Jack Yeats - the most notable connection was with Lissadell House at Drumcliff, the former home of the Gore-Booths, of whom the best known was Constance Gore-Booth who, as Countess Markievicz, was much involved with the Easter Rising of 1916; since the sale of Lissadell in 2003, the house and gardens are open to the public. The nearby Enniscrone & Rosses Point championship golf courses provide a tough test for golfers of all abilities. **ROSSES POINT**, a few minutes' drive from Sligo town, has views across to Oyster Island and Coney Island (after which the island off New York was named); Rosses Point is renowned for golf and has a lovely beach. There are several

Georgina Campbell's Ireland

restaurants and bars to choose from: Joe Grogan's bar/restaurant **The Waterfront** (071 917 7122) offers some of the best food in the area and it can be outstanding when on top form; **Austies** (071 917 7020) is a fine old bar with a maritime theme and views over Sligo Bay - there's an informal restaurant attached.

WWW.IRELAND-GUIDE.COM FOR THE BEST PLACES TO EAT, DRINK & STAY

Sligo
CAFÉ
The Atrium Café

The Niland Model Arts Centre The Mall Sligo Co Sligo **Tel: 071 914 1418**
info@modelart.ie www.modelart.ie

féile bia If you are planning a visit to Sligo town, the Model Arts Centre is well worth a visit and it could make sense to arrange your day around a break here. Well-known chef Brid Torrades runs the delightful daytime restaurant, an open-plan café that spills out into the bright atrium area of the gallery - stylish, yet accessible, the perfect spot for seriously tempting, simple food with an emphasis on good quality and flavour: superb soups, for example, delicious omelettes or tuna & black olive bruschetta (both prettily presented with herbs and leaves from Rod Alston's Organic Centre, nearby) and hot daily blackboard specials. Pretty compôtes topped with cream - rhubarb, blackberry - are simply delicious, and there's good coffee too. *Brid Torrades has a second Sligo venue, Ósta Café Wine Bar (see entry) and, at the time of going to press, another 2-storey restaurant called Tobergal Lane is due to open across the river from Ósta, just off O'Connell Street. Parking (up the steep hill, behind the gallery). Meals: Tue-Sat 12-3 (Sun Brunch 11-3), Veg menu avail. Closed Mon, 23 Dec-4 Jan, Easter weekend, 17 Mar. **No Credit Cards. Directions:** Sligo town centre; prominent building on The Mall. ◈

Sligo
HOTEL
Clarion Hotel Sligo

Clarion Road Sligo Co Sligo **Tel: 071 911 9000**
info@clarionhotelsligo.com www.clarionhotelsireland.com

This large hotel in Sligo town actually dates back to 1848 but, since being given 'the works', it has emerged as a modern classic with the contemporary style that is associated with the new Clarion hotels. The warm-toned reception area has a welcoming atmosphere and accommodation is well up to the usual standard, with a high proportion of suites (including a penthouse suite) and good-sized rooms, high quality bedding, smart bathrooms, broadband, and irons & ironing board as standard. Dining options offer the now familiar choice between the well-appointed Sinergie restaurant (crisp white linen, international menu, attentive service) and casual dining Asian style in the Kudos Bar. Leisure and pampering facilities include a 20m pool, gym and spa treatments. Business and conference facilities offer meeting rooms for groups of 4 to 400, and a business team to co-ordinate events if necessary. **Rooms 316** (91 suites). Sinergie seats 160 (private room, 35); D daily 6-10; Sun: L 1-3, D 6-9.30; Set Sun L about €30; Set D about €35. House wine from €24. Food served in Kudos Bar & Rest 12.30-10 daily. Amex, Diners, MasterCard, Visa, Laser. **Directions:** Follow N16 signs for Enniskillen. ◈

Sligo
RESTAURANT/PUB
Coach Lane Restaurant @ Donaghy's Bar

1-2 Lord Edward Street Sligo Co Sligo
Tel: 071 916 2417

féile bia The restaurant over Orla and Andy Donaghy's pub is approached by an attractive side alley, with a menu board displayed on the street. It's a long narrow room, furnished in a comfortable mixture of traditional and contemporary styles, with well-appointed white-clothed tables, soft lighting and neatly uniformed waitresses in black polo shirts and trousers with white aprons all creating a good impression. Andy's menus are lively and attractive, the cooking is confident and, an active supporter of local produce, he does a great line in well-aged steaks, and seafood. There's also a wide choice of salads, pasta dishes and chicken - and the cooking style ranges from traditional (steak with home-made fries, crispy onion rings & HP sauce) to spicy (cajun chicken with a fresh fruit salsa). This attractive well-run restaurant has earned a well-deserved place as one of the best in the area. **Seats 120** (plus 40 on an outside terrace, weather permitting). Air conditioning. D daily 3-10, à la carte. House wine from €20.50; service discretionary except 10% on parties of 8+.Closed 25 Dec, Good Fri, 2nd week Feb. Amex, MasterCard, Visa, Laser. **Directions:** N4 to Sligo, left at Adelaide Street, right into Lord Edward Street.

Montmartre

Sligo
RESTAURANT

1 Market Yard Sligo Co Sligo **Tel: 071 916 9901**
edelmckeon@eircom.net

féile bia French run and staffed, this is the area's leading restaurant and has a strong local following, so reservations are strongly advised, especially at weekends. After a long closure following a fire it re-opened in summer 2007 and, to the delight of all, has hardly changed at all. Although not big, there is a little bar area that doubles as reception and a bright and airy feeling, with potted palms, white crockery and smartly uniformed staff all emphasising the French style. Proprietor-chef Stéphane Magaud's varied menus offer imaginative French cuisine in a light, colourful style with local produce featuring in some dishes, especially seafood - Lissadell oysters and mussels, for instance, there may also be game in season, and there will always be imaginative vegetarian dishes. Sound cooking, attractive presentation and reasonable prices have brought this restaurant many friends some say the service is slow, but to the French eating is a leisurely pastime. The wine list, which is mostly imported directly from France, includes an unusually good selection of half bottles and wines by the glass. An early dinner menu offers exceptional value. **Seats 50.** Children welcome. Air conditioning. Toilets wheelchair accessible. D Tue-Sun, 5-11pm. Early D about €16 (5-7pm), D a la carte. House wines from €18. Closed Mon, 24-26 Dec. Amex, Diners, MasterCard, Visa, Laser. **Directions:** 200 yards from Hawks Well Theatre & Tourist Office. ◇

Osta Café & Wine Bar

Sligo
CAFÉ/WINE BAR
Ⓝ

Garavogue Weir View (near Hyde Bridge) Stephen Street Sligo Co Sligo
Tel: 071 914 4639 info@osta.ie www.osta.ie

The Garavogue river sweeps past this bright and airy café in the centre of Sligo town, and the floor to ceiling glass frontage makes it a delightful spot for coffee (organic and fairly traded) or a more substantial meal. Run by Brid Torrades (see Atrium Café), who is a leader in the Euro-Toques and Slow Food campaigns for better food, and well-known for her ardent support of local organic food and small producers, the food here has immediacy and real depth of flavour; breads and pastries from Brid's bakery at Ballinafad are a speciality, also Irish cheeses and charcuterie. Menus include modestly described soups which are very good indeed, quite complex in flavour and with a nice texture, and interesting options like Tullynascreen goat's cheese and caramelised onion crostini or an exceptionally fresh and crunchy chicken and toasted almond salad with a light creamy dressing. Daily specials appearing on a chalk board include pannini and wraps - usually with a bit of a twist, such as chicken with jalapeno relish and cream cheese. The soups have a quality and come with home-made brown bread. And it would be difficult to leave without sampling something from a spectacular array of home-made cakes including, coconut muffins, almond croissants, raspberry tarts and cream sponges. A small bar area makes for a good spot to sip wine from a short but perfectly formed list and tapas are also on offer in the evening. *At the time of going to press, a third restaurant called Tobergal Lane is due to open across the river from Osta, just off O'Connell Street. **Seats 30.** Mon-Sat, 9am- 8.30pm (Thurs-Sat, to 9.30pm), Sun 12- 5pm. Lunch from €4.50, cakes from €4. Bottle of wine from €15, per glass from €3.50. No SC. **No credit cards. Directions:** On Stephen Street, near Hyde Bridge.

Radisson SAS Hotel Sligo

Sligo Area
HOTEL

Ballincar Rosses Point Sligo Co Sligo **Tel: 071 914 0008**
info.sligo@RadissonSAS.com www.radissonsas.com

This fine contemporary hotel is out of town, towards Rosses Point; it is not especially attractive from the road but, once inside the door it's a different story as it has a light and appealing atmosphere that the new Radisson hotels seem to achieve especially well, and a huge welcoming flower arrangement in the large foyer to win over any waiverers. Staff are keen to make guests feel at home, and clearly take pride in the hotel - and it's easy to see why. Simple lines and classy contemporary decor in quality materials and warm tones create a pleasing ambience, without distracting from the hotel's great attraction - the views over Sligo Bay. Bedrooms are well-sized and very comfortable, with all the facilities now expected (TV options, voicemail, safe, mini bar, iron/ironing boar as well as trouser press, and so on), and there are various room combinations offered, including family rooms. The Classiebawn Restaurant, which is an open-plan dining area along the front of the hotel (and the gains in smart design and, especially, views are greater than anything it loses in lack of privacy) is an especially pleasant place for a weekend lunch, or dinner on a long summer evening, when the views can be enjoyed to the full. Conference/banqueting (950/470); business centre, free broadband wi/fi. Leisure centre, swimming pool, spa. Golf nearby. **Rooms 132** (7 junior suites, 3 executive rooms, 6 disabled). 24 hr room service, lift, turndown service offered. Children welcome (under 16 free in parents' room; cots available without charge, baby sitting arranged). B&B €80pps, ss €45. **Restaurant:** D daily 6.30-10.30, L sat & Sun 12.30-3. Set Sun L €35. House wine, €21. Bar meals also available, 12-7 daily. No SC. *Short breaks offered; golf breaks are a speciality (3 championship courses nearby). Open all year. Amex, MasterCard, Visa. **Directions:** From Sligo town, follow signs for Rosses Point; the hotel is on the right after 3km (2 m).

Strandhill
RESTAURANT/PUB

Strand House Bar
Strandhill Co Sligo
Tel: 071 916 8140

Just ten minutes drive from Sligo, close to the airport and one of Europe's most magnificent surfing beaches, this well-known bar has a big welcoming turf fire, cosy snugs and friendly staff. No children after 9pm. The first floor restaurant **Triskell** (071 912 8402) is operated separately, currently by Catherine Byrne and Marie-Claire Danguy, who have recently made this a destination for discerning diners in the Sligo area, who love the simplicity of their flavoursome food. Bar meals served all day (12-3pm). Restaurant: D Tue-Sun 6.30-9.30 (from 6pm Sun); value D all evening Sun-Fri, 2/3 courses, €20/25; also a la carte & specials; house wine from €17. Closed 25 Dec & Good Fri. MasterCard, Visa, Laser. **Directions:** Follow signs to Sligo airport (Strandhill). Strand House is situated at the end near the beach.

COUNTY TIPPERARY

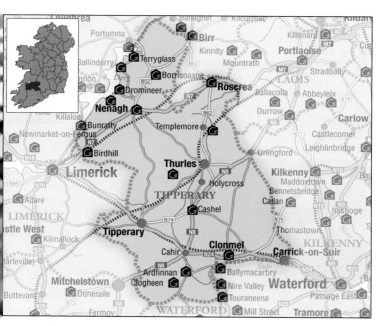

The cup of life is overflowing in Tipperary. In this extensive and wondrously fertile region, there's an air of fulfillment, a comfortable awareness of the world in harmony. And the place names reinforce this sense of natural bounty.

Across the middle of the county, there's the Golden Vale, with prosperous lands along the wide valley of the River Suir and its many tributaries, and westwards towards County Limerick across a watershed around Donohill. The Vale be so named because the village of Golden is at its heart, but then it could be the other way round - that's the kind of place it is

The county's largest town, down in the far south under the Comeragh Mountains, is the handsome borough of Clonmel - its name translates as "Honey Meadow". Yet although there are many meadows of all kinds in Tipperary, there's much more to this largest inland county in Ireland than farmland, for it is graced with some of the most elegant mountains in the country.

North of the Golden Vale, the Silvermine Mountains rise to 694m on Keeper Hill, and beyond them the farming countryside rolls on in glorious profusion to Nenagh - a town much improved by by-passes on either side - and Tipperary's own riviera, the beautiful eastern shore of Lough Derg. Inevitably, history and historic monuments abound in such country, with the fabulous Rock of Cashel and its dramatic remains of ancient ecclesiastical buildings setting a very high standard for evoking the past.

But Tipperary lends itself every bit as well to enjoyment of the here and now. Tipperary is all about living life to the full, and they do it with style in a place of abundance.

Local Attractions & Information

Cahir Cahir Castle	052 41 011
Cahir Farmers Market Sats 9am-1pm	086 648 2044
Carrick-on-Suir Ormond Castle	051 640 787
Carrick-on-Suir Tipperary Crystal Visitor Centre	051 641 188
Cashel Bru Boru Culture Centre	062 61 122
Cashel Rock of Cashel	062 61 437
Cashel Tourism Information and Heritage Centre	062 61 333
Clonmel Clonmel Racecourse	052 22 611
Clonmel Theatre & Arts Festival (July)	052 29 339

Clonmel Tourism Information	052 22 960
Nenagh Heritage Centre	067 31 610
Nenagh Tourism Information	067 31 610
Roscrea Roscrea Heritage - Castle & Damer House	0505 21 850
Thurles Holy Cross Abbey	0504 43 124 / 43 118
Thurles Race Course	0504 23 245
Tipperary Race Course (Limerick Junction)	062 51 357
Tipperary Town Tourism Information	062 51 457

Ballinderry
RESTAURANT
🍴🍷 Ⓔ

Brocka-on-the-Water Restaurant
Kilgarvan Quay Ballinderry Nenagh Co Tipperary
Tel: 067 22038

Anthony and Anne Gernon's almost-waterside restaurant has attracted a following disproportionate to its size over the years and, although it has been extended at the back to include a high-ceilinged conservatory style room which opens on to a garden patio, it is still basically carved out of the lower half of a family home that is by no means huge. The atmosphere is very much a "proper restaurant" - yet with all the warmth of welcome that the family situation implies. There's a reception room with an open fire, comfy chairs, interesting things to read and look at (Anthony's a dab hand at wood carving) - and aperitifs served in generous wine glasses, while you read a menu that promises good things to come in the adjoining dining room and conservatory. Guests arriving in daylight will notice hens clucking around a garden well-stocked with fruit and vegetables - promising the best of all possible beginnings for your dinner. Seasonal menus depend on availability of course, but there are always some specialities retained by popular demand, including Cooleeney cheese croquettes with home-made chutney (Cooleeney is one of Ireland's finest cheeses, made by Breda Maher on the family farm near Thurles). **Seats 30** (private room, 30). Air conditioning. Toilets wheelchair accessible. Reservations strongly advised. D 6.30-9 Mon-Sat in summer (call to check opening times off-season). Set D about €40, also à la carte & Vegetarian Menu. SC discretionary. House wine about €22. Closed Sun. **No Credit Cards. Directions:** Lough Derg drive, half way between Nenagh and Portumna. ◇

CARRICK ON SUIR

This beautifully located medieval town is set in the ancient Golden Vale (Gleann an Oir), with the Comeragh Mountains to the south and the Walsh Mountains to the southeast making this unspoilt area a wonderful base for outdoor activities. The river has always been central to the life and development of the town, formerly for trade and now mainly for pleasure. Although tidal, Carrick-on-Suir is navigable from any part of Ireland's inland waterways and a landing pontoon has recently been built adding to the of the amenities of the town. The **Carraig Hotel** (051 641455; www.carraighotel.com, on Main Street is the centre of community activities, and the new Blarney Woollen Mills/Meadows & Byrne development, Dove Hill Design Centre (3 miles outside town on the N24/Clonmel road, now brings shopper to the area and refreshment is available there at **The Passionate Cook** (051 645603), a large and attractively designed restaurant offering quality informal food.
WWW.IRELAND-GUIDE.COM FOR THE BEST PLACES TO EAT, DRINK & STAY

CASHEL

Visitors flock here to see the famous the Rock of Cashel, a site hosting a ruined church and fortifications, formerly the seat of the Irish kings of Munster; King Cormac built his superb Royal Chapel in the 12th century and it can be seen on the Rock - nearby were Cistercian, Dominican and Franciscan abbeys two of which may still be viewed. And the town itself also has much to offer, including archaeology and architecture of great historical significance (information available at the Heritage Centre on Main Street) but also some of the best food and hospitality to be found in Ireland including - right beside the Rock - the renowned restaurant **Chez Hans** and its highly regarded informal younger brother, **Café Hans** (see entries). Nearby **Legends Townhouse** (062 61292; www.legendsguesthouse.com) with access to the ock of Cashel carpark - is a neat owner-run guesthouse with open fires that makes a comfortable base r visiting the area's many sites. In the town, **The Spearman** (062 61143) bakery and café is a simple nd charming old-style place to take a break and buy some home-bakes to take home.

WW.IRELAND-GUIDE.COM FOR THE BEST PLACES TO EAT, DRINK & STAY

---

ashel

OTEL/BAR/RESTAURANT

R

Bailey's Cashel

Main Street Cashel Co Tipperary **Tel: 062 61937**
info@baileys-ireland.com www.baileys-ireland.com

Set back from the road, with a very attractive planted plaza set up with seating and umbrellas in front, this fine early 18th century building in the heart of Cashel was previously a seven-bedroom guesthouse but a cleverly-concealed, extension has allowed it to grow, gracefully, into a fully-fledged family-run hotel (with 14 new bedrooms, a spacious restaurant, a cosy cellar bar, and a lovely swimming pool and leisure centre). There's a comfortable residents' drawing room ('The Library') and, although the attractive contemporary bedrooms have no ea/coffee facilities (available in The Library), otherwise they tick all the right boxes: good lighting, uality furnishing, efficient air conditioning, windows that open, comfortable chairs, flat screen TV, irons nd boards, hair-dryers, safes broadband and plenty of connection points for laptops, chargers and so n - and well-designed, if compact, bathrooms. Banqueting (80). Children welcome (under 3s free in arents' room, cot available free of charge); **Rooms 19** (1 suite, 1 for disabled, all no smoking); lift, oom service (limited hours); B&B €80 pps, ss €15. **Restaurant Number 42:** Gently contemporary, with vell-spaced tables and comfortable chairs, this is a pleasant place to relax and enjoy a good dinner. Balanced menus combining modern Irish and European cuisine, feature some local ingredients and ffer a wide choice. Appealing dishes on the evening à la carte might include starters like twice baked heddar & chive soufflé or warm potato pancake with smoked salmon & chive crème fraîche, and main ourses include excellent beef fillet or a tender rack of lamb with champ. The bar menu, which offers n extensive range of more casual dishes, provides a casual option and good value. This is a well-run lace that delivers the goods in friendly Irish style... Free private parking in an underground car park nakes this a particularly attractive all-purpose stop for business people and visitors alike. **Seats 80** outdoors, 15); air conditioning; children welcome before 7pm; bar food served daily 12.30-9.30; Sun , 12.30-4, Sun D 6-9.30; set Sun L €25; also a la carte L&D; house wine €19. Establishment closed 23-27 Dec. Amex, MasterCard, Visa, Laser. **Directions:** Centre of town, on Main Street.

Cashel

CAFÉ

R

Café Hans

Moor Lane Cashel Co Tipperary
Tel: 062 63660

Hans and Stefan Matthia's smashing little contemporary café is the perfect complement to the parent establishment, Chez Hans, next door. A neat renovation job has been done with clean-lined style, creating a bright and airy space out of very little; bare-topped tables are laid café-style and a canny little menu offers just the kind of food that's needed during the day: colourful, sassy dishes including lots of salads - several versions of Caesar salad include a vegetarian one, and there's an irresistible house salad with pear Cashel Blue cheese what else?) and Parma ham; open sandwiches come with home-made French fries and there are half a dozen hot dishes - grilled lamb cutlets with mushroom sauce, poached salmon with new potatoes, green beans and salsa verde. Good desserts and afternoon tea (2-5.30), lovely coffee; wine list. Well worth planning a journey around a break here - everyone travelling the Dublin-Cork route should make a note of this place and its hours. But get there early or be prepared to wait, as the secret about Café Hans is well and truly out. There is some menu overlap with Chez Hans, where, together with Jason Matthia, Stefan is also responsible for the early dinner. Children welcome. **Seats 30.** Open Tue-Sat, 12-5.30 (advisable to check off-season). Closed Sun & Mon. No reservations. **No Credit Cards. Directions:** Off N8 in Cashel, 50m in Rock of Cashel direction. ◊

Cashel
HOTEL/RESTAURANT

Cashel Palace Hote|

Main Street Cashel Co Tipperary **Tel: 062 6270|**
reception@cashel-palace.ie www.cashel-palace.|

One of Ireland's most famous hote|
and originally a bishop's residenc|
Cashel Palace is a large, graciously proportione|
Queen Anne-style house (dating from 1730), s|
well back from the road in the centre of Cash|
town. The beautiful reception rooms and some |
the spacious, elegantly furnished bedrooms ove|
look the gardens and the Rock of Cashel at th|
rear. The present owners, Patrick and Susa|
Murphy, took over the hotel in 1998 and, sinc|
then, have been gradually renovating and refu|
bishing both public areas and bedrooms; the whole hotel has been redecorated, and a new functio|
room opened - but it still exudes that old fashioned atmosphere and hospitality that modern hote|
simply cannot emulate. Conference/banqueting (85/94). Children welcome (Under 3 free in parent|
room, cot available without charge, baby sitting arranged). No pets. Garden. **Rooms 23** (5 suites). Li|
Room service (limited hours). B&B from €105, ss about €35. Closed 24-26 Dec. **The Bishop|
Buttery:** Lunch and dinner are served every day in this atmospheric vaulted basement restaurant an|
bar, which successfully juggles the various demands of a mixed clientèle ranging from passing trad|
to local business people, corporate guests, families out for a treat - and, of course, residents; there |
also a formal ground floor dining room, overlooking the gardens, which is used for breakfast an|
Sunday lunch. New head chef Robin O'Connell is doing a good job, offering well-balanced and we|
cooked meals that include the traditional choices like steak and chicken breast alongside more adver|
turous ones, and tasty bar fare - home-made lamb sausages with black pudding mash & red onio|
confit, for example; the cooking is quite modern and well-presented, with the generosity expected i|
country areas. Food available all day; D €48. House wine about €20 *Food is also available in th|
Guinness Bar, 10.30am-8pm (Fri & Sat to 6pm). Amex, Diners, MasterCard, Visa, Laser. **Directions|**
On N8 which runs through Cashel; hotel is just off main road.

Cashel
RESTAURANT

Chez Han|

Moore Lane Cashel Co Tipperar|
Tel: 062 6117|

Although many others have since followed suit, th|
idea of opening a restaurant in a church was high|
original when Hans-Peter Matthia did so in 1968|
The scale - indeed the whole style of the place - i|
superb and provides an unusual and atmospheri|
setting for the seriously fine food which peopl|
travel great distances to sample. Hans-Peter's son|
Jason (who brought experience in great kitchen|
like Le Gavroche and La Tante Claire) joined him i|
the business several years ago and this - togethe|
with the more recent opening of their exceller|
daytime restaurant, **Café Hans**, next door (see entry) - brought renewed energy, confirming the statu|
of Chez Hans as the leading restaurant in a wide area. Ably assisted by restaurant manager Louise|
Matthia and a strong kitchen brigade, Jason offers menus that include an early dinner menus, offerin|
some of the best value to be found in Ireland and an extensive à la carte, either of which is definitel|
worth travelling for. Guests arrive into the bar, and look at menus over a drink there: the à la cart|
offers an outstanding choice of nine excellent dishes on each course, including many specialities |
their famous cassoulet of seafood (half a dozen varieties of fish and shellfish with a delicate chive|
velouté sauce), for example, imaginative vegetarian dishes - and, of course, the great lamb and bee|
for which the area is renowned. Finish perhaps with lemon tart & lime tart with raspberry sorbet o|
chocolate mousse with vanilla ice cream and candied oranges then tea or coffee with home-made|
petits fours. Service, under Louise Matthia's direction, is quick and pleasant. A wine list strong o|
classic old world wines offers some treats for the deep-pocketed as well as two pages of recommended|
wines under €40, some from Hans-Peter's sister's vineyard in Germany. Booking ahead is essentia|
Seats 70. D Tue-Sat, 6-9.30. Early D 2/3 courses, €27.50/33 (6-7.15); also à la carte. House wine|
from €24.50. Closed Sun, Mon, 16 Sep-8 Oct, also 2 weeks in Jan. MasterCard, Visa, Laser|
Directions: First right from N8, 50m on left; at foot of Rock of Cashel.

Hill House

Cashel
B&B

R

Palmer Hill Cashel Co Tipperary **Tel: 062 61277**
hillhouse1@eircom.net www.hillhousecashel.com

Carmel Purcell's lovely Georgian house was built in 1710 and has great character. It is set well back from the road in large gardens, with plenty of parking and a magnificent view of the Rock of Cashel and a welcoming hospitable atmosphere, noticeable immediately on arrival in the spacious entrance hall, which has fine Georgian features and fresh flowers. While Carmel shows guests to one of the large rooms (some with four posters), she gives the lowdown on local attractions and settles you in; rooms are very comfortable, with television, radio and tea/coffee facilities and good bathrooms. Breakfast is a high point, served at a large communal table very nicely set up with good linen, baskets of freshly-baked breads and scones and home-made preserves; a side table offers fruits and cereals and the cooked breakfasts are delicious. Not suitable for children under 8 years. No pets. Garden. **Rooms 5** (all shower only & no smoking, 1 family room). B&B €50, ss €25. MasterCard, Visa, Laser. **Directions:** 2 minutes from Cashel town centre; from Dublin, bear left after the turn signed Rock of Cashel - Hill House is opposite the next juntion.

Carron House

Cashel Area
FARMHOUSE

R

Carron Cashel Co Tipperary **Tel: 052 62142**
hallyfamily@eircom.net www.carronhouse.com

Mary Hally's country home is on an award-winning farm, in a peaceful location in the heart of the Golden Vale, yet only minutes from Cashel and just an hour from Kilkenny. Approached up a long, well-maintained drive, first impressions are very encouraging, as there's a lovely front garden in front of the large, modern house - and separate entrances for the house and farm. Large individually decorated bedrooms include one triple room (with double and twin beds) and are very comfortably furnished, with generous beds, television, tea/coffee facilities, hair dryers and neat en-suite shower rooms. Housekeeping throughout is immaculate and there's a guest sitting room with antique furniture and interesting books, which is always available to guests. Mary, who is a friendly, attentive and informative hostess, gives guests a good send-off in the morning, with a generous, well-cooked and nicely presented breakfast in a large sun room overlooking the garden. Not suitable for children. **Rooms 4** (all with en-suite shower & all no smoking). B&B €36pps, ss €19. Closed 1 Oct-1 Apr. MasterCard, Visa, Laser. **Directions:** Take N8 south bound from Cashel for 2.5 miles. Signposted left at crossroads; follow signs.

Dualla House

Cashel Area
FARMHOUSE

R

Dualla Cashel Co Tipperary **Tel: 062 61487**
duallahse@eircom.net www.duallahouse.com

Set in 300 acres of rolling Tipperary farmland in the "Golden Vale", Martin and Mairead Power's fine Georgian manor house faces south towards the Slievenamon, Comeragh, Knockmealdown and Galtee Mountains. Just 3 miles from the Rock of Cashel, this is a convenient base for exploring the area but its special appeal is peace and tranquillity which, together with comfortable accommodation in large airy bedrooms (with tea/coffee trays), great hospitality and Mairead's home cooking, keep guests coming back time and again. An extensive breakfast menu includes local apple juice as well as other fresh fruits and juices, farmhouse cheeses, porridge with local honey, also free-range eggs and sausages from the local butcher in the traditional cooked breakfast - and home-made bread and preserves. Children welcome (under 3s free in parents' room, cot available without charge). **Rooms 4** (3 with en-suite shower, 1 with private bathroom, all no smoking). B&B €50 pps, ss €10/15. Closed Nov-Mar. MasterCard, Visa. **Directions:** 5km (3 miles) from Cashel on R691. Coming from Dublin signed from N8, 5 miles after Horse & Jockey. Sign on left. 2.5 miles to house.

The Old Convent Gourmet Hideaway

Clogheen
RESTAURANT/B&B

Mount Anglesby Clogheen Co Tipperary **Tel: 052 65565**
info@theoldconvent.ie www.theoldconvent.ie

COUNTRY HOUSE BREAKFAST AWARD

Dermot and Christine Gannon's restaurant with rooms, styled a 'gourmet hideaway', is in one of the most beautiful and unspoilt yet relatively little known - parts of the country: just the place for couples 'seeking a short getaway from it all experience'. It's an unusual, very comfortable, beautifully designed and decorated, country house with mountain views across the famously scenic 'Vee' - emphatically not for 'family weekends', bookings are not accepted for children under 12. A lofty double drawing room with large windows and a mixture of antiques and good modern furnishings makes a relaxing reception area, and the spacious, airy restaurant is in what was once the convent refectory and adjoining sacristy - now one large area, but still complete with stained glass windows. An unusual setting, for an exceptional meal: only a 9-course Tasting Menu is offered, plus an optional cheese platter of seven Irish cheeses with Trass Farm fruit and plum jam. Ingredients are sourced locally (and organic) when possible and, as anyone who has experienced a meal cooked by this talented chef will testify, the cooking is stunningly accurate: the discernible difference between beautiful pieces of Irish beef cooked 'rare' and 'very rare' a joy to behold, for example. Sensitive seasoning is another highlight there is no cheffy arrogance here and a (tiny) salt and pepper set is offered on tables, but Dermot has such a sure palate that it will almost certainly be unnecessary to use it. Many diners might be wary of the Tasting Menu, but servings are well-judged - it certainly isn't a marathon and, on the other hand, could never be described as 'grudging' or 'mean'; furthermore, in deference to Irish taste, the meat course is very generous indeed. And at €58 it is very good value for an exceptional meal: skilfully cooked, generous and beautifully presented. **Accommodation** (ITB approval pending): The bedrooms, all individually styled, are sumptuously appointed and have wonderful views although no tea and coffee making facilities; bathrooms are also stylishly appointed, and have separate bath and shower. This is a lovely place that is definitely 'itself' - and you could very quickly become fond of it; there are several major golf courses nearby, and their culinary reputation preceded them from their previous restaurant in Cahir, so the Gannons have already earned a following. Everything they do at The Old Convent is not just done superbly well, but done differently - the wonderful breakfast that is a further treat in store for overnight guests, for example, begins with a beautiful fruit martini with yogurt, honey & toasted pistachios, presented to your table in a martini glass on arrival - delightful; and, of course, everything that follows is equally special, including brown bread and beer bread baked in the Aga, Ballybrado eggs and Graham Roberts' organic smoked salmon. Simply superb. Free Broadband wi/fi. **Seats 50;** children over 12 years welcome; D Thu-Sun, 8pm (at 7.30pm Sun); Set 8 course gourmet D €58. House wine from €22. SC 10% on groups 6+. Closed Mon-Wed and 2 weeks Nov / 2 weeks Spring. **Rooms 7** (4 suites, 1 shower only, all no smoking); B&B from €75 pps, ss €30. House avail for private rental for conferences, weddings etc. MasterCard, Visa, Laser. **Directions:** From Clogheen take the Vee/Lismore road, 0.5km on right.

Befani's Mediterranean & Tapas Restaurant

Clonmel
RESTAURANT

6 Sarsfield Street Clonmel Co Tipperary **Tel: 052 77893**
info@befani.com www.befani.com

This stylish new Mediterranean and tapas restaurant is in a recently restored listed building just up from the quays, and it's a very welcome arrival in Clonmel. Co-owner and chef, Adrian Ryan, and business partner and restaurant manager, Fulvio Bonfiglio, are thorough professionals who have quickly won the hearts of discerning diners in the locality. Spacious and simply furnished, the restaurant has a small bar, and a pleasant ambience; appealing menus are deliberately restricted and include a tapas menu which, together with the high quality of ingredients, cooking and service, and real value for money, has won them a lot of friends. Local organic ingredients are sourced where possible and vegetarians are well catered for. Look out for the 'fish of the day' and also a monthly special offer on the carefully chosen wine list. Befani's is a delightful experience with a southern European atmosphere and the long opening hours are a great bonus. **Seats 55** (outdoors, 15); children welcome; wheelchair access to courtyard only; air conditioning. Food served daily, 9am-9.30pm; L 12.30-3. D 6-9.30; set D about €31.50, set Sun L about €21.50, also a la carte L&D; house wine €18.50. Closed 25 Dec, 1 Jan. MasterCard, Visa, Laser. **Directions:** Town centre.

Clonmel
HOTEL
R

Hotel Minella

Coleville Road Clonmel Co Tipperary **Tel: 052 22388**
hotelminella@eircom.net www.hotelminella.ie

Sparky, the Old English sheepdog, establishes a friendly tone from the outset as he welcomes arriving guests to this pleasant hotel, which is attractively located in its own grounds, overlooking the River Suir. The original house was built in 1863 and was purchased in 1961 by the current owners, the Nallen family. They've extended the hotel several times over the years, most recently to add a further 22 rooms, and the existing rooms have been refurbished and upgraded; all are furnished to a high standard with smart bathrooms - and housekeeping is exemplary. This is the main hotel in the area, popular for weddings, with conference facilities and a fine leisure centre. The public areas in the old house include a cocktail bar, restaurant and lounge areas. Leisure centre with 20 metre swimming pool and outdoor Canadian hot tub, jacuzzi, steam room and gym; Broadband. Children welcome (under 16 free in parents' room, cot available without charge, baby sitting arranged). Tennis, fishing. Garden. **Rooms 90** (4 suites, 5 junior suites, 80 no smoking, 3 for disabled, 13 ground floor, 10 family rooms). B&B from about €90 pps. Closed 23-29 Dec. Amex, MasterCard, Visa, Laser. **Directions:** Edge of Clonmel town. ◇

Clonmel
CHARACTER PUB
R

Sean Tierney

13 O'Connell Street Clonmel Co Tipperary
Tel: 052 24467

This tall, narrow pub is packed with "artefacts of bygone days", in short a mini-museum but one with a giant screen which is discreetly hidden around the corner, for watching matches. Upstairs (and there are a lot of them this is a four storey building) there's a relaxed traditional family-style restaurant. Expect popular, good value food like potato wedges, mushrooms with garlic, home cooked lasagne, steaks and grills rather than gourmet fare; however, although it is unlikely there will be many surprises, the evening restaurant menus are more ambitious. This is a pub of character and toilets are at the very top, but grand when you get there. Children welcome before 8.30 pm (high chair, childrens menu). Air conditioning. Food served daily, 12.30-9; set 3 course L €25; set Sun L €30. Closed 25 Dec, Good Fri. MasterCard, Visa, Laser. **Directions:** Situated ¹/₂ way down O'Connell St. on the left opposite Dunnes Stores.

Clonmel Area
FARMHOUSE
🏆 ⊜ ⊙ 🍸 ✍

Kilmaneen Farmhouse

Ardfinnan Newcastle Clonmel Co Tipperary **Tel: 052 36231**
kilmaneen@eircom.net www.kilmaneen.com

As neat as a new pin, Kevin & Ber O'Donnell's delightfully situated farmhouse is on a working dairy farm, surrounded by three mountain ranges - the Comeraghs, the Knockmealdowns and the Galtees - and close to the rivers Suir and Tar, making it an ideal base for walking and fishing holidays. Kevin is trained in mountain skills and leads walking groups, and trout fishing on the Suir and Tar on the farm is free (hut provided for tying flies, storing equipment and drying waders). It's an old house, but well restored to combine old furniture with modern comforts. Bedrooms are not especially big, but they are thoughtfully furnished (including tea/coffee facilities and iron/trouser press) and, like the rest of the house, immaculate. There's a great welcome and guests feel at home immediately - especially once they get tucked into Ber's delicious dinners. Don't expect any fancy menus or a wine list (you are welcome to bring your own wine), what you'll get here is real home cooking, based on fresh farm produce: home-produced beef, perhaps, or chicken stuffed with ricotta, spinach & parmesan and wrapped in cured ham, then apple pie for afters, perhaps - and breakfast are equally delicious, with stewed fruits from the garden and home-made breads and preserves as well as lovely porridge or the 'full Irish'. Genuinely hospitable hosts, homely comforts - including a log fire to relax beside after dinner and a large, well-maintained garden, where guests can enjoy the peaceful setting - all add up to a real country break. Kilmaneen was our Farmhouse of the Year in 2005. **Rooms 3** (2 shower only, all en-suite & no smoking). B&B €45 pps, ss €10. Children welcome (under 2s free in parents' room, cots available without charge). Pets permitted by prior arrangement. Dining room seats 12. Residents' D 7pm except on Sun (must book in advance); Set D €27.50. No SC. Closed 1 Nov - 1 Mar. MasterCard, Visa, Laser. **Directions:** In Ardfinnan, follow signs at Ryan's Hill Bar.

DROMINEER

Dromineer is an appealing little place on Lough Derg, with a pretty harbour and lovely woodland walks. It's a popular destination for Shannon cruisers, sailing folk and families out for the day at weekends. **The Whiskey Still** (067 24129), an attractive pub with a deck overlooking the harbour, offers good food. **WWW.IRELAND-GUIDE.COM FOR THE BEST PLACES TO EAT, DRINK & STAY**

Fethard
COUNTRY HOUSE

Mobarnane House

Fethard Co Tipperary **Tel: 052 31962**
info@mobarnanehouse.com www.mobarnanehouse.com

Approached up a stylish gravel drive with well-maintained grass verges, Richard and Sandra Craik-White's lovely 18th century home has been restored to its former glory and makes a wonderfully spacious retreat for guests: the aim is to provide peace and quiet in great comfort, with very personal attention to detail. A large, beautifully furnished drawing room has plenty of comfortable seating for everyone when there's a full house - and the dining room, where Richard's good country cooking is served (usually at a communal table, although separate tables can be arranged on request), is a lovely room; everything served for dinner is freshly prepared on the day, allowing for any preferences mentioned at the time of booking. Accommodation is of the same high standard: all rooms have lovely views and comfortable seating (two have separate sitting rooms), quality bedding and everything needed for a relaxing stay, including tea/coffee making facilities, phones and television - and fresh flowers from the garden. Bathrooms vary somewhat (bedrooms without sitting rooms have bigger bathrooms), but all have quality towels and toiletries. An excellent breakfast gets the day off to a good start - and, as well as being well-placed to explore a large and interesting area blessed with beautiful scenery, an interesting history, local crafts and sports, there is tennis and croquet on site, and lovely lake and woodland walks in the grounds. Not suitable for children under 5 except babies (cot available without charge), children aged 5-10 stay free in parents room. Pets by arrangement. **Rooms 4** (2 junior suites, 2 superior, all no smoking). B&B €75 pps, ss €30. Residents' 4-course D 8pm, €45; advance reservation essential. House wine €15. SC discretionary. Closed Nov-Mar. MasterCard, Visa. **Directions:** From Fethard, take Cashel road for 3.5 miles; turn right, signed Ballinure and Thurles; 1.5 miles on left.

Garrykennedy
PUB

Larkins

Garrykennedy Portroe Nenagh Co Tipperary **Tel: 067 23232**
info@larkinspub.com www.larkinspub.com

You can't miss this pretty white cottage pub with its cheerful red paintwork, and it's a great asset to the charming little harbour at Garrykennedy. Good food includes an excellent house chowder, and traditional daytime bar menus move up a notch or two for dinner, when you can look forward to dishes like succulent duckling and great steaks, with lovely fresh vegetables - good service too. Maura and Cormac Boyle took over ownership of Larkins in 2006 and, have done a little gentle modernisation but, thankfully, the atmosphere has not changed much. Music at weekends and every Wed in summer. Food available 10.30 am- 9.30 pm daily (12.30-9.30 Sun); set Sun L €25. Closed Good Fri, 25 Dec. MasterCard, Visa, Laser. **Directions:** 12km (7 m) from Nenagh.

R NENAGH

This thriving town in the heart of Ireland's best farmland can provide a convenient base within easy reach of many attractions in the mid-west, including Lough Derg, or makes a handy place to break a journey - the modern **Abbey Court Hotel** (067 41111; www.abbeycourt.ie) is located on the edge of town, with ample parking and good facilities. Interesting places in the town that might be handy to know about include **Roots** (19a Pearse Street 067 42444) a quirky casual restaurant with a chess set for customers, newspapers and a selection of books on alternative healing and therapy to browse through, and **Café Q** (067 36445) on Pearse Street, the headquarters of a small chain of quality ingredients-led cafés connected with Quigley's bakery, who supply all the baked goods (*Also at: Limerick, Roscrea, Thurles, Tullamore). Near Nenagh, an unusual and hospitable farm B&B with 'cows, trees and total quiet' is **Bayly Farm** (067 31499; www.baylyfarm.ie) at Ballinaclough. And, between Cloughjordan and Nenagh, locals are warming to **The Fairways Bar & Orchard Restaurant** (067 41444), in new ownership.

WWW.IRELAND-GUIDE.COM FOR THE BEST PLACES TO EAT, DRINK & STAY

Nenagh
CAFÉ

Country Choice Delicatessen & Coffee Bar

25 Kenyon Street Nenagh Co Tipperary **Tel: 067 32596**
info@countrychoice.ie www.countrychoice.ie

Food-lovers from all over the country plan journeys around a visit to Peter and Mary Ward's unique shop. Old hands head for the little café at the back first, fortifying themselves with simple home-cooked food that reflects a policy of seasonality - if the range is small at a particular time of year, so be it. Meats, milk, cream, eggs, butter and flour: "The economy of Tipperary is agricultural and we intend to demonstrate this with a finished product of tantalising smells and tastes." Specialities developed over the years include Cashel Blue and broccoli soup served with their magnificent breads savoury and sweet pastry dishes and tender, gently-cooked meat dishes like Irish stew and Hereford beef (from their own farm) and Guinness casserole. The shop carries a very wide range of the finest Irish artisan produce, plus a smaller selection of specialist products from further afield, such as olive oil and a range of superb dried and glacé fruits that are in great demand for Christmas baking. Specialities that make this place so special include a great terrine, made from the family's saddleback pigs; the preserves - jam (Mary Ward makes 12,000 pots a year!) and home-made marmalade, based on oranges left to caramelise in the Aga overnight, producing a runny but richly flavoured preserve; then there is Peter's passion for cheese. He is one of the country's best suppliers of Irish farmhouse cheeses, which he minds like babies as they ripen and, unlike most shops, only puts on display when they are mature: do not leave without buying cheese. As well as all this, they run regular art exhibitions in the shop, wine courses and poetry readings. Definitely worth a detour. [Country Choice was the winner of our Natural food Award in 2004]. **Seats 35.** Picnic service available. Open all day (9-5.30); L 12-3 daily, à la carte; house wine - any bottle in the shop + €5 corkage; Vegetarian Menu available. Children welcome. Closed Sun. MasterCard, Visa, Laser. **Directions:** Centre of town, on left half way down Kenyon Street.

Nenagh
RESTAURANT

The Pepper Mill

27 Kenyon Street Nenagh Co Tipperary
Tel: 067 34598

Mairead and Robert Gill's popular restaurant recently moved into much-needed larger new premises next door, and now, behind an elegant grey-green frontage, you'll find a smart but comfortable wine bar downstairs and a fine contemporary restaurant on the first floor. A giant crystal chandelier lights the wide atrium beside the stairs; elsewhere in the elegantly appointed soft brown and cream restaurant, lighting is discreet and soothing. With a mixture of banquette seating and upholstered chairs, a vase of fresh flowers on each bare-topped table (no linen napkins, alas, but that is the only fault) and light modern jazz playing softly in the background, the scene is set for an enjoyable evening. Excellent breads make a good impression, arriving with a slab of fresh butter on a glass plate, and tap water is brought to the table in bottles. Refreshingly straightforward menus offer about eight choices on each course and, although there are world influences, there's a welcome leaning towards Irish themes: chicken in a creamy cider sauce is served on apple mash with Clonakilty black pudding and caramelised apples; new season lamb shank comes with colcannon mash & red wine jus; and Irish Hereford fillet beef has an Irish whiskey and mushroom cream sauce. Fresh seafood is delivered daily, and you might start with delicious crab cakes (little chunks of crabmeat and a real crab flavour) with cucumber & dill relish, and have a main course of moist and flavoursome organic salmon with spicy Asian flavourings, perhaps, and a lime cream; vegetables, served separately, are equally good (and more varied than most Irish restaurants). Gorgeous puddings are another highlight, including home-made ice cream, old favourites like crushed meringues with raspberries and cream, and a delectable bread and butter pudding. A well chosen wine list is reasonably priced and includes wines by the glass. With interesting, well-sourced food, good cooking and good value with a sense of occasion, The Peppermill is doing a great job. * Due to open for lunch downstairs, and introduce an Early Bird menu at the time of going to press. Children welcome before 8pm. **Seats 75** (private room, 30). Reservations recommended. Air conditioning. Toilets wheelchair accessible. L Tue-Sat, 12-4pm; D Tue-Sun, 5-10 (Sun 4-9). House wine €18.50. Closed Mon, 24-26 Dec & Good Fri. Amex, Diners, MasterCard, Visa, Laser. **Directions:** Nenagh town centre.

Nenagh Area
COUNTRY HOUSE

Ashley Park House

Ardcronney Nenagh Co Tipperary **Tel: 067 38223**
margaret@ashleypark.com www.ashleypark.com

From the moment you turn off the busy Nenagh-Borrisokane road, you enter a time warp. Margaret and P J Mounsey's home, Ashley Park, is one of those beautiful 18th century houses where all is elegance and comfort. This old house breathes an old-fashioned order, comfort and charm, with stunning views of Lough Ourna and the distant Slieve Bloom Mountains. You can walk down to the lakeshore or through the walled garden; the house is surrounded by 76 acres of woodland and walks are being created through it. Whichever room you stay in, you are guaranteed a fine view, a good night's rest, and a hearty breakfast the next morning in the splendour of the double dining room and dinner can be booked by arrangement in advance. Highly recommended if you want peace and comfort in really splendid surroundings. **Rooms 5** (all with private bathrooms, 2 shower only, 2 family, 4 no smoking, 1 for disabled). B&B €60, ss €10. Residents L&D available by prior arrangement only, €30-38.45. Open all year. **No Credit Cards. Directions:** On the N52, 7km (4 miles) north of Nenagh. Heading north, look for the lake on the left and go through the stone archway, past the gatehouse.

Nenagh Area
HOTEL

Coolbawn Quay Lakeshore Spa

Coolbawn Nenagh Co Tipperary **Tel: 067 28158**
info@coolbawnquay.com www.coolbawnquay.com

Spas and retreats are appearing all over Ireland at the moment, but few could rival the beauty of this magic place. This unique resort on the eastern shores of Lough Derg is modelled on the lines of a 19th century Irish village with quietly understated luxurious accommodation scattered throughout the cottages in the village. The shoreside situation is truly lovely and there is a sense of being very close to the changing moods of nature, partly because the main building - which has a small traditional bar and a country style dining room - is only a few feet from the water. Rooms do vary considerably, but all are simple in style and furnished well, and - a very nice touch this - many have a turf-burning stove which is set up in advance, matches at the ready, so you can have your own real fire whenever you like. The contrasts are wonderful here: whether you want to pamper yourself at the mini spa, hold a small conference - or simply unwind with style - this unusual village could be the ideal destination. Excellent cooking is provided by chef, Rob Oosterbaan. This is a romantic location for weddings, which are held in a luxury banqueting marquee set by the water's edge. [*Coolbawn Quay was our Hideaway of the Year in 2005.] (Small conference/banqueting (40/190). Destination Spa, sauna, steam room; beauty treatments. Walking, fishing. Children welcome (under 2s free in parents room, baby sitting arranged). Garden. No pets. Wheelchair accessible. **Rooms 48** (9 suites, 7 shower only, 1 family room, 20 ground floor, 1 for disabled, all no smoking). Room service (all day). B&B €115 pps, ss €35. *Short / off-season breaks offered. Restaurant Seats 35. Non-residents welcome by reservation if there is room (not suitable for children after 7pm). D Tue-Sat, 7-9; Set D €45, also small à la carte menu. Bar food daily in high season, 12.30-2.30 (residents & members only); also barbecues. House Wine from €18.95. *Luxury 3 & 4 bed cottages available with hotel-style service. Closed Christmas. Amex, Diners, MasterCard, Visa, Laser. **Directions:** From N7, Nenagh, N52 heading to Borrisokane for approximately 1.5km (1 mile) until you reach a factory on the right. Take the turn left (opposite the AIBP factory) on to the Lake Drive Route through the village of Puckane & Coolbawn village, located exactly 3.2km (2 miles) past Coolbawn village.

ROSCREA

Roscrea (Ros Cré - "wood of Cré") is a small town in the south midlands where, in ancient times, the five main routes in Ireland, or the Slighe Dhála, converged, and is quite near the Slieve Bloom Mountains. Designated a Heritage Town, it has many architectural features of note, including the Round Tower, Roscrea Castle and Damer House Complex (0505 21850). The town grew around its monastery and The Round Tower, on Church Street, has a doorway 15 feet from the ground and is the oldest surviving part of the ancient monastery. The Coughlan family's **Tower Bar** (0505 21774; www.thetower.ie) on Church Street has olde-world character with warm hospitality and makes a useful place to break a journey.

Roscrea Area
RESTAURANT

Fiacrí Country House Restaurant & Cookery School

Boulerea Knock Roscrea Co Tipperary **Tel: 0505 43017**
fiacrihouse@eircom.net www.fiacrihouse.com

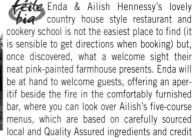

féile bia Enda & Ailish Hennessy's lovely country house style restaurant and cookery school is not the easiest place to find (it is sensible to get directions when booking) but, once discovered, what a welcome sight their neat pink-painted farmhouse presents. Enda will be at hand to welcome guests, offering an aperitif beside the fire in the comfortably furnished bar, where you can look over Ailish's five-course menus, which are based on carefully sourced local and Quality Assured ingredients and credit suppliers on the first page. Menus are balanced, to include fish, poultry and vegetarian choices, but local meats are especially good, and generous portions of seasonal vegetables are served separately. Like the bar, the restaurant has an open fire and, with red walls, white ceiling, mahogany furniture and crisp white linen, it is cosy and pleasingly traditional, making a special yet relaxed setting to enjoy a good meal. House specialities include lovely breads, a delicious starter salad of baked Clonakilty black pudding & caramelised apple, and fairly traditional main courses like rack of Tipperary lamb, or the ever-popular grilled sirloin steak Diane. If a long list of tempting desserts makes decisions difficult, you could try the excellent Assorted Dessert Plate or farmhouse cheeses. Ailish's cooking is excellent and, under Enda's supervision, caring service makes it a special experience and a compact, informative wine list offers good value and includes some half bottles. Ailish also offers cookery classes throughout the year. This is a very popular restaurant and advance booking is essential. *Fiacri was selected for our Féile Bia Award in 2004. Toilets wheelchair accessible. **Seats 80.** Reservations required. Not suitable for children under 12. D Wed-Sat, 7-9.15. Set 5 course D €55. House wine €20. Full bar licence. Closed Sun, Mon, Tue and 25 Dec, Good Fri. *Cookery classes held Tue night, over a 5 week period (€140pp). 1 day courses (c. €100) are also held at other times as Christmas and Easter. Also BBQ evenings in the summer with Q&A. Accommodation is available locally for the cookery classes. MasterCard, Visa, Laser. **Directions:** 10 km (6.5 miles) from Roscrea; Signed from Dublin-Limerick road (N7); Dublin side of Roscrea.

Templemore Area
COUNTRY HOUSE

Saratoga Lodge

Barnane Templemore Co Tipperary **Tel: 0504 31886**
saratogalodge@eircom.net www.saratoga-lodge.com

In a particularly unspoilt and peaceful part of the country, just below the famous Devil's Bit in the Silvermine mountain range, Valerie Beamish's lovely classically proportioned house on a working stud farm is well-situated on an open, sunny site looking out over the hills. A greeting by Valerie and a friendly Irish wolfhound sets the tone for a very relaxing and peaceful stay in this lovely country house, where large traditionally furnished reception rooms open off a spacious hall, and good equestrian paintings reflect the family interest. Bedrooms are very comfortably furnished and peaceful, with no tv - and all now have lovely new en-suite bathrooms. Valerie takes great pride in giving guests a good breakfast, and she's also willing to cook 4-course dinners on request, and make picnics - this is extremely hospitable house all round. Children welcome (under 3s free in parents' room, cots available free of charge, baby-sitting arranged).

Pets by arrangement. Garden, walking, cycling, tennis. Golf, fishing, horse riding, hiking, racing (horses, greyhounds), cheesemakers and garden visits all nearby. **Rooms 3** (all en-suite, 1 shower only, 1 family room, all no smoking). B&B €55 pps, no ss. Residents' D €30, on request. House wine €12-18. Closed 23 Dec-3 Jan. MasterCard, Visa, Laser. **Directions:** From Templemore, take the Nenagh road for 3km (2 m); take 2nd turn right at the B&B sign. Take left at next junction (2.5km/1.5m); house is on the left.

Terryglass
BAR/RESTAURANT/PUB

The Derg Inn

Terryglass Co Tipperary **Tel: 067 22037**
sales@derginn.ie www.derginn.ie

féile bia Tables set up outside Michael and Joyce Soden's popular Derg Inn please the summer crowd and a crackling fire is a welcome sight on a cold day - like many country pubs, this is a place perhaps seen at its best off-season. This is one of the area's best pubs for food and the sight of tables set up for the comfortable enjoyment of a good meal quickly gets hungry guests into a relaxed mood (especially boating visitors, after the walk up from the harbour). Everything is sourced with care, using the best of local produce including organic food when possible; sea fish is more prominent on the menu than might be expected in a river and lakeland area, and traditional Irish dishes like bacon & cabbage and beef & Guinness pie are always a treat here. Evening menus are quite wide-ranging with a choice that usually includes delicious house specialities like home-made paté with Derg Inn mango chutney & garlic bread and salmon in filo pastry with lemon & caper sauce - and maybe fillet steak with wholegrain mustard sauce along with more-ish desserts like praline parfait with cinnamon syrup. Sunday lunch is also quite a speciality, but you don't have to eat at the Derg - there's an interesting little wine list to enjoy with or without food, and a very pleasant bar. Music in summer - Friday, Saturday and Sunday, various styles; Sunday night is the one for traditional music enthusiasts. **Seats 150** (private function room, 70+). Toilets wheelchair accessible. Open daily: food available 11-10. Breakfast from 11 am, L 12-5, D 6-10. A la carte. House wine €19. SC discretionary. Closed Good Fri, 25 Dec. Amex, MasterCard, Visa, Laser. **Directions:** In the heart of Terrryglass Village. ◇

Terryglass Area
COUNTRY HOUSE

Kylenoe House

Balinderry Terryglass Nenagh Co Tipperary **Tel: 067 22015**
ginia@eircom.net

Virginia Moeran's lovely old stone house on 150 acres of farm and woodland offers homely comfort and real country pleasures close to Lough Derg. The farm is home to an international stud and the woodlands are a haven for wildlife, including deer, stoats, red squirrels, badgers, rabbits and foxes as well as many varieties of birds and flowers. With beautiful walks, riding (with or without tuition), golf and water sports available on the premises or close by, this is a real rural retreat. Spacious, airy bedrooms are furnished in gentle country house style, with antiques and family belongings, and overlook beautiful rolling countryside; recent refurbishment has included new super-comfortable beds. Downstairs there's a delightful guests' sitting room and plenty of interesting reading. Virginia enjoys cooking, her breakfasts are a speciality and dinner is available to residents by arrangement. Importantly for people who like to travel with their dogs, this is a place where man's best friend is also made welcome and Kylenoe was our Pet Friendly Establishment of the Year in 1999. Children welcome (under 8 free in parents' room; cot available, baby sitting arranged). Pets welcome. Garden, walking. ITB approval pending. **Rooms 4** (3 en-suite, 1 with private bathroom, all no-smoking) B&B €60 pps, ss €10. Residents D 7-8pm, €38 (book by noon). Wines from €16. Closed 18-30 Dec. MasterCard, Visa. **Directions:** N7 to Moneygall, Cloughjordan, Borrisokane, leave Egans shop on right and straight 10km (6.5m) on right. ◇

Thurles Area

Inch House Country House & Restaurant

COUNTRY HOUSE/RESTAURANT

Bouladuff Thurles Co Tipperary **Tel: 0504 51348**

mairin@inchhouse.ie www.inchhouse.ie

Built in 1720 by John Ryan, one of the few landed Catholic gentlemen in Tipperary, this magnificent Georgian house managed to survive some of the most turbulent periods in Irish history and to remain in the Ryan family for almost 300 years. John and Norah Egan, who farm the surrounding 250 acres, took it over in a state of dereliction in 1985 and began the major restoration work which has resulted in the handsome, comfortably furnished period house which guests enjoy today. Reception rooms on either side of a welcoming hallway include an unusual William Morris-style drawing room with a tall stained glass window, a magnificent plasterwork ceiling (and adjoining library bar) and a fine dining room which is used for residents' breakfasts and is transformed into a restaurant at night. Both rooms have period fireplaces with big log fires. The five bedrooms are quite individual and are furnished with antiques. Small weddings. Equestrian, golf, fishing (coarse) and hunting/shooting all nearby. Walking. Children welcome (under 10 free in parents' room; cot available without charge). No Pets. **Rooms 5** (all en-suite, 1 shower only, 1 family room). B&B €65 pps, ss €10. Closed Christmas & New Year. **Restaurant:** The restaurant, which is open to non-residents by reservation, has polished wood floors, classic country house decor and tables laid with crisp white linen and fresh flowers, which provide a pleasing setting for dinner, especially when the atmosphere is softened by firelight and candles. Dinner menus offer a well-balanced choice of about six dishes on each course, in a fairly traditional style that combines French country cooking and Irish influences, and makes good use of local produce. Dishes like smoked salmon terrine, for example, and the ever-popular entrecôte steak with mushroom & whiskey sauce illustrate the style. Anyone with special dietary needs, including vegetarians, should mention this on booking to allow for preparation of extra dishes. Not suitable for children after 7 pm. Seats 50. D Tue-Sat 7-9; Set D €50-55; house wine €17; sc discretionary. Closed Sun & Mon, Christmas week. MasterCard, Visa, Laser. **Directions:** Four miles from Thurles on Nenagh Road.

COUNTY WATERFORD

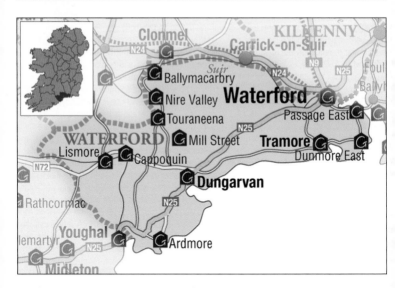

Waterford's past has become very much part of its present with the discovery - during road excavation works to the west of the city - of the remains of a major Viking settlement at Woodstown. It may indeed be the site of the Norse raiders' original main base in the area, from which today's river city eventually emerged.

On the quays of Waterford city, we are witness to a trading and seafaring tradition which goes back at least 1,150 years. But this sense of history also looks to the future, as Waterford - the city of crystal and quality glassware – is popular as a Tall Ships assembly port. Today's larger commercial ships may be berthed downstream on the other side of the river at Belview, but the old city-side quays on the south bank retain a nautical flavour which is accentuated by very useful marina berthing facilities in the heart of town.

This fine port was founded in 853 AD when the Vikings - Danes for the most part - established the trading settlement of Vadrefjord. Its strategic location in a sheltered spot at the head of the estuary near the confluence of the Suir and Barrow rivers guaranteed its continuing success under different administrators, particularly the Normans, so much so that it tended to overshadow the county of Waterford, almost all of which is actually to the west of the city.

But for many years now, the county town has been Dungarvan, which is two-thirds of the way westward along Waterford's extensive south coast, which includes the attractive Copper Coast - between Fenor and Stradbally - in its midst. This spreading of the administrative centres of gravity has to some extent balanced the life of the Waterford region. But even so, the extreme west of the county is still one of Ireland's best kept secrets, a place of remarkable beauty between the Knockmealdown, Comeragh and Monavullagh mountains, where fish-filled rivers such as the Bride, the Blackwater, and the Nire make their way seawards at different speeds through valleys of remarkable variety and beauty, past pretty towns and villages such as romantic, castle-bedecked Lismore which has been an overall winner in the Tidy Towns awards, and is architecturally all of a piece.

West Waterford is a place of surprises. For instance, around the delightful coastal village of Ardmore, ancient monuments suggest that the local holy man, St Declan, introduced Christianity to the area quite a few years before St Patrick went to work in the rest of Ireland. And across the bay from Ardmore, the Ring neighbourhood is a Gaeltacht (Irish-speaking) area with its own bustling fishing port at Helvick.

Dungarvan itself is enjoying the fruits of an attractive revival. It has relinquished its role as a commercial port, but is enthusiastically taking to recreational boating and harbourside regeneration instead. Along the bluff south coast, secret coves gave smugglers and others access to charming villages like Stradbally and Bunmahon. Further east, the increased tempo of the presence of Waterford city is felt both at the traditional resort of Tramore, and around the fishing/sailing harbour of Dunmore East.

ocal Attractions & Information

rdmore
RESTAURANT

White Horses Restaurant
Ardmore Co Waterford **Tel: 024 94040**
whitehorses@eircom.net

téile bia Christine Power and Geraldine Flavin's delightfully bright and breezy café-restaurant on the main street of this famous seaside village is one of those places that changes its character through the day but always has style. They're open for all the little lifts that visitors need through the day - morning coffee, afternoon tea - as well as imaginative lunches (plus their tradi-tional Sunday lunch, which runs all afternoon) and a more ambitious la carte evening menu. Vegetarian dishes feature on both menus - a pasta ish during the day perhaps, and spinach & mushroom crêpe with toasted brie in the evening - and here's a good balance between traditional favourites like steaks and more adventurous fare: a daytime sh dish could be deep-fried plaice with tartare sauce, for example, while its evening counterpart night be grilled darne Helvick salmon on asparagus, with a wine & cream sauce. Attractive and leasant to be in - the use of local Ardmore pottery is a big plus on the presentation side, and empha-ses the sense of place - this is a friendly, well-run restaurant and equally good for a reviving cuppa nd a gateau or pastry from the luscious home-made selection on display, or a full meal. Even when ery busy, service is well-organised and efficient. **Seats 50.** Air conditioning. In summer (May-Sep) pen: Tue-Sun 11-'late'; L 12.30-3.30, D 6-10. In winter (Oct-Apr) open weekends only: Fri from 6 m, Sat 11-11 & Sun 12-6. A la carte except Sun - Set L €27. Licensed; House Wine €18.50; sc iscretionary. Closed Mon all year, except bank hols (bank hol opening as Sun), 1 Jan-13 Feb. lasterCard, Visa, Laser. **Directions:** Centre of village. ◇

allymacarbry
ARMHOUSE

Glasha
Glasha Ballymacarbry via Clonmel Co Waterford **Tel: 052 36108**
glasha@eircom.net www.glashafarmhouse.com

téile bia Paddy and Olive O'Gorman's spacious farmhouse is set in its own gardens high up in the hills and makes a very comfortable and hospitable base for a relaxed rural break. Fishing is a major attraction (the Nire runs beside the farm-house and permits are available locally), also walking (Glasha links the Comeragh and Knockmealdown sections of the famous Munster Way), pony trekking, golf (available locally), and painting this beautiful area. Olive thinks of every-

493

thing that will help guests feel at home and bedrooms - which are extremely luxurious for a farm sta - have lots of little extras including TV/radio, hair dryers, electric blankets, tea/coffee-making, sprin water and magazines; most rooms have king size beds, all are en-suite, and the newer ones have love bathrooms with jacuzzi baths. There's plenty of comfortable lounging room for guests' use, too including a conservatory - and the nearest pub is just 3 minutes' walk from the house. Olive makes delicious home-cooked dinner for guests, by arrangement, and it is served in a comfortable big dinin room; her 3-course menus change daily and you might begin with something that showcases loca seafood, like Dungarvan mussels in a creamy basil sauce, then a main course of Comeragh lamb - rack, perhaps, served with apple & mint chutney and a rosemary sauce - and finish with rhubarb & strawberry crumble, or warm apple fudge cake, then tea or coffee and chocolates in the conservatory or in beside the fire on chilly evenings. The food is gorgeous with its farmhouse simplicity, and you' get a good breakfast to set you up for the day too. This is a lovely place to stay, and a perfect antidot to the stresses of urban life. Children welcome, cots available. **Rooms 6** (4 with jacuzzi bath, 2 showe only, 1 family room, 2 ground floor, all no-smoking). B&B €60 pps, ss €10. Residents' D Mon-Sat 7.30 by arrangement (short à la carte), €25-35. Closed D Sun, 20-27 Dec. MasterCard, Visa, Lase **Directions:** Off 671 road between Clonmel and Dungarvan, 3.5km (2 m) from Ballymacarbry; signe on 671.

Ballymacarbry
GUESTHOUSE/RESTAURANT

Hanora's Cottage

Nire Valley Ballymacarbry Co Waterford **Tel: 052 3613** hanorascottage@eircom.net www.hanorascottage.com

The Wall family's gloriously remote country guest house is now a very substantial building, yet the still actively nurture the spirit of the ancestra home around which Hanora's is built. This a ver special place - equally wonderful for foot-wear walkers, or desk-weary city folk in need of som clear country air and real comfort - and the genuin hospitality of the Wall family is matched by th luxurious accommodation and good food the provide. Comfortably furnished seating areas wit sofas and big armchairs provide plenty of room t relax, and the spacious thoughtfully furnished bedrooms all have jacuzzi baths (one especiall romantic room is perfect for honeymooners); there's also a spa tub in a conservatory overlooking th garden, with views of the mountains. Overnight guests begin the day with Hanora's legendary break fast buffet, which was the National Winner of our Irish Breakfast Awards in 2002; it takes some tim to get the measure of this feast, so make sure you get up in time to make the most of it. Local produc and exotics (some of which you may not previously have encountered) jostle for space on the beauti fully arranged buffet: fruits and freshly squeezed juices (including luscious Crinnaghtaun Apple Juic from Lismore), home-made muesli and porridge... a whole range of freshly-baked breads, includin organic and gluten free varieties... local farmhouse cheeses, smoked salmon, home-made jams - an all the cooked breakfast options you could wish for. This is truly a gargantuan feast, designed to se you many miles along the hills before you stop for a little packed lunch (prepared that morning) an ultimately return for dinner... Small weddings (40). **Rooms 10** (1 suite, 3 junior suites, all n smoking). Not suitable for children. No pets. B&B from €85 pps. Closed Christmas week. **Restaurant** One of the best things about Hanora's is that people travel from far and wide to dine here, which add to the atmosphere. It is pleasant for evening guest to mingle with residents at the fireside, have a aperitif and ponder on Eoin and Judith Wall's imaginative, well-balanced menus - then, difficu choices made, you move through to the restaurant, which overlooks a secluded garden and riversid woodland. Enthusiastic supporters of small suppliers, Eoin and Judith use local produce whenever possible and credit them on the menu - fresh fish from Dunmore East, free range chickens fror Stradbally and local cheeses, for example. There's a separate vegetarian dinner menu on request a well as an à la carte which offers about seven dishes on each course, usually including some vege tarian options. Popular dishes include starters of sautéed lambs kidneys on a croustade wit mushroom cream, and stuffed mushrooms with walnuts, blue cheese & garlic mayonnaise; mai courses include beautifully fresh and accurately cooked fish and, as lamb is so abundant locally, th all-time favourite is roast rack of lamb (served, perhaps, with a delicious mint hollandaise). Dessert include well made classics like lemon tart with crème anglaise and good home-made ice creams - anc of course, there's always an Irish cheese selection. Not suitable for children under 12. **Seats 30/40** Mon-Sat, 7-9, Set D about €40, also à la carte. House wine about €14.50. Closed Sun. MasterCarc Visa, Laser. **Directions:** Take Clonmel/Dungarvan (R671) road, turn off at Ballymacarbry.

Cappoquin
COUNTRY HOUSE/RESTAURANT

Richmond House

Cappoquin Co Waterford **Tel: 058 54278**
info@richmondhouse.net www.richmondhouse.net

Genuine hospitality, high standards of comfort, caring service and excellent food are all to be found in the Deevy family's fine 18th century country house and restaurant just outside Cappoquin - no wonder this is a place so many people like to keep as a closely guarded secret. For returning guests, there's always a sense of pleasurable anticipation that builds up as you approach through parkland along a well-maintained driveway, which is lit up at night; after a brief pause to admire the climbing plants beside the door, you're into the fine high-ceilinged hall with its warming stove and catch the scent of log fires burning in the well-proportioned, elegantly furnished drawing room and restaurant opening off it. Claire or Jean Deevy will usually be there to welcome arriving guests, and show you to one of the nine individually decorated bedrooms; they vary in size and appointments, as is the way with old houses - some guests love the smallest cottagey bedroom, while others may prefer the larger ones - but all are comfortably furnished in country house style with full bathrooms. As well as serving wonderful dinners in the restaurant (see below), the Deevys make sure that you will have a memorable breakfast to see you on your way - it is a wonderful area to explore, and Richmond House makes an excellent base. Children welcome (under 3 free in parents' room, cot available without charge, baby sitting arranged). No pets. Garden; walking. Golf, garden visits nearby. **Rooms 9** (1 junior suite, all with full bathrooms & no smoking). B&B €75 pps, ss €20. Closed 22 Dec-10 Jan. **Restaurant:** The restaurant is the heart of Richmond House and non-residents usually make up a high proportion of the guests, which makes for a lively atmosphere. Warm and friendly service begins from the moment menus are presented over aperitifs - in front of the drawing room fire, or in a conservatory overlooking the garden. Paul is an ardent supporter of local produce and sources everything with tremendous care: Quality Assured meats (beef, lamb, bacon and sausages) come from his trusted local butcher, fresh seafood is from Dunmore East and Dungarvan while herbs, fruit and vegetables are home grown where possible, and extra organic produce is grown nearby. There is a sureness of touch in Paul's kitchen, seen in stimulating menus that offer a balance between traditional country house cooking and more adventurous dishes inspired by international trends; dinner menus offering about five choices on each course are changed daily, and a slightly shorter separate vegetarian menu is also offered. House specialities include Helvick prawns (tempura, perhaps) and - a dish it would be hard to resist at Richmond House - roast rack of delicious West Waterford lamb, a memorable dish presented on braised puy lentils and buttered green beans, with home-made mint jelly and rosemary & garlic jus; vegetables, served separately, are invariably imaginative and cooked 'au point'. Classic desserts are always a treat too, including plenty of imaginative and beautifully executed fruit-based choices to balance the richness of a fine meal here - orange pannacotta with orange segments, perhaps - and, of course, there will always be Irish farmhouse cheeses with home-made biscuits. Service, under Claire's direction, is attentive and discreet. A carefully selected and fairly priced wine list includes about twenty offered by the glass, several wines of the month, and a good choice of half bottles. The early dinner menu offers particularly good value. Richmond House received the Féile Bia Award in 2006. Children welcome. **Seats 45** (private room, 14). D 6.30-9.30 daily; Set D €50, Early Bird €35 (Vegetarian Menu also avail); house wine €20; sc discretionary. Closed 22 Dec-10 Jan. Amex, Diners, MasterCard, Visa, Laser. **Directions:** 1km (0.5 mile) outside Cappoquin on N72.

Cheekpoint
RESTAURANT

The Cottage Bistro

Cheekpoint Village Co Waterford **Tel: 051 380 854**
cottagebistro@eircom.net www.cottagebistro.com

Aidan and Marian McAlpin's neat cottagey restaurant is spick and span and the style is pleasingly simple, with a small bar area and plain, handsomely-laid tables softened by warm lighting and fresh flowers. Good home-made brown bread and iced water are served promptly, along with hand written menus that offer plenty of choice, although local seafood is a speciality, along with steaks, chicken and a tempting speciality vegetarian shepherd's pie. A side salad is served after the main course, and desserts are home-made. What you get here is Marian McAlpin's sound home cooking, simply presented - and prices are reasonable, especially for seafood, including an excellent Seafood Platter which could include ten different fish and shellfish. An interesting,

informative and well-priced wine list includes unusual house wines and an equally carefully selecte
choice of half bottles. Children welcome before 7pm. **Seats 45** (+10 outside). Reservations required
Toilets wheelchair accessible. D Tue-Sat, 6-9.30 (Sun, June-Aug only, 5.30-8.30). A la carte. Hous
wine €18. SC discretionary. Closed Mon (also Sun off-season), last week Sept, all Jan. Amex
MasterCard, Visa, Laser. **Directions:** 7 miles east of Waterford city; in village, above the harbour.

Cheekpoint
RESTAURANT

The Suir Inn

Cheekpoint Co Waterford **Tel: 051 382 22**
frances@mcalpins.com www.mcalpins.com

This immaculately maintained black-and-white painted inn is 300 years old an
has been run by the McAlpin family since 1972. It's a characterful, country styl
place with rustic furniture, cottagey plates and old prints decorating the walls - more like a traditiona
bar than a restaurant. Seasonal menus offer a choice of about six starters (mostly seafood) and te
main courses, including several cold dishes and two vegetarian ones, again all moderately priced
specialities include a generous and reasonably priced seafood platter and home-made seafood pie. A
meals come with brown soda bread and butter, and a side salad and a nice little wine list includes
choice of eight moderately priced wines. No children after 9pm. **Seats 62.** D Tue-Sat, 5.30-9.45; a
la carte; sc discretionary. House wine from €13.50. SC discretionary. Closed Sun, Mon. MasterCard
Visa, Laser. **Directions:** 7 miles east of Waterford, on harbour front.

DUNGARVAN

This is the county's main town outside Waterford city and is beautifully located on Dungarvan Harbou
(renowned for its wildlife), with much of interest nearby: the Gaeltacht of Ring is just a few miles awa
for example, and the lovely Nire Valley (walking, pony trekking) runs deep into the Comerag
Mountains north of the town. West of Dungarvan, the Heritage Town of Lismore, with its fairytale castl
and gardens, is just a short drive. The main hotel in Dungarvan is the Flynn family's **Park Hotel** (058
42899; www.flynnhotels.com), which is just on the edge of town overlooking the Colligan Rive
esturay; spacious and comfortable, with leisure centre/swimming pool.
WWW.IRELAND-GUIDE.COM FOR THE BEST PLACES TO EAT, DRINK & STAY

Dungarvan
B&B/COUNTRY HOUSE

Cairbre House

Strandside North Abbeyside Dungarvan Co Waterford **Tel: 058 4233**
cairbrehouse@eircom.net www.cairbrehouse.com

Brian Wickham's fine old house is just across the bridge from Dungarvan town centre - it is of grea
historical interest, and set in wonderful gardens, right on the water. The house has a homely feel wit
a lounge and fire for guests, and lots of local information. Bedrooms are a little old-fashioned bu
spacious and comfortable, with beautiful views out over the water; they include rooms for families o
groups and, as well as en-suite facilities, there's an extra communal bathroom. Breakfast is a hig
point - and includes a hot vegetarian special, with the option of bacon for non-vegetarians! In fin
weather, Brian is happy to serve breakfast in the back garden, where there are some wooden table
and benches. The gardens, which enjoy a micro-climate that allows many 'impossible' plants to surviv
here, are Brian's greatest love and a source of great pleasure to guests; and there will be a new conser
vatory too - it was under construction at the time of the Guide's summer 2007 visit. Garden visits, go
and sea angling nearby. Free broadband wi/fi. Children welcome (under 4s free in parents' room, co
available free of charge). **Rooms 4** (all shower only, 3 en-suite, 1 with private bathroom, 1 family room
3 no smoking, 1 ground floor); B&B €50 pps, ss €6. Closed Nov-mid Feb. Amex, Diners, MasterCard
Visa. **Directions:** From Waterford take right exit off N25 at Strandside roundabout, house 200m up o
the left.

Dungarvan
GUESTHOUSE

Powersfield House

Ballinamuck West Dungarvan Co Waterford **Tel: 058 4559**
powersfieldhouse@cablesurf.com www.powersfield.com

You could be forgiven for thinking that Edmund and Eunice Power's fine guesthouse ha
been here for a long time - although new, the garden has matured well and this, togethe
with traditional country house style furnishing, gives it an unexpected sense of age. Antiques and inter
esting fabrics create a soothing and relaxing atmosphere throughout the house, including
comfortable, homely sitting room as well as bedrooms which have been individually decorated an
finished to a high standard, with smart bathrooms and all the necessary comforts. Eunice is an enthu

siastic cook and offers dinner to residents by arrangement; menus are based on local produce and, as a new vegetable garden is well under way, Eunice hopes to be self-sufficient in seasonal produce during the summer. This is a lovely, friendly place to stay and would make a good base for exploring the area. Children welcome (under 4 free in parents' room; cot available without charge; children's playground, baby sitting arranged); Dogs allowed in some areas by arrangment (kennel in garden); **Rooms** 5 (all en-suite and no smoking, 4 shower only, 1 family, 1 ground floor, 1 for disabled). Room service (limited hours). B&B €65 pps, ss €10. Residents' D by arrangement €25-35; house wine €20-30; sc discretionary. *Cookery Courses available, details on application. Amex, MasterCard, Visa, Laser. **Directions:** Take the Killarney road R672 from Dungarvan at Kilrush roundabout; second turn left, first house on right.

Dungarvan
CAFE/BAR/RESTAURANT

Quealy's Café Bar & Restaurant Q82

82 O'Connell Street Dungarvan Co Waterford
Tel: 058 24555 info@quealys.com www.quealys.com

Just off the main square in Dungarvan town, Quealy's has recently had an extensive makeover and has clearly won the hearts of locals and visitors of all ages. It's a friendly buzzy place, with simple but good quality table settings, and the food served in the smart bar is very much a cut above the usual expectation of "bar food" in terms of sourcing, cooking and presentation. They offer a modern menu of good dishes at very reasonable prices, many of them available either as starters or as main courses, and there is always a good traditional "specials of the day" menu on blackboards; examples recently enjoyed include a very good mixed seafood platter, and a St Tola goat's cheese salad with pine nuts & piquillo peppers. Well turned out staff are superbly efficient, and the ambience in this busy bar is relaxed even when people are being turned away because there are no tables available. Q82 Restaurant is above the bar but has a separate entrance; this stylish contemporary restaurant offers a more formal alternative to the bar for evening meals, and has earned a following in the town. Toilets & bar wheelchair accessible; children welcome before 8/9pm (high chair, childrens menu in bar); air conditioning; Bar meals: Mon-Sat, 12-3pm, Tue-Fri, 5-8pm, Sun 12.30-4.30pm; Restaurant: D only Tue-Sat, 6-10pm (early D 6-7.30, €29). House wines €20-25; SC 10% on groups 6+. Restaurant closed Sun, Mon & 1 week Sept; 2 weeks end Jan/start Feb. MasterCard, Visa, Laser. **Directions:** Town centre, west of the main square.

Dungarvan
RESTAURANT WITH ROOMS
♨ ★ ♟

The Tannery

10 Quay Street Dungarvan Co Waterford **Tel:** 058 45420
tannery@cablesurf.com www.tannery.ie

CHEF OF THE YEAR

Discerning diners from all over Ireland (and beyond) make a beeline for Paul and Maire Flynn's stylish contemporary restaurant, which is in an old leather warehouse - the tannery theme is echoed throughout the light, clean-lined interior, creating a pleasingly historic atmosphere in a modern setting. Arriving guests can see Paul and his team at work in the open kitchen on their way upstairs to the first-floor dining area, which is bright and welcoming, with dramatic paintings, fresh flowers and smart, simple table settings. Ten years after opening both the style and the room itself feel fresh, which is rarely the case with minimalism. Menus are also wonderfully simple but the food tastes very exciting; while inspired to some extent by global trends and regional cooking, particularly of the Mediterranean countries, menus have a strongly Irish feeling and are based mainly on local ingredients, which Paul supports avidly and sources with care - notably local seafood of course, also meats including pork and bacon supplied by renowned local butcher JD Power. Simplicity is of the essence here, and there are no amuse bouches; what is certain to be an outstanding meal cuts straight to the chase with superb starters (a perfect marinière of mussels and clams, perhaps, with a few garlicky herby crumbs thrown on top and a delicious wine and herb broth with spoon provided; one of many classics revisited). An unusual main course that illustrates the skill of this exceptional chef is described simply as slow cooked beef: it is in fact ox cheek and arrives under a salad of shallot and leaves - tender enough to eat with a spoon, it is still gelatinous enough to not be in the least dry. A triumph of a dish. Even hardened food critics are continually surprised by Paul Flynn's cooking which, as one fellow chef put it, "makes dishes which one thought one knew taste as if one was eating them for the first time". Presentation is good and all the better for being plain - not too much height, and not too many useless drops about the plate; occasionally a dish may look a little bizarre - a lasagne of rabbit shredded like rillettes, for example - but you can be sure that it will taste extremely good. An Irish farmhouse cheese platter is invariably a highlight, and the dessert menu offers plenty of treats - but, here too, the maverick genius is at work and you will find novelty alongside the conventional chocolate confections - anyone for mango ice cream on a piece of toasted bread and cheese? But, yes, it works - and you will love it. And giving good value has always been a notable feature of The Tannery: the à la carte is very fairly priced for food of this quality, but the lunch and early evening menus (both changed daily) are outstandingly good value. Attentive and efficient service, an interesting and kindly-priced wine list (which offers lots of cheaper choices for this style of restaurant, also a welcome page of half bottles) and, above all, Paul's exceptional cooking, make for memorable meals. *The Tannery was our Restaurant of the Year in 2004. ** Paul Flynn is the consultant chef for the new restaurant, **Balzac**, in Dublin (see entry). Toilets wheelchair accessible. Children welcome. **Seats 60** (+ 30 downstairs, private room, 30). L Tue-Fri & Sun, 12.30-2.15 (Sun to 2.30); D Tue-Sat, 6.30-9.30. Early D €28 (Tue-Fri, 6.30-7.15); Set Sun L €30; house wine €22; sc discretionary (10% on parties of 6+). Closed Mon, Sat L, also D Sun; annual closure 2 weeks end Jan, 1 week Sept. **Rooms:** Accommodation is offered in a boutique guesthouse just around the corner in Church Street; while not quite up to the exceptionally high standard of the restaurant, it is comfortable and very convenient. Public areas of the house are very bright and funky but, while also contemporary, the seven double rooms and a self-catering apartment are furnished more calmly; a continental breakfast is organised so that you can have it in your room. **Rooms 7** (all en-suite, 2 shower only), children welcome (under 4s free in parents' room, cots available at no charge); B&B €60 pps or €80 pps for superior room, ss €10. Amex, Diners, MasterCard, Visa, Laser. **Directions:** End of lower main street beside old market house.

Dungarvan area — An Bohreen
B&B
Killineen West Dungarvan Co Waterford **Tel: 051 291 010**
mulligans@anbohreen.com www.anbohreen.com

Just a few miles outside Dungarvan, off the Waterford road, Jim and Ann Mulligan's striking contemporary house has panoramic mountain and coastal views, and you'll get a warm welcome from Jim, who will show you to a compact bedroom furnished with an antique bedstead (with modern mattress), old style furniture and neat en-suite shower room. Guests also have use of a furnished outdoor patio for warm weather, and the spacious, open plan sitting room has everything that you need to relax indoors, including an open fire, television, radio, CDs, books and a comfortable seating area; a couple of steps up from it, the dining room has wall-to-wall windows overlooking the garden to the sea at Helvick Head, a fine setting for Ann's good cooking. Dinner is by arrangement and meals are cooked to order: preferring to concentrate on one set of guests at a time, you are asked when booking to agree a time and choose, from a short menu, what you would like for a main course at dinner as ingredients are bought freshly on the day of arrival. Ann takes pride in sourcing local ingredients and a typical dinner might include a home-made seasonal soup (an excellent and unusual leek and pear, perhaps), a simple salad, lamb chops with a wine sauce, barbary duck breast or fillet of salmon and, to finish, the superb house dessert of New York cheesecake and good coffee. For breakfast (you agree a suitable time on arrival), there's a good menu that includes fresh fruit, fresh orange juice, freshly baked scones and bread and, in addition to the usual porridge, full Irish, smoked salmon and scrambled eggs, there are crêpes with a strudel-style apple filling. Not suitable for children under 12. Free broadband wi/fi. Fishing, golf and walking nearby. **Rooms 4** (all shower only, no smoking and ground floor). B&B €45-50 pps, ss about €20. Residents D €40, 6.30-8.30pm daily. Closed Oct 31-Mar 21. MasterCard, Visa. **Directions:** Off N25. Look for town of Lemybrien; look for resume speed sign, 5km later there is a right turn; house signed after 220m.

Dungarvan Area — Gortnadiha Lodge
FARMHOUSE
Ring Dungarvan Co Waterford
Tel: 058 46142

Eileen and Thomas Harty's house is west of Dungarvan in the Ring Gaeltacht (Irish speaking) area, and it is in a lovely setting, with woodland gardens and sea views. Accommodation in the family home is comfortable, hospitality is warm and breakfasts offer a very wide selection of local and home produce, including fresh fish in season. Children welcome (under 5 free in parents' room, cot available without charge, baby sitting arranged). Pets permitted. **Rooms 3** (2 shower only, 1 ground floor) B&B room rate €90. Closed 21 Dec - 21 Jan. Visa. **Directions:** N25 Rosslare to Cork, 3 km from Dungarvan: follow the sea.

DUNMORE EAST

Dunmore East is a picturesque village and a major fishing port, known for its pretty well-maintained thatched cottages. A recent addition which is proving successful is the attractive **Spinnaker Bar** (051 3831331); a sister establishment to **Chez K's** (see entry) in Waterford City, it serves informal food, especially local seafood, in atmospheric surroundings.

WWW.IRELAND-GUIDE.COM FOR THE BEST PLACES TO EAT, DRINK & STAY

Dunmore East   Beach Guesthouse
GUESTHOUSE   1 Lower Village Dunmore East Co Waterford **Tel: 051 383316**
beachouse@eircom.net   www.dunmorebeachguesthouse.com

Breda Battles' smart modern guesthouse has easy accessibility to the beach, and offers good value, making this a good, moderately priced base for exploring the area. Rooms to the front - including the pleasant breakfast room and lounge, as well as some of the bedrooms - have a sea view. Everything is very clean and well-maintained and, although hard flooring throughout can be noisy, bedrooms have plenty of hanging space and a writing desk as well as TV/radio and tea/coffee making. Tasty breakfasts include lovely scones and preserves, well-made traditional Irish and some other options, such as scrambled egg with smoked salmon. Free broadband wi/fi; not suitable for children under 6. No pets. **Rooms 7** (1 suite, 2 shower only, 1 family room, 1 ground floor, 1 for disabled, all no smoking). B&B €45, ss €10. Closed 1 Nov - 1 Mar. Amex, MasterCard, Visa, Laser. **Directions:** Left after petrol station in village; house facing sea wall.

Dunmore East   Strand Inn
PUB/RESTAURANT WITH ROOMS   Dunmore East Co Waterford **Tel: 051 383 174**
strandin@iol.ie   www.dunmoreeast.com

Right on the beach, and with sea views out towards the Hook Lighthouse, The Strand goes back a good few hundred years but today it is the first choice for many when it comes to seafood. 'Fish, fish, fish' is how they describe their menu, and so it is - up to a point: non-seafood eaters will be glad to know that there are some concessions, including a roast perhaps, or poultry such as traditional duck with orange sauce. But it is mainly for the seafood that people head for the Strand - and it couldn't be fresher as much of it comes from the nearby harbour, which is one of Ireland's main fishing ports. Toilets wheelchair accessible. **Seats 70** (outdoor, 40); children welcome before 8pm; L daily in summer, 12.30-4.30 (to 2.30 Sun); set L about €22.50; D daily all year, 6.30-10; early D about €22.50, 6.30-7.30; House wine from €17; SC 10% on parties 8+. Restaurant closed all of Jan and Mon-Tue in Nov-Mar. Amex, Diners, MasterCard, Visa, Laser. **Directions:** Left after petrol station in village; beachside building. ◇

Dunmore East Area   Gaultier Lodge
HISTORIC HOUSE   Woodstown Co Waterford **Tel: 051 382 549**
gaultierlodge@yahoo.ie   www.gaultier-lodge.com

Beautifully located right beside the beach at Woodstown Strand and snugged down in sand dunes for shelter, Sheila Molloy's early 19th century lodge is built on the mezzanine plan, with reception rooms on the upper floor and bedrooms beneath and it has wonderful views from the upper windows right across the Suir estuary, to Duncannon and the Hook Peninsula in County Wexford. Set in large and very private gardens, it has the feeling of a secret place on arrival you almost wonder if you are in the right place at all and, although Sheila describes it modestly as 'comfortably furnished' it has great style and, like Sheila herself - who is an artist and a warmly hospitable person - this lovely house will lift the spirits. Reception rooms and bedrooms are all large and well proportioned, providing a good framework for her inspired modern classical décor and guests will be pleased to find that, along with other interests including gardening and horses, she enjoys cooking and entertaining. Dinner is available on most nights by arrangement (book 24 hours in advance); when unavailable you can go to Dunmore East, just three miles away. On site there is swimming and beach or coastal walks, and other activities like sea fishing, sailing, riding and golf are all available nearby. Not suitable for children under 8. Dogs permitted by arrangement; equestrian, fishing, hunting and golf all nearby. Wallking, cookery courses, art courses. **Rooms 3** (all en-suite and no smoking, 1 shower only). B&B €75 pps, ss €20. D €50 by arrangement (book 24 hours in advance; not always available Sun or Thu). Closed Nov-May. MasterCard, Visa, Laser. **Directions:** From Waterford take R684, Dunmore East road. Take left for Woodstown after 4km. Right at beach, last house on left.

Lismore   # Ballyrafter Country House Hotel
HOTEL

Lismore Co Waterford **Tel: 058 54002**
info@waterfordhotel.com ballyrafter@waterfordhotel.com

Fishing is perhaps the big draw to Joe and Noreen Willoughby's welcoming country house hotel, but a relaxing laid-back atmosphere, log fires and good home cooking also add up to a very attractive package. The bar, where informal meals are served, is lined with photographs of happy fisherfolk - if you are dining in the restaurant, it's an enjoyable place to have an aperitif while looking at the menu, or you can go in beside the fire in the drawing room. The spacious bedrooms are simple and comfortable and one side of the courtyard area has been thoughtfully developed to provide five new executive bedrooms in keeping with the old house. On the ground floor, an attractive conservatory area is available for small functions. **Rooms 14** (5 shower only). B&B about €60 pps, ss about €20. Closed Dec-Feb. Restaurant: An open fire, family antiques and flowers from the garden create a caring atmosphere in the restaurant and the Duke of Devonshire's fairytale castle looks magical from window tables when floodlit at night. Appetising home-cooked meals are based on local ingredients, with friendly and helpful service. **Seats 30.** D daily, L Sun only 1-3 pm. SC 10% sc. Bar Meals: 12-6.30 daily (L 1 2.30). Closed Dec-Mar. Amex, Diners, MasterCard, Visa. **Directions:** On the edge of Lismore town, from Cappoquin direction. ◇

Lismore Area   # The Glencairn Inn & Pastis Bistro
BAR/RESTAURANT WITH ROOMS

Glencairn Lismore Co Waterford **Tel: 058 56232**
info@glencairninn.com www.glencairninn.com

téile bia Husband-and-wife team Stéphane and Fiona Tricot fulfilled a dream by buying this pretty pub just outside Lismore in 2006, and the restaurant - which they renamed Pastis French Bistro quickly earned a following. Three delightful old-world dining rooms ooze charm and cosiness and, just off the small bar, there is an alcove for intimate dining for four. Fiona manages front-of-house while Stéphane produces wonderful food using plenty of local produce, and offering menus with about five choices on each course, plus a weekly special on the board. Well-chosen starters may include a flavoursome salad like pear & blue cheese salad with roasted walnuts and balsamic & honey vinaigrette, and pan seared seabass provençale is a speciality main course. A very nice dessert menu includes classics like tarte tatin and pot de crème au chocolat, offered with liqueur coffees, dessert wine or a digestif. A tapas bar menu is also available - tasty little dishes like fried calamari with saffron aioli; prawn & anchovy crostini, and piquillo peppers stuffed with Ardsallagh goat's cheese and at four for €12 with a basket of freshly baked baguette they're good value. A compact, carefully chosen wine list, offers a surprisingly wide range and includes some real treats, also half a dozen wines by the glass. Service is excellent, with friendly and knowledgeable staff - a rare treat. Free broadband wi/fi; lawn bowls, walking; equestrian fishing (fly & coarse), golf and garden visits all nearby. Accommodation: Upstairs there are four delightful en-suite rooms, all no smoking (€60 pps, ss €20). Not suitable for children under 12. **Seats 45** (private room, 15, outdoors, 24). L Sun only, 1-6pm, set Sun L €28. Tapas (5-7pm) & D Tue-Sun high season 6.30-8.30pm (to 9.30 Fri/Sat), à la carte; house wine from €21; SC disc. Closed Mon Tue off-season (Oct-Apr), Christmas period & 2 weeks Nov, 2 weeks Jan. MasterCard, Visa, Laser. **Directions:** 3.5km (2 m) from Lismore off N72 Lismore/Tallow Road.

Millstreet
FARMHOUSE/CASTLE

The Castle Country House

Millstreet Dungarvan Co Waterford **Tel: 058 68049**
castlefm@iol.ie www.castlecountryhouse.com

FARMHOUSE OF THE YEAR

Set in several acres of landscaped gardens encompassing a circular walk overlooking the River Finisk, the Nugent family's unusual and wonderfully hospitable farmhouse is a substantial 18th century farmhouse built around remains of a 16th century castle. Although most of the house seems quite normal inside, it blends into the original building in places - so, for example, the dining room has walls five feet deep and an original castle archway. Outside you can visit the cellar of the original castle and, on the other side, view the rock on which the house and castle are built and, as befits a farmhouse, you may watch the milking and whatever other farm activities are in season. Spacious, comfortably appointed rooms have king size beds, television, tea/coffee facilities and neat shower rooms Well equipped with a selection of toiletries; (there is also a full bathroom available for any guest who prefers a bath). Bedrooms have comfortable easy chairs, good lighting, lots of books and the full history of the house in an information pack. Meticulous housekeeping, a very pleasant guests' sitting room (more books, games, an open fire), interesting pictures and fresh flowers everywhere all add up to a very appealing farmhouse indeed, and Joan and her daughter and daughter-in-law provide excellent breakfasts beginning with a wide selection of home grown fresh fruit, fruit compôtes and fruit juices, porridge and home baked bread. In addition to the traditional Irish breakfast you may choose from dishes like smoked salmon and scrambled free-range eggs, French toast with bacon and maple syrup. Dinner is served at separate tables in the lovely dining room, set up with crisp white linen and silver, more like a small restaurant than a farmhouse dining room; it is only available by arrangement so you must book when making a reservation, when you will be asked about your likes and dislikes. The menu changes daily and might include home-made soups with freshly baked bread, poached salmon with hollandaise sauce and a rhubarb, ginger and orange crumble followed by good coffee; some well chosen wines are available, around €19. The family are constantly improving the house - decorating, renewing furniture and linen and re-doing bathrooms. Children welcome (under 5s free in parents' room, cot available without charge, baby sitting arranged). Pets permitted by arrangement. Garden, walking, fishing (fly). **Rooms 5** (all en-suite, shower only and no smoking). B&B €50pps, ss €20. **Dining Room: Seats 20** (+5 outside); Residents D 7pm €30, House wine €16. Closed 1 Nov-31 Mar. MasterCard, Visa, Laser. **Directions:** Off N25 on R671.

Passage East
COUNTRY HOUSE

Parkswood Country House

Parkswood Lower Passage East Co Waterford **Tel: 051 380 863**
info@parkswood.com www.parkswood.com

Roger and Terrie Pooley's lovely house is very near the car ferry linking Waterford and Wexford and is beautifully situated in six acres of grounds overlooking the River Suir. The house has been fully refurbished since the Pooleys took it on in 2002, and the four of the very pleasing guest rooms have estuary views, three of them with walk out balconies; all have power showers except one family room, with a private bathroom. Part of the house dates back to the early 17th century, and later additions have been made in keeping with the house; some are hundreds of years old, the latest is a sunroom which was recently added to the front of the house, allowing guests to enjoy the view fully whatever the weather and making a lovely dining room; breakfast and evening meals for residents (including those in a self-catering cottage in the grounds) are served here, and local residents too, on request and, although they do not consider themselves a restaurant, they're open for afternoon teas and light refreshments during the day in summer. They make their own jams and cakes, which are also for sale, and use local, preferably organic produce as much as possible. As if all this is not enough they also undertake small functions (weddings, parties), are building a new sun terrace and have plans to convert a 200-year old barn in the grounds

Parkswood is a lovely, welcoming place, and a stay here should be very relaxing. Children welcome (under 2s free in parents room); Equestrian, fishing, golf and garden visits nearby. Walking, tennis. Pets permitted in certain areas. **Rooms 4** (all en-suite & no smoking, 1 family); B&B €65pps, ss €15. Discounts available for stays longer than one night. Closed Christmas. **Directions:** R684 from Waterford City (Dunmore East road); 5 km left to Passage East; 5 km on left hand side.

Tallowbridge
RESTAURANT/PUB

The Brideview Bar & Restaurant

Tallowbridge Tallow Co Waterford
Tel: 058 56522

Noel and Annmarie Costello's attractive roadside bar and restaurant is in a beautiful setting just outside Tallow, beside an old stone bridge over the River Bride and with wonderful views from a fine informal dining area and a new deck overlooking the river and bridge. Ongoing renovations in recent years have made big improvements and adding a gently contemporary tone to all aspects of the building, while retaining character in the older bar - which is along the road side of the building and has a welcoming open fire and adding a snug-like after dinner lounge with original artwork, and library. Whether you call in for an informal bite in the bar or go for the full dining experience, food will be carefully sourced and prepared, and menus which are quite contemporary include a great selection of local seafood (the seafood platters are very popular), and home grown fruit and vegetables. To complement the food, a short but carefully selected wine list offers a balanced choice, and lists a selection of lesser known wines including Thomas Walks red wine, from Kinsale. One big recent change is very noticeable on arrival, as two of the old stables have been converted to make a food, wine and homeware/kitchenware shop, which opens at the same time as the restaurant so people dining can browse before or after their meal; they sell as much local produce as possible including their own excellent brown bread and hampers based on their own food range, Bride View Foods. Noel and Annmarie's dedication and hard work over nearly a decade has transformed this bar into a fine establishment that is offering something different from others in the area including an exceptional location, of course, as well as good food and very long opening hours all year round. Lifestyle gift shop (homeware, food, wine); Toilets wheelchair accessible; Children welcome (baby changing facilities). Outdoor seating (28). Food available Mon-Sat, 12.30-9pm (to 9.30pm Fri/Sat; no food 2.30-5.30pm Mon-Thurs off-season). Set Sun L, 12.30-2.30pm; then a la carte 2.30-8.30pm. Closed 22-27 Dec & Good Fri. Amex, MasterCard, Visa, Laser. **Directions:** Near Tallow on N72; 12 miles east of Fermoy - 3 from Lismore.

Touraneena
FARMHOUSE

Sliabh gCua Farmhouse

Touraneena Ballinamult Dungarvan Co Waterford **Tel: 058 47120**
breedacullinan@sliabhgcua.com www.sliabhgcua.com

Breeda Cullinan's lovely creeper-clad farmhouse is in a beautiful area for lovers of the rural life; it is not as old or as large as it looks, but it was built with the classical proportions that create handsome, light-filled rooms, and has a happy atmosphere. There's a delightful drawing room (just completely refurbished) and bedrooms, individually furnished and decorated with great care by Breeda, are very comfortable and have tea/coffee making facilities. Wholesome food, based on fresh farm produce, is served in a lovely dining room overlooking the garden (where walks are planned): there are home-made cereals, fruit salads, freshly baked breads, local cheeses and hot cooked dishes to set guests up for the day. People love this place, and it is easy to see why. Dogs permitted. Children welcome (under 3 free in parents' room, cot available without charge, baby sitting arranged, playground). Walking; garden. Fishing, golf & hunting all nearby. **Rooms 4** (all en-suite, shower-only & no smoking, 1 family). B&B €40 pps, ss €5. Closed Nov-Mar. **No Credit Cards. Directions:** 16km off the N25, signposted on main Dungarvan- Clonmel Road(R672).

Tramore
CHARACTER PUB/RESTAURANT

Rockett's of The Metal Man

Westown Tramore Co Waterford **Tel: 051 381 496**
rockettsofthemetalman@eircom.net

Open fires and a friendly, welcoming atmosphere will always draw you into this unusual pub but it's the speciality of the house, Crubeens (pig's trotters) which has earned it fame throughout the land. Crubeens (cruibíns) were once the staple bar food in pubs everywhere in Ireland but, as they've been supplanted by crisps, peanuts and lasagne & chips, Rockett's is one of the few places to keep up the old tradition. Two bars are set up with tables for the comfortable consumption of these porcine treats, served with cabbage and colcannon. Other traditional foods like boiled bacon & cabbage, spare ribs, colcannon and apple pie are also very much on the menu at Rockett's - and all prepared freshly. Children welcome (high chair, childrens menu, baby changing facilities). Toilets wheelchair accessible. **Seats 150** (outdoors, 20). Air conditioning. Food served daily 12-8.30 (Sun to 9). A phone call is advised to check times off-season. Closed 25 Dec & Good Fri. MasterCard, Visa, Laser. **Directions:** From Waterford, straight through Tramore, 1.5km (one mile) far side.

WATERFORD

Waterford City is most famously home of the Waterford Crystal Glass Centre, which is certainly worth a visit. Only recently designated a city, the centre is now developing attractively around the river - which, with a marina and walkways along the quays, is a pleasant place to explore. Of its many cultural events, the most famous is the Waterford International Festival of Light Opera, which is held in September. And hospitality is very much alive and well in Waterford too notably, with a number of French restaurants providing healthy competition, there is an unusually good choice of eating places offering quality and value for money. Other Irish towns and cities might take note. Travellers requiring spacious modern accommodation outside the city at a reasonable room rate may be interested in the **Ramada Viking Hotel** (051 336933; www.vikinghotel.ie) on the Cork road, which has business facilities and family/interconnecting rooms.
WWW.IRELAND-GUIDE.COM FOR THE BEST PLACES TO EAT, DRINK & STAY

Waterford
HOTEL

Athenaeum House Hotel

Christendom Waterford Co Waterford **Tel: 051 833 999**
info@athenaeumhousehotel.com   www.athenaeumhousehotel.com

Guests feel very much at home in this boutique hotel, which is set amidst 10 acres of parkland overlooking the River Suir, just outside Waterford city - and owner-managed by Stan Power, a previous General Manager of Mount Juliet House in County Kilkenny, and his wife Mailo. Chic contemporary decor, luxurious suites and deluxe rooms and a welcome emphasis on service are the characteristics that will appeal most to discerning travellers. The restaurants of Waterford city are just a short taxi ride away, but you can dine in-house at the hotel's Zaks Restaurant, where you should get an enjoyable meal and good service. **Rooms 28.** B&B from about €90. **Seats 65** (private room, 40; also outdoor area, 20). Toilets accessible by wheelchair; Live Music Sat pm. Food served all day 7.30-9.30; D Tue-Sun (7- 9 on Sun), Early Bird D €23 (5.30-7.30), also a la carte; L Sun, 12.30-3; Set Sun L about €21. House Wine from €22. Rest closed Mon, House closed 25-27 Dec. MasterCard, Visa, Laser. **Directions:** Leaving railway station on N25 in the direction of Wexford, take the first right after the traffic lights on to Abbey Road, half a mile later take the first right. ◇

Waterford
PUB/RESTAURANT
Ⓝ

Becketts Bar & Restaurant

Dunmore Road Waterford Co Waterford
Tel: 051 873 082

A well maintained garden with lots of comfortable seating make a good impression on arrival at this large pub on the outskirts of the city; inside it is big and airy the décor is very simple, with some black and white photos and quotations from Irish authors on the walls, and high tables with tall chairs and minimal pub style place settings (knife and fork in a paper napkin). Pleasant staff make you feel very welcome and immediately offer menus which, with about a dozen main courses, are perhaps too long for the kitchen to handle well; however there is also a set menu with a very short choice (about €12.50 for main courses) which is great value for a family tea and, on the à la carte, it is a pleasant surprise to find a dish like lamb's liver and lambs kidneys as a starter (and, while not exactly pink, in our experience it tasted very good), also a huge bowl of mussels in tomato & scallion sauce. Main courses include staples like cod in beer batter with mushy peas and pasta dishes and, although perhaps less successful than the starters, prices are very reasonable and, with very good staff and pleasing surroundings, this is a useful place to know about. Toilets wheelchair accessible. Children welcome (high chair, childrens menu, baby changing facilities); Food served daily 12.30-9.30pm (to 8.30pm Sun). House wine €19.95. Closed 25 Dec, Good Fri. Visa, Laser. **Directions:** Follow Dunmore East signs out of city.

Waterford
RESTAURANT/WINE BAR

Bodéga!

54 John St. Waterford Co Waterford **Tel: 051 844 177**
info@bodegawaterford.com www.bodegawaterford.com

With its warm Mediterranean colours, this place would bring the sun out on the darkest of days: interesting artwork, pine tables, covered with the occasional oilcloth, a mix'n'match collection of seating. Menus are quite extensive and offer a wide range, but the chef is French and you will find many favourites like beef bourguinon, Toulouse sausage with choucroûte and moules frites mingling with the international dishes. A written menu offers everything from lunchtime dishes like soup of the day and quiche of the day to Bodega fish pie and steaks, to dinner specialities such as roast magret & confit de canard with sweet red cabbage & apple There are also blackboard specials, which are likely to be the best bet - and friendly staff are well-informed to advise. At lunch time the place fills up with young people, some with children - who are made especially welcome - and there are lots of regulars. Dinner is a little more structured and the prices heat up a bit too, but it's still good value - and at €21/26 for 2/3 courses, the early dinner is a snip. Regular live music too, with big names including Mary Coughlan, Freddie White, Eleanor McCoy. Children welcome (high chair). **Seats 80.** L Mon-Fri, 12-5pm & D Mon-Sat 5-10pm (to 10.30pm Fri/Sat). Early D 2/3 course, €21/26, Mon-Fri 5.30-7pm. Also a la carte. House wines from €19.50. SC discretionary. Closed Sat L, Sun (except bank hol w/ends), bank hol Mons, Good Fri, 25/26 Dec, 1 Jan. Amex, MasterCard, Visa, Laser. **Directions:** A few doors down from the Applemarket, in city centre.

Waterford
GUESTHOUSE

Diamond Hill Country House

Slieverue Waterford Co Waterford **Tel: 051 832855**
info@stayatdiamondhill.com www.stayatdiamondhill.com

The Smith-Lehane family's long-established and moderately-priced guesthouse just outside Waterford city is set in one and a half acres of landscaped gardens; it would make a good base for exploring the area, and will appeal to anyone who wants to be quietly located yet handy to the city. The house has been completely refurbished and most of the well-equipped bedrooms have king-size beds as well as power showers and all the other usual amenities (phone, TV, tea/coffee facilities etc). With ten courses including Mount Juliet, within half an hour's drive it's ideal for golfing breaks; other sporting activities nearby include fishing and horse riding. **Rooms 17** (14 shower only, all no smoking). Children welcome (under 5s free in parents' room, cot available without charge). No pets. Gardens. B&B about €40, ss €5. Closed Dec. MasterCard, Visa, Laser. **Directions:** Off the N25 - 0.5 miles outside Waterford. ◊

Waterford
FARMHOUSE

Foxmount Country House

Passage East Road Waterford Co Waterford **Tel: 051 874 308**
info@foxmountcountryhouse.com www.foxmountcountryhouse.com

For those who prefer a country house atmosphere rather than an hotel, the Kent family's 17th century home on the edge of Waterford city is a haven of peace and tranquillity. The house is lovely with classically proportioned reception rooms, and accommodation in five very different rooms which are all thoughtfully, and very comfortably, furnished - but, as peace and relaxation are the aim at Foxmount, don't expect phones or TVs in bedrooms, or a very early breakfast. However Margaret Kent is a great cook and she loves baking

as guests quickly discover when offered afternoon tea in the drawing room - or in the morning, when freshly-baked breads are presented at breakfast. David and Margaret celebrated forty years in business in 2007 and say they are "delighted to have survived through the era of tax incentives, venture capital leisure centres & spas, and still have guests coming from all parts of the world to enjoy the homely comforts and experiences of a family run country house on a working farm." They are right - it is a very special place and no amount of investment in new developments can recreate what Foxmount, and other like them, do so well. No evening meals are offered, but the restaurants of Waterford and

Cheekpoint are quite close - and guests are welcome to bring their own wine and enjoy a glass at the log fire before going out for dinner. Children welcome (under 2s free in parent' room, cot available without charge). No pets. Garden. **Rooms 4** (all with en-suite or private bathrooms, all no-smoking, 1 family room). B&B €65 pps, ss€10. Closed Nov-mid Mar. **No Credit Cards. Directions:** From Waterford city, take Dunmore Road - after 4 km, take Passage East road for 1.5 km.

Waterford
PUB

The Gingerman
6/7 Arundel Lane Waterford Co Waterford
Tel: 051 879522

In the old Norman area of the city, this hospitable pub is in a pedestrianised lane just off Broad Street. It can be very busy but, at quieter times it's a pleasant place, with welcoming open fires in several bars - and this lovely ambience together with pleasant staff, a good-humoured hands-on owner and a commitment to serving wholesome food has earned The Gingerman a loyal local following. A useful place to drop into for a drink, a cuppa, or a casual bite to eat. Parking in nearby multi-storey carpark. Open 10am-11.30pm. Food served Mon-Sat, 12-6. No food on Sun. Closed 25 Dec, Good Fri. Amex, Diners, MasterCard, Visa, Laser. **Directions:** Off John Roberts Square.

Waterford
HOTEL

Granville Hotel
The Quay Waterford Co Waterford **Tel: 051 305 555**
stay@granville-hotel.ie www.granville-hotel.ie

One of the country's oldest hotels, this much-loved quayside establishment in the centre of Waterford has many historical connections with Bianconi, for example, who established Ireland's earliest transport system, and also Charles Stuart Parnell, who made many a rousing speech here. Since 1979, it's been owner-run by the Cusack family, who have overseen significant restoration and are continuously renewing the old building, and it has that indefinable ambience of the well-run privately owned hotel, the sense of being cosseted in an old fashioned way unlike the slick informality of modern "concept" establishments. It's a large hotel, bigger than it looks perhaps, with fine public areas including a spacious bar/lounge where both residents and locals congregate, and well-appointed if, perhaps, slightly dated bedrooms (all with well-designed bathrooms, with both bath and shower). This is a good choice for business guests and would also make a comfortable and friendly base for touring the area - how many hotels today would inspire comments like this: "I loved the Granville; having tea and a sandwich in the afternoon I was asked by a caring local bar lady: 'more tea dear?'." And, aside from being very conveniently situated for exploring this interesting city on foot, the many activities available locally include boating, fishing, golf, walking and horse riding. off-season value breaks available. Conference/banqueting (200). Parking nearby. Children welcome (under 3s free in parents' room; cots available without charge). No pets. **Rooms 98** (3 junior suites, 60 executive rooms, 90 no-smoking). Lift. B&B about €80 pps, ss €35 (winter rate from about €55pps, ss €20). Meals: D daily, L Sun-Fri (except bank hol Mons); bar meals 10.30-6 daily. Closed 25-27 Dec. Amex, Diners, MasterCard, Visa. **Directions:** In city centre, on the quays opposite Clock Tower.

Waterford
CHARACTER PUB

Henry Downes
8-10 Thomas St Waterford Co Waterford
Tel: 051 874 118

Established in 1759, and in the same (eccentric) family for six generations, John de Bromhead's unusual pub is one of the few remaining houses to bottle its own whiskey. Although not the easiest of places to find, once visited it certainly will not be forgotten. Large, dark and cavernous with a squash court on the premises as well as the more predictable billiards and snooker it consists of a series of bars of differing character, each with its own particular following. It achieves with natural grace what so-called Irish theme pubs would dearly love to capture, and friendly, humorous bar staff enjoy filling customers in on the pub's proud history and will gladly sell you a bottle of Henry Downes No.9 to take away. Not suitable for children. Open from 5pm to normal closing time. No food. Closed 25 Dec & Good Fri. **No Credit Cards. Directions:** Second right after Bridge Hotel, halfway up Thomas Street on right.

Waterford
RESTAURANT

L'Atmosphère

19 Henrietta Street Waterford Co Waterford **Tel: 051 858 426**
latmosphererestaurant@hotmail.com www.restaurant-latmosphere.com

The closely packed tables in Arnaud, Mary and Patrice Garreau's well-named French restaurant don't matter too much - the decor is basic, with pine tables, paper napkins, and menus that double as paper mats, and it all adds up to a cheerful bistro atmosphere. Three menus are offered, an early bird, the day's specials and an à la carte. The early dinner menu (5.30 to 7) is extremely good value, and even includes a glass of house wine, which is unusually generous. Expect typical French cooking: for starters there are good soups (fish, perhaps) and excellent breads (Arnaud has a French Bakery in the town), then maybe chicken liver terrine or tender seared scallops on spinach Main courses could include a classic cassoulet with duck confit, Toulouse sausage and tender little haricot beans, or braised French rabbit, served in its own casserole with good chunky vegetables and potatoes The offering is different from other restaurants in the area - there is a high level of skill here and a good old fashioned sense that cheaper cuts of meat will be used and properly; menus may also offer luxurious items like foie gras, or lobster, but the same philosophy applies. Finish, perhaps with a classic hot chocolate soufflé (wonderful liquid chocolate insides, served with vanilla ice cream) or cream slice made with superb vanilla ice cream. With delicious, keenly priced, food and friendly service from French and Irish waiting staff, the whole impression is of eating in a good French bistro, rare today even in France. **Seats 48**; air conditioning; children welcome; Open for L&D Mon-Fri; D only Sat; early D €20, 5.30-7; set D €25/33, 2/3 course; House wine €18, Closed Sat L, Sun and Bank Hol Mons. MasterCard, Visa, Laser. ◊

Waterford
RESTAURANT

La Bohème

2 George St Waterford Co Waterford **Tel: 051 875 645**
labohemerestaurant@eircom.net

Eric and Christine Thèze's restaurant is in the basement of one of Waterford's most prestigious buildings, the Chamber of Commerce. The cellar has been beautifully converted, with the original high arched ceilings retained but all painted white; it seems very bright and there are plenty of flowers, some nicely restrained art on the walls and French music in the background. Well spaced white-clothed tables are set with good glasses, heavy silver and a flower on each, and a nice touch mismatched old crockery. It is a very French restaurant - nearly all of the staff are French, and the welcome is friendly but formal as you are shown to the bar for your aperitif. The menu, which is not overlong but offers plenty of choice, changes seasonally and is modern classic French: good fish choices, lamb and beef, with daily specials and the soup pinned on the menu; an Early Bird is also available and - with dishes like a superb crab brulée, a crisp, unctuous confit of duck with a rich duck sauce and impeccable puy lentils, and perfectly matured French cheeses with quince paste among the options it offers remarkable value at €29. Seafood offered includes a speciality of lobster smothered in beurre blanc sauce, and other luxurious treats may include duck foie gras. Pleasingly, for Irish tastes, main courses are accompanied by some good mashed potatoes and vegetables, and in addition to the all-French cheese board, there are excellent classic desserts. Good wines - strongly French, as you would expect, but including some cheaper regional French wines - and very good service. This is a restaurant that is serious about its food and is a great asset to Waterford city; although the à la carte gets a little pricey, it is worth it and the early table d'hôte is excellent value for money. Stair lift. Not suitable for children under 10 years. **Seats 70** (private room, 10 & 20); air conditioning; reservations required; D Tue-Sat (& Bank Hol Sun), 5.30-10pm; Early D €29, 5.30-7 Tue-Fri; gourmet menu €70; house wine from €26; SC 10% on groups 6+. Closed Sun (except on Bank Hol weekends), Mon. MasterCard, Visa, Laser. **Directions:** Across from the Bank Bar on O'Connell Street, parallel to the quays.

Waterford
RESTAURANT

La Palma on the Mall

20 The Mall Waterford Co Waterford **Tel: 051 879 823**
info@lapalma.ie www.lapalma.ie

Claudio, Rachel and Dario Cavilieri's popular Italian restaurant is in a graceful Georgian building on Waterford's Mall. The reception is upstairs in a tall navy and beige drawing room, now working as a cock-tail bar, where guests are greeted and seated, and offered a drink while you look at the menu. As well as an à la carte, there's a very good value mid week "Treat" menu available. The restaurant is downstairs in a series of pleasant high-ceilinged Georgian rooms. Meals begin with a little amuse bouche and a choice of breads. Service is very pleasant and attentive, and the wine waiter is happy to give a good recommendation for the perfect bottle to accompany your meal. Rustic dishes might include hearty bruschetta, pasta or confit of duck, and classic tiramisu. Good coffee to finish, and an agreeably reasonable bill. [The old Palma is now called the Espresso and serves pizzas and pasta.] Children welcome; toilets wheelchair accessible. **Seats 75** (private room, 35, outdoors, 10); D only Mon-Sat, 5.30-10.30pm; early D €25, 5.30-7pm Mon-Sat; house wine from €19. Closed Sun and 25-26 Dec. Amex, Diners, MasterCard, Visa, Laser. **Directions:** In city centre opposite Bishop's palace & Theatre Royal.

Waterford
RESTAURANT
N

Restaurant Chez K's
20-22 William Street Waterford Co Waterford **Tel: 051 844 180**
info@chez-ks.com www.chez-ks.com

This smart centrally located restaurant is well-maintained, with very large windows making it appealing from the street. There's a pleasant reception area with relaxing couches and low tables - and also and a bar, where you can enjoy an aperitif while considering the menu. The restaurant is stylish, too, with an open kitchen and well-spaced tables attractively set up with linen napkins, good glasses and cutlery and fresh flowers - and a piano placed promisingly in the centre of the room; it needs a good crowd to fill the rather large spaces and then a good buzz builds up. A new head chef, Mark Gunnip, took over the kitchen in 2007 and the change has been dramatic: a good and interesting à la carte is offered, also a mid week menu at €25, which is remarkable value. The dishes offered sound familiar enough, and there are no flowery descriptions - starters of smoked salmon with fromage frais potato, or confit of duck salad with rocket, perhaps, and main courses like rib eye steak with pepper sauce or monkfish with spring vegetables but, although this is conventional food, it is cooked by someone who appreciates the value of taste and contrasts on the plate. And you should end on a high note, as dessert is likely to be the pièce de resistance: imagine a large glass with a warm tart rhubarb compôte in the bottom covered with a layer of light vanilla mousse... with a scoop of fresh strawberry sorbet on top of that: all the contrasts (warm/cold, tart/sweet, smooth/bite) work excellently. Result: one of the best desserts you're ever likely to find anywhere. Service is pleasant, the wine list unexceptional. *The **Spinnaker Bar** (051 383133) in Dunmore East is under the same management. Not suitable for children after 8pm. **Seats 90.** Reservations advised.Toilets wheelchair accessible. D daily 5.30-10 (Sun 4-9). Early D about €25 (Mon-Fri, 5.30-7). D also à la carte. House wine about €20. Open all year. MasterCard, Visa, Laser. **Directions:** Left at traffic lights at Tower Hotel - on the left 400m. ◇

Waterford
HISTORIC HOUSE

Sion Hill House & Gardens
Sion Hill Ferrybank Waterford Co Waterford
Tel: 051 851 558

George and Antoinette Kavanagh have been welcoming guests to their lovely hillside house above Waterford city since 1996 and the story of how they came to be here is an interesting one. The Kavanagh family were devastated when their three acre garden in Waterford city was compulsorily purchased some years ago, and this house on the opposite hill became the focus of their dreams; it was built in 1746 and is one of five houses built by the Pope family, who made their fortune as wine merchants during the Napoleonic embargo, and

George and Antoinette managed to buy it in 1995 and moved in, transplanting 2,000 plants from their previous garden. They also planted 20,000 daffodils and over 400 species roses and - thanks to a map in the National Archives - rediscovered the original paths in the upper part of the garden, which lies in Kilkenny. And they have been restoring and replanting ever since. So this is more a garden with a house in it, rather than a house with a garden attached but what a house, all the same. Immaculately maintained and with classically proportioned rooms furnished with fine antiques, anyone who enjoys beautiful old things will find this a wonderful place to stay and George and Antoinette are great hosts, who really enjoy sharing their home and garden with visitors. Children welcome (under 8s free in parents' room, cot available free of charge, baby sitting arranged). Gardens; walking. Equestrian, fishing & hunting all nearby. **Rooms 4** (all en-suite & no smoking, 2 shower only, 3 family); B&B €58 pps, ss €12. MasterCard, Visa. **Directions:** 300 metres from Waterford Bridge roundabout and rail station on the N25 to Wexford/Rosslare.

Waterford

HOTEL

Tower Hotel Waterford

The Mall Waterford Co Waterford **Tel: 051 875801**
reservations@thw.ie www.towerhotelwaterford.com

A central location within easy walking distance of everything in the city, ample secure private parking, large conference/banqueting capacity and excellent on-site leisure facilities are all reasons for staying at this big hotel. Considerable investment over the last few years has seen an improvement in standards throughout the hotel: a smart bistro, a carvery restaurant and a state-of-the-art conference centre and the lobby and reception area have been renovated, and bedrooms have also been refurbished - with a big difference between old and new rooms. Conference/banqueting facilities (450/350). Leisure Centre, indoor swimming pool. Children welcome (cots available free of charge). Own parking. No pets. **Rooms 136** (3 suites, 6 junior suites, 15 executive, 38 no smoking, 3 for disabled). Lift. B&B from about €70 pps, ss €20. Closed 24-26 Dec. Amex, Diners, MasterCard, Visa, Laser. **Directions:** Waterford city centre overlooking the marina. ◊

Waterford

HOTEL/RESTAURANT

Waterford Castle Hotel & Golf Club

The Island Ballinakill Waterford Co Waterford **Tel: 051 878 203**
info@waterfordcastle.com www.waterfordcastle.com

IRISH BREAKFAST AWARD - NATIONAL WINNER
BEST HOTEL BREAKFAST AWARD

féile bia This beautiful hotel dates back to the 15th century, and is situated on its own 310 acre wooded island (complete with 18-hole golf course), reached by a private ferry. The hotel combines the elegance of earlier times with modern comfort, service and convenience - and the location is uniquely serene; its quietness (and the golf facility for off-duty relaxation) makes the castle a good venue for small conferences and business meetings, but it is also a highly romantic location and perfect for small weddings. All guest rooms have been refurbished and, although they inevitably vary in size and outlook (and may have some of the little quirks that are typical of old buildings), all are very comfortably furnished in a luxurious country house style, and discreet, well-trained staff look after guests magnificently. And you may be sure of an excellent breakfast, offering a well presented buffet with fresh juices and prepared fruit, yoghurts, muffins, smoked salmon, local cheeses, Waterford Blas (the local bread rolls), and cooked offerings of Flavahans porridge, excellent dry cured bacon and sausages in a full breakfast, or other hot dishes including omelettes and scrambled eggs & smoked wild Irish salmon and breakfast service is excellent too. Conference/banqueting (30/80). Golf, archery, clay pigeon shooting, fishing, tennis, walking, gardens. Pool table. Children welcome (under 4 free in parents' room; cots available; bay sitting arranged). **Rooms 19** (5 suites, 3 junior suites, 2 family, 4 ground floor, all no smoking). Lift. 24 hr room service. Turndown service. Room rate from about €195. Closed 2 Jan - 8 Feb. **Munster Dining Room:** This beautiful room is appointed to the highest standard and head chef Michael Quinn and a fine kitchen brigade continue to create superb meals. Michael demonstrates through all his menus the true spirit of sourcing the best local and Irish foods, and using them in a very imaginative and creative way - this includes rearing his own Saddleback pigs and using the pork on menus which, as well as his own Saddleback brawn, may include Paul Crotty's chicken broth, croquettes made with Sally Barnes smoked haddock, local man Tom Cleary's vegetables, and cheeses from nearby areas including Knockalara Sheep's and Crozier Blue. The setting, staff and the cooking, in a modern classical style, are all excellent and a meal here is sure to be a very special experience. A set dinner menu is offered, but considerately priced by course, allowing for a semi à la carte selection. Children welcome. **Seats 60.** D daily, 7-9 (to 8.30 Sun), L Sun only (12.30-2); Set D about €59, à la carte and vegetarian menu also available; Set Sun L about €30. House wines from €28. SC 10%. Pianist at dinner. Amex, Diners, MasterCard, Visa, Laser. **Directions:** Outskirts of Waterford City just off Dunmore East road. ◊

Waterford
RESTAURANT

The Wine Vault

High Street Waterford Co Waterford **Tel: 051 853 444**
ddfw@eircom.net www.waterfordwinevault.com

Situated in the medieval part of the city, in an 18th century bonded warehouse with the remains of a 15th century tower house, David Dennison's informal little wine bar and restaurant includes a vaulted wine merchant's premises, and has great atmosphere. A range of menus offers a combination of the classic dishes enjoyed by the original clientèle (an excellent duck liver parfait on brioche, for example) and modern dishes like Thai spiced confit of duck - and there is a list of daily specials, which may offer the best choices. Sadly a former policy of naming artisan products and suppliers is lacking, and in recent experience the cooking has been mixed. Wine is available by the glass (albeit rather expensive) and, although staff may be too rushed to chat, service is efficient. Toilets wheelchair accessible. Children welcome. **Seats 50** (private room 20). L& D Mon-Sat, 12.30-2.30 & 5-10.30. Early D about €22 (5-7.30 only), otherwise a la carte. House wines (26) about €18-€22. sc discretionary. Closed Sun (except bank hol weekends), 25 Dec, Good Fri. Amex, MasterCard, Visa, Laser. **Directions:** Take right turn off quay - City Square car park. Take next left to High Street, 100m on the right. ◇

Waterford Area
HOTEL

Faithlegg House Hotel

Faithlegg Co Waterford **Tel: 051 382 000**
reservations@fhh.ie www.faithlegg.com

Set in wooded landscape with magnificent views over its own golf course and the Suir estuary, this lovely 18th century house has a splendid Waterford Crystal chandelier to set the tone in the foyer, and public areas are elegant throughout. Accommodation, in the old house and a discreetly positioned new wing, is furnished to a high standard; the large, graciously proportioned rooms and suites in the old house are really lovely, while those in the new wing are more practical. (Self-catering accommodation is also offered in the grounds.) Aside from golf, the range of activities available on site includes a swimming pool, and numerous health and beauty treatments. There is a choice of restaurants nearby (Waterford city, or Cheekpoint, are each only a few minutes' drive), and the hotel's fine dining restaurant, **The Roseville Rooms**, offers classical cuisine The restaurant is shared between two lovely classical, formally appointed dining rooms and it is a very pleasant place to enjoy an evening meal. **Rooms 82.** B&B from about €95 pps. Restaurant seats 90 (private room 40). Not suitable for children after 8.30pm. D daily, 6.30-9.30; L Sun only, 12.30-2.30. Set D about €50, Set Sun L about €30. House wines from €18. Amex, MasterCard, Visa, Laser. **Directions:** Off Dunmore East Road 6 miles outside Waterford city. ◇

COUNTY WESTMEATH

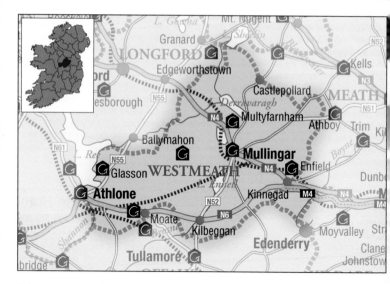

As its name suggests, in the distant past Westmeath tended to be ruled by whoever held Meath, or perhaps it was the other way around. But today, Westmeath is a county so cheerfully and successfully developing its own identity that they should find a completely new name for the place. For this is somewhere that makes the very best of what it has to hand.

Its highest "peak" is only the modest Mullaghmeen of 258 m, 10 kilometres north of Castlepollard. But this is in an area where hills of ordinary height have impressive shapes which make them appear like miniature mountains around the spectacularly beautiful Lough Derravaragh, famed for its association with the legend of the Children of Lir, who were turned into swans by their wicked step-mother Aoife, and remained as swans for 900 years until saved by the coming of Christianity.

Westmeath abounds in lakes to complement Derravaragh, such as the handsome expanses of Lough Owel and Lough Ennell on either side of the fine county town of Mullingar, where life has been made even more watery in recent years with the continuing work to restore the Royal Canal, which loops through town on its way from Dublin to the north Shannon.

Meanwhile, Athlone to the west is confidently developing as one of Ireland's liveliest river towns, its Shannonside prosperity based on its riverside location, and a useful manufacturing mixture of electronics, pharmaceuticals and the healthcare industry. Following a period of riverside development, Athlone's waterfront has become a mixture of old and new, with the traditional quayside area below the bridge on the west providing a haven from modern buildings.

Despite modernity, this remains a very rural place - immediately south of the town, you can hear the haunting call of the corncrake coming across the callows (water meadows). Athlone itself has a real buzz, and north of it there's the wide lake expanse of Lough Ree in all its glory, wonderful for boating in an area where, near the delightful village of Glasson, the Goldsmith country verges towards County Longford, and they have a monument to mark what some enthusiasts reckon to be the true geographical centre of all Ireland. You really can't get more utterly rural than that.

Local Attractions & Information

Athlone All Ireland Amateur Drama Festival (May)	090 647 8303
Athlone Athlone Castle Visitor Centre	090 649 2912
Athlone River Festivals	0902 94 981
Athlone Tourism Information	090 649 4630
Ballykeeran MV Goldsmith Lake & River Cruises	090 648 5163
Castlepollard Tullynally Castle & Gardens	044 966 1159

Clonmellon Ballinlough Castle Gardens	046 943 3268
Kilbegggan Locke's Distillery Museum	057 933 2134
Kilbeggan Race Course	057 933 2176
Moate Dun na Si Folk Park	090 648 1183
Mullingar Belvedere House, Gardens & Park	044 934 9060
Mullingar Tourism Information	044 934 8761
Mullingar Westmeath Tourism Council	044 934 8571

ATHLONE

R

Athlone makes a perfect break for anyone crossing the country, but it's much more than a handy stopover: it is now a destination town for discerning travellers. This bustling, youthful centre town of Ireland has much of historical interest - and, although other towns along the mighty Shannon will no doubt be keen to mount a challenge, Athlone is presently seen as the culinary capital of the inland waterways, with a cluster of good eating places in the town itself and surrounding area. And there's a growing supply of quality accommodation in and around the town too; **The Prince of Wales Hotel** (090 647 7246; www.the princeofwales.ie) re-opened in the centre of the town fairly recently, after a complete re-build; just out of town on the Roscommon side, the large beautifully located waterside **Hodson Bay Hotel** (090 644 2000) serves the area well by offering extensive conference and leisure facilities - and it gets bigger all the time. The town is gaining a reputation for good ethnic restaurants too: lovers of spicy foods should check out the authentic **Saagar Indian Restaurant** (090 647 0011) on Lloyds Street.
WWW.IRELAND-GUIDE.COM FOR THE BEST PLACES TO EAT, DRINK & STAY

Kin Khao Thai Restaurant

Athlone
RESTAURANT
N R

1 Abbey Lane Athlone Co Westmeath **Tel: 090 649 8805**
kinkhaothai@eircom.net www.kinkhaothai.ie

You can't miss this restaurant on the western side of Athlone, near the castle - its vivid yellow exterior walls on two sides of a street corner and red doors and windows mark it out very easily. Reception is on first floor at the top of stairs a small area without seating, but if you have a reservation your table (simple but very neat, although only paper napkins) should be ready. It's a pleasant room in soft tones and warm colours, with large working ceiling fans adding to the atmosphere - you may not have been transported to Thailand, but it's a good try. Kin Khao Thai is run by Irishman Adam Lyons and his Thai wife Janya - Janya's family is steeped in the restaurant and food tradition, with recipes and techniques passed from generation to generation. The choice is enormous, neatly broken down into the various headings such as curry, soups, starters etc and with each dish accompanied by a short but useful explanation of the dish - the best initial choice is a starter platter for two of various finger items, and perhaps ask one of the attentive and charming staff for their recommendations. Authenticity is their mantra, and the chefs are from several regions in Thailand so whether you're looking for a creamy coconut curry from the south or a sharp spicy dish from the north, you'll find it here; with the exception of Adam, all the waiters, chefs, and managers are Thai - in fact, the kitchen is a real family affair with Head Chef Num and his little sister Song working side by side. This is a deservedly popular restaurant and good value for money estimate around €18 for a main course; an extensive wine list is also offered. D daily 5.30-10.30; L Wed-Fri, 12.30-2.30 & Sun from 1.30. MasterCard, Visa, Laser.
Directions: Behind Athlone Castle, west side of the Shannon. ◇

The Left Bank Bistro

Athlone
RESTAURANT
W E R

Fry Place Athlone Co Westmeath **Tel: 090 649 4446**
info@leftbankbistro.com www.leftbankbistro.com

A growing number of peope are now seeing Athlone as a destination for holidays or short breaks and, for many, it would be unthinkable to visit the area or even pass through it without a visit to Annie McNamara and Mary McCullough's elegantly informal contemporary restaurant, where architectural salvage materials and interesting, subtle colours combine well with the simplicity of bare tables and paper napkins to suit the lively modern food. Short, keenly-priced menus - plus specials chalked up on a blackboard - offer a wide range of delicious-sounding dishes with a multi-cultural stamp which, together with carefully sourced ingredients and snappy cooking, make this the number one choice for an informal meal in Athlone Wraps, bruschetta, focaccia and pasta are typical lunch time dishes and vegetables are always colourful and full of zing. Fresh fish has always had its own separate menu here, and vegetarians can choose between blackboard specials and dishes from the regular menu, including favourites like Left Bank Salad and vegetable spring rolls. Dinner menus are more extensive and tend to be based on more expensive ingredients, but the style is similar; delicious desserts are high point, and all home made - and, of course, there's a farmhouse cheese plate too. A concise, well-chosen wine list offers a fair choice of half bottles and several champagnes. For the quality of food and cooking, not to mention the style of the place, a meal here is always good value. * A range of speciality products is sold at the Left Bank: salamis, pestos, house dressing, oils, olives, pastas, and coffee are just a few examples - and breads, dressings, chutneys and desserts from the restaurant too. **Seats 60.** Air conditioning. Toilets wheelchair accessible. Open Tue-Sat L 12-5 & D 5.30-9.30; Early bird D €25 (5.30-7.30), also à la carte; house wine about €19. SC 10% on groups 8+. Closed Sun & Mon, bank hols & 10 days Christmas/New Year. Amex, MasterCard, Visa, Laser. **Directions:** Behind Athlone Castle, west side of the Shannon.

Athlone   The Olive Grove Restaurant

RESTAURANT   Bridge Street Custume Place Athlone Co Westmeath **Tel: 0902 76946**

R   info@theolivegrove.ie www.theolivegrove.ie

Garry Hughes and Gael Bradbury celebrated a decade in their charming restaurant in 2007, and it is very much a part of the Athlone dining scene - popular for its pleasant, informal atmosphere (seasoned with a colourful style), excellent home-cooked food from noon until late (light food in the afternoon), good value and a great willingness to do anything which will ensure a good time being had by all. The cooking style is Mediterranean-influenced international and youthful as seen in starters such as traditional Greek salad and lunchtime pastas like prosciutto & ricotta tortellini; vegetarians have particularly good choice here on both lunch and the more ambitious evening menus although this is beef country and the speciality of the house has always been chargrilled steaks. The entire restaurant was refurbished recently, and more extensive new menus introduced. Children welcome. Parking nearby. **Seats 50.** L &D Tue-Sun,12-4 & 5.30-10); à la carte (average main course about €10 (L); €18-20 (D) house wine €16.95, sc discretionary. Closed Mon, 24-28 Dec. Amex, MasterCard, Visa, Laser. **Directions:** Travelling from Dublin, take the left before the bridge in Athlone town centre. ◇

Athlone   Radisson SAS Hotel Athlone

HOTEL   Northgate Street Athlone Co Westmeath **Tel: 090 644 2600**

R   Info.Athlone@RadissonSAS.com www.athlone.radissonsas.com

féile bia Magnificently located right on the river and bang in the middle of town, this hotel has impressive public areas and great style: an expansive foyer leads off to an informal split level restaurant one side, conference and meeting rooms on the other - and opens out on to a huge riverside deck; overlooking the marina and set up with teak furniture, umbrellas and patio heaters, this is a great asset to a town centre hotel. The usual Radisson attributes of contemporary chic and eco awareness apply throughout the hotel, and also a choice of room styles - Urban if you like warm tones, Ocean if you prefer a cooler, watery theme; all rooms have excellent facilities, including mini-bar, hospitality tray and broadband internet access - and some have great views of the River Shannon and the town. Athlone has character and is well-placed to explore an interesting area that deserves to be better known for those who like a town centre location this would be hard to beat as a short break destination. Golf nearby (golf breaks offered). Conference/banqueting (700/500). Children welcome (under 17 free in parents' room, cots available). No pets. **Rooms 124** (1 suite, 4 junior suites, 4 executive, 7 disabled). Lift. 24 hr room service. Turndown service offered. Conference/banqueting 750 business centre; video conferencing. B&B from about €77.50 pps (various packages and offers available). Meals available all day. Open all year. **Directions:** Town centre, east side of the bridge. ◇

Athlone   Restaurant Le Chateau

RESTAURANT   St. Peter's Port The Docks Athlone Co Westmeath **Tel: 090 649 4517**

🍸 🌿 **R**   lechateau@eircom.net www.lechateau.ie

féile bia Steven and Martina Linehan's quayside restaurant is in a converted Presbyterian Church and it makes a two-storey restaurant of character which complements their well-earned reputation for good food and hospitality. Designed around the joint themes of church and river, the upstairs section has raised floors at each end, like the deck of a galleon, while the church theme is reflected in the windows notably an original "Star of David". Food is available all day and at formal meal times fine dining is offered, notably at their renowned Candlelight Dinners. The team works hard to maintain standards, and local and speciality produce is very much in evidence - notably organic goat's cheese, Clare Island organic salmon, certified Irish Angus beef and roast rack of midland lamb. Early dinner and Sunday lunch menus are popular, and offer especially good value. Broadband wi/fi; children welcome. **Seats 100** (private room, 25, outdoor, 8) Air conditioning. Open 12.30-10 daily (Sun to 9.30): L 12.30-3 , D 5.30-10; Set 2 course L €14.50, Set Sun L €27.50, Early D €27.50 (5.30-6.30 only); also à la carte; house wines from €22; SC10%. Full bar. Closed 25-26 Dec. Amex, MasterCard, Visa, Laser. **Directions:** Heading west through Athlone,over Shannon and left at castle, left again and on to bank of Shannon.

Athlone
CHARACTER PUB
R

Sean's Bar
13 Main Street Athlone Co Westmeath
Tel: 090 6492358

West of the river, in the interesting old town near the Norman castle (which has a particularly good visitors' centre for history and information on the area, including flora and fauna of the Shannon), Sean Fitzsimons' seriously historic bar lays claim to being the pub with the longest continuous use in Ireland, all owners since 900 AD are on record. (It has actually been certified by the National Museum as the oldest pub in Britain and Ireland - and the all-Europe title is under investigation.) Dimly-lit, with a mahogany bar, mirrored shelving, open fire and an enormous settle bed, the bar has become popular with the local student population and is very handy for visitors cruising the Shannon. The sloping floor is a particularly interesting feature, cleverly constructed to ensure that flood water drained back down to the river as the waters subsided. A glass case containing a section of old wattle wall original to the building highlights the age of the bar, but it's far from being a museum piece. Food is restricted to sandwiches (Mon-Sat), and they serve a good pint. Closed 25 Dec & Good Fri. **Directions:** On the west quayside, just in front of the castle.

Athlone Area
HOTEL

Glasson Golf Hotel
Glasson Athlone Co Westmeath **Tel: 090 648 5120**
info@glassongolf.ie www.glassongolf.ie

Beautifully situated in an elevated position over-looking Lough Ree, the Reid family's impressive hotel has been developed around their fine old family home; although the golfing dimension has earned an international reputation as one of Ireland's premier inland courses, the hotel is equally geared to business guests and non golfers, and it is a lovely place to stay. Bright and contemporary, with a welcoming atmosphere, it has spacious bedrooms, that are thoughtfully furnished and decorated in an attractive modern style, and have excellent views of the lough or over the golf course at the back. Both the bar and restaurant have been recently refurbished, and in these areas the style is warmly traditional. Conference/banqueting (100/130); free broadband wi/fi, secretarial services, video conferencing. Children welcome (under 5 free in parents' room, cots available without charge, baby sitting arranged). Walking, fishing. Garden. Pets by arrangement. **Rooms 65** (3 suites, 6 junior suites, 13 executive, 3 disabled, 25 ground floor, 15 family rooms, all no smoking). Lift. Room service (all day). B&B €100pps, ss€40. Special breaks offered. *Golf breaks are offered - details on application. Closed 25 Dec. Amex, Diners, MasterCard, Visa, Laser. **Directions:** 10km (6 miles) north of Athlone, off the N55 Cavan-Longford road.

Glasson
RESTAURANT
R

Glasson Village Restaurant
Glasson Co Westmeath **Tel: 090 648 5001**
michaelrosebrooks@gmail.com www.glassonvillagerestaurant.com

In an attractive stone building which formerly served as an RIC barracks, chef-proprietor Michael Brooks opened the Village Restaurant in 1986, making his mark as a culinary pioneer in the area, there's a real country atmosphere about the place, with a pleasant conservatory overlooking fields. The style is imaginative - traditional French meets modern Irish perhaps; unusually for the area (especially in 1986) fresh fish has always featured strongly, and wide ranging seasonal menus include treats like lobster and scallops - also other less usual dishes such as roast wild rabbit and game, in season, and there are always popular dishes like midland lamb and a couple of interesting vegetarian dishes. There is a true love of food which, together with caring service and good value, has earned a loyal following. A balanced and informative wine list includes seven house recommendations (€20-28) and nearly a dozen half bottles. Toilets wheelchair accessible. Parking (25). Children welcome. **Seats 60** (private room, 16). D Tue -Sat 6-9.30; L Sun only 12.30-2.30. Set D €40, also à la carte; early D €29 (Tue-Fri, 6-7pm). Set Sun L €25. House wines €20-28; SC discretionary. Closed D Sun, all Mon, 3 weeks mid Oct-early Nov, 3 days at Christmas. Amex, MasterCard, Visa, Laser. **Directions:** 8 km (5 miles) from Athlone on Longford/Cavan road (N55).

Glasson

PUB

R

Grogan's Pub
Glasson Co Westmeath
Tel: 090 648 5158

It's hard to cross the Midlands without being drawn into at least a short visit to this characterful pub in Goldsmith's "village of the roses". It's one of those proudly-run, traditional places with two little bars at the front (one with a welcome open fire in winter) and everything gleaming; it was established in 1750 and feels as if the fundamentals haven't changed too much since then. Good food is served in the back bar and, on Wednesday nights, there's traditional music when three generations of the same family play and visiting musicians are also welcome. Food served Mon-Sat 12.30-3.30 & 5-9, Sun 2-5 Closed 25 Dec, Good Fri. MasterCard, Visa, Laser. **Directions:** Centre of village.

Glasson

RESTAURANT WITH ROOMS

Wineport Lodge
Glasson Co Westmeath **Tel: 090 643 9010**
lodge@wineport.ie www.wineport.ie

Ray Byrne and Jane English's lovely lakeside lodge styles itself 'Ireland's first wine hotel' and the accommodation - which now offers nearly thirty beautiful rooms, hot tub and treatment rooms - is nothing less than stunning. A covered lakeside boardwalk leads to the front door: you enter your guest key card and step into a different world. A lofty residents lounge with a stove and its own bar simply oozes style and comfort, a hint of the high pamper quota waiting above in spacious suites and guest rooms, all with private balconies overlooking the lake. Superbly comfortable beds with goose down duvets and extra large pillows face the view, and seriously luxurious bathrooms have separate double-ended bath and walk-in shower. Wineport has a huge amount to offer discerning guests and has quickly become a hot choice for business and corporate events. Luxurious, romantic, beautiful, businesslike, this boutique hotel is a place of many moods: Wineport has everything. Ray and Jane were the Guide's Hosts of the Year in 1999, and Wineport was our Hideaway of the Year in 2003. Conference /banqueting 100/140. Free broadband wi/fi, laptop sized safes in bedrooms. Children welcome (under 2 free in parents room, cot available free of charge, baby sitting arranged). Walking; fishing; garden; jacuzzi; treatment rooms; relaxation room. No pets. Heli-pad. **Rooms 29** (5 suites, 8 junior suites, 3 superior, 2 family, 15 ground floor, 2 disabled, 2 shower only, all no smoking). B&B €97.50pps, ss €47.50; SC discretionary. Lift. Turndown service. All day room service. Closed 24-26 Dec. **Restaurant:** Wineport Lodge began life as a restaurant, and faithful fans continue to beat a path to the door at the slightest excuse, to be treated to a fine meal, served with warmth and professionalism in this lovely contemporary restaurant - and what a setting! Regular guests find the combination of the view, the company and a good meal irresistible, and many return bearing additions to the now famous Wineport collections (nauticalia, cats)... A new head chef Linda Martin, took over the kitchen shortly before the Guide went to press but, as she was previously sous chef at Wineport, a major change of style is unlikely; Wineport is known for well-balanced and strongly seasonal menus which are quite international in tone but based on Quality Assured and local ingredients including game in season, eels, home-grown herbs and wild mushrooms; a tasting plate of McGeough's cured & turf smoked charcuterie is an unusual starter, served with celeriac & spiced red cabbage roulade, and signature dishes include slow roast confit of lamb with creamy cannelloni beans, smoked garlic and sundried organic tomatoes. A lovely dessert menu is teamed with a list of pudding wines and a very informative cheese section offers seven ports, all offered by the glass even a Grahams 40 year Tawny, at €250 per bottle (glass, €27.50). An impressive and informative wine list charts a wine connection with the area going right back to 542AD, and makes very interesting reading; Jane English and wine consultant Tim Sacklin constantly make mprovements to the list, which offers special treats and many more affordable wines, and includes a good selection of wines by the glass and six well chosen half bottles. **Seats 100** (private room, 50; outdoor seating, 50). Toilets wheelchair accessible. Children welcome. Food service: Mon-Sat, 6-10pm; Sun 3-5pm & 6-10pm; set Sun L €45; set D €69, gourmet menu €90; otherwise à la carte; wines from about €25. Closed 24-26 Dec. Amex, Diners, MasterCard, Visa, Laser. **Directions:** Midway between Dublin and Galway: take the Longford/Cavan exit off the Athlone relief road; fork left after 2.5 miles at the Dog & Duck; 1 mile, on the left.

R ## KILBEGGAN

Kilbeggan is a handy place to break a journey across the country, and famous for its old distillery. Even if you do not wish to do the tour, **Locke's Distillery** (0506 32134) is a good place to stop for a civilised bite to eat in the café, which is open during the day.

WWW.IRELAND-GUIDE.COM FOR THE BEST PLACES TO EAT, DRINK & STAY

Moate
COUNTRY HOUSE/RESTAURANT
👑 **R**

Temple Country Retreat & Spa
Horseleap Moate Co Westmeath **Tel: 057 933 5118**
reservations@templespa.ie   www.templespa.ie

Declan and Bernadette Fagan's well known well-being retreat is on its own farmland in the unspoilt Westmeath countryside, where guests are welcome to walk close to peat bogs, lakes and historical sites, and outdoor activities such as walking, cycling and riding are all at hand. Wellbeing programmes and healthy eating have been available at Temple since 1987, but the magnificent new facility which opened some twenty years later has made it possible for many more people to enjoy and benefit from their philosophy of calm relaxation, which is unchanged and, despite the much larger scale of the operation, the essence of its origins in their charming and immaculately maintained 200 year-old farmhouse remains at its heart. Impressive spa facilities include18 treatment rooms with over 80 restorative treatments; a hydrotherapy pool, steam room, sauna and relaxation room; stress management and guided relaxation; yoga; personal training centre with fully equipped gym and on-site personal trainer. But Temple is not just a spa it also well equipped for business meetings, training programmes and seminars (up to 48 delegates), and you do not in fact need any special reason to come here: it is a lovely place to stay, with very comfortable accommodation, and there is no obligation to take part in activities. However, once there, casual guests tend to be drawn in to the spirit of the place, and many return as soon as possible to enrol in specific activities. An atmosphere of calm, good food, comfortable surroundings, gentle exercise and pampering therapies all contribute to a relaxing experience here - and the wide range of programmes offered include pampering weekends, 24 hour escape breaks, mother & daughter breaks, maternity breaks, and his & her weekends. Small Conferences/Banqueting (48/60). Destination Spa (hair dressing, massage, fitness room, treatment rooms, jacuzzi, sauna, steam room etc), garden, cycling, equestrian nearby. **Rooms 23** (all en-suite, 1 shower only, 1 junior suite, 1 suite, 1 for disabled, all no-smoking). B&B about €115 pps, ss €50. Spa Package about €235 pps, (min 2-night stay at weekends). Spa weekends from about €300 pps (ss about €40). **Garden Room Restaurant:** Temple is a member of the Health Farms of Ireland Association, which means that special attention is given to healthy eating guidelines, and vegetarian, vegan and other special diets are catered for. However, head chef Jamie Hagan has much more than healthy eating in mind when creating the wonderful menus which make this lovely contemporary restaurant a dining destination for non-residents, as well as an experience for spa or corporate guests to look forward to at the end of each day. Top quality ingredients, local and organic where possible - including lamb from the farm, garden vegetables, organic midland beef, cheese and yoghurts - are the sound foundation on which seriously tasty and beautifully presented meal are based. As one reader put it "The food was fantastic what impressed us most was that there were so many low fat options, and yet this was beautiful and substantial - 'real' food". It may seem strange to dine in a spa, but you would need to travel a very long way before finding a restaurant to match it. Organic wines. Not suitable for children. **Seats 55;** D Tue-Sat 7-8.30 & L Sun. 12.30-2. Reservations essential. Establishment closed Christmas. Amex, MasterCard, Visa, Laser. **Directions:** Signed off N6, 1.6km (1 m) west of Horseleap. ◇

R R

MULLINGAF

This thriving midland town that is encircled by the Royal Canal is really booming at the moment. Th town contains some early 19th century style architecture and is dominated by the cathedral, dedicate in 1939, and imposing renaissance-style structure. The attractive old town-centre hotel, the **Grevill Arms Hotel** (Tel 044 934 8563) continues to be the hub of local activities although, with the openin of both Mullingar Park Hotel and, more recently, the town centre Annebrook House Hotel (see entries the choice of facilities has grown dramatically of late which is good news for the growing number c city folk who find the town is a perfect short break destination. In the town centre, **Canton Casey's** pu is a place for those who appreciate traditional bars (at its best at quiet times - it can get very busy upstairs, over the bar, **Fat Cats Brasserie** (044 934 9969) offers informal dining. New restaurants including several ethnic ones - are opening all the time, so it's worth taking a browse around the towr Lovers of Indian food should check out **Saagar** (044 934 0911) which is near the Dublin Bridge an is the parent restaurant of the highly-regarded Saagar in Dublin (see entry). Mullingar is also know for the neighbouring lakes, Lough Owel and Lough Ennell, which attract many anglers, as well a Lough Derravaragh. Lough Derravaragh is best known for its connection with the Irish legend of th Children of Lir. Having been turned into swans, the four children of King Lir spent three hundred year on Lough Derravaragh before moving to other locations around Ireland. Nearby **Belvedere House an Gardens** (044 934 9060) is a lovely place to spend a few hours, while a testing round of golf is avail able in Mullingar Golf Club. It is also a great area for cycling.

WWW.IRELAND-GUIDE.COM FOR THE BEST PLACES TO EAT, DRINK & STAY

Mullingar
HOTEL
N R R

Annebrook House Hote

Pearse Street Mullingar Co Westmeath **Tel: 044 935 330**
info@annebrook.ie www.annebrook.i

If you haven't been to Mullingar for a while, this fine town centre hotel will be a pleasant surprise, jus off the main street and yet built around a beautiful old house situated elegantly in spacious surround ings, with the town park on the doorstep and the River Brosna flowing through the grounds - it's a distinctly fairytale. The original house has an interesting history, having been built around1810 as residence for the County Surgeon and, surprisingly perhaps, was still lived in as a family home for it original use until recently; however its most famous historical connection is with the author Mari Edgworth, who is said to have stayed here in the early 19th century. The old house is now used mainl for its impressive public rooms, including the atmospheric Brook Restaurant (good food and service lovely ambience), the Old House Bar, and also a very pleasant reading room and drawing room Accommodation is in the new part of the hotel, entered over a little bridge into reception, an bedrooms are very comfortably furnished in an easy modern style and soothing colours that won't dat too quickly. Certain to be popular for weddings and business/conferences, it's also an ideal destina tion for a weekend away. Staff are friendly and helpful and there's a welcome emphasis on service Conferences/Banqueting (300), free broadband wi/fi; Children welcome (cot available, baby sittin arranged); **Rooms 111** (2 suites, 26 executive, +36 apart-hotel suites, 1 disabled); B&B €75-95 pps ss €20-30. **Brook Restaurant:** D Tue-Sat,7-10 (early D 6-7). Brosna Bar: carvery L daily, à la carte ba meals every evening. Amex, MasterCard, Visa, Laser. **Directions:** On main street. ◇

Mullingar
RESTAURANT
R R

The Belfry Restaurant

Ballynegall Mullingar Co Westmeath **Tel: 044 934 248**
belfryrestaurant@eircom.net www.belfryrestaurant.cor

féile bia The tall spire will lead you to this unusual restaurant in a magnificently converted churc near Mullingar. The design is brilliant, with (excellent) toilets near the entrance, perfect fc a quick freshen up before heading up thickly carpeted stairs to a mezzanine lounge which is luxuri ously furnished. A second staircase descends to the dining area, which is very striking and extremel atmospheric, especially when seen in candlelight, with background music from the grand piano wher the altar used to be. Everything has been done to the very highest specifications, colours schemes ar subtle and elegant - and the whole set-up is highly atmospheric. Head chef Damian Martin and fror of house manager and sommelier Florence Servieres, have been operating The Belfry since 2005 an have a well-deserved reputation well beyond the immediate area for their modern classical cooking an warm, professional and efficient service. Damian offers well-priced lunch and early dinner menus, an a more sophisticated à la carte; he is not afraid to have traditional dishes like oxtail, confit of bell pork or braised lamb neck on menus - and of course this is beef country, so offering tip top qualit roast beef with Yorkshire pudding for Sunday lunch is a must. This down to earth quality in the cookin has won friends for the restaurant - and he has succeeded admirably in balancing the demand fo generous portions with the requirements of the fine dining guest. Florence is responsible for the wine list, which offers both treats and some interesting middle range bottles. Catering offered for private parties, small weddings (up to 75); private room for meetings. Cookery classes are offered - call the restaurant for details. **Seats 65** (private room 20); air conditioning; children welcome. D Wed-Sat, 6-9 (to 9.30 Fri-Sat); L Wed-Sat 12.30-2; Sun L only, 1-3.30. Early D about €28.50 (6-7.30pm), otherwise D à la carte, Set Sun L about €30; house wine from €21. SC 10% on groups 6+. Closed Mon,Tue & may close for 2 weeks in Jan. MasterCard, Visa, Laser. **Directions:** Castlepollard road, off the Mullingar bypass. ◊

Mullingar

Gallery 29 Café

CAFÉ   16 Oliver Plunkett St Mullingar Co Westmeath   **Tel: 044 934 9449**

R R   corbetstown@eircom.net

Ann & Emily Gray's smart, black-painted, traditionally-fronted premises is really bright and welcoming - and the buzz of an open kitchen and beautiful freshly cooked food on display draws people in. They're great bakers and, although there's much more on offer than that, their food reflects that interest - freshly baked breads, scones, muffins, baked puddings, tarts and gateaux are all on display. Good soups, salads, savoury tart of the day "tailor-made" sandwiches, fashionable focaccia with every imaginable filling and hot main courses, like oven-baked salmon with sweet chilli sauce, champ & salad and steak sandwich on ciabatta, with spicy salsa & mixed salad. It's a good place for any time of day, including breakfast (with freshly squeezed juice) and afternoon tea; it's very popular and often busy, but well-trained staff seem well able to cope. Outside catering, picnics and freshly made dishes for home freezing are also offered. **Seats 50.** Children welcome. Open Mon-Sat 9.30am-5.30pm (late opening with a bistro menu Thu-Fri evenings). All a la carte. Wine licence. Closed Sun, Christmas/New Year. **No Credit Cards. Directions:** From Dublin through traffic lights at Market Square in town centre. About 60m on right hand side. ◊

Mullingar

Ilia A Coffee Experience

CAFÉ   28 Oliver Plunkett Street Mullingar Co Westmeath   **Tel: 044 934 0300**

R R   juliekenny@eircom.net

féile bia   Julie Kenny's delightful 2-storey coffee house and informal restaurant in the centre of Mullingar is attractively set up - the first floor area is particularly pleasing, with a seating area of sofas, low tables and plants at the top of the stairs setting a relaxed tone. The rest is more conventionally furnished in café style - and a more comfortable height for eating a real meal. Menus cater for all the changing moods though the day, beginning with an extensive breakfast, including the full traditional, then there are the mid-day bites like home-made soup, panini, steak baguettes, and much more. More predictably, there's a nice little drinks menu offering everything from big glasses of freshly squeezed orange juice through iced teas, smoothies, teas - and, of course, coffees (Java Republic), any way you like, including flavoured coffees. Everything is deliciously fresh and wholesome, staff are charming and efficient, with reasonable prices. Takeaway also available. Wine licence. ****"Ilia Gourmet"** specialist food store (and hampers and outside catering) is across the road. **Seats 60.** Children welcome. Toilets wheelchair accessible. Air conditioning. Open Mon-Sat 9am-6pm. Closed Sun, Christmas & bank hols. Amex, MasterCard, Visa, Laser. **Directions:** Centre of Town. ◊

Mullingar

Mullingar Park Hotel

HOTEL   Dublin Road Mullingar Co Westmeath   **Tel: 044 934 4446**

R R   info@mullingarparkhotel.com   www.mullingarparkhotel.com

This large hotel on the Dublin side of Mullingar brought quality accommodation and welcome facilities to the town when it opened in 2002 - and it makes a very convenient journey break when travelling across the country. Although not especially appealing from the road, it is a spacious and friendly place - and has an unexpectedly pleasant outlook at the back, where the bar and conference areas open on to a large and sheltered courtyard style garden, well away from the road. The Hotel's Terrace Restaurant attracts diners from the town and beyond; pleasingly simply worded menus offer mainly classic dishes on a well-priced set dinner (€42.50) and a sensibly short à la carte. Conference/banqueting (1000/700); secretarial services, video conferencing, free broadband wi/fi. Children welcome (under 2s free in parents' room, cot available without charge, baby sitting arranged). No pets. Garden, walking; leisure centre, swimming pool, spa, beauty salon. **Rooms 95** (1 junior suites, 2 disabled, 67 no smoking). 24 hr room service. B&B €100 pps, ss €30, no SC.*Short breaks offered. Restaurant open daily: B'fst 7.30-10.30; L 12.30-2.30; D 6-10pm. Bar meals available 12-6 daily. Amex, Diners, MasterCard, Visa, Laser. **Directions:** Off the N4 - take exit no. 9.

Mullingar
RESTAURANT

R **R**

Oscars Restaurant

21 Oliver Plunkett Street Mullingar Co Westmeath
Tel: 044 934 4909

This smartly painted centrally located restaurant is extremely popular locally, pleasing people of all ages with its lively atmosphere and mix of traditional and contemporary favourites at reasonable prices. This is beef country, so a section of the menu given over to steaks should come as no surprise, but there's much else besides, ranging from '80s' classics like deep-fried mushrooms with garlic & cucumber dip, through spicy chicken wings to simple smoked salmon. Main courses include steaks various ways, honey glazed lamb shanks, chicken Oscars style and crispy Silver Hill duckling. Pastas and pizzas too - this is popular food, well executed at fair prices - and with cheerfully efficient service to match. Oscars offers an affordable outing with something for everyone, and wines (from an accessible and informative list, with details on grape varieties as well as a well-balanced selection) starting at under €20. **Seats 70.** Air conditioning. D daily, 6-9.30 (to 10 Fri/Sat, to 8.15 Sun), L Sun only, 12.30-2.15. A la carte D. Set Sun L about €25. House wine €18.50. Closed 25/26 Dec, first 2 weeks Jan. MasterCard, Visa, Laser. **Directions:** Centre of town opposite town mall.

Mullingar Area
PUB

R **R**

Mary Lynch's Pub

MacNead's Bridge Coralstown Nr. Mullingar Co Westmeath
Tel: 044 937 4501

John and Mary Moriarty's charming old-world pub a short distance east of Mullingar is tucked between the N4 and the Royal Canal, with a grandstand view of the new harbour works from the back of the bar. A blackboard menu offers traditional home-cooked dishes like soup of the day, fish pie, roast of the day and steak sandwiches, and there's likely to be live music at weekends too. It's a popular destination for locals, and a useful place for travellers to know about. Meals from noon daily. **Directions:** Between the N4 and the canal.

Multyfarnham
COUNTRY HOUSE

👑 👁 **R** **R**

Mornington House

Mornington Multyfarnham Co Westmeath **Tel: 044 937 2191**
stay@mornington.ie www.mornington.ie

Warwick and Anne O'Hara's gracious Victorian house is surrounded by mature trees and is just a meadow's walk away from Lough Derravarragh where the mythical Children of Lir spent 300 years of their 900 year exile - the lough is now occupied by a pleasing population of brown trout, pike, eels and other coarse fish. This has been the O'Hara family home since 1858, and is still furnished with much of the original furniture and family portraits - and, although centrally heated, log fires remain an essential feature. Bedrooms are typical of this kind of country house - spacious and well-appointed, with old furniture (three have brass beds) but with comfortable modern mattresses. Anne is well-known for her skills in the kitchen, and cooks proper country breakfasts and country house dinners for residents, using fresh fruit and vegetables from the walled garden and local produce (Westmeath beef cooked in Guinness is a speciality), while Warwick does the honours front-of-house. There is a wealth of wildlife around the house, and there are gardens and archaeological sites to visit nearby - this is a tranquil and restorative place for a short break. Pets allowed by arrangement. Garden, croquet; fishing, canoes, boats & bicycles can be hired. Equestrian: trekking & a cross-country course nearby. Golf nearby. Children welcome (under 3s free in parents' room, cot available without charge). **Rooms 5** (4 en-suite, 1 with private bathroom, 2 shower only, 1 family room, all no smoking). Turndown service. B&B €75 pps, ss €20. Set residents D €45, at 8pm (book by 2pm). House wine about €16. *Short breaks offered: 3-day stay (3 DB&B) from €275pps. Closed Nov-Mar. Amex, Diners, MasterCard, Visa, Laser. **Directions:** Exit N4 for Castlepollard.

COUNTY WEXFORD

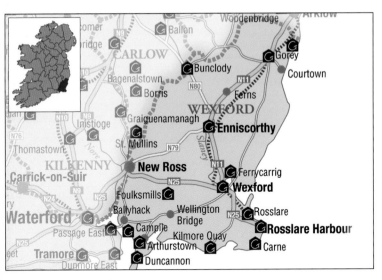

The popular view of Wexford is beaches, sunshine and opera. The longest continuous beach in all Ireland runs along the county's east coast, an astonishing 27 kilometres from Cahore Point south to Raven Point, which marks the northern side of the entrance to Wexford town's shallow harbour. As for sunshine, while areas further north along the east coast may record marginally less rainfall, in the very maritime climate of the "Sunny Southeast" around Wexford, the clouds seem to clear more quickly, so the chances of seeing the elusive orb are much improved.

And opera.....? Well, the annual Wexford Opera Festival (2007's was in June) is a byword for entertaining eccentricity - as international enthusiasts put it, "we go to Wexford town to enjoy operas written by people we've never heard of, and we have ourselves a thoroughly good time."

But there's much more to this intriguing county than sun, sand and singing. Wexford itself is but one of three substantial towns in it, the other two being the market town of Enniscorthy, and the river port of New Ross. While much of the county is relatively low-lying, to the northwest it rises towards the handsome Blackstairs Mountains. There, the 793m peak of Mount Leinster may be just over the boundary in Carlow, but one of the most attractive little hill towns in all Ireland, Bunclody, is most definitely in Wexford.

In the north of the county, Gorey is a pleasant and prosperous place, while connoisseurs of coastlines will find the entire south coast of Wexford a fascinating area of living history, shellfish-filled shallow estuaries, and an excellent little harbour at the much-thatched village of Kilmore Quay inside the Saltee Islands.

Round the corner beyond the intriguing Hook Head, the peninsula marked by Ireland's oldest lighthouse, Wexford County faces west across its own shoreline along the beauties of Waterford estuary. Here, there's another fine beach, at Duncannon, while nearby other sheltered little ports of west Wexford - Arthurstown and Ballyhack - move at their own sweet and gentle pace.

In New Ross, the authentic re-creation of a 19th Century emigrant ship - the impressive Dunbrody - is proving to be a very effective focal point for the revival of the picturesque waterfront. It's a fitting place for the lovely River Barrow to meet ships in from sea in an area with strong historical links to President John F Kennedy – his great-grandparents sailed from New Ross to America on the original Dunbrody.

Local Attractions & Information

Ballygarrett Shrule Deer Farm	053 942 7277
Ballyhack Ballyhack Castle	051 389 468
Campile Kilmokea Gardens	051 388 109

Georgina Campbell's Ireland

Dunbrody Abbey & Visitor Centre	051 388 603
Duncannon Duncannon Fort	051 388 603
Enniscorthy National 1798 Visitor Centre	053 923 7596
Enniscorthy Tourism Information	053 923 4699
Enniscorthy Wexford County Museum	053 924 6506
Ferrycarrig National Heritage Park	053 912 0733
Gorey (Coolgreany) Ram House Gardens	0402 37 238
Hook Head Hook Head Lighthouse	051 397 055
Johnstown Castle Demesne & Agricultural Museum	053 914 2888
Kilmore Quay Saltee Island Ferries	053 912 9684
New Ross Dunbrody - re-creation of 19th C ship	051 425 239
New Ross Galley River Cruises	051 421 723
New Ross John F Kennedy Arboretum	051 388 171
New Ross John F Kennedy Homestead, Dunganstown	051 388 264
New Ross Tourism Information	051 421 857
Rosslare Ferry Terminal	053 916 1560
Tintern Abbey (nr Saltmills)	051 562 650
Wexford North Slobs Wildfowl Reserve	053 912 3406
Wexford Opera Festival (October)	053 912 2400
Wexford Tourism Information	053 912 3111

Arthurstown
HOTEL/RESTAURANT

Dunbrody Country House Hotel & Cookery School

Arthurstown Co Wexford **Tel: 051 389 600**
dunbrody@indigo.ie www.dunbrodyhouse.com

Set in twenty acres of parkland and gardens on the Hook Peninsula, just across the estuary from Waterford city, Catherine and Kevin Dundon's elegant Georgian manor was the ancestral home of the Chichester family and the long tradition of hospitality at this tranquil and luxurious retreat is very much alive and well. Well-proportioned public rooms, which include an impressive entrance hall and gracious drawing room, are all beautifully furnished and decorated with stunning flower arrangements and the occasional unexpectedly modern piece that brings life to a fine collection of antiques. Spacious bedrooms, including those in a newer wing which blends perfectly with the original building, generally have superb bathrooms and offer all the comforts expected of such a house - and fine views over the gardens. Converted outbuildings house what must be Ireland's most stylish cookery school and, alongside it, a beautiful spa. An outstanding breakfast offers a magnificent buffet - fresh juices, fruit compotes, cheeses - as well as hot dishes from a tempting menu - and was the national winner of our Irish Breakfast Awards in 2004. While Dunbrody provides a wonderfully relaxing place for a leisure break, they also cater for business meetings, small conferences, product launches and incentive programmes (full details available on request). Conference/banqueting (30/110). Secretarial services; video conferencing. Cookery school. Spa & beauty salon. Garden, walking. Children welcome (under 5s free in parents' room; cot available without charge, baby sitting arranged). No pets. **Rooms 22** (7 suites, 7 junior suites, 7 superior). B&B about €125 pps; ss €25. *A range of special breaks is offered (weekend, midweek, cookery, New Year); details on application. Open all year except Christmas. **The Harvest Room at Dunbrody:** The restaurant looks out on to a pleasure garden and, beyond, to a promisingly productive organic vegetable and fruit garden. The dining room is a lovely well-proportioned room, with an open fire in winter and stunning flower arrangements all the time; it presents a striking blend of classic and contemporary style. Likewise, Kevin Dundon and his head chef, Gary Bourke, offer tempting a la carte and set menus that combine classical and international influences with local produce and Irish themes - and suppliers are given full credit: fresh fish is delivered daily from nearby Duncannon harbour, and shellfish from Kilmore Quay, and meats are supplied by Wallace's butchers, of Wellington Bridge - and organic fruit, vegetables and herbs are, as far as possible, home grown. Starters - which tend to showcase some unusual ingredients and to be pretty and light - might include a lovely Wexford strawberry salad with a peppered Blackwater cheese basket: a perfect summer first course. Seafood dishes tend to the contemporary, as in Dublin Bay prawns with mead salsa, and Kevin Dundon's 'eat local' philosophy comes through on all his menus, and local meats like rack of Wexford lamb often top the bill - in a terrific house speciality, Roast Rack of Lamb with an Irish Stew Consommé, for example, which is a modern twist on a very traditional theme. And meals at Dunbrody always end on a high note so make sure you save a little space for a spectacular dessert... Catherine leads a well-trained and efficient dining room staff with the charm and panache that typifies all aspects of the hospitality at this exceptional country house. An informative wine list which leans towards the classics includes a nice selection of half bottles and wines by the glass. The early dinner menu and Sunday lunch offer particularly good value. [Kevin Dundon's cookery book, 'Full On Irish', features many of the dishes from the restaurant and cookery school at Dunbrody.] *Constant improvement is the on-going quest at Dunbrody, where the most recent change is the introduction of the new all-day **Dundon's Champagne & Seafood Bar**, a stylish contemporary area with a temperature controlled wine cellar and another drawing room off it, and a lovely outside eating area under a white canopy. A smart menu offers 16 items, all served in starter-sized portions, plus desserts and cheese; the food is delicious and served with the usual Dundon style: Hook Head smokies come with grilled bread; fish and skinny chips, are tartare sauce and a pea shot and a trilogy of panna-cotta is also served in large shot glasses. Introducing this stylish, casual food at reasonable prices is a great move and will introduce many new guests to this lovely house. **Harvest Room Seats 70** (private room, 18). Reservations required. Toilets wheelchair accessible. D Mon-Sat 6.30-9.15. L Sun only 1.30-2.30. Set D €48/€60; 'Full On Irish' Tasting Menu about €75, changes daily, offered with or without matching wines. House wines from €21. SC discretionary. Not suitable for children after 8pm. Closed 22-26 Dec. Amex, Diners, MasterCard, Visa, Laser. **Directions:** N11 to Wexford, R733 from Wexford to Arthurstown. ◇◈

Arthurstown

FARMHOUSE/B&B

🛏️ 🍴 € 👁️ 🌿

Glendine Country House

Arthurstown New Ross Co Wexford **Tel: 051 389 500**
glendinehouse@eircom.net www.glendinehouse.com

Ann and Tom Crosbie's large nineteenth century farmhouse is approached up a driveway off the main road to Arthurstown, and has magnificent views across the estuary. It is a spacious house and makes a very comfortable and hospitable place to stay at a reasonable price; it would be ideal for a family holiday as there are sandy beaches nearby and there's a safe, enclosed playground for children beside the house - and they also enjoy the highland cows, Jacob sheep and horses which the Crosbies keep in paddocks around the house. A pleasant guest drawing room has plenty of comfortable seating with excellent views down to the harbour and across the estuary, and the immaculately maintained bedrooms are very large, as are the en-suite bathrooms. Guest rooms are of two types: the newer ones are, bright and individually decorated in quite a contemporary style, with smart bathrooms; the original rooms are more traditional, with a cosy atmosphere, and all nine rooms have sea views. Service at Glendine House is a priority; the Crosbies take pride in giving their guests personal attention and lots of advice on local amenities and a full dinner menu, with a choice of three dishes on each course, is offered on some nights; this includes local seafood, of course - but also, in true farmhouse tradition, their own lamb and beef, eggs and vegetables. And the Crosbies also believe in sending everyone off well-fed for the day after a really good breakfast that offers home-baked breads, fresh and cooked fruits, organic porridge and a range of hot dishes include smoked salmon & scrambled eggs and French toast as well as the full Irish. *Glendine House was our Farmhouse of the Year in 2006. Free broadband wi/fi. Children welcome (under 1s free in parents room, cot available, baby sitting arranged; children's playground), but not in dining room after 8.30pm. Pets allowed by arrangement. Equestrian, fishing & golf all nearby. Garden, walking. **Rooms 6** (1 suite, 2 family rooms, all no smoking; turndown service offered; B&B €65 pps, ss €15. Room service (limited hours). Light meals (soup & home-baked bread, open sandwiches) available all day. *Off-season breaks offered. 2 self-catering cottages are also available - details on application. Closed at Christmas. MasterCard, Visa, Laser. **Directions:** From Wexford, turn right before Talbot Hotel, on to R733; 35km (22 m) to Arthurstown; entrance on right before village.

Arthurstown
B&B

Marsh Mere Lodge

Arthurstown New Ross Co Wexford **Tel: 051 389 186**
sta@marshmerelodge.com www.marshmerelodge.com

The McNamaras' friendly almost-waterside bed and breakfast is beautifully located just outside Arthurstown and has lovely views out toward the Hook Head lighthouse. When you see the sign beside the car parking spaces that fresh eggs are for sale - and you see the chickens running around the yard - you know that you are in for something special, so just enjoy Maria Mc Namara's warm welcome and let yourself relax in this beautiful part of Wexford. There's a cosy and relaxing sitting room, with DVDs and books for guests' use; the spacious, individually decorated en-suite rooms are very comfortably furnished, and you'll get a lovely breakfast too. Marsh Mere complements other accommodation in the area and, as some rooms are suitable for families, this warm and welcoming place would make a relaxing base for a family break. Children welcome. Garden. Pets permitted. **Rooms 4** (all en-suite). B&B about €40 pps; family rooms from about €90. **Directions:** from Wexford, R733 to Arthurstown via Wellingtonbridge; from Waterford, take Passage East-Ballyhack car ferry - coming off ferry turn right. House 1 km om left. ◇

Bunclody
HOTEL

Carlton Millrace Hotel

Carrigduff Bunclody Co Wexford **Tel: 053 937 5100**
info@millrace.ie www.millrace.ie

N **R**

téite bia The picturesque town of Bunclody is set in wonderful rolling countryside on the edge of the Hall-Dare estate, with magnificent parkland and riverside walks along the River Slaney. Ideally located for a break to explore this beautiful area, Bunclody is not much more than an hour's drive from either Dublin or Rosslare. This large hotel offers a wide range of facilities and, despite its size, is tucked quite neatly into a wooded site and does not dominate the village too much. Individually furnished guest rooms, suites and family apartments are spacious and comfortably furnished for leisure and business guests, and there are full spa facilities. A modern bar on the ground floor attracts local people as well as guests, and there is an impressive restaurant at the top of the building, which overlooks the town and opens on to a balcony - very pleasant on a summer evening, and handy for smokers. There's salmon fishing on site, walking in parkland and the nearby hills, and a number of championship golf courses are within an hours drive. Business facilities. Spa. **Rooms 60.** B&B from €70. Midweek specials from €129 (3 nights). Closed 24-27 Dec. MasterCard, Visa. **Directions:** On the N80 between Carlow and Enniscorthy. ◇

Campile
COUNTRY HOUSE/CAFÉ

Kilmokea Country Manor & Gardens

Great Island Campile Co Wexford **Tel: 051 388 109**
kilmokea@eircom.net www.kilmokea.com

Mark and Emma Hewlett's peaceful and relaxing late Georgian country house is set in 7 acres of Heritage Gardens, including formal walled gardens. The house is elegantly and comfortably furnished, with a drawing room overlooking the Italian Loggia, an honesty library bar, and a restaurant in the dining room. The individually-designed and immaculately maintained bedrooms command lovely views over the gardens and towards the estuary beyond and in an adjoining coach house there are newer rooms and self-catering suites, with some offering a contemporary atmosphere. Mark and Emma continue with their ongoing programme of improvements to the property - there is now a tennis court and an indoor swimming pool, plus a gym and aromatherapy treatment rooms. And work continues on a large organic vegetable garden, planted in the old potager design. Conferences/banqueting (60/55). Children welcome (under 2s free in parents' room, cots available without charge; baby sitting arranged, playground, high chair, childrens menu). Pets allowed in some areas by arrangement. Gardens, fishing, tennis, croquet, walking; swimming pool, gym, mini-spa, aromatherapy. **Rooms 6** (5 en-suite, 1 with private bathroom; 1 suite, 1 junior suite, 1 shower only, 2 ground floor, 1 family room, 1 disabled, all no smoking). B&B €95 pps; ss €30. Self-catering also available. Light meals in conservatory Pink Teacup Café, 12-3 daily when house and gardens are open; gift shop. Open weekends only 5 Nov- 1 Feb. **Peacock Dining Room:** The dining room overlooks the lovely gardens at the back, and is a delightful place. Emma looks after the cooking herself at present, and the emphasis is on organic and home-made fare. There is also n unusually extensive wine list, including some real treats. **Seats 24** (private room, 14). Reservations equired (non-residents welcome). Children welcome. Toilets wheelchair accessible. D daily, 7-9.15; Light meals in conservatory Pink Teacup Café, 12-3 daily when house and gardens are open; gift shop. A la carte. House wines from about €24.95. Amex, MasterCard, Visa, Laser. **Directions:** Take R733 outh from New Ross to Ballyhack, signposted for Kilmokea Gardens.

Campile
RESTAURANT

The Shelburne
Campile New Ross Co Wexford
Tel: 051 388 996

féile bía Chef Denise Bradley already well known in the area from her time as head chef at Sqigl in Duncannon has taken over this neat restaurant in Campile village, and is pleasing her loyal ollowing with its hospitable atmosphere and good cooking. It's a simple enough place: a rectangular room broken up by low room dividers has a little bar, tiled floor, white tablecloths and napkins, night-ghts and plain good quality cutlery and glasses; but there's a speedy greeting on arrival, excellent breads served with pesto and a welcoming amuse-bouche of salmon & potato cake. Quite an exten-sive and wide ranging menu is offered and, of course the seafood for which the area is well known is well respresented; and the fish dishes are especially attractive a dish of pan-fried Duncannon sea bass with fennel, in a crisp parmesan cheese crust with an aniseed cream sauce attracted special praise on the Guide's visit - there is plenty else to choose from including good steaks, tasty stuffed pork fillet, guinea fowl and duck. Presentation, on modern white plates of various shapes, is attractive but portions are generous so remember to save a little space for dessert summer berry pudding, perhaps, or a very good chocolate fondant and there are petits fours with the coffee too. **Seats 40** (private room 20). Reservations advised. Childen welcome. Air conditioning. Toilets wheelchair accessible. D Tue-Sun, 6-9.30, L Sun only 12-2.30. A la carte. House wine about €18. MasterCard, Visa, Laser. **Directions:** In centre of Campile.

Carne
CHARACTER PUB/RESTAURANT

The Lobster Pot
Ballyfane Carne Co Wexford
Tel: 053 913 1110

Near Carnsore Point and just over 5 miles from Rosslare ferry port, Ciaran and Anne Hearne's good-looking country pub in elegant dark green with lots of well-maintained plants is a welcome sight indeed. Inside the long, low building several interconnecting bar areas are furnished in simple, practical style, with sturdy furniture designed for comfortable eating. For fine summer days there are picnic tables outside at the front. One room is a slightly more formal restaurant, but the atmosphere throughout is very relaxed and the emphasis is on putting local seafood to good use, providing good value and efficient service. Daily deliveries ensure fresh fish supplies and, the catch dictates daily specials. Simple but carefully prepared meals are served all day in the bar, typically including an outstanding seafood chowder (salmon, crab, prawns, cod, cockles & mussels in a rich fish base), a wild Irish smoked salmon platter and delicious fresh crab salad. An extensive laminated evening menu (with the names of 21 fish listed in eight different languages) offers treats like River Rush oysters and lobsters from the sea tank, crab mornay and, for non-seafood lovers, crispy duckling and various steaks, pork fillet and ever-popular rack of lamb. Friendly service, a relaxing atmosphere and carefully prepared fresh food should ensure an enjoyable visit here - and, on Wednesday nights off-season (Sep-May), a special dinner menu offers great value. No reservations in high season (Jun-Aug) or bank hol week-ends, so avoid busy times if possible. **Seats 100** (private rooms 16/28; outdoor seating, 20). Children welcome, but not under 10 after 5pm. Bar menu Tue-Sat, 12-9 (to 8.30 Sun, 7.30 off-season). A la carte menu 6-9 (to 8.30 Sun, 7.30 off-season). Closed Mon except bank hols, 25 Dec, first 5 weeks of the year. Good Fri. MasterCard, Visa, Laser. **Directions:** 8 km (5 miles) south of Rosslare port; follow route to Carnsore Point.

Duncannon
RESTAURANT WITH ROOMS

Aldridge Lodge

Duncannon New Ross Co Wexford **Tel: 051 38911**
info@aldridgelodge.com www.aldridgelodge.com

féile bia Euro-Toques chef Billy Whitty and his partner Joanne Harding's modern stone fronted dormer home overlooks the picturesque fishing village of Duncannon, with lovely views of the beach and mountains - and has earned a reputation for excellence in fine modern Irish cooking. The restaurant is bright and airy, with patio doors out on to a deck area, tables smartly set up with white linen runners and comfortable high backed leather chairs. Billy's fine training shows through in the many delightful dishes on dinner menus which are changed daily and offer six or eight appealing dishes on each course, including steak, poultry and some imaginative vegetarian options, although the emphasis is on seafood. First class ingredients are cooked with skill - a moist, flavourful and deliciously crumbly Hook Head crab cake could make a wonderful starter, for example, and lobster is a treat of a main course, perfectly baked and served with lemon & saffron butter sauce. Soups, breads and side vegetables are all lovely, and a tasting plate of half a dozen desserts rounds off a meal here nicely. The wine list is sensibly limited and offers good value. **Seats 32** (+12 outdoors;private room, 14). Reservations required. Children welcome before 7pm. D daily in summer, 6-9.30 (to 9pm Sun). Set D €35; à la carte; vegetarian menu also available. SC discretionary. Closed Mon (& Tues Sept-Jun), 24-28 Dec, 3 Jan-8 Feb. **Accommodation:** Three well appointed bedrooms (one with full bath and shower, the others with shower only) are quiet and comfortable, with a residents lounge area on the landing. *Aldride Lodge was our Newcomer of the Year in 2006. Not suitable for children under 7. Small conferences/banquets (30/34). **Rooms 3** (all en-suite, 2 shower only, 1 junior suite, all no smoking, 1 family room). Turndown service. Pets allowed by arrangement. Garden. B&B €50 pps, no ss. Closed Mon (& Tues Sept-Jun), 24-28 Dec, 3 Jan-8 Feb. MasterCard, Visa, Laser. **Directions:** 1/4 mile outside Duncannon, overlooking beach on Fethard on-Sea road.

Duncannon
RESTAURANT

Sqigl Restaurant & Roches Bar

Quay Road Duncannon New Ross Co Wexford **Tel: 051 389 18**
sqiglrestaurant@eircom.net www.rochesbar.com

féile bia Bob and Eileen Roche's fine traditional bar in the centre of Duncannon village serves the local community (and discerning visitors) well. There's an old bar at the front, pleasingly free of improvements, and it gradually develops more towards the back which keeps the younger crowd and the oldies in their preferred spaces. The bar food menu offers a selection of hot dishes, salads and sandwiches, plus some daily specials, including traditional chowder and panini. There is something for everyone - and if the weather is fine, you can now enjoy out in the beer garden. Bar Food served 12.30-6 daily (to 7 Sun). Pub closed 25 Dec, Good Fri, 3-4 weeks Jan. **Restaurant: Sqigl** (pronounced Squiggle) is located in a converted barn beside the pub and is run by Bob and Eileen's daughter Cindy Roche supported by head chef Aidan Kelly, who joined the team in 200 and is cooking very interesting dishes with confidence - his fish dishes, especially, are well cooked, flavoursome and nicely presented and local seafood is the star: a very good dish of the Guide's visit was fillet of John Dory with roasted garlic risotto, crisp pancetta and a beurre noisette. Sqigl aims to make the most of local produce and does it well with a sensibly limited menu, not only with the white fish landed at the harbour round the corner, but also Wexford beef and lamb. Decor is light, bright and modern and the cooking style is modern too, except that portions are aimed at generous Wexford appetites: cream South-East seafood chowder, for example, makes a fine substantial starter. A set dinner at €45 offers good value, including a glass of sparkling wine and canapés and tea or coffee with petits fours, as well a choice of about half a dozen dishes on each course and dishes are priced individually too, so you don't have to have the full dinner. Well-made classic desserts will round off a good meal nicely, and good cooking, good service from a friendly and efficient front of house team under Cindy's supervision

nd good value for money make for a very attractive package. The wine list is due to be changed at
he time of going to press. **Seats 36** (outside seating, 12). Reservations advised. D Tue-Sat, 7-9.30;
ouse wines from €15. Restaurant closed Sun (except bank hol Suns), Mon (& Tue off-season), 24-
7 Dec & 3-4 weeks in Jan. MasterCard, Visa, Laser. **Directions:** R733 from Wexford & New Ross.
entre of village.

ENNISCORTHY

he aptly named **Riverside Park Hotel** (Tel 053 92 37800; www.riversideparkhotel.com) has a
easant riverside path in a linear park beside the hotel, this can be a useful place to break a journey
● stretch the legs and have a bite. If you enjoy finding an unusual place to stay, **Woodbrook** (053 925
114) is a large late Georgian house a few miles from Enniscorthy which is open for guests in the
ummer months; set in its own parkland under the Blackstairs Mountains, it is owned by the
tzHerbert family and has a spectacular 'flying' spiral staircase.
WW-IRELAND-GUIDE.COM FOR THE BEST PLACES TO EAT, DRINK & STAY

---

nniscorthy
OUNTRY HOUSE

Ballinkeele House

Ballymurn Enniscorthy Co Wexford **Tel: 053 913 8105**
john@ballinkeele.com www.ballinkeele.com

Set in 350 acres of parkland, game-filled woods and farmland, this historic house is a listed building; designed by Daniel Robertson, it has been the Maher family home since it was built in 1840 and remains at the centre of their working farm. It is a grand house, with a lovely old cut stone stable yard at the back and some wonderful features, including a lofty columned hall with a big open fire in the colder months, and beautifully proportioned reception rooms with fine ceilings and furnishings which have changed very little
nce the house was built. Nevertheless, it is essentially a family home and has a refreshingly
ospitable and down-to-earth atmosphere. Large bedrooms are furnished with antiques and have
onderful countryside views - all are large and comfortably furnished but one has been upgraded to a
ore luxurious standard, and now has a bath and shower. Margaret, who is a keen cook and a member
f Euro-Toques, enjoys preparing 4-course dinners for guests (nice little wine list to accompany too).
here's croquet on the lawn, a long sandy beach nearby at Curracloe, and bicycles (and wellingtons!)
e available for guests' use; horse riding, fishing and golf can be organised nearby - and work
ontinues in the leisure grounds, including a lake that is to be stocked for coarse fishing. Garden.
hildren welcome (cot available, €15). No pets. **Rooms 5** (all en-suite, 2 shower only, all no smoking).
&B €85 pps; ss €20. Residents Set D €45 at 7.30 (book by 11am); house wine from €19.50.
rivate parties up to 14. Closed 1 Nov-28 Feb. MasterCard, Visa, Laser. **Directions:** From Wexford
11, north to Oilgate Village, turn right at signpost.

---

nniscorthy
ESTAURANT

Via Veneto

58 Weafer Street Enniscorthy Co Wexford **Tel: 053 923 6929**
viavenetoristorante@hotmail.com

Just off the main square in Enniscorthy, you'll encounter the unexpected - an authentic Italian restaurant, run by Paolo Fresilli, who is President of the Irish Delegation of the Italian Chefs' Federation, no less. It's buzzy and homely Italian in style, with the ingredients they prize, wines and Italian liqueurs all on shelves open to view; the welcome is warm and efficient, white clothed tables are simply laid and a generous basket of good bread is left on the table throughout the meal, along with two carafes of home-flavoured olive oils
● dress your salad to taste. As you'd expect, the menu is divided into antipasti, pasta, main dishes,
zza, and also an intriguing page of house specials for all courses all written in Italian, with accurate
escriptions in English; you'll find dishes here that rarely feature on Irish/Italian menus, and top

quality Italian cheese, salami, cured hams and other speciality foods feature. With seating for over 60 it's broken up into 3 areas by a central bar and semi-open kitchen. This is a hive of good humoured activity and the three chefs cook everything to order. Dishes are prepared and served Italian style, without fussy presentation a salami selection with marinated olives comes simply but stylishly on wooden platter, for example and the emphasis is on good cooking and real flavour; gnocchi comes with delicious gorgonzola cheese, sage & cream, and jump in the mouth veal rolls with sage and parma ham are cooked in a rich white wine and olive oil sauce, then served with mashed potatoes - wonderful. The dessert menu offers home-made traditional delights like ice creams, tiramisu, Italian meringues, gateaux, biscotti and ammareti. An all-Italian wine list offers over 120 wines, including both special bottles and many more affordable wines. The locals have taken this place (which is very family friendly) to heart, so it's wise to make a reservation - especially if you want to dine after 7.30 or 8.00 pm. Children welcome (high chair, baby changing facilities); Toilets wheelchair accessible; **Seats 7** (private room, 20); D Wed-Mon, 5-10pm. Closed Tue. MasterCard, Visa, Laser. **Directions:** Enniscorthy centre, market square.

Enniscorthy Area   # Monart Destination Spa
HOTEL   The Still Enniscorthy Co Wexford **Tel: 053 923 899**
R   info@monart.ie www.monart.i

Nestled on a hundred acres of private mature woodland and only an hour and a half from Dublin airport, south-east Ireland's first purpose-built destination spa is an adults only facility in a magical location, offering world class Spa facilities and treatments, accommodation in luxurious guest room and suites, personalised and attentive service, and exceptional dining. Whether to address a specific health or wellness need (such as detox, inch-loss, anti-ageing, post surgery recovery, athlete rejuvenation) or simply to rest, relax and rejuvenate, Monart is a wonderful destination. A 2400 sq. m Thermal Suite includes a Swedish sauna with ice grotto among its facilities, and day programmes are available to non-residents - who are also welcome to share a very special dining experience - enhanced by wonderful gardens, designed by Chelsea Flower Show gold medallist, Mary Reynolds. Not suitable for children; broadband wi/fi;garden, fitness room, destination spa, indoor 'pool, walking, hairdressing, massage. **Rooms 70** (2 suites, all executive & no smoking); lift; B&B about €230 pps, ss €40. Closed 24-27 Dec. Amex, MasterCard, Visa, Laser. **Directions:** N11 from Dublin, then right on to N80, first left and follow the signs.

Foulksmills   # Horetown House
HISTORIC HOUSE   Foulksmills Co Wexford **Tel: 051 565 63**
N   horetownhouse@eircom.net www.horetownhouse.i

téite bia   Situated in beautiful unspoilt rolling pastures about 20 minutes from Wexford town (and half an hour from Waterford), this remarkable 17th century house came into new ownership in 2004 and, following extensive restoration and refurbishment, has now re-opened for guests. Impressive public rooms include an atmospheric Cellar Restaurant and elegant reception rooms, and the ten bedrooms which vary considerably according to their position in the house are all individually designed and named after people who have had a connection with the house. There was a change of chef at an early stage after opening, and the Cellar Restaurant will be assessed at a later stage. Children welcome (under 5s free in parents room, baby sitting arranged); Equestrian, fishing and golf nearby. Garden, walking. **Rooms 10** (3 suites, 3 junior suites, 4 family, 3 shower only); No lift; Limited room service; B&B €160 pps, ss €40. MasterCard, Visa, Laser. **Directions:** N25 from Wexford, turn for Taghmon, in Taghmon take turn for Foulksmills, approx. 4km turn right immediately after bridge.

R   # GOREY

Conveniently situated midway between Dublin and Wexford, Gorey is a good shopping town and hand to the many sandy beaches for which the area is famous. The **Ashdown Park Hotel** (053 948 0500; www.ashdownparkhotel.com) offers quality accommodation and good facilities including a Leisure Centre; a smart sister hotel **Amber Springs Hotel & Health Spa** (053 948 4000; www.amberspring shotel.ie)) has recently opened on the edge of Gorey; within easy walking distance of the town centre, makes a very comfortable place to stay. Nearby, Courtown Harbour is a popular family resort with an attractive harbour, and walks in the surrounding countryside. **Stack's** (053 942 1271) formerly Poole Porterhouse, on the main street, could be good place to break a journey as Warren Gillan, previously of the famed La Riva restaurant in Wexford, is cooking here at the time of going to press. Near Gorey, the new **Seafield Hotel & Spa** (053 942 4000; www.seafieldhotel.com) has recently opened (see entry) and has attractive opening offers. Gorey has a vibrant cultural life, with a very active Theatre Group, producing

everal plays through the year, and bringing plays in performed by visiting groups. They also host an
nnual week long Drama Festival. In the summer months, they put on a twice weekly play, which is
opular with locals and visitors alike. Molumney Art Centre is open daily in summer. There are numerous
ther activities available locally including championship standard golf, walking, watersports, horse riding
nd angling. For garden lovers the **Ram House Gardens** at Coolgreany (0402 37238) are a 'must visit'.
WWW-IRELAND-GUIDE.COM FOR THE BEST PLACES TO EAT, DRINK & STAY

Gorey
COUNTRY HOUSE/RESTAURANT

Marlfield House

Courtown Road Gorey Co Wexford **Tel: 053 942 1124**
info@marlfieldhouse.ie www.marlfieldhouse.com

téile bia Often quoted as 'the luxury country house hotel par excellence', this impressive house was once the residence of the Earls of Courtown, and is now an elegant oasis of unashamed luxury offering outstanding hospitality and service, where guests are cosseted and pampered in sumptuous surroundings. It was first opened as an hotel in 1978 by Mary and Ray Bowe who have lavished care and attention on this fine property ever since - imposing gates, a wooded drive, antiques and glittering chandeliers all

romise guests a very special experience - and, although Mary and Ray are still very much involved,
heir daughters Margaret and Laura Bowe now continue the family tradition of hospitality established
y their parents. The interior is luxurious in the extreme, with accommodation including six very grand
tate rooms, but the gardens are also a special point of interest: there is a lake and wildfowl reserve, a
ormal garden, kitchen garden, and beautiful woodland with extensive woodland walks - and a number
f gardens open to the public are within easy access, including Mount Usher, Powerscourt, Altamont
nd Kilmokea. Conference/banqueting (30/40); broadband wi/fi; secretarial services. Dogs may be
ermitted by arrangement. Children welcome by prior arrangement (under 2s free in parents room, cots
vailable without charge, baby sitting arranged). Tennis, cycling, walking, croquet, garden. Golf nearby.
leli-pad. **Rooms 20** (6 state rooms, 14 superior, 8 ground floor, all no smoking). B&B €140pps, ss
€17.50. Room service (limited hours). Closed mid Dec-29 Dec, 3 Jan-end Jan. **Restaurant:** Dining is
lways an exceptional experience in Marlfield's fine restaurant, where the graceful dining room and
urner-style conservatory merge into one, allowing views out across the gardens, including a fine kitchen
arden that is a delight to the eye and provides a wide range of fresh produce for the restaurant. The
onservatory, with its hanging baskets, plants and fresh flowers (not to mention the occasional statue),
s one of the most romantic spots in the whole of Ireland, further enhanced at night by candlelight a
onderful setting in which to enjoy chef Colin Byrne's accomplished cooking. His strongly seasonal
nenus are changed daily and outline the produce available in the kitchen garden (which is Ray Bowe's
articular point of pride), and the origin of other ingredients used. Although contemporary in style and
resentation, there is a strong classical background to the cooking, and it is all the better for that.
pecialities that indicate the style include an elegant starter terrine of braised ham and foie gras with
eleriac roulade & toasted brioche, and a luxurious main course of roasted Dunmore East lobster with
asil potatoes, sauce vierge, and sautéed green beans - and the ready supply of fresh garden produce
nspires imaginative vegetarian choices too. Lovely puds reflect the best fruit in season at the time, and
cheese selection from Sheridans cheesemongers is served with a delectable little salad, caramelised
alnuts and apple cider jelly. Then it's off to the drawing room for coffee and petits fours to round off
he feast. Very professional service is a match for this fine food and an informative wine list, long on
urgundies and clarets, offers a wine of the month, a page of special recommendations and a very good
election of half bottles. Not suitable for children under 8 at D. **Seats 90** (private room, 20; outdoor,20).
eservations advised. Air conditioning. Toilets wheelchair accessible. D daily, 7-9 (Sat to 10, Sun to 8
L Sun only 12.30-2. Early D €42 (Sun-Thu, 6.30-7.45), also à la carte; Set Sun L about €42. House
ine €29. SC for parties 6+. Light à la carte lunches are served daily in Library, 12.30-5. Amex, Diners,
lasterCard, Visa, Laser. **Directions:** 1 mile outside Gorey on Courtown Road (R742).

Gorey
CAFÉ

Partridges Artisan Café & Fine Food Shop

93 Main Street Gorey Co Wexford **Tel: 053 948 4040**
christian@partridgelodge.com www.partridgelodge.com

welcome arrival to the bustling town of Gorey, this centrally located new daytime café is a buzzy
lace, popular with locals and visitors alike. It is located at the back of a speciality food shop selling

artisan foods from Ireland and beyond, and there will be plenty to tempt you on your way in and out
ingredients used in the café are on sale in the shop, which is useful for picking up a picnic. The menu
features simple, unpretentious dishes that allow the high quality of the ingredients to take pride
place - enjoy, amongst other treats, good soups served with freshly home-baked bread, unusual past
dishes, tasty savoury tarts, flavoursome salads, an excellent farmhouse cheese and oatcake plate, an
an enticing selection of home-baked cakes and tarts. There is a coffee menu and a short "by the glass
wine list. It does get busy (especially at lunchtime), but service is friendly and willing. Good valu
considering the high quality of the food. Children welcome (high chair); **Seats 30;** no reservation
accepted; open all day Mon-Sat, 10am-7pm; house wine from €6 per glass. Closed Sun. MasterCard
Visa, Laser. **Directions:** Main Street Gorey town.

Gorey Area   Seafield Hotel & Oceo Spa
HOTEL/RESTAURANT   Ballymoney Gorey Co Wexford **Tel: 053 942 400**
R   sales@seafieldhotel.com www.seafieldhotel.com

Set in lush parkland adjacent to Seafield Golf Club with its 18 hole Peter McAvoy designed cours
this new hotel enjoys a fine location with views of Irish Sea. It is a stylish property with extensive faci
ities, including a spa, and luxurious contemporary accommodation; some rooms have terraces and a
are furnished to a high standard with very comfortable beds and many extras, including complimen
tary WiFi, and well-designed bathrooms with bath and monsoon shower. Although destined to becom
a very popular short break destination (it is only about an hour from south Dublin), it is also we
equipped for business and conferences and sure to be in demand. Spa, golf (18), walking. **Restauran**
The dining room is a surprising, lovely, spacious, high-ceilinged room of individual design and déco
A classic French menu is (relatively) short, yet offers something to suit every taste, and is describe
in plain English, and apparently led where possible by locally sourced ingredients. Cooking is to a ve
high standard and beautifully presented without being fussy or "artistic"; special highlights on a rece
visit included a lovely fricassée of rabbit in a wine sauce; rack of Wicklow lamb with a classic reduce
jus, galette of potato and superb parsnip crisps - simple but delicious and lamb perfectly cooked (a
requested) very pink - and a classic lemon tart to finish, accompanied by a perfect soft berry compôt
delicious. Meticulously turned-out, very professional staff provide excellent service and (at least in th
early evening) are swift to welcome children and to provide tub or high chairs. Amex, MasterCard, Vis
Laser. **Directions:** On coast north of Gorey, signed from N11. ◇

KILMORE QUAY

This picturesque fishing village is noted for its thatched cottages, as a base for sea angling and for th
Maritime Museum in the harbour, which is in a lightship - the Guillemot - previously used by Iris
Lights, and still with all the original cabin furniture and fittings. It is a popular place for family hol
days, and the nearby Saltee Islands are home to Ireland's largest bird sanctuary. There are sever
attractive pubs and restaurants in the village, notably the characterful **Kehoe's Pub & Maritim
Heritage Centre** (053 912 9830), which is well known for its seafood. Kilmore Quay and the are
around it has many unspoilt beaches which offer miles of the finest sand dunes in the south-east.
WWW-IRELAND-GUIDE.COM FOR THE BEST PLACES TO EAT, DRINK & STAY

Kilmore Quay   Hotel Saltee
HOTEL/RESTAURANT   Kilmore Quay Co Wexford **Tel: 053 912 960**
                     info@hotelsaltees.ie www.hotelsaltees.ie

The pretty fishing village of Kilmore Quay is popular for family holidays and, wi
moderate prices and comfortable accommodation - all rooms are en-suite, with a
the necessary facilities this modest, friendly hotel would be a relaxing choice, especially as there is
very pleasant bar, the Coningbeg, and an unusually good restaurant for a small hotel (see below
Children under 3 are free in parents' room (baby sitting arranged). **Rooms 10** (all shower only, a
ground floor, 3 family rooms, 4 no smoking). TV, tea/coffee-making, iron/trouser press in rooms. A
day room service. B&B from €55 (also special offers). Open all year except Christmas. **Le Saffro**
Dominique Dayot, who is well known the area, set up this French restaurant in the hotel in 2005, ar
it has become a magnet for food lovers visiting the area. There's an hospitable atmosphere an
although not too fancy, it has classy white linen, high backed chairs and fresh flowers - a comfortab
setting for some good French cooking. Menus are well-judged to allow for varying tastes so - althoug
you'll find a leaning towards local seafood in dishes like its trademark 'Rendez-vous de Poissons'
combination dish of cod, salmon, lemon sole with Kilmore scallops and prawns, with a basil sauce
classic black sole, and lobster, when available - there are lots of Slaney Valley steak and lamb dishe

ist duckling and several vegetarian dishes to choose from. Vegetables are charged separately, but e freshness of ingredients, generous portions and good cooking ensure value for money. Staff are ry willing and helpful, and it's a relaxing place to enjoy good food. **Seats 52;** not suitable for chil-en after 8pm; non-residents welcome by reservation; D daily 6-9pm, L Sun only, 12.30-2.30pm; set n L €26, value D €34, 6-7.45pm, also a la carte; house wine €18.95. Bar meals available daily. tablishment closed 25 Dec. MasterCard, Visa, Laser. **Directions:** N25 out of Wexford towards sslare, turn right on R739 for Kilmore Quay. ◇

---

lmore Quay
IESTHOUSE

Kilmore Quay Guest House

Quay Road Kilmore Quay Co Wexford **Tel: 053 912 9988**
quayhome@iol.ie www.quayhouse.net

obhan McDonnell's pristine guesthouse is centrally located in the village and is especially famous
* its support of sea angling and diving there's an annexe especially geared for anglers with
ying/storage room, fridges and freezers, live bait and tackle sales. Packed lunches can be provided
d non-residents are welcome for breakfast. The whole place is ship shape, with attractive, slightly
utical bedrooms ("a place for everything and everything in its place"), practical pine floors and neat
-suite rooms (most shower only). Children welcome (under 2s free in parents' room, cots available
thout charge). Pets by arrangement. Garden. Walking; cycling. **Rooms 7** (all en-suite, 4 shower-only).
&B €50 pps. *Self-catering also available. Open all year. MasterCard, Visa, Laser. **Directions:**
exford 14 miles, Rosslare Ferry route. ◇

NEW ROSS

is old town on the estuary of the River Barrow has much of interest to the visitor - especially, of urse, its key attraction, the recreation of the nineteenth century sailing ship the Dunbrody. For good od and good value (even if the exterior and carpark are a little rough), head to **The Hillside Bar** (051 21155) Camblin, where Gilles Laforges and Jacques Carrera are cooking hearty carvery lunches that gulars are happy to queue for, and more sophisticated evening menus. For comfortable accommo-tion in a pleasant environment the **Brandon House Hotel** (Tel 051 421703; ww.brandonhousehotel.ie), just outside the town, is on a hillside site with river views; it has been veloped around a house of character and offers some surprises (including an interesting art collec-n) as well as much-needed facilities (conference; leisure centre; new spa). Signage from the road n be a little off putting, but it is worth going up the drive to take a closer look. The **Kennedy Centre d Arboretum** (051 388171) just a few miles from the centre of New Ross are well worth a visit, you n picnic in the gardens or just stroll around many acres of parkland. New Ross is an ideal base for king in a drive around the scenic Ring of Hook which features many historical sites including inbrody Abbey, Tintern Abbey and The Hook Lighthouse. The famous and reputedly haunted Loftus all is also located nearby. There are also many fine beaches and many other activities such as Angling d Charters, Diving and Snorkelling, Canoeing, Windsurfing, Golf and River Cruises (Galley River uises; 051 421723).
WW-IRELAND-GUIDE.COM FOR THE BEST PLACES TO EAT, DRINK & STAY

---

ew Ross
FÉ
E

Café Nutshell

In A Nutshell 8 South Street New Ross Co Wexford **Tel: 051 422 777**
inanutshell8@gmail.com

A walk through the town to find Philip and Patsy Rogers' Emporium will be very rewarding for lovers of good food. The concept is a natural evolution from Philip's background in farming, and Patsy's love of cooking: traditional country methods, handed down recipes and a respect for fresh produce are at the heart of this delightful shop and café, where everything is freshly made every day - and 'chemically treated or pre-prepared foods are not welcome'. Choose from a wide range of deli-cious freshly-prepared dishes beginning with licious breakfasts and fresh bakes for elevenses, then moving on to soups, panini, wraps and abattas, warm salads, quiche of the day, and classic platters (fresh seafood, charcuterie, Irish farm-use cheese) - and lots of other seasonal produce - and, perhaps, a perfectly brewed Illy coffee - then ke time to browse around the shop, which has a vast range of goodies to take home, including complimentary medicines like homeopathic ad herbal remedies. Anyone staying in self-cater accommodation in the area should also check out the food to go, which offers the same high st dards of genuinely home-cooked foods as Patsy serves in the café. A little treasure. **Seats 50;** conditioning. No reservations. Children welcome (supervised). Open Mon-Sat 9-5.30, L 12.3 3.30pm; house wine €20. Closed Sun, Mon, 1 week May, Oct & Jan. MasterCard, Visa, Las **Directions:** Town centre.

Rosslare Area   Castleview Heigh
RESTAURANT   Our Lady's Island Broadway Co Wexf
Tel: 053 913 11

Set on a hill overlooking the old castle ruins and the pretty inlet around Our Lady's Island, this fam run restaurant is worth a stop on the way to or from Rosslare Harbour - not only is the food good, the views are wonderful too. You can sit at a window table in the bright, spacious dining room, or one of the outdoor seats, and watch the golfers while sipping a glass of wine or choosing from tempting menu. Seafood features strongly, as you would expect, probably including a good hou chowder, and a wide variety of fish and shellfish, including mussels, calamari, smoked salmon, bass and cod. Seafood salad includes a generous quantity of prawns, smoked salmon and wonder hickory smoked trout. Homemade lasagne topped with Wexford Cheddar, steak, duckling and ch grilled chicken are the kind of non-fish meals you can expect, and there's a vegetarian option children's menu and a variety of freshly made sandwiches. A short wine list includes some quar bottles, also bottled beer. As well as the restaurant, there's a good craft shop - and crazy golf and 18-hole Par 3 golf course are part of the business, so if you have time to spare before your ferry, y could happily while away an afternoon here. In good weather there is a trampoline and bouncing cas to keep children amused too. Toilets wheelchair accessible; children welcome (high chair, childre menu, baby changing facilities); **Seats 56** (outdoors, 16); Food served all day, 10-9pm; L 12.30-4p D 5-9pm (4-8pm Sun). Set Sun L €20; house wine €18.50. Closed Mon & Tues off-seas MasterCard, Visa, Laser. **Directions:** N25 Wexford to Rosslare, take right after Tagoat, to our Lad Island. 300m on right after village.

Rosslare Area   Churchtown Hous
COUNTRY HOUSE   Tagoat Rosslare Co Wexford **Tel: 053 913 25**
                                    info@churchtownhouse.com www.churchtownhouse.c

Although situated very near the coast, Patricia a Austin Cody's fine Georgian house is set in ab eight and a half acres of wooded gardens a makes an ideal destination for anyone seeking ru tranquillity. The house dates back to 1703 but has been completely renovated and elegar furnished by the Codys, to make a comfortar country house retreat spacious sitting rooms ha antique furniture and open fires, and the la bedrooms are equally pleasing, with genero beds, phones, TV and well-finished bathrooms. would make a beautifully relaxing base for a few days exploring the area, and there is no shortage things to do. Golfers have no less than six championship links and parkland courses to choose fr (two are only a few minutes' drive away), for example, sea and shore angling are a big attraction, a walking the long sandy beaches, and horse riding - there's a choice of equestrian centres nearby. A there's so much to visit too the great Victorian revival Johnstown Castle and demesne is not to missed, for example, also unspoilt Hook Head and the Hook Lighthouse which are just a short dr away, and there's much more besides. The Codys are renowned for their hospitality and, if you're luc enough to arrive at this well-run house at around teatime, you'll be served delicious home-made ca and tea in the drawing room - other edible highlights include the fine Irish breakfast served in bright dining room, also home-cooked dinners, which are available to residents by arrangeme Midweek breaks, weekends and golf breaks all offer very good value. Garden. Children welcome (un 3s free in parents' room, cot available, €15). No pets. **Rooms 12** (2 junior suite, 3 executive, 6 sho only, all no smoking, 1 family room). Dining room closed Sun-Mon. House closed Nov - M MasterCard, Visa, Laser. **Directions:** On R736 1 km (half mile) from N25, at Tagoat.

osslare Strand
OTEL/RESTAURANT

Kelly's Resort Hotel & Spa

Rosslare Co Wexford **Tel: 053 913 2114**
info@kellys.ie www.kellys.ie

téte bía With its special brand of relaxed professionalism, the Kelly family's renowned
beachside hotel sums up all that is best about the
sunny south-east for many regular visitors. Perhaps
it's because its history in the same family spans
three centuries, so there's not a lot they don't know
about keeping guests happy - quite simply, the
hotel has everything, for both individuals and families. Its special qualities are so wide-ranging that
it's hard to know where to begin - will it be with the
stunning art collection they have built up over the
ears, the exceptional leisure and pampering facilities (constantly updated), or perhaps the unusual
mount of 'personal space' offered in a series of comfortable lounging areas around the hotel; for some
e highlight of the hotel is the two excellent restaurants (see below). It's known as the 'hotelier's hotel'
ecause so many others in the hospitality industry choose to come here to relax (praise indeed!) and,
ong with exceptional hospitality (and a no conference/event policy), its key appeal is that there is
enuinely something for everybody, so people with different interests can do their own thing (or nothing
: all) then meet up with friends and family over dinner to chat about their day. In summer it's the in-
ace for family holidays there's a crèche, playroom and a children's playground - but people travelling
ithout children will be glad to know that the number permitted at any one time is limited, to prevent
eating an imbalance. Many of the bedrooms have sea views (the best have balconies), and even now,
hen so there is so much competition between hotels to offer the best leisure facilities, Kellys remains
ght up there at the top, with two indoor swimming pools, a 'SeaSpa' well-being centre (11 treatment
oms, seawater vitality pool, steam room, rock sauna and much else besides), indoor tennis, and - a
t of fun for Francophiles - boules. Lots to do nearby too, including golf of course. Outside the summer
oliday season (end June-early Sept), ask about special breaks (including special interest breaks),
hen rates are reduced. No conferences or functions are accepted. Free broadband wi/fi. Fishing (sea).
hooker, pool table. Hair dressing. Children welcome (under 3 months free in parents' room, cot avail-
ble without charge, baby sitting arranged). Supervised playroom & children's playground. Destination
pa; Leisure centre ('pool, fitness room, sauna, steam room, jacuzzi); Walking, cycling, croquet, lawn
owls, tennis, pitch & putt. Garden. No pets. **Rooms 118** (2 suites, 2 junior suites, 2 superior, 20
round floor, 2 disabled). Lift. Room service (limited hours). Turndown service offered. B&B €95, ss
10; SC10%. Hotel closed 10 Dec-mid Feb. **Beaches Restaurant:** This L shaped room, which has
een run under the eagle eye of Pat Doyle since 1971, has a sense of traditional opulence yet with a
esh, almost gallery-esque approach - an ideal home for some favourites from the hotel's famous art
ollection. Executive Chef Jim Aherne has been pleasing guests with his classic cuisine for over thirty
ars now - and his menus reflect the value placed on fresh local produce, with ingredients like
exford beef, Rosslare mackerel, Slaney salmon and locally sourced vegetables used in daily-changing
enus. The hotel's renowned wine list is meticulously sourced, always changing, and excellent value.
ighly informative, most wines are directly imported and there are many treats in the collection, which
cludes organic and bio-dynamic wines, and an exceptional choice of half bottles - and a page of
agnums (2 bottles), jeraboams (4 bottles) and imperials (8 bottles), which are ideal for big parties
d special celebrations. **Seats 200** (private room 40); air conditioning. L &D daily: 1-2.15pm, 7.30-
pm; Set L €28; Set D €50. House wine from €20; SC discretionary. **La Marine:** This informal
staurant has its own separate entrance and offers a relaxed alternative to the dining experience in
eaches Restaurant. A zinc bar imported from France is the focal point of the rather pubby bar, where
u can have an aperitif - although the turnover in La Marine is brisk and it is better to go directly to
ur table if it is ready. Fashionably sparse tables have fresh flowers, good quality cutlery and paper
apkins, but space is at a premium. Head chef Eugene Callaghan's ingredients are carefully sourced,
sing local seasonal produce as much as possible, and a finely judged balancing act between tradi-
nal and contemporary fare is achieved on menus offering plenty of choice: a starter of grilled bell
epper with mozzarella cheese, basil oil & bread sticks rubs shoulders with classic grilled Bannow Bay
ussels with garlic & parsley butter, while main courses include an upbeat version of roast rack of
mb - with roast aubergine & Moroccan coucous - and also offer some retro dishes like sole
éronique'. Desserts are deliciously updated-classics lemon possett with raspberry jelly & white
ocolate cookie perhaps perhaps, and there's always a carefully selected trio of Irish cheeses. Service
swift and friendly and Sunday lunch, which is very good value, tends to be a little more traditional.
oking strongly advised, especially at weekends. A light bar menu is also available every afternoon,

531

12.30-5.30. Well chosen wines reflecting the style of food, are fairly priced. **Seats 70.** L daily, 12.3(
2pm; D 6.30-9pm. Amex, MasterCard, Visa, Laser. **Directions:** Take the signs f(
Wexford/Rosslare/Southeast. 20 km from Wexford Town alongside Rosslare Strand beach.

WEXFORD

Wexford is a fascinating old town and offers much of interest, notably the annual Opera Festival whic
usually takes place every autumn; pending redevelopment of the Theatre Royal, the 2007 festival wa
held in the summer at nearby Johnstown Castle, as a one-off event. The new building, which will b
open for the 2008 Festival (16 Oct -2 Nov), is on the site of the old theatre, and it has been conceive
as a secret opera house, nestling into Wexford's medieval street setting. It has a larger capacity ma
auditorium (750 seats) with excellent acoustics, a second theatre and many other greatly enhance
facilities and, although focused on the autumn festival, the new building will operate as a year rour
arts venue for both additional Wexford Festival productions and visiting companies. On a mo
workaday note, anyone who is looking for moderately priced good quality accommodation with leisu
facilities and does not want to be in the town, might try the **Quality Hotel & Leisure Club** (053 91
2000; www.qualitywexfordhoel.com) on the edge of town, which offers a room rate from €79 and ha
good facilities, including a swimming pool.

Wexford
RESTAURANT

Forde's Restaurant
Crescent Quay Wexford Co Wexfo(
Tel: 053 912 383

Happy customers and good lighting create a good atmosphere at this informal restaurant in a ren
vated building near the Ballast Office; on the first-floor, overlooking the harbour it has mirro
reflecting lots of candles and, as darkness falls, lights twinkling across the harbour are highly atmo
pheric. Although set up in the pared-down modern style, fresh flowers and candles on well-space
polished tables create a caring feeling, and Liam Forde's varied seasonal set and à la carte menus off(
value and a wide choice, with vegetarian (and vegan) options listed although there's an understand
able leaning towards local seafood. Steaks and Wexford mussels are popular options and servings a(
generous. More-ish desserts might include a more-ish dark chocolate mousse. Everything is made c
the premises and well-trained, knowledgeable staff are courteous and efficient. Interesting, inform
tive wine list. Sunday lunch and the short dinner menu offer especially good value. **Seats 8(**
Reservations advised. Air conditioning. Children welcome. D daily, 6-10, L Sun only, 12-6pm. Ear
D about €22 (2-course); Set Sun L about €22. Also à la carte. House wine from €18.50; SC discre
tionary. Closed 22-25 Dec. Diners, MasterCard, Visa, Laser. **Directions:** On the quay front, opposi
statue. ◇

Wexford
CAFÉ/RESTAURANT

La Dolce Vit;
6/7 Trimmers Lane Wexford Co Wexfo(
Tel: 053 917 08C

In a quiet side street just off North Main Stree
one of Ireland's favourite Italian restaurateurs ha
a smashing daytime restaurant and deli that s
popular with the locals that lunchtime hopefu
must arrive early, or be prepared for a long wai
You'll spot the trademark striped awning (ar
tables outside in summer) from either end of th
unexpected oasis in the centre of town, then se
through the big window a bright spacious eatir
area set up with smart lighted tables and chair
surrounded by shelves stacked with Italian goodie:
Good glasses and elegant tableware heighten the sense of anticipation - and so to Roberto Pons's ser
ously tempting menus, in Italian with English translations, including home-made Italian bread wi
oil, fresh soup of the day, or risotto of the day. Excellent salads are offered and a range of pasta dishe
Then there are some more 'serious' dishes, like grilled seabass with salmoriglio dressing or Italia
sausage with lentils. Don't leave without tasting at least one of Roberto's lovely desserts too - a perfe
pannacotta, orange & lemon tart perhaps and, of course, a classic tiramisu, with a really good coffe
But, anyway, there's still the shopping to do - all sorts of Italian treats, including wines (with pler
offered by the glass) are imported directly by Roberto and, should you be lucky enough to live near
(or staying in self-catering accommodation), there's even a short takeaway menu. **Seats 45;** Toile

Wheelchair Accesible; Open Mon-Sat, 9-5.30pm, L 12-4pm, no evening meals. Set L about €10-12; House Wine from €13. Closed Sun, Mon, Bank Hols & 4 days Christmas. MasterCard, Visa, Laser. **Directions:** Off the northern end of the main street - look out for the big green, red & white canopy. ◇

Wexford
RESTAURANT

Mange 2
@ Crown Bar Monck Street Wexford Co Wexford
Tel: 053 914 4033

A real taste of France awaits you in this first floor restaurant above a well known pub, The Crown, which has two entrances, one from the quayside (close to the Admiral Barry statue) the other on an adjoining side street. Decorated in a simple but elegant manner with very comfortable tables, good tableware and glasses and a relaxing atmosphere, this is a place with the confidence not to court fashion but to do their own thing, and do it well. A fairly brief but well constructed menu offering French cooking with a creative contemporary spin, is delivered with simple style. Expect interesting starters, good lamb and beef with intense sauces and well chosen accompaniments, classic fresh fish dishes and excellent breads and desserts. A la carte, plus an early bird set menu that is good value for the quality of food and cooking. Service is attentive and professional. Short but carefully chosen wine list. L & D Tue-Sun, 12.30-2.30pm & 5.30pm-'late'. Early bird D, 5.30-7pm. MasterCard, Visa, Laser. **Directions:** Just off Custom House quay, west of Wexford bridge.

Wexford
B&B

McMenamin's Townhouse
6 Glena Terrace Spawell Road Wexford Co Wexford **Tel: 053 914 6442**
mcmem@indigo.ie www.wexford-bedandbreakfast.com

B&B OF THE YEAR

Seamus and Kay McMenamin's B&B has been one of the most highly-regarded places to stay in this area for many years, making a useful first or last night overnight stop for travellers on the Rosslare ferry (15 minutes), as a base for the Wexford Opera, or for a short break exploring this fascinating corner of Ireland. This hospitable duo has upped sticks and moved around the corner to a beautiful Victorian terrace house that has been completely restored and beautifully furnished, with quality beds and bedding, and everything that you need to be comfortable away from home, including TV and tea/coffee-making facilities.The McMenamins' extensive local knowledge is generously passed on to guests and this, together with a really good breakfast, gets you off to a good start and helps to make the most of every day: quite extensive menus include a range of fruits and juices, home-made yoghurts, old-fashioned treats like kippers and also fresh local fish such as delicious fillets of plaice, lambs' kidneys in sherry sauce, omelettes & pancakes - all served with a choice of several freshly baked breads and home-made preserves, including an excellent marmalade and unusual jams such as loganberry. A McMenamin breakfast is always beautifully prepared and presented, and cooked dishes served piping hot: you will want to return as soon as possible! Hunting, shooting, fishing & walking all nearby. Also scenic drives, historic walks, racing, boating, swimming & tennis. Children welcome (under 2s free in parents' room, cots available without charge). No pets. **Rooms 4** (2 family rooms, all en-suite, shower only & no smoking, 1 disabled). B&B €45 pps; ss €10. Private parking. Closed 20 Dec - 1 Mar. MasterCard, Visa. **Directions:** In town centre opposite county hall.

Wexford
HOTEL

Riverbank House Hotel
The Bridge Wexford Co Wexford **Tel: 053 23611**
info@riverbankhousehotel.com www.riverbankhousehotel.com

Away from the bustle of the town, this pleasant hotel just across the bridge has an encouraging approach, with well-tended gardens and a welcoming reception area with lovely flower arrangements and candles. An attractive Victorian style bar and restaurant enjoys views of the river, and an adjacent conservatory area has character and interesting plants. Renovations have been done with deference to the character of the building so, although comfortable, guest rooms tend to be a little small. A very nice breakfast is served in Windows restaurant - a good range of juices, excellent coffee, lovely breads and good hot dishes. This hotel offers a pleasingly personal style of hospitality and food service. Conference/banqueting 350/260); business centre. **Rooms 23** (14 shower only, 1 disabled, 8 no smoking, 6 family rooms, 8 ground floor). 24 hr room service, Lift. Children welcome (under 4s fre in parents' room, cot available free of charge, baby sitting arranged). No pets. Garden, walking. *Sho breaks, including golf breaks, offered. B&B €85pps, ss €25. No SC. Restaurant open Fri/Sat (dai Jul, Aug, Dec) L 12.30-2.30, D 6.30-9.30 (Sun to 9). Bar meals available 12-10 daily. Closed 2 Dec. Amex, Diners, MasterCard, Visa, Laser. **Directions:** Directly across the bridge in Wexford town.

Wexford   Rosemount Hous
B&B
Spawell Road Wexford Co Wexford **Tel: 053 912 46C**
N   info@rosemounthouse.ie   www.wexfordbedandbreakfast.

Having run their B&B on Auburn Terrace for many years, Carol and Tim Kelly agreed to the loc council's request to relocate to allow for road expansion there, and have now opened Rosemount Hous on Spawell Road. The new premises is an 18th century period residence, on a quiet road, with walking distance of the town centre. All the original features have been retained, allowing for brigh spacious and comfortable rooms, which are beautifully decorated and furnished with antique furnitu throughout. Although some exterior work still remains to be done, the interior has been fully complete and this is a lovely place to stay. Not suitable for children under 6. **Rooms 3** (all en-suite & no smokin 2 shower only). B&B €60 pps, ss €10. Closed 18 Dec - 2 Jan. MasterCard, Visa, Laser. **Direction** Follow N25 into town centre, on Spawell Road (signed).

Wexford   Talbot Hote
HOTEL
Trinity St Wexford Co Wexford **Tel: 053 912 256**
sales@talbothotel.ie talbothotel.

féile bia Sister to the Stillorgan Park Hotel in Dublin, this 1960s hotel originally dates back to 190 and has recently undergone massive renovation. It is well-located on the harbour-front, ar also convenient to the town centre - indeed, so many activities revolve around it that many would sa the Talbot is the town centre. A warm welcome from friendly staff, plus the contented crowd tha always seems to be milling around the foyer, immediately sets arriving guests at ease - and one immediately struck by the range and quality of original paintings, which is a feature of great intere throughout the hotel. Bedrooms are inevitably somewhat limited by the age and style of the buildin, but are pleasant and comfortable, with phone, TV and tea/coffee trays as standard. The baseme leisure centre is an unexpectedly characterful area, confirming the feeling that the Talbot will alwa spring a few surprises. Short breaks offered. Conference/banqueting (450/400); free broadband wi/ business centre, secretarial services). Leisure centre ('pool, jacuzzi, sauna, steam room); Sp (massage, beauty salon). Children welcome (under 4s free in parents room, cot available free charge, baby sitting arranged, creche, playroom). Wheelchair access. Own parking. No pets. **Room 109** (1 suite, 2 junior suites, 8 family, 4 disabled) Lift. Limited room service. B&B €100 pps, ss €2C Closed 24-25 Dec. Amex, Diners, MasterCard, Visa, Laser. **Directions:** On quay front.

Wexford   Westgate Desig
CAFE/RESTAURANT
22 North Main Street Wexford Co Wexfo
Tel: 053 912 378

féile bia Locals know how to find this popular daytime café - the entrance is through Westga Design and downstairs. It's a big bustling self service café, with plenty of rustic b comfortable seating and a friendly atmosphere. Food quality is very good and the menu wide-rangin, from home-made soups and a varied selection of salads (20 per day) to hot dishes of the day - lasagr and braised lamb shank with chive champ, or fish pie are all typical. It's contemporary Irish hom cooking, but with international favourites taking their place alongside traditional Irish dishes. Th baking is exceptionally good, with delicious cakes and desserts. Everything is served in generou portions and it's family friendly. Take-out dishes are available and outside catering is also on offer f parties. Good food at very reasonable prices is a winning combination for day time meals. **Seats 14** Air conditioning; Children welcome; Open Mon-Sat, Food served all day, L11-5.30; Wine from €4.5 per glass. Closed Sun, Bank Hols, 25/6 Dec. Visa, Laser. **Directions:** Accessible from the main stre or, through the lower level, at the back. ◇

Whites of Wexford

Wexford
HOTEL

Abbey Street Wexford Co Wexford **Tel: 053 912 2311**
info@whitesofwexford.ie www.whitesofwexford.ie

Wexford's most famous hotel, Whites re-opened in June 2006 after total reconstruction and you certainly won't miss it as it is a very large building, with obvious signage which can be seen from all around the town. Very different from the higgledy-piggledy building we had all grown fond of, this new development does not have quite the character expected of an hotel that goes back to 1795, but it is comfortable, and the unbroken tradition of hospitality lives on. The consolation is that what is now a very large hotel has excellent facilities in all areas, including on-site leisure activities and pampering treatments; White's now has the first Cryotherapy Clinic in Ireland, and an impressive swimming pool and Spa. Smart contemporary guest rooms and suites have all the bells and whistles: in addition to the usual facilities, all rooms have plasma screen television, in house movie & satellite channels, broadband in room safe and minibar. And, although the food side of the operation had not fully settled down at the time of our 2007 visit, there's a choice of bars and restaurants too, and extensive conference facilities. Conference/banqueting (1,000/800); broadband wi/fi; secretarial services. Parking. Leisure Centre ('pool, fitness room, sauna, steam room); Spa; beauty salon; Walking; Children welcome (under 4s free in parents' room, cots available free of charge, baby sitting arranged). No pets. **Rooms 157** (all en-suite); Lift, 24hr room service. B&B €75 pps; ss €25. Closed 24-26 Dec. Amex, Diners, MasterCard, Visa, Laser. **Directions:** Follow signs when leaving N25 or N11.

Ferrycarrig Hotel

Wexford Area
HOTEL/RESTAURANT

Ferrycarrig Wexford Co Wexford **Tel: 053 912 0999**
info@ferrycarrighotel.com www.ferrycarrighotel.ie

FAMILY FRIENDLY HOTEL OF THE YEAR

This stylish modern hotel is in a lovely location overlooking the Slaney estuary and has excellent amenities, including a superb health and fitness club. Public areas include an appealing contemporary bar, the Dry Dock, which has a large riverside deck where you can relax and enjoy the view and also lunchtime barbecueing at the Courtyard Grill (Mon-Sat); it is a popular meeting place for local people as well as residents, and appeals to all ages. Good food is served here - real beef burgers, steak, ribs, pasta and fish, and desserts like pear and almond tart and rhubarb & mascarpone fool, also an excellent cheese board with John Hempenstall's Blue Brie and Wicklow Bán cheeses; a separate children's menu includes spaghetti bolognese and chicken curry as well as old favourites. Alternatively Reeds (see below) offers a fine dining option which is more appropriate for adults. Accommodation is contemporary in style, and very comfortable - unusually, all of the well-appointed bedrooms have splendid views across the water, and some also have balconies with wooden loungers; well-equipped family rooms have bunk beds or adjoining rooms, depending on your requirements, and there's a private baby station room for guests. It's a very family-friendly and child-friendly hotel, especially in July and August when children between four and 12 can enjoy 'Crazy Clubbers' facilities in the leisure centre, which offers a programme of daytime activities and evening entertainment but it is not a babysitting service, as an adult must be on the hotel premises at all times; there's an excellent swimming pool for younger swimmers, with its own fountain and Jacuzzi jets, and a separate room for 'baby clubbers' where parents can entertain babies and toddlers. Staff are exceptionally welcoming and friendly, and special breaks are offered. Conference/banqueting (400/320); broadbandwi/fi; business centre. Leisure centre (swimming pool, jacuzzi, fitness room, sauna, steam room), beauty salon. Garden, walking. Fishing and golf nearby. Children welcome (cots available, baby sitting arranged; playroom & creche - limited hours). No pets. Heli-pad. **Rooms 102** (5 junior suites, 4 executive, 2 for disabled, all no smoking). Lift. 24hr room service. B&B about €120 pps; ss €40. Open all year. **Reeds Restaurant:** Good food has always been a strong point at the Ferrycarrig, and Reeds offers adult guests accomplished modern cooking in the atmosphere of an independent restaurant rather than an hotel dining room. It has its own reception/bar area, and formally appointed tables are arranged to make the most of the waterside position. Imaginative and well-balanced à la carte menus are interesting and, although the style is international, there is real emphasis on local foods - Killurin lamb, fresh fish from Duncannon, and speciality cheeses from Wexford and Wicklow are likely to be among the produce named, for example. Food presentation is fashionable but not over the top, and service is pleasant and professional, ensuring a relaxing evening. **Seats 160.** Toilets wheelchair accessible; air conditioning; children welcome. D daily 6.00-9.45pm (to 9.15pm Sun; limited opening in winter); early D €23, 6-7pm; also a la carte. House wines from about €20 sc discretionary. Amex, Diners, MasterCard, Visa, Laser. **Directions:** Located on N11, 2 miles north of Wexford Town.

Wexford Area
FARMHOUSE

Killiane Castle

Drinagh Wexford Co Wexford **Tel: 053 915 8885**
killianecastle@yahoo.com www.killianecastle.com

The past and present mix effortlessly in Killiane Castle, the Mernagh family's farm B&B. The farmhouse and Towerhouse are 17th century and some of the 13th century Norman Castle still stands. Killiane is just a few miles from Wexford town so it's ideal for an overnight on the way to or from Rosslare Harbour (about 10 minutes). Inside there's a spacious entrance hall, an elegant, comfortably furnished residents' sitting-room with an open fire and a small room down a few steps is a TV room. Climb up the 17th century staircase to the second and third floors where individually designed bedrooms have comfortable beds, en-suite facilities and great views over the countryside. The working farm, allows visitors to see a modern dairy in action and their own hens supply the eggs for the delicious breakfasts that Kathleen Mernagh serves her in a warm, cosy dining-room, buffet style. No dinners are offered but the restaurants of Wexford are very close, ot Kathleen will advise guests on the best local choices. 10 bay driving range (4 more to be added at time of going to press), croquet, cycling, tennis, garden, walking. Golf and equestrian nearby. Children welcome (cots available free of charge). **Rooms 8** (1 shower only, 2 family rooms, all no smoking). B&B €50 pps, ss €15. *Self catering also available in 3 courtyard apartments. MasterCard, Visa, Laser. **Directions:** 6km (3 m) outside Wexford town on Rosslare Road.

COUNTY WICKLOW

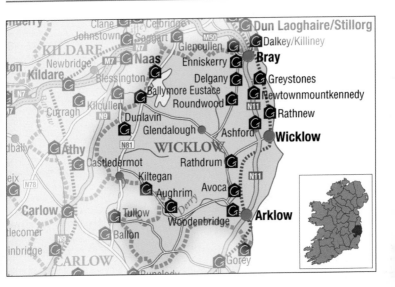

Wicklow is a miracle. Although the booming presence of Dublin is right next door, this spectacularly lovely county is very much its own place, an away-from-it-all world of moorland and mountain, farmland and garden, forest and lake, seashore and river. It's all right there, just over the nearest hill, yet it all seems so gloriously different.

In times past, the official perception of Wicklow – as seen from the viewpoint of the authorities in Dublin Castle – was the complex story of mountain strongholds where rebels and hermits alike could keep their distance from the capital. But modern Wicklow has no need to be in a state of rebellion, for it is an invigorating and inspiring place which captivates everyone who lives there, so much so that while many of its citizens inevitably work in Dublin, they're Wicklow people first, and associate Dubs - if at all - an extremely long way down the line.

Their attitude is easily understood, for even with today's traffic, it is only a short drive on notably handsome roads to transform your world from the crowded city streets right into the heart of some of the most beautiful scenery in all Ireland. This building of roads into Wicklow was a Dublin thing. One of the most scenic in the country – the old Military Road along the top of the hills to the Sally Gap – was originally built for the enforcement of rule from Dublin Castle Today, it is one of Wikclow's assets, as is the elegant dual carriageway sweeping through the Glen of the Downs, a masterpiece in itself which improves life in the county, and augments the scenery.

Such scenery generates its own strong loyalties and sense of identity, and Wicklow folk are rightly and proudly a race apart. Drawing strength from their wonderful environment, they have a vigorous local life which keeps metropolitan blandness well at bay. Thus the hill town of Aughrim in southeast Wicklow has so much community spirit at it topped the 2007 Tidy Towns awards.

While being in a place so beautiful is almost sufficient reason for existence in itself, they're busy people too, with sheep farming and forestry and all sorts of light industries, while down in the workaday harbour of Arklow in the south of the county - a port with a long and splendid maritime history - they've been so successful in organising their own seagoing fleet of freighters that there are now more cargo ships registered in Arklow than any other Irish port.

Local Attractions & Information

Arklow Tourism Information	0402 32 484
Ashford Mount Usher Gardens	0404 40 116
Avoca Tourism Information	0402 35 022

Blessington Russborough House & Gardens	045 865 239
Bray Kilruddery House & Gardens	01 286 3405
Bray National Sealife Centre	01 286 6939
Derrynamuck Dwyer McAllister Traditional Cottage	0404 45 325
Enniskerry Powerscourt House & Gardens	01 204 6000
Glendalough Tourism Information	0404 45 688
Glendalough Visitor Centre	0404 45 325
Kilmacanogue Avoca Handweavers Garden	01 286 7466
Kilquade Nat. Garden Exhibition Centre	01 281 9890
Macreddin Organic Market (first Suns month)	0402 36 444
Rathdrum Avondale House	0404 46 111
Rathdrum Kilmacurragh Arboretum	01 804 0300
Wicklow County Gardens Festival (May-July)	0404 20 100
Wicklow Mountains National Park	0404 45 425
Wicklow Town Wicklow Historic Gaol	0404 61 599
Wicklow Town Tourism Information	0404 69 117

Arklow
RESTAURANT/PUB

R

Kitty's of Arklow

56 Main Street Arklow Co Wicklow
Tel: 0402 31669

A big blue double-fronted building in the centre of town, Kitty's is something of an institution in Arklow. Large and airy ground floor bar areas are decorated in retro '50s style
and there's a lofty first floor restaurant with a slightly olde-world feel. It's very popular with locals,
who like the informal atmosphere and affordable prices. Menus offer a range of seafood and
descriptions aren't too fussy: typical starters may include traditional deep fried mushrooms, while
main courses include perennial favourites likes steaks and rack of lamb, and several fish dishes.
There is a separate vegetarian menu, and coeliac options are also available on request. Cooking can
be a little hit and miss, but generous portions and friendly, efficient and professional staff keep 'em
coming back. Children welcome before 9pm. **Seats 110** (private room 24). Reservations recommended;air conditioning. D in restaurant daily 5.30-8.45pm (Sat, 6-10pm), early D daily
5.30-7.30pm, 2/3 courses €21/26; set D €39, also à la carte. Food also served in the Lounge;
L12-3, D 6-9. House wine about €19. Closed Sun L, 25 Dec & Good Fri. Amex, Diners,
MasterCard, Visa, Laser. **Directions:** Off N11; centre of town, beside car park.

Arklow
COUNTRY HOUSE

R

Plattenstown House

Coolgreaney Road Arklow Co Wicklow **Tel: 0402 37822**
mcdpr@indigo.ie www.plattenstownhouse.com

About halfway between Dublin and Rosslare and overlooking parkland, this quiet, peaceful place is set
in 50 acres of land amidst its own lovely gardens close to the sea - and Margaret McDowell describes
her period farmhouse well as having "the soft charm typical of the mid-19th century houses built in
scenic Wicklow". The garden is lovely (a new fernery and waterfall were added last year) and there is
plenty to do in the area, with the sea, golf, riding stables and forest walks all nearby, and places such
as Glendalough and Avondale House to visit. There's a traditional drawing room furnished with family
antiques overlooking the front garden, a TV lounge and a lovely dining room where breakfast is served
- and evening meals are also offered by arrangement. Comfortable bedrooms vary in size and outlook
according to their position in the house and have interestingly different characters. Garden, walking,
croquet. Equestrian, fishing, golf & garden visits all nearby. French spoken. Children welcome (under
3s free in parents' room, cot available without charge); no pets. **Rooms 4** (3 en-suite with shower only,
1 with private bathroom, all no smoking); limited room service; B&B €49 pps, ss €8. Weekend / midweek breaks - details on application. Closed 23 Dec-2 Jan. MasterCard, Visa. **Directions:** Top of Arklow
town, small roundabout, straight on to Coolgreaney Road. 5 km on left.

Ballyknocken House & Cookery School

Ashford
FARMHOUSE
♨ ✿ R

Gleanealy Ashford Co Wicklow **Tel: 0404 44627**
info@ballyknocken.com www.ballyknocken.com

Perfectly placed for walking holidays in the Wicklow Hills, playing golf, or simply for touring the area, Catherine Fulvio's charming Victorian farmhouse provides comfort, cosiness, home-cooked food and hospitality. The farm has been in the Byrne family for three generations and they have welcomed guests for over thirty years - Catherine took over in 1999, and she has since refurbished the house throughout in old country style. A gently Victorian theme prevails: bedrooms have been charmingly done up, with antique furniture and very good beds - and pretty bathrooms, five of which have Victorian baths. The dining room, parlour and sitting room are in a similar style and her energetic quest for perfection also extends to the garden, where new fruit tree, roses and herbs were planted, and her cookery school - which is in a renovated milking parlour in the grounds. Catherine cooks four course dinners for guests, based on local produce, including vegetables and herbs from the Ballyknocken farm (with wine list, including some specially imported wines). The cooking style is modern Irish. All this, plus extensive breakfasts and great picnics - and a relaxing atmosphere ensure guests keep coming back for more. Short breaks are offered, also self-catering accommodation; details on these, and Ballyknocken Cookery School, on application. *Ballyknocken was our Farmhouse of the Year in 2004. **Rooms 7** (all en-suite, 1 shower only, 1 family room, all no smoking). B&B €59-67 pps, ss €32. Residents D Tue-Sat, at 7.30. Set 4-course D €42.00; Lighter suppers also served midweek; houses wines €20.95. No D on Sun or Mon. Closed Mid Dec & Jan. MasterCard, Visa, Laser. **Directions:** From Dublin turn right after Texaco Petrol Station in Ashford. Continue for 5.5km (3 m). House on right.

The Garden Café

Ashford
CAFÉ
N R

Mount Usher Gardens Ashford Co Wicklow **Tel: 0404 40205**
info@mountushergardens.ie www.mount-usher-gardens.com

The River Vartry is the central feature of these magnificent gardens planted in the Robinsonian (informal) manner, and it's a veritable garden of Eden where, throughout 20 acres, visitors are treated to a series of glorious prospects and to a magnificent collection of trees, plants and shrubs in sylvan settings - a place to revisit in celebration of the changing seasons. And, now that Avoca has recently taken on the stewardship of these wonderful gardens, there are likely to be changes in the shop and Garden Café there in the near future. Since taking on the lease, Simon Pratt has sought to reassure those who fear a rush of commercialisation but, while the jury may be out on that, the food and ambience is sure to be good. **Directions:** Mount Usher gardens are in the centre of Ashford, just off the N11. ◇

Clone House

Aughrim
COUNTRY HOUSE

Aughrim Co Wicklow **Tel: 0402 36121**
stay@clonehouse.com www.clonehouse.com

The oldest part of Carla Edigati Watson's rambling country house in the lovely unspoilt south Wicklow countryside goes back to the 1600s - today this elegantly furnished and hospitable house is full of comfort, providing a quiet, relaxing haven. Landscaped gardens surround the house and are under continuous development, and open fires in every room are a particularly attractive feature - and no television to intrude into this tranquil retreat. Three comfortable guests' sitting rooms are comfortably furnished for relaxing in, and dinner is served in an elegant period dining room. Carla, who is Italian, loves cooking and prepares traditional Tuscan dinners by arrangement - set menus are changed daily and, although there is no choice, special dietary requiremnts can be met with advance notice. Carla's food is simple and full of flavour - black risotto with squid & chili; thick Tuscan bean & vegetable soup; a salad course; ossobucco with porcini & tomato sauce are all typical, with a classical dessert to finish - and service is friendly and willing. A mainly Italian wine list complements the food. *Short breaks are offered. Banqueting (24). No pets. Gym, weight room, sauna, table tennis, garden, walking; free broadband wi/fi; Children welcome (under 3s free in parents' room, cot available free of charge). **Rooms 7** (5 en-suite & shower only, 2 with private bathrooms, all no smoking) B&B €85pps, ss €40. Dinner at 8pm by arrangement, €55-65. Wines from €23 (BYO corkage €8). 10% SC on dinners. Open all year. MasterCard, Visa, Laser. **Directions:** Follow brown house signs from Aughrim or Woodenbridge.

Avoca
Avoca Handweavers
CAFÉ

R

téite bia Avoca handweavers, established in 1723, is Ireland's oldest business. It's a family owned craft design company which now has half a dozen branches throughout Ireland (most of which feature in this Guide) and the business originated here, at Avoca village, where you can watch the hand weavers who produce the lovely woven woollen rugs and fabrics which became the hallmark of the company in its early days. Today, the appeal of Avoca shops is much broader, as they are known not only for the high standard of crafts sold (and their beautiful locations) but also for their own ranges of clothing, restaurants with a well-earned reputation for imaginative, wholesome home-cooked food - and delicious deli products and speciality foods to take home. Garden. Parking. Children welcome. Pets allowed in some areas. Seats 75. Open all day (10-5) Mon-Sun. House wine about €12.50. No service charge. Wheelchair access. Closed 25-26 Dec. Amex, Diners, MasterCard, Visa, Laser. **Directions:** Leave N11 at Rathnew and follow signs for Avoca. ◇

Avoca Village Co Wicklow Tel: 0402 35105
info@avoca.ie www.avoca.ie

Blessington
Grangecon Café
CAFÉ

Kilbride Road Blessington Co Wicklow **Tel: 045 857 892**
grangeconcafe@eircom.net

Wholesome aromas will draw you into Jenny and Richard Street's smashing cafe, which retained its name when re-locating from the charming village of Grangecon to the bustle of Blessington. Here they are in an old building that has been given new life by a lovely renovation job, with gentle modern decor and natural materials that should never date. But the fundamentals remain unchanged: the stated aim has always been "to provide you with a really good food stop", and this they continue to do brilliantly. Everything on the menu is made on the premises, including the breads, pastries and ice cream; the ham hocks for the quiche lorraine are cooked here, the pork meat used in the sausage rolls is organic, fruit and vegetables come from Castleruddery organic farm, and all other ingredients are of the very best quality, many of them also organic and/or free range. The menu is fairly brief, but that's the beauty of it, allowing the cooking to be this good, and flavours superb: the quiche, for example, is a little classic and comes with a scrumptious salad; similarly moist, freshly-baked brown bread arrives with home cooked ham, farmhouse cheese (Sheridan's) and home-made chutney, also garnished with salad: simple and excellent - not for the first time, we say: why aren't there more places like this? Delicious chilled Crinnaughton apple juice is offered, which comes from Cappoquin, and B-Y-O wine is fine. Luscious Illy coffee to finish and maybe a slice of chocolate cake. This is not cheap food - how could it be when the ingredients are of such high quality - but is extremely good value for money. **Seats 30.** Open all day Mon-Sat, 9am-5pm. Toilets wheelchair accessible; children welcome (high chair, baby changing facilities); party Service; Closed Sun, Bank Hols & 25 Dec - 1 Jan. MasterCard, Visa, Laser. **Directions:** Centre of Blessington village, just off main street (Kilbride turning).

Delgany
Glenview Hotel
HOTEL

R

Glen O' The Downs Delgany Co Wicklow **Tel: 01 287 3399**
pkavanagh@glenviewhotel.com www.glenviewhotel.com

Famous for its views over the luxuriantly green and leafy Glen O'The Downs, this well-located hotel has all the advantages of a beautiful rural location, yet is close to Dublin and offers a wide range of facilities, including an excellent Health and Leisure Club and a state-of-the-art conference centre. All bedrooms are attractively furnished in warm colours and an undemanding modern style. Public areas include a comfortably furnished conservatory bar, which is well situated for a casual meal (Conservatory Bistro menu, international cooking,12.30-9), and Woodlands Restaurant offers quite ambitious, formal cooking. All this, together with special breaks offering good value, make the hotel a valuable asset to the area. Conference/banqueting (250/180). Secretarial services, ISDN lines, video conferencing. Leisure centre (indoor swimming pool); beauty salon. Snooker room (adults only). Garden, woodland walks. Children welcome (under 2s free in parents' room, cots available without charge, play room). No pets. **Rooms 70** (all en-suite, 1 suite, 12 executive rooms). Lift. B&B from about €90, ss about €40. Restaurant seats 90; not suitable for children after 7.30pm; D daily, L Sun only; air conditioning; pianist some evenings. Open all year. Amex, Diners, MasterCard, Visa, Laser. **Directions:** On N11, turn left 2 miles southbound of Kilmacanogue. ◇

Rathsallagh House, Golf & Country Club

Dunlavin
COUNTRY HOUSE

Dunlavin Co Wicklow **Tel: 045 403 112**
info@rathsallagh.com www.rathsallagh.com

This large, rambling country house is just an hour from Dublin, but it could be in a different world. Although it's very professionally operated, the O'Flynn family insist it is not an hotel and - although there is an 18-hole golf course with clubhouse in the grounds - the gentle rhythms of life around the country house and gardens ensure that the atmosphere is kept decidedly low-key. Day rooms are elegantly furnished in classic country house style, with lots of comfortable seating areas and open fires. Bedrooms, as in all old houses do vary - some are spacious with lovely country views, while other smaller, simpler rooms in the stable yard have a special cottagey charm; and there are newer rooms, built discreetly behind the main courtyard, which very big and finished to a high standard, with luxurious bathrooms. Rathsallagh is renowned for its magnificent Edwardian breakfast buffet which was, for the second time, the overall national winner of our Irish Breakfast Awards in 2005. Breakfast at Rathsallagh offers every conceivable good thing, including silver chafing dishes, full of reminders of yesteryear. A large sideboard display offers such an array of temptations that it can be hard to decide where to start - fresh juices, fruits and home-bakes, local honey and home-made jams and chutneys... Irish farmhouse cheeses, Rathsallagh ham on the bone, salamis and smoked salmon... then there are the hot dishes, including the full Irish, and then some - less usual dishes like smoked salmon kedgeree, and Kay's devilled kidneys are specialities worth travelling for, and there's another whole menu devoted to the Healthy Option Breakfast. If golf is not your thing, there are plenty of other ways to work off this remarkable meal - the Wicklow Hills beckon walkers of all levels, for example, or you could at least fit in a gentle stroll around the charming walled gardens. Great food and service, warm hospitality, and surroundings that are quiet or romantic to suit the mood of the day - Rathsallagh has it all. Conference/banqueting (130), free broadband wi/fi. Swimming pool, jacuzzi, steam room. Golf (18), gardens, tennis, cycling, walking. Pool table. Beauty salon. Pets allowed by arrangement. Helipad. **Rooms 29** (1 suite, 9 ground floor, 2 shower only, 2 for disabled, all no smoking). B&B about €135 pps, ss €45. *Short breaks (incl golf breaks) offered, details on application. Open all year. **Restaurant:** Have an aperitif in the old kitchen bar while considering daily-changing menus based on local and seasonal produce, much of it from Rathsallagh's own farm and gardens. Head Chef John Kostuik clearly relishes everything that is going on at Rathsallagh; his menus, which are interesting and change daily, are based on local and seasonal produce, much of it from Rathsallagh's own farm and walled garden. Menus are not over-complicated but offer a well-balanced range of about five dishes on each course, changed daily: Duncannon scallops with Waldorf salad & carrot oil makes a lovely starter, for example, while main courses will usually include Wicklow lamb from Doyle's butchers - a roast rack, perhaps, served in summer with warm potato salad and red wine jus. Choices made, settle down in the graciously furnished dining room overlooking the gardens and the golf course to enjoy a series of dishes that are well-conceived and visually tempting but especially memorable for flavour. Leave room for luscious desserts, often based on fruit from the garden, which are served (generously) from a traditional trolley, or Irish farmhouse cheeses, before relaxing with coffee and petits fours in the drawing room or bar. An informative wine list offers many interesting bottles, notably in the Rathsallagh Cellar Collection, and includes a good choice of recommended wines under about €30. **Seats 120** (private room, 55). Reservations essential. D daily, 7-9.30. Set D 2/3+ course €38/50; gourmet menu €65; house wine €25; SC discretionary. *Not suitable for children under 12. Non-residents welcome for dinner, by reservation. Lunch is available only for residents (12-4), but food is served at Rathsallagh Golf Club, 9-9 daily (to 7pm in winter). Amex, Diners, MasterCard, Visa, Laser. **Directions:** 24km (15 miles) south of Naas off Carlow Road, take Kilcullen Bypass (M9), turn left 3km (2 miles) south of Priory Inn, follow signposts.

Powerscourt Terrace Café

Enniskerry
CAFÉ/RESTAURANT

R

Powerscourt House Enniskerry Co Wicklow **Tel: 01 204 6070**
simon@avoca.ie www.avoca.ie

In a stunning location, overlooking the famous gardens and fountains of Powerscourt House, the Pratt family of Avoca Handweavers operate this appealing self-service restaurant. It is a delightfully relaxed space, with a large outdoor eating area as well as the 160-seater café, and the style and standard of food is similar to the original Avoca restaurant at Kilmacanogue: everything is freshly made, using as many local ingredients as possible including organic herbs and vegetables with lots of healthy food. Avoca cafes are renowned for interesting salads, home-bakes and good pastries, and also excellent vegetarian dishes many of which, such as oven-roasted vegetable and goat's cheese tart, have become specialities. Parking (some distance from the house). Children welcome. **Seats 160** (indoors; additional 140 outside terrace; private room 20-90). No-smoking area. Toilets wheelchair accessible. Open daily 10-5 (Sun to 5.30). House wine about €13. Closed 25-26 Dec. Amex, Diners, MasterCard, Visa, Laser. **Directions:** 2 miles from Enniskerry Village. ◇

Enniskerry
HOTEL/RESTAURANT

The Ritz Carlton Powerscourt

Powercourt Estate Enniskerry Co Wicklow **Tel: 01 274 0101**
www.ritzcarlton.com/resorts

A short drive south of Dublin city, in one of Ireland's most scenic locations in the beautiful Wicklow Hills, this long-awaited deluxe hotel set in the 47 acre Powerscourt Estate opens as we go to press. It promises to bring an unprecedented level of luxury and outstanding facilities to the area and unusually for a new opening all facilities are available from the outset. Entry to the crescent shaped building is on the first floor, with palatial public areas designed to make the most of the wonderful location overlooking formal landscaped gardens and the Sugarloaf mountain beyond. Accommodation, in traditionally furnished suites and rooms, is to a predictably luxurious level throughout, with items like signature linens and marble bathrooms as standard and a special emphasis on service, including details like twice-daily housekeeping and evening turndown service; and then there is the Ritz-Carlton Club Level, with separate lounge, dedicated concierge staff and a range of complimentary refreshments offered throughout the day. Resort amenities include the existing 36-hole championship-quality Powerscourt Golf Club golf complex, and a new 30,000 square foot spa with VIP suites, 20 treatment rooms and beauty salon, and an equally impressive Fitness Centre and a children's activity programme and babysitting services. With such an exceptional location and state-of-the-art meeting and event amenities, this is also set to become the venue for a wide range of events, both corporate and private and it is certain to be a highly sought after wedding venue. And, of course, the hotel offers a range of dining experiences, covering every possible occasion and mood, from Afternoon Tea or casual meals in The Pub bar to fine dining on the terrace. But what everyone really wants to know is how Gordon Ramsay's first Irish venture will work out to find out what we think, visit www.ireland-guide.com. Conferences/Banqueting; broadband wi/fi; business centre, secretarial services, video conferencing, laptop sized safes in bedrooms. Golf (36), walking, gardens, leisure centre ('pool, fitness room, steam room, jacuzzi); Destination Spa (treatment rooms, massage etc); Equestrian, fishing (fly, coarse & sea), garden visits & hunting/shooting all nearby. Children welcome (under 5s free in parents room, cot available, baby sitting arranged, high chair, childrens menu, baby changing facilities). Wheelchair friendly. **Rooms 200.** Restaurant open for L & D daily; 11.30-2pm, 6-10pm. Bar food also available from 4pm daily in McGills pub. Open all year. Amex, Diners, MasterCard, Visa,, Laser. Heli-pad. **Directions:** M50/N11 from Dublin, turn for Enniskerry, go through village following signs to Powerscourt.

Greystones
RESTAURANT

Backstage @ Bels

Church Road Greystones Co Wicklow **Tel: 01 201 6990**
backstage@bels.ie

Formerly Bel's Bistro, the new owners Jeff and Tara Nolans' theatrical theme is now seen in objets d'art on the walls, menus that are organised like the acts of a play - and special pre- and post- theatre meals planned in conjunction with the new local theatre (not yet open at the time of the Guide's visit). The newly refurbished restaurant has large windows looking out on to outdoor tables and the busy street outside, which diners can watch from window tables; the front room is elegant and relaxing, and a few steps lead down to the back room and the open kitchen where Jef (who was previously head chef at Roly's in Dun Laoghaire) presides. At the time of the Guide's visit they had been opened just three months, but everything was working seamlessly... Menus that reassuringly carry Euro-Toques and Féile Bia logos also state that dishes are adaptable for both coeliac and vegetarian diets very down to earth, and considerate and the general cooking style, of fresh variation on old favourites, is appealing. Good breakfast and light lunch/terrace menus are offered but, like the theatre, the kitchen really comes into its own in the evening. 'Act One' offers a good choice of eight promising starters including, for example, crispy fried coconut coated wedges of Wicklow Brie with a plum and ginger chutney, and while catch of the day for 'Act Two' could be classic Dover sole on the bone, you may also find rump of Wicklow lamb with champ, spring carrots, olive and rosemary jus - and a vegetarian dish of Ardsallagh goat's cheese, tomato, courgette and aubergine tart with wild rocket and pepper fondue would be a contender for best dish of the night. Luscious 'Act Three' desserts offer very seasonal dishes such as Wexford strawberries, or rhubarb crumble vanilla ice cream, or there's an Irish farmhouse cheese selection. A nice wine list offers daily wine specials as well as house wines, but no tasting notes. Staff, under Tara Nolan's direction, are particularly warm, friendly and knowledgeable. It's little wonder that Backstage@Bel's is already carving out a well-deserved niche in Greystones. Toilets wheelchair accessible; Children welcome (high chair, childrens menu, baby changing facilities); **Seats 60** (outdoors, 18); reservations recommended; Food served daily 10am-10pm (12-8pm Sun); B 10-12pm, L 12-4pm, D 5-10pm. Value L €9.95; Value D €19.95, 5-7pm; house wine from €20. SC 10% on groups 10+. Closed Mon, 25 Dec, Good Fri. MasterCard, Visa, Laser. **Directions:** Middle of Greystones.

Greystones
RESTAURANT

Chakra by Jaipur

1st Floor Meridian Point Church Road Greystones Co Wicklow
Tel: 01 201 7222 info@jaipur.ie www.chakra.ie

This delightful younger sister to the successful Jaipur restaurants in Dalkey, Dublin & Malahide (see entries) occupies a custom-designed restaurant space in and overlooking a modern shopping mall just off the main street of Greystones, and opened to some well-deserved acclaim a couple of years ago. It has a comfortable bar/reception within a spacious and very attractive high-ceilinged dining room, with lovely subdued warm-toned décor and, from the moment of arrival, service is unobtrusively attentive and charmingly friendly. The cooking maintains Jaipur's crisp, modern contemporary take on traditional Indian food - colourful, delicious, well-flavoured dishes with a lot of eye-appeal. The vegetarian choices are numerous and appealing, and old favourites like tandoori prawns and succulent biryanis are served with splendid breads and delicious sauces. Unusually for an Indian restaurant, even the dessert menu is worth exploring and, like all the restaurants in the group, a fairly priced wine list has been carefully selected to complement Indian food. The shopping mall car park is available free for diners. Toilets wheelchair accessible; children welcome (high chair); **Seats 95** (private room, 12); air conditioning; D daily, 5-11pm; Early D €22, 5.30-7pm; Set D €30-45. House wine €18-20. Closed 25-26 Dec. MasterCard, Visa, Laser. **Directions:** Just off main street in new shopping centre, 2 minutes from DART station.

Greystones
BAR/RESTAURANT

Diva Restaurant and Piano Bar

The Harbour Greystones Co Wicklow
Tel: 01 201 7151

In a town rapidly becoming a food mecca, Tara O'Grady's Italian restaurant has an enviable harbourside location - where, until such time as the new marina comes on-stream, waves still gently lap on the shore. At the top of the stairs, double doors open into the pleasant bar with comfortable sofas, where a fire blazes in winter. The two rooms that make up the restaurant are busy, with tables full of contented diners, including a number of children; the back room is where the pianist plays and sings while you dine. The menu has all the Italian favourites, plus some variations- and, unusually, gluten free pasta is available and there is no flour in any of the sauces. Bruschetta, authentic minestrone soup, or mussels on the half shell in a tomato and red wine sauce make good starters, and main courses include classics like lasagne al forno, and spaghetti bolognese, alongside less usual dishes like scallopine Anna Bolena sautéed scallops in fresh pasta, in a white wine sauce with sundried tomatoes. All the popular varieties of pizza are available, also a choice of chicken dishes. But do leave space for dessert a chocolate and orange mousse, perhaps, profiteroles, tiramisu or a seasonal strawberry mascarpone cheesecake. The wine list is shortish, with good value house wines. Diva has all the ingredients that make for a good night out great location, excellent mid range food, a lively atmosphere and friendly, welcoming staff. **Seats 120;** Open Mon-Thur 5-11pm (last orders) Fri-Sun 12-11pm. MasterCard, Visa, Laser. **Directions:** On the harbour front. ◈

Greystones
CAFÉ/RESTAURANT

The Happy Pear

Church Road Greystones Co Wicklow **Tel: 01 287 3655**
info@thehappypear.ie www.thehappypear.ie

Twins David and Stephen Flynn run this cheerfully ethical vegetable shop, with smoothie bar, café and an evening tapas bar with wine and beer available. If that all sounds a lot for a vegetable shop, it is but it is also very small, and there are plans to expand the shop and café/restaurant on the current site in the near future. Food is simple and tasty try the house salad, for example, with sprouted mung bean, watercress, radicchio in a pumpkin seed & parsley dressing: very good. A telling detail about this pair they run their van on local rapeseed oil. Now that is walking the walk. Children welcome (high chair); Toilets wheelchair accessible. **Seats 40** (outdoors, 30); Vegetarian; food served daily 9-6pm (from 11am Sun); house wine €17. MasterCard, Visa, Laser. **Directions:** Main Street Greystones.

Greystones
RESTAURANT

The Hungry Monk

Church Road Greystones Co Wicklow **Tel: 01 287 5759**
info@thehungrymonk.ie www.thehungrymonk.ie

Well-known wine buff Pat Keown celebrates 20 years of running this hospitable first floor restaurant on the main street in 2008, and his warmth and enthusiasm are undimmed. Pat is a great and enthusiastic host; his love of wine is infectious, the place is spick and span and the monk-related decor is a bit of fun- and a combination of hospitality, great wines and interesting good quality food at affordable prices are at the heart of this restaurant's success. Seasonal menus offered include a well-priced all-day Sunday lunch and an evening à la carte menu, with fish the speciality in summer, and game in winter. Blackboard specials guaranteed to sharpen the appetite include the day's seafood dishes, any special wine offers - and, perhaps, a special treat like suckling pig. Menus give a slight nod to current trends, but there is no pretence at cutting edge style and you will also be pleased find faithful renditions of old favourites, like lambs kidneys Madeira and roast fillet of Irish pork. Vegetarian dishes are highlighted on the menu and there is emphasis on high quality ingredients, including Angus steaks and Wicklow lamb as well as seafood, both local and from Castletownbere. The famous wine list ('The Thirsty Monk') is clearly a labour of love and, in turn, gives great pleasure to customers, especially as prices are very fair; affordable favourites include a whole page of house wines listed by category and of course, offers many special bottles for connoisseurs. Two pages of half bottles too, and a couple of dozen pudding wines. Children welcome. **Restaurant Seats 35.** Reservations advised. Air conditioning. Food served Wed-Sun 12.30-9. à la carte; also Vegetarian Menu; Set Sun L €27. House wines from €19, SC 10%. Restaurant closed Mon & Tue. Closed 24-26 Dec. *Downstairs, **The Hungry Monk Wine Bar** offers an informal menu of bistro style dishes (Monk's famous burger, Dublin Bay prawn scampi & chips...) and a carefully selected short wine list. Wine Bar open daily, 5-12. Closed 25-26 Dec. Amex, MasterCard, Visa, Laser. **Directions:** Centre of Greystones village beside DART.

Greystones
RESTAURANT

The Three Q's

Gweedore Church Road Greystones Co Wicklow **Tel: 01 287 5477**
thethreeqs@gmail.com

The Three Qs is a small, stylish restaurant on the main street run by three brothers, Brian, Paul and Colin Quinn, who bring together local foods and international inspiration to create innovative menus with real style. The dinner menu has a smart edge, including dishes such as saddle of rabbit with sage and black pudding stuffing, with the lunch and brunch menus a more relaxed affair, offering tasty fresh tasting combinations like a dish of corn fritters with crispy pancetta, avocado and tomato Attention to detail is seen in good side orders, including proper freshly cut chips. The flavours of North Africa and Arab cooking are seen in delicious desserts like Medjoul dates soaked in espresso, star anise and cinnamon, and served with vanilla mascarpone and shortbread. There's welcome originality here also well informed service and fair pricing on both food and wine. Not suitable for children after 6pm **Seats 30** (outdoors, 8); food served daily 9am-11.30pm (Sun 9-3); L 12-4.30, D 6-10. A la carte (Starters €4.95 to €9.95, main courses €16.95 to €26.95, desserts €6.95.); house wine €19 Closed Sun D, Christmas week. Amex, MasterCard, Visa, Laser. **Directions:** Main street Greystones 100m from the Dart station. ◇

Greystones
RESTAURANT

R

Vino Pasta
Church Road Greystones Co Wicklow
Tel: 01 287 4807

féile bia Attractive awnings and clear signage make a good impression at this popular Italian restaurant and, once past the tiny bar/reception area (which has just two seats), you'll find a warmly decorated room with bistro-style table settings - paper cloths & napkins - and a moderately priced menu, majoring in pastas and pizzas plus daily specials on a blackboard menu: lambs kidneys in a creamy mustard sauce with tagliatelle, perhaps, and fresh fish such as cod with a spicy chilli jam, or salmon with a herb crust. Efficient, friendly service, sound cooking and generous portions make this the kind of place that locals pop into frequently. Limited wine list. The early dinner is good value, and can include a fish special of the day. **Seats 60;** reservations required; air conditioning. Amex, MasterCard, Visa, Laser. **Directions:** End of Main Street beside DART station. ◇

Kilmacanogue
CAFÉ

Avoca Handweavers
Kilmacanogue Bray Co Wicklow **Tel: 01 286 7466**
reception@avoca.ie www.avoca.ie

féile bia This large shop and restaurant, off the N11 south of Dublin, is the flagship premises of Ireland's most famous group of craft shops and, they have become almost equally well known for the quality of their food - people come here from miles around to shop, and to tuck into wholesome home-cooked food, which is based as much as possible on local and artisan produce, and there is a commitment to using products from recognised Quality Assurance Schemes. (In recognition, Avoca Cafes were the recipients of the Féile Bia Award in 2003). The style at Avoca is eclectic and, although they are especially well-known for great baking and traditional dishes like beef and Guinness casserole, their salads and vegetables are also legendary. In addition to the large self-service area, a delightful new table service cafe, The Fernhouse, opened in 2007, making this an even more attractive destination and there is also a wide range of excellent delicatessen fare for sale in the shop.*Also at: Avoca, Powerscourt, Rathcoole & Suffolk Street, Dublin 2 (see entries). Now also at The Garden Café, Mount Usher Gardens, Ashford. Toilets wheelchair accessible; Children welcome. **Seats 170** (+Outdoor Dining, 80). Air conditioning. Open daily, 9.30-5 (Sun 10-5). House wine from €20. No s.c. Closed 25-26 Dec. Amex, Diners, MasterCard, Visa, Laser. **Directions:** On N11 sign posted before Kilmacanogue Village.

Kilpedder
CAFÉ

N R

Organic Life
Tinna Park Bower Kilpedder Co Wicklow
Tel: 01 201 1882

A long avenue of trees leads to a large glass-house where Marc Michel's organic restaurant and shop nestle amongst working fields. Exquisite breads and dips can double as starters though more substantial starters can include warm salad of tiger prawns and Aran Victor potato salad (a rare variety of potatoes popular in the 1950s). Superb home home-made burgers come with a tangy tomato salsa, tossed salad and home-made fries, and other main courses can include Spanish fish stew of seasonal seafood tossed with onion and olives in a robust tomato reduction topped with garlic aioli - or organic lamb patties with cucumber, chilli and lemon crème fraîche. Interesting desserts reflect both the quality of ingredients and traditional tastes such as the orange and vanilla pannacotta or fruit crumble with spiced apple. The restaurant is only open at lunch time but is a firm favourite for those seeking a country escape so near the capital. **Seats 60.** Open L only Tue-Sun, 12 4, scones and teas from 10 am Tue-Sat, shop open 10 to 5pm. Starters €6.95, average main course €15, average dessert €6.50. Short wine list of organic wines from €19.95 a bottle, €4.95 a glass. ◇

Kiltegan
COUNTRY HOUSE
👑 € 👁

Barraderry Country House
Barraderry Kiltegan Co Wicklow **Tel: 059 647 3209**
jo.hobson@oceanfree.net www.barraderrycountryhouse.com

Olive and John Hobson's delightful Georgian house is in a quiet rural area close to the Wicklow Mountains and, once their family had grown up the whole house was extensively refurbished and altered for the comfort of guests. Big bedrooms with country views are beautifully furnished with old family furniture and have well-finished shower rooms - and there's a spacious sitting room for guests' use too. Barraderry would make a good base for touring the lovely counties of Wicklow Kildare, Carlow and Wexford and there's plenty to do nearby, with six golf courses within a half hour drive, several hunts and equestrian centres within easy reach and also Punchestown, Curragh and Naas racecourses - and, of course, walking in the lovely Wicklow Mountains. Garden; walking. Children welcome (cot available). Pets permitted in certain areas by arrangement. **Rooms 4** (all en-suite, shower only & no smoking). B&B €50 pps; ss €5. Closed 15 Dec-15 Jan. MasterCard, Visa. **Directions:** N81 Dublin-Baltinglass; R 747 to Kiltegan (7km).

Macreddin
HOTEL/RESTAURANT
👑 👁 🍽

The BrookLodge Hotel
Macreddin Village Co Wicklow **Tel: 0402 36444**
brooklodge@macreddin.ie www.brooklodge.com

Built on the site of a deserted village in a Wicklow valley, this extraordinary food, drink and leisure complex exists thanks to the vision of three brothers, Evan, Eoin and Bernard Doyle. The driving force is Evan, a pioneer of the new organic movement when he ran The Strawberry Tree restaurant in Killarney. Here in Wicklow their hotel and restaurant has earned a national recognition for its strong position on organic food (BrookLodge won the Guide's Natural Food Award in association with Euro-Toques, in 2003), and their little "street" is thriving, with an olde-worlde pub (Actons), a café, a micro-brewery and gift shops selling home-made produce and related quality products. Organic food markets, held on the first Sunday of the month (first and third in summer) have also proved a great success. Spacious and welcoming, the hotel has elegant country house furnishings, open fires and plenty of places to sit quietly or meet for a sociable drink - and there are accommodation choices between the original rooms, which are furnished with quite traditional free standing furniture, and state-of-the-art mezzanine suites, which will please those who relish very modern high-tech surroundings. A luxurious spa centre, The Wells, features an indoor to-outdoor swimming pool, gym, juice bar and a wide variety of exclusive beauty and health treatments Midweek, weekend and low season special offers are good value, and staff are friendly and helpful *Recent developments include The River Mews (4 conference suites and 8 bedrooms) a short stroll from the main hotel; also Macreddin Golf Club, designed by Irish Ryder Cup hero Paul McGinley and open in June 2007 and also Brook Hall, a self-contained area for weddings and large functions (up to 200) with dedicated reception, mezzanine bar, large south facing deck, 24 new rooms and a swimming pool. Conference/banqueting (350/200); business centre, broadband wi/fi, secretarial services video conferencing (by arrangement). Equestrian centre, archery, clay pigeon shooting, falconry, golf (18), snooker, garden, walking, lawn bowls, fitness room, spa, swimming pool, hot tub. Children welcome (under 3s free in parents' room, cot available without charge, baby sitting arranged). Pets allowed in some areas by arrangement. Heli-pad. **Rooms 66** (13 suites, 3 junior suites, 4 ground floor 27 family, 4 disabled, 27 no smoking). Lift. 24 hr room service; B&B €130 pps; ss €50. Open all year. **Strawberry Tree:** This is Ireland's only certified organic restaurant, reflecting the BrookLodge philosophy of sourcing only from producers using slow organic methods and harvesting in their correct season. Menus are not too long or too fussy: dishes have strong, simple names and, except when underlined on the menu as wild, everything offered is organic. Typical dishes might include starters like home smoked beef, with figs and balsamic dressing or grilled wild pollock with roast red pepper and main courses such as slow cooked spring lamb with roast celeriac & garlic jus, or a vegetarian dish of wild mushroom and brie tart with wild garlic pesto. There's a great buzz associated with the commit ment to organic production at BrookLodge, and it makes a natural venue for meetings of like-minded groups such as Euro-Toques and Slow Food, especially on market days. Dining at the Strawberry Tree is a unique experience - and good informal meals can be equally enjoyable at The Orchard Café and Actons pub (both open noon-9pm daily). Given the quality of ingredients used and the standard of cooking, meals at BrookLodge represent very good value. **Seats 145** (private room, 60, outdoor, 10). Air conditioning. Toilets wheelchair accessible. D daily 7-9.30 (to 9 Sun). L Sun only 1.30-3.30. Set D €60, Set Sun L €40. House wines €25. SC discretionary. *William Actons Pub - Bar food daily, 12.30-9; The Orchard Café, light meals in summer 12.30-9. Amex, Diners, MasterCard, Visa, Laser. **Directions:** Signed from Aughrim.

Newtownmountkennedy

HOTEL/RESTAURANT

Marriott Druids Glen Hotel & Country Club

Newtownmountkennedy Co Wicklow **Tel: 01 287 0800**
mhrs.dubgs.reservations@marriotthotels.com www.marriottdruidsglen.com

téite bia Just over 30 km south of Dublin, in a stunning location between the sea and the mountains and adjacent to Druids Glen Golf Club, this luxurious hotel has a feeling of space throughout - beginning with the marbled foyer and its dramatic feature fireplace. Suites and guest rooms, many of them "double/doubles" (with two queen sized beds), are all generously-sized, with individual 'climate control' (heating and air conditioning), and all bathrooms have separate bath and walk-in shower. A wide range of recreational facilities on site includes the hotel's spa and health club (recently refurbished and extended), and two championship golf courses, while those nearby include horse riding, archery, quad biking - and, of course, the gentler attractions of the Wicklow Mountains National Park are on the doorstep. When dining in, choose between Flynns' Steakhouse (see below) and the bigger Druids Restaurant (where breakfast, carvery lunch and dinner are served daily). Bar meals also available in 'The Thirteenth' bar or, in fine weather, on a sheltered deck outside the two restaurants. Druids Glen Marriott was our Business Hotel of the Year in 2003 - and this is a place to relax and unwind, as well as do business. Conference/banqueting 250/220; business centre, secretarial services. Golf (2x18); leisure centre, swimming pool; spa, beauty/treatment rooms, walking, garden. **Rooms 148** (11 suites, 137 executive, 6 disabled). Lift. Children welcome (under 12s free in parents' room, cots available without charge; baby sitting arranged). 24 hr. room service, turndown service, laundry/valet service. B&B about €115, ss €30. **Flynn's Steakhouse:** Quite small and intimate, with an open log fire and candlelight, Flynn's has more atmosphere than the bigger daytime Druids Restaurant, and reservations are essential. American style steaks and grills are the speciality but, demonstrating a welcome commitment to using Irish produce, a supply of Certified Irish Angus is contracted for the hotel; just remember that American-style means big - 24oz porterhouse and ribeye, for example... Rack of Wicklow lamb is another speciality and there's a sprinkling of other dishes with an Irish flavour which might not be expected in an international hotel, like Dingle crab cakes, Guinness braised mussels - and an Irish cheese platter. **Seats 75** (private room 16). Reservations essential. Not suitable for children after 8. D daily, 6-10.30. Set D €40/50 2/3 course, also à la carte. House wine, from about €22; SC discretionary. *The larger Druid's Restaurant serves breakfast, lunch & dinner daily; L carvery, Druids Irish D Menu à la carte. Bar meals also available in 'The Thirteenth' bar or, in fine weather, on a sheltered deck outside the two restaurants. Amex, Diners, MasterCard, Visa, Laser. **Directions:** 32 km (20 miles) south of Dublin on N11, at Newtownmountkennedy. ◇

Newtownmountkennedy

HOTEL

Parkview Hotel

Main Street Newtownmountkennedy Co Wicklow **Tel: 01 201 5600**
info@parkviewhotel.ie www.parkviewhotel.ie

This quietly contemporary privately owned hotel opened in the village of Newtownmountkennedy in 2007, and it is a useful addition to the accommodation options in this beautiful area. Public areas include an attractive modern bar, where informal food is served, and facilities for small business meetings of up to 20 people are available. The spacious and pleasingly furnished bedrooms include four suites and four family rooms, and this would make a very comfortable base for exploring the area, golfing, or any of the many other activities available locally. Staff are extremely helpful and friendly and smart. Conferences/Banqueting (400/250); lap top sized safe in bedrooms; jacuzzi, walking; children welcome (under 2s free in parents' room, cot available free of charge, baby sitting arranged); **Rooms 60** (4 executive, 4 family, 3 disabled); Lift; all day room service; B&B €80 pps, ss €40. MasterCard, Visa, Laser. **Directions:** N11, Newtownmountkennedy, in village on Main Street.

Rathnew
HOTEL/RESTAURANT

Hunter's Hotel

Newrath Bridge Rathnew Co Wicklow **Tel: 0404 40106**
reception@hunters.ie www.hunters.ie

ATMOSPHERIC ESTABLISHMENT OF THE YEAR

A rambling old coaching inn set in lovely gardens alongside the River Vartry, this much-loved hotel has a long and fascinating history - it's one of Ireland's oldest coaching inns, with records indicating that it was built around 1720. In the same family now for five generations, the colourful Mrs Maureen Gelletlie takes pride in running the place on traditional lines with her sons Richard and Tom. This means old-fashioned comfort and food based on local and home-grown produce with the emphasis very much on 'old fashioned' which is where its charm and character lie. There's a proper little bar, with chintzy loose-covered furniture and an open fire, a traditional dining room with fresh flowers from the riverside garden where their famous afternoon tea is served in summer - and comfortable country bedrooms. There is nowhere else in Ireland like it. Conference (30). Garden. Parking. Children welcome. No pets. **Rooms 16** (1 junior suite, 1 shower only, 1 disabled). Wheelchair access. B&B from about €95 pps, ss about €20. **Restaurant:** In tune with the spirit of the hotel, the style is traditional country house cooking: simple food with a real home-made feeling about it - no mean achievement in a restaurant and much to be applauded. Seasonal lunch and dinner menus change daily, but you can expect classics such as chicken liver paté with melba toast, soups based on fish or garden produce, traditional roast rib beef, with Yorkshire pudding or old-fashioned roast stuffed chicken with bacon and probably several fish dishes, possibly including poached salmon with hollandaise and chive sauce. Desserts are often based on what the garden has to offer, and baking is good, so fresh raspberries and cream or baked apple and rhubarb tart could be wise choices. Delightful. **Seats 50.** Toilets wheelchair accessible. L daily, 1-3 (Sun 2 sittings: 12.45 & 2.30). D daily 7.30-9. Set D about €40. Set L about €22. No s.c. House wine about €16. Afternoon tea about €7.50. Closed 3 days at Christmas. Amex, Diners, MasterCard, Visa. **Directions:** Off N11 at Ashford or Rathnew. ◇

Rathnew

Tinakilly Country House

The well known hotel Tinakilly Country House at Rathnew (0404 69274; www.tinakilly.ie) was sold as a going concern shortly before the Guide went to press, and will be re-assessed. For further details contact the hotel directly, or log on to www.ireland-guide for an independent review.

Roundwood
RESTAURANT/PUB

Roundwood Inn

Roundwood Co Wicklow
Tel: 01 281 8107

féile bía Jurgen and Aine Schwalm have owned this atmospheric 17th century inn in the highest village in the Wicklow Hills for over 25 years and, during that time, caring hands-on management backed up by dedicated long-serving staff have earned this unique bar and restaurant a lot of friends. There's a public bar at one end with a snug and an open fire and, in the middle of the building, the main bar food area has an enormous open fireplace with an ever-burning log fire, and is furnished in traditional style. Together with head chef Paul Taube, who has also been in the kitchen here for over 20 years, the style that the Schwalms have developed over the years is their own unique blend of Irish and German influences: excellent bar food includes Hungarian goulash, fresh crab bisque, Galway oysters, smoked Wicklow trout, and hearty meals, notably the delicious house variation on Irish stew. The food has always had a special character and this, together with the place itself and its own special brand of hospitality, has earned the Roundwood Inn an enviable reputation. Bar meals 12-9.30 daily. Bar closed 25 Dec, Good Fri. **Restaurant:** The restaurant is in the same style, only slightly more formal than the main bar, with fires at each end of the room, and is open by reservation. The menu choice leans towards more substantial dishes such as rack of Wicklow lamb, roast wild Wicklow venison, venison ragout, pheasant and other game in season. German influences are again evident in long-established special-ities such as smoked Westphalian ham and wiener schnitzel, but there are also classic specialities such as roast stuffed goose on winter menus, and roast suckling pig. An interesting mainly European wine list favours France and Germany, with many special bottles from Germany. Not suitable for chil-dren after 6.30. **Seats 45** (private room, 25). D Fri & Sat, 7.30-9; à la carte. L Sun only, 1-2. (Children welcome for lunch). House wine from about €16; SC discretionary; reservations advised. No SC. Restaurant closed L Mon-Sat, D Sun-Thu. Amex, MasterCard, Visa, Laser. **Directions:** N11, follow sign for Glendalough. ◊

Woodenbridge

HOTEL

R

féile bia

Woodenbridge Hotel

Vale of Avoca Arklow Co Wicklow **Tel: 0402 35146**

info@woodenbridgehotel.com www.woodenbridgehotel.com

This pleasant country hotel lays claim to the title of Ireland's oldest hotel, with a history going back to 1608, when it was first licensed as a coaching inn on the old Dublin-Wexford highway - and later came to prominence when gold and copper were mined in the locality. Today, it is very popular for weddings and golf, and makes a friendly and relaxing base for a visit to this beautiful part of County Wicklow. Older bedrooms in the hotel have all been refurbished and are comfortably furnished, and many of them overlook Woodenbridge golf course; Woodenbridge Lodge offers forty newer en-suite rooms overlooking the River Aughrim. As well as a more formal restaurant, food is available in the lively bar (traditional Irish music in summer). *Golf breaks are a speciality and discounted green fees are offered on a number of local golf courses, with other activities for non-golfing partners if required. Children welcome (under 12s free in parents' room; cots available without charge). No pets. **Rooms 62** (8 family rooms, 45 no smoking, 3 for disabled). B&B €50pps, ss €20. Food available 12.30-9. Amex, Diners, MasterCard, Visa, Laser. Directions: N11 to Arklow; turn off - 7km (4 miles). ◊

BELFAST

The origins of the cities of Ireland are usually found in 5th Century monastic centres which were overrun by the Vikings some four hundred or so years later to become trading settlements that later "had manners put on them" by the Normans. But Belfast is much newer than that. When the Vikings in 823AD raided what is now known as Belfast Lough, their target was the wealthy monastery at Bangor, and thus their beach-heads were at Ballyholme and Groomsport further east. Then, when the Normans held sway in the 13th Century, their main stronghold was at Carrickfergus on the northern shore of the wide sea inlet which was known for several centuries as Carrickfergus Bay. In the tumult of the 17th Century, with the Plantation of Ulster, the Cromwellian campaign, and the WilliamiteWars, Carrickfergus with its powerful Norman Castle continued as a major historical focus.

At the head of Carrickfergus Bay beside the shallow River Lagan, the tiny settlement of beal feirste - the 'town at the mouth of the Farset or the sandspit' - wasn't named on maps at all until the late 15th Century. But Belfast proved to be the perfect greenfield site for rapid development as the Industrial Revolution got under way. Its rocketing growth began with linen manufacture in the 17th Century, and this was accelerated by the arrival of skilled Huguenot refugees after 1685.

There was also scope for ship-building on the shorelines in the valleymouth between the high peaks crowding in on the Antrim side on the northwest, and the Holywood Hills to the southeast, though the first shipyard of any significant size wasn't in being until 1791, when William and Hugh Ritchie opened for business. The Lagan Valley gave convenient access to the rest of Ireland for the increase of trade and commerce to encourage development of the port, while the prosperous farms of Down and Antrim fed a rapidly expanding population.

So, at the head of what was becoming known as Belfast Lough, Belfast took off in a big way, a focus for industrial ingenuity and manufacturing inventiveness, and a magnet for entrepreneurs and innovators from all of the north of Ireland, and the world beyond. Its population in 1600 had been less than 500, yet by 1700 it was 2,000, and by 1800 it was 25,000. The city's growth was prodigious, such that by the end of the 19th Century it could claim with justifiable pride to have the largest shipyard in the world, the largest ropeworks, the largest linen mills, the largest tobacco factory, and the largest heavy engineering works, all served by a greater mileage of quays than anywhere comparable. And it was an essentially Victorian expansion - the population in 1851 was 87,062, but by 1901 it was 349,180 - the largest city in Ireland.

Growth had become so rapid in the latter half of the 19th Century that it tended to obliterate the influence of the gentler intellectual and philosophical legacies inspired by the Huguenots and other earlier developers, a case in point being the gloriously flamboyant and baroque Renaissance-style City Hall, which was completed in 1906. It was the perfect expression of that late-Victorian energy and confidence in which Belfast shared with conspicuous enthusiasm. But its site had only become available because the City Fathers authorised the demolition of the quietly elegant White Linen Hall, which had been a symbol of Belfast's less strident period of development in the 18th Century.

However, Belfast Corporation was only fulfilling the spirit of the times. And in such a busy city, there was always a strongly human dimension to everyday life. The City Hall may be on the grand scale, but it was nevertheless right at the heart of town. Equally, while the gantries of the shipyard may have loomed overhead, they did so near the houses of the workers in a manner which somehow softened their sheer size. Admittedly this theme of giving great projects a human dimension seems to have been forgotten in the later design and location of the Government Building (completed 1932) at Stormont, east of the city. But back in the vibrant heart of Belfast, there is continuing entertainment and accessible interest in buildings as various as the Grand Opera House, St Anne's Cathedral, the Crown Liquor Saloon, Sinclair Seamen's Church, the Linenhall Library, Smithfield Market, and some of the impressive Victorian and Edwardian banking halls, while McHugh's pub on Queen's Square, and Tedford's Restaurant just round the corner on Donegall Quay, provide thoughtful reminders of the earlier more restrained style.

Today, modern technologies and advanced engineering have displaced the old smokestack industries in the forefront of the city's work patterns, with the shipyard ceasing to build ships in March 2003. Shorts' aerospace factories are now the city's biggest employer, while parts of the former shipyard are being redeveloped as the Titanic Quarter in memory of the most famous ship built in Belfast, although it's a moot point if all the people of Belfast wish to be reminded on a daily basis of the Titanic disaster, which occured as recently as 1912.

The energy of former times has been channeled into impressive urban regeneration along the River Lagan. Here, the flagship building is the Waterfront Hall, a large concert venue which has won international praise, and is complemented by the Odyssey Centre on the other side of the river. In the southern part of the city, Queen's University (founded 1845) is a beautifully balanced 1849 Lanyon building at the heart of a pleasant university district which includes the respected Ulster Museum & Art Gallery, while the university itself is particularly noted for its pioneering work in medicine and engineering.

There's a buzz to Belfast which is expressed in its cultural and warmly sociable life, and reflected in the internationally-minded innovative energy of its young chefs. Yet in some ways it is still has marked elements of a country town and port strongly rooted in land and sea. The hills of Antrim can be glimpsed from most streets, and the farmland of Down makes its presence felt.

They are quickly reached by a developing motorway system, relished by those in a hurry who also find the increasingly busy and very accessible Belfast City Airport a convenient boon, while access to the International Airport to the west beside Lough Neagh is being improved. So although Belfast may have a clearly defined character, it is also very much part of the country around it, and is all the better for that. And in the final analysis, Belfast is uniquely itself.

Local Attractions & Information

Arts Council of Northern Ireland	028 90 385200
Belfast Castle & Zoo	028 90 776277
Belfast Crystal	028 90 622051
Belfast Festival at Queens (late Oct-early Nov)	028 90 971034
Belfast Visitor and Convention Bureau	028 90 246609
City Airport	028 9093093
City Hall	028 90 270456
Citybus Tours	028 90 626888
Fernhill House: The People's Museum	028 90 715599
Grand Opera House	028 90 241919
International Airport	028 94 484848
Kings Hall (exhibitions, concerts, trade shows)	028 90 665225
Lagan Valley Regional Park	028 90 491922
Linenhall Library	028 90 321707
Lyric Theatre	028 90 381081
National Trust Regional Office	028 97 510721
Northern Ireland Railways	028 90 899411
Odyssey (entertainment & sports complex)	028 90 451055
St Anne's Cathedral	028 90 328332
Sir Thomas & Lady Dixon Park (Rose Gardens)	028 90 320202 / 90603359
Tourism Information	028 90 246609
Ulster Historical Foundation (genealogical res.)	028 90 332288
Waterfront Hall (concert venue)	028 90 334455
West Belfast Festivals	028 90 313440

BELFAST

Ireland's fastest changing city has a huge buzz about it and, whatever your reason for visiting, you'll be glad to find plenty of great places to eat, drink and chill out. Belfast abounds with bars, coffee shops and informal eating places and, as well as those listed, some worth keeping an eye open for include the smart **Clements Coffee Shops** throughout the city, which are well known for quality and ethical standards they use Fairtrade coffee in their trademark cappuccinos, make their own crisps and let the staff choose the music (Donegall Square West, Castle Street, Royal Avenue & Rosemary Street, all open all day; and Botanic Avenue, Stranmillis Road and Lisburn Road, also open at night). In the city centre **The Linen Hall Library** on Donegall Square North (Tel: 028 9032 1707; www.linenhall.com) is a hidden gem, and it has a coffee shop overlooking the City Hall with an old world feeling and serene, restorative atmosphere and Waterstones, almost next door on Fountain Street, has more substantial fare on offer and you can browse the books, and have a quick read over coffee. For wholesome fast food in the city centre, the crêperie **Flour** (028 9033 9966) on Upper Queen Street offers 45 sweet & savoury crêpes and filled baguettes too. Garden centres are often great places for a bite to eat, and Belfast is no exception; should you find yourself out Gilnahirk way, the huge **Hillmount Garden Centre** (028 9044 8822; www.hillmount.co.uk) is well worth a visit for many reasons, including its café, **The Gardeners Rest**, where you'll find wholesome home cooked food every day (Mon-Fri 10-7.30, Sat 10-5, Sun 12.30-4.45). And, if attending an event at **The Waterfront Hall**, it may be useful to know that pre-theatre menus are available at their brasserie, **Arc** (028 9024 4966), from 5pm until 30 minutes before curtain up (also open for lunch). Food lovers visiting the city will of course want to go to **St George's Market**, which is one of Belfast's oldest attractions; since its refurbishment in 1997, the Friday (variety, including clothes, books and antiques) and Saturday (food and garden) markets held in this atmospheric Victorian building are among the most interesting things to visit in Belfast. In 2002 the Saturday market won the Irish Food Writers' Guild Supreme Award for Contribution to Food in Ireland Portavogie fish, venison and pheasant in season, local beef and pork, local organic vegetables, herbs and fruit, and farmhouse cheeses are among the delicious things you'll find here.

WWW.IRELAND-GUIDE.COM FOR THE BEST PLACES TO EAT, DRINK & STAY

Belfast
RESTAURANT
👑 ☆ Ⓔ

Aldens Restaurant
229 Upper Newtownards Road Belfast Co Antrim BT4 3JF
Tel: 028 9065 0079
info@aldensrestaurant.com www.aldensrestaurant.com

A neat aubergine canopy highlights the discreetly distinctive public face of Jonathan Davis's fine contemporary restaurant, an indication of the genuine quality you will find here: Aldens was at the forefront of Belfast's first wave of chic, uncluttered modern restaurants when it opened in 1998 and, although the choice of location seemed unlikely at the time, it immediately attracted a strong business following and became a destination address for food lovers visiting Belfast, as well as a favourite with residents and, these days, its proximity to the government buildings at Stormont is a big plus. Competition in the city centre has grown dramatically of late but Aldens serves its area extremely well and head chef Denise Hockey, who took over from the founding chef Cath Gradwell in 2006, is doing a great job in the kitchen and retaining the restaurant's position at the forefront of the Belfast dining scene. Under Jonathan Davis's personal supervision, this has always been an especially hospitable restaurant, with comfortable seating and pleasing details - fresh flowers, choice of olives, newspapers and food guides to browse over a drink in the welcoming bar/reception area, and caring, knowledgable service throughout. Opaque glass windows soften the light and give a sense of privacy, with strips of mirror adding reflections on painted walls, and tables are set up smartly with linen napkins, tapenade, olive oil and butter, along with several types of bread. The style is lively and admirably simple, allowing the quality of carefully sourced seasonal ingredients to speak for itself, and with special emphasis on fish and local produce. The cooking is accomplished and executed with flair, with well-judged flavour combinations and giving good value is also a point of honour here, with several daily changing international menus offered, including an extremely reasonable midweek menu and great lunch specials. Menus are not overlong yet offer plenty of choice, and include some luxurious dishes - seared foie gras is a speciality, served with mixed leaves and caramelised shallots, perhaps; updated classics, like chicken liver paté with hot toast & red onion marmalade and steamed mussels with white wine, parsley and garlic sit happily alongside prime fish and meats (roast hake, ribeye steak), and simpler everyday foods like twice-baked mushroom soufflé with truffle and herb sauce (one of several mainstream vegetarian choices), served with imaginative side dishes. Consistency at a very high level over a decade is not an easy thing to achieve, yet Jonathan Davis's personal direction of a fine team safeguards Aldens' place at the top of Northern Ireland's dining scene. An well selected, fairly priced and informative wine list includes a god range of house wines and half bottles. *A range of Aldens gift items, including tapenade, red onion marmalade and Caesar salad dressing, is available. **Seats 70.** Children welcome. No smoking area; air conditioning. L Mon-Fri,12-2.30; D Mon-Thu 6-10, Fri & Sat 6-11; Set D from about £20 (Mon-Thu), à la carte. House wines from about £11.95; sc discretionary. Closed L Sat, all Sun, Public Holidays, 2 weeks July. Amex, Diners, MasterCard, Visa, Switch. **Directions:** On the Upper Newtownards Road at junction with Sandown Road. ◈

An Old Rectory

148 Malone Road Belfast Co Antrim BT9 5LH **Tel: 028 90 66 7882**
info@anoldrectory.co.uk www.anoldrectory.co.uk

Conveniently located near the King's Hall, Public Records Office, Lisburn Road and Queen's University, Mary Callan's lovely late Victorian house is set well back from the road in mature trees, with private parking. A former Church of Ireland rectory, it has the benefit of being in the Malone conservation area and retains many original features, including stained glass windows. There's a lovely drawing room with books, sofas, comfortable armchairs with cosy rugs over the arms - and a very hospitable habit of serving hot whiskey in the drawing room at 9 o'clock each night. Accommodation is on two storeys, every room individually decorated (and named) and each has both a desk and a sofa, magazines to browse, also beverage trays with hot chocolate and soup sachets as well as the usual tea and coffee; better still there's a fridge on each landing with iced water and fresh milk, helpful advice on eating out locally is available (including menus) and, although they don't do evening meals, pride is taken in providing a good breakfast. Children welcome (under 5 free in parents' room). Garden, walking. No pets. **Rooms 5** (3 en-suite, 2 with private bathrooms - 2 shower only, all no smoking). B&B £37.50 pps, ss £11.50. Closed Christmas-New Year & Easter. **No Credit Cards. Directions:** 3km (2 miles) from city centre, between Balmoral Avenue and Stranmillis Road.

The Bank Gallery @ The Edge

The Edge May's Meadow Belfast Co Antrim BT1 3PH
Tel: 028 9032 2000

Right on the Lagan and just a short stroll along a walkway from the Waterfront (and only 10 minutes walk from Royal Avenue), this popular establishment known as The Edge operates on three levels, with the smart Port Bar at lower ground level, a gently contemporary restaurant The Bank Gallery above it, and a function/hospitality area on the top floor; food is served at all levels and, at busy times in summer, people tend to migrate from one to another and there are tables set up outside, and even in the car park in good weather. With views of the famous Harland & Wolf cranes, Samson & Goliath, and doors opening onto a small outside seating area on both bar and restaurant levels it a pleasant spot which, thanks to consistently good cooking, has earned a following. The decor is appealing: portholes in the double doors are repeated on chair backs and, with lightwood everywhere, recessed wall lights and dusky pinks and beiges used in voile curtains and upholstery, there's a softness that offsets the industrial exterior. Tables are set up smartly with black rubber mats and simply folded damask napkins, and professional black-aproned servers move speedily to bring delicious warm breads with tapenade (£2.50). Scottish head chef Duncan Millar (formerly of Cayenne and Rain City) and, although wide ranging, there is a little more in the way of Asian and Fusion touches, and less emphasis on fish and shellfish than formerly. Menus offered include snacks and light lunches in the Port Bar and, in the Bank Gallery, an individually priced lunch menu, a midweek Meal Deal (3 course dinner for two with a bottle of wine for £35), a Saturday Fixed Price Menu (pre-theatre) which is also excellent value at £13/£16 per person for 2/3 courses. There are also more expensive set dinner (à la carte on Saturday) menus, and some dishes appear on several different menus, with prices varying according to time and day of the week rather than the dish itself; overall the value is very keen although side orders charged extra can be annoying. Dishes attracting praise on recent visits included a truly delicious sweet potato soup with coriander & sesame seeds and a succulent and aromatic dish of coconut chicken with Asian salad & lime leaf, offered as either a (generous) starter or main course portion (£5.50/ £7.50). Other appealing dishes may include wild Irish venison with Clonakilty black pudding, creamed celeriac & caramelised red onion, or roast cod with mash, confit of tomato & saffron. This is a super place, where good food combines with caring service and value for money - a great combination by any standards. Parking (8). Disabled access; lift. Open Mon-Sat 11-'late'. L Mon-Fri 12-2.30; D Mon-Sat, 5.30-9.30; early D 5.30-6.45. D reservations advised. Pianist - baby grand (Fri Sat from 9pm). Closed Sun. MasterCard, Visa. **Directions:** Laganside. ◊

Belfast
RESTAURANT

Beatrice Kenned

44 University Road Belfast Co Antrim BT7 1NJ **Tel: 028 9020 229**
www.beatrice.kennedy.co.

Named after the lady whose home it once was, the dining area of this unusual restaurant begins
what would have been her front room and extends into adjoining areas towards the back, retaini
something of the authentic lived-in feeling of a private period residence; although now furnished w
white-damasked tables, it has a Victorian atmosphere with a small open fireplace and mantelpiece a
a few books and leftover personal effects: softly-lit, atmospheric, intimate, it exudes an atmosphere
calm in which to enjoy proprietor-chef Jim McCarthy's accomplished cooking. Ingredients are carefu
sourced, dishes are smoked on the premises and breads, desserts and ice creams are all home-mad
The style is modern, with some Thai and Chinese influences, but also flavours closer to home in roa
cod. Presentation is very special, especially the desserts - which are minor works of art. This delight
place is very much itself and offers a welcome contrast to the mainly contemporary restaurants of t
city. **Seats 80** (private room 25). D Tue-Sun, 5-10.15 (Sun to 8.15pm); L Sun only 12.30-2.15. Ea
D (5-7), Set Sun L about £15. Closed Mon, 24-26 Dec, 11-14 Jul. Amex, MasterCard, Visa, Switc
Directions: Adjacent to Queen's University.

Belfast
HOTEL

Benedict's Hotel Belfas

7-21 Bradbury Place Belfast Co Antrim BT7 1RQ **Tel: 028 9059 199**
info@benedictsHotel.co.uk www.benedictshotel.co.

Very conveniently located in Bradbury Place, just off Shaftesbury Square, this reasonably priced c
centre hotel is situated in the heart of Belfast's "Golden Mile", and a wide range of attraction
including the Botanic Gardens, Queen's University, Queen's Film Theatre and Ulster Museum, a
within a few minutes walk. Benedicts combines comfort and a degree of contemporary style with ve
moderate prices; the comfortable beds invariably come in for special praise, as do the warm a
friendly staff; on the downside, it can sometimes be noisy and there is no on-site parking, althoug
the hotel has an arrangement with a nearby carpark. Children welcome (cot available without charg
No private parking (arrangement with nearby car park); no pets; free broadband WI/FI. **Rooms 32 (**
executive rooms, 2 for disabled, all no smoking). Lift; all day room service. B&B from £37.50 pps,
£27.50. Closed 24-25 Dec. Amex, Diners, MasterCard, Visa, Switch. **Directions:** City centre hotel sit
ated in Bradbury Place - just off Shaftesbury Square in the heart of Belfast's "Golden Mile."

Belfast
RESTAURANT

Bourbo

60 Great Victoria Street Belfast Co Antrim BT2 7BB **Tel: 028 9033 212**
info@bourbonrestaurant.com www.bourbonrestaurant.co

Behind an unassuming entrance lies an amazingly theatrical interior: totally at home alongside neig
bouring buildings like the Crown Liquor Saloon and the Grand Opera House, it features pillars, palm
ornate plaster work and wrought iron, chandeliers and statues - everything, in short, to convey sumpt
ousness. Not to everybody's taste, to be sure, but it works, and this 'taste of New Orleans' is one
Belfast's most popular restaurants. But don't expect pristine white linen, silver and crystal: what y
actually get is bare table tops, the ubiquitous black rubber place mats, and paper napkins. So it shou
come as no surprise that menus are modern, written in a no-nonsense style and offering a wide ran
of mainly international contemporary crowd pleasers: starters of spicy chicken wings and an extensi
selection of main courses includes half a dozen poultry dishes, pizzas and pasta, and steaks vario
ways, and homemade burgers. But vegetarians do get some choice from the pizza and pasta range
and there will be several main course fish dishes. Helpful staff, competent cooking and an amazi
atmosphere make this a place worth visiting. Open daily; air con. L Mon-Fri 12-2.3; D Mon-Sat 5-1
(to 11pm Fri/Sat); Express L £6-7.50; early D 5-6.45pm Mon-Sun, £12.95; set 3 course meal £2
House wine £14.50. Closed Sat & Sun L; 25-26 Dec. MasterCard, Visa, Switch. **Directions:** City centr

---

Belfast
CAFE/RESTAURANT

Café Conc

11A Stranmillis Road Belfast Co Antrim BT9 5/
Tel: 028 9066 32(

Just across the road from the Ulster Museum, Manus McConn's unusual high-ceilinged room was or
inally the William Conor studio (1944-1959) and is bright with natural light from a lantern roof. T
art theme is carried through to having original work always on show - there's a permanent exhibiti
of Neill Shawcross's bold and colourful work. Open for breakfast and brunch, through coffee, lunc
afternoon tea and eventually dinner, this is a casual place with a distinctive style - light wood boot

ong the walls and a long refectory-style table down the centre. Good coffee, home-baked scones, formal food such as warm chicken salad, hot panini with mozzarella, modern European dishes cluding lots of pastas, comfort food and classic dishes such as paté à la maison and steak & uinness pie are all worth dropping in for. Popular with locals, this place is a real find for those visiting e Museum (especially on Sundays); the only downside is that background music is sometimes too ud, which can make it difficult to converse. **Seats 50.** Open daily 9am-11pm, L menu from noon, specials from 5pm. A la carte. Licensed. Closed July fortnight. MasterCard, Visa, Switch. **Directions:** pposite Ulster Museum. ◇

---

elfast
AFÉ

Café Paul Rankin
27-29 Fountain Street Belfast Co Antrim BT1
Tel: 028 9031 5090

afé Paul Rankin offers informal quality food (notably their speciality baking) throughout the day - be for a quick cup of coffee or a more leisurely bite with a glass of wine, this is the in place for a shop-ng break. The breakfast menu is available all day and includes Jeanne's toasted muesli & yoghurt, hile a wider range hot food on offer after 11 am includes the Rankin club sandwich and a range of uiches and salads. Smart pavement tables for fine weather - and food to go too. **Seats 50** (outside ating, 12). No reservations. No smoking. Open 7.30-5.30 (Thu to 7.30). Closed Sun; 25 Dec, 1 an, 12 Jul. MasterCard, Visa, Switch. **Directions:** Town centre, near City Hall. ◇

---

elfast
AFÉ/RESTAURANT
🅝

Café Renoir
95 Botanic Avenue Belfast Co Antrim BT7 1JN
Tel: 028 9031 1300

usband and wife team Lindsay and Karen Loney's Café Renoir restaurant and shop have a great local llowing, especially among young professionals, for wholesome homemade food, both in this stylishly formal premises and in the original Queen Street daytime café in the city's main shopping area, hich has been in business since 1991. Here on Botanic Avenue, European bistro is the stated style nd they've earned respect for their support of local and organic produce as well as for delicious ooking with real home flavour. Open throughout the day with varying offerings, the café begins early ith a breakfast menu and is open right through until late at night home baking is a speciality and eir cakes, tray bakes and scones are popular for in-between times lunchtime is busy and the menu cludes a wide selection of vegetarian dishes, then at night it takes on a bistro atmosphere and menu. eside it, the newer pizzeria (with wood fired pizza oven) offers keenly priced informal evening meals. rivate rooms available; outside catering also offered. *Also at: 5-7 Queen Street. **Café/Bistro: Seats 00.** Licensed. Open 8am -11.30pm (Fri & Sat to 11.30). Pizzeria: Seats 100. Unlicensed (BYO). pen 5pm 'late'; early bird 5-7pm; on Mon & Tue all pizzas are £8. MasterCard, Visa. **Directions:** Near otanic Gardens, at back of Queen's University. ◇

---

elfast
AFÉ

Cargoes Café
613 Lisburn Road Belfast Co Antrim BT9 7GT **Tel: 028 9066 5451**
www.cargoescafe.co.uk

adha Patterson's very special little delicatessen and café has maintained a great reputation over more an a decade in business - fine produce for the delicatessen side of the business is meticulously urced, and the same philosophy applies to the food served in the café. Modern European cooking orks well with some Thai and Indian influences here, and simple preparation and good seasonal gredients dictate menus. Smoked & fresh salmon terrine, Mediterranean tapas selection and beef & uinness are regulars, also vegetarian dishes such as goat's cheese & tarragon tart. There are classic esserts like lemon tart or apple flan, also delicious bakes like cinnamon scones and Moroccan orange ake and a range of stylish sandwiches. Children welcome; toilets wheelchair accessible; air condi-oning. **Seats 36** (new outdoor seating area, 12). Open Mon-Sat 9 am-4.15 pm, L 12-3.30; Sun 0-3pm. A la carte; sc discretionary. MasterCard, Visa, Switch. **Directions:** On the Lisburn Road.

---

elfast
ESTAURANT
🄵 ☆

Cayenne
7 Ascot House Shaftesbury Square Belfast Co Antrim BT2 7DB
Tel: 028 9033 1532
belinda@rankingroup.co.uk www.rankingroup.co.uk

ter almost two decades as pioneers of Northern Ireland's food scene, Paul and Jeanne Rankin's flag-ip restaurant continues to offer Belfast diners a great mix of interesting and fashionable food in a cool urban atmosphere. Longstanding former head chef Danny Millar has recently handed over the reigns to Winston Mathews, who now has the kitchen running sweetly - and, as his eclectic menu demonstrate, the Rankins' influence is still very much alive and well too. Friendly, smartly uniformed staff are quick to settle arriving guests in and offer menus that are likely to feature many of the Cayenne signature dishes - the ever-popular salt'n'chilli squid with Napa slaw, chilli jam and aioli, for example, or perhaps a more European tone in a delectable combination of pan seared foie gras with toasted brioche, caramelised peach, ginger and five spice jus - but nothing stands still here. and even the most popular dishes are under constant review. There are a few dishes with a broadly international/Mediterranean tone Fresh tagliatelle of Strangford lobster with a lobster and basil cream perhaps - but Asian flavours are dominant throughout the savoury sections of the menu, bringing new dimension to local ingredients: loin of Irish lamb comes with black mustard seeds, garlic purée and boulangère potatoes and a mustard miso sauce, for example, and marinated pork belly is served with Shanghai noodles, Asian vegetables and a black bean sauce. A separate vegetarian menu is offered too although a conservative example, delicious) steamed asparagus with poached free range egg and lemon butter is typical. Excellent desserts too - fresh strawberries set in Lemon cello jelly with buttermilk ice cream and milk crisp, for example, makes a refreshing end to a most enjoyable meal. The cooking here can be really exciting, and is generally backed efficiently up by smart, well-trained young staff who work tirelessly to ensure guests receive first class service. A very good wine list, organised by grape variety and style, offers a wide choice in both range and price, and includes a good choice of wines by the glass and half bottles, and also some fine wines; extensive drinks menu too. **Seats 120** (private room, 16). Reservations advised; children welcome. No smoking area; air conditioning; Toilets Wheelchair Accessible. L Mon-Fri 12-2.15, Set 2/3 course L from £12/15.50. Set 2/3 course D £15.50/10.50. D Sun- Fri 5- 'late', Sat 6- late. A la carte & Vegetarian Menu. House wine from £17 sc discretionary (except 10% recommended on parties of 6+). Closed L Sat & Sun, 25-2? Dec, 1 Jan, 12 July. Amex, Diners, MasterCard, Visa, Switch. **Directions:** 5 mins from Europa Hotel a top of Great Victoria St. ◇

Belfast
HOTEL/RESTAURANT

The Crescent Townhouse

13 Lower Crescent Belfast Co Antrim BT7 1NR **Tel: 028 9032 334**
info@crescenttownhouse.com www.crescenttownhouse.com

This is an elegant building on the corner of Botanic Avenue, just a short stroll from the city centre and is a good choice for business visitors. The reception lounge is on the first floor and the ground floor is taken up by the Metro Brasserie and a stylish club-like bar, Bar/Twelve, that is particularly lively and popular at night - so noise could be a problem in front bedrooms. Spacious bedrooms include suites and superior rooms, that are more elaborate and have luxurious bathrooms (some with Victorian roll top baths and walk-in showers), but all are comfortably furnished, with good tiled bathrooms. Breakfast is taken in the contemporary split-level Metro Brasserie on the lower ground floor, which is open for all meals and has a following for its good value contemporary cooking. Children welcome before 7pm (under 14s free in parents' room, cots available without charge, baby sitting arranged). No pets.*Weekend breaks offer good value. **Rooms 17** (1 suite, 2 junior suites, 5 superior, 6 shower only 1 disabled, 2 no smoking). Wheelchair lift. Room service (limited hours). B&B from £60 pps, ss £30 Metro Brasserie Seats 70. D daily from 5.45 (Sat from 5.30, Sun from 5pm). Early D & Vegetarian menus available. Lunch also at BarTwelve: Mon-Sat 12-3. Amex, MasterCard, Visa, Switch. **Directions:** Opposite Botanic Railway Station. ◇

Belfast
CHARACTER PUB
🍺🍷

Crown Liquor Saloon

46 Great Victoria Street Belfast Co Antrim BT2 7 B
Tel: 02890 279 90

Belfast's most famous pub, The Crown Liquor Saloon, was perhaps the greatest of all the Victorian gi palaces which once flourished in Britain's industrial cities. Remarkably, considering its central location close to the Europa Hotel, it survived The Troubles virtually unscathed. Although now owned by the National Trust (and run by Bass Leisure Retail) the Crown is far from being a museum piece and attracts a wide clientèle of locals and visitors. A visit to one of its famous snugs for a pint and half dozen oysters served on crushed ice, or a bowl of Irish Stew, is a must. The upstairs restaurant section "Flannigans Eaterie & Bar", is built with original timbers from the SS Britannic, sister ship to the Titanic. Crown: bar food served Mon-Sat 12-3. Flannigans: 11-9. Closed 25-16 Dec. Diners MasterCard, Visa. **Directions:** City centre, opposite Europa Hotel. ◇

Deanes at Queens

Belfast
BAR/RESTAURANT

36-40 College Gardens Belfast Co Antrim **Tel: 028 9038 2111**
www.michaeldeane.co.uk

With its stylish contemporary interior enhanced by original work from local artist Oliver Jeffers and an alfresco eating area overlooking 'Methody' (as the school, Methodist College, is known locally), this all day bar and grill is the latest addition to the Deane empire - and, as well as Deane's trademark good food, it brings a refreshing contrast to the mainly traditional atmosphere that the fine Victorian archi-tecture of the university brings to the area. Menus through the day begin with casual brunch fare, then light food in the afternoon and follow with more structured evening meals; many of the dishes are Deanes classics that will be familiar to anyone who has visited Deanes Deli in the city centre. It's child friendly (children's menu available up to 7pm) with the outside seating area being non-smoking. An accessible wine list includes a good choice by the glass and a high proportion of half bottles. The Common Rooms are available for private parties, either singly or together. Open daily 1-10 (except: Sun 11.30-3; Mon & Tue 11.30-9). L Menu 12-3; Afternoon Specials 3-5; D from 5pm. **Directions:** just up from Queen's University and to the right, Deane's at Queens is at the QUB Common Rooms on College Gardens, overlooking Methodist College.

Deanes Deli

Belfast
RESTAURANT

44 Bedford Street Belfast Co Antrim BT2 7FF **Tel: 028 9024 8800**
info@michaeldeane.co.uk www.michaeldeane.co.uk

Just around the corner from Deanes Restaurant, this smashing New York style all day deli-dining expe-rience is a smart-casual venue serving great bistro food and given an extra twist by the sumptuous retail deli store adjacent to the restaurant. Deanes Deli chicken Caesar, mussels à la crème with pommes frites and local roast chicken with braised potato cake, smoked bacon & pan juices are all typical dishes, and they'll taste as good as they sound. The evening menu gears up a bit but it's still very informal and there are loads of tempting things to take home from the deli, including Deanes own label range. Well chosen drinks list to match, including g beer and cocktails as well as accessible wines. **Seats 80** (outdoors, 16); reservations advised; children welcome; toilets wheelchair accessible; air conditioning. Open all day Mon-Sat, 11.30-9pm (to 10pm Wed-Sat); L 11.30-3, D 5.30-9/10; à la carte. SC discretionary except 10% on parties of 6+. Closed Sun; 25 Dec. Amex, MasterCard, Visa, Switch. **Directions:** City centre.

Deanes Restaurant

Belfast
RESTAURANT

36-40 Howard Street Belfast Co Antrim BT1 6PF **Tel: 028 9033 1134**
info@michaeldeane.co.uk www.michaeldeane.co.uk

RESTAURANT OF THE YEAR

Devoted followers of Northern Ireland's most exceptional dining experience, Restaurant Michael Deane, feared the worst during the recent closure of the prolific chef's brasserie and fine dining restaurant and, unsurprisingly, the rumour machine went into overdrive, predicting the immi-nent demise of this esteemed chef's business. But, following a major makeover, the two former city centre hot spots merged, transformed into one elegant fine dining restaurant - how Mr Deane must now be smiling at his doubters as, once again, he has established himself as one of Ireland's foremost chefs and restaurateurs. The renovations have in no way compromised on comfort, and diners can enjoy pre-dinner drinks in the elegant bar and lounge area before exploring the brightly lit, minimalist dining room. The smart, attentive and knowledgeable staff, under the direction of affable Maître d', Alain Ker'loch provide unobtrusive professional service while, behind the open kitchen service hatch, head chef Derek Creagh works his magic, and what magic! And, as always, the ever-present Deane meticulously controls the pace of events and timing of food to perfection. An evening à la carte menu offers six choices on each course and reads deceptively simply, yet it is anything but basic and offers many luxury ingredients, artistically prepared in dishes of great refinement. As ever, wonderful breads come with tapenade, olive oil and balsamic vinegar, leading you into a meal that is sure to be a memorable experience by any standards and is, if anything, enhanced by the limited choice and simple menu offering. Typically, you will find creative, perfectly judged starters like John Dory in crisped cous cous, with basil tapenade and tomato & fennel broth, or carpaccio of Oisin venison, with panfried sweetbreads and summer mushrooms, baby leaves almond butter vinaigrette, and an irresistible speciality of saddle back pork belly with roast langous tine, savoy cabbage, black pudding & apple caramel. Main courses may include a stunning poache and roast fillet of dry-aged Fermanagh beef with braised ox cheek, triple cooked chips and sauc Bordelaise with bone marrow executed to perfection, and with great depth of flavour (the highlight a recent visit) and, perhaps an updated classic of grilled whole Dover sole served with cured cucumbe brown shrimp, capers and lemon & parsley butter; every dish is brilliantly executed, eye-catching an - something which is missing in too many restaurants - has real depth of flavour. Desserts are also strong point, including such treats as warm pistachio tart with a sublime blood orange & rose wate sorbet, and a warm peach tart fine with a subtle white pepper ice cream. Lunch menus offer a goc range of more informal dishes, but the same high standards apply. The new restaurant certainly mark a departure from the more formal style of Restaurant Michael Deane - it is more open and airy, an extras such as the Menu Prestige, amuse bouches and pre-desserts are no longer offered; howeve this in no way makes the dining experience any less enjoyable and cooking by Deane and Creag remains the yardstick against which all serious cooking in Northern Ireland and, indeed, further afiel should be judged. An appropriate wine list includes a champagne menu and many classic treats, a well as some more accessible bottles and a page of wines available by the glass and, as always, th discreet advice given to match wines with the food is outstanding. The first floor restaurant is avai able by arrangement for private parties. **Seats 60** (private room, 40); air conditioning; toile wheelchair accessible; children welcome. L Mon-Sat 12-3, D Mon-Sat 5.30-10.30. Set L £16.5C early D £16.50/22.50, 2/3 courses, 5.30-7pm; also A la carte; SC discretionary (10% on parties c 6+). Closed Sun; 24-26 Dec, Jul 12-14. *'**Deanes Deli**', a New York style all day deli dining expe ence is around the corner at 44 Bedford Street (see entry). Amex, MasterCard, Visa, Switc **Directions:** From back of City Hall, about 150m towards M1, on left.

Belfast
RESTAURANT

Ginge

7-8 Hope Street Belfast Co Antrim BT12 5EE **Tel: 028 9024 442**

www.gingerbistro.co

A flyer proclaims "Where there is life there is Hope Street, where there is Hope Street there is th Ginger Bistro" and that nicely sums up the attitude at redhead Simon 'Ginger' McCance's chic an cheerful bistro just off Great Victoria Street. Simon McCance has a great following so he lost no tim when the opportunity arose recently to expand into the building next door, roughly doubling th number of happy punters he can accommodate, and making the restaurant easier to work too. Far fro grand except for a lovely mahogany floor and, perhaps, a tall window beautifully dressed with soft smoky leather trimmed voile it's a quirky place with two dining spaces, a partially visible kitchen, an décor 'a bit like home' with a mix'n'match of furniture and light fittings and acid green and dee mauve/purple accents. Carefully sourced ingredients have always been at the centre of this likeab' chef's philosophy and, although you will find wide ranging influences on his constantly changin menus, you can be sure that the food that tastes so good will be local if possible. Menus are balancec offering a good choice of vegetarian dishes alongside appealing meat dishes like braised pork bell with creamy mash & rosemary jus, but seafood is what he likes to cook best grilled sardines, fc example or beautifully cooked crisp-skinned seabass with an unusual celeriac and pea casserole anc although they don't take themselves too seriously (there's a light-hearted tone on blackboard notice etc), there's no doubt that this is a place that is serious about the quality of both food and wine. Finis with a classic dessert (crème brulée with raspberry compôte, perhaps) or an Irish cheese selectior Prices are reasonable and lunch/pre-theatre menus offer especially good value. In addition to carefully chosen wines, there's a full bar list. Children welcome; reservations required. **Seats 60**; L & D Tue-Sat 12-3pm, 5-10pm; A la carte L&D; house wine £12.50. Closed Sun, Mon, 2 weeks Jul, 2 week Christmas. MasterCard, Visa, Switch. **Directions:** Off Great Victoria street, 5 mins from Europ Hotel. ◇

Belfast
RESTAURANT

Harbour View Teppanyak

1 Lanyon Quay Belfast Co Antrim BT1 3LG **Tel: 028 9023 882**

booking@harbourviewbelfast.co.uk www.harbourviewbelfast.co.u

At this scenic Lagan side location beside the Waterfront Hall, the ever popular Japanese dining expe rience, Teppanyaki, is alive and well. Very friendly professional staff greet customers arriving at th spacious lounge and reception area overlooking the river and, after choosing from the extensiv Japanese menu, one is led to the Teppan and seated comfortably to watch the chef's deft displays, a he cuts, stirs and flambés various seafood and meat dishes on the Teppan. The menu offers an exce lent selection of superbly fresh seafood, sushi and sashimi, with some meat dishes such as duck, bee and chicken also available, all served with wonderfully fluffy fried rice and Japanese noodles. After such an impressively cooked meal, the desserts (ice cream list) are somewhat less appealing, so one may find oneself returning to the lounge to relax, enjoy the view and finish drinks. Teppanyaki is an entertaining night out and is especially suited to larger parties, but be warned: it does come at a premium. Toilets wheelchair accessible; open for food all day; L 12-2.30; a la carte from 2.30 to 11pm; house wine £15. Closed Christmas Day only. Amex, MasterCard, Visa, Switch. **Directions:** By the Waterfront Hall.

Belfast	Hastings Europa Hotel
HOTEL	Great Victoria Street Belfast Co Antrim BT2 7AP **Tel: 028 9027 1066**
	res@eur.hastingshotels.com www.hastingshotels.com

This landmark 1970s city centre building is the largest hotel in Northern Ireland and particularly striking when illuminated at night. It has undergone many changes since first opening in the '70s and has been renovated and refurbished to a high standard, including the addition of executive rooms. Off the impressive tall-columned entrance foyer is an all-day brasserie and the lobby bar, featuring live musical entertainment and, upstairs on the first floor, you'll find the Gallery Lounge and a cocktail bar. However, perhaps the hotel's greatest assets are the function suites and the staff, who are excellent, ensuring high standards of service, housekeeping and maintenance. Nearby parking can be added to your account. Conference/banqueting (750/600); business centre; secretarial services. Beauty salon; hairdressing. Children welcome (under 14s free in parents' room; cots available without charge, baby sitting arranged). Pets permitted by arrangement. **Rooms 240** (1 presidential suite, 4 junior suites, 56 executive rooms, 115 no smoking, 2 for disabled). Lifts. B&B about £100 pps, ss about £30. Piano Bar Restaurant: D Mon-Sat (closed 24 Dec-2 Jan); Brasserie open all day 6am-11pm (Sun from 7 am). *Short breaks offered - details on application. Hotel closed 24-25 Dec. Amex, Diners, MasterCard, Visa, Switch. **Directions:** Located in the heart of Belfast. ◇

Belfast	Hastings Stormont Hotel
HOTEL	Upper Newtownards Road Belfast Co Antrim BT4 3LP **Tel: 028 9067 6012**
	sales@stor.hastingshotels.com www.hastingshotels.com

A few miles east of the city centre, the hotel is directly opposite the imposing gates leading to Stormont Castle and Parliament Buildings and suits the business guest well. There's a huge entrance lounge, with stairs up to a more intimate mezzanine area overlooking the castle grounds, and the main restaurant and informal modern bistro are both pleasantly located. Spacious, practical bedrooms have good workspace and offer the usual facilities; several rooms are designated for female executives, and there is a relatively new executive floor. The hotel also has eight self-catering apartments with their own car parking area, featuring a twin bedroom, lounge and kitchen/dinette, available for short stays or long periods. The self-contained Confex Centre, comprising ten trade rooms, complements the function suites in the main building. Weekend rates and short breaks are good value. Conference/banqueting 500/350. Own parking (255). Wheelchair accessible. No pets. **Rooms 105** (2 suites, 23 executive rooms, 52 no-smoking, 1 for disabled). Lift. B&B about £50 pps, ss £20. Open all year. Amex, Diners, MasterCard, Visa, Switch. **Directions:** 3 miles east of Belfast city centre; take A20 towards Newtownards - directly opposite Stormont Parliament Buildings. ◇

Belfast	Hawthorne Coffee Shop & Espresso Bar
CAFÉ/RESTAURANT	Fulton's Fine Furnishings Balmoral Plaza Boucher Road
	Belfast Co Antrim BT2 6HU **Tel: 028 9038 4705**

Not only has The Hawthorne café/restaurant retained pride of place on the first floor of the new Fulton's furniture store, now relocated to the Balmoral Plaza development on Boucher Road, it has spawned a downstairs espresso bar as well, with splendid leather seats where you can have a restorative coffee and something to tempt the sweet tooth. The shop's stairwell - of cathedral proportions, like the shop itself - incorporates a double escalator leading to the first floor where the Hawthorne now has floor to ceiling windows and a number of pleasant seating areas, some with elevated views over the Boucher Road and beyond to the Black Mountain. If you're shopping or have business in the area (generous parking) this is a great place to know about as, thanks to Sylvia, there's a pride in real home cooking and the art of scone making is alive and well. There's nothing flashy about the food: expect lovely flavoursome dishes like home-made soup with wheaten bread, quiches - asparagus & salmon, vegetable - seafood pie and steak & mushroom hot-pot and several casseroles daily. There's always a large selection of salads, and home-made desserts like banoffee and lemon meringue pie- and free refills of coffee. An added attraction between 12 and 2 is to listen to the resident pianist play on the

Steinway baby grand. **Seats 210.** Open Mon Sat 9.15-5.15. A la carte. Espresso bar open to 8 pm Thu, for late night shoppers. Master Card, Visa, Switch. **Directions:** Off M1, take Stockman's Lane exit off roundabout, left into Boucher Road. (At Fultons Fine Furnishings Store). ◇

Belfast   # Hilton Belfast
HOTEL   4 Lanyon Place Belfast Co Antrim BT1 3LP   **Tel: 028 9027 7000**
hilton_belfast@hilton.com

Occupying a prominent position on a rise beside the Waterfront Hall, the interior of this landmark hotel is impressive: the scale is grand, the style throughout is of contemporary clean-lined elegance - the best of modern materials have been used and the colour palette selected is delicious - and, best of all, it makes the best possible use of its superb waterside site, with the Sonoma Restaurant and several suites commanding exceptional views. Outstanding conference and business facilities include the state-of-the-art Hilton Meeting service tailored to individual requirements and three executive floors with a Clubroom. All rooms have air-conditioning, in-room movies, and no-stop check-out in addition to the usual facilities, and recreational facilities are also excellent; however, although there is a multi-storey carpark next door, it is not owned by the hotel. Conference/banqueting (400/260); secretarial services; business centre; video conferencing; ISDN lines. Leisure centre; indoor swimming pool; beauty salon. Children welcome (cots available). **Rooms 195** (6 suites, 7 junior suites, 38 executive rooms, 68 no-smoking, 10 for disabled). Lifts. Room rate (max. 2 guests) from about £100. Open all year. Amex, Diners, MasterCard, Visa, Switch. **Directions:** Belfast city centre, beside Waterfront Hall. ◇

Belfast   # Holiday Inn Belfast
HOTEL   22 - 26 Ormeau Avenue Belfast Co Antrim BT2 8HS   **Tel: 028 9032 8511**
belfast@ichotelsgroup.com   www.belfast.holiday-inn.com

Conveniently located near most of the main city centre attractions, this contemporary hotel offers luxurious modern accommodation, with excellent business and health and leisure facilities. The style is classy and spacious; bedrooms are designed particularly with the business guest in mind - the decor is unfussy and warm, with comfort and relaxation to match its use as a workbase; superior rooms all have air conditioning, modem points, fridge, interactive TV with on-screen checkout facility and Sky Sports, trouser press, power shower, cotton bathrobe and quality toiletries, while suites have a hallway as well as a separate sitting/dining room. 'The Academy' offers state-of-the-art conference and training facilities, and business support. Conference/banqueting (120/100); business centre, secretarial services, video-conferencing. Children welcome (under 16s free in parents' room, cot available without charge). Leisure centre; swimming pool; beauty salon. **Rooms 170** (2 suites, 36 executive, 102 no smoking, 10 for disabled). Lift. 24 hour room service. B&B from about £85pps. Special weekend rates available. No private parking (NCP car park behind hotel). Open all year. Amex, Diners, MasterCard, Visa, Switch. **Directions:** Opposite BBC, 2 minutes walk from City Hall via Bedford Street. ◇

Belfast   # James Street South
RESTAURANT   21 James Street South Belfast Co Antrim BT2 7GA   **Tel: 028 9043 4310**
info@jamesstreetsouth.co.uk   www.jamesstreetsouth.co.uk

Just across the road from the Europa Hotel, Niall and Joanne McKenna's elegant modern restaurant has tall arched windows overlooking James Street South and it is well-appointed in a beautifully understated style with white walls and crisp white linen, relieved by contemporary Irish artwork, fresh flowers and effective lighting. Since opening in 2004, this talented team has not only brought something fresh and exceptionally good to Belfast, but their gem of a restaurant has thrived and they have earned a loyal following. Niall McKenna, who has worked for respected names like Gary Rhodes, Marco Pierre White and Nico Ladennis, has confidently stamped his own authority on the Northern Ireland food scene, serving modern classics with an Irish twist - and continues unfalteringly to delight diners in Belfast city centre. This is deceptively simple food using only the best of fresh, local ingredients cooked with an assured elegance, and a welcome absence of fusion influences. Although menus are simply presented, there are plenty of very tempting options - including lovely vegetarian dishes like chicory tartlet with goat's cheese, pear and walnuts, luxurious starters like sautéed foie gras with caramelised saffron pear and candied almonds, great local lamb loin served perfectly pink with a celeriac and turnip gratin complemented by a sublime red wine jus - and utterly irresistible desserts including a delectable house fondue (to share), trio of petits crème brulées, or perhaps a rich hot chocolate fondant with a gooey centre. The dining room has an exciting, lively ambience, and well choreographed service from the smartly-dressed staff should ensure a memorable meal here. Lunch and pre-theatre menus offer exceptional value. The wine list is arranged mainly by grape variety and includes regional varieties; although mainly under £30, there is also a short selection of fine wines; gourmet wine evenings are sometimes held. **Seats 70.** Reservations advised. Air con. No smoking area (bar). Children welcome. L Mon-sat, 12-2.45; D daily, 5.45-10.45 (Sun 5.30-9.30). Set L about £15. Pre theatre D Mon-Thu 5.45-6.45 about £16, also A la Carte. Closed 25-26 Dec, 1 Jan, 11-12 July. Amex, MasterCard, Visa, Switch. **Directions:** City centre: located behind Belfast City Hall, between Bedford Stree and Brunswick street. ◇

Belfast
BAR/RESTAURANT

The John Hewitt Bar & Restaurant

51 Donegall Street Belfast Co Antrim BT1 **Tel: 028 9023 3768**
info@thejohnhewitt.com www.thejohnhewitt.com

The in-place pub for discerning Belfast people, who like the combination of traditional interior and good quality sassy modern food, The John Hewitt is owned by the Unemployment Resource Centre next door, which was originally opened by the poet and socialist John Hewitt in the 1980s. Some years ago they decided to open the premises as a bar, and all profits go back to that worthy cause. High-ceilinged, with a marble bar, a snug and an open fire, there's a pleasing preference for conversation and civilised relaxation. It operates more or less as a restaurant by day - they serve lunch every day except Sunday, and offer a light afternoon 'Talking Bowls' snack menu on Friday & Saturday afternoons. There are traditional music sessions three nights a week (Tue, Wed & Sat), live music every Thursday and jazz on Fridays - which leaves Mondays free for exhibition launches. The day's menu is posted on their website. A short wine list includes four wines by the glass and two bubblies. Open daily; food served Mon-Thu, 12-3pm, also short menu Fri & Sat 3.30-6pm. MasterCard, Visa, Switch. **Directions:** Belfast city centre; 3 doors from St Anne's Cathedral.

Belfast
HOTEL

Jurys Inn Belfast

Fisherwick Place Great Victoria Street Belfast Co Antrim BT2 7AP
Tel: 028 9053 3500
jurysinnbelfast@jurysdoyle.com www.book@jurysinn.com

Located in the heart of the city, close to the Grand Opera House and City Hall and just a couple of minutes walk from the major shopping areas of Donegall Place and the Castlecourt Centre, Jurys Belfast Inn offers comfortable accommodation in a central location at very reasonable prices. The high standards and good value of all Jurys Inns applies here too: all rooms are en-suite (with bath and shower) and spacious enough to accommodate two adults and two children (or three adults) at a fixed price. Rooms are well-designed and regularly refurbished, with good amenities for a hotel in the budget class. **Rooms 190.** Room rate from about £69, (max 3 guests w/o b'fst). Restaurant. Closed 24-26 Dec. Amex, Diners, MasterCard, Visa. **Directions:** City centre, close to Opera House. ◇

Belfast
HOTEL

Malmaison Hotel

34-38 Victoria Street Belfast Co Antrim BT1 3GH **Tel: 028 9022 0200**
belfast@malmaison.com www.malmaison-belfast.com

This beautiful building (especially striking when lit up at night) is now owned by the stylish UK group Malmaison who introduced a new wow factor to Belfast accommodation choices, beginning with the reception area where everything is black and white, with opulent drapes and large church candles. Although it may seem a bit overwhelming notably the bar, which can be very noisy - friendly, efficient staff at reception set arriving guests at their ease and guest accommodation - spacious, contemporary, luxurious, with all the technical gizmos you could possibly want - is given a human dimension with the offer of early morning delivery of a quarter pint of fresh milk. The Brasserie offers simple wholesome fare (steaks from The Duke of Baccleuch's Scottish Estate, for example), and good breakfasts are smartly served here too. The bar, with extensive cocktail menu, flat screen television, huge leather sofas, flickering lights, and loud music, is an in-place at night. Multi storey car park nearby, but check details when booking as it is may not be possible to access your car at certain times. Multi storey car park nearby. **Rooms 62;** Room rate from £140. Brasserie: L & D daily. Amex, MasterCard, Visa, Switch. **Directions:** Centre of Belfast. ◊

Belfast   # Malone Lodge

HOTEL   60 Eglantine Avenue Malone Road Belfast Co Antrim BT9 6DY **Tel: 028 9038 8000**

info@malonelodgehotel.com   www.malonelodgehotel.com

This reasonably priced townhouse hotel near Queen's University is very pleasantly located if you like to be in a quiet area, yet convenient to the city centre. It offers comfortable accommodation in spacious well-maintained en-suite rooms, with all the facilities required by business guests, both in-room and in the hotel itself. There are good conference and meeting facilities and plenty of parking space, and yet it is within walking distance of city centre restaurants and entertainment. Bar. Conferences (9 rooms, biggest caters for 140 delegates); Banqueting (30-140); ample parking (access to back of hotel from carpark), fitness suite, broadband. **Rooms 51** (standard or executive), B&B from £45, suites from £150. Weekend specials from £99. Open all year. *Malone Lodge also has 22 apartments comprising of one, two and three bedroom suites. MasterCard, Visa, Switch. **Directions:** Between the Lisburn and Malone Roads in South Belfast. ◊

Belfast   # McHugh's Bar & Restaurant

PUB/RESTAURANT   29-31 Queen's Square Belfast Co Antrim BT1 3FG **Tel: 028 9050 9999**

info@mchughsbar.com   www.mchughsbar.com

This remarkable pub is in one of Belfast's few remaining 18th century buildings; built in 1711, it is the city's oldest listed building. It has been extensively and carefully renovated allowing the original bar (which has many interesting maps, photographs and other memorabilia of old Belfast) to retain its character while blending in a new café-bar and restaurant. It is worth a visit for its historical interest, and the modern food offered includes an interesting lunch menu ('open flame' wok cooking is a speciality), a slightly more formal evening menu and light food through the day; a dedicated head chef, Gerard Lawlor, has been here for nine years, ensuring consistent standards.Seats 75 (private room, 35); children welcome (high chair, childrens menu); toilets wheelchair accessible; air conditioning. Food served daily, 12-10pm (Sun to 9); Set D £16/23, 2/3 courses, also à la carte. Bar food 12-7 daily. House wine from £12.95. Parking in nearby carpark. SC 10% on groups 8+. Closed 25 Dec, 1 Jan, 12/13 Jul. Amex, MasterCard, Visa, Switch. **Directions:** Turn right at Albert Clock.

Belfast   # The Merchant Hotel

HOTEL/RESTAURANT   35-39 Waring Street Belfast Co Antrim BT1 2DY **Tel: 028 9023 4888**

info@themerchanthotel.com   www.themerchanthotel.com

The grandeur of a larger than life Victorian banking building is a fit setting for Belfast's most dramatic and beautiful hotel. The exterior of the building is Italianate in style, with sculptures depicting Commerce, Justice and Britannia, looking down benignly from the apex of the magnificent façade. The entrance is up two flights of steps, through tall mahogany and glass revolving doors and then into a room of epic proportions with high ceilings, a central glassed dome with Tyrone crystal and brass chandelier, Corinthian columns, very tall doors painted black with bevelled glass panes and lovely windows with stained glass features at the back (where chunky bamboo plants give at least the appearance of garden outside). The lobby - furnished with comfortable sofas and chairs, rich autumnal fabrics, antiques and curiosities - sets the tone for the whole hotel, which has an authentic period feeling throughout and, although very luxurious, is not ostentatious. The adjacent cocktail bar is equally beautifully furnished in the same style, with red velvet and deep fringing and more of that autumnal velvet too on soft chairs; here, there are two beautiful windows overlooking the street. (On the other side of the front door, also with two beautiful windows, a residents' bar with modern furnishings seems less successful.) The bedrooms and suites are all named after a literary figure with Belfast associations (MacNeice, Heaney, Brian Friel, C.S. Lewis, Larkin etc); the geography of the building means there are features like lovely marble fireplaces with comfy chairs in lobbies and quaint corners en route to somewhere else - a world away from purpose built hotel accommodation with long corridors of doors. All guest rooms are elegantly and opulently appointed and offer air conditioning, black out curtains, WiFi, flat screen television, and spacious marbled bathrooms with many extras. Everything at the hotel is about luxury and indulgence - including the offer of The Merchant Bentley, which you can book to collect you from the airport or elsewhere. Meeting rooms (18); free broadband wi/fi. Children welcome (under 4s free in parents' room, cot available free of charge). **Rooms 26** (5 suites, 2 junior suites, 19 executive, 2 shower only, 7 ground floor, 2 disabled, all no smoking). Room rate from £160-220. 25 hr room service; lift; laundry service. **The Great Room Restaurant:** Three central steps take you from the lobby up to the restaurant, where a small antique reception desk and menu signal the transition; here, despite the great height and scale, low dividers give a sense of more intimate spaces without interrupting the view - and a bold choice, carried throughout the hotel, is the striped carpet. Well balanced set and à la carte menus are offered at various times; the style is upbeat classic and, typically, you might expect to find starters like duck and foie gras terrine with Sauternes jelly, toasted brioche & fig jelly, and dressy main courses including local Finnebrogue venison - saddle, perhaps, with turnip & vanilla purée and confit leg pithivier & hazelnut foam. Desserts include house versions of many favourites and there's an informatively described French and Irish cheeseboard. Coffee is beautifully served in art deco style silver pot with wicker handles and matching bowls (but no little treats petits four are extra, at £3.75). **Seats 65** (private room, 18); air conditioning; open daily, L 12-2.30pm; D 6-10.30pm; open all day Sun, 12-9pm; value menu £25; also a la carte; house wine from £18; SC 10%. Bar food also available in the hotel and in the Cloth Ear pub-bar nearby. Parking on site (35); valet parking offered. Closed 25 Dec. Amex, Diners, MasterCard, Visa. **Directions:** City centre.

Belfast
RESTAURANT

Molly's Yard

1 College Green Mews Botanic Avenue Belfast Co Antrim BT7 1LW
Tel: 028 9032 2600 www.mollysyard.co.uk

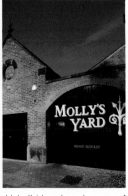

This atmospheric restaurant on two floors - informal ground floor bistro with a more elegant dining room above - is in the former stables of College Green House and there is nothing clichéd about it, giving an intriguing feeling that this place is a 'find'. Menus have a pleasingly down to earth tone - casual bistro fare downstairs with more 'grown up' versions upstairs. Barry Smyth, previously of the much-praised restaurant The Oriel of Gilford, in County Down, was head chef during the set-up phase and established a fine reputation for both the cooking and the philosophy of using carefully sourced ingredients, including (and naming) as much local produce as possible. Current head chef Matthias Llorente worked with him prior to taking over and, judging by the Guide's 2007 visit and consistently good local reports, the transition was effected very smoothly and the original philosophy of food remains in place; menus are kept relatively small with the emphasis on making everything freshly, and the cooking is really delicious. An interesting drinks list has always been one of the attractions here - including real ales from the renowned Hilden Brewery in Lisburn and Molly's Yard now includes Belfast's first (and Ireland's smallest) micro-brewery. At the time of the Guide's visit there were plans to introduce a crêperie downstairs, with more focus on fine dining upstairs in the evening. Children welcome before 6pm; toilets wheelchair accessible. Outdoor seating for 20; L Mon-Fri, 12-2.30pm, D Mon-Fri, 5-9.30pm, Sat all day, 12-9.30pm; set D 2/3 course about £20/25; house wine from about £12.50. Closed Sun, 25-26 Dec, 1 Jan, 12-13 Jul. MasterCard, Visa, Switch. **Directions:** Beside Dukes hotel at back of Queen's University.

Belfast
BAR/RESTAURANT

Mourne Seafood Bar Belfast

34-36 Bank Street Belfast Co Antrim BT1 1HL
Tel: 028 9024 8544

A sandwich board sign will lead you to the Mourne Seafood Bar, which is also a fish shop and owned by Andy Rae previously head chef with Paul Rankin at Roscoff and Cayenne - and business partner Bob McCoubrey, of the original Mourne Seafood Bar in Dundrum, Co Down (see entry), who have their own shellfish beds on Carlingford Lough. You enter past a well-stocked display of fish (including lobster, oysters etc), through a dark brown painted door which opens onto a long bar with an authentic Belfast feel; a world away from your designer bar concept, the old walls are a mixture of red brick and black areas acting as large blackboards for the menu and cocktail list, floorboards have been roughly painted black, tables are simply set and there's more of the same upstairs for overflow at weekends.

Georgina Campbell's Ireland

Andy's passion for seafood is evident - starting with the sourcing, he uses less popular local fish rather than trendy imports and, of course, mussels and oysters from Carlingford - everything is home made and the menu, which offers a mix of dishes at varying prices, changes daily according to the catch (a steak option is also offered). A daily specials board might offer 15 dishes, including potted herrings, seafood casserole or roast hake. Nice desserts, good coffee to finish and lovely service. Children welcome; toilets wheelchair accessible. **Seats 75** (private room, 30); air conditioning; food served Mon-Sat, 12-9.30pm, Sun, 1-6pm; vegetarian menu, also a la carte; housewine about £12.95. Closed 25-26 Dec, 1 Jan. MasterCard, Visa, Switch. **Directions:** Near Kelly's Bar - turn off Royal Avenue onto Bank Street. 100 metres on left. ◇

Belfast
RESTAURANT
🖐 ⓔ

Nick's Warehouse

35-39 Hill Street Belfast Co Antrim BT1 2LB **Tel: 028 9043 9690**
info@nickswarehouse.co.uk www.nickswarehouse.co.uk

Nick and Kathy Price's long established restaurant was originally a whiskey warehouse (built for Bushmills Whiskey in 1832), and when they opened here over 150 years later they were very much the culinary pioneers in this now popular area of Belfast. It's a clever conversion on two floors, with interesting lighting and an open kitchen, which is intended to be theatrical and adds to the buzz. This was Belfast's first wine bar and, although the layout has changed a little, wine is an even more important element these days, as they now have their own wine business. Both lunch and dinner are served on the informal ground floor (Anix) and also the restaurant upstairs, which is slightly more formal; menus change daily in both areas, depending on the fresh produce available from a network of trusted suppliers. The style is lively and contemporary, with menus offering a wide range of dishes which are consistently interesting and often include unusual local items Owen McMahon's steak sausages, perhaps, served on roast garlic mash with red wine lentils - and game in season. There's always an imaginative selection of vegetarian dishes and menus are considerately marked with symbols indicating dishes containing nuts or oils and also shellfish. There's a sense of fun about the place ("Why not try one of our 'Seductive Money Saving Offers'" pudding and a glass of dessert wine or cheese with port") and it's no wonder that Nick's has a loyal clientèle who love the good food, attentive, friendly service and the buzz. A well-priced and entertaining wine list offers a carefully selected range of house/by the glass wines, a small selection of (very good value) fine wines, and a special Spanish list. Children welcome before 9 pm; toilets wheelchair accessible; air conditioning. **Seats 130** downstairs (+ 55 upstairs, available as private room at night). L Mon-Fri 12-3, D Tue-Sat 6-9.30 (Fri & Sat to 10). House wines from about £12.95. Closed Sat L, all Sun, D Mon; 25-26 Dec, 1 Jan, Easter Mon/Tue, May Day, 12 July. Amex, Diners, MasterCard, Visa, Switch. **Directions:** Behind St.Anne's Cathedral, off Waring St. ◇

Belfast
BAR

Northern Whig

2 Bridge Street Belfast Co Antrim BT1 1LU **Tel: 028 9050 9888**
info@thenorthernwhig.com www.thenorthernwhig.com

Located in the former offices of the Northern Whig newspaper and convenient to the city's now fashionable Cathedral Quarter, this is an impressive bar of grand proportions. The high ceilings of the old press hall have been retained - and now look down on several gigantic statues salvaged from Eastern Europe that are in keeping with the scale of the building. A long bar has comfortable contemporary seating in coffee and cream, where Belfast's trend-setters meet for drinks or a bite to eat - or you can take a pavement table on a sunny afternoon and watch the world go by, sipping cocktails or sampling something from the reasonably priced menu. Very popular with the local business fraternity for lunch and for a relaxing drink after work. Expect upmarket bar food and good service from black-clad young staff. **Seats 160** (private room 40). No smoking area; air conditioning; toilets wheelchair accessible; children welcome. Open 10am-1am; bar food 12-9. MasterCard, Visa, Switch. **Directions:** From front of City Hall: walk to 2nd set of traffic lights, turn right, left at next lights; cross road - Northern Whig is on the corner. ◇

Belfast
CAFÉ

The Olive Tree Company

353 Ormeau Road Belfast Co Antrim BT7 3GL **Tel: 028 9064 8898**
www.olivetreecompany.com

This unique delicatessen/café specialises in freshly marinated olives, handmade cheeses and salamis - and also sells an exclusive range of French specialities, notably from Provence. The café offers authentic French patisserie and food with a Mediterranean flavour, mainly based on the best of local Irish produce: think sandwiches with tapenade (olive paté with vine-ripened tomatoes & spring onions, or dolmades (vine leaves) salad with organic natural yoghurt and ciabatta bread and you'll get the flavour. Hot dishes include specialities like 'brodetto' a traditional Italian fish stew, or contemporary dishes such as warm duck salad with chilli & lime dressing. **Seats 26.** Shop open daily: Mon-Sat 9am-6pm (café to 4.30pm), Sun 11-5. Hot food available Mon-Fri, 8.30-3.45pm, Sat, 9-3.45pm; (No wine but BYO allowed.) Closed 8-15 July, 24 Dec-2 Jan. **No Credit Cards. Directions:** From Belfast City Centre, take the direction for Newcastle/Downpatrick, cross the Ormeau Bridge - spot the Ormeau Bakery landmark and The Olive Tree Company is on the right.

Belfast
RESTAURANT

Oxford Exchange Bar & Grill

1st floor, St George's Market Oxford Street Belfast Co Antrim BT1 3NQ
Tel: 028 9024 0014
info@oxfordexchange.co.uk www.oxfordexchange.co.uk

Dining in an historically interesting building has a certain cachet at any time, but this stylish venue over the renovated glass-roofed St. George's Market is particularly fascinating The market is a redbrick listed Victorian building and Paul Horshcroft's successful conversion has created a pleasing restaurant with views of either the daytime market scene below or, at night, the attractively lit Laganside area. There's a small bar area, with comfortable seating, and a large restaurant with some striking features where menus reflecting the produce available in the market below are offered; interesting good-value lunches are served and, later, a more ambitious dinner menu takes over it's quite convenient to the Waterfront Hall for pre-theatre meals. Interesting wine list. **Seats 110.** Opening hours: L Mon-Sat 12-2.30; D Mon-Sat from 5pm; Express D Menu, 5-7pm, 2/3 course £14.95/17.95; also Breakfast on the balcony Fri & Sat 10am-midday;also à la carte. House wine from £13.95. SC discretionary (except 10% on parties of 8+). Closed Sun; 25 Dec, 1 Jan, public holidays. MasterCard, Visa, Laser, Switch. **Directions:** Opposite Waterfront Hall.

Belfast
HOTEL

Radisson SAS Hotel, Belfast

The Gasworks 3 Cromac Place, Ormeau Road Belfast Co Antrim BT7 2JB
Tel: 028 9043 4065 www.radissonsas.com

The hard red brick high-rise exterior may not be immediately pleasing, but you are in for a pleasant surprise on entering this uncompromisingly modern hotel. Most strikingly, seen through a glass wall, a highly original water feature has been created from the old 'grave dock' that was once a turning space for the boats coming up to the gasworks to deliver coal; both restaurant and bar overlook this extraordinary feature, and it is worth a journey to see this alone. Accommodation is designed and finished to the same high standard as other Radisson hotels; suites and rooms have everything that the modern traveller could need, and more and the friendly ad helpful staff clearly take great pride in this hotel. Conference/banqueting (150/40); secretarial services. Children welcome (cot available without charge, baby sitting arranged). No pets. **Rooms 120.** (1 suite, 7 junior suites, 18 executive, 94 no smoking, 6 disabled). Lift. 24 hour room service. B&B about £95pps, ss about £20. *Special offers / short breaks available. **Filini Restaurant:** L Mon-Sat, 12.30-2.30; D Mon-Sat, 6-10. Closed Sun. Bar meals 12-9 daily. Hotel open all year (not L 25 Dec). Parking (60). MasterCard, Visa, Switch. **Directions:** Belfast city centre, in the Cromac Wood Business Park development. ◊

Belfast
HOTEL

Ramada Hotel Belfast

117 Milltown Road Shaws Bridge Belfast Co Antrim BT8 7XP **Tel: 028 9092 3500**
mail@ramadabelfast.com www.ramadabelfast.com

This modern hotel near Shaws Bridge enjoys a beautiful setting in the Lagan Valley Regional Park, overlooking the River Lagan. Bedrooms are decorated in a fairly neutral modern style and have all the facilities expected of a new hotel, including in-room safes, TV with satellite and movie channels, telephone with voicemail and either a king-size bed or two singles. There are also executive suites available, intended mainly for business guests, and good conference and banqueting facilities. Leisure centre; steam room, spa and fitness suite; indoor swimming pool. Conference/banqueting 900/550.

Georgina Campbell's Ireland

Garden, walking. No pets. Children welcome, (under 5s free in parents' room, cot available without charge). **Rooms 120** (4 suites, 116 executive, 83 no smoking, 6 for disabled). Lift. 24 hour room service. Room rate from £85. Belfast Bar & Grill, L&D daily. Parking (300). Open all year. Amex, Diners, MasterCard, Visa, Switch. **Directions:** In Lagan Valley Regional Park, near Shaws Bridge. ◇

Belfast
GUESTHOUSE

Ravenhill House

690 Ravenhill Road Belfast Co Antrim BT6 0BZ **Tel: 028 9020 7444**
info@ravenhillhouse.com www.ravenhillhouse.com

Although it is beside a busy road, the Nicholson family's late Victorian redbrick house has some sense of seclusion, with mature trees, private parking and a quiet tree-lined street alongside. A comfortable ground floor lounge has an open fireplace, a big sofa, lots of books and a PC for guests who want to use the internet (at a modest charge). Bedrooms, which are a mixture of single, twin and double rooms, are comfortably furnished with style - beds and other furniture have been specially commissioned from an Islandmagee craftsman; all are en-suite, with tea/coffee making facilities and TV. After a good night's sleep, breakfast is sure to be the highlight of a visit here: served in a bay-windowed dining room with white-damasked tables, the breakfast buffet is displayed on the sideboard in a collection of Nicholas Mosse serving bowls - a feel for craft objects that is reflected elsewhere in the house. A printed breakfast menu shows a commitment to using local produce of quality and includes a vegetarian cooked breakfast; the Nicholsons buy all their fresh goods from local framers/producers who they deal with directly via the weekly St George's Farmers' Market, and they make what they can on the premises, including marmalade and wheaten bread for breakfasts. All these good things, plus a particularly helpful atti-tude to guests, make this an excellent, reasonably priced base for a stay in Belfast. Children welcome (under 2s free in parents' room, cot available without charge); free broadband wi/fi. No pets. Garden. Rooms 5 (all en-suite, 3 shower only, all no smoking). B&B £35 pps, single room £50. Open all year. MasterCard, Visa, Switch. **Directions:** Follow signs for A24 to Newcastle. 2 miles from city centre, located on corner of Ravenhill Road and Rosetta Park, close to junction with Ormeau Road (A24).

Belfast
RESTAURANT

Roscoff Brasserie

7-11 Linenhall Street Belfast Co Antrim BT2 8AA **Tel: 028 9031 1150**
belinda@rankingroup.co.uk www.rankingroup.co.uk

Modelled on Paul and Jeannie Rankins' original flagship restaurant (now Cayenne, see entry), which deservedly earned them great critical acclaim, Roscoff Brasserie opened some 3 years ago to the delight of many who admired the Rankins' fine cooking but not the style of the newer restaurants. Avoiding sharp contemporary style, the decor is timelessly classic: with white linen-clad tables, soft neutral toned furnishings, effective lighting and artwork by Peter Anderson, the overall effect is attrac-tively subdued and low key. A little reception bar is the perfect place to sip aperitifs and choose from à la carte or set menus which are basically classic French, although new head chef Paul Waterworth allows more local influence the cuisine, in starters like smoked haddock with creamed leeks, poached quail egg and hollandaise, or smoked eel with roast beetroot & horseradish cream. Simple main courses may include a loin of lamb with honey, garlic, thyme and potato rosti, maybe a steamed symphony of seafood with a caper and saffron butter vinaigrette - or, perhaps, breast of duck with aubergine caponata, potato pancakes and balsamic vinegar. There's a good cheese plate and desserts, which have always been a Roscoff tour de force, may include good home-made ice creams and a dessert du jour - a boon for regular diners. The wine list offers a large well selected range from around the world with several excellent 'by the glass options' and interesting half bottles. Roscoff Brasserie offers a complete contrast to the funky Rankin flagship restaurant, Cayenne and, at its best, a meal here is a very pleasant and relaxed experience, although it can also feel rather serious - and, on the Guide's most recent visit, staff had poor knowledge of the menu and the earlier wow factor created by simple excellence was disappointingly absent. **Seats 86;** toilets wheelchair accessible; children welcome. L 12-2.15pm; D 6-10.15pm (to 11.15 Fri/Sat). Separate vegetarian à la carte menu avail-able. Closed Jan 1, Jul 12, Dec 25/26, Easter Sun/Mon. Amex, Diners, MasterCard, Visa. **Directions:** Near the City Hall.

566

Shu

Belfast
RESTAURANT

253 Lisburn Road Belfast Co Antrim BT9 7EN **Tel: 028 9038 1655**
eat@shu-restaurant.com www.shu-restaurant.com

Set back somewhat from the main road, tall arched windows and a smartly painted Victorian frontage exude warmth, providing a vivid contrast to the stainless steel efficiency of the bar and de rigeur 'on view' kitchen of Alan Reid's fashionable restaurant. After a courteous welcome, guests are led into a large and atmospheric L shaped room which is light and airy, with shiny metal softened by terracotta pillars and discreet covers. Headed up by the fervent Brian McCann since 2004, a seriously talented team of chefs are in serious pursuit of gastronomic excellence here - McCann's training with chefs of distinction, like the legendary Marco Pierre White, Philip Howard at London's celebrated Square restaurant, and his experience as head chef at the late Robbie Millar's Shanks restaurant is very evident in his menus at Shu. Superb freshly baked breads (still warm), served with delicious oils and olives offer a small taste of what is to follow, in menus that really do have something to suit every taste and pocket, combining classics with much-loved brasserie favourites. A choice of à la carte and set menus at lunch and dinner offer exceptional value, and illustrate this chef's dedication to seasonal provenance. Typically you may find that a starter of smoked salmon, potato salad, fine herbs and horseradish is pretty and refreshing, although perhaps upstaged by a beautifully creamy summer vegetable and mascarpone risotto with very fresh vegetables (peas, beans, butternut squash) topped with fine shavings of summer truffle, which is offered as a starter or main course (£4.50/£9.00). Of the main courses what seafood lover could resist spankingly fresh and perfectly cooked roasted wild hake, with new potatoes, braised fennel and a light fish broth the broth like a bouillabaisse, packed with flavour but perfectly light for lunch time. But the dish that stole the show on the Guide's most recent visit was crispy pork belly, with cauliflower purée, potato gratin and cider soaked raisins - a sublime flavour combination with real depth and apparently effortlessly executed. A refreshing salad might then be a good choice, or delicious dessert such as blueberry clafoutis with mascarpone, yoghurt and honey or a rich chocolate pudding with chocolate sauce and vanilla ice cream. Under the supervision of restaurant manager Julian Henry, an enthusiastic, friendly restaurant team offer very professional service - and a comprehensive wine list with many choices available by the glass also matches the food. Downstairs **Shubar** provides a good place to enjoy pre or post dinner drinks, and an upstairs room is available for private parties. With great food, service and atmosphere Shu continues to up the ante on the Belfast restaurant scene. Lucky old Belfast! Children welcome; air conditioning. **Seats 80** (private room, 24). L Mon-Sat, 12-2.30, D Mon-Sat 6-9 (Sat to 9.30). L £7-13, 1-3 courses; value D £17.50, Mon-Thu, 6-10pm (also available in Shu Bar Fri, Sat); otherwise à la carte; house wine from £15.50; s.c. discretionary (10% on parties of 6+). Bar open Fri & Sat 7-1. Closed Sun, 24-26 Dec, 11-13 Jul. Amex, MasterCard, Visa, Switch. **Directions:** Half mile south on Lisburn Road.

Sun Kee Restaurant

Belfast
RESTAURANT

42-47 Donegall Pass Belfast Co Antrim BT7 1BS
Tel: 028 9031 2016

The Lo family's restaurant just off Shaftesbury Square has earned widespread recognition as one of Ireland's most authentic Chinese restaurants and, as it became more famous, it became almost impossible to get a table so they moved to bigger premises across the road. Old hands may miss the squeeze but what you still get here is the classic Chinese dishes which are already familiar - but created in uncompromising Chinese style, without the usual "blanding down" typical of most oriental restaurants. They also offer more unusual dishes, which offer a genuine challenge to the jaded western palate: be prepared to be adventurous. Children welcome. Open for food daily, 12-11.30pm; house wine from £10.50; MasterCard, Visa, Switch. **Directions:** Opposite Police Station.

Swantons Gourmet Foods

Belfast
CAFÉ

639 Lisburn Road Belfast Co Antrim BT9 7GT **Tel: 028 9068 3388**
swantonsh@aol.com www.swantons.com

Run by husband and wife team Stewart and Gloria Swanton, this speciality food store and café has earned a following amongst discerning Belfast people - even in an area that is especially well served with good places to shop and eat, it stands out for dedication to quality and value. As well as offering a carefully selected range of deli fare, the food freshly cooked on site is delicious. You can see the chefs at work in the kitchen at the back, and a changing selection through the day begins with break fasts that include lovely options such as fruits with yoghurt and so on then, from late morning the lunch menu offers really good home made soups, custom made sandwiches in a variety of good breads salads, hot dishes like quiches and spinach & filo pastry layer, plus one or two specials. Baking is a speciality - beautiful home baked desserts and tarts - and tray bakes with tea and coffees on the after noon menu. It's a small place, so you may have to wait for a table at peak times, but you are not hurried or hassled once you get served. Toilets wheelchair accessible. **Seats 24** (+ outdoors, 10). Open Mon Sat, 9-5; L 11.30-3. D Thurs-Fri in summer only; set 2 course L £10.95. Closed Sun, 1 week 12 Jul 1 week Christmas. Amex, MasterCard, Visa, Switch. **Directions:** On the Lisburn Road.

Belfast
BAR/RESTAURANT

Ta Tu

701 Lisburn Road Belfast Co Antrim BT9 7GL
Tel: 028 9038 0818

This fashionable bar and grill found an immediate niche when it opened in 2000, and is always packed at weekends. The design incorporates an ultra-modern high-roofed 'warehouse' with a long bar where the bright young things meet and greet and, at the rear, a more intimate restaurant area; at the time of the Guide's 2007 visit a major refurbishment was imminent, to include an extension of the dining area; a new head chef, Martin Wilson, has taken over since out visit, but regardless of who is in the kitchen, they have always done a good job here and it is certain to remain one of Belfast's most popular informal dining spots. Various menus are offered, with dishes changing monthly, and the food is youthful and well presented; there's an all-day menu, also a reasonably priced evening Bistro Menu with an option of 1/2 carafe house wine and a recent introduction is the Sunday Lunch deal offering a choice of roasts at £7.95 with a complimentary Movie Lounge to keep the kids busy. And tradition alists who think of this as a trendy place that they may not like could be in for a surprise, as wel trained staff who know the menus are extremely friendly and make it a place for all ages; the wine list offers carefully chosen wines at very fair prices and there's plenty to choose from by the glass. Cocktai menu. DJ music. No children after 7pm. *The very trendy Bar Bacca in Franklin Street is in the same ownership. No children after 7pm. *The very trendy Bar Bacca in Franklin Street is in the same owner ship. **Seats 90.** Air conditioning. Food served daily all day. L 12-6, D 6-9.45 (Sun to 8.45). All day menu and a la carte. House wines from £13.95. Bar food served 12-9.30 daily. Closed 25 Dec MasterCard, Visa. **Directions:** From the city centre, take Lisburn Road - about 1 mile on the right.

Belfast
RESTAURANT

Tedfords Restaurant

5 Donegall Quay Belfast Co Antrim BT1 3EF **Tel: 028 9043 4000**
tedfordsrestaurant@btinternet.com www.tedfordsrestaurant.com

Sailing folk may remember this listed building as a ship's chandlers and, although the maritime theme is now less pronounced than formerly, there are still reminders of its history. Since proprietor-chef Alan Foster took over as sole owner a couple of years ago, the interior has been refurbished and the ground floor now has a more contemporary feeling to match the more sophisticated private dining room upstairs - and, although seafood is still the star here, it is now a seafood restaurant and steakhouse there's plenty to choose from - especially speciality fish and seafood dishes, of course, and the certi fied Irish angus steaks, and also vegetarian options. The food is imaginative and well cooked, and service is caring; as it is close to the Waterfront Hall and Odyssey Area, this is a good choice for a pre theatre meal. An extensive and reasonably priced wine list includes half a dozen house wines. **Seats 45.** Reservations required. L Tue-Fri, 12-2.30; D Tue-Sat, 5-9.30. Pre-theatre D Tue-Sat, about £19.95 (5-6.30). House wine from about £14; sc discretionary. Toilets wheelchair accessible. Children welcome. Parking in multi-storey carpark next door. Closed Sun-Mon, July fortnight, 1 week Christmas. Amex, MasterCard, Visa, Switch. **Directions:** 3 minute walk from Waterfront Hall, next to multi storey car park. ◊

Belfast
HOTEL/RESTAURANT

Ten Square Hotel

10 Donegall Square South Belfast Co Antrim BT1 5JD
Tel: 028 9024 1001
reservations@tensquare.co.uk www.tensquare.co.uk

This delightful boutique hotel has established a special niche for discerning visitors to Belfast: it is situated in a particularly attractive listed Victorian building and the location - just opposite the City Hall, and within walking distance of the whole city centre area - is superb. Although the interior is contemporary, it has been achieved with sensitivity to the original building: a striking feature, for example, is the lovely old stained glass in many of the original windows, which is now subtly echoed in the interior design. Accommodation - in generous high-windowed rooms, theatrically decorated in an uncompromisingly modern style - is simple yet very luxurious; even the most dyed-in-the-wool traditionalist would be won over by the sheer style of these rooms and they have wonderful bathrooms to match. Features include well-planned lighting, state-of-the-art entertainment systems and - going a stage further than the usual mini-bar (which, however, includes fresh milk for your freshly brewed tea or coffee) - a collection of drinks, nibbles and bits and pieces that would be worthy of a small corner shop, all neatly tucked away out of sight. Conference/banqueting 100/150. Children welcome (under 10s free in parents' room, cot available free of charge). No pets. **Rooms 22** (13 junior suites, 2 executive, 2 for disabled). Lift. 24 hour room service. Turndown service. Air conditioning, safe, ISDN, TV/DVD/video channel, tea/coffee-making facilities, iron & trouser press. B&B room rate £175 (max 2 guests). Closed 24-25 Dec. **The Grill Room & Bar:** This stylishly informal area, which occupies the whole of the ground floor, has become one of Belfast's most popular restaurants and meeting places, and is always busy with non-residents, which gives the hotel a great buzz; the Grill Room is the perfect antidote to other fashionable restaurants in the city, as the focus is firmly on wholesome traditional all-day fare and very reasonable prices. The theme is colonial and, although there is actually quite a wide range offered on menus that smack of retro, red meat is king here (and very good meat it is too); char-grilled steaks and burgers are served with super chips and well-made classic sauces, and other comforting dishes include 'knife & fork' barbecued ribs. Staff are warm, welcoming and generally efficient, with none of the stuffiness sometimes encountered in exclusive hotels. All round, this accomplished hotel is retaining its well-earned its reputation as a top destination in Belfast for discerning travellers. **Seats 120** (private room, 30, outdoor, 72); Live music Wed & Sun. Food served daily 12-10pm (Sun, 1-10pm); L 12-3, D 6-10. A la carte. SC discretionary. Amex, MasterCard, Visa, Switch. **Directions:** Corner of Linenhall Street at rear of City Hall.

Belfast
RESTAURANT

The Water Margin

159-161 Donegall Pass Belfast Co Antrim BT7 1DP
Tel: 028 9032 6888

This 200-seater emporium in a converted church at the bottom of the Ormeau Road is the biggest Chinese restaurant in Ireland. Inside, East meets West - a comfortable reception lounge with red leather sofas leads into the large open dining space with tables of various sizes, lots of artificial plants and garish stained glass windows. An open bar runs the length of the inside wall and the dining area is divided between the ground floor and a gallery with a purple painted vaulted ceiling and an adjoining opaque glass walled function room. The menu is massive and it pays to either know Chinese food really well, or have inside information to find your way about. An extensive Dim Sum menu offers uncompromising authentic Chinese dishes, but also includes set banquets with familiar dishes - at this level, the food is pretty average (and by no means cheap), but there is plenty of noisy atmosphere to experience. [The original sister restaurant is in Coleraine, Co. Londonderry (see entry).] Seats 200. Open daily, 12-11pm. Set menus from about £20 per person. House wine about £20. Open all year. MasterCard, Visa, Laser. **Directions:** Bottom of Ormeau Road. ◊

Belfast
HOTEL

The Wellington Park Hotel

21 Malone Road Belfast Co Antrim BT9 6RU **Tel: 028 9038 1111**
info@wellingtonparkhotel.com www.wellingtonparkhotel.com

Located in the fashionable Malone Road area close to the University, this friendly, family-owned and managed hotel is quite a Belfast institution. It is well located near most of the city's cultural attrac-

Georgina Campbell's Ireland

tions and is also a popular choice for business guests and as a conference venue, with all the most up to date audio-visual equipment and facilities. The spacious foyer and public areas are comfortably furnished, as are the refurbished bedrooms, featuring the usual facilities. A new patio area and restaurant **'Wellie Bar & Grill'** (reflecting the affectionate local nickname for the hotel) were added in 2007. Guests have free use of Queen's University sports centre, a few minutes from the hotel. *The Dunadry Hotel & Country Club, a fifteen minute drive from the city, is in the same ownership, also the **Armagh City Hotel** (see entries). Conference/banqueting (400/300); business centre, broadband wi/fi, secretarial services; video conferencing. Parking. Wheelchair accessible. Children welcome (under 12 free in parents' room; cots available without charge, baby sitting arranged). No pets. **Rooms 75** (all en-suite, 30 no smoking, 2 for disabled). Lift. 24 hour room service. B&B from about £40 pps. Restaurant open for L&D daily; *Short breaks offered. Closed 24-26 Dec. Amex, Diners, MasterCard, Visa, Switch. **Directions:** From Queen's University, head south up Malone Road, hotel is on the right hand side.

Belfast   **Zen**
RESTAURANT   55-59 Adelaide Street Belfast Co Antrim BT2 8FE
Ⓝ   **Tel: 028 9023 2244**

It would be interesting to know what the original owners of this 19th centry redbrick mill would make of its recent transformation by proprietor Eddie Fung into an ultra modern, stunningly cool Japanese restaurant. To call it spectacular would be an understatement - with acres of glass and mirror to contend with if you wish to eat in the upstairs area, where you can dine in booths or hunkered down Japanese style, traditionalist may opt instead to try the downstairs dining area, where you can choose your food at the sushi bar if you wish. In keeping with its setting, this is a place where they talk about 'food design' although more familiar Asian food is offered as well as cutting edge Japanese cuisine. Now one of Belfasts's most popular ethnic restaurants, Zen offers a unqiue dining experience and especially known for the authenticity of their fresh sushi and sashimi. L Mon-Fri, 12 -3; D Mon- Sat 5-11 (Sat from 6). Closed L Sat, all Sun. Amex, MasterCard, Visa. **Directions:** Behind City Hall. ◈

BELFAST INTERNATIONAL AIRPORT

Although dining out at airport restaurants was once all the rage, airports and good food have not often been seen together recently - but Paul & Jeanne Rankin have done their best ensure that passengers going through Belfast can look forward to something a cut above the rest at **Café Paul Rankin** (028 9445 4992), which is in the Departure Lounge and offers wide range of quiches, salads, gourmet sandwiches and pasta dishes, and an upmarket all-day breakfast menu: Eggs Benedict, home-made pancakes, free range scrambles egg & toast, as well as their version of the traditional fry. For accommodation near the airport, **Hilton Templepatrick** (028 944 3500; www.templepatrickhilton.com) is nearby, on the Castle Upton Estate; it has excellent facilities, including golf.
WWW-IRELAND-GUIDE.COM FOR THE BEST PLACES TO EAT, DRINK & STAY

COUNTY ANTRIM

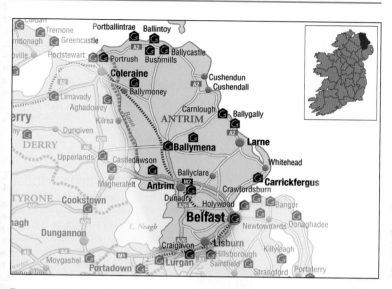

The Antrim Coast may be timeless in its beauty, but today its picturesque ports are enjoying the fruits of restoration and development at places as various as Ballycastle, Glenarm and Carrickfergus.

With its boundaries naturally defined by the sea, the River Bann, the extensive lake of Lough Neagh, and the River Lagan, County Antrim has always had a strong sense of its own clearcut geographical identity. This is further emphasised by the extensive uplands of the Antrim Plateau, wonderful for the sense of space with the moorland rising to heights such as Trostan (551m) and the distinctive Slemish (438m), famed for its association with St Patrick.

The plateau eases down to fertile valleys and bustling inland towns such as Ballymena, Antrim and Ballymoney, while the coastal towns ring the changes between the traditional resort of Portrush in the far north, the ferryport of Larne in the east, and historic Carrickfergus in the south.

In the spectacularly beautiful northeast of the county, the most rugged heights of the Plateau are softened by the nine Glens of Antrim, havens of beauty descending gently from the moorland down through small farms to hospitable villages clustered at the shoreline, and connected by the renowned Antrim Coast Road. Between these sheltered bays at the foot of the Glens, the sea cliffs of the headlands soar with remarkable rock formations which, on the North Coast, provide the setting for the Carrick-a-Rede rope bridge and the Giant's Causeway. From the charming town of Ballycastle, Northern Ireland's only inhabited offshore island of Rathlin is within easy reach by ferry, a mecca for ornithologists and perfect for days away from the pressures of mainstream life.

Local Attractions & Information

Antrim Town Maid of Antrim Cruises	079 6992 7089
Antrim Town Shanes Castle	028 94 428216
Antrim Town Tourism Information	028 94 428331
Ballycastle Carrick-a-Rede Rope Bridge	028 20 731855
Ballymena Tourism Information	028 25 660300
Ballymoney (Dervock) Benvarden Garden	028 20 741331
Ballymoney Leslie Hill Open Farm	028 27 666803
Bushmills Antrim Coast and Glens	028 20 731582
Bushmills Irish Whiskey-World's Oldest Distillery	028 20 731521
Carrickfergus Castle	028 93 351273
Carrickfergus Waterfront	028 93 358049
Carrickfergus Andrew Jackson Centre	028 93 358049
Dunluce Castle Visitor Centre	028 20 731938

Giants Causeway	028 20 731855
Giants Causeway & Bushmills Railway	028 20 732844
Glenariff Forest Park	028 2955 6000
Larne Carnfunnock Country Park	028 28 270541
Larne Ferryport	028 28 872100
Larne Tourism Information	028 28 260088
Lisburn Irish Linen Centre & Lisburn Museum	028 92 663377
Lisburn Tourism Information	028 92 660038
Portrush Tourism Information	028 70 823333
Rathlin Island Ferries	028 20 769299
Rathlin Island Visitor Centre	028 20 762024
Templepatrick Patterson's Spade Mill	028 94 433619

Ballintoy

B&B

Whitepark House

150 Whitepark Road Ballintoy Ballycastle Co Antrim BT54 6NH **Tel: 028 2073 1482**

bob@whiteparkhouse.com www.whiteparkhouse.com

GUESTHOUSE OF THE YEAR

A warm welcome from chatty and well-informed hosts Bob and Siobhán Isles awaits visitors to this pretty old house which is tucked away in well-maintained gardens and has stunning views of Whitepark Bay, and a path down to a beautiful beach just across the road. Arriving guests, welcomed to the cosy sitting room - furnished with couches, easy chairs and an extraordinary array of antiques and Asian mementos - could easily lose themselves in hours of relaxation at the open fire while indulging in homemade pastries and bottomless cups of perfect tea. The bedrooms have just been redesigned to allow for en-suite bathrooms (which are gorgeous, some with bath and separate shower, and some have views - in one you can lie in the bath and soak in the beauty of the garden); one front bedroom is exceptionally large and another has windows on three sides. You may be lucky enough to have a four-poster bed and seating area, but all are beautifully decorated with distinctive colour themes and lots of exotic touches to give each its special personality, and there is that warm feeling of being surrounded by a well-loved garden. They have also added a huge conservatory at the back, where breakfast is served, and there are comfy couches to relax on. Bob likes to see guests well prepared for the day ahead - there is much to explore, notably of course, the beautiful north coast and the Glens of Antrim - and, as a vegetarian, he's well placed to make a great vegetarian breakfast in addition to a perfect rendition of the traditional Ulster Fry. Bob and Siobhán are exceptional hosts, giving guests plenty of space to relax but ensuring they never want for anything and they have apparently unlimited local knowledge of the area, attractions and restaurants to help you enjoy your stay. A treasure indeed. Not suitable for children under 12. No pets. Garden, walking. Beach, fishing (fly, sea angling) & golf all nearby. **Rooms 3** (one bathroom for all; all no smoking). B&B from £45 pps, ss £15. 5% surcharge on credit card payments. MasterCard, Visa. Open all year. **Directions:** On Antrim coast road A2, 9km (6m) East of Bushmills; on east side of Whitepark Bay.

BALLYCASTLE

Ballycastle, a friendly market town on the beautiful north-eastern corner of Co Antrim, has a museum (028 207 62942) on Castle Street which will be of interest to visitors who are curious about the folk and social history of the Glens of Antrim (open daily Jul-Aug, otherwise by arrangement; free entry), and a growing number of restaurants and bars. The **Central Bar & Restaurant** (028 2076 3877), on Ann Street, is a friendly recently renovated premises with a new bar serving snacks downstairs and a large brasserie style restaurant above, offering good quality food at fair prices very popular, so reservations are recommended, regular music too; across the road you'll find **O'Connors** (028 207 62123), an old bar that has been restored keeping some of its old charm and with a good atmosphere that, attracts a young crowd (folk nights on Thursdays). On the Diamond, **The Cellar Restaurant** (028 2076 3037; www.thecellarrestaurant.co.uk), with barrel vaulted roof and cosy snugs separated by traditional etched glass dividers, is known for its atmosphere; expect traditional cooking with good fish and surf'n'turf; open 12-10 daily in summer and open just after the Guide's 2007 visits **Quay 26 Restaurant** (028

2076 1133) on Bayview Road overlooking the marina, with lovely views towards Fairhead - is already making waves for its interesting menus and a speedily earned reputation for excellent seafood.

Ballycastle
CHARACTER PUB

The House of McDonnell

71 Castle Street Ballycastle Co Antrim BT54 6AS **Tel: 028 2076 2975**
toms1744@aol.com www.houseofmcdonnell.com

The House of McDonnell has been in the caring hands of Tom and Eileen O'Neill since 1979 and in Tom's mother's family for generations before that, they can even tell you not just the year, but the month the pub first opened (April 1766). Tom and Eileen delight in sharing the history of their long, narrow premises with its tiled floor and mahogany bar: it was once a traditional grocery-bar, and is now a listed building. The only real change in the last hundred years or so, says Tom, was the addition of a toilet block. They have a good traditional music session every Friday and love to see musicians coming along and joining in. As Tom and Eileen rightly take pride in the fact that this is the only old bar in Ballycastle to have resisted 'refurbishment and makeover', you can rest assured that any changes will be completed with a very light touch. Not suitable for children after 8pm. They're usually open from 11 am until "late" at weekends, but only in the evenings midweek, although times might vary in winter; it's worth checking out at weekends anyway, all year. **Directions:** Town centre, near the Diamond.

Ballyclare
RESTAURANT

Oregano

29 Ballyrobert Road Ballyrobert Ballyclare Co Antrim **Tel: 028 9084 0099**
oregano.rest@btconnect.com www.oreganorestaurant.co.uk

A Victorian house in the small village of Ballyrobert is the setting for this rural restaurant. It's run by Dermot and Catherine Reagan, a young couple whose passion for good food is evident from the moment you enter their delightful, spacious, high-ceilinged dining room: with three white walls and one in warm raspberry, and classic wooden tables perfectly set off by smart white leather seats, it's clear that a lot of thought has gone into the décor - but it's the menu that takes centre stage. Dermot offers both à la carte and set menus (lunch and early dinner), based mainly on locally sourced foods including fish, duck, beef and venison, which he cooks to perfection. Lunch menus usually include homemade soup and a couple of other appealing starters - a well made Caesar salad with char-grilled chicken, perhaps, or pretty goats' cheese with mixed leaves and a balsamic roasted beetroot & hazelnut dressing. Main courses may offer a good mainstream vegetarian dish such as organic butternut and chilli risotto with nut brown butter and crispy fried sage, and tasty 'Bangers n Mash' - pork & leek sausages with buttery mash and onion gravy. A la carte menus offer more luxurious options, with an emphasis on seafood, including treats such as Kilkeel prawn risotto or tagliatelle with Glenarm smoked salmon in a light curry cream, and you'll also find dishes based on local ribeye beef, rack of Northern Irish lamb and local chicken. Desserts feature unusual homemade ice creams, such as fig and balsamic, alongside old favourites like lemon tart. A global wine list includes excellent house wines, also available by the glass. Children welcome. Garden. Parking. L Sun & Tue-Fri; D Tue-Sat. 2/3 course L/early D, about £14.95/17.95 (Tue-Fri); also à la carte. Closed Mon, 24-26 Dec & 1 Jan, 11-13 Jul. **Directions:** M2 north from Belfast, then A6 to Sandyknowes roundabout; take Larne exit to Corrs Corner roundabout; turn left to Ballyclare. Oregano is 1.5 miles on the right. ◇

Ballygally
HOTEL

Hastings Ballygally Castle Hotel

Coast Road Ballygally Co Antrim BT40 2QZ **Tel: 028 2858 1066**
res@bgc.hastingshotels.com www.hastingshotels.com

This coastal hotel really has got a (very) old castle at the heart of it - and they've even got a ghost (you can visit her room at the top of the castle). The whole thing is quite unlike any of the other Hastings hotels and, although recent investment has improved standards dramatically, the hotel still has character; some of the older rooms are literally shaped by the castle itself, and are quite romantic. Cosy chintzy wing chairs and open fires make welcoming lounge areas to relax in - and the beach is just a stone's throw away, across the road. Conference/banqueting (200/120). Children welcome; (under 14 free in parents' room; cots available without charge). Wheelchair accessible. Parking. No pets. **Rooms 44** (3 junior suites, 4 executive, 4 shower only, 5 family rooms, 8 no smoking, 1 for disabled) B&B

£65pps, ss £35; no SC. Meals: Rest D, 5-9; buffet L 12.30-2.30. *Short breaks offered - details on application. Open all year. Amex, Diners, MasterCard, Visa, Switch. **Directions:** Situated on the coast road between Larne and Glenarm (5km/3 miles from Larne on A2). ◇

Ballygally
RESTAURANT

Lynden Heights Restaurant

97 Drumnagreagh Rd. Ballygally nr Larne Co Antrim BT40 2RR
Tel: 028 2858 3560

On a clear day, the Doran family's restaurant high up above the coast road has the most amazing views - and the dining room is in a conservatory, to make the most of it. There's a cosy bar, where orders are taken by friendly, neatly uniformed waiting staff. Well-balanced menus offer a wide choice of dishes on every course, with seafood the main strength, and also game in season. On the carte, three of the seven starters and three main courses will probably be seafood dishes, cooked in a fairly classic style and given the occasional contemporary twist. Steaks get a predictably good showing too, and also Ballymoney ham; vegetarian dishes are available on a separate menu. Good carefully sourced ingredients, sound cooking, hearty portions and efficient service all complement this restaurant's natural appeal. An interesting, informative and well-priced wine list is changed monthly. * Lynden Heights also offers B&B accommodation, from spring 2008. Parking. **Seats 60** (private room, 26). Reservations advised. D Thu-Sun, 5-9 (Sun to 8); L Sun only, 12.30-3. Set D from about £20, also à la carte; Set Sun L about £17.50. Children welcome. House wine £14.50. Closed Mon-Wed. Amex, MasterCard, Visa, Switch. **Directions:** Situated between Larne and Glenarm - signed off the coast road.

Ballymena
HOTEL

Galgorm Manor Hotel

136 Fenaghy Road Ballymena Co Antrim BT42 1EA **Tel: 028 2588 1001**
sales@galgorm.com www.galgorm.com

Set amidst beautiful scenery, with the River Maine running through the grounds, this former gentleman's residence is now a country house hotel and a sister establishment to TENsq in Belfast (see entry). Approaching through well-tended parkland, guests pass the separate banqueting and conference facilities to arrive at the front door of the original house, which is a mere 100 yards from the river. The hotel has been greatly extended recently but the original house still has a very pleasant atmosphere, with a welcoming fire in the foyer, an elegant drawing room and characterful socialising spaces in Gillie's Pub & Bollinger Garden and Gillies Bar & Grill (where meals are also served). Accommodation includes 48 new deluxe bedrooms in the old walled garden area, and some suites and rooms in the old house; most of these have views over the river and are potentially special although, on the guide's 2007 visit, the original rooms (and bathroms) were in need of renovation. Also at this stage, the food side of the operation had not settled down. Conference/banqueting (500); golf (9/18); spa; fishing; horse-riding; walking; garden. Children welcome (under 4s free in parents room, cot £10, babysitting arranged). Wheelchair accessible. No pets. **Rooms 75** (9 suites, 6 junior suites, 2 disabled) B&B from £65 pps. L &D available daily. Open all year. Amex, Diners, MasterCard, Visa. **Directions:** From the Galgorm roundabout, take the third exit for Cullybackey (Fenaghy road). About 2 miles, on the left. ◇

Ballymena
COUNTRY HOUSE

Marlagh Lodge

71 Moorfields Rd Ballymena Co Antrim BT42 3BU **Tel: 028 2563 1505**
info@marlaghlodge.com www.marlaghlodge.com

Robert and Rachel Thompson took on this neglected early Victorian house on the edge of Ballymena in 2003 and then painstakingly restored it to make an unusual and very comfortable haven for guests and, although close to the road, the result is truly impressive. Originally built as the Dower House for the O'Hara family of nearby Crebilly House, the Lodge is a classic of its era, double fronted with spacious, high-ceilinged reception rooms of human proportions on either side of the entrance hall, and bedrooms which have lent themselves remarkably well to the architectural gymnastics needed in order to provide en-suite bathrooms in an old house. The three rooms - The Blue Room, The Chintz Room and The Print Room - are all large and comfortably furnished with interesting antiques, but otherwise very different. Robert and Sarah also offer dinner for residents - and non-residents are welcome too, by reservation. The repertoire is quite extensive, with local and artisan produce used in some unusual dishes - a typical 6-course spring menu might include lemon risotto with asparagus & pecorino, locally made Dundermotte Farmhouse sorbet, monkfish en papillotte with Thai butter, dark & white chocolate marquise, cheeses with home made chutney and tea or coffee with 'homemade goodies'... Special gourmet evenings are sometimes held, with wine paired with each course. Marlagh Lodge is within easy reach of the main airports and ferry ports, and all the attractions of the north Antrim coast. Banqueting (20). Children welcome (u 5s free in parents' room, cot available, free of charge). No pets. Golf, equestrian & fishing all nearby. **Rooms 3** (2 en-suite, 1 with private bathroom, all no smoking). B&B £40 pps, no ss. D Mon-Sat, 8pm (book by noon); Non residents welcome on Fri-Sat by reservations; Set D £31.50. Wines from about £15. "Closed occasionally," please ring ahead off-season. MasterCard, Visa, Switch. **Directions:** On A36, 1km (0.6 m) from Larne Road roundabout and visible from the road.

BUSHMILLS

Most people visiting Bushmills do so to see the world's oldest licensed whiskey distillery - and this interesting and immaculately maintained distillery and visitor attraction is certainly worth a detour. The village is also well-placed for a break when exploring the beautiful North Coast and, as it can be surprisingly difficult to get a meal here when there are coach loads of other visitors on the same trail, a good new restaurant is especially welcome: **Sixteenoeight** (028 2073 2040; Open L&D Tue-Sun 12-3pm, 5-9.30pm) is a contemporary restaurant, bistro & café on the main street, and when it opened in 2007 it was immediately welcomed by local residents and visitors alike, for its tempting modern menus, good cooking, friendly staff and good value. You will also find "old-fashioned home-style of the highest order" at **Bushmills Garden Centre** (028 2073 0424; www.creativegardens.net) on Ballyclough Road (see also, Donaghadee, Co Down). **WWW-IRELAND-GUIDE.COM FOR THE BEST PLACES TO EAT, DRINK & STAY**

Bushmills
HOTEL/RESTAURANT

Bushmills Inn

9 Dunluce Rd Bushmills Co Antrim BT57 8QG **Tel: 028 2073 3000**
mail@bushmillsinn.com www.bushmillsinn.com

Originally a 19th-century coaching inn, developments have been undertaken with sensitivity, improving amenities without loss of character. The tone is set by the turf fire and country seating in the hall and public rooms - bars, the famous circular library, the restaurant, even the Pine Room conference room carry on the same theme. Bedrooms are individually furnished in a comfortable cottage style and even have "antiqued" bathrooms but it's all very well done and avoids a theme park feel. Although quite expensive, it's hard to think of a better base for a holiday playing the famous golf courses of the area (Royal Portrush is just four miles away) - or simply exploring this beautiful coastline and its hinterland; taking the Magilligan-Greencastle ferry, day trips can comfortably include a visit to the beautiful Inishowen peninsula in Co. Donegal. Garden. Fishing (fly). Broadband wi/fi; children welcome (cot available, £10). No pets. **Rooms 32:** 22 in Mill House, 10 in Coaching Inn; (6 superior, 7 shower only, all no smoking, 2 family, 1 for disabled) B&B from £89 pps.*Short breaks offered. **Restaurant:** The inn is known for its wholesome food and makes a good place to plan a break when touring, as it offers both day and evening menus in cosy surroundings (the only disadvantage is that coaches often make a lunchtime stop here for the same reasons). Pride in Irish ingredients is seen in A Taste of Ulster menus that offer a range of traditional dishes with a modern twist: an unusual speciality, for example, is Dalriada cullen skink, a 'meal in a soup bowl' based on smoked haddock and topped with an (optional) poached egg; another is onion & Guinness soup, which is topped with a cheese croûton like the French soup that inspired it - and, of course 'Bushmills coffee', which is better than a dessert any day. Wheelchair accessible. **Seats 110** (private room, 40, outdoor, 14). Reservations advised. Not suitable for children after 6pm. L&D á la carte; D daily 6-9.30; L daily, Day Menu 12-6.00; (Sun: carvery from 12.30-2.30pm and day menu to 6pm); bar food Sun only 12-4 (soup & sandwiches). House wines from £14; SC discretionary. Closed 24/25 Dec. MasterCard, Visa. **Directions:** On the A4 Antrim coast road, in Bushmills village, as it crosses the river.

Bushmills
The Distillers Arms

BAR/RESTAURANT 140 Main Street Bushmills Co Antrim BT57 8QE **Tel: 028 2073 1044**
simon@distillersarms.com www.distillersarms.com

Simon Clarke's stylish modern bar and restaurant is housed in a renovated 18th century building which was once the home of the distillery owners. The bar - which leads through into the restaurant at the far end - has smart modern lightwood bar stools with comfortable curved backs, comfy sofas, table lamps and a warm atmosphere; the restaurant is more rustic by comparison, with open stonework and a fireplace. As much as half of the menu could be seafood, including a speciality dish of salmon cured with old Bushmills whiskey; main courses also offer a good choice of seafood, with some good meat and poultry dishes, and mainstream vegetarian dishes. Lunch and early evening menus offer particularly good value and the wine list, which offers many bottles sourced directly from auction and sold with only a small mark up, includes a fair choice of house wines and half bottles. Toilets wheelchair accessible. Children welcome before 7.30pm. **Seats 80** (outdoor seating, 6, private room, 25). Open daily in summer: L12.30-3, D 5.30-9 (to 9.30 Fri/Sat). House wines from £13. Closed Mon-Tue off-season (Oct-Mar); 25 Dec. MasterCard, Visa, Switch. **Directions:** 300 yards from Old Bushmills Distillery.

Carnlough
Londonderry Arms Hotel

HOTEL 20 Harbour Road Carnlough Co Antrim BT44 0EU **Tel: 028 2888 5255**
lda@glensofantrim.com www.glensofantrim.com

The Londonderry Arms Hotel, built by the Marchioness of Londonderry in 1848 as a coaching inn, was inherited by her great grandson, Sir Winston Churchill, in 1921 and retains great character to this day. Since 1948 it has been in the caring hands of the O'Neill family, and they do good home-made bar meals, or afternoon tea, which you can have in the bar or beside the fire in an old fashioned lounge; as well as dinner, High Tea is still served in the restaurant on Sunday afternoons. Bedrooms are comfortable and well-furnished; many of the older rooms have sea views and it is worthwhile discussing the type and location of your room when booking, as some have been refurbished recently and one or two are badly positioned for a restful night's sleep. This is a delightful place in a lovely old-fashioned village, and a refreshing contrast to today's streamlined new hotels. Conferences/banqueting (100/80); secretarial services. Parking. Wheelchair accessible. Children welcome (under 2s free in parents' room; cots available without charge). No pets. Walking.*Off season short breaks offered - details on application. **Rooms 35** (all en-suite, 4 executive, 6 family, 1 for disabled). Lift; limited room service. B&B £55 pps, ss £15. Restaurant: D 7-9 (5-8 Sun), L Sun only, 12-3. Bar food served daily, 10am-8.30pm. Closed 24-25 Dec. Amex, MasterCard, Visa, Switch. **Directions:** On the A2 Antrim coast road, 24km (14 miles) north of Larne.

Carrickfergus
Clarion Hotel

HOTEL 75 Belfast Road Carrickfergus Co Antrim BT38 8BX **Tel: 028 9336 4556**
info@clarioncarrick.com www.clarioncarrick.com

Conveniently located to Belfast airport (10 miles) and the scenic attractions of the Antrim coast, this modern hotel makes a comfortable base for business and leisure visitors. It has good conference facilities (600), meeting rooms (max. 60) and in-room amenities (desk, fax/modem line) for business guests. Bedrooms include three suitable for disabled guests, two suites, two junior suites and 20 non-smoking rooms; all are furnished to a high standard with well-finished en-suite bathrooms (all with bath and shower). **Rooms 68.** B&B from about £45 pps, ss about £30. Open all year except Christmas. Amex, MasterCard, Visa, Switch. **Directions:** Main Coast Road exit Belfast North (8 miles). ◊

Dunadry
HOTEL

Dunadry Hotel & Country Club

2 Islandreagh Drive Dunadry Co Antrim BT41 2HA **Tel: 028 9443 4343**
info@dunadry.com www.dunadry.com

This attractive riverside hotel is well-located close to Belfast International Airport and only about 15 minutes from the city centre. It was formerly a mill and it succeeds very well in combining the character of the old buildings with the comfort and efficiency of an international hotel. It has excellent facilities and stylish, spacious bedrooms include three suites and eleven executive rooms all have good amenities. There's a choice of dining in The Linen Mill Restaurant or the informal Mill Race Bistro, which makes the most of its situation overlooking the river. Leisure facilities within the grounds include a professional croquet lawn, fun bowling, trout fishing and cycling, as well as a leisure centre. *Sister hotel to the **Wellington Park Hotel** in Belfast city and the **Armagh City Hotel** (see entries). Conference/banqueting 350/300. Children welcome (under 12s free in parents' room cot available without charge, baby sitting arranged). **Rooms 83** (all en-suite, 2 for disabled). No pets. Garden, walking, fishing, cycling; leisure centre, beauty salon. B&B from £82pps; room-only rate also available.*Short breaks offered. Linen Mill Restaurant (fine dining): D Sat only, 7.30-10.30. **Bistro:** open all day. Closed 24-26 Dec. Amex, Diners, MasterCard, Visa, Switch. **Directions:** Near Belfast airport; look for signs to Antrim/Dunadry. ◊

Portballintrae
HOTEL
Ⓝ

Bayview Hotel

2 Bayhead Road Portballintrae Bushmills Co Antrim **Tel:028 2073 4100**
info@bayviewhotelni.com www.bayviewhotelni.com

This simple and well maintained hotel on the seafront has great views, and a modern bar and restaurant area with an open fire. It would make an ideal base for tourists, families, couples and for short breaks. **Rooms 25.** B&B from £40 pps (off season breaks from £55). Open all year. MasterCard, Visa, Switch. **Directions:** On the seafront. ◊

Portballintrae
BAR/RESTAURANT

Sweeney's Public House & Wine Bar

Seaport Avenue Portballintrae Co Antrim BT57 8SB
Tel: 028 2073 2404 seaport@freeuk.com

Seymour Sweeney's bar is in an attractive stone building is on the sea side of the road as you drive into Portballintrae, and is very handy to both the Royal Portrush Golf Club and the Giant's Causeway. It's a pleasant place, with a welcoming open fire in the bar and a choice of places to drink or have a bite to eat. Unpretentious food is in the modern international café/bar style; seafood platter and 'Wellington Bomber' are specialities. Although likely to suit all age groups during the day, it can get very busy during the evening, especially on live music nights (folk & country; there is a late licence to 1 am on Friday and Saturday). A useful place to break a day exploring the area, although a phone call is advised. Children welcome, wheelchair accessible. **Seats 120** (+50 outside, +32 private room). Air con. Food daily, 12-9. Set L about £10, set Sun L about £15, also A la carte. Closed 25 Dec. Amex, Diners, MasterCard, Visa, Switch. **Directions:** Centre of village overlooking bay & harbour. ◊

PORTRUSH

Portrush is a popular seaside holiday resort, golfing destination and a good base for exploring the beautiful Antrim coast. The most spectacularly located hotel in the area is the **Royal Court** (028 7082 2236; www.royalcourthotel.co.uk) on the coast road and, in the town, those in the know head for the smart **Comfort Hotel Portrush** (028 782 6100; www.comforthotelportrush.com). Nearby, the popular **'55 North'** (028 7082 2811; www.55-north.com) is in an attractive modern building with sea views, offering a useful all-day café on the ground floor and a restaurant with beautiful views serving eclectic food above it.

WWW-IRELAND-GUIDE.COM FOR THE BEST PLACES TO EAT, DRINK & STAY

Portrush
B&B/FARMHOUSE

Maddybenny Farmhouse

Loguestown Road Portrush Coleraine Co Antrim BT52 2PT
Tel: 028 7082 3394
beds@maddybenny.com www.maddybenny.com

Just two miles from Portrush, the White family's Plantation Period farmhouse was built before 1650. Since extended, and now modernised, it makes a very comfortable and exceptionally hospitable place to stay, with a family-run equestrian centre nearby (including stabling for guests' own horses). There is also snooker, a games room and quiet sitting places, as well as a garden and an area for outdoor children's games. The accommodation is just as thoughtful. The bedrooms are all en-suite and there are all sorts of useful extras electric blankets, a comfortable armchair, hospitality tray complete with tea cosy, a torch and alarm clock beside the bed, trouser press, hair dryer and, on the landing, an ironing board, fridge and pay phone for guest use. Across the yard there are also six self-catering cottages, open all year (one wheelchair friendly). No evening meals, but guests are guided to the local eating places that will suit them best - and the breakfasts here are legendary, so make sure you allow plenty of time to start the day with a feast the like of which you are unlikely to encounter again. Maddybenny was the Guide's Farmhouse of the Year in 2000. Equestrian, garden, walking; snooker. Golf, fishing, tennis and pitch & putt nearby. Children welcome (cot available £2 charge). No pets. **Rooms 3** (all en-suite, 2 family rooms) B&B £32.50pps, ss £5 (children £10). Closed 25-26 Dec. MasterCard, Visa, Switch.
Directions: Signposted off A29 Portrush/Coleraine road.

Portrush
RESTAURANT

The Ramore Oriental Restaurant

6 The Harbour Road Portrush Co Antrim BT56 8BN **Tel: 028 7082 6969**
www.ramorerestaurants.co.uk

The wonderful Ramore Restaurant was once the leading light of cosmopolitan fine dining in Northern Ireland and, after a long spell concentrating exclusively on quality fast food, George and Jane McAlpin promised to being back something of the spirit of the old Ramore in an 80-seater fine dining restaurant that now complements their three existing casual eating places (The Wine Bar, Coast Pasta & Pizza and Harbour Bistro). Things are not quite what they were of course although the smart modern design is perhaps in tune with the hopes of longtime followers, the fact that the name has already been changed from 'Restaurant & Wine Bar' to 'Oriental Restaurant' indicates how different the current Ramore really is. On the top floor, above the wine bar, the new restaurant is in two areas - one a large square room overlooking the harbour, which is very noisy, and a quieter area in a room along the bar. The very long menus offer a wide range of broadly oriental dishes and would sound a warning note in any but the most accomplished hands - but here the cooking is as good as ever, presentation is very attractive and service is quick and attentive. Wine service, especially, is impressive and the drinks menu includes a tempting range of cocktails. This is a fun place, with many of the dishes designed for sharing, and it is executed with flair. **The Wine Bar:** This informal restaurant is on the first floor, underneath Ramore Oriental, and above Coast, the pasta restaurant; it remains very popular with the holiday market and with the young who appreciate the fun and friendly atmosphere, the speed and reasonable prices. Menus offer a wide selection of contemporary dishes ranging from home baked breads with nuts, olives and dips, through bang bang chicken, or chilli steak in pitta, to roast fillet of salmon with champ. Prices are very accessible - but the downside is noise, discomfort and scanty service. *The famous old **Harbour Bar** nearby is in the same ownership; the front section retains its original character and, behind it the **Harbour Bistro & Wine Bar** offer mainly contemporary food, and roasts for Sunday lunch. (L&D served daily). Ramore Wine Bar **Seats 300.** L&D daily: L12.15-2.15pm, D 5-10 (Sun,12.30-3 & 5-9); Coast Italiano Seats 90 (Mon-Sat 4-10.30, Sun 3-9.30). Wine bar & toilets on ground floor wheelchair accessible. Harbour Bistro - Mon-Sat, 5-10pm, Sun 4-9pm. Closed 25 Dec. MasterCard, Visa, Switch.
Directions: This complex of four linked establishments is at the harbour in Portrush.

COUNTY ARMAGH

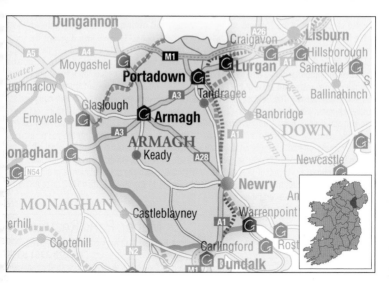

Mention Armagh, and most people will think of apples and archbishops. In the more fertile northern part of the county, orchards are traditionally important in the local economy, with the lore of apple growing and their use a part of County Armagh life. And the pleasant cathedral city of Armagh itself is of course the ecclesiastical capital of all Ireland, and many a mitre is seen about it.

But in fact Armagh city's significance long pre-dates Christian times. Emhain Macha - Navan Fort- to the west of the town, was a royal stronghold and centre of civilisation more than 4,000 years ago. Marking the county's northern coastline, the inland freshwater sea of Lough Neagh provides sand for the construction industry, eels for gourmets, and recreational boating of all sorts. In times past, it was part of the route which brought coal to Dublin from the mines in Coalisland in Tyrone, the main link to the seaport of Newry being the canal from Portadown which, when opened in 1742, was in the forefront of canal technology.

That County Armagh was a leader in canal technology is only one of its many surprises. The discerning traveller will find much of interest, among the undulating farmland and orchards, the pretty villages, or the handsome uplands rising to Carrigatuke above Newtownhamilton, and on towards the fine peak of Slieve Gullion in the south of the county, down to Forkhill and Crossmaglen and the Gaelic football heartlands.

Local Attractions & Information

Annaghmore (nr Portadown) Ardress (NT house)	028 38 851236
Armagh County Museum	028 37 523070
Armagh Planetarium	028 37 523689
Armagh Observatory	028 37 522928
Armagh Palace Stables Heritage Centre	028 37 521801
Armagh St Patrick's Trian Visitor Centre	028 37 521801
Bessbrook Derrymore House	028 30 830353
Forkhill (Slieve Gullion)Ti chulainn Cultural Centre	028 30 888828
Loughgall Loughgall Country Park	028 38 892900
Lough Neagh Discovery Centre, Oxford Island	028 38 322205
Markethill Gosford Forest Park	028 37 551277
Moy The Argory (NT Mansion)	028 87 784753
Portadown Moneypenny's Lock (Newry Canal) C/O Armagh Tourist Office	028 37 521800
Scarva Newry Canal Visitor Centre	028 38 832163
Slieve Gullion Forest Park	028 337551277

Armagh City Hotel

Armagh
HOTEL

2 Friary Road Armagh Co Armagh BT60 4FR **Tel: 028 3751 8888**
info@armaghcityhotel.com www.armaghcityhotel.com

Located at the heart of the "orchard county" of Armagh, this modern hotel is a sister establishment to the Dunadry Inn, Co. Antrim and Wellington Park Hotel, Belfast (see entries). Although the functional lines of the building are disappointingly out of place in this historic location, it has brought welcome facilities to the area, notably Northern Ireland's largest hotel conference facility. A cafeteria style 'Deli' and informal dining area located in the foyer give a poor impression on arrival - but the bar and more formal restaurant areas at the back of the hotel look out onto pleasant landscaped gardens, and a new beer garden 'The Balcony' opened in 2007. Bedrooms are practical and well-equipped for business guests, with good amenities. Children welcome (under 10s free in parents' room, cot available without charge, baby sitting arranged). Conference/banqueting (1,200/700); business centre, secretarial services, broadband wi/fi. Leisure centre with swimming pool, steam room, jacuzzi. *Special breaks offered - details on application. **Rooms 82** (10 executive, 30 no smoking, 4 for disabled). B&B from £48.50 pps; ss 35.50. Closed 24-26 Dec. Amex, Diners, MasterCard, Visa, Switch. **Directions:** From Dublin take A28 to Armagh City, when the police station is in sight, follow the road round to the left to the hotel. From Belfast take M1 to Junction 11, then M12 on to A3, hotel is situated just before Palace Stables.

Manor Park Restaurant

Armagh
RESTAURANT

2 College Hill The Mall Armagh Co Armagh BT61 9DF
Tel: 028 3751 5353
manorparkrestaurant@yahoo.ie www.manorparkrestaurant.com

An attractive early nineteenth century stone-fronted building beside the entrance to the Observatory is home to this well known French restaurant; it is a building of character - low-ceilinged, with a period fireplace and antique furnishings. Arriving guests are greeted by the French staff, and may have an aperitif in the bar, or go straight to their table. Several different menus are offered at various times, and they make a good read - ingredients are very good quality and include local seafood, beef and lamb, and also black Lyon duck. Although dinner may seem expensive, lunch and early dinner menus generally offer good value for money. The full à la carte is much grander, and offers game in season. The wine list is extensive and offers good value, also an unusually wide selection of half bottles. Children welcome. **Seats 60** (private room 26). Reservations required. Open for food daily: 12.30-10; L 12.30-2.30, D 5.30-10. Carvery L £5.95; early D £19.95 (Mon-Fri, 5-6.30), Set D £35. L & D also à la carte. House wines from £15. Closed 24 & 26 Dec & 1 Jan. MasterCard, Visa, Laser, Switch. **Directions:** On the mall, beside the Courthouse.

Newforge House

Craigavon
COUNTRY HOUSE

58 Newforge Road Magheralin Craigavon Co Armagh BT67 0QL
Tel: 028 9261 1255
enquiries@newforgehouse.com www.newforgehouse.com

John and Louise Mathers' fine Georgian country house is less than half an hour's drive south west of Belfast, and handy to both Belfast International and City airports and Ferry Terminal - yet, in a wonderful setting of mature trees, gardens and green fields on the edge of the quiet village of Magheralin, it feels like worlds away. The property - which is substantial - was built around 1785 and has been in the Mathers family for six generations; after major renovations the Mathers opened John's former family home as a guesthouse in 2005, and it now offers luxurious en-suite accommodation in stylish, individually decorated rooms (all with beautiful bathrooms, five of which have separate bath & shower), a period drawing room with an open log fire and a fine dining room where John takes pride in presenting meals based mostly on local and organic produce - which can be taken at separate tables or as a group. It is a lovely spot for a short break (various special offers are available) and makes a perfect setting for special occasions, including weddings (which can be in a marquee in the garden for larger numbers), smaller celebrations, or corporate events. Free Broadband Wi/FI. **Rooms 6** (5 with separate bath & shower, 1 shower only, all no smoking). B&B £65 pps, ss £15. Wheelchair accessible on ground floor, including toilet facilities;

bedrooms are upstairs & not wheelchair accessible. **Dining Room seats 22.** D daily 7-8.30 (to 9 Fri/Sat); Sun & Mon light dinner only; Set 2/3 course D £25/29.50; Vegetarian meals on request; House wine £14. No smoking house. Closed 24 Dec - 8 Jan. MasterCard, Visa, Switch. **Directions:** M1 from Belfast to Craigavon until junction for A3 to Moira; through Moira to Magheralin then turn left at Byrnes Pub (on the corner) onto Newforge Road. Continue for 2 minutes until the National Speed Limit signs; black and white sign for Newforge House on the left. Next left through entrance in stone wall; take first right turn and park in front of the house.

Lurgan
RESTAURANT

The Brindle Beam Tea Rooms
House of Brindle 20 Windsor Avenue Lurgan Co Armagh BT67 9BG
Tel: 028 3832 1721

This in-store self-service restaurant is a real one-off. Nothing is bought in and the kitchen team, puts the emphasis firmly on real home cooking. There are two freshly-made soups each day and hot dishes like beef stew, made with well trimmed fat-free chump steak - with no onions. None of the pies or casseroles contain onions as some customers don't like them, but they're still full of flavour. Their salad cart is a special attraction, with anything up to 30 different salads served each day, and several different hot dishes including baked or grilled chicken breasts, salmon and always some vegetarian dishes too. There's also a huge variety of tray bakes and desserts - and only real fresh cream is used. Scrupulously clean, with reasonable prices (not cheap, but good value for the quality) and real home cooking, this place is a gem. **Seats 110** (private room 50). Open Mon-Sat, 10-5, L 12-2.30, Afternoon Tea 2-4.30 (Sat to 4.45). A la carte self-service except special set menus, e.g. Christmas. Unlicensed. Closed Sun, 25-26 Dec, Easter, 12-13 Jul. MasterCard, Visa. **Directions:** Town centre; located in The House of Brindle Store.

Portadown
HOTEL
R

Seagoe Hotel
Upper Church Lane Portadown Co Armagh BT63 5JE **Tel: 028 3833 3076**
info@seagoe.com www.seagoe.com

Attractively situated in its own grounds on the edge of Portadown, this fine hotel has been in the same ownership for many years but underwent a complete makeover a few years ago. The design is innovative and exceptionally easy on the eye and, once inside, the tone of the whole development is set by stylish public areas which are outstanding for wheelchair access throughout the building, which has been thought through in detail. In the contemporary bedrooms warm, rich fabrics are teamed with good work space for business guests; executive rooms also have modem and fax facilities. Business/conference facilities are equally special and there's also a separate function entrance, with its own dramatic lobby/reception area - and there are two superb honeymoon suites. Bar and restaurant areas are designed with equal care, looking on to a delightful courtyard garden. Conferences/Banqueting (600/450); business centre. Own parking. Garden. Children welcome (under 5s free in parents' room, cot available free of charge). **Rooms 34** (all en-suite, 2 junior suites, 2 executive, 2 family, 17 ground floor, 2 disabled). Room only £65 single, £96 double. Lift. Limited room service. Restaurant open for lunch and dinner daily. 12-2.30 & 5-9.30 (Sun 6-9) and bar meals (panini, ciabatta, steak etc.) are available at the same times. Closed 25 Dec. Amex, Diners, MasterCard, Visa, Switch. **Directions:** Off A27 (Old Lurgan Road).

Portadown
CAFÉ

Yellow Door Deli, Bakery & Café

74 Woodhouse Street Portadown Co Armagh BT62 1JL **Tel: 028 3835 3528**
info@yellowdoordeli.co.uk www.yellowdoordeli.co.uk

The energetic and very talented Simon Dougan is one of the luminaries of the Northern Ireland food scene, and his Yellow Door Deli celebrates a decade of success in 2008. It has an in-house bakery, producing some of the finest bread in Northern Ireland (an area renowned for good home baking) and, as well as retailing a wide selection of the best speciality foods from Ireland and abroad, they also have a number of home-made specialities, including patés, terrines, chutneys, salads and ice cream, which are sold in the shop and served in the café - discerning customers from all over the north home in on this smashing shop, to top up with goodies and have a tasty bite of lunch. Hot smoked Irish salmon with grilled soda bread, wild rocket and lemon dill cream is a house speciality - go for it! There is a also an extensive, very interesting and keenly priced wine list, and a soft seating area, complete with cookery book library, where customers can relax. (Also at: 427 Lisburn Road, Belfast.) **Café seats 75.** Breakfast from 9am, L 12-2.30pm, otherwise food from deli all day until 5pm; house wine £8. Closed Mon, 12-13 Jul, 25-26 Dec, "some" Bank Hols. MasterCard, Visa, Switch. **Directions:** Off Main St. on left only street on left as the traffic flows one way.

COUNTY DOWN

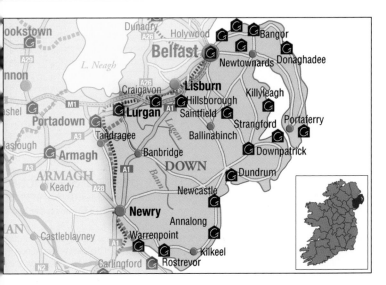

County Down rings the changes in elegant style, from its affluent shoreline along Belfast Lough - the "Gold Coast" - through the rolling drumlin country which provides Strangford Lough's many islands, and on then past the uplands around Slieve Croob, with the view southward being increasingly dominated by the purple slopes of the Mountains of Mourne.

The Mournes soar to Northern Ireland's highest peak of Slieve Donard (850m), and provide excellent hill-walking and challenging climbing. When seen across Down's patchwork of prosperous farmland, however, they have a gentleness which is in keeping with the county's well-groomed style. In the same vein, Down is home to some of Ireland's finest gardens, notably Mount Stewart on the eastern shore of Strangford Lough, and Rowallane at Saintfield, while the selection of forest and country parks is also exceptional.

Within the contemporary landscape, history is much in evidence. St Patrick's grave is in Downpatrick, while the Ulster Folk and Transport Museum at Cultra near Holywood provides an unrivalled overview of the region's past. The coastline is much-indented, so much so that, when measured in detail, County Down provides more than half of Northern Ireland's entire shoreline. Within it, the jewel of Strangford Lough is an unmatched attraction for naturalists and boat enthusiasts, while Portaferry has one of Ireland's longest-established saltwater aquariums in Exploris.

In the south of the county, the increasingly prosperous town of Newry on the river inland from Carlingford Lough is – with Lisburn in County Antrim – one of Ireland's two newest cities under a re-designation of 2003, Newry is responding with enthusiasm to its enhanced status, and the urban regeneration of this interesting canalside centre is intriguing to watch., while the Ship Canal down to the sea has been restored and was re-opened in 2006.

Local Attractions & Information

Bangor Events Office	028 91 278051
Bangor Tourism Information	028 91 270069
Bangor North Down Heritage Centre	028 91 271200
Castle Espie Wildfowl and Wetlands Centre	028 91 874146
Cultra Ulster Folk & Transport Museum	028 90 428428
Downpatrick Down Cathedral	028 44 614922
Downpatrick St Patrick Centre	028 44 619000
Dromore Kinallen Craft Centre	028 97 533733
Dundrum Murlough National Nature Reserve	028 43 751467
Greyabbey Mount Stewart House	028 42 788387

Hillsborough Hillsborough Castle Gardens	028 92 681300
Kilkeel Nautilus Centre	028 41 762525
Millisle Ballycopeland Windmill	028 90543033
Mourne Mountains Guided Wildlife Walks	028 43 751467
Newcastle Tollymore Forest Park	028 43 722428
Newtownards Armagh Down Tourism Partnership	028 91 822881
Portaferry Exploris Aquarium	028 42 728062
Portaferry Strangford-Portaferry Car Ferry	028 44 881637
Rathfriland Bronte Interpretive Centre	028 40 623322
Saintfield Rowallane Gardens	028 97 510131
Strangford Castle Ward	028 44 881204
Strangford... Strangford-Portaferry Car Ferry	028 44 881637
Strangford Lough Wildlife Centre	028 44 881411

Ardglass
RESTAURANT/PUB
N 🚬

Curran's Bar & Seafood Steakhouse

83 Strangford Road Chapeltown Ardglass Co Down BT30 7SB
Tel: 028 4484 1332 www.curransbar.net

Originally the Curran family home, this well known establishment dates back to 1791 and has been renovated and extended over the years. An ideal location opposite the local church, and at a junction with five roads, ensured brisk business with wakes, weddings, funerals in the early years and now it's a centre of hospitality for appreciative locals - and also the fortunate visitors who get to know about its more recently earned reputation for fine food, under the guidance of Paula Mahon, (née Curran). Today, it not only has a 60-seater restaurant, a comfortable bar and outdoor area to offer but the premises also holds a licence for civil weddings, with an outdoor arch used for the ceremony; receptions are held in the restaurant - which has a large fireplace as its centrepiece, with original family photographs and memorabilia. Outside, there's a covered, heated smoking area, a walled beer garden and barbecue area, and a play area for children and the old milking parlour has been converted into The Stables Bar and function room. Seafood has always played a central role here, of course, and menus - which are written in French and Spanish as well as English offer a wide range including the ever-popular Seafood Platter (a splendid collection of clams, smoked mackerel, mussels, crabcakes, prawns, dressed crabs and langoustine, served with homemade wheaten bread) along with other delights such as Ardglass prawns, crab claws, poached salmon, Dundrum Bay mussels, and crayfish risotto. Alternatively, there's a daily roast dinner, prime sirloin or fillet from local butchers and homemade steakburger. Children are well catered for with a half rack of barbecue ribs, southern fried chicken fillets, mussels in garlic cream sauce or they can have the roast dinner. The wine list, though short, is well chosen. Toilets wheelchair accessible; children welcome (high chair, childrens menu, baby changing facilities; playground); free broadband wi/fi; Seats 100 (outdoors, 44); reservations recommended; food served all day, 7 days, 12.30-9pm; set Sun L £14.95; value L £4.95, 12.30-5pm; also a la carte; house wine from £11. Live music (trad & modern) Fri/Sat, 9.30-1; Sun from 7.30pm. Closed 25 Dec. MasterCard, Visa, Switch. **Directions:** Main road between Ardglass (2 miles) and Strangford (6 miles).

Banbridge
CAFÉ
N **R**

Greenbean Coffee Roasters

11 Townsend Street Banbridge Co Down BT32 3LF **Tel: 028 4062 9096**
info@greenbeanroasters.com www.greenbeanroasters.com

Hidden behind a stylish frosted glass frontage and contemporary logo in the relative calm of Banbridge's Townsend Street, a treat awaits famished shoppers and caffeine addicts alike. Since opening their Greenbean Coffee Shop and Barista training school here in August 2006, the renowned coffee roasters Deirdre and Pat Grant, long celebrated for supplying quality coffees to the catering trade, have already built up a loyal following of discerning locals. A comfortable and well spaced mixture of high and low level seats at round and oval tables provide the perfect resting place to re-fuel and watch the world go by. Coffee is, of course, their speciality and very much in evidence, with glass topped tables and casks filled with beans, and freshly roasted coffee delivered twice daily - it doesn't get much fresher than this! Greenbean offer a rich or smooth option with all coffees, to suit varying tastes. The food is unfussy and homely: delicious French toast with crispy bacon and maple syrup is a speciality on the inviting breakfast menu, and lunch specials include freshly prepared quiches, soups, salads, sandwiches and pastas. A large selection of homemade desserts and sweet and savoury pastries is on display, and just too good to resist. Deirdre is very much hands on, along with the other friendly staff, providing cheerful informal but efficient service. This reasonably priced gem is the perfect spot for a brunch, lunch, snack or caffeine hit, and children are welcome. Children welcome (high chair); toilets wheelchair accessible; MasterCard, Visa, Switch. **Directions:** Centre of Banbridge town, go down Rathfriland Street; take right turn up Townsend Street.

Banbridge
RESTAURANT
N R

Simply Deanes
Unit 1 Cascum Road Banbridge Co Down BT32 4LF
Tel: 028 4062 7220

Located just outside Banbridge on the main Belfast - Dublin Road, The Outlet discount designer centre is billed as 'the ultimate shopping destination' and here you will find the latest addition to the expanding Deanes portfolio (see Belfast entries). Seasonal, locally sourced ingredients are used for a carefully constructed all day menu and daily blackboard specials that offer everything from snacks, salads and sandwiches 'to go'. Open: B Mon-Sat, 9.30 11.30; L Mon-Sat, 11.30 5.30 (Sun 1-5); D Thu & Fri 6 9 (Sat 6-9.30). MasterCard, Visa, Switch. **Directions:** Well-signed on the main Dublin-Belfast road. ◊

BANGOR

A thriving shopping town and popular seaside resort easily accessible from Belfast, Bangor has a three mile seafront with extensive promenades, and a large marina. The first franchised Rankin Café is a more recent addition the High Street; the café, operated by Robert Craig, comes complete with a soundproof play area facilitating up to 40 children. For a pleasing informal dining experience, head for **Coyle's pub** (028 9129 0362) on High Street, where you will find good midday bar food and more structured meals in the evening or, at the top of High Street, try the recently opened **Back Street Bistro** (028 9145 4741) on Holborn Avenue, which offers appealing modern cooking during the day and evening every day except Sunday. For those who prefer quality family run accommodation in a more intimate environment rather than an hotel, **Hebron House** (028 91 463126; www.hebron-house.com) is a 5* B&B on Princetown Road, near the marina.

WWW-IRELAND-GUIDE.COM FOR THE BEST PLACES TO EAT, DRINK & STAY

Bangor
RESTAURANT
N

Jeffers by the Marina
7 Grays Hill Bangor Co Down BT20 2BB **Tel: 028 9185 9555**
www.stephenjeffers.com

Although not large, clever use of mirror creates a feeling of space in Stephen Jeffers' smart little harbour front restaurant overlooking the marina - bare tables, café chairs and uncurtained windows make for an uncluttered look too, although the downside is that there's not a lot to absorb noise. Friendly staff are quick to settle new arrivals in with the wine list (informative, interesting, good value) and everything is very relaxed, with unstructured menus offering an eclectic choice of modern dishes. Although there are constants through the year, there's always a seasonal twist, such as a winter dish of richly flavoured Portavogie Estate game sausage, with creamy colcannon. Menus change throughout the day - there's an afternoon tea menu, with a good choice of teas and coffees and treats like Victoria sponge - and a proper children's menu, offering real food. Sunday brunch is especially popular here, but this really is an any-time pace. [*Stephen Jeffers also operates **The Boat House** (028 91469253) on Seacliff Road at the other side of the marina.] Open Tue-Sat, 10am-10pm, Sun, 11-8pm. A la carte D. Closed Mon. MasterCard, Visa, Switch. **Directions:** At the bottom of Grays Hill, overlooking the marina.

Bangor
HOTEL

Marine Court Hotel
18-20 Quay Street Bangor Co Down BT20 5ED **Tel: 028 9145 1100**
marinecourt@btconnect.com www.marinecourthotel.net

Excellent leisure facilities at the Marine Court's Oceanis Health & Fitness Club are this hotel's greatest asset these include an 18 metre pool, steam room, whirlpool and sunbeds, plus a well-equipped, professionally-staffed gym. The hotel overlooks the marina (beyond a public carpark) but the first-floor Lord Nelson's Bistro restaurant is the only public room with a real view. Only a few bedrooms are on the front - most overlook (neatly maintained) service areas - but all rooms are regularly refurbished and they are spacious, with plenty of worktop and tea/coffee tray, hair dryer and trouser press as standard in all rooms. Conference/banqueting (350/220). Leisure centre; swimming pool. Children welcome (cots available without charge; baby sitting arranged). Private parking 30. No Pets. **Rooms 52** (3 junior suites, 15 executive rooms, 3 family rooms, 16 no smoking, 1 for disabled). Lift. 24 hour room service.

B&B about £50pps, ss about £20. *Short/off season breaks offered - details on application. Closed 25 Dec. Amex, Diners, MasterCard, Visa, Switch. **Directions:** 23km (14 miles) from Belfast/ 16km (10 miles) Belfast City Airport, A2. ◇

Bangor
HOTEL

Royal Hotel

26/28 Quay Street Bangor Co Down BT20 5ED **Tel: 028 9127 1866**
royalhotelbangor@aol.com www.the-royal-hotel.com

This old hotel near the marina came into new ownership some years ago, but is still family-run and has lost none of its friendliness or old-fashioned charm. There's a warm personal welcome and a clear willingness to help guests in any way possible and, although, alas, the early 20th century lift with folding grille doors and a mind of its own, has long since been replaced by a sleek new early 21st century one, the building has some endearing idiosyncrasies. Rooms vary, but all have been refurbished - the best are the new ones on the front, overlooking the marina. Public areas include The **Crown Bar** pub, with original coal fire, photographs of old Bangor and access to a landscaped garden area, a cosy oak-lined **Library Bar**, (also with open fire) and a new modern cocktail bar, **The Windsor**. This is a pleasant and characterful place to stay and there is a large public carpark just across at the marina. Small conferences (40); Children welcome (under 5s free in parents' room; cots available). No Pets. **Rooms 50** (7 executive, 8 shower only, 1 for disabled). Lift. B&B about £30-40pps, ss about £15. Special offers sometimes available. Nearby parking. Closed 25-26 Dec. Amex, Diners, MasterCard, Visa. **Directions:** A2 from Belfast, at bottom of Main Street turn right (keeping in left lane). Hotel is 300 yards on right facing marina. ◇

Bangor Area
HOTEL

Clandeboye Lodge Hotel

10 Estate Road Clandeboye Bangor Co Down BT19 1UR **Tel: 028 9185 2500**
info@clandeboyelodge.co.uk www.clandeboyelodge.com

Set in woodland on the edge of the Clandeboye estate, this comfortable modern hotel fits in well with its rural surroundings. With a welcoming fire and plentiful seating areas the foyer creates a good impression and the recently redesigned restaurant, where breakfast is also served, is now part of this stylish open plan area. Good-sized bedrooms are comfortably furnished with neat, well-planned bathrooms (suites have whirlpool baths) and all the expected amenities. A country-style pub, The Poacher's Arms, is in an original Victorian building beside the hotel. Conference/banqueting (450/350); free broadband wi/fi, business centre, secretarial services. Children welcome (under 12s free in parents' room; cots available at no charge, baby sitting arranged). No Pets. Credit card numbers are taken when booking - and the deduction may be made before your arrival. Parking. **Rooms 43** (all en-suite & no smoking, 2 junior suites, 13 executive, 2 family, 13 ground floor, 2 disabled) Lift; 24 hr rooms service. B&B £57.50 pps, ss £25. Closed 24-26 Dec. Amex, Diners, MasterCard, Visa, Switch. **Directions:** 15 minutes from Belfast, on outskirts of Bangor off A2.

Bangor Area
BAR/RESTAURANT
😋 Ⓔ Ⓝ

Thyme

Blackwood Golf Club 150 Crawfordsburn Rd Bangor Co Down BT19 1GB
Tel: 028 9185 3394

This new restaurant is in the premises previously occupied by the renowned restaurant, Shanks; smart new signage at the Golf Club entrance, and frosted glass doors with the name in elegant black capitals, create a sense of anticipation that should not be disappointed. Conor Mc Cann, formerly head chef at Roscoff in Belfast, had only recently opened here at the time of the Guide's visit yet, with a manageable menu offering just six choices on each course, the cooking was already impressive - and conveying a sense that this young team are at the beginning of a culinary journey. Upstairs a grill bar offers informal meals, downstairs you will find the more serious fine dining on white linen; the dining room has been given a makeover in understated browns and whites but, with much the same layout and glass fronted kitchen, it will feel familiar to old hands. Top quality produce is used, much of it local, and the well-balanced menu is clear and concise, demonstrating this chef's maturity through dishes and flavours that are uncomplicated. Luxury ingredients are prepared with knowledge and skill in dishes like a starter of lightly smoked lobster, with asparagus, broad beans & citrus beurre blanc, or raviolo of quail with sautéed foie gras &

caramelised orange salad. Main courses might typically include dishes such as seared wild seabass, spiced aubergine caviar, sauce vierge, lobster cream & basil (perfectly cooked and with lovely flavours, although a little busy perhaps) and a very successful, delicately flavoured, combination of turbot cooked, unusually, on the on the bone - steamed with ginger and lemongrass, asparagus and spring onions and tomato consommé. Great flavour and appealingly simple presentation are the key characteristics and this applies equally to delicious desserts (a lovely peach parfait with red wine poached pear, perhaps) and chocolate truffles served with espresso, in a trinket box. Very professional service - friendly yet not at all intrusive adds to the experience, as does an extensive and well chosen wine list, and it offers good value for the quality of food and culinary skill. **Seats 60.** L Wed-Fri 12-3, D Wed-Sat 6-11; Sun12-7. Closed Mon & Tue. Mastercard, Visa, Maestro. **Directions:** 2km off main Belfast-Bangor road, opposite Clandeboye Estate. ◊

Comber

B&B

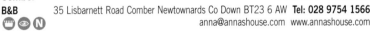

Anna's House

35 Lisbarnett Road Comber Newtownards Co Down BT23 6 AW **Tel: 028 9754 1566**

anna@annashouse.com www.annashouse.com

Anna and Ken Johnson's charming house near Strangford Lough looks over their own ten-acre wildfowl lake to the rolling north Down countryside, and it makes a wonderfully comfortable and hospitable base for exploring this beautiful area. There is a cosy sitting room for guests' use and, for the most part, accommodation is quite simple and cottagey - who could fail to be charmed by real Irish linen on the beds and uninterrupted rural views, especially when two of these pretty rooms have seating areas and their own balconies? But the pièce de résistance in this surprising house is a large room with a mezzanine floor (allowing two private sitting rooms for the adjoining bedrooms) that has recently been added; the floor of this truly astonishing room is polished granite and the 45ft length of 15ft high windows look out over the lake and meadows to the Mountains of Mourne. And garden lovers will find it a particularly interesting place to stay: visits to the major County Down gardens are a must when staying here, especially in summer (three National Trust gardens are nearby, including Mount Stewart) and they have a wonderful garden of their own as well - although Anna has had less time than she would like to care for it recently, and is worried that some guests may be disappointed. Breakfast - an organic feast with freshly baked breads and scones - is normally the only meal offered, but it is sometimes possible to share an evening meal with Anna and Ken. **Rooms 3** (all en-suite and no-smoking, 2 shower only, 1 equipped for disabled). B&B from £35 pps, ss, £10-15. MasterCard, Visa. **Directions:** From Lisbane, follow the brown B&B signs. ◊

Crawfordsburn

HOTEL/RESTAURANT/PUB

The Old Inn

11-15 Main Street Crawfordsburn Co Down BT19 1JH
Tel: 028 9185 3255

info@theoldinn.com www.theoldinn.com

The pretty village setting of this famous and hospitable 16th century inn - the oldest in continuous use in all Ireland - belies its convenient location close to Belfast and the City Airport, and also the Ulster Folk & Transport Museum and the Royal Belfast Golf Club which are both nearby. Oak beams, antiques and gas lighting emphasise the natural character of the building, an attractive venue for business people and private guests alike. A welcoming fire and friendly staff in the cosy reception area set the tone for the whole hotel, which is full of charm, very comfortable - and always smartly presented. Bedrooms are individually decorated and, due to the age of the building, vary in size and style - most have antiques, some have romantic four-posters and a few have private sitting rooms; 12 new junior suites are soon to be added. There are several dining options in the hotel: '1614' is the fine dining restaurant, informal evening meals are served in the Churn Bistro, and food is also served in the newly refurbished Parlour Bar during afternoon and early evening. Conference/banqueting (120/125); broadband wi/fi, business centre, secretarial services. Ample parking. Garden, walking. Golf, fishing (sea angling, coarse) & equestrian all nearby. Children welcome (cot available, £10, baby sitting arranged). Dogs permitted by prior arrangement. **Rooms 31** (7 junior suites, 18 executive, 6 family, 8 ground floor, 1 disabled, all no smoking). Limited room service. Room rate about £85. Open all year except 25 Dec. **Restaurant '1614':** After an aperitif in the bar or the large and comfortable residents' lounge, a meal in this characterful old-world dining room should be very enjoyable. Interesting menus offer plenty of choice and a high standard of cooking, in an updated classic style. Typical dishes might include chicken liver parfait or a tian of local smoked salmon and perhaps an unusual and attractively presented main course of local Finnebrogue venison, served pink, with Savoy cabbage, bacon & morel cream. A nice dessert menu offers more refreshing fruit-based dishes than usual, and coffee is served in the lounge. An informative wine list is organised by country and includes a well-selected page of house wines and half a dozen half bottles. **Seats 64** (private room, 25, outdoors, 50); toilets wheelchair accessible; children welcome (high chair, childrens menu, baby changing facilities); D Mon-Sat, 7-9.30, D Sun 5-10, L Sun only 12.30-2.30. Set Sun L £18.75; set 2/3 course D £26/30; house wine £13.75. Bar meals: 12 noon-7pm daily. *Short breaks offered. Closed 25 Dec. Amex, MasterCard, Visa, Switch. **Directions:** Off A2 Belfast-Bangor, 6 miles after Holywood (exit B20 for Crawfordsburn).

DONAGHADEE

Donaghadee is a charming seaside town situated on the east coast of County Down; about 18 miles from Belfast it is about five miles south east of Bangor on the Ards Peninsula and is best known for its attractive little harbour lighthouse. According to the Guinness Book of Records, **Grace Neills** (see entry) claims to be Ireland's oldest public house, opened in 1611 as the 'King's Arms'. Another pub of character is the Waterworth family's **Pier 36** (028 91 884 466), a lively place with a good buzz and friendly staff that is known for its food, especially local seafood, and is atmospheric in the evening. And garden lovers in search of a wholesome bite to eat will be delighted with the food at Creative Gardens at **Donaghadee Garden Centre** (028 9188 3237; www.creativegardens.net) on Stockbridge Road, between Bangor and Donaghadee (and also at Bushmills, Co Antrim 028 2073 0424); the range of wholesome homemade fare offered in their coffee shop is impressive by any standards, and the opening hours are long (Mon, Tue, Sat 9.30-5; Wed, Thu, Fri 9.30-8, and Sun 12.30-5).
WWW-IRELAND-GUIDE.COM FOR THE BEST PLACES TO EAT, DRINK & STAY

Donaghadee   Grace Neill's
RESTAURANT/CHARACTER PUB   33 High Street Donaghadee Co Down BT21 0AH
                    Tel: 028 9188 4595 info@graceneills.com www.graceneills.com

Dating back to 1611, Grace Neill's lays a fair claim to be one of the oldest inns in all Ireland; Grace Neill herself was born when the pub was more than two hundred years old and died in 1916 at the age of 98. Extensions and improvements in recent ownership have been completed with due sensitivity to the age and character of the original front bar, which has been left simple and unspoilt this is one of Ireland's best-loved pubs and, even without serving as much as soup and sandwiches, it would be on the must-visit list for visitors to Donaghadee.

But, by a happy chance, there is also a restaurant in a bright, high-ceilinged contemporary area at the back of the old pub and this stylish informal restaurant with elegant, nautically-inspired, decor has become a magnet for diners who relish the easy-going food and relaxed atmosphere - especially at Sunday Brunch which is a speciality, with live jazz. Children welcome before 8pm. Live Jazz Fri-Sat, 9.30-12.30, Sun,1.30-4.30. **Seats 80.** L & D daily (early D about £30 Mon-Thurs 5.30-7, also à la carte, set Sun L about £20); sc discretionary. Closed 25 Dec, 12 Jul. MasterCard, Visa, Switch. **Directions:** Centre of Donaghadee. ◇

Downpatrick   Denvirs
CHARACTER PUB   14 English Street Downpatrick Co Down BT30 6AB
                                                              Tel: 028 4461 2012

What a gem this ancient place is. It's a wonderful pub with two old bars and an interesting informal restaurant, genuinely olde-worlde with an amazing original fireplace and chimney discovered during renovations. There's also delightful accommodation in sympathetically updated rooms. And there's a first floor room, with some remarkable original features, suitable for meetings or private parties. Go and see it - there can't be another place in Ireland quite like it. Private room available for conferences/meetings etc. (70). Wheelchair accessible. Children welcome. Accommodation offered. **Bar/Restaurant:** Food served L daily & D Mon-Fri. Closed 25 Dec. Amex, Diners, MasterCard, Visa. **Directions:** On same street as Cathedral and Courthouse in Downpatrick.

Downpatrick
COUNTRY HOUSE

Pheasants Hill Farm

37 Killyleagh Road Downpatrick Co Down BT30 9BL
Tel: 028 4461 7246

info@pheasantshill.com   www.pheasantshill.com

Pheasants' Hill was a small Ulster farmstead for over 165 years until it was rebuilt in the mid-'90s - and is now a comfortable country house on a seven-acre organic small-holding within sight of the Mourne Mountains. The property is in an area of outstanding natural beauty and, although very close to the road, it is otherwise an idyllic spot. The bedrooms differ in character and outlook but are all comfortably furnished with generous beds and modern facilities; rooms at the back are quieter. Breakfast is a major event and worth factoring in as a main meal in your day, including dry-cured bacon and home-made sausages made with their own free range Tamworth pork; vegetarians are also well catered for. *Farm shop: rare breed free range pork, bacon, lamb, beef & organic poultry, fruit, vegetables sold. Open Mon-Sat 9-6 & Sun 12-6. Delivery service available. Also farm shop & butchers shop in Comber, Mon-Sat 9-6. Children welcome (cot available free of charge). Garden, fishing, walking. Golf & equestrian nearby. **Rooms 5** (2 en-suite & 1 with private bathroom, 1 ground floor, 1 family room, 3 shower-only, all no smoking). B&B about £32. Closed 1 Nov-16 Mar. Amex, MasterCard, Visa, Switch. **Directions:** On A22, 4km (2.5 miles) north of Downpatrick, 4km south of Killyleagh.

Dundrum
RESTAURANT/BAT

The Buck's Head Inn

77 Main Street Dundrum Co Down BT33 0LU **Tel: 028 4375 1868**
buckshead1@aol.com   www.thebucksheaddundrum.com

Michael and Alison Crothers have developed this attractive, welcoming place from a pub with bar food and a restaurant, to its present position as a restaurant with bar. Alison is in charge of the kitchen and sources local produce, especially seafood, including oysters from Dundrum Bay, which might be baked with a garlic & cheddar crust and Kilkeel cod, with mushy peas and chips. Well-balanced and interesting menus have a pleasing sense of place - aside from the seafood, County Down beef is used for the Sunday roast sirloin and steaks on the dinner menu, lamb is from the Mournes, the famous butchers McCartneys of Moira supply sausages for the traditional bangers & champ; many tempting dishes are offered, also a short but imaginative vegetarian menu - and the range of styles ensures there is something to please all tastes. At lunch time there's a shortish à la carte (often including excellent salads - try the fresh Dublin Bay prawns...) and daily blackboard specials - and they are open for high tea as well as dinner. Cooking is consistently good (and continues to become more interesting) and service under the direction of the proprietor Michael Crothers, is friendly and efficient. The atmosphere is always relaxed and each dining space has its own personality and is quite intimate - a dining room at the back (formerly a conservatory) overlooks a walled garden and is particularly pleasant. This is a fine restaurant, providing an exceptionally comprehensive service: well worth planning a journey around. Interesting wines are supplied by the highly respected Co Down wine merchant James Nicholson. Children welcome. *Ask about accommodation - a previous owner, Maureen Griffith, offers B&B next door. **Seats 80** (private room, 50) No smoking area L 12-2.30, High Tea 5-6.30, D7-9 (Sun to 8.30). Set Sun L from about £15; Set D from about £20, otherwise à la carte. House wine from £11; sc discretionary. Closed Mon off-season (Oct-Apr); 25 Dec. Amex, MasterCard, Visa, Switch. **Directions:** On the main Belfast-Newcastle road, approx 3 miles from Newcastle. ◇

Dundrum
B&B

The Carriage House

71 Main St. Dundrum Co Down BT33 0LU **Tel: 028 437 51635**
inbox@carriagehousedundrum.com   www.carriagehousedundrum.com

Maureen Griffith, a previous owner of The Buck's Head Inn, offers well-hidden bed and breakfast accommodation in her unusual house which is next door to the inn. Her home has great style, and is furnished mainly with antiques but she has an eye for unusual items and you will find modern pieces amongst them, and also quirky decorative little bits and pieces among the lovely paintings and prints - and some not so little too, as a full size horse sculpture at the back of the house is the item that guests find most fascinating. The three guest rooms include one away from the road at the back of the house, and all are quietly luxurious with beautiful bedding and delightful details. No dinner is offered but a lovely breakfast is served in a sun room overlooking a walled garden, prettily planted with wild flowers and herbs. Fishing, equestrian, garden visits, walking and golf nearby (Royal County Down Golf Club). Fishing, equestrian, garden visits, walking and golf nearby (Royal County Down golf club). **Rooms 3** (all en-suite and no smoking); B&B about £30 pps, ss about £10 **No Credit Cards. Directions:** A24 from Belfast, Dundrum. The violet blue house next to The Bucks Head (no sign: name etched in glass on top of front door). ◇

Dundrum
RESTAURANT

Mourne Seafood Bar

10 Main Street Dundrum Co Down BT33 0LU **Tel: 028 4375 1377**
bob@mourneseafood.com www.mourneseafood.com

A prominent black and white 19th century terrace building in the centre of Dundrum, Robert and Joanne McCoubrey's lively and informal seafood restaurant and fish shop is appreciated by the many happy punters who relish ultra fresh seafood and who now have more space to enjoy it since the new upstairs eating area opened recently. They specialise in fresh fish from the local ports of Keel and Annalong, and mussels, oysters and cockles from their own shellfish beds on Carlingford Lough - and, like the new sister restaurant run by Andy Rae in Belfast (see entry), they use local fish that is not under threat such as gurnard and ling, helping to take the pressure off species like cod, so their extensive menu changes according to what is caught. Very friendly, family-tolerant staff deserve special mention, and the wine list is short and interesting - and the sparkling water offered is San Pelligrino. Children welcome before 8pm (high chair); toilets wheelchair accessible. **Seats 45** (private room, 20, outdoors, 20). Food served daily, 12-9.30pm; a la carte; house wine £11. Closed Mon in winter. Amex, MasterCard, Visa, Switch. **Directions:** Main Street of village.

Hillsborough
RESTAURANT/PUB

The Plough Inn

3 The Square Hillsborough Co Down BT26 6AG
Tel: 028 9268 2985 www.barretro.com

Established in 1752, this former coaching inn is owned by the Patterson family who have built up a national reputation for hospitality and good food, especially seafood. Somehow they manage to run three separate food operations each day, so pleasing customers looking for a casual daytime meal and more serious evening diners. The evening restaurant is in the old stables at the back of the pub, and renowned for seafood and fine steaks; booking is required. Developments and makeovers mercifully left the characterful old bar intact (fairly traditional bar food is still available there) and also the original **Plough Restaurant**, which has a separate entrance from the carpark. However the rest of the pub, including the adjacent building, is now stylishly contemporary and comprises the trendy **Barretro Café & Bistro**, which is open most of the day. The stylish bistro is above the old bar and offers more substantial international dishes; bookings are taken there for business lunches, but not in the evening. While there is obvious youth appeal, people of all ages feel comfortable here and the staff, who are clearly very proud of it, are friendly and helpful. It is very extensive, so allow yourself time to have a good look around and get your bearings before settling down to eat. [The Plough Inn was our Pub of the Year in 2004]. *The Pheasant Inn at Annahilt is a sister establishment (see entry). **At the time of going to press, some areas of The Plough had not yet reopened following a fire; however the premises will be fully restored. Toilets wheelchair accessible; Restaurant not suitable for children, but they are welcome in the bistro (high chair, childrens menu, baby changing facilities). Sun terrace. Parking. **Seats 40** (private room, 28, outdoors, 60); L daily, 12-2.30; D 5-9.30 daily (to 8pm Sun). Bar Retro Bistro/Café: Seats 150; food served all day, daily. Closed 25 Dec. Amex, Diners, MasterCard, Visa, Switch. **Directions:** Off the main Dublin-Belfast road, turn off at Hillsborough roundabout; in village square.

Hillsborough Area
RESTAURANT/PUB

The Pheasant

410 Upper Ballynahinch Road Annahilt Hillsborough
Co Down BT26 6NR **Tel: 028 9263 8056**

A sister to the well known **The Plough Inn** (see entry) in Hillsborough, this welcoming cottage style bar and restaurant is discreetly tucked away in the green County Down countryside and has earned a following locally for its tasty food served at very reasonable prices. Everyone loves an old world pub, and this quaint exterior has a pleasant country charm, with old carts and memorabilia from bygone days beside the excellent parking facilities. Inside, the busy and atmospheric restaurant has a traditional and relaxed feeling, with friendly and efficient staff greeting guests and quickly taking orders from an extensive à la carte menu with daily specials. Starters such as Moroccan spiced chicken with yogurt and warm potato salad, or green and black pepper beef in filo pastry with a Chinese spice dressing are typical of an Asian influence, while a house main course speciality of suckling hog medallions with cabbage, champ, caramelised pineapple & cider jus demonstrates a more Irish feel; there's a separate menu section dedicated to dry aged local beef, and also very attractive vegetarian, gluten free and children's menus offered, so there really is something for everybody. The food is well prepared, tasty and (very) generous, and a low to mid priced wine selection offers great value; all this plus good service and a children's play area which makes this a excellent place for a family outing. A private function room on the first floor is available for parties. Fully wheelchair accessible; children welcome before 9pm (high chair, childrens menu, baby changing facilities, playground); **Seats 75** (private room, 16, outdoors, 40); reservations recommended; food served all day Tue-Sun, 12-9pm; L 12-2.30 (to 3pm Sun), D 5-9 (to 8pm Sun). Value L £7, value D £24, 5-7pm. Set 2 course L £10; Sun L £13.95; set 2/3 course D £19.95/23.95; also a la carte; house wine £12. Closed Mon (restaurant); 25-26 Dec; 12-13 Jul. Amex, Diners, MasterCard, Visa, Switch. **Directions:** 7km (4 miles) from the A1 Hillsborough.

Holywood
CAFÉ/RESTAURANT

Bay Tree Coffee House & Restaurant
118 High Street Holywood Co Down BT18 9HW
Tel: 028 9042 1419 suefarmer@utvinternet.com

Since 1988, The Bay Tree has been attracting customers from miles around to its delightful craft shop and coffee house on the main street. The craft shop, which sells exclusively Irish wares, is a busy, colourful place specialising in pottery. There is also a gallery exhibiting the work of Irish artists and, perhaps best of all, Sue Farmer's delicious food. Baking is a strength, especially the cinnamon scones which are a house speciality, and there's quite a strong emphasis on vegetarian dishes and organic salads, especially in summer, when you can also eat out on a patio in fine weather. No reservations for lunch, but they are required on Friday evenings, when the Bay Tree is open for dinner. *Sue Farmer has published a book of Bay Tree Recipes, available directly from the restaurant. Children welcome. Parking. Wheelchair accessible (not to toilets). **Seats 55** (outdoors, 8). Open all day: Mon-Sat, 8-4.30, (Sat from 9.30); D Fri only, 7-9.30. L Mon-Sat,12-3; Set D Fri only 2/3 course about £20/£23. Sun Brunch 10-3. House wine about £12.50. SC 10% on Fri D. Closed Christmas 4 days, Easter 3 days & 12 July 4 days. MasterCard, Visa, Switch. **Directions:** Opposite the police station. ◊

Holywood
RESTAURANT

Fontana Restaurant
61A High Street Holywood Co Down BT18 9AE
Tel: 028 9080 9908

A first floor restaurant over a classy kitchen shop, Fontana is fresh and bright perfectly in tune with the lovely zesty Cal-Ital cooking that proprietor-chef Colleen Bennett offers. Starters and main courses tend to overlap on her interesting and loosely structured menus, with small and large portions of some dishes offered; a popular dish like Caesar salad with char-grilled chicken might come in two sizes, for example, and appear on both the lunch and dinner menus. Imaginative use of fresh produce is a striking characteristic of the food at Fontana: vegetables and salads are used with great panache and seafood is usually strongly represented - consistently accomplished cooking, stylishly simple presentation and clear flavours make an appealing combination. Outside eating area. Toilets wheelchair accessible. On street parking. Children welcome. Seats 54 L Mon-Fri 12-2.30 (Sun brunch 11-2.30), D Mon-Fri 5-9.30, D Sat, 6.30-10pm. Set 2/3 course D about £13.50/16.50, otherwise à la carte (average meal about £25); house wine about £12.50; SC discretionary, except 10% added on tables of 6+. Closed L Sat, D Sun, all Mon, 25-26 Dec & 1 Jan. MasterCard, Visa, Switch. **Directions:** Three doors from Maypole flag pole. ◊

Holywood
HOTEL/RESTAURANT

Hastings Culloden Estate & Spa
Bangor Road Holywood Co Down BT18 0EX **Tel: 028 9042 1066**
guest@cull.hastingshotels.com www.hastingshotels.com

Formerly the official palace for the Bishops of Down, Hastings Hotels' flagship property is a fine example of 19th-century Scottish Baronial architecture with plasterwork ceilings, stained glass windows and an imposing staircase. It is set in beautifully maintained gardens and woodland overlooking Belfast Lough and the County Antrim coastline. Period furniture and fine paintings in spacious high ceilinged rooms give a soothing feeling of exclusivity, and comfortable drawing rooms overlook the lough. Spacious, lavishly decorated guest rooms include a large proportion of suites and a Presidential Suite, with the best view; all are lavishly furnished and decorated with splendid bathrooms and details such as bathrobes, a welcoming bowl of fruit, and nice touches like ground coffee and a cafetière on the hospitality tray. Wireless internet access is available in all areas, and there are video/DVD players in suites. The hotel has an association with The Royal Belfast Golf Club, four minutes away by car (book the complimentary hospitality limousine) also a fine health club; the **'Cultra Inn'**, a bar and informal restaurant in the grounds, offers an alternative to The Mitre Restaurant. The hotel is licensed to hold weddings on the premises. Conference/banqueting (1,000/600); business centre; secretarial services. Leisure centre (swimming pool; spa; beauty salon; hairdressing). Garden. Children welcome (under 3s free in parents' room; cot available without charge, baby sitting arranged). No pets. **Rooms 79** (2 suites, 17 junior suites, 22 executive rooms, 2 disabled, 40 no-smoking). Lift. Air conditioning. 24 hr room service B&B about £100 pps, ss about £60.* Short breaks offered. Parking (500). Helipad. Open all year. **The Mitre Restaurant:** The fine dining restaurant is in a long room overlooking the lough, with a discreet and luxurious ambience - and, with well-padded and very comfortable upholstered chairs, conducive to lingering. Tables are beautifully appointed in classic style, and extensive menus that live up to their promise may include a speciality main course, of tender saddle of venison from nearby Clandeboye Estate, with crushed root vegetables and buttered greens. Classic cooking, lovely surroundings and correct, attentive service all make this a restaurant with a sense of occasion. Extensive wine list to match. **Seats 110** (private room, 50). Reservations required. Children welcome. Toilets wheelchair accessible. Piano & Jazz Fri/Sat/Sun. D daily, 7-9.30, Set D £32.50; L Sun only, 12.30-2.30. Set Sun L, £28. House wine £17. Amex, Diners, MasterCard, Visa, Switch. **Directions:** 6 miles from Belfast city centre on A2 towards Bangor. ◊

Holywood
COUNTRY HOUSE/RESTAURANT

Rayanne Country House
60 Demesne Road Holywood Co Down B18 9EX
Tel: 028 9042 5859
rayannehouse@hotmail.com www.rayannehouse.co.uk

Situated almost next to the Holywood Golf Club and Redburn Country Park, and with views across Belfast Lough, the McClellands' family-run country house is a tranquil spot in which to unwind, and a fine alternative to impersonal hotels. Bedrooms, some with views of Belfast Lough, are individually decorated to a high standard with phones and television - and little extras like fresh fruit, spring water, sewing kit, stationery and a hospitality tray with bedtime drinks and home-made shortbread as well as the usual tea & coffee facilities. It's a relaxing place, with friendly staff and a great breakfast, offering a wide range, including unusual dishes such as prune soufflé, French toast topped with black and white pudding & served with a spiced apple compôte, grilled kippers and a 'healthy house grill' (with nothing fried). Friendly staff are helpful and make families with children most welcome; beach, shops and restaurants are all just a few minutes' walk away. **Restaurant:** Conor McClelland, who returned to take over Rayanne with 15 years as an international chef under his belt, cooks for up to 30 guests in their restaurant D'Vine Dining, which is open to non-residents by reservation (closed only 24-25 Dec). Small conferences/banqueting (15/34); free broadband wi/fi. Parking (14). Children welcome (under 2s free in parents room, cot available without charge, baby sitting arranged). Pets allowed by arrangement. Garden, walking. **Rooms 11** (4 shower only, 2 family, 1 ground floor, 1 disabled, all no smoking). B&B £45pps, ss £22.50. D about £39.50, by reservation. Short breaks offered. Closed 24/25 Dec, 31 Dec, 1 Jan. MasterCard, Visa, Switch. **Directions:** Take A2 out of Belfast towards Holywood 10km (6 miles), up to top of My Ladys Mile; turn right; 200 metres.

Sullivans Restaurant

Holywood
RESTAURANT

2 Sullivan Place Holywood Co Down BT18 9JF **Tel: 028 9042 1000**
www.sullivansrestaurant.co.uk

Simon Shaw's bright, friendly and informal restaurant is now well over a decade in business - and consistently excellent food, varied menus, a good atmosphere and fair prices are the secret of his success. Lively lunch and sandwich menus are offered, based on the quality ingredients which have always been the building blocks of his cooking, and he seeks out interesting produce from trusted suppliers like Helen's Bay Organics and Finnebrogue (venison); vegetarians do well here, too, with interesting choices on the regular menus as well as a separate vegetarian menu. A 2-course early evening menu with a choice of three dishes on each course is outstanding value at £9.95 (extra side dishes £1) and the evening à la carte is refreshingly down to earth and also keenly priced. The wine list is not very informative (no tasting notes) but is well chosen and good value. **Seats 60.** L daily 12-2.30, D Tue-Sun, 6-9.30 (from 5pm Fri-Sun, to 8.30pm Sun). Value D £9.95 before 7pm; set D from £16.50, also à la carte; house wine from £12.50; sc 10%, on parties of 8+. Closed D Mon, 2 days Christmas,12-13 Jul. MasterCard, Visa, Switch. **Directions:** Just off main Belfast-Bangor dual carriageway.

Beech Hill Country House

Holywood Area
B&B

23 Ballymoney Road Craigantlet Holywood Co Down BT23 4TG
Tel: 028 9042 5892 info@beech-hill.net www.beech-hill.net

Victoria Brann's attractive Georgian style house is set in the peaceful Holywood Hills. It has great style - and the benefit of an exceptionally hospitable hostess, who does everything possible to ensure that guests have everything they need. Ground floor bedrooms have panoramic views over the North Down countryside and are furnished with antique furniture - and, believe it or not, the beds are made up with fine Irish linen; all also have good in-room facilities including laptop size safes - and lovely en-suite bathrooms with lots of special little extras. Breakfast is a meal worth allowing time to enjoy - and it is served in a spacious conservatory overlooking a croquet lawn. **Rooms 3** (all en-suite, 1 shower only, all no smoking, all ground floor). B&B £40.00pps. ss £15.00. Pets permitted by arrangement. Open all year. *Self-catering accommodation or B&B also offered in The Colonel's Lodge (£280-£380 per week self catering, £70 per night B&B). Amex, MasterCard, Visa, Switch. **Directions:** A2 from Belfast; bypass Holywood; 3km (1.5 miles) from bridges at Ulster Folk Museum, turn right up Ballymoney Road signed Craigantlet - 3km (1.5) miles on left.

Balloo House

Killinchy
PUB/RESTAURANT

1 Comber Road Killinchy Co Down BT23 6PA **Tel: 028 9754 1210**
info@balloohouse.com www.balloohouse.com

This famous old 19th century coaching inn fell into great hands when Ronan and Jennie Sweeney took it over in 2004 with extensive experience in the hospitality industry behind them (Ronan had worked front of house with Paul Rankin at both Cayenne and Roscoff, then as restaurant manager at Bill Wolsey's Ta Tu, and Jennie has left a career in the wine trade). They were determined to restore Balloo's reputation as one of the finest country dining pubs in Northern Ireland - and this, as a growing band of loyal followers would testify, they are achieving very nicely. The place has oodles of genuine character and the old kitchen bar, with its flagstones and traditional range, makes a great setting for excellent bistro fare like fresh Kilkeel scampi & chips, dry-aged locally reared steaks and home-made burgers. A separate entrance from the bar leads up to the first floor, which resembles a quaint and cosy converted loft, and has a small snug reception area with open fire and comfy seats beside a well stocked bar with many liqueurs on display. The décor is quite traditional in style, with beautiful exposed stone walls the main feature; the restaurant is beautifully laid out with tall backed chairs around white linen clad tables with sparkling crystal wine glasses - and despite the cosy appearance, there's plenty of space between tables. Head chef Danny Miller, who was formerly at Cayenne and has recently joined the team at Balloo, is a well known advocate of local seasonal produce and this is reflected in his menus, typically in dishes such as warm lobster salad with Comber potatoes, broad beans, rocket and truffled lobster mayonnaise; grilled Strangford Lough langoustines with garlic, parsley and lemon butter; rump of Finnebrogue venison with wild mushroom risotto cake, roast parsnips and sun dried cranberries - and a house speciality of Balloo House chocolate tart with autumn berries and crème fraiche. The cooking is accomplished, as would be expected of this highly regarded chef, and with the confidence to 'faites simple' and allow the quality of ingredients to shine through. An impressive wine list includes wines by glass and service is professional, helpful and efficient in our midweek experience, although it may come under pressure on busy weekend nights. Overall, the lovely relaxed ambience make Balloo the perfect place to kick back, unwind and enjoy quality food and very reasonable prices. The dining room only seats 35 and booking in advance is essential. Children welcome; toilets wheelchair accessible; free broadband WI/FI; air conditioning. Downstairs bistro **seats 60** (private room, 40, outdoors, 12); live music (Blue Grass) Wed 9pm. Bistro: Food served daily 12-9 (to 8.30pm on Sun, Mon); house wine from £11.95. Restaurant: open Tue-Thurs, 6-9pm, Fri-Sat, 6-9.30pm, also available for functions and private dining. SC 10% on groups 6+. Closed 25 Dec. MasterCard, Visa, Switch. **Directions:** At Balloo crossroads on main road from Comber to Killyleagh.

Killinchy
PUB
Ⓝ

Daft Eddies

Sketrick Island Whiterock Killinchy Co Down BT23 6QB
Tel: 028 9754 1615

A scenic coastal drive along Strangford Lough brings you to a causeway that curves behind trees to reach this unassuming but beautifully located pub, which has lovely views of Sketrick Castle, Whiterock marina and the lough, and is a popular summer destination. A comfortable old world bar leads into a cosy restaurant decorated with maritime memorabilia, where well balanced menus offer plenty of choice, with particular strength in local seafood: fresh local oysters served with a shot of perfectly zingy bloody Mary really hit the spot on a recent visit, and a wonderfully fresh and perfectly executed dish of pan roasted sea bass with tomato confit, lemon, prawn and dill dressing was equally impressive. There is no shortage of choice for the non seafood lover however you might try local rack of lamb with grilled aubergine, and rosemary jus perhaps or, from the lunch menu, Daft Eddy's burger with bacon and cambazola, which could prove more than a match for the largest appetites. But the homemade desserts are good too, so don't forget to leave a little space for a sweet ending to your meal. Good food, cheery staff and a relaxing atmosphere make this a first-rate casual dining destination. Open Mon-Fri 12-2.30 & 5-9; Sat 12-9.30. Sun 12.30-9 (set menu). Weekday Bistro Menu; Fri & Sat night à la carte. MasterCard, Visa, Switch. **Directions:** From Killinchy drive to shore and turn left for 1/2 mile - pub is on island over causeway. ◇

KILLYLEAGH

This charming village in north County Down is best known for its castle, which is built in the style of a Loire valley chateau and believed to be the oldest inhabited castle in the country. Just beside the castle, **Picnic** (028 4482 8525) is a smashing little deli and café which is well worth knowing about: lovely simple daytime food to enjoy while you're there - and a great range of carefully sourced goodies to take home. (Open Mon-Fri 7am-6.30pm, Sat 10-4; closed Sun off season). And, nearby, the 200 year old **Dufferin Arms** (028 4482 1182; www.dufferincoachinginn.com) is an inn in the true sense of the word, offering food, drink and shelter to travellers. It's full of old-world character, and known for music too.

WWW-IRELAND-GUIDE.COM FOR THE BEST PLACES TO EAT, DRINK & STAY

Kircubbin
RESTAURANT WITH ROOMS

Paul Arthurs Restaurant

62-66 Main Street Kircubbin Newtownards Co Down BT22 2SP
Tel: 028 4273 8192 www.paularthurs.com

Paul Arthurs has built up a great reputation for this little restaurant on the main street of his home town and it serves the area and visitors to it well. There are plans to expand into the premises next door but, meanwhile, the restaurant is currently a simple modern room on the first floor, with an open kitchen and simply laid tables. Menus are interesting and local produce features strongly, often including mussels and various shellfish, and there is always a catch of the day, however the wide range of dishes usually offers more meat (including beef from the family farm) and poultry than fish and ou're also likely to find local game in season; vegetarian options are listed separately, and there's even vegan choice. The cooking is good, prices are very fair and there are some tables in the garden too, allowing for al fresco dining in fine weather. **Accommodation:** Seven simply furnished en-suite bedrooms are offered, including 2 for disabled guests. **Seats 55** (outdoor, 20), air conditioning. D Tue-Sat, 5-9.30; L Sun only, 12-2.30. A la carte. House wine £12.95. Rooms 7 (all en-suite, 3 ground floor, 2 disabled); B&B £35pps, ss £15.Closed D Sun, all Mon, 25 Dec & Jan. Amex, MasterCard, Visa, Switch. **Directions:** On main street, 1st floor, opposite supermarket.

Moira
PUB

Pretty Mary's

Main Street, Moira Co Down
Tel 028 9261 1318

The new modern lounge of this family-run pub has been nicely done up and is not at all pretentious. The staff are very friendly and they're serving really good quality pub food. Open for lunch and evening meals every day, also through the afternoon at weekends.

Newcastle
HOTEL

Burrendale Hotel & Country Club

51 Castlewellan Road Newcastle Co Down BT33 0JY **Tel: 028 4372 2599**
reservations@burrendale.com www.burrendale.com

Just outside the traditional seaside holiday town of Newcastle, and close to the championship links of the Royal County Down golf course, this friendly hotel on the edge of the Mourne mountains has a pleasingly remote atmosphere and spacious public areas, including the homely Cottage Bar with an open log fire, welcome on chilly days. Well-appointed accommodation includes some family rooms and some newer superior rooms that have lovely views and are furnished to a higher standard, including air conditioning, but all rooms are well-equipped with the usual amenities. Golf is a major attraction in the area, and the hotel is also a popular conference venue. Well-trained, efficient staff are courteous, making this a pleasant place to stay. Conference/banqueting (350 /250); business centre; secretarial services; video conferencing available, broadband WI/Fi. Leisure centre (swimming pool, steam room, jacuzzi, sauna, fitness room); beauty salon, treatment rooms, massage. Children welcome (under 2s free in parents' room; cots available without charge, baby sitting arranged). Garden, walking, cycling, pool table. **Rooms 69** (3 suites, 18 executive, 6 family, 20 no smoking, 19 ground floor, 10 disabled). Lift. 24 hour room service. B&B £60 pps, ss £20. Bar and restaurant meals available daily (phone to check restaurant times). Open all year. Amex, Diners, MasterCard, Visa, Switch. **Directions:** on A50 Castlewellan Road.

Newcastle
HOTEL

Hastings Slieve Donard Hotel

Downs Road Newcastle Co Down BT33 0AH **Tel: 028 4372 1066**
res@sdh.hastingshotels.com www.hastingshotels.com

This famous hotel stands beneath the Mournes in six acres of public grounds, adjacent to the beach and the Royal County Down Golf Links. The Victorian holiday hotel par excellence, the Slieve Donard first opened in 1897 and has been the leading place to stay in Newcastle ever since. Bedrooms are finished to a high standard and all the bathrooms sport one of the famous yellow Hastings' ducks. The hotel is well known for its wide range of special short breaks, which can be very good value - excellent on-site facilities include the hotel's Elysium health club, and the nearby Tollymore Forest Park provides excellent walking. Golf nearby (18). Conference/banqueting (825/440). Business centre; secretarial services. Leisure centre, swimming pool, spa, beauty salon. Pitch & putt. Ample parking. Children welcome (under 4s free in parents' room; cots available without charge, baby sitting arranged). No pets. **Rooms 124** (8 junior suites, 2 executive rooms, 3 for disabled). 2 Lifts. B&B about £87.50 pps, ss about £25. Open all year. Helipad. Amex, Diners, MasterCard, Visa, Laser, Switch. **Directions:** situated 32 miles south east of Belfast. ◇

Newcastle
CAFÉ/RESTAURANT

Sea Salt Bistro

51 Central Promenade Newcastle Co Down BT33 0HH
Tel: 028 4372 5027

A good meal will add greatly to your enjoyment of a visit to this traditional holiday town on the sea edge of the Mountains of Mourne, so make a point of seeking out this unusual seafront restaurant. Sea Salt has a found renewed energy under new proprietor Aidan Small, who has reduced the number of choices to focus more on quality and local produce. Expect simple quality dishes cooked with flair and an attention to flavour: certain menu items feature an "FU" symbol, which means flavours unleashe and applies to particularly tasty dishes. Aidan is very passionate about what he is doing and hopes get involved with farmers markets when better established. The shelves are packed with interesti deli goods, many produced locally - and, although they are competing with an ice cream parlour one side and chip shop/café on the other, an interested middle market, seeking quality, will surely fi them here. **Seats 30.** Air conditioning. Open daily in summer. MasterCard, Visa, Switch. **Direction** Seafront Newcastle, foot of Mournes. ◇

Newcastle Area
RESTAURANT/COUNTRY HOUSE

Glassdrumman Lodg

85 Mill Road Annalong Co Down BT34 4R
Tel: 028 4376 845
info@glassdrummanlodge.com www.glassdrummanlodge.co

In a dramatic hillside location just outside the coastal village of Annalong, and close to the great fore parks of Tollymore and Castlewellan, Glassdrumman Lodge is in the heart of one of Ireland's mo picturesque mountain districts, the ancient 'Kingdom of Mourne'. Graeme and Joan Hall have deve oped the building into an unusual country house, where comfortable guest rooms and suites offer peaceful base for golfers wishing to play the Royal County Down Golf Course - and for fishing folk, w may prefer casting for trout on the well-stocked lake, to other more energetic outdoor activities li walking and climbing. The fine dining restaurant is also open to non-residents, by reservation, a fresh produce for dinner comes from their own gardens, and local seafood from nearby ports. **Memori Restaurant seats 45** (private room, 20); D Daily at 8pm about £40. Small conferences/banqueti 16/50; Rooms 10 (all en-suite, 2 junior suites, 2 suites, 1 ground floor); Children welcome (cots av free of charge); B&B about £50 pps, ss about £30. Amex, Diners, MasterCard, Visa, Switc **Directions:** A2 coast road between Newcastle and Kilkeel. Take right at Halfway House pub, 1.6km mile) up Mill road. ◇

R

NEWR

Newry - now a city - has a canal as its central feature, and **Canal Court Hotel** (028 3025 123 www.canalcourt.com) is the leading establishment of the area. An interesting dining option in the tov is **The Graduate** restaurant (reservations: 028 3025 9611) at Newry College (now the Southe Regional College, Newry Campus), hospitality and tourism department. Experienced lecturers all wi quality industry backgrounds run the restaurant on different days of the week, and the whole ope tion is a realistic training environment for student chefs and waiters. Lunch is £6.95 for 4 course and 6 course dinner, Tuesday nights only, is £10.

WWW-IRELAND-GUIDE.COM FOR THE BEST PLACES TO EAT, DRINK & STAY

Newtownards
B&B/COUNTRY HOUSE

Edenvale Hous

130 Portaferry Road Newtownards Co Down BT22 2A
Tel: 028 9181 48
edenvalehouse@hotmail.com www.edenvalehouse.cc

Diane Whyte's charming Georgian house is set peacefully in seven acres of garden and paddock, w views over Strangford Lough to the Mourne mountains and a National Trust wildfowl reserve. The hou has been sensitively restored and modernised, providing a high standard of accommodation and hos tality. Guests are warmly welcomed and well fed, with excellent traditional breakfasts and afterno tea with homemade scones. For evening meals, Diane directs guests to one of the local restaurar Edenvale is close to the National Trust property Mount Stewart, renowned for its gardens, and a convenient to Rowallan and Castle Ward. Children welcome (under-5s free in parents' room; cots ava able without charge). Pets permitted by arrangement. Garden. **Rooms 3** (all en-suite, 1 junior suite superior, 1 shower only, 1 family room, all no-smoking). B&B £40 pps, ss £10. Closed Christm MasterCard, Visa. **Directions:** 3.5 km (2 m) from Newtownards on A20 going towards Portaferry.

Portaferry Hotel

°ortaferry
IOTEL/RESTAURANT

The Strand Portaferry Co Down BT22 1PE **Tel: 028 427 28231**
info@portaferryhotel.com www.portaferryhotel.com

This 18th-century waterfront terrace presents a neat, traditional exterior overlooking the lough towards the attractive village of Strangford, and the National Trust property, Castleward. The inn is now one of the most popular destinations in Northern Ireland - not least for its reputation for good food, including their excellent lunchtime bar meals. The ground floor bar, a comfortable sitting room, and the restaurant have a cosy, well-kept old-fashioned feeling to them and, while not luxurious, accommodation is comfortable and most of the individually decorated en-suite bedrooms have views of the water - those on the front attract a small supplement. he hotel is beautifully kept and maintained, a lovely place with personality, and friendly, helpful staff. mall conference/private parties (35/80); parking. Children (Under 16s free in parents' room; cots available at no charge). No pets. **Rooms 14** (all en-suite, 2 shower only, 4 family rooms, all no-smoking) &B about £65 pps, ss about £20. **Restaurant:** A slightly cottagey style provides the perfect background or good unpretentious food. Local produce features prominently in prime Ulster beef, Mourne lamb and ame from neighbouring estates but it is, of course, the seafood that takes pride of place. Well-balanced able d'hôte lunch and dinner menus are offered, plus a short à la carte, providing plenty of choice lthough majoring on local seafood. Excellent breakfasts are served in the restaurant - a particularly ood menu is offered, giving plenty of choice including fresh and smoked fish as a feature. This may ot be the gargantuan spread that some country houses lay on for guests, but it is all freshly cooked to rder and really delicious - and efficiently served by friendly staff: exactly what the perfect hotel breakast should be. **Seats 65.** Children welcome. L daily, 12.30-2.30; D daily 5.30-9 (to 8.30 Sun). D Value Menu nightly 5.30-6.30. Set menu; Sun L about £18.50. Á la carte and childrens menu also available; ouse wine from about £10.50; sc discretionary. Toilets wheelchair accessible. Open all year except Christmas. Amex, Diners, MasterCard, Visa. **Directions:** On Portaferry seafront. ◊

Edgars Restaurant

5aintfield
RESTAURANT

11-15 Main Street Saintfield Co Down BT24 7AA
Tel: 028 9751 1755

n an attractive traditional terrace at the centre of Saintfield, Colin and Emma Edgar's smart contemporary café-style restaurant is in a lovely double-height room simply furnished with wooden tables, and omfortable chairs and offers a wide-ranging bistro style menu all day. Depending on the time of day ou can order anything from fry-ups and other breakfast dishes, through an interesting lunchtime election including open sandwiches, and salads; a bistro menu offers dishes such as fresh cod, campi, homemade burgers, rib-eye steak and chicken, all served with thick-cut homemade chips. hen, at the weekends (Friday and Saturday nights from 6-9.30), it shifts up a gear and an enticing contemporary à la carte dinner menu comes on stream - starters like shellfish linguini and and mains ncluding slow roasted cannon of Mourne lamb with colcannon mash & red wine jus. Edgars is a harming place (the kind every small town deserves) and run by an enthusiastic young couple who ffer friendly service, good quality, freshly prepared and correctly cooked food. Children welcome efore 8pm; **Seats 30;** reservations recommended; L & D Tue-Sat, 10am-2.30pm, 6-9.30pm; Sun .0am-6pm; value D £30, Tue-Thur 6-8.30pm, also a la carte; house wine from £10. Closed Mon, 25 Dec, 12-13 Jul. MasterCard, Visa. **Directions:** 18km (11 miles) south of Belfast on the A7.

The Cuan

5trangford Village
PUB/GUESTHOUSE

6-10 The Square Strangford Village Co Down BT30 7ND
Tel: 028 4488 1222 info@thecuan.com www.thecuan.com

)n the square, just up from the car ferry that goes over to Portaferry, Peter and Caroline McErlean's riendly village inn presents a neat, inviting face to the world. Over a century old, it has character with pen fires, cosy lounges and a homely bar (due for refurbishment at the time of going to press), where ood is available every day. Bedrooms, including two family rooms, are comfortably furnished with telesion and tea/coffee making facilities, and most of the bathrooms have bath and shower. Short breaks ffered. Small conferences/banqueting (60/80); free broadband wi/fi. Children welcome (under 2s free n parents' room, cots available without charge, baby sitting arranged). **Rooms 9** (3 shower only, all no moking, 3 family). Limited room service (on request). B&B £42.50 pps, ss £10. Short breaks offered;

SC discretionary. Closed 25 Dec. MasterCard, Visa, Switch. **Directions:** 11km (7 miles) from Downpatrick on the A25; on the square, near the ferry.

Warrenpoint
RESTAURANT

Copper Restaurant

4 Duke Street Warrenpoint Co Down BT34 3JY **Tel: 028 4175 304**

info@copperrestaurant.co.uk www.copperrestaurant.co.u

Just off the diamond in the centre of Warrenpoint, Neil and Sarah Meaney's appealing restaurant lie behind a smart understated façade. Inside, there's a bar and a fine high-ceilinged dining room, wit tables welcomingly set up with classic white linen and all the nice little touches that convey a qualit feeling. Neil offers imaginative but admirably concise set menus as well as a more extensive à la carte and typically delicious summer offerings might include a deeply-flavoured soup (white onion with blu cheese croûtons, perhaps); an unusual seafood starter like crisp tuna roll with melon & ginger an pickled radish and a great meat dish, such as spiced roast rump of lamb with crushed new potatoes roast aubergine and baked tomatoes & basil. Neil is clearly a talented chef who likes to send customer away happy and, time permitting, there's a flexible approach to orders taken from the short menus, wit generous portions. A separate vegetarian menu is offered and also a Tasting Menu (£50) which need to be prebooked on Saturdays. An interesting and fairly priced wine list, great coffee and charmin, service under Sarah's direction ensure an enjoyable experience, at a fair price. Well worth a detour, an special dining deals are often offered. Toilets wheelchair accessible. **Seats 42.** Air conditioning; chil dren welcome. L Tue-Fri & Sun 12-3; D Tue-Sun 5.30-9.30 (to 10.30 Fri/Sat). Set L £16; Earl dinne £16, 5.30-7; Set 2/3 course D £19.50/23.50, also á la carte L&D. House wine from £13. Closed Sa L, Mon & 25-26 Dec. Amex, MasterCard, Visa, Switch. **Directions:** Just off main square in Warrenpoint

---

Warrenpoint
RESTAURANT

The Duke Restaurant

7 Duke Street Warrenpoint Co Down BT34 3JY **Tel: 028 4175 208**

www.thedukerestaurant.com

Seafood straight from Kilkeel harbour and most other produce also sourced with a ten mile radius is the foundation for Ciaran Gallagher's success at his popular restaurant, which occupies the whole of the first floor over pleasantly traditional pub, The Duke. Guests are met promptly and efficiently, seated a contemporary laid tables, with a comfortable mixture of traditional and modern styles, the busy atmos phere and friendly service all add up to a relaxed ambience. Like the surroundings, menus are balance and well-tailored to the clientèle; the midweek set menu is exceptionally good value and goes down well Crowd pleasers like surf'n'turf and chicken kiev take their regular places alongside some more ambi tious dishes for discerning diners, like hake fillet grilled, or roast venison with roast vegetables. Cookin, is accomplished and generous, the staff cheerful and attentive and the value is terrific. **Seats 65.** Ai conditioning. D Tue-Sun, 6-9.30pm. Midweek Special Set D £12.95, also à la carte. House wine from £8.95. No SC. Closed Mon. Amex, MasterCard, Visa, Switch. **Directions:** Just off town square. ◇

Warrenpoint
RESTAURANT

Restaurant 23

23 Church Street Warrenpoint Co Down BT34 3HN **Tel: 028 4175 3222**

restaurant23@btconnect.com www.restaurant-23.co.u

Right in the busy town centre of Warrenpoint, once part of a very large traditional pub, a long L-shape room is now part of a beautifully crafted contemporary restaurant. The proprietors, Raymond McArdle and his wife, Andrea, have assembled a great team led by talented head chef Trevor Cunningham, who offers enticing menus based on carefully sourced, quality ingredients. The style is broadly upbea modern classical (which allows for some of the currently fashionable Asian influences) and, despite the stylish surroundings and accomplished cooking, it's an accessible place and a number of menus are offered to please all tastes including a separate vegetarian menu and a seafood listing. Expect tast lunchtime food like smoked salmon Caesar salad or comforting Cumberland sausage & champ, and more sophisticated evening dishes like a house speciality of pressed confit foie gras, and mussels with chilli, ginger & white wine, or lovely crisp spiced belly of pork. Excellent attention to detail includes delicious freshly baked breads, tempting desserts and homemade petits four with your after dinne coffee. The same care is reflected in a well chosen wine list, and the service brings an easy blend o Northern friendliness and professional skill. With a talented and confident chef in the kitchen, a lovel ambience and good value, it is not surprising that this restaurant has earned a following in its first yea of business. Toilets wheelchair accessible. **Seats 60** (private room, 30); air conditioning; open Tue Sat, L 12.30-3, D 6.30-9.30 (to 10 Fri/Sat), Sun 12.30-8. Set Sun 2/3 course meal £12.95/15.95 gourmet menu £50; also a la carte; House wine about £12-14. Closed Mon, Tue, 25 Dec, 9-16 Jan Amex, MasterCard, Visa, Switch.

COUNTY FERMANAGH

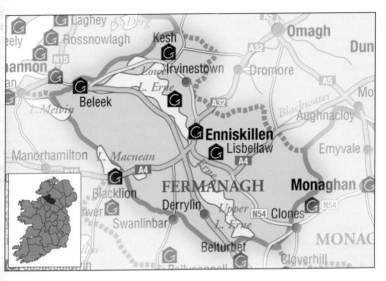

Ireland is a watery place of many lakes, rivers and canals. So it's quite an achievement to be the most watery county of all. Yet this is but one of Fermanagh's many claims to distinction. It is the only county in Ireland through which you can travel the complete distance between its furthest extremities entirely by boat.

Rivers often divide one county from another, but Fermanagh is divided - or linked if you prefer - throughout its length by the handsome waters of the River Erne, both river and lake. Southeast of the historic county town of Enniskillen, Upper Lough Erne is a maze of small waterways meandering their way into Fermanagh from the Erne'e source in County Cavan.

Northwest of characterful Enniskillen, the river channels open out into the broad spread of Lower Lough Erne, a magnificent inland sea set off against the spectacular heights of the Cliffs of Magho. Through this broad lake, the River Erne progresses to the sea at Ballyshannon in Donegal by way of a rapid descent at Belleek in Fermanagh..

It's a stunningly beautiful county with much else of interest, including the Marble Arch caves, and the great houses of Castle Coole and Florence Court, the latter with its own forest park nestling under the rising heights of Cuilcagh (667m) – beyond it, the River Shannon emerges to begin its long journey south.

For those who think lakes are for fishing rather than floating over, in western Fermanagh the village of Garrison gives access to Lough Melvin, an angler's heaven which is noted particularly for its unique sub-species of salmon, the gillaroo. You just can't escape from water in this county, and Fermanagh is blessed as much of the rest of the world contemplates water shortages.

Local Attractions & Information

Belleek Porcelain and Explore Erne Exhibition	028 68 659300
Bellanaleck Sheelin Lace Museum	028 66 348052
Enniskillen Ardhowen Lakeside Theatre	028 66 325440
Enniskillen Castle Coole House & Parkland	028 66 322690
Enniskillen Enniskillen Castle	028 66 325000
Enniskillen Lakelands Tourism	028 66 346736
Enniskillen Lough Erne Cruises	028 66 322882
Enniskillen Tourism Information	028 66 323110
Enniskillen Waterways Ireland	028 66 323004
Florence Court House and garden	028 66 348249

Georgina Campbell's Ireland

Florencecourt Marble Arch Caves	028 66 348855
Garrison Lough Melvin Activity Holiday Centre	028 68 658142
Kesh Castle Archdale Country Park	028 68 621588
Newtownbutler Crom Castle	028 67 738118

Belleek
CAFÉ
R

The Thatch
Belleek Co Fermanagh BT93
Tel: 028 6865 8181

This coffee shop is really special: a listed building dating back to the late 18th century, it's the only originally thatched building remaining in County Fermanagh. Home-made food has been served here since the early 1900s and the tradition is being well-maintained today, with home-made soups, a range of freshly made sandwiches and toasted sandwiches all made to order, hot specials like stuffed baked potatoes and (best of all) delicious bakes like chocolate squares, carrot cake and muffins. Drinks include a coffee menu and, more unusually, you can also buy fishing tackle, hire a bike - or even a holiday cottage here. Open Mon-Sat. 9-5 (from 10 off-season). Closed Sun. **Directions:** On the main street. ◇

Enniskillen
RESTAURANT/PUB
R 🖑

Blakes of the Hollow (Café Merlot / Restaurant Number 6)
6 Church Street Enniskillen Co Fermanagh BT74 6JE
Tel: 028 6632 0918

One of the great classic pubs of Ireland, Blakes has been in the same family since 1887 and, up to now, has always been one of the few places that could be relied upon to be unchanged. Not a food place, a pub; maybe a sandwich, but mainly somewhere to have a pint and put the world to rights. This original Victorian bar still remains untouched after 120 years, but major changes have taken place elsewhere in this historic establishment of late. Recent additions include **Café Merlot** (serving reliable informal, bistro-style food) on the lower ground floor, and **The Atrium**, a gothic style bar spread over two floors. But the most interesting aspect of this new development is right up at the top of the house, where you will find one of Fermanagh's most interesting dining experiences at **Number 6:** This is an attractive space, with a comfortably furnished reception area where you can wind down and ponder the choices on a concise à la carte menu. The restaurant is elegantly appointed for fine dining and brings together the talents of two personalities well known in the hsopitality of the area, head chef Gerry Russell and front of house manager Johnny Donnelly. As a team they present ambitious cooking, a relaxed fine dining atmosphere and caring, knowledgeable service with all the little extra that gives guests that pampered feeling all of add which adds up to something very special. Imaginatively updated classics may include charred dry aged fillet (beef), a deliciously modern take on the nation's favourite dish, and you may find a speciality of roast belly of pork with langoustines, black pudding, creamed cabbage & puy lentils doing something similar to surf'n'turf. Fish cookery is very accomplished, and side dishes are taken unusually seriously too. Wine is Johnny Donnelly's passion, and this is reflected in both an interesting list, and interested guidance and service. Café Merlot (casual dining), L daily 12-3.30; D daily 5-9.30; a la carte, also 2-course early D about £12 (5.30-7.30). No 6: D Fri-Sat 6-10; A la carte; will open any day for parties 12+. Open all year. MasterCard, Visa, Laser, Switch. **Directions:** Town centre. ◇

Enniskillen
RESTAURANT
R

Franco's Restaurant
Queen Elizabeth Road Enniskillen Co Fermanagh BT74
Tel: 028 6632 4183

If what you want is buzz and relaxed bustle, this is the place for you - there is no other restaurant in town that can even begin to match the ambience. You get a fair hint of this on arrival, as the exterior facing the Queen Elizabeth Road is always attractively maintained, with a pleasing mix of red brick and glass, and an eye-catching display of plants and creepers - and all expertly lit after dark too. Informal meals, including pizzas, pastas and barbecues, are the order of the day - and it's all done with great style, using quality ingredients. More sophisticated items include seafood, lamb and dry aged beef. No side vegetables, except potato dishes, alas, but vegetarians have plenty to choose from in every section of the menu. Smart staff, efficient service and fairly reasonable prices keep this place busy, all the time. Popular wine list too (mainly under about £15). **Seats 140** (private room, 60). Toilets wheelchair accessible. Children welcome. Open Mon-Sat, 12-11 (Sun to 10.30 pm). A la carte. Houses wines from about £10. Closed 25 Dec Amex, MasterCard, Visa, Switch. **Directions:** Prominent orange coloured building by the river. ◈

Killyhevlin Hotel

Enniskillen
HOTEL
R

Killyhevlin Enniskillen Co Fermanagh BT74 6RW **Tel: 028 6632 3481**
info@killyhevlin.com   www.killyhevlin.com

Just south of Enniskillen, on the A4, this spacious, modern hotel on the banks of the Erne is a popular choice for business guests and would make a comfortable and relaxing base from which to explore this fascinating and unspoilt area. Recent developments have added 27 new rooms and a state-of-the art health and beauty spa with gymnasium & fitness suite, indoor swimming pool, hot tub, hydro therapy pool, treatment suites, sauna, and steam room. Fishing and river cruising are particular attractions and the hotel gardens reach down to the riverbank and their own pontoon, where visiting cruisers can berth - food is available in the Boathouse Grill. Golf and horse riding nearby Lakeshore self-catering chalets also available, , with private jetties and full use of hotel facilities. Conference/banqueting facilities (400/300); secretarial services; broadband wi/fi. Garden, cycling, walking, leisure centre ('pool, jacuzzi, sauna, fitness room); Spa. Golf & equestrian nearby. Ample parking. Children welcome (under 12s free in parents' room; cots available free of charge; baby sitting arranged). Wheelchair accessible. Pets permitted by arrangement. **Rooms 70** (4 suites, 3 junior suites, 22 ground floor, 2 for disabled, 50 no smoking). B&B £72.50 pps, ss £30; No SC. Closed 24-25 Dec. Amex, Diners, MasterCard, Visa, Switch. **Directions:** On the A4 just south of Enniskillen.

Rossfad House

Enniskillen
COUNTRY HOUSE

Killadeas Ballinamallard Enniskillen Co Fermanagh BT94 2LS
Tel: 028 6638 8505 rossfadhouse@aol.com

Lois and John Williams' lovely house is approached up a curving drive, lined with mature trees, with horses grazing in the paddock. The present house is Georgian, built in 1776 on the site of an older Plantation house, and guest accommodation is in a Victorian wing, overlooking the garden and lake. The accommodation is very comfortable and there is a period feel with some nice antique pieces. Breakfast is served in a light, airy room overlooking the garden and lake, which is attractively furnished and doubles as a sitting room. It would be of special interest to anyone with a feel for history - it's very close to Lough Erne Yacht Club (the oldest racing sailing club in the Ireland) and, Castle Archdale is nearby. Children welcome (babies free; cot available without charge, baby siting arranged). Pets allowed in some areas. Garden, walking, equestrian. **Rooms 2** (1 en suite, 1 with private bathroom, both no smoking). B&B about £25 pps, ss £5. Closed Nov-Feb. **No Credit Cards. Directions:** 5 miles from Enniskillen on Kesh Road, A32, for 2 miles to Trory Cross; then take B82 for 3 miles; entrance on left, opposite the Whitehill Cross road. ◈

Scoffs Restaurant & Uno Wine Bar

Enniskillen
RESTAURANT/WINE BAR
R

17 Belmore Street Enniskillen Co Fermanagh BT74 6AA
Tel: 028 663 42622 info@scoffsuno.com   www.scoffsuno.com

Just a few minutes walk from the town centre, proprietor-chef Gavin and Linda Murphy's popular two-storey bistro-style restaurant and wine bar has now been pleasing a wide range of customers for eight years. Early evening opening and Gavin's wide-ranging menus - offering everything from inexpensive pastas to more serious (but still moderately priced) 'dinner' dishes such as pan fried Blacklion duck breast - partly explain the wide appeal, but consistent cooking, friendly, attentive staff and an atmos-phere of relaxed informality are equally attractive. Although menus may include some choices from afar such as kangaroo, local produce features and there are some interesting vegetarian options and they have recently installed a saltwater tank so they can offer fresh lobster and oysters, reflecting an increase in seafood offered overall, usually on the daily specials. Modern classics like fillet steak with dauphinoise potato, grilled plum tomato & beanaise sauce are well cooked and stylishly presented, and the only down-side is that side dishes charged extra at £2.90 can add significantly to the costs of a meal. **Seats 147** (private room, 57). Reservations accepted. Toilets wheelchair accessible. Children welcome. D only daily, 5-'late'. D à la carte, from about £20. House wine about £10. Closed 24-26 Dec. Diners, MasterCard, Visa, Laser. **Directions:** Access from main shopping centre. ◈

ENNISKILLEN AREA

Beautifully situated between two channels of the river joining Upper and Lower Lough Erne, Enniskillen has developed as a holiday centre in recent years, and is especially popular with fisherfolk and anyone with an interest in life on the river. Interesting waterside establishments nearby include the aptly-named **Waterfront Restaurant**, at Rossigh (028 686 21938) which has come into the energetic new ownership of Lisa Little, who is originally from Kesh, and is attracting a local clientèle, and the famous old thatched place, **The Sheelin** (028 6634 8232) at Bellanaleck, which has been run as a restaurant for some year but, at the time of going to press, is expected to become more of a country pub/ tea rooms doing informal food, which will please visitors to the adjacent Lace Museum. Enniskillen is also famously associated with Oscar Wilde, who attended Portora Royal School; **Oscar's** (028 6632 7037) restaurant celebrates that connnection (with menus that, appropriately, read well and praise local ingredients) while, nearby, **Picasso's** (028 6632 2226) develops a different artistic theme.
WWW-IRELAND-GUIDE.COM FOR THE BEST PLACES TO EAT, DRINK & STAY

Enniskillen Area
FARMHOUSE

Arch House
Tullyhona Florencecourt Enniskillen Co Fermanagh BT92 1DE
Tel: 028 6634 8452 info@archhouse.com www.archhouse.com

Located near Marble Arch Caves and Florencecourt House, Rosemary Armstrong's friendly farm guest house has six pretty en-suite bedrooms and a big comfortably furnished sitting room with lots of room for guests to relax. Good food is very important at Arch House - a varied breakfast is served in the big dining room, and quite an extensive à la carte evening menu is offered too, which is available to non residents by arrangement. And, not only does Rosemary do meals for guests, but she also has scone and bread making demonstrations in her kitchen - and home produce is on sale in their own shop as well. A good place for a family stay as children are very welcome, and there's a children's menu and high chair available. Broadband wi/fi. Farm shop, walking, table tennis; Fishing (fly & coarse), golf tennis, equestrian, boating and marble arch caves nearby. **Rooms 6** (3 family rooms, 2 twin, 1 double, all en-suite), children welcome (play ground, toys & games, baby listening); B&B about £25 pps £10ss. Open all year. MasterCard, Visa, Switch. **Directions:** From Enniskillen follow the A4 (Sligo Road) for 4km (2.5 m) on to A32 (Swanlinbar road). Follow signs for the Marble Arch Caves. Turn right at posting for National Trust Property at Florencecourt, 3km (2m) on.

Kesh
HOTEL

Lough Erne Hotel
Main Street Kesh Co Fermanagh BT93 1TF **Tel: 028 6863 1275**
info@loughernehotel.com www.loughernehotel.com

In a very attractive location on the banks of the Glendurragh River, this pleasantly old-fashioned and friendly town centre hotel has comfortable accommodation in rooms that are not large but have everything you need including en-suite bath/shower rooms, TV and tea/coffee facilities. The hotel is understandably popular for weddings, as the bar and function rooms overlook the river and have access to a paved riverside walkway and garden. Wholesome fare is available for most of the day and helpful staff, good value and a soothing view make this a relaxing place to break a journey. Popular for fishing holidays, it would also make a good base for a family break; there is plenty to do in this lovely, unspoilt area, including golf, watersports and horse-riding. Conference/banqueting(200/180). Fishing, cycling, walking. Off-season breaks and self-catering accommodation in one and two bedroom cottages (from about £250 pw) also on offer. Garden. Limited wheelchair access. Own parking. Children welcome. Pets permitted in some areas. **Rooms 12** (all en-suite) B&B about £35pps, ss about £5; sc discretionary. Bar L Mon-Sat, 12.30-2; Grill Menu daily 2.30-8 (Sun 5-8). Restaurant D only except L Sun. Light snacks available all day. Closed 25 Dec. Amex, Diners, MasterCard, Visa, Switch. **Directions:** From Dublin N3 to Belturbet, A509 to Enniskillen, A35 to Kesh. ◇

Kesh
B&B/RESTAURANT/PUB

Lusty Beg Island
Boa Island Kesh Co Fermanagh BT93 8AD **Tel: 028 6863 3300**
info@lustybegisland.com www.lustybegisland.com

If you arrive by road, a little ferry takes you over to the island , or of course, you can call in by boat. It's an unusual place and worth a visit, if only to call into the pleasant waterside pub for a drink, a cup of tea or an informal bite. However, you could stay much longer as accommodation is available in lodges, chalets and a motel, all spread relatively inconspicuously around the wooded island. Conferences, corporate entertaining and management training are specialities and all sorts of activity breaks are offered. Visiting boats are welcome; phone ahead for details of barbecues and other theme nights; music Saturday nights. Bar food available daily in summer, may be weekends only off season (phone ahead or details). Conference/banqueting (300/200). **Rooms 40** (all shower only, 23 family rooms, 10 ground floor, 2 for disabled, all no smoking) Children welcome (under 5s free in parents' room; cot available €5). Leisure centre: swimming pool, sauna, tennis, pool table. Football pitch, canoes, bike hire, archery, clay pigeon shooting, equestrian & fly fishing nearby. B&B £45 pps. ss £20. Closed Christmas week. MasterCard, Visa, Switch. **Directions:** Located off the main Kesh - Belleek Road A47.

Manor House Resort Hotel

Killadeas
HOTEL/RESTAURANT

Killadeas Co Fermanagh BT94 1NY **Tel: 028 6862 2211**
info@manor-house-hotel.com www.manor-house-hotel.com

This impressive lakeside period house makes a fine hotel. The scale of the architecture and the style of furnishings and decor lean very much towards the luxurious in both public areas and accommodation. Spacious bedrooms range from interconnecting family rooms to deluxe doubles and romantic suites with canopied four-poster beds and front rooms have stunning views. Recent changes have included extensive refurbishments, most recently to the foyer and adjacent areas, and the addition of an impressive new conference and banqueting area with its own separate entrance, which has been discreetly added to the side and rear of the original building and, despite its large size and more contemporary approach, in no way detracts from the appeal of the old house. Conference/banqueting. Leisure centre, indoor swimming pool; beauty salon. Children under 3 free in parents' room. No pets. **Rooms 81** (all en-suite, 6 suites) B&B about £55pps, ss about £30. Special breaks offered. **The Belleek Restaurant:** Formally appointed in the old style, the restaurant is well positioned to make the most of the lovely view. Quite classical dinner menus are offered and, while not aiming to be cutting edge, cooking is accomplished and presentation well-judged (simple but attractive). Service from a well-trained team is exemplary and, like the food, in tune with the grand surroundings, making this a good choice for a special evening out. Bar meals available 12.30-9 pm daily, 12.30-3.30 and 6.30-9.30. **Seats 65** (private room 30). Air Conditioning. L&D daily. Set D about £25. Set Sun L about £25. [*Information on the nearby Inishclare restaurant, bar & marina complex is available from the hotel, which is in common ownership.] Open all year. Amex, MasterCard, Visa. AmexMasterCardVisa**Directions:** 6 miles from Enniskillen on the B82. ◇

Belle Isle Castle

Lisbellaw
COUNTRY HOUSE/CASTLE

Belle Isle Estate Lisbellaw Co Fermanagh BT94 5HG
Tel: 028 6638 7231
accommodation@belleisle-estate.com www.belleislecastle.com

Belle Isle is owned by the Duke of Abercorn, and magically situated on one of eleven islands on Upper Lough Erne that are owned by the Estate; the original castle dates back to 1680 and has mid-19th century additions, including a courtyard and coach house which have been converted to make very appealing self-catering accommodation. The castle itself has a delightfully exclusive away-from-it-all country house atmosphere and is impressively furnished with antiques, striking paintings and dramatic colour schemes (the work of the internationally renowned interior designer, David Hicks); in addition to the eight romantic bedrooms, which all have their special character, guests have use of a magnificent drawing room and also the Grand Hall, complete with minstrels' gallery, where dinner is served. Under the eagle-eyed supervision of hosts Charles and Fiona Plunket, maintenance and housekeeping are immaculate throughout - and full central heating has recently been installed in the dining room and the four bedrooms above it. This romantic place could be the perfect choice for a small wedding: they are licensed to hold civil weddings and the courtyard accommodation is available to guests. There are many wonderful things to do in this idyllically beautiful area - fishing is an obvious first choice but there are also golf courses nearby, field sports can be arranged and there are historic houses and gardens to visit. But, most tempting of all, perhaps, might be a course at the Belle Isle School of Cookery, which is very professionally operated and offers an extensive range of courses of varying lengths throughout the year. **Cookery School:** Tel 028 6638 7231; www.irishcookeryschool.com. Small weddings (30). Children welcome (under 5s free in parents' room, cot available without charge; playground). Pets allowed in some areas. Garden, walking, fishing, tennis. **Rooms 8** (1 en-suite, 7 with private bathrooms, 1 shower only, all no smoking). B&B £70 pps, ss £15. No SC. Residents D daily, 8pm, £28/30; wines from £10.45. *Self-catering also offered in 10 apartments & 3 cottages, with 1-3 bedrooms; larger groups may use both castle & apartments. Open all year. Amex, Diners, MasterCard, Visa, Laser, Switch. **Directions:** From Belfast, take A4 to Lisbellaw - follow signs to Carrybridge.

LONDONDERRY

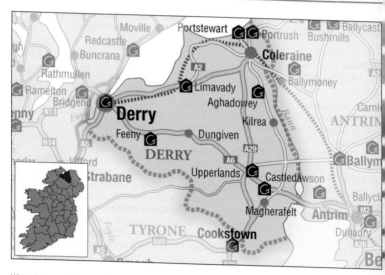

When its boundaries were first defined for "modern" times, this was known as the County of Coleraine, named for the busy little port on the River Bann a few miles inland from the Atlantic coast. It was an area long favoured by settlers, for Mountsandel - on the salmon-rich Bann a mile south of Coleraine - is where the 9,000 year old traces of the site of some of the oldest-known houses in Ireland have been found.

Today, Coleraine is the main campus of the University of Ulster, with the vitality of student life spreading to the nearby coastal resorts of Portstewart and Portrush in the area known as the "Golden Triangle", appropriately fringed to the north by the two golden miles of Portstewart Strand. Southwestward from Coleraine, the county - which was re-named after the City of Derry became Londonderry in 1613 - offers a fascinating variety of places and scenery, with large areas of fine farmland being punctuated by ranges of hills, while the rising slopes of the Sperrin Mountains dominate the County's southern boundary.

The road from Belfast to Derry sweeps through the Sperrins by way of the stirringly-named Glenshane Pass, and from its heights you begin to get the first glimpses westward of the mountains of Donegal. This is an appropriate hint of the new atmosphere in the City of Derry itself. This lively place could reasonably claim to be the most senior of all Ireland's contemporary cities, as it can trace its origins directly back to a monastery of St Colmcille, otherwise Columba, founded in 546AD. Today, the historic city, its ancient walls matched by up-dated port facilities on the River Foyle and a cheerfully restored urban heart, is moving into a vibrant future in which it thrives on the energy drawn from its natural position as the focal point of a larger catchment area which takes in much of Donegal County to the west in addition to County Londonderry to the east.

The area eastward of Lough Foyle is increasingly popular among discerning visitors, the Roe Valley through Dungiven and Limavady being particularly attractive. The re-establishment of the ferry between Magilligan Point and Greencastle in Donegal across the narrow entrance to Lough Foyle has added a new dimension to the region's infrastructure, as does the up-grading of the increasingly busy City of Derry Airport at Eglinton.

Local Attractions & Information

Bellaghy Bellaghy Bawn (Seamus Heaney centre)	028 79 386812
Castlerock Hezlett House	028 70 848567
City of Derry Airport	028 71 810784
Coleraine Guy L Wilson Daffodil Garden	028 70 324431 / 324431
Coleraine Tourism Information	028 70 344723
Derry City The Fifth Province - Celtic culture	028 71 373177
Derry City Foyle Cruises (year round)	028 71 362857
Derry City Foyle Valley Railway Centre	028 71 265234
Derry City The Guildhall	028 71 377335

Aghadowey
HOTEL/RESTAURANT

The Brown Trout Golf & Country Inn

209 Agivey Road Aghadowey Co Londonderry BT51 4AD
Tel: 028 7086 8209 jane@browntroutinn.com www.browntroutinn.com

Golf is one of the major attractions at this lively family-run country inn, both on-site and in the locality, but it's a pleasant and hospitable place for anyone to stay. Golfers and non-golfers alike will soon find friends in the convivial bar, where food is served from noon to 10 pm every day - and outside in a pleasant barbecue too, in fine weather. Accommodation is not especially luxurious, but very comfortable, in good-sized en-suite rooms which are all on the ground floor, arranged around the main courtyard, and have plenty of space for golfing gear. Newer cottage suites overlooking the golf course (just 100 yards from the main building) were the first of this standard to be completed in Northern Ireland. As well as bar food, there's an evening restaurant up a steep staircase (with chair lift for the less able), overlooking the garden end of the golf course. A dedicated kitchen team produces good home cooking with local fresh ingredients for daytime food (soups, freshly made sandwiches and open sandwiches, baked potatoes, pasta) and evening meals like hot garlic Aghadowey mushrooms or ribeye steak with a Bushmills whiskey sauce. Free Broadband WI/FI. Small conference/private parties (50). Tennis, horse-riding, golf (9), fishing. Gym. Children welcome (under 4s free in parents' room; cots available without charge, baby sitting arranged). Pets permitted. Garden, walking. Traditional music in bar (Sat). **Rooms 15** (all en-suite; 1 for disabled & most wheelchair friendly). B&B about £50 pps, ss about £20. Stair lift. Toilets wheelchair accessible. No smoking house. Bar meals, 12-9.30 daily (to 10 in summer). Restaurant D only, 5-9.30. A la carte; house wine about £10; sc discretionary. Open all year. Amex, Diners, MasterCard, Visa, Switch. **Directions:** Intersection of A54/B66,11km (7 m) south of Coleraine. ◇

Aghadowey
FARMHOUSE

Greenhill House

24 Greenhill Road Aghadowey Coleraine Co Londonderry BT51 4EU
Tel: 028 7086 8241

greenhill.house@btinternet.com www.greenhill-house.co.uk

Framed by trees with lovely country views, the Hegarty family's fine Georgian farmhouse is at the centre of a large working farm. In true Northern tradition, Elizabeth Hegarty is a great baker and greets guests in the drawing room with an afternoon tea which includes a vast array of home-made teabreads, cakes and biscuits - and home baking is also a highlight of wonderful breakfasts that are based on tasty local produce like bacon, sausages, mushrooms, free range eggs, smoked salmon, strawberries and preserves. There are two large family rooms and,

Georgina Campbell's Ireland

although not luxurious, the thoughtfulness that has gone into furnishing bedrooms makes them exceptionally comfortable everything is in just the right place to be convenient - and Elizabeth is constantly maintaining and improving the decor and facilities. Bedrooms have direct dial telephones, and little touches - like fresh flowers, a fruit basket, After Eights, tea & coffee making facilities, hair dryer, bathrobe, good quality clothes hangers and even a torch - are way above the standard expected of farmhouse accommodation. There's also internet access, a safe, fax machine, iron and trouser press available for guests' use on request. Guests have been welcomed to Greenhill House since 1980 and, wonderfully comforting and hospitable as it is, Elizabeth constantly seeks ways of improvement, big and small: this lovely house and the way it is run demonstrate rural Irish hospitality at its best. [Greenhill House was our Farmhouse of the Year Award for 2003.] Children welcome (under 2s free in parents' room, cot available). No pets. Garden Fishing (coarse) & golf nearby. **Rooms 6** (all en-suite, 2 shower only, 2 bath only, 2 family rooms, all no smoking). B&B £30 pps, ss £10. Closed Nov-Feb. Amex, MasterCard, Visa, Switch. **Directions:** On B66 Greenhill Road off A29, 10.5km (7 miles) south of Coleraine, 5km (3 m) north of Garvagh.

Castledawson
CAFÉ

Ditty's

44 Main Street Castledawson Co Londonderry BT1
Tel: 028 7946 8243

Renowned throughout the Ireland for their excellent home baking, this great craft bakery has received widespread recognition through the years (including a Good Food Award from the Irish Food Writers Guild) for the quality of their products, and their bakeries in both Castledawson and Magherafelt make a great place for a journey beak and you can pick up a few loaves of their speciality breads and other treats to take home, or to your self-catering accommodation. The in-store café serves a range of baked treats to have with a cup of tea or coffee - and several hot dishes are offered every day. Ditty's baked products most famously the delicious oatcakes that are so good with cheese (now sold at Waitrose stores throughout England) are also widely available in good food stores, and appear on many restaurant menus. Also at: 33 Rainey Street, Magherfelt (028 7963 4644). Open daytime (shop hours 8am-5.30pm). **Directions:** On the Main Street. ◇

Castledawson
RESTAURANT/GUESTHOUSE

The Inn at Castledawson

47 Main Street Castledawson Co Londonderry BT45 8AA
Tel: 028 7946 9777
info@theinnatcastledawson.co.uk www.theinnatcastledawson.co.uk

Built around the 200 year old Castledawson House, Simon Toye and Kathy Tully's latter day inn is a delightful place - and, thanks to Simon's excellent cooking and their 'nothing is too much trouble' policy, a visit here sure to be memorable and relaxed. The Inn is most attractive, with a modern bar where smart informal dining is offered at neat round darkwood tables with cream leather armchairs and banquettes and, beyond it, a lovely tiered light-filled restaurant with a huge arched window looks over the garden to the River Moyola and has doors leading out to a decked balcony. Concise, well-constructed à la carte bar menus with daily-changed specials offer a tempting choice including seriously good soups and breads, lovely pasta dishes and outstanding fish cooking, as in a memorable fish pie with creamy mash. The deceptively simple restaurant menu offers a fine choice of 6-8 dishes on each course, some of them dressier developments of the delicious bar food specialities to look out for include smoked salmon and other fish from Walter Ewing's renowned Belfast fishmongers, Finnebrogue 'Oisin' venison from Downpatrick, and rare breed pork dishes. The restaurant conveys a natural sense of occasion and is stylishly furnished, with hardwood flooring, warm red high-backed chairs, crisp white linen and gleaming glasses - it is a beautiful room in which to enjoy the good food and service for which the Inn already has a well-earned reputation. And it is a true inn, offering food, drink and a (very relaxing) place to lay your head: there are twelve chic contemporary bedrooms with river or courtyard views, including a suite with its own riverside balcony. With a spa next door, and golf, equestrian and fishing all nearby, this is a very appealing place for a short break. Small conferences/banqueting (90/80); secretarial services, video conferencing. Children welcome (under 5s free in parents' room, cot available free of charge); wheelchair accessible. **Rooms 12** (6 shower only, 6 ground floor, all no smoking, 2 disabled); B&B £39.95, ss £10. **Restaurant Seats 80** (+20 outside). L Sun-Fri 12-2.30; D Mon-Sat 5-10, D Sun 5-8. House wine £11.95. Restaurant closed Sat L; establishment closed 12 Jul. MasterCard, Visa, Switch. **Directions:** On main street of Castledawson, on the main Belfast-Derry road (M2-M22-A6).

Water Margin

Coleraine
RESTAURANT

The Boat House Hanover Place Coleraine Co Londonderry BT52 1EB
Tel: 028 7034 2222

An impressive first floor restaurant above the Boat Club, this magnificently located Chinese restaurant predated its famous Belfast sister (the largest Chinese restaurant in Ireland) by many a year and, with its fine river views, plush bar and a rather luxuriously appointed dining room to enhance cooking which has enjoyed a great reputation in the area over a long period, it has all the ingredients for a special meal out. Extensive menus offer all the familiar set 'banquets' and western favourites like aromatic duck, sesame toast, sweet & sours and sizzling dishes, but the more adventurous diner will find that there are many unusual dishes available too - and made all the more enjoyable by good service, provided by helpful, smartly-dressed staff. L Mon-Sat, 12.30-2pm, D daily,5-10.30pm, Sun 1-10pm. MasterCard, Visa, Switch. **Directions:** Above the boat club in Coleraine. ◇

Arbutus

Kilrea
RESTAURANT
Ⓝ

13 Bridge Street Kilrea Co Londonderry BT51 5RR
Tel: 028 2954 0140

In the beautiful Bann Valley, on the South Derry/Antrim border, this well known restaurant is in the centre of Kilrea in an elegant mid terrace town house. Following its closure in 2006, local chef Barry Dallat took on the challenge and is earning a well-deserved following for good cooking, a relaxing ambience and value for money. Inside it is a characterful place, with a series of intimate dining rooms on two storeys, open fires, a bar and lounge, and an attractive roof garden (complete with arbutus tree) which Barry added recently and is ideal for aperitifs and smokers. Traditional décor, low lighting and gentle background music create a relaxing atmosphere, and an extensive à la carte dinner menu offers a very wide choice, with no less than 17 main courses under various headings, including two vegetarian dishes. Prawn cocktail with passion fruit and mango sorbet, fillet steak with mature cheddar & Diane sauce, and fresh apple pie with crème anglaise are the kind of dishes to expect, along with a range of meat, poultry, fish dishes and traditional desserts. A reduced choice high tea menu is also available. A well thought out selection of wines supplied by James Nicholson is in the £10-£35 range, and includes four half bottles. Arbutus is a charming restaurant offering good value and a relaxing dining experience enhanced by professional friendly staff. **Seats 50.** Open Wed-Sun D 6-10pm. Closed Mon, Tue. MasterCard, Visa, Switch. **Directions:** Diamond Centre - follow signs for Ballymena. ◇

Lime Tree Restaurant

Limavady
RESTAURANT

60 Catherine Street Limavady Co Londonderry BT49 9DB
Tel: 028 7776 4300

info@limetreerest.com www.limetreerest.com

Loyal customers come from far and wide for the pleasure of dining at Stanley and Maria Matthews' restaurant on the handsome, wide main street of this attractive town. And no wonder, as Stanley is a fine chef and Maria a welcoming and solicitous hostess. Ingredients are carefully sourced, many of them local; menus are generous, with a classical base that Stanley works on to give popular dishes a new twist. Specialities include their own home-made wheaten bread, which is the perfect accompaniment for a chowder of Atlantic fish & local potatoes, or Irish smoked salmon (supplied by Donegal Prime Fish), with cucumber salad, while main course favourites include Sperrin lamb (with classic onion white sauce) fillet or sirloin steak (from the award-winning local butcher, Hunters) and seafood thermidor (Stanley's selection of fresh fish with a mild cheese & brandy sauce). Menus are not over-extensive, but change frequently to suit different occasions - there's an attractive early dinner menu which is exceptional value, followed by a dressier late dinner for the main evening menu, which also has an accompanying (and more adventurous) à la carte. Stanley's cooking is refreshingly down-to-earth - new dishes are often introduced, but if it's on the menu it's because it works: there are no gimmicks. Good cooking and good value go hand in hand with warm hospitality here and it is always a pleasure to visit The Lime Tree - indeed, many discerning guests enjoy it so much that they plan journeys around a meal here. A concise, interesting wine list also offers predictably good value. **Seats 30.** Children welcome (high chair,

607

childrens menu); toilets wheelchair accessible. D Tue-Sat, 6-9 (Sat to 9.30). Early D £14.95 (6-7pm, Tue-Fri). Set D £22.95; also à la carte; house wine £12.50; sc discretionary. Closed Sun & Mon, 25/6 Dec, 1 week around 12 July. Amex, MasterCard, Visa, Switch. **Directions:** On the outskirts of town, main Derry-Limavady road.

Limavady
HOTEL/RESTAURANT

Radisson SAS Roe Park Resort

Roe Park Limavady Co Londonderry BT47 2 AH **Tel: 028 7772 2222**
reservations@radissonroepark.com www.radissonroepark.com

Built on rising ground in lovely rolling countryside, this imposing hotel dates back to the eighteenth century when a Captain Richard Babington built the original house from which today's extensive hotel has grown. There is a pleasant air of relaxed luxury - the tone is set in an impressive foyer, with columns and a curved gallery overlooking a seating area smartly set up with comfortable sofas and armchairs. Conferences play a major part in present-day business - and the surrounding greensward provides relaxation for delegates, along with many others who come here specifically to enjoy the excellent leisure facilities. Spacious bedrooms are designed in the modern classic mode, with double and single beds and all the features expected of this type of hotel (all have desk areas, some with computers) and well-finished bathrooms - and all look out over the golf course or a courtyard garden. Dining options allow for different moods: formal dining in Greens Restaurant (dinner daily and lunch on Sunday) or a more relaxed style in The Coach House Brasserie; healthy options and dishes suitable for vegetarians or coeliacs are highlighted on menus. Conferences/banqueting (450/275). Leisure centre (indoor swimming pool, spa). Golf (18 hole), fishing, garden, walking, cycling. Children welcome (under 5 free in parents' room; cot available, baby sitting arranged, playroom). No pets. **Rooms 118** (7 suites, 3 junior suites, 108 executive, 15 family, 2 disabled). Lift. 24 hr room service. B&B £60 pps, ss £25. *Wide range of special breaks offered. Open all year. **Greens Restaurant:** Seats 150; air conditioning; children welcome; D Tue-Sat, 6.30-9.30; L Sun only, 12-2.30. Closed for D Sun & Mon. Amex, Diners, MasterCard, Visa, Laser, Switch. **Directions:** On the A2 L'Derry-Limavady road, 1 mile from Limavady (Derry City 16 miles).

LONDONDERRY / DERRY CITY

The City of Londonderry, also known as Derry, is the economic centre for the northwest of Ireland and a vibrant modern city with a fascinating history and rich cultural life. It is a very hospitable place and, for a city of its size, it has an exceptionally wide range of hotels, cafés, restaurants and pubs to suit every taste, budget and occasion. In addition to the recommendations below, other establishments which are useful to know about include the popular **Ramada Da Vincis Hotel** (028 7127 9111; www.davincishotel.com), about a mile from the city centre on the Culmore Road; it has private car parking and a pleasant riverside walkway into the city from the hotel. If you are attending an event at **The Millennium Forum** (Theatre and Conference Centre), you will be very glad to find the Derry Theatre Trust's stylish **Encore Brasserie** (028 7137 2492;ww.encorebrasserie.com), which offers interesting, fairly-priced food and a well-chosen wine list and is open for lunch and dinner; its location between the city's two main shopping centres widens the appeal, especially as children are very well catered for. Lovers of Italian food will find authentic Italian cooking at **La Sosta Ristorante** (028 7137 4817; www.lasostarestaurant.com) which is one of Derry's most popular restaurants and just a few minutes walk from the city centre.
WWW.IRELAND-GUIDE.COM FOR THE BEST PLACES TO EAT, DRINK & STAY

Londonderry
HOTEL/RESTAURANT

Beech Hill Country House Hotel

32 Ardmore Road Londonderry Co Londonderry BT47 3QP
Tel: 028 7134 9279 info@beech-hill.com www.beech-hill.com

Beech Hill is just a couple of miles south of Londonderry, beautifully set in 42 acres of peaceful woodland, waterfalls and gardens. Built in 1729, the house has retained many of its original details and proprietor Patsy O'Kane makes an hospitable and caring hostess. Comfortable bedrooms vary in size and outlook - many overlook the gardens, but all are thoughtfully and attractively furnished with Mrs O'Kane's ever-growing collection of antiques. Public rooms include a good-sized bar, a fine restaurant (in what was originally the snooker room, now extended into a conservatory overlooking the gardens) and, unusually, a private chapel, now used for meetings, private parties or small weddings. All the main public areas have recently been refurbished, but changes are always undertaken sensitively, in keeping with the building. American visitors, especially, will be interested to know that US Marines had their headquarters here in World War II and an informative small museum of the US Marine Friendship Association is housed within the hotel. Facilities include picnic areas in the grounds for fine weather and a fitness suite with sauna, steam room, jacuzzi and weight room. Conference/banqueting (100); business centre, broadband wi/fi, secretarial services. Beauty salon, massage & treatments, walking, tennis, garden. Golf, fishing & equestrian nearby. Children welcome (under 3s free in parents' room cot available without charge, babysitting arranged). Pets allowed by arrangement. **Rooms 27** (2 suites, 3 junior suites, 10 executive rooms, 10 shower only, 1 for disabled, all no smoking). Lift. B&B £67.50pps, ss £22.50; SC discretionary. Closed 24/25 Dec. **Ardmore Restaurant:** The restaurant is a particularly attractive feature of this charming hotel; it is elegantly appointed and well-positioned overlooking gardens (which is a particularly pleasant outlook at breakfast time). Head chef Raymond Moran is a member of Euro-Toques, the European community of chefs who work together to defend the integrity and diversity of their ingredients, and he and sous chef Paul Curry have also partnered with the North West Organic Association for supply of their seasonal organic vegetables. The first page of the menu is a hymn to quality ingredients the freshest local seafood, dry-aged local meats, free-range pork and chickens from County Down, award-winning cheeses from the acclaimed Five Mile Creamery in Co Tyrone, The Causeway Coast Cheese Company and the Tiernan family's Glebe Brethan, which has been making waves at all the artisan food shows recently. Similarly, the ingredients of the dishes themselves are described in detail, all of which is interesting and confidence-inspiring. The cooking style is modern classic, with a strong Irish twist and the pride taken in each dish is palpable, adding greatly to the enjoyment for the guest. A vegetarian menu is offered, and also an early dinner menu, which is very good value. An informative, well chosen wine list includes tasting notes and makes interesting reading. **Seats 100.** Reservations accepted; children welcome; toilets wheelchair accessible. L daily, 12-2; D daily 6.30-9. Set L £19.95, Set Sun L £19.95. Set 2/3 course D, £24.95/29.95. A la carte and vegetarian menu also available. House wines (6), about £12.95. SC discretionary. Amex, MasterCard, Visa, Switch. **Directions:** Main Londonderry road A6.

Londonderry
RESTAURANT

Browns Restaurant, Bar & Brasserie

1-2 Bonds Hill Londonderry Co Londonderry BT47 6DW **Tel: 028 7134 5180**
eat@brownsrestaurant.com www.brownsrestaurant.com

The city's leading contemporary restaurant has a devoted local following. Always immaculate, inside and out, it's a relaxed space with subtle blends of natural colours, textures and finishes - proprietor-chef Ivan Taylor's cool cooking keeps them coming back for more; his approach to food never stands still, and the cooking is consistently creative. Wide-ranging menus offer a range of fresh-flavoured dishes, including delicious starters like spiced crumbled beef served in a light vegetable broth with pecorino, and a perfectly judged main dish of char-grilled rare-breed sirloin steak on a fine balsamic onion gravy with a horeshradish Yorkshire pudding & pea purée and braised root vegetables - one of several examples of classics that have been modernised without forgetting the basics. Desserts also ring some changes with the classics - or espresso, vin santo & home-made biscotti might make a pleasing alternative. All round, there's imagination, a certain amount of style, dedication and consistency - not bad after more than 20 years in business. *Browns2Go* service offered, for boardroom lunches and corporate entertaining. L Tue-Fri, 12-2.15; D Tue-Sat, 5.30-Late. Early Set D Tue-Fri, about £12 (5.30-7.15). House wine about £12. Closed Sun & Mon, 1st 2 weeks Aug. Amex, MasterCard, Visa, Laser, Switch. **Directions:** In a cul-de-sac pposite the old Waterside railway station: Belfast-Derry road (A6), turn left at Melrose Terrace & branch right at sign. (Or park at station and walk across). ◇

Londonderry
HOTEL

City Hotel

Queens Quay Londonderry Co Londonderry BT48 7AS **Tel: 028 7136 5800**
res@derry-gsh.com www.gshotels.com

Centrally located on a quayside site overlooking the River Foyle, this modern hotel is bright and contemporary, and would make an equally attractive base for a leisure visit or for business - executive rooms have a workstation with modem/PC connections, voice mail, interactive TV systems and mini-bar and there's a business centre providing secretarial services for guests. Well-located close to the old city, business districts and main shopping areas, it also has free private parking for guests and on-site leisure facilities. Conference/banqueting (450/350). **Rooms 145** (1 suite, 4 junior suites). Lift. 24 hour room service. Children welcome (under 2s free in parents' room, cot available without charge). Leisure centre: swimming pool, Jacuzzi, steam room, sauna, dance suite, gym, hydrotherapy). B&B about £50pps. Room rate about £100 (max 3 guests). Amex, Diners, MasterCard, Visa, Laser. **Directions:** In Derry city centre, overlooking River Foyle. ◇

Londonderry
RESTAURANT

Exchange Restaurant & Wine Bar

Queens Quay Londonderry Co Londonderry BT48 7AY
Tel: 028 7127 3990

Just outside the walled city, the contemporary design of this popular bar and restaurant makes a great contrast to the age of nearby landmarks. Although seriously modern, this is a friendly and welcoming place that appeals to all age groups and their colourful, fresh-flavoured food suits the mood perfectly. They seem to have a winning formula here as prices are reasonable, ingredients are sourced locally as far as possible and the cooking hits the mark. At first glance the menu seems very international but close examination reveals plenty to please traditionalists too and blackboard specials reflect the same desire to please a wide range of customers. **Seats 120.** Toilets wheelchair accessible. Children welcome. Air conditioning. L Mon-Sat, 12-2.30; D daily 5.30-10 (Sun to 9.30). A la carte. House wine about £10. SC discretionary. Closed L Sun, 25 Dec. Amex, MasterCard, Visa, Laser, Switch. **Directions:** Opposite City Hotel. ◇

Londonderry
RESTAURANT/WINE BAR

Fitzroys Restaurant

2-4 Bridge Street 3 Carlisle Road Londonderry
Co Londonderry BT48 6JZ **Tel: 028 7126 6211**
info@fitzroysrestaurant.com www.fitzroysrestaurant.com

This large modern restaurant beside the Foyle Shopping Centre is on two floors and very handy for shoppers, visitors or pre- and post-theatre meals. Refurbishment has revamped the interior, but the central philosophy of providing good quality, reasonably priced food in enjoyably informal surroundings remains unchanged. Menus change through the day and offer a wide range of food in the current international fashion - lamb cutlets with herb crust, champ, red onion confit, and red wine jus indicates the evening style while the daytime menu ranges from soup of the day and designer sandwiches (sweet chilli chicken & roast peppers panini) to house favourites like Cajun chicken tagliatelle. A conveniently located, family-friendly restaurant - handy to know about. The wine list includes a useful flavour key, indicating style. **Seats 80.** Reservations accepted. Open daily, 11-10pm (Sun 12-'late'). Value D Mon-Thurs 7-10 about £12.95, also à la carte; Sun brasserie menus all day. House wine from about £11. Closed 25 Dec. MasterCard, Visa, Switch. **Directions:** City centre, opposite main entrance to Foyleside Shopping Centre. ◇

Londonderry
HOTEL

Hastings Everglades Hotel

Prehen Road Londonderry Co Londonderry BT47 2NH **Tel: 028 7132 1066**
res@egh.hastingshotels.com www.hastingshotels.com

Situated on the banks of the River Foyle, close to City of Derry airport and quite convenient to the city, this blocky modern hotel is well located for business and pleasure. Warm and welcoming staff are very hospitable and helpful and, as at all the Hastings Hotels, an on-going system of refurbishment and upgrading pays off as the spacious public areas never feel dated. The well-maintained bedrooms are all very comfortable, with good amenities and most of the bathrooms have also been renewed. The hotel is quietly situated which, together with a high standard of accommodation and friendly staff, makes it a very pleasant place to stay and they do a particularly good breakfast (from 7am). Although probably most popular for business guests, it is well located for golf, with the City of Derry course just a couple of minutes away and six other courses, including Royal Portrush, within easy driving distance. Conference/banqueting (400/320); secretarial services; video conferencing (on request). Wheelchair accessible. Own parking (200). Children under 14 free in parents' room; cots available; baby sitting arranged. No pets. **Rooms 64** (2 suites, 1 junior suite, 4 executive, 40 no-smoking, 1 for disabled). Lift. B&B about £60 pps, ss about £15; no sc. *Short breaks & golfing breaks offered. Closed 24-25 Dec. Amex, Diners, MasterCard, Visa, Switch. **Directions:** From Belfast follow M2; hotel is on A5 approx 1 mile from city. ◇

Londonderry
RESTAURANT

Mange 2

2 Clarendon Street Londonderry Co Londonderry BT48 7ES
Tel: 028 7136 1222 dine@mange2derry.com www.mange2derry.com

John O'Connell and Kieran McGuinness's restaurant off the Strand Road is one of the best in the area and has recently been refurbished, providing a better setting for Kieran's creative good cooking - and an outside seating area offers an alternative in good weather when the interior can seem a little dark. Keen, knowledgeable staff are quick to welcome guests, offering menus with plenty of choice, in a pleasingly straightforward modern style - there are some real classics alongside the spicy dishes, a very good French onion soup, for example, and you may well find other old favourites, like bacon & cabbage. There is some emphasis on fish and seafood, which will probably include fresh mussels from County Down, offered in a choice of five classic and modern styles; vegetarians have a fair choice too, but you will also find less usual ingredients, perhaps including game in season - Finnebrogue venison is a speciality. Everything is home made, including desserts, and prices are reasonable - what you get here is wholesome food, served in generous portions. Look out for special value promotions, such as a midweek early dinner menu offering a 3 course meal for two for £31.95, with a bottle of house wine. The wine list is limited but well priced. Toilets wheelchair accessible. **Seats 55;** air conditioning; children welcome. Open daily (all day in summer): D, 5.30-10; L, 12-3. A la carte; Set Sun L £11.95. Value D £31.95 for two people, D & bottle of wine, Mon-Thur 5.30-7pm. House wines £11.95. Closed 3 days Christmas. Amex, MasterCard, Visa, Switch. **Directions:** Off Strand Road.

Londonderry
HOTEL

Tower Hotel Derry

Off The Diamond Londonderry Co Londonderry BT48 6HL **Tel: 028 7137 1000**
reservations@thd.ie wwwtowerhotelderry.com

This attractive hotel has the distinction of being the only one to have been built inside the city walls and, while this does have its disadvantages (the constraints of the site restricted the amount of parking provided, for example), these are offset by wonderful views over the river and a real sense of being at the real heart of the city. Accommodation and facilities have obvious appeal for both leisure and business visitors - the style throughout is bright and sassy, and rooms are pleasingly decorated, with all the necessary modern facilities, including phones/ISDN, hospitality trays, TV, trouser press etc (also a safe in suites). An attractive bistro restaurant off the lobby has the potential to appeal to non-residents as well as hotel guests. A fitness suite with gym and sauna has a great view across the city. Conference/banqueting 250/180). Parking (limited). **Rooms 90** (3 suites, 4 disabled). Lift. Room service (limited hours). Children welcome (cot available without charge). Room rate £85-99. Closed 24-27 Dec. Amex, Diners, MasterCard, Visa, Laser. **Directions:** City centre - old town. ◇

Magherafelt
RESTAURANT

Gardiners Restaurant

7 Garden Street Magherafelt Co Londonderry BT45 5DD
Tel: 028 7930 0333 gardiners2000@hotmail.com www.gardiners.net

Local man Sean Owens opened this impressive restaurant with his wife Helen in 1999 and a redesign of the original premises has produced a smart and atmospheric dining room, with a proper bar. The stated aim is to bring quality local food and service to the people of the area, and this is achieved remarkably well, through accessible menus that offer really good variations of many popular dishes: ever-popular prawn cocktail, for example, deep fried Ulster button mushrooms with garlic aoili and (who could resist?) real spaghetti bolognaise with parmesan croûte... Sean is a committed supporter of local produce and suppliers, and you will find some unusual specialities here too - Lough Neagh smoked eel, for example (a parfait, perhaps, on roasted soda bread), and dishes inspired by traditional rural products, like blackthorn gravad lax with sloe gin and sweet Swedish senap mustard. All menus are good value (including a Celebrations Menu, offered occasionally to give the kitchen a good stretch, which is also keenly priced), and an early dinner menu offering plenty of choice with nothing over £9.95 is a snip. But it's not just good food that attracts people to Gardiners - it's a good night out. Gardiners is a great neighbourhood restaurant - and plenty come from other neighbourhoods to enjoy a night out here, especially at weekends. A carefully selected (and thoroughly tasted) wine list is also well priced. Children welcome; toilets wheelchair accessible; air conditioning. **Seats 90** (private room, 105); D Tue-Sun, 5.30-10pm; Sun L about £15, value D about £15, 5.30-7pm, set D about £20, also a la carte; house wine from £11.95. Closed Mon, 25-26 Dec, 12-13 Jul. MasterCard, Visa, Switch. **Directions:** To diamond in Magherafelt, down Rainey St., first right into Garden St.

PORTSTEWART

Probably best-known for its sandy beach, this popular seaside resort is popular with surfers and golfers - and generally regarded as quieter version of neighbouring Portrush. **Cromore Halt Inn** (028 7083 6888; www.cromore.com) is a friendly, family-owned 12-room guesthouse and restaurant on Station Road and would make an equally good base for a business or leisure visit, as the rooms are furnished to hotel standard and prices are reasonable. For more specialist accommodation, Ernestine and Claire McKeever's **Strand House** (028 7083 1000; www.strandhouse.com) on Strand Road (first road coming from Portstewart Strand and Golf Course) offers a stylish alternative, with lovely views and many special features.

WWW.IRELAND-GUIDE.COM FOR THE BEST PLACES TO EAT, DRINK & STAY

Upperlands
COUNTRY HOUSE

Ardtara Country House

8 Gorteade Road Upperlands Maghera Co Londonderry BT46 5SA
Tel: 028 7964 4490 valerie_ferson@ardtara.com www.ardtara.com

Former home to the Clark linen milling family, Ardtara is now an attractive, elegantly decorated Victorian country house and, in the caring hands of manager Valerie Ferson, has a genuinely hospitable atmosphere. Well-proportioned reception rooms include a proper bar which has access to the conservatory and garden, and there are antique furnishings and fresh flowers everywhere. All the large, luxuriously furnished bedrooms enjoy views of the garden and surrounding countryside and have king size beds, original fireplaces and LCD TV and DVDs, while bathrooms combine practicality with period details, some including free-standing baths and fireplaces. Breakfast should be a high point, so allow time to enjoy it. Ardtara would make an excellent base for exploring this beautiful and unspoilt area. Tennis, golf practice tee. Pets allowed by arrangement. Garden, woodland walk. Conferences/Banqueting (50). **Rooms 8** (3 suites) B&B about £75pps, ss about £10. *Short breaks offered. **Restaurant:** Although meals may also be served in the conservatory or bar, the main dining room was previously a snooker room and still has the full Victorian skylight and original hunting frieze, making an unusual setting for fine dining. Daily-changed menus offer three or four choices on each curse, typically including starters like pheasant terrine, or smoked salmon with prawns, and main courses like rack of lamb, or fillet of halibut, served with champ and spinach. A selection of Irish cheeses is offered (with the famous locally-made Ditty's biscuits) as well as classic desserts like pear and almond tart. The food is excellent, and guests enjoy the intimacy of the small house which allows the time to build up a rapport with staff. **Seats 65** (private room,30). Reservations required. Children welcome. Toilets wheelchair accessible. L Daily 12-2.30, Sun L 12-4. Set L about £25, Set Sun L about £25. D daily 6.30-9.30 (to 9 Sun). Set D about £33. House wines from about £12. Amex, MasterCard, Visa, Switch. **Directions:** M2 from from Belfast to A6. A29 to Maghera. B75 to Kilrea.

TYRONE

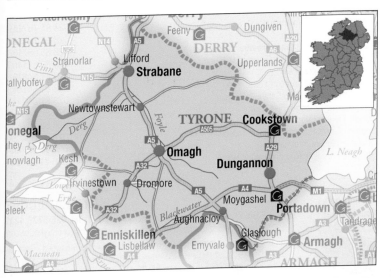

People in Ireland identify strongly with their counties. This is as it should be. The county boundaries may have evolved in many ways over a very long period, often in obscure ways. But in the 21st Century, Irish counties – for all that they vary enormously in size – seem to provide their people with a sense of place and pride which survives modern efforts to create newer administrative structures.

The enduring spirit of Tyrone well expresses this, and never more so than when a county team is playing in a national final at Corke Park in Dublin. In 2003, Tyrone went all the way to win the senior All-Ireland Football. The seniors failed to reach the finals in 2004, but the young men of Tyrone's Minor Team put in a determined performance on September 26th 2004 to wrest the championship from Kerry's Minor Team, a hopeful pointer for future achievement.

Tyrone is Northern Ireland's largest county, so it is something of a surprise for the traveller to discover that its geography appears to be dominated by a range of mountains of modest height, and nearly half of these peaks seem to be in the neighbouring county of Londonderry.

Yet such is the case with Tyrone and the Sperrins. The village of Sperrin itself towards the head of Glenelly may be in Tyrone, but the highest peak of Sawel (678 m), which looms over it, is on the county boundary. But much of the county is upland territory and moorland, giving the impression that the Sperrins are even more extensive than is really the case.

In such a land, the lower country and the fertile valleys gleam like jewels, and there's often a vivid impression of a living - and indeed, prosperity - being wrested from a demanding environment. It's a character-forming sort of place, so it's perhaps understandable that it was the ancestral homeland of a remarkable number of early American Presidents, and this connection is commemorated in the Ulster American Folk Park a few miles north of the county town of Omagh.

Forest parks abound, while attractive towns like Castlederg and Dungannon, as well as villages in the uplands and along the charming Clogher Valley, provide entertainment and hospitality for visitors refreshed by the wide open spaces of the moorlands and the mountains.

Local Attractions & Information

Ardboe Kinturk (Lough Neagh) Cultural Centre	028 86 736512
Benburb Benburb Castle and Valley Park	028 37 548241
Castlederg Visitor Centre (Davy Crockett links)	0044 16626 70795
Clogher Clogher Valley Rural Centre	028 85 548872
Coagh Kinturk Cultural Centre	028 86 736512
Cookstown Drum Manor Forest Park	028 86 762774

Georgina Campbell's Ireland

Cookstown Wellbrook Beetling Mill (Corkhill)	028 86 748210
Cranagh (Glenelly) Sperrin Heritage Centre	028 81 648142
Creggan (nr Carrickmore) Visitor Centre	028 80 761112
Dungannon Heritage Centre	028 87 724187
Dungannon Tourism Information	028 87 767259
Dungannon Tyrone Crystal	028 87 725335
Dungannon Ulysses S Grant Ancestral Homestead	028 85 557133
Fivemiletown Clogher Valley Railway Exhibition	028 89 521409
Gortin Ulster History Park	028 81 648188
Newtownstewart Baronscourt Forest Park	028 81 661683
Newtownstewart Gateway Centre & Museum	028 81 662414
Omagh Ulster-American Folk Park	028 82 243292
Omagh Tourism Information	028 82 247831
Strabane Gray's Printing Press (US Independence)	028 71 884094
Strabane Tourism Information	028 71 384444
Strabane President Wilson Ancestral Home	028 71 381348

Dungannon   # Grange Lodge
Country House
7 Grange Road Dungannon Co Tyrone BT71 7EJ **Tel: 028 8778 4212**
stay@grangelodgecountryhouse.com www.grangelodgecountryhouse.com

Norah and Ralph Brown's renowned Georgian retreat offers comfort, true family hospitality and good food. The house is on an elevated site just outside Dungannon, with about 20 acres of grounds; mature woodland and gardens (producing food for the table and flowers for the house) with views over lush countryside. Improvements over the years have been made with great sensitivity and the feeling is of gentle organic growth, culminating in the present warm and welcoming atmosphere. Grange Lodge is furnished unselfconsciously, with antiques and family pieces throughout. Bedrooms (and bathrooms) are exceptionally comfortable and thoughtful in detail. Norah is well known for her home cooking and they will cater for groups of 10-30. Grange Lodge is fully licensed and dinner menus change daily (in consultation with guests). Residents dinner (from £32) must be pre-booked, especially if you want to dine on the day of arrival. Breakfasts are also outstanding, so allow time to indulge: a fine buffet beautifully set out on a polished dining table might typically include a large selection of juices, fruit and cereals and porridge is a speciality, served with a tot of Bushmills whiskey, brown sugar and cream - and that's before you've even reached the cooked breakfast menu, served with lovely fresh breads and toast and home-made preserves. *"Cook with Norah" cookery classes have been running since 2002, and are very successful; details on application. Conferences/banqueting (20/30). Garden, walking, snooker. Not suitable for children under 12. Pets allowed by arrangement. **Rooms 5** (3 shower only, all no smoking). Room service (limited hours). Turndown service. B&B £39 pps, ss £20. Residents D Mon-Sat, 7.30pm, by arrangement; Set D from £32. Closed 13 Dec-1 Feb. MasterCard, Visa, Switch. **Directions:** 1 mile from M1 junction 15. On A29 to Armagh, follow "Grange Lodge" signs.

Dungannon   # Stangmore Town House
RESTAURANT WITH ROOMS
24 Killyman Road Dungannon Co Tyrone BT71 6DH
Tel: 028 8772 5600
info@stangmoretownhouse.com www.stangmoretownhouse.com

Anne and Andy Brace will be remembered by many visitors to Dungannon from their previous business, Stangmore Country House. Now they have moved to new premises about a mile and a half away, and it didn't take their followers very long to catch up with them as both their new rooms and the restaurant are already very busy. Here, once again, guests will find very comfortable accommodation Anne's trademark hospitality and immaculate housekeeping - and, of course, Andy's cooking. As before, quite extensive menus are offered, always based on local produce wherever possible, including steaks from award winning Cloughbane Farm, 5 miles away, and there's a carefully chosen and fairly priced wine list to accompany. Small conferences/meetings (20); free broadband wi/fi; wheelchair access to restaurant & toilet; children welcome (high chair, childrens menu, baby changing facilities under 12s free in parents' room, cot available); **Seats 50**; L 12-2pm; D 6.30-9pm; a la carte; house wine £12.50. Rooms 5 (all en-suite & no smoking, 1 shower only); limited room service; B&B £40pps; ss £25. Restaurant closed Sun; house closed 1 week Jul & 1 week Christmas. Amex, MasterCard, Visa, Switch. **Directions:** Junction 15 off M1, 2 set of traffic lights take a right down Gortmellon Links road. At the end of the road take a left, 3km (1.5 miles) on the right.

Deli on the Green

Moygashel
RESTAURANT
Ⓝ Ⓡ

The Linen Green Moygashel Co Tyrone BT71 7HB **Tel: 028 8775 1775**
info@delionthegreen.com www.delionthegreen.com

Across the yard from The Loft @ The Linen Green (see entry), the stylish Deli on the Green offers table service and a slightly more leisurely pace. Glasgow-born chef Bob McDonald, highly respected in Ulster food circles, is head chef and ideas man. Besides a classy deli (choose your lunch or pick up the makings of a picnic from the selection of quality local and more exotic foodstuffs) there are sofas and café style seating, inside and out, for coffees and snacks, and a brasserie, where the contemporary cuisine is reflected in a stylish combination of bare stone and glass, blond wood tables and high-backed cream leather chairs. Changed daily, the menus reflect Bob's commitment to profiling quality local produce including Kettyle's dry-aged beef, Moyallon sausages, Ditty's oatcakes and Tickety Moo Jersey Ice Cream - and there's a guarantee of no GM foods. Lunch can be as simple as you want to make it, from the salad and cooked meats display (incl. Bob's home made corned beef), or wholesome hot dishes. Then in the evening the tea lights and relaxing music herald a mood move: an ambitious menu, stylish presentation, comprehensive wine list and good service from well-trained, smartly turned out staff all create a sense of occasion. Begin with deli breads with dipping oils, or seared scallops with summer pea velouté & crispy pancetta, perhaps, then follow with Carlingford seafood medley with a lemon and chive veloute, classic chargrilled steaks, or Chinese red roast pork fillet, with interesting side orders. Finish with a delicious dessert such as coconut panna cotta, with caramelised pineapple & sorbet or Irish Cheeses with Ditty's Oatcake. An early dinner menu on Thu & Fri offers especially good value. **Seats 45**. Open all day Mon-Sat 8.30 am to 5.30 pm, D Thu, Fri & Sat 6-9.30 (booking advisable). Early Bird Thu & Fri, 5.30-7. 2/3 courses £13.50/ £16.50. **Directions:** Just off main Belfast road, follow signs to Moygashel. ◇

The Loft @ The Linen Green

Moygashel
CAFÉ
Ⓡ

Moygashel Co Tyrone BT71 7HB
Tel: 028 8775 3761

In the heart of Ulster, near the Dungannon end of the M1 motorway and just three minutes off the main Belfast road (look for the sign to Moygashel village) is The Linen Green discount designer outlet and retail park, its phenomenal success testimony to the lure of retail therapy in its most pleasurable guise. Developed on the site of a former textile mill, the complex retains an historic feel and hosts names such as Paul Costelloe, Foxford, Helen McAlinden and Ann Storey as well as shops offering luxury lingerie, textiles and treats for the house and garden. Add to that generous parking and a choice of two contrasting restaurants, The Loft, and **Deli on the Green** (see entry), both run by Claire Murray, and it makes an attractive refuelling stop. Upstairs in the main building, The Loft is an attractive café with high ceilings, lots of light and some memorabilia from Moygashel's days as a textile mill. Head up the stairs (lift access too) for a pick-me-up cappuccino and, perhaps, a generous scone, a tray bake or lemon meringue, or a quick lunch - sandwiches on good bread made to order from the salads and meats selection, or a tasty panini, with a good choice of hot and cold drinks too. Open Mon-Sat, 10am-5pm. **Directions:** Just off main Belfast road, follow signs to Moygashel. ◇

Dublin - Belfast

Distance:
166 km (103 miles)

Travel Time (approx):
2 Hours

Roads:
M1 / N1 / A1

⊖ – EAT   ⓓ – DRINK   Ⓢ – STAY

DUBLIN

	Town	County	Road	Km from Dublin	Km from Road	Category
1	Malahide	Dublin	M1	12	5	⊖ ⓓ Ⓢ
	Swords	Dublin	M1	12	3	⊖ ⓓ Ⓢ
2	Skerries	Dublin	M1	18	15	⊖ ⓓ Ⓢ
3	Drogheda	Louth	M1	46	3	Ⓢ
	Temonfeckin	Louth	M1	46	10	⊖
4	Clogherhead	Louth	M1	53	16	⊖
5	Collon	Louth	M1	60	8	⊖
6	Dunleer	Louth	M1	70	2	⊖

BELFAST

	Town	County	Road	Km from Dublin	Km from Road	Category
7	Ardee	Louth	M1	75	9	⊖ ⓓ
8	Blackrock	Louth	M1	80	5	⊖ ⓓ Ⓢ
9	Dundalk	Louth	M1	90	2	⊖ ⓓ Ⓢ
10	Warrenpoint	Down	A1	106	11	⊖
	Rostrevor	Down	A1	106	15	⊖
11	Portadown	Armagh	A1	125	17	⊖ ⓓ Ⓢ
12	Hillsborough	Down	A1	150	3	⊖ ⓓ

Dublin - Derry

Travel Time (approx.):
3.5 Hours

Distance:
231 km (145 miles)

Roads:
N2 / A5

ⓔ – EAT   ⓓ – DRINK   ⓢ – STAY

DUBLIN

25% | 50% | 75% |

DERRY

	Town	County	Road	Km from Dublin	Km from Road	Category
1	Ashbourne	Meath	N2	22	0	ⓔ ⓢ
2	Navan	Meath	N2	47	13	ⓔ ⓓ ⓢ
	Slane	Meath	N2	47.5	0	ⓔ ⓓ ⓢ
3	Collon	Louth	N2	56	0	ⓔ
4	Ardee	Louth	N2	66	0	ⓔ ⓓ
5	Carrickmacross	Monaghan	N2	86	0	ⓔ ⓓ ⓢ

	Town	County	Road	Km from Dublin	Km from Road	Category
6	Monaghan	Monaghan	N2	123	0	ⓔ ⓓ ⓢ
	Clones	Monaghan	N2	123	25	ⓢ
	Glaslough	Monaghan	N2	124	10	ⓔ ⓢ
7	Dungannon	Tyrone	A5	167	7	ⓢ
	Moygashel	Tyrone	A5	167	9	ⓔ

Dublin - Donegal

Travel Time (approx):
4 Hours

Distance:
235 km (146 miles)

Roads:
N3 / A509 / N3 / N15

Ⓔ – EAT   Ⓓ – DRINK   Ⓢ – STAY

DUBLIN

25% — 50% — 75%

DONEGAL

	Town	County	Road	Km from Dublin	Km from Road	Category
1	Dunboyne	Meath	N3	14	10	Ⓔ Ⓓ Ⓢ
	Kilmessan	Meath	N3	16	22	Ⓢ
2	Navan	Meath	N3	50	0	Ⓔ Ⓓ Ⓢ
	Athboy	Meath	N3	50	19	Ⓔ Ⓢ
3	Tara	Meath	N3	61	0	Ⓓ
4	Kells	Meath	N3	66	0	Ⓔ
5	Virginia	Cavan	N3	85	0	Ⓔ Ⓓ Ⓢ
	Mount Nugent	Cavan	N3	85	20	Ⓢ
	Bailieborough	Cavan	N3	85	13	Ⓔ

	Town	County	Road	Km from Dublin	Km from Road	Category
6	Cavan	Cavan	N3	113	0	Ⓔ Ⓓ Ⓢ
7	Cloverhill	Cavan	N3	122	3	Ⓔ Ⓓ Ⓢ
8	Belturbet	Cavan	N3	130	0	Ⓔ Ⓓ Ⓢ
	Ballyconnell	Cavan	N3	130	12	Ⓔ Ⓓ Ⓢ
9	Blacklion	Cavan	N3	162	16	Ⓔ Ⓓ Ⓢ
10	Enniskillen	Fermanagh A509		166	0	Ⓔ
11	Belleek	Fermanagh A509		204	0	Ⓔ
12	Ballyshannon	Donegal	N3	212	0	Ⓔ Ⓓ

JOURNEY PLANNER - WITH SUGGESTED PLACES FOR A BREAK...

ⓔ – EAT   ⓓ – DRINK   ⓢ – STAY

Dublin - Sligo

Travel Time (approx):
3.25 Hours

Distance:
208 km (130 miles)

Roads:
M4 / N4

DUBLIN → DONEGAL

	Town	County	Road	Km from Dublin	Km from Road	Category
1	Lucan	Dublin	M4	15	2	ⓔ ⓢ
2	Leixlip	Dublin	M4	16.5	2	ⓔ ⓢ
	Celbridge	Kildare	M4	16.5	8	ⓔ
	Clane	Kildare	M4	16.5	20	ⓔ
3	Maynooth	Kildare	M4	24	3	ⓔ ⓓ ⓢ
	Straffan	Kildare	M4	24	11	ⓔ ⓢ
4	Enfield	Kildare	M4	37	9	ⓔ
	Moy Valley	Kildare	M4	37	2	ⓔ ⓓ ⓢ
5	Mullingar	Westmeath	N4	76	3	ⓔ ⓓ ⓢ
6	Multyfarnham	Westmeath	N4	86	5	ⓔ ⓢ
7	Granard	Longford	N4	106	12	ⓔ
8	Longford	Longford	N4	119	0	ⓔ ⓓ ⓢ
	Tarmonbarry	Roscommon N4		119	9	ⓔ ⓓ

	Town	County	Road	Km from Dublin	Km from Road	Category
9	Rooskey	Leitrim	N4	137	3	ⓢ
10	Jamestown	Leitrim	N4	146	3	ⓔ
11	Carrick on Shannon	Leitrim	N4	153	0	ⓔ ⓓ ⓢ
	Drumshanbo	Leitrim	N4	153	15	ⓢ
	Keshcarrigan	Leitrim	N4	153	7	ⓔ ⓓ
12	Knockvicar	Leitrim	N4	153	15	ⓔ
13	Cootehall	Roscommon N4		158	3	ⓔ ⓓ
14	Castlebaldwin	Roscommon N4		165	3	ⓔ ⓓ ⓢ
15	Riverstown	Sligo	N4	181	0	ⓔ ⓓ ⓢ
16	Collooney	Sligo	N4	189	2	ⓢ
	Ballygawley	Sligo	N4	195	0	ⓢ
		Sligo	N4	195	5	ⓔ ⓢ

PLANNER - WITH SUGGESTED PLACES FOR A BREAK...

ⓔ – EAT   ⓓ – DRINK   ⓢ – STAY

Dublin - Westport

Travel Time (approx): 4 Hours

Distance: 253 km (157 miles)

Roads: M4 / N4 / N5

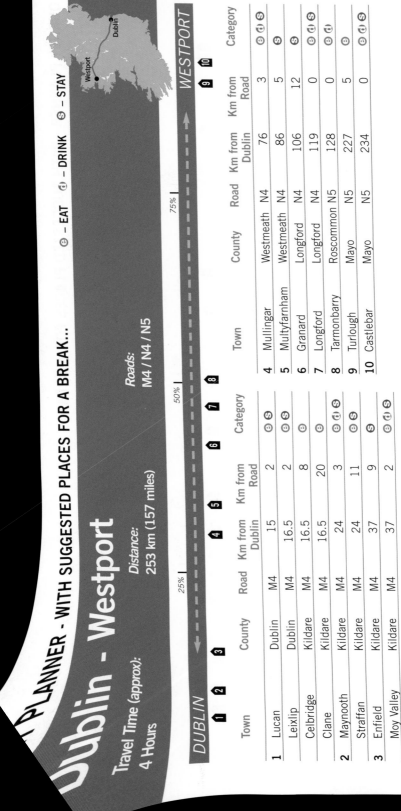

DUBLIN

	Town	County	Road	Km from Dublin	Km from Road	Category
1	Lucan	Dublin	M4	15	2	ⓔ ⓢ
	Leixlip	Dublin	M4	16.5	2	ⓔ ⓢ
	Celbridge	Kildare	M4	16.5	8	ⓔ
	Clane	Kildare	M4	16.5	20	ⓔ
2	Maynooth	Kildare	M4	24	3	ⓔ ⓓ ⓢ
	Straffan	Kildare	M4	24	11	ⓔ ⓢ
3	Enfield	Kildare	M4	37	9	ⓢ
	Moy Valley	Kildare	M4	37	2	ⓔ ⓓ ⓢ

WESTPORT

	Town	County	Road	Km from Dublin	Km from Road	Category
4	Mullingar	Westmeath	N4	76	3	ⓔ ⓓ ⓢ
5	Multyfarnham	Westmeath	N4	86	5	ⓢ
6	Granard	Longford	N4	106	12	ⓢ
7	Longford	Longford	N4	119	0	ⓔ ⓓ ⓢ
8	Tarmonbarry	Roscommon	N5	128	0	ⓔ ⓓ ⓢ
9	Turlough	Mayo	N5	227	5	ⓔ
10	Castlebar	Mayo	N5	234	0	ⓔ ⓓ ⓢ

25%   50%   75%

Westport

Dublin

ⓔ – EAT   ⓓ – DRINK   ⓢ – STAY

Dublin - Galway

Travel Time (approx):
3 Hours

Distance:
215 km (133 miles)

Roads:
M4 / N6

DUBLIN ← - → GALWAY

25% | 50% | 75% |

	Town	County	Road	Km from Dublin	Km from Road	Category
1	Lucan	Dublin	M4	15	2	ⓔ ⓢ
	Leixlip	Dublin	M4	16.5	2	ⓔ ⓢ
	Celbridge	Kildare	M4	16.5	8	ⓔ
	Clane	Kildare	M4	16.5	20	ⓔ
2	Maynooth	Kildare	M4	24	3	ⓔ ⓓ ⓢ
	Straffan	Kildare	M4	24	11	ⓔ ⓢ
3	Enfield	Kildare	M4	37	9	ⓔ ⓢ
	Moy Valley	Kildare	M4	37	3	ⓔ ⓓ ⓢ

	Town	County	Road	Km from Dublin	Km from Road	Category
4	Tullamore	Offaly	N6	93	10	ⓔ ⓓ ⓢ
5	Moate	Westmeath	N6	100	0	ⓢ
6	Glasson	Westmeath	N6	120	10	ⓔ ⓓ ⓢ
7	Athlone	Westmeath	N6	123	0	ⓔ ⓓ ⓢ
8	Shannonbridge	Offaly	N6	146	10	ⓔ ⓓ
9	Ballinasloe	Galway	N6	150	2.5	ⓔ ⓓ ⓢ
10	Craughwell	Galway	N6	202	4	ⓔ ⓢ
11	Clarinbridge	Galway	N6	206	6	ⓔ

...NER - WITH SUGGESTED PLACES FOR A BREAK...

ⓔ – EAT   ⓓ – DRINK   ⓢ – STAY

...lIn - Limerick - Killarney

Distance: 305 km (190 miles)

...el Time (approx): 4.5 Hours

Roads: N7 / M7 / N20 / N21 / N23

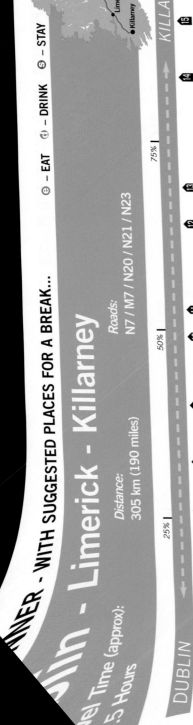

DUBLIN →

#	Town	County	Road	Km from Dublin	Km from Road	Category
1	Red Cow R/about	Dublin	N7	9	0	ⓢ
2	Newlands Cross	Dublin	N7	12	0	ⓢ
	Liffey Valley	Dublin	M7	12	0	ⓔ ⓢ
3	Saggart	Dublin	M7	17	1	ⓢ
4	Naas	Kildare	M7	30	3	ⓔ ⓓ ⓢ
5	Newbridge	Kildare	M7	47	3	ⓢ
6	Killenard	Laois	M7	60	13	ⓔ ⓢ
7	Portlaoise	Laois	M7	80	5	ⓔ ⓢ
8	Mountrath	Laois	N7	100	0	ⓢ

→ KILLARNEY

#	Town	County	Road	Km from Dublin	Km from Road	Category
9	Roscrea	Tipperary	N7	123	2	ⓔ
10	Nenagh	Tipperary	N7	151	6	ⓔ ⓓ ⓢ
	Garrykennedy	Tipperary	N7	151	11	ⓔ ⓓ
11	Dromineer	Tipperary	N7	162	18	ⓔ ⓓ
12	LIMERICK	Limerick	N7	197	3	ⓔ ⓓ ⓢ
13	Adare	Limerick	N20/N21	212	0	ⓔ ⓓ ⓢ
	Ballingarry	Limerick	N21	212	11	ⓔ ⓢ
14	Listowel	Kerry	N21	257	16	ⓔ ⓢ
15	Tralee	Kerry	N23	280	17.5	ⓔ ⓓ ⓢ

25%   50%   75%

JOURNEY PLANNER - WITH SUGGESTED PLACES FOR A BREAK...

Dublin - Cork

Travel Time (approx):
4 Hours

Distance:
257 km (167 miles)

Roads:
N7 / M7 / N8

ⓔ – EAT   ⓓ – DRINK   ⓢ – STAY

	Town	County	Road	Km from Dublin	Km from Road	Category
1	Red Cow R/about	Dublin	N7	9	0	ⓢ
2	Newlands Cross	Dublin	N7	12	0	ⓢ
	Liffey Valley	Dublin	M7	12	0	ⓔ ⓢ
3	Saggart	Dublin	M7	17	1	ⓢ
4	Naas	Kildare	M7	30	3	ⓔ ⓓ ⓢ
5	Newbridge	Kildare	M7	47	3	ⓢ
6	Killenard	Laois	M7	60	13	ⓔ ⓢ
7	Portlaoise	Laois	N8	87	1	ⓔ ⓢ
8	Abbeyleix	Laois	N8	98	0	ⓔ ⓓ ⓢ

	Town	County	Road	Km from Dublin	Km from Road	Category
9	Durrow	Laois	N8	107	0	ⓔ ⓢ
10	Thurles	Tipperary	N8	137	15	ⓔ ⓢ
11	Cashel	Tipperary	N8	156	3	ⓔ ⓓ ⓢ
12	Clonmel	Tipperary	N8	176	20	ⓔ ⓓ ⓢ
	Clogheen	Tipperary	N8	176	15	ⓔ ⓢ
13	Mitchelstown	Cork	N8	203	0	ⓔ
	Doneraile	Cork	N8	203	23	ⓢ
14	Fermoy	Cork	N8	218	0	ⓔ ⓢ

DUBLIN

1 2 3 4 5 6   7 8 9   10   11   12   13 14

25% | 50% | 75% |

CORK

JOURNEY PLANNER - WITH SUGGESTED PLACES FOR A BREAK...

@ – EAT   @ – DRINK   @ – STAY

Dublin - Kilkenny - Waterford

Travel Time (approx): 2.5 Hours	*Distance:* 160 km (100 miles)
	Roads: N7 / M7 / M9 / N9

DUBLIN

	Town	County	Road	Km from Dublin	Km from Road	Category
1	Red Cow R/about	Dublin	N7	9	0	@
2	Newlands Cross	Dublin	N7	12	0	@
3	Liffey Valley	Dublin	M7	12	0	@ @
3	Saggart	Dublin	M7	17	1	@
4	Naas	Kildare	M7	30	3	@ @ @
4	Ballymore Eustace	Kildare	M7/M9	30	11	@ @
5	Dunlavin	Wicklow	N9	54	3	@ @ @
6	Castledermot	Kildare	N9	73	5	@
6	Athy	Kildare	N9	73	15	@ @ @

WATERFORD

	Town	County	Road	Km from Dublin	Km from Road	Category
7	Carlow	Carlow	N9	83	0	@ @ @
8	Leighlinbridge	Carlow	N9	97	1.5	@ @ @
9	Bagenalstown	Carlow	N9	100	2	@
9	Borris	Carlow	N9	100	15	@ @ @
10	Maddoxtown*	Kilkenny	N9*	105	14	@
10	KILKENNY CITY*	Kilkenny	N9*	105	18	@ @ @
11	Inistioge	Kilkenny	N9	125	9	@
11	Thomastown	Kilkenny	N9	125	0	@ @

* Turn on to N10 for Kilkenny

JOURNEY PLANNER - WITH SUGGESTED PLACES FOR A BREAK...

ⓔ – EAT   ⓓ – DRINK   ⓢ – STAY

Dublin - Wexford

Travel Time (approx):
2 Hours

Distance:
138 km (58 miles)

Roads:
N11

DUBLIN ➊ ➋ ➌ ➍ ➎ ➏ ➐ ➑ ➒ ➓ **WEXFORD**

25% | 50% | 75% |

	Town	County	Road	Km from Dublin	Km from Road	Category
1	Enniskerry	Wicklow	N11	23	3	ⓔ ⓓ ⓢ
	Kilmacanogue	Wicklow	N11	24	2	ⓔ
2	Greystones	Wicklow	N11	29	4	ⓔ ⓓ
	Delgany	Wicklow	N11	29	0	ⓢ
3	N/twnmtkennedy	Wicklow	N11	32	3	ⓔ ⓢ
4	Ashford	Wicklow	N11	40	3	ⓔ ⓢ
5	Rathnew	Wicklow	N11	43	2	ⓔ ⓢ

	Town	County	Road	Km from Dublin	Km from Road	Category
	Rathdrum	Wicklow	N11	43	15	ⓢ
6	Avoca	Wicklow	N11	55	10	ⓔ
7	Woodenbridge	Wicklow	N11	66	10	ⓢ
	Arklow	Wicklow	N11	66	10	ⓔ
8	Gorey	Wexford	N11	86	0	ⓔ ⓓ ⓢ
9	Bunclody	Wexford	N11	100	15	ⓔ ⓢ
10	Enniscorthy	Wexford	N11	114	0	ⓔ ⓓ ⓢ

Wexford ●   ● Dublin

90 MINUTES
...from the Red Cow

County	Town	Establishment	Category	Distance*
Kildare	Leixlip	Courtyard Hotel	Hotel	7
Dublin	Leixlip	Becketts Country House Hotel	Hotel	12
Dublin	Lucan	Finnstown Country House Hotel	Hotel	12
Kildare	Maynooth	Glenroyal Hotel	Hotel	16
Kildare	Maynooth	Maynooth Campus	Accommodation	16
Kildare	Maynooth	Carton House Hotel	Hotel	16
Kildare	Maynooth	Moyglare Manor	Country House	16
Meath	Dunboyne	Dunboyne Castle Hotel & Spa	Hotel	20
Kildare	Naas	Osprey Hotel & Spa	Hotel	21
Kildare	Naas	Killashe House Hotel & Villa Spa	Hotel	21
Kildare	Naas	Keadeen Hotel	Hotel	21
Dublin	Killiney	Fitzpatrick Castle Hotel	Hotel	22
Meath	Ashbourne	Broadmeadow Country House	Guesthouse	25
Dublin	DunLaoghaire	Rochestown Lodge Hotel	Hotel	25
Kildare	Straffan	Barberstown Castle	Hotel	26
Kildare	Straffan	K Club	Hotel	26
Dublin	Portmarnock	Portmarnock Hotel	Hotel	26
Kildare	Moyvalley	Moyvalley Estate	Hotel	27
Dublin	Malahide	Belcamp Hutchinson	Country House	27
Dublin	Swords	Roganstown Golf & Country Club	Hotel	28
Dublin	Howth	Ann's	B&B	30
Dublin	Howth	King Sitric Fish Restaurant & Acc	Restaurant with Rooms	30
Wicklow	Enniskerry	Ritz Carlton Powerscourt	Hotel	31
Wicklow	Delgany	Glenview Hotel	Hotel	34
Wicklow	Newtnmkedy.	Marriott Druids Glen Hotel	Hotel	38
Meath	Enfield	Marriott Johnstown House Hotel	Hotel	39
Meath	Kilmessan	The Station House Hotel	Hotel	39
Kildare	Curragh	Martinstown House	Country House	40
Dublin	Skerries	Red Bank House & Restaurant	Guesthouse/Restaurant	40
Wicklow	Dunlavin	Rathsallagh House	Country House	41
Meath	Trim	Trim Castle Hotel	Hotel	43
Meath	Trim	Knightsbrook Hotel & Golf Resort	Hotel	43
Meath	Navan	Killyon House	B&B	45
Meath	Navan	Bellinter Country House	Country House	45
Wicklow	Rathnew	Tinakilly Country House	Country House	48
Wicklow	Rathnew	Hunter's Hotel	Hotel	48
Wicklow	Ashford	Ballyknocken House & Cookery Sch.	Farmhouse	50
Wicklow	Glendalough	Derrymore House	B&B	54
Louth	Collon	Forge Gallery Restaurant	Restaurant with Rooms	58
Louth	Drogheda	Boyne Valley Hotel & Country Club	Hotel	58
Louth	Drogheda	D Hotel	Hotel	58
Kildare	Athy	Carlton Abbey Hotel	Hotel	61
Kildare	Athy	Bert House Hotel & Leisure	Hotel	61
Kildare	Athy	Coursetown Country House	Country House	61

Distance in kilometres. Travel times are traffic dependent.

County	Town	Establishment	Category	Distance*
Wicklow	Rathdrum	Avonbrae	Guesthouse	62
Wicklow	Kiltegan	Humewood Castle	Hotel	62
Wicklow	Kiltegan	Barraderry Country House	Country House	62
Meath	Athboy	Frankville House - The Blue Door	B&B	64
Laois	Killenard	The Heritage Golf & Spa Resort	Hotel	65
Kildare	Castledermot	Kilkea Castle	Hotel	65
Wicklow	Arklow	Plattenstown Country House	Country House	73
Carlow	Carlow	Barrowville Townhouse	Guesthouse	73
Carlow	Tullow	Mount Wolseley Hilton Hotel	Hotel	76
Laois	Portlaoise	Ivyleigh House	Guesthouse	76
Laois	Portlaoise	Portlaoise Heritage Hotel	Hotel	76
Wicklow	Woodenbridge	Woodnebridge Hotel	Hotel	80
Westmeath	Mullingar	Mullingar Park Hotel	Hotel	80
Carlow	Leighlinbridge	Lord Bagenal Inn	Hotel	84
Cavan	Kingscourt	Cabra Castle Hotel & Golf Club	Hotel	86
Westmeath	Multyfarnham	Mornington House	Country House	87
Carlow	Ballon	Ballykealey Manor Hotel	Hotel	88
Carlow	Ballon	Sherwood Park House	Country House	88
Wicklow	Aughrim	Clone House	Country House	90
Carlow	Bagenalstown	Kilgraney House	Country House	90
Carlow	Bagenalstown	Lorum Old Rectory	Country House	90
Monaghan	Carrickmacross	Nuremore Hotel & Country Club	Hotel	90
Louth	Dundalk	Ballymascanlon House Hotel	Hotel	92
Wicklow	Macreddin	BrookLodge	Hotel	95
Offaly	Tullamore	Tullamore Court Hotel	Hotel	96
Offaly	Tullamore	Annaharvey Farm	Farmhouse	96
Laois	Durrow	Castle Durrow	Hotel	99
Laois	Mountrath	Roundwood House	Country House	100
Cavan	Mountnugent	Ross House	Farmhouse	100
Westmeath	Moate	Temple Country Retreat & Spa	Country House	103
Carlow	Borris	The Step House Hotel	Hotel	104
Offaly	Kinnity	Ardmore Country House	Country House	110
Offaly	Kinnity	Glendine Bistro	B&B	110
Offaly	Kinnity	Kinnitty Castle	Hotel	110

Georgina Campbell's Ireland

Georgina Campbell's Ireland

Georgina Campbell's Ireland

Georgina Campbell's Ireland

Georgina Campbell's Ireland

INDEX

Georgina Campbell's Ireland

Georgina Campbell's Ireland

Georgina Campbell's Ireland

INDEX

How to Use the Guide

Location /Establishment name

- Cities, towns and villages are arranged in alphabetical order within counties, with the exception of Dublin, Cork, Belfast, Galway and Limerick where the city comes ahead of other towns
- Establishments arranged alphabetically within location
- In Dublin city, postal codes are arranged in numerical order. Even numbers are south of the River Liffey, and uneven numbers on the north, with the exception of Dublin 8 which straddles the river. Dublin 1 and 2 are most central; Dublin 1 is north of the Liffey, Dublin 2 is south of it (see map). Within each district, establishments are listed in alphabetical order.

Telephone numbers

- Codes are given for use within the Republic of Ireland / Northern Ireland. To call ROI from outside the jurisdiction, the code is +353 (or +44 for NI), then drop the first digit (zero) from the local code.
- To call Northern Ireland from the Republic, replace the 028 code with 048.

Reading the text

Our aim is to lead readers to the best places in Ireland, to suit their needs, allowing for regional variations in standards - and differing requirements, depending on the occasion. Please read the text for each establishment and consider what it is about them that we are recommending. The longer narratives tend to be for the better establishments as they have more positive and interesting things to say about them e.g. if we only highlight the business and conference facilities about a particular hotel then this may not be the best choice for those seeking a romantic break.

Categories

We have multiple categories including Hotel, Restaurant, Café etc, and we highlight the aspects of a particular establishment that we recommend. Where only one category is highlighted, that is the main recomendation, for example 'Hotel' is recommend as a placce to stay. If there is a restaurant and it is recommend, the category becoomes 'Hotel/Restaurant'.

Abbreviations

SC	Service Charge
SC incl	Service Charge Included
B	Breakfast
L	Lunch
D	Dinner (evening meal)
PP	Per Person
PPS	Per Person Sharing
PN	Per Night
Power Shower	A shower that has an electric pump that increases the water flow
Double	A bedroom with a bed that sleeps two people
Twin	A bedroom that has two separate beds
Family Room	Contains multiple beds suitable for a family, contact establishment for more information

Rating for outstanding cooking, accommodation or features

- Best Establishment: selected for overall excellence and/or specific special qualities - e.g. 'Outstanding Location'
- ☆ Demi star: for cooking and service well above average
- ★ Restaurants offering consistent excellence overall
- ★★ One of the best restaurants in the land
- ★★★ The highest restaurant grade achievable
- Outstanding accommodation of its type
- Deluxe hotel
- Pub star: good food and atmosphere
- Denotes establishment committed to the Féile Bia Charter
- Identifies inclusion in the BIM Seafood Circle programme
- € 'Best Budget' denotes moderately priced establishment (max approx €50 pps for accommodation, €35 for 3-course meal without drinks)
- Outstanding location, building or atmosphere
- E Editor's Choice; a selection of establishments outside the standard categories that should enhance the discerning travellers experience of Ireland
- N Establishments that are new to this edition of the Guide
- Previous award winner in earlier editions of our guides
- ◇ Confirmation of times/prices not received at time of going to press

Route indicators:

Throughout the Guide, we have highlighted establishments which are on or close to National Primary routes. Further details are contained within the 'Routes' Section towards the back of this book. Each colour denotes a route as follows:

R – Dublin to Belfast		R – Dublin to Derry
R – Dublin to Donegal		R – Dublin to Sligo
R – Dublin to Westport		R – Dublin to Galway
R – Dublin to Limerick / Killarney		R – Dublin to Cork
R – Dublin to Kilkenny / Waterford		R – Dublin to Wexford

Maps are intended for reference only: Ordnance Survey maps are recommended when travelling; available from Tourist Information Offices.

PRICES & OPENING HOURS
PLEASE NOTE THAT PRICES AND OPENING HOURS ARE GIVEN AS A GUIDELINE ONLY, AND MAY HAVE CHANGED; CHECK BEFORE TRAVELLING OR WHEN MAKING A RESERVATION.

Prices in the Republic of Ireland are given in Euro (€) and those in Northern Ireland in pounds Sterling (£).

RECOMMENDED ESTABLISHMENTS THAT ACCEPT OUR DISCOUNT VOUCHERS...

DUBLIN 2
Aya
Clarence Hotel & Tea Room
Jacobs Ladder
Tulsi Restaurant

DUBLIN 4
French Paradox
Poulot's Restaurant
Schoolhouse Hotel & Restaurant

DUBLIN 6
Ranelagh — Eatery 120
Rathgar — Poppadom

DUBLIN 18
Foxrock — The Gables Restaurant

CO DUBLIN
Howth — Deep
Howth — Ella
Howth — The Oar House
Skerries — Red Bank House & Restaurant

CO CARLOW
Bagenalstown — Lorum Old Rectory
Ballon — The Forge Restaurant
Ballon — Sherwood Park House
Tullow — Ballyderrin House

CO CLARE
Ballyvaughan — Drumcreehy House
Ballyvaughan — Rusheen Lodge
Carron — Burren Perfumery Tea Rooms
Doolin — Ballinalacken Castle Country House
Doolin — Stonecutters Kitchen
Ennis — Zucchini
Kilkee — Murphy Blacks
Kilkee — The Strand Restaurant & Guesthouse
Lahinch — Barrtra Seafood Restaurant

CORK CITY
Café Gusto
Hotel Isaacs & Greenes Restaurant
Liberty Grill

CO CORK
Ahakista — Hillcrest House
Ballylickey — Seaview House Hotel
Baltimore — Casey's of Baltimore
Bantry — Organico
Blarney — Blairs Inn
Carrigaline — Carrigaline Court Hotel
Castletownshend — Mary Ann's Bar & Restaurant
Clonakilty — Gleeson's
Clonakilty — O'Keeffe's
Nr. Clonakilty — Deasy's Harbour Bar & Seafood Restaurant
Cobh — Knockeven House
Crosshaven — Cronin's Pub
Durrus — Blairs Cove House
Goleen — The Heron's Cove
Kilbrittain — The Glen Country House
Mallow — Longueville House Hotel
Oysterhaven — Oz-Haven Restaurant

Schull — Grove House
Skibbereen — Kalbo's Bistro
Youghal — Ballymakeigh House

CO DONEGAL
Bruckless — Bruckless House
Laghey — Coxtown Manor
Malin — Malin Hotel
Ramelton — Ardeen
Rossnowlagh — Sand House Hotel
Tremone — Trean House

GALWAY CITY
Courtyard by Marriott
Heron's Rest B&B
Killeen House

CO GALWAY
Aran Islands — An Dún
Barna — Twelve Hotel
Cashel — Cashel House Hotel
Clifden — Ardagh Hotel & Restaurant
Clifden — The Quay House
Furbo — Connemara Coast Hotel
Leenane — Delphi Lodge
Recess — Lough Inagh Lodge

CO KERRY
Ballybunion — Teach de Broc
Caherdaniel — Derrynane Hotel
Dingle — Dingle Benners Hotel
Dingle — Dingle Skellig Hotel
Kenmare — Bácús Bistro
Killarney — Kathleens Country House
Killarney — Killarney Lodge
Killarney — Killarney Royal Hotel
Listowel — Allo's Restaurant
Tralee — Brook Manor Lodge
Tralee — Meadowlands Hotel
Valentia Is. — Seabreeze Coffee Shop
Waterville — Brookhaven House

CO KILDARE
Ballymore Eustace:
  Ballymore Inn
  Ardenode Hotel
Leixlip — Leixlip House Hotel
Moyvalley — Moyvalley Estate

CO KILKENNY
Kilkenny — Butler House

CO LAOIS
Mountrath — Roundwood House
Portlaoise — Kingfisher Restaurant

CO LEITRIM
Carrick-on-Shannon:
  Victoria Hall
Rossinver — Grass Roof Café

CO LIMERICK
Limerick — Brulees Restaurant

CO LONGFORD
Longford — Viewmount House

CO LOUTH
Dundalk — Restaurant Number 32

CO MAYO
Crossmolina — Enniscoe house
Ballinrobe — JJ Gannons
Claremorris — Old Arch Bar & Bistro
Mulranny — Park Inn Mulranny
Westport — Hotel Westport

CO MONAGHAN
Clones — Hilton Park

CO OFFALY
Birr — Stables Emporium
Kinnitty — Ardmore Country House

CO ROSCOMMON
Shannonbridge — The Old Fort
Tarmonbarry — Keenans Bar & Restaurant

CO SLIGO
Riverstown — Coopershill House

CO TIPPERARY
Cashel — Hill House
Newcastle — Kilmaneen Farmhouse

CO WATERFORD
Ballymacarbry — Glasha
Ballymacarbry — Hanora's Cottage
Cheekpoint — The Cottage Bistro
Dungarvan — Cairbre House
Dungarvan — Powersfield House
Lismore — Glencairn Inn & Pastis Bistro
Tallowbridge — The Brideview Bar & Restaurant
Waterford — Sion Hill House & Gardens

CO WESTMEATH
Athlone — Restaurant le Chateau
Glasson — Wineport Lodge

CO WEXFORD
Campile — Kilmokea Country Manor & Gardens
Enniscorthy — Ballinkeele House

CO WICKLOW
Arklow — Plattenstown House
Greystones — Backstage @ Bels

BELFAST
Ravenhill House
Swantons Gourmet Foods

CO ARMAGH
Craigavon — Newforge House

CO DOWN
Annahilt — The Pheasant
Ardglass — Curran's Seafood Bar & Steakhouse
Holywood — Beech Hill Country House
Killinchy — Balloo House
Warrenpoint — Copper Restaurant

CO LONDONDERRY
Limavady — Lime Tree Restaurant

- €5 (£5 NI) discounted off either a 3 course meal for two, or 1 night's B&B for two
- Can only be redeemed in establishments that have the  symbol on their entry in the "Georgina Campbell's Ireland 2008 - the Guide" guidebook
- Guidebook must be presented with the voucher
- Only one voucher per group

€5

£5 in Northern Ireland

VALID UNTIL 30/11/2008

- €5 (£5 NI) discounted off either a 3 course meal for two, or 1 night's B&B for two
- Can only be redeemed in establishments that have the symbol on their entry in the "Georgina Campbell's Ireland 2008 - the Guide" guidebook
- Guidebook must be presented with the voucher
- Only one voucher per group

€5

£5 in Northern Ireland

VALID UNTIL 30/11/2008

- €5 (£5 NI) discounted off either a 3 course meal for two, or 1 night's B&B for two
- Can only be redeemed in establishments that have the symbol on their entry in the "Georgina Campbell's Ireland 2008 - the Guide" guidebook
- Guidebook must be presented with the voucher
- Only one voucher per group

€5

£5 in Northern Ireland

VALID UNTIL 30/11/2008

- €5 (£5 NI) discounted off either a 3 course meal for two, or 1 night's B&B for two
- Can only be redeemed in establishments that have the symbol on their entry in the "Georgina Campbell's Ireland 2008 - the Guide" guidebook
- Guidebook must be presented with the voucher
- Only one voucher per group

€5

£5 in Northern Ireland

VALID UNTIL 30/11/2008

This voucher may be redeemed to offset the cost of either a 3 course meal for two,

or 1 night's B&B for two. If you are being presented with this voucher

please check that the ✐ symbol is highlighted on your entry in

"Georgina Campbell's Ireland - the Guide 2008"

This was authorised by the proprietor/manager/sales & marketing department
when they signed and returned a form in early summer 2007

Georgina Campbell Guides
PO Box 6173, Dublin 13 - info@ireland-guide.com

This voucher may be redeemed to offset the cost of either a 3 course meal for two,

or 1 night's B&B for two. If you are being presented with this voucher

please check that the ✐ symbol is highlighted on your entry in

"Georgina Campbell's Ireland - the Guide 2008"

This was authorised by the proprietor/manager/sales & marketing department
when they signed and returned a form in early summer 2007

Georgina Campbell Guides
PO Box 6173, Dublin 13 - info@ireland-guide.com

This voucher may be redeemed to offset the cost of either a 3 course meal for two,

or 1 night's B&B for two. If you are being presented with this voucher

please check that the ✐ symbol is highlighted on your entry in

"Georgina Campbell's Ireland - the Guide 2008"

This was authorised by the proprietor/manager/sales & marketing department
when they signed and returned a form in early summer 2007

Georgina Campbell Guides
PO Box 6173, Dublin 13 - info@ireland-guide.com

This voucher may be redeemed to offset the cost of either a 3 course meal for two,

or 1 night's B&B for two. If you are being presented with this voucher

please check that the ✐ symbol is highlighted on your entry in

"Georgina Campbell's Ireland - the Guide 2008"

This was authorised by the proprietor/manager/sales & marketing department
when they signed and returned a form in early summer 2007

Georgina Campbell Guides
PO Box 6173, Dublin 13 - info@ireland-guide.com